W. L. Sharkey

MISSISSIPPI STATE

MISSISSIPPI STATE CASES:

BEING CRIMINAL CASES DECIDED

IN

The High Court of Errors and Appeals,

AND IN THE

SUPREME COURT,

OF

THE STATE OF MISSISSIPPI;

From the June Term 1818 to the First Monday in January 1872, inclusive.

WITH

EXPLANATORY NOTES OF ENGLISH AND AMERICAN DECISIONS AND
AUTHORITIES; AND A MANUAL OF FORMS FOR MAKING
UP RECORDS, ENTRIES, CRIMINAL
PLEADINGS, ETC.

BY J. S. MORRIS,
ATTORNEY GENERAL OF MISSISSIPPI.

IN TWO VOLUMES.
VOLUME I.

JACKSON, MISS.,
PUBLISHED BY THE COMPILER,
1872.

95095

HOSFORD & SONS,
STATIONERS AND PRINTERS,
NEW YORK.

WILLIAM LEWIS SHARKEY.

In connection with the elegant and life-like portrait, which embellishes this volume, of one of the most distinguished living Jurists of Mississippi, it will not be improper to mention some of the leading events of his history.

Born in that cradle of great lawyers, the State of Tennessee, WILLIAM L. SHARKEY immigrated with his parents, in 1803, to the Territory of Mississippi, and was raised on a farm near Warrenton, then the seat of justice of Warren County, on the Mississippi river, a few miles below the spot on which Vicksburg now stands. His opportunities for early education were limited to those afforded by the primitive schools of that day. To the other apparent hardships of his childhood was superadded the loss of both his parents by death, before the future Chief Justice had reached the age of fifteen years. But his few advantages, such as they were, were earnestly and patiently improved. With but little means of education or support, and few friends, and they not wealthy, he labored industriously as a manual laborer on the farm, devoting all his leisure hours to study, till he had accumulated enough of money to obtain the rudiments of English and classical learning. This he did partly at Greenville college, Tennessee, and partly by the tuition of Mr. John Hall, an eminent scholar of Sumner County in that State.

That gentleman, besides being the principal of an Academy, was also a lawyer and the fortunate owner of a law and miscellaneous library ; and it is to his kindness and skill that the country is indebted for laying in the mind and character of his orphan pupil, the foundations of that profound learning and professional integrity which have contributed so much to the usefulness and fame of the bench and bar of the South-west.

The course of study commenced with Mr. Hall was completed with Messrs. Turner and Metcalfe, a distinguished law firm of Natchez ; and in 1822 Mr. Sharkey was admitted to practice at the bar of the Supreme Court, and located for practice among the scenes of his early boyhood, at Warrenton. In 1825 he followed the county seat of Warren County in its removal from that place to the village of Vicksburg. Rising rapidly in professional reputation and fortune, he was married to her who is still the sharer of the unpurchasable honors of his upright and useful life—the unbounded respect and esteem of a wide circle of society and friends.

In 1827 Mr. Sharkey was elected to the State Legislature from Warren County, and was made Speaker of the House of Representatives, in which position he won a high reputation, not less for his inflexible honesty, impartiality and firmness, than for his thorough and accurate knowledge of, and ability to perform, all his complex duties as a legislator and as presiding officer.

Under the Constitution of 1832, Mr. Sharkey was elected by the people as one of the three judges of the High Court of Errors and Appeals of the State, and was immediately appointed Chief Justice. To this high office he was chosen for four terms of six years each. And these repeated proofs of the popular esteem appear the more significant when it is remembered that in politics Judge Sharkey was always an ardent and inflexible Whig, while his constituency were intensely Democratic.

In 1850, Judge Sharkey resigned his office as Chief Justice and returned to practice, locating for this purpose at Jackson. He was induced to this course by pecuniary embarrassments, growing out of the insufficient salaries at that time allowed to the judiciary of the State—the bar being far more remunerative. Very soon afterwards he was invited by President Fillmore to go as Consul to Havana to adjust complications which had grown out of filibustering expeditions between this and the Spanish Government. Finding that his expectations respecting the emoluments of that position had been exaggerated, he resigned and returned to his profession.

Throughout the Secession agitation and the war which followed, Judge Sharkey remained a steadfast unionist. In 1865 he was appointed by President Johnson to be Provisional Governor of the State. The manner in which the duties of this anomalous position were performed is too fresh in the memory of the public to require any notice here. On the organization of the State Government upon Mr. Johnson's plan, Judge Sharkey was elected to the United States Senate ; but, with all the other Senators and Representatives of the Seceded States at that time, he was refused a seat.

Without attempting even the slightest critical examination of Judge Sharkey's career on the bench, or of that system of State

Jurisprudence to the development and preservation of which his labors and his integrity have contributed so much, we may observe in passing, that, although he is conceded by all to be a jurist of profound attainments in the technical erudition of legal science, he is believed to be less remarkable in this respect than for those peculiar native powers which have adapted comparatively but few judges to the task of applying and of limiting the application of the ancient maxims and principles of the common law to American ideas and institutions.

If it be true that the grand system of Equity Jurispr dence of England and America is merely the creature of successive generations of chancellors, and that the common law itself is only the perfection of human reason, it may be safely concluded that judicial inquiry has done more for both systems than has ever been done by legislation and by all other temporal influences combined. And whatever value may be attached to the maxim, *Stare Decisis*, it were absurd to suppose that such a result could have followed a rigid adherence by the courts, in all cases, to established precedent. In the history of civilization, those men who have been long recognized by their contemporaries as the leaders of parties, were never so great as those who have been recognized as the founders of parties; and, in like manner, may it not be said, in reflecting upon the history of a refined and exalted system like that of the common law, as it comes down to us hallowed by the experience of many generations in the mother country, and by the more fruitful experience of other generations under the written constitutions of this Republic, that those judges who, not content with merely treading upon the heels of precedent, have themselves become the authors of the best precedents, occupy a higher rank among the benefactors of mankind than any mere followers of precedents? These are not the mere imitators of the wise and the good; but they are themselves the great exemplars, whom the wise and the good delight to imitate. Their acts are the precedents themselves, which grow brighter with receding years; and to them the advocate of the oppressed shall turn in ages to come and find encouragement and strength in the struggle for the right. It is upon this foundation that must forever rest the pure fame of a Hardwicke and a Mansfield. And upon it, with still more commanding consequences to those respectively concerned, must rest the claims of such men as John Marshall and WILLIAM L. SHARKEY.

PREFACE.

By an Act of the Mississippi Legislature, approved February 24, 1854, the Attorney General was "authorized to report anew the decisions in criminal cases," contained in these twenty-five volumes of Mississippi Reports. When the compiler of the present volumes succeeded to the office of Attorney General, in the winter of 1869–'70, the work so authorized had not yet appeared. He was informed that Mr. Attorney General Glenn had, in his life-time, commenced it ; but the result of his labors had been lost then, and it was not known, even by the most intimate friends of that distinguished gentleman, to what extent it had progressed. In the meantime the number of the volumes of the current series of the decisions of the appellate court, from which the criminal cases for the compilation were to be taken, had increased from twenty-five to forty-three. Recognizing the increased demand for the work, the legislature passed "An Act to authorize a compilation of criminal laws," approved July 17, 1870, the provisions of which are in all respects similar to the first, except that the cases to be reported anew are the cases "contained in all the volumes of Mississippi Reports, or such and so many of said decisions, as the Attorney General shall deem of sufficient importance," etc.

It is under the authority of the act last mentioned that these two volumes of "Mississippi State Cases" are presented to the profession. The two volumes contain in a condensed and convenient form for reference and use, all the criminal cases of value ever reported, from the first term of the Supreme Court, in June, 1818, to the October term, 1871.

It will, of course, be very apparent that the current of decisions in this state, during the last fifty-three years, has not been exempt from the mutations, and even contradictions, which have always marked the affairs of men, and prove the infirmity of man's purest purposes and highest attainments. But it is humbly submitted that such *a variety* of rulings upon given questions as are to be found in the adjudications of any one court in a period of over half a century, instead of militating against them as authority, really enhance their value. The *overruled* cases are frequently found by subsequent reflection, criticism and experience, to be more in accordance with authority, reason and justice, than are the cases by which a new doctrine has been introduced.

Though the decisions here presented are those of a single state only, the compiler ventures to hope that they will be found to possess a general value to the profession in all the states. The common law is the same everywhere, and, so far as felonies are concerned, the judicial and statutory modifications of the common law have been strikingly similar in all the states.

The PRECEDENTS FOR PLEADINGS IN CRIMINAL CASES, and for ENTRIES in making up RECORDS in criminal proceedings, which are appended to the second volume, have been compiled with care, and it is hoped will be found convenient to prosecuting officers, to the clerks of courts of criminal jurisdiction, and to the profession generally. The forms of Indictments and Pleas inserted have been taken in most instances, in substance at least, from the latest edition of Mr. Wharton's valuable work on that subject, sustained, as I believe they are, by the older standards of English and American practice.

The matter of these two volumes has been prepared amidst severe personal affliction, and a constant routine of official and professional engagements. Under these circumstances he has pleasure in acknowledging his obligations to Mr. Wm. T. Deason, a law-student in the compiler's office, whose ambition, industry and fine natural talents have been of great value in the compilation.

JACKSON, MISS., *February*, 1873.

TABLE OF CASES.

(ix)

MISSISSIPPI STATE CASES.

The State *v.* Blennerhassett, et al., Walk. Miss. Rep., 7.

Assault and Battery.

A prosecutor in an indictment for an assault and battery, with intent to murder, who has commenced a civil suit for the injury, will not be compelled to elect or abandon the civil suit, or the prosecution; but both may be sustained, the first for damages to the injured individual, the second to avenge the public wrong.

A prosecutor in an indictment is a competent witness for the state upon the trial, though liable for costs if the prosecution be frivolous or malicious.

Defendants separately indicted for the same assault and battery, may be tried jointly, although they may have claimed the right to be tried separately.[1]

Where two defendants are tried together on indictments for the same assault and battery, one of the defendants is not a good witness for the other upon the trial, unless no proof of guilt is offered against the defendant proposed as a witness.[2]

The voluntary withdrawal, during the trial, of a witness subpoenaed, but not examined on behalf of the state, is not sufficient ground to grant a new trial, especially where his testimony is not shown to be material for the defendant.

Where the jury assess a fine, the court will not grant a new trial, unless the amount of the fine is so excessive as to evince partiality or corruption in the jury.

THE defendants were separately indicted, at the March term, 1818, of the Claiborne Superior Court, for an assault and battery, with an intent to murder one John Hays, on the 4th of February, 1818. In each indictment there was also a separate and distinct count for a simple assault and battery. Upon the affidavit of the defendants that they did not believe they could have a fair and impartial trial in Claiborne county, by the reason

[1] 1 Term Rep., 163; 5 Johns., 256; 1 ib., 490; 4 Term, 17. [2] 4 Johns., 296.

of the exertions of John Hays, the prosecutor, to influence and excite the public mind against them, of the prejudices of many men of weight and influence, and of the malice and ill-will of the sheriff of the county against the defendants, the indictments were transferred to Jefferson county, to be tried by a jury of that county. The defendants were tried jointly upon their several pleas of not guilty, although they claimed the right to be tried separately; and were both found guilty by the jury, and a fine of eight hundred dollars assessed against Harman Blennerhassett and of two hundred dollars against Dominic. The defendants moved the court for a new trial, and assigned the following reasons, viz:

1. Because the court ruled the said defendants into a trial of the indictments found against them in the above cases, without compelling the prosecutor, John Hays, who had instituted a civil suit for damages for the same assault and battery, to make his election either to proceed in the civil or criminal cases, but not in both, though an application to that effect was made by defendants' counsel and overruled by the court.

2. Because the court admitted the said John Hays, who is indorsed on the indictments as the prosecutor, and who may be liable for the costs, to be sworn and examined as a witness upon the trial of said indictments, though the counsel for the defendants took and urged an exception against his competency.

3. Because the court ruled the said defendants to be tried jointly and by the same jury, though the indictments were several, and though they claimed and urged by their counsel a right to be tried separately on the several indictments against them.

4. Because the court refused to permit the said Dominic Blennerhassett to be examined as a witness on behalf of the said Harman Blennerhassett who produced the said witness and claimed that he should be examined on his behalf.

5. Because the defendants were surprised at the trial by the absence of Thomas Rogers, a witness summoned on behalf of the state, who was material for them, and who, they believe, was procured to absent himself by the malpractice of the prosecutor, John Hays.

6. The verdict was contrary to law and the evidence.

This motion for a new trial was, by the Superior Court of Claiborne county, referred to the Supreme Court for their decision.

Reed, for the defendant.

It is not denied, that an individual who has sustained an injury, such as the prosecutor in this case is alleged to have received, has a right to call in the public arm to avenge his wrongs; but he ought not to be permitted, at the same time, to pursue the defendant by a civil suit, to recover damages for the same injury. Neither reason, policy, nor authority will sanction such a proceeding. If an individual be permitted to carry on a public prosecution and a civil suit, against the same defendant for the same offense, and be also permitted to testify in behalf of the state in the public prosecution, will not the testimony which he shall then give, disguised and disfigured by his real or imaginary sense of injury, have a tendency to operate greatly to the prejudice of the defendants on the trial of the civil suit? If the court tolerate a proceeding of this kind, they will afford but too much scope and too much encouragement for the exercise of malignant and vindictive passions. No man ought to be twice punished for the same offense; and although it may be said that the fine in the public prosecution is a punishment for a breach of the peace, and for the violation of the majesty of the laws, and that the verdict in the civil suit is a remuneration to the prosecutor for the injury which he has sustained; yet, both are in fact punishments upon the defendant, and he has in truth committed but one offense. The case of Rex v. Fielding, 2 Bur., 719–20, goes strongly to support the doctrine contended for. The court refused to grant an information against the defendant, a justice of the peace, for malpractice in office, until the prosecutor would discontinue a civil suit which he had instituted for the same offense. And the court then observe, that if the prosecution had been commenced in a manner strictly legal, by indictment, the attorney general would, and ought, to enter a *nolle prosequi* upon the indictment, unless the prosecutor would enter a discontinuance of the civil suit. In the case of State v. Blythe, 1 Bay, 166–7, the court declare it to be the settled practice in South Carolina to compel the prosecutor to make his election. That was an assault and battery. In Rex v. Storrs, 3 Bur., 1702, the attorney general admits that it is the practice in assault and battery, etc., for the prosecutor to elect whether he will proceed by indictment or civil suit. In the case of the Territory of Mississippi v. Peper, Judge Simpson decided that the prosecutor must make his election. I think, therefore, that in our first point we are fortified both by reason and authority.

2. If the prosecutor were absolutely liable for costs upon failure of the prosecution, he would unquestionably be an incompetent witness. A liability to pay costs goes to the competency, and not to the credibility of a witness. Hence a *prochein ami*, by whom an infant sues, cannot be a witness for the infant, nor the bail for his principal, because, being liable for costs, he is interested. 2 Stra., 1026. He has a direct interest in the event of the suit. 1 Term R., 164; 2 Esp. N. P., 347, 703; 1 Bin., 444. By our statute, it is made the duty of the attorney general, to indorse the name of the prosecutor upon all bills of indictment; and if the government fails in the prosecution, and it appears to be frivolous or malicious, it is the duty of the court to render a judgment for costs against the prosecutor. Dig., 237. It is a general rule, that he who is to be the gainer or loser by the event of a suit cannot be a witness. 2 Haw., 610; 2 Hale, 279, 280; 1 Hale P. C., 302-3. And that which exempts a witness from a charge or loss which he may incur on the event of the suit, is as much an interest, as the prospect of positive advantage. 2 Esp. N. P., 347, 703. In this case the prosecutor may, upon a conviction of the defendant, avoid the payment of costs, which he might incur by failure of the prosecution; he is, therefore, directly interested, and his interest renders him an incompetent witness.

3. In this case the attorney general might have indicted the defendants jointly. Had he done so, the court, in their discretion, might, perhaps, have directed them to be tried together; but as he has caused several indictments to be found against them, they are entitled to separate trials. No case, it is believed, can be produced, in which two defendants who have been seve-

rally charged in distinct indictments, have been compelled, against their will and consent, to unite in their trial. By our constitution, every man accused of a crime or misdemeanor, is entitled to a speedy and public trial, by an impartial jury of his country. Although in this case, the right to challenge any number of jurors peremptorily does not exist, the offense not being capital, yet each defendant might challenge any number of jurors against whom he could show good cause of challenge. If one defendant show good cause of challenge against a juror, to whom the other defendant has no legal objection, and in whom he has the utmost confidence, what course would the court pursue? They must deprive one of the defendants of that fair and impartial trial secured to him by the constitution. If the challenge be disregarded, the challenger is tried by a juror who is not impartial; and if it be allowed, the other defendant is deprived of a juror in whose uprightness and integrity he has great confidence, and to whose services as a juror he had an unquestionable right from the moment that the name of the juror was entered on the panel, and he was called to be sworn. Where several individuals are indicted for a joint offense, either a joint or several *venire facias* issues, but it is not the preferable mode to issue a several one. 2 Hale P. C., 173, 263; 2 Haw., 407; Trials *Per Pais*, 46, 47. By ruling the defendants to be tried jointly, one defendant was deprived of the testimony of the other on his trial. If it can be shown, that one of these defendants would have been a competent witness for the other, if they had been tried separately, and that this right was denied them upon a joint trial, it would seem to follow as a legal deduction, that the court erred in compelling them to be tried together, and, therefore, a new trial ought to be granted.

4. No good reason can be assigned why an accomplice, who is indicted separately, shall not, before conviction, be a witness for his associate. He is not interested in the event of the trial; the judgment of acquittal or conviction of his associate could not be given in evidence for or against him on the trial, and he is not rendered infamous until after conviction. Why, then, should his testimony be rejected? His credibility may be impeached from the circumstances of his being an accomplice, but

his competency cannot be denied.   An accessory before or after the fact may be a witness, for or against the principal felon, unless tried with him by the same jury, which he is not bound to submit to, if they were indicted separately.   If three persons be separately indicted for perjury in swearing falsely to the execution of a bond, and one traverse the indictment and be put on his trial, the other two may be witnesses for him.   If two persons be severally indicted for the same assault and battery, they may be witnesses for each other.   Foster, 360 ; 2 Esp. N. P., 393, 726 ; 2 Hale P. C., 280 ; 2 Haw., 620 ; McNal., 204 ; Peake Ev., 144 ; 1 Term, 301 ; 1 Wash., 187.

5. It appears from the affidavit of the defendants that the testimony of Thomas Rogers was material for them, of which they were deprived without any fault in themselves.   Rogers had been summoned by the state, and had been attending during the trial, but left the court without the knowledge of defendants, before the testimony on behalf of the state was closed, and before the defendants could call upon him to testify.   The defendants knowing he had been summoned by the state, and seeing him in attendance upon the court during the trial, could not deem it necessary for them to summon, and were, therefore, taken by surprise when they discovered that he had left the court.   Surprise is a good ground for granting a new trial.   If the absence of Rogers was procured by the prosecutor, it is such a fraud upon the defendants that the court will grant a new trial.   6 Bac. Abr. 671–2.

6. If the court are satisfied that the verdict is against law or evidence, or that justice has not been done the defendants, they will not hesitate to grant a new trial.   1 Bur. 390 ; 3 Black. Com. 387.   If death in this case had ensued, the defendants would, at most, have been guilty of manslaughter only.   In that case the defendants could not have been mulct in a larger sum than five hundred dollars.   Dig. 244.   And the jury in this case having assessed a fine against Harman Blennerhassett of eight hundred dollars, affords very good reason for the conclusion, that the verdict is so unjust, and the fine so unreasonable, that the court willl grant a new trial.

Harding, attorney general.

1. It is important to every government that all breaches of its penal laws should be punished.   It would be better not to enact laws, than to permit them, when enacted, to be violated with impunity.   This is a much more penal offense than a simple assault and battery.   It was attended with circumstances of peculiar aggravation and atrocity.   The prosecutor was very severely wounded, and it was little less than a miracle that he escaped with his life.   Can it be seriously contended that the government ought to wink at offenses of this kind, because the prosecutor is seeking a pecuniary remuneration for the atrocious injury which he has sustained?   Should such be the decision of the court, there will be no longer any security for life or liberty; the government and laws will justly fall into contempt, and become a "laughing stock, and a bye-word among the people." The prosecution is not carried on for the benefit of the prosecutor alone; the whole community are deeply interested in it. It is important for them that offenders, like the present defendants, should be severely punished, that others of similar dispositions may be deterred from committing the like outrages.   The prosecutor cannot be deprived of his action for damages.   It is secured and guaranteed to him as well by the principles of eternal justice, as by the express provisions of the constitution. 3 Black. Com. 121; 4 ib. 156; 3 Bac. Ab. 156, Ass't and Bat. D.

The cases cited by the counsel for the defendants do not support the principles for which they contend.   The case of Rex v. Fielding is very distinguishable from the present.   That was an application to the court for leave to file an information against a magistrate, who had conducted illegally in the execution of his office.   The court was satisfied that the magistrate had acted honestly, that no corrupt or evil intention could be imputed to him, that application was made by the prosecutor from malicious and vindictive motives, and, therefore, in the exercise of a just discretion, they rejected the application, until the prosecutor should discontinue a civil suit which he had instituted for the same misconduct or misdemeanor.   There is no English case, where the prosecution was by indictment, in which the court have required the prosecutor to make his election.   In some cases of a trifling nature, or where the prosecutor appears to be instigated by malice, the attorney general will enter a *nolle prosequi*, unless the prosecutor will discontinue the civil suit.   The case in Bay's Reports cannot be considered as entitled to much weight, when put in competition with several English cases, and a decision of the Supreme Court of Massachusetts expressly in point.   1 Bac. Abr. 245–6; 1 Bos. & Pul. 191; 2 Mass. R. 372.

2. It is generally true in criminal as well as civil cases, that a person who may gain or lose by the event of the suit cannot be admitted as a witness; but in robbery or larceny, where the prosecutor is entitled, upon conviction of the defendant, to a restitution of the goods stolen, and in cases where a reward is offered to the prosecutor, by statute, by proclamation, or by a private person, he is, notwithstanding, a good witness.   Phil. Ev. 86, 91; 1 McNal. 61.   It is not pretended, that the prosecutor in this case is interested in the event of the suit, except that he may be liable for costs, upon certain contingencies, if the state should not succeed in the prosecution.   He is not entitled to any reward, in case the defendants shall be convicted, nor can the verdict and judgment be given in evidence for him in the civil suit.   Should the state fail in the prosecution, he is not liable for costs unless, in the opinion of the court, the prosecution is frivolous or malicious.   His liability then depends upon two contingencies, future and remote.   This is not such a liability as will disqualify him from being a witness, or exclude his testimony.   To render a witness incompetent, his interest must be legal and fixed, not depending on any contingency.   Phil. Ev. 39; Salk. 283; 1 Term R. 163.

3, 4. All offenses are several as it respects the offenders.   If two or more individuals are jointly concerned in the commission of the same offense, the attorney general may, at his pleasure, indict them jointly or separately.   2 Hale's P. C. 173; 2 Haw. 342.   It is not denied by the counsel for the defendants, that they might have been tried together, if they had been jointly indicted.   What good reason can be given, why two persons jointly indicted, may, in the discretion of the court, be tried together when, if they had been charged with the same offense, in separate indictments, they must be separately tried. It is conceived there is none. It is not the circumstance of their being jointly indicted that authorizes the court to put them upon trial together; but that of their being jointly concerned in the commission of the offense. The evidence against the one, goes to disclose the guilt or innocence of the other. No injury can, therefore, result to either of the defendants from a joint trial. But it is said, that by denying the defendants a separate trial they are deprived of the testimony of each other. It is very clear that one defendant cannot be a witness for another, unless there is no evidence given against him; and in that case, when they are tried together, the court will send up an issue for the one against whom no evidence has been given, and upon the return of a verdict of acquittal, his testimony will be received on behalf of the other defendant. 1 McNal. 56; Phil. Ev. 74. Belmore's case is very distinguishable from the present. The perjury of one man is not that of another; and although they may have sworn falsely in regard to the same circumstance, they cannot be joined in the same indictment. As to the other principles relied on by the defendants' counsel on this point, they are the mere *dicta* of McNally and the American editor of Espinass' *Nisi Prius*, not supported by any adjudged cases.

5. It does not appear from the affidavit of defendants that the testimony of Rogers, if it could have been procured, would have been material for their defense. They swear that they could have proved by him, an offer of a compromise or reference with the prosecutor, prior to the assault for which they are indicted, and an assault upon them by the prosecutor, on the morning of the same day on which they committed the assault upon him. These facts, if true, would not be material for their defense, nor could they be legally given in evidence upon the trial; and if they could have been given in evidence, the verdict must have been the same. There is no evidence that the absence of Rogers was procured by the prosecutor, except the belief of the defendants; and the affidavit of Mills goes strongly to show the fallacy and improbability of that belief. The defendants did not summon Rogers; and if they relied upon him, they were guilty of *laches* in this respect. The attorney general is

not bound to keep, till the end of the trial, all the witnesses whom he may have summoned. He may dismiss them when he pleases, and the adverse party will have no cause of complaint.

6. The verdict is neither against the law nor the evidence. The assault was most atrocious and aggravated, and the jury showed their good sense by inflicting a heavy fine upon Harman Blennerhassett.

Per Curiam :

1. The doctrine contended for by the defendants' counsel, that a prosecutor is bound to make his election, and cannot, at the same time, be the prosecutor in an indictment, and the plaintiff in a civil suit, for the same assault and battery, is not recognized by the court. The prosecution is not carried on for the benefit of the prosecutor only ; the whole community is interested in the execution of the criminal laws. Any individual may become the prosecutor in an indictment as well as the injured party. The object of public prosecution is to give force and vigor to the laws, by showing the community that they cannot be violated with impunity ; to reclaim the offender, if possible, by the salutary restraint of punishment, and to secure and protect all the citizens in the enjoyment of their rights and privileges, by deterring the wicked and abandoned, through the fear of punishment, from the perpetration of similar offenses. The public, therefore, cannot be deprived of their right to prosecute for every violation of the penal or criminal laws. Nor can we refuse to the injured individual a remedy for the wrongs which he has received. The government guarantees to all its citizens, security in their lives, liberty and property. If either of these essential rights is violated, the suffering party has a right to call upon the courts of justice to aid him in obtaining remuneration for the injury which he has received. If a public prosecution and a civil suit could not be carried on at the same time, for the same offense, it would be in the power of the injured party to compound any offense. This the law does not authorize.

The only case in point cited by the defendants' counsel is

from Bay's reports. Although that case may be considered of binding authority in South Carolina, yet we do not think it has sufficient weight to overrule or even to counterbalance the cases referred to by counsel for the prosecution, so that upon the score of both reason and authority, we feel ourselves bound to overrule the first reason for a new trial.

2. It is a general rule, that when a person is to be a gainer or loser by the event of a suit, he is not an incompetent witness. But in many cases in criminal prosecutions, an individual is admitted as a witness, although he may be a gainer by the conviction of the defendant, as in robbery, burglary, and larceny, where, upon conviction, there is a restitution of the goods stolen, and in all cases where a reward is given to the informer or prosecutor, upon conviction, whether given by statute, proclamation, or by a private person. In all these cases, and in many others, where the witness may seem to have an interest in the conviction of the defendant, he is, nevertheless, admitted, and his credibility is left to the jury. The courts in modern times, are much more liberal in the admission of witnesses, than they were a century ago. Nothing now renders a witness incompetent but the infamy of his character, or an absolute and direct interest in the event of the suit, or, unless the verdict and judgment in the suit in which he is to testify, can be given in evidence for or against him, in some future trial. The interest of the witness, to exclude his testimony, must be legal and fixed, absolute and direct, not remote and indeterminate, nor depending upon a contingency. Phil. 39; N. Y. Term R. 271. Thus a surety in an administration bond, is a good witness for the administrator in a suit brought against him as such. Term R. 163. A deputy sheriff who has taken a prison bounds bond, is a competent witness for the sheriff in a suit brought against him for an escape. 5 Johns. 256. A person liable to be assessed in the poor rates, may be a witness in settlement cases. 1 Johns. 490; 4 Term 17. So an agent is a witness, though he may by possibility gain or lose by the event of the suit. In these and many other cases, where the liability of the witness is remote or contingent, he is uniformly admitted, and this possibility of interest is considered as going to his credibility, not to his competency.

What interest has the prosecutor in this case? He may be obliged to pay costs if the prosecution fail, and appear to be frivolous or malicious. This liability is too remote, and depends upon too many contingencies, to render him an incompetent witness.

3. On the third point, the court had at first some doubts, but upon reflection, and an examination of the authorities, those doubts were removed. It is very clear that when two or more persons are guilty of the same offense, they may be indicted jointly, and when jointly indicted, may be tried together, although they sever in pleading, unless the court, in their discretion, direct them to be tried separately. The only good reason why two or more, joined in the same indictment, may be tried together, is conceived to be, that their offense is the same, committed at the same time, and the evidence against the one, is equally applicable to the other. These reasons apply equally to several indictments, where the offense is the same, and committed at the same time. Two persons whose offense is not precisely the same, as a principal and accessory, may be tried together, if they are indicted jointly; and it is conceived, that there are stronger reasons for trying two persons together who are guilty of precisely the same offense, although they may be severally indicted. The court have the power in either case to direct a separate trial when the circumstances require it, or injustice would otherwise be done. In this case such necessity does not seem to exist. The defendant cannot, as a matter of right, claim a separate trial, unless, from the nature of the offense, they are entitled to peremptory challenges. 4 Johns. 296, etc. But it is said, that it puts it in the power of the attorney general, to deprive a party of his witnesses. He could as easily do this by indicting them jointly. It is the circumstance of both defendants being indicted for the same offense that excludes the one from giving testimony for the other. It makes no difference, in that respect, whether they are indicted jointly or severally. No inconvenience can, on that account, result to them from a joint trial; for if no evidence be given against the one, the court may direct the jury to inquire first as to him, and upon his acquittal, he may be received as a witness for the other.

The arguments and authorities on this point apply equally to the fourth reason assigned for a new trial.

5. As to the ground of surprise urged by the defendants' counsel, the court do not think it tenable. It is not shown by the defendants' affidavit, that the testimony of Rogers would have been material, and if they considered it so, it was their duty to have summoned him.

There is no evidence that the absence of Rogers was procured by the prosecutor, or by any one concerned in the prosecution, and the affidavit of Mills affords strong reason to believe that it was not the case, but that Rogers withdrew without the knowledge of the prosecutor or of the attorney general.

It is said that the fine against Harman Blennerhassett is excessive. It is the duty of the jury to assess the fine according to the nature and aggravation of the offense. The court will not in such a case interfere and grant a new trial, unless the fine is so excessive as to evince partiality or corruption of the jury. The evidence in this case proves that the offense was highly atrocious and aggravated. The circumstances attending the assault, and the weapons used, leave no doubt of the intention of the defendants. It must ever be a consolation to them, that that intention was not carried into effect. The court do not think the fine so excessive as to demand their interference.

Motion for a new trial overruled and judgment to be executed in Claiborne county. *Turner, Reed* and *Davis* for defendants, —Attorney General, *Harding* and *Rankin* for State.

MOORE *v.* THE STATE, Walk. Miss. Rep., 134.

GRAND LARCENY.

On an indictment for grand larceny, the jury not being able to agree, up to the last moment, when the term of the court ceases by limitation of law, may be discharged without the consent of the accused, and he may be lawfully remanded to jail for trial at the next term of the court.[1]

[1] Price's case, 36 Miss., 531; People v. Olcott, 2 Johns. Cases, 301; 18 Johns. 200; 9 Mass., 494; 12 ib., 313; 8 Day, 504; 2 Caine, 100; 2 Johns. Cases, 275; 9

Even in capital cases, when a striking necessity exists, the jury may be discharged. The clause in the constitution of the United States, "Nor shall any one be subject for the same offense to be twice put in jeopardy of life or limb," is binding in the courts of the States, as well as of the United States. Under this clause in the constitution, the prisoner is not put in jeopardy till after verdict.

ELLIS, J. :

From the record in this case it appears, that at the last term of the circuit court of Adams county, the following order was spread upon the minutes : " At twelve o'clock on Saturday night, the last day of the term, the jury in the prosecution not having agreed upon their verdict, were discharged by the court, without the consent and against the wish of the prisoner, and the prisoner is forthwith ordered to be remanded to the prison of Adams county." The first authority upon the question, now submitted for the consideration of the court, is to be found in Coke on Littleton, sec. 366, letter (F), where the principle is laid down in broad terms :

" A jury sworn and charged in case of life or member, cannot be discharged by the court or any other, but they ought to give a verdict."

The same doctrine is to be found in 3 Institutes, 110, where Lord Coke says : " To speak it here once for all, if any person be indicted of treason or of felony, or of larceny, and plead not guilty, and thereupon a jury is returned, and sworn, their verdict must be heard, and they cannot be discharged, neither can the jurors in those cases give a privy verdict ; but, ought to give their verdict openly in court." It seems to have been admitted at bar in the argument, that the only case referred to by Lord Coke to support the rule he laid down, had no applicability, for it was the case of an approver to be found in the year books during the reign of Edward III. in which it was adjudged, " that a person indicted for larceny, and who had pleaded not guilty, and put himself upon his country, should not afterwards, when the jury was in court, be admitted to become an approver, because by solemnly denying the fact by his plea, he had lost all credit, and ought not to be received as a witness against others." Sergeant Hawkins and Mr. Justice Blackstone adopted

Wheat., 580 ; 13 Wend., 56 ; 2 Pick., 521 ; 2 Scam., 396 ; 2 Sumner, 19 ; 2 McLean, 114 ; 4 Wash. C. C. R., 409 ; Whar. Am. Cr. L., 205–218 ; 1 Archb. Cr. Pl., 171–173.

the rule in the Institutes, and refer to those books as authority. I find, from an examination of the case of the two Kinlocks, Foster, 27, the judges did not consider the resolution as reported in Carthew, entitled to much respect, as there was no authentic report of the case. So far as we have been able to understand this case as reported by Chief Justice Eyre, Holt is reported to have said : " I have had occasion to consider of this matter. In criminal cases a juror cannot be withdrawn but by consent. And in capital cases it cannot be done even with consent." It is evident the learned judge did not intend to lay down a general rule upon this subject; but, to prevent the exercise of an unreasonable and oppressive claim on the part of the prosecutor, who, it seems, after the jury had been charged with the deliverance of the accused, found his evidence insufficient to produce a conviction, prayed to have a juror withdrawn, and the case to be continued, until such time as he might be prepared with his testimony. An application so unprecedented, even in those days, could not fail to strike the court as unwarranted by precedent and principle, and contrary to the known and established rights of every subject of the realm. Subsequent to the resolution reported in Carthew, many cases can be found where the courts have discharged juries where the crown was not prepared with its testimony. This was done in the case of Whitebread and Fearnwick, reported in the state trials, and deemed by all humane and enlightened judges of the present day, an arbitrary and unjustifiable exercise of discretionary power. Mr. Justice Foster, in his able and elaborate review of all the authorities in the case of the Kinlocks, does not deny the general position, that a jury can be discharged under particular circumstances, when he says: " It seems that an opinion did once prevail, that a jury once sworn and charged in any criminal case whatsoever, could not be discharged without giving a verdict ;" but he says this opinion is exploded in Ferrars' case, and it is there called a common tradition, which had been held by many learned in the law.

An information was exhibited against Ferrars for forgery, and it was resolved by all the justices, that although the jury be charged and sworn in the case of a plea of the crown, yet a

juror may be drawn, or the jury dismissed, contrary to common
tradition, which hath been held by many learned in the law.
Sir Thos. Ray, 84. From this view of the old authorities, without resorting to the numerous cases in Kelyng's, it will be admitted, the court has the power of discharging juries in capital
cases under circumstances of great necessity. What circumstances of necessity will be considered as sufficient to warrant
our interposition in the exercise of high discretionary powers in
such cases, is a matter of great doubt and delicacy. I am fully
persuaded it will be difficult and dangerous to establish any
general rule upon this subject, therefore we shall confine ourselves to the record before us, and not hazard the establishment
of a precedent which may in its operation turn loose the murderer upon society, or sacrifice the innocent to the inflexibility
of its principles.

It was urged with considerable force and ability that the defendant is entitled to his discharge, because the jury separated
contrary to his consent, before they agreed on their verdict; and
secondly, the fact of their not being able to agree, raises such a
presumption in favor of his innocence, as ought to be tantamount
to an acquittal. These positions cannot be sustained without
incurring all the evils resulting from a general rule, hence we
have thought it prudent to confine ourselves to the particular
circumstances of this case. So far as the American authorities
touch this case, I think there can be no doubt as to the result of
our conclusion. In the case of the Commonwealth v. Bowden, 9
Massachusetts Reports, the court was clearly of opinion, that a
juror could be withdrawn in a case of felony without operating
as an acquittal; but I believe the exercise of discretionary
power in that case, uncontrolled by any circumstance of absolute or inevitable necessity, extended the doctrine too far.
The court declares " the ancient strictness of the common law
upon this subject, has very much abated in the English courts;
nor would it be consistent with the genius of our government
or laws, to use compulsory means to effect an agreement among
jurors. The practice of withdrawing a juror, where there existed no prospect of a verdict, has frequently been adopted at
criminal trials in this court, and the exception taken in this

case cannot prevail." The same doctrine was held in the case of the Commonwealth v. Wood & Sherborn, on an indictment for larceny. The case of the People v. Olcate, ruled by Mr. Justice Kent, in 2 Johnson's Cases, is very full upon the subject, which extends not only to misdemeanors, but capital cases. He says, "With respect to misdemeanors, we may with perfect safety and propriety adopt the language of Sir M. Foster, 27, which he, however, applies to capital crimes, that it is impossible to fix upon any single rule which can be made to govern the infinite variety of cases that may come under the general question touching the power of the court to discharge juries sworn and charged in criminal cases, which evidently implies, if the court is satisfied the jury have made long and unsuccessful efforts to render a verdict, and in all human probability there be but little prospect of their agreeing, every principle of humanity and public justice would seem to require they should be delivered of their charge, and the prisoner remanded. I believe there is not a single case to be found in the books, where the court is precluded from the exercise of a discretionary power in discharging the jury, if the prisoner should put himself upon the country in a fit of insanity—so in the case of the jury becoming intoxicated —so if one of the jurors fall down in a fit of apoplexy—so if one of the jurors be mentally diseased, or incurably prejudiced against the accused—so if the jury be separated and dispersed by any force—and so, also, if the judge be incapacitated from presiding over the trial; in all these cases, I presume it will not be pretended, the prisoner would go without day. If such a doctrine be established, and declared to be the law of the land, the ends of justice would be defeated, and the most abandoned and depraved villains would be virtually licensed in the commission of the most unparalleled atrocities. Every principle of public policy and expediency protests against such a state of things, and I think the corrective must, from the very nature of things rest in the breast of the court, in the exercise of a sound discretion, controlled by the case cited, for the protection of the prisoner, from unreasonable and oppressive prosecutions." The defendant's counsel relied much upon the 5th article of the amendment to the constitution of the United States, which contains the following provision : " Nor shall any person be subject, for the same offense, to be twice put in jeopardy of life or limb." I must confess, this amendment to the constitution of the United States created the only doubt I have ever entertained upon this important question. It was properly admitted in argument, that this provision of the constitution was binding in the United States, as well as the state courts of the Union, for I take it, it has never been questioned, but that the constitution of the United States is the paramount law of the land, any law, usage, or custom of the several states to the contrary notwithstanding. What was intended by the framers of the constitution, when they declared, " Nor shall any person be twice put in jeopardy of life or limb for the same offense ?" Chief Justice Spencer, in the case of the People v. Goodwin, 18 Johnson, gives a very learned and able opinion upon the subject, and shows what must have been the intention of those who framed this article. But it is asked, Why insert a provision in the constitution for the protection of the citizen, which had been repeatedly and unequivocally recognized by the whole current of English authorities ? This question will be satisfactorily answered by a recurrence to the history of the times, not very long after the establishment of our independence, when every State, and every individual in the community were jealous of their rights and liberties—privileges which they had rescued at the hazard of their lives and fortunes, from the throes of the revolution, and secured by a solemn recognition in the charter of their political freedom. They did not wish to leave anything in doubt, when they looked back with horror and indignation upon the judicial despotism of a Jeffries. The prisoner was in jeopardy from the very moment the jury was empanelled to try him. I cannot persuade myself that such is the fair construction to be given to the amendment. The forms prescribed by law to ascertain the guilt or innocence of the accused, cannot properly be considered that kind of jeopardy contemplated by the constitution of the United States ; but, the means used by courts of law in attaching the jeopardy, which can never take place until after the rendition of the verdict by the jury charged with the deliverance of the accused. Such I conceive to be the construction which ought to be placed upon this word.   A prisoner must in all cases answer to his offense before he can be considered in jeopardy.

And will it be contended, if any one of the facts necessary to constitute the whole of an answer be wanting, that the others will be sufficient in contemplation of law ?   But we are met by this objection—suppose the court place it out of the power of the prisoner to answer, by discharging the jury,—then I will answer and say, if the discharge has taken place unadvisedly, the cases controlling the undue exercises of such a power will protect him, and the court will in all such cases be compelled to consider his answer as full and perfect, upon a plea of *autrefois acquit*. How stands the case here ?   The defendant Moore was arraigned, and he pleaded not guilty, and put himself upon the country for trial, and a jury was regularly charged with his deliverance.

After hearing the evidence and counsel on both sides, the jury retired to consider of their verdict, and not being able to agree, they were discharged at the very last moment of the term, when the powers of the court and jurors ceased. Was this the exercise of a discretionary power, used for the purpose of oppressing the prisoner ? Certainly not.   It was a case of inevitable necessity, which grew out of the operation of the law, known to the prisoner, and over which the court could have no control. I cannot distinguish this case, of inability in the jury to act, from those I have already mentioned, where the jury, either from intoxication, or if they be bodily or mentally diseased, are incapacitated from the discharge of their duties.   The case of Cooke et al., cited from Pennsylvania, does not deny the power of the court, under imperious cases of necessity, to discharge the jury. Chief Justice Tilghman, in giving his opinion, said it was the duty of the justices who tried the case to receive separate verdicts, although the jury could not agree as to the other.   There was no facts on the records to show which of the parties were entitled to the verdict the jury were ready to give in, therefore, the learned judge correctly observed, he would not jeopardize the lives of innocent men, who had a right to claim their verdict, on the trial below, more especially as it did not appear to the court there was an absolute necessity of discharging the jury at the time they separated.   He observes, when speaking of Goodwin's case, "This argument, it must be confessed, reached to all cases of felony, but still he prudently confined his opinion to the case before the court, in which there was an ingredient of some weight, not found in any other case, and that was, that the time of the court sitting was to expire in half an hour, and there was a moral certainty the jury would not agree in so short a time." The case decided by Mr. Justice Story, 2 Gallison, 364, lays down the position: the courts have the power of discharging juries under striking circumstances of necessity.

We are of opinion the judge acted in conformity with the well-established principles of the law, in discharging the jury, and remanding the prisoner to take his trial at the next term.

BRADLEY *v.* THE STATE, Walk. Miss. Rep., 156.

ASSAULT AND BATTERY.

Although, at common law, a husband has the right to chastise his wife, he may still be convicted of an assault and battery upon her.

ELLIS, J. :

This case was tried in the circuit court before the Honorable Judge Turner, at the April term, 1824. The defendant was indicted for a common assault and battery, and upon his arraignment, pleaded not guilty, *son assault demesne,* and that Lydia Bradley was his lawful wife, etc. Issue was taken upon all the pleas. After the evidence was submitted, and before the jury retired, the counsel for the defendant moved the court to instruct the jury, "If they believed the person named in the bill of indictment, and upon whom the assault and battery was committed, was the wife of the defendant, at the time of the assault and battery,—that then and in such case they could not find the defendant guilty." The court refused to give the instructions prayed for by the defendant, and charged the jury that a husband could commit an assault and battery on the body of his wife, to which opinion of the court a bill of exceptions was filed, and the case comes up by writ of error upon petition.

The only question submitted for the consideration of the court is, whether a husband can commit an assault and battery upon the body of his wife. This, as an abstract proposition, will not admit of doubt. But I am fully persuaded, from the examination I have made, an unlimited license of this kind cannot be sanctioned, either upon principles of law or humanity. It is true, according to the old law, the husband might give his wife moderate correction, because he is answerable for her misbehavior; hence it was thought reasonable to intrust him with a power, necessary to restrain the indiscretion of one for whose conduct he was to be made responsible. Strange, 478, 875, 1 H. P. C. 130. Sir William Blackstone says, "during the reign of Charles the First, this power was much doubted,——notwithstanding the lower orders of people still claimed and exercised it as an inherent privilege, which could not be abandoned without entrenching upon their rightful authority, known and acknowledged from the earliest periods of the common law down to the present day. I believe it was in a case before Mr. Justice Raymond, where the same doctrine was recognized, with proper limitations and restrictions well suited to the condition and feelings of those who might think proper to use a whip or rattan, no bigger than my thumb, in order to enforce the salutary restraints of domestic discipline." I think his lordship might have narrowed down the rule in such a manner as to restrain the exercise of the right within the compass of great moderation without producing a destruction of the principle itself. If the defendant now before us could show, from the record in this case, he confined himself within reasonable bounds when he thought proper to chastise his wife, we would deliberate long before an affirmance of the judgment.

The indictment charges the defendant with having made an assault upon one Lydia Bradley, and then and there did beat, bruise, etc.—and the jury have found the defendant guilty, which never could have taken place, if the evidence supporte either the second or third pleas of the accused. It was necessary for the defendant below to introduce his second third pleas, as we think he could have made a full and defence, upon the same matter, under the plea of the issue. However abhorent to the feelings of every member of the bench, must be the exercise of this remnant of feudal authority, to inflict pain and suffering, when all the finer feelings of the heart should be warmed into devotion, by our most affectionate regards, yet every principle of public policy and expediency, in reference to the domestic relations, would seem to require the establishment of the rule we have laid down, in order to prevent the deplorable spectacle of the exhibition of similar cases in our courts of justice. Family broils and dissensions cannot be investigated before the tribunals of the country, without casting a shade over the character of those who are unfortunately engaged in the controversy. To screen from public reproach those who may be thus unhappily situated, let the husband be permitted to exercise the right of moderate chastisement, in cases of great emergency, and use salutary restraints in every case of misbehavior, without being subjected to vexatious prosecutions, resulting in the mutual discredit and shame of all parties concerned.

Judgment affirmed.

THE STATE *v.* McGRAW, Walk. Miss. Rep., 208.

An indictment for stealing a negro man not called a slave is insufficient. A trial and acquittal on an indictment for stealing a negro *man*, is no bar to a subsequent prosecution for stealing a negroman, *slave*. A conviction or acquittal, or an invalid indictment, is no bar to a second prosecution.

TURNER, J.:

It appears by the record, that at the October Term, 1823, of Pike circuit court, the defendant was indicted for stealing a negro man, on which charge he was tried on the plea of not guilty, and acquitted. At the same time he was also indicted for stealing one negro man, *slave*, named Emanuel, etc., of the goods and chattels of one William B. Heath, etc. On his arraignment, he pleaded a former acquittal for the same offense, to which the state replied *nul tiel* record of a former acquittal; and the court doubting the law, referred the case to this court, on the issue of *nul tiel* record.

It appears by the record that the district attorney appeared to enter a *nolle prosequi* on the first indictment, and informed the prisoner and his counsel, that he considered that indictment invalid, and had preferred another, and submitted to them, whether they would risk a trial on the first indictment—whereupon the prisoner and his counsel would not move to quash the first indictment, but claimed a trial by jury. A trial was had, and verdict for the defendant.

I am of opinion that the first indictment was insufficient to warrant a conviction, and on which no sentence could have been passed against the prisoner. It charges the prisoner with having stolen a negro man, nowhere called a slave in the whole indictment; and it is obvious that the attorney of the state aimed at an indictment under the statute, for stealing a slave. The authorities summed up in the first volume of Chitty's Criminal Law, p. 453, etc., show clearly, that a conviction or acquittal on an invalid indictment, cannot be pleaded in lieu of a second, on subsequent prosecution. Wherefore, let judgment be entered for the state, on the issue joined on the plea of *autrefois acquit;* and it is ordered that the cause be remanded for further proceedings in the circuit court of said county of Pike.

THE STATE *v.* DOTY, Walk. Miss. Rep., 230.

The judge of the criminal court may re-examine the causes of commitment, and remand or discharge the prisoner, according to his own belief of his innocence or guilt.

CHILD, J. :

I have looked into the papers in this case, referred to the supreme court for its decision, on doubts of the judge of the criminal court.

It was discretionary with that court, sitting as a re-examining magistrate, to have inquired into the causes of the arrest and detention of the prisoner, and either to have discharged or remanded to custody, as the existence or absence of the evidence of guilt might determine his own judgment.

The arrest appears to have been founded on an affidavit of one Henry Earl, which does not even charge the commission of any act made criminal by our laws, unsupported by other evidence ; and I see no regular *mittimus* to the jailor authorizing the detention of the prisoner.

The bare naked suspicions of two magistrates, on the charge of vagrancy, unsupported by other testimony, ought not to weigh a moment with the court, to deprive a citizen of his liberty, who stands free of other criminal charges. I have been utterly unable to ascertain how a constitutional question can arise in this case, either directly, incidentally, or collaterally ; and should have had no hesitation in discharging the prisoner, if the case was legitimately before the court.

The statute establishing the criminal court, gives to the judge the power of reference on doubt, only in case of the consent of the accused. In this case, the consent of the accused does not appear of record, and the case must, therefore, be remanded to the criminal court for further proceedings.

Cause remanded.

THE STATE *v.* FLOWER, Walk. Miss. Rep., 318.

HOMICIDE.

A juror cannot be asked, either by the State or the accused, whether he has formed or expressed an opinion as to the guilt or innocence of the prisoner before he is challenged.

A hypothetical opinion, or one formed upon rumor, subject to be changed by the evidence on the trial, does not disqualify a person from serving as juror in the case.

E. & F. Huston, for defendant.

Gaines, attorney general.

TURNER. C. J.:

All the errors assigned in this case, except one, are deemed unsustainable, and, indeed, were not relied on by the counsel of the plaintiff in error in their second argument. The error mostly relied on by them, is presented in the following part of

the bill of exceptions, to wit : " That on the trial of said indictment, S. D. Roberts was called, and tendered by the state, to
the prisoner, as a juror, and the prisoner requested the said
Roberts to be sworn to answer questions.   The court then asked
the said Roberts whether he had formed and expressed an opinion as to the guilt or innocence of the prisoner ?   And he answered that he had.   The court then asked him whether he had
formed this opinion from rumor or from statements of the witnesses ?   He stated that his opinion was formed from common
report.   The court then asked him if he had formed an opinion
as to the truth of said report ?   He said he had not, and stated
that, if the evidence turned out as it had been represented to
him, he thought the prisoner guilty.   The court then permitted
the said Roberts to be sworn in chief, to which opinion the
counsel for the defendant excepts."

The first thing which strikes my mind, on reading this exception, is that the court allowed the juror to be sworn to answer
questions *before he was challenged.*   It is a settled rule that
neither party has a right to *interrogate* a juror before he is
challenged.

The form of doing this is laid down in 1 Chitty's Crim. Law,
p. 546 ; and in Burr's trial, the chief justice said, " Unless the
challenge is made, it will be improper to draw out any expression from the juror ;" and further, " that the court must undoubtedly direct the same mode of challenge on the part of the
U. S. as on the part of the prisoner."   Pages 70, 71 and 72 of
Vol. 2, by Carpenter.

But, as the court below treated this as a challenge, we will
waive the informality, and proceed to consider the substance of
the matter as if the challenge had been made by the prisoner.

Both the American and the English law declare that the
accused shall have an *impartial* trial ; that " the jurors shall
stand indifferent as they stand unsworn."   It is certainly desir-
able that the accused have a jury composed of men wholly free
from prejudice or bias for or against him.

How this matter really is, in practice, we all know, who know
anything of trials and prosecutions for public offenses in our
country.   The accused must be tried in the county where the

offence is alleged to have been committed ; he is entitled to a
jury of the vicinage where a crime is committed, and more
especially where one is accused thereof.   When arrested and taken
before the examining magistrate, whether the accused be bound
over to court or discharged, the affair excites public attention ;
the people take an interest in the case ; they cannot help listening to reports, and will indulge in conversation about the case ;
and, in our free country, they will express opinions among each
other.   They think they have a constitutional right to do so ;
and men often express opinions, in such cases, on hearing one
story, and change them on hearing another story ; and finally,
after having formed and expressed opinions pro and con, when
they come to court, witness the trial, hear the evidence, the
arguments of the counsel and the opinion of the judge, they will
forget or abandon their preconceived opinions, and decide impartially between the accused and the state.   Men are more
likely to act thus in our country than in England, where the
judges declare it a *misdemeanor* for a man to prejudge another's
cause.

Hence, some decisions, recited in Hawkins and repeated in
more modern days, that the formation of such loose, out-of-door
opinions, will not disqualify, unless they are formed *maliciously;*
and hence the remarks of Ch. J. Marshall as reported in Burrr's
trial : " This general principle of law is, that a juror whose
mind is prepared to go upon the case to receive his convictions
of the guilt or innocence of the accused from the testimony, and
that only, is the only proper person to be called an *impartial*
juror.   But, a different character, the law cannot trust.   It ap-
prehends danger from the result, and therefore declares him not
to be fit to stand between the accused and the country.   This is
the general view which the courts have had with respect to
qualification, that where a man has formed and expressed an
opinion upon the case itself, upon a view of the whole case, he
is not esteemed an impartial juror ; but where a man has formed
an opinion upon only part of a case, from testimony, such as he
has seen or heard, or when the impression made is extremely
slight, it merits a different treatment.   The court has not said,
nor will it say, that slight impressions should disqualify," etc.,

p. 63, 4. Again, in p. 66, the Ch. Justice said, " Now here is one of these jurors who has said, that if the public mind was true, the prisoner was guilty. Now the court thought this man a good juror, because he had left his mind open to conviction," etc., and he draws a distinction between an *active* and a *passive* opinion. The one excludes; the other does not.

Hence, also, in England, the court will not allow the juror to be asked whether or not he has formed and expressed an opinion, but if the prisoner challenges on the ground, he must adduce his proofs to the court to sustain his objections. See State Trials, Hawkins, Chitty, etc.

Our courts, however, do not consider this a misdemeanor; and do allow the juror to be examined on oath, to ascertain the state of his mind by this sort of evidence, as well as by the evidence of others.

The object of this investigation is to ascertain the state of the juror's mind; not whether he has heard of the case; heard rumors; heard the evidence, formed loose opinions and expressed them; but to ascertain whether the juror stands without malice, settled hate, or fixed, active prejudice against the accused; and whether he is a man who can be trusted to give a true verdict, according to the evidence. To do this, the juror may, after being challenged, be examined on oath, and if he shows clearly on his examination, that he is prejudiced either for or against the accused, the court should sustain the challenge. If it does not so appear on his examination, witnesses may be called and examined to ascertain the fact, and if the challenge is not sustained by the court, and the prisoner shall claim a different mode of inquiry, triers may be sworn to say on oath, whether the juror stands indifferent or not; 6 Cowen, 557; or the juror may be examined before the triers, and the prisoner may call and examine his witnesses before them, and when they decide their decision is final.

On this occasion the prisoner appears to have been almost passive; he exercised but a small portion of his privileges. It is expected that the accused will at least attempt to protect his own rights in every stage of the cause, and if he neglects to do so, it may be fatal to him. After the questions which were put in this case had been answered, the juror's partiality or prejudice not clearly appearing, the prisoner might have requested triers to be called, or he might have requested the court to let the juror stand aside for the present, to ascertain whether a full jury could not have been made up without him; or he might have challenged peremptorily. He did neither, and the record states that the court *permitted* the juror to be sworn, because the judge was not convinced that the juror was incompetent.

I am not satisfied, by what is stated in the bill of exceptions, that the juror was incompetent. I think it at least doubtful. But I consider, that in so important a case, the judge should have directed the juror to stand aside for the present until it could have been ascertained whether a full jury could have been obtained without him; and as some of my brothers are clearly of opinion that the juror was disqualified, I am not disposed to preclude the prisoner from another trial, and to pass sentence of death against him on a divided court, upon a doubtful case.

I will add, that the most respectable decisions show that a hypothetical opinion will not disqualify a juror. Sec. 8, John. Rep., 445, Burr's trial, and numerous other authorities. Nor will an opinion formed merely on report; 7 Cowen, 110.

I cannot acquiesce in the opinion that, after a juror says he has formed and expressed an opinion as to the guilt or innocence of the accused, the inquiry stop there. It is the duty of the court, in such case, to ascertain, fully, the state of the juror's mind, and for this purpose to question him, to ascertain whether the juror understands the question, the nature of the accusation, the object or view he had in so forming his opinion. This practice is manifest by the report of Burr's trial, and in State trials, etc.

It is deemed proper to state, that these rules are made as well for the accused as for the state. We do not interrogate a juror to ascertain whether his opinion or bias is in favor of the accused or the state. He should stand indifferent as to both; and, in practice, I have nearly as often known the objection to come from the side of the one as the other party.

Judge Child concurs.

E. & F. Husten for the defendant; *Gaines*, Attorney General for the state.

Challenges of jurors.—1 Cowen, 432; 6 do., 557, 564; 7 do., 108, 113; 2 Johns., 194; 1 do., 316; 8 do., 445; 2 Tidd, 779, 780; Bacon, title juries (E. 5); Bull N. P., 307; Hale's Com. Law, 138; 1 Co. Litt. 155–6; 2 Swift's System, 232; Trial *per pais*, 122–8; Chace's trial, App. 4, 19; Fire's trial, 177, App. 42; 1 Burr's trial, 43, 46, 370, 371; 2 Hawk. P. C. Ch., 43, Sec. 27, 28; 13 Mass., 221; 1 Chitty Cr. L., 542, 544; 1 Const. Rep. of So. Car., 289 to 321; 3 Dall., 518; 7 Cranch, 291.

THE STATE *v.* COMMISSIONERS OF PUBLIC ROADS, ETC., OF ADAMS COUNTY, Walk. Miss. Rep., 368.

The commissioners of public roads are liable to a criminal prosecution for any neglect of duty.

TURNER, C. J.:

The defendants were tried and found guilty, on a presentment, in the criminal court of Adams county, for unlawfully suffering a bridge over St. Catherine's creek to be and remain for a long space of time, out of repair, and in a dangerous condition. A motion was made for a new trial, and a motion in arrest of judgment. The judge of the criminal court, doubting as to the rule of decision, referred those motions with the consent of the defendants to this court, and sent up a statement of the evidence given on the trial, and of the points on which the court doubted.

As both these motions were entertained by the court, and were sent up for the purpose of having the law settled, we will just consider, whether the commissioners of roads are liable to this mode of prosecution. These officers are created by statute, and all their duties are prescribed by statute; they are not commissioned, nor are they judicial officers. They are vested with important powers, and the highways of the county are entirely and exclusively under their care. The statute is silent as to the mode of punishment, for neglect of duty. They are certainly not impeachable before the legislature. Are we to consider them irresponsible for neglect of duty toward the public? We think not. Judging by analagous cases, we have abundant authority for sustaining this presentment.

Overseers of roads and the road-commissioners in the other counties of the state have ever been liable to this mode of prosecution; and if these commissioners should be considered exempt therefrom, we should not be enabled to enforce the provisions of the statute. The road law would become a dead letter, or be left dependent, for its due execution, on the irresponsible will and pleasure of the commissioners.

Reason, authority, and public convenience, all unite in sustaining this mode of prosecution.

As to the second point, the evidence supports the verdict, and we see no ground on which to disturb it.

It is therefore considered that the motion for a new trial be overruled, and also the motion in arrest of judgment; and the court, being required by law to give judgment, it is ordered that the defendants pay a fine of ten dollars each, and pay the costs of prosecution.

THE STATE *v*. CHACE, Walk. Miss. Rep., 384.

LIBEL.

The office of an indictment is to connect the libel with the extrinsic facts, to show the meaning and bearing of words and phrases used in it, and is necessary, when the words published would not be libellous, unconnected with such facts.[1]

The court will regard the use of fictitious names and disguises, in a libel, in the sense that they are commonly understood by the public.[2]

BLACK, J.:

The song written in doggerel rhyme, charged in the first count of the indictment, is of a most obscene and exceptionable character. The name used in the song is a fictitious one—Goody Two Shoes—and is directed to her. The indictment, in the

(1) Commonwealth v. Childs, 13 Pick., 198. So with the declaration in a civil suit. Bloss. v. Toby, 2 Pick., 320; Carter v. Andrews, 16 Pick., 1.

(2) Edsall v. Brooks, 3 Rob., 284; King v. Horne, Cowper, 672; King v. Lawrence, 12 Wood, 311; Goodrich v. Woolcot, 3 Cow., 231; Demarest v. Haring, 6 Cow., 76.

first count, charges that this scandalous piece was published by the defendant, of, and concerning the prosecutrix, Nancy Irvin; recites the libel verbatim; states that it was directed to Goody Two Shoes, meaning thereby the said Nancy Irvin. It is questioned whether this innuendo is proper, and it is said, that in order to have made this innuendo a proper one, the indictment should have charged that this publication was made of, and concerning the prosecutrix, by the name of Goody Two Shoes.

The office of indictments is to connect the libel with extrinsic facts, to show the meaning and bearing of words and phrases made use of in it, and necessary, when the words published would not be libellous, unconnected with such facts.

This publication was unquestionably libellous in itself, and the only question was, whether it had relation to the prosecutrix.

This was the only fact besides publication, necessary to be averred and proven to fix the defendant. After an examination of the authority and the forms of indictments in criminal, and declarations in civil cases, there is no doubt in my mind that the previous averment in this indictment, that this libel was published of and concerning the prosecutrix, is sufficiently full and certain for the innuendo to refer to, without any such averment as is contended to be necessary.

In no case I can find, has it been thought to be necessary. In King v. Horne, Cowper, 672, are many such innuendos. The indictment reciting the publication, where the name of Mr. Horne is introduced, contains invariably this innuendo, (meaning the said John Horne,) and the king, (meaning thereby his majesty.) In King v. Lawrence, 12 Wood, 311, the words were to Sir John Pigot, "to moderate his zeal, for that the king," (meaning thereby King James II.) In King v. Baxter, 3 Mad., 60, where the word bishop is mentioned, there is an innuendo, (meaning thereby Bishop of England).

It is seldom libels contain the name of the individual concerning whom it is published, in full; generally a part of the name, or a fictitious one, or some of the letters of the name. Slanders conveyed under such disguises, are as injurious, and often more so, than in a more open and bold way. In such cases, it is only necessary, by proper averments, to show their relation to the prosecutor, and the court will not be hoodwinked to allusions which every other person can understand, but will also exercise its common understanding with others. I should have thought this too plain a question to need anything more than a statement of it, if it had not been urged with so much apparent earnestness.

As to the second point raised, whether there is sufficient evidence of publication, there can be as little doubt. One of the witnesses swore, that the song was handed to Chace, the defendant, who took it, read it to the company present, and laughed at it with others. Afterwards he repeated it to another person, and spoke it over to a third. If this was done maliciously, there can be no doubt but that it amounted to a publication, and from the jury having found a verdict against the defendant, it is to be presumed they were satisfied on that head. He knew after he first read it that it was a libel; his repeating it afterwards to a second and a third person, is evidence of publication.

The attorney general is entitled to demand judgment for the state.

THE STATE *v.* JOHNSON, Walk. Miss. Rep., 392.

An indictment commencing with the words " The State of Mississippi" and concluding " against the peace and dignity of the same," is sufficient.

If the words " then and there" precede every material allegation, it is sufficient, though these words may not precede the conclusions drawn from the facts.

If the accused pleads not guilty, and proceed to trial, he waives the privilege given him by statute of having a copy of the indictment and venire two days before the trial.

A juror being examined on his *voire dire*, was asked, " Have you formed an opinion as to the guilt or innocence of the prisoner at the bar ?" Answer, " I have." " Have you formed or expressed that opinion from common report, or from the witnesses, or either of them ?" Answer, " From common report only. I have never heard any of the witnesses say anything on the subject." " Will anything you have heard respecting the prisoner, have any influence on your mind, as a juror, in determination of this cause ?" " It will not. I feel free to decide the case according to the evidence which may be produced on the trial :" *Held*—Such an individual is a competent juror.

It is not necessary, to exclude a juror, that he should have formed and expressed his opinion against the accused, with malice or ill-will; but a mere hypothetical opinion, from rumor only, and subject to be changed by the testimony, does not disqualify.

If a juror has formed a fixed opinion, he ought to be excluded, though he may never have expressed that opinion.

R. M. Gaines, attorney general.

The formation and expression of an opinion does not disqualify a juror, without express favor or express malice. The English authorities on this point are full and uniform. Co. Litt., 157, *a*; Trials *per pais*, 185, 189; 4 Hawk., b. 2, ch. 43 § 28; 3 Bacon, 757; 1 Chitty, Cr. Law, 442, top of page; 4 B. & A., 470; 6 Eng. C. L. R., 502. In this country the same doctrine is sanctioned by the highest authority; and no case can be produced which overrules it. The case in Cowen goes farther, perhaps, than any other that can be produced. But, on examination, the case at bar will be found not to come within the rule laid down in that case. Burr's Trial, 416; 6 Cowen, 557; 7 ib., 108.

In the case in Cowen, (6 Cowen, 557,) the juror stated that he had been present at a former trial, and heard all the evidence, and had made up his opinion, perfectly, that the defendants were all guilty; and had frequently expressed it. 4 Wend. 240-4.

As to a hypothetical opinion, see 8 Johns., 445; Case in Va., 5 Am. Dig., 181, § 120. As to the necessity of the case, 1 Burr's Trial, 419. Abuse of discretion is no ground of error. Flower's case. Supra 318.

E. & F. Huston for defendant.

Making up and expressing an opinion as to the guilt or innocence of the prisoner, disqualifies a juror. In all the English books, this is laid down as a general rule. There is considerable contrariety of opinion as to its application to particular cases. This difference of opinion will be found, on examination, to grow out of the exercise of discretion in the triers or judges; a discretion now controlled by the emphatic language of our constitution. 1 Johns., 316; 7 Cowen, 121; 1 Burr's Trial, 414; 3 Bacon, 756; 4 Hawk., b. 2d, chap. 43, § 28.

Favor or ill-will is not necessary to be proved. 6 Cowen, 564; 7 ib., 128.

Making up and expressing an opinion upon rumor, disqualifies, etc. 7 Burr's Trial, 370; 4 Wend., 241.

For definition of impartiality or indifference, see 7 Cowen, 122.

The law attaches the disqualification to the forming and expressing of an opinion; and does not go beyond, to examine the occasion, or weigh the evidence on which that opinion is formed. 4 Wend., 242; 1 Burr's Trial, 419. Expression of an opinion indicates bias. 6 Cowen, 465; 7 ib., 128.

The disqualifying bias which the law regards, is one which, in a measure, operates unconsciously on the mind of the juror, and leads him to indulge his own feelings, when he thinks he is influenced by the weight of evidence. 4 Wend., 245; 1 Chitty Cr. Law, 544; 3 Bacon, 756.

Making up and expressing an opinion, is a principal cause of challenge; and the judgment of the inferior court is revisable on error. 4 Wend., 204, *et seq.;* 1 Cowen, 432; 6 ib., 564; 7 ib., 121; King v. Edwards, 4 Barn. & Ald. 470; 7 Cowen, 125–129:

"Common law required the juries to be brought from the vicinage, because they were supposed to know the facts, etc. But by statutory provisions, and legal adjudications, this is changed, because it is found that such jurors were apt to intermix their prejudices and partialities in the trial of right." 3 Black. Com., 390.

The inference to be drawn is that, as at common law, there certainly was a principal challenge allowed for express malice, or express favor. See 1 Co. Litt., 157 *a*, 157 *b;* 3 Black. Com., 363; 4 Wend., 229. The prejudices and partialities which arose from a knowledge of the facts; or (7 Cow., 127), a part of the fact; or from rumors, etc. (for all these may cause prejudice), were held by Blackstone in his time. 8 Johns., 445; 6 Cowen, 554; 7 ib., 122, cited and commented upon.

The juror's expression of a willingness and capacity to do justice, etc., is not to be relied on. Where there is cause to suspect a bias of mind, etc., the law will not trust a juror, etc. 4 Wend., 244.

The question to be tried on challenge of a juror is, whether he stands altogether indifferent, as he stands unsworn. 1 Chitty, Cr. Law, 544; Co. Litt., 157 *b*; 3 Bacon, 756.

It is better to trust a juror who has made up and expressed

an opinion, than one who makes it up on rumor. 1 Burr's Trial, 370 ; 4 P. William, 242. The formation and expression of an opinion, by a juror, is, of itself, evidence that he does not stand indifferent.

NICHOLSON, J. :

This case is brought before us by a writ of error to the circuit court of Greene county.

There are four assignments of error :

First, That the indictment is not drawn in conformity to the constitution, which requires that the style of all process shall be : " The State of Mississippi," and all prosecutions shall be carried on in the name, and by the authority of the " State of Mississippi ;" and shall conclude " against the peace and dignity of the same."

The second assignment is, that the words " then and there" are wanting before the words " feloniously, wilfully, and of malice aforethought," in the concluding part of the indictment.

The third assignment is, that it does not appear by the record, that a copy of the indictment and a list of the venire was furnished the accused two days previous to his trial.

And the fourth assignment, which is embraced in the bill of exceptions, is, that the court erred in deciding that Matthew Moody was a competent juror to pass upon the trial of the prisoner.

A passing remark is a sufficient notice of the first assignment.

The indictment commences with " the State of Mississippi," and concludes " against the peace and dignity of the same."

This has been considered sufficient, according to the practice of fourteen years under the constitution. The assignment, I consider, however, as having been abandoned by the counsel, inasmuch as it was not insisted on in the argument.

The second assignment is equally untenable. If the words " then and there " preceded every material allegation, it is sufficient; and, in drawing the conclusion from the preceding facts, these words may be omitted ; 3 Chitty's Criminal Law, 736–7, 751.

The third assignment is, That it does not appear from the record that a copy of the indictment and a list of the venire was furnished the prisoner two days before his trial. But it appears from the record in this case, that on finding the indictment, the court ordered a venire of one hundred jurors to be summoned, returnable on Thursday following; that on Thursday, a venire of fifty more were ordered; after which the case was continued till the next term.

At the subsequent term, on the first day of the term, a venire for thirty-six jurors was issued, returnable on the next day.

At the preceding term he had pleaded not quilty, and, although the trial began on Tuesday, and although this is a privilege which the law, in its benignity, extended to criminals in capital cases, yet it is a privilege which the prisoner may waive; and his pleading not guilty, and not having claimed this privilege, amounts to a tacit waiver, and he cannot afterwards take advantage of it; for his pleading has caused the objection; Chitty's Crim. L., 405; 4 Hargrave's St. Trials, 746. There is no error, then, in the third assignment.

The fourth and last assignment of error, is, that the court erred in deciding that Matthew Moody was a competent juror to pass upon the trial of the prisoner. The juror was sworn on his *voir dire*, and the court interrogated him as follows: "Have you formed or expressed an opinion as to the guilt or innocence of the prisoner at the bar?" *Answer:* "I have." *Question:* "Have you formed or expressed that opinion from common report, or from the witnesses or either of them?" *Answer:* "Common report only. I have never heard any of the witnesses say anything on the subject." *Question:* "Will anything you have heard or said respecting the prisoner have any influence on your mind as a juror, in the determination of this case?" *Answer:* "It will not. I feel free to decide the case according to the evidence which may be produced on the trial."

Upon which the court decided that he was a competent juror.

The question which is raised by this exception is one of great import, not only to the accused but to the community at large. The great difficulty of laying down a fixed and determinate rule in the selection of jurors, by which the guilty may be punished and the innocent acquitted, has agitated the courts for centuries back.

The old English authorities laid down the rule, that, to incapacitate a juror from sitting upon the trial, he must have formed and expressed his opinion against the accused, with malice or ill-will. This rule has been much softened, and, indeed, such is not the doctrine in the courts of this Union, although the common law is opposed to trying an individual by men who have prejudged his case ; yet, in most of the States of the American Union, we have constitutions which guarantee to the accused a fair and impartial trial.

Lord Coke has laid down the rule that a juror must stand in-indifferent, as he stands unsworn ; Coke Litt., 155.

By the constitution of Mississippi, declaration of rights, section 10, a speedy public trial by an impartial jury of the country is given to the accused. But how are we to ascertain the fact whether a juror stands indifferent between the parties ?

This must either be drawn from the juror on his *voir dire* or shown by evidence *aliunde*.

I believe the first important decision on this subject in the American courts, is to be found in the trial of Col. Burr for high treason.

The decision of Chief Justice Marshall in that case, has been looked to by the State courts as the pole star by which they were to be guided.

Judge Marshall says (Burr's trial, 1, vol. 44), " that to have formed and delivered an opinion was sufficient to exclude from the jury, but that slight impressions on the mind are not sufficient."

In the case of Vermilyea, *ex parte*, 6 Cowen, 563, Justice Woodworth says : " That to have formed and expressed an opinion from a knowledge of the facts is good cause of challenge." And the learned judge goes on and says, that it cannot be material from what source the opinion is derived ; if the bias proceeds from a preconceived opinion, it equally affects the accused.

Chief Justice Spencer, in the case of Vanalstyne, decided, that if a juror had formed and expressed his opinion from a knowledge of the facts, or from the information of those acquainted with the facts, it was good cause of challenge; but if the opinions of jurors were formed on mere rumors and reports, that such opinions were not sufficient to disqualify. On an application for a new trial in the case of Fries, Judge Iredell put the question on this ground, "that whenever a predetermined opinion is formed, from whatever motives, it creates an improper bias, extremely difficult to get rid of." And the same doctrine is held forth by Justice Maxcy in the case of the People v. Mather, for the abduction of William Morgan. 4 Wendell, 229.

The rule, then, to be drawn from these authorities, I think, amounts to this, that if the juror has made up and expressed an opinion, either from a knowledge of the facts, or from the information of those acquainted with the facts, or a decided opinion from report, that he does not stand indifferent between the parties and should be excluded from the jury; and the situation of the juror must be ascertained by triers appointed for that purpose, or by the court, and when referred to the court it stands as a demurrer to evidence.

In the case of Flowers, decided in this court, December term, 1829, I am satisfied that I went too far in laying down the rule, with respect to the examination of the juror on his *voir dire.* I there stated, that if the juror, on being interrogated, answered *positively* and *affirmatively,* that he had formed and expressed his opinion, the court should set him aside without further inquiry. Since the decision of that case, I have presided on the circuit at the trial of seven capital cases, and experience has fully satisfied my mind, that jurors frequently answer the question without understanding its true meaning.

It is frequently the case, that a juror, who has barely heard the case from report, and has but a slight impression on his mind, will answer affirmatively, that he has formed and expressed opinions, but upon further examination, it will be discovered to amount only to a *hypothetical,* and not a *decided* opinion. In fact, there are but few jurors who understand the difference between a fixed and predetermined opinion, and a hypothetical one. Besides, much is often ascertained from the manner in which the juror answers the questions: whether he shows a sober indifference, an agitation of feeling, or signs of ill-will. In fact, it is almost impossible, from the nature of things, to lay down any *invariable* rule on this subject.

From the necessity of the case much must be left to the discretion of the presiding judge, who is "*pro hac vice*" of counsel for the accused, to see that he has a fair and impartial trial. Let us apply the law as laid down, to the case, as shown by the bill of exceptions. The juror, Matthew Moody, was asked if he had formed or expressed an opinion, as to the guilt or innocence of the accused; he said he had; he was then asked whether that opinion was formed from report, or from hearing the witnesses; he said from report only, that he had never heard any of the witnesses say anything about it.

He was then asked, whether anything which he had heard or said, would have any influence on his mind in the determination of the case, as a juror; he said it would not, that he felt free to decide the case according to the evidence which might be introduced at the trial. It will be observed that the disjunctive conjunction is used instead of the copulative. The question is, have you formed, or expressed, instead of, have you formed *and* expressed. I have not been able to find a solitary case in the American decisions, where the form of interrogating has been practiced upon, which is set forth in this bill of exceptions.

The reason given in the books is, that a man who has made up his opinion, and expressed it aloud, will be much more apt to adhere to it, than if he had only formed it and kept it concealed.

This reason is not entirely satisfactory to my mind. I think if a juror has made up a fixed opinion from a knowledge of the facts, although he has kept that opinion locked up in his own breast, he is not a competent juror; but if he has only fashioned in his mind an opinion from report, and has not given utterance to that opinion, it would not be sufficient to exclude him.

It is uncertain from the bill of exceptions whether Moody had barely formed his opinion from report, or whether he had expressed that opinion. But I am willing to give to it its most extended sense, and admit that he had both formed and expressed his opinion, and then taking all his answers together, to my mind it shows nothing more than a hypothetical opinion. If the report which he had heard was true, he thought him guilty; if it was not true, he thought him innocent. In fact, his answers taken altogether, show clearly that he had not formed a decided opinion. His opinion had extended no farther than the law. The law had said that if the prisoner had committed the crime of murder, he should be punished; and yet this law was competent to try him. And I will here premise, that when establishing rules by which the community is to be governed—whether in the legislative hall or on the judicial bench, we must lay down rules for man as he *is*, and not as he *should be.* And the idea of selecting jurors as pure and uncommitted as if they had just dropped from another planet at the moment of trial, is entirely Utopian.

When an outrageous crime is committed, it is immediately wafted on the swift pinions of rumor to every corner of the country, and men take up slight impressions which they frequently call opinions, but which readily yield to the evidence produced on the trial; and it is but rarely the case, that one of those rumor-formed opinions amounts to anything more than hypothetical. And if jurors are to be excluded, on whose minds slight impressions only are made, and that from report, we may as well blot out from our criminal code, all those crimes of deep and malignant dye; and I do not consider the establishment of such a rule as above laid down, in any way jeopardizing the rights of the citizen. There are so many safeguards thrown around the accused in this country, that there is no danger of innocence being punished. Every member of the community is interested in protecting the innocent.

Although in England, the venire belongs to the king, yet in this country it may be said to belong to the accused; and is so often the case, that it is made out with a view to the acquittal of the prisoner. And while we are cautious to protect the innocent, we must be careful not to let the guilty escape.

Neither do I think the establishment of the above rule at all in opposition to the true intent and meaning of the constitution.

The framers of that instrument certainly did not understand the words *impartial jury*, to mean anything more or less, than that the accused should not be tried by men who had prejudged his case; he is to be tried in the county where the offense is committed, and it is stretching presumption too far to suppose, that an atrocious deed can be committed and a jury obtained within the limits of the county, who have never heard of the transaction.

An impartial juror is one whose mind is open to receive the impression to be made by the testimony; one whose mind is poised upon the scales of indifference, and capable of weighing the testimony adduced on trial, in opposition to floating rumors.

I again repeat, that the case at bar, to my mind, shows nothing more than a hypothetical opinion; it amounts to the same thing as saying, if the reports were true, he thought the prisoner guilty, but if they were false, he thought him innocent. I am, therefore, of opinion that the court below did not err in deciding that Matthew Moody was a competent juror, and that the judgment below must be affirmed.

Judges Turner and Montgomery concur.

THE STATE v. CRAFT, Walk. Miss. Rep., 409.

In an indictment, under the act of 1830, prohibiting any person other than Indians, from making settlements within their territory, it is necessary to aver that the defendant is not an Indian.

R. M. Gaines, attorney general.

In this case the only question is, whether the court erred in overruling the motion for a new trial. There was but one motion made, and that was for arrest of judgment, and for a new trial, which was treated by the court below simply as a motion for a new trial.

Whether any offense is stated in the indictment, or whether the law is constitutional, are questions which only can arise upon a demurrer, or on a motion in arrest of judgment, neither of which courses was adopted by the defendant.

The ground chiefly insisted on in support of the motion for a new trial, is newly discovered evidence, and it appears from the record that the newly discovered evidence was only cumulative. This constitutes no ground for a new trial. 4 Am. Dig., 446, § 28 ; 2 Caine R., 129, 151 ; 8 Johns., 84.

The whole evidence is not spread upon the record, to enable the court to judge whether a new trial ought to be granted. The court will not hear or give sentence in a criminal case, where the punishment is corporal, unless the accused is present, or at least under recognizance ; or unless his presence is waived. See Chitty Cr. Law.

George Winchester for defendant.

The offense charged is, " That Whitwell Craft, on the 18th of September, 1830, did improve, clear, clean up, and build houses on, plant and cultivate, and fence certain lands within the boundary of that part of said county, (to wit, Covington,) lying and being within the lands occupied by the people called Indians." Acts of 1830, 39. Congress shall have power to regulate commerce with the Indian Tribes. Rev. Code, 492.

Trial of crimes, jurisdiction of—page 492, sec. 2, 3.

Judicial powers of the United States, Revised Code, 496, sec. 1.

Laws of the United States, and treaties ; Graydon's Digest, 230, 423–5–6.

Gordon's Digest, 264, (1604,) page 267, (art. 1615) ; page 761, and note 2, K.

It is necessary to show his negative averments, and that defendant is not within the exceptions of the statute. Chitty, 234.

Motion for a new trial, on affidavits for a new trial ; the affidavits stating that Craft cultivated the ground under the authority and by virtue of a contract with Susan Nabby, an Indian authorized to cultivate said lands.

NICHOLSON, J. :

This is an indictment under the act of 1830, page 38, which inflicts the penalties of fine and imprisonment on any person other than Indians, for attempting to make settlements or cultivate any lands within the boundary of the Indian territory.

The clause under which the indictment was framed is in the following words: "It shall not be lawful for any person or persons, *other than the aforesaid Indians*, to make any settlement, or attempt to cultivate any land or lands within the boundaries of the said Indian territory," etc. The indictment states that "Whitwell Craft, late of said county, laborer, on the first day of September, in the year aforesaid, with force and arms, at the county aforesaid, did improve, clear up, build houses, plant, cultivate, and fence certain lands within the boundary of that part of said county, being and lying within the lands occupied by the persons called Indians," &c.

Three grounds were taken by the defendant's counsel in the argument of this case.

1st. That the offense is not sufficiently described.

2d. That it is not alleged in the indictment that the said defendant is not an Indian; and,

3d. That the act of the legislature creating this offense is in opposition to the articles of cession and agreement between the State of Georgia and the United States; hostile to the acts of Congress on this subject; at war with the Indian treaties which have been made since 1776; and in direct violation of the constitution of the United States.

1. With respect to the first ground, that the offense is not sufficiently charged—formerly it was said that the fullest description of an offense, where it even amounted to a legal definition, would not be sufficient without keeping close to the expressions of the statute—1 Chitty Cr. Law, 282. This ancient canon, however, is somewhat relaxed at the present day; for the present rule seems to be, that if the variations consist in the introduction or alteration of words purely superfluous and unnecessary, it will not be material, unless the alteration render the whole repugnant to the intent of the statute; in such case, the superfluous words cannot be rejected, 1 Chitty Cr. Law, 280. Now apply this rule to the description of the charge in the present case; the words of the statute are, "It shall not be lawful for any person, etc., to make any settlement, or attempt to cultivate," etc. The charge in the indictment is, "that the defendant did improve, clear, clean up, build houses, plant, cultivate and fence," etc. Here

are several superfluous and unnecessary charges; yet I can see no repugnancy to the true intent and meaning of the statute.

2. It is not alleged in the indictment that the defendant is not an Indian, etc.   It is laid down in Chitty's Cr. Law, 284, that if exceptions are stated in the enacting clause, it will be necessary to negative them, in order that the description of the crime may in all respects correspond with the statute; but that when a statute contains provisos and exceptions in distinct clauses, it is not necessary to state in the indictment that the defendant does not come within the exceptions, or to negative the provisos it contains. Chitty Cr. Law. 283.   In the case of King v. Jarvis, 1 Bur., 148, Lord Mansfield says, "it is now settled, by the uniform course of authorities, that the qualifications be all negatively set out."   In the present case, the exception is interwoven with the offense; the language is, "It shall not be lawful for any person or persons, *other than the aforesaid Indians,* to make any settlement, or attempt to cultivate," etc.

Suppose the case had been against Susan Nabby, who, it seems, was the Indian proprietor of the land in question, could the prosecution have been successfully sustained without proving that Susan Nabby was a person other than Indian.   I apprehend not.   So, in the present case, it was necessary, before the state could fix the offense on the defendant, to prove that he was *other than an Indian.* And his not being an Indian being the very gist of the charge, and absolutely necessary so to be proven, I think it ought to have been so laid in the indictment.   And for this defect in the indictment, the judgment below must be reversed. It is not necessary to decide the question raised by the third ground taken in the argument.   We will, therefore, not attempt a pacification of the act in question with the several acts of Congress of the United States, nor awake from their slumbers the Indian treaties.

Let the judgment be reversed.

Judges TURNER, CAGE, and MONTGOMERY concur.

BYRD *v.* THE STATE, 1 Howard, 163.

ACCESSORY TO MURDER.

No questions can be adjudicated by an appellate court which were not subjects of decision in the inferior court, or which do not appear upon the record in a proper and tangible form. The judgment of every court of competent jurisdiction will be holden to be correct, unless by the record itself, the error is made manifest.[1]

Where a prisoner had a right to demand a discharge upon showing that he had been imprisoned for two stated terms of the court, without having been prosecuted by indictment and trial, it would be presumed, if the court refused to discharge, that there was no evidence before the court to support the application; or that the contrary was established.[2]

The *habeas corpus* act is, in every particular, of a highly remedial character, and should be construed, like all statutes of that class, with a view to the advancement of the objects of its enactment. All laws are obligatory only in the sense in which they are intended by the law-making power to operate.

Where the prisoner was held in confinement on a charge of being accessory to murder, from Feb., 1833, to Feb., 1834, and was not indicted and tried, the two intermediate regular terms of the Circuit Court having failed to be held, he is not entitled to be discharged under the 14th section of the *habeas corpus* act. That act contemplates terms of the court which shall have been *held;* and the object of the legislature was to provide against unnecessary or oppressive delays.[3]

The language of the statute shows that in order to entitle the prisoner to a discharge, the state must have been in default; but as to the fact whether the term has been held or not, is wholly beyond the power of the state, the presumption of default cannot arise.

By the common law every man was entitled to a trial by his peers—good and lawful men of the county in which the offense was charged. This principle is recognised and established by the constitution of this state, and the right thus secured should be beyond legislation. The caption of the indictment, thus, "The grand jurors of the State of Mississippi, empanelled and sworn in and for the county of Warren," etc., is sufficiently certain to show that were of the proper county. The county court was a court of general jurisdiction for the trial of slaves. The jurisdiction of a court of general jurisdiction will be presumed until the contrary appear; that of a court of limited jurisdiction must be made to appear by the record. The record of the county court showing the conviction of the principal of murder, may be properly admitted on the trial of the accessory, as evidence of the guilt of the principal.

It is necessary to the competency of jurors that they shall be freeholders or householders, but no length of citizenship is required.[4] The qualification of jurors to serve on a special *venire*, are the same as those for the regular *venire*. If a juror declare on his *voire dire* that he is neither a freeholder nor a householder, it is ground of challenge for cause.

Although the constitution is silent as to the number and qualification of jurors, yet it recognizes the number twelve, as known at common law, and although the legislature cannot abolish or substantially change the jury, it can prescribe the qualification of those who compose it.

1 Waters v. Travis, 8 Johns., 566; Campbell v. Stokes, 2 Wend., 137; Houghton v. Star, 4 ib., 175; Davis v. Packard, 6 ib., 327; Driggs v. Rockwell, 11 ib., 504; Hause v. Carroll, 87 Mo., 578; Brown v. Scott, 5 Penn. St., 357; Alexander v. Polk, 39 Miss., 737.

2 Vide State v. Segar, T. U. P. Charlt., 24.

3 See note 2 supra.

4 Changed by statute. See Acts of 1857,   ; Const. Miss., Art.   , § .

This cause came up on writ of error from Warren county. The prisoner, a free man of color, was indicted at the Warren court as an accessory to the murder of Joel Cameron, committed by a slave named Daniel. The indictment further charged, that said Daniel had been convicted at a previous term of the county court, and that said Byrd did counsel, hire and procure said slave, Daniel, to murder the deceased.

The indictment against Byrd was filed at the February special term of the Warren court, 1838, to which the counsel for the prisoner demurred, and assigned the following causes:

1. It does not appear that the persons composing the grand jury named in this indictment were citizens of Warren county, and that they were sworn.

2. It does not appear that the court, at which the slave, Daniel, was convicted as alleged, was legally constituted and had jurisdiction of said offense.

3. It does not appear from said indictment, that the said slave, Daniel, was convicted by the verdict of a jury, of the murder of Joel Cameron, or that the judgment of the court, sentence or order of execution has yet been pronounced against him, said Daniel, or that said conviction is yet in force or unreversed.

4. It does not appear with sufficient certainty, how said court was constituted, or whether a competent court was present, or whether it was at a regular term of the county court, or a special court convened for the trial of said slave, Daniel.

5. It does not appear that twenty-four good and lawful men of the vicinage had been summoned by the sheriff of Warren county, of whom twelve were slaveholders in their own right, to try said Daniel, and out of which number twelve were selected for the trial of Daniel.

6. It does not sufficiently appear that the indictment in the case was found a true bill by twelve of the grand jury.

7. It does not appear from said indictment, that the grand jury who passed upon the same were good and lawful men of Warren county.

8. It does not appear from the record and proceedings, that the circuit court of Warren county, at its special term, ordered

in February, 1833, had any right or jurisdiction to try said cause; nor have the grand jury any right at said term to act on the defendant's case; whereas everything necessary to confer jurisdiction should appear.

Which said demurrer was, by the court, overruled.

This cause was continued at the above-mentioned term. There was no circuit court held in Warren county, in May, 1833, nor in the following November, which were the regular terms appointed by law. By the act of the legislature, approved November 25th, 1833, the circuit court for said county was held on the first Monday in February, 1834, when the counsel for the prisoner moved, that he be discharged from custody, on the following grounds:

1. Because he had been held in custody on the above charge four stated terms, and one special term of the circuit court for Warren county, and has, during the whole of that time, been urging the trial of said cause.

2. That he was not indicted or tried within the two first stated terms of the circuit court of Warren county.

3. That he has not been indicted or tried on the above cause, though he has been confined four stated terms, and one special term of the Warren circuit court.

This motion was overruled by the court. At this term of the court, there was a mis-trial, owing to the disagreement of the jury; subsequently, another *venire facias* was ordered, and the prisoner convicted.

A bill of exceptions was tendered to the opinion of the court, admitting the record of the county court in the case of the slave Daniel, to be read in evidence in this cause.

Four of the jurors tendered to the prisoner, declared, on examination, that they were neither householders nor freeholders; the counsel for the defendant objected to them for that cause. The court overruled the objection, and admitted them as legal jurors, to which opinion of the court, the defendant excepted.

There were other proceedings in the cause not necessary to be mentioned.

Coalter and *Warren* for plaintiff in error.

T. F. Collins, attorney general, contended,

1. That the prisoner should not have been discharged under the *habeas corpus* act upon a motion in the court below. Revised Code, 224, 103; McCord, 564, 565.

2. That the court below did not err in admitting the record of the trial of Daniel, a slave, to be read on the trial.   2 Peter's R., 163.

3. That there was no error in the jury.   Revised Code, 136, 1830.

4. That the grand jury were of the county of Warren.   Revised Code, pointing out the mode of selecting a grand jury.

5. As to the foreman of the grand jury, the point was abandoned by the prisoner's counsel.

6. As to the *venue*, see Acts of 1831, and the affidavits in the record.

Smith, J. :

This cause comes before us upon a writ of error to the circuit court of Warren county.

Questions of a highly interesting character and of the deepest importance to the criminal jurisprudence of this state, are presented by the record, and require the decision of this court.

In the examination of the principles involved in this case, the desire to arrive at true results has been powerfully stimulated by the conviction, that upon the conclusion to which I have come, depends not only the fate of the unfortunate man now in charge of the court, but to some extent, at least, the repose and wellbeing of this community.

In the examination of the different topics discussed by the counsel, I shall pursue, as most convenient, the order in which they were presented.   But before I proceed to investigate the correctness of the position assumed first by the counsel for the plaintiff, it may be necessary to notice an objection made by counsel for the prosecution, that the first point relied on by the plaintiff cannot come before the court in such a shape as to admit of decision.

No question can be adjudicated by an appellate court which was not a subject of decision in the inferior court, or which does not appear upon the record in a proper and tangible form. In the record will be found a motion for the discharge of the prisoner, under the 14th section of the act in relation to the writ of *habeas corpus*, with the reasons which were filed, and the judgment of the court overruling the said motion.

There does not appear a bill of exceptions to have been taken to the opinion of the court, on the motion, which would have embodied the evidence adduced in support of the application, and spread it upon the record, to be judged of by this court. Admitting the motion itself, with the judgment thereon, to be correctly upon the record, or rather to constitute a part of it, what appears from the record to invalidate the decision or to show it erroneous? It is very true, the reasons manifestly brought the case within the 14th section of the *habeas corpus* act; but there appears no evidence by which they are sustained.

The judgment of every court of competent jurisdiction must be holden to be correct, unless by the record itself the error is made manifest. The court would be presumed to be cognizant of the fact that the prisoner was remanded to jail on the 15th February, 1833, and that the court was not held for the two succeeding stated terms thereof. But it by no means follows that the judge before whom the motion was made, knew, without proof of the fact, that the prisoner, in the meantime, remained in the custody of the sheriff.

Admitting that the prisoner had a right to demand a discharge upon showing that he had been imprisoned for two stated terms of the court, without having been prosecuted by indictment and trial, would it not, if the court refused the application for a discharge of the prisoner, be presumed that there was no evidence before the court to support the application? or that the contrary was established? And this presumption exists in favor of every judgment of a court, that it is correct. Where the evidence in support of the application, that by which alone the correctness of the decision could be tried, is not before us, this question, therefore, is not properly before this court. But as it is one of deep interest and great importance, demanding an early decision, I will proceed to give what I conceive to be the legitimate construction of the law out of which this question springs.

The *habeas corpus* act, in every particular, is of a highly remedial character, and is to be construed, like all other statutes of the same description, with a view to the advancement or furtherance of the objects of its enactment.

It is, however, contended, though acknowledged to be of this character, that it is in language so clear and distinct, as to be susceptible of deriving no aid from constructions as to what were the objects of the legislature; that it has fixed the limit of imprisonment when there is no delay or default on the part of the prisoner; and in language, clear, unambiguous and impartial, has declared, that, unless the default is on the part of the prisoner, he shall be discharged from imprisonment.

To this interpretation I cannot assent. Can that act be so clear, distinct and unambiguous, whose construction has been mooted in almost every court in the state, and upon which there is the greatest diversity of opinion?

The question raised in this case, and which has been discussed with great ingenuity by the counsel, and which, in its decision, necessarily involves the construction of this act, is this: Was the prisoner, who, having been held in confinement, upon a charge of being accessory to murder, from the special term in February, 1833, to February 1834, the two intermediate stated terms of the circuit court of Warren county having failed, entitled to a discharge upon the ground that he was not prosecuted by indictment and trial at the next second stated term, November previous thereto?

All laws are obligatory, only in the sense in which, by the law-making power, they are intended to operate. And if courts of justice, in exploring, by the first rules of interpretation, the intentions of the legislature, arrive at an interpretation of a law different from its verbal import, which construction will be enforced by them? But here there will be no necessity to carry the construction beyond what may be considered the common sense meaning and legal import of the words of the section.

What object in view had the legislature in the passing of this law? What evil did they intend to suppress—what remedy supply?

It cannot be doubted but that the object of the legislature was to guard the personal liberty of the citizen, by throwing around it this additional protection against oppressive and unnecessary delays in the prosecution of persons charged and imprisoned.

It established a rule for expediting state prosecutions, by providing for the discharge of the prisoner where the default at the second term shall be on the part of the state. The language of the statute, I think, shows that in order to entitle the prisoner to a discharge, the state must have been in default.

Can this presumption arise on the part of the state when there has been no term of the court holden? The fact whether the term has been holden or not, is wholly beyond the power of the state; in no way subject to its control. Not so the prosecution, and the witnesses over which the law presumes the state to have complete command. It is provided that the court shall, on the last day of the first stated term, admit the prisoner to bail, etc.; and it is evident that the law contemplated the actual holding of a court; for how could the court be required to admit to bail, when no court was in session?

The technical meaning of the word term is relied upon, to show that the legislature meant that the prisoner should be tried at all events, at the time designated for holding the second stated term.

This word is used not only to designate the time appointed for holding court, but to convey the idea of a court actually held, or in session.

Thus in section 5, page 10, Revised Code, the word term is used to designate the time appointed for holding the court. But in the 14th section of the *habeas corpus* act, it evidently means a term at which a court was holden; otherwise, the provision requiring the enlargement of the prisoner, if he shall not be prosecuted by indictment and trial at or before the stated term, on the last day of the term, would be absurd and unintelligible. This meaning must also be applied to the second member of the section, where the same words are used in the same combination. 1st. The interpretation here given to this statute is sustained by an authority in 1 M'Cord's Rep., 154.

This case there arose, vol. 1, 22, under the *habeas corpus* act of South Carolina, which in substance in this particular, is very similar to our own.   It was there held, "that it was the unquestionable intent of the act to require the state to bring the prosecution to trial on the first or second term, or else the prisoner shall be discharged.   In other words, the trial must not be in *default for two terms*."   In that case the prisoner demanded his trial at the first term, and was tried; but a mistrial ensued. The court held, "that the state committed no default; the mistrial being a *misfortune*, attributable neither to the state nor to the defendant.   The court and jury were *equally for both parties*, and both were ready at the court, and the trial had.

At the second term, the state was not ready.   And there was the first default; "and the prisoner, under the terms of the act, might demand to be bailed, and if the state should not be ready at another term, then to be discharged."   In the case now before the court, the state committed no default.   The holding of the court did not depend upon the state.   The state can indict and try when there is a term of the court; but the holding of a court is not more within the power of the state than of the prisoner.

The case read to the court from 1 Stewart, 31, does not decide directly the question here involved, although broad enough to embrace the case here presented.   In that case, there were two terms of the court actually held, so that the state was twice in default.   But I regard this authority as of no weight, however highly respectable some of the decisions of the supreme court of that state unquestionably are.   No reason is assigned for the construction given to the act upon which the question arose, except that the act was too plain and unequivocal to derive any aid from considering what might be the views of the legislature.   And further, it was contended, that as a necessary incident of a discharge under this act, the prisoner would be thereafter forever free from prosecution for the same offense.

I am compelled to dissent from this proposition.   What was the intention of the legislature?   Was it to establish an act of limitation for the prosecution of felons, or to lay down a rule to expedite state prosecutions, the better to preserve the liberties of the citizen? This act constitutes a component part of a system of law, adopted at the same time, and which to some extent, for the purposes of construction at least, must be regarded as the same act. It must then be construed with direct reference to the other provisions of the other portions of the law having relation to the same subject. But there is no confliction between this question and any other portions of the law. An effect cannot be given to words beyond their obvious meaning, unless it be necessary to effectuate the intentions of the legislature.

What then is the intent of its application? The language is, that "if such prisoner be not prosecuted by indictment and trial at the second stated term, or some special term prior thereto, of the court where the offense is properly cognizable, he or she shall be discharged from further imprisonment, in all cases whatever, unless the delay was occasioned by the default, or on the application of the prisoner." The utmost extent to which this law can be carried, considered, too, as remedial, is to a total discharge from imprisonment for the same offense, and cannot go to bar a prosecution for the crime charged. But if, by any process of reasoning, such a construction could be maintained, it would operate as a repeal of the 52d section of the statute in relation to crimes and misdemeanors, by which the limitation in prosecutions for criminal offenses is established.

A discharge upon motion under this section, can have no greater effect than a discharge for the same cause upon a writ of *habeas corpus*, which only goes to free the prisoner from imprisonment for the same cause, unless by the order of a court of competent jurisdiction, he shall be ordered into custody. See Revised Code, page 223, section 8. Upon this point there can be no reasonable doubt entertained.

2. The second question is, does the caption of the indictment show with sufficient certainty that the grand jurors, who found the indictment, were of the county of Warren? By the common law, every man was entitled to a trial by his peers; which peers were good and lawful men of the county in which the offense was charged.

This principle of the common law is recognized and established

by the constitution of this state; and the right thus secured,
should be beyond legislative action.

It should appear, then, with reasonable certainty in the caption of the indictment, that the grand jurors empanelled and
sworn to inquire of, and presentment make, of the guilt or innocence of the party charged, were of the proper county.

And if it does not, it will be a fatal defect.

The caption of the indictment in this case, is in the following
words, to wit:

"The grand jurors of the State of Mississippi, empanelled
and sworn in and for the county of Warren," etc. The grand
jury is constituted to inquire on the part of the state, into the
commission of felonies, etc., in their county. The grand jury
of any county may, therefore, with strict legal correctness, be
styled the grand jury of the State of Mississippi.

And when the words are added, that they "were empanelled
and sworn *in* and *for* the body of the county," it appears with
that degree of certainty required in indictments, that they were
of the county for which they are sworn. This legal certainty,
so far, at least, as the prisoner's safety is involved, is strengthened by the presumption that the court could not issue a *venire*
to any other county in the state; and that it could have issued
to summon only the householders and freeholders of the county.
Courts of justice are disposed to relax the rigor of the ancient
forms, when no injury can possibly result to the liabilities or
rights of the accused.

Under the process of summoning and drawing the grand
jury, the accused can always ascertain whether the persons
drawn are good and lawful men of the county, by referring to
the list which the clerk is required to keep of those from whom
the grand jury must be drawn. See act of November session,
1830, page 25. I am therefore of opinion, that in this respect,
there is no error.

3. The third question presented to the consideration of this
court is, whether the indictment is not defective, inasmuch as it
does not appear that the slave, Daniel, was legally tried and convicted by a court of competent jurisdiction. This question is

again raised, by the bill of exception to the opinion of the judge, admitting the record of the trial and conviction of the said Daniel to be read as evidence on the trial of the prisoner.

I will consider the question as arising on the admissibility of the record to the jury.

The slave, Daniel, who was the property of Joel Cameron, of whose murder he stood charged, was tried by the county court, prior to the adoption of the amended constitution, and convicted of the murder of said Cameron; and received the judgment of the court.

The record of the trial, conviction and sentence of the said Daniel, was offered to the jury as evidence of his guilt, as a necessary step to charge Byrd, the prisoner, with the crime of being accessory before the fact to the murder of Cameron. This record was objected to upon the ground, that the county court, in respect to its powers to try slaves for felonies, was a court of special as well as limited jurisdiction. That the record did not show that the court had jurisdiction of the subject matter; that it did not pursue strictly its authority; that its acts were irregular, and its judgment erroneous; and that as such, it could be no evidence of the conviction of Daniel, but a mere nullity.

These objections I think wholly untenable as applied to this record. The county court, in reference to its authority or jurisdiction over felonies committed by slaves, was not a court of special jurisdiction. It was a permanent judicial tribunal; limited, it is true, in its jurisdiction over a particular class of persons; but general as to felonies committed by them. A special, as well as a limited jurisdiction, is confined, not to classes, but to individuals and special cases; such, for instance, as a court martial, " which has power to hear and determine in the particular inquiry, and upon the particular cases, with a view to which they are organized;" 19 Johnson's Reports, 32. But even jurisdictions of this character are sustained, and their judgments incapable of collateral investigation, although erroneous, so long as they confine themselves within the line of their jurisdiction; 2 Sir W. Blackstone's Reports, 1145. It may be regarded as well settled, that the judgment of any court of however limited or special jurisdiction, when it appears that it had jurisdiction of the person and the subject matter, cannot be disputed collaterally. Nor will the judgment of any court of general jurisdiction be regarded as proof of any fact, unless it appears from the record that the court had actual jurisdiction of the person ; 15 Johnson's Reports, 181.   The only difference between the judgment of a court of general jurisdiction, and one of special and limited jurisdiction, is this : in the one case the jurisdiction of the court is presumed until the contrary appear ; in the other, a party claiming a right under it must know affirmatively that the court had jurisdiction ; 1 Johnson's Reports, 34.

In the case of the record before the court below, the jurisdiction of the court was established by law, and the record showed that it had jurisdiction as well over the person as the subject-matter.   Whatever errors there may be, (and I am inclined to think that there are none) the judgment will not affect its validity, and cannot in this collateral manner be examined.   As to the position assumed by counsel, that this record formed " a part of the gist of the prosecution, and comes directly before the court," I wholly dissent.   It is only evidence ; and of a necessary fact to convict the party charged before the court of the crime of being accessory to the murder of Cameron.   It was only introduced as evidence of the guilt of Daniel.

4. The fourth question is, did the court err in overruling the plaintiff's challenge for cause to certain persons named in the bill of exceptions?   The bill of exceptions shows that neither of the jurors were householders nor freeholders ; and one of them, though a citizen of the United States, had resided in the State of Mississippi but eleven months.   The statute law of this state, Revised Code, 136, provides that no person under the age of twenty-one nor above the age of sixty years, nor any person who is not a citizen of the United States, (except when a jury *de mediatate linguæ*), nor any person who has been convicted of felonies, perjury, forgery, or any other offense, etc., shall be capable to serve on a jury for the trial of any case, civil or criminal, whatsoever.

Was it the intention of the legislature by this provision simply to designate and enumerate the causes which would incapacitate from serving as jurors?   May it not with much greater reason be said that the legislature, by enumerating the persons disqualified, intended to establish that all others not enumerated, should be deemed legal jurors? If the legislature, instead of pointing out the circumstances of disqualification, should have declared what were the necessary qualifications of a juror, would not all who could not have shown the required qualifications, be incapacitated by the mere force of an exclusion? This interpretation is to my mind materially strengthened by the 133d section of the circuit law, which provides that the petit jury, where the title to land is put in issue, must be freeholders. For is not this statute evidently based upon the supposition, that without this provision, those who were not freeholders would be competent jurors? This view is aided, in no small degree, by the terms of the 1st section of the Bill of Rights. For who does not regard the right of serving on juries, as well as the right of being tried by jury, as an immunity of great importance, constituting a portion of the common birthright of the freemen of the State of Mississippi? The length of residence is not material as a qualification of a juror, for there is no practical rule now in existence in this state by which it can be ascertained when he became a citizen of the state. The constitution does not define citizenship, and there is no law, if it were competent for the legislature to pass one on this subject, defining the qualifications of a citizen. And as the legal presumption is, that these jurors were residents of the county of Warren, the contrary not appearing from the record, I am disposed to regard them as legal jurors.

5. The fifth ground taken by the counsel having been abandoned, I have not noticed it.

6. But I will proceed to the sixth and last point which requires the attention of the court. The question arising upon a motion for a change of *venue*, was argued with much force and ingenuity by the counsel for the prisoner, and sanguinely relied on for a reversal of the judgment below. It, however, does not come before this court in a manner to authorize the adjudication of the court upon it. The affidavit upon which the motion was based, and by which alone the correctness of the judgment of the court could be tested, is not part of the record. The pris-

oner, for the purpose of reversing the decision of the court upon his motion for a change of *venue,* should have excepted to the opinion of the court, and, embodying the affidavit and the motion in the bill, made both a part of the record.

Having examined all the points which required investigation, I have come to the conclusion that the judgment must be affirmed.

Judge WRIGHT dissented as to the objection to the jurors.

JANUARY TERM, 1835.—A re-argument of this case having been granted, the opinion of the court was delivered at this term by Mr. Chief Justice SHARKEY.

This case was argued at the last term, and is again before us by an order for re-argument, granted in consequence of a division in the court, only two of the judges having heard the argument. The opinions delivered at the last term are adhered to, and the unpleasant task of deciding on the point of difference devolves on me. This circumstance of itself, independently of the importance of the question, is well calculated to produce in me a distrustfulness as to the correctness of the conclusion to which my mind has been drawn, and has, in a high degree, contributed to induce a scrupulous investigation of the principles which are to be regarded in this decision. The most of the points raised in argument were decided at the last term by the united opinion of the judges who were present. Several of them are of a high importance, and I have only to add my entire concurrence in the views then taken, so far as they are again raised in argument.

The qualifications requisite for a juror, being the only point of difference, remains to be considered, and it is not a little surprising that a question of such magnitude should have been permitted to remain so long without adjudication. In the examination of the question, under the particular structure of our government and laws, we must necessarily recur back to the principles of the common law, as the great fountain from which we originally derived the trial by jury, and, indeed, from which the body of our municipal law is mainly drawn. The various statutory provisions in England, prescribing the qualifications

of jurors, have existed so long and with such a variety of modifications by succeeding enactments, that, to rescue the common
law principle from the obscurity thus created, is a task not entirely clear of difficulty.   The learned commentators on the
laws of England have not treated this subject with as much
clearness as we could have wished, resting satisfied, doubtless,
with the full enjoyment of the privilege as permanently secured ;
but I think they fully show that, according to the common law,
in all courts of general jurisdiction, it was necessary that the
jurors should possess a freehold qualification—to what amount
seems to have been a point unsettled, if any particular amount
was necessary.   Perhaps the better opinion is that anything
which would constitute a freehold was sufficient ; but I take it
to be clearly shown that a freehold was necessary.   3 Bacon's
Abridgment, 751–2 ; 4 Blackstone, 302 ; Littleton's, 464.   As
the law stood at the time of the formation of the federal government, both the common and statute law of England required
the possession of a freehold as necessary to qualify a juror, and
the right of trial by jury, being of the highest importance to
the citizen, and essential to liberty, was not left to the uncertain
fate of legislation, but was secured by the constitution of this
and all the other states as sacred and inviolable.   The question
naturally arises, how was it adopted by the constitution ?   That
instrument is silent as to the number and qualifications of jurors.
We must, therefore, call into our aid the common law for the
purpose of ascertaining what was meant by the term jury.   It
is a rule that when a statute or the constitution contains terms
used in the common law, without defining particularly what is
meant, then the rules of the common law must be applied in
the explanation.   The framers of the constitution must have
meant, therefore, to secure the right of trial by jury as it existed
in England, either by the statute or common law, and the constitution, in the absence of all subsequent legislation, would have
secured to the citizen this mode of trial and all its incidents not
incompatible with the republican form of our government.   The
legislature cannot abolish or change substantially the panel or
jury, but it may, it is presumed, prescribe the qualifications of
the individuals composing it.   Our statute nowhere defines the

number necessary to constitute a jury; but the number twelve,
known as the number at common law, is no doubt what is meant
by the constitution and all the statutes, when a jury is mentioned.   If we have thus derived the number and consider it
secured by the constitution, is it not also a fair inference that
the incidents, such as the mode of selecting and the qualifications of the individual jurors, should also follow as necessary to
the perfect enjoyment of the privilege?   I think it does; and
if the position be correct, any juror not possessing the qualifications required in that country from which our constitutional
privilege was taken, and to the regulations and laws of which
the constitution must be supposed to have referred, could have
been successfully challenged, in the absence of a statutory regulation.   It becomes necessary, therefore, to inquire how far the
qualifications requisite for jurors have been fixed by statute.
There are several statutes which must be noticed, the first of
which is in the Revised Code, p. 133, beginning at the 122d
section.   This section provides that the assessor and collector of
taxes of each county shall once in two years furnish to the clerk
of the circuit court, a list of the "freeholders and householders
who are citizens of the United States."   The names on the list
are to be put in a box, and the clerk is required to draw from it,
in term time, one by one, "the names of thirty-six persons to
serve as jurors at the next succeeding term."   A *venire facias*
is to be issued for the persons drawn, and they are to be summoned by the sheriff; and a penalty is imposed if they fail to
attend.   The 125th section of the same act requires the clerk
to keep another box, into which the names drawn shall be
placed, and when they are all drawn out of the first box, he is
to begin again.   To ascertain the intention of the legislature
in passing a law, is the primary object in construing it, and if
that intention can be discovered, the statute should be so construed, as to carry it into effect.   The first prominent feature
of the statute before us, is the classes of citizens, whose names
the tax collector is required to furnish.   They are required to
be freeholders and householders and to be returned with a view
to a particular service.   Citizen is a more general term than
freeholder and householder, and we cannot suppose that the

latter terms were used as more convenient. They convey distinct and definite meanings to the mind and are less comprehensive than several terms which would strike us as more appropriate, if intended to be used for the purpose of including all the inhabitants of a county. It is difficult to perceive why these words were used if not intended to fix a qualification, and direct from what class of citizens the jury should come. It will not do to suppose that the legislature intended by the words freeholder and householder, to comprehend all the male inhabitants of a county, for they must have been aware that in this and every other community, there is a large proportion of the population who are neither freeholders nor householders. We cannot suppose either, that those terms were used uselessly ; nor are we to conclude that they were used to designate a portion of citizens who would be likely to be known to the assessors, for it is equally his business to assess every individual, whether householder or not. The name of every male citizen above the age of twenty-one, and under fifty, is bound to appear on the tax list, as being subject to a capitation tax, whether they have property subject to taxation or not, and why should the assessor be required to make a selection from his list, of freeholders and householders, leaving out the other class, if it be not for the purpose, and with the sole object of pointing out what qualifications should be possessed by those required to be returned for the discharge of a duty. Is it also not obvious that the legislature considered the jury service as a duty to be performed, and that they intended to equalize the burden amongst those selected for the performance of it? This is manifest from the mode prescribed in drawing juries as contained in the 125th section act. Each individual liable to serve, is protected from an undue proportion of duty by the rotation resulting from the provisions of this statute ; but this rotation, and the whole of the duty, is confined to a particular class of individuals.

If the legislature intended that all citizens should be qualified to serve on juries, I cannot perceive why the burthen is thrown upon freeholders and householders, whilst those not so situated are privileged from the duty. Certainly, the favor is not the result of assessment, for he who has acquired by industry and economy, a freehold or household, to say the least, is as much entitled to the favorable consideration of the law-makers as he that has not given these evidences of merit and industry. In the due course of summoning juries under the law, the consequence would be a total exemption to those least entitled to it ; and I infer that such could not have been the intention of the legislature, but rather that they intended to disqualify them, by requiring the jury to be selected from such as possessed the evidences of a more permanent interest in the welfare of the community.

The act approved 16th December, 1830, contains the same provisions as the one above mentioned in regard to the list of names to be returned by the assessor and collector, but there is an additional provision in the first section which, I think, goes very far to show that the legislature intended to prefix a qualification as necessary to a competent juror. The language of the act is, that "it shall be the duty of the assessor of taxes, within each county of this state, once in every year, to take and return to the circuit court in term time, or to the clerk thereof at his office in vacation, a list of the names of all freeholders and householders (being citizens of the United States), within his county, liable to serve as jurors ; and for the better ascertaining who are liable, the said assessor, whenever he shall have doubts as to such liability, is hereby authorized and required to take the statement of such person or persons under oath (to be administered by him), as to his or their liability to serve." This act is directory only so far as regards persons liable to serve on juries, which necessarily presupposes that there are some who are not liable. On which class does that liability fall? It must of course be that class whose names the assessor is required to return, and all of that class is liable to serve, unless especially exempted or especially excluded. For what purpose is he authorized to administer the oath, if he doubts as to the liability? He cannot be authorized to administer the oath, to ascertain who are exempt from liability, for that is a mere privilege which the individual may or may not claim. It is true, there are many persons exempt from serving on a jury, such, for instance, as physicians, postmasters, preachers of the gospel, and perhaps many others; but they may exercise their privilege at discretion, and if they do not choose to be excused, it forms no ground for challenge. Nor can the assessor administer the oath to ascertain who are expressly excluded, for this, in most cases, would be authorizing him to inquire whether the individual have been disgraced; an inquiry which even the court could not make. I think, therefore, that the principal thing intended to be ascertained by administering the oath, is the freehold and household qualification; and if this be the case, it seems to me to follow that the legislature intended to make a freehold or household interest a requisite; and in order to obtain a performance of the duty, they have provided that the citizen shall not avoid it by a mere denial of his freehold or household interest.

It is argued for the state, that the 138th section Revised Code, 136, by declaring that no person under twenty-one, or above sixty years, nor any person who is not a citizen of the United States, nor any person who has been convicted of felony, perjury, or forgery, or other offenses punishable with stripes, &c., shall be capable to serve on a jury, is an evidence that all others are to be considered as qualified, and that by making the exception, the legislature intended that all others should be qualified. The disqualification of particular persons and for particular causes by no means shows that there is not a particular rule prescribing a qualification. The section referred to creates only exceptions to the general qualifications as attaching to particular individuals, who, although they possess the general requisites, yet, in consequence of some particular disability, are declared to be incompetent. It is evident that there must be a qualifying rule somewhere, either in the common or statute law, otherwise we should be led into gross perversions of the law. The language in this section is "no person," &c., and it would not do to say that every other person, except those expressly excluded, is qualified to serve.

It has also been said that serving on juries is a privilege, and cannot be taken away without express legislation. Considering it as a privilege to the juror merely, it might be questionable whether even express legislation could take it away from those in whom it had vested, but it is also certainly a privilege of no ordinary kind vested in the individuals interested in the trial, to have a jury of good and lawful men, and certainly this privilege is placed beyond the range of legislation.

The 133d section, Revised Code, 136, requires that the petit jury, when the title of land is in issue, shall be composed of freeholders. From this, I do not think it can be inferred that jurors in other cases need not be freeholders nor householders. The term freeholder in this section is no doubt used in contradistinction to householder, and is considered a higher qualification, required by the nature of the controversy.

From the view that I have taken of the several statutes, it appears to me that the legislature intended that jurors should possess certain qualifications, and it is a subject of regret that the law is not more explicit in this particular. The right of trial by jury stands so conspicuous in the Bill of Rights, and its value is so directly instrumental in the protection of the life, liberty, and prosperity of the citizen, that I could not but regard any legislation tending to impair it as injudicious. And it would be unfair to attribute to the legislature that has acted on this subject, any other than a desire to preserve it inviolate. It is then fair to conclude that the legislature, with a due regard for its value, intended to protect it from abuse on the one hand, by requiring the duty to be discharged by citizens exhibiting the most usual evidences of permanency and worth, and to relieve it on the other from a feature at variance with the spirit of our government. I do not think any particular length of residence is necessary to constitute a competent juror, as the counsel have insisted. The jurors are to be taken from the list returned by the assessor, taken, as we may presume, at the time of making the assessment. So soon as the assessment is made, therefore, the individual's name may be returned, and he may be drawn to serve on a jury. It is, to be sure, necessary that he should be permanently located, and so soon as he is so, he becomes a citizen, entitled to all the privileges not expressly prohibited to him, and is bound to perform all the duties from which he is not expressly exempt.

The jurors to whom the exception was taken in this case were on the special *venire*, and it is an invariable rule that jurors brought in by special *venire* must possess the same qualifications necessary to make them competent to serve on the regular panel.

One of the jurors, on being asked after he was sworn on his *voire dire,* declared that he was neither a freeholder nor householder, and the counsel for the prisoner challenged him for cause, which was overruled by the court, and a bill of exceptions taken, which brings the question fairly before this court as a defect appearing affirmatively on the record.

The judgment of the court below must be reversed.

SHAFFER *v.* THE STATE.—1 Howard, 238.

MURDER.

By the statute, the panel of jurors is to be drawn in term time, or in vacation, and a *venire* is directed to be issued, returnable to the next term. The grand jury is to be drawn from the number appearing; the balance are to be sworn as petit jurors for the term. These jurors were not intended exclusively to form the panel for the trial of criminal cases.

The circuit courts derive their criminal jurisdiction and the powers necessary to enforce it from the sixteenth section of the Circuit Court Law, which declares that they shall "have and exercise all the powers incident or belonging to a court of oyer and terminer, and general jail delivery." This statute vests in the circuit courts, without further legislation, the subject matter pertaining to courts of oyer and terminer, and of general jail delivery, and also confers on them all the incidents and necessary means of enforcing their jurisdiction.

The *venire* may be for a greater number of jurors than twelve, and may be made returnable the same day it is issued, or any day during the term.

Alleging the grand jurors to be the grand jurors of the State of Mississippi, is a sufficient averment, and it is not necessary to allege in the caption of the indictment that they were "then and there" sworn.

A return of "served a true copy of the indictment, *venire facias* and the *venire* on the prisoner," is a sufficient service of the panel.

A command to the sheriff, embraced in the special *venire*, to summon the jury "residing as near as may be to the place where the murder was committed," is erroneous, and ground for a reversal of the judgment.

Error to Wilkinson circuit court.   SMITH, J.

The plaintiff in error was indicted in the court below for the murder of Benjamin Turbeville, and on trial thereof, was convicted, and he brings the case to this court. He made a motion in arrest of judgment, which was overruled, and for error assign the following:

VOL. I.—5.

1. The writ of *venire* is defective in this : The sheriff is commanded to summon a jury from a particular part of the county. The sheriff summoned the jury without its having been drawn as directed by statute.

2. The indictment is defective in both counts. The assault is not alleged in the first count with sufficient certainty. The time the person killed died, is not alleged with sufficient certainty in the second count.

3. The verdict is general; it ought to have specified upon which count the prisoner was found guilty.

The indictment alleged that the defendant, "on the 24th day of September, 1832, with force and arms, at Woodville, in said county of Wilkinson, in and upon said deceased, did feloniously," etc., "of his malice," etc., etc., "did make an assault," with the usual description of weapon, wound, etc. The indictment also alleged that Turbeville, from the 24th to the 25th of September, 1832, at Woodville, in said Wilkinson county, "did languish," etc., "and then" (repeating the time and place) "of said mortal wounds did die."

There was also a motion for a new trial, upon the ground that, previous to the investigation, one of the jurors had expressed an opinion from rumor. Both of the foregoing motions were overruled, bills of exception tendered to the opinion of the court, and an appeal was also prayed by the defendant, which was refused by the court below. And this action of the court is assigned as error.

Gildart for plaintiff in error, contended, that the indictment was defective. When or where the assault was made, is not alleged with sufficient certainty.

The assault is material; time and place must be added to every material circumstance. 7 Dana, 268.

When the person slain died, is material. 4 Comyn, 393.

2. The verdict is general. The reason why this is error, is that the court may know how to give judgment, and that the party, if indicted a second time for the same offense, may he plead an acquittal or conviction in bar.

3. The caption forms a part of the indictment, and a copy

must be furnished the prisoner.   U. S. *v.* Insurgents, 2 Dall., 342.

4. It does not appear in the caption when and where the grand jurors were sworn.   6 Wentworth Pl., 2 ; Guernsey v. People, 3 Johns. Cases, 265.

5. The prisoner was entitled to appeal.

6. The jurors who were called to try the prisoner were selected by the sheriff without being drawn.   See statute prescribing the mode of summoning jurors ; 3 Bacon, 729 ; Hale's Hist. Com. Law, 286, ch. 12.

7. When the *venire* was exhausted, the court erred in directing the sheriff what particular jurors to present to the prisoner ; and a bare order of the court was not sufficient to summon talesmen.

If the sheriff have any right to summon tales-jurors, it must be from by-standers.   He must exercise his own discretion, and that discretion cannot be controlled by the judge.

A tales can only be summoned by writ, and then only after return of *distringas.*   3 Bacon, 774 ; 2 Hawkins, 576.

8. The court erred in directing the sheriff to summon a jury from a particular part of the county ; although this was the old common law form, it was found to be an evil, and abolished. Hale's Com. Law Notes to 12th chap., note B. ; Wentworth Pl., 2.   The jurors were to come from the hundred.   Ib.

The prisoner could, by common law, challenge for want of hundredors.   3 Thomas' Coke, 606, note 3.   A hundred is a political division of a government.   There is no such division known to our law.   Such parts of the common law only were adopted as were necessary, useful and adapted to our institutions.   It is not the practice.   The constitution, Rev. Code, 541, repeals it.   None of these errors are cured by statute of jeofailes or amendments.   3 Bacon, 773 ; 2 Hawkins, 429, ch. 27, §§ 108—9—10.

SHARKEY, C. J.:

There are several points made in the argument of this case, principally in relation to the legality of the jury and the jury process.

First. It is contended that the petit jury were neither drawn according to the statute nor the common law. The *venire* was issued in term time, for thirty-six jurors, returnable in six days, and tested of the same time. By the statute, the panel of jurors is to be drawn in term time, or in vacation, and a *venire* is directed to issue, returnable to the next term. The grand jury is to be drawn from the number appearing, and the balance are to be sworn as petit jurors for the term, according to the form of the oath prescribed. To my mind, it is obvious that these jurors were not intended exclusively to form the panel for the trial of criminal causes. There is a different section of the statute from which the circuit courts derive criminal jurisdiction, and the powers necessary to enforce it. By the sixteenth section of the circuit law, it is declared, that they shall " have and exercise all the powers incident, or belonging to a court of oyer and terminer and general jail delivery."

The terms used in the statute are sufficiently broad, in the absence of express legislative provision, to vest in the circuit courts, not only the subject-matter of jurisdiction pertaining to courts of oyer and terminer, and general jail delivery, but also to confer on them all the incidents or necessary means of enforcing their jurisdiction.

The judges at the assize in England sit by virtue of five different commissions or authorities, two of which are mentioned in our statute, as conferred upon the circuit courts, to wit, oyer and terminer, and general jail delivery. By the first, they are to inquire, hear and determine, of all felonies and misdemeanors found by indictment at the same term, and cannot try indictments previously formed. By the second, they can try every prisoner that is in custody when the term commences. In order to exercise jurisdiction under the first-named commission, it is proper, and, indeed, especially necessary, that they should have power to summon and empanel a jury at the same time, otherwise their powers could not be enforced. It is even said that they cannot issue jury process until issue joined ; but it is clear that they may issue a *venire* and make it returnable the same day, or any day during the term, according to common law ; and the same power may be exercised as a court of jail delivery.

1 Chitty Cr. Law, 508, 513 ; 4 Hawkins, P. C., 376, 377 ; Cro. Car. 315 ; 3 Bacon Abr., 736.   There is, thus far, no irregularity in the *venire* in this particular, and this may answer also the objection made to the test of the *venire.*

It is next urged that the *venire*, at common law, could only issue for twelve jurors ; but this position is not sustained by the authorities.   They are clear that a greater number might, and, indeed, should be summoned.   3 Thomas' Coke, 459 ; 1 Chitty Cr. Law, 505 ; 2 Dallas, 341.

There is an objection taken to the caption of the indictment, because it is not shown that the grand jury, were " then and there" sworn.   Lord Hale, in the form which he has given, 1 Chitty Cr. Law, 327, has omitted the words "then and there," which he probably would not have done, if he had deemed them material.   Chitty himself is more explicit on this subject, and says in express terms, that these words are unnecessary, and cites many authorities in support of his position.   1 Chitty Cr. Law, 334.   The caption as it is made up in our courts, is the mere ministerial act of the clerk in making out his record and I know of no rule that requires it to be completed before the trial.

Justice Kent, in the case cited from 3 Johnson's cases, admits it to be an objection to form, merely resting on positive authority ; and with due deference, I think the weight of authority is against it.   The case cited, was removed to the Supreme court, by *certiorari,* and was then to be tried at the circuit court, such being the course in that state.

It is also said that it does not appear with sufficient certainty, that the grand jury were of Wilkinson county.   As a principle it is evidently true that they should appear to be of the county, and I think the record is within the rule.   The *venire* by which the grand jury were summoned, is set out at length, and shows that the persons drawn, were of the county, and I do not think that that showing can be wholly disregarded, it being a part of the record.   But the indictment itself as fully shows them to be of the county, as did the indictment in Byrd's case, 1 How. R., 163, 247.   That they are called the grand jurors of the State of Mississippi, can be no objection, it being true.   They are emphatically, the grand jurors of the state, being authorized to inquire concerning offenses against the state. This is the form given in the books, and pursued in the United States courts, and I think it without objection.

Another objection is, that it does not appear that a list or panel of the jury was served upon the defendant. I do not think the record sustains the objection. The language of the record is this: "Served a true copy of the indictment, *venire facias*, and *venire* on the prisoner." The word " venire," was no doubt intended to mean the panel, but this question is not now open to decision, unless the defect could be made clearly to appear, since it was decided in the case of the State v. Johnson, Walker's R., 396, that by going to trial, the prisoner waived the privilege. The only remaining point which deserves notice, arises out of the language used in the special *venire*, which commanded the sheriff to " summon thirty-six good and lawful men of his county, and who are in nowise of kin to James Shaffer, and residing as near as may be to the place where the murder was committed," etc. It is argued with much plausibility, that the direction to summon the jury " as near as may be," to the place of the offense, was an abridgment of the prisoner's constitutional right to be tried by a jury of the county.

The common law was particularly careful in securing to individuals a trial by the jury of the neighborhood or *visne*, and hence it required, that the jury, or at least a part of them, should be of the hundred in which the cause of action or offense occurred, and if they were not, it was a cause of challenge. The rule proceeded from the reason, that the inhabitants of the neighborhood, were more intimately acquainted with the merits of the cause of controversy, and, therefore, better prepared to decide. This was found in some cases, to be productive of mischief and delay, because, at times, a sufficient number of hundreders could not be obtained, and because jurors permitted their prejudices to have an influence in the formation of their verdict. The courts, therefore, relaxed the rule, and it was ultimately changed in civil cases, by the 4 and 5 Anne, ch. 16, which authorized the taking the jury from the county.

Under this statute it was held to be no cause of challenge that part of the jury were not from the *visne*, or neighborhood; and certainly, it was never held to be cause of challenge, after the enactment, that the jury, or any part of it, were from the hundred and not from the body of the county generally.

The statute mentioned, did not extend to criminal cases, and afterwards, another was passed, in the reign of George II., which included prosecutions on penal statutes leaving prosecutions for crimes still unaltered. But the practice in criminal prosecutions also changed, and the direction in the *venire* was looked upon as mere form, and the jury were selected from the body of the county, without the least regard to the *visne* of the indictment. 3 Thomas' Coke, 464, note 8. So far as the law was altered by statute, the principal object seems to have been to prevent captious objections after trial, for the want of hundredors, and the statutory provisions commenced by making a verdict cure the defect, and ultimately authorized the taking of the jury from the body of the county. The practice in criminal cases was made to conform to it, and objection to want of hundredors discontinued, until it went out of use, and was ultimately abolished by statute. The rule of the common law evidently had its origin in a spirit of justice and humanity toward the accused party, and the abuse of its just and humane indulgence, was one cause of this change. In regard to juries, therefore, in most cases, the *visne*, or neighborhood, or hundred, is no longer regarded by the laws of England, as it is with us, a county is the smallest subdivision of territory known in the summoning of juries. We are to consider the nature of the privilege secured by our constitution, and for this purpose it may not be amiss to recur to the reasons, independently of those of convenience and justice, which superinduced the security of it in a permanent manner. The taking of our citizens from their homes and friends to be tried by strangers, without the means of a fair investigation, had no doubt due weight in the constitutional arrangement. It was made in the spirit of the common law, to secure to the accused a trial by his neighbors, by constituting the citizens of the county as triers, and excluding such as were of a different county. It is true that there is nothing which confers a right to select from a particular neighborhood, and I think such a construction should be given, as to prevent the selection of a jury from a particular neighborhood, and I think such a construction should be given, as to prevent the selection of a jury from a particular part of a county, by definite description ; but it may be questioned whether the general terms used in this *venire facias*, are to be understood as confining the sheriff to any certain limit.   Certainly, if the common law be founded in reason, the taking of a jury from a neighborhood cannot be an objection, and the common law principle may serve in some degree to illustrate the spirit of the constitutional provision.

The words used do not necessarily and of themselves comprehend any particular district, but they might be used for oppressive purposes.   The words *visne* or neighborhood are interpreted to mean the county, and they do not seem to be more explicit than the language of the *venire*.   Although the common law principle had its origin in reasons the most favorable to the accused, yet it was found to be attended with bad consequences, as bringing into the jury-box the prejudices and animosities of juries, and Lord Hale gives this as the main reason for the gradual change in the law.   It is certainly the object in the law to give to the accused an impartial jury, and any rule which would tend to impair the object should not be sanctioned.

I do not think the term used imposed a restraint on the sheriff, yet he might so use the power to the injury of the party. I strongly incline, on the whole view of this question, to think that the words of the *venire* did not direct, necessarily, the sheriff to the particular neighborhood, but as my brother judge is very positive on the other side of the question, and as I entertain strong doubts, I will yield in favor of him.

The other points in the case I do not think sustainable ; the authorities are, to my mind, clear.

Judgment reversed.

BYRD *v.* THE STATE, 1 Howard, 247.

ACCESSORY TO MURDER.

The records of the old county court are public documents, and when that court was abolished, the clerk of the probate court was appointed as the officer to take charge of those records; and the register of the orphan's court was directed to deliver to him all books, records, &c., pertaining to the office of register. He is therefore the proper certifying officer of all such records. See act of 1833, p. 136.

The rule is well settled in this state, that a party may pursue such order, as he thinks proper, in the introduction of his testimony, unless where a foundation is necessary to be laid for the introduction of secondary evidence. [1]

The district attorney is the proper person to prosecute, and so far as official acts in prosecutions are required by law to be done in a particular way, or to assume permanent character, he is required, and is the only one authorized, to discharge such duties; such as signing indictments, and all other proceedings of an official character on the part of the state. When these have been performed, it is not error for the district attorney to withdraw from the prosecution, and for other counsel to appear on the trial in his stead.

The jurisdiction of the county court, under the old constitution, for the trial of slaves, was only concurrent with that of the circuit court. The new constitution took effect, from the time of its adaption, in all cases, unless specially excepted, and by it the jurisdiction in the trial of slaves was taken from the county court and transferred to the circuit court, and the county court abolished.

Where the *venue* is changed, it is not the duty of the clerk to send any but the original papers in the case; [2] and a writ of error to the circuit court of the county in which the trial was had, will not reach an error in the proceedings of the court of the county from which the *venue* has been changed. Quære—Can a writ of error be issued to the circuit court of such county?

In Missouri, in a change of *venue* in a criminal cause, the original indictment must be retained in the office of the clerk in the county in which it is found. A copy only should be included in the transcript of the record and proceedings. Ruby *v.* State, 7 Mo., 206.

The *venire* is no part of the record, and if an objection exists as to it, or to the panel of jurors summoned under it, the party, to avail himself of it, must place it upon the record by bill of exceptions.

Special terms of the circuit court, like the regular terms, are regulated by law; and the certificate of the clerk, and the allegations in the indictment that it was found at a special term, will be deemed by this court sufficient evidence of that fact.

It is the province of the caption of an indictment to show when the indictment was found, and before what court. And where the record states that " the grand jury was empanelled and sworn to inquire in and for the body of the county of Warren, viz. J. C., foreman," &c.; this is sufficient evidence that the grand jury was sworn, Castleman as foreman; and the swearing him as foreman was a sufficient appointment.

Where a former judgment of the circuit court has been reversed for errors occurring during the trial, and not affecting the plea, and the cause remanded, it is not necessary to arraign the prisoner again on his second trial, inasmuch as the former plea still remained.

[1] Dyson *v.* State, 26 Miss., 362.

[2] Changed by statute. Rev. Code, 621, art. 299. See also Rev. Code, 1871. Browning *v.* State, 30 Miss., 656; Bishop on Cr. Proceedure, 108–119; and notes.

Error to Hinds circuit court.

This case originated in the circuit court of Warren county, at the February special term, 1833, thereof, and was brought to this court from the February term, 1834, of said circuit court, and reversed and remanded by this court to the circuit court for further proceedings. A change of *venue* was obtained to the circuit court of Hinds county, and the trial took place therein, in which the plaintiff in error was convicted, and he brings his case again to this court, and assigns the following errors:

1. A paper purporting to be a record of the conviction of the slave, Daniel, was improperly admitted to be read in evidence on the trial of said cause.

2. The court erred as set out in the bill of exceptions.

3. The court erred in not arresting the judgment.

4. The court erred in not granting a new trial in the above cause.

5. The court erred in permitting the district attorney to withdraw from the prosecution of said cause and to abandon it, and give it up to the entire management and control of counsel employed by an individual to prosecute said case.

6. It erred in refusing to permit the counsel for the defendant to conclude the argument of said cause before the jury.

7. It erred in suffering the case to be put to the jury without causing the defendant to be arraigned, and demanding of him to plead.

8. It erred in putting the case to a jury without calling upon the defendant for his plea, and, in fact, without his pleading; and in refusing to discharge defendant upon *habeas corpus.*

Coalter and *Warren* for plaintiff in error.

T. F. Collins, attorney general, and *S. S. Prentiss,* contra.

SHARKEY, C. J.:

All the points arising in this case are embraced in the assignment of errors and will be considered in the order of assignment.

It is said, first, that the court below erred in permitting a paper purporting to be a record of the conviction of Daniel to be read to the jury.   The ground of objection taken to the admissibility of this record is, that it was not certified by the proper officer.   It is a record of proceedings in the county court of Warren county previous to the adoption of the present constitution, in a prosecution against a slave, Daniel, for the murder of Joel Cameron, and is certified by John A. Marsh, as clerk of the probate court of Warren county.   For the prisoner, it is contended, that the board of county police succeeded to the jurisdiction of the county court, not specially distributed to another tribunal by the constitution ; and that, therefore, the police clerk is the proper certifying officer of matters on the records of the former county court.   It is true that, by the act of 1833, the board of police have all jurisdiction which formerly belonged to the county court, with the exception of such powers as may have been given to different tribunals by the constitution and laws.

Under our former organization, the county courts had jurisdiction in the trial of slaves for capital offenses, and that part of its jurisdiction is now vested in the circuit courts by the constitution.   The former register of the Orphan's court *was ex officio* clerk of the county court.   And the present clerk of the probate court is *ex officio* clerk of the board of police.   The records of the county clerk are public documents, and when the court was abolished, an officer was appointed to take the custody of those records, and that officer is the clerk of the probate court.

By an act passed in 1833, page 136, the register is directed to deliver to the clerk of the court of probate, all books, records, papers, and all other matters pertaining to the office of register. This act must have been designed to include every thing, especially as there is no other law that directed him to deliver any part of his records to any other officer, and without such direction, he would not be authorized to deliver them to any person, and as his office ceased, of course, it was not the intention of the legislature that records of public utility should remain in his hands when he ceased to be a certifying officer.   The record is properly certified, and was, therefore, properly admitted.   *Secondly,* "That the court erred as set out in the bill of exceptions." The first bill of exceptions must be understood as an objection to the order of the testimony.   Dr. Hagaman was asked if he was present at the finding of Cameron's watch, which he answered in the affirmative ; and was then asked if the prisoner was present ; which question was objected to by the prisoner's counsel, on the ground that no testimony had then been introduced to prove the conviction of Daniel, the principal named in the indictment.

The court very properly overruled the objection.   It is a rule well settled, in this state at least, that a party may pursue such order as he thinks proper, in the introduction of his testimony, unless where a foundation must be laid for the introduction of secondary evidence.   The first point raised by the second bill of exceptions is, as to the propriety or legality of permitting the district attorney to withdraw from the prosecution, and leave it to be managed by others.   During the trial the district attorney stated that he was willing to withdraw from the prosecution, and leave the management of it to Mr. Prentiss, which the court permitted him to do, and the prisoner excepted.   It is true, that the district attorney is the officer appointed to prosecute, and so far as official acts in prosecutions are required by law to be done in a particular way, or to assume permanent character, he is required, and, indeed, the only one authorized to discharge such duty ; for instance, the indictment must be signed by him, and all other proceedings when an official act on the part of the state is necessary.   But when all the preliminaries to trial have been duly performed, I do not think it error that other counsel should appear on the trial in his stead.   Nor do I think the authorities relied on in support of this position show the existence of any such rule.   The authority, cited from 3 Haywood, goes no further than to decide that an indictment must be signed by the district attorney.   That is necessary in this state by positive enactment, and this indictment is properly signed by the district attorney.   It is also set out in this bill of exceptions, that certain witnesses were then introduced and sworn.   If this was intended to be included as a part of the objectionable proceeding, the objection is not set out, nor is it perceived.   The next feature in this bill of exceptions, is as to the admissibility of the record of the county court of Warren county, which has been already noticed under the first assignment.   It also appears by this bill, that the defendant's counsel, having introduced no evidence, claimed the right of opening and concluding the argument to the jury, which was properly refused by the court.

The only remaining point made by this bill of exceptions, arises out of the request made by prisoner's counsel to the court to charge the jury.   The counsel for the prisoner requested the court to charge the jury, that they must be satisfied from the evidence in the case, that Mercer Byrd was a free man, or they could not find a verdict of guilty.   And that from personal inspection of the prisoner, if they believed he was of negro blood and extraction, they would be authorized to presume him to be a slave in the absence of all testimony to the contrary.

There are three very conclusive reasons why this objection was not good.   In the first place, by the old constitution, the circuit courts had general jurisdiction in all matters civil and criminal, but in civil cases only when the matter in controversy exceeded fifty dollars.   This was a general grant of power, and the subsequent section authorizing the legislature to establish a court of probate, for the granting of letters testamentary and of administration for orphans' business, for county police, and the trial of slaves, cannot be construed as making an exception to the general grant, but only as conferring power to establish a particular court with concurrent jurisdiction in the trial of slaves. In the next place it was clearly, both by the constitution and statute, a court of general jurisdiction in criminal matters, and if slaves were persons who formed an exception to its general powers, the exception could only have been taken by plea to the jurisdiction, and the plea of not guilty admitted the jurisdiction;   Chitty's Criminal Law, 438.   And lastly, the new constitution went into operation in all cases, unless specially excepted, from the time of its adoption, and by it the jurisdiction in the trial of slaves was taken from the county court and given to the circuit court, and the county court was abolished; because there was no provision for continuing it, and its jurisdiction was also repugnant to the constitution.   By the 3d section of the Schedule it was provided, that all officers then holding offices should continue to hold them " until they should be superseded, pursuant to the provisions of the constitution, and until their successors be duly qualified."

There are no successors to the judges of the county court, and we have already decided in this court that, when there was no provision in the constitution for the appointment or election of successors, the office was abolished.   The county courts after the adoption of the constitution, could not have continued to exercise the powers; because all their jurisdiction had been vested in tribunals entirely different.   Even if the prisoner had been a slave, therefore, he was not triable by the county court, as that branch of jurisdiction had been transferred to the circuit court, which was kept in operation by the constitution.   It was, therefore, unnecessary for the state to prove his freedom.   This disposes of the points raised by the bill of exceptions, and brings us to the remaining errors assigned.

Thirdly, that the court erred in not arresting the judgment. Several reasons were assigned in support of this motion: First, it does not appear from the indictment, or in the caption thereof when said indictment was found, or before whom.   It is the province of the caption to contain those particular statements, and when the record is returned on a writ of error it should be complete.   On looking into this record, some facts appear which may readily account for any defect mentioned, if there is any. It cannot be overlooked that the offense was committed in Warren county and the prosecution originated there.   That after one trial in that court the *venue* was changed to the county of Hinds, on the application of the prisoner, when a second trial took place, and he was convicted, and took his writ of error to the proceedings in Hinds county on the last trial.   The writ of error is directed to the clerk of the circuit court of Hinds county and by him the record is returned.   When the *venue* was changed, I am not aware that it was the duty of the clerk of Warren county to send anything more than the original papers and pleadings in the case, and if so, this writ of error cannot reach any defect in the record from that county.   The clerk of the circuit court of Hinds county could only make up his record from the original papers in the case which came into his possession, and the proceedings that took place in his court.   If there be any foundation for the first reason in arrest of judgment, it must have originated in the proceedings in Warren, and could not have been noticed by the judge in Hinds.

The reason, however, is not sustainable on its merits. It does appear from the indictment, that it was found by the grand jury, empanelled and sworn in and for the body of the county of Warren, which has been held sufficient by this court, in this same case, on a previous trial.

The second reason is, "that it does not appear where the jury came from, constituting the pretended grand jury, empanelled at said pretended February term, or by what authority they came there or were empanelled, nor but that it might have been made up of bystanders." The first branch of this reason is untenable, by a decision of this court already referred to. As to their competency, and the authority by which they were summoned, it is now out of our power to question it. The *venire* did not constitute any part of the proceeding that could be reached by this writ of error, nor do I think, under any circumstances, it necessarily formed a part of the record. It is laid down in 1 Chitty's Criminal Law, 308, that if a disqualified juror be returned on the grand jury, he may be challenged, or the prisoner may plead it in avoidance, but it is even doubted whether such exception can be taken after trial. It is also clearly inferrible from the case cited from Martin and Yerger's Reports, that the *venire* is not considered as a part of the record. If there had been any objection to the *venire* or the jurors summoned, the prisoner might have placed it on the record, and the objection would have come fairly up. The case cited from 1 Wendell, evidently alludes to the *venire* for a petit jury, and in that case it was certified to the court by the return on a *certiorari*, that no *venire* issued.

The third reason is, that by law the courts in Warren are held in May and November, and the indictment was found at February special term, without any authority on the record for holding such term. We are here again met by the fact that this is only a writ of error to Hinds circuit court, and there is nothing to justify a decision as to the records of Warren county unless they were properly and fully before us. It is believed that this in itself would justify the overruling of the reason assigned. But independently of this, there are strong objections to sustaining it, which of themselves would be considered sufficient.

A special term of the circuit court is as much a matter regulated by a general law as the regular term. It is provided in certain cases, that a special term may be called. If it be not called in pursuance of law, it cannot be a special term, or any term at all, and to decide that this was not a special term, would give a flat contradiction to the record before us. The clerk has certified that the indictment was found at a special term, and the indictment itself, in every count, distinctly sets out the term as being special, held in February, 1833. If the clerk had set out the order by which the court was convened, it would have been liable to the same objection. Its validity would have been equally questionable. The order for that term was made matter of record in the supreme court, of which this court is but a continuation, under a different name, and of course, to us, it must be matter of public notoriety, such as we are bound to notice. One of the judges now presiding, was also presiding at that time, and if the order be a material part of the record, I should not feel warranted in deciding it to be a defect, knowing it to exist on the records of our own courts. It was placed there by virtue of a law, and became the means by which the law was enforced, and was, of course, a part of the general regulation.

The fourth reason in arrest of judgment is, "That it does not appear that Joseph Castleman, whose name purports to be signed or indorsed on said indictment, was by the court appointed foreman, and who indorsed said indictment a true bill." I do not think this reason is supported by the fact as it appears on the record. It appears that a "grand jury was empanelled and sworn to inquire in and for the body of the county of Warren, to wit : Joseph Castleman, foreman, etc." By this it appears that a grand jury was sworn, Castleman as foreman, and the swearing him as foreman was certainly a sufficient appointment within the meaning of the statute.

The fifth and last reason in arrest of judgment is, that it does not appear that the prisoner was charged on the indictment, or that he was called on to plead since the reversal of the judgment by this court. The reversal of the judgment could affect none of the proceedings which took place previous to the commission of the error. The error for which it was reversed, occurred during the progress of the trial after issue joined, and did not in any degree affect the plea, which remained unimpaired by the reversal. The arraignment is nothing more than calling on the defendant to answer the accusation; 1 Chitty, 414; 4 Blackstone, 322. The prisoner had been arraigned, called on in the first trial, and pleaded not guilty. So long as this plea stood, it was not only unnecessary, but would have been improper to arraign him a second time. He was arraigned before the first trial, and pleaded; that trial was determined to have been irregular, and of course, was as though no trial had taken place, and it was certainly unnecessary that he should a second time be arraigned, when he could have pleaded nothing without a withdrawal of his first plea.

The *fourth* error assigned is, that the court erred in not granting a new trial, which was abandoned in the argument, and need not be noticed.

Fifthly, That the court erred in permitting the district attorney to withdraw from the prosecution and give it up to the management of counsel employed to prosecute. This point has been noticed under the second assignment, as arising in the bill of exceptions.

Sixthly, That the court erred in refusing to permit counsel for the prisoner to conclude the argument. This has already been decided.

The *seventh* and *eighth* errors are substantially the same, to wit: That it was error to try the prisoner without a second arraignment, and calling on him to plead. This question I have also already noticed.

After an examination as thorough as I have been able to give to the various points raised in an argument conducted with much zeal and ability, I am unable to discover any reason that would justify a reversal of the judgment, and however much I may regret that any individual should be found obnoxious to the criminal laws of the country, yet those laws must be enforced.

The judgment must be affirmed.

SERPENTINE v. THE STATE.   1 Howard, 256.

MURDER.

It is a well recognized principle of law, that the confessions of the accused cannot be given in evidence against him, when they appear to have been forced from the mind by fear, or obtained by the influence of hope; [1] and testimony is admissible to show under what circumstances confessions or gestures of the accused were made. [2] Nor are such confessions, made before a magistrate, admissible, if made through fear of bodily harm, or induced by the persuasion of hope. [3]

Where the prisoner offered to introduce witnesses to prove that, on the night previous to the examination before the magistrate, he had been taken from his bed after night, bound to a tree, and lashed in the severest manner, and also to prove that the actors in the scene were present at the time the prisoner made his confession before the magistrate, such proof was competent, and to reject it was error. [4]

An allegation in an indictment that the prisoner committed the act in A.D. 1030, presupposes the life of the accused to have continued over eight hundred years, and contradicts a known law of nature and vitiates the indictment.

Error to Warren circuit court, MONTGOMERY, J.

The facts of the case are sufficiently stated in the opinion of the court.

Coalter & Warren for plaintiff in error.

T. F. Collins, attorney general.

SMITH, J. ;

The evidence, upon which the jury who tried the issue between the State of Mississippi and the prisoner at the bar, grounded their verdict, appears embodied in the bills of exceptions which were taken at the trial.   The evidence thus presented establishes the following facts, to wit : That John Coun, Alexander Montgomery, and others, on the night of the 30th of September, 1833, proceeded to the house of the late John Dubois, with whose murder the prisoner stood charged, when they found the prisoner in bed.   That the prisoner was taken from his bed and severely whipped, so badly so, that John Coun

---

[1] Peter's case, 3 How., 433; same case, 4 S. & M., 33; see Keithler's case, 7 S. & M., 192; McCann's case, 13 ib., 471; Coon's case, ib., 246; 30 Miss., 593; Jordan's case, 32 Miss., 382; Alfred's case, 37 ib., 296; Simon's case, ib., 288; Frank's case, 39 ib., 705; Pitt's case, 43 ib., 472.

[2] Jordan's case, 32 Miss., 382; Belote's case, 36 ib., 96; State v. Guild, 5 Halst., 163.

[3] Peter's case, 4 S. & M., 83; Jordan's case, 32 Miss., 382; Van Buren v. State, 24 Miss., 512; Com. v. Harman, 4 Barr, 269.

[4] 32 Miss., 382; Com. v. Knapp, 10 Pick., 477; State v. Roberts, 1 Dev., 259; State v. Gould, 5 Halstead, 163; Van Buren v. State, 24 Miss., 512.

did not recollect to have seen any one so badly abused.   That a
rope was then fastened to the prisoner, and one of the witnesses
taking hold of it, followed the prisoner to the north-west corner,
of the field, where Dubois had been found murdered about three
weeks previous thereto, and that a gun was then placed in the
hands of the prisoner, " who put his finger in the muzzle,
handed it back and nodded his head."   And further, that none
of the persons present understood the expressions used by the
prisoner, as he spoke in a foreign language.   That on the morning following, before the committing magistrate, prisoner voluntarily confessed " to the murder."   That the prisoner was informed " of his right to make a confession."   That the witness,
William J. Read, " apprised defendant of the law, and that he
need not make any statement that would criminate himself."
That the confession was made in the French language, which was
translated and taken down by the magistrate.   That the witness
Read " understood the French language indifferently, but sufficiently to enable him to transact ordinary business ; " but that he
" would not be positive he understood the prisoner correctly, but
at the time was positive he understood him."   That at the time
of the examination before the magistrate he heard no threats or
menaces of any kind, and that John Coun and Alexander Montgomery were present at the said examination before the committing magistrate.

It also appears from the exceptions taken at the trial, that the
counsel for the defendant offered several witnesses who were not
permitted to be sworn, to prove that during the night preceding
the examination before the magistrate, the witnesses who were
then offered went to the house of the late John Dubois, where
finding the prisoner, they took him from his bed, bound him to
a tree, and, while naked, he was whipped by four persons suc-
cessively ; that, having suffered the severest inflictions of the
lash, " he was told to confess about the murder of Dubois."
That afterwards, he, the said prisoner, was again informed
through an interpreter, " that their object in whipping him was
to make him confess what he knew about the murder of Dubois,"
and that they, the persons, who had thus, by this extraordinary
method, attempted to coerce a confession from the prisoner,

were present at the examination before the magistrate who took prisoner's confession.

Upon the state of facts here presented, two questions present themselves for the consideration of the court, to wit:

1. Were the acts of the prisoner on the night of the 30th of September, 1833, under the circumstances above detailed, and the confession made on the following morning before the magistrate, admissible as evidence to charge him with the murder of Dubois?

2. And was the testimony offered on the part of the defendant properly excluded?

It does not appear from any part of the evidence adduced in support of the prosecution, that the prisoner was informed or knew that the treatment which he had received was connected with his alleged guilt as the murderer of Dubois.

It is, however, fairly to be inferred, that, informed by his guilty fears, or the language of those who had thus unceremoniously put him to the torture, he but too well knew the motives which influenced them. His act, then, in proceeding to the scene of the murder, of putting his finger in the muzzle of the gun, which was there presented to him, and nodding his head, may, by a very strained construction, be interpreted to mean an acknowledgment of his guilt. But regarded as an explicit avowal of the deed, it is clearly inadmissible as evidence of the crime with which he stood charged. It is a well-recognized principle of law that the confessions of the accused cannot be given in evidence against him, when they appear to have been forced from the mind by fear or obtained by the influence of hope. See Lord Hale, P. C., 234; McNally's Ev., 42, Rules 4 and 9; Hawk., P. C., 234, § 36. It is impossible to conceive a case where the rule applies with much greater force. Every circumstance was calculated to excite the most agonizing impressions of fear. Taken from his bed after night, bound to a tree, and lashed in the severest manner, he may well have supposed that the only alternative by which he could relieve himself from his calamities was an acknowledgment of the crime of which he was accused. But I do not think the acts of the prisoner, on that occasion, can be considered a confession of his guilt; at most, they are very equivocal, and may have been intended by the prisoner, who, it appears, did not speak the English language, to convey not an admission of his guilt, but a knowledge of the fact of Dubois' murder, and the weapon used in the perpetration of the crime.   The first confession of the prisoner was on the morning following, as appears from the evidence in support of the prosecution.   The confession made at that time was voluntary, uninfluenced by the persuasion of hope, or the suggestions of fear, and after he had been, in the language of the witness, " informed of his rights, and that he need not make any statement that would criminate himself."   There is, however, a vagueness in the confession of the prisoner, and the admission on the part of Read, who acted as interpreter before the committing magistrate, that, from his imperfect knowledge of the French language, in which the prisoner spoke, he may not have correctly understood the prisoner's meaning; which strongly incline me to the opinion that his testimony should have been refused.   I do not, however, deem it necessary to decide the question of its admissibility.

2. The witnesses tendered by the prisoner to prove the transactions of the night, previous to the examination before the magistrate, and also to prove that the actors in the scene were present at the time the prisoner made the confession before the magistrate, were, I am inclined to believe, improperly excluded. If it is assumed that the acts of the prisoner, on the night of the 30th of September, were, in effect, an acknowledgment of the crime charged, the testimony here offered was clearly competent to prove the circumstances under which that confession was obtained, and that the subsequent confession was made under the same inducement.   But taking it as granted that no confession was made on that night, yet it was competent to establish facts which, in their direct effect, would raise legal presumptions that the mind of the prisoner in making his confession was operated upon by a strong sense of impending danger, which he hoped thereby to avoid.   The witnesses offered by the accused, and who were excluded by the court, were introduced to prove that several persons, who were present at the time when the prisoner's confession was made, had, on the

preceding night, greatly abused the prisoner, and severely scourged him, informing him, at the same time, that their object was to make him confess what he knew about the murder of Dubois; and that the prisoner, under the infliction of the lash, attempted to express himself, but was unintelligible. Had these facts been established in the court below, would not the presumption most clearly have arisen, that the prisoner, at the time of making his confession, surrounded as he was by those who, but a few hours before, had manifested a purpose of coercing a confession; without assurance of safety, or warning of the consequences of a confession, ignorant of the language of those who surrounded him, and unintelligible to all save the witness Read, labored under an impression that he had been brought before the magistrate for the purpose of acknowledging the murder of Dubois?   If so, the confession of the prisoner ought not to have been given in evidence against him, under a rule of law universally recognized to be founded, not only in the dictates of humanity, but upon the soundest principles of reason.

3. A third objection not embraced by the special assignment of errors, but which is properly presented under the general assignment, merits the consideration of the court. The objection is, that the indictment does not show any crime to have been committed against the State of Mississippi, and that the assumption of the truth of the allegations contained therein, is inconsistent with a known law of nature. The crime charged against the prisoner, is alleged to have been committed on the 30th day of September, A. D. one thousand and thirty-three; whether it is a mistake which occurred in the indictment, which substantially contradicts a known law of nature, regulating the duration of human life, it is clearly defective, and cannot be the legitimate foundation of a judgment of a court. All knowledge of the laws of nature which govern the material world, is primarily derived from experience, and our belief in their permanency rests upon the same foundation. An allegation which presupposes the life of the accused to have endured for upwards of eight hundred years, as it contradicts the experience of the whole world, must be considered as impossible. Again, an

offense committed at that date, though not barred by any statute of limitations, is not an offense against the State of Mississippi. Courts of justice will judicially notice the great epochs in the history of the country, as well as the laws of the land; this court is, therefore, bound to know that the State of Mississippi did not exist at the time at which the murder is alleged to have been committed, and that, therefore, it could have been no infraction of her laws.

The judgment will, therefore, be reversed, and the prisoner discharged.

DAMEWOOD *v.* THE STATE,—1 Howard, 262

LARCENY.

The felonious taking and carrying away of the mere personal goods and chattels of another with the criminal intent to apply them to the party's own use, constitutes the crime of larceny, and is its technical definition [1] ; and, although it is usual to use the terms "did feloniously steal, take and carry away, etc.," the omission of the word "steal" will not vitiate the indictment.[2]

At common law, bank notes, bank bills, and bills of credit were not subjects of larceny, but they are made such by our statute, which provides that, "Robbery, or simple larceny, may be committed, of obligations, bonds, bills obligatory, or bills of exchange, *promissory notes for the payment of money,* or notes for the payment of specific property, etc." [3] In an indictment for larceny of a bank note, it should be described as a promissory note for the payment of money, purporting to be a bank note. [4]

Error to Hinds circuit court.

This was an indictment against Damewood for larceny of a pocket-book and certain bank notes on the Planters' Bank, the property of J. Caldwell. The facts are sufficiently set forth in the assignment of errors, and the opinion of the court.

The counsel for plaintiff in error assigned the following errors:

[1] Starkin Cr. Pl., 84 ; 2 East, 836, 784 ; Commonwealth v. James, 1 Pick., 375.

[2] 2 Wills v. The State, 4 Blacks., 457.

[3] People v. Cook, 2 Park. Cr. Cases, 12 ; Thompson v. Commonwealth, 2 Virg. Ca., 135.

[4] Rev. Code, 1857, 604, art. 193. See also Boyd's case, 1 Rob., 691; see also Culp v. The State, 1 Porter, 33.

Sed vide, The State v. Route, 3 Hawks, 618 ; Commonwealth v. Richards, 1 Mass., 337.

1. That the first count in the indictment (if for anything) is a count for grand larceny, and the second count (if for anything) is for robbery, which two counts cannot be joined in the same indictment.

2. The first count is bad and insufficient in this, that it does not describe the bank notes with sufficient certainty.

3. That notes on the Planters' Bank are not subjects on which larceny can be committed at common law, nor made so by statute.

4. That the second count is bad and insufficient, in not averring that the said Caldwell was first put in fear.

5. That the notes on the Planters' Bank are not sufficiently described.

6. That the notes on the Planters' Bank are not subjects of larceny.

7. That the court erred in overruling the motion of his counsel to put the district attorney to his election, to introduce evidence alone with regard to the bank notes or to the pocket-book.

8. That the court erred in overruling the objection of the defendant's counsel to the introduction of evidence on the part of the state with regard to the supposed felonious taking, stealing, and carrying away the notes on the Planters' Bank.

9. The court erred in refusing to charge the jury, that, notwithstanding, of their own knowledge, they might know the notes on the Planters' Bank, named in the indictment, or the pocket-book named in the indictment, were of some value; yet, unless the state had proved that the said notes were of some value, or that the pocket-book was of some value, the jury was bound to find the defendant not guilty. And the court also erred in charging the jury that, if they saw the pocket-book, they might judge of its value.

10. That the court erred in refusing to correct the minutes, by inserting the words, " We, the jury, believe the defendant guilty as charged in the indictment," instead, and in lieu of the words, " We find the prisoner guilty in manner and form as charged in the indictment."

11. The court erred in overruling the motion in arrest of judgment for the reasons assigned on the record.

R. W. & C. W. Webber for plaintiff in error.
T. F. Collins, attorney general, contra.

SMITH, J. :

The indictment upon which the prisoner was tried in the court below contains two counts ; the first, for feloniously stealing, taking and carrying away, one leather pocket-book, of the value of one dollar and fifty cents, and two bank notes on the Planters' Bank of the State of Mississippi, of the value of one hundred dollars each ; and the second, for feloniously taking and carrying away one leather pocket-book, of the value - of one dollar, and five one hundred-dollar bank notes on the Planters' Bank of the State of Mississippi, of the value of one hundred dollars each.

The exception which I shall first notice, is that which is embraced in the first assignment of errors, and necessarily involves in its decisions the question presented by the 4th assignment. This exception presents the question of misjoinder of the counts in the indictment.

It is stated in the assignment, and was insisted on in the argument at bar, that the first count, if good, is for grand larceny, and the second, if unexceptionable, is for robbery ; and the conclusion sought to be deduced is, that, as the crimes of grand larceny and robbery are distinct in their nature, and the character and degrees of punishment affixed to them by the law, it is error to join them in the same indictment. But this exception appears to be based on an erroneous conception of the character of the second count, which is for larceny and not for robbery, as assumed in the exception, and good, if the notes of the Planters' Bank, by that description, can be the subject-matter of larceny. The omission of the word " that " in the second count, does not change its character, or render it defective. It is well settled that the indictment should technically describe the offense of which the party stands charged, and an imperfection in this respect would be fatal.

The felonious taking and carrying away the mere personal goods and chattels of another with the criminal intent to apply them to the party's own use, constitutes the crime of larceny, and is its technical definition. It is true that this offense is

usually described in the entries by the terms "feloniously stealing, taking, and carrying away, etc.," but it is no defect if the
word "that" is omitted.   See Starke's Crim. Pl., 84 ; 2 East.,
336, 784.

But were the premises assumed good, the conclusion sought
to be established would nevertheless be erroneous.   Numerous
authorities sustain the propriety of joining, in the same indictment, counts for robbery and larceny.   See 1 Hale, 5, 6, 534,--
5 ; 2 East., 736, 754.

The validity of the 2d, 3d, 5th, 6th and 8th assignments of
error depends upon the solution of the foregoing proposition,
and, therefore, need not be separately considered.

At common law, it is admitted that larceny could not be committed of bank notes, bank bills, or bills of credit.   But it is
contended that the state has thrown around these objects of
property the protection of her laws, and made it, by statute,
felony for any person to steal them.   Upon the construction of
this statute depends the validity of the indictment.   The question to be settled is one deeply important to the state, and I
regret that I have had neither the time nor means of thorough
investigation.   The statute referred to, is in the following words,
viz. :   Robbery, or simple larceny, of obligations, bonds, bills
obligatory, or bills of exchange, *promissory notes for the payment of money*, or notes for the payment of any specific property, lottery tickets, *paper bills of credit, etc.*   See Rev. Laws,
299, sec. 20.

The words "promissory notes for the payment of money,"
and "paper bills of credit," are, it is insisted, fairly construed,
so as to embrace bank notes of the Planters' Bank, or of any
banking corporation.

It is a uniform principle in the construction of penal statutes,
that they are to be taken in their most restricted sense, in favor
of the rights of the accused.   Was it, then, the evident intent of
this section to make the theft of a bank note the crime of larceny ?

It is unquestionably true that a bank note is a promissory
note by a banking corporation to pay a specific sum of money,
and comes, therefore, strictly within the meaning of the generic

term "promissory note." And I am, therefore, impressed with the conviction that, although the statute has not expressly enumerated bank notes, and made them subjects of which larceny could be committed under that description alone, yet as they are in verity promissory notes, possessing all the properties which constitute a promissory note, a count charging the larceny of a promissory note for the payment of money purporting to be a bank note, would be sustained by proof of the felonious taking, etc., of a bank note of the Planters' Bank; and by a similar decision in the case of the Commonwealth of Virginia v. Hersley, 2 Virg. Laws, 153.

But in the case before us, neither count of the indictment charges the taking of promissory notes for the payment of money, purporting to be a bank note, nor in any respect conforms to the offense created by the 20th section of the act in relation to crimes and misdemeanors. I am, therefore, compelled to regard each count of the indictment as defective. In strict accordance with this opinion, will be found the decision in the case of The King v. Richard Craven, (2 East. P. C., 601), which was an indictment upon the statute of 2 Geo. 2, C. 25.

As this defect goes to the foundation of the indictment, I will not notice the other questions arising upon the record.

The judgment must be reversed and the prisoner discharged.

BRYANT *v.* THE STATE, 1 Howard, 351.

PRACTICING MEDICINE WITHOUT A LICENSE.

By the constitution of 1833, the terms of all officers were limited, respectively, to some specified time; and consequently abrogated the law providing for the appointment of a board of medical censors, whose term of office was unlimited. Consequently, an indictment for practicing medicine without a license from said board, cannot now be maintained.

Error to Wilkinson circuit court.

This was an indictment in Wilkinson county, against Bryant, for practicing medicine without a license from the board of medical censors, and came up to this court on writ of error. To the indictment, the defendant below made plea of confession and evidence, viz., that he did practice medicine by administering to divers sick persons, at the times charged in the indictment; but that said medicines, and the administration of them were the same, and none other than is authorized by patent rights of Samuel Thompson and his assigns, and by the said Thompson and his assigns, and by the said Thompson permitted to be used and administered by the defendant. To which plea there was a demurrer, which was sustained by the court.

Henderson for plaintiff in error.

The defendant had full and ample authority to compound and administer the medicines, as by his plea alleged, and that the law of the state, on which his conviction is based, and his punishment demanded, was as to him and his acts confessed, *null and void.* 2 Peters' Reports, 251–2; 2 Wheaton, 405–6; ib. 421–5; ib. 431–2.

This charge was preferred against defendant at the April term, 1833, and since the new constitution has repealed the repugnant statute in the Revised Code. There was, therefore, no such offense known to the law, as is charged in the indictment, and hence, the judgment below should be reversed and given for the defendant. 2 Peters' R., 251–2; Rev. Code, p. 416, sec. 2. 5; Statute of 1827, 25, 26, 27; New Const., p. 6, sec. 30; p. 26, sec. 4; Const. U. S. Rev. Code, p. 492–3, art. 1, sec. 8, par. 8; p. 498, art. 6, par. 2; Gordon's Dig. p. 547, secs. 2811, 2816, 2820, 2825.

T. F. Collins, attorney general.

SHARKEY, C. J.:

Bryant, the plaintiff in error, was indicted in the circuit court of Wilkinson county at the November term, 1833, for practicing medicine without a license.

To the indictment, he pleaded that he was authorized so to practice by virtue of a patent issued by the proper department of the Federal government, to one Samuel Thompson, under whom, the plaintiff claims by transfer, or as having a special authority to use the invention. The privilege secured to the patentee and his assigns, is that of using, compounding, mixing, preparing and administering certain medicines according to the schedule attached to the patent, which is commonly denominated the "Thompsonian System." There was a demurrer to the plea, and various causes assigned, which was sustained by the circuit court.

We are precluded from any inquiry as to the merits of the plea, by an interposing question which goes directly to the foundation of the indictment, and that is, was the act stated as the offense, a violation of an existing law of the state? The act of 1819, incorporated into the revised code, 416, provided for the appointment of a board of medical censors, who were authorized and required to decide on the qualifications of applicants, for license to practice medicine, and to grant such license to those who might be qualified. The first act was found to be imperfect, and several amendments were subsequently passed, by which it was made an indictable offense, subjecting the offender to heavy penalties, to practice medicine without a license. Under these provisions, the plaintiff in error was indicted, at a period subsequent to the adoption of the revised constitution; we must necessarily determine how far these several laws are in confliction with the constitution, and consequently inoperative. There is but one feature in the law, that tends to place it in conflict with the paramount authority of the revised constitution, and that arises from the tenure of office conferred on the members of the board. They went into office by appointment by the governor, and were to hold during good behavior, and had power to fill vacancies. The mode of appointment, and their holding during good behavior, and the object of the appointment being to carry into effect a general law of the state, go very far to show that they must be considered as officers. They were doubtless subject to impeachment for malconduct in office, because they hold their office during good behavior, which necessarily implies that a power of inquiry into their conduct was reserved to the authorities of the state. If we consider them as officers, the provisions of the constitution must bear on them. The first provision which must be considered relates to the term of office, and is contained in the 30th section of the Bill of

Rights. It declares "that no person shall be appointed or elected to office in this state for life, or during good behavior, but the tenure of all offices shall be for some limited time." This section may be considered as more properly relating to officers, thereafter to be appointed or elected, but it very clearly shows the spirit of the constitution to an unlimited tenure of office, and must have its due weight in the investigation of a constitutional question. The fourth section of the schedule shows conclusively, that the convention did not intend to permit any law which was repugnant to the constitution, to remain in force, and for that reason, particular care was taken to perpetuate all laws that were not repugnant, leaving no other conclusion, than that they intended to abolish all that were of a different character. The provisions of this law are manifestly in opposition to the spirit as well as the declared provisions in the constitution, and must be considered as void.

It is true the third section of the schedule provides that officers then in office should remain in until their successors should be qualified; but neither the convention nor the legislature contemplated the continuance of the board by making provisions to fill the offices of the members. We cannot, therefore, consider it, as the legislature may by possibility continue it, but must look at it as it is, and contrast it with the constitution. The several amendments must be taken as a part of the general law, and must altogether depend for their validity on the powers of the board, for the provisions of the law are nugatory without the essential officers, who alone are authorized to perform the duties required. A law containing the same provisions in regard to the particular officers necessary to the enforcement of it could not now be constitutionally passed by the legislature; and by parity of reasoning, I do not think it can constitutionally exist in the face of the fourth section of the schedule by having been in operation at the adoption of the constitution. The act charged in the indictment was, therefore, no violation of law, and the judgment must be reversed.

Woodsides *v.* The State, 2 Howard, 655.

Murder.

Where the caption of the indictment was: "The State of Mississippi, Wilkinson county, ss.   The circuit court of Wilkinson county, October Term, 1835, thereof, in the year of our Lord, 1835.   The grand jurors of the State of Mississippi, empanelled and sworn, in and for the county of Wilkinson and the State of Mississippi, at the term aforesaid, in the name and by the authority of the State of Mississippi, upon," &c., it was held a sufficient allegation that the grand jurors were of the State of Mississippi, and of the county of Wilkinson; and also that they were *then* and *there* sworn. [1]   If the record show that A. B. *was sworn as foreman*, it is sufficient evidence that he was *appointed* foreman.

The circuit courts, as courts of oyer and terminer, have power to issue writs tested and returnable within the same term ; and it is no objection to a *venire facias*, that it commands the sheriff to summon a jury *from the county*, instead *of the county;* the word "from" not authorizing him to summons persons out of his county.

The *venire facias* in capital cases, is not a writ within the contemplation of the 20th section of the circuit court law, and is not required to bear test on the first day of the term next preceding that to which the same may be made returnable.   The authority to issue this writ and to fix the day on which it shall be returned, vested in the circuit courts, not by virtue of the above statute, but as incident to their powers as courts of oyer and terminer at common law.   The act of 1833, prescribing the mode of summoning and empanelling juries in capital cases, was simply declaratory of the powers which those courts before possessed; and did not in any respect, modify their authority as it then existed.

Challenge to the array is an irregular form of pleading, whereby the party excepts to all the jurors returned upon the *venire*, for some original defect in making the return thereto; and must relate to the acts of the sheriff, and should charge a particular default or partiality in forming the array.   Consequently, the want of legal qualification in a juror, placed upon the panel, is no ground of challenge to the array.

Where it is stated in the indictment that the wounds of which the deceased died, were inflicted on the 8th day of September, 1835; and "that from said day he, the said H. P. S., until the 13th day of September, 1835, in the county of W., did languish, and languishing did live, on which said 13th day of September, 1835, &c., *he died;* and the said Alexander Woodsides, *then and there*, &c., was present, aiding and abetting the said Samuel Woodsides, and Robert Woodsides, in the felony and murder aforesaid, in manner and form aforesaid," Held, that these allegations in the indictment are sufficiently certain, and form no ground for reversing the judgment.

A party, in order to present the question of error in the decision of the court upon the competency and relevancy of evidence, offered on the trial of a cause, or of any matter of fact brought to the consideration of the court, not appearing by the pleadings, should except to the opinion and embody the evidence or facts in the bill of exceptions.   If this be not done, the judgment of the court below upon the subject, will be regarded as correct.

The *venire facias* directed the sheriff to summon fifty jurors, but the panel contained the names of fifty-one.   The sheriff returned that he had served the prisoner with a true copy of the indictment and a list of the jurors; but the name of one had been erased from the panel, leaving the fifty, still.   The affidavit of the prisoner, affirming the identity of the list, and denying that a true one had been delivered to him, cannot be received by the court as conclusive that he had not been regularly notified of the jurors who were to pass upon his trial.   If the sheriff has returned that he has delivered to the prisoner a correct copy of the indictment, and a list of the jury, the truth of such return cannot be collaterally questioned.

[1] State v. Price, 6 Halst., 203.

It is a common law doctrine that the declarations of deceased persons, made after the reception of the mortal wound, and under the declared apprehension of death, are admissible as evidence on the trial of the accused; and the 10th section of the bill of rights, declaring " that in all criminal prosecutions the accused hath a right to be heard by himself and counsel, to demand the nature and cause of the accusation, and to be confronted by the witnesses against him," &c., is but an affirmance of this long cherished principle of the common law.

Presumption of a malicious intent, may arise from the character of the weapon used in the perpetration of the deed.

W. was convicted of murder in the circuit court, but owing to some cause not appearing of record, sentence was not executed. At a subsequent term of the court, certain proceedings were had in the case. Held, that errors in the subsequent proceedings cannot affect the validity of the judgment previously entered against the prisoner.

Error to Wilkinson circuit court. WILLIS, J.

The opinion of the court contains a sufficient statement of the facts of the case.

John Gildart, for plaintiff in error.

Cited Rev. Code, 134; 1 Chitty, 270; 4 Hawkins; Peck's R 310; Rev. Code, 116; 1 Chitty, 419; Jury Law, Acts Legislature 1830; 1 Coke, 156, A; Leach 87; Chitty, 165.

J. F. Collins, attorney general.

SMITH, J.

At the October term, 1835, of the circuit court of Wilkinson county, Samuel Woodsides, the prisoner at the bar, was tried and convicted of the murder of Hudson P. Liscomb, and having received sentence, he has, by writ of error, removed his cause into this court, and asks a reversal of the judgment against him, for several errors and irregularities alleged to exist in the proceedings of the court below.

As the questions which are presented by the record, and which it will be necessary to determine, are disconnected and independent, we will pursue the order in which they stand in the assignment of errors. It is insisted in the first place, that there is error in the record, because it is not shown that the court in which the prisoner was tried was holden within the state of Mississippi, nor where the jury were empanelled, nor the indictment found. These objections are valid, and, if they exist in point of fact, would require a reversal of the judgment.

But the record shows conclusively that they are without foundation. The caption of the indictment sets out with certainty each of these particulars. It is in the following words, to wit: " The State of Mississippi, Wilkinson county, ss. The circuit court of Wilkinson county, October term, thereof, in the year of our Lord one thousand eight hundred and thirty-five. The grand jurors of the State of Mississippi, empanelled and sworn, in and for the county of Wilkinson, and State of Mississippi, at the term aforesaid, in the name and by the authority of the State of Mississippi, upon, &c." It is contended in the second place, that there is error, because it does not appear in the record, that a foreman of the grand jury was appointed by the court.

Assuming that it is necessary that the appointment of the foreman should appear upon the record, in order to confer validity upon the finding of a grand jury, we are of opinion that such appointment appears with the requisite degree of certainty. It is true, that it is not expressly stated that a foreman was appointed by the court. The record shows that fifteen persons were drawn, according to the statute, from the jurors summoned for the first week of court and sworn and empanelled as a grand jury for the body of the county, of which Daniel Bass was sworn as foreman. This statement on the record, that Bass was sworn as foreman of the grand jury, necessarily implies his appointment as such by the court. And it is sufficient if that which is omitted be implied in common understanding from that which is expressed. 3 Bac. Abr. 574. But we understand that the administration of the oath required by the statute to be taken by the foreman of the grand jury, is in effect the appointment, and, in fact, the only appointment ever made by a court of the foreman of a grand jury.

The third objection is, that it does not appear that the grand jury were then and there sworn. This objection is answered by what is above remarked. It is also clear from authority that the words " then and there" need not appear in the caption, for if it is by the record shown that the jurors were sworn, it will be sufficiently intended that they were " then and there" sworn. Chitty Cr. Law, 334 ; 3 Bac. Abr. 574. The fourth and fifth exceptions may be considered under the same head, and present the question of error in the decision of the court overruling the motion to quash the special *venire.*

Several grounds were assumed in support of the motion to quash the *venire*, to wit:

1. That by the precept of the writ of *venire facias*, the sheriff was not required to summon good and lawful men "*of*" his county.

2. That the writ shows a prosecution pending between the State of Mississippi and Robert Woodsides, Alexander Woodsides and Samuel Woodsides, and the jury were required to determine only, whether the said Samuel be guilty of the crime whereof he stands charged.

3. That the writ does not bear test at the term next preceding that to which the same is made returnable.

4. That the return upon the said writ does not show at what time the jurors mentioned therein were summoned.

5. That the writ does not show upon whom the murder was committed, of which the prisoner stands charged.

In relation to the first ground, it was contended in the argument at bar, that the writ varies from the proper form and necessarily violates the rights of the accused. The particular variance insisted on, is, that by the writ, the sheriff was required to summon the jury "from the county," and not "of the county." It is unquestionably the intention of the law that the accused shall be secure in his right of an impartial trial by a jury of his county; and if it could be shown that a precept to the sheriff, directing him to summon "fifty good and lawful men from his county" would authorize him or require him to summon individuals as jurors who were not of his county, the exception would be held valid. But as the writ is not varied according to common understanding or in its legal import by the insertion of the word "from," instead of the word "of," we cannot see that the objection has any validity whatever.

The second, fourth and fifth grounds of objection to the *venire* were not urged in argument, and as they do not constitute a defect in the *venire* which should induce this court to reverse the judgment of the circuit court, will not be particularly examined.

The objection that the writ which was issued to bring in the jury for the trial of the prisoner was not tested at the next term preceding that at which it was made returnable, is equally without foundation.   It is clearly not a writ contemplated by the 20th section of the circuit court law, Revised Code 106, by which it is directed generally, that all writs or process shall bear test on the first day of the term next preceding that to which the same may be made returnable; and that all original process, and all subsequent process thereupon, to bring any person or persons to answer any action, suit, bill, or complaint in any state, shall be made returnable on the first day of the term next succeeding that at which the same shall bear test, and shall be executed at least five days before the return day thereof; and that any writ or process, except as above described, which shall be issued within five days before the commencement of any term of a court, shall be made returnable to the next term after that to be held within five days.

The special *venire* in the case under consideration, issued after the arraignment of the prisoner, and in term time, and if it be governed by the general provisions of any law regulating the test and return of process from the circuit courts, it should have been made returnable on the first day of the preceding term, and not, as it was, on a day within the term at which it issued.

The authority to issue this writ and to designate the time at which it is to be returned, vested in the circuit courts, as incident to their power as courts of oyer and terminer at common law.

The act of 1833, prescribing the mode of summoning and empanelling in capital cases, was but declaratory of the powers which those courts before possessed, and imposed no restriction, nor in any respect modified their authority as it then existed. But as the writ emanated during term time, it was properly tested at the commencement of the term.   For, if it be held that the testing of the special *venire* is to be regulated by the general law in regard to process, it should have been tested at the same time at which it ought to have been, if made returnable at the preceding term of the court.

And there can be no doubt, under the law of the Revised Code, that process emanating during term time, and made returnable on the first day of the preceding term, should be tested on the first day of the term at which it shall issue.

The next exception is taking to the ruling of the court below upon the demurrer to the prisoner's challenge to the array.

A challenge to the array is an irregular form of pleading, by which the party excepts to all the jurors returned upon the *venire,* for some original defect in making the return thereto. 1 Chitty Cr. Law, 537.

It must relate, therefore, to the acts of the sheriff or some other officer, and should charge him with a particular default or partiality in arraying the panel. Coke Litt., 156 A.

The array of the panel is the placing in order the names of the jurors who are returned for the trial of the issue. Coke Litt., 156, A.

The want of qualification in a juror placed upon the panel, or arrayed, is consequently no ground of challenge to the panel. This is conclusively shown from the fact, that the coroner may return the same jurors immediately after the array has been quashed for partiality or default on the part of the sheriff in making his returns, or in arraying them.

Anciently it was held good cause of challenge to the array, that a sufficient number of hundredors were not returned on the panel; but the want of qualification which constitutes an objection to the polls, was never considered a cause of challenge to the principal panel. The causes assigned for the challenge in the case under consideration, are not predicated upon any default or act of partiality in the officer who returned the *venire.* The court was, therefore, correct in sustaining the demurrer to the challenge.

The next objection is to the decision of the court overruling the motion in arrest of judgment. Several of the reasons assigned in support of the motion have been commented upon in the consideration which we have seen to the third assignment of error, and will in this place require no further elucidation.

The indictment is alleged to be repugnant and inconsistent. And in support of this position, it is said that the "time and place, as set forth, of the aiding and abetting on the part of the accessory is long subsequent to the time laid when the principal committed the act."

It is stated in the indictment, that the wounds of which Hudson P. Liscomb, the murdered individual, died, were inflicted on the 8th of September, 1835 ; and " that from said day he, the said Hudson P. Liscomb, until the 13th day of September, 1835, in said Wilkinson county, did languish, and languishing did live, on which said 13th day of September, 1835, &c., *he died ;* and the said Alexander Woodsides, *then and there*, &c., was present, aiding, &c., the said Samuel Woodsides and Robert Woodsides, in the felony and murder aforesaid, in the manner and form aforesaid."

In Catherine Graham's case (Leach, Crown Law, 87), which was referred to by counsel, the indictment contained two counts, charging two distinct felonies against the principals ; and in the same indictment, Catherine Graham was charged as accessory after the fact, at common law, for harboring the principal felons, she well knowing that they had committed the felony aforesaid. Catherine Graham was convicted, and the judgment arrested ; the court holding that it was uncertain to which of the felonies the charge referred.

In the case before us, there is but one offense with which the prisoner stood charged ; and the allegations of the indictment in respect to that offense are clear, distinct, and unequivocal ; and upon the principle of the decision referred to, although there might be uncertainty with respect to the time in the charge against Alexander Woodsides, it would afford no ground for arresting the judgment against the prisoner at the bar.

But it does not appear to us that this part of the indictment is obnoxious to the objection of uncertainty.

The indictment alleges, that the said Alexander Woodsides, *then and there*, etc., was present, aiding, etc., the said Samuel Woodsides, and Robert Woodsides, in the felony and murder aforesaid, in the manner and form aforesaid, to do, and commit, etc. The latter part of the count explains the time to which reference is made by the words " then and there." The deed which terminated in the death of Liscomb, was perpetrated on the 8th of September, but he did not expire till the 13th of the same month.

The circumstances attending the murder, "the manner and form," are stated; and it being alleged that the accessory was "then and there" present, aiding and assisting "in the manner and form aforesaid," in the commission of the murder, there is no room for uncertainty as to which of the antecedents reference is made.

The next error assigned, is to the judgment of the court overruling the motion for a new trial. But there is nothing on the record by which we can examine into the correctness of that decision. The testimony adduced on the trial, does not appear in it, nor do any of the grounds upon which the decision was predicated. The facts detailed in the affidavit of the prisoner, if they constituted a sufficient showing to have required the judge to award a new trial, cannot be noticed by this court.

The party, in order to present the question of error in the decision of a court upon the competency and relevancy of evidence offered on the trial of a cause, or of any matter of fact brought to the consideration of the court, not appearing by the pleading, should except to the opinion and embody the evidence or facts in the bill of exceptions. This not having been done in the present case, we are bound to regard the judgment of the court upon the motion as correct.

The prisoner, when put upon trial, objected to being tried by the jury empanelled, upon the alleged ground that he had not been served with a correct list of jurors returned by the sheriff. The court overruled the objection; to which decision of the court, the prisoner by his counsel excepted, and filed his bill of exceptions in the following words, to wit: "Be it remembered, that on the trial of this cause, and during the progress thereof, Robert Semple was called as a juror, whose name appeared upon the panel; it also appeared upon the copy furnished the prisoner, that the name of Robert Semple was erased, and that without his name, there were fifty jurors named. In the original, there were only fifty jurors named. The prisoner, by his counsel, objected on the ground that a correct copy of the list of jurors who were to pass upon his trial, had not been furnished him."

The fact that the prisoner was not furnished with a correct list of the jury who were to try him, is not directly stated in this bill of exceptions.

The facts presented by the court, and upon which it is to be presumed its decision was based, is that the name of Robert Semple, who was one of the panel, appeared erased from the list which had been furnished to the prisoner, and that without his name, the copy or list contained the names of fifty jurors, the number which, by the award of the court, should have been summoned. But it is not stated, nor can it be inferred from the bill of exceptions, that the list, at the time it was presented to the prisoner, did not contain the name of Semple, or that without his name more than fifty were included.

But assuming that the bill of exceptions stated directly that the list referred to was the one which had been delivered to the prisoner, and that it was incorrect in not containing the names of all the jurors who had been summoned upon the special *venire*, would the list itself, supported by the affidavit of the prisoner, affirming the identity of the list and denying that a true one had been delivered to him, have constituted evidence which the court should have regarded as conclusive of the fact that the prisoner was not notified, as the law requires, of the jurors who were to pass upon the trial?

The rule of evidence does not require the strongest possible evidence of the matter in contest, but only that evidence shall not be admitted, which from its character supposes a higher degree of evidence to exist. It is the duty of the sheriff as the ministerial officer of the court, upon making his return to the *venire* in any case where the party has been indicted for a capital offense, to deliver to the prisoner a copy of the indictment and a list of the jury, and to make a return thereof to the court.

If the sheriff, failing to deliver to the prisoner a list and copy as required, or having done so, neglect to make a return, it would be proper to inquire into the matter upon affidavit, or otherwise upon suggestion to the court that such was the fact. 3 Johns. R., 529 ; 1 Munf. R., 269. But if the sheriff has returned that he has delivered to the prisoner a correct copy of the indictment, and a list of the jury, the truth of such return, we apprehend, could not be collaterally questioned. The return of the sheriff that he has served the prisoner with a list of the jury, must be conclusive of the fact, as his return to any process issuing from the court and properly directed to him. In the case of Stayton v. The Inhabitants of Chester, 4 Mass. Rep., 479, it was held to be "clear that when a writ appears by the return, indorsed by the officer, to have been legally served, the defendant cannot plead in abatement of the writ by alleging matter repugnant to the return." And when a writ is duly returned and filed, the return is so far evidence of the facts stated in it, as not to be disputed incidentally; and hence, if the sheriff return a rescue or a summons on a writ of *scire facias*, the parties cannot dispute it on affidavit. Norris' Peake, 82; Phillips v. Hyde, 1 Dallas, 439.

In the case under consideration, the officer's return, which appears of record, shows that the prisoner was furnished with a list of the jurors. Upon the principle, therefore, that the return of the sheriff cannot be questioned by alleging matter repugnant to it, the decision of the court overruling the objection of the prisoner must be regarded as correct.

An objection to the judgment of the court overruling the motion for a new trial, although it is not properly presented by the record, will be noticed. It is in effect, this, that the declaration *in extremis* of the murdered person, as to the fact of murder, should not be admitted as evidence against the accused.

It is not denied, that by the common law, the declarations of deceased individuals, in prosecutions for murder, made after the reception of the mortal wound, and under the declared apprehension of death, are admissible as evidence.

But the objection is rested upon the assumption that this principle of the common law has been abrogated by the 10th section of the bill of rights, which declares "that in all criminal prosecutions, the accused hath a right to be heard by himself and counsel, to demand the nature and cause of the accusation, to be confronted by the witness against him," etc.

This point was ably and ingeniously argued by the counsel for the accused, but we cannot assent to the proposition sought to be established. The bill of rights in respect to the rights of the accused, of being confronted by the witnesses for the prosecution, is but an affirmation of a long cherished principle of the common law.   By the bill of rights the accused is secured in the right of an oral examination of the opposing witnesses, and of the advantages of a cross-examination.   This privilege is placed beyond legislative action.   The same right belongs to the subjects of England, but there they have no constitutional provision guarantying its perpetuity.

The argument proceeded upon the supposition that the deceased party was the witness, and as he could not be confronted or cross-examined by the prisoner, it was a violation of the prisoner's rights by the sovereign will of the state to allow the dying declarations of the deceased to be given in evidence.

But it is upon the ground alone that the murdered individual is not a witness, that his declarations, made *in extremis*, can be offered as evidence upon the trial of the accused. If he were, or could be a witness, his declaration, upon the clearest principle, would be inadmissible.   His declarations are regarded as facts or circumstances connected with the murder, which, when they are established by oral testimony, the law has declared to be evidence.   It is the individual who swears to the statements of the deceased that is the witness, not the deceased.

In the case of implied malice, the presumption of a malicious intent may arise from the weapon used in the perpetration of the deed.   Thus if A, without any provocation or declaration of preconceived hatred, deliberately draw his sword and inflict a mortal wound upon B, it will be murder, and the fact that a weapon calculated to produce death was employed in the assault, will be the circumstance from which the law presumes the existence of malice.   Evidence applied to proceedings in courts of justice consists of those facts or circumstances connected with the legal proposition which establishes its truth or falsehood.   The use of the weapon in the case supposed, is the fact or circumstance which establishes or manifests the criminal intention.

In a case where the declarations of the deceased are offered to the jury, they constitute facts or circumstances to which the law imparts verity, and tend to establish the truth of the matter to which they relate.   The position, therefore, that the declarations of the deceased, in prosecutions for murder, are not admissible as evidence to establish the murder, is wholly without foundation.

The sentence of death which was pronounced upon the prisoner at the October term of the circuit court of Wilkinson county, from some cause not appearing of record, was not carried into execution at the time appointed. He was therefore ordered before the same court at its March term, in 1836, to have execution awarded on the judgment previously pronounced, at which time certain proceedings took place which it is not now important to notice, for if, in those proceedings, errors had intervened, it cannot affect the validity of the judgment which had previously been entered against the prisoner.

Having carefully examined every question presented by the record, and having come to the decided conclusion that there is no error which can authorize this court to reverse the judgment of the court below, we have affirmed it.

————

YOUNG v. THE STATE, 2 Howard, 865.

An indictment may be found at the special terms of the circuit court. Byrd v. State, 1 How., 163, cited and approved.

Error to Copiah circuit court.

At the January special term of the Copiah Circuit Court, 1835, the grand jury found a true bill against William P. Rose for an assault committed on the 25th of said month, on which a bench warrant issued. Rose was taken on the 16th of January, 1836, and entered into bond with the defendant, Young, as surety, in the sum of two hundred dollars. At the May term of said court, 1836, a scire facias issued against Young. At the May term, 1837, a judgment final was rendered against said Young for the amount of the recognizance. Upon petition of the defendant, the clerk of the circuit court granted a writ of error returnable to the last December term of this court.

Harris & Bowie for plaintiff in error.

T. F. Collins, attorney general.

SHARKEY, C. J.:

The only question to which our attention has been directed in this case is, whether an indictment can be originated at a special term of the circuit court.   The same question was raised before this court in the case of Byrd v. State, 1 How., 163, 238, and not regarded as error.   The jurisdiction of the circuit court is fixed by the constitution, and whenever such court can be legally held it must possess all its constitutional jurisdiction.   The constitution requires that two circuit courts in each year shall be held in every county, leaving it thus discretionary with the legislature to appoint more terms, if necessary, and by law special terms may be held as often as occasion requires.   Although the act providing for the holding of special terms may seem to limit, to some extent, their jurisdiction with regard to the cases to be tried, yet it is believed that the law did not intend (nor could it do so) to interfere with the undoubted jurisdiction of the court in criminal cases.

The judgment must be affirmed.

CODY *v.* THE STATE, 3 Howard, 27.

MURDER.

The statute points out the method by which those who are to compose the panel shall be selected, and prescribes their qualifications; and it will be presumed that the court intrusted with this duty has performed it, by placing on the panel none but such as are good and lawful men of the county, in accordance with the provisions of the act. The party can only rebut this presumption by challenge and proof before trial. The question cannot afterwards be raised in another court.

It must appear by the record that the grand jurors were sworn; and if the record shows that one of them was "sworn as foreman," it will be sufficient evidence of *appointment* as such.[1]

The record, without any notice of the original *venire*, stated that fifteen persons, naming them, were drawn as a grand jury, and that A. E. D. (one of the number) was sworn as foreman of the same. There is no statement that he was appointed foreman by the court, nor that the remainder of the jurors took the oath required by law of grand jurors.   Held, that the indictment was fatally defective

The 69th section of the act "for the punishment of crimes and misdemeanors," Rev. Code, 309, requires the district attorney to mark on all bills of indictment, the name of the prosecutor; an omission to do so is fatal to the indictment.

[1] Woodsides v. State, 2 How.

Where a juror, upon being interrogated by the court, "denied that he had formed or expressed any opinion of the prisoner's case;" and it was proved that, after he had been summoned by the officer to attend as a juror, he had said that, if he should be on the jury, "he did not think he could clear him, but should be bound to find him guilty," he was held to be clearly incompetent as a juror, and a new trial ought to be granted on that ground.

Error to Perry circuit court.

Hays & McClung for plaintiff in error.

T. F. Collins, attorney general.

Cited Chitty Cr. Law, 333–4–5 ; Woodsides v. State, 2 How., 655 ; Chitty Cr. Law, 266 ; Walk. R., 392.

Trotter, J. :

This case stands upon a writ of error to the circuit court of the county of Perry. The record states that at the October term of that court, held in the year 1837, a bill of indictment was found by the grand jury, charging the plaintiff in error with the murder of one Henry Rodgers. That at the April term following, a special *venire facias,* for twenty jurors to try the prisoner, was awarded. That a jury at the same term was empanelled and sworn to try the issue made upon the plea of not guilty, which had been filed by Cody at the preceding term, and that said jury found a verdict of guilty against him at the same term. That the court thereupon proceeded and pronounced final judgment of death against him with the usual order of execution.

The first error complained of in the proceedings of the court below in this cause is, that the grand jury who found the indictment were not good and lawful men of the county of Perry. The grand jurors in each county of this state are directed to be selected by lot from the whole number of jurors summoned and attending the court under the *venire* of the term. The statute points out the method by which the jurors who are to compose the *venire* shall be selected, and prescribes their qualifications. They are to be selected by the sheriff and clerk, under the direction and control of the court, from the return of the assessor and collector of taxes, and are to be freeholders or householders of the county in which they are required to serve. It is to be presumed that the court entrusted with the selection of the *venire* has done its duty by placing none upon it except such as are good and lawful men of the county, according to the directions of the act. It is competent for any party, whose rights are to be affected by the action of the jury, to destroy this presumption by challenge and proof tendered at the time. If he is silent, however, he cannot afterwards raise the objection in another court. All exceptions to the jurors must be taken at the time of the trial. To sustain this position, the court might refer to many adjudications of the highest courts in other states. 1 Chitty Cr. Law, 333.

We do not deem this assignment of error sufficient to affect the judgment.

It is insisted in the second place, that there is no evidence upon the record, that the grand jury were ever sworn by the court. The record, without any notice of the original *venire*, proceeds to state that fifteen persons, naming them, were drawn as a grand jury, and that A. E. Denham (one of the number) was sworn as foreman of the same. There is no statement that A. E. Denham was appointed foreman by the court, nor is there any statement that the remainder of the jurors took the oath required by law of grand jurors.

This we deem a fatal objection to the indictment. The constitution of this country provides that no man shall be held to answer for any capital or infamous offense until he shall have first been charged with the same by a grand jury of the proper county. Our laws have, with great precision, prescribed the method by which this body, entrusted with such high powers over the life and liberty of the citizens, shall be organized. They are required to be selected by lot, under the direction of the court, from the whole number of jurors summoned, and in attendance, by virtue of the *venire facias*, for the term. When thus selected, they shall take an oath, the form of which is particularly prescribed by law. In order to give system and certainty to their proceedings, the court is directed to appoint one of their number to act as foreman. This appointment constitutes him the organ through which their inquisitions and proceedings are reported to the court, and particular duties are devolved upon him distinct from those of the other members of the jury. He must report all bills which may be submitted to the jury and state, over his name to be endorsed on the same as foreman, whether they are *true* or *not.* His functions are, therefore, highly important, and it should clearly appear from the record that he has been designated by the court, and sworn to act in this capacity. It is his return as foreman, which places the bill of indictment in possession of the court, and apprises it that the grand jury have found it to be true. It is not deemed necessary for us to decide, whether, if the record or caption of the indictment should show that the grand jury in a body returned the bill of indictment into court with their findings endorsed upon it or specially entered of record, it would not be sufficient. In the absence of such a statement, it must appear of record that the foreman returned the bill, and of course that he was authorized to act as such. And it is an inference which is deemed consistent with the record that he was appointed. His appointment is included in the fact of his taking the oath. This was the determination of this court in the case of Woodsides v. State, 2 How., 655, decided at the January term in 1837, and we do not feel inclined to disturb it. But there is no statement that the other members of the grand jury were sworn, and we do not feel authorized to infer it from anything on the record. The fact that A. E. Denham was sworn as foreman of the grand jury cannot by any rule of construction or inference known to us, include the other and distinct fact that the residue of the panel took an oath also. The recital of this fact in the bill of indictment cannot supply the omission of it in the record. The record may aid the indictment, but not *e converso.* For the authority of the jury to find the indictment must be contained in the record, and the bill becomes no part of the record until it is acted upon and returned into court in the manner prescribed by law.

We will proceed to notice two of the other assignments of error relied on by the plaintiff. One is that the indictment is defective, because there has not been endorsed upon it the name of the prosecutor or prosecutors. The 69th section of the act "for the punishment of crimes and misdemeanors," Rev. Code, 309, makes it the duty of the attorney general to mark upon all bills of indictment the name of the prosecutor or prosecutors. This statute was designed to protect the state against the payment of costs for frivolous and malicious prosecutions by affording certain record evidence of the *person* who had perverted the criminal jurisprudence of the country from its true objects, and sought to make it a means to gratify his malice and revenge. It was manifestly designed to operate as auxiliary to a previous provision contained in the 67th section of the same act, by which it is provided that, if the state fail in the prosecution of any inferior offense, the court may, if the prosecution appear to be frivolous or malicious, order the prosecutor to pay costs, etc. This act had another most important and salutary object in view, and that was to enable a party against whom a malicious and vexatious prosecution is instituted, to ascertain, with certainty, the hand from whence the injury to his reputation has proceeded. 2 Bibb. R., 210 ; 1 ib., 355. But these objects may be defeated by a neglect on the part of the officers of the state to comply with the directions of the statute. We are of opinion, therefore, that this indictment is bad for that reason.

We are clearly of opinion that, on the other ground which it was proposed to examine by the court, the circuit court ought to have awarded a new trial to the defendant. The juror R. J. Patrick was not competent to try the defendant. This is made manifest from the affidavit of William Snow, which is a part of the record. Jurors should be, in the language of the law, *exceptione majores*. That was not the condition of the juror in this instance. He had formed and expressed an opinion against the prisoner. It will not do to say in answer to this objection that his opinion may have been a mere hypothetical one, founded on mere loose rumor. When examined on his *voire dire*, he should have stated the fact, and the court would have been enabled to determine upon the character of it, whether his mind was laboring under any undue bias, unfavorable to an impartial examination and decision of the case of the prisoner. But the record shows that he denied, when asked by the court, that he had formed or expressed any opinion of the prisoner's guilt ; yet, we are furnished by the same record with proof that he had formed an impression highly prejudicial to Cody. He declared, and that too, after he was summoned by the officer to attend the court as the juror, that if he should be upon the jury, "he did not think he could clear him, but should be bound to find him guilty." A due regard to the sanctity of the trial by jury, and the constitutional right which has been guaranteed to every man, to a trial, in all cases of the kind before the court, by an impartial jury of his country, demand, as we conceive, a new trial. McKinley v. Smith, Harding R., 167.

The judgment of the court below must, therefore, be reversed, and the cause remanded, and a new trial granted by the circuit court of Perry county.

OVERSTREET *v.* THE STATE, 3 Howard, 328.

FORNICATION.

The general rule is that hearsay evidence is not admissible. The exceptions to this rule are grounded alone upon necessity. The offense of fornication, charged in the indictment, is one of a specific character, not falling within those exceptions, and must be proved in the mode pointed out by law. [1]

Error to Holmes circuit court.

This was an indictment against Overstreet for living in fornication. Plea, not guilty. On the trial the attorney for the state proposed and offered to prove, that it "was common report in the neighborhood, that the defendant and one Sarah Hamilton lived together in fornication," which proof was objected to by the prisoner's counsel. The objection was overruled and exceptions taken to this opinion of the court.

Objections were also made to the indictment, but it is unnecessary to state them.

Fitch, for plaintiff in error, contended:

1. It was error in the court below, to refuse to quash the indictment.

[1] Wharton Am. Cr. Law, 668.

2. It appears from the record that the indictment was found under the direction, and signed by Robert S. G. Perkins, district attorney *pro tem.*, and not by the legal district attorney.

3. The court admitted improper and illegal testimony to go to the jury, as stated in the bill of exceptions; wherefore the said plaintiff in error prays, that said judgment for the errors aforesaid, and other errors in the record and proceedings aforesaid, may be set aside, and reversed, &c.

Thomas F. Collins, attorney general.

The record may not show that the jurors were good and lawful men, or that they were freeholders or householders. For all men are presumed to be good and lawful men unless the contrary appear. Woodsides v. State, 2 How., 247; Farish v. State, ib., 826.

Hearsay testimony may be admitted to prove the general character in which parties live together, so the party introducing it, does not undertake to prove any particular facts or fact by the hearsay testimony, but only the general reputation of the manner in which the parties lived. Norris' Peake, 27. If the bill of exceptions showed that the hearsay testimony was the only proof offered by the state, there would be some ground for doubt on the subject.

TROTTER, J.:

The plaintiff in error was indicted in the circuit court of Holmes county, for the offense of fornication. On the trial the attorney for the state offered, in support of the prosecution, testimony that it was the general reputation in the neighborhood of the defendant's residence, that the defendant and Sarah Hamilton did live together in a state of fornication as charged in the indictment. This proof was objected to, but admitted by the court to go to the jury. The error assigned is, the admission of this testimony. The charge in the indictment is of a specific offense, and must be proved as all other offenses are established; that is, by proof pointed out by law. It is a general rule that hearsay evidence is not admissible; and the cases which have been made exceptions to this rule, have proceeded upon the ground of necessity alone. This is not a case which falls within any of the reasons of the exceptions. And besides, in this case, the witness states the strongest possible reason excluding it, which is, that he believed the neighbors who had spoken of the cohabitation knew nothing about it.

Let the judgment be reversed, and a *venire de novo* awarded.

FRIAR *v.* THE STATE, 3 Howard, 422.

NEGRO STEALING.

The 22nd section of the act establishing the criminal court, provides that the judge may, when he deems it necessary, hold a special term on giving twenty days notice thereof. No formal order is necessary for holding such term, and the propriety thereof is wholly within the discretion of the judge.

The twenty days notice by advertisement, required by the statute, is for the information of the public, but is not necessary to confer jurisdiction; the statute being merely directory.

Where the record shows that the indictment was endorsed a true bill by one of the grand jurors, and that it was returned into court by the authority of the whole fifteen jurors who composed the panel, it is sufficient without the special appointment of a foreman.[1]

The sheriff, as one of the officers of the court, is competent to serve the prisoner with a copy of the indictment and the *venire.*

Where, by the assent of the accused and the state, entered on the record, the jury were allowed by the court to bring in a sealed verdict and deposit it with the clerk, and to separate until a certain day; and they did so, and appeared on the day named, when their verdict was opened by the clerk and read to them, and they "severally, upon their oaths in open court, confirm their sealed verdict," and say, " We the jury find the prisoner guilty in manner and form, as he stands charged in the bill of indictment," the conviction was held to be regular and valid. And where the judge directs the jury to bring in a sealed verdict, and gives them permission to separate after agreeing on the same, the parties will be deemed to have assented to such permission, if no objection appear, and it is no cause of objection to the verdict.

The mere affidavit of a third person, that the prosecutor had declared that there was in existence a bill of sale of the property charged to be the subject of the larceny, which bill of sale went to establish title in the prisoner, is not a sufficient ground for a new trial, unless the affidavit be supported by the oath of the prisoner, alleging sufficient reason why such bill of sale was not produced on the trial, and an expectation that it could be procured on a subsequent trial.[2] The affidavit of a juror will not be received to impeach the verdict of the jury.

The bill of exceptions should set forth the precise grounds of exception, otherwise the court cannot take cognizance of the subject matter.

A general verdict of guilty will be sustained, although all the counts of the indictment are bad but one.

[1] Peter v. State, 3 How., 433; Wharton's Am. Cr. Law, 502.

[2] Wharton Am. Cr. Law, 3170; State v. Harding, 2 Bay, 267; Com. v. Drew, 4 Mass., 599.

Error to Adams circuit court.

Jennings & Webber for plaintiff in error.

T. F. Collins, attorney general.

Cited, Acts of 1836, p. 25; Rev. Code, 106; 1st Session of Acts of 1830, ch. 15. § 5; Chitty Cr. Law, 640; 1 Salk, 384; 1 Comp. 276; Rev. Code, 109.   •

TROTTER, J.:

This case was brought up by writ of error to the circuit court of Adams county. The indictment was found at a special term of that court, which was holden on the fourth Monday of June, 1838. It charged the plaintiff in error with the crime of negro stealing under the statute of this state, and contained two counts which varied with each other only in the description of the slave, the subject of the larceny. The prisoner was arraigned on the indictment and pleaded not guilty.

At the trial the prisoner objected, that he had not been served with a copy of the indictment, and a list of the *venire*, two entire days before the trial, according to law. The objection was, however, overruled, and the jury returned a general verdict of guilty on both counts of the indictment. The plaintiff then moved the court for a new trial on the grounds stated in the record, and which will be presently noticed, but the motion was refused, and he now assigns as error:

1. That the record shows no order for the holding of the special term of the court below. By the 22d section of the act to establish the criminal court of this state, it is provided, that whenever it shall be deemed necessary, the judge of said court may hold special terms, upon giving twenty days notice thereof. The question of the necessity and propriety of directing a special term, is thus referred entirely to the discretion of the judge, and with it we can have nothing to do. No formal order is necessary, nor is any required to be shown on the minutes. The twenty days notice of the time of holding any such special term, is required for the information of those who may have causes or business in the same, but it is not necessary to confer jurisdiction. In this respect the act is merely directory, without the

publication of notice as required the proceedings could only be held as irregular. But it is contrary to well settled principles to decide the proceedings of a court of record to be irregular without any proof that they are so. The presumption is in their favor, and must be indulged until the contrary clearly appears.

It is secondly, assigned as error, that the record does not show the appointment of any foreman of the grand jury. To this objection it may be answered, that the record states that the grand jury presented the bill of indictment in open court. It is endorsed, a "true bill" by one of the body, and it is shown independently of this endorsement, that it was returned by the authority of the whole fifteen jurors who composed the panel. The caption of the record states that "by the oaths of the jurors (naming them in full), it was presented as follows," and then sets forth the bill of indictment at length. This is surely as satisfactory as to the finding of the jury, and the identity of the bill, as the simple endorsement of a regularly appointed foreman. The objection is wholly contradicted by the record.

3. The next ground of error is, that the plaintiff in error was not served with a copy of the indictment and a list of the *venire* two entire days before the trial as required by law. This is certainly a right to which he is strictly entitled by the statute of this state to enable him to prepare his defense, and to make his challenge to the jurors. But the record shows that a copy of the indictment and a list of the *venire* were both furnished him by the sheriff on the 29th day of June, and the trial did not take place until the 3rd day of July. But it is insisted that the sheriff was not authorized by law to furnish such copies. The statute simply provides that the accused in capital cases shall be entitled to have a copy of the indictment and of the *venire*, two entire days before his trial, and is silent as to who shall serve them. He has, therefore, a right to look to the court, and it is surely the duty of the court to see it done by some one of its officers, and we can see none more proper than the sheriff.

4. It was next assigned as error, that the court permitted the jury to separate and return a sealed verdict. The record states that it was agreed by prisoner and his counsel, that the verdict of the jury when agreed upon, might be sealed by the jury and

left in charge of the clerk until Thursday, as agreed upon. The record then proceeds to state that on Thursday, the 5th day of July, the parties appeared, and that the jury were called into court, and that they "severally and upon their oath do say in open court, and by their sealed verdict aforesaid, opened and read to them by the clerk ; we of the jury find the prisoner guilty in manner and form as he stands charged in the indictment." It has been repeatedly held that the court will not set aside a verdict for irregularity when the jury have separated after agreeing to a sealed verdict, if agreed to when they deliver it. Such was the case of Douglass v. Tousey, 2 Wend., 352. And where the judge directs the jury to bring in a sealed verdict, and gives them permission to separate after agreeing to the same, the parties will be deemed to have assented to such permission, if no objection is made, and it is no cause of objection to the verdict. Ib. In the case of the People v. Douglass, 4 Cowen, 26, it was held in a civil suit to be perfectly clear that the separation of a jury without and even contrary to the directions of the court, would not of itself warrant the court in setting aside the verdict. The same principle is established in the case of Burns v. Hoyt, 3 Johns. R., 255. In the last case the jury had deliberated several hours, sealed their verdict and separated, and next morning brought it into court. On being polled one of them disagreed, and Judge Kent sent them out again, and the disagreeing juror ultimately assented to the verdict as it had been sealed up. It was held, that until it was received it was no verdict, and the jury had a right to alter it. 6 Johns. R., 68. This is precisely the case before us ; the verdict though sealed, was not binding until it was delivered into court. When read, if it is not objected to, it is then emphatically their verdict; for when read, either party has a right to poll the jury to ascertain if they all assent. Blakeney v. Sheldon, 7 Johns. R., 32. In this case the verdict was opened in the presence of all the parties, and read aloud by the clerk to the jury. The prisoner was thus afforded ample opportunity to poll the jury. It was then a public verdict spoken by the jury ; and we can see no reason for disturbing it on that ground.

5. The next objection is rested on the refusal of the court to

grant the prisoner a new trial. The grounds relied on in support of the motion besides some which have already been considered, were the affidavits of Thomas Mackin, one of the jurors, and Farmer. The affidavit of Mackin states, that he would not have consented to the verdict of guilty in this case, "but upon the drawing up and signature by the jury of the communication addressed to and received by the court recommending a new trial, and that he believed said letter would have a great influence upon the mind of the court." We forbear all comment upon the singular ground taken by this member of the jury for his verdict. He does not state that he entertained doubts of the guilt of the prisoner, or that he was moved by any other consideration than the hope or expectation that the court would set aside what he and his fellows had solemnly and deliberately agreed upon. This is not ground, however, for setting aside a verdict. The letter of the jury was one thing and their verdict another. Their verdict was upon oath. If there were reasons known to them sufficient to grant a new trial, then the verdict should not have been rendered. The letter was inconsistent with the verdict and the latter must prevail. But be this as it may, the court had no authority to notice the affidavit of the juror, which tended to impeach his conduct and repudiate his verdict. It is not competent for one of the jury to prove the misbehavior of his brethren. Dana v. Tucker, 4 Dana, 486. Nor can the affidavit of jurors be received to impeach their verdict. Ib. This is a well settled rule, and so well settled, as we conceive, upon the clearest principles of justice and public policy; if it were otherwise there would be opened the widest door for protracted litigation, fraud and perjury. We are not at all satisfied with the reasoning of Judge White in the case of Crawford v. The State, reported in 2 Yerger. His conclusion is not warranted by the authorities to which he refers; for we find Lord Mansfield deciding against the admissibility of such proof, in all cases cited, except the one which arose a short time after he came to preside in the court of King's Bench. But the case decided by Judge White was an extreme one, the jurors then declaring that they did not believe the prisoner guilty. The affidavit of Farmer stated simply that the prosecutor told him that there was a bill of sale to the prisoner for the negro he was charged with stealing; that the bill of sale was mailed and directed to affiant at Natchez, with a view of getting him, affiant, to establish the verity of it, and he further inquired of affiant whether he had received it, to which he had answered that he had not. And this was all he stated. This was addressed to the court as a reason for a new trial, on the ground of newly-discovered evidence. But it does not state that this fact was not known to the prisoner before the trial. It does not show at what time the prosecutor communicated the information, whether before or after the trial. It is not accompanied by any affidavit of the prisoner himself of the fact. It is a naked statement of a fact furnished by the prosecutor, who appears to have been the owner of the slave. Can it be possible that the prisoner could have gone to trial on a charge so deeply affecting his reputation, and in which his life must be the forfeit of his conviction, without having insisted upon time to procure testimony so important to his defense as a bill of sale, establishing his title to the property? But he does not offer any statement of his own to explain what certainly deserves explanation. If he had an authentic bill of sale to the slave, he surely could not have been ignorant of it, and if it was out of his possession, he should have notified the court of the fact, and moved a continuance of the cause until he could procure it. But it does not appear from this affidavit where it now is, nor does the witness profess to state that such a paper in fact exists. How was it sent to him? By mail. For what purpose? He says that he might establish the verity of it. But how could he establish its verity? If he was a subscribing witness and had seen it, he need not have depended, as it seems he did, on the information of the prosecutor. But he does not furnish the court with any ground for any expectation he has that the paper can ever be procured, or used in the event of a new trial. It is totally insufficient.

6. It is next insisted, that the court erred in refusing to notice, without affidavit, facts which transpired under the eye of the court. The only criterion furnished us of what those facts were, is the statement in the bill of exceptions, that they were those

set forth in some of the reasons filed in support of the motion for a new trial. And yet what they were we cannot tell, unless they be the affidavits of Mackin the juror, and of Farmer, which have been noticed. It is impossible for this court to decide upon such an objection. The general statement, that they were facts which had been offered in support of some of the reasons filed for a new trial is not sufficient. It is incumbent on the party who excepts to the decision of the court to place in his bill of exceptions the precise ground of exception. But this can only be done by embodying in the bill the facts on which the exception rests. This is done, and we should be acting upon a very loose principle to decide under such circumstances that there was error in the action of the court in that case.

7. It is also objected that the verdict is general not referring to the particular count on which it was rendered. This is totally unfounded. A general verdict of guilty will be sustained, though all the counts in the indictment be bad but one. Chitty Cr. Law, 640.

But both the counts in this indictment are good under the statute, and are properly framed.

Let the judgment be affirmed.

LOPER *v.* THE STATE, 3 Howard, 429.

MURDER.

If the caption of the record fails to show in what county and at what place the court was holden, the record of the subsequent proceedings may be referred to, and considered in connection with the caption, to remove the uncertainty. The whole record should be considered together, and that which is uncertain in one part, may be rendered clear by that which is certain in another part.

Where the accused submits his affidavit, fortified by that of another, setting forth grounds, and praying for a change of *venue*, and the court makes the order changing the *venue* accordingly, he will not be subsequently heard to criticise the regularity of his own proceedings. The court had full jurisdiction to make the order, and this court will not presume against its regularity.

The *venue* was changed from Lafayette county to Marshall; the transcript of the record of the circuit court, certified and transmitted with the papers by the clerk, were found to be imperfect; there is no doubt that the circuit court of Marshall county had authority to award a *certiorari* to the clerk of Lafayette circuit court to forward an amended record.

The statute requires that the prisoner shall be furnished with a copy of the indictment and a list of the *venire*, two entire days before the trial; and he cannot be compelled to go to trial without it. But if he goes to trial without this, making no objection, he will be deemed to have waived this right, and will not be allowed to object here.

Error to Marshall circuit court.

Robert Hughes for plaintiff in error.

T. F. Collins, attorney general.

TROTTER, J. ·

This was a prosecution for murder, commenced in the circuit court of Lafayette county. The indictment was found the May term of that court, 1838. After pleading not guilty, the plaintiff applied to the court to change the *venue*, and in support of his application presented his affidavit and that of Alexander McFarland, which, in substance stated, that from the prejudice existing in the public mind in the county of Lafayette, the plaintiff could not have a fair trial, etc. The *venue* was ordered to be changed to Marshall county. And at the September term of the circuit court of that county he was tried and convicted. On a motion for a new trial, grounded on alleged defects in the original transcript of the record in Lafayette county, the court, on a suggestion of diminution awarded a *certiorari*, in obedience to which the clerk of the Lafayette circuit court forwarded an amended record. The principal errors assigned in this cause arise out of the matters presented on the motion.

1. The first error assigned is, that the record on which the defendant was tried was defective, and that it was not competent for the court to amend it. That amendments are not allowed in criminal cases, nor are they embraced by the statute of jeofaile. The caption of the record to which this objection is in part directed, is very informal and inartificial, and is, unaided by the other parts of the record, defective, as it does not state in what county nor at what place the court had opened its session. The subsequent proceedings, however, very satisfactorily remove the uncertainty in this respect, and may very properly be referred to, and considered in connection with the caption. It is a well-settled rule in the construction of deeds, statutes, and records, that all the parts of the deed and all statutes in *pari materia*, as well as the whole of the record, must be viewed together. And

that which is uncertain in one part may be rendered clear by that which is certain in another part. In other parts of the record it is stated in direct terms that the court was holden at the town of Oxford, in the county of Lafayette. It is objected, however, that the certificate of the clerk is not as full as the requirements of the statute, which directs him to send a transcript of all the minutes of the court, and of the papers in the cause. The general certificate referred to as the ground of this objection is perhaps not full enough. But he has given a separate certificate of each of the papers mentioned in the descriptive list made out by him, and we think this is as well as if the general certificate objected to had referred to them aggregately. He has, to be sure, called these papers originals, but that is evidently a mere clerical blunder, which cannot change the character of the record. But the court certainly had the power to supply any diminution of the record. The power is unconnected with the question of amendments. In awarding a *certiorari*, the court only aims to get the whole record as it exists. Its office is not to change the record, but to perfect it. It is, therefore, technically speaking, no amendment. And the power to award *certioraries* has always been conceded to the courts as well in criminal as in civil cases.

2. It is insisted in the second place, that the order to change the *venue* was illegal, and therefore, conferred no jurisdiction of the cause upon the circuit court of Marshall county. But there does not appear upon the record any foundation for this objection. The affidavit of the prisoner, which states the ground of his belief, that he cannot have a fair and impartial trial in the county of Lafayette, and also that of McFarland to sustain and corroborate it, are both shown upon the record as a portion of the proceedings in the cause. It is objected, however, that it does not appear that they were sworn in open court, and that the clerk before whom the jurat was taken, had no authority to administer an oath in such a case out of court. But we think it sufficiently appears that they were sworn in open court, and at all events, that they were sufficient to persuade the court of the necessity for a change of *venue*. We can draw no other conclusion, from anything apparent upon the record. But it strikes the court that this is a novel objection. The defendant below makes an affida-

vit containing grounds for removing his trial, and for his benefit the court awards the change. How, then, can he be heard to criticise the regularity of his own proceedings? But a conclusive answer to this objection is, that the court below had full jurisdiction to make the order. It has done so, and we should be acting in violation of well-established principles to presume against the regularity of the order in the absence of any proof that such was the case. The sufficiency of the proof was a question for the determination of that court. It deemed the proof sufficient, and we have nothing to do with it. Surely it will not be contended that the judgment of a court of competent jurisdiction can be attacked because the record does not show all the proof upon which it was rendered. But the record in this case does state that the prisoner applied in person for change of *venue*, and this shown by a distinct averment of the order itself. It states that the defendant's application, supported by his affidavit and that of Alexander McFarland, came up, etc.

3. The last objection taken is, that the prisoner was not furnished with a copy of the bill of indictment and a list of the *venire* two entire days before the trial, as required by law. The statute requires this to be done to enable the prisoner to prepare his defense and his challenge to the jurors; and he cannot be compelled to go to trial without it. He may waive this, however, and consent to a trial immediately; and if he does, he cannot afterwards object. As the prisoner made no objections in the court below, he cannot object here. Such was the decision of the supreme court in the case of Johnson v. The State, Walk. R., 396; of this court in the case of Shaffer v. The State, 1 How., 238. The same doctrine is recognized in Chitty Cr. Law, 405.

The judgment of the court below must, therefore, be affirmed.

PETER, A SLAVE, *v.* THE STATE, 3 Howard, 433.

MURDER.

Where it appears that neither the witness nor any one else, at the time, placed any particular motive of temporal advantage or fear before the mind of the prisoner, but simply told him to tell all he knew concerning the murder of the deceased, and he then, without any compulsion or any promise, made his statements, they were held to be competent evidence to go to the jury, It is a well-settled rule, and it must clearly appear to the court, in order to exclude them, that the confessions were superinduced by promises of temporal advantage or threats of temporal punishment. 2 Starkie, 27.

Where the record shows that the indictment was found and returned into court by the whole panel, the special appointment of a foreman is not necessary.[1]   The indictment, however, will be fatally defective if it have not the name of the prosecutor endorsed upon it.[2]

Where the appellate court reverses the judgment of the court below for the want of form in the indictment, the indictment will be considered sufficient *prima facie* evidence of guilt to remand the prisoner.[3]

Error to Franklin circuit court.

Vannerson & Baker for plaintiff in error.

Thomas F. Collins, attorney general.

TROTTER, J.:

This was an indictment for murder, found in the circuit court of Franklin county. There are numerous errors assigned as grounds for reversing the judgment of the court below, none of which, however, we deem necessary to notice, except the following:

1. That the court below improperly admitted the confessions of the prisoner.

2. That the juror, whose name appears endorsed on the bill of indictment as foreman of the grand jury, was not appointed or designated as such by the court.

3. That the name of the prosecutor is not endorsed upon the indictment.

1. The grounds in support of the first objection, are disclosed in the bill of exceptions. A witness was introduced to prove certain confessions made by the prisoner of his guilt, and his

[1] Friar v. State, 3 How., 422; Wharton Am. Cr. Law, 502, and cases cited in note.

[2] Cody v. State, 3 How., 433.

[3] Indictment is *prima facie* evidence of guilt. See Street v. State, 43 Miss., 1, and cases cited in note.

testimony was objected to on the ground that the prisoner, at the time of making the confessions, was in custody, and surrounded by an exasperated crowd, and that he was under the influence of hope of being benefited by the confessions. But it is not stated that the witness to the confessions, or any one else, at the time placed any particular motive of temporal advantage or punishment before the mind of the prisoner. The witness simply told him to tell him all he knew concerning the murder of the deceased. He then, without any compulsion, or promise, made his statements. It is impossible to decide upon the force of this objection under this bill of exceptions. The statements made by the prisoner are not embodied in the bill. It merely avers that they were such as tended to establish his guilt. But it does not appear whether they were naked confessions of guilt, or whether they disclosed facts which proved the confession to be true. The rule is well-settled on this subject, and it must appear clearly to the court, in order to exclude them, that the confessions were superinduced by promises of temporal advantage or threats of temporal punishment. 2 Starkie, 27. But it does not appear that such was the case here.

2. It is objected that there was no foreman of the grand jury. To this we answer that the bill of indictment was found and returned into court by the whole panel of the jury, and this is sufficient.

3. The third and last objection has already been decided by this court, and held to be fatal. The name of the prosecutor must be marked on the bill of indictment.

The judgment of the court below must, therefore, be reversed, the indictment dismissed, and, as the indictment is merely defective in point of form, and affords *prima facie* evidence of the guilt of the prisoner, he must be remanded for further proceedings.

CARPENTER *v.* THE STATE, 4 Howard, 163.

PERJURY.

At common law the number of the jury, for the trial of all issues involving the personal rights and liberties of the subject, cannot be less than twelve. In all cases where the term "jury" is used in our statutes, it is regarded as one of fixed and determined meaning, ascertained by the paramount law. A trial and conviction by a jury of less than twelve is therefore a nullity.

It should appear by the caption of the record, not only that the court was holden for the proper county, but that it was holden at the proper place within the county; and the omission of any material statement in the caption or record cannot be supplied by recitals in the indictment, which becomes no part of the record until it is returned into court in the manner prescribed by law.

The caption of the indictment was as follows: "The State of Mississippi, county of Hancock, the circuit court of Hancock county, August term thereof, in the year of our Lord one thousand eight hundred and thirty eight. The grand jurors of the State of Mississippi, empanelled and sworn in and for the county of Hancock and State of Mississippi, at the term of the court aforesaid, upon their oaths present," &c. Held, that it does not show with legal certainty that the grand jury was taken from the body of good and lawful men of Hancock county.

In an indictment for perjury it is not necessary to allege that the false affidavit charged an offense upon any particular individual, in order to constitute the crime of willful perjury.

Error to Hancock circuit court.

The defendant, Samuel A. Carpenter, was tried and convicted of perjury, at the August term of the Hancock circuit court. The foundation of the indictment was an affidavit made by Carpenter before a justice of the peace, of Hancock county. The affidavit stated that certain articles of household furniture had been stolen from the possession of affiant, and the affiant suspected and believed that the said articles of furniture were secreted in and about the premises of one Michael Eldridge, at Pass Christian, in the county aforesaid.

Several objections were made to the caption of the indictment, which was as follows: "The State of Mississippi, county of Hancock, August term thereof, in the year of our Lord one thousand and eight hundred and thirty-eight. The grand jurors of the State of Mississippi, empanelled and sworn in and for the county of Hancock and State of Mississippi, at the term aforesaid, upon their oaths present," &c.

The sufficiency of the record was also objected to on the ground, that it did not show that the court in which the cause was tried was held at the court-house, the place appointed by law for holding the court.   The caption was as follows : " The State of Mississippi v. Samuel Carpenter, pleas in the circuit court of Hancock county, before the Honorable B. Harris, judge presiding, the term of August, in the year of our Lord one thousand eight hundred and thirty-eight."   The record showed also, that the jury which convicted defendant was composed of only eleven men.

The following errors in the proceedings of the court below are assigned by the counsel for plaintiff in error.

1. The issue in the case was tried by only eleven jurors.

2. That there is nothing in the record showing that the court in which defendant was tried, was held at the place appointed by law, for holding the same.

3. The grand jury are not shown by the record to be elected and drawn from the county of Hancock.

4. The said bill of indictment does not show in what manner the said Michael Eldridge was intended to be aggrieved and vexed, or in what way he was to be subjected to the pains and penalties and punishment of the laws of the state.

Mitchell, for plaintiff in error.

It seems agreed that, if the caption of the indictment either set forth no place at all where the indictment was found, or do not show with sufficient certainty that the place set forth is within the jurisdiction of the court before which it was taken, as when it sets forth the indictment as taken at a session of the peace, holden for such a county, at B., without showing in what county B. is, otherwise than by putting the county into the margin, is insufficient.   2 Hawk. P. C., ch. 25, § 128 ; Peck's Tenn. R., 166.

Therefore, in every prosecution on the statute, you must set forth in the record the place wherein you suppose the perjury to have been committed, and must prove at the trial that there is such a record, either by actually producing it, or an attested copy.   Also, in the pleading, you must set forth the point wherein the false oath was taken, but must also show that it conduced to the proof or disproof of the matter in question.   1 Hawk. P. C., ch. 27, § 17.

When the grand jury have heard the evidence, if they think it a groundless accusation, they endorse upon the indictment, "not a true bill;" if they are satisfied of the truth of the accusation, they then endorse upon it, "a true bill." 4 Black. Comm., 305.

It is necessary to constitute the offense of perjury, that the false oath be taken wilfully, viz: with some degree of deliberation, and it must be also corrupt, that is, committed *malo animo;* it must be willful, positive, and absolute; not merely owing to surprise or inadvertency, or a mistake of the true state of the question. 5 Modern R., 350; 4 Com. 137; 1 Ferm R., 69; 1 Hawk. P. C., ch. 27, § 2.

The oath must be taken absolutely and directly; therefore, if a man swears only as he thinks, remembers, or believes, he cannot be guilty of perjury. 1 Hawk. P. C., ch. 27, § 7. 3 Inst., 166.

The thing sworn ought to be some way material; for if it be wholly foreign to the purpose and immaterial, and neither pertinent to the matter in question, nor tending to aggravate or extenuate the damages, nor likely to induce the jury to give credit to the substantial part of the evidence, it cannot be perjury. 1 Hawk., ch. 27, § 8.

The truth of every accusation, whether preferred in the shape of indictment, information, or appeal, should be confirmed by the unanimous suffrage of twelve of his equals or neighbors, indifferently chosen, and superior to all suspicions. 4 Black. Com., 350.

Perjury is defined to be a crime committed when a lawful oath is administered in some judicial proceeding, to a person who swears wilfully, absolutely and falsely, in a matter material to the issue or point in question. 4 Black. Com. 137. From this definition the following things are necessary.

1st. It must be false.

2d. The intention must be wilfull.

3d. It must be in some judicial proceeding.

4th. The party must be lawfully sworn.

5th. The assertion must be absolute.

6th. The falsehood must be material to the matter or issue in question.

A general affidavit could only authorize the issuing of a general warrant, and, therefore, void under *magna charta.* 3 Burr, 1742. 1 Chitty 34, 268–327. See also, Constitution of Mississippi, Art. 1, § 9.

Thomas F. Collins, attorney general.

SMITH, J. :

At the August term, in the year A.D., 1838, in the circuit court of Hancock county, Samuel A. Carpenter was indicted, tried and convicted of the crime of perjury; and having received sentence, has by writ of error removed his cause to this court, and asks a reversal of the judgment against him for several errors and irregularities alleged to exist in the record of the proceedings and judgment of the court below.

It appears by the record, that the issue in the cause was submitted to eleven persons, who were empanelled and sworn as a jury; and that as such they found the prisoner guilty as charged in the indictment.

In all prosecutions by indictment or information, the accused is entitled to " a speedy public trial by a jury of his country." This right, justly regarded as the palladium of the liberties of the citizen, is guaranteed by the fundamental law of the land, and is placed by express provision beyond the control of legislative authority. But neither by the Federal constitution nor by that of our own state, have the qualifications of a juror been defined; or the number necessary to constitute " a jury" been fixed.

It is a general rule that where terms used in the common law are contained in a statute or the constitution, without an explanation of the sense in which they are there employed, they should receive that construction which has been affixed to them by the former. To ascertain then, in what the right of trial by jury consists, we must necessarily recur to the provisions of the common law defining the qualifications, and ascertaining the number of which the jury shall consist; as the standard to which, doubtless, the framers of our constitution referred. At common law, the number of the jury, for the trial of all issues involving the personal rights and liberties of the subject, could never be less than twelve ; though there are some precedents which show that a verdict by a greater number would not on that account be void.   The legislation of the state has left this particular topic untouched.   It has in no instance prescribed the number of the jury, if it were at all important for it to have done so ; but in all cases where the term " jury," is used in our statute, it is regarded as one of fixed and determined meaning, ascertained by the paramount law.   Our courts have also proceeded on the assumption, that the constituents of the jury, at least so far as the number is involved, have been fixed by the constitution as they existed at common law, at the time of its adoption.   Byrd v. State, 1 How., 177.

The finding in the case before us, therefore, cannot be considered as the verdict of a jury, upon which the court was warranted in pronouncing judgment.   For this cause the judgment of the circuit court should be reversed and a new trial awarded ; but it is insisted that other objections exist, which strike at the foundation of the indictment, and require not only a reversal of the judgment, but also the discharge of the prisoner.   These objections apply to the caption of the indictment, as well as the subject matter charged.   We do not deem it important to notice all of them in detail, but shall confine our examination to some of the most obvious.

1. It is insisted that the caption does not show a place at which the court was holden, the indictment found, or the prisoner tried.

To test the validity of this exception, we must refer to the caption of the indictment as it is presented in the record.   It is set out in the following words, to wit : The State of Mississippi v. Samuel A. Carpenter ; pleas in the circuit court of Hancock county ; B. Harris, Judge, presiding ; the term of August, in the year of our Lord, one thousand eight hundred and thirty-eight.   Be it remembered that on the second day of the present term, being the 30th day of August, A. D., 1838, the grand jury of the State of Mississippi being duly empanelled, sworn, and charged, to-wit : (Asa Russ, foreman,) Antoine Field, etc., came into court and presented the following indictment to-wit :"

The fact that the court was holden for the county of Hancock, is stated with sufficient certainty, and also that it was held at the time appointed by law; but does this statement in the caption necessarily include the additional fact, that it was holden at the place in the county designated by the statute? It is not directly expressed, and no presumption can be indulged which contradicts the record; nor are we warranted in the assumption of any fact which is not necessarily included in that which is expressed. In the case of Woodsides v. State, the record showed that one of the grand jurors was sworn as foreman; and it was considered tantamount to a direct statement, that he had been appointed as such by the court; as he could not have been sworn in that capacity without having been appointed. Here the court may have been holden in Hancock county, and yet it be true that it was not held at the court house. If the court was holden at any other place in the county, other than that designated by law, it is obvious that it could rightfully have exercised no jurisdiction in the cause and therefore requires no argument to show that all of its proceedings were irregular. It is clear from authority that it should appear not only that the court was holden for the proper county, but also that it was holden at the proper place within the county. To show this fact is part of the appropriate office of the caption. See. 1 Chitty Cr. Law, 327; 2 Hawk. P. C. ch. 25, § 128; 2 Hale, 166. This omission, therefore, in the caption, to state the place where the court was holden and the indictment found, must be considered as a valid objection.

The omission of any material statement in the caption or record, cannot be supplied by the recital in the indictment, which becomes no part of the record until it is returned into court in the manner prescribed by law. The record in the case now under investigation, does not directly state that the grand jurors who returned the bill of indictment into court, were the grand jurors of the county where the court was holden; and this is the ground of the second objection which we deem necessary to notice.

The grand jurors for any county duly selected and empanelled, according to the directions of the law, may with strict legal propriety, be termed the grand jurors of the state; as it is on behalf of the state and by its authority that they are required to discharge the duties assigned to them.   But it is objected that the record which describes the grand jury who returned the bill into court, as the "grand jurors of the State of Mississippi, duly empanelled, charged and sworn," does not show by that description that they were selected from the proper county.

No man can be held to answer for any criminal violation of the law, unless he shall be first charged by a grand jury of the county where the offense may have been committed.   This fact must be shown by the caption of the indictment, or it will be presumed that the court has proceeded without authority.   The forms of proceeding in prosecution for public offenses are designed to protect the life and liberty of the citizen, and are justly regarded as a valuable appendage to the right of trial by jury. Objections of a merely technical character may sometimes impede, instead of advance the cause of justice; and although courts of justice have very properly manifested a disposition to relax the rigor of ancient forms, where no injury could result to the accused, yet there must be some limit beyond which judicial innovations should not be permitted to advance.   Upon the principle of this relaxation, this court in Byrd's case, and subsequently in that of Woodsides, where the record showed the grand jurors were "sworn in and for the body of the county," held that it was equivalent to a statement that they were grand jurors of the proper county.   But it appears to me that it would be extending this principle too far, to hold that the description of the grand jury in the record before us necessarily evinces the fact, that they were selected from the county where the prisoner was charged with the offense.

The other objection which we shall notice is in effect this, that the act charged does not amount in law to the crime of willful and corrupt perjury.

The argument in support of this exception proceeded on the ground, that the affidavit of the prisoner set out in the indictment, charged no particular individual with the commission of an offense, and that therefore, although the affidavit may have been false, it did not constitute the crime of perjury.

It is not denied that the magistrate before whom the affidavit was sworn to, was legally authorized to administer an oath. The affidavit charges unequivocally that a felony had been committed by some person, and was made for the purpose of obtaining a search warrant for the recovery of the property alleged in it to have been stolen. We cannot perceive that it makes the slightest difference that no particular person was averred to have committed the felony. We therefore think that this objection is untenable; but for the errors before noticed we are bound to reverse the judgment of the circuit court, and order the prisoner to be discharged.

HARE v. THE STATE, 4 Howard, 187.

MURDER.

Where a person who was not a sworn officer was permitted to go into the jury room after the jury had retired to make up their verdict, in a capital case, and to have charge of them in the absence of the bailiff, it was held a sufficient ground for a new trial.[1]

The well established rule is, that wherever the circumstances of irregularity attending the deliberations of a jury *might* have affected the correctness or purity of the verdict, the verdict cannot be sustained; on the contrary, where those circumstances could *not* have influenced the jury in its determination, the verdict shall stand.[2]

TROTTER, J. Dissenting.

Error to Hinds circuit court.

At the May term of said court, 1839, William Hare, the plaintiff in error, was tried and convicted of the murder of Robert Sharp. A motion was made for a new trial by the prisoner, which was overruled.

The motion was supported by affidavits which disclosed these facts. When the case was submitted to the jury, they were placed in charge of a sworn officer, who took them to a hotel in the town of Raymond, at which there were many guests, and

[1] McCann's case, 9 S. & M., 465.

[2] Cornelius v. State, 7 Eng. 782; Ned & Taylor v. State, 9 S. & M., 465; Nelms v. State, 13 ib., 500; Boles v. State, ib., 398; Browning v. State, 33 Miss., 48; State v. Preston, 7 N. H., 287; State v. Fox, 1 Ga. Decisions, 35; State v. Peter, ib., 46; McLain v. State, 10 Yerg., 241; Hines v. State, 11 Humph., 597; 1 Iredell, 513; Wesley v. State, 11 Humph., 502.

the placed them in a room which did not admit of being fastened except on the outside. After they had been there some
time, how long was not stated, a man by the name of Woodley
came into the room unnoticed by the bailiff. That whilst he,
the bailiff, withdrew to obtain water for the jury, he left them
in the charge of Woodley; that he was absent seven or eight
minutes and that he left the door unfastened. It was proved
further that Woodley was not a deputy sheriff, nor was he sworn
to take charge of the jury. How long he continued in the room
with them, did not appear. By the bill of exceptions it appears
that a motion was made because Woodley was in the room
with the jury, and conversed with them on the subject of the
prisoner's guilt, and to establish this, the affidavit of one of the
jurors was offered, which the court below rejected, and although
the affidavit had a place designated in the bill of exceptions, yet
by some omission, it was not copied.

Before the indictment was found, or the grand jury were
sworn, the counsel for the prisoner filed a plea, challenging the
array of the panel, on the ground that the same was not drawn
at the regular term of the circuit court, or otherwise in pursuance of the statute. The court refused to receive this plea.

The prisoner also tendered a plea, setting out in substance
that he had before been arraigned and tried for the same offence "which was charged in the bill of indictment." This plea
was likewise rejected and the opinion of the court excepted to.

The following errors in the proceedings of the court below
were assigned by counsel for plaintiff in error:

1. The refusal of the court to hear the plea of the defendant
challenging and objecting to the array of the panel for the reason that they were not drawn at the preceding regular term of
the court, and recorded for the instruction of the prisoner according to the statute.

2. That there was no regular writ of *venire facias* upon which
to bring in the panel.

3. That the writ of *venire facias*, whereon the said panel was
brought into court, was issued without authority, and was therefore null and void.

Wilson for plaintiff in error.

The first point to be considered is, whether there was a lawful grand jury. The first assignment brings into review the array of the panel, the *venire facias* service and return, and the rejection of the plea to the array. Indeed, the plea itself presents the prominent objection. It was offered when the persons selected for a grand jury were about to be sworn. It is stated that the sheriff and clerk on the 18th of March, 1839, which will be judicially recognized as a day of the recess between the fall and spring terms of the circuit court, drew a number of persons to serve as jurors at the next term; and the clerk issued a written command to the sheriff to summon them accordingly. That they were freeholders or householders of the county, or were drawn out of the box *one* or *two*, or that the names were registered, does not appear.

It is surely no vain assumption that the grand jury is an essential auxiliary of the court of oyer and terminer, and jail delivery, and that without its preliminary action a prosecution and conviction for murder could not be sustained. The constituent elements of the grand inquest, as well as that of trial by jury, were, by our national and state constitutions, engrafted upon our civil polity; and, though the forms and modes of these institutions, owing to differences in our condition, habits and circumstances, differ from those of the nation from whom we derived them, the substance of them must be preserved. It cannot be too often or too urgently repeated, that they are the foundation pillars of that noble fabric of civil liberty which was reared by the Saxon race, and which each successive generation of that race has delighted to beautify and adorn.

But what are those constituent elements thus planted on constitutional foundations, and that must be preserved? There must be an authoritative and responsible source from which the panel is to emanate; each one in the array must be a freeman, at least in the civil division over which the court is to preside, and the inquest is to be taken; the panel must be registered or so published previously, as that those who are suitors, or to be tried, can have opportunity to make up knowingly challenges to the array or polls. 3 Black. Com., 355; 6 Bacon, 523–4.

In England, the sheriff arrayed the panel, and hence the

challenge to the array for his neglect, partiality or corruption; 6 Bacon, 551, 552; 1 Chitty Cr. Law, 536, 537. Here, it is essential to the existence of the grand inquest that some officer, commission, or tribunal should be designated and empowered to select the jurors to be summoned. The act of 1830, Reprint, 304, gave a sure, safe and perfect mode of originating the panel; and adjudications of this court had scrupulously enforced its provisions. The freeholders and householders of the county were to be procured from the assessment rolls and deposited in a box. Then, at the court preceding that to which the *venire facias* was returnable, the sheriff and clerk, in open court, in the presence of the judge, were to draw the required number of names, rejecting the removed and ineligible. The panel thus drawn could not be a shuffled one. The public eye was open upon its inception. On this the *venire facias* issued, and the panel was registered for inspection. If the circuit court failed to sit, the sheriff and clerk repaired to the probate court, and the record-box was opened, and so the *modus operandi* excluded the probability of abuse. But the act of 1836 abrogated the challenge to the array and forbid a *venire facias* being quashed for any cause whatever in any court. Reprint, 578. Let us carry this stolid act into operation. No challenge to the array is to be had, and no *venire facias* to be quashed. What then? Where are we to go for the panel? To the act of 1830? We are constrained to do so because it is a dead letter. If we invoke it as a rule of action, no violation of its provisions, however monstrous, can be noticed. If a sheriff should return a panel of free negroes and mulattoes as good and lawful men, the judge, in obedience to the act of 1836, would make up his grand jury out of them. Would he reject a plea to the array? He could not. Would he quash the *venire?* Thus, then, it is we are putting our fellowmen upon trials of life and death, under a statute that gives us no panel out of which to form a grand jury, or on which to build petit juries for the trials of issues of traverse and of civil controversies.

  Again, another element of the grand inquest to be preserved as we would sustain the institution itself, is that the jurors should have at least the qualification of being freemen. 6 Bacon,

524. The act of 1830 requires freeholders or householders who are free white citizens. But if this requisition be disregarded, under the latter act, it is no vice. If the sheriff were to return a panel of young men, or such as were neither householders nor freeholders, a grand jury could be selected out of them, and under the latter act it would be quite sufficient. Here, those on the panel are called *persons.*

So, too, it is necessary that the panel should be composed of citizens of the county. 6 Bacon, 559. But as the challenge to the array no longer exists, and as no *venire facias* is to be vacated for any cause, a panel from Rankin or Warren would have answered to have passed on the indictment in this case, as well as if from Hinds. There was nothing prior to the plea to the array to show from what county those persons came.

Abuses, at each step in the application of the statute in review, multiply and aggravate. Our constitutions in bringing from Britain the institution of the grand jury, assuredly contemplated an *impartial inquest.* But allow it possible, or even probable, that in some county there may be some temporary excitement, or some undue and formidable conspiracy, and that the sheriff, or whoever may choose to make a panel (for the act of 1836 appoints no person or mode for its emanation) should be very much prejudiced, or somewhat base, and should cull out a trained band to his own notion, your circuit judge is obliged to submit to it. He is constrained to elect his grand inquest out of such material. These illustrations could be readily increased.

There is still another important consideration. It was a portion of the British scheme of grand and petit juries, that the panel should be arrayed and returned "weeks and months before the jurors were to appear," and for the very important reason and motive that the suitors and accused should have inspection of the names; that partialities, corruptions, affinities and the like, might be ascertained—and thus the trial, through the grand and petit juries, should be kept pure and sacredly devoted to the administration of public justice. But what is the practice under the late act? It is to make the list at any time—in any manner—no one knows or can know whether even the clerk and sheriff coöperate.   In the present instance, the list was made in March for May, instead of being drawn at the preceding term, and of being enrolled according to the act of 1830. Instances have occurred where the judge gave an oral order, after taking his seat, and a jury was got up for him in an hour. Is this to be borne? Is it not plain that with such flagrant violations of the act of 1830, which is really the law in force, the institutions of the grand jury and jury trial will sink into the most shameful abuses, the extremest contempt, and become too mean or too hurtful to be preserved? If you enforce the act of 1836, you are obliged to consider the act of 1830 as suspended and inoperative. You cannot enforce the former with the power to declare infractions of it illegal and void; and that you cannot do unless you have the power to entertain a challenge to the array and to substantial defects in the *venire facias*. But as it has been shown that an enforcement of the latter act necessarily involves a subversion of the constituents and essential elements of the grand inquest and trial by jury, as secured to us by the fundamental law, this court is constrained to declare it unconstitutional and void. And this being done, it will be plain that the panel was illegal, the *venire facias* void, the grand jury unlawful, and that the indictment in this case must fall.

Challenge to the array may be made by the prisoner before the finding of the indictment; and the proper time is between the appearance and swearing of the grand jury. So it was made here.   1 Chitty Cr. Law, 309, 544, 545; 1 Burr's trial, 38; Ross v. State, 1 Blackf., 318; Hudson v. State, ib., 318; Commonwealth v. Clark, 2 Brown, 323; People v. Jewett, 3 Wend., 314; Commonwealth v. Smith, 9 Mass., 109; McClure v. State, 1 Yerg., 206; Commonwealth v. Knapp, 10 Pick., 477; Hooker v. State, 4 Ohio, 450; Gardner v. Turner, 9 Johns., 261; Pringle v. Hughs, 1 Cowen, 435, 436, note 1; Commonwealth v. Leppard, 6 Searg. & Rawle, 395; Crane v. Dygett, 4 Wend., 675.

II. The plea of former trial, etc., ought not to have been rejected.

III. A new trial ought to have been granted.   After the jury retired under charge of a sworn officer, they, according to his oath, ought to have been kept together in a convenient place (separated from the rest of the world) without meat, drink or fire, candles and water excepted, suffered to speak to no one, nor to the officer, nor he to them unless to ask if they had agreed, without leave of the court.   They were conducted to a room in a tavern ; the door for a period left open ; they were put under the charge of one who was not an officer, nor sworn. He spoke to them.   If these deviations are to be allowed, anything may be.   King v. Moseley, etc., 18 Eng. C. & R., 115 ; Cochrane v. Street, 1 Wash., 79, 103 ; Howle v. Dunn, 1 Leigh, 455 ; Hale v. Cove, 1 Strange, 642 ; Metcalf v. Dean, Cro. Eliz., 189, 411 ; Blair v. Chambers, 1 Searg. & Rawle, 169 ; People v. Douglass, 4 Cowen, 26 ; Brant v. Fowler, 7 Cowen, 562.

Foote, on same side.

Thomas F. Collins, attorney general.

SHARKEY, C. J.:

Whilst the law is rigidly vigilant in guarding and preserving the purity of jury trials, yet it will not, for light or trivial causes, impugn the integrity of juries, or question the impartiality of their verdicts.   But if the verdict be given under circumstances which might conduce to an improper influence, or the natural tendency of which might be to produce bias or corruption, it cannot then be said to be above suspicion ; and if it be not, it must fall short of that perfection which the law requires, and which, under a more guarded administration, it is capable of producing.   It is not necessary that any attempt should be made to bias the minds of jurors, or that any pernicious influence should be exerted.   The door to tampering is to be closed ; this is the only security ; for if it be left open, it may be predicted with certainty that the evil consequences will fall somewhere.

This question has received repeated adjudications, and it will be sufficient for me to refer to some of the decided cases, in which the reasoning is, to my mind, conclusive, and the rule clearly defined.

In the case of the Commonwealth v. Roby, 12 Pick., 496, the question was very fully considered, and it is made so clear that

I shall give the language of the chief justice somewhat at length. In giving the general rule he says : " It is a well settled rule of practice incident to all jury trials, that after the jury are charged and have left the court to consider of their verdict, they are to be kept by themselves, without refreshment and without communication with others, until they have agreed. Any departure from this rule is an irregularity ; but it is not every irregularity which will render the verdict void, and warrant setting it aside. This depends upon another and additional consideration, namely, whether the irregularity is of such a nature as to affect the impartiality, purity, and regularity of the verdict."

I might here pause and inquire, what irregularity will, and will not vitiate the verdict ? The object of jury trials suggests the answer. Common reason dictates to us what might affect the "impartiality, purity, and regularity" of a verdict, and whatever might have that effect, will vitiate it, as will appear from the conclusions of Judge Shaw. After he has reviewed many of the authorities, he concludes by saying, "the result of the authorities is that when there is an irregularity which may affect the impartiality of the proceedings, as where meat and drink or other refreshments have been furnished by a party, or where the jury have been exposed to such influence, as where they have improperly separated themselves, or have had communications not authorized, there, inasmuch as there can be no certainty that the verdict has not been improperly influenced, the proper and appropriate mode of correction and relief is by undoing that which was improperly and may have been corruptly done; or where the irregularity consists in doing that which may disqualify the jurors from proper deliberation and exercise of their reason and judgment, as where the act done is contrary to the ordinary forms, and to the duties which jurors owe to the public, the mode of correcting the irregularity is by animadversion upon the conduct of the jurors or of the officers, but such irregularity has no tendency to impair the respect due to such verdict." To me it seems that the line of distinction is here so clearly drawn, that it is impossible to mistake it, and so fortified by reason as to place it beyond doubt. It is briefly this : If the purity of the verdict *might* have been affected, it must be set aside: if it could not have been affected, it will be sustained. A verdict upon which doubts might rest cannot be good. The same learned judge says, " it must command entire confidence."

The reasons here given run through all the decided cases. In the case of the Commonwealth v. McCall, 1 Va. Cases, one of the jurors separated from his fellows, but for a few minutes, and spoke to no one about the trial, yet a new trial was granted. So in the case of McLain v. State, 10 Yerger, 241, in which a part of the jury separated from the balance for fifteen or twenty minutes pending the trial ; this was held sufficient ground for a new trial. In neither of these cases was any such thing as a tampering with a jury shown. The courts both held that to be unnecessary, and say that is sufficient that they might have been subject to improper influences. In the last case the court said " there would be no safety in a different rule of practice, for it would be almost impossible ever to bring direct proof of the fact that it was done." These decisions are evidently based upon the same principles with that first cited, to wit, that the purity of the verdict might have been affected.

In the case of Knight v. Inhabitants of Freeport, 13 Mass. R., 218, the verdict was set aside because a party indirectly interested spoke to one of the jurors and told him he was deeply interested in the case, and that it was a spiteful thing on the part of the plaintiff. This case is only cited to show the degree of strictness necessary to make a valid verdict. The court said " too much care and precaution could not be used to preserve the purity of jury trials." This strictness is necessary to give due confidence to the parties in the results of their causes ; and every one ought to know that for any, even the slightest inter-meddling with jurors, a verdict will be set aside.

In the case of Perkins v. Knight, 2 N. H., 474, the court say that " it is of the highest importance that jurors should be preserved not only from all improper bias in causes, but even from the suspicion of improper bias."

It only remains to make an application of these principles to the case before us. If, for a separation of the jury, which occasions a mere exposure to improper influence, a new trial will be granted, why should it not in the present case? The thing to be guarded against is improper influence. Can it not be as well exercised in the jury-room by an individual who has the art and capacity to exercise it, as it can anywhere else? Woodley was with the jury, how long it is not known; who can say that he did not speak of the guilt of the prisoner? Who can say that he had not influence, and that his influence was not exerted to procure a verdict of guilty? If it was legal for Woodley to be with the jury, it would also be legal for any one else to be there. Suppose that he had been the prosecutor, and an influential man, could it be said, under such circumstances, that the verdict was free from suspicion? Could every one rely on it as the voice of an impartial jury? Can there be any difference between admitting a stranger into the jury-room, and admitting him into the company of the jury after they had dispersed?

To me it seems that all the evils are fully incurred by letting an unauthorized person into the jury room, that could be incurred by letting them separate. It seems to be a proposition too clear to admit of a doubt, that in this way the verdict *might* be tainted with corruption or bias. If so, the rule which I have before stated will apply. It applies with all its force. If the sanctity of the jury room may be violated by an intruder, there is an exposure to his influence, and when the opportunity has been offered, no one can say that it has not been used. The verdict is opened to suspicion, and does not, nor cannot command respect and confidence. An artful man might infuse the poison in a few words. We cannot know that Woodley did not do so; or even if we could be satisfied that he did not, another person, on another occasion, might, and the law is to operate by general rules. If it were lawful for him to be there, it would also be lawful for another person. If lawful for one person, why not for two or more? One man may effect as much as more could. It is the duty of the court to swear an officer to take charge of the jury; his oath is, that he will not speak to them or permit others to do so. How useless is this ceremony, if the officer may commit the jury to the keeping of one who is not sworn. Suppose the court had called a mere by-stander who was not sworn, to go out with the jury, would a verdict under such circumstances be good? It would not; and yet, are we to permit the officer to leave the jury in an exposed room under the charge of any intruder that may thrust himself into the presence of the jury? Suppose twelve men had been admitted, who could say whether the verdict was the voice of those who had been sworn, or those who had not? and if one be admitted, certainly twelve might with the same propriety. One man could exert all the art, ingenuity, and malice, that twelve could. I must think that this verdict is within the rule. The irregularity might have affected its purity. I am therefore led to the conclusion that a new trial should be granted.

SMITH, J. concurred.

TROTTER, J. dissenting:

William Hare was indicted in the circuit court of Hinds county for the murder of Robert Sharp.

Before the indictment was found and the grand jury were sworn, the counsel for the prisoner presented a plea challenging the array of the panel from which the grand jury were selected, on the ground that the same was not drawn at any regular term of the circuit court, or otherwise in pursuance of the statute. The court refused to receive this plea. The prisoner afterwards tendered a plea stating in substance, that he had *before been arraigned and tried* for the same offense which was charged in the bill of indictment. The court refused to receive this plea likewise. The cause was then submitted to a jury, who returned a verdict of guilty. The prisoner moved the court to grant him a new trial. It appears that after the evidence was closed, the jury retired under the care and charge of a bailiff, who conducted them to a room in one of the hotels in the town of Raymond, where the court was held. That after they had been engaged some time in their deliberations, a man by the name of Woodley came into their room unobserved by the bailiff. Woodley had occasionally acted as a special deputy of the sheriff, and the officer who had charge of the jury was under the impression that he was then one of the deputies. It appears, however, that he had no authority to be with the jury at that time. Woodley remained with the jury a few minutes whilst the bailiff retired to get them some water. There is no proof that Woodley did or said anything calculated to have any influence against the prisoner. The motion for a new trial was refused by the court.

The errors assigned are: 1st. The rejection of the plea which challenged the array. 2d. The rejection of a special plea of a former arraignment and trial for the same offense. 3d. The judgment of the court on the motion for a new trial.

1st. The record states that the panel of jurors for the term was drawn by the sheriff and clerk in vacation, without the assistance of any officer. This was irregular, for the act of 1830 provides that the *venire* shall be drawn, if in the circuit court, in open court, in presence of the judge, by the clerk and sheriff; but if this shall be omitted, the same may be afterwards done by the clerk and sheriff in the presence of the judge of probates. The plea should, therefore, have been received, unless the act of 1836 can be considered as an answer to the objection which was stated and relied on. The first section of that act provides that no challenge to array shall be sustained, nor shall any *venire facias* be quashed by any court of justice in this state. There is a proviso that in capital cases any *venire facias* may be quashed for partiality or corruption in the officer summoning the jury, etc. This act is a direct authority for the rejection of the challenge in this case. This court was zealously invoked to disregard the provisions of this law, which were denounced in the argument as an unconstitutional and dangerous infringement on the right of jury trials. The constitution of our state has asserted the importance of this institution, and guarded it with emphatic terms from the danger of violation. In this day, and in this country, there can be, I apprehend, but one sentiment on the subject. The right of trial by jury is universally looked upon as the most valuable and effectual bulwark of human rights. And no law which should deprive the citizen of this safeguard of his life, liberty and property, could receive the sanction of any court of justice. But I cannot regard the act of 1836 as subject to this objection. It does not take away the right, but only provides the method of enjoying it. It is true that its provisions are open to some observations on the score of policy. Abuses may sometimes grow out of it. But the remedy for this lies with the legislature, and not with this court. It is not deemed unconstitutional, and under the liberal indulgence of the right of challenge to the polls, peremptory as well as for cause, it will not often happen that this law will have the effect to deprive the party of a jury not free from objections. The frequent instances in which the whole panel for the term had been set aside on account of some mere technical objection to the form of process of *venire facias*, by which justice was defeated, and litigation was increased, was the cause of this law, and although it is very broad in its terms, has yet proved highly salutary to the administration of justice. It has served to extricate justice from the web of mere technical form, in which she is too often entangled. In the case before the court, I can discover no ground for arresting the regular operation of the act. Should one of these extreme cases, which were supposed by the prisoner's counsel, ever occur, it will be the duty of the courts to pause and consider whether it is within the spirit and meaning of the law, and to give to it such interpretation as will vindicate the constitutional right of the citizen, and uphold the public policy and justice of the country.

2. Very few remarks are deemed sufficient to dispose of the second ground of error. The plea alleges, in substance merely, that the prisoner had before been arraigned and tried for the same offense. It does not aver either a conviction or acquittal. It is, therefore, neither a plea of *autrefois acquit* or *autrefois convict.* The plea was attempted in the argument to be sustained on the authority of that great principle applicable to criminal jurisprudence, that no man shall twice be put in jeopardy for the same offense. There is no question as to the principle, and it has been expressly sanctioned in this country by a constitutional enactment. In the constitution of the United States it is thus expressed: "Nor shall any person be subject for the same offense to be twice put in jeopardy of life or limb." This phrase is well known in the law, and is considered as descriptive of the class of punishments inflicted for crimes amounting to a felony, whether the punishment be loss of life or limb. And hence this clause in the constitution is considered as equivalent to a declaration that no man shall be twice tried for the same offense. In the application of this maxim, it is important, however, in each case to consider, whether the party who claims its benefits, has

been really put in jeopardy, and for the same offense. For a man may have been tried, and yet have been in no jeopardy, in the sense in which this term is understood at common law, and in the constitution. Thus if the court have no jurisdiction, no valid judgment could be rendered, and the maxim does not apply to a trial before such a tribunal. Or if the indictment was defective, so that no punishment could be awarded upon a conviction, or, if during the trial, a juror is suddenly taken ill, or dies, or the prisoner becomes so indisposed as not to be able to attend his trial, or from any other urgent necessity the progress of the trial is interrupted, another jury may be empanelled, and the prisoner again put upon his trial. And so when the prisoner has been convicted, and the judgment has been arrested at his instance, and likewise, when the jury cannot agree after the proper efforts, and there is no prospect of a verdict, and the powers of the court are about to terminate, and under this necessity they are discharged, the prisoner may again be put upon his trial. In all these cases, the prisoner may be said to have been in jeopardy by the first trial, and yet as the event has shown that there was no legal trial, he was not in jeopardy in the true sense of the maxim. See the case of the Commonwealth v. Roby, 12 Pick. R., 502; Bowden's case, 9 Mass. R., 494; People v. Goodwine, 18 J. R., 187; United States v. Perez, 9 Wheat, 579. Hence it is necessary in every plea which seeks for the prisoner the benefit of this maxim, to aver a conviction or acquittal, on a former trial for the same offense. This was so expressly held by the court of appeals of Kentucky, in the case of the Commonwealth v. Olds, 5 Lit. R., 139, in which a very lucid and satisfactory explanation is given of the maxim under consideration. Upon the two grounds of error which I have noticed, the other judges fully concur in opinion with me.

3. I come now to consider the objection to the verdict, which is the only remaining subject of inquiry; and regret that I cannot agree with the other judges on this point. This objection is rested on the single ground that Woodley was in the jury-room for a few moments, whilst they were consulting about their verdict. This man was an entire stranger to the prisoner, from aught that appears from the record, and there is no fact pre-

sented to the court upon which any imputation can be made against him on the score of interest or feeling.   He is not shown to have had any motive to prejudice the cause of the prisoner, and he neither did nor said anything for or against him.   The jury had no agency in procuring his absence, nor are they charged in anything with impropriety or misbehavior.   Woodley was a mere intruder, nor is it shown that his presence was at all countenanced by the jury.   Is this naked, dry fact, standing by itself on the record, sufficient to destroy the deliberate and solemn determination of the jury?   I confess that I can see no pretext for giving it such influence either in principle or adjudged cases.   On that principle I do not see how any verdict can stand.   Verdicts may and should be set aside for a mistake in the jury, by which injustice has been done, or for corruption or partiality in any of the members of the jury; or for such misbehavior as naturally tends to affect the impartiality, purity and regularity of the verdict.   It will not do to determine that every irregularity on the part of the jury will avoid their verdict.   It is important to the welfare of society and the ends of justice, that impartiality and purity should mark the action of juries.   Their verdict should command entire confidence.   But it is equally essential to the harmony of society, that verdicts should not be lightly set aside.   The law must repose some confidence in the honesty of juries, and the integrity of their verdicts, so much, at any rate, as not to presume any vice in them as such, until it is established by proof.   To set aside the present verdict, this reasonable presumption must be entirely disregarded; nay, the court must indulge the contrary presumption.   This I cannot consent to do.   Nor have I been able to find one adjudged case which would require me to do it.   For I have seen no case in which the verdict has been set aside, unless some misconduct or irregularity of the jury has been shown.

The ground on which the court is asked to vacate this verdict, is the mere impropriety of Woodley, a stranger.   The case of the Commonwealth v. Roby, 12 Pick. R., 516, fully sustains the views which I have here expressed; and as this is the case on the authority of which the majority of the court have considered themselves bound to reverse the judgment in the present case, I will notice at length.

Roby was indicted for murder, and convicted. A motion was made to set aside the verdict, on the ground of irregular conduct in the jury. The irregularity complained of consisted of the following facts : After the jury had retired to consider of their verdict, and after they had been for some time engaged in their deliberations, some of them told one of the constables that they were faint, and asked him whether they could not obtain some refreshments ; and the constable thereupon went to a grocer's shop and procured crackers and cheese, and two bottles of cider, which were carried into the jury-room by the constable and the grocer's boy ; that while the constable and the boy were in the room, one of the jurors said that two bottles were not enough, and the constable told the boy to bring two more ; the boy brought them and delivered them to the constable, who carried them into the room, etc. The court refused to set aside the verdict, on the ground that though it might have been an irregularity to drink cider and admit the boy in the room, yet it was not an irregularity for which the verdict could be avoided.

There was in that case an irregularity charged against the jury ; in this case there was none. In that case the judge says, that the question whether misbehavior in the jury shall set aside their verdict, depends upon another question, and that is, whether the misbehavior or irregularity is of such a nature as to affect the impartiality, purity, and regularity of the verdict. Here the judge gives the rule and also a practical illustration of it, and he did not consider the irregularity complained of in that case as necessarily tending to affect the verdict. How, then, can this court hold that the irregularity of a mere stranger, in which the jury in no way participated, can affect the verdict ?

In the conclusion of his opinion, Judge Shaw observes, that the result of the authorities is, that when the jury have so acted as to expose themselves to influences which may affect their verdict, as when they have improperly separated themselves, or had communications not authorized, then, as there can be no certainty that the verdict has been improperly influenced, the proper mode of correction is to set aside the verdict.

The rule is here laid down in terms as broad as possible for the prisoner at the bar, and in terms much broader than what the judge in the preceding part of his opinion had allowed himself. For he has cited several authorities in his opinion to show that an unauthorized separation of the jury is no ground to reverse the judgment; and amongst others that of the King v. Kinnear, 2 Barn. & Ald., 462; St. John v. Abbott, Barnes, 441. He might also have referred to many other cases, to show the same doctrine, and where the judges have determined, that though it is a misdemeanor of the jury, for which they may be fined, yet it will not of itself vitiate their verdict. In the King v. Moseley *et al.*, 18 Eng. C. L. R., 115, this point was fully settled after full argument. But as there was no separation of the jury in this case, it is unnecessary to consider this point further. And it is quite evident to me that Judge Shaw could only have intended, at most, by the irregularity referred to in his concluding remarks, some positive act, such as an unjustifiable separation of the jury, or some actual unauthorized communication under circumstances tending to expose the jury to undue influences.

This case cannot, therefore, in my opinion, come within the rule thus laid down, any more than the case he was considering. The case of Park, in 2 Rolle R., 85, is identical in principle with the one at bar. In that case a juror was challenged and withdrawn, but went on with the jury and remained with them above half an hour; and yet the judges held that this, though a misdemeanor in the juror, for which he might be punished, yet of itself was not sufficient to set aside the verdict. This was as strong a case as the one at bar. That was surely a case where there was as much room for conjecture that improper influence had been exerted, as in the present case; yet the court very properly, as I conceive, refused to indulge in conjecture, or to visit upon the jury the impropriety or misbehavior of a stranger.

I am clearly of opinion that there is no ground for reversing the verdict.

KLIFFIELD *v.* THE STATE, 4 Howard, 304.

RETAILING WITHOUT LICENSE.

A count in an indictment on the statute, charging that the defendant did unlawfully sell and retail vinous and spirituous liquors, to wit: wine, rum, gin, brandy and whiskey, in a less quantity than one gallon, to persons to the jurors unknown; and that the said defendant did then and there suffer and permit the said vinous and spirituous liquors, so retailed and sold in less quantities than one gallon, as aforesaid, to be drank and used in and about the house of him, the said C. contrary, to the form of the statute, etc., was held to be good.

A count charging that the defendant, as a tavern and inn-keeper, did unlawfully, and without special charge therefor, offer, give, and deliver vinous and spirituous liquors, etc., in less quantity than one gallon, to divers persons to the jurors unknown; which said persons were then and there the guests of the said C. contrary to the statute, etc., was held to be good.

A count charging that the defendant, inn-keeper, etc., did then and there, by evasion, etc., violate the plain intent and meaning of an act, etc., is too vague and uncertain, and will not warrant a conviction. When the indictment contains several counts, and one of them is good, it will sustain the verdict of "guilty."

It is a well established rule of law, that a hypothetical opinion of the court, given in its instructions to the jury, is no ground of error.

No one can excuse himself from the operation of penal statutes, on the mere ground that he acted only as agent for another person.

Error to Jefferson circuit court.

Saunders for plaintiff in error.

T. F. Collins, attorney general.

TURNER, J. :

The plaintiff in error was indicted, tried and convicted under the statute commonly called the gallon law, and received the sentence of the court at the December term, 1839.

The plaintiff in error assigns the following errors:

1. The criminal court erred in refusing a new trial, as prayed for.

2. The criminal court erred in the instruction given on motion of the attorney for the state.

3. The indictment is wholly defective in substance, and the judgment in the case unlawful and defective.

We will notice the last error first.

There are three several counts in the indictment. The first count charges that the defendant below by the name of George H. Cliffield, yeoman, did unlawfully sell and retail vinous and spirituous liquors, to wit, wine, rum, gin, brandy and whiskey, in a less quantity than one gallon, to persons to the jurors unknown, and that the said defendant did then and there suffer and permit the said vinous and spirituous liquors, so retailed and sold in less quantity than one gallon, as aforesaid, to be drank and used in and about the house of him the said Kliffield, contrary to the form of the statute, etc.

The second count charges that George H. Cliffield, tavern keeper and inn-keeper, did "unlawfully, gratuitously and without special charge therefor, offer, give and deliver vinous and spirituous liquors, viz: wine, gin, rum, brandy, and whiskey, in less quantity than one gallon, to divers persons to the jurors aforesaid unknown, which said persons were then and there the guests of the said George H. Cliffield, contrary," etc.

The third count charges "that George H. Kliffield, tavern-keeper and inn-keeper, etc., did then and there by evasion, subterfuge and chicanery, violate the plain intent and meaning and law of the State of Mississippi, bearing date, etc., entitled ' an act for the suppression of tippling houses, and to discourage and prevent the odious vice of drunkenness,' contrary," etc.

The defendant below being arrested and brought into court, pleaded "not guilty," and for trial put himself upon the country.

In some parts of the indictment, the plaintiff in error is described as George H. Cliffield, "yeoman;" in others, as "tavern - keeper and inn - keeper;" and in some parts of the record his name is spelled "Cliffield," in others, "Kliffield," and it is contended that these variations amount to errors, fatal to the recovery, had or sought by the state. In answer to this, it is sufficient to state, that on the plea of "not guilty," there was a conviction on the merits, and no question raised on the record, as to the identity of the person of the defendant.

The first and second count in the indictment are unquestionably good. The third count is too general, and cannot be considered as charging the accused with lawful certainty. To indict a person for violating the whole of any particular statute without specifications, is not sufficient to call for a conviction. But the rule is, after a verdict of "guilty" on an indictment containing several counts, if there be one good count, it is sufficient to sustain the conviction.

The next error assigned, in the order proper to be followed, is the second, viz : the supposed error of the court below in its charge to the jury.

After the evidence, both on the part of the state and of the accused, had been closed, the district attorney, on the part of the state, requested the court to give the following instructions to the jury, to wit :

1. The court will instruct the jury that, if from the testimony they believed that Cliffield sold vinous or spirituous liquors in less quantities than one gallon, as the agent of Noe, they will find him guilty.

2. If they believe the defendant permitted vinous liquors to be drank in his house of which the defendant was not the owner, but the barkeeper, they will find him guilty.

3. If they believe from the testimony, that the defendant delivered eighty drinks, by the drinks, it is immaterial whether there was more or less than a gallon in the aggregate ; the defendant is equally guilty.

4. That there can be no clerks, barkeepers or agencies in crime, and the agent is as guilty as the principal.

5. If the defendant is guilty on one count of the indictment, it is sufficient to convict.

All of which instructions the court gave to the jury, in the words stated as above.

The above charges may be considered, in some measure, as hypothetical, as it is not stated in the record what evidence was before the jury ; for instance, in the first charge, we see for the first time the term *agency*, and the name of Noe introduced. It is the well settled law, that a hypothetical opinion given by a court to a jury, is not error, but, so far as the charge may be considered as having any bearing upon the case, it is not in violation of the rules of law. No one can excuse himself in criminal cases, by showing that he acted in the matter as the agent of another person.

The second and remaining charges have relation to the same matter of agency, and as these charges were all in writing, and given together at the same time, they may be considered as having reference to the case before the court, and are substantially correct.   As to the last charge, I have already stated that, if there is one good count in the indictment, it is sufficient to warrant a conviction.

The first error assigned is, that the court below erred in not granting a new trial, which was moved for, for the following reasons, to wit: 1st. Because the court misdirected the jury, and because the jury empanelled, and that tried this case, were not impartial jurors.

We have already expressed our opinion on the first ground of the motion for a new trial, and there is no evidence before us of any want of impartiality in the jurors who tried the cause. We are, therefore, of opinion that the judgment of the court below be affirmed.

NOE *v.* THE STATE, 4 Howard, 330.

RETAILING WITHOUT LICENSE.

The indictment in this case is substantially the same as that in the case of Kliffield, decided in this court, containing three counts, two of which are good and one bad.   Our opinion in that case is applicable to this.   See Kliffield v. The State, ante, p. 304.   There being two good counts, it is sufficient to warrant the conviction.

The continuance of a cause is a matter in the sound discretion of the court; and putting the prisoner upon his trial for violating a penal statute at the same term of the court at which the indictment has been found against him, is not ground of error.

Mere impressions as to the guilt or innocence of the prisoner do not disqualify one as a juror.   To *disqualify*, the juror must have formed and expressed an opinion, or have such acknowledged prejudice or bias, as would render him incapable of doing justice, according to the evidence, between the state and the accused.

Error to Jefferson criminal court.

Saunders for plaintiff in error.

Thomas F. Collins, attorney general.

TURNER, J.:

The plaintiff in error was indicted, tried and convicted under the statute commonly called the gallon law, and received the sentence of the court at the December term, 1839.

The plaintiff in error assigned the following errors, to wit :

1. The criminal court erred in refusing to the prisoner a new trial as prayed for.

2. The court below erred in overruling the challenge of the prisoner to the juror, Lewis C. Watson.

3. The court below erred in compelling the prisoner to submit to a trial at the term of the court at which the indictment is supposed to be found.

4. The indictment is wholly defective in substance, and each order and judgment in the cause is unlawful and defective.

The record in this case contains an indictment of three counts, substantially the same as those contained in the case of the State v. George H. Kliffield, already decided in this court, and the same opinion is entertained by this court in this as in that case, as to the form and substance of the indictment. The two first counts are considered good ; third, bad. But, as already decided, if there is one good count in an indictment consisting of several counts, it is sufficient to warrant a conviction. We therefore find nothing in the fourth error assigned to warrant a reversal of the judgment as it respects the indictment ; and we have not found any " order or judgment in the record either unlawful or defective."

It seems that the indictment was found at the same term at which the defendant was arrested, tried and convicted, and this is assigned for error. There is no law or usage against such a proceeding. The defendant below moved for a continuance, but did not succeed in satisfying the judge that justice required a continuance of the cause. A continuance of a cause ready for trial is a matter in the discretion of the court, and it is not the subject for a writ of error or an appeal. Such a matter cannot be re-examined in an appellate court. But if it could, the affi davit for a continuance is wholly insufficient, in not showing due diligence to procure the testimony of the witnesses, and in not stating that he expected to procure the attendance of the witnesses at the next term.

The 2d error assigned is for overruling the challenge of the appellant to the juror S. C. Watson.

It appears by the bill of exceptions that this juror was challenged for cause, and being examined on oath stated "that he had not formed or expressed any opinion as to the guilt or innocence of the defendant, that in the case of the State *v*. George H. Kliffield, indicted for the same offense, and just tried in this court, he heard the testimony of the witnesses, which created an *impression* upon his mind as to the guilt or innocence of the defendant in this case, the witness therein speaking of the defendant in this case as to his connection with the said Kliffield, which it would require testimony to remove, but that he believed he could impartially decide between the State and the defendant, or that he had no settled or fixed opinion," whereupon the court overruled the objection and permitted the said Watson to be sworn upon the jury.

We do not consider that we should be warranted by the authorities of adjudged cases in deciding that Watson was not an impartial juror. He says that he had not formed or expressed any *opinion*, etc., but that being a listener in court, he heard evidence given in another case which made an *impression* on his *mind*, which it would require testimony to remove, but that he believed he could impartially decide, etc., etc., that he had no settled or fixed opinion. Slight impressions made on the mind, in this way, are of such common occurrence, that it cannot be considered as disqualifying a juror. To *disqualify*, the juror must have formed and expressed an opinion, or have such acknowledged prejudice or bias as would disable him from doing justice, according to the evidence, between the state and the accused. If this were a capital case, the question might be different.

There is nothing in the case to show that the first error assigned should prevail; that the court overruled a motion for a new trial. The evidence given in the case is not embodied in the record.

With respect to the legislative act in question, we consider that there is no constitutional difficulty. The provisions of that law are such as the General Assembly are entirely competent to enact. They are the peculiar judges of the acts necessary to promote public order, public morals, and the public good.

Let the judgment of the court below be affirmed.

DAINGERFIELD v. THE STATE, 4 Howard, 658.

FORFEITURE OF RECOGNIZANCE.

Judgment on the forfeiture of a recognizance for appearance, will be reversed if there is a material variance between the recognizance, the *scire facias*, and the judgment of the court.

Error to Jefferson circuit court.

Clark for plaintiffs in error.

T. F. Collins, attorney general.

TURNER, J.:

At the December term, 1837, of the circuit court of Jefferson county, Henry M. Jones was presented by the grand jury for stealing a negro woman named Louisa, and her child named Rachel, of the value of $1200, of the goods and chattels of one George Torrey. A bench warrant issued to bring in the body of said Jones, which was returned executed, during said term, he was admitted to bail, and entered into recognizance,—himself in the sum of $500, and his bail, Young and Daingerfield in the sum of $250 each, for the appearance of said Jones at the (then) next term of said court. At the June term, 1838, the accused, Jones, was called out, together with his bail, and forfeitures taken according to the recognizance *nisi*.

On the 18th of September, 1838, a *scire facias* issued, reciting that at the June term, 1838, the said Jones was presented for the offense aforesaid; that a bench warrant issued; the accused arrested, who gave bail in five hundred dollars with the above sureties, conditioned for the appearance of said Jones at the court of said county to be holden on the 2d *Monday of December*, 1887; that at the *June term*, 1838, Jones was called to appear, etc., but wholly failed to do so, and requiring the said Jones and Young to appear on the 2d Monday of December (then) next, 1838, to show cause why the state should not recover of them, and each of them, the sum of $500, which *scire facias* is endorsed by the sheriff, "made known to Young and Daingerfield on the 11th October, 1838."

At the December term, 1838, the said Young and Daingerfield were called out, making default, whereupon it was ordered that the judgment heretofore entered against said defendants, to wit : at the June term, 1838, on a forfeiture of their recognizance " for the sum of five hundred dollars, be made final, and that the state recover against said defendants the sum of $500, the penalty named in said *scire facias,* also the costs of suit," etc.

The said Young and Daingerfield sued out this writ of error, to the December term, 1839, of this court.

The above statement of the case, shows such palpable variance between the recognizance, the *scire facias,* and the judgment of the court thereon, that the same must be reversed, the *scire facias* be quashed, and the cause remanded for further proceedings in the court below.

OLIVER *v.* THE STATE, 5 Howard, 14.

LARCENY.

The time of the commission of the offense laid in the indictment is not material, and it does not confine the proof within the limits of that period ; the indictment will be satisfied by proof of the offense at any anterior day.[1]

The act of 1839 guards against the effect of repealing the act of 1823, but expressly providing that it shall not affect any case subject to punishment under the act of 1822, or any former law.

When reference is made in the bill of exceptions to a paper by a particular mark, as being part of the bill of exceptions, this reference must clearly appear, or the court will not presume the paper in the record to be the same referred to in the bill. The evidence, if to be reviewed by the appellate court, must be certified by the court below.

On the trial of the prisoner on an indictment, the evidence taken before the committing magistrate cannot be legally introduced.

Where a prisoner has been found guilty on a charge of larceny, and the court below pronounced an illegal sentence, the appellate court will reverse the sentence, and pronounce judgment in conformity to the statute.

[1] Wharton Am. Cr. Law, 261, 599 ; Com. v. Alfred, 4 Dana, 496 ; People v. Santvoord, 9 Cow., 660 ; 1 Chitty Cr. Law, 557 ; State v. Munger, 15 Verm., 291 ; Com. v. Braynard, Thacher's C. C., 146 ; Johnson v. United States, 3 McLean, 89 ; State v. Woodman, 3 Hawks. 384 ; Jacobs v. Com., 5 S. & R., 316 ; State v. Baker, 4 Reding. 52 ; Com. v. Dillane, 1 Gray, 483 ; U. S. v. McCormick, 4 Cranch C. C. R., 104 ; Com. v. Kelly, 10 Cush., 69 ; State v. Hewson, Jones Law (N. C.), 173 : Medlock v. State, 18 Ark., 363 ; People v. Littlefield, 5 Cal., 355 ; State v. Porter, 10 Rich. Law (S. C.) 145 ; People v. Jenness, 5 Mich., 305 ; McDade v. State, 20 Ala., 81 ; State v. Baker, 34 Maine, 52 ; Archb. Cr. Pr. & Pl., 276–279 ; ib., 389, 1018, notes ; Wharton's Prec. Idict., 2 notes : Bishop Cr. Procedure, 250, 253 ; Loftus v. Commonwealth, 3 Gratt., 631 ; State v. Rollett, 6 Iowa, 535 ; Miazza v. State, 36 Miss, 603 ; Charnack's case, Holt, 801–802 ; State v. Grey, 39 Me., 52 ; Cook v. State, 11 Ga., 53 ; 2 Hale P. C., 179 ; 1 Phill. Ev. (Cow. & Hill's notes), 854, notes ; Kelyng, 16 ; 3 Greenl. Ev. 152, notes.

TROTTER, J.:

The plaintiff in error was indicted in the circuit court of the county of Marshall for larceny. The indictment contains four counts. The first charges the stealing, etc., of one promissory note on McEwen, King & Co. for the payment of fifty dollars. The second is for stealing five promissory notes, but does not state that they were promissory notes for the payment of money. All the notes are alleged to be the property of Gideon Blythe and Benjamin Blythe. The jury found a verdict of guilty against the prisoner, and assessed the value of the property at sixty dollars. The offense is laid in each counts of the indictment to have been committed on the 1st day of September, 1839. Two bills of exceptions were taken, and appear upon the record. One of these bills recites that the prisoner moved the court to exclude from the jury all the evidence on the part of the prosecution, on the ground which is recited, that it appeared from this evidence that the offense was committed anterior to the time when the act of 1839 upon the subject of crimes and punishments and the penitentiary went into operation. The court refused to allow the motion. The prisoner then moved for a new trial and an arrest of judgment on the grounds contained in the first bill of exceptions, and also, because it was alleged the act of 1839, which changed the law of 1822, operated as a pardon of the offense. The court overruled both motions.

Several errors have been assigned, but it is not deemed necessary to notice any, except the following, the others having been disposed of.in the opinion given by this court during the present term in the case of Greeson v. State, (infra. p. 33.)

1st. The court erred, it is said, in refusing to exclude the evidence on the ground stated in the bill of exceptions. 2d. The court erred in overruling the motion in arrest of judgment; and 3d. In not deciding that the act of 1839 operates as a statutory pardon.

1st. It is said the court should have rejected the evidence. Taking it for granted, as assumed by the prisoner, that the evidence objected to established the commission of the offense before the time at which the act of 1839 went into operation, it yet by no means follows, that the evidence should have been excluded. The time laid in the indictment is not material, and does not confine the proof within the limits of that period. The indictment was satisfied by proof of the offense at any anterior day. This is well settled, and it is not necessary to refer to authorities to sustain it. The court had nothing to do with the act of 1822 or that of 1839 in deciding upon this motion. The proof was equally competent whether the act of 1839 or the act of 1822 was the law under which the defendant was to be punished if found guilty. It is true that if the act of 1839 had repealed that of 1822, the defendant might have claimed the benefit of the statutory pardon. But the act of 1839 expressly guards against that consequence by providing that it shall not affect any cases subject to punishment under the act of 1822, or any former law. The only question then for the court was, whether the proof tended to establish the guilt of the prisoner as stated in the bill of indictment, and if so, it could not be excluded. The effect of a verdict of guilty was another. But we cannot notice the objection, for the reason that the evidence which went to the jury is not stated in the record. It is true that the bill of exceptions refers to some extrinsic paper or document which is said to be marked B, and to be considered as a part of the bill of exceptions. But what that document is, we do not know; for, on looking through the record, we find no document which has such a mark, or is otherwise identified. It is true there is in the subsequent history of the cause, a document which appears to be an exemplification of the warrant of arrest, and of the depositions taken before the justice of the peace. But this document has no mark of identity with the one referred to by the judge in the bill of exceptions. And we cannot presume that this was the paper or document referred to, because it was not competent evidence before the jury. The depositions taken before the magistrate are not evidence on the trial in the circuit court. We cannot, therefore, presume that it was the instrument of evidence indicated in the bill by the letter B. This case fully illustrates the policy of the rule which excludes from the consideration of the court matter of exception so loosely presented. The bill of exceptions must contain the matter of exception, and this court has so held repeatedly. Berry v. Hale, 1 How., 318;

Cox Dig., 104. The judge has not certified to this court what the evidence was—and it is by his certificate alone that we can learn it. There is a certain method of communication between an appellate and an inferior tribunal. The evidence which formed the subject of the motion now under consideration has not been made known to us in any of the modes recognized by law. We cannot, therefore, notice it. 2d. This view of the subject is a sufficient answer to the other assignments of error; because it leaves us with no criterion by which to determine, save the bill of indictment and the verdict of the jury. The law requires us to presume that the verdict was fully sustained by the proof. How does the question then stand? The verdict finds the defendant guilty of the larcenies charged in the indictment, which are there charged to have been committed on the 1st day of September, 1839, and finds the value of the property stolen to be sixty dollars. What is the judgment of the law on these facts? This question is easily answered. The 63d section of the act of 1839, "to amend the acts of this state concerning crimes and punishments and the penitentiary," provides that any person who shall be convicted of the feloniously taking and carrying away the personal property of another, of the value of more than twenty-five dollars, shall be adjudged guilty of grand larceny, and shall be imprisoned in the penitentiary for a term not exceeding five years. The judgment of the court below must therefore be reversed, and rendered here in pursuance of this opinion, that the prisoner be confined in the penitentiary of this state for the term of one year, as the law directs.

Joseph Thomas and Pendleton Thomas *v*. The State, 5 Howard, 20.

Burglary.

The criminal court for the counties of Warren, Claiborne, Jefferson, Adams, and Wilkinson, established by the act of 1836, was a court of inferior and limited jurisdiction under the constitution, and one which the legislature was clearly empowered to establish by the 24th section of the 4th article of the constitution.

Since the passage of the act of 1836, to amend the jury laws, no challenge to the array shall be sustained, nor shall any *venire facias* be quashed by any court of justice in this state, for any cause whatsoever, except for corruption in the officer who may summon the jury.

Where the prisoner had been tried and convicted at the June term of the criminal court, and, for some cause, sentence of the law was delayed till the next term, and in the meantime, one of the counsel who had assisted the state on the trial, had been elected judge of said court, there is no legal objection to his sitting as judge in the case, and pronouncing the sentence of the law upon the prisoners, whatever may be the propriety or impropriety of such action. The objection is one which cannot be raised and adjudicated in this court.

The plea of *non-identity* is to be pleaded *ore tenus*, and is never allowed except in cases where the prisoner has escaped after verdict and before judgment, or after judgment and before execution. On review, to render the plea valid, the record must show an escape.

To constitute the crime of burglary, it is necessary that it should be committed in *the night time*, and whether, or not, there be light enough to distinguish a man's face, is immaterial to the offense.

It is the office of the caption of an indictment, to state with sufficient certainty, not only the style of the court, the judge there presiding, but the time and place, when and where it was found, and the names of the grand jurors by whom it was found. Where the caption of the indictment, after stating the style of the court, and the term, proceeds to state that "the grand jury came into court and presented the following bill of indictment, and say they are content that the court shall alter therein anything, the same being matter of form and not of substance," it was held to be insufficient and uncertain, and the indictment should be quashed.

Where the statute creates several degrees of the same offense, and graduates the punishment according to the degrees, the verdict must designate the degree, or else no judgment can be pronounced.

Error to the criminal court of Adams County.

RAWLINGS, J. :

At the December term, 1837, of the criminal court, the plaintiffs in error were indicted for burglary. The *venue* was changed to Jefferson county, and at June term, 1838, they were tried and found guilty. Sentence was respited, and at December term following, when they were brought to the bar of the court to receive sentence, and were asked what they had to say why judgment should not be pronounced against them, they tendered their plea of *non-identity*, upon which issue was joined. After several fruitless efforts to procure a jury to try this question, the case was continued until the succeeding term; at which the judge treated the plea as a nullity, and pronounced the usual sentence of death against the prisoners.

In the errors assigned, it was objected, 1st. That the criminal court which tried the prisoners, had no jurisdiction; that the legislature had no authority to establish it, and, therefore, all its acts were void.

VOL. I.—11.

2d. The refusal of the court to set aside the special *venire facias* issued from the Jefferson Circuit Court.

3d. That the judges overruled the exception taken to his presiding in the case on the ground of bias and interest. He had, while practicing at the bar, been retained, and prosecuted as counsel on the part of the state, at the trial at a previous term.

4th. The court erred in striking out, and treating as a nullity, the plea of *non-identity* tendered by the accused, when asked what they had to say why the sentence of the law should not be pronounced upon them.

5th. The refusal of the court to instruct the jury on the request of the prisoners, "that if at the time of committing the burglary laid in the indictment, there was light enough to discern a man's face, it was not burglary."

6th. That the record, or caption of the indictment did not state by what judge, or at what place in Adams county, the court was holden at which the indictment was found, nor by what jurors, nor by what number it was found.

7th. The act of 1839, in force when the indictment was found, altered the penalty of the offense of burglary, substituting, instead of capital punishment, confinement in the penitentiary for a term according to the degree specified. The verdict in this case did not specify the degree of the offense.

Baker for the plaintiff in error.

The first error assigned is the unconstitutionality of the act organizing the court below. The first section of the 4th article of the constitution provides, "that the judicial power of this state shall be vested in one High Court of Errors and Appeals, and such other courts of law and equity as are hereafter *provided* for in this constitution." The 13th section of the same article provides, "that the state shall be divided into convenient districts, and each district shall contain not less than three nor more than twelve counties." The term *district* being used synonymously with circuit. The 14th section provides that "the circuit court shall have *original* jurisdiction in all matters, *civil* and *criminal*, within the state," etc. The 16th section *provides* for the establishment of a "Court of Chancery," section 18th for a "Court of Probates," etc.

By the 24th section it is declared that "the legislature may from time to time establish such other *inferior* courts as may be deemed necessary." By this section the legislature supposed it had power to establish the criminal court. Now the constitutionality of this court depends upon the question whether it is or is not, in the sense contemplated by the framers of the constitution, an *inferior* court.

The mere fact that it is styled in the act an *inferior* court, does not make it such. To determine its grade and dignity, resort must be had to the matters over which it has jurisdiction. It is invested with jurisdiction, concurrent with the circuit courts, in all matters of a criminal nature, and thus becomes co-ordinate and co-equal in its powers over all matters confided to its jurisdiction, with the circuit court, and cannot, therefore, be said to be inferior to it. The mere fact of its being *limited* in jurisdiction to a certain portion of the matters confided to the circuit courts, does not *per se* render it *inferior*. If an appeal lay from the criminal court to the circuit court, then it will be admitted that the former would be inferior to the latter; the power of revisal being the true test of superiority. Such is, however, not the case, an appeal lying from both these courts alike, to the High Court of Errors and Appeals, they having concurrent jurisdiction over the same criminal matters.

2d. The record should show the *names* of the grand jurors, and that the indictment was found by at least twelve men. 1 Chitty's Crim. Law, 333; 2 Hale P. C., 167; Cro. Eliz., 654; 1 Chitty's Crim. Law, 202; Peck's Rep., 166; ib., 140. The record should show the return of the *venire facias*. Peck's Rep., 140–166. The record should show that the grand jurors were sworn *then* and *there*. 3 John. Cases, 265. The record should show that a "foreman" was sworn, and that the bill was returned through *him*, or else by the whole grand jury, with their return *specially* endorsed thereon. 3 How., 29; 1 How., 254; 1 Chitty's Crim. Law, 313; 4 Com. Dig., 643, 644, 645; 1 Chitty's Crim. Law, 330. The record should show the *place* as well as the *county* where the court was held. 3 How., 430.

3d. The court should have quashed the special *venire facias* issued in Jefferson county.   18 John. R., 212.

4th. The indictment ought to have been signed by the district attorney of the first judicial district.   1 How., 250 ; 3 Haywood, 98 ; Acts 1833, p. 88.

5th. The court erred in refusing the instruction asked for on behalf of the prisoner.   In the crime of burglary, time is of the essence of the offense ; it must be alleged to have been committed in the night time and so proved on the trial.   If there had been light enough to discern a man's face, it would not have constituted burglary.   1 Chitty's Crim. Law, 219, 293 ; 1 Hale, 549, 550 ; 10 Petersdorf, 504, 505 ; 4 Black. Com., 224 ; 4 Petersdorf, 744.

6th. It was not competent for the judge presiding (Hon. C. Rawlings, he not having been in commission at the time of trial before the jury), to pronounce judgment on the prisoners, at a subsequent term.   He could not judicially know that they were the same persons supposed to have been convicted at the previous term.   2 Hale, 401, 402, 403, 406, 407, note (C).

7th. The Hon. C. Rawlings having, previous to his election as judge of said court, been consulted and retained as counsel by the prosecutor, and having assisted the state on the trial of the prisoners, became interested in the prosecution, and unduly biased, and was therefore equally disqualified to preside in the case.   See act of 25th Dec., 1833.

8th. The prisoners should have been permitted to plead their *non-identity.*   1 Chitty's C. L., 443, 777 ; 3 Burrows, 1810 ; 2 Hale, 407.   This was the more necessary in this case, as the judge pronouncing the sentence, did not preside at the trial, and could not know with legal, judicial certainty that the prisoners were those supposed by the record to stand convicted.

9th. It was error in the court to sentence the prisoners capitally on the verdict of the jury in this case.   The act of 1839 had changed the punishment from capital to confinement in the penitentiary, and had also created several degrees of the crime of burglary, and the verdict did not specify of what degree the jury convicted.

Thomas F. Collins, attorney general.

It was competent for the legislature to create a criminal court. See Constitution, art. 4, sec. 24. The plea of not guilty admits the jurisdiction of the court. Chitty's C. L. Though the caption of the record is incomplete, the record will be adjudged sufficient, if it appear in other parts of the same to contain the matter usually stated in the caption. That which is uncertain in one part, may be rendered certain by that which is clear in another part. 3 How., 429.

A *venire facias* can in no case be quashed, except for partiality or corruption in the officer summoning the same. See Republished Statutes of Miss., p. 578.

The act which prohibits circuit judges from presiding in cases wherein they were interested as counsel, does not apply to the criminal court. There is no other judge with whom the criminal judge could interchange. Condensed Statutes of Miss., 548–9; the statute prohibiting judges of criminal courts from presiding, is only directory; and the error cannot be available in this court.

The plea of *non-identity* will not be regarded by the court, unless the record and plea show that the prisoner was out of custody after conviction and before sentenced. 1 Chitty Crim. Pl., 776; 3 Burrows, 1810; 1 Hale, 368; 1 Black. Rep., 4; Foster, 40.

Upon change of *venue* the clerk of the court should send only the original papers, and a writ of error to the county where the trial was had, will not reach an error in the proceedings in the county from which the *venue* was changed. Byrd v. The State, 1 Howard, 248; and see Woodsides v. The State, 2 How., 666.

Trotter, J. :

The statute of 1836 regards the criminal court as an inferior court, and so designates it. It makes it an inferior court to the circuit court by conferring upon the latter the authority to bring the record of any prosecution pending in the former, before them by a writ of *certiorari* whenever it is made to appear that injustice is likely to be done in the criminal court, and the cir-

cuit court, upon the removal of the record into it, is vested with
full power to hear and determine the cause.   Thus the circuit
courts are vested with full superiority and controlling power
over this court, and is thus superior to it, according to the rule
insisted on by the counsel for the prisoners.   But the criminal
court is inferior in point of jurisdiction in another sense, and in
the sense of the constitution as we think.   It is a tribunal of
limited jurisdiction, its powers being confined exclusively to
criminal proceedings.   It has no civil jurisdiction, and is therefore inferior to the circuit courts.   It is inferior to the high court
of errors and appeals, because a writ of error lies directly to it
from the appellate court.   In this point of view the circuit
courts are also inferior, and are so termed in the constitution.
It is not essential in order to sustain the authority of the legislature to create this court to consider it inferior in relation to the
circuit courts, or to any other courts created by the constitution,
save that of the court of errors and appeals.   For we apprehend that the power to establish and to abolish " all such inferior courts" as the legislature may deem necessary, is unlimited,
save by the enumeration, which the constitution itself has made
of particular courts.   Such as are included in the enumeration,
are, of course, beyond the reach of legislative control.   Beyond
the enumeration the power is plenary, to create as many jurisdictions inferior to the court of errors and appeals as may be
deemed expedient.   The constitution of 1817 vested the judicial power of the state in one supreme court, and such inferior
courts of law and equity as the legislature should from time to
time, establish.   The legislature afterwards created a chancery
court, and also a court of probates.   The power to establish the
orphan's court and court of probates under the old constitution,
was never doubted, notwithstanding it was vested with a very
large portion of the mass of powers confessedly cognizable in a
court of chancery.   It was inferior to the chancery court.   It
was inferior to the chancery court in the amount of its jurisdiction, and because that court possessed the power to revise its
decrees ; and it was inferior in its relation to the supreme court.
It was, therefore, one of the inferior courts authorized by the
constitution.   The new constitution of 1832, has by express

enactment, established the probate court and defined its jurisdiction. Yet it will scarcely be insisted, it is presumed, that if it had not done so, the hands of the legislature would be tied up against its creation. And yet, in regard to many subjects of its jurisdiction, it bears the same relation to the chancery court, which the criminal court does to the circuit courts. We are, therefore, clearly of opinion that this is fairly embraced in the provision of the twenty-fourth section of the fourth article of the constitution, and is a constitutional court.

2. It is next assigned for error, that the court below refused to set aside the special *venire facias* which is issued from the criminal court of Jefferson county. The first section of the act of 1836, entitled an act to amend the jury laws of this state, enacts " that no challenge to the array shall be sustained, nor shall any *venire facias* be quashed by any court of justice in this state for any cause whatsoever, except for corruption in the officer who may summon the jury. But there was no objection made to the sheriff, nor any improper conduct charged against him. The objection was merely to the form of the process, and was, therefore, properly disregarded.

3. The next error which we deem proper to notice, is the refusal of the judge who presided on the trial of this prosecution, to notice the exception taken to him on the ground of interest. He had previously, and whilst engaged in the practice of the law, been consulted and retained as counsel for the state by the prosecutor. The trial and conviction were had before he came upon the bench, and he did not consider himself precluded either by law or official delicacy from pronouncing the mere judgment of the law. Whatever might have been the more discreet course for the judge to pursue in these circumstances, or whether the reasons which influenced him were good, we are not required to decide. It is very clear that it was a question of discretion which belonged to him, and for the exercise of which his course is not subject to review in this court. We recognize the soundness and utility of the maxim that a judge should never sit to hear any cause when he is interested, nor when from any other circumstances, his mind may likely have received any bias or prejudice for or against either party. And

we may be indulged to remark that a judge should never act when there can be any just ground to impute partiality or prepossessions either way. For, as was very justly remarked by the judge who delivered the opinion of the court in the case of Lyon v. The State Bank, reported in 1 Stewart's Ala. R., 464, where the same question was before the court, "The spirit of the law, the dignity of the state and the reputation of the judiciary demanded purity in the arbiters and impartiality in the administration of justice." It was in view, no doubt, of these considerations, that the statute law of this state has prohibited the judges from deciding causes in which they may have previously been interested as counsel. But sensibly as we may feel the influence of these reflections, and much as we may deplore the example, if it shall ever be set up of a judge who will boldly venture to sit in judgment upon the life, the liberty, or the property of the citizen, in circumstances calculated to create an interest deeper than that which arises out of a sense of the duty and responsibility of his station, we, yet, have no power to interpose. Redress by the party injured, can only be had in other forms, and the evil whenever it shall happen, can only be cured by an application of the powers of the other departments of the government. It is highly probable, in this case, that the judge did not conceive that there was any scope for the exercise of any power in which his discretion as a judicial officer was involved. But be this as it may, his judgment cannot for that reason be reversed. For it is well settled, that a "judge shall not be excepted against or challenged or have an action brought against him for what he does as judge." 1 Inst., 294. The supreme court of Alabama held this principle in the case before noticed, of Lyon v. the State Bank. The action was brought in the county court by the bank, and the judge who tried the cause then was one of the directors of the bank. The defendant challenged him on the ground of interest, but he refused to notice the objection and gave a judgment for the bank. This was assigned as error on an appeal to the supreme court, but it was not sustained; and there is a very obvious reason for it. There is no tribunal adequate to decide a challenge to the judge when made in his own court.

4th. The next error we shall notice is the conduct of the judge in refusing to allow the plea of non-identity. The correctness of this assignment of error depends upon the goodness of the plea. This plea, which in practice is interposed *ore tenus* at the bar of the court, is never allowed except in cases where the prisoner has escaped after verdict and before judgment, or after judgment and before execution. In this case it should not have been received, because the record does not show any escape. The prisoners were constantly in custody. It was, therefore properly treated as a nullity. 1 Chitty Cr. Law, 776 ; 3 Burr, 1870.

5th. The next assignment of error in the order we choose to consider them, is the refusal of the court below to instruct the jury as asked by the prisoner "that if at the time of committing the burglary laid in the indictment, there was light enough to discern a man's face, it was not burglary." The only question in regard to time in prosecutions for this crime, is whether it was committed in the *night time*. The instruction asked does not present that question. The light of the moon may sometimes be sufficiently brilliant, even at the still hour of midnight, to enable a man to discern another's face and to recognize his features. The instruction was properly refused.

6th. It is next assigned, as error, that the record or caption, of the indictment does not state by what judge, or at what place in Adams county the court was holden at which the indictment was found, nor by what number of jurors it was returned. The caption after giving the style of the court, and the term, proceeds to state that " the grand jury came into court and presented the following bill of indictment, and say they are content that the court shall alter therein anything, the same being matter of form and not of substance ;" and then it terminates. Nor does the record show in any other part of it of what number the grand jury consisted, or who they were, or how they were brought into court. It is the business of a caption of an indictment to state with sufficient certainty, not only the style of the court, the judge then presiding, but the time and place when and where it was found, and the jurors by whom it was found. 1 Chitty Cr. Law, 326 ; 2 Hawk., 346. There is wanting in this record a statement of facts essential to confer jurisdiction upon the court below. And little as we feel disposed to entertain objections to form, yet we feel constrained in cases highly penal like this, to insist upon the observance of those rules which the constitutional law of this state has prescribed. No court is authorized to put the most humble citizen upon his trial for any capital or infamous crime, until a grand jury of the proper county, organized as the law directs, has preferred a formal accusation against him. Does the record in the Jefferson criminal court inform that court that these prisoners had been thus accused? It does not. And we therefore conclude that the indictment is bad for that reason. There are some errors assigned which we do not deem necessary to notice. It is proper, however, for us to observe, that the judgment must be reversed on another ground. The act of 1839 which was in force when the judgment was rendered in the court below, alters the penalty of this offense, and for the capital punishment under the old law, substitutes confinement in the penitentiary for a longer or shorter period according to the degree in which it has been committed. The statute defines three degrees of this crime, by particularly declaring the circumstances which constitute one or the other and before any judgment can be pronounced, it must be ascertained by verdict, in which of these degrees the defendants are guilty. The judgment must be reversed, and the prisoners remanded for further proceedings.

GREESON *v.* THE STATE, 5 Howard, 33.

ROBBERY.

Where it appears from the whole record that the prosecution was in the name of the state, a formal statement in the indictment, that it was found by the authority of the state, is not necessary.[1]

Where it appeared by the record that a foreman was appointed, and that the indictment was returned, signed by him, and the caption stated that the grand jury returned the bill into court by their foreman, it was held sufficient evidence that the bill was returned by the authority of the grand jury.[2]

[1] Wharton Am. Cr. Law, 233.

[2] Wharton Am. Cr. Law, 228, 497; State v. Davidson, 12 Vir., 300; State v. Elkins, 1 Meigs, 109; Bennett v. State, 8 Humph., 118; 1 Chitty Cr. Law, 324: Archb. Cr. Pr., 59; Spratt v. State, 8 Mo., 247; McDonald v. State, ib., 283; Gardner v. People, 3 Scam., 83; Harriman v. State, 2 Greene (Iowa), 270; State v. Ohumat, 20 La., 196, Hopkins v. Commonwealth, 14 Wright, 9.

At common law, bank notes are property, and are the subject of larceny or robbery. Were it otherwise, they are made so by the 20th section of the act of 1822, which provides " that robbery or simple larceny of obligations, or bonds, bills obligatory, or bills of exchange, promissory notes for the payment of money, etc., shall be punished as simple larceny or robbery of goods and chattels, etc. Bank bills or bank notes are promissory notes of the corporation which issues them.[1]

Where the record states at what court, at what term, and in what county the grand jury were empanelled and sworn, it sufficiently appears that they were sworn in and for the county, and the omission to state that they were *then* and *there* sworn, is immaterial, and does not affect the validity of the indictment.

Where the property feloniously taken was laid in the indictment as the property of Richard Gaines, but was afterwards recited as the property of the said Robert Gaines, it was held to be a mere clerical error, and that it did not constitute repugnance.

Error to the circuit court of Tishomingo county.

The defendant was indicted in the circuit court of Tishomingo county for the crime of robbery. The indictment contained but one count, and charged that the defendant, on the 1st day of June, 1838, with force and arms in and upon one Richard Gaines, feloniously did make an assault; and him, the said Richard Gaines, in bodily fear and danger of his life, then and there feloniously did put, and the following bank bills, to wit: One, one hundred dollar bank bill, payable at the branch of the Bank of Alabama at Mobile, for the payment of one hundred dollars, and of the value of one hundred dollars, the property of the said Richard Gaines; one bank bill of the Agricultural Bank of the State of Mississippi, for twenty dollars, and of the value of twenty dollars, the property of the said Richard Gaines, then and there being found, the said sum of one hundred dollars, and the said sum of twenty dollars, secured and payable by and upon the said bank bills, being then and there due and unpaid to the said Richard Gaines, from the person, and against the will of the said Richard Gaines, then and there feloniously and violently did steal, etc.

On this indictment the defendant was convicted.

The 1st error assigned is that the indictment did not state that it was found in the name and by the authority of the State of Mississippi. The record stated the county, the term of the court, the time and place, and the presence of the presiding

---

[1] Damewood v. State, 1 How., 262; Wharton Am. Cr. Law. 337.

judge.   It then states that Hogue, the sheriff, returned into court the *venire facias*, executed on the following persons (naming them), out of whom the following persons were drawn, elected, empanelled and sworn as a grand inquest to inquire in and for the body of the county aforesaid.   (Then follows the names.)   The record contained the following statement : " The State of Mississippi v. John L. Greeson.   This day, the fourth day of June, 1838, the grand jury returned into open court a bill of indictment in the case of the state against John L. Greeson on a charge of robbery, a true bill by Reuben Boone, their foreman."   The caption of the indictment, after reciting the state, county, circuit and term, proceeded as follows : " The grand jurors of said state, elected, empanelled, sworn and charged to inquire for the body of Tishomingo county, aforesaid, upon their oaths present," etc.

2d error assigned was, that it did not appear upon the record that the same was returned into court by the grand jury themselves, or under their authority.

3d. That there was no offense charged in the indictment which was known to the law.

4th. That the words *then* and *there* are not prefixed to the word *sworn*, so as to show that the grand jury were sworn in the proper court or county, and at the proper time.

5th. That the indictment is repugnant in alleging the bank bills specified to be the property of Richard Gaines, and afterwards of Robert Gaines.

Mayes for plaintiff in error.

1st. The indictment is defective in that it does not purport to have been found by the grand jury " in the name and by the authority of the State of Mississippi.   The State v. Johnson, Walker's R., 395 ; Allen v. the Commonwealth, 2 Bibb. 210.

2d. The act charged by the bill of indictment is not an offense by the laws of the State of Mississippi.

3d. The charge is for robbing, in taking from the person, etc. bank bills of value, without describing the things taken, as promissory notes purporting to be bank bills of great value, etc. How. v. Hulch, 666 ; Starkie's Crim. Pl. 244 ; Damewood v.

The State, 1 How. 262 ; 2 Russell on Cr., 186–8 ; 2 East, 601 ; 2 Russell 143–4; Stat. 2 Geo. 2, C. 25.

4th. The bill of indictment is repugnant in this, that in one part thereof, the bank bills alleged to be taken are averred to be the property of Richard Gaines, and in another part in the same count, to be the property of Robert Gaines. See 6th assignment.

5th. There is no venue as to swearing the jury. Am. C. L. Rep. 6, p. 14 ; 3 Johnson's cases, 265. As to the inferior court, 1 Johnson's cases, 179.

6th. The indictment is repugnant in alleging that the bank notes were the property of *Richard Gaines*, and that the money thereby promised was due and unsatisfied ; that said money was the property of *Robert Gaines*, and that the money, not the bills, was stolen from the person of Richard Gaines. Starkie's Crim. Pl. 229, 273.

Hughes, on the same side.

Collins, attorney general.

The record in this case shows all that the laws require. The grounds taken by the prisoner to reverse the judgment of the court below, are those taken in his motion in arrest, to wit : repugnance in the indictment. This is not repugnance in the eye of the law. The indictment throughout speaks of the bills as belonging to Richard Gaines, until near the close, it once only uses the name Robert Gaines, and prefixes the word "said" to it ; thus showing clearly a mere clerical error. Certainly to a certain intent in general, is all that the law requires. Arch. Crim. Pl. 4, 3. And see Chit. Crim. Law, 697, note. That part of the record or indictment which is certain may be referred to to explain and make certain another part of the same record or indictment. Loper v. The State, 3 How. 428.

Bank notes are considered personal property, and as such may be the subject of robbery, like any other species of property. An individual convicted after the passage of the act of 1839, on an indictment commenced before its passage, is properly sentenced to the punishment inflicted by the penitentiary law. Thomas v. The State, Ante. p. 20. The court will not discharge a prisoner on the quashing of the indictment. Hare v. The State, 4 How. 187.

TROTTER, J.:

1. The first assignment of error was not seriously insisted upon in the argument, and it will be sufficient to observe that the question which it presents has been decided by the supreme court of this state, in the case of State v. Johnson, Walk. R., 395. That court held that it was sufficient if it appeared in the record that the prosecution was in the name of the state, and that a formal statement of the fact that the indictment was found by its authority was not necessary. The only object which our constitution had, in requiring that all prosecutions should be in the name, and by the authority of the state, was to exclude any other or foreign power from the exercise of this authority; and to assert the sovereignty and supremacy of the state as paramount. In this case the indictment is in the name of the state, and, of course, conducted under its authority; and this appears as fully as if there had been a formal averment of that proposition. In the case of Allen v. The Commonwealth, 2 Bibb, 210, the Court of Appeals of Kentucky considered the same objection, made under a similar provision of the constitution of that state, and decided it to be untenable. 2d. The second ground of objection is not supported by the record, that Reuben H. Boone was appointed foreman of the grand jury, and the bill is returned endorsed by him, a true bill, as such foreman. But besides this evidence of the finding of the bill, it is stated in the caption that the grand jury returned the bill into open court by their foreman, which is sufficiently certain. 3d. The third assignment of error presents a very interesting question, and one which is not entirely free from difficulty. It is, whether *bank bills, eo nomine,* are the subjects of larceny or robbery. It has been contended that bank bills are choses in action, being species of promissory notes, and that as such, they are not the subject of larceny at common law, and that they are not embraced by the 20th section of the act of 1822, " for the punishment of crimes and misdemeanors;" or if embraced under the term "*promissory notes for the payment of money,*" they

have not been so described in the indictment as to fall under the operation of that act. The validity of the objection depends, therefore, upon three questions: 1st. Whether bank notes or bills be mere choses in action at common law. 2d. Whether they are included in the enumeration of written securities in the statute of 1822; and 3d. Whether the description in the indictment is sufficient. It has long been settled, that by the common law, choses in action are the subjects of larceny, on the ground that they had no intrinsic value, and did not import any property in the possession of the person who held them. At the time of the adoption of this rule, bank bills had no existence. After they came into use, they were treated and considered as imparting to the holder or bearer something more than a *bare right*, existing only in action. The courts began to regard them as having an intrinsic value, and as equivalent to cash or money. Thus in Miller v. Race, 1st Barron, Lord Mansfield, with the entire concurrence of the other judges of the Court of King's Bench, held these notes to be money or cash, and not mere securities or documents for debts. He says they were treated as *cash* or *money*, in the ordinary course and transactions of business by the general consent of mankind, which give the credit and *currency* of *money*, etc. In the case of King v. Deane Leach's C. Cases, they are regarded in the same light. In the case of the King v. Vyse, 1 Ryan & Moody, C. C., 218, it was holden that bankers' notes were not the subjects of larceny at common law, but that they might be described in the indictment as goods and chattels of the owners; and there are some other cases in the English courts in which the same doctrine has been maintained. It is true that some of the earlier cases in that country settle the point differently, but I take the weight of authority to be decidedly in support of the principle settled in Miller v. Race, supra. In the case of United States v. Moulton, 5 Mason's C. C. R., 537, this very question arose; and upon a very full review of all the English cases, and many American, Judge Story comes to the same conclusion which the king's bench expressed in the case of Miller v. Race. He says in the conclusion of his opinion, " Can it be truly said that bank notes, payable to bearer, and passing as currency, have no present value in possession? They pass as money, are received as money—in courts of justice they are treated as money," etc. It seems, therefore, he observes, that it would be an over-refinement to hold that they are not personal goods, etc. The case of The People v. Holbrook, 13 J. R., 90, is to the same effect. The court there say that bank bills are to be considered as goods and chattels. The statute of New York, under which that indictment was found, is in these words: " If any person shall steal," etc., "any bill of exchange, bond, order, warrant, bill, or promissory note, for the payment of money, etc., being the property of another person, it shall be deemed felony of the same nature, and in the same degree, and in the same manner, as it would have been, if the offender had stolen any other goods of the like value, with the money due thereon," etc. The indictment was for stealing bank notes, alleged to be of *the goods and chattels of the owner.* An objection was made to the indictment for stating the notes to be of the goods and chattels of the owner. But the court held the allegation sufficient deciding that they were goods and chattels. In Richards' case, 1 Mass. R., 337, the same principle is settled. It has been held in New York that bank notes may be levied under an execution as the goods and chattels of the defendant. Handy v. Dobbin, 12 J. R., 220. I think, therefore, it may be safely laid down as a proposition resulting from all the authorities considered in one view, that at common law bank notes are property, and are the subject of larceny. But if this is otherwise, I am of the opinion that they are embraced by the act of 1822. The 20th section of that statute provides, that robbery or simple larceny of obligations or bonds, bills obligatory or bills of exchange, promissory notes for the payment of money, etc., shall be punished as simple larceny, or robbery of goods and chattels, etc.

A bank bill or note is a promissory note of the corporation which issues it. This I take to be a proposition not susceptible of controversy. I have attempted to show that it is not only a promissory note, but it is a species of a note to be regarded on a higher ground, and imparting higher value than a private note. It is, at any rate, a promissory note, and so expressly held by the Supreme Court of Massachusetts, in 6 Mass. R., 182, and 9 Ib.,

557; and has just been shown by the court in New York, in the People *v.* Holbrook. This being the case, it follows that they are the subject of larceny by the statute. This was so held by this court, as I understand the case, in Damewood v. The State, 1 How., 262; for the judge remarks, that it is unquestionably true that a bank note is a promissory note by a corporation, etc., and comes, therefore, strictly within the meaning of the generic term "promissory note." The conclusion of the judge, from this is, that if the note charged to have been stolen had been described by proper averments, the indictment might have been sustained.

I concur in this case fully, so far as it treats bank notes as promissory notes, and regret that I feel compelled to differ, as I do, entirely from the conclusion at which the court arrived. It is certain that it might have been properly described as a promissory note, commonly called a bank note; and yet I apprehend that unless a bank note be a promissory note, the styling it so could not give it that character; and *vice versa,* if it be a well-known species of promissory note, the omission to style it so in the pleadings, would not divest it of that character, any more than in declaring upon a due bill, and stating it to be simply such, the pleader would be bound to style it a promissory note, commonly called a due bill. I apprehend it would be sufficient in the latter instance to describe the note as a due bill; and for the same reason, if a bank note, in law, is a promissory note, it is so, independent of any averment to that effect. The note in that case was termed in the indictment a bank note of the Planters' Bank, and, because it was not styled a promissory note, the indictment was held bad, and the prisoner discharged. I cannot consent to the judgment in that case, nor do I think it warranted by the principles stated in the opinion of the court.

The case, however, fully recognizes bank notes as subjects of larceny, under the statute, and the judgment proceeded on the ground of a defective statement and description of the subject of the larceny. It is evident that the court, in that case, found their judgment on the decision in the case of The King v. Craven, 2 East. Cr. Law, 601. But I am clearly of the opinion that Craven's case is not an authority for the judgment in Damewood's case. That was an indictment under the act of George II., and that act expressly mentions bank notes, and the judgment was arrested solely on the ground of a defective description of the note; and I will now proceed to show that that case is not supported by principle or authority.

In Milne's case, 2 East. C. L., 602, the indictment charged the defendant with stealing a promissory note for the payment of one guinea, and also one other note for the payment of five guineas. It was moved in arrest of judgment after a conviction upon this indictment, that the description was too general. But all the judges held the indictment well laid. In the case of the Commonwealth v. Richards, 1 Mass. R., 337, the charge was stealing from the person of A. B. one bank note, of the value of ten dollars, of the goods and chattels of the said A. B. And it was objected that the bank bill was not sufficiently described, it not appearing to have been issued by any bank authorized to issue bills, or that it contained any promise by any person to pay the sum of ten dollars, or that it contained such promise to pay that sum to any person, or that it was signed by the president of any bank, or countersigned by the cashier, and that from this uncertainty, the prisoner was unable to defend himself, and because a conviction would be no bar to a second prosecution, etc. But the court held the description to be sufficient. In delivering the opinion of the court, the judges observe that "if a more particular description were necessary, it would be extremely difficult, and in most cases, impossible to convict, because ordinarily a person cannot testify as to the bank which issued the note. He can prove nothing more than the amount." Holbrook's case, 13 L. R., 90, which was before noticed, very fully illustrates the doctrine laid down in Richard's case. In that case the indictment charged the defendant with stealing "four promissory notes, commonly called bank notes, given for the sum of fifty dollars each, by the Mechanics' Bank of the City of New York, which were there and then due and unpaid, of the value of two hundred dollars," etc. This was held a sufficient description. The court say in answer to the objection that the description was too general, that the "notes being in the hands of the defendant, it was impracticable to state them *in hæc verba*." A general description is all that is necessary in trover. And that the form of the proceeding gave the defendant notice to be prepared to produce the notes if it should be necessary, in order to falsify the plaintiff's evidence.

In the case of the United States v. Moulton, before noticed, the indictment charges the stealing of "one bank bill of the New Haven Bank, of the denomination of five dollars, and of the value of five dollars; one other bill of the State Bank of Boston, of the denomination," etc., pursuing the same description as in the case of the bill on the New Haven Bank. But there was no objection to this description. Hence, I conclude that the objection which has been taken to the indictment in this case is not maintainable.

4th. In regard to the objection that there is no *venue* stated in the indictment as to the swearing and charging of the grand jury. I deem it only necessary to observe that the record states at what court, at what term, and in what county the grand jury were empanelled and sworn. In 1 Chitty's Cr. Law, 334, he observes that it was formerly held necessary to prefix the words *then and there* to the word *sworn*, as it would show that the grand jury were sworn in the proper county, and at the proper time. But this, he observes, is not usual, and in none of the modern and approved forms does it appear to have been thought necessary.

5th. It is lastly objected that the indictment is repugnant in the description of the offense. It is too evident to require argument that the use of the name of Robert in one clause of the indictment instead of Richard Gaines, was a mere clerical mistake of the draftsman. It could not prejudice the defendant, and if that member of the sentence in the indictment were stricken out, it would appear yet very manifest that the bank bills are laid to be the property of Richard Gaines. And so I conclude that the objection cannot prevail.

Let the judgment be affirmed.

TUOMY v. THE STATE, 5 Howard, 50.

RETAILING WITHOUT LICENSE.

In criminal cases, an appeal does not lie to the High Court of Errors and Appeals. Such cases can only be removed by writ of error.

Appeal from Adams circuit court.

No counsel marked for plaintiff in error.

T. F. Collins, attorney general.

TURNER, J. :

The defendant, in the court below, was indicted for retailing spirits, etc., in less quantity than one gallon, and being convicted and sentenced to fine and imprisonment, he prayed for and obtained an appeal to this court.

It has become necessary for the court to decide whether an appeal is given by our statute in criminal cases, as the practice of allowing appeals in such cases in the superior and inferior courts of the state is becoming common.

We are of opinion that our statutes do not provide for appeals in such cases, and it is very certain that the common law does not. Our several courts of justice are constituted, and the proceedings therein regulated, by our constitutional and statute laws. The common law comes in aid of the statute law by furnishing rules of construction; rules founded in reason, and sanctioned by usage time out of mind.

The circuit court, under both the old and new constitutions of this state, had general jurisdiction, both civil and criminal; and the acts of 1822, Rev. Code, provided in ch. 13, for the mode of trial, appeal, writs of error, and all other remedial writs and proceedings in the most ample and satisfactory manner.

The 148th sec. of the act of 1822, Rev. Code, 138, is as follows : " The said circuit courts, when a new or difficult question arises, on which the judge may doubt as to the rule of decision, - may adjourn such question or matter of law, to the next supreme court; or any party thinking himself or herself aggrieved by the judgment of the said courts, may appeal therefrom, as of right ; and the party praying such appeal shall enter into bond with good and sufficient security, to be approved of by the court, in such penalty as such court shall direct, with condition to pay the amount of the recovery, and all costs and damages awarded, in case the judgment be affirmed; and where several appeal, bond and security being given by any party, shall be sufficient; and the judge of any circuit court may, at his discretion, with the consent of the person accused, on a point reserved, motion in arrest of judgment, or for a new trial, in any criminal case, respite the judgment or sentence, and reserve such point or motion for the consideration and decision of the supreme court, at their next succeeding term, which may there be argued and decided, though such accused person be not present; and the supreme court shall pronounce such sentence or judgment as the circuit court ought to have pronounced, and in case the same be against the person accused, to award execution accordingly. (By the 9th sec. of the supreme court law, 151, the sheriff of the *proper county* shall be charged with the execution of such sentence.)   And in all cases not capital, so removed into the supreme court, the defendant shall enter into recognizance, with one or more good and sufficient securities, to be approved of by the judge of the circuit court in which the prosecution is pending, in such sum as shall be directed by said court, to appear before the supreme court at their next succeeding term, and abide the sentence or judgment which may be there pronounced against him."

The same act gives full power to the judges to grant writs of error in all cases.

The act of March 2, 1833, organizing the circuit courts under the new constitution, again provides for appeals "in all controversies in law and equity depending in the circuit courts to every suitor and party litigant," and refers generally to the act of 1822, as to the rules and regulations for the government of the courts thus newly organized.

Here we find ample authority and provision for appeals, in civil and criminal cases, and the general words of those acts have been construed by some to give an appeal in all cases. But when the terms and conditions on which appeals are allowed, are examined, we find terms and expressions showing that appeals are only allowable in civil cases.   The condition of an appeal bond, for instance, and the bond itself, show the sense and meaning of these several acts, and the intention of the legislature.   Such as a bond to the opposite *party;* and the conditions thereof to *pay* and *satisfy* the judgment *damages and costs.*   This certainly cannot be construed to apply to judgments and sentences of imprisonment, whipping, hanging, etc.

In the section first above quoted, we find provisions for *appeal bonds* for civil suits, and of *recognizances,* for criminal cases. Also, in writs of error, the judge or clerk granting a writ of error and *supersedeas,* in a civil case, will take a bond payable to the opposite party; and in criminal cases recognizances to the state.   The condition of an appeal or writ of error bond in a civil case is quite different from the condition of a recognizance in a criminal case.

There are some loose and general expressions in one or more of the acts of assembly, which, at first sight, might be so construed as to give an appeal in a criminal case.   Such is a section in the act establishing the late criminal court, which reads as follows: " All the provisions in relation to appeals and writs of error in criminal cases in the circuit courts of this state shall be applicable to said criminal courts in the same manner, and under the rules, restrictions, and regulations as they are now applicable to said circuit courts."   How. & Hutch. Dig. 497, § 64.

But these general terms are not deemed sufficient to give the right of appeal.   This last statute refers generally to the acts giving appeals, etc., and these have been already shown and explained.

If the general words used in these several acts could be considered as giving appeals in criminal cases, the *state* would have an equal right with the "opposite party."   But this would be incongruous, and probably unconstitutional, as a party accused of a crime has a right to a speedy trial; and, by the act of 1822, above quoted, sentence could be respited, in a case proposed to be sent up on doubts, *only with the consent* of the accused.   And again, in case the state could be considered as having a right to appeal, she could not give " bond and security."

The provisions of the law are ample, in affording criminals the benefit of writs of error to have their cases reviewed by this court, whenever they claim the right.

This suit and all others of the kind now before us, must be stricken from the docket, as having been improvidently brought here.

AINSWORTH *v.* THE STATE, 5 Howard, 242.

ASSAULT WITH INTENT TO KILL AND MURDER.

Where the indictment charged that the prisoner, "with force and arms in the county aforesaid, in and upon the left arm of him, the said Alson Shelby, then and there feloniously and maliciously did, with a certain drawn knife, stab and wound, with intent, then and there, feloniously, wilfully, and of his malice aforethought, the said Alson Shelby, to kill and murder," the indictment was held bad, because it did not allege that the prisoner "did *assault and beat*, and because it did not charge that the instrument was a *deadly weapon.*

Error to the circuit court of Clarke county.

The prisoner was indicted under the act of 1839, in the words following, to wit: "That Sampson Ainsworth, late of the county aforesaid, laborer, on the 20th day of September, 1839, with force and arms in the county aforesaid, one Alson Shelby, in and upon the left arm of him, the said Alson Shelby, then and there feloniously and maliciously did, with a certain *drawn knife*, stab and wound, with intent then and there, feloniously, wilfully, and of his malice aforethought, the said Alson Shelby, to kill and murder, contrary to the form of the statute," etc.

The language of the statute is: "Every person who shall be convicted of shooting at another, or of attempting to discharge any kind of fire-arms, or any air-gun, at another, or of any *assault and battery* upon another, by means of any *deadly weapon*, or by such other means or force as was likely to produce death, with intent to kill, maim, ravish, or rob such other person, or in the attempt to commit burglary, larceny, or other felony, etc., shall be punished by imprisonment," etc.

Forrester for plaintiff in error.

The offense charged in the indictment is unknown to our criminal code. At common law the offense was an assault with intent to kill, etc. The offense described in the penitentiary code is an "*assault and battery* upon another, with a *deadly weapon*, or by such other means as was likely to produce death, with intent to kill," etc. How. & Hutch., 698, sec. 33.

1st. There must be an *assault and battery*. The words "stabbing and wounding" are not descriptive of the offense named in the statute; although stabbing and wounding may, under certain circumstances, be an assault and battery. If these words were used synonymously, it would still be fatal where technical words are used in the statute, because in such cases no words can be substituted as exactly descriptive of the offense. 1 Chit. Crim. Law, 283, note A ; United States v. Batchelder, Gallison's Rep. 18 ; 1 Haywood, 403 ; 9 Pick., 143 ; 6 Am. Com. Law Rep. 12, letter B ; 11 C., 589.

2d. The offense must be committed with a deadly weapon, or such other means or force, as was likely to produce death. The indictment should, but does not, show the weapon used to be deadly, or such other means or force as was likely to produce death. Starkie's Crim. Pl., 244, Gillespie's case. In an indictment under a statute, the offense must be brought within all the material words of the statute. Nothing is to be taken by intendment. 6 Am. Com. Law Rep., 34, letter A ; 1 Baily S. C. Rep., 144. All knives are not deadly weapons, nor would the use of one not calculated to produce death, come within the province of the statute. Starkie's Crim. Pl., 249.

The caption of the indictment is defective in stating that it was found in a circuit court of law, of Jasper county ; no such court being known to the law of this state. 15 sec. Constitution.

Although the caption is no part of the indictment, it must show with sufficient certainty the court before which it was found, so as to show that the court had jurisdiction of the offense charged. 6 Am. Com. Law Rep. 12 and 13, letter C, 2 n. ; also 3 Johnson's cases, People v. Guernsey, 266, and cases cited.

A. L. Hays, on same side.

T. F. Collins, attorney general.

The first cause for quashing the indictment is, that it states the grand jurors *for* the state, etc., instead of the grand jurors

of the state, etc.   This is not error.   See Arch. Cr. Pl., 418.
The two words, *for* and *of*, in legal intendment, mean the same
thing.   Byrd v. The State, 1 How., 172.

The crime of stabbing, with intent to kill and murder, is fully
embraced in the act of 1839.   The terms felony and feloniously
apply to crimes, the punishment of which is death, or confinement in the penitentiary.   Act 1839, sec. 24.

The expressions in the indictment, " with intent to kill and
murder," convey only the idea of committing murder, and are
not double.   Arch. Crim. Pl., 54.   The indictment is certain to
a certain intent in general, which is all the law requires.   Arch.
Crim. Pl., 43 ; Coke Lit., 303 ; Act 1839, sec. 3.

TURNER, J. :

The exception to this indictment is, that the supposed offense
is a statutory offense, and not an offense at common law, and is
not described in the substantial language of the statute.

It is said, in our law authorities, that it is in general necessary,
not only to set forth on the record all the circumstances which
make up the statutable definition of the offense, but also to pursue the precise and technical language in which they are expressed.   1 Chitty Cr. Law, 283 ; and other authorities there
cited.   See also Starkie Cr. Pleading, 248.

The statute speaks of an assault and battery, by means of a
deadly weapon.   The indictment does not state that there was
an assault and battery, neither does it state that the supposed
stabbing was with a deadly weapon.   The substance of the charge
in the indictment is, that the accused stabbed and wounded
Shelby with a drawn knife.   The indictment should have alleged
that the accused did assault and beat, and it should also have
alleged that the assault was made with a deadly weapon.

The act aforesaid further provides that " if by such other means
or force as was likely to produce death, with intent to kill, etc.,
shall be punished," etc.

If this clause is relied on, the same particularity and certainty,
as to the assault and battery, and the means used, should be observed in the indictment.

Judgment reversed, and prisoner remanded for further proceedings in the court below.

MILLER *v.* THE STATE, 5 Howard, 250.

SELLING LIQUOR IN LESS QUANTITY THAN ONE GALLON.

The act of 1839, which declares that "it shall not be lawful for any person to sell or retail any vinous or spirituous liquors in less quantities than one gallon, nor suffer the same, or any part thereof, to be drank or used in or about his or her house," creates two distinct offenses; and hence an indictment which charges the defendant with "selling or retailing less than one gallon," and "permitting the same to be used in and about his or her house," is bad for duplicity.

Where the indictment contains some good counts and some bad, and the verdict of the jury is general, the verdict will be sustained, upon the presumption that it was found under the good count.

Error to the criminal court of Adams county.
D. S. Jennings for plaintiff in error.
Collins, attorney general.

TROTTER, J. :

The plaintiff in error was indicted in the criminal court of Adams county for selling spirituous liquors in less quantities than one gallon, in violation of the act of 1839. The indictment has three counts; in the first of which the defendant is charged with having unlawfully sold and retailed vinous and spirituous liquors in less quantities than one gallon ; and also with having then and there suffered the same so sold, as aforesaid, to be drunk in and about his house. The second count charges that the defendant did unlawfully and gratuitously, and without special charge therefor, offer, give and deliver said liquor in less quantity than one gallon to persons who were the guests of the said defendant. The third count contains a general charge of a violation of the act, but specifies no instance. The jury found the defendant guilty; when he moved to arrest the judgment, which was overruled, and final judgment rendered against him.

Two errors have been assigned : 1st, That the indictment is defective ; 2d, That the record does not show that the grand jury were sworn as required by law.

1st. The objection to the indictment is confined chiefly to the structure of the first count, which, it is said, contains two distinct offenses; the one for selling in less quantities than one gallon, and the other for suffering the spirits to be drank in and about the house of the defendant.

The section of the indictment under which this count of the indictment was framed, is in the following words : " It shall not be lawful for any person to sell or retail any vinous or spirituous liquors in less quantities than one gallon, nor suffer the same to be drank or used in and about his or her house."

This section does, evidently, embrace two separate and distinct offenses. The first member of the section makes it unlawful to sell in a less quantity than one gallon. The violation of the act is completed by the sale of the prohibited quantity ; and it is immaterial, in that case, whether the spirits are drank about the house of the vendor or elsewhere. The second member of the section makes it unlawful for the person selling the spirits to suffer the same to be drank about his house, whatever may be the quantity which is sold. A person may hence be guilty under the second member of the section who has committed no violation in the first. For instance, it is lawful to sell one gallon under the act, but it is not lawful, when so sold, for the vendor to suffer it to be drank in or about his house. This count is, therefore, manifestly bad for duplicity and uncertainty.

It is impossible for the defendant to ascertain what violation of the law he is charged with under this count. He could not, therefore, be prepared, from any information which it communicates, to make his defense. For this reason it is bad. The second count is a charge of violating that section of the statute which provides that it shall not be lawful for any innkeeper to offer any spiritnous liquors to his guests, either gratuitously, or without special charge therefor, in less quantities than one gallon (How. & Hutch., Dig., 187); and contains a statement of the offense with sufficient certainty to justify a conviction. It is alleged that the defendant is a tavern-keeper and inn-keeper, and as such did offer and give spirits to his guests, without charge for the same, in less quantities than one gallon. This being the case, the general verdict of guilty will be sufficient to warrant the judgment. For the principle is well settled, that if there be one or more good counts in a bill

of indictment, the verdict will be supposed to have been found
under them, and judgment will not be reversed because there.
may be one faulty count. This point has been frequently settled
by this court.

The objection that it does not appear from the record that
the grand jury was sworn, must have been taken under a misapprehension of the record, for it shows that fact fully.

The judgment must be affirmed.

Rockhold v. The State, 5 Howard, 291.

Forgery.

Power of clerk to grant writ of error in criminal cases.

Clerks of the circuit court cannot grant writs of error in criminal cases; the writ
in such cases can only issue upon the fiat of a judge, or court of competent jurisdiction.

Error to Adams criminal court.

Saunders for plaintiff in error.

Thomas F. Collins, attorney general.

Turner, J.:

These cases come up on writs of error granted by the clerk of
the criminal court.

The defendant below, plaintiff in error, was indicted and convicted of the crime of forgery in the criminal court sitting in
and for the county of Adams, and sentenced to imprisonment in
the penitentiary. He thereupon petitioned the clerk of that
court to grant him a writ of error to this court, which was done,
and bond and security taken, as in case of appeals from the circuit courts in civil cases, in the penal sum of one hundred dollars, payable to the state, with a condition to prosecute this writ
to effect, or in case of failure to pay and satisfy the judgment of
this court, together with all such damages, interest, costs, etc.

We are of opinion that these cases must be stricken from the
docket, inasmuch as the clerks of courts are not authorized to

grant writs of error in criminal cases, and can only *issue* them
on the fiat of a judge, or court of competent jurisdiction, for
the reasons given in the case of Tuomy v. State, in case of an
appeal in state cases.

The act of 1837, How. & Hutch., Code, 541, § 50, is considered
as applying to civil cases only.

KING v. THE STATE, 5 Howard, 730.

HOMICIDE.

Since the passage of the act of 1836, regulating the proceedings in criminal cases,
the special *venire facias* in criminal cases will not be quashed for any cause, except
for partiality or corruption of the officer summoning the jury by virtue of such special
venire facias.

If there be a deficiency of jurors present, summoned by virtue of said *venire facias,*
it is competent for the court to order the sheriff to summon others from the by-
standers until the jury is completed.

The foreman of the grand jury is competent as a prosecutor, and may be marked
as such upon the indictment.

It is not necessary that the grand jury should return with the indictment, the
names of the witnesses, or the evidence taken before them.   The only return required
of them is, whether or not they find a true bill.   Nor is it necessary that the record
should show that the witnesses were sworn; the presumption will be that they were.

A juror who, being sworn and challenged, answered that he had formed an opinion with regard to the guilt or innocence of the prisoner, from rumor only, and that
his mind was free to act upon the testimony that might be adduced before him, is
competent. [1]

A juror must be sworn and challenged before he can be interrogated as to his
competency as a juror.[2] Chit. Cr. Law, 546; 2 Burr's Trial, by Carpenter, 70, 71, 73.

On an indictment for murder, the prisoner may be acquitted of the murder and
found guilty of manslaughter.[3] The old rule not being affected by the criminal code
of 1838.

[1] Ogle v. State, 33 Miss., 383; State v. Johnson, Walk., 392; Wharton Am. Cr. Law,
3004, 3011, 3026; Nelms v. State, 13 S.& M.; Same v. State, 13 S.& M.,500; Cotton v.
State, 31 Miss., 504; State v. Potter, 18 Conn., 166; Spence v. Commonwealth, Virg.
Cases, 375; Brown v. Commonwealth, 11 Leigh, 769; Pollard v. Commonwealth, 5
Randolph, 659; Heath v. Commonwealth, 1 Robinson, 735; State v. Benton, 2 Dev.
& Bat., 196; State v. Ellington, 7 Iredell, 61; Hudgins v. State, 1 Kelly, 193; John
v. State, 16 Georgia, 200; State v. Williams, 3 Stew., 454; Hewenton v. State, Meigs,
342; McGregg v. State, 4 Blackf., 106; Smith v. Eames, 3 Scam., 78; Gardner v.
People, ib., 88; Sellers v. People, ib., 414; Baker v. People, 3 Gilman, 368; State v.
Flower, Walk., 318; Armstead v. Commonwealth, 11 Leigh, 657; Heath v. Common-
wealth, 1 Robinson, 735; People v. Rathbun, 21 Wend,, 509; 1 Burr's Trial, 416.

[2] Wharton's Am. Cr. Law, 3027; Johnson v. State, Walk., 392; State v. Flower,
ib., 318; Commonwealth v. Jones, 1 Leigh, 598; 12 East., 231; Commonwealth v.
Webster, 5 Cush., 298; Gillespie v. State, 8 Yerg.; 507.

[3] State v. Gafney, Rice, 431; People v. Doe, 1 Manning, 451; Commonwealth v.
Gale, 7 S. & R., 423; Brooks v. State, 3 Humph., 25; State v. Dowd, 19 Conn., 388;
Hurt v. State, 25 Miss., 378; Reynolds v. State, 1 Kelly, 222.

Error to the circuit court of Hinds county.

The plaintiff in error was indicted for the murder of James M. Farrar, and found guilty of manslaughter at the November term, 1839.

Michell, Mayes & Foote, for plaintiff in error.

Collins, attorney general.

TURNER, J.:

This case comes before us by a writ of error from the circuit court of Hinds county. The plaintiff assigns fourteen errors, which are as follows, to wit:

1. That the original writ of *venire facias* returnable to the term of the circuit court of Hinds county, Mississippi, and the same at which the bill of indictment in this case was found, does not command the sheriff of Hinds county to summon such a number of good and lawful men, *citizens and freeholders and householders of said county.*

2. That the said writ is not under the seal of said court.

3. That the said sheriff does not, in his return, show that the persons summoned by him as jurors, were citizens of the county of Hinds, in said state.

4. That part of the grand jurors were not legally summoned by any writ of *venire facias*, with or without seal, but made up of the *by-standers* by mere verbal authority.

5. That the plea to the *venire facias* ought to have been sustained, and not overruled, as it was by the court.

6. That the special *venire facias* issued in this case was not under the seal of the court.

7. That the said special *venire facias* does not command the sheriff to summon one hundred good and lawful *men*, citizens and freeholders and householders of Hinds county.

8. That the return of the sheriff does not show that the jury summoned by him were good and lawful men, citizens of said county, and freeholders and householders.

9. There is no one marked as prosecutor on said bill of indictment, except by mere intendment.

10. That the foreman of the grand jury cannot rightfully

mark his name on the back of a bill of indictment found and endorsed, or to be found and endorsed by him, a true bill.

11. That the record nowhere shows that the bill of indictment was found by the grand jury, on any evidence whatever, from witnesses sworn at the clerk's table, and sent to them by the order of the court or otherwise.

12. That the prisoner, on his trial, was by the court deprived of his right of challenge for partiality in the juror Lord Ware, who said he had formed and expressed an opinion, from rumor, as to the guilt or innocence of the prisoner, and of several others in the same situation, and was compelled to challenge them peremptorily.

13. That the court erred in not arresting the judgment in this case.

14. That there is manifest error in this, that the court overruled the motion for a new trial.

The first eight of these assignments of error, relate to the *venire facias* and matters pertaining thereto; none of which do we consider sufficient to arrest or reverse the judgment.

The act of 1836, found in How. & Hutch. Statute Laws of Mississippi, 498, § 67, provides, that "hereafter no challenge to the array shall be sustained, nor shall any *venire facias* be quashed by any court of justice in this state for any cause whatsoever; provided, however, that in capital cases any *special venire facias* may be quashed, for partiality or corruption in the officer summoning the jury, by virtue of such special *venire facias*, but for no other cause whatsoever."

This statute has received the judicial construction of this court in the case of Hare v. the State, and other cases decided at the last January term; and according to those decisions there is no error in the record as to the *venire facias*. The proceedings appear to have been regular, according to law, and the usage of the court. The usual mode of drawing took place, a *venire facias* issued, and was returned, and a grand jury was drawn, a foreman appointed, and they were all sworn. It is true there appears to have been a deficiency of jurors in attendance, and the court ordered others to be summoned from the by-standers. We perceive no irregularity in this course of proceeding, and the prisoner appears to have had a fair trial by a jury of his county. If, on the trial, a person should be called, to be sworn on the jury, the prisoner as well as the state, has a right to challenge the juror, and try the matter before the court, and if the court makes an illegal decision, it should appear by a bill of exceptions taken at the time. None such appears in the record. The plea filed to the *venire* was overruled, as it was contrary to the statute above cited.

The ninth assignment of error, and the tenth, state that there was no prosecutor marked on the indictment, except by mere intendment, and that the foreman of a grand jury cannot rightfully be a prosecutor in the case.

It appears by the record, that Edwin Shumway was marked as the prosecutor, and that Edwin Shumway acted under the appointment of the court, as foreman of the grand jury.

We do not think there is anything illegal in this. We see no reason why the person appointed by the court as foreman of the grand jury, may not be a prosecutor, as well as any other one of the grand jury. Unless expressly disqualified by law, he is as competent to prosecute as any other person. Any one member of a grand jury may be a prosecutor or an informer. It is their peculiar province to inform against, and present all offenders against the criminal laws of the state.

The eleventh assignment of error sets forth, "that the record nowhere shows that the bill of indictment was found by the grand jury, on any evidence whatever, from the witnesses sworn at the clerk's table, and sent to them by order of the court or otherwise."

It is not necessary that the grand jury should make return of the witnesses examined, or the evidence taken before them. The only return they are required to make, is whether they find a true bill or not. But the record does show, and gives the names of several witnesses, immediately above the return and signature of the foreman. If there had been any question, whether the witnesses were sworn, the fact should have been brought to the notice of the court, and the opinion of the court taken. The prisoner's counsel, in the grounds taken for a new trial, say, that "it does not appear that the witnesses who were carried before the grand jury, were actually sworn to give evidence."

It is not alleged that *they were not sworn*, it only says that "*it does not appear* that the witnesses were sworn." Well, the court, no doubt, knew that they were sworn, as that ceremony takes place in open court, at the clerk's table, and the same course of proceeding takes place in relation to the witnesses sworn on the trial. It is not the practice of our courts to make a record of the names, or of the swearing of the witnesses, called to testify in trials at bar, or before our grand juries; and all the ends of justice, and of fair and legal trials, can be attained without such record being made.

The twelfth assignment of error is this: "That the prisoner on his trial, was by the court deprived of his right of challenge for partiality in the juror Lord Ware, who said he had formed and expressed an opinion from rumor, as to the guilt or innocence of the prisoner, and several others in the same situation, and was compelled to challenge them peremptorily."

The bill of exceptions, as to this point, states, "that on the trial of this cause, when the first juror, Lord Ware, was called, the court asked him if he was a householder or a freeholder, and if he had formed or expressed an opinion as to the guilt or innocence of the defendant. To the first branch of the question the prisoner answered in the affirmative; and to the second, he answered that he had formed an opinion from rumor. The court then asked him if his mind was free to act upon the testimony that might be adduced before him. And he answered that it was. The court decided that the juror was competent, and that the defendant could not object to him without cause. The juror was then challenged peremptorily by the prisoner. The same, as above, occurred in regard to several other jurors, all of whom the court decided to be competent jurymen."

On looking into this ground of error the same view occurs to me as did in the case of the State v. Flower, reported in Walker, 318. The juror was not challenged by either party, nor sworn to answer questions. It is a settled rule that neither party has a right to interrogate a juror until he is challenged. 1 Chitty Cr. Law, 546. 2 Burr's Trial, by Carpenter, 70-1-2.

But, supposing the challenge to have been made, and the juror sworn to try the issue, which he was not, being after-

VOL. I.—13.

wards challenged peremptorily by the prisoner, did the court err in its opinion? We think not. The principles of law which apply to and govern this case, have been well ascertained and settled, on the most satisfactory and rational grounds, in this, and in other states, and we do not deem it necessary to sum them up or to discuss them again. See Walker's R., 318, 392, in which cases, four of the judges of the old supreme court of this state concur in opinion, that a hypothetical opinion, formed on rumor, subject to be changed by evidence on the trial, does not disqualify a person from sitting on a jury. 3 Stewart's R., 465.

In this case the juror did not state that he had *expressed* his opinion ; and for this reason, likewise, the case is not as much in favor of the positions assumed by the prisoner, as those which have heretofore been decided.

The 13th and 14th assignments of errors, are that the court erred in overruling the motions for a new trial and in arrest of judgment. These points are disposed of in the foregoing remarks, with one exception ; and that is, that on an indictment for murder, it is not competent for the jury to find the prisoner guilty of manslaughter ; and the statute found in Howard & Hutchinson Code, 726, § 22, as well as the constitution of our state is relied on by the prisoner's counsel.

By the common law, there are several classes of criminal cases, where the accused may be acquitted of the crime charged, but found guilty of an inferior degree of the same offense ; as in the case of murder, burglary, grand larceny, and assault and battery ; and the statute in question having created several new degrees of offenses, it was reasonable and proper, that the provisions contained in the said twenty-second section should have been made ; and the rule there laid down, merely carries out, extends and recognizes the rules and principles of the old law, and adapts them to the new grades of offense created, for the first time, by the provisions of the new criminal code, passed in 1838.

The language of the twenty-second section is general : " Upon an indictment for any offense, consisting of different degrees, the jury may find the accused not guilty of the offense in the degree charged in the indictment, and may find such accused person guilty of any degree of such offense inferior to that charged in the indictment, or of an attempt to commit such an offense." If this statute had declared explicitly that this provision should apply only to cases arising under the statute, and to no other case, the old law on the subject would probably have been abolished. But it is not so ; and we know of no rule of construction which would justify a different interpretation, of the twenty-second section.

The judgment must be affirmed.

ISHAM, A SLAVE, *v.* THE STATE, 6 Howard, 35.

MURDER.

On the trial of a slave on an indictment for murder, his owner was a competent witness for him. [1]

Error to the circuit court of Adams county.

Indictment against Isham, a slave, for the murder of Wilford Hoggatt. On the trial, Richard R. Sessions, the owner of Isham, was offered as a witness for the prisoner, but was excluded by the court on the ground of interest. The counsel for the accused excepted to the action of the court.

Cox and *Davis* for the plaintiff in error.

The chief question is, whether Sessions, the owner of the defendant, and who was offered as a witness for the prisoner, was properly excluded. The rule, excluding as a witness, a party having a direct interest in the event of the suit, does not apply to criminal cases where life is at stake. The law should be leniently construed *in favorem vitæ.*

A case somewhat similar to, but distinguishable from, this is found in the Law of Slavery, 214. *There* the master was offered as a witness *against* the slave, but objected to testify. Upon appeal it was determined that he was not a competent witness.

[1] State v. Elijah, 1 Humphreys, 102 ; Austin v. State, 14 Ark., 355 ; Pleasant v. State, 15 Ark., 625.

The question there, was simply whether he could be *compelled to* testify. The decision beyond that point was extra judicial, and is not authority. In North Carolina (where this case was decided) the master, on conviction of the slave, is liable for costs. In Mississippi, *contra*. How. v. Hutch., 179, sec. 87 ; and 171, sec. 58. Courts in modern times, lean to the *admissibility* of witnesses, leaving their *credibility* to the jury.

If a witness after suit brought, acquire an interest in the suit it does not deprive the party of the benefit of his testimony. If Sessions, therefore, had bought the defendant after the time of the alleged crime, or after indictment, he was compelable to testify. Shall the accidental fact, then, of ownership *before* the time, alter the case ? In Kentucky (and some other states) the master is allowed one half the value of his slave, and yet is a competent witness. This is not a release of interest, but compensation for the consequences of an act beyond his control.

Informers, persons robbed, and those entitled to a reward upon conviction, are competent witnesses. The interest in those cases is as direct, and may be as great as in the present. But this will, it is said, rest upon *necessity*. Does not that reason apply as strongly in the present instance ? Take this case for example : A master and his slave are in the dwelling-house ; a burglar enters and in the commission of his felony, is killed by the slave. The homicide, itself, can be proved, but the circumstances under which it was committed cannot be proved except by the master. Shall not the master be permitted to show that it was done to prevent the perpetration of a felony ? 1 Mass., 7 ; 3 Ib., 82 ; 1 Dallas, 110 ; 2 Ib., 239 ; 1 Yeates, 401 ; 2 Ib., 1. Upon indictment for forgery, the party whose signature is alleged to be forged, is competent to prove it a forgery. The effect in a criminal prosecution of allowing him to show, by his own testimony, that it is a forgery, is a discharge of the whole amount, for the forged instrument is usually cancelled by an order of the court, and filed among the records. See 2 Black. Com., 93, 94 ; Litt. Sec., 177 ; Law of Slavery, 6, 229, 230 ; Hump. Tenn. Rep., 102. On the evidence, vide 1 Leach, 263 ; Roscoe's Crim Evi., 36, et seq., 1 McNally, 43 ; 2 Starkie's Ev., 48 ; 1 How., 286.

Freeman, attorney general.

1st. The evidence of the master was rightly excluded on account of his interest in the slave as property. Law of Slavery, 214.

2d. The motion for a new trial was rightly overruled because the same was based solely on the supposed insufficiency of this evidence, of which the jury were the sole judges. 1 Starkie's Ev. 474 ; Margin. The jury are the sole judges of probabilities. Same authorities. If a person not interested, and not clothed with authority, obtains confessions by threats, or otherwise, it will not render them inadmissible. Archbold, 117. Although a confession may be inadmissible, any discovery that takes place in consequence of the same, is admissible. Archbold, 119.

Montgomery & Boyd, in reply.

From the testimony it appears that the strongest circumstantial evidence against Isham was, that his shoes and pantaloons had blood on them; and that when questioned about his shoes, he said they were in Washington, which was not true. At this time the investigation was not only progressing, and this slave had not only been accused, but a proposition had been made in his presence to try him and hang him, and some of the company were actually punishing Dick with great severity to make him confess; and his groans and prayers were distinctly heard by all the company where Isham was. His shoes being of a common size, and such as were usually worn by negroes and laboring white men, it was natural that he should deny they were at home, for fear they might fit the tracks found about the place where Hoggatt was hid. When the shoes and pants were found with the marks of blood upon them, no opportunity was given Isham to explain how it came there, but those slight circumstances were considered by the company sufficient evidence of his guilt to justify immediate punishment; and but for the moderation of a brother of deceased, no doubt the defendant would have fallen a victim to the blind fury of the excited mob.

A part of this company took him to a strange quarter, away from his comrades and his master, keeping him in ignorance of the course they intended to pursue, keeping his shackles so severe as to cramp him and cause great pain, and under these circumstances he made a confession. We contend that this confession was improperly permitted to go to the jury. There is abundant evidence of *threats* of punishment, and of *actual* punishment, and no assurance that he should receive the protection of the law, to clearly show that the confessions were not *voluntary*, but the result of fear that his punishment would be protracted to an indefinite period, and perhaps end in his destruction, unless he could say or do something to divert the attention of the multitude to some other object. He had seen the effect of that kind of stratagem when used by Dick, who, by accusing him, had been relieved altogether, and the whole weight of public indignation had centered on him. Under such circumstances, nothing was more natural than for him to suppose that if he could satisfy them that he had done the act under the orders of his master, he would be excused, for the reason that he was obliged to obey his master. This case in many of its features, resembles that of Serpentine, 1 How., 256.

The slave, habitually accustomed to submit, not only to the command of his master, but to the orders of all white persons who undertake to control him; naturally timid and submissive, and frequently subjected to unjust and severe punishment upon slight suspicion, cannot be expected to show that firmness and independence when accused of crime, which is usually displayed by the weakest and most unprotected freeman. Yet the law regards the general weakness of human nature as incapable of resisting the influences of hope or fear, and will not give credit to the confessions of an individual when there is reason to believe either of these motives influenced his conduct. 1 Phil. Ev., 111; 2 Ib., 235.

As to the competence of Sessions, the master, to testify in his behalf, we refer to but one authority, which is directly in point, that on a trial for a capital offense, the master is a competent witness in favor of his slave. 1 Humphrey's Tenn. Rep., 102.

Sharkey, C. J.:

The plaintiff in error was indicted in the circuit court of Adams county, for the murder of Wilford Hoggatt. In the course of the trial, Richard R. Sessions, the master of the slave, was offered as a witness for the prisoner; but his testimony was ruled out, on the ground of interest, to which exception was taken. After the jury returned a verdict of guilty, a motion was made for a new trial, which being overruled, the evidence was reduced to writing, and another bill of exceptions taken; and the matters set out in the bill of exceptions are now assigned for error.

The first point is entirely new in this state. As a general rule, it is undoubtedly true that no one can testify in his own favor, when he has an interest in the event of the suit. The question, however, here presented, has received direct adjudication in other states; and if those adjudications are not repugnant to principle, we shall be inclined to adopt them.

The first case to which we shall refer is the case of Elijah v. The State of Tennessee, reported in 1 Humphrey's Rep., 102. The case was in every particular like the present, the offense being capital. The prisoner was indicted for an assault with intent to commit murder. On the trial the master of the slave was offered as a witness, but the court refused to allow him to testify. This judgment was reversed in the supreme court, and the opinion of the court is based, as we conceive, upon sound and humane principles. The interest of a master in his slave was compared with the interest which the master has in the labor of his apprentice, in which case the master is always a competent witness. It was considered also as a question of common humanity. The master has the custody of his slave and owes to him protection, and it would be a rigorous rule, indeed, if the master could not be a witness in behalf of his slave. What would be the condition of the slave, if that rule, which binds him to perpetual servitude, should also create such an interest in the master as to deprive him of the testimony of that master? The hardship of such a rule would hardly comport with that humanity which should be extended to that race of people. In prosecutions for offenses, negroes are to be treated as other persons; and although the master may have had an interest in his servant, yet the servant had such an interest in the testimony of his master as will outweigh mere pecuniary considerations; nor could he be deprived of the benefit of that testimony by the mere circumstance that, in a civil point of view, he was regarded by the law as property. In the decision of the court which we have mentioned, a reference was made to a case which had been decided in New Jersey in the same way.

We are referred to a case by the attorney general, reported in 2 Devereux's Reports, 543, which inclines the other way. The case is, however, not analogous, and there was also a dissenting opinion. A master was called to prove the confessions of his slave, but he objected to giving testimony, and the slave also objected to his testifying as to the confessions. The majority of the court was of the opinion that he was not bound to testify.

As the judgment, for this reason, must be reversed, we have not thought it necessary to examine the other grounds taken.

The judgment is reversed, and a new trial granted.

Moss et al. *v.* The State, 6 Howard, 298.

Retailing.

Where a bench warrant has been issued in term time, returnable to a subsequent day of the same term, the sheriff may take a recognizance for defendant's appearance at that day.

Where the recognizance requires the party to appear at a certain day of the term, a forfeiture cannot be taken at a subsequent term without notice for that purpose. 2 Hawkins Pl. of the Crown, 173, and note (5); Barbour's Criminal Treatise, 507. This rule would probably not apply to recognizances returnable generally at a particular term, if the forfeiture was taken during that term.

The statute provides that recognizances shall continue from term to term, as other processes; and requires that recognizance shall contain a condition, that the accused and his sureties shall be liable thereon, until the principal shall be discharged by due course of law. Still it seems that, if a forfeiture be not taken on the day for the appearance, it cannot be taken at a subsequent term without notice, and such notice should appear by the record.

Error to the circuit court of Hinds county.

Moss and Gwin were indicted in the circuit court at November term, 1839. A bench warrant issued returnable during the same term, commanding the sheriff to have the defendants before the court on the 12th of December, (a day of the same term), and fixing the amount of bail at two hundred dollars.

Moss was taken, and released upon his recognizance in that sum, with Hughes as surety; conditioned for his appearance on that day, *and not to depart thence until he was discharged by due course of law.* Moss was not called at the November term, to which his recognizance was returnable; but at the March term thereafter, and a forfeiture taken, *scire facias* issued returnable to the following term, reciting that a recognizance was given for his appearance, to answer the charge at the November term, but the condition *that he should not depart* thence was omitted. Defendant moved to quash this *scire facias*, motion was over-ruled, and judgment *nisi* made absolute. This action of the court is assigned for error.

W. Yerger for plaintiffs in error.

Insisted that the court erred, because, first, the sheriff or his deputy, has no power to take a recognizance upon a bench warrant issued from the circuit court in term, and returnable at the same term. See Rev. Code, 252, sec. 13, Chap. 44, title sheriff. It clearly gives no authority to the sheriff to do that which was done. The power is expressly limited to cases returnable to a subsequent, from a preceding term; he is to recognize to the *next* term. In cases returnable forthwith he can take no recognizance, but brings the offender into court.

2d. The *scire facias* should have been quashed, for it did not show upon its face such a case as authorized a judgment. The recognizance recited in the *scire facias*, was conditioned for defendant's appearance on the 12th of December, and not for his appearance on that day, and that he should not depart, etc. Act of 1824, Ch. 70, sec. 2–3., Miss. Laws, p. 36.

The contract of a surety is to be construed strictly, and must not be extended by implications, beyond its very terms. To that extent he is bound, and no further. 5 Cond. R., 727. It is essential to a breach of the condition af a recognizance, that the party who is to appear, should be solemnly called before default is taken. 2 Wash. C. C. R. 422.

Attorney General, contra.

Sharkey, C. J.:

The plaintiff in error was indicted in the circuit court of

Hinds county, for retailing spirituous liquors in less quantities than one gallon. A bench warrant issued which was executed by the sheriff and the defendant entered into a recognizance for his appearance at a subsequent day of the same term at which the indictment was found. At a subsequent term a forfeiture was taken, and on the return of a *scire facias*, the defendant failing to appear the judgment *nisi* was made final, to reverse which, this writ of error is brought.

The first objection taken is, that the sheriff had no power to take the recognizance, because the bench warrant was issued in term time, returnable at a subsequent day of the same term; and it is insisted that the sheriff can only take recognizances in vacation returnable to the next term.

The language of the statute on which this objection is predicated is as follows: " He (the sheriff), is hereby authorized to take recognizances, with good and sufficient security, of any person or persons whom he may arrest on the process of a circuit court of law, charged before said court with any crime or misdemeanor not punishable with death, in a reasonable penalty, conditioned for the appearance of the offender or offenders, to the next term of said court, unless such process be made returnable forthwith during the term of the court at which the same is awarded." A general rule is here laid down, but there is also an exception created by the latter clause of the statute. The general provision must prevail, unless the case comes within the exception. The only exception is, where the process is made returnable forthwith to the same term of the court at which it was awarded. This process was returnable to the same term, but it was not returnable forthwith. The reason why the sheriff is not allowed to take recognizance when the process is returnable forthwith is, that it is his duty to take the prisoner immediately into court, according to the command of the writ. But when the prisoner is only required to appear at a distant day, it is competent for the sheriff to take his recognizance. The reason of the exception then fails, and the object of the law is answered. The recognizance taken by the sheriff is equally as binding as if it had been taken in open court. Hence we think the recognizance was well taken.

The objection is, that the forfeiture was not taken on the day when the defendant was bound to appear at a subsequent term of the court. This circumstance, of itself, would not vitiate the forfeiture; but the rule seems to be, that where a defendant is recognized to appear on a particular day, a forfeiture cannot be taken at a subsequent term without notice for that purpose. 2 Hawk. P. C. 173, note 5; Barbour, Cr. Treat., 507. This rule would probably not apply to recognizances returnable generally at a particular term, if the forfeiture was taken during that term.

There is a further statutory provision by which recognizances are continued from term to term, as other process, in which there is also a provision that recognizances shall contain a condition, that the accused and his sureties shall be liable thereon until the principal shall be discharged by due course of law. This provision is little more than declaratory of the common law, by which, on recognizance, the defendant was bound to appear from time to time, until discharged by due course of law; and still it seems if a forfeiture was not taken on the day for appearance, that it could not be taken afterwards without notice. It is therefore reasonable to conclude, that although the recognizance was continued by statute from term to term, a forfeiture could not be taken at a subsequent term without notice. And if a notice be essential to the forfeiture, it is but right that it should appear to have been given; and as no such thing appears in the record, we think the forfeiture was improperly taken. The recognizance is unexceptionable, and under the statute will continue in force, but the judgment on the *scire facias* must be reversed, and the cause remanded.

Peter, a Slave, v. The State, 6 Howard, 326.

Murder.

The statute, authorizing the parties in a suit to select a member of the bar to preside in civil cases, when the presiding judge has been interested in the cause, does not apply to criminal cases.

Error to the circuit court of Franklin county.

The prisoner was indicted, tried and convicted at the May term, 1841, of said court, of the murder of Samuel Harvey.

The presiding judge of the court having been formerly interested as counsel for the accused, by consent of counsel for the prisoner and for the state, C. McClure, Esq., was selected, under the acts of 1840 and 1841, to preside at the trial of the cause; and that is now assigned as error.

Vannerson & Webber for plaintiff in error.

T. F. Collins, attorney general.

TURNER, J.:

This case will be disposed of on the ground of the incompetency of the person who presided as judge at the trial of the plaintiff in error. The attorney general, in argument, admitted that in capital cases no such substitution can take place, as was done in this case, and this court is of that opinion. A circuit judge, regularly elected and qualified, is the only person qualified to sit in criminal cases. The constitution and laws of the state have made ample provision for the trial of all cases. Where a circuit judge is rendered incompetent to preside in any particular case, a judge from another circuit can be called in.

The constitutional modes of appointment must be observed strictly; and we do not consider that the legislature, by the act of 1841, 217, in prescribing that the provisions of the act of 1840, made in relation to the chancery court, which has jurisdiction only in civil cases, intended to apply the provisions of that act to criminal cases; and jurisdiction in capital cases cannot be taken or exercised by mere inference or analogy.

If this point was seriously controverted, it might be proper for the court to give a more full and detailed opinion.

The judgment is reversed, and the prisoner remanded to Franklin county, and a *venire de novo* awarded.

DAVIS *v.* THE STATE, 6 Howard, 399.

LARCENY.

It is competent for the circuit court, in all offenses, except those of a capital nature to take bail after conviction, to secure the appearance of the prisoner, to receive and abide the sentence of the law. The power to take bail in certain cases after conviction existed at common law.

Error to the circuit court of Hinds county.

At the November term, 1836, of the circuit court, an indictment was found against I. G. Davis for larceny; upon which he was tried and convicted. After conviction, the court admitted him to bail, taking his recognizance, with William Davis as his surety, conditioned that he would attend upon the court from day to day and abide by and perform the judgment of the court when rendered.

On the 26th November, 1836, the prisoner, I. G. Davis, upon being called, made default, forfeiture of his recognizance was taken, and judgment *nisi* rendered against said William Davis, his surety; and *scire facias* ordered to be issued. At January special term, 1838, *scire facias* was returned, served on William Davis, plaintiff in error, who demurred thereto, assigning but one cause of demurrer;—that the court had no power to admit the accused to bail after conviction and before judgment.

Foute for the plaintiff in error.

The statute regulating the taking of recognizances, clearly expresses that they shall be for the *appearance of the party charged, for trial*, or to *answer the charge;* and provides for the "continuance of them as other process," and that they shall remain in full force and effect until disposed of by the court, "without a renewal of the same."

The record shows that the appellant surrendered his principal, Isaac G. Davis, to the circuit court of Hinds county, in discharge of himself before trial; this surrender was accepted by the court; the principal ordered into custody of the sheriff, and he was therefore no longer in the custody of his bail. The *scire facias*, judgment, etc., in this case, against the appellant, cannot

therefore be based upon the first recognizance given.   2 Bay
S. C. Rep. 34; 5 Cowen, 39.

The recognizance given after trial and conviction of the principal, Isaac G. Davis, is unauthorized by any statute in this
state, and is void.   But if not void, and has been taken in pursuance of law, the proceedings thereon, by judgment *nisi, scire
facias,* etc., as taken in this case, are without authority, and unsupported by the provisions of the statute.   How. & Hutch.
672, section 40.

The 6th error assigned is certainly well taken, the *scire facias*
was joint against I. G. Davis, principal, and William Davis appellant, surety, and the sheriff made no return whatever as to
said I. G. Davis.

Freeman, attorney general.

The principal question arising on the error assigned is, whether
the court had power to take the recognizance on which the *scire
facias* and judgment are founded.   The recognizance was taken
after conviction of the crime of grand larceny, and is conditioned
for the appearance of the principal, and that he will abide the
judgment, etc.   This was forfeited, judgments *nisi* and final rendered, and execution issued.

The power exists in the circuit court, at common law, to admit the accused to bail, in all bailable cases, after conviction
and before sentence : at least with the consent of the attorney
general.   Chit. Crim. Law, 93; 4 Burrows Rep. 25; Rex v.
Wilkes.

In the case at bar the state is prosecutor; no objection to
granting the bail was made by the state; the district attorney
stood by and permitted the bail to be granted.   This is equivalent to the common law consent of the attorney general.

The case cited from 2 Bay's S. C. Rep. does not alter the rule.
There the attorney general *resisted* the motion to bail; in this
case both parties consented.   The case in 15 Mass. Rep. is not
in point.   The case in 5 Cowen, 39, does not involve the issue
in this case.   There the question was, whether the defendant
was guilty of manslaughter or of murder; here the question is
as to the power of the court to bail after conviction of grand
larceny, until the court shall pronounce sentence.

With regard to the return of the *scire facias*, there was a separate judgment against both principal and surety, and a failure to return the *scire facias* as to one of the parties would not discharge the other.

DAVIS, J. :

The only question which this court can properly consider, is the one raised by the demurrer in the circuit court. Does (as is insisted by counsel) the 17th section of the 1st article of the constitution of the State of Mississippi, which declares that all persons, before conviction, shall be bailable by sufficient securities, except for capital cases, operate as an inhibition upon the powers of the circuit court to take bail from prisoners after conviction and before judgment? We think not. It is believed that that clause of the constitution was intended by its framers for the better security of the citizen against an improper exercise of discretion, with which the common law clothed the judges of the courts; and to take from them all discretion whatever before conviction, only when it becomes necessary to discriminate between capital and minor offenses; leaving the discretion of the judges to take bail after conviction and before judgment as it stood at common law. There was a great necessity for that provision of the constitution, originating in the fact that judges, under the common law, were in the daily practice of committing prisoners to jail for offenses less than capital.

It is insisted by the counsel for the plaintiff in error that the cases of the Commonwealth v. Trask, 15 Mass. R., 277 ; Ex parte Taylor, 5 Cow., 39 ; State v. Conner, 2 Bay S. C. R., 35, settle the doctrine that, at common law, the power to bail after conviction did not exist, and that all discretion ceased on the part of the judges. After a very careful examination of these cases, we believe they do not warrant such a construction, but establish the very reverse of the proposition, so far as they are analogous to this case. The only point raised in the case of Trask, was in relation to the power of the court to allow bail to the prisoner before conviction, upon the facts presented by the testimony. The same question arose in the case of ex-parte

Taylor. It must, therefore, be true that they cannot be relied on to deprive the courts of the country of a power founded in justice, and intended, in many instances that may arise, to protect the citizens of the country from manifest oppression.

Conner's case is in all its features the same with the case now before the court, and must be conclusive in establishing the power of the court, to grant bail after conviction and before judgment, when, from any peculiar circumstances, the court may think justice requires its interposition. Conner was convicted ; and before sentence was pronounced upon him, the attorney general moved the court to order him to jail. The application was resisted by the prisoner upon the grounds that he desired an appeal to the supreme court of the state. The prisoner's right to bail was fully considered by the court and refused. It was not denied in that case, however, even by the attorney general, but that the court possessed the power to grant bail after conviction, nor did the court so determine. But, on the contrary, the court determined that, in cases where the punishment was only fine and imprisonment, the court would exercise its discretion so far as to allow bail when the peculiar circumstances of the case would seem to justify it. While we admit the power of the judges to take bail after conviction, we think it should be exercised with great caution, and only in minor offenses, where the peculiar circumstances of the case render it necessary and proper.

In the case of Conner, the supreme court, to which an appeal was taken, after confirming the judgment of the circuit court, remarked, that they would take an opportunity of expressing their opinion in favor of the refusal of the circuit court to admit a defendant to bail after his conviction in a case so highly criminal, but admitted the necessity of the exercise of a sound discretionary power, even after conviction. The power of the court to admit to bail after conviction is nowhere denied in cases which are the legitimate subject of bail.

We think the court did right in overruling the demurrer in this case. The judgment must be affirmed.

White *v.* The State, 1 Smedes & Marshall, 149.

PERJURY.

The affidavit, as a foundation for the issuance of a writ of *habeas corpus*, can be legally made before a justice of the peace; and if it falsely alleges matter material to the order for the writ, the party may be convicted of perjury. But if the false matter be wholly immaterial as a foundation for ordering the writ, it is otherwise. It is sufficient for one in custody to make affidavit that he is illegally so detained, and he is entitled as a matter of right to the writ.

Error to the circuit court of Madison county. ROLLINS, J.

R. Hughes, for plaintiff in error.

John White was indicted for perjury, in this, that he, in a petition to the judge, which was sworn to before a justice of the peace, stated that on a trial of him, said White, before said justice, for harboring a negro, " that he was forced into a trial late on Saturday night, without giving him an opportunity to produce his witnesses," when in fact, he was not so forced into trial, but that he demanded a trial at the time specified. A motion to quash the indictment was overruled, a jury empanelled, and defendant put upon his trial. It was proved that said White was apprehended and brought before James Priestly, Esq., late on Saturday, upon a charge of harboring a negro. When the defendant appeared, his counsel, without consulting him, insisted upon a trial immediately, supposing the state was not ready; but the justice waited for the arrival of the state's witnesses,— the counsel for defendant then left, saying when the testimony was taken, he would return and address the court upon it. Defendant seemed distressed and bewildered by the charge, and seemed to have nothing to do with the course of his counsel. The swearing to the petition, without producing it, was proved by the justice who administered the oath. The judge who tried the case testified that, on hearing the writ of *habeas corpus*, he paid no attention to the allegations of the petition, although he did, upon the application for the writ. There was a verdict of guilty, and motions for a new trial and in arrest of judgment, severally overruled.

It is now assigned for error,

1. That the court erred in refusing to quash the indictment.

2. In refusing a new trial.

3. In refusing to arrest the judgment.

1. 3. These two assignments will be considered together, as under both the question arises, admitting the allegations in the indictment to be true, was the defendant guilty of perjury? The question can only be answered in the negative. As to what constitutes perjury, see Hutch. Code, 711, § 1. A concurrence of these things is necessary to constitute perjury. 1. The oath must be false. 2. The intention willful. 3. The proceedings judicial, or before some of the officers, or in some of the proceedings mentioned in the statute. 3. The party must be lawfully sworn. 5. The assertion absolute; and 6. The falsehood must be material to the matter in question. 2 Chit. Crim. Law, 302.

Of the essential ingredients of that offense, two are wanting here. 1. The oath was not legally administered. 2. The falsehood was not material to the matter in question. The taking of the oath before a justice of the peace was extra judicial and voluntary. Shaffer v. Kentzer, 1 Binney, 512. 2. The falsehood alleged as perjury was not *material* to the matter in question. It was only necessary then to aver in the petition, that the party was in jail, having been committed for a bailable offense, and praying a writ of *habeas corpus*; and it was not necessary to make the allegation charged as perjury. The writ would have been issued without the false allegation, and therefore it must be held as immaterial to the matter in question.

2. A new trial should have been granted, because, as has been already shown, the offense charged and proved was not perjury. The fact that the judge testified that he regarded the allegation complained of as material on the application for the writ of error, does not make it so. And it is plain that the petition without this allegation, was sufficient to require the issuance of the writ. But it was not proven on the trial that the allegation of White in his petition,—if material and legally sworn to,—was false. He swears that he was forced into trial late Saturday evening, in the absence of his witnesses. The testimony in the bill of exceptions fully sustains the fact. As to the grounds of the motion to quash, and in arrest of judgment, see Hutch. Code, 221; Chit. Crim. Law, 302; 4 Black. Com., 137, note 35.

J. D. Freeman, attorney general.

The record shows a conviction of John White for the crime of perjury. The errors assigned are as follows:

1. The court erred in refusing to quash the indictment. The perjury is alleged to have been committed in falsely swearing to a petition for a writ of *habeas corpus*, and the facts falsely sworn to are cited in the indictment, as follows: "Said petitioner having been forced into a trial late Saturday night, without giving him an opportunity to produce his own witnesses, was thereof convicted by a justice of the peace." The record discloses the fact that White was arrested on a charge of harboring a slave, and that his counsel demanded an immediate trial in the presence of White, who did not object, but was silent. The justice of the peace waited an hour for the state's witnesses, proceeded to trial, and recognized him in the sum of $500. White refused to give the bail and was sent to jail. He then petitioned a judge of the circuit court for a writ of *habeas corpus*, which petition was sworn to before a justice of the peace, and the writ was granted.

A justice of the peace is a constitutional officer, and by our statute has all the powers of a justice of the peace in England. Our statute on the subject of perjury, includes false swearing before any officer of any court of law or equity. A justice of the peace certainly is an officer of a court of law. How. & Hutch., p. 711. The *habeas corpus* act provides that the petitioner may show probable cause that he is unlawfully detained in custody by affidavit or otherwise. There is no particular officer designated to administer the oath. The case of Shaffer v. Kentzer, 1 Binney, 542, is not in point. There the affidavit was voluntary, here it is required by law. Perjury may be assigned on an oath administered by a justice of the peace on an investigation by arbitrators. 4 Ind., 165; 1 Va. Cases, 130; 3 Carr & Payne, 419; Chit. Crim. Law, 304; H. & H. Dig., p. 711, title 5, § 1, 2.

As to the materiality of the facts sworn to in the petition, the writ of *habeas corpus* is a writ of right. (Constitution, art. 1, § 17.) White was in jail for a bailable offense, as the record shows, and he was entitled to a writ of *habeas corpus*, independent of the fact that he was forced into trial without the benefit of his own witnesses. Whether White was forced into trial or not, could not influence the circuit judge one way or the other in granting the writ of *habeas corpus*. It is, therefore, submitted that facts falsely sworn to were not material to the granting of the writ of *habeas corpus*. This being the main point in the case, other assignments of error will not be discussed.

PER CURIAM.

The affidavit administered by the justice of the peace in this case, as a foundation for obtaining the writ of *habeas corpus*, was within the scope of the powers of a justice of the peace; and had the matter alleged to have been falsely sworn been material to the obtainment of the writ of *habeas corpus*, the defendant below might with propriety have been convicted. We are clearly of the opinion, however, that the oath, which it is said is false, was of a matter wholly immaterial to the end contemplated, and not calculated in any degree either to forward or retard the application. It is sufficient for one in custody to make affidavit that he is illegally so detained, and he is entitled, as a matter of right, to the issuance of a writ of *habeas corpus*. Whatever else he may state in his affidavit, by way of inducement, though it be false, cannot be made the foundation of a conviction for perjury.

Let the indictment be quashed and the prisoner discharged.

NOONAN v. THE STATE, 1 Smedes and Marshall, 562.

SELLING SPIRITUOUS LIQUOR TO SLAVE.

On the trial of an indictment for selling liquor to a slave, the statement of one present at the sale, "that the defendant did let the negro man have the whiskey," although made in the presence of the defendant, is not competent evidence, and being admitted, should have been excluded by the court from the jury.

The act of 1842, entitled "An act to regulate the mode of obtaining license, etc., and to amend an act entitled An act for the suppression of tippling houses, etc.; approved February 9th, 1839," is constitutional.

The common law is recognized by the constitution as a part of the law of this state, but it may be altered or abolished by the legislative power.

On the trial of a person for the violation of this statute, it is not necessary to prove the particular kind of spirituous liquors by name; nor is it necessary to the proof of a person being a slave, to prove his master's name.

Under the plea of *autrefois acquit* or *convict*, the evidence is not necessarily and exclusively of record, but may be by parol, to the extent demanded by the circumstances of the case.

Error to the circuit court of Madison county.

The defendant was indicted at the November term, 1842, of the Circuit Court of Madison county, for "unlawfully retailing spirituous liquor to a negro man slave, without the permission then and there, of the master, etc., of said slave, contrary to the statute," etc. Plea "not guilty," and verdict "guilty." A motion was made to set aside the verdict, which was overruled, and the exceptions and evidence were embodied in the bill of exceptions.

The testimony is as follows:

John D. Scott testified on the part of the state, that a negro man of Captain Grigsby came to the store of witness and asked for plaintiff in error, stating that he wanted to get a flask or bottle of whiskey; the flask was empty; the negro went into defendant's store, followed by witness; when the negro entered the store, witness heard footsteps in the back room, and in a short time saw, at the front door of the store, the negro man, Noonan, and one or two other white men; the negro's flask was filled with whiskey; it was the same flask the negro had in the store of witness; witness asked the negro where he got it, who said "Noonan let him have it," which Noonan denied, looking down, however, and coloring in the face. One Hoyle was present at this conversation, and said "Noonan did let the negro have the whiskey." "Here the court (recites the bill of exceptions) rejected as testimony what the negro man had told or said to witness, and also rejected the denial made by Noonan, that he let the negro man have the whiskey, but refused to exclude the statement of Hoyle." This was all the evidence.

The errors assigned are:

1. The illegal testimony as to the statements of Hoyle, and
2. The unconstitutionality of the license law.

Geo. Calhoun for plaintiff in error.

The attention of the court is requested to the 5th and 8th sections of the statute, under which the indictment was found. The indictment is general, that defendant did unlawfully sell by retail, spirituous liquors to a negro man slave, without permission of his master.

Counsel contended that the provisions of the above act, at once destroy all the rules of law in criminal prosecutions, as regards offenses under it.   Two things have always been deemed necessary to a legal conviction.   1. That the offense should be found by a grand jury; and 2. That the party should be found guilty by a petit jury, of the same offense.   If this is necessary, it becomes a matter of mere accident for the party to get a fair trial, when prosecuted under this act.   The old rule, that the indictment must so describe the offense, that the party will be enabled to prepare his defense, is abolished, and the grand jury may find the offense of selling to one slave, and the petit jury may convict the party for selling to another; the indictment being in general terms, the petit jury cannot ascertain from it, the offense found by the grand jury.   1 Chitty's Cr. Law, 169; Bac. Abr., title Indict, G.

But the 8th section of the act is unconstitutional.   The 10th section of the bill of rights provides, that the accused shall have the right to demand the nature and cause of the accusation; to be confronted by the witnesses against him, etc.   Here the charge is retailing to a negro man slave.   How was it possible for the party to know what negro man he was charged with retailing to ?   The prosecutor could direct the evidence to a sale to any negro slave, and it would be impossible for defendant to know what one, until it should be developed by evidence adduced on the trial.   Then, and then only, could the defendant *prepare* for his defense.   We feel confident that, upon a thorough investigation of this subject, the 8th section of this act will be found to be unconstitutional, that all the requisites of indictments in other cases, will be held necessary under it, and that the indictment in this case is defective.

John G. Ott on same side.

1. It is contended that the indictment is not sufficient for uncertainty; giving defendant no kind of notice of what he is charged with, so that he may prepare his defense.   " In all criminal prosecutions, the accused hath a right to demand the nature and cause of the accusation."   Const. Miss., art. 1, § 10.   Nor

does the 8th section of the act cure the defect, because it is likewise contended that that act is unconstitutional. If this 8th section is to be enforced as it stands, it is manifest that it gives no kind of information to the accused, of the nature and cause of the accusation, which the constitution secures to him.

At common law, the indictment would be bad for uncertainty, and also for not having the name of the prosecutor marked thereon. Cody v. The State, 3 How., 27. Indictments must be certain as to the facts, circumstances, and intent constituting the offense. Arch. Crim. Pl., 41. It must be positive. Ib., 55. This 8th section attempts to take away that protection designed by the bill of rights, and gives him no opportunity of preparing his defense. The common law was in force in this state before the adoption of the constitution. Dig. Miss. Territory, p. 30. And see Kent's Com., 463, note a.

As to the evidence, it may be justly said that there is none. Scott only swears what he hears from Hoyle, a person present, when the defendant denies having sold the liquor to the negro man. Hoyle's statement is but hearsay at best. Scott proves nothing, for he knows nothing. A witness must testify from his own knowledge of the facts, not from hearsay. 1 McNally's Ev. 262, margin ed., 1811.

J. D. Freeman, attorney general.

THACHER, J.:

This case appears in this court by writ of error to the circuit court of Madison county.

The plaintiff in error was indicted at the November term, 1842, of the said circuit court, under the statute of 1842, entitled an "Act to regulate the mode of obtaining license to sell vinous and spirituous liquors, and to amend the act entitled an 'act for the suppression of tippling houses, and to prevent the odious vice of drunkenness,' approved February 9th, 1839." The indictment was framed upon the 5th section of said act, by which it was enacted, " that if any person, either with or without license to retail, shall sell any vinous or spirituous liquors to any slave, without permission of his or her master, mistress, owner or overseer, he, she or they offending shall be subject to indictment or presentment, and upon conviction thereof, shall pay a fine of five hundred dollars, and shall be imprisoned in the common jail of the county for a period of not less than thirty nor more than ninety days ; and upon the trial of any indictment under this section, if it be proven, the person to whom the liquor was sold was a negro or mulatto, that fact shall be received as *prima facie* evidence of his or her being a slave." Upon this indictment, the jury found a verdict of guilty.

Various points are made to this court, and insisted upon, as showing error in the judgment of the court below. We shall confine ourselves to one only for the purpose of judgment herein, but for general purposes, and to explain our judgment, we propose likewise to remark upon another point that was fully reviewed by counsel in the argument here.

It was objected below, that the court, upon the trial, refused to rule out a portion of the testimony of John D. Scott, who was introduced as a witness on the part of the state. That portion of his testimony where the part referred to occurs, is set forth in the bill of exceptions, thus : " Witness asked the negro man where he got it (a bottle of whisky)? and he said that Noonan had let him have it, and Noonan denied having sold the whisky to the negro man. That Noonan looked down and colored in the face greatly. That one Hoyle was present at this conversation, and said that Noonan did let the negro man have the whisky." This latter statement of what Hoyle said, the court below, upon application of defendant's counsel there, refused to rule out from the evidence.

The propriety of the judgment of the court below upon this application is fairly questionable here, as this court is not advised and cannot say how much the weight of that testimony might have affected and influenced the jury in finding their verdict. It is now insisted by the plaintiff in error, that the statement of Scott in relation to what Hoyle said, is hearsay evidence, and of a kind inadmissible on the trial ; and by the state, to have constituted a part of the *res gestæ*, and therefore legitimate evidence for the jury.

To explain the character of a transaction, not only what was done, but what was said by all the parties during the transaction is admissible. In the celebrated trial of Lord George Gordon, the cries of the mob accompanying him were pronounced admissible to show the intention of its leaders. The principle, however, seems to depend upon the existence of two attendant circumstances—that the testimony must relate to what was said by one connected with the act in question and during its progress. The individual, Hoyle, was merely present at a conversation, in which he volunteered his remark about what defendant below had done ; and it does not appear that Hoyle was in anywise connected with the transaction save as an uninterested listener to a conversation. What he is declared to have said, shows also that he would have been a witness to a material fact in the case, to wit, the delivery of the article alleged to have been sold ; and there is nothing to show that he might not have been produced on the trial. It is well settled in 1 Starkie Ev., 31 (Phila. ed., 1834), that " where a witness to facts might be produced and examined on oath, little doubt can be entertained that hearsay evidence of his mere declaration, heard and detailed by another, ought to be excluded, so infinitely inferior in degree must such hearsay evidence be when compared with direct testimony delivered in open court." In this connection, we would again remark, that as in the daily transactions of life, men are apt to receive and credit without scruple the statement by one man of what was said by another, and as the jury, in the instance under review, might have been directed to their conclusions solely by Scott's repetition of Hoyle's statement, if it was erroneously admitted by the court below, we cannot suffer the plaintiff in error to be prejudiced to that extent. Considering it, then, abstractedly, as a question of testimony, we are forced to the conclusion that it was illegal evidence in this case, and should have been ruled out by the court below upon the application of the defendant's counsel.

In the argument of this case, great stress was made, and much reliance seemed to be placed by the counsel for the plaintiff in error upon the insufficiency of the indictment growing out of a supposed unconstitutionality of the statute under which it was framed. As the attorney general expressed his own doubts upon the point, the court feels called upon to advance its opinion.

It is very true that under our constitution, no person can be accused, arrested or detained, except in cases ascertained by law, or deprived of his life, liberty or property, but by due course of law, and that every accused hath a right to demand the nature and cause of his accusation, and that his right to a trial by jury shall be inviolate. In what does this statute infringe either of these personal rights and privileges? It is said that at the adoption of our constitution there was included the common law as a part of the law of the land, and that it would now be an unconstitutional act to alter or repeal by legislature any principle, rule, or law, that was then a part of the common law. That, indeed, which was the common law at that juncture, was in fact incorporated into our constitution, and, consequently, not subject to any power short of that of the people themselves, in the exercise of their inherent political power, to alter or abolish their form of government. This view of the subject does not meet the approbation of this court, nor does it for the purpose intended, require its elaborate examination. The language of the constitution rebuts the presumption of such a meaning or intention. That the common law, like the common atmosphere around every living being, is gladly received by all framers of a government, is certainly very true; but that it was adopted to remain perpetual, unaltered and unalterable, and not to be tempered to our habits, wants and customs, was never designed by the wisdom of those who established our fundamental law. The constitution everywhere allows, and in some places exacts, the enactment of laws directly contravening the long established rules of the common law; and when it enjoins that the rights of persons shall be "ascertained by law," and protected "by the common law," it intends to sanction only that species of legislation which shall, in its assertion in criminal cases, be equal and general, and not partial and particular. The common law was the product of the experience of time and the necessities of men living under a form of government. Many of its rules are now vexatious and have become unnecessary and unfitted to our occasions, and are properly repealed when they are found to obstruct the current of justice or the interests of the whole people. Many are "unseemly niceties," which Sir Matthew

Hale declares to be "a reproach to the law, a shame to the government, and encouragement to villainy, and a dishonor to God." And our constitution has wisely provided for us the means to obtain what he desired to see, when he adds, "that it were very fit that by some law this overgrown curiosity and nicety were reformed, which is now become the disease of the law, and will, I fear, in time grow mortal, without some timely remedy."

The statute runs against several *mala prohibita*, which were unknown to the common law. The substance of the offense is the selling of vinous or spirituous liquors to a slave without the master's permission, and not necessarily the selling of a particular kind of vinous or spirituous liquor to the slave of a particular individual. Every offense consists of the omission or commission of certain acts, under certain circumstances, and all which are its necessary ingredients, must be stated. It certainly is not material to the proof of spirituous liquors to define its particular kind by name, or to the proof of a person being a slave, to show his master's name. Nor is this a parallel case with those uncertain charges enumerated in being "common thieves, common evil-doers," and such like. It cannot be well said that no one can well know how to defend himself from so general a charge, as it is deemed, when the statute provides it in the permit of the master of the slave to whom the article is sold, nor that he cannot plead the charge in bar or abatement of a subsequent prosecution. The evidence under a plea of *autrefois acquit* or *convict*, is not exclusively of the record, but may be oral to the extent required in the circumstances. And where the law departs in one particular from a previous rule, it necessarily admits a proportionate relaxation in all particulars growing out of that departure.

The judgment of the court below must be reversed, and a new trial granted by the circuit court of Madison county.

DEAN *v.* THE STATE, 2 Smedes & Marshall, 200.

LARCENY.

The mayor of the city of Vicksburg is authorized by the charter to take recognizances of persons, to appear before the circuit court, to answer for offenses with which they stand charged.

No particular form of words is required for the validity of a recognizance, provided it contains the essential requisites of such an instrument. A recognizance requiring the party to appear before "the judge" of the circuit court, etc., is sufficient. If it set forth sufficiently the cause for which it was taken, it need not describe specifically the circumstances of the offence.

Where the principal in a recognizance was recognized to appear in the sum of fifteen hundred dollars, and his two sureties in the sum of seven hundred and fifty dollars each, it is error to render joint judgment against the sureties for fifteen hundred dollars; the judgment should have been against each for seven hundred and fifty dollars. A suggestion to the high court of errors and appeals, that the principal in the recognizance, against whom the judgment was rendered in the court below, was dead before the judgment was rendered, cannot be inquired into by that tribunal.

Error to the circuit court of Warren county.

On the 14th day of August, 1840, M. C. Folkes, as mayor of Vicksburg, took the recognizance of N. J. Dean, as principal, and of David Dean and J. H. Vannoy as sureties, the former in the sum of 1500, and the latter in the sum of $750 each, conditioned for the appearance of said N. J. Dean "before the judge" of the circuit court of Warren county, at the court house thereof, on the third Monday of October following, to answer the charge of feloniously taking, stealing, etc., about the 3d day of August, 1840, in the town of Canton in Madison county, State of Mississippi, of about $200 in bills or notes of sundry banks, the property of etc., as appears on record in the said Mayor's court, etc.

Afterward, on the 12th day of November, 1840, in and by the circuit court of Warren county, a judgment *nisi* was rendered against David Dean and J. H. Vannay, the sureties, and a *scire facias* ordered to be issued. At the same term defendants moved to quash the recognizance. 1st, Because it requires the appearance of N. J. Dean "before the judge" of the circuit court of Warren county. 2d. Because it requires the appearance of Dean in Warren county to answer to an offense charged therein to have been committed in Madison county. The motion was overruled.

To this ruling of the court, exceptions were taken; the bill of exceptions setting out substantially, that on the 24th of April, 1841, a motion was made by said sureties, on whom *scire facias* had been served, to quash the recognizance and *scire facias ;* because,

1. Said recognizance requires N. J. Dean to appear to answer the court of Warren county for an offense stated to have been committed in the county of Madison.

2. It requires the appearance of N. J. Dean "before the judge" of the circuit court of Warren county.

3. There is no judgment *nisi* upon the recognizance, on which a *scire facias* could or ought to have been issued, commanding said sureties to appear, etc.

On the hearing of said motion, the recognizance, the *scire facias* and the indictment were submitted, and which was all the proof before the court on said hearing. This motion was overruled, and judgment rendered on the *scire facias* against David Dean and J. H. Vannay, as follows, to wit : It is considered by the court, that the State of Mississippi have execution against the goods and chattels, lands and tenements of the said David Dean and the said J. H. Vannay, for the sum of fifteen hundred dollars, etc., and costs, etc.

The errors assigned are,

1. The court erred in overruling the motion to quash the *scire facias* and recognizance.

2. The recognizance was not taken by one having legal authority to do so.

3. The recognizance was conditioned for the appearance of Dean "before the judge" of the circuit court of Warren county, on the 3d Monday in October, 1840, and the record does not show that the condition was not complied with. The court erred in rendering judgment of forfeiture, on default of Dean to appear before the circuit court of Warren county on the 12th day of November, 1840.

4. The condition of the recognizance shows that the circuit court of Warren county had no jurisdiction to inquire into the offense with which said Dean stood charged, (alleged to have been committed in Madison county,) and no other proceedings were had which gave such jurisdiction to the court.

5. The court erred in awarding execution against the bail, because the recognizance states that the amount acknowledged to be due is "now rendered," instead of *to be rendered* for the use of the state.

6. The final judgment against David Dean and Vannay on said *scire facias*, is a joint judgment for $1500, which is contrary to the tenor and meaning of the recognizance.

Tupper for the plaintiff in error.

The validity, form and effect of the recognizance, are the only points for the consideration of the court. Has the mayor power under the law, to take a recognizance for appearance before the circuit court? We think no such power exists. But if such power does exist, the recognizance was informal and valid. But the court erred in taking a forfeiture on the 12th of November, because the condition of Dean's recognizance required his appearance, not before the circuit court to be holden, etc., but before the judge of the court.

As to the 4th assignment of error, we contend that the circuit court of Warren county had no jurisdiction of an offense committed in Madison county. An offense must be tried in the county where committed, unless there be a change of *venue* as provided by statute. The condition of the recognizance, then, requiring the performance of an act contrary to law, was illegal and void.

The 6th error assigned, is also a valid objection to the judgment, to require its reversal. The judgment against the sureties is joint and for the sum of $1500, whereas they are each only bound for the sum of $750. If they are liable at all, it is certainly the individual and separate liability of each.

J. D. Freeman, attorney general.

The assignment of errors in the bill of exceptions is not well taken. The offense was larceny, and the defendant was, therefore, indictable in Warren county, where he was found with the money on his person, although the original taking was in Madison county. There is no error in the judgment, *nisi*, but it is submitted to the court, that the judgment final against the sureties should have been several, for seven hundred and fifty dollars, each, and not joint, for fifteen hundred dollars.

THACHER, J. :

A judgment was awarded in the Warren county circuit court upon a *scire facias,* upon recognizance against David Dean and Joseph H. Vannay, sureties of Nathan J. Dean charged with larceny.

The first objection offered in the court below, as a reason to quash the recognizance and *scire facias,* is, that the mayor of Vicksburg is not authorized by law to take recognizances. The charter of that city, section 41, conferred in 1839, fully conveys that power in all "criminal and penal cases" conferred upon justices of the peace.

The next objection was taken to the phraseology of the recognizance which required the appearance of the party before "the judge" of the circuit court of Warren county, at the term next succeeding its date. No form of words is required for the validity, provided it contains the essential requisites of such an instrument. The recognizance in this respect was more than sufficient.

It was next objected, that the crime is alleged in the recognizance to have been committed in Madison county of which the circuit court of Warren county had no jurisdiction. It is very true, that to legally convict the defendant in one county, when the original taking is proved to have been in another, it must be shown that the accused carried the property stolen into the county where he is indicted ; because, in contemplation of law, he is guilty of, not only a carrying away, but also a taking in every county through or into which the goods have been carried by him. 1 Hale, 507 ; 1 Hawk., ch. 33, sec. 52. But whether this was so or not, is immaterial to the validity of the recognizance. The statute makes it the duty of those authorised to act in such cases, to issue their warrant for the arrest of such persons as are charged on oath of having committed a felony, crime, or misdemeanor ; and where the offense is bailable, to take the recognizance of the deceased, with sufficient security, to appear when and where, etc., to answer the same. The record shows all these preliminaries to the recognizance sufficiently.

The last error assigned is that the judgment on the *scire*

facias is a joint judgment against the said David Dean and Joseph H. Vannay, for the sum of fifteen hundred dollars, while their obligation in the recognizance was not joint but several, each for the sum of seven hundred and fifty dollars. Upon inspection of the record this objection seems to be well taken.

The judgment of the circuit court of Warren county is, therefore, reversed, and, as this is a case calling upon this court to pronounce the judgment, which the court below should have done, it is directed by this court that judgment be entered up severally against the said David Dean and Joseph H. Vannay, each for the sum of seven hundred and fifty dollars, and costs.

On the 20th January, 1844, after the foregoing opinion was delivered, the counsel for Dean filed his petition for a re-hearing, based upon the affidavit of the counsel, who stated that to the best of his knowledge and belief, the defendant, N. J. Dean died in the city of New Orleans in the year 1841. This belief rests upon the facts, that in 1841, Daniel W. Dean, brother of said N. J. Dean, returned from New Orleans to Madison county, his former place of residence, and reported the death, by yellow fever, during that year, of his said brother in New Orleans, and that he was with him at the time of his death, and the fact is generally believed in the community where he formerly resided. Whether his death occurred before or after the 10th May, 1841, affiant does not positively know.

The petition asks a re-hearing on the following grounds: When the cause was called on the first week of the term, the papers were in the hands of the attorney general, who, it was understood by petitioner, would prepare a brief to which petitioner might reply, if he chose so to do, and that the case should then be submitted. On this understanding, counsel for defendant returned home, and on his arrival here yesterday learned, for the first time, that the cause had been already submitted and decided. That said N. J. Dean, the principal of defendants, David Dean and J. H. Vannay, is now dead, and as counsel is informed and believes, died before the final judgment in this case was rendered, of which fact, however, they were unapprised, or it would have been suggested to this honorable court before the cause was submitted. The judgment of the court below was reversed;

no valid judgment then existed against Dean and Vannay, and if N. J. Dean was not dead at the rendition of the judgment by the court below, he was, undoubtedly, before the rendition of the judgment by this court.

Counsel for plaintiff in error respectfully again calls the attention of the court to the 4th error assigned, to wit : That the recognizance was illegal and void, because the cause for taking it, as therein set forth, the commission of an offense in Madison county, did not authorize the magistrate to require the prisoner to enter into a recognizance to appear at the circuit court of Warren county. 16 Mass. Rep., 447 ; 9 Mass. Rep., 520. If a recognizance is void, that it does not contain the cause for taking it, then, *a fortiori*, a recognizance setting forth a cause which does not authorize the taking of it is also void.

THACHER, J., overruling application for a re-argument :

This case comes up on a petition and motion for a re-hearing.

As a general rule we cannot regard, after the submission of a cause, any misunderstanding that may occur between counsel in reference to the agreement of submission. It does not seem that in this case any injury accrued to the plaintiff in error from a want of inspection of the attorney general's brief by his counsel. That brief submitted all the points with but little argument and no reference to authorities. The brief of the counsel for plaintiff in error brought all the points fully to the consideration of the court.

It is urged that, since judgment was rendered by this court, information of the death of the principal in the recognizance has come to the knowledge of counsel, and also that the death took place anterior to the final judgment in the court below. This is a fact concerning which we cannot inquire. This tribunal is strictly appellate, and our only inquiry can be whether the judgment below, as disclosed by the record, is correct. The judgment of the court below in this case was final, and the judgment of this court decreeing such judgment, as the court below should have pronounced, is a judgment *nunc pro tunc*.

A rehearing of argument upon the 4th error assigned, we imagine, would give us no cause for a change in our opinion.

A recognizance should always set forth a cause for which it was taken, but it does not require a specific description of the circumstances of the offense. State v. Rye & Dunlap, 9 Yerger, 386. If it shows a *corpus delicti* upon its face, it is sufficient. The recognizance in the case at bar gives a recital of the oath of him by virtue of which the warrant of arrest issued, and has reference, also, to previous proceedings before the magistrate, in his office of record. It charges a larceny. And the recognizance need not set forth the evidence nor the course of reasoning by which the magistrate arrived at his conclusion to require it. Though the original asportation was in Madison county, the removal of the accused, with the stolen goods into another county, would constitute a new taking in that county. The case of the Commonwealth v. Daggett, 16 Mass. R., 446, shows a recognizance " to answer to such matters and things as should be objected against" the principal, and contained no reference "to any previous proceedings before the magistrate." This was indefinite and bad. The recognizance in the case at bar sets forth, it is true, the oath of complainant to a charge of larceny, in which the original taking was alleged to have occurred in Madison county; but it likewise refers to antecedent proceedings which authorized the taking of it, and an intelligible object for which it was entered into and the jurisdiction of the magistrate follows from the transitory nature of the offense charged. Commonwealth v. Daggett, 9 Mass. R., 492. We cannot but consider the recognizance valid.

Motion overruled.

Nixon *v.* The State, 2 Smedes & Marshall, 497.

Murder.

By the words "speedy trial," as used in the constitution of this state, in guarantying to every one indicted a speedy trial by an impartial jury, is meant a trial regulated and conducted by fixed rules of law; and any delay created by the operation of those rules, is not within the meaning of the constitutional provision.

The statute which gives the accused the right to have a "copy of the indictment and a list of the jurors " at least two entire days before his trial, intends thereby two entire judicial days.   In computing, therefore, the two days, the fraction of the day of its service must be excluded.

Where a prisoner, indicted for murder, cannot, by the rules of law, be put upon his trial until the last judicial day of the then term of the court has partially elapsed, it will not be an infraction of the constitution entitling him to a speedy trial, for the court, upon the application of the state, to postpone the trial to the next term.

The certificate of the clerk of the probate court that the list of jurors, by whom a bill of indictment was found, was drawn in open probate court, in the mode prescribed by law, when the clerk of the circuit court has failed to draw the jurors as required, is evidence to the circuit court that the panel has been properly drawn.

Error to the circuit court of Pontotoc county.

This case is brought, by writ of error, from the judgment of the Hon. Stephen Adams, judge of the ninth judicial district, upon a writ of *habeas corpus*, upon the application of the prisoner, then in custody of the sheriff of Itawamba county.   The petition for the writ was dated April, 1843, and stated that the prisoner was in custody, under the charge of having murdered Geo. W. Wiley, late of Pontotoc county.   That the indictment was preferred against him, under which he was then in prison, at March term, 1843, of the Pontotoc circuit court ; and that he had been imprisoned, under the same charge, since September, 1841 ; and made the record a part of the petition.   The writ was returned with the prisoner on the 19th April, 1843, and the investigation was held in Fulton, in Itawamba county.

An indictment was found against the prisoner by the grand jury of Pontotoc county, November 16th, 1841, for the murder of George W. Wiley, on which the defendant was arraigned before the circuit court on the 16th day of November, 1841, and to which he pleaded not guilty.   At the same term of the court, on the showing and application of the defendant, the *venue* was changed, by order of the court, to the county of Itawamba, to answer the charge on the third Monday of April, 1842, at which term the cause was continued, on the application of the prisoner, until the next term of the court.   At that term the defendant moved to quash the indictment.   This motion was sustained, and the indictment quashed, and defendant removed to the county of Pontotoc, to answer the charge at the then next April term.

The certificate of the clerk of the probate court, that the clerk of the circuit court, the sheriff and the judge of the probate court, drew the jurors in open probate court, at the November term, 1842, of said court, is filed with the record, and appears as part of it. The jurors thus drawn found the second indictment for the same offense, March term, 1843, of the circuit court of Pontotoc county. On the 23d March, 1843, defendant was arraigned on said indictment, and again pleaded " not guilty," and demanded his trial, but refused to waive his right to a copy of the *venire* and indictment for two entire days ; and there not being sufficient time remaining of the term, his motion, for that reason, was overruled. The defendant was in the custody of the sheriff during the entire term of the court. The *venue* was, on application of defendant, again changed to Itawamba county, no affidavit or other cause appearing of record.

Before the trial, defendant moved to quash the indictment, because it was improperly found, and by an irregular grand jury. He moved, also, to have the case stricken from the docket of that county for want of jurisdiction, no affidavit for the change of *venue* having been filed. The motion was overruled. On the trial under the writ of *habeas corpus,* no other evidence was adduced than the record of the proceedings in the circuit court. The application for discharge was overruled, and the prisoner remanded.

Davis for the prisoner.

Cited the 10th section of the first article of the constitution, which declares, " that in all prosecutions, by indictment or otherwise, the accused shall have a speedy and public trial by an impartial jury of the county where the offense was committed ; and insisted that it was imperative in its mandates, absolute in its effect upon the action, both of the courts and the legislature, and that no discretion was vested by it, either in the judiciary or in the legislature.

If the circuit courts can absolutely refuse a trial at one term, can they not do so for ten, or any number of terms ? If they can commence the exercise of a discretion, what power of the government can limit them ? what power restrain them ? None but the power which gave them existence, and it has already fixed that restraint by withholding the power. That power has, in effect, said, that this is a substantial power, intended for the protection of the citizen, and that one refusal by the court to grant a trial, is a failure to furnish a speedy and impartial trial, in accordance with the spirit of the constitution, and for which the prisoner shall be discharged. Green v. Robinson, 5 How. 100. The record shows default and unjustifiable delay on the part of the state. After eighteen months' confinement of the prisoner in a dungeon, the proceedings against him by the prosecution are found by the court to be so irregular and illegal, that it is constrained to quash the whole proceedings. The whole fault was on the part of the state, whereby it failed to furnish the prisoner that speedy trial guaranteed to him by the constitution, and the defendant should have been then discharged. But oppression does not stop at this point; he is remanded to the jail of Pontotoc county for further proceedings.

Three years have now been passed by the prisoner in chains and a dungeon. The question is, shall he be discharged? There is not in the record anything to be found which shows the jury to have been drawn in accordance with the statute. How. & Hutch., 491, sec. 46. Neither of the modes prescribed in the first part of that section was pursued. In default of pursuing these modes, another is prescribed, to wit : they shall be drawn by the clerk and sheriff in presence of the probate judge. This the probate clerk testifies has been done ; but his certificate is a nullity, because he has no authority in law to make it. Hence we insist that the prisoner is illegally detained, and ought to be discharged.

John D. Freeman, attorney general.

THACHER, J. :

This was a writ of error from the judgment of the judge of the ninth judicial district, upon an investigation, by virtue of a writ of *habeas corpus.*

The plaintiff in error is under indictment for murder. He claimed his discharge upon two grounds : that he had been deprived, through the default of the state, of his constitutional privilege of a speedy trial ; and that the indictment by process, under which he was now held in imprisonment, is null and void.

One who is prosecuted by indictment or information has, by the constitution, his right to a speedy and impartial trial. He shall not be unnecessarily hindered and delayed, in his efforts to relieve himself from the burden of an onerous charge of crime. But the constitution also declares that he shall not be deprived of his life or liberty, but by due course of law. Const., art. 1, § 10. Delays growing out of the established mode of proceeding, which has been so established by law, equally for the protection of the accused, and to accomplish the design of the scheme of laws, are evils, necessarily attendant upon all human systems of jurisprudence. They are evils to which all may be subjected alike, and which constitute a part of the price paid for the advantages, far greater in proportion, thereby derived. By a speedy trial is then intended a trial conducted according to fixed rules, regulations, and proceedings of law, free from vexatious, capricious, and oppressive delays, manufactured by the ministers of justice.

In examining the record, we can see but one cause of delay, which did not originate, directly and immediately, from the accused himself; and that exception seems to be the one most urgently pressed upon this court. The state of facts relied upon most forcibly in the argument, as exemplifying the state's default was, that the pending indictment was found by the grand jury of Pontotoc county, on Tuesday, the 21st day of March, 1843; that the accused was arraigned thereon on Thursday, the 23d day of the same month, and plead thereto; and that he thereupon demanded his trial, which was refused him, as he declined to waive his statutory right to a copy of the indictment for two entire days before his trial. H. & H., 667, § 15.

The trial, under the circumstances, could not have taken place at that term of the court. The Circuit Court of Pontotoc county could continue in session six judicial days, and no longer. Laws of 1842, 221, § 2. The statute gave the accused a right to an examination of the indictment "at least two entire days before the trial." The service of copy must have been made some time on Thursday, and he would have been entitled to the days of Friday and Saturday for its examination, with the advice of counsel. The statute intends two entire judicial days. The fraction of the day of its service must be excluded in the computation, not only for the reason already given, but because the greatest liberality of construction should be accorded to an accused in passing upon his rights and privileges before, during, and after his trial. Had a different estimate been made, by including the portion of Thursday which, as we have said, would have been erroneous, then the trial could not have commenced until some time during Saturday, the last of the judicial days of that term. It must, necessarily, have been precipitated with haste, and without that deliberation and reflection on the part of the court, which is due, as a right, in the course of law, to an accused, in so solemn and awful a position.

The main reason urged against the validity of the indictment is based upon an alleged informality of the certification of the manner in which the jurors for the term of the court, at which the indictment was returned, were drawn. There having been an omission by the clerk of the circuit court, and sheriff of the county of Pontotoc, to draw the jurors, as required by the general circuit court law, in such case provided; the certificate of the clerk of the probate court shows in the record, that the clerk of the circuit court, and the sheriff of the county, in presence of the judge of probate, and during the term time of his court, did draw the requisite number of jurors for the said March term, 1843, of that circuit court. H. & H., 491, § 46. The inspection and supervision of this proceeding shows a judicial exercise of the duties of the judge of probate, which is properly, and must necessarily, under such circumstances, be certified unto by the clerk of that court. If done in vacation, the certificate may be by the judge of probate himself, but when done in term time, it must be certified by the clerk.

After a careful and elaborate examination of the record in this case, we can see nothing that calls for a reversal of the judgment of the judge of the ninth judicial district.

The judgment is therefore affirmed.

M'Ewin et al. *v.* The State, 3 Smedes & Marshall, 120.

Unlawful Retailing.

A party indicted under the statute for retailing spirituous liquors in less quantity than one gallon, may be punished by imprisonment as well as fine; therefore it is not error to issue a *capias* for his arrest, that being the proper process in such cases.

The sheriff acquires his authority to take recognizances of those whom he may arrest, on process from the circuit courts, from the statute, H. and H., 294, sec. 13, which invests him with discretion respecting the amount of security. The fact that the clerk, without the order of the court, directed the sheriff in the writ, as to the number and amount of bail, is immaterial.

Judgment was rendered on a recognizance made returnable to the 3rd Monday after the 4th Monday in April, at a court held on the 3rd Monday in March, the legislature having changed the time of holding the court from the former to the latter day, and directed all process to be returned to the latter; held not to be error.

When the parties have agreed to consider a plea as filed, and issue as joined, it is error to render judgment by default.

Appeal from the circuit court of Pontotoc county.

Indictment November term, 1841, of circuit court of Pontotoc county, against William Mann, for selling spirituous liquors in less quantities than one gallon. The clerk issued a *capias* and endorsed thereon, "Let the defendant be recognized, himself in the sum of $250, with two sureties in the sum of $125 each, conditioned as the law requires." On 3rd March, sheriff arrested Mann and took his recognizance in the sum of $200, and that of Wardlaw and M'Ewin, his sureties, in $190 each. On 23rd March, 1842, court having commenced its session on the 3rd Monday of that month, the defendant being called and making default, judgment *nisi* was taken, and *sci. fa.* ordered. At the next term the defendants appeared, and pleaded as follows: "*Nul tiel record*, and issue in short by consent;" to which the district attorney replied: "Replication and issue in short by consent." At the March term, 1843, the court rendered judgment against the defendants, by default, from which they appeal to this court.

C. D. Fontaine, for appellants.

The first error relied on is, that a *capias* issued on the indictment instead of a summons, or *venire facias* in nature of a summons, the proper process on all indictments for offenses inferior to felony or mayhem. 2 Hawkins, 395; 4 Black. Com., 318, Tucker's Edition.

The second error is, the clerk had no authority, in the absence of an order of the court, to command the sheriff to recognize the defendants, and require two sureties for his appearance in court.

The third error is, the variance between the amounts in which the defendant and sureties are respectively recognized, from those mentioned in the endorsement on the writ.

The fourth error is, the court had no right to render judgment by default, it appearing by the record that the defendants had filed the plea of *nul tiel record*, and issue taken thereon, by the district attorney.

Lastly, that the court erred in rendering a judgment on a recognizance, made returnable to the 3rd Monday after the fourth Monday in April, when in truth and in fact, the court was held on the 3rd Monday in March.

John D. Freeman, attorney general.

The first error assigned is that a *capias* issued. This process is proper on all indictments for offenses punishable by imprisonment as well as by fine. The defendant could not be tried unless he was brought personally into court, and a summons would not have effected this object. The sheriff had power, under the statute, to take the recognizances in the manner he did, and in the respective penalties. The order of the clerk on the writ was but directory, and had no binding effect on the sheriff.

The fourth error is, that the default was taken, when the record showed a plea. The record shows an agreement of counsel to file a plea of *nul tiel record* in short, but none such was filed, the default, therefore, was properly taken. The last error assigned is, that the recognizance was made returnable to the April term, when the court was held in March. The legislature after the giving of the recognizance, altered the time of the term from April to March, making all process, etc., returnable to that term. Laws of 1842, page 221.

THACHER, J.:

This was an appeal from the Circuit Court of Pontotoc county.

The first objection stated is that a *capias* issued on an indictment for retailing spirituous liquors in less quantity than one gallon, when the proper process was a summons or *venire facias* in the nature of a summons.   The offense is punishable by imprisonment as well as fine, and a *capias* was the proper process to bring the body into court.   Such process has long been in practice in England, after indictment, in the case of misdemeanors, and is the practice here, except in cases punishable by fine only.   This, however, could not constitute error in any event.

It is next objected, that the clerk had no authority, without an order of the circuit court, to command the sheriff to recognize the defendant, and require two sureties for his appearance at court.   This, also, even admitting it to be true, could not constitute an error that would affect the judgment below upon the *scire facias*, which has caused this appeal.   A sheriff acquires his authority to take recognizances of persons whom he may arrest on the process of the circuit courts, from the statute H. H. 294, § 13.   He is thereby invested with discretion respecting the amount of the security.

The objection that a variance exists between the amounts in which the defendant below and security are respectively recognized from those mentioned in the endorsement of the writ, cannot avail by reason of the power invested in the sheriff by the statute.   Neither does it affect the judgment on the *scire facias*.

Again, it is urged, that a judgment was rendered on a recognizance, made returnable to the 3d Monday after the 4th Monday in April, at a court holden the third Monday in March.   This resulted from a change by the legislature of the time of holding the terms of the circuit court of Pontotoc county, and in the returns of recognizances and process to that court.   Acts of 1842, p. 221.

In fine, it is objected that the court rendered a judgment by default, while a plea of *nul tiel record* and issue, joined thereon, was filed in the action.   There seems to have been an agreement by the representative of the state and the attorneys for the defendant, to consider such a plea and issue filed.   In such a view, and it is a mode of making up pleadings in short, which we reluctantly recognize, the judgment by default was erroneous.

The judgment, for this reason, must be reversed, and the cause remanded for further proceedings.

KELLY AND LITTLE *v.* THE STATE, 3 Smedes & Marshall, 518.

MURDER.

The caption of the indictment stated, that the court was held for the county of Smith, at the court-house, in the town of Raleigh; and the town of Raleigh, in Smith county, was incorporated, by act of the legislature, in 1838, and by another act of the legislature, passed in 1836, the county site of the public buildings of Smith county was located in what is now a part of the town of Raleigh; *held*, that the caption of the indictment sufficiently showed that the court was held at the place designated by law.

Numerical figures may be used in an indictment to express numbers and dates; if, however, they are illegible, the indictment will be bad for uncertainty.[1]

It is sufficient if the record shows that the jurors, who tried the defendant, were summoned by the deputy sheriff, his acts as such deputy being, in legal effect, the acts of the sheriff; and it cannot be objected to the verdict that the court *dismissed* the sheriff from the duty of summoning *tales* jurors, as such order or action of the court would be null and void.

Where a slave has been killed by his master and overseer, or either, in inflicting chastisement upon him, the rules of the common law, upon the subject of murder, will regulate the character of the offense.

Under the laws of this state, the master is liable to be indicted for an assault and battery upon his own slave, when he has inflicted cruel and unusual punishment on him; and it is for the jury to determine what constitutes such cruel and unusual punishment.

Intoxication may be a circumstance proper for the consideration of the jury upon the question of intention or malice on the part of the offender, but it is no legal excuse or extenuation of the crime.[2]

[1] State v. Peck, 165; Com. v. Adams, 1 Gray, 481; State v. Raiford, 7 Porter, 101; State v. Hodgeden, 3 Vermont, 481; State v. Seamon, 1 Iowa, 418; State v. Eagan, 10 La., 699; Cody v. Commonwealth, 10 Gratton, 776; Lazier v. Commonwealth, ib., 708; State v. Reid, 35 Me., 489; State v. Lane, 4 Iredell, 113; State v. Haddock, 2 Hawk., 461; State v. Dickens, 1 Haywood, 406; State v. Smith, Peck 165; Wharton's Am. Cr. Law, 408; *sed vide contra*, State v. Voshall, 4 Indiana, 590; Finch v. State, 6 Blackf. 533; Berrian v. State, 2 Zabriskie 9; though see ib., 679; in New Jersey this is corrected by statute; Johnson v. State, 1 Dutch., 313.

[2] Pa. v. McGall, Add., 257; Swan v. State, 4 Humpt., 136; People v. Balencia, 21 Cal., 544; Mooney v. State, 33 Ala., 419; Golden v. State, 25 Ga., 527; Jones v. State, 29 Ga., 595; Keenan v. Commonwealth, 8 Wright, 55; Commonwealth v. Hawkins, 3 Gray, 463; State v. Harlowe, 21 Mo., 446; People v. Robinson, 2 Parker Cr. R., 235; People v. Hammill, ib., 223; Haile v. State, 11 Humpt., 154; U. S. v. Roundenbush, 1 Bald., 514; Pirtle v. State, 9 Humph., 663; State v. McCants, 1 Spear, 384; Cornwall v. State, Mart. & Yerg., 147; State v. Bullock, 13 Ala., 413; Wharton Am. Cr. Law, 41–4; Rex v. Crusoe, 8 C. & P., 541; 3 Greenl. Ev., 6148; Eastwood v. People; 3 Parker Cr. R., 25 (4 Kern, 526); Rogers v. People, ib., 632; 1 Russell v. Crimes, 8; Rex v. Grindley, Worcester Sum. Ass.. 1819 M.S.; Rex v. Carroll, 7 C. & P., 145, 32 Eng. Com. Law R., 471; Rev. Thomas, 7 C. & P., 817; Pearson's case, 2 Lewin, 145; Marshall's case, ib., 76; Goodier's case, ib.; Pigman v. State, 14 Ohio, 555.

[2] U. S. Clarke, 2 Cranch, C. C. R., 158; U. S. v. McClue, Curtis C. C. R., 1; People v. Pine, 2 Barbour, 566; State v. Bullock, 13 Ala., 413; State v. Stark, 1 Strob., 479; U. S. Cornell, 2 Mason, 91; U. S. v. Forbes, Crabbe, 558; State v. Harlow, 21 Mo., 446; Cornwall v. State, Mar. & Yerg., 147; Pirtle v. State, 9 Humph., 663; State v. John, 8 Ired., 330; State v. Turner, 1 Wright, 30; People v. Wilby, 5 Parker Cr. R., 19; Porter v. State, 12 Tex., 500; Mercer v. State, 17 Ga., 146; People v. Robinson,

Motions by the state, in the absence of the accuser, to quash the *venire facias* and for the issuance of an alias *venire facias*, made after arraignment and before trial, and which were overruled, will not vitiate the verdict of the jury.   The absence of the accused may have been the reason for overruling the motions.

Upon conviction of manslaughter, the prisoner must be present in court when sentence is pronounced; without such presence, the sentence would be invalid.‡

The sentence of the court, inflicting the punishment of imprisonment, must fix the date of its commencement, or otherwise it will be erroneous.§

Where the verdict of the jury, finding the accused guilty of manslaughter, is regular and valid, but the sentence of the court is erroneous, the judgment of the court may be reversed without disturbing the verdict, and the cause remanded with directions to the court below, to pronounce a correct judgment.

Error to the circuit court of Smith county.

At the April term, 1844, of the Smith county circuit, the grand jury found a joint bill of indictment against Kelly and Little for the murder of " Jack, a slave of said Kelly ;" and at the same term were tried and convicted of manslaughter in the first degree ; and were sentenced to confinement in the penitentiary for a term of seven years.   The indictment was in the common law form for murder, except that in the caption the grand jurors are not stated to have been sworn to enquire for the " State of Mississippi."

The bill of exceptions shows, that the special *venire* for the trial of prisoners and residue of the regular panel were exhausted, without obtaining the requisite number of jurors ; and thereupon the court being satisfied, as it alleged, that the sheriff " was grossly ignorant of his duties as sheriff," dismissed him from service in summoning *tales* jurors, and there being no coroner in the county, directed the sheriff to summon *tales* jurors.   The reason of this action of the court was, that the sheriff had summoned on the *venire* several of the grand jurors by whom the indictment was found, and also many of the original *venire*, and several of the jury of inquest.   Before this action was had, the district attorney moved the court to quash the special *venire*, and for an *alias special venire facias*, on the ground of partiality and corruption in the sheriff, in summoning

2 Parker Cr. R., 235; People v. Hammill, ib., 223; Smith v. Commonwealth, 1 Duvall, 224; Kenney v. People, 4 Tiffany, 330; Commonwealth v. Hawkins, 3 Gray (Mass.), 463; People v. Robinson, 1 Parker C. C. 649; Schaller v. State, 14 Mo., 503; Wharton, on Homicide, 369; Wharton Am. Cr. Law, 40-4; 1 Archbold Cr. Pr. & Pl., 81, et seq.; see also note (1) p.   supra.

‡ Archbold Cr. Pr. & Pl., 277; notes.

§ Wharton v. State, 41 Miss. 680; Rex v. Kenworthy, 1 Barn. & Cress., 711; Rex v. Nichols, 1 Barn & Ald., 21.

improper jurors; but these motions were overruled by the court. The prisoners excepted to the discharge of the sheriff, and to the direction to the deputy to summon talesmen. The same was afterwards assigned as ground for the motion for a new trial, which was overruled; and for this the prisoners also excepted. It does not appear by the record that the prisoners were present in court when sentence was pronounced against them, nor at what time the punishment was to commence.

Motion in arrest of judgment, because,

1st. The indictment does not charge any offense known to the laws of this state.

2d. Because it is not stated in the indictment that the grand jury was empanelled, sworn and charged to inquire for the State of Mississippi. Motion overruled and prisoners excepted thereto. The jury who tried the case were " sworn to speak the truth of and concerning the premises." The prisoners asked the court to give the following instructions to the jury :

2. "There being no system of domestic slavery known to the common law of England, the relation of master and slave known in this state, as well as that between slave and overseer not having existed in England, there is nothing in the common law, on the subject of murder, that has strict and complete application to a case of killing, as arising from the chastisement of a slave by his master or overseer or both."

6th Instruction. " The first description of killing is the only one that the jury can regard as applicable to the present case." (This has reference to the description of the three cases of killing declared to be murder in the penitentiary codes.)

7th Instruction. In determining whether the act of killing was or was not murder, if the jury, find from the evidence that the defendants were in a state of serious intoxication, they are entitled to regard this fact as elucidatory to the point of intention, as evidence more or less strong, according to their view of the real circumstances of the case, as proof of the absence or that premeditated design required by our statute in the first description of murder, as stated in the 5th instruction, as an indispensable ingredient of murder.

9th Instruction. More especially if they entertain reasonable doubts of the malicious intention with which the act was done, that doubt must weigh in favor of the prisoners, and the jury must acquit them.

13th Instruction. "One who is indicted for murder cannot be convicted of manslaughter; or if, on such indictment, the offense proved is involuntary manslaughter, the defendants should be acquitted;" all of which 2d, 6th, 7th, 9th and 13th instructions were refused by the court; and the prisoners excepted. It appeared by the record fully proved that the prisoners, at the time of the act charged, were both drunk.

On the part of the state, the court charged as follows: "That drunkenness is no excuse for crime, and that, in this respect, there is no difference between the common law and the law of this state; that although the master has the right to chastise his slave, yet he is responsible for the proper and rational exercise of that right; and if he exceeds the bounds of moderation, and punish in a manner which evinces a cruel and depraved mind, regardless of human life, and death results from such cruel, reckless and immoderate punishment, that is murder; that if there be no other evidence of insanity in the accused but that kind of disorder of mind which is common to all men under the influence of ardent spirits, it is not such insanity as will excuse the commission of crime; that if the death of the negro was the immediate and necessary result of the means employed by the accused, they are, in law, presumed to have intended his death; that the statute of this state has not altered the common law in respect to drunkenness and insanity; that, under the indictment, it is competent to the jury to find the accused guilty of manslaughter." To which the prisoners also filed their exceptions, and now prosecute this writ of error.

The prisoners assigned the following errors:

1. The circuit court erred in giving the order to James Sommers to summon *tales* jurors to be passed in chief as jurors, and in discharging and prohibiting the sheriff from performing that duty, as set forth in the first bill of exceptions.

2. The court erred in refusing to give the second instruction asked by the prisoners.

3. It erred in refusing the sixth instruction, so asked.

4. It erred in refusing the seventh instruction, so asked.

5. It erred in refusing the ninth instruction, so asked.

6. It erred in refusing the thirteenth instruction, so asked.

7. It erred in refusing to grant a new trial.

8. It erred in overruling the reasons assigned in arrest of judgment.

9. It erred in granting the instructions asked by the state, as set out in the third bill of exceptions.

10. The record does not show that the prisoners were put to the bar of the court pending trial, or at the rendition of the verdict, or at the time sentence was pronounced.

11. The sentence is uncertain in not showing any day at and from which the punishment should commence.

12. The record does not show in the caption that the court was held in the place designated by law.

13. The day and year in which the court was held, and the indictment found, is in figures; and the whole caption, in relation to the empanelling of the jury and the finding of the indictment, is in the past tense.

Foote & Swann for the plaintiffs in error.

The sheriff cannot be removed from office unless in cases specified in the constitution and laws. Const., art. 4, sec. 28; art. 5, sec. 19.

The persons summoned and objected to by the court were not absolutely disqualified by law to serve as jurors, so as to evince gross ignorance on the part of the sheriff. Rev. Code, 136, sec. 138. 1 How., 174 establishes the doctrine that all persons are qualified, in this regard, not specially excluded by the statute. If the sheriff was disqualified to act, there being no coroner, a justice of the peace should have been summoned for the occasion. How. & Hutch., 304, sec. 46. If the sheriff was incompetent, so was Sommers his deputy.

The prisoners had a right to that trial with all the forms of law, and administered by the appointed officers. How. & Hutch., 690, tit. 1, sec. 1. The statute requires the sheriff to summon talesmen. Acts 1833, p. 412.

3d Assignment. " Law of Slavery," 244.

5th Assignment. How. & Hutch., 722; 4 How., 168.

7th Assignment.   1 Russ. on C., 421, 428; Addison's Rep., 257.

8th Assignment.   1 Chitty's Crim. Law, 551.

10th Assignment.   How. & Hutch., tit. 2, p. 690, sec. 1, as to first ground; as to second, 2 Hale's P. C., ch. 23, 167; 4 Black. Com. App.; 4 Hawk. P. C., 76; 2 Keble, 471.

12th Assignment.   2 Hale's P. C., 293; 18 Johns., 212. Prisoner waives no right.   Lofft, 400; 1 Chitty's Cr. Law, 799, 712; 7 Cow., 525; 1 Wend., 91; 2 Ala. Rep., State v. Hughes.

For the following errors, which go to the foundation of the indictment, the prisoners ought to be discharged: It does not show in the caption that the court was held at the place designated by law. 2 Hawk. P. C., 350, sect. 128; Acts, 1836, p. 399; Acts, 1838, pp. 95, 96, sec. 2; also, Carpenter's case, 4 Howard.

2d. The day and year when the court was held and the indictment found are stated in figures; and the whole caption in relation to the empanelling of the jury and the finding of the indictment is in the past tense. This is not allowable. 2 Hale's P. C., 170; 2 Hawk, P. C. 360, sec. 127; Starkie's Cr. Pl., 269.

THACHER, J.:

This was an indictment preferred in the circuit court of Smith county against the plaintiffs in error for the murder of a slave, the property of the plaintiffs in error, Kelly, which, upon trial, resulted in a verdict of manslaughter in the first degree.

We shall proceed to notice such points made by the plaintiffs in error, which we deem to be at all in doubt.

The first objection insisted upon is, that the caption of the indictment does not show that the court was held in the place designated by law. It shows that the circuit court, at which the indictment was found, was held for the county of Smith, and at the court-house in the town of Raleigh. The town of Raleigh in Smith county was incorporated by act of the legislature, 1838, which is sufficient to authorize this court to take notice of it as a place within that county. 9 Yerg. R., 381, Hite v. State. By the act of 1836, the county site for the public buildings of Smith county was located in what is now a portion of the town of Raleigh. We think, therefore, the description in the caption is made with reasonable certainty, and as much so as can be required to designate the place where the court was held.

It is objected to the validity of the indictment, that numerical figures are used in it to express numbers and dates. The rule in England restraining the expression of numbers by figures was not a regulation of the common law, but made by a statute which has since been repealed. There must be certainty in an indictment, in order to furnish a bar to another prosecution for the same offense. But figures are a part of the English language, and are admissible in indictments. 3 Vermont R., 431, State v. Hodgden. If, however, the figures are illegible, the indictment is bad for uncertainty.

The objection that the court below erred in dismissing the sheriff from the duty of summoning *tales* jurors, we think is ineffectual. Any such act or order was void, and it is enough that the record shows the jurors to have been summoned by the deputy sheriff, which in the eye of the law is the act of the sheriff himself.

Several points have been urged growing out of the refusal of the court below to charge the jury as requested by the prisoner's counsel.

1st. The court below declined to charge the jury as follows: "There being no system of domestic slavery known to the common law of England, the relation of master and slave known in this state, as well as that between slave and overseer, not having existed in England, there is nothing in the common law on the subject of murder that has strict and complete application to a case of killing, as arising from the chastisement of a slave by his master or overseer, or both." This instruction, we think, was properly refused. The system of slavery, as controlled by the laws of this state, is peculiar, and differs in some respects from the system in other states of the Union. It is unlike the system as it existed among the Jews, the Greeks, the Romans, and differs materially from the villanage of ancient England.

Among the Jews the death of the slave by whipping, under the hand of the master, was merely punishable by a fine. Exodus xxi. 20, 22. Among the Greeks, the young Spartans were occasionally compelled to kill all the Helots they could meet, in order to prevent their great increase. Plutarch's Life of Lycurgus. Among the Romans there was an uncontrolled power by the owner over the life of his slave. Just. Inst. B. 1 tit. 3, § 3. In ancient England the life and limb of the slave were protected against his master, because, as Lord Coke says, 127 a, he was subject to the king,—"*Vita et membra sunt in manu regis.*" Yet in several other respects, his condition did not at all resemble the condition of the slave here.   But in this state, the killing of the slave by the master, feloniously, is murder. Walker, R. 83, State v. Jones.   By the statute H. & H., 162, § 28, the master, or any other person entitled to the service of the slave, shall not inflict upon such slave cruel or unusual punishment, under the penalty, upon conviction thereof, of a fine of five· hundred dollars.

In this state the master is therefore, under the above circumstances, liable to an indictment for a battery committed upon his slave.   In the absence of similar legislation, it has been elsewhere otherwise decided. 2 Dev. R. 263 ; State v. Mann ; 5 Raud. R. 678 ; Commonwealth v. Turner.   But anywhere in this country the attempt to take the slave's life by the master, or any other person, feloniously, may rightfully be resisted by him. 1 Dev. & Batt. R. 171, State v. Will.   Now, by the common law of England, masters were allowed to punish their servants with moderation. 1 Hale's P. C. 454.   What was moderation at common law, was a question of fact for a jury who might be masters ; and here, what is a cruel and unusual punishment, is likewise, in all cases, a question of fact for a jury who most generally are slave owners.   It is not contended that a greater degree of punishment may not be inflicted here by the master upon his slave than by the master upon the servant at common law, because such here may be usual from necessity, but the same general principle of law holds in both cases, so that the court did not err in refusing the instruction.

2d. The court below declined to charge the jury as follows : " In determining whether the act of killing was, or was not murder, if the jury find, from the evidence, that the defendants were in a state of serious intoxication, they are entitled to regard this fact as elucidatory of the point of intention, as evidence, more or less strong, according to their view of the real circumstances of the case, as proof of the absence of that premeditated design, required by our statute in its first description of murder, as an indispensable ingredient of murder." As, in this case, the finding of the jury was manslaughter, no injury accrued to the prisoners from the denial of the charge by the court. It is true that our statute, H. & H., 722, § 2, has enacted, that no person can be punished for an offense committed in a state of insanity; but, in doing so, it has done no more, as all writers on criminal law show, than to re-enact the common law. It is to be noticed, that the instruction under review has reference only to a single instance of intoxication, and has no reference to well-defined and unmistakable insanity, produced by a long-continued or excessive use of intoxicating stimulants. Legal writers, from the earliest times to the present, agree, that mere drunkenness is no extenuation or excuse for crime in the view of the law. "He who is guilty of any crime whatever, through drunkenness, shall be punished for it, as much as if he had been sober." 1 Hawk. P. C., 3. "A drunkard," says Lord Coke, "is *voluntarius dæmon*, and hath no privilege thereby." Judge Story, commenting on the same subject, says: "If persons wilfully deprive themselves of reason, they ought not to be excused one crime by the voluntary perpetration of another." In this connection, it is insisted by counsel that, as our statute, in one of its definitions of murder, declares, that it must be perpetrated from "a premeditated design to effect the death of the person killed, or some other person," and as intoxication "steals away the brain," such is a circumstance to infer the want or absence of a premeditated design to commit a felonious act. The fact of the party being intoxicated has, indeed, been holden to be a circumstance, proper to be taken into consideration, where the sole question is, whether an act was premeditated, or done only with sudden heat and impulse. The same may as truly be said of the passion of anger, or any other excitement arising from sudden provocation or peculiar circumstances. But how slight that consideration should be in the instance of intoxication, is readily conceived from the as equally just presumption, that the design to commit a crime may have previously existed or been contemplated, and the intoxication have been employed "to screw the courage to the sticking place." Hence it is that the law discriminates between the delusion of intoxication, and the insanity which it may ultimately produce. For, if the mere fit of drunkenness is always to be held as an excuse for crime, there is at once established a complete emancipation from criminal justice. And, generally, to sustain a defense on the ground of insanity, a comparison of the best authorities concludes, that it must be clearly proved that, at the time of committing the act, the party accused was laboring under such a defect of reason, from disease of the mind, as not to know the nature and quality of the act he was doing, or, if he did understand them, that he did not know he was doing what was wrong.

In looking through the record, we observe, that in the interval, after the arraignment and before the trial, two motions were made in behalf of the State, and in the absence of the prisoners. These were motions to quash the special *venire facias*, and for an *alias venire facias*, and they were overruled by the court. These proceedings wrought no injury to the defendants, as they did not preclude them from preferring similar motions at the trial, had they so desired, nor does it appear, but that the two motions were overruled on account of the absence of the prisoners.

But it does not appear in the record that the prisoners were personally in court at the time of pronouncing the sentence. The presence of the prisoners is considered absolutely necessary, both in England and in this country, in all cases where judgment of corporal punishment is to be pronounced. 1 Chit. C. L., 695; 12 Wend., 344; 7 Cowen, 525.

Finally; the sentence or judgment of the court below is defective, in not setting forth the time from whence the commencement of the imprisonment shall date. This is generally from the day of the sentence.

For the two errors just pointed out, the judgment of the court below is reversed, without disturbing the verdict, and the cause remanded, with directions to the court below to pronounce its judgment in accordance herewith, having first duly required of the defendants whether they have anything further to urge why its judgment should not then be pronounced.

VAUGHAN *v.* THE STATE, 3 Smedes & Marshall, 553.

SHOOTING WITH INTENT TO KILL AND MURDER.

When the bill of exceptions purports to contain all the evidence adduced on the trial, and is so certified by the judge of the court below, this court will presume it to be true.

On the trial of persons indicted for criminal offenses, the prosecution must prove the offense to have been committed in the county as charged in the indictment, to bring it within the jurisdiction of the court.

Where the indictment charges a shooting with a felonious intent, it must be proved on the trial that the gun was so loaded as to be capable of doing the mischief alleged to be intended.

Error to the circuit court of Lowndes county.

The defendant was indicted in the circuit court of Lowndes county for shooting with intent to kill and murder one Henry R. Owen. The weapon alleged to have been used was a shotgun, loaded with gun powder and divers leaden shot. The plea was " not guilty." The evidence is substantially stated in the opinion of the court. The verdict was " guilty," and a motion was made in arrest of judgment, which was overruled by the court.

Wm. Yerger for the plaintiff in error.

The record presents four distinct grounds for reversal.

1. No prosecutor was marked on the bill of indictment. This is required by statute.   How. & Hutch., 669 ; 3 How. Rep., 27.

2. The record does not show that the grand jury acted upon and returned as a " true bill " the indictment on which the prisoner was tried and convicted. This is necessary.   The record only shows that a " true bill " for an " assault with intent to kill " was found against the defendant ; while he was tried on an indictment for an " assault with intent to kill and murder," which are very different offenses.   Hite v. The State, 9 Yerger, 198 ; Chappel v. The State, 8 Yerger, 166 ; Chit. Cr. Law., 266.

3d. No *venue* was proved on the trial ; this is essential to conviction.   6 Yerger, 364 ; 1 Chit. Cr. Law., 176.

4. The proof made out on the merits no case of offense against the defendant, and the court erred in refusing a new trial.

THACHER, J. :

This case comes into this court by writ of error to the circuit court of Lowndes county.

It was an indictment under the statute for shooting with intent to kill, and upon trial resulted in a verdict of guilty.

We shall notice two grounds upon which the judgment of the court below must be reversed.

The record does not show that the offense was committed in the county of Lowndes. The bill of exceptions is certified by the court below to contain all the evidence adduced upon the trial. It is to that alone, therefore, that we can look for the evidence. The bill of exceptions contains nothing that sufficiently meets the requirements of the law, as proof of the *venue*. It is scarcely necessary to add, that the offense must be proved to have been committed in the county, as charged in the indictment, in order to bring it within the jurisdiction of the court.

Again, from the evidence, as detailed in the bill of exceptions serious doubts arise in our minds that the defendant below entertained felonious intentions at the time of the alleged assault. A dispute had existed between the defendant below and his neighbors about the right of the latter to use a part of his lands as a highway for travel. Upon the day mentioned in the indictment, certain boys, returning from school, undertook this road, not without some design, as they themselves confess, to annoy the defendant below. They were pursued by the defendant, who, when at the distance of sixty yards from one of the boys, who was then getting over a fence, discharged his gun. The boy against whom the gun is alleged to have been discharged, was uninjured, and no marks of shot could be discovered in the immediate neighborhood of the place where he was at the time. Subsequently, marks of shot were found in some bushes, and traced to a sapling in a somewhat different direction from that which the boy had occupied, and were discovered to be small bird shot. There was other testimony that went to prove that the bird shot were most probably the contents of the gun which was discharged. If they were not so, there is no evidence that the gun contained anything more than a charge of powder. It has been held, in cases decided under statutes similar to our own, that it must appear that the firearms were loaded, so as to be capable of doing the mischief intended. If loaded with powder and wadding only, but if fired so near an individual and in such a direction that it would probably kill him, it would come within the statute.   But it would be absurd to say that the discharging a gun, even loaded with ball, at so great a distance as could not possibly effect injury to the person against whom it was directed, evinced an intention to kill; and the same may be said of anything else wherewith the gun may be loaded.   There was evidence before the jury of experiments having been made with the gun used by the defendant, that went to show that at the same distance at which he stood from the boy when the gun was discharged, and with a charge of the same kind of bird shot, the gun was incapable of taking life.   Now, as a man's motives and intentions are to be inferred from the means which he uses, and the acts which he does, we are inclined to the belief that no serious damage was intended by the defendant, but that his object was rather to alarm than to injure.

The judgment of the court below must be reversed, and a new trial awarded by the circuit court of Lowndes county.

THE STATE v. ANDERSON, 3 Smedes & Marshall, 751.

LARCENY.

In criminal prosecutions, after the verdict of a jury, and a judgment of acquittal, neither a new trial nor a writ of error can be granted to the state.

Application for a writ of error to the circuit court of Hinds county, made to this court by the district attorney for the seventh judicial district, in a criminal prosecution, wherein the jury found the defendant " not guilty."

The petition for the writ submitted by the district attorney, stated that at the June term, 1843, of the Hinds circuit court, an indictment was found by the grand jury against the defendant, Anderson, for stealing, etc., upon the testimony of one Theodore Younger, whose name was marked on the indictment as prosecutor.   That at the March term, 1844, of the court, said cause came on to be tried, the defendant having plead " not guilty " to the indictment.   That said Younger then stated on oath to the court that he was not prosecutor in said case, and that he had never authorized his name to be marked on the indictment as such prosecutor, and that thereupon the defendant by his counsel moved the court to quash said indictment for want of a prosecutor, and to discharge him from custody, which motions were sustained by the court.

Thacher, J. :

This is an application made by the district attorney of the 7th judicial district, for a writ of error in behalf of the state, in a state prosecution.

Our statutes do not expressly grant the state a writ of error in criminal prosecutions, after a verdict of a jury and judgment of acquittal, nor has such been the practice in this state. Any such practice would seem to contravene that provision of the constitution, art. 1, § 13, which provides that " No person shall for the same offense be twice put in jeopardy of life or limb." Upon the plea of " not guilty," the accused puts himself upon the country for his deliverance, and when so found by a jury, it must be considered to be final. No new trial can be granted by our laws, after such a result, which is the only judgment which could be made upon a writ of error. The adoption of the practice of permitting the state writs of error in criminal prosecutions, would work a vexatious hardship that is repugnant to the principles of criminal justice. 6 Yerger, 360 ; The State v. Solomons. Besides, the statute, H. & H., 725, § 20, which provided that when a defendant shall have been acquitted on trial, on the merits and facts, he may plead such an acquittal in bar of any subsequent accusation of the same offense, taken in connection with another provision of the same statute, H. & H., 725, § 19, which provides that when a defendant shall have been acquitted of a criminal charge upon trial, on the ground of a variance between the indictment and the proof, or upon an exception to the form or substance of the indictment, he may be tried and convicted upon a subsequent indictment for the same offense, affords, not only the defendant a complete protection from the vexation of a writ of error in favor of the state, but also gives the state an ample remedy by re-indictment, when the defendant escapes justice by any informality of the proceedings, and without a trial upon the merits of the case.

The application is therefore overruled.

PETER, A SLAVE, v. THE STATE, 4 Smedes & Marshall, 31.

MURDER.

Where a justice of the peace, upon a preliminary examination of the accused before him, took down in writing, his confessions made at the time, it is error to permit him, upon the final trial of the accused, to testify from his recollection, in relation to such confessions ; the production of such written statements, being unaccounted for.[1]

The general rule of law is, that confessions when made under the influence of a sufficient threat, or of a sufficient promise, are not admissible as evidence. Subsequent confessions, however, are admissible, if made under such circumstances as create a reasonable presumption that the threat or promise had ceased to have any influence upon the mind of the accused.[2]

The presumption of law is, that the influence of a threat or promise, once made, continues to operate ; this presumption may be rebutted by other proofs, showing that it had ceased to operate.[3]

Where a slave, who had been charged with crime, and was threatened by a party armed with guns, that if he did not confess he would be hanged, did therefore confess his guilt ; and shortly afterwards, was taken before a magistrate, accompanied by some of these same persons, and was interrogated by the magistrate as to his guilt, without being previously cautioned by the magistrate of the effect of his replies, and he again made confessions of his guilt, held, that the last confessions of the accused were not properly admissible as evidence against him.

Error to the circuit court of Franklin county.

Peter, the slave of James Harrington, was indicted at the April term, 1837, for the murder of Samuel Harvey. The case upon change of venue was tried at the Lawrence circuit court, and a mistrial resulted. The presiding judge at a subsequent term, having been of counsel in the case, the venue was again changed to Copiah county. The case not having been transferred, at a subsequent term, by consent of parties, a member of the bar presided. The jury on this trial found the accused guilty, a motion for a new trial was overruled and sentence of death pronounced. The cause was removed to the High court, and judgment was reversed and cause remanded. See 6th How. 326. Again the venue was changed to Lawrence county, where another trial was had, and the prisoner again convicted.

[1] State v. Parish, Bush. (N. C.) R., 289; Archbold Cr. Pr. and Pl., 427, notes.

[2] State v. Carr, 37 Vermont, 191 ; State v. Hash, 72 La. Ann., 895 ; 2 Russ. on Cr. 824, 835; State v. Roberts, 1 Dev. 259; Wharton Am. Cr. Law, 696 ; Archbold Cr. Pr. and Pl., 416, 417, notes ; ib. 478; Rex v. Sexton, 6 Peters, 88 ; Commonwealth v. Knapp, 10 Pick., 477 ; Milligan & Welshman's case, 6 City Hall Recorder, 69, 77, 78.

[3] Commonwealth v. Knapp, 10 Pick., 477 ; State v. Roberts, 1 Dev., 259 ; State v. Gould, 5 Halstead, 163 ; Commonwealth v. Harmon, 4 Barr, 296 ; Simon v. State, 37 Miss., 288 ; Deathridge v. State, 1 Smedes, 75 ; 2 Russ. on Crimes, 882.

The evidence adduced at this trial was as follows : John P. Stewart, testified that he was an examining justice of the peace, when the prisoner, shortly after his arrest and before his commitment, was brought before him ; when the prisoner confessed that he and another negro, named Tom, agreed to kill the overseer for Tom's master ; that the deceased, with a gun on his shoulder, passed through the woods where he and Tom were, when Tom killed him, by beating him to death with his own gun ; he, the prisoner, not assisting, but standing by, ready to assist if it had been necessary ; that it was not necessary, Tom killing the deceased without difficulty. That he, the prisoner, did not know the name of the overseer of Tom's master, or Harvey, the deceased, and did not know that Tom had killed the wrong man, until informed by Tom. The witness further testified, that before interrogating the prisoner he gave him the instruction laid down in the Revised Code of 1822, in the fifth section of an act with reference to justices of the peace ; and informed him that he had a right to ask any question he might wish, but gave him no other charge or caution ; that these confessions were taken down by him in writing at the time.

Witness further testified that the slave was brought before him by several persons who remained and were present during his examination of the prisoner ; that these persons were, some of them, armed with guns, and had, so armed, conveyed the prisoner from his master's place, where he had been arrested, to the magistrate, and that they formed part of a party who had gone to the master of the slave, had arrested the slave, and had in the prisoner's presence made preparations to hang him, if he did not confess ; at which time and place when so threatened and surrounded, the prisoner had confessed to the same effect that he had confessed before the magistrate.

The prisoner's counsel moved to exclude this evidence, but the motion was overruled and exceptions taken, and the prisoner was again sentenced to be hung ; whereupon this writ of error was sued out.

The plaintiff in error assigned the following causes of error.

1. The court erred in permitting parol testimony of the prisoner's confessions to go to the jury, as the said confessions were

taken down in writing by the magistrate to whom they were made.

2. The court erred in admitting the confessions of the prisoner under the circumstances.

H. Cassidy for plaintiff in error.

Both the errors complained of are so contrary to the long established and indisputable principles of law, that a simple reference to authorities will be sufficient. The confessions were taken down in writing, and without showing a loss of the writings, parol testimony was inadmissible to prove their contents; the rule being that the best evidence the case admits of shall be adduced. 2 Starkie on Ev., 28, admissions; 1 Hale, 284; 1 Phillip's Ev., 113; 2 Cowen & Hill Notes, 243, note 213.

With regard to the second error, the authorities are equally clear. The confessions before the magistrate ought not to have been admitted without its clearly appearing that the magistrate had given those cautions required to put the prisoner on his guard relative to the legal consequences that might result from his confessions. No confessions can be considered voluntary, so long as any influence of hope, or fear of consequences, operates on the prisoner's mind. Roscoe's Crim. Ev., 37. The law is that the evidence must be very strong and clear of an explicit warning by a magistrate not to rely on any expected favor, and that it ought most clearly to appear that the prisoner understood such warning, before his confessions can be given in evidence. Roscoe's Crim Evi., 41. There should be strong evidence to show that the impressions of hope or fear, under which the first confessions had been made, were afterwards removed, before the second confessions can be received. Roscoe's Crim. Ev., 42, 43; 1 Phillip's Ev., 112. The facts of this case are very similar to those in the case of Serpentine v. The State, in relation to the confessions made. 1 Howard, 259, 260.

J. D. Freeman, attorney general.

THACHER, J.:

This was an indictment for murder upon the trial of which a verdict of guilty was found by the jury.

It is admitted by the attorney general that the court below

erred in permitting a justice of the peace upon the trial, to tes
tify from his recollection of the confessions of the accused upon
the preliminary examination had before him, when it also ap
peared in evidence that the same justice of the peace had taken
that confession in writing, and there was no evidence of the los
of that confession so taken in evidence, and no other satisfactory
legal reasons given for its non-production. This court is in
clined to take a similar view of the law upon this point.

This court, nevertheless, is desired, in view of a new trial, to
express its opinion upon another ground insisted upon as error
in the trial below.

It appears, from the bill of exceptions in the record, that
shortly after the arrest of the prisoner, and before any commitment had taken place, he was brought before the justice of the
peace, whose testimony is above referred to, for examination on
a charge of murder. In his testimony, the justice of the peace
says, that upon the accused being brought before him, he informed him of his privilege to ask any questions he might think
proper, but that he gave him no further caution or charge, as he
recollected. He then proceeded to take the information of the
accused in writing. It likewise appears from the bill of exceptions, that a number of persons had collected at the house of the
owner of the accused, who, in the presence of the accused,
threatened him with death by hanging, by which means confessions had been extorted from him; and that some of those persons, armed with guns, were among those who escorted the
accused to the office of the aforesaid justice of the peace, and
were present there during his examination.

The general rule of law upon the subject of confessions, is,
that when made under the influence of a sufficient threat, or a
sufficient promise, they are inadmissible as evidence. So it has
been the common practice, when a prisoner has been once induced to confess upon a promise or a threat, to reject any subsequent confession of the same or like facts, though at a subsequent
time. East's P. C., 2, 658. But it has been further and frequently held, that notwithstanding such threat or promise may
have been used, the confession is admissible if made under such
circumstances as to create a reasonable presumption that the

threat or promise had no influence, or had ceased to have any influence upon the mind of the party. Roscoe's C. E., 30. In this case, the original confession of the accused made to the persons collected at the house of his owner, as we gather them from the whole record, had, in law, an effect against himself though perhaps not so designed by him. This was ruled out of the evidence in the court below, as having been improperly obtained.

It remains, then, to inquire whether the confession made before the justice of the peace was induced by the original threats for if otherwise induced, and from voluntary information, it was good. Moore v. The Commonwealth, 2 Leigh, 701. The presumption is, that the influence of the threats continues, and such presumption must be overcome. State v. Guild, 5 Halst., 163. But such presumption may be removed by the length of time intervening between the threats and the examination, from proper warning of the consequences of such confession, or from any other circumstances that might reasonably be considered sufficient to dispel the fears induced by the threats. Ib. Was, then, the second confession, in this instance, made under the same influence that produced the first? The lapse of time between the two confessions would seem not to have been great, since the bill of exceptions informs us that the prisoner was brought before the justice of the peace "shortly after his arrest." The effect of time in effacing the influence upon the mind, cannot fairly be supposed to have operated upon the accused. Next, when brought before the justice of the peace, it appears that no caution was given to the accused, respecting the effect of his confessions, and that thus unwarned, he proceeded to detail statements that fatally criminated himself. Upon this point, it is laid down in East's P. C. 2, 658, quoting the opinion of Buller, J., that there must be very clear and strong evidence of explicit warning by the magistrate of the consequences of confession, after the fact is known, of the existence of either the influence of hope or fear superinducing confession; and it should likewise be manifest that the prisoner understood such warning, before his subsequent confession could be given in evidence. Lastly, there was nothing in the circumstances attending the subsequent confession that would have had the effect to dispel the fears previously created in the mind of the accused. Being a slave, he must be presumed to have been ignorant of the protection from sudden violence, which the presence of the justice of the peace afforded him, and he saw himself surrounded by some of those before whom he had recently made a confession. As we gather from the whole record, he then reiterated his previous confession. This court has before, under similar circumstances, refused to acknowledge such confessions as evidence. Serpentine v. The State, 1 H., 256. It is true, that by adopting this rule, the truth may sometimes be rejected; but it affects a greater object in guarding against the possibility of an innocent person being convicted, who, from weakness, has been seduced to accuse himself, in hopes of obtaining thereby more favor, or from fear of meeting with immediate or worse punishment. We conclude that, as the facts are disclosed in the record, the confession was improperly admitted in evidence.

The judgment of the court below is reversed, and a *venire de novo* must be awarded by the circuit court of Lawrence county.

RANDALL *v.* THE STATE, 4 Smedes & Marshall, 349.

LARCENY OF A SLAVE.

If one lose his goods and another find them and convert them to his own use, not knowing the owner, it is not larceny; but if the finder knew the owner, or had the means of knowing him, it would be larceny. [1]

Under the laws of this state, a negro *prima facie* is presumed to be a slave; and if he be found in the possession of one other than his owner, under suspicious circumstances, it will be sufficient to put such person upon the explanation of the circumstance of his possession. And it is the duty of every citizen who finds a slave at large, without a permit from his owner, to deliver him to the nearest justice of the peace for commitment.

[1] State of Pennsylvania v. Myers, Addison, 320; State v. Brewster, 7 Vermont, 118; State v. Jones, Dev. & Bat., 544; Engleman v. State, 2 Carter, 91; State v. Williams, 9 Iredell, 140; State v. Weston, 9 Con., 527; State v. Williams, 2 Jones, 194; State v. Shaw, 4 Jones, 440; State v. Clark, 4 Strobh., 311; Hughes v. State, 8 Humph., 75; Archbold Cr. Pr. & Pl., 397 *et seq.*; Tyler v. People, Breeze, 227; State v. Roper, 3 Dev., 473; State v. Ferguson, 2 McMullen, 502; Lane v. People, 9 Gilman, 305; Coon v. State, 13 S. & M., 246; People v. Swann, 1 Parker, 9; Wharton Am. Cr. Law, 1780, 1792-3-4, 1800; People v. Cogdell, 1 Hill, 94; State v. Pratt, 20 Iowa, 267; Rex. v. Moore, L. & C., C. C. 1; 8 Cox, C. C., 416; State v. Jenkins, 2 Tyler, 379; Lane v. People, 5 Gilman. 305.

Randall was indicted for stealing the slave of Bridges. It was proved that the slave ran away, and was absent five months, when he was found in the woods; that during this absence, Randall was seen traveling along the road with a negro very much resembling the slave of Bridges, and whom the witness believed to be the slave of Bridges, though he was not sure. Witness did not know the slave, and had only seen him once. Randall, when seen with the slave, was going in the direction of Bridges's residence. *Held* that the evidence was not sufficient to warrant a verdict of guilty, nor to put the defendant on proof in explanation, and that a new trial should have been granted.

Error to the circuit court of Jasper county.

The prisoner was indicted at the November term, 1844, of the circuit court of Jasper county, for stealing a negro, Sam, slave of William Bridges. Plea, "not guilty." On the trial, Wm. Bridges testified, on the part of the state, that Sam, the person named in the indictment, is his slave; that he ran away from his overseer in February or March, 1844, in the county of Jasper, and remained absent about five months, when he was caught in the woods up in a tree. Martin Walker testified, on the part of the state, that in June, 1844, he met the defendant in the public road about 9 o'clock in the morning, a few miles on the other side of Raleigh, in Smith county, and spoke to him. There was a negro with the defendant at the time, riding a mule and carrying a gun in his hand, the defendant being on foot. The negro passed on without stopping. From general appearance, witness thought Sam to be the same negro, but he was not certain. Believed he had on black or blue pantaloons, but was not sure; could not say whether he had on a dress or frock coat, nor the color of it. The negro was traveling openly in the public highway in the direction of Bridges's residence, some twenty-seven miles distant. Never saw the negro before nor afterwards, but once, until he saw him in court. Another witness for the state testified that, in June, 1844, defendant came to his house after night, and brought with him a negro, but what negro he did not know, as he stood out in the lane while the defendant came into the house; and that, when they started away, the negro mounted a mule. Did not see the negro have a gun; did not know him, nor could he say defendant ever had Sam in his possession. Witness lives in Jasper county, about twenty-seven miles from Mrs. Campbell's, and about fifteen from Mr. Bridges's, the owner of Sam. This was all the evidence, and upon it the jury returned a verdict of guilty.   A motion for a new trial was overruled, and the case is here upon writ of error.

Marshall and McDougald for plaintiff in error.

THACHER, J. :

This was an indictment in Jasper county circuit court for the larceny of a slave.

The plaintiff here claimed as error that the court below refused a new trial, though the evidence was insufficient to warrant a conviction by the jury.

It is insisted that there is no evidence of the *corpus delicti.* The testimony of the owner of the slave charged to have been stolen, shows that the slave had run away from his possession, and after having been absent several months, was discovered and captured by him in the woods.

It is a settled principle of law, that if one lose his goods and another find them, and convert them to his own use, not knowing the owner, this is no larceny.   But if the latter knew the owner, or had the means of knowing him, it would be larceny.   2 Leach, 952 ; 17 Wend., 460.   The laws of this state presume a negro *prima facie* to be a slave, and if a slave be found in the possession of one other than his owner, and under suspicious circumstances, it will be sufficient evidence to compel that person to explain the circumstances of his possession.   It is the duty of every good citizen who finds a slave at large, without a permit from his owner, etc., to deliver him to the nearest justice of the peace for commitment.   A runaway slave, therefore, may be a subject of larceny.

In this case, however, neither of the two witnesses who testify to the fact of seeing the plaintiff in error in company with a negro at a period during the absence of the runaway abovementioned, speak positively as to the identity of that negro with the slave charged to have been stolen ; and it also appeared that the accused, when thus seen, was traveling in the direction of the house of the owner of the slave.   All the circumstances of the case, as described in the bill of exceptions, fail to make out a sufficient case for the state to warrant a conviction, or, indeed, to put the accused upon proof in explanation.

Our statute properly affixes an exemplary punishment to the offense of slave stealing; it may extend to the confinement of the convicted in the penitentiary for the term of his life, and it therefore especially should remind us to require proof, to a reasonable certainty, that the party accused has been guilty of the offense charged.

The judgment of the court below is reversed, and a *venire de novo* awarded.

GOODWIN *v.* THE STATE, 4 Smedes and Marshall, 520.

MURDER.

The record showed the following entry: "On the 3d day of April, 1844, the following entry was made on the minutes of the court, to wit: The grand jurors returned into court an indictment against William S. Goodwin, endorsed thereon a 'true bill;' Wm. M. C. Mirus, foreman of the grand jury, and returned to consider of further presentment. Said indictment is in the words and figures following, to wit:" Held, that these words show, with sufficient certainty, that an indictment was returned into court by the grand jury, and that the accused was indicted in due form.

Where the minutes of the court omit to state the character of the offense charged in the indictment, such omission forms no ground of error, if it be supplied by the other parts of the record. The rule is well settled that what is uncertain in any part of the record may be explained and rendered certain by reference to another part which is certain.

Where, it being in evidence that the deceased came to his death by means of the discharge, by the accused, of a shot gun loaded with duck shot, the court was asked to charge the jury, "That if they believed, from the evidence, that the deceased came to his death by means of the shot aforesaid, and not by one leaden bullet discharged from said shot gun, as alleged in the bill of indictment, they must find for the accused, and the court refused to give said charge, but did charge the jury, "That the said proof was sufficient to sustain the said bill as alleged in said indictment," the court properly refused to give said charge, and was clearly justified in the one which was given, as it referred solely to the proofs of the contents of the shot gun, and was not intended as a charge generally upon the evidence.

Error to the circuit court of Lowndes county.

The plaintiff in error was indicted by the grand jury of Lowndes county, at the April term, 1844, for the murder of Edmund N. Abbott. On the 14th February, 1844, a *venire facias* was issued by the clerk of the circuit court of Lowndes county, commanding the sheriff to summon, etc., and that on the first day of April term of said court, fourteen of the jurors summoned were drawn by lot and sworn as grand jurors. The record states : "And afterwards, to wit, on the 3d day of April, 1844, the following entry was made upon the minutes of said court, to wit : The grand jurors returned into court an indictment against William S. Goodwin, endorsed thereon a true bill, Wm. M. C. Mirns, foreman of the grand jury, and returned to consider of further presentments. The indictment is set out in full. The prisoner was arraigned and plead not guilty, whereupon a special *venire facias* was issued to the sheriff, commanding him to summon fifty good and lawful men, etc., to serve as jurors on the trial of the prisoner.

The trial came on at the October term 1844. Geo. M. Mullins testified on the part of the state, that he was at home about candle-light, on the evening of the 21st of March, 1844, when he heard the report of two fire-arms ; he opened his door and heard Abbott, the deceased, setting his dogs on some one. He went out, and saw some one get on a horse and go off at a rapid rate, the dogs following him, and a loose horse which ran off at the same time. Went out and saw Abbott, the deceased, lying on the ground, on his face, about fourteen yards from the middle of the road, in an open lot on the north side of the road or street, with his left hand under him, and a revolving pistol, with five or six barrels, lying a little to his right and near his right hand, and two or three barrels of which had been discharged, the others being still loaded. The reports of the fire-arms were not simultaneous, but several seconds apart. Could not say which was the loudest sound, nor could the wife, with whom he immediately after conversed on the subject. The lot where the deceased was found is immediately north of witness's house, on the Tuscaloosa road. Deceased was wounded in the left side, just above the hip, and died in a very short time after witness reached him. On next morning witness found upon the ground a ramrod, and the deceased's whip, lying near together ; nearly opposite to each other to left of deceased, as he was lying when witness found him. Deceased owned a large pack of dogs, twelve or fifteen, and used to run negroes with them ; they were very fierce. From the nature of the wound, deceased could not have gone from the road to the spot where he was lying ; he had time after he was shot. The firing seemed to witness to be over the road from witness's house, and in the lot where deceased was lying. The ramrod was indented on one side as though it had been bruised in the thimble of the gun in coming out. A person, in traveling the road to Swearengen's, on the upper Tuscaloosa road to Columbus, would not have passed through the lot where the deceased was found.

Mrs. Swearengen testified that she was out in her yard, a mile from Columbus, on upper Tuscaloosa road, between sundown and dark, and saw two gentlemen meet,—defendant and deceased. Deceased was going towards Columbus. Defendant meeting him, they conversed sometime together on their horses. She started towards her house, when a negro called to her to look. She turned round, saw the defendant off his horse, and running round and flourishing his arm, and got on his horse and rode by. Witness heard him say, "I'll be God Almighty God damned, if I don't have your life, at the risk of my own." Witness was alarmed and remained in the yard, and soon saw the negro, who had gone towards Columbus with deceased, after Goodwin, the defendant, had left and gone towards Columbus, returning on horseback at full speed, the dogs and a loose horse following him. Witness is rather deaf and could not hear what passed between defendant and deceased; could not hear them talk at all. The dogs neither attempted to bite nor bark at defendant. After defendant rode off towards Columbus, deceased followed slowly with the negro and dogs.

Mrs. Morris,—she was called by the negro to look, and had not observed the deceased and defendant before. Heard defendant say, as he rode off, "I'll be damned if I don't have his life at the risk of my own." Heard no other remarks. Defendant was not addressing any one when he made these remarks. Heard the guns. The first report was loudest. Her attention was directed to the sound. Anticipating, from what Mrs. S. and the girl had told her, that there would be murder, stood in the door fifteen or twenty minutes listening. This was on 21st March, 1844.

Wm. Lester testified that before he heard the report of the guns, defendant came to his father's lot, in a gallop, on the upper Tuscaloosa road, and inquired if he had seen Ned Abbott, the deceased, pass there; and being told that he had not, went on towards Swearengen's. Shortly afterwards he came back in a gallop, and before he reached him, said, " William, William! Sterling, Sterling! have you got a gun?" Witness told him he had a gun, but neither powder nor shot. Defendant then rode towards Wallace's in a gallop; and soon afterwards, witness heard the report of two guns, and saw a negro on horseback, with the dogs and a loose horse following. Witness went to Mr. G. M. Mullin's, and there found the deceased dead. The report of the gun did not appear to come from the road, but from the open lot where deceased was found. Dr. Liscomb was called by the jury of inquest to make a *post mortem* examination. The wound was in the flank, just above the hip bone, a little anterior thereto; the shot ranging at a little elevation towards the back-bone, from the left side; that the clothing was torn, and the wadding of the gun and clothing were forced into the wound. The shot extracted were duck shot. The clothing about the wound were powder burnt. A man might have gone ten steps after receiving such a wound.

Mr. Riddle testified, that he was passing by defendant's house on the evening of the death of deceased; heard him call defendant, though he did not see the latter. Deceased was sitting on his horse at defendant's gate, some one being with him, whom witness took to be a negro. Witness came to town by Major Downing's house, on the Tuscaloosa road; was overtaken by defendant, who, after speaking about some fish witness had, inquired of him if he had seen Ned, or Ned Abbott (deceased.) Defendant was riding fast towards town. Afterwards, when witness got to the edge of the town, he again saw defendant cross the military road in a gallop, going towards Joseph Wallace's. In a few minutes afterwards, witness heard the report of two guns, a few seconds apart, and heard deceased's voice setting on his dogs, and some one riding off towards Lester's, the dogs in pursuit, and horse following. Went to the place whence the gun shot reports came and saw deceased dead. Was about one hundred and fifty yards off when he heard the reports, but could not distinguish between them. C. Frazer confirms the statements of the above witness.

Mr. Wallace testified, that he was with Riddle and Frazer; confirms their statements, and further, that after hearing the defendant coming to his father's gate, with his (witness) gun, defendant called witness, and set the gun down beside the gate. Witness had not used the gun for some time, and did not know that it was loaded. It did not have the ramrod in it then; identified the ramrod spoken of by G. M. Mullin as having been found near the deceased, as the ramrod belonging to his gun, which was a common single-barrel shot gun. Defendant resides two or three miles from town, has a double-barrel shot gun and a pistol which he usually kept at home.

Joseph Wallace testified, that he had loaded the gun some days previous, with middling size shot, (goose or duck shot), and it had not been discharged since. Defendant owned a double-barrel shot gun and one or two pistols. Saw the defendant after the killing of the deceased. Defendant was wounded in the right shoulder with a ball; the ball descended from the shoulder towards the back-bone. Tail of defendant's coat was torn. Eli Abbott is sheriff of Lowndes county. On the 21st March, 1844, appointed deceased special deputy to levy an execution against defendant, endorsed: E. N. Abbott is hereby authorized to levy this *fi. fa.* this 21st March, 1844, E. Abbott, sheriff. [SEAL.] This evidence defendant objected to, but the objection was overruled, and exceptions taken. Witness stated that it is 1150 yards from Mullin's house to Swearengen's; 600 from Lester's to Joseph Wallace's; 400 from Mullin's to Wallace's; had examined the ground where deceased was killed; saw a horse-track across the ditch; that the same negro deceased had in custody when killed, was in custody some twelve months ago, and got away after court. Deceased caught him, and he was afterwards released by the plaintiff in execution. Deceased usually went armed; that he kept dogs to hunt negroes, and white persons, also. He weighed about 145 pounds, and was strong and active. Witness sent deceased to levy on the negro, because the negro knew him, witness, and his other deputies.

Mr. Nell, testified that some twelve months since, defendant took him to his house, told him the negro remained there several days, that he had taken him away from the state, to avoid the execution against him; did not intend to run him off, but only wanted to get a witness who was absent, by whom he could prove the negro was not subject to the execution; that as soon as that witness returned he intended to deliver the negro again to the sheriff.

Mr. Thomas; has hunted with defendant several times, and he always shot left-handed, when he saw him shoot.

Mr. Moore testified, was present when the ball was taken out of defendant's back; when Dr. Winter attempted to probe the wound, the probe not entering readily, defendant said, "let me raise my arm, doctor; it was raised when I was shot."

Doctor Wharton, first witness on the part of the defence, stated that the dogs had pursued the defendant and himself, on one occasion, when they had to get on a fence; the defendant appeared to be agitated; that on the arrival of the deceased, the dogs noticed them no farther. Mr. Leverett and Maxey Hall stated substantially the same thing in relation to themselves.

Mr. Graham, said that on the evening of the killing, and before, one of the dogs caught him by the pantaloons in the street. S. G. Mills also testified to the ferocity of the dogs. Dr. Winter examined the wound on defendant's shoulder, on the evening deceased was killed; the ball entered his right shoulder near the point and ranged back towards the spine. Probed the wound, took out the ball, which, upon deceased's pistol being shown to him, he said was of a size about suited to that. Defendant's arm must have been raised when he received the wound. Dr. Smith saw the wound on defendant, and agreed with Dr. Winter in his description of it.

Miss Wallace, (daughter of Joseph Wallace), testified that on the evening deceased was killed, between sundown and dark, defendant came to her father's house and asked for a gun, and a servant handed him her brother's gun. As he turned off she asked defendant, "what he wanted with it?" He replied, "nothing much; I only want to shoot a dog," and rode off.

The defendant's counsel asked the court to instruct the jury, "that if they believed from the evidence, that the deceased came to his death by means of the shot aforesaid, and not by one leaden bullet discharged from said shot gun, as alleged in said bill of indictment, that they must return a verdict for the prisoner of not guilty as charged in the bill of indictment;" the court refused to give this instruction, but instructed the jury, "that the said proof was sufficient to sustain the said bill, as alleged in the indictment." To which opinion of the court, refusing to give the instruction asked, and in giving the charge which it did, the defendant's counsel excepted, and filed his second bill of exceptions. The verdict was "guilty of manslaughter in the second degree," and the sentence seven years in the penitentiary.

Harris & Harrison, for plaintiff in error.

1. The deceased was not an officer, and all his acts done under color of office was void. How. & Hutch. Dig.. 292, § 6. Ib. 296, § 22. At common law the sheriff had the right to appoint both regular and special deputies, and our statute was intended 1st, to *limit* and define to a certain extent, the powers and duties of the sheriff himself; for at common law, he · was a judge, keeper of the peace, a ministerial officer of the superior courts and the King's bailiff. 1 Black. Com. 343. 2nd. To authorize and empower the deputies to do and perform *all* the several acts and duties injoined upon their principals. Not so in England. 1 Black. Com. 345. 3rd. The common law did not prescribe that the appointment should be in writing, etc., this our statute has done, and declares that, unless it is so done, "all acts and proceedings done under color of office, shall be absolutely void."

It is contended on the part of the prosecution, that deceased was not a deputy sheriff; but was deputed to do a particular act only; and that said section 6, has no application to such a case. But it is insisted that the two sections are not only parts of the same statute, but that the second clause referred to, makes direct mention of the first, and dispenses only with part of its requirements, that the latter clause is a mere limitation of the former one; and that both classes are spoken of as deputy sheriffs, that when it is enacted that "no person who shall be deputed to do a particular act only, shall be required to take the oath directed by the act to be taken by deputy sheriff," it is declaring *in totidem verbis,* that the other directions and requirements of the statute, are to be complied with; that the express exclusion of one by direct terms, is a direct inclusion of the other. See Welsh v. Jamison, 1 How., 160; Montgomery v. Scanland, 2 Yerger, 337.

2nd. The mortal wound is alleged to have been given with a gun loaded with powder and *one leaden bullet.* The proof was, that it was loaded with powder and a *great number of small shot.*

" If it be alleged that the gun was loaded with powder and a leaden bullet, it must be proved to have been loaded with a bullet, otherwise the defendant must be acquitted. Rex v. Hughes, 5 O. & P. 126; Archb. on Indict. 422 (4th Amer. ed., 1840;) see title Murder; Ib. 382, 383; 24 Eng. Com. Law Rep., 241; Rosc. Crim. Ed. 651. As to the necessity of the proofs corresponding strictly with allegations in the indictment, see Rex v. Thompson, 1 Mood. C. C., 139; Archb. on Indictment, 382; Rex v. Kelly, 1 Mood. C. C. 113; Arch. on Indict. 383. See the form in Archbold, 421, 422.

John D. Freeman, attorney general.

Contended that the facts shown by the record clearly proved a regular finding and return into court of the indictment by the grand jury of Lowndes county, against the defendant for murder.

With regard to the venue, several witnesses state, that the offense was committed near Columbus; that deceased was deputy sheriff of Lowndes county, and was in the act of executing a *fi. fa.* on defendant's slave at the time the killing occurred. There is but one Columbus in this state, and the court judicially knew that, that Columbus is the seat of justice of Lowndes county. Kelly v. The State, 3 S. & M., 518. The bill of exceptions does not pretend to give all the evidence in the case, this court will therefore presume that the venue was fully proven.

4th. The point made for the defense, that the deceased was not a deputy sheriff, is not sustained by the facts. The fact clearly appears, that deceased was appointed a special deputy to do a particular act, the appointment being endorsed in the process he was appointed to execute.

5th. There was no error in the refusal of the court to give the charge asked on behalf of the accused, nor in the charge actually given by the court. Arch. Crim. Pl. 332. See also, Gill Ev., 231; 9 Co. 67, a; 2 Hale, 115, 185; 2 Hawk. C. 23, sec. 84.

William Yerger, in reply.

1. The record does not show that the indictment, upon which the defendant was tried, was found by the grand jury. The record of the court should show that the indictment was found by the grand jury. This point has been expressly adjudicated in Tennessee. Chappel v. The State, 8 Yerger, 166.

2. There is no prosecutor marked on the indictment. This court has decided this to be error, for which the judgment must be reversed. Cody v. The State, 1 Howard.

3. The venue is not sufficiently proven. There is no evidence that the offense was committed in Lowndes county.

4. The court erred in permitting the testimony of Eli Abbott in relation to the appointment of deceased as deputy sheriff, to be given to the jury.

5. The evidence did not justify the conviction. It is impossible to say from the evidence, whether the defendant killed in self-defence, or not; it is all vague, indefinite and uncertain.

6. The court erred in charging the jury that the " proof given before them sustained the indictment." It was a charge upon the force of the facts, the weight of the evidence, and an attempt to form for the jury, conclusions which it was their special province to form for themselves.

7. It was error to permit the execution against plaintiff, in favor of Saltonstall, to be read to the jury. Nothing but the judgment should have been read.

THACHER, J.:

This was an indictment for murder, preferred against the plaintiff in error, in the circuit court of Lowndes county, which, upon trial, resulted in a verdict of manslaughter in the second degree.

The first ground of error taken is, that the record does not show that the indictment in this case was found by the grand jury. The record states, that "on the 3d day of April, 1844, the following entry was made upon the minutes of said court, to wit: The grand jurors returned into court an indictment against William S. Goodwin, endorsed thereon a true bill, William M. C. Mirus, foreman of the grand jury, and retired to consider of further presentments. Said indictment is in the words and figures as follows, to wit," etc. These words show that an indictment was returned in court by the grand jury, which shows that the accused had been indicted in due form by the grand jury. This entry is in the usual form, with the omission of the character of the offense charged in the indictment. This is always in general terms, as " for murder, for larceny," etc., and does not further particularize the offense, and is not important. An indictment is no part of the minutes of the court. The clerk, in making up the record, of which the minutes and the indictment both form parts, must necessarily connect them together in the order of their occurrence in the court below. It appears from the record that an indictment, therein recited, was returned into court on the 3d day of April, 1844, against the accused ; the record further states that " on the said 3d day of April the following entry was made upon the minutes of said court, to wit : this day came, as well Henry Gray, Esq., the district attorney, who prosecutes in behalf of the state, as the said William S. Goodwyn, who was led to the bar in the custody of the sheriff of Lowndes county, and being arraigned upon the indictment in this case, upon his arraignment pleads not guilty," etc. ; it also further appears in the record, that on the same day a *venire facias* was ordered to summon jurors to serve on the trial of said William S. Goodwin, indicted for murder. It is a rule well settled that, if there be an uncertainty in any part of a record, it may be explained by any other part of the record. If it really be error in the first entry of the minutes not to state the character of the offense charged in the indictment, the subsequent entries in the minutes, on the same day, in the same case, and in reference to the same indictment, are too explicit to leave any doubt upon the minds of this court upon this point.

The only other technical objection which we deem requires

comment, is that which has reference to the instruction given by the court below to the jury. It was in evidence, that the deceased came to his death by means of a discharge, by the accused, of a shot-gun, loaded with shot, between the size of squirrel-shot and small sized buck-shot, commonly known as duck-shot. Upon this evidence, the court was desired to charge the jury, " that, if they believed from the evidence, that the deceased came to his death by means of the shot aforesaid, and not by one leaden bullet discharged from said shot-gun, as alleged in the bill of indictment, they must find a verdict for the accused." This charge the court refused, but charged the jury " that the said proof was sufficient to sustain the said bill as alleged in the indictment." The charge requested was clearly, properly refused. The instrument by which the death is caused need not necessarily be strictly proved as laid in the indictment, and proof of its having been caused by any other instrument capable of producing death in a similar mode, satisfies the indictment in that respect. The charge given by the court was but the negative of the charge requested. The language of the court, referring to " the said proof," refers solely to the proof of the contents of the shot-gun, and its language, when declaring the said proof " sufficient to sustain the said bill, as alleged in the indictment," refers to the allegation in the indictment of the contents of the shot-gun. It was not, in our view, intended as a charge generally upon the evidence in the case, and from the finding of the jury could not so have been understood by them.

There is nothing in the circumstances attending the commission of the fatal act by the accused, as they are to us presented, that seems to warrant us to interfere with the judgment. The accused parted from the deceased before the event, with a deadly threat against some one, shortly returned to him armed, and an affray ensued, in which he shot the deceased. The evidence shows an inducing cause for excited, but inexcusable feelings of passion in the arrest of his property, in execution by the deceased, in his capacity as deputy sheriff, a threat, and finally an act of violence, that resulted in the death of that officer by the hand of the accused. The chain of evidence links the circumstances so together, that it is impossible for the mind to separate them, or to divert them of the stain of guilt. We are disposed to adopt the more mild interpretation of the jury, which mitigated the offense into a lesser degree of crime than the one charged in the indictment, but we find ourselves, after an anxious investigation of all the facts, unable to behold them in any other light.

The judgment of the circuit court of Lowndes county is therefore affirmed.

OVERAKER *v.* THE STATE, 4 Smedes & Marshall, 738.

SELLING LIQUOR TO SLAVES.

Where a party was indicted in four different cases at the same term of the court, and recognizances given in each case, which were severally forfeited, and the clerk recites in the *scire facias*, the forfeiture as having been taken *in these four cases* without specifying which cases, or their titles, or identifying them in any way; *held* to be erroneous.

Where the sheriff executes a bench warrant, and takes bail, he should so state it, and return the facts in full to the court.

Where the sheriff returns a bench warrant, "executed," and says nothing of any recognizance or bail taken by him, the mere fact that a recognizance is recited in the record, there being nothing but its own recitals to connect it with the case, will not be sufficient to uphold a judgment for a forfeiture upon it.

Error to the circuit court of Jefferson county.

There were four records filed in this court against the same parties; the condition of the records in the several cases is nearly the same, and the opinion delivered in each case is nearly a transcript of the opinion in each of the others. One case only is therefore reported.

The facts are fully stated in the opinion of the court.

The plaintiffs assigned the following errors:

1. That there is no offense against the laws of Mississippi charged against said Overaker, either by presentment or indictment.

2. There is no return of the sheriff showing and identifying any recognizance on which to charge the plaintiffs in error.

3. There is no legal recognizance on which to charge the plaintiffs in error.

4. The judgment of the court is not in conformity with the previous parts of the record and proceedings, but is a departure therefrom, and not justified thereby.

Lea & Kennedy for plaintiffs in error.

1st Error. No offense is charged either by presentment or indictment. 1. December 16th, 1837, is the time stated of the supposed offenses; but this date is long after the term at which the presentment was made; and the supposed offenses were impossible at the date of the accusation. Serpentine v. The State, 2 How. 256. 2. The supposed offenses are not indictable, but are subjects of penalty by civil or *qui tam* proceeding. Rev. Code, 390, Ch. 74. S. 4: 1 Chitty Cr. Law, 162. This is not among the offenses enumerated in chapter 73, and therein referred to the criminal jurisdiction of the courts.

2d Error. No return of the sheriff as to any recognizance. On the *capias* his only return is, "Execution, November 14th 1838," a date, by the way, long subsequent to the date of this pretended recognizance. But if at a proper time the return should show that a recognizance had been taken if true.

3d Error. No legal recognizance. 1. Because no crime or misdemeanor is charged. Rev. Code, 252, 253. 2. Because the *capias* and recognizance purport to be on a charge by indictment for entertaining slaves; but no such charge is otherwise found in the record.

4th Error. Judgment—a *non sequitur* from the record. 1. Because, without an offense charged, possible, and indictable, all the subsequent proceedings are erroneous. 2. Because the subsequent parts of the record are not connected by the sheriff's return with the proceedings. 3. Because the latter and former parts of the record are incongruous in several particulars already cited. As there is no *prima facie* case against the accused, he will expect a final discharge.

Collins, attorney general.

The only point in these cases is the legality of a recognizance taken before the sheriff of the county when he has taken a prisoner on a bench warrant, with directions to take a recognizance from the party: the acknowledgment of the indebtedness to the state is sufficient.

The record shows a presentment by the grand jury of Jefferson county, a return of it into court, a bench warrant executed thereon, and a recognizance entered into by Overaker, with Wilcox as surety. They acknowledge themselves indebted to the state in the penal sum therein specified. This was done before the sheriff. A forfeiture is taken against the parties; *scire facias* issues and is made final.

TURNER, J.:

The record in this case represents in the caption, that an indictment was found by the grand jury of Jefferson county at the June term, 1837, against George Overaker, which is in the words, etc., following, to wit, etc. Then follows a presentment, as of December term, 1837, and not an indictment, charging that the said George Overaker, late of the county of Jefferson, grocer, on the 10th day of December, 1837, did sell and give to certain negro slaves, naming their owners, spirituous liquors, without the permission of their master, etc. The record further states, that thereupon *capias* issued, and the *capias* is copied, requiring the sheriff to arrest Overaker, etc., to answer to " the indictment " preferred against him for " entertaining slaves " at the June term, 1837. This warrant issued the 21st September, 1837, requiring bail in five hundred dollars. The sheriff's return reads as follows : " Received November 13, 1837. Executed November 14, 1838. George Torrey, sheriff. Nothing is said in this return about having taken a recognizance. But a recognizance immediately follows, purporting to have been taken on the 14th November, 1837, of George Overaker and G. H. Wilcox, by said sheriff, in the sum of five hundred dollars, for the appearance of said Overaker to answer to an indictment preferred against said Overaker at the June term, 1837, for " entertaining slaves," and not to depart, etc., but continue to attend from term to term, etc.

The next entry in the record shows proceedings at the June term, 1838, by which it appears that the district attorney came on the part of the state " in the four cases," and the said Overaker, though called, came not, neither did Wilcox, the security

in the recognizance, bring into court the body of the said Overaker; whereupon a forfeiture of their recognizance "in these
four cases," was by proclamation taken *nisi*. Then follows a
scire facias reciting, "Whereas George Overaker was, at the
June term, 1837, of the circuit court of said county, for selling
and giving to two negro men, to wit: Peter and Ben," etc.,
without naming either presentment or indictment, and going on
with other recitals appearing to have relation to the previous
proceedings, and requiring the sheriff to make known, etc., to
said Overaker and Wilcox to appear, etc., and show cause why
judgment, etc., which *scire facias*, has returns of "Received
November, 1838, executed, etc., November, 1838;" and at the
December term, 1838, the judgment was made final for five
hundred dollars against said Overaker and Wilcox.

The errors assigned four in number, are, in substance, that
there is no offense charged either by presentment or indictment;
that there is no return of the sheriff, identifying and showing
any recognizance on which to charge the plaintiff in error; that
there is not any legal recognizance; and that the judgment of
the court is not in conformity with the previous parts of the
record and proceedings, but is a departure therefrom, etc.

It is very apparent that this record is full of errors, both in
form and substance, and it is not made up with that care and in
that order which the law requires. A record should be a united,
properly connected and true history of the case. Some of the
errors and omissions in this case could have been corrected in the
court below. For instance, when the grand jury made a presentment of a misdemeanor, which was within their own knowledge,
the district attorney might have preferred an indictment thereon,
if he considered the accusation sustainable, and had a proper
finding with the name of the prosecutor endorsed. See Chit.
Crim. Law, 163. "After the presentment has been delivered
into court by the grand inquest, in general an indictment is
framed upon it by the officer of the court; for it is regarded
merely as instructions for an indictment, to which the party accused must answer." This is the general law. But in the Revised Code, 367, 368, this offense, and the mode of proceeding,

are pointed out. The act authorizes proceedings by presentment, without indictment; and this presentment might have
been returned to the grand jury which made it, for correction.

The offenses charged are stated to have been committed at a
day *subsequent* to the presentment. Whether this was a mistake
or not, it is fatal. The offense of selling spirituous liquors to
slaves, and entertaining them without permit, etc., is an offense
presentable by the grand jury, by the act Rev. Code, p. 368. I
am not informed of any decision of this court on the subject, or
of the repeal of that act.

The bench warrant, or *capias* which issued, sets forth an indictment "for entertaining slaves," when no indictment is
shown, and "entertaining slaves" is not a proper designation of
the offense set forth in the presentment.

The return on the *capias*, as made by the sheriff, states it to
have been executed on the 14th November, 1838, when it was
received in 1837, and made returnable to December term, 1837;
and the return does not state what was done by the sheriff with
the body of Overaker, which he was required to take; but the
record contains a recognizance taken of Overaker by the sheriff,
with Wilcox as his surety, reciting that the said Overaker was
to appear and answer "to an indictment for entertaining slaves."
No proceedings appear to have been had in the case at the
December term, 1837, but at the June term, 1838, it is stated
in the record, that this day came the district attorney on the
part of the state, "in these four cases" (without stating what
cases), and that said Overaker, being called, came not, neither
did the said Wilcox, etc., and forfeited their recognizances "in
these four cases." *Scire facias* issued to December term,
1838, was returned executed, and judgment final taken against
the plaintiffs in error, on their default, for five hundred dollars.

The sheriff should have stated in his return on the bench warrant, what he had done on it; if he took bail he should have
stated it. The bench warrant and the recognizance, and the
scire facias should have contained the true cause of the prosecution, with certainty, at least to a common intent. What the
clerk meant in the court below, by "these four cases," we are
left to conjecture. But, certain it is, that we have now before

us *four cases* between these same parties; and they are all
pretty much alike as to parties and forfeitures, but very different
as to the grade of crime.

The judgment must be reversed, bench warrants and all subsequent proceedings quashed, and case remanded for further
proceedings in the court below, on the presentment of the grand
jury.

Pagaud v. The State, 5 Smedes & Marshall, 491.

Forgery.

The words "bill of credit," as used in the constitution of the United States, mean
"a paper medium, intended to circulate between individuals and between the government and individuals, as money, for the ordinary purposes of society." 4 Peters,
431; Briscoe v. Bank of Ky., 11 Peters, 257.

The statute of this state (How. & Hutch., 270), provides that "it shall be the duty
of the auditor of public accounts to examine, settle and audit all accounts, claims
or demands whatsoever, against the state, arising under any act or resolution of the
legislature, and to grant to every claimant authorized to receive the same a warrant
on the state treasury." These warrants are not "bills of credit" within the meaning of the constitution of the United States, although they may have been sometimes
used by individual holders as a circulating medium and a substitute for paper money.
Vide note, supra.

Whether an instrument is or is not a "bill of credit," depends upon the intention
of the legislature, in the act authorizing its issue, but that intention can only be ascertained by reference to the act itself. Testimony *aliunde* to explain the motives,
or to point out the object of the law-makers, is inadmissible.

On the trial of a party indicted for the forgery of auditor's warrants, the prosecution will not be allowed to prove, with a view of showing that they are bills of
credit, that at the time they were issued, there was no money in the treasury to pay
them, that warrants were not then redeemed, were under par, and circulated from
hand to hand as money.

On the trial of the accused for forgery of auditor's warrants, besides the proof
of the handwriting of the accused, there being no positive proof of the forged
warrant having been seen in the possession of or uttered by the prisoner; the state
proved that he was the clerk of the auditor, had official custody of his books, free
access at all times to the registry, and that the forged warrants, in all material respects, corresponded with the genuine ones in the register; whereupon the prisoner
proposed to prove that the registry was not always, or generally, in his custody,
but was carelessly thrown about the office, accessible to all who might casually
enter it, and often with auditor's office itself, for a considerable time, in the care
of a single servant; *held*, that the testimony offered by the accused was proper rebutting testimony and should have been admitted.

Error to the circuit court of Warren county.
Three cases against the accused were submitted together.
At the circuit court of Hinds county, the grand jury found a

true bill of indictment against the prisoner for forgery of an auditor's warrant. The warrant was in these words :

No. 48. $115.
State of Mississippi, Auditor's Office.

Pay to Daniel Thomas, or order, the sum of one hundred and fifteen dollars, on account of the appropriations for 1840 department, and for so doing this shall be your warrant.

Given under my hand and seal of office, this 5th day of March, Anno Domini, 1840.

A. B. SAUNDERS,
Auditor Public Accounts.

To the State Treasurer.

The prisoner was found guilty, and on the trial the following exceptions were taken and made part of the record :

" Be it remembered, that these causes came on to be tried, by consent, together ; and considerable evidence having been adduced on both sides, touching the handwriting upon the warrants described in the indictments as forged, and on other points ; it having been explicitly proved in particular, that the defendant had been before the date of said warrants, and that he was at the time, and for some time thereafter, a deputy in the auditor's office, whence said warrants emanated, and as such had held custody of the books and papers of said office severally, and was familiar with the proceedings occurring in the same ; the evidence in regard to the signatures upon said warrant being of a conflicting character, a portion of the same consisting of the belief of witnesses that the signatures were defendant's, whilst another part consisted of statements of an opposite belief ; it having been likewise proved that a certain book offered in evidence as the *Register* of said office, and containing a specific description of all the warrants issued from the same, including name of payee, amount, date, etc., etc., was chiefly in the handwriting of accused, and that he had the official custody of said books, enjoyed free access to it at all times ; it having been also proved, at this stage of the case, that the warrants described in the indictment corresponded in all material respects with the descriptions of the genuine warrants in said register ; it was proposed by counsel for the prisoner to introduce testimony of said auditor's office having been generally kept during the time of A. B. Saunders, the principal of defendant, in a loose and careless manner; that said register book was not always, or generally, in the strict custody and keeping of said defendant, but usually to be found negligently thrown about the office, sometimes in one place, and sometimes in another, and accessible to all who might casually enter the office; that said Saunders was in the habit of leaving blank-printed warrants at the office, signed by him, to be filled up and used in his absence; that there were numerous occasions when said auditor's office was open for a considerable time under the care of a single servant. Appropriate questions were asked by prisoner's counsel for the purpose of bringing out this testimony, with a view of rebutting the presumption that the prisoner was the guilty person. When these questions were thus propounded, no witness had proved, nor did any witness prove at any subsequent period of the trial, that he had seen the defendant execute any of the writings in question; nor did any witness prove that he had known of said Pagand's selling or disposing of any of said warrants, or that any of them were either found in, or directly traced by positive evidence to his possession. But the court refused to permit said questions to be answered, or said evidence to be given. Defendant's counsel, with a view of proving said warrants to be bills of credit, in the sense of the federal constitution, and consequently nullities, the forgery of which could not be legally criminal, offered evidence that, at the time of the issuance of said warrants there was no money in the state treasury for their redemption; that the redemption of them by the government did not go on at all; that they were generally under par in the market, but circulated from hand to hand as money; they were of convenient denominations, so as to be suited to currency purposes; and that various statutes of the State of Mississippi evidenced on the part of the government of the same, a recognition of said warrants as money, and recognized the fact that they were not expected to be redeemed on demand or according to their face, but the court acceded that no proof beyond the face of the warrants themselves, could be properly adduced to establish their legal character, and would not permit suitable questions propounded by counsel, to be responded to;" to which various opinions and refusals of the court exceptions were taken and signed.

Motion for a new trial, and motion in arrest of judgment were made, and were overruled.

L. Lea, H. S. Foote, and *Geo. S. Yerger* for the plaintiff in error.

Jno. D. Freeman, attorney general.

CLAYTON, J.:

This was an indictment for the forgery of certain instruments, termed auditor's warrants, purporting to have been issued by the State of Mississippi.

The bill of indictment was found in the county of Hinds, but the *venue* was charged to Warren, where a trial was had, which terminated in the conviction of the prisoner. Various errors have been assigned, and many grounds taken to reverse the judgment, but we do not deem it necessary to notice them all.

It was urged in argument, with great zeal and earnestness, that the auditor's warrants of this state, are bills of credit emitted by the state, that they thus come within the prohibition of the Constitution of the United States; that they are void, and that it is no crime to counterfeit them.

To determine this point, it is necessary to ascertain what is the precise meaning of the term "bill of credit." There is no better means of doing this than the adoption of the definition, or rather description, of a bill of credit, given by the supreme court of the United States, in the case of *Craig, et al. v. The State of Missouri,* 4 Peters, 431. That court says: "In its enlarged, and perhaps literal sense, the term bill of credit may comprehend any instrument by which a State engages to pay money at a future day; thus including a certificate given for money borrowed. But the language of the Constitution itself, and the mischief to be prevented, which we know from the history of our country, equally limit the interpretation of the terms. The word emit is never employed in describing those contracts, by which a State binds itself to pay money at a future day, for services actually received, or for money borrowed for present use; nor are instruments executed for such purposes, in common language, denominated bills of credit. To emit bills of credit, conveys to the mind the idea of issuing paper, intended to circulate through the community for its ordinary purposes as money, which paper is redeemable at a future day. This is the sense in which the terms have been always understood."

Again, in the same opinion, the court says, "The term has acquired an appropriate meaning; and bills of credit signify a paper medium, intended to circulate between individuals, and between government and individuals, for the ordinary purposes of society." In the farther progress of the opinion, the term seems to be regarded as synonymous with paper money issued by a state.

The law of this state, which authorizes the issuance of auditor's warrants, is in these words: "It shall be the duty of the auditor of public accounts to examine, settle, and audit all accounts, claims, or demands whatsoever, against the state, arising under any act or resolution of the legislature, and to grant to every claimant, authorized to receive the same, a warrant on the state treasury." H. & H., 270. Upon this warrant or certificate of the auditor, the treasurer is authorized to make payment, and in no other way.

A comparison of this law of our state, with the definition of a bill of credit, above given, satisfies us entirely that an auditor's warrant, issued according to the law, is not a bill of credit, within the prohibited sense of the term. It is not issued to form a circulating medium for the community, nor to operate as a substitute for paper money. That they have been sometimes so used by the individual holders, cannot alter their legal effect. They are invariably an acknowledgment of indebtedness for services actually rendered, and to say that they are repugnant to the constitution, and void, would deprive the state of an important means which it has adopted to prevent frauds and impositions upon the treasury. That the law has not fully answered this end, tends only to prove the imperfection of all human legislation when directed against fraud.

It was also urged as error upon this branch of the case,

that the court erred in rejecting the testimony, which was proposed to be introduced, in order to show that at the time the warrant was issued, there was no money in the treasury to take it up, that warrants were not then redeemed, that they were under par, but circulated from hand to hand, as money, and thus to show that they were bills of credit. It is said by counsel that the issuing of bills of credit is a question of intent, and that evidence was admissible to show the intent. It may be conceded that the intent is an essential point of inquiry in this case, and yet it will not follow that the evidence offered was admissible to show the intent. The intent, which must stamp the character of this instrument, is that of the legislature, which enacted the law; not of the officers who were to execute it, or of the persons who received the warrants. The legislative intent can be deduced from the legislative acts alone. In construing statutes, courts may look to the history and condition of the country as circumstances from which to gather the intention. Testimony to explain the motives which operated upon the law-makers, or to point out the objects they had in view, is wholly inadmissible. It would take from the statute law every semblance of certainty, and make its character depend upon the varying and conflicting statements of witnesses. We think, therefore, the evidence was properly excluded.

The next point we shall notice, likewise grows out of the exclusion of testimony in the court below. There was no direct evidence on the part of the prosecution of the guilt of the prisoner. In other words, no one had ever seen him execute any one of the instruments, nor had any of them been seen in his possession, nor was there any proof that he had ever uttered or passed one of them. The evidence in regard to the signature upon the warrants was of a conflicting character; a part of the witnesses believed that the signatures were in the handwriting of the prisoner, and others expressed an opposite belief. It was also in evidence that the prisoner was a clerk in the auditor's office, that he had the official custody of the books of the office, including the register, in which a description of all the warrants which were issued was inserted; that he had free access to them at all times, and that the warrants described in the indictment corresponded in all material respects with the description of the genuine warrants in the register. The counsel for the prisoner then proposed to prove, in order to rebut the presumption of his guilt, that the register was not always, or generally in the strict custody or keeping of the prisoner, but usually to be found negligently thrown about the office, sometimes in one place, sometimes in another, and accessible to all who might casually enter the office; and that there were numerous occasions when the auditor's office was open for a considerable time under the care of a single servant. This evidence was objected to by the counsel for the state, and excluded. Its admissibility depends solely upon the point whether it is to be regarded as rebutting testimony or not.

There was no positive evidence, according to the bill of exceptions, of the prisoner's guilt. The testimony as to his handwriting was contradictory. Had the prosecuting attorney submitted the case upon that testimony, this question could not have arisen. But to strengthen the case for the state, he proved the opportunities to commit the crime, and the facility of doing so with probable impunity and exemption from detection. This was no more than presumptive testimony. To rebut the presumption of guilt thence arising, the prisoner offered to prove that similar opportunities were presented to others. This offer was rejected.

In this, we think, the court erred. The circumstances thus proven against the prisoner were calculated to have weight against him, and it would be but just and proper to hear the rebutting proof. We cannot tell what influence they had with the jury. If the state proved even more than was necessary to produce a conviction, still, if part of the testimony were illegal, the judgment must be reversed. If the presumptive proof last introduced were wholly unnecessary to the prosecution, it cannot deprive the defendant of his right to offer rebutting testimony. For this error the judgment will be reversed, and a new trial granted.

As the result is thus in favor of the prisoner, we shall not consider the exceptions to other portions of the proceedings.

Judgment reversed, new trial granted, and prisoner remanded.

Dowling *v.* The State, 5 Smedes & Marshall, 664.

Murder.

Where, in organizing the grand jury, a sufficient number is not obtained before the regular *venire* is exhausted, it is not error to complete the necessary number from by-standers summoned by the sheriff under the authority of the court.

Sharkey, C. J., *dissenting.*

Whether objections to the personal qualifications of grand jurors, or to the legality of the returns, can affect indictments found by them, after such indictments have been received by the court and filed. *Query.*

Where a sufficient number of the regular *venire* did not attend to form the grand jury, and the deficiency was supplied from by-standers, summoned by the sheriff by order of the court, and it does not appear by the record that they had the requisite qualifications, the law will presume, until the contrary is made to appear, that they had.

The statute (How. & Hutch. 674, sec. 46,) which limits the number of peremptory challenges in capital cases, on the part of the prisoner, to twelve, is not an infringement of that clause of the constitution which provides, "that the right of trial by jury shall remain inviolate."

"Trial by jury" means a trial by twelve free and lawful men, of kin to neither party, for the purpose of establishing, by their verdict, the truth of the matter in issue between the parties; and legislation which merely regulates the mode of attaining this object, and does not take from it any of its essential attributes, will not be considered as infringing on that right.

D being indicted for the murder of a slave, and it being proved that D was acting in the capacity of overseer for B, a witness on the part of the state was permitted, although objected to by the prisoner's counsel, to testify as to the prisoner's general habit, as overseer, in punishing slaves upon the plantation of the owner of the slave killed; *held*, by the court, that such evidence was inadmissible, being calculated to prejudice the jury against the prisoner, and not being responsive to any charge in the indictment.

Error to the circuit court of Warren county.

Caption of the record.

"State of Mississippi. Pleas before, etc., at a circuit court held in and for Warren county, at the court-house, on 24th May, 1845. Be it remembered, that at a circuit court begun, etc., on 21st Oct., 1844, a grand jury of inquest for the body of this county was empanelled, viz: John G. Parham, (and nine others,) of the regular *venire*, which being exhausted, the following persons, by-standers, were summoned by the sheriff, viz: Robt. L. Matthews and Thos. Rigley. The court thereupon appointed John G. Parham foreman; said grand jury were then sworn according to law, and having received their charge, retired," etc. On 30th October, 1844, the grand jury, thus constituted, returned into the court an indictment against the accused for murder, "a true bill."

The indictment charges the prisoner with having, in August,

1844, " in and upon one Dick Smith, a negro man (slave of one R. C. Ballard), in the peace, etc., feloniously, wilfully, and of his malice aforethought, made an assault, and that the said Thos. Dowling, with both his hands and feet, the said Dick Smith, negro, etc., as aforesaid, to and against the ground, then and there, feloniously, wilfully, and of his malice aforethought, did cast and throw; and that said Thos. Dowling, with a certain wooden paddle" inflicted divers mortal blows, etc., of which, on the 6th day of September, he died; and so the grand jury pronounced him guilty of murder.

At April term, 1845, a special *venire facias* for fifty men was ordered, and out of them a jury was empanelled. In organizing this jury, Dowling having peremptorily challenged twelve of the panel, further peremptorily challenged E. Grammar, tendered him by the state. This was objected to by the state, and the objection sustained, and Grammar received and sworn as one of the jury, to which exception was taken and filed.

On the trial Puckett, a witness on the part of the state, was asked by the state, " Did the accused ever tell you what was his usual and general habit of punishing slaves on Ballard's plantation?" Objected to, but the court overruled it and permitted the answer, " that prisoner told him his usual habit was to punish slaves with a paddle," which the witness stated was a piece of white oak timber about two and a half inches thick and as broad as his hand. To this question and answer, exceptions were taken and filed.

Another bill of exceptions recites, " that the only proof offered to the jury that the slave Dick Smith was the property of R. C. Ballard, was the testimony of one Dickson, on the part of the state, who, to the question by the state, " Do you know the slave Dick Smith, the property of R. C. Ballard?" replied, " yes;" and the proof that Dick Smith was on the plantation of R. C. Ballard at the time of the alleged beating and wounding, and had been there for several months previous; and had been attended to in his last illness on the plantation, and had died there. The verdict is as follows: " The said Thomas Dowling is not guilty of murder as he stands indicted, but is guilty of manslaughter in the second degree."

Motions for new trial and in arrest of judgment, because 1st. The court had permitted Grammar to be sworn upon the jury. 2d. Because the testimony of Puckett was improperly admitted. 3d. Because the grand jury was not empanelled according to law. 4th. Because the petit jury was not organized according to law. These motions were both overruled and exceptions taken.

John I. Guion and *S. C. Cox* for plaintiff in error.

Insisted upon the following errors, to wit:

1st. The grand jury was not organized and empanelled according to law; the grand jury could be selected from the original panel or *venire* only; the court had no power to summons bystanders and add them to the ten persons of the original *venire* in attendance, for the purpose of forming a grand jury. How. & Hutch., p. 490, sec. 44, 45; ib., 492, sec 49; Byrd v. The State, 1 How., 163. The statute provides, that "if none of the regular jurors summoned to such term attend, the court shall forthwith award a special *venire* to bring a sufficient number, etc., to serve as jurors at such term of the court." How. & Hutch., 498, sec. 66. If any one of the grand jury who returned the indictment into court, was not possessed of the legal qualifications of a juror, the indictment was void. 1 Chitty's Cr. Law, 307; 4 Bacon's Ab., title juries, 525; The State v. Bennett, Mart. & Yerger, 135; The State v. Duncan & Trott, 7 Yerger, 271; Byrd v. The State, 1 How., 163. The two bystanders placed upon the grand jury, may or may not have possessed the legal qualifications. On a failure of a sufficient number of the regular *venire*, it was the duty of the court to bring them in by compulsory process. 4 Bacon, title juries, 528; 2 Hale P. C., 265; 2 Hawk., 565.

2d. The second error assigned, and upon which a new trial should have been granted is, that the court restricted the number of peremptory challenges to twelve. The act of 1836, How. & Hutch., 674, reducing the number of such challenges to twelve, deprives the accused in a capital case of a most valuable and important constitutional right, and is, therefore, void. The constitution of the United States guarantees to every citizen a speedy public trial by an impartial jury. The constitution of this state declares, that "the right of trial by jury shall remain inviolate." Declaration of Right, sec. 28. By the common law, a party accused of a capital crime, was entitled to challenging peremptorily thirty-five of the regular panel. Bacon Ab., title juries, 569; 2 Hale P. C., 268; 2 Hawk. P. C., ch. 43, sec. 5. This number was reduced to twenty by the statutes of England; except in treason and misprisions of treason. Thus stood the right of trial by jury in England, at the time of the adoption of the federal constitution. The constitution of this state, when admitted into the Union, and that of 1833, both guarantee to the citizen the right of trial by jury, and which for many years remained unimpaired; and the court, in the case of The State v. Byrd, 1 How., 163, clearly recognized the right of trial by jury as it existed at the time of the adoption of the constitution. At that time one of the most important incidents of the trial by jury, in capital cases, was the right to challenging peremptorily twenty of the panel.

3d. The third error is, that the court permitted proof of the general habit of the accused in punishing slaves on the Ballard plantation, to go to the jury for the purpose of establishing his guilt in this particular case. This was a violation of the well-known rules of evidence. The general rule is, that every species of evidence should be rejected which is foreign to the point in issue, and should be more rigidly enforced in criminal than in civil cases. 1 Phillips Ev., 178; Greenl. Ev., 61, 62. The character of the accused, as a cruel overseer, was not in issue. On such trials it is not permissible to show even that accused has a general disposition to commit this sort of crime. 1 Phil. Ev., 181. The general character of one accused of crime, cannot be given in evidence to establish his guilt. Greenl. Ev., 61, 62. For this error the court ought to have granted a new trial. Roscoe's Cr. Ev., 57, note 1. Cruelty to slaves is a distinct offense, for which the accused was indictable. Norris's Peake, 13, 14; Bul. Nisi Prius, 296; Rosc. Ev., 89; 2 Mass. Rep., 317; 7 How., 631; Cow. & Hill's Notes, 459.

4th. The fourth error assigned is, that there was not sufficient proof before the jury, that Dick Smith, the deceased, was a slave or the property of R. C. Ballard. Every material aver-

ment in the indictment must be established by legal and sufficient evidence. The averment, that Dick Smith was a slave
and the property of Ballard, we contend, were material averments. An averment in an indictment, although unnecessary,
yet if it be pertinent to the point in issue, must be proved;
and greater strictness will be required in the proof in criminal than in civil cases. Rosc. Cr. Ev., 86; United States v.
Porter, 3 Days' Cases, 283. Descriptive averments must be
proved as laid. Rosc. Cr. Ev., 78, 82. This fact, as laid, was
not sufficiently proved to authorize the verdict rendered by
the jury.

Sanders & Price, on same side.

The errors relied on question the correctness of the finding
of the jury; the refusing of the peremptory challenge of juror
Grammar; the admission of Puckett's testimony; the refusal
of a new trial; and the overruling of the motion in arrest of
judgment. The finding of the jury is defective and erroneous.
Under our constitution, which gives the accused the right "to
demand the nature and the cause of the accusation," and exempts him from arrest or detention, except in cases ascertained
by law; and which prescribes a different punishment for manslaughter, dividing it into different degrees, the right of the
jury to find the accused guilty of any other offense than that
directly charged, is prohibited. In England, murder and manslaughter were alike punishable with death; here they are not;
and the reason of the rule not existing here, the rule itself
ceases. The finding of the jury, "but guilty of manslaughter
in the second degree," without other qualification connecting
it with the person killed, is too general, and ought not to be
sustained.

It was error to admit the testimony of W. R. Puckett. A
detail of a conversation with the accused, touching his usual or
general habit of punishing slaves on the Ballard plantation, was
clearly irrelevant, foreign to the issue, and calculated to excite a
prejudice in the minds of the jury towards the prisoner. Chitty's Crim. Law., 564; see also, Ib., 573, 575; but *Nisi Prius*;
Hawkins b. 2 c., 46, § 206. The declarations of a party, criminally prosecuted, are received with great caution, even when

pertinent. Chitty's Crim. Law, 571. Also, Buller on trials, 294; 1 Chitty's Crim. Law, 556, 557, and authorities there cited.

The court erred in refusing a new trial on the ground of denying the prisoner his peremptory challenge to the juror, Grammar. The constitution declares that, "the right of trial by jury shall remain inviolate." Art. 1, § 28. At common law, in capital cases, the prisoner could challenge thirty-five peremptorily. The English statutes reduced this number to twenty, in capital cases, except in treason and misprision of treason. The right of trial as thus regulated, was guaranteed by our constitution of 1832, 3 Bacon's Ab., title juries, 263 and 264; How. & Hutch., 667, § 17. Thus it is manifest, that at the time of the adoption of the constitution, by the common law, the right to challenge twenty jurors peremptorily in capital cases, existed. This common law right was guaranteed by the constitution, and the legislature has no power to change or impair it. See Byrd v. The State, 1 How., 163.

Lastly, we insist the circuit court erred in refusing to arrest the judgment, as well upon the particular finding of the jury, as for the defect in the indictment, and especially in the caption. It is the office of the caption of an indictment to state with sufficient certainty, not only the style of the court, the judge then presiding, but the time and place, when and where it was found, and the grand jurors by whom it was found. Thomas v. The State, 5 How. 20—32.

G. Baker, on same side.

1st. In order to effect a regular conviction, all the requirements of law, applicable to the case, should be strictly observed in the court below.

2d. The record should show, and it is presumed does show, every thing material which transpired during the progress of a cause to its final result.

3d. This court will presume that the circuit court kept a true and faithful record of its acts, and that the transcript of the record, certified to this court is correct.

4th. That, if the record fails to show that every thing material to a regular conviction has been observed in the court below, or if it shows error in the ruling of the court in any material matter, then this court will pronounce the conviction irregular, and will reverse the judgment of the court.

The errors which will be noticed are,

1st. The grand jury, by whom the indictment purports to have been found, was not summoned or organized according to law. The statute provides that the clerk and sheriff shall draw the names of the requisite number of jurors, and that the names so drawn shall be entered on the minutes of the court, and a *venire facias* to issue, etc., and that the sheriff shall summon them at least five days before the return, and make due return of the same. H. & H., 492, § 48, 49. From this number so drawn and summoned, the grand jury shall be drawn by lot. To organize a grand jury legally and regularly, all these acts should have been performed substantially as required by the statute; this, it is insisted, was not done; inasmuch as the record is silent upon the matter. Where the existence of a fact *should* appear by the record, but does not so appear, the legal presumption is that it did not take place.

These principles have been recognized by this court in the case of Thomas v. The State, 5 How., 32. "In cases highly penal no court is authorized to put the humblest citizen upon his trial, until the grand jury of the proper county, organized as the law directs, has preferred a formal accusation against him." There is nothing in the record to show that the grand jurors were drawn by lot, or indeed, how they were drawn. The record, after the caption and term, simply states that, "A grand jury of inquest, etc., was empanelled, viz: John G. Parham, etc., of the regular *venire* to the number of ten, which *venire* being exhausted, the following persons, by-standers, were summoned, to wit; R. L. Matthews, etc." This is all that the record shows relative to the organization of the grand jury. The record does not show "a grand jury of the proper county, organized as the law directs," as defined by the court in the above case.

2d. Although the record shows an *order* of the court for a special *venire* of fifty men, as traverse jurors, yet no such *venire* appears by the record to have been issued by the clerk, or returned by the sheriff; nor does it appear by what authority the jurors were brought into court. The statute (How. & Hutch. 673, § 45,) makes it the duty of the court, where any person is charged with felony, the punishment of which is death, to award a special *venire*, etc., commanding the sheriff to summon, etc., any number, etc.," requiring them to attend on a particular day, to be mentioned in said *venire*, etc. The record does not show the issuance or return of any such process. It has been decided by the supreme court of New York, whose statute upon this subject is very similar to our own, that in a capital felony, a special *venire facias* is necessary to authorize the summoning of a petit jury to try the case, and that if the record does not *show* that one has been issued, and duly served and returned, the judgment will be reversed. The People v. McKay, 18 Joshns. 212. See also, 2 Hawk. P. C., look 2 ch. 41, sec. 1 ; 2 Hale's P. C., 260, 261 ; 1 Chit. Crim. Law, 505. The record should show all necessary facts, otherwise it will be presumed the court below proceeded without proper authority. Carpenter v. The State, 4 How. 168.

3d. The court erred in permitting testimony to be given to the jury as to defendant's usual mode of punishing slaves on the Ballard plantation. The testimony of Puckett had not the most remote tendency to prove the issue between the state and the defendant ; but it had a tendency to create an unfavorable impression on the minds of the jury towards the prisoner, and was therefore improper, and should not have been admitted.

4th. The evidence adduced to prove the slave, Dick Smith, charged to have been killed, was the property of R. C. Ballard, as charged in the indictment, was not sufficient to authorize the verdict of guilty ; and therefore the court erred in refusing a new trial. There were but two witnesses who testified as to the matter of ownership. Dickson, to the question by the state " Do you know the slave, Dick Smith, the property of Rice C. Ballard ?" answered " Yes ; and that at the time of the alleged beating, etc., the said Dick was on the plantation of said Ballard." This answer proves two things, and nothing more, viz., witness knew Dick Smith, and that at the time of the beating, etc., charged, he was on the plantation of R. C.

Ballard. He does not say that he knew the boy to be the property of Ballard, nor was the question put to him. Again, the testimony of Puckett had not the remotest tendency to prove ownership in Ballard. Witness says he heard the testimony of witness, Dickson, that he knew the boy, Dick Smith, spoken of by Dickson, and that he had visited him during his last illness on the plantation of Ballard, and had administered medicine to him there. The assumption by the district attorney, of ownership in Ballard, is no evidence of the fact, and there is, therefore, no proof of property to support the allegation in the indictment.

8th. The court erred in overruling the motion in arrest of judgment, it appearing that there was no prosecutor marked on the indictment. The statute, in explicit terms, requires this. Cody v. The State, 3 How., 27; Peter (a slave) v. The State, 3 How. 434.

John D. Freeman, attorney general.

Error 1st. In drawing the grand jury, the *venire* was exhausted, and two talesmen were summoned and put upon the jury. The statute provides that talesmen may be empanelled as grand jurors, and that they shall serve until discharged by the court. H. & H., 499.

The common law affords the same rule in cases where the *venire* was exhausted before the grand jury was complete. It is a discretionary power of all courts of general criminal jurisdiction, without which designing persons summoned on the *venire,* by refusing to attend court, might prevent the formation of a grand jury at every term of the court, and so defeat the ends of justice. Huling v. The State, How., 6.

The issuance of an attachment for contempt by failure of a juror to attend, is discretionary with the court, and if not resorted to is no cause of error.

2d. The law reducing the peremptory challenges from twenty to twelve is unconstitutional. The constitution secures the right of trial by jury. The number and qualification of jurors has ever been the subject of legislation under *Magna Charta* in England, and under the constitution of the United States. The statute of this state now brought in question, was decided to be constitutional by Mr. Justice Trotter. 4 How. 196, 197. The points made in the bill of exceptions are submitted without comment.

THACHER, J.:

This was an indictment for murder preferred in the Warren county circuit court, which resulted, upon a trial, in a verdict of manslaughter in the second degree.

The first ground claimed for error is, that the grand jury which found the indictment was composed in part of by-standers, of which ten persons were taken from the regular *venire*, and it having then become exhausted, two persons were taken from by-standers summoned by the sheriff.

It has been held that objections to the personal qualifications of grand jurors, or to the legality of the returns, cannot affect any indictments found by them after they have been received and filed by the court; but such objections, if any exist, must be made before the indictments are found, and may be received from any person who is under a presentment for any crime whatsoever, or from any person present who may make the suggestion as *amicus curiæ*. Commonwealth v. Smith, 9 Mass., 107. But assuming that this objection is well taken in point of time in this case, it is not clear that it is well taken in point of fact.

The first inquiry which grows out of this assignment of error is, the legality of completing a grand jury by means of tales grand jurors, in cases of an exhaustion of the jurors returned upon the regular *venire facias*.

The constitution of this state has provided that " the right of trial by jury shall remain inviolate ;" and it has further provided, that " before an individual shall be held to answer for a capital, or otherwise infamous crime, except in cases not now pertinent to enumerate, there must be a presentment or indictment for such crime by a grand jury." It is contended that, by thus adopting modes of legal proceedings, we have adopted them with all their incidents, as known to the common law, or, at least, so far as not changed by absolute legislation. The history of this country, and the opinions of some of its most eminent jurists, show that this position, when generally claimed, must be taken with restrictions.

Mr. Justice Story in his Commentaries on the Constitution, vol. 1, p. 132, § 148, enlarges those limitations to a great degree, and excludes all rules repugnant to our local and political circumstances. The historical fact is, that the early colonists of this country were more learned in divinity than in jurisprudence; and Hutchinson, the best colonial historian observes, in his history of Massachusetts, 1399, that its "judicial proceedings were in as summary a way as could well consist with the preservation of any tolerable method or order." None would contend, at this day, in a trial of a writ, for the extraordinary jury called the grand assize, composed of four knights, "girt with swords," and who chose twelve other persons to be joined with them. It has been deemed necessary in this State, to secure by enactment, the privilege of a jury *de mediatate linguæ.* Yet both these juries were known to the original common law. It will be observed that the modifications in this country of the English forms of legal proceedings have not always been formally made, as by legislation, but have sprung naturally from our circumstances. The old common law has been insensibly changed and tempered to our situation and institutions, and thus practice, custom and usage, which are always as potent as legislation in such cases, have made a common law for the individual states.

Thus, while the constitution must be construed to have adopted the generous privilege of the common law trial by jury in its essential elements, it reasonably follows that whatever was an accidental, and not an absolute part of that institution, the mere superfluous forms and complicated proceedings of the English courts, is not necessarily included to have been guaranteed in the right by the clause of the constitution. It was, therefore, competent for legislation to point out the mode of empanelling juries, both grand and petit, so long as it did not intermeddle with the constituents of those bodies; and, whenever legislation is silent, we must presume an intention to adopt the forms of the common law, unless they are found to be repugnant to our local or political circumstances, and well established usages. In this state the mode of empanelling grand juries, differs in many respects from the mode existing at common law. One of the marked differences is, that at common law, jurors duly served

with process under a *venire facias*, were compellable to appear,
and their appearance in the common pleas was enforced by writs
of *habeas corpora* and *distringas juratores*, and in the Kings
Bench and exchequer, by the writ of *distringas juratores* alone.
Bac. Abridg. tit. Juries.   With us, jurors duly served with process under a *venire facias*, and failing to attend, are liable to a
fine unless good cause be shown for their non-attendance, on or
before the first day of the regular term of the court next after
their default, or before a final judgment on *scire facias* issued
according to law against them.   H. & H., 492, § 48.   They are
not compellable to appear at the return term of the *venire facias*.
The statute has affixed the penalty and the whole penalty for
such non-attendance.   The *scire facias* against a defaulting
juror in this state, corresponds to the *distringas juratorem* of
common law, the latter having been returnable immediately,
and the former being returnable to a subsequent term of the
court.   In this interpretation of the statute the legal maxim
that *Expressio unius est exclusio alterius*, applies with much
force.   It is a legitimate mode of ascertaining the meaning of a
statute to compare it with others of a similar character.   For
instance, the statutes of this state respecting the summoning and
attendance of witnesses upon trials, resemble the rules governing
jurors ; they are subject to the same penalty and same process
of its recovery.   H. & H., 599, § 2 and 4.   In the case of witnesses, however, there is a special statute authorizing the issuance of a warrant or attachment to compel their attendance,
which does not exist in the case of defaulting jurors.   H. & H.,
605, § 21.   In further confirmation of this view of the law upon
this point, it may be observed that the statute, H. & H., 492,
§ 49, provides that the grand jury shall be constituted from the
whole number of the jurors summoned by the *venire facias*,
and attending thereon, which seems plainly to anticipate the
contingency of the non-attendance of some of the jurors summoned by the regular *venire facias*.   In reply to that branch
of the assignment of error which would appear to hold that,
under the circumstances, a special *venire facias* should have
been awarded to complete the grand jury, it is enough to observe that the statute providing for such an order, (H. & H.,

498, § 68), authorized it only when not any of the regular jurors summoned to a particular term shall be in attendance. This is but a re-enactment of the common law, as will be hereafter seen.

Then, there existing no means of enforcing the appearance of the defaulting jurors of the regular *venire facias*, and it not having been a case for the award of a special *venire facias*, what was the proper course to be adopted to complete the number of jurors necessary for a legal grand jury? Our statutes, although they do not expressly point out the mode, point it out by inference, by acknowledging the legal existence of tales grand jurors. H. & H., 499, § 70. At common law, if a jury did not attend on the *habeas corpora* or *distringas juratores*, which were to bring them into court, there was a writ of *undecim*, *decim*, or *octo tales*, according to the number deficient, to force others into court; and also subsequently, 35 H., viii, 6, the court could cause a supply to be made of so many men as were wanting, of them as were standing about the court," and hence the act itself was styled a *tales de circumstantibus*. The *tales de circumstantibus* was given by statute to trials by assize and *nisi prius*. In this state the *tales* and the *tales de circumstantibus* have been indifferently used by custom of the courts.

It occurs here to notice the objection, that the two persons, by-standers, do not appear to have been competent jurors, although this objection is likewise involved in the difficulty of having been taken too late in point of time, as before sustained by authority, it is not well made in point of fact. The two persons were summoned from the by-standers to sit upon the grand jury. The circumstances show that they were summoned as *tales de circumstantibus*. The word *tales* is similitudinary, and has reference to the resemblance, which there ought to be in *esse*. Thus, at common law, if the array were quashed, or all the polls challenged, or absent, a new *venire facias* was awarded, and not a *tales*, because there were no *quals*. The mode of proceeding shows, therefore, that the persons summoned were "such as those" of the jury already empanelled, and who, nothing to the contrary appearing, must be considered to have been good and lawful men, and invested with all the necessary qualifications.

Upon the examination of the second assignment of error, some remarks are equally applicable to the one just considered. The second ground claimed as error is, that the circuit court erred in refusing to allow the prisoner to challenge peremptorily a greater number than twelve of the jurors tendered to him by the state for his trial.

Our statute (H. & H., 674, § 46) limits the number of peremptory challenges in capital cases to twelve. At common law, in capital cases, the prisoner could challenge thirty-five peremptorily. By statute 38, H. VIII., c. 3, peremptory challenges were reduced to twenty, but by 1 & 2, W. & M., c. 10, the challenge of thirty-five in treason and petit treason was restored. In this state, formerly, by act June 11th, 1822, peremptory challenges were allowed to the number of twenty. The origin of peremptory challenges shows that the reason for the common law rule has ceased at this day. The trial by the petit jury was introduced to do away with the trial by ordeal; the jury of twelve being after the manner of the canonical purgation of accusation. Among the canonists, the whole *pares* were not upon the jury, but only a select number was brought in and chosen by the accused himself. A middle way was therefore adopted, and the accused had liberty to challenge peremptorily any number under three juries; four juries being as many as generally appeared to make the total *pares* of the county. Gilbert's Com. Pleas, 99; Bacon's Abridg. Title Juries, E. It might be extremely inconvenient, and indeed, in some instances work a complete denial of public justice, under our local circumstances, of a sparse population, to adhere implicitly to this feature of the common law. The trial by jury is by twelve free and lawful men, who are not of kin to either party, for the purpose of establishing, by their verdict, the truth of the matter, which is in issue between the parties. It is called a trial by one's peers; that is, by men who have that concern for the party on trial, which naturally flows from a parity of circumstances, common to him and his judges. 3, Black. Com., 361. The jurors should be as impartial and independent as the lot of humanity will admit, and be allowed to judge upon the matter submitted to them freely and without fear or favor.

Such is the trial by jury, guaranteed by the Constitution, and originally secured by the *Magna Charta* of England. Any legislation, therefore, which merely points out the mode of arriving at this object, but does not rob it of any of its essential ingredients, cannot be considered an infringement of the right.

The third point relied upon as error is, that a witness, on the part of the state, was permitted to testify as to the general habit of the prisoner, in his capacity of overseer, in punishing slaves upon the plantation of the owner of the slave charged to have been killed.

It is not necessary to prove strictly, as laid in the indictment, the instrument or means by which the crime of murder has been committed; for if it be proved to have been effected by any other instrument, capable of producing the same kind of death, it will be sufficient. But the mode in which the death is alleged to have been effected, must be proved to a reasonable degree of certainty. In this case the answer of the witness was a response to the allegation in the indictment, of the instrument used to inflict the wounds, but was general in its character, and had no other than a general reference to the individual slave charged to have been killed. It cannot, therefore, be viewed as evidence in this case of killing, even though we supply the fact that this slave was upon the plantation. The primary rule in relation to evidence is, that the evidence must correspond with the allegations, and be confined to the point in issue. A principal reason for this rule is, that a party, having had no notice of such a course of evidence, may not have prepared himself to rebut it. It is not an answer to this to say, that the matter in evidence having no relation to the point in issue, cannot therefore influence the mind upon it. It may have the effect to withdraw the minds of the jury from the point in issue and thus mis-lead them. If the admitted evidence tend to prove that the prisoner has committed another distinct offense, it may thus excite prejudice, and even raise the inference of the commission of the offense alone in question. It is of the last importance to a person charged with an offense, that the facts laid before the jury should consist exclusively of the transaction, not only because he cannot be expected to come prepared to answer them alone, but because, even should he happen to be so prepared, it is so much irrelevant matter tending to confuse the minds of the jury, and to take from him the benefit of their exclusive consideration of the merits of the matter solely in issue. The customary manner of the prisoner's punishing slaves upon the plantation under his control, was not the point in issue, nor a collateral fact of that point, nor did it constitute any part of the transaction to which that point related. The prisoner was not necessarily prepared to prove his customary mode of punishing slaves. Such a matter involved an inquiry into circumstances that might draw away the minds of the jurors from the true merits of the investigation submitted to them. It might have tended to prove that the prisoner had committed the offense of cruel and unusual punishment upon a slave, which is a misdemeanor under our statutes, and thus have excited an improper prejudice against him in the minds of his jury. There was error, therefore, in permitting the question complained of to be asked and answered by the witness.

With the foregoing view of this case, its remaining points relied upon by counsel need not be reviewed.

The judgment of the court below is therefore reversed, and a new trial awarded.

SHARKEY, C. J.:

One of the objections raised in this case is, that the grand jury was illegally organized. It seems that after the *venire* was called, only ten of the jurors, who had been summoned, appeared, whereupon the court ordered the sheriff to summon two by-standers to serve on the jury, who were accordingly sworn. The regularity of this proceeding seems to me to depend entirely upon the sixty-eighth section of the circuit court law, which is in this language: " If at any regular or special term of any court in this state, there shall not be in attendance any of the regular jurors summoned to such term, it shall be the duty of the court to award forthwith a special *venire facias*, directing the proper officer to summon without delay, persons, freeholders or householders of the county in which the court shall be sitting, to serve as jurors at such term of the court," etc. Now the question is, does this section authorize the court to exercise this power only when all the grand jurors fail to attend, or is the special *venire facias* to issue to bring in a less number than a full panel? I think the statute is not to be read as providing only for the non-attendance of the whole panel, but if any part fail to attend, then a *venire* shall issue to make up the requisite number. The sense of the statute is made apparent by reading it thus: "If there shall not be in attendance any one or more of the regular jurors," etc., or "any number of the jurors," then it shall be the duty of the court to issue a special *venire.* The word "any" means every, either, whosoever. By giving to it either of the latter significations, my construction is sustained, and the statute leaves no contingency unprovided for. It would seem singular, indeed, that the legislature should have intended to authorize the court to issue a special *venire* only in the event of the non-attendance of the whole jury, a contingency that is least likely to occur, and that they should have overlooked the difficulty, which is most probable, and which must, in the nature of things, often occur, by the non-attendance of part of the jury. Thinking, then, that the statute provides for supplying the deficiency, in case any one or more of the jurors should fail to attend, the question is narrowed down to this: may the court disregard the mode prescribed by the statute, by pursuing a different method? I think not. The statute must be followed. As well might the court dispense with the *venire facias* entirely, and summon the whole of the grand jury from the by-standers. It is not for the court to say, that the provision of the law is useless, or that its object may be accomplished without process, when process is required. The law requires, that the special *venire facias* shall direct the sheriff to summon freeholders or householders of the county, but under a mere order, verbally given, the defendant has no security that competent persons will be summoned. It is safe to follow the law, but dangerous to depart from it. If my construction of the statute be the true one, then the indictment was bad, and the judgment ought to have been arrested.

I concur with the majority of the court in holding that improper evidence was permitted to go to the jury. The testimony which tended to show the defendant's treatment of other slaves should have been excluded.

JOHNSTON v. THE STATE, 7 Smedes & Marshall, 58.

UNLAWFUL GAMING.

A grand jury composed of twelve men of the panel summoned under the *venire facias*, being all who were in attendance of the panel, and two by-standers summoned by the sheriff, under an order of the court, constitute a good and legal grand jury. The case of Dowling v. the State, 5 S. & M., 664, cited and confirmed.

In an indictment under the act "further to suppress and discourage gaming" (Act of 1839, ch. 26), it is not necessary to state the particular game of cards played; it being sufficiently definite for all reasonable or legal purposes to charge that the defendant "did play at a game of cards for money."

Error to the circuit court of Hinds county.

The defendant, Peter G. Johnston, was indicted by the grand jury of Hinds county; the indictment charged, "That Peter G. Johnston, late of the county of Hinds, aforesaid, laborer, on the 30th day of May, A. D. 1843, in, etc., did play at a game at cards for money, contrary to the form of the statute." Verdict, guilty; sentence, a fine of twenty dollars. The bill of exceptions in the record shows the following facts, to wit: On the call of the regular *venire*, but twelve persons summoned, answered; whereupon the sheriff, under the order of the court, summoned two by-standers, who, together with the twelve *venire*-men, were sworn and charged as a grand jury, etc. On the trial the state proved that at sundry times in 1842 and 1843, defendant had played at games of cards, at Cayuga, in said county; playing, as witness considered it, for pastime or amusement; the game was usually seven-up, and the bet from a dime per game to several dollars, which was generally laid out in a treat. This being all the evidence, the defendant asked the court to instruct the jury, "that they ought to find for the defendant." The court refused and defendant excepted. The defendant moved the court to arrest the judgment, but the motion was overruled.

Daniel Mayes for the plaintiff in error.

1st. The indictment should have been quashed, because there was no grand jury, legally empanelled and constituted, and cited Laws of Mississippi, from 1824 to 1838; Nay's Maxims, 9th ed., p. 4; Staniland v. Hopkins, 9 M & W., 192; Devarris on Statutes, 48; Rex v. Daniel, 5 B. & C., 569; Rex v. Ramsgate, 6 B. & C., 712; Rex v. Inhabitants of Great Bentley, 10 B. & C., 527; Best, J., in 3 Bing.; 196.

2d. The indictment is bad on its face, because it does not charge the general name of the game at which the defendant may have played. If the statute dispenses with all identifications of the offense, it is unconstitutional. 10th sec. 1st art., Cons. of Miss.; 3 Story's Com. on Const., 661; 2 Kent's Com., 3d ed., 12; Const. of Miss., sec. 12, art. 1; 2 Russell on Cr., 659; 3 Story on Const., 658, 662.

Franklin Smith for the state.

Indictments making the charge in the language of the statute creating the offense, in general language, are good. 6 Cowen, 293, 296; 12 Wend., 431; King v. Holden, Crown Cases, Reserved, 116; see also Noonan v. The State, 1 S & M., 562, 563; 1 Chit., 281, 282, 286, 288; 3 Gill & John. Rep., 310, 311.

At common law the *terms* require the species of game to be stated; to obviate this, the statute, How. & Hutch., 684, sec. 85, was passed, which declares that it shall be sufficient to charge the general name of the game. There are three general names mentioned in the 79th section, to wit: cards, dice, and billiards.

This court, in Noonan v. The State, 1 S. & M. 562, ruled that it was not necessary to state, in the indictment for a violation of the license law of 1842, the *kind* of spirits sold, or the *name* of the master. These acts against unlawful gaming are remedial, not penal statutes, and should be therefore liberally construed. 6 Cowen, 693; 15 Wend., 280. See same act, sec. 85; 1 Chitty, 303. The sole point in this case is, is the law, How. & Hutch., 684, sec. 85, constitutional? And upon this point, see. 1 S. & M., 562.

THACHER, J.:

The plaintiff in error was indicted in the Hinds county circuit court, under the act of 1839, ch. 26, entitled "an act further to suppress and discourage gaming." A verdict of guilty was rendered upon the indictment.

The first point made in the case was considered and decided by this court in the case of Thos. Dowling v. The State, 5 S. & M., 664. This point had reference to the mode in which the grand jury were empanelled, and was determined unfavorably to the position assumed by the plaintiff in error in this case.

Another point in this case is made as to the sufficiency of the indictment. The indictment charges that the defendant " did play at a game at cards for money." It is objected that this description of the offense is not sufficiently certain, and that it should have set forth the name of the game at cards played by the defendant. The statute H. & H., 683, § 79, enacts that, " if any person or persons shall encourage or promote any game or games, or shall play at any game or games at cards, etc., for money," etc.; and the same statute, H. & H., 684, § 85, provides, that in all cases arising under this or any other act to suppress gaming, it shall be sufficient to charge the general name of the game at which the defendant may have played, without setting forth or describing with or against whom he may have played or bet. In Tennessee, the statute against gaming, Act 1799,-ch. 8, § 2, is nearly word for word similar to that of Mississippi. In the case of Dean v. The State of Tennessee, Martin & Yerg. R., 1, 127, the indictment charged that Dean " did unlawfully encourage and promote a certain unlawful game and match at cards for money, and unlawfully did play for and bet money at the said game and match at cards," etc. An objection was raised to the insufficiency and uncertainty of the charge in the indictment, in not specifying the particular game played at for money, and the amount of money bet. The court held the allegation in the indictment to be sufficient. In the case of Montee v. The Commonwealth, 3 J. J. Marshall's R., 135, it was decided that the word " cards " identifies the specific game played, and that the individual game of cards played need not be stated.

We are disposed to think that the allegation in the indictment that the defendant " did play at cards for money," is sufficiently defined for any reasonable or legal purpose ; for " it may be," as was said by Judge Peck, in the case quoted above, from Martin & Yerger's Reports, " that adepts at gaming play for money without any game, where their invention for names has been exhausted." [1]

Judgment affirmed.

[1] On the point here decided, see Webster v. State, 8 Blackford, 400; Ewbanks v. State, 5 Mo., 450; State v. McBride, 8 Humph., 66; Commonwealth v. Crupper, 3 Dana, 466; State v. Ross, 7 Blackf., 322.

MOUNT *v.* THE STATE, 7 Smedes & Marshall, 277.

PERMITTING UNLAWFUL GAMING.

Where a party is indicted and tried for suffering a faro bank to be exhibited in the house occupied by him, it is not error to refuse to instruct the jury, "that if the defendant had let the rooms in his house in which the exhibition of the faro bank took place, to certain persons, and that at the time when he let them, he had no knowledge or expectation that they would be used for that purpose, they must find for the defendant."

The tenants of the accused, so renting the rooms or tenements from him, were equally subject to indictment and punishment under the statute.

Error to the circuit court of Hinds county.

On the trial, Robert Brown testified on the part of the state, that he saw faro-dealing in three rooms of the Eagle Hotel, in Jackson, kept by the defendant, during the previous winter, while the legislature was in session; saw the dealing both day and night, but did not see defendant in either of the rooms or about when the dealing took place. Charles W. Hart testified, that he saw the faro dealt in that hotel, both up stairs and down stairs, at the same period of time spoken of by the foregoing witness; no guard was kept about the room, which seemed to be accessible to any one wishing to enter; did not see defendant in either of the rooms or about when the dealing took place but once, when a negro, belonging to the establishment, was in the room, and was called out by the defendant who came near the door but did not enter. It was not proved by any witness that defendant was in the rooms, or knew of the dealing.

It was proved that defendant had leased the rooms to the occupants for a month, at $150 per month, and during which time the dealing took place. The defendant asked the court to instruct the jury, "that before they could find the defendant guilty, it must have been proved to them that he knew of the unlawful gaming in his hotel," which was given, with the addition "that the jury were authorized to infer such knowledge from circumstances which would authorize the inference."

Defendant then asked the court to instruct the jury, "that, if they believed from the evidence that the defendant rented the rooms in which the exhibition took place, and that during that tenancy the exhibition occurred; and that he rented the rooms in good faith, without any knowledge or expectation that they would be used for the exhibition of a faro bank, he was not responsible for their exhibition during the continuance of such tenancy." This instruction the court refused to give, and exceptions were taken.

Howard & Foote, for plaintiff in error.

John D. Freeman, attorney general.

THACHER, J.:

This was an indictment against the plaintiff in error, for knowingly suffering a gaming table, called a faro bank, to be exhibited in the house occupied by him.

The court below declined to instruct the jury to the effect that, if the accused had let the rooms of his house, in which the exhibition of the faro bank is proved to have taken place, to certain persons, and that at the time when he let them, he had no knowledge or expectation that they would be used for the purpose of such an exhibition, the jury must find for the defendant.

This charge, we think, was properly refused, for, if the accused, after he had let the rooms in good faith and without any knowledge of the unlawful purposes for which they would be used, knowingly permitted them to be occupied and improved for such an exhibition, he would still be answerable under the statute.[1] The tenants of the accused would be equally subject to the statute. Regina v. Pierson, 2 Ld. Raym., 1197.

In the other respects of this case the evidence seems to warrant the finding of the jury, and upon close examination the remaining assignments of error are not found to embrace any thing that would warrant a reversal of the judgment.

Judgment affirmed.

[1] See 2 Archbold Cr. Pr. & Pl., 1013, note.

DOMINGES *v.* THE STATE, 7 Smedes & Marshall, 475.

MURDER.

The substitution of depositions for oral testimony belongs to civil proceedings. In no state of circumstances under our constitution can the deposition of a witness be used against the defendant in a criminal prosecution; and the same rule holds as to the deposition of a witness in his favor, unless by his consent; and therefore, where a defendant makes an affidavit for a continuance, on account of the absence of witnesses, setting forth what they will prove when present the state cannot force him into a trial by admitting the truth of what the absent witness would testify.

In criminal cases it should not be allowed or encouraged, except in very extreme cases, to admit what the prisoner, in his application for a continuance, stated he expected to be proved by the absent witness; but when such admission has been once made, it constitutes an admission, not merely that the absent witness would have sworn to certain alleged facts, but, also, that the facts alleged are absolutely true.

Error to the circuit court of Wilkinson county.

John Dominges, having been indicted for the murder of James H. Holmes, was tried and found guilty at the April term, 1845, of the circuit court.

When the case was called for trial, the defendant filed his affidavit for a continuance, in which he stated that Haley, Hodge and Ferguson were important witnesses for him, and were absent; that by Haley he would prove that in killing Holmes he had acted in self-defence; and by the other witnesses that deceased had threatened his life, and went armed for the purpose of taking it. The district attorney stated that he would admit that if the witnesses named in the affidavit were present, they would swear to the truth of the facts deposed to therein; and thereupon the court compelled the defendant to go into trial, and he excepted.

After the evidence for the state was closed, and also that for the prisoner, which it is not deemed necessary to notice further, the state introduced witnesses who testified that they knew Haley's general character for truth and veracity in the community in which he lived, and that they would not believe him on oath.

The prisoner then asked the court to instruct the jury, "that the admission of the counsel for the state, that the facts contained in the prisoner's affidavit for a continuance, should be considered as sworn to by the witnesses therein named, was an

admission of the truth of those facts, and that unless the jury **can convict** the prisoner of the charge in the indictment consist-**ently with the** admitted truth of these facts, they must find for **the prisoner.**" The prisoner asked for other instructions to the **like effect, all** of which were refused.

Farish for plaintiff in error.

1. That the practice of allowing concessions in cases like the **present, was** novel and not calculated to advance justice, but **if encouraged,** the prosecutor was bound to admit the truth of **the facts** proposed to be proved. People v. Vermilyea, 7 Cowen. **388; Brill v.** Lord, 14 Johns., 341; 7 Cowen, 390; Graham Pr., **285, and auth**orities cited.

2. That the admission of the truth of what the witnesses would **swear to, was** also an admission of all that might be fairly de-**duced theref**rom.

3. That even if Haley be impeached, yet what he deposed to, **taken in conn**ection with the testimony of Hodge and Ferguson, **as corroborat**ing it, was entitled to weight by the jury. People **v. Vane, 12** Wendell, 78; 2 Phil. Ev. (Cow. & Hill's notes,) **779.**

John D. Freeman, attorney general.

THACHER, J.

The plaintiff in error was indicted in the Wilkinson county **circuit court** for the murder of one Holmes. Upon his being **called to the** bar for trial, he filed his affidavit for a continuance **of the cause** on the ground of the absence of material witnesses **in his behalf.** This affidavit was in legal form, and set out that **an absent witn**ess, Haley, would prove that the accused acted in **self-defence in** the matter with which he was charged, and that **absent witne**sses, Hodge and Ferguson, would prove that the **deceased, alleg**ed to have been murdered by the accused, threat-**ened to take** the life of the accused, and went armed for that **purpose. At** the filing of this motion for a continuance, sup-**ported by an** affidavit of the foregoing character, the state, by **the district** attorney, agreed to admit upon the trial, that if the **witnesses nam**ed in the affidavit were present, they would swear **to the truth** of the facts deposed to therein. The motion for a continuance was overruled below and an exception to that judgment taken by the accused. On the trial the affidavit for the continuance was read to the jury, and it was admitted, that if the witnesses named therein had then been present, they would have sworn to the truth of the facts therein set forth. The state thereupon introduced witnesses to impeach the credibility of the said Haley, one of the witnesses named in the affidavit for a continuance. A number of instructions to the jury were requested, upon the behalf of the accused, to the effect, that the foregoing admission by the state, in reference to the testimony of the witnesses described in the affidavit for a continuance, was an admission of the truth of the facts therein set out, and that full weight to that extent should be given to them by the jury in weighing the evidence of the case. These instructions were refused by the court, and a verdict and judgment of guilty according to the indictment were rendered against the accused.

The substitution of depositions for oral testimony belongs to civil trials. In no state of circumstances, under our constitution, can a deposition of a witness be used against the accused in a criminal prosecution, and a similar rule seems to hold as to depositions of witnesses in his favor, unless by his consent. The system of criminal jurisprudence appears to require the presence of the witnesses, both for and against the accused. Very often, in such prosecutions, much depends upon the appearance, manner and mode of testifying of a witness, and it is this that adds the superior character and importance to oral testimony.

The practice in criminal cases of proposing to admit what was expected to be proved by absent witnesses, is not calculated to advance the ends of public justice; and if, indeed, regular and competent should not be allowed or encouraged except in very extreme cases. But when such an admission has been once made it constitutes an admission, not merely that the absent witnesses would have sworn to certain alleged facts, but also that the facts alleged are absolutely true. Such an admission is an absolute concession of the facts stated by the accused upon his part, because that alone would be a fair substitute for what might have been the result of the evidence upon an oral examination of the witnesses whose actual presence was sought to be obtained.

Judgment reversed, and a new trial directed to be allowed by the court below.

TOUMEY *v.* THE STATE, 8 Smedes & Marshall, 104.

RAPE

Questions are leading, which suggest to the witness the answer desired; or which embody a material fact, and may be answered by a mere negative or affirmative; or which involve an answer bearing immediately upon the merits of the cause, and indicating to the witness a representation which will best accord with the interests of the party propounding them.

On the examination in chief, it is irregular and improper to propound a question which assumes a fact to be proved which is not proved;—whether such a question is or is not a leading question.—*Quære !*

It is a well-established general rule, that leading questions should not be propounded to a witness on the examination in chief; but there are exceptions to this general rule; as where the witness is manifestly reluctant and hostile to the interest of the party calling him; or where he has exhausted his memory without having stated the particular required, as a proper name or other fact, which cannot be arrived at by a general inquiry; or where the witness is a child of tender years, whose attention cannot be otherwise called to the subject matter.

The circuit court before which the examination is had, is allowed to exercise a certain discretion in permitting leading questions to be propounded to a witness on the examination in chief; that discretion, however, is not an absolute or arbitrary one, but is subject to revision in the appellate court; and if it appear that leading questions were propounded under circumstances that did not justify them, and that the party against whom they operated excepted to them at the time, this court will reverse the judgment, and grant the injured party a new trial. Mr. Justice Clayton dissenting as to the power of the appellate court to revise the discretion exercised by the court below in permitting the leading questions.

This discretion of the court to permit leading questions on the examination in chief, is allowed to be exercised alone in the cases forming exceptions to the general rule, and where these do not exist, the discretion is not allowed; as where the witness is a willing witness, of competent age, or favorable to the party calling him; in these cases, to allow leading questions will be a fatal error.

On the trial of the prisoner for a rape, the victim of the outrage being a witness for the state, testified that the crime had been committed about seven months before indictment found, which, as far as appeared by the record, was the first disclosure by the witness of the commission of the crime; it also appeared that the prisoner had been the guardian of the witness from early orphanage, and was her step-father; and that she was, at the time of the alleged offense, sixteen years of age;—she was then asked; "Did the prisoner then, or at any subsequent time, say anything to you in relation to this matter to dissuade you from disclosing it? State when, where and what he said." This was held to be a leading and illegal question. Mr. Justice Clayton, dissenting, held the question to be legal and proper.

Under the same circumstances, the following question propounded to the same

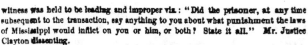

witness was held to be leading and improper viz.: "Did the prisoner, at any time subsequent to the transaction, say anything to you about what punishment the laws of Mississippi would inflict on you or him, or both? State it all." Mr. Justice Clayton dissenting.

Under the same circumstances, the question to the same witness, "If the prisoner, in any of his antecedent conversations offered property, or any other advancement to you in order to attach you to him, say so;" was held to be illegal and inadmissible. Mr. Justice Clayton dissenting.

On the trial of a prisoner for a rape upon his ward, the entire record of his proceedings, as guardian, in the probate court, including his accounts and settlements and appropriations of the ward's property, is evidence to establish the continuing guardianship of the prisoner over the ward; and if the prisoner desire to exclude any portion of the record as irrelevant, he should move to exclude the irrelevant part, and not the whole record; in default of which the admission of the whole record will not be error, though the prisoner except to it at the time. Chief Justice Sharkey dissenting, and holding that the whole record was inadmissible, as calculated to prejudice the jury against the prisoner, inasmuch as it showed that he had squandered the property of his ward, besides having despoiled her of her virginity.

The prisoner was on trial for a rape, and a witness was asked if he had not at a certain time authorized his wife to offer the victim of the outrage a home, and in what manner he had authorized it; and the record, without setting forth the answer of the witness, stated in general terms that he answered the question in the affirmative, and stated the reasons which he had stated to his wife; it was held that, the record not disclosing what the testimony was which the witness gave, the court could not determine as to its legality. Chief Justice Sharkey dissenting, and holding that, let the testimony be what it might, it was inadmissible, being a conversation between a man and his wife, not in the presence of the prisoner, and forming no part of the *res gestæ.*

On the trial of a prisoner for a rape, if the victim of the outrage be a witness in the cause, it is competent for the prosecution to prove her good character, by way of confirming her credibility before the jury.

Error to the circuit court of Claiborne county.

At the May term, 1845, of the circuit court of Warren county, Isaac Toumey was indicted by the grand jury, for a rape upon the person of Mary Folkes, on the first day of September, 1844. The venue was changed to Clairborne county, where at the June term of the circuit court, he was tried and found guilty, and sentenced to twenty years in the penitentiary.

The bill of exceptions, made part of the record in the case, shows substantially as follows: Mary Folkes, on behalf of the prosecution, testified that about the first day of September, 1844, the defendant committed a rape upon her in Warren county, near a bridge in the main road from Vicksburg to Warrenton; the rape was committed ten or twelve steps from the road, behind an embankment about two miles from Warrenton. She was then just sixteen years old. The counsel for the state then asked the witness, "Did Mr. Toumey then, or at any subsequent

time, say anything to you in relation to this matter to dissuade
you from disclosing it? state when, where and what he said."
To this question the counsel for the prisoner then and there objected, but the objection was overruled, and the prisoner excepted.   The record proceeds—in answer to this question the
witness stated that the prisoner had charged her not to tell it,
that it would ruin her, and her friends would desert her, that it
would hurt her mother's feelings, (who was the prisoner's wife),
and she would not be believed ; the witness further testified
that the prisoner had always been very affectionate towards her,
and said he loved her better than any child he ever saw.   She
had lived with him as her guardian and stepfather from eight or
nine years old to 1842."   The counsel for the state then asked the
following question, to wit : " If in any of his antecedent conversations he offered property or any other advancement to you, in
order to attach you to him, say so."   (The objection to this
question being made, overruled, and exceptions taken, the record proceeds), " The witness answered, the prisoner had talked of
adopting her and of leaving her half of his property ; that on
their way to Vicksburg on the morning of the day the rape was
committed, he offered to give her a gold watch and fifteen dollars, to induce her to consent to his desires."   The counsel for
the state then asked witness the following questions, viz : " If at
any time subsequent to this transaction, he said anything about
what punishment the laws of Mississippi would inflict on him,
or you, or both ?   State it all."   (To this question a like objection was made, and exceptions taken to its admission).   The
witness answered that the prisoner said it would penitentiary
him and her, both ; this was said about the first of March, last.

The record of the probate court of Warren county was offered,
showing the proceedings in the matter of guardianship of Mary,
Florida,   and Virginia Folkes.   The prisoner, in November,
1836, took letters of guardianship, of these three children, (minor
heirs of Henry Folkes, deceased), in right of his wife, widow of
said Henry and mother of the children.   In February, 1837,
the prisoner presented his annual account as guardian, in which
he charged each of his wards $144 a year for board; besides
separate charges of their clothing.   In August, 1837, he applied

by petition to the probate court, to sell the slaves of his wards, six in number; aged 20 years, 16, 13, 5, 4, respectively, and one 10 months.   He states in his petition that it would be greatly to the benefit of the heirs to sell the slaves, and that if the order were granted, he would maintain and educate the minors at his own expense until they attained an age when they could maintain themselves.   The sale was ordered on a credit for twelve months, and at January term he reported it; amounting to about $4,000, of which $1,115 belonged to Mary.   At same term, in his annual account as guardian, he charged each of his wards $144 a year for board, which was allowed.   At March term, 1840, he gave a new guardian bond.   At March term, 1841, he presented another annual account showing amount in his hands, and which he was to retain, and pay lawful interest for it.   At November term, 1842, filed his petition, stating that he educated, boarded and clothed the children, and in consideration thereof asked to be exonerated from payment of interest; this was granted.   At February term, 1845, reported to the court that he held the ward's money in his hands, neither paying interest nor charging board, etc.   At May term 1845, on his own petition showing that circumstances connected with the guardianship were of such a nature as to compel him to relinquish it, and that he was in the jail of Warren county, and was unable to say when his confinement would end; court discharged him from his guardianship.   This is the substance of the whole record.   The defendant objected to the admission of the record as illegal and incompetent, but the court overruled the objection, it was read, and the exceptions taken.

Samuel Luckett was then called for the state, who testified that Mary Folkes was half sister of his wife; and was asked by the prosecution, "Please tell whether or not, you last fall, or at any other time, offered Mary Folkes a home at your house, or authorized your wife to do so; if so, state in what manner and when."   This was objected to, allowed, and exceptions taken. "The witness stated that he had authorized his wife to offer Mary Folkes a home in his house, and proceeded to state the reasons which induced him to do so, and which he stated to his wife;" "to which testimony, as to the reason, etc., of the wit-

ness, the prisoner's counsel objected," but it was admitted and
exceptions taken.

The prosecution then asked, " From your knowledge of Mary
Folkes, has she maintained the reputation of a lady of good
fame ? This was also objected to, and being admitted, exceptions were taken. Witness answered, "she has, and he had
heard several ladies speak well of·her."   This was also objected
to.

Benjamin Folkes, brother of Mary, called by the prosecution,
stated that on the 9th or 10th of April, 1845, prisoner told him
he had taken Mary Folkes to Hendersonville, Ky., and left her
with a Mrs. Taylor, a relation of his ; witness went to Hendersonville, and not finding her there, returned to Vicksburg, where,
learning from another source, that his sister was at Newburgh,
Indiana, he went for and found her with the prisoner's brother-
in-law, and brought her back to Vicksburg.   This was objected
to, but admitted, and exceptions taken.

Miles C. Folkes, on the part of the state, said Mary Folkes
was his half sister by the same father ; prisoner married Mary's
mother in 1835 or 1836 ; he was then asked, " After the prisoner married your step-mother, on what terms was the intercourse between him and the half-brothers of Mary Folkes regulated, whether friendly or otherwise ?" Exceptions were taken
·to its admission, and he answered that until the year 1842, it
had not been cordial, but since that period it had been of a social
and·friendly nature.   Witness also stated the conversation he
had with his brother when he first heard the rumors about his
sister's condition, and the language of rebuke to the persons who
first communicated it.   These conversations and language are
not inserted in the record, but their admission was made the
subject of exception.   Same witness detailed the interview between his brother Benjamin and himself, as to the reports in cir-
culation about their sister, and only of putting a stop to them ;
also of facts relative to his brother's trip to Hendersonville, and
Indiana and the reasons which led to it.   These conversations,
etc., are not set out in the record, but were admitted to the jury,
and excepted to.

James C. Goodwin, stated that Bullitt was the brother-in-law of Toumey, prisoner, etc., had at one time worked in the witness's shop; and stated the history of some tools belonging to witness, which had been found in Bullitt's chest, and the conversation between Toumey, Bullitt and witness about them. This conversation was also made the subject of an exception.

William T. Martin, on the part of the state, testified that the general reputation and standing of Mary Folkes was as good as that of any girl; her associates and her character were good; he never heard her chastity or truth questioned.

The prisoner's counsel asked the witness if he knew the general reputation of Miss Folkes for veracity; witness responded, that he had never heard it spoken of, or called in question; the question was repeated, and a similar reply given. Prisoner's counsel insisted on a more distinct and direct answer being given, but the court decided the reply to be sufficient, and exceptions were taken.

Foote & Hutchinson, for plaintiff in error.

John D. Freeman, attorney general.

THACHER, J.:

An indictment for rape was preferred by the grand jury of Warren county against Isaac Toumey, at the April term, 1845, of the circuit court of that county. Under the statute a change of venue was allowed, and the indictment was tried in the county of Claiborne, whereupon a verdict of guilty was rendered, and the defendant sentenced to imprisonment in the penitentiary for the term of twenty years.

The defendant below brings the cause into this court by a writ of error, sued out upon exceptions reserved to the ruling of the court, in admitting and rejecting testimony upon the trial.

The first exceptions exhibited in the record relate to the mode of examination pursued with the witness for the state, Mary Folkes. This witness, having previously testified that about the first day of September, 1844, at which time she was just sixteen years of age, the defendant committed a rape upon her, was then permitted by the state to be asked upon her examination in chief, this question: " If Mr. Toumey then, or at any subsequent time, said anything to you in relation to this matter to dissuade you

from disclosing it? State when, where and what he said."
Again, the witness having testified that she was the defendant's
step-daughter, and had lived with him as her guardian from the
age of eight or nine years to the year 1842, during which time
he had treated her very affectionately, was also permitted to be
asked by the state: "If, in any of his antecedent conversations,
he (Toumey) offered property, or any other advancement to you,
in order to attach him to you, say so?" Again, the following
question was permitted to be put to the same witness: "If, at
any time, subsequent to the transaction, he (Toumey) said anything about what punishment the laws of Mississippi would inflict on him, or you, or both?—state it all." These questions
were answered affirmatively.

It is well settled that in the inquiry into the nature of a transaction, whatever was said by both parties, as well as what was
done during the continuance of the transaction, is admissible.[1]
Roscoe's Cr. Ev., 22. But in this case the objections are directed
to the form of the questions, upon the ground of their being
leading questions.

It is often extremely difficult to distinguish such questions as
should not be allowed because of their leading tendency, from
those which, though in form leading, in effect only draw the
mind of the witness to the subject of inquiry. But, while it is
impossible to lay down any fixed rule, which will serve in all
cases, there are yet certain established rules upon the subject of
leading questions, which afford a good test by which to discriminate in cases not very doubtful. For instance, that is a leading
question which suggests to the witness the answer desired.[2] 1
Stark. Ev., 124; 2 Phill. Ev., 722; The People v. Mather, 4
Wend., 249. And that is also a leading question which assumes
a fact to be proved, which is not proved. A question is also
leading which, embodying a material fact, admits of an answer
by a simple negative or affirmative. The latter constitutes an
argumentative or pregnant cause of interrogation, which the law
holds objectionable.[3] 1 Greenl. Ev., § 434.

[1] See 1 Archbold Cr. Pr. & Pl., 577.
[2] 1 Greenl. Ev., 434, 435, 437; Hill v. Coombe, 1 Ev., 163, note qq; Hanley v.
Ward, Ib.; Roscoe Nisi Prius Ev., 171; 2 Phill. Ev., 888–889; Roscoe Cr. Ev., 130,
et seq.
[3] See note 2 supra.

On the other hand, however, there are exceptions to the rule,[1] which forbids leading questions to be put to a witness in his examination in chief; as when he is manifestly reluctant and hostile to the interest of the party calling him,[2] or when he has exhausted his memory[3] without stating the particulars required, where it is a proper name, or other fact, which cannot be arrived at by a general inquiry, or when the witness is a child of tender years, whose attention cannot be otherwise called to the subject matter.[4] Moody v. Rowell, 17 Pick., 498.

It is also to be observed upon this subject, that much discretion is confided to a court in regulating and controlling the examination of witnesses, which is to be governed by the circumstances of each case;[5] and that some courts have gone so far as to hold that the subject, under what circumstances a leading question may be put, is a matter resting in the sound discretion of the court presiding over the examination, and is not a matter upon which to base a motion for a new trial, or which can be assigned for error. Greenl. Ev., § 435; 17 Pick., 498; Stratford v. Sanford, 9 Conn. R., 275.

In order the better to scrutinize the character of the questions propounded in this case to the witness, Mary Folkes, we must bear in mind the state of the evidence at the different periods when they were severally proposed to her. Before the first question now objected to was asked, it had been shown that about seven months had elapsed between the time when the act of violence was alleged by her in her testimony to have been committed, and the finding of the indictment, which, for all that appears, was the first disclosure of the offense charged. It was, therefore, a material fact for the state to explain satisfactorily the cause of this long concealment by Mary Folkes, of the enormity alleged to have been perpetrated upon her. A sufficient

1 Stringfellow v. State, 26 Miss., 157; Gunter v. Watson, 4 Jones, 455,

2 Bank of Northern Liberties v. Davis, 6 Watts & Serg., 285; Towns. v. Alford, 3 Ala., 378; 1 Greenl. Ev., 434-5, notes.

3 Huckins v. People's M. F. Ins. Co., 11 Foster, 238.

4 People v. McNair, 21 Wend., 608.

5 Colclough v. Rhodes, 2 Pick., 76; Sears v. Shaffer, 1 Barb., 408; Donnell v. Jones, 13 Ala., 490; West v. State, 2 N. J., 212; Gayle v. Bishop, 14 Ala., 552; State v. Lull, 37 Maine, 246; York v. Pease, 2 Gray, 282; Budlong v. Van Nostrand, 24 Barb., 25; Walker v. Danspaugh, 20 N. Y., 170; Green v. Gould, 3 Allen, 465; Steer v. Little, 44 N. H., 613; Barton v. Kane, 17 Wis., 122.

explanation of this long silence might be established by proving that the defendant dissuaded the witness from disclosing the deed by promises or threats, or altogether prevented it by a removal from her friends. It had already appeared in evidence, that, from year to year from a very early period of the orphanage of the witness, he had with constant assiduity insinuated himself into her confidence, and it was fair to presume that by the accomplished arts of such a deliberate scheme of remorseless and calculating villainy, he had succeeded in becoming the master and tyrant of her mind, and rendered her the slave either of his promises or threats. Under these circumstances, the witness is asked to reply whether the defendant dissuaded her from disclosing the act, and also whether he informed her what punishment the laws of Mississippi would inflict upon either or both of them in consequence of it. It is clear that both of those questions embody a material fact in the case, and are capable of a conclusive answer affirmatively or negatively. They are likewise interrogatories pregnant with circumstances indispensable to be proved for the success of the prosecution. Had the witness simply rejoined that the defendant did dissuade her from disclosing the matter, and did inform her that the laws of Mississippi affixed a punishment upon her for her part in the transaction ; such answers, in view of the high degree of abused confidence already shown to repose in the mind of the witness towards the defendant, must have most satisfactorily accounted for the long delay in bringing the dark atrocity to the exposure of light. But, while the principle of law fortunately is fixed, that it being often necessary, it is, therefore, admissible to bring the mind of a witness into contact with the subject of inquiry, especially when a witness is examined as to any conversation or admission ; still it is also a principle of law equally fixed, and beyond the control of the indignation of public justice, that, in such questions, the witness should not be prompted to give a particular answer, or be asked any questions to which the answer "Yes" or "No" would be conclusive. 1 Stark. Ev., 124 ; Nicholls v. Dowding, 1 Starkie's C., 81 ; opinion of Lord Ellenborough. It is undoubtedly more convenient to ask a witness whether such a thing was said or done ; and questions so framed might, in many cases, be asked without danger of perjury, even involuntary, and we do not deny that such was the result in the very case under consideration; and there are also instances when such leading questions are proper, as have been before alluded to; but, in ordinary cases, it is certainly most consistent with fairness and justice, both to the witness and the defendant, to ask the witness *what* was done, and *what* was said, rather than whether a particular and material thing was done and said. We are compelled, therefore, to the conclusion that the questions propounded to Mary Folkes, and which have been examined, conform to the legal definition of *leading questions.*

It comes next in order to inquire whether there were any of those peculiarities surrounding this witness which warranted leading questions to be asked in the direct examination. It does not appear that the witness was hostile to the interests of the state in the prosecution. On the contrary, every witness so unfortunately situated as this one was, must be presumed, if supposed to indulge any sentiment upon the subject, other than a desire to simply state the facts of the occurrence, to entertain deep feelings of profound indignation and horror towards her violator. Keeping in mind that the witness had already deposed as to the perpetration of the actual violence at the point of time when the questions objected to were propounded, it necessarily became a subject of great moment to her reputation and good fame to vindicate her purity of mind and chastity of heart. It is not unreasonable to conceive that any one so unfortunate might be willing to adopt and assent to whatever might be suggested for her own benefit; and it is wisely provided, that whenever a witness, from peculiar situation, has, or upon interrogation, shows a bias in favor of the examining party, a court should prohibit leading questions, even upon cross-examination. Further, the facts sought to be obtained from the witness were not such as could not significantly be pointed to by general interrogations, or which could not have been extracted from the witness by a skillful and legitimate mode of interrogation. And lastly, upon this branch of the subject, while it may with propriety be inferred that the witness was very naturally confused, and perhaps confounded, by the peculiarity of her position, in being required to testify in public to facts so repugnant to female delicacy, it yet appears that the most dreaded and abhorrent details had been communicated; and it does not appear from the course of examination that repeated unsuccessful efforts had been first attempted in the proper mode to call forth what was supposed to exist in point of fact. In conclusion, nothing appears to show that the purposes of justice required the exercise of the discretionary power to vary the general rule controlling direct examinations, but rather the contrary.

It having been determined then, that leading questions were addressed to this witness, and that they were not essential to the ends of justice in this substance, it remains solely to inquire in this connection, whether this court will undertake to interfere with the discretionary power which is admitted to subsist with the courts who preside over the examination of witnesses.

It is true that it has been held in the *nisi prius* courts of England, that the rules of evidence are exactly the same in civil and in criminal cases, and that in both, it is in the discretion of the judge how far he will allow the examination in chief of a witness to be by leading questions, or, in other words, how far it shall assume the form of a cross-examination.[1] Regina v. Murphy and Douglas, 8 C. & P., 297. But the decisions above quoted from this country, wherein it was held that the matter of judicial discretion respecting the examination of witnesses, was not such as upon which to base an application for a new trial, or which can be assigned for error, were made in civil and not in criminal cases. Yet, in the case of Duncan v. McCullough, Admr., 4 Serg. & Rawle, 482, which was a civil action, the supreme court of Pennsylvania admitting the rule, that the manner of examining witnesses as a matter very much in the discretion of the court presiding upon the trial, intimate that they would entertain the question, whether that court would reverse for error on a point in which the law permits the court below to exercise their discretion, provided it appeared that there had been any abuse of discretion. In the case of The People v. Mather, 4 Wend., 247, which was the case of an indictment for a conspiracy in the abduction of William Morgan, the court,

[1] See note 1J, p. 312; 1 Greenl. Ev., 435, notes; Clarke v. Saffrey, Ry. & M., 126.

while it also admits the doctrine that considerable discretion is left to a judge who presides at a trial to control and regulate the examination of witnesses, and that appellate courts should cautiously avoid encroaching upon the proper exercise of this discretion, yet held, that if an established rule of law has been violated, the party injured has an undoubted right to belief, and that the court would feel no reluctance to grant it. The rule thus laid down by the Supreme Court of New York seems most consonant to the object of public justice, which is more the protection of the innocent than the punishment of the guilty.

Upon other points relied upon in the case, it now becomes necessary to speak but generally.

In regard to evidence of the actual guardianship of the defendant over the person of Mary Folkes, the chief witness, it was, perhaps, only necessary to have produced the copy, or a certificate of the grant of letters. This would have been enough to have established the existence of such guardianship during the minority of the ward, unless the contrary was made to appear by proof of a resignation or removal from the trust. Yet, I am not prepared to say, that the state could not be permitted to anticipate any such presumption, and establish the continuance of the guardianship up to any period necessary to be shown by means of the records of the probate court granting the letters.

Evidence was introduced as to the good fame of the person violated. This was competent, because she was made a witness in the cause. The party ravished is a competent witness to prove the fact, but the credibility of her testimony must be left to the jury. It is legitimate to support her credibility by evidence of her good fame, or to attack it by evidence of her evil fame. Such evidence tends to show that the connection with the woman was had against or with her consent. 4 Bl. Com., 213.

In consequence of the inadmissibility of the questions propounded to the chief witness, and the objection to them by the defendant upon the trial below, the judgment must be reversed, and a new trial awarded by the circuit court of Claiborne county.

Sharkey, C. J., *dissenting:*

I concur in the opinion, that there was an error committed in

permitting leading questions to be asked and answered, and as
the question is one of great importance in the present case, I
will briefly state some of the grounds on which my conclusion
is based.   It is very clearly laid down by elementary writers,
that leading questions, that is, such as instruct a witness how to
answer, are not allowed on the examination in chief, because by
directing witnesses in their evidence, the bias which they generally feel towards the interest of the party who calls them, would
be strengthened.   The strictest observance of this rule is said
to be necessary for the discovery of truth and the administration
of justice.   1 Phillip's Evidence, 268.   Starkie says, that the
principal rule to be observed upon the examination in chief is,
that *leading questions* are not to be asked; that is, questions
which suggest to a witness the answer he is to make; he also
says, that objections to questions of this nature are of the highest
importance.   1 Starkie, 123.   But a witness may be examined
in an introductory manner, so as to lead his mind to the subject;
hence it is often difficult to decide whether a question propounded
is objectionable.   These questions resemble so much the question which was decided to be objectionable as a leading question, in the case of Courteen v. Touse, 1 Camp., 43, as to entitle them to be held liable to the objection.   The rule against
the admissibility of leading questions is said to be most important, when the question is asked in reference to any conversation, admission, or agreement, as there is danger, that the witness should by design or mistake be guilty of some variance,
and give a false coloring to the transaction.   Again, there are
cases, in which leading questions will be allowed.   The instances
given are, where the witness appears to be in the interest of the
opposite party, or unwilling to give evidence, or when he is so
young, that it is necessary, to enable him to understand the subject.   If the rule is to be relaxed in cases of this kind, it must
be enforced with more strictness, when a willing witness is to
be examined.   Whilst it may be relaxed in the case of an unwilling witness, for the purpose of extracting truth, it must be rigor-
ously enforced against a willing witness, for the purpose of sup-
pressing falsehood.   The reason of this rule seems to be, that a
bias is supposed to exist in the mind of the witness towards the

party who calls him. If such a supposed motive has been deemed a sufficient foundation for the rule, then if there be palpable additional motives, the rules must acquire a corresponding importance, and require to be more rigidly enforced. If the law does not allow a leading question to be asked merely because of a supposed bias on the mind of the witness, arising from the circumstance that he was called by the party for whom he is about to testify, where there are considerations and motives personal to the witness, the danger of perjury is increased tenfold, and leading questions become too manifestly improper. Was there any such thing as a personal motive to operate on this witness? The crime had been perpetrated on her seven months before it was disclosed; a circumstance powerfully calculated to induce suspicions, that she had been a willing victim to the perfidy of a seducer, rather than a resisting subject of a brutal outrage. These suspicions were fatal to her character. Her good name was at stake; it was necessary to redeem it from the imputation of unchastity; this could only be done by giving some plausible excuse for the unaccountable delay which had preceded the disclosure; the question suggested the means of escape; it led to an answer, which might account for that delay, and save the reputation of the witness. When the motive to commit perjury is so powerful, the strictest administration of the law is necessary, and even that may fail to prevent it. This witness must have been fully aware, that her long silence would operate against her character, by causing a belief that she had yielded to importunities, and she must have felt a deep interest in removing such belief. Under circumstances like these, it was peculiarly improper that leading questions should be asked. I think it more than likely, that the witness told the truth, but that does not alter the case. The law must so operate as to meet all contingencies, and other witnesses under similar circumstances, to whom the rule would equally apply, might be induced to swear falsely. It would be tolerating a temptation to commit perjury. Besides the motives which may have operated on the witness, these questions were put in reference to conversations, admissions, and agreements of the accused, in which cases it is said in the books, the rule must be strictly enforced.

But it is said to be within the discretion of the court, before which the examination is had, to allow leading questions to be propounded or not, and that it cannot be assigned as error. The authorities on this subject are contradictory; by some it is holden to be error, by others it is said to be a matter of discretion. It is of the greatest importance in legal proceedings that truth should be ascertained, and this is one of the rules that the law employs to reach that end; it is said to be a rule of the highest importance, and that the strictest observance of it is essential to the discovery of truth and the due administration of justice. It seems to involve a contradiction to hold, that the rule is so important, and at the same time to hold, that it rests solely in the discretion of the court before which the examination takes place. If it be so important for the discovery of truth and the administration of justice, every means should be allowed of enforcing it. The exceptions to the rule show, that it is in some instances a rule of discretion, but they by no means prove, that it is always to be so regarded. Leading questions may be asked a reluctant witness or one who seems to be in the interest of the opposite party, or one who is so young as to make it necessary. In such cases the court has a discretion. If, in the opinion of the court, the witness testifies reluctantly, or seems to favor the interest of the opposite party, leading questions may be allowed. The court, in its discretion, is to judge of the necessity for such questions. In this we perceive the reason for classing it as a rule of discretion. But is it still a rule of discretion, when it is manifest that the witness favors the party by whom he is called? It would seem not. The discretion is to be exercised in deciding when the questions of a leading character are to be permitted, but when it is perfectly manifest that they are not necessary, then the court has no discretion; it must prohibit them. This is a matter which cannot, in many cases, be made to appear in an appellate court; and hence it is often said to be matter of discretion to allow such questions or not. But there are cases in which the record will enable the appellate court to judge of the necessity or impropriety of such questions. When it is perfectly manifest from the language of the witness and from the relation which he bears towards the person against whom he is testifying, that he is and must be hostile to the interest of that party, and must, in the nature of things, desire that the verdict should be against him, then leading questions are certainly improper, and if such a state of things is exhibited by the record, it must be competent for an appellate court to correct an error which has occurred by permitting leading questions to be asked. Under such circumstances the court has no power to allow a leading question to be asked; the law forbids it; and if it should be allowed, is an abuse of discretion, and if the facts can be made to appear in the appellate court, the error may be corrected. It is because the appellate court cannot, as a general rule, be advised of the temper of the witness, of his bearing and manner, that it will not undertake to control the court below in the matter of leading questions. But where it can be fully informed, where the record furnishes the means of judging of the propriety of such questions, I see no reason whatever why the appellate court should not exercise its judgment. It would seem to be peculiarly proper that it should do so, when a rule, confessedly important for the discovery of truth and the due administration of justice, has been violated. Now what is the state of facts exhibited by this record? They need not be repeated. It is perfectly apparent that the witness was not favorably disposed towards the prisoner. In the nature of things she must have desired his conviction; she was not reluctant to testify against him. Of these facts we are fully informed by the record, and therefore capable of judging of the propriety or impropriety of leading questions. As a general rule, I would admit that leading questions are to be regulated by the discretion of the circuit court; but when it is apparent that there was a powerful motive personal to the witness, beyond the mere bias supposed to arise in favor of the party who calls the witness, and where it is also apparent from the record that there was no necessity for allowing leading questions to be put, but, on the contrary, powerful reasons why they should not have been allowed, then I shall be willing to hold that it is a matter which may be assigned as error; then the error can be shown, and ought to be corrected. I would also advert to the fact that the legislature has gone very far to limit the discretion of the circuit courts

over the evidence given at the trial, by allowing parties to reduce the evidence to writing, and take appeals from motions for
new trials.

But to my mind this record exhibits other errors, on which a
judgment of reversal may rest with even less doubt than that
above referred to. After the witness, Mary Folkes, was examined, the state introduced a transcript from the records of the
probate court, of Warren county, containing the appointment
of the accused as guardian of Mary Folkes and her two sisters,
and exhibiting every step taken in the progress of guardianship,
and every order of court made in relation thereto, beginning in
November, 1836, and ending with his removal, in May, 1845.
It contains his annual accounts which specify every item charged
to each of his wards, and every order of the court made in relation
thereto. It contains the petition of the accused that he might
be permitted to sell all the slaves of his wards, on pretence that
it be for their benefit, and the order of court granting the petition, and also the return of sales. It is but too manifest that
the sale was to their prejudice. The slaves were but few in
number, and mostly young and valuable. No good reason was
shown for the sale, but still the court allowed it under a promise
tendered in the petition, that the accused would support his
wards at his own expense. But when the sum of $4000 came
to his hands, we find him violating this pledge by asking to be
permitted to hold it without interest, on the ground that he was
sending the girls to school. This record then exhibits his solemn
pledge and his violation of that pledge. It also shows that his
surety became alarmed, and he was cited and required to give
other sureties. He was formally removed, but the money of his
wards was not accounted for; that was doubtless squandered;
at least it was not surrendered. The witness was not only despoiled of her virginity, but of her fortune also. What but
prejudice could be excited by an examination of this record, in
connection with the facts before the jury; and what had these
proceedings to do with the issue before the jury. Was it necessary that the jury should know how he had managed the estate
of his ward, in order to enable them to determine whether he
had committed a rape on her? Even if this record did not ex-

cite a prejudice, still it was so much irrelevant matter. The prisoner had a right to have the whole mind of the jury directed and confined to the single inquiry of guilty or not guilty. But instead of that their attention was divided and directed to an examination of his management as guardian. They could but see that he had contrived to cheat his wards out of their property. It will not do to urge the necessity of this whole record as proof; it was not necessary. If it was necessary to prove the fact that he was guardian, which I admit it was competent for the prosecution to do, a mere extract from the order of appointment, or a certificate from the proper officer that he had been appointed, was all that was necessary. This is the way that the appointment of an administrator is proved, and it is all that is necessary. 1 Phillips Ev., 398. A party cannot introduce the various settlements with the probate court in reference to a particular estate, and the orders made by the court during a period of nine years, merely because a single entry happens to be an important item of proof. It was not necessary to introduce this record to prove that he continued guardian. It followed as a necessary presumption from his appointment, that he continued guardian, as a guardian is appointed to continue in office during the minority of his ward. In any point of view, then, this record seems to me to have been inadmissible. If it contained matter that was calculated to excite a prejudice, without having any bearing on the issue, it was of course inadmissible; and if it contained matter apparently innocent, if it was irrelevant, it was inadmissible.

I also think that the examination of Samuel Luckett was foreign to the issue. This question was propounded to him: " Please tell whether or not, you, last fall, or at any other time, offered Mary Folkes a home at your house, or authorized your wife to do so? if so, state in what manner and when." We are informed by the bill of exceptions, that the witness answered in the affirmative, and proceeded to state the reasons which induced him to do so, and which he stated to his wife; but the language of the witness is not given; it is therefore difficult to show its objectionable character; but this much I am free to say, I cannot imagine any possible motive which dictated the conversation between the witness and his wife that would have been proper as evidence, or that could justify the admission of the conversation which passed between *them* as evidence. Such conversation was not part of the *res gestæ*, but it seems to have been a disclosure of reasons which prompted the witness to offer Mary Folkes a home at his house. If a conversation held between the witness and his wife, the prisoner not being present, was admissible as evidence in this trial, it would seem to be difficult to say what would not be admissible. There is other testimony of the same character. M. C. Folkes was called as a witness, and proceeded to state a conversation which passed between him and his brother in reference to Mary Folkes. This conversation is set out in the bill of exceptions, and speaks its own condemnation. If it was admissible, there seems to be no limit to the admissibility of conversations between third persons. On the whole I am of opinion that the judgment should be reversed, and a new trial awarded.

CLAYTON, J.

I cannot concur in the reversal of this cause. I am not satisfied that the questions considered objectionable fall within the class of questions denominated leading. I fully concur with the court in Mather's case, 4 Wend., 247, " that it is often a matter of extreme difficulty to distinguish such questions as ought not to be tolerated, because they are leading, from those which, though in their form leading, are in effect only calculated to draw the mind of the witness to the subject of inquiry."

This difficulty is very apparent, from the various definitions or descriptions which have been attempted of leading questions. The most usual definition is, that they are those which may be answered by a mere affirmative or negative, and in which consequently the answer is fully suggested by the question. Another is, that they embody a material fact, and admit of an answer by a simple negative or affirmative. Another, that the question propounded involves an answer bearing immediately upon the merits of the cause, and indicating to the witness a representation which will best accord with the interests of the party. Two other objections to questions are likewise stated in the books, though they do not partake of the character of leading questions. One is, that an argumentative or pregnant course of examination is as faulty as the like course in pleading; the other, that the interrogatory must not assume facts to have been proved which have not been proved. 1 Greenleaf, § 434 ; 2 Pothier on Ob. by Evans, 203, 205.

Tried by any or all of these tests, and the questions in this case are not *clearly* and *certainly* objectionable. The first of them was this: " If Mr. Toumey, then or at any subsequent time, said anything to you in relation to this matter to dissuade you from disclosing it, state when, where and what he said." This could not be answered by a simple negative or affirmative, nor does it suggest to the witness the answer which is desired. The objection presupposes, or it is of no force, that the witness is ignorant, and would not, without prompting in some shape or other, know how to tell a story or frame an answer that would be favorable to the party for whom he is called. It will require no little sagacity to discover from this question any representation which will not best accord with the interests of the party. Unless the mind of the witness had been previously directed to this point, and unless she had learned the necessity of explaining away her silence, this question could not have instructed her what answer to give. If she had been previously crammed for the occasion, the question was harmless, and the utmost latitude of cross-examination was allowable to detect and expose the fact that it was a fabricated tale. The witness no doubt stood in a suspicious attitude; she must have felt a deep interest in the result, and the jury had a right to take into view all these considerations, and to receive her testimony with allowance. But when all this is conceded, I cannot see that this question suggested what answer she was to give, or put words into her mouth which she was to echo back again.

The next question was this: " If in any of his antecedent conversations he offered property or any other advancement to you, in order to attach you to him, say so." It is not easy to see how this question could have assumed a less exceptional shape. All the authorities say, you may bring the mind of the witness to the precise point, about which you wish to inquire.

Could this have been done in a less objectionable mode? The last question was this: "If at any time subsequent to this transaction, he said anything about what punishment the laws of Mississippi would inflict on him, or you, or both, state it all." This question is perhaps more free from objection, than either of the others. In one sense all questions are leading, they point the attention of the witness to the subject about which he is requested to testify. Judge Cowen, in his notes to Phillips on Ev. after a careful review of the subject, thus states the general rule: "In cases of conversations, admissions and agreements, you may draw the witness' attention to the subject, occasion, time, place, person and ask directly, whether such a person said anything on the subject thus brought under attention; and if yea, what did he say," Vol. 2., p. 724. These questions in my view, do not fall under condemnation by this rule.

In Watson's case, 3 C. L. R., 280, it was held, that the prosecutor might point to the prisoner, and ask the witness, if he were the person meant. In the case of the People v. Mather, 4 Wend., 247, the question objected to was, "how did you address the defendant in respect to his being one of the persons concerned," in the abduction of Morgan? The court said, "this question assumes the fact as true, which it was the object of the question to prove. It assumed that the witness did address the defendant, as one of the persons concerned in carrying off Morgan, and only asked him to tell the manner of the address." Now the questions were to be regarded as leading, their admission rests in the sound discretion of the court, and is not error, for which a reversal can be had. There is not in the English books, so far as I have seen, and none certainly was produced upon the argument, a case in which such objection has been taken in the appellate court. Every one, that I have been able to find, occurred in the progress of the trial at *nisi prius*, and was put finally to rest by the judge who presided. Greenleaf and the American editors of Phillips on Evidence, lay down the rule, that it is a matter resting in the sound discretion of the court, and which cannot be assigned for error. 1 Greenl., § 435; 2 Phill., 725. This rule is distinctly recognized in Stratford v. Sandford, 9 Conn., 275, and in Moody v. Rowell, 17 Pick., 498.

It is true, that in the case of The People v. Mather, 4 Wend., 247, a different rule is propounded. Indeed, there are but few points in the whole circle of the law, on which conflicting opinions of American courts may not be found. In all such instances of conflicting opinions as to the common law, the only true source to which we can resort for a resolution of doubts in the English authorities, and in them, this point seems never to have been urged as a ground of error.

All the writers, admit, that the asking of a leading question, rests in the sound discretion of the court, in which the trial is had. It is a settled principle of common law, that the exercise of discretionary power, is not in general, if indeed under any circumstances, a matter examinable upon a writ of error. Comyn. Dig. Error A.; Barr v. Gratz, 4 Wheat. 213. There may be exceptions, to which reference will hereafter be had; but this court has repeatedly recognized this as the general rule. Because this was the law, the legislature of this state enacted that a writ of error, should lie, for the granting or refusing a new trial. Before this statute, that was a matter resting in the sound discretion of the court, which tried the case, and was not ground of error. The legislature has passed other acts trenching upon the discretionary powers of the courts. These acts must be obeyed; but it does not thence follow, that the restriction is to be carried beyond the limit indicated by the legislature. I have just stated, that there might be exceptions to this rule; though many courts have refused to allow of any. I think it safer to admit, that the wrong exercise of legal discretion may be matter of error, "but the error must be gross and palpable, and not subject to hesitation or doubt; and must have produced flagrant and oppressive injustice." This is the language of the cases. Smith v. Britton, 4 Hump., 202; People v. Mather, 4 Wend. 247; 5 Hump., 568; 2 Rob. Va. Rep. 849; 10 Leigh, 692.

This case does not fall within such rule. It is matter of much doubt, whether the questions are liable to the objection at all. The books lay down various cases, which constitute exceptions to the general rule as to leading questions, and in which they are admissible. One of these is, when the witness is a reluctant one as to the party calling him, or manifests a bias against such party. All the evidence in this case is not set out ; it is impossible then for this court to know whether the witness was willing or reluctant, or whether the state of the case did not exist which authorized such mode of interrogation. The manner and bearing of the witness cannot be transferred into the bill of exceptions. The presumption is in favor of the acts of the court below. If in one state of circumstances the question was proper, and in a different state improper, and if this court has not the means to determine which was the true state of the case in this instance, this presumption sustains the decision of the court below. We cannot reverse unless we see there is error.

In most cases of exceptions, the objection is to the *answer*, not to the interrogatory. The court excludes or admits the answer, as may be right. But here the objection is to the *question*, because it may teach the witness, what answer to give. It subjects him to suspicion. The objection goes not to the competency, but to credibility of the witness. For, if he means to tell the truth, the mode of examination will not induce him to tell a falsehood. Starkie says, " that answers extracted by such improper means, are of little advantage in general to the party, in whose favor they are given, since evidence, obtained from a partial witness, by unfair means, must necessarily be viewed with the utmost jealousy." " Such evidence is very unsatisfactory, and open to much remark." 1 Starkie, 150, 162. It is the province of the jury to decide upon the credibility of the witness, and no court can invade that province. Yet, I cannot see how a judgment is to be reversed because a leading question is asked, without infringing the right of the jury to determine upon the credibility of all testimony. If the question be not answered, all will agree that it will do no harm; if it be answered, it is only objectionable because it may lead the witness to tell an untruth. Whether he does so or not, is matter for the jury, and it seems to me, that by reversing a judgment for this reason, we place ourselves in the proper position of the jury.

It has been shown that the erroneous exercise of a discretionary power by a court will not be ground of reversal, unless it be productive of flagrant and oppressive injustice. Is the asking of a leading question likely to work such a result? Starkie says, they are of little advantage to the party. Mr. Evans, in his edition of Pothier on Contracts, lays even less stress on them. Vol. 2, p. 203. Lord Ellenborough said, "If questions are asked, to which the answer yes or no would be conclusive, they would certainly be objectionable, but in general, no objections are of less moment than those which are made to questions as leading ones." Nicholls v. Dowding, 1 Starkie, N. P. C. 81; 2 Com. Law Rep., 305. It is not probable, therefore, that injury or injustice was done to the prisoner by these interrogatories; and it would extend the rule beyond the limit indicated in any case, that I have seen, so to hold.

This point was the one mainly discussed in the argument, and after having bestowed so much time upon it, I shall dwell but briefly upon the others.

The record of the probate court perhaps contained some matters which were irrelevant. Parts of it, however, were clearly legal and proper testimony; indeed the only legitimate testimony of facts which it was important to establish. The counsel for the prisoner did not move for the exclusion of those parts of the record which they deemed objectionable, but of the *whole.* This motion could not have been sustained, because a part was clearly legal and necessary proof. As to the presumption, that when the guardianship was once established, it continued until its determination was shown, the reply is, that a party cannot be required to rest his case upon presumptions, when he has positive proof in his power. On this point I concur with Judge Thacher.

In regard to the other exceptions, a few words will form my answer to them all. They all rest upon the ground, that the testimony offered was irrelevant, and ought not to have been admitted.

This court has decided, on more than one occasion, that although testimony ought, in strict practice, to appear to be irrelevant at the time it is offered, yet if it appear to be so at any time during the trial, it is sufficient. If it do not, then it should be excluded, when the testimony is closed. Lake v. Munford, 4 S. & M., 312.

The bill of exceptions in this case does not purport to set out all the testimony; there was at the close of the testimony no motion to exclude that in question, nor any motion for a new trial. It was an important point upon the part of the prosecution to account for the long silence of this ruined girl. To do so, it might have been important to unravel the web of cunning and falsehood, by which the prisoner, after having spoiled her of all that gives pride and purity to womanhood, had made her the slave of his will, and to conceal his guilt, had removed her to a distance from her friends and counsellors. The testimony excepted to might have been relevant and pertinent for that object. It was manifestly introduced for that purpose. If it were not pertinent, the bill of exceptions should have disclosed the whole evidence, and furnished the means of determining its propriety, in connection with all the proof, not on partial and garbled extracts. An exception for the exclusion of testimony rests upon a different footing. Worten *v.* Howard, 2 S. & M., 530.

It is my conclusion, that if there be error, the judgment is irreversible, because the record does not furnish the necessary means of enabling us to decide whether the evidence was irrelevant.

JOLLY *v.* THE STATE, 8 Smedes & Marshall, 145.

SELLING LIQUOR TO A SLAVE.

On the trial of a man, under the statute against selling liquor to slaves without permission of the master, it appears that some persons, who suspected the defendant of a violation of the statute, sent a negro belonging to one of them, with money and a jug, and told him to get some whisky, and the defendant sold him the whisky; whereupon the court instructed the jury, "that permission to the slave to buy liquor of any one, did not satisfy the statute, which required permission to the seller." This instruction was erroneous, as a permission to buy implied a permission to the vendor to sell; the fact should have been left to the jury to say, whether the master gave the slave permission to buy, or whether the slave was sent to ascertain and fix the fact that the vendor would sell without permission, and did so sell. If the jury believe the former, they should find for the defendant; if the latter, they should find against him.

The delivery of money to a slave by his master, with instructions to buy whisky with it from a person whom he suspects of having sold whisky in violation of the statute to his slaves, for the purpose of detecting the offender, if guilty, does not excuse the sale of whisky to the slave for money; it is not such permission to the slave as was contemplated by the statute.

Error to circuit court of Marshall county.

Joseph Jolly was indicted for having sold spirituous liquors to a certain slave, named John, without permission of his master, etc. He was tried and found guilty, and thereupon moved for a new trial, but the motion was overruled, and exceptions taken. Armstead, a witness for the state, testified that in November, 1845, suspecting the defendant of unlawful dealings with slaves, he and several others, for the purpose of detecting him, went at night to the house of defendant, taking with them the negro man John, the slave of one of the party, and some spun-thread and other articles, which they concealed near by. The negro roused defendant from his sleep, and offered to trade with him for liquor. He refused to trade liquor for the articles, but would sell it to the negro for money. John went to the party and got the money from one of them in presence of his master, and was directed to take it, and a jug, and get the whisky in it. The slave did so, and returned with the whisky. Another witness testified to the same effect. The court was asked by the state to instruct the jury that "permission to the slave to buy spirituous liquors of any one will not satisfy the statute; that it requires permission to be given the seller thereof, to make the act justifiable in the eye of the law; that the owner of the slave being willing, for the purpose of detection, for his slave to buy spirituous liquor of any one, will not, in the eye of the law, justify that one in selling to such slave; that if the jury believe from the testimony that the defendant sold the liquor to the slave without permission of the master, etc., given to the defendant, and not to the slave, they must find the prisoner guilty." These charges were given and excepted to by the defendant, who asked the court to instruct the jury, that if they "believed from the evidence that the slave was furnished with the money to purchase the liquor by the master, owner, or overseer, and was instructed by them or either of them, to purchase the liquor from the defendant, in that case the sale to the slave was not a violation of the statute." This charge was refused, and exceptions taken.

D. S. Jennings for the plaintiff in error.

1. The court erred in giving the charges they did give, and in refusing that asked by defendant.

2. The court erred in refusing to grant a new trial.

There are but two questions for the court to consider.

1. Was there a sale to the slave within the true intent and meaning of the act of 1842? The testimony shows that the sale was made to the slave *as the agent* of the master, to whom, consequently, the sale was really made. "A sale or exchange is a tranfer of property *from* one man *to* another in consideration of some *price* or recompense in value." Chit. on Con. 107, 108; Shep. Touch., 218. A slave may be an agent. Story's Agency, 9; 9 Yerg. R., 205, 206. And the slave, in this case, purchased in that character. See also Story's Agency, 291 (in note), 9 B. & Cres., 78.

2. The other question supposes the one already discussed to be decided affirmatively. It is, was this sale without the permission of the master," etc., and within the prohibition of the statute on which the indictment is founded. The facts make it necessary to determine what meaning the legislature attached to the word " permission" in the act of 1842. As the word has no technical meaning, it must be taken in its usual acceptation. Webster thus defines the word " to permit," " to allow, to grant leave or liberty by express consent, to allow by silent consent or by not prohibiting, to suffer without giving express authority." The slave, then, to constitute a violation of the act, must be against the will, *in invito domino*, of the master, etc.; in other words, it must be without the assent of the master, etc Meigs's Rep., 84.

John D. Freeman, attorney general.

CLAYTON, J. :

This is an indictment framed upon the act of 1842, made to prevent the selling of vinous or spirituous liquors to a slave without permission of his master. The defendant was found guilty in the court below, and the case comes by writ of error to this court.

The proof was, that several persons suspecting the defendant of a violation of this statute, went in the night near to his house and sent a negro belonging to one of them with money and a jug and told him to get some whisky. The witnesses were concealed. Defendant sold the whisky to the negro.

Upon this state of facts, the court charged the jury, "that permission to the slave to buy spirituous liquors of any one will not satisfy the statute, which requires permission to be given to the seller. That the owner of the slave being willing, for the purpose of detection, for his slave to buy spirituous liquors of any one, will not justify the sale to such slave; the permission must be given to the seller." The defendant asked the court to charge the jury, "that if the slave was furnished with the money to purchase the liquor by his master, and was instructed to buy the liquor from the defendant, then the sale thereof by the defendant does not make him guilty." This charge the court refused.

The first part of the charge given by the court lays down the law too broadly, even with the qualification which seems to be contained in the other part. A permission to the slave to buy, in itself implies a permission to the vendor to sell.

But, in this case, the question arises, was there a permission given to the slave to buy, or was it merely an experiment to see if the defendant would sell without permission? In other words, was it not a plan to detect the defendant in a violation of the law, by seeing him sell spirituous liquor without a permission to the slave to buy. The true point is, whether the master was willing for the slave to buy the liquor of the defendant, and gave him permission to do so. This point is for the determination of the jury. If, from the evidence, they should be of opinion that permission was given to the slave by the master, mistress, owner or overseer to buy the liquor, then the offense is not committed, though the permission were given to the slave and not to the seller. But if they should be of opinion that permission was not given to buy, but that the slave was sent to ascertain and fix the fact that the defendant would sell without permission, and the sale took place under these circumstances, then the offense would be consummated.

In the case of The State v. Anone, 2 Nott & M'Cord, 30, the law is thus laid down upon a similar statute: "It has long been decided that the master's delivery of any article to a slave, and standing by for the purpose of detecting an offender who may trade with the slave, does not legalize the trading." "When the owner goes in order to detect, and for that purpose merely eyes the traffic carried on, giving to the offender no real or apparent intimation of his assent, there can be no inference that he assents to the traffic; and the policy of the law sanctions a practice so essential to the exposure of skillful traders."

The object of the statute under consideration cannot be mistaken. It is to prevent the demoralizing influence of drunkenness and its attendant vices upon the slaves, which constitute so large a portion of our population. As one of the guards for the security and well-being of society, a traffic in this article with slaves is prohibited unless with the consent of the master. It is a traffic which it is hard to detect, and it would be singular if a resort to almost the only means of detection should have the effect to legalize the transaction. Such traffic, without the consent of the master, mistress, owner or overseer, is a breach of the statute; and the consent must be to a sale of the liquors, not merely to an experiment to detect a violation of the law.

For the error in the charge of the court below, the judgment will be reversed, and a new trial granted in accordance with the principles here laid down.

Cause remanded and a new trial granted.

WILBORNE v. THE STATE, 8 Smedes & Marshall, 345.

GRAND LARCENY.

Grand larceny in this state consists in the stealing, taking, and carrying away of any property of greater value than twenty dollars, and where a prisoner has been indicted in two counts, each charging this offense, the verdict of the jury finding him guilty, generally, without specifying the value of the stolen property, will be sufficient to warrant a sentence and judgment for the offense of grand larceny; although the jury *might*, under the indictment, have found a verdict for *petit* larceny.

Error to the circuit court of Monroe county.

Ephraim E. Wilborne was indicted for grand larceny; the indictment contained two counts; the first charged him with feloniously stealing, taking, and carrying away, one gray mare, value seventy dollars; saddle, value ten dollars, money, bank-notes, and other articles. The second count charged him with stealing, etc., one promissory note for $2,200, etc.

The verdict of the jury was as follows: "We the jury find the defendant guilty." The defendant moved in arrest of judgment, but it was overruled, and the prisoner was sentenced to a term of five years in the penitentiary. To the ruling and action of the court exceptions were taken and made part of the record.

Coopwood & Herbert for plaintiff in error.

1. The punishment annexed to the crime of grand larceny is imprisonment in the penitentiary. H. & H. Dig., 709, sec. 63. That for petit larceny may be for a shorter term in the penitentiary, or in the county jail, and fine, etc. Ib., 722, sec. 21. Prior to the passage of the penitentiary code, the punishment of the former was whipping and the pillory; of the latter, whipping only. Ib., 666, sec. 13.

We thus perceive that a clear and well-defined distinction is drawn, not only by the common law, (4 Black. Com., 237,) but by our legislature by positive enactment. These distinctions existing in the description of the two offenses, and in the punishment annexed to each, it is important that the court, who is to pronounce the sentence of the law, should be clearly advised by the finding of the jury, of the particular grade of the offense, to enable it to apply or annex the proper punishment.

2. But the indictment contains two counts, and the court below, from the finding of the jury, was not informed, nor can this court now be informed, by that finding, to which of the two counts the verdict was intended to be applied. The fact that each count contains allegations sufficient, if proved, to sustain the verdict, can make no difference, because the law, not dealing in vague generalities, requires, in highly penal cases like this, at least reasonable certainty. This is important to the prisoner in view of his liability for the value of the property alleged to have been stolen. His liability would certainly be less, if the verdict pointed to the first count, than if it referred to the second. As the verdict stands, he is liable for the property described in both counts.

3. The verdict of the jury should have found the value of the separate articles charged in the indictment to have been stolen,

in order that the court could render judgment that defendant return the articles, or pay the value thereof to the owner.

John D. Freeman, attorney general.

There is no bill of exceptions, and no statement of the evidence. The finding of the jury is not questioned on the evidence, and the finding being general, the presumption of law is that defendant stole all the articles mentioned in the counts. The indictment does not, as assumed by counsel, contain two grades of offense. It is true there are various articles of different values charged to be stolen, but the taking, as it occurred at the same time and from the same person, constituted but one larceny. The jury might have found the value of the articles charged to have been stolen of less value than twenty dollars, if the testimony had justified it; but in the absence of the evidence, the finding of the jury making the offense grand larceny will be presumed to be correct.

THACHER, J.:

This was an indictment for larceny, preferred in the circuit court of Monroe county. The indictment contained two counts, the first for the larceny of a gray mare of the value of seventy dollars, a saddle of the value of ten dollars, a bridle of the value of one dollar, a saddle-blanket of the value of one dollar, ten dollars in specie, and a bank-note for ten dollars; the second count was for the larceny of a promissory note for the sum of twenty-two hundred dollars. The jury found a verdict of guilty; without assessing any value to the property or any portion of it charged to have been the subject of the larceny. The ground of error taken is, that the verdict is too vague and uncertain, upon which to predicate a judgment.

The statutes of this state make a distinction between grand and petit larceny, accordingly as the value of the property alleged to be stolen be over twenty-five or under twenty dollars, and in regard to the kind and amount of punishment. H. & H., 666, § 13; ibid., 709, § 63; ibid., 722, § 21.

The jury in this case found a general verdict of guilty upon an indictment containing two counts, both charging grand larceny. This was sufficient to warrant a sentence and judgment for the crime of grand larceny, although it be true the liberty remained with the jury, under the indictment, to have found a verdict of petit larceny, or guilty of feloniously taking and stealing and carrying away property, under the value of twenty dollars. 1 Chit. Cr. L., 640; Poindexter v. The Commonwealth, 4 Rand. R., 668.[1]

Judgment affirmed.

McDaniel *v.* The State, 8 Smedes & Marshall, 401.

Murder.

The statute, H. & H., 610, §37, provides that upon every application for a continuance, the party shall set forth in his affidavit the facts which he expects to prove by his absent witness or witnesses, in order that the court may be able to judge of the materiality of such facts to the issue or issues in the case; this rule applies also to criminal cases.

The continuance of a cause is matter resting in the sound discretion of the court, and an appellate tribunal will never interfere to control the exercise thereof but with extreme reluctance and caution. To justify such interference there must have been some palpable error committed, without the correction of which manifest injustice will result.

When an application for a new trial is made, the judge is supposed to know nothing of the testimony which will be adduced; he can, therefore, only determine the materiality of the facts stated in the affidavit, by the consideration of what might be urged in the defence, if they should be established. His means of judging are less satisfactory at that stage than at the close of the trial; therefore, if at the conclusion the court is convinced that the continuance should have been granted, it should allow a new trial; and if it refuse a new trial, the party asking it, should give all the testimony in his bill of exceptions, that the appellate court may see the bearing of the whole evidence, and thus be able to judge of the force of the application for a continuance.

The dying declarations of one who has been killed, are admissible in evidence against the slayer, notwithstanding the constitutional provision that the accused "shall be confronted with the witnesses against him;" their admissibility is confined to cases of homicide only.

It is essential to the admissibility of dying declarations, and it is preliminary to be proved by the party offering them in evidence, that *they were made under a sense of impending death;* but it is not necessary that they should be stated at the time, to be so made. It is enough if it satisfactorily appears, in any mode, that they were made under that sanction, whether it be proved directly by the expressed language of the deceased, or be inferred from his evident danger, or the opinion of the medical or other attendants, stated to him, or from his conduct, or other circumstances of the case.

Dying declarations under the following circumstances were admitted in evidence.

[1] See State v. Summerville, 8 Shep., 20; Jones v. State, 13 Ald., 153; State v. Smart, 4 Rich., 356. But see Ray v. State, 1 Greene, 316; Sawyer v. People, 3 Gilman, 513; Highland v. People, 1 Scam., 392; Gilbert v. Steadman, 1 Root, 403; Locke v. State, 32 N. H. R., 106.

On the day the mortal stroke was given, the witness told the deceased that he thought his deposition ought to be taken, as, in the opinion of the witness, he must inevitably die before morning; the deceased replied he thought so too; and afterwards exclaimed, "O Lord! I shall die soon." His declarations were reduced to writing, and read over to him twice, and signed by him. The attending physician on the evening previous, had held out to the deceased some hope of recovery, but told him his chance was bad. Deceased lived some ten days after making the declarations.

On the trial of a prisoner for murder, where the fact of the killing by the prisoner has been clearly proved, evidence as to the character of the prisoner for peace or violence, is inadmissible; but if the guilt of the prisoner be doubtful, such testimony is admissible, and is not confined to the general character of the prisoner, but have reference to the nature of the charge against him; but rebutting testimony as to character may be introduced by the prosecutor, and the presumption arising from such evidence of general character is of little weight.

Where, on the trial of a prisoner for murder, the court charged the jury that "every homicide is presumed to have been committed with malice aforethought, and it devolves on the prisoner to prove the circumstances which excuse the act;" the charge was held to be too broad and unrestricted; that it should have been qualified by adding, "unless they arise out of the evidence produced against him."

Every indictment of murder charges that the prisoner did feloniously, wilfully, and of his malice aforethought, kill and murder the deceased. The fact of killing, and the intent, must concur to constitute the crime of murder; and if the jury from the whole evidence doubt either of these facts, the prisoner is entitled to the benefit of such doubt; or to be either acquitted or convicted of a crime of less grade than murder, according to the circumstances. But in cases where the killing is proved, and no circumstances appear to the contrary, the law presumes malice in the slayer; and these presumptions, if unopposed, may amount to full proof of the fact.

No trespass on the personal property of a person will justify the killing of the trespasser; and any such killing with a deadly weapon will constitute murder.

To constitute larceny, it must be proved that the goods were wrongfully or fraudulently taken and carried away, with the intent of the taker to convert them to his own use. If there be no such intention, it amounts to a trespass only. If the taking be open and in the presence of the owner or other persons, it is only a trespass. But if the goods be taken either by violence, or by putting the owner in fear, it is sufficient to constitute robbery.

Instructions containing only mere propositions of law, when refused by the court, is no ground of error.

Error to Hinds circuit court. Coalter, J.

James M. McDaniel was indicted in the court below for the murder of Alexander Frazier, was arraigned and pleaded not guilty at the April term of the court, 1846.

He made application for a continuance on the ground that two witnesses, residents of the county of Hinds, were absent without his procurement or consent, whose evidence would be material for him, as they would testify to facts which he could not prove by others. The court overruled the application, and the prisoner excepted.

On the trial, R. O. Edwards, for the state, testified that he was called to see Frazier after he was wounded, some ten or eleven days before his death; and during his conversation between them, he told Frazier his depositions ought to be taken, as in his (Edwards') opinion, he (Frazier) would die before morning; the deceased replied that he thought he would die before morning; and afterwards that he would die soon. He exclaimed, "Oh, Lord! I shall die soon." The witness had never seen the deceased before; and the subject of his approaching death was not alluded to until the witness introduced it. The statements of the deceased were drawn up in writing, which was twice read over to him in his hearing and sanctioned by him, and his signature affixed to it. Upon this preliminary proof, the court decided that the statements of the deceased, as thus drawn up, were admissible as his dying declarations. To this paper was affixed the certificate of a magistrate, of the oath of the deceased to the truth of the statements contained in it. Exception was taken to the admission of this paper as the dying declarations of the deceased.

The dying declarations of the deceased disclosed these facts:

That as he was traveling on the road from Raymond to Vicksburg, about between the hours of twelve and two o'clock, he met a man of light complexion, who said his name was McDaniel, and that he persuaded him to turn back and go with him to his residence. The offer of McDaniel, which induced him to accompany him, was to pick out cotton; that McDaniel inquired of him if he had any money, and he answered that he had some; they did not proceed far when they left the main road, being informed by McDaniel that he would go a nearer route to his residence than the usual one. That deceased was on foot and the prisoner on horseback; but the prisoner dismounted and accompanied him on foot, leading his horse; that the deceased traveled in front and McDaniel followed behind him; they did not proceed far when they reached a creek bottom; they followed that some distance when McDaniel drew a pistol and shot him in the back; deceased fell to the ground, and cried out, and saw McDaniel mount his horse and ride off in a gallop; the beast McDaniel was riding was a small mare pony, with white legs and feet, with a flaxen mane and tail, with a large white spot in her face.   The pony was presented to the deceased, and he said that it was the same.

In the course of the examination of Edwards, he was asked by the district attorney: "Do you know what became of McDaniel after the killing?" which he answered in the negative.   He was then asked: "Do you know anything touching the whereabouts of the defendant, and whether he absconded?"   This question was objected to by the prisoner's counsel, as leading.   The objection was overruled, and the prisoner excepted.

Dr. Thompson, who was the only physician who attended deceased, testified that he examined the wound described in the indictment, on the day it was inflicted and often afterwards; that he had repeatedly conversed with the deceased on the prospects of his recovery, and prior to taking down his dying declarations had told him his chances were bad, his recovery very doubtful, and not until after the dying declarations were made did he tell him his case was desperate.

Brooks, a witness for the state, testified, that before the dying declarations were made, he heard Dr. Thompson tell Frazier that he would not recover.

The following instructions were given at the instance of the state, to wit:

1. Every homicide is presumed to have been committed with malice aforethought; and it devolves upon the prisoner to prove the circumstances which excuse the act.

2. No trespass upon personal property will authorize the killing of a man; any such killing would be murder if committed with a deadly weapon.

3. To constitute the crime of larceny, there must be a felonious taking as well as carrying away; and it is necessary to constitute larceny, that the property should be taken in order to be converted to the defendant's own use.

4. To constitute robbery, the person robbed must have been first in fear of his person or property.

5. A man who takes property, claiming it for himself or another, commits no larceny.

The following are the instructions asked for by the prisoner, and refused.

1. If the jury believe from the evidence that the statement of the dying declarations of the deceased was not designed as a dying declaration, and that the same is not satisfactorily proved to have been drawn up at his instance or subscribed by him with a perfect knowledge of its contents, and under a strong sense of his being about to die, or that he was on the verge of immediate dissolution, they are bound to disregard it in making up their verdict.

2. If the jury believe from the evidence in the case, that the deceased did not actually make dying declarations, designing them to operate as such, under a strong sense of impending dissolution, they are bound to disregard all such evidence.

3. If the jury believe from all the evidence in the case, that McDaniel killed Frazier, whilst the latter was carrying off his pony without his consent, with a view of permanently depriving the owner of the same; and for the purpose of preventing a fraudulent scheme of taking and carrying away said pony, without his, the said owner's, consent; and that the means employed by McDaniel were actually necessary to such prevention, they are bound to acquit.

4. If the jury conceive, upon considering all the evidence that there is one or more material facts of a character inconsistent with the hypothesis of guilt, they are bound to acquit.

This instruction was refused as asked, and modified by striking out the word "hypothesis," and adding after "guilt" the words "of accused."

5. And this they must do, though they find there are circumstances, however material, produced before them satisfactorily, which do not harmonize with the hypothesis of innocence.

6. It is lawful to exert such force against a trespasser who comes to take the goods of another, as is necessary to make him desist; and if the jury believe from the facts that the deceased had taken the horse of the accused and was riding him off beyond the reach of probable recapture, that the accused, after having repeatedly hailed him, slew the trespasser, he is not guilty of murder.

7. If the jury believe from the evidence, that at the time of killing Frazier the prisoner had reasonable grounds to apprehend

a design on the part of the deceased to commit a felony, or to do the prisoner some great personal injury, and there was imminent danger of such design being accomplished, they are bound to acquit him.

The jury retired to consider of their verdict, and returned into court that they could not agree, and being asked by the court if they wished to hear any further testimony, replied that they did not, but wished to know whether they could find the prisoner guilty of murder or manslaughter in the first degree. The prisoner objected to this intercourse between the court and jury and to any further instruction from the court to them on any point on which they had not been previously instructed.

The court decided not to give them any further instructions, but would give them any information on any point of law that they desired, but proceeded to instruct them as follows : " The jury are exclusive judges of what is proven before them and from the testimony before them, it is for them to say whether or not the defendant is guilty of any offense on this indictment ; they can say he is not guilty ; or they can say he is not guilty of murder but is guilty of manslaughter, according to the testimony."

The jury found the prisoner guilty of murder, the court sentenced him to be hung, and he prosecuted this writ of error.

The following errors are assigned :

1. In refusing a continuance of the cause, on affidavit of the prisoner, and forcing him to a trial in the absence of testimony disclosed in his affidavit.

2. In admitting the dying declarations of the deceased on the preliminary proof adduced.

3. In permitting the district attorney to propound to the witness, Edwards, several leading questions, as disclosed in the bill of exceptions.

4. In excluding the interrogatory propounded by prisoner's counsel by Mrs. McDaniel, a witness for the defense, touching the declarations and threats of Atwell.

5. In excluding the investigation of the character of the accused for peace or violence, in manner and form as defendant's counsel ought to conduct such examination.

6. In giving the second, third, fourth and fifth instructions for the state.

7. In refusing to give the first, third, fourth and seventh instructions asked for by the prisoner's counsel.

8. In instructing the jury after the retirement from the bar, and in opposition to the remonstrances of prisoner's counsel.

9. In modifying the fifth instruction asked for by prisoner's counsel.

10. In disregarding the sixth instruction asked by prisoner's counsel, and neither giving nor refusing the same.

11. The court erred in passing sentence upon the prisoner.

A. R. Johnston and *H. S. Foote* for the plaintiff in error.

The paper called the "dying declarations of the deceased" ought not to have gone to the jury; because the preliminary proof required was not adduced prior to its introduction; because the magistrate who attested it, and administered the oath to the deceased, was not produced; and because the whole mass of testimony relating to that document shows that it ought not to have been admitted as an instrument of evidence. 1 Greenl. Ev. 186, 188, 189, 190 ; 1 Phil. Ev. 235 ; 1 Starkie Ev. 28, 29 ; 2 Phil. Ev. 606, and notes.

It was error to permit the state to propound leading questions to its own witnesses on direct examination.   1 Greenl. Ev. 481 ; 1 Starkie Ev. 149, notes, and cases cited.

It was error in the court below to refuse to admit testimony touching the general character of the prisoner, for peace or violence. 1 Greenl. Ev. 61 ; 2 Starkie in Ev. 314, 315 ; notes and cases cited.

The second, third, fourth and fifth instructions for the state were manifestly wrong. 4 Black. Com. 180 ; 2 Starkie Ev. 524, 443, 444 ; 4 Black. Com., 232, note 8 ; Russ. & Ry. C. C. 307, 18 ; Burns's Jus., 24th ed. 209 ; 2 Russ. on Crimes, 94 ; ib. 61, note A ; How. & Hutch., 708.   The fifth instruction need only to be read to show that it should have been refused.   If it is correct, all rogues would escape punishment.

The court improperly refused instructions for the prisoner. See 1 Greenl. Ev. 186, 188, 189, 190 ; 1 Phill. Ev. 235 ; 1 Starkie Ev., 28, 29 ; ib., 191, note 1 ; 1 Greenl. Ev. ; 4 Black. Com. 180 ; 1 Starkie 523 ; How. & Hutch., 694.

The court cannot legally instruct the jury after they have retired to consider of their verdict. How. & Hutch. Dig. 482, § 9 ; ib. 493.

R. A. Clarke, on same side.

J. D. Freeman, attorney general.

Cited 1 Peter's Dig., 593 ; 1 Greenl. Ev. 188, 189, 190 ; Roscoe Cr. Ev. 31, 33 ; 1 East P. C. 357, 358 ; 1 Starkie Ev. 523 ; 1 Leach, 503 ; 6 Car. & Payne, 157, 386 ; 9 ib., 157 ; 7 ib., 187 ; 1 Har. Dig., 1943 ; 1 Chitty Cr. Law, title " Dying Declarations ;" Phillip's Ev. Cow. & Hill's notes ; Black, Com., title " Larceny ;" Chitty Cr. Law, title " Larceny ;" 5 Humph., 383.

CLAYTON, J.

This was an indictment for murder in the circuit court of Hinds, which resulted in the conviction of the defendant. A great number of errors have been assigned as causes of reversal.

The first is, that there was error in overruling an application for a continuance upon the affidavit filed. Our statute upon this subject lays down a very explicit rule. It provides that upon every application for a continuance, the party shall set forth in his affidavit the facts which he expects to prove by his absent witness or witnesses, in order that the court may judge of the materiality of such facts to the issue or issues in the case.[1] H. & H., 610, § 37.

The continuance of a cause is matter resting in the sound discretion of the court, and an appellate tribunal will never interfere but with extreme reluctance and caution.[2] To justify such interference, there must have been a palpable error committed, without the correction of which manifest injustice will be wrought. 5 Humphreys, 568 ; Bellew v. The State, 2 Rob. Virginia Rep. 849 ; 10 Leigh, 692 ; 4 Humph., 202.

[1] Revised Code of 1857, 503, art. 151.
[2] Bohr v. Steamboat Baton Rouge, 7 S. & M., 715; Lindsay v. State, 15 Ala, 43; State v. Duncan, 6 Iredell, 98; Green v. State, 13 Mo., 382; Wharton Am. Cr. Law, 2936; People v. Thompson, 4 Cal., 238; Bledsoe v. Commonwealth, 6 Randolph, 67†; State v. Hildreth, 9 Iredell, 490; Fiolt v. Commonwealth, 12 Grattan, 564; State v. Thomas, 8 Rich., 295; McKinney v. People, 2 Gilman, 540; Baxter v. People, 3 ib., 368; State v. Patterson, 1 McCord, 177; Wood v. Young, 4 Cranch, 237; 1 Archbold, Cr. Pr. & Pl., 567.

When the application for a continuance is made, the judge is supposed to know nothing of the testimony which will be adduced, he can therefore only determine the materiality of the facts stated in the affidavit by the consideration of what might be urged in the defence, if they should be established. His means of judging are less satisfactory at that stage than at the close of the trial. When a continuance has, in the opinion of counsel, been improperly refused, it is the regular course of practice to move for a new trial, after the verdict has been rendered, when the judge can see more clearly the bearing of the testimony sought to be introduced, and can have an opportunity of correcting his error, if convinced that he has committed one. If he refuse the new trial, the bill of exceptions embodying the whole testimony will furnish this court with the means of forming a correct conclusion. This is safer than merely to bring up the affidavit for a continuance, without all the other testimony in the cause. Whether the continuance was improperly refused in this case, we need not determine, as the judgment will be reversed upon another ground.

The next alleged error which we shall notice, is the admission of the dying declarations of the deceased. The admission of such declarations in any case is an exception to the general rule of evidence. It is only permitted in cases of homicide, and the exception stands upon the ground of the public necessity of preserving the lives of the community, by bringing manslayers to justice.[1] 1 Greenl., 193.

It is essential to the admissibility of these declarations, and is a preliminary fact to be proved by the party offering them in evidence, that *they were made under a sense of impending death ;*[2] but it is not necessary that they should be stated at the time to be so made. It is enough if it satisfactorily appears, in any mode, that they were made under that sanction, whether

[1] Wharton Am. Cr. Law, 669, *et seq.;* and cases cited ; 2 Russell on Crimes, 752, *et seq.;* 1 East P. C, 353, § 124 ; 1 Archbold Cr. Pl., 449, *et seq.*, notes ; Rex v. Van Butchell, 3 C. & P. 629 ; Rex v. Mead, 4 D. & R. 120, 1 Greenl. Ev., 156.

[2] See note (*) supra. and cases cited, Rex. v. Mead, 4 D. & R. 120 ; 2 B. & C, 605 ; 1 Greenl. Ev. 156–162, 346 ; 3 ib., 296 ; Rex v. Hutchinson, 2 B. & C., 608, note ; 1 East. P. C., 353 ; King v. Commonwealth, 1 Va. Cases, 78 ; Woodsides v. State, 2 How., 655 (supra.,   ) ; Campbell v. State, 11 Ga., 353 ; Nelson v. State, 7 Humph. 542 ; Smith v. State, 9 Humph. 9 ; Hill v. Commonwealth, 2 Gratt., 594 ; Moore v. State, 12 Ala., 764 ; People v. Green. 1 Denio, 614.

it be directly proved by the express language of the declarator or be inferred from his evident danger, or the opinions of the medical or other attendants stated to him, or from his conduct or other circumstances of the case, all of which are resorted to in order to ascertain the state of declarant's mind.[1] 1 Greenl., 195. The objection to their admission in this case is, that it does not sufficiently appear, that, at the time, the dying declarations were made, the deceased was sufficiently impressed with a sense of his impending dissolution. Upon this point the evidence is, first, that of R. O. Edwards, who testified, that on the night when the declarations were made, he told Frazier, the deceased, that he thought his deposition ought to be taken, as, in the opinion of witness, he must inevitably die before morning. The deceased replied, he thought so too. Afterwards deceased exclaimed, O Lord! I shall die soon! His declarations were reduced to writing, read over to him twice, and signed by him. The attending physician was examined, who stated, that, in the preceding evening, he had held out some hopes of recovery to the deceased; but told him his chance was bad. The interview with Edwards was during the following night; the deceased lived some ten days afterwards. It seems to us that every requirement of the law was fully satisfied. The situation of the deceased, the opinions of those around him, his own solemn declarations, all show, that, at the time, he believed he was on the very threshold of death. In Rex. v. Mosley, 1 Moody Cr. Cases, 97, the declarations were made some eleven days before death, at a time when the surgeon did not think the case hopeless, and told the patient so; but the patient thought otherwise, and the declarations were received. 1 Greenl. 195, n.

We cannot yield our assent to the position that the introduction of such testimony violates the provision of the federal constitution, which secures to the accused the right "to be confronted with the witnesses against him." Such evidence has been admitted in many of our sister states, and excluded in none, so far as we know. It would be a perversion of its meaning to exclude the proof, when the prisoner himself has been the

[1] Smith v. State, 9 Humph., 9; vide cases cited in notes 2, 3, supra.

guilty instrument of preventing the production of the witness by causing his death. This was expressly decided in Woodsides v. The State, 2 How., 656.

The objection that some of the questions propounded to the witnesses were leading, need not be the subject of remark. That point has already been sufficiently discussed in the case of Toumey.

An objection is taken to the excluding of an inquiry on the part of the defendant, as to his general character for peace or violence; the court holding that the inquiry must be directed to the general character, without reference to particular traits. The rule is, that where evidence touching the general character of the party is admitted, it ought manifestly to bear reference to the nature of the charge against him. But this evidence of good character, in relation to the particular crime charged, seems to be only admissible in cases where the guilt of the party accused is doubtful. The prosecutor may introduce opposing testimony, and the presumption arising from such evidence of general character is said to be of little weight. 1 GreenL., 65; 2 Starkie, 214; Roscoe, 89.

We shall now pass to the charges given by the court. The first given at the instance, is in these words: "Every homicide is presumed to be committed with malice aforethought; and it devolves upon the prisoner to prove the circumstances which excuse the act." This charge is too broad and unrestricted. It contains only a part of the rule, as usually stated in the books, and omits the important addition, "unless they arise out of the evidence produced against him." 1 Russ., 338; Foster, 255.

Every indictment for murder contains the charge, that the prisoner did "feloniously, wilfully, and of his malice aforethought, kill and murder the deceased." The fact of killing, and the intent, must both concur to constitute the crime of murder. They are both charged by the state, and if, from the whole evidence in the cause, the jury doubt either of the fact of killing, or of the malice of the act, the prisoner is entitled to the benefit of such doubt, and to be either acquitted, or convicted of a crime of less grade than murder, according to the circumstances. The jury must be satisfied, that he is guilty of murder, before they pronounce him so.   This, by no means, excludes a resort to presumptions in certain cases.   When the fact of killing, with all its attendant circumstances, is clearly proved, and the testimony either shows express malice, or that there was no malice at all, there is no room for presumption.   But in cases where the killing is proved, and no accompanying circumstances appear in the evidence, the law presumes the killing was done maliciously. So, where the killing is proved, and the circumstances attending it are shown, though no express malice may appear from the proof, it may be presumed from some attending fact; as if a deadly weapon were used, the law presumes malice.   So, if there be circumstances of barbarity and cruelty, the law presumes malice.   These presumptions of law, if unopposed, may amount to full proof of the fact.   They stand until the contrary is proved or until such facts are proved, as are sufficient to raise a contrary and stronger presumption.   1 Stark. Ev., 452; Coffee v. The State, 3 Yerg., 283; Woodsides v. The State, 2 How., 666. From the presumptions of law, and the whole evidence in the cause, as well as for the state, as for the accused, the jury must make up their verdict.   In its definition of murder, our statute, instead of "*malice aforethought*," uses the words "*premeditated design*."   In legal effect we regard them as the same.   2 Va. Ca., 88.

The second charge given by the court is in these words: "No trespass upon the personal property of another will authorize the killing of a man; any such killing would be murder, if committed with a deadly weapon."   This charge was correct.   The kind of weapon used in such cases, determines the intent, and fixes the degree of guilt.   If it be a deadly weapon, the killing will be murder.   Commonwealth v. Drew, 4 Mass., 396; State v. Tellers, 2 Hals.; Roscoe Cr. Tr., 718; 2 Stark. Ev., 524.

The third charge given is likewise free from objection.   It corresponds very nearly with the definition of larceny at common law.   To constitute the offense, the goods must have been wrongfully or fraudulently taken and carried away, with the intent to convert them to the taker's own use, and make them his own property.   If there be no such intention, it amounts to a trespass only, and not to a felony.   If the taking be open, and in the presence of the owner or of other persons, this **carries with** it evidence, that it is only a trespass. Rosc., 531, **536.** The definition in our statute amounts to the same.

The fourth charge, which purports to give a definition of robbery, is not quite full enough. If the goods be taken **either by** violence, or by putting the owner in fear, it is sufficient **to render** the felonious taking a robbery. Rosc., 832. To the **same effect** is our statutory definition.

The fifth charge given on the part of the state, is **likewise in**accurate in some degree. It is not enough to do away **with the** criminal intent, that there should be a mere false claim **of prop**erty in the article stolen. But, if there be a fair, *bona fide* claim of property or right in the prisoner the offense amounts but to a trespass. Rosc., 537, 829.

The first and third charges asked for by the counsel of the prisoner, have been already sufficiently elucidated in **the remarks** as to the admission of the dying declarations of the **deceased.** It is for the court to determine whether, under the circumstances, they are competent testimony ; when admitted, it is **for the jury** to judge of the weight to be attached to them, precisely, **as they** judge of all other testimony.

The second charge requested on the part of the **prisoner was** given, and there is no complaint of it.

The fourth charge requested by the prisoner's **counsel, was** properly refused. It has been sufficiently explained **in what has** been said of the second charge upon the part of the **state.** A mere trespass, or a larceny, will not justify an intentional killing. Our statute declares homicide to be justifiable, **when com**mitted in resisting any attempt to murder such **person, or to** commit any felony upon him or her, or upon, or in **any dwelling** house, in which such person shall be. H. & H., 694.

The fifth and sixth instructions asked on the part **of the pris**oner were properly refused. They contained mere abstract propositions, bearing but remotely, if at all, upon the case, **and their** relevancy is not perceived. They propound a rule laid **down by** Starkie, in reference to cases dependent entirely **upon circum**stantial proof; a rule, however, which does not apply **to a case in** which there is *positive* proof.

The seventh charge asked for by defendant, was also properly refused. A portion of it consisted only of abstract propositions, having no perceptible connection with the testimony. If there be any part not liable to this objection, it is that which asks the court to instruct the jury, "that if they believe the deceased had taken the horse of the accused, and was riding him off beyond the reach of probable recapture, and that the accused, after having repeatedly hailed him, slew the trespasser, he is not guilty of murder." If, under such circumstances, the killing was with a deadly weapon, we have already seen it would be murder. We have thus adverted to nearly all the prominent points made in the argument, in order to have the principles settled by which the next trial will be governed.

The judgment is reversed, and cause remanded for another trial.

COVEY v. THE STATE, 8 Smedes & Marshall, 573.

GRAND LARCENY.

MOTION IN ARREST OF JUDGMENT.

A motion in arrest of judgment is confined to defects upon the face of the record itself, and which make the proceedings apparently erroneous; and no defect in evidence, or improper conduct on the trial can be urged under this motion.

Error to Warren circuit court. COALTER, J.

The opinion of the court contains a sufficient statement of the facts of the case.

The plaintiff in error assigned as cause of reversal, the overruling by the court below of the motion in arrest of judgment, which motion was made on the following grounds, to wit:

1. Because the court, from inspection of the defendant, will find that he is a descendant from the African race, and therefore, *prima facie* a slave.

2. Because the indictment does not correctly describe the person of the defendant as a slave, a free man of color, and is therefore defective.

3. Because the court cannot pronounce the judgment of law upon a slave.

4 Because there is no evidence upon the trial rebutting the presumption of law that the defendant was a slave.

The motion was overruled by the court, and the defendant excepted. The defendant was sentenced to two years' imprisonment in the penitentiary. To reverse this judgment, the defendant now prosecutes this writ of error.

E. G. Walker for plaintiff in error.

1st. The plaintiff in error is a descendant of the African race, and *prima facie* a slave.

2d. The *descriptio personis* is not set out in the record.

All Africans are presumed to be slaves until the contrary appears. Hudgins v. Wrights, 1 Henn. & Munn., 137, 141; Gregory v. Baugh, 2 Leigh, 696; 7 ib., 448, 451; Pollock on Slavery, 406, notes and cases cited.

As to who is deemed a mulatto, see How. & Hutch., 137, § 12. Free negroes are to be registered. See How. & Hutch., 168, § 51; ib., 176, § 81. As to how free negroes are to be tried, see How. Hutch., 737.

J. D. Freeman, attorney general.

It does not appear that any person claimed the prisoner as a slave. His own declarations on this subject, together with the fact that he was at large in the community without the guardianship or restraint of any one, was evidence which he had no right to object to. The presumption of slavery arising from color was rebutted by his own declarations and the absence of any master or owner. The *profert* of a colored skin was not sufficient to rebut this evidence, and hence he was properly sentenced. Had he proved himself to have been a slave, he would not have been the less guilty, but his presentment would have been different.

Thacher, J.:

This was an indictment for larceny, preferred against Charles Covey by the grand jury of Warren county. The defendant below pleaded not guilty, and the jury found a verdict of guilty, as charged in the indictment. Upon being brought to the bar for sentence, the defendant pleaded in arrest of judgment, and assigned the following reasons, to wit: First, because the court, from inspection of the defendant, will find that he is a descendant from the African race, and therefore, *prima facie* a slave. Second, because the indictment does not correctly describe the person of the defendant as a slave or a free man of color, and is therefore defective. Third, because the court cannot pronounce the judgment of the law upon a slave. Fourth, because there was no evidence upon the trial rebutting the presumption of law that the defendant was a slave.

A motion in arrest of judgment is confined to defects apparent upon the face of the record itself, and which make the proceedings apparently erroneous; and therefore no defect in evidence, or improper conduct on the trial can be urged under this motion.[1] 1 Chit. C. L., 661; Barbour's C. T., 330. The grounds upon which the motion in arrest of judgment in this case is made have clearly reference to matters *dehors* the record, and even if the motion was improperly overruled upon their intrinsic merits, which is very questionable, it was rightly overruled upon the principles of law governing such motions.

Judgment affirmed.

SWINNEY *v.* THE STATE, 8 Smedes & Marshall, 576.

LARCENY.

It is not necessary that all the averments in an indictment should be proved as laid, in order to warrant a conviction. The general rule is that every material averment must be proved, yet it does not follow that it is necessary to prove the offense charged to the whole extent as laid. It is enough if so much of a charge be proved as constitutes an offense punishable at law.

Where an accusation includes an offense of inferior degree, the jury may acquit of the higher crime, and convict the defendant of a degree less atrocious.

Upon a conviction of larceny of property of value under twenty dollars, the court has unlimited jurisdiction as to the length of imprisonment, provided it be not less than two years in the penitentiary.

[1] Wharton Am. Cr. Law, 3043–45; Whitehurst v. Davis, 2 Hay, 113; 1 Sid., 65; 1 Salk., 77, 315; 1 Lord Raymond, 281; 4 Burr, 2287; Horsey v. State, 3 Harris & Johns., 2; Commonwealth v. Linton, 2 Va. Cases, 476; Commonwealth v. Watts, 4 Leigh, 672; State v. Allen, Charlton, 518; Newbell v. Adams, 8 Taunt., 335; Rex v. Ramsbottom, 5 Price, 447; Carter v. Bennett, 15 How., P. C., 354; United States v. Hammond, 1 Cr. C. C., 15; United States v. White, 5 Ib., 73; United States v. Peaco, 4 Cr. C., 601.

Error to Copiah circuit court. WILLIS, J.

This was an indictment in the court below, **found by the** grand jury of Copiah county, at the November **term, 1846,** against Joel Swinney. At the same term of the **court the pris-** oner was arraigned, and plead not guilty, and issue **joined there-** upon he was tried, and the jury returned the following **verdict:** " We, the jury, find the said defendant, Joel **Swinney, guilty,** and that he did feloniously take, steal and carry **away the saddle** in the indictment mentioned, in manner and form **as charged in** said bill of indictment; and we do assess the value of **said sad-** dle to the sum of twelve dollars."

The counsel for the prisoner then moved in **arrest of judg-** ment on the following grounds:

1st. Because the jury failed to find whether the **prisoner, the** said Joel Swinney, was guilty or not of stealing the **horse, bridle** and blanket, charged in the indictment to have been **feloniously** taken and carried away by the said Swinney.

2d. Because the jury failed to find the whole **issue submitted** to them.

The court overruled the motion, and the prisoner **excepted.** The defendant was sentenced to ten years' **imprisonment in the** penitentiary. Whereupon he sued out a writ **of error to this** court, and assigns the following errors, to wit:

1st. Neither the record nor the caption of **the indictment** shows from what county the grand jury were taken.

2d. The record does not show of what number **the grand jury** consisted.

3d. The record does not show that the grand **jury were sworn** by the court.

4th. The verdict of the jury finds only part of **the issue sub-** mitted to them, and is so defective that no judgment **can legally** be rendered upon it.

5th. The sentence to ten years' imprisonment is **not warranted** by law.

E. G. Peyton, for plaintiff in error.

1. Every caption of an indictment that the grand **jury were** of the county for which the court was holden. 5 **Bacon, Abr.,** 93, (Amer. ed., 1844). Rex v. Kilderby, 1 Saund. **R., 308. If**

the caption does not state that the grand jury are of the county for which the court had jurisdiction to inquire, the whole will be vitiated.   1 Chitty Cr. Law, 327, 333.

2. It must be shown on the face of the record that the bill was found by at least twelve jurors, or it will be insufficient.   1 Chitty Cr. Law, 333 ; Cro. Eliz., 654 ; 2 Hale, 167 ; Hawkins, 126 ; Falkner's case, 1 Saun. R., 248, note 1.   Andr., 230 ; 5 Bac., 93 ; State v. Carpenter, 4 How., 163.   In the case of Thomas v. State, 5 How. 32, the court say that it is the business of the caption of the indictment to state the jurors by whom it was found.

3. The indictment must in all cases be shown to have been taken on oath, and if this allegation be admitted, the caption cannot be supported, 1 Chitty, 333.   It should appear upon the record that the grand jury were sworn by the court.   Cody v. State, 3 How., 28.

4. The verdict of the jury must respond to the whole issue or matters in the issue submitted to them, 2 Murphy, 571.   The jury may acquit the defendant of part, and find him guilty of the residue, 1 Chitty, 638 ; Barbour Cr. Treatise, 325.   The whole issue must be answered by the verdict, 1 Chitty, 638 ; Durham v. State, 1 Blackf., 33.   As to the incorrectness of this verdict, see 2 East P. C., 516—518 ; 2 Hale, P. C., 302.

Where the accusation includes an offense of inferior degree, the jury may discharge the defendant of the higher crime and convict him of the less atrocious.   Thus upon an indictment for murder, he may be convicted of manslaughter.   In Barley's case, Cro. Eliz., 296, upon a charge of murder, the jury found the defendant "not guilty of murder, but that he was guilty of manslaughter."   Chitty says that on an indictment for grand larceny, the offense may be reduced to petit larceny.   This, however, disposes of the whole issue.   But in the case at bar, the indictment charged the defendant below with stealing four distinct articles in one count, and the value of each alleged ; and the jury find him guilty as to only one of the articles, and assess the value of it, and say nothing as to the rest.   This verdict would not sustain a plea of former acquittal in case the prisoner were again indicted for stealing the same articles ; and if it would not the verdict is so defective, that no judgment could be properly founded upon it.

There are so many instances in which a verdict, taking no notice of aggravation, has been regarded as sufficient, that it does not seem to be necessary at the present day. 1 Chitty, 641. The cases in 9 Coke, 67, and 4 ib., 46, are special verdicts; and Hale says that, where an indictment for felony includes a felony of inferior degree, the jury may acquit the defendant of the higher crime, and find him guilty of the less. 2 Hale P. C., 302; also Stephen's Cr. Law, 313; 27 Law Library, 183. In the case of Rex v. Haynes, 2 Strange, 843, 845, the defendant was indicted for three distinct offenses. 1. For forging a bond; 2. For publishing such forged bond; 3. For publishing a bond knowing it to be forged; and upon the plea of not guilty the jury found that he forged the bond, and that he published the same, but they say nothing as to the third offense. This case clearly shows that a general verdict finding the defendant guilty of forging and publishing a bond, without finding not guilty as to the rest, would have been insufficient. But the verdict being special, the court undertook to give it proper form according to the evidence. Had the verdict been a general one, the opinion of the court shows that no judgment could have been given upon it. It is believed, however, that the court possesses no power at the present day, even upon a special finding, to shape a verdict according to the evidence in the case; it being the province of the jury to find the facts in a special verdict and not the evidence, and of the court to pronounce the law arising upon those facts.

The jury must answer to the whole issue with which they have been charged. Kerr v. Hawthorne, 4 Yeates, 295. If a verdict find only part of what is in issue, it is bad; because the jury have failed in their duty, which was to find all that was in issue. 10 Bac. R., 327 (Amer. Ed., 1846). In an action of trespass, the plaintiff declared for breaking his close, for beating his servant, and for carrying away his goods. The jury found the defendant guilty of breaking the close, but were silent as to the rest. Upon motion in arrest of judgment the verdict was held bad, because it does not find all that is in issue. 10 Bac.,

328. If this be so in a civil case, a *multo fortiori* does it apply in a criminal case. Rex v. Simons, Sayer's R., 36; 10 Bac., 328; State v. Arrington, 2 Murphy, 571.

A verdict which does not clearly find the whole matter in issue cannot be helped by intendment. Jewett v. Davis, 6 N. H., 518; 3 Salk., 372; 1 Ld. Raym., 324; Graham's Pr., 276; Hanly v. Levin, 5 Ohio, 238; Patterson v. United States, 2 Wheat., 221; 4 Peter Con. R., 100. This court has also decided that a verdict is bad, if it find only a part of that which is in issue; and no judgment can be rendered upon it. McCoy v. Rives, 1 S. & M., 592. Where the indictment charged a riot and assault, and the jury found " guilty of a riot," this was held a partial finding on the entire count, and, therefore, void. State v. Creighton, 1 Nott & McCord, 256; 1 Chitty Cr. Law, 638, note, In the case at bar there was but one count in the indictment. and the verdict is void, as it shows but a partial finding of the jury upon the issues submitted to them in that count. Nothing can be taken by intendment or implication in a criminal case. Highland v. the People, 1 Scam., 394.

5. It was error in sentencing the prisoner to two years' imprisonment in the penitentiary. The legislature could never have intended to punish petit larceny to a greater extent than grand larceny.

John D. Freeman, attorney general.

A jury has a right to find part of a count. 1 Chitty Cr. Law, 250–2, and notes, 251, note f. The verdict of the jury was in response to the whole issue. There was but one count, and the charge was grand larceny; the jury found petit larceny which they had a right to do.

It is true that nothing can be taken by intendment against the prisoner, but all intendments shall be in his favor. The presumption is, that the jury intended to discharge the prisoner of all that part of the count not found; and this finding in law is an acquittal to that extent. Had there been two counts, one of which the jury had not disposed of, the question would have assumed a different attitude.

The sentence is in accordance with the penitentiary code.

THACHER, J.

The three errors first assigned, to wit: that the **record does** not show from what county the grand jury were ta**ken, nor of** what number of jurors it consisted, nor that the gra**nd jury were** sworn by the court, do not seem, from an inspe**ction of the** record, to be well taken in point of fact. Those fac**ts are found** in the statement of the proceedings prior to the fi**nding of the** indictment, the whole of which statement comprises **the caption.**

The remaining error assigned is, that the verdict **of the petit** jury finds only part of the issue submitted to them**, and is so** defective that no judgment can legally be rendered **upon it, and** that the sentence of ten years' imprisonment in the **penitentiary** is not warranted by law.

It was an indictment for larceny consisting of bu**t one count,** and charging the accused with stealing one saddle h**orse, of the** value of fifty dollars; one saddle, of the value of **five dollars;** one saddle blanket, of the value of one dollar; and o**ne bridle, of** the value of three dollars; all the property of the same **individual.**

The verdict of the jury was as follows: " We, th**e jury, find** the said defendant, Joel Swinney, guilty, and that **he did felo-** niously steal, take and carry away the saddle in the **indictment** mentioned, in manner and form as charged in said b**ill of indict-** ment, and we do assess the value of said saddle to **the sum of** twelve dollars."

The defendant was sentenced to imprisonment in **the peniten-** tiary for the term of ten years.

It is not necessary that all the averments in an **indictment** should be proved as laid, in order to warrant a **conviction.**[1] The general rule is, that every material averment mus**t be proved,** yet it does not follow that it is necessary to prove **the offense** charged to the whole extent laid. It is enough if so **much of a** charge be proved as constitutes an offense punish**able by law.** In the case of Rex v. Hunt, 2 Campb., 585, Lord **Ellenborough** says, that it is invariably enough to prove so much **of the indict-** ment as shows that the defendant has committed a **substantive** crime therein specified.

[1] John v. State, 24 Miss, 569; 1 Bishop Cr. Law, 880; State v. Coleman, 3 Ala., 14; Nabors v. State, 6 Ala. 200; Weinzorpflin v. State, 7 Blackf., 186; 1 Bishop Cr. Procedure, 837.

The substance of the crime, in this case, is larceny, and this is a substantive offense, although the accused was guilty of stealing but one of the articles laid in the indictment. The finding would have been free from doubt or criticism, had the jury added to their verdict, not guilty of the larceny of the residue of the articles charged in the indictment. 1 Chit. C. L., 638; Durham v. The State, 1 Blackf., 33.

It is well settled also, that where an accusation includes an offense of inferior degree, the jury may discharge the defendant of the higher crime, and convict him of the less atrocious. 2 Hale P. C. 302; Hawk. b. 2, c. 47, § 6. The form in which a verdict which thus partially convicts and acquits should be given, has been somewhat contradicted; but it is now put at rest, that it is sufficient if the jury find a verdict of guilty of the inferior offense, and take no notice of the aggravation. 1 Chitt. C. L. 640.

In still later times, a practice has obtained of not requiring a formal finding upon all the issues presented, provided enough be found upon which to warrant judgment against the accused, and of considering a finding of a part of the issues to be the negativing of the rest. In the case of Stoltz v. The People, 4 Scammon's R. 168, the accused was indicted in two counts. The first count charged the accused with keeping a gaming house; and the second with keeping open a tippling house on Sunday. The verdict was guilty on the first count, but no finding on the second. The court said, "It is insisted, that the verdict of the jury was void, and that the court erred in rendering judgment upon it. The general rule is, that the verdict must be as broad as the issues submitted; and it was formerly held, with much strictness, that a failure to find on all the issues vitiated the verdict. The tendency of modern decisions, however, has been to relax the severity of the rule and sustain the verdict, where the intention of the jury can be ascertained. What is the reasonable view to be drawn from this verdict, and the circumstances under which it was rendered? The people prefer two charges of criminal offenses against the defendant; he is arraigned on them and the question of his guilt submitted to the jury for determination. They hear the testimony adduced to substantiate both charges, and find, affirmatively, that he is guilty of one.   Is not the inference irresistible, that the prosecution failed to establish his guilt on the other charge, and therefore the jury find negatively on it ?   We are of opinion that the verdict should be regarded as an acquittal of the defendant on the second count.   If such be the effect of the verdict, he certainly has no right to complain.   He can never again be put on trial for the same offense.   He has once been put in jeopardy, and the charge against him adjudicated.   This reasoning applies still more forcibly to cases where the several issues are embraced in but one court as in the case before us.   The doctrine seems equally applicable to every grade of offense, and appears to be a rational deduction or corollary of the established principle, that the finding of the inferior is a discharge of the superior offense, which holds even in indictments for murder.

. We have had occasion already at this term, in the case of Wilborne v. The State, ante, 345, to remark upon the distinction existing in this state between grand and petit larceny.   By a reference to that case, or to the statutes How. & Hutch., 666, § 13; ib., 700, § 63; ib., 722, 21, it will be observed, that upon a conviction of larceny of property of the value of under twenty dollars, there is an unlimited discretion as to the length of the imprisonment, provided it be not less than two years in the penitentiary.   We have nothing to do with the policy of legislation. " Quod scriptum, scriptum."

There being no error in the proceedings, the judgment of the circuit court must be affirmed.

McQuillen *v.* State, 8 Smedes and Marshall, 587.

Assault with Intent to Commit Robbery.

It is the duty of the circuit court to charge the grand jury when empanelled, in regard to the nature of the duty which they are required to perform, and the motives which should govern them in the discharge of that duty.   But the charge is not to be placed upon the record; nor can it be essentially necessary that the record should state that it was given at all, as the matter charged does not constitute ground of error.   The charge must be presumed to have been given unless the contrary appears.

In criminal as well as civil cases, the rule is that the party who complains of the judgment must make the error apparent; and if it is some part of the proceedings not appearing on the face of the record, it must be placed there by the bill of exceptions.

In criminal cases, the prisoner must plead in person; any plea by attorney is a nullity.

It is incompetent for the clerk at a subsequent term, to make any entry of what transpired at a previous term.

When a juror is elected, he must remain under the charge of the court or an officer before, as well as after he is sworn, and it is error to permit the jury to disperse without the consent of the prisoner. And it is immaterial whether improper influences have been exerted or not.

A prisoner has the right to question by plea in abatement, the competency of the grand jury by whom he was indicted; he cannot be called to answer a charge unless it has been preferred according to law.

Pleas in abatement must be made at the proper time; by denying the charge the accused waives matter in abatement.

Error to Washington circuit court.   Coalter, J.

The record in this case discloses the following facts, to wit:

On the 13th day of September, 1845, the clerk of the circuit court, and the sheriff of Washington county, drew from the box containing the names of persons liable to sit on juries, the names of thirty-six persons to attend and serve as jurors at the October term, 1845, of the circuit court of Washington county; that a writ of *venire facias* was issued, and the same was returned executed. At the October term the sheriff and clerk drew from the persons summoned, who were present at the court, a sufficient number to serve as a grand jury. And the court having appointed Aaron Wickliffe, foreman, the whole number were sworn and empanelled according to law, and proceeded to the discharge of their duties; and on the second day of the term returned into court and presented an indictment against John P. McQuillen for an assault with intent to rob, and an assault with intent to kill. The indictment contained four counts; 1st. For an assault with a stick upon Michael Carroll with intent to steal; 2d. An assault with a knife upon Michael Carroll with intent to steal; 3d. An assault upon Michael Carroll, with a knife, with intent to rob; 4th. An assault with a knife upon Michael Carroll with intent to kill.

On the third day of the term the following entry was made, to wit: " The defendant, by S. C. Cox, saith he is not guilty in manner and form as in the indictment against him is alleged, and of this he puts himself upon the country, and the attorney for the commonwealth likewise, and the trial of the issue is deferred until next court."

At the March term, 1846, the following entry was made, on the third day of the term, to wit: "This day came by Fulton E. Anderson, district attorney, and the defendant in his own proper person, and the said defendant having been arraigned at a former term of the court pleaded not guilty, and put himself upon the country, and the district attorney likewise, and therefore the following persons were selected from the regular panel, to wit: James Reidheimer, and Turner Joyner, and the regular panel being exhausted, the sheriff was directed to summon from the by-standers a sufficient number of the good and lawful men of the county of Washington, to complete said jury," etc. A sufficient number was not found among the by-standers, the sheriff was directed by the court to summon a sufficient number from the county, of good and lawful men to complete the jury on the next day at ten o'clock. "And thereupon the persons selected as jurors were charged according to law, and required to be in attendance next morning at ten o'clock."

On the fourth day of the term, came the plaintiff by the district attorney, and the defendant in his own proper person, when five other jurors were tendered by the district attorney on behalf of the state, and accepted by the defendant in his own proper person; and the whole number of jurors in this case were sworn, and empanelled according to law. Before the jury were sworn, the defendant at the March term, 1846, moved the court to quash the indictment, for the following, reasons, to wit:

1st. Because the writ of *venire facias* returnable to the October term, 1845, of the Washington circuit court was defective in this, that the jurors drawn to serve at the said term, were not drawn in the presence of the probate judge of Washington county.

2d. Because said jurors were drawn by the sheriff and clerk of Washington county, without the presence of the said judge of probate, to wit: on the 13th day of September, 1845.

3d. Because the said jurors were not drawn by the said clerk and sheriff in the term time of the circuit court, of the county of Washington, as required by law.

4th. Because the said grand jurors were not, nor was any or either of them, at the said October term, 1845, of said court, sworn to inquire in and for the body of the said county of Washington, as required by law.

5th. Because the writ of *venire facias* aforesaid, returnable to the October term, 1845, of the said circuit court, was defective in this, that it did not command the sheriff of said county to summon householders or freeholders, as required by law, who are competent to serve as grand jurors.

6th. Because neither the record nor any paper filed in said circuit court shows, that the names of the persons mentioned in the said *venire facias* were drawn from box No. 1, as the law directs.

The motion was overruled and the prisoner excepted.

The defendant then, before the jury were sworn, moved the court for leave to file three pleas in abatement, which are in substances as follows, to wit: That the grand jurors, by whom the indictment was found, were not, nor was either of them sworn to inquire in and for the body of the county of Washington, as required by law; that the grand jury were composed of persons drawn by the clerk and sheriff, without the presence of the probate judge of said county; and that the foreman of the grand jury which preferred the indictment, was not sworn as such, either before or at the time of returning the indictment into court. The court also overruled this motion, and the prisoner excepted. The jury were then sworn, the cause tried, and the defendant found guilty as charged on the first and third counts, as charged in the indictment; and not guilty as to the second and fourth. The defendant was sentenced to five years' imprisonment in the penitentiary. To reverse which judgment he prosecutes this writ of error, and assigns the following errors, to wit:

1. The record does not show that the grand jury who found the indictment, were charged by the court.

2. The record does not show that the defendant, the plaintiff in error, ever pleaded to the indictment, or that any issue was made up for the jury to try.

3. It appears from the record that seven of the jurors, by whom the plaintiff in error was tried, were not sworn until the day after their selection, and in the meantime were allowed to disperse.

4. It does not appear from the record, that the jury were sworn to try any issue between the state and the defendant, or what they were sworn to do.

5. The court erred in refusing to permit the accused to file the pleas in abatement to the indictment by him tendered.

6. The first instruction to the court is erroneous.

7. The court erred in refusing to give the instructions asked by the accused, and in giving one in lieu thereof, uncertain and vague in its terms, and calculated to mislead the jury.

8. The court erred in refusing to reduce to writing the instructions given to the jury.

9. There are other errors manifest in said record, all which the plaintiff in error is ready to verify.

John I. Guion and *E. G. Walker,* for plaintiff in error.

1. The record should show that the grand jury were charged by the court before they retired to consider of presentments or indictments. 1 Chitty Cr. Law, 313.

2. There is no plea to the indictment. The plea by an attorney is a nullity. A defendant charged with a felony, must plead in proper person upon his arraignment. Chitty Cr. Law, 416, 436, 472; Stephen's Cr. Law, 290; Barb. Cr. Treat., 300, 304; Archb. Cr. Prac., 93.

3. There was no arraignment of the prisoner. Arraignment is necessary, and it is error not to state it in the record. Chitty Cr. Law, 415–419; Stephen's Cr. Law, 279; 4 Com. Dig., 701.

Seven persons elected as jurors were not sworn until the day after their selection, but were permitted by the court to disperse until the next day. They should have been sworn and empanelled as they were elected. Chitty Cr. Law, 552.

5. The record does not show what persons were sworn on the jury, or what they were sworn to do. They should have been sworn "well and truly to try the issue joined, and a true deliverance make between the state and the prisoner at the bar." Chitty Cr. Law, 552.

6. No plea of not guilty having been entered, the prisoner had a right to plead abateable matter.   The pleas contain abateable matter of defense.   Chitty's Cr. Law, 422, 435, 437 ; 5 Porter, 130, 474 ; 7 Yerger, 271 ; 4 Dev. 305 ; 7 Leigh, 747 ; Meig's R. 192.

7. The court below should either have given or refused the instructions.   Acts 1846, 125.

John D. Freeman, attorney general.

1. It is admitted that the grand jury should be charged, but the charge is no part of the record, and is no part of the proceedings in this case to which the prisoner could except.

2. It is true that the record shows that the defendant plead by attorney, but it is also stated that the defendant appeared in his own proper person, and (having been arraigned at a former term), pleaded not guilty, and put himself upon the country, and a jury was elected, etc.   This is sufficient.   See 1 How. R., 167.

3. An arraignment is merely placing the prisoner at the bar to answer the charge preferred in the indictment.   1 Chitty, 419 ; Com. Dig., indictment M.   It is sufficient if the prisoner pleaded "not guilty," first by his counsel, and secondly *ore tenus,* in his own proper person.   1 How. 167.

4. This court must presume that the jury were selected according to law, unless the contrary appears in the record.   1 How., 498 ; 2 ib., 655 ; 4 S. & M., 579.

5. A plea in abatement is properly rejected, when offered after the jury has been empanelled and sworn to try the issue joined on the plea of not guilty.   3 How., 27 ; 1 Chitty, 309 ; Bacon Abr. Jury, A ; 9 Mass. 107, 116 ; 1 Blackf., 318, 390 ; 2 Brown. 323 ; 2 Pick., 563 ; 1 Burr's Trial, 38–41 ; 2 S. & M., 497 ; 5 ib., 681.   Challenge to the array is denied, but individual jurors may be removed by challenge.   H. & H., 498.

The law of 1846 does not apply to criminal cases, the same being a statute to regulate the practice in civil cases only ; hence the meaning of the terms used in the statute must be construed with reference to the subject matter of legislation.   Dwarris on Statutes, 2 S. & M., 17.

Sharkey, C. J.:

The plaintiff in error was indicted for an assault committed with intent to rob, and found guilty on the first **and third counts**, and not guilty on the second and fourth. The **case is brought** up on a writ of error, and a number of errors **are now assigned** for reversing the judgment. We shall proceed **to consider of** the sufficiency of such as seem to require to be **noticed.**

1st. It is said that the record does not show **that the grand** jury were charged. It is the duty of the **circuit courts to** charge the grand jury, when empanelled, in regard **to the nature** of the duty which they are required to perform, **and the motives** which should govern them in the discharge of **that duty; but** the charge so given is not to be placed upon the **record, nor can** it be essentially necessary that it should appear **by the record** that it was given, as the matter charged does **not constitute a** ground of error. But as it constitutes part of **the duty of the** court to give it, we must presume that it was given, **unless the** contrary is shown. In criminal, as well as in **civil cases, the** rule prevails that the party who complains of **the judgment** must make the error apparent,[1] and if it is **committed in refer-** ence to a matter which does not constitute a part **of the record,** it must be placed there by bill of exceptions.[2]

2nd. The second error assigned is, that it does **not appear that** the accused ever pleaded to the indictment. The **law undoubt-** edly is, that the defendant must plead in **person.**[3] **In this** instance, there was a plea by attorney, but that **was a nullity.** But there may be some doubt whether he did **not plead at the** subsequent term when he was tried. The **record contains an** entry in these words: " This day came the **plaintiff, by Fulton** E. Anderson, Esq., district attorney, and the **defendant in his** own proper person, and the said defendant having **been arraigned** at the last term of this court, pleaded not guilty, **and put him-** self upon the country and the district attorney, **likewise. It** would seem quite probable that this entry has **reference to the** plea entered at the former term. The true sense **is rather ob-** scure for want of punctuation. But it does **appear from this**

[1] Greenl. Ev., 74 et seq. and notes; Bishop Cr. Procedure, 496, **502, 503**; Archbold Cr. Pr. & Pl., 385-6.

[2] Ingram v. State, 7 Mo., 293; Wade v. State, 11 S. & M., 120.

[3] Wharton Am. Cr. Law, 534; 1 Archb. Cr. Pl., 355; Bishop **Cr. Procedure, 683**; Sperry's case, 9 Leigh, 623.

entry, that the defendant had been arraigned at the previous term.   By looking at the record of the previous term, no arraignment is mentioned.   It was incompetent for the clerk, at a subsequent term, to make any entry of what had transpired at the preceding term.   The consequence is, that it does not legally appear that the accused ever was arraigned, which was error. 2 Hale's Pleas of the Crown, 217.   The regular time for pleading is, when the prisoner is arraigned ;[1]   it is the more probable, therefore, that the plea by attorney, which was doubtless put in at that time, is the plea referred to in the entry, quoted as having been pleaded at a former term.

3d.   It is thirdly assigned, that seven of the jurors were tendered to the prisoner and elected, and permitted to disperse until next day, without having been sworn, and that they were not sworn until next day, when the panel was completed.   The record shows this to have been the fact, and it was a palpable error.   When a juror is elected, he must remain under the care of the court or an officer, before as well as after he is sworn,†　and it is error to permit the jury to disperse without the consent of the prisoner.[2]   By permitting them to go at large, they were liable to be tampered with, and to imbibe prejudices against the accused.   It is immaterial whether improper influences have been exerted or not ;[3]   the only safety is in keeping the jury free from a liability to such influences.   These persons, although not sworn, had been selected by the prisoner, they were known as part of the jury, and, by mixing with the crowd, which is usually in attendance on a court, they were exposed to the dan-

[1] Wharton Am. Cr. Law. 530.

[2] 1 Bishop Cr. Proceedure, 823; Wharton Am. Cr. Law, 3112; et seq. ; Wiley v. State, 1 Swan, 256 ; Sam v. State, ib., 61.

[3] Wharton Am. Cr. Law, 3112, et seq. ; 1 Bishop Cr. Proceedure, 823; 1 Archbold Cr. Pr. & Pl., 638 ; People v. Douglas, 4 Cowen, 26 ; State v. Prescott, 7 N. H. 287 ; State v. Sherbourne, Dudley, 29 ; McLain v. State, 10 Yerg., 241 ; Hines v. State, 8 Humph., 597 ; Boles v. State, 13 S. & M., 398 ; Sam v. State, 1 Swan, 61 ; McCann v. State, 9 S. & M., 465 ; Woods v. State, 43 Miss., 364 ; 4 Black. Com. (by Sharswood), 359 ; Commonwealth v. Roby, 12 Pick., 496 ; Hare v. State, 4 How., 187 ; Commonwealth v. McCall, 1 Va. Cases ; McLean v. State, 10 Yerger, 24 ; Perkins v. Knight, 2 N. H., 474 ; Eastwood v. People, 3 Park., 25 ; McCann v. State, 9 S. & M., 465 ; Lewis v. State, 9 S. & M., 115 ; People v. Hartung, 4 Park., 265 ; Nelms v. State, 13 S. & M., 500 ; 4 How., 187 ; 10 Yerg., 141 ; Westley v. State, 11 Humph., 502 ; Wiley v. State, 1 Swan, 256 ; 7 Cow., 562 ; 12 Pick., 496 ; 1 Va. Cases, 271 ; 13 Miss., 220 ; 36 Miss., 121 ; Organ v. State, 26 Miss. 83 ; Caleb v. State, 39 Miss., 721.

ger of receiving a bias against the prisoner, if any one happened to desire to bring about his conviction by unfair means. Or, if prejudices existed against him in the community, as is sometimes the case, there was danger that their might be communicated to the minds of these jurors, without they being aware of the motive or the effect. Perhaps the prisoner had a right to object to them the next day before they were sworn; if so, they should have been retendered to him. But even if he had such rights, it did not cure the error in permitting them to disperse.

It is also assigned as error that the court refused to allow the accused to file three pleas in abatement, the first of which avers that the grand jurors were not sworn according to law; the second, that they were not drawn according to law; and the third, that the foreman was not sworn as such. It is said these pleas were tendered before the prisoner pleaded not guilty. We have already seen that it is doubtful whether the accused ever did plead in person to the indictment. If he did not, these pleas were offered in time; but if he had previously pleaded not guilty, of course he could not afterwards plead in abatement.[1] We are uninformed as to the precise ground on which these pleas were rejected. Before us the question has been argued, as though the pleas were rejected, because no exception can be taken to the competency of the grand jury by plea in abatement. The law requires, that grand jurors shall possess certain qualifications. From the list returned by the assessor, the jurors' names are to be placed in a box and drawn in a particular manner, either before the circuit court, or before the probate court, and a *venire* is to issue containing the names so drawn. From the number of jurors summoned as directed, the grand jurors are to be drawn by lot, who, when so drawn, shall constitute the grand jury. In view of these several provisions, it is believed that a grand jury composed of members who do not possess the requisite qualifications, or who have not been drawn, summoned, and empanelled in accordance with the law, have no power to

[1] Bishop Cr. Law, 843; 1 Cr. Procedure, 429, *et seq.*; State v. Butler, 17 Vermont, 145; Smith v. State, 19 Conn., 493; State v. Rickey, 5 Halst., 53; Archbold Cr. Pl. & Pl., 359; Palmer v. Green, 1 Johns. Chey., 104; Palmer v. Everston, 2 Cow., 457; Commonwealth v. Dedham, 16 Mass., 141; Commonwealth v. Lewis, 1 Metc., 151; Turno v. Commonwealth, 6 Metcalf, 224.

find a valid indictment.[1]   These restrictions and requisites have
been imposed for wise purposes.   They are guards thrown round
the liberty of the citizen.   They constitute an important part
of the right of trial by jury.   A grand jury does not, by our
law, consist of thirteen or more men, congregated by the mere
order of court, or by accident, in a jury box; but it consists of
the requisite number of competent individuals, selected, summoned, and sworn, according to the forms of law, and if the
law be not followed, it is an incompetent grand jury.   If this be
so, it results as a necessary consequence, that any one indicted
by such a jury, may question their power.   He cannot be called
to answer a charge against him, unless it has been preferred according to the forms of law.   The question is, how is this to be
done?   A prisoner who is in court, and against whom an indictment is about to be preferred, may undoubtedly challenge for
cause; this is not questioned.   But the grand jury may find an
indictment against a person who is not in court.   How is he to
avail himself of a defective organization of the grand jury?   If
he cannot do it by plea, he cannot do it in any way; and the
law works unequally by allowing one class of persons to object
to the competency of the grand jury, whilst another class has
no such privilege.   This cannot be.   The law furnishes the same
security to all, and the same principle which gives to a prisoner
in court the right to challenge, gives to one who is not in court
the right to accomplish the same end by plea, and the current of
authorities sustains such a plea.   True, some may be found the
other way, but it is believed that a large majority of the decisions are in favor of the plea.   To the list of authorities cited
by counsel, may be added the name of Sir Matthew Hale, which
would seem to be sufficient to put the question at rest.   2 Hale's

---

[1] Wharton's Am. Cr. Law, 472; Wharton's Precedents, 1158; Jackson v. State,
11 Tex., 261; Vanhook v. State, 12 Tex., 469; State v. Symmonds, 36 Me., 128;
Rawle v. State, 8 S. & M., 599; Barney v. State, 12 S. & M., 68; State v. Brooks, 9
Ala., 10; State v. Bryant, 10 Yerg., 271; State v. Duncan & Troll, 7 Yerg., 527;
State v. Martin, 2 Iredell, 101; State v. Duncan, 6 Iredell, 98; 2 Hale, 155; 3 Inst.,
34; 4 Dev., 305; State v. Carver, 49 Me., 588; State v. Freeman, 6 Blackf., 248;
Vattler v. State, 4 Blackf., 73; State v. Herndon, 5 Blackf., 75; State v. Lamon, 3
Hawks., 175; State v. Martin, 2 Iredell, 101; People v. Griffin, 2 Barb., S. C., 427;
1 Chitty Cr. Law, 309; Bacon Abr. Juries, A.; 2 Hawks P. C. Ch., 25, §§ 18, 26, 29,
30; Cro. Car., 134, 147; 1 Archbold Cr. Pr. & Pl., 535, notes; 1 Bishop Cr. Proc.,
748-9.

Pleas of the Crown, 155. *Vide* also Sir William Withpole's Case, Cro. Car., 134–147. A different doctrine seems to have been holden in the case of The Commonwealth v. Smith, 9 Mass. R. 107, but that case was very much doubted afterwards, in the case of The Commonwealth v. Parker, 2 Pick. R., 550. In the latter case the court suggested the difficulty that might arise in the application of such a rule to a prisoner who was not present. In such cases, it was intimated, that the rule would not be followed. The conclusion is, that these pleas were improperly rejected; that is, assuming that they were tendered before the prisoner had pleaded not guilty. Pleas in abatement in criminal as well as in civil cases, must be pleaded at the proper time. By denying the charge, the accused waives matter in abatement. [1] We do not, of course, decide on the technical sufficiency of these pleas. That is a question which could only be raised by demurrer, after they were received. It is true that a plea, which is a mere nullity, may be rejected, but these are not so obviously defective and inappropriate as to require them to be so treated.

It is not deemed necessary that we should notice particularly the instructions given or refused, as the other points dispose of the case, and the same difficulties may not again rise.

Judgment reversed, and cause remanded for a new trial.

Rawls *v.* The State, 8 Smedes & Marshall, 599.

Exhibiting Faro Bank.

When the judge of the circuit court refuses to sign a bill of exceptions, it may be signed by two of the attorneys of said court, and be in compliance with the statute.

A plea in abatement that the indictment was found by men who were not a part of the original panel, is good, and should be received; and on the trial of the plea it is competent for the defendant to read in evidence the original *venire*, for it is conclusive proof on the point.

A record is conclusive evidence, but what is, or what is not a record, is matter of evidence, and may be proved like other facts.

Incompetency of the grand jury may be pleaded in abatement, and if true it will defeat the indictment.

There is no law which authorizes the court to take substitutes for any portion of the regular panel. If it can for one, it can for the whole. And if the court do re-

[1] *Vide* note 1, p. 367.

ceive substitutes, the indictment found by them will be quashed by plea in abatement.

When a plea in abatement to an indictment is demurred to, and the demurrer overruled, the judgment of the court should be that the indictment be abated. '

Error to Warren circuit court, COALTER, J.

The opinion of the court contains a sufficient statement of the facts of the case.

E. G. Walker for plaintiff in error.

1. It was error to exclude (upon the trial of the plea in abatement) the writ of *venire facias,* and the testimony of the witnesses offered by the defendant. The plea was a good defense in avoidance of the indictment, and evidence in support of it should have gone to the jury. 4 Bac. Abr., 525, 530, tit. A; 1 Chitty Cr. Law, 309, note 83; 6 Binn., 447; 2 Pick., 563; 5 Porter, 130, 447; 4 Dev., 305; 7 Leigh., 747; 7 Yerger, 271; 4 Black. Com., 302, 306, and notes.

2. It was error to strike out, on motion, the plea of misnomer. The plea was a good defense, but if defective in any way the district attorney should have demurred to it specially, setting forth specifically the causes of demurrer. 1 Chitty Cr. Law, 202; 1 Pick., 388; 3 ib., 262, 263; 2 Chit. R., 335; 11 East., 83; 5 Porter, 236; 3 N. H., 31.

3. The court erred in sustaining the plea in abatement, which averred that six of the grand jurors, who found returned into court, the indictment, had been substituted by the court for six of the regular *venire.* For neither at common law, nor by statute, can jurors be summoned or selected by the judge, but must be summoned by the sheriff or his legally authorized deputy. 4 Bac. Abr., 530, tit. Jury, A; 1 Chitty Cr. Law, 310; Commonwealth v. Barry, Hardin's R., 229; H. & H. Dig., 450, §§ 44, 45, 46, 48, 49, 68, 69. See also § 11 of Bill of Rights, Const. of Miss.

4. There was error in the judgment. The defendant was sentenced to imprisonment in the penitentiary, when, according to the act of 1839, he should only have been fined. H. & H. Dig., 680, 683.

G. S. Yerger on same side.

1. The indictment is returned a true bill, but is not signed by

the foreman.   The law requires the endorsement on the indictment, that it is a true bill, and signed by the foreman.   H. & H., 487, 492 ; Nomaque v. People, 1 Breeze, 109 ; Webster's case, 5 Greenl., 432 ; *Dictum Contra*, State v. Calhoon, 1 Dev. & Batt., 374 ; also, 1 Nott & McCord.

2. The plea of misnomer was a good plea in abatement.   1 Chitty Cr. Law, 202 ; Bac. Abr., Misnomer, A ; Commonwealth v. Perkins, 1 Pick., 388 ; Commonwealth v. Hall, 3 Pick., 262, 263 ; 3 N. H., 31, 36 ; 1 Marsh. R., 477, or 4 Eng. C. L. R. ; 2 Chitty R., 335, or 18 Eng. C. L. R.

The case in 5 Johns., 84, was not a criminal case ; it was a question of variance, and moreover it is not supported by any authority.   It asserts that a man can have but one Christian name.   That is true ; but John J., James J., John Thomas, etc., constitute but one Christian name.   The authority in Co. Litt. does not support it.   See 3 Co. Litt., 3 a.

3. The plea in abatement alleging that the court discharged the grand jurors of the regular *venire*, and substituted other persons in their stead, was sufficient to abate the indictment. H. & H. Dig., §§ 44, 45, 46, 48, 49, 68, ·69 ; Chitty Cr. Law, 309, 310 ; 7 Yerger R. ; 5 Porter, 130 ; 7 Leigh, 747 ; 4 Dev., 305 ; 2 Pick., 550 ; 3 Blackf., 37 ; 6 Binn., 447 ; 6 S. & M., 680 ; 3 How., 27 ; 1 Blackf., 318.

4. The fact that it is stated in the record that the grand jury was composed of good and lawful men, does not preclude proof to show they were not, upon the trial of a plea in abatement alleging the contrary.

5. If an indictment concludes contrary to the statute it is defective.   Archbold's Cr. Law ; State v. Paul, 2 Dev., 202.

J. D. Freeman, attorney general.

Sharkey, C. J. :

To an indictment for having exhibited a faro bank, the accused filed three pleas in abatement, two of which go to the competency of the grand jury who found the indictment, and the other is a plea of *misnomer*.

The first plea is that six of the grand jurors were not legally qualified to serve, inasmuch as they had not been drawn by the clerk and sheriff in either of the modes prescribed by law from a list of freeholders and householders, returned by the assessor. nor had they been summoned as persons liable to serve on juries by virtue of a special writ of *venire facias*, nor were they summoned as tales jurors, nor had the regularly summoned jurors failed to attend, nor had the panel been exhausted, nor were they summoned from the by-standers.   The plea is full and specific in stating, that these grand jurors were not summoned and empanelled in any mode prescribed by law.   The district attorney took issue.

The second plea to the competency of the grand jury is in substance, that the six persons named in the first plea, were substitutes, who were received by the court to serve in place of so many of the jury summoned under the *venire*, and who were there in attendance on the court, and who had procured the six persons to serve in their places.   To this plea, there was a demurrer which was sustained.

On the trial of the issue taken on the first plea, certain evidence was offered and ruled out, to which the accused excepted. but the court refused to sign the bill of exceptions, and it was signed by two attorneys of the court.   The sufficiency of the bill of exceptions, as a preliminary question, is denied, but it seems to have been signed in strict accordance with the statute: it states that the judge refused to sign it, and also that the persons who did sign it, were practicing attorneys of the court, and present at the trial.   The question then arises, was the evidence properly ruled out?   The defendant offered to read the original *venire facias*, returnable to the April term, 1845, together with the sheriff's return.   If this evidence was relevant, it was surely competent.   It was the process of the court, and competent to prove any fact stated on its face, if such fact was in issue.   The defendant pleaded, that six of the grand jurors, who found the indictment, were not competent, not having been drawn and summoned according to law.   On this plea issue had been taken.   If the names of the objectionable persons did not appear in the *venire*, the first point in the plea was established.   This made it manifest, that they had not been summoned under the original *venire facias*, and after establishing that fact, if by other proof it could be shown, that they had not been summoned according to either of the other modes provided by law to supply a deficiency caused by the non-attendance of a sufficient number of the original panel, the defence was made out. The process was not inadmissible because it contradicted the caption of the record, which had been read by the district attorney. The caption, after reciting the term of the court, proceeds in these words: "A grand jury of inquest for the body of this county, was drawn and empanelled from the regular *venire*, viz., Joseph N. Craddick, etc.," beginning the list with the name of one of the persons named in the plea, as having been irregularly empanelled. No such name is found in the process, which was the foundation of the record, and no record could be true, which did not follow it. One or the other was untrue, and as the process was referred to as furnishing the names of the persons mentioned in the recital or caption, it must control, and prove that the caption was untrue. By the plea, it is said, that the indictment was found by men, who were not a part of the original panel, and the *venire* was conclusive proof on this subject, and ought to have been received.

The defendant next offered to prove by Henry Green, who was deputy sheriff, and the court officer, that when he called the list of jurors regularly summoned, a sufficient number answered to their names, and were present in court, to constitute a grand jury, and that the six persons mentioned in the plea were, by the order of the judge, substituted for six of the regular panel, who were then in attendance, who had brought in their substitutes and tendered them, whereupon the court received the substitutes and discharged the original jurymen, and the witness was instructed to insert the names of the substitutes on the panel. The regular jurors, who had employed the substitutes, were also offered to prove the fact of substitution; but this testimony was all excluded. It furnishes the key to the discrepancy between the caption of the record and the *venire facias*, and shows beyond doubt the truth of the matter pleaded. We can see no reason whatever, for its exclusion. True, it contradicts a recital in record, but better evidence had been offered, to wit: The *venire facias*, to prove that the recital of the record was not true. The fact of its untruth being established, it was competent to show how the variance had occurred. An alteration had been made in the panel, and from the panel so altered, the record was made up. "It cannot be doubted," says Chief Justice Parker, "that anything produced as a record may be shown to be forged or altered; if it were not so great mischief might arise. A record is conclusive evidence, but what is or is not a record, is matter of evidence, and may be proved like other facts; otherwise there would be no remedy." Brier v. Woodbury, 1 Pick. Rep., 362. We are not called on to say, whether parol evidence in a case like this, may be introduced to falsify the record. The proof in this instance tended only to account for a discrepancy between different parts of the record. The recital would have been shown to be untrue by the *venire*. A question of power was raised, and the proof showed a want of power in the court. The evidence was pertinent to the issue, which was not an immaterial one. We have already decided that the incompetency of the grand jurors is a matter, which may be pleaded in abatement; and we conclude that this evidence ought to have been admitted, as if true it defeated the indictment. McQuillen v. The State, ante, 587.

It is agreed that there was another plea in abatement, which averred the substitution of the grand jurors in the manner above stated, to which a demurrer was sustained. This brings up fairly the legality of the course pursued in taking substitutes for part of the regular panel. In the case above referred to, it was decided that the law must be followed in forming the grand jury, and that an indictment found by an incompetent grand jury may be quashed on plea. We will only add that there is no law which authorizes the court to take substitutes for any portion of the regular panel. If it can for one, it can for the whole. It is useless to comment on the consequences which might result; the effect would be to break down the provisions of the law. In the case of Davis v. The Commonwealth, a report of which was cited in Commonwealth v. Parker, 2 Pick. Rep., 550, it was discovered, after a verdict of guilty against the prisoner, that one Locke, who served on the grand jury, had not been chosen a grand juror, but that the name of one Burr, who had been chosen, had been erased from the return of the *venire*, and Locke's name inserted in its place. The court of common pleas arrested the judgment, and this decision seems to have met the approbation of the supreme court. This case is in point, and if it be right to arrest the judgment, surely it cannot admit of question, whether such matter is pleadable in abatement. The demurrer in this plea should have been overruled, and the judgment would then have been, that the prosecution should abate. Stephen on Pleading, 107. And as we are to give the judgment, which the court below should have given, that must be our judgment.

DONNAHER *v.* THE STATE, 8 Smedes & Marshall, 649.

NUISANCE.

The statute of 1832 reserves to the legislature the right to dispose of the entire two sections of land designated by the commissioners to locate the seat of government, except the streets and lots which may be sold from time to time. This vests the title to the streets in the corporation of the city, and deprives the legislature of the power to dispose of them, except so far as the *jus publicum*, or right of domain may authorize it. This right of domain always exists, unless the state has absolutely parted with it by grant.

There is a necessary exception in the title of all property, that if it be necessary for public use, it may be taken for such purpose, provided that just compensation shall be made to the owner.

The property of a corporation is not less liable to the exercise of the *jus publicum* than the property of a private individual. A corporation is an ideal individual, and is to be treated as other individuals.

Error to Hinds circuit court. COALTER, J.

This was an indictment preferred by the grand jury of Hinds county against Patrick Donnaher for a nuisance, in digging and subverting large quantities of dirt in the streets of Jackson, and thereby obstructing the same. The defendant pleaded not guilty. The case was submitted on the following state of facts, to wit:

In 1836, the legislature passed an act incorporating the president and directors of the Jackson and Brandon Railroad and Bridge Company. The eleventh section of this act is as follows: "Be it further enacted, That the said company shall have the privilege of extending said road, and of constructing branches in any direction whatever, that they may intersect or unite with any other road terminating in or passing through the town of Jackson ; provided the said railroad be so constructed as not to interfere with the passage of any public street of said town. And so much of the land donated to the state by the act of Congress, passed February 20th, 1819, for the seat of government, as may be necessary for the passage of said railroad, and as may be selected by the commissioners, with the consent of the governor of the state, and which yet remains unsold, is hereby donated to said company during the continuance of this charter ; provided that not more than one acre shall be donated for the erection of warehouses or a place of depot, and that said acre of said land, shall only be located within two hundred yards of the place where the said road shall pass Pearl river." It was agreed on the trial, that the foregoing act, or any part thereof, or any other act in relation to said railroad, whether mentioned in the case or not, might be read in evidence from the pamphlet acts as printed by the state printers.

By virtue of this and other similar acts the said railroad company claimed the right to extend the railroad from the termination of the Vicksburg and Jackson railroad through the city of Jackson to Brandon, and through the eastern part of the state, to connect with the Charleston railroad.   It was further agreed that the land on which the city of Jackson now stands, at and before the laying off of the said city of Jackson, belonged to the State of Mississippi.   By another act the city of Jackson was laid off by commissioners, into lots with public streets, etc.   A plan of said city was referred to and part of the case on the trial. It was also agreed that all the acts laying off the said city of Jackson, or amending the same, should be considered a part of the case and read in evidence from the statute-book.   It was also agreed that the various acts incorporating the city of Jackson, and amending and modifying its charter, may be read in the case from the statute-books.   It was further agreed that the lots in the said city of Jackson were sold by authority of the state, according to said plan, and were then held by individuals ; that the president and directors of the Jackson and Brandon Railroad

Company laid out the railroad to pass through the city of Jackson to Brandon, from the west side of State street, commencing at a point where the railroad from Vicksburg to Jackson had been completed, to the piers on Pearl river, where the bridge is to be built, which route as laid out passes across State street in the city of Jackson to and across South street, thence part of an acre lot 1, south, into and down Commerce street to the lot on which the saw-mill is situated, whence said route passes through individual property. The right of way has been secured by the company. It was further agreed that Commerce and State streets are each one hundred feet wide, and South street eighty feet wide, through which streets alone the track will run. The track of the road was to be twelve feet wide on the surface, and the rails will be five feet apart. The track when completed to be used by either horse or steam cars. The line of road on Commerce street to be about a quarter of a mile in length, and about one hundred and twenty feet on State street, and about one hundred feet on South street. It was further agreed that the defendant was and continued to be employed by said railroad company to grade the road through the city of Jackson, in pursuance of which contract he was digging and grading on said streets in said city of Jackson, over which said line of road as laid off by said company is to run. It was agreed that the acts of said defendant in digging and grading said streets, constitute a nuisance in law, if said company had no power to run their said road through and over the said streets in said city; but if said company had such power, it was agreed that said acts are necessary to make said road through said streets, and did not constitute a nuisance. It was further agreed that the lots in said city of Jackson situated on said streets were sold by the state to individuals, some of which have been built on and improved; the said individual purchasers purchased with reference to the plan of said city, and with a reference to the use of said streets, etc., in accordance with said plan. In running the road through said streets the value of the property thereon would be lessened to some extent, and the use and enjoyment of said streets would be impaired to some extent, that is to such an extent as railroad trains, propelled either by steam or horse power, passing through a street, necessarily impair its use.   It was further agreed that said streets have not been condemned, or damages assessed against said company for the right of way through them; that the corporate authorities of the city of Jackson never agreed to, but resisted the right and power of the railroad company to use the streets of the city for the railroad.   It was further agreed, that if upon the foregoing facts, the court should be of opinion that the said company had the power and right to run said railroad, through said streets of Jackson, then and in that case, judgment should be entered up for the defendant.   But if the court be of opinion that said company had no such right, then judgment was to be rendered for the state.

The court was of the opinion that the railroad company had no right to use the streets of the city of Jackson in the manner claimed by them, and rendered judgment against the defendant. To reverse which, he has sued out a writ of error, and brings the case to this court.

George S. Yerger for plaintiff in error.

1. The company undoubtedly has the power, delegated from the state, to run their road through Jackson, so as to join the railroad from Vicksburg.   See Acts of 1836, 163, 196; Acts of 1838, 82; Acts of 1840, 198; Acts of 1841, 138; Acts of 1842, 123; Acts of 1846, 126.   The act incorporating the Southern Railroad Company, gives the Jackson and Brandon Railroad and Bridge Company the power of building and completing their road from where it unites with the Southern railroad at Brandon to a point "*at* or *near* the city of Jackson, and B. R. & B. Co., shall unite with the Vicksburg and Jackson railroad," etc. See § 7, Acts of 1846, 142.

Not merely the local public, but the community at large have a right to use the streets of Jackson, which were dedicated as public streets and highways in any manner not inconsistent with the public use, or contrary to the original purposes for which they were given to the public.

The use of the streets for running railroad cars is precisely in accordance with the uses of a public street or highway.   If the streets are not for the sole use of the town but for the public, what right have the local authorities of Jackson to prevent the public from traveling over them in an improved or different mode of traveling than that which was known at the time of the dedication.

The consent of a municipal corporation to use and appropriate the streets in a way inconsistent with their original use, would not give validity to such use. 8 Dana, 289. Neither the original proprietor nor the city can appropriate or use property dedicated for public use, to a different use.

The use must be consistent with the dedication, and if the streets are permitted to be used in a way inconsistent with the use originally intended, it is clear that any citizen or citizens of the town, or any member of the community can in equity enjoin such use. City of New Orleans v. The United States, 10 Peters, 662; 1 Wharton, 469; 3 Vermont, 279, 519; ib. 378; 2 Greenl. Ev., § 662; 6 Peters, 507. It is settled that property may be dedicated to public use without grant. See cases in 6 and 10 Peters R.

It is clear that the owners of property have no right to damages, for they do not own the soil. Neither has the corporation, for the city only holds the street as a right of way; and if the streets were condemned, the damages would have to be for the use of the original proprietor, the state. 11 Leigh, 42; 6 Peters, 507. And if the use of the streets by running the cars was inconsistent with their original dedication, it follows, that the court, notwithstanding the consent of the corporation, ought to have enjoined such inconsistent use. 8 Dana, 289.

To constitute a nuisance, there must not only be an obstruction of the street, but it must be an unlawful obstruction. It cannot be an unlawful obstruction to grade the streets for the purpose of carrying into effect the right of way given to the public by the original dedication of the streets and by the act of 1846.

William Yerger for the state.

The constitution of this state declares, that "No person's property shall be taken or applied to public use without the consent of the legislature, and without compensation being first made therefor."

It has been decided that a charter to a railroad company, authorizing them to pass over lands without the consent of the owner, upon an assessment of damages being made, and a judgment and execution therefor, was unconstitutional. The land must not only be condemned for public uses ; but it must be first paid for before it can be used.   Thompson v. Grand Gulf Railroad, 3 How., 240.

Wherever the owner of land lays it out in lots, with streets, etc., for the purpose of being used as a town, and sells lots in it with reference to such plan, he cannot afterwards deprive the grantees of the benefits of the streets, etc., so laid out.   4 Paige, 510.

All public dedications are to be considered with reference to the use for which they are made.   6 Peters, 438.

The purchasers of lots in the city of Jackson bought them in reference to the plan of the city then laid out, and have a right to the use of the streets as easements to the full extent of the dimensions of the streets so laid out.   2 Wend., 472.

Under the grant of a thing, whatever is parcel of it or necessary to its beneficial enjoyment or, in common intendment, is included in it, passes to the grantee.   3 Mason, 280.

Wherever the owner of lands in a city sells building lots, bounding them by streets of a specified width, as laid down on a map, but not actually opened, the purchasers acquire a legal right against the grantor to have the streets kept open to the width delineated on the map.   8 Wend., 85.

The state, having laid out the city of Jackson with various streets, squares, etc., and sold lots therein with reference to such plan, cannot by any subsequent legislation appropriate the streets or squares of said city for any other purpose than such as was originally intended, or do any thing which will impair the use and enjoyment of the same by the owners thereof.   6 Peters, 431, 498, 738 ; 10 ib., 662, *et seq.* ; 1 Wend., 268 ; 2 ib., 475 ; 8 ib., 95 ; 11 ib., 493 ; 17 Mass., 415 ; 4 Paige, 510 ; 3 Mason, 280.

CLAYTON, J. :

The agreed state of facts contained in this record, presents this as the prominent question for investigation : whether the

Jackson and Brandon Railroad and Bridge Company have a right to construct a railroad through the streets of the city of Jackson without an assessment and payment of damages for such use of the streets.

The statute incorporating this company, passed February 5th, 1836, gives power to it to extend its railroad so as to intersect or unite with any other railroad terminating in or passing through the city of Jackson, provided the road be so constructed as not to interfere with the passage of any public street of said city. There has been various legislation on the subject of this railroad since, but the above provision has been retained.

The statute of 1823 reserves to the legislature the right to dispose of the entire two sections of land, designated by the commissioners to locate the seat of government, except the streets and the lots which may be sold from time to time. How. & Hutch., 60, § 11; Poin. Rev., 486. This vests the title to the streets in the corporation of the city, and deprives the legislature of the power to dispose of them, except so far as the *jus publicum* or the right of eminent domain may authorize it. This right of eminent domain always exists, unless the state has absolutely parted with it by grant. There is a necessary exception in the title to all property, that if it be wanted for public use, it may be taken for such purpose. But this is always upon the condition that just compensation shall be made to the owner. The principle has its origin in the common law, The King v. Ward, 31 Com. Law R., 96, and is enforced by our constitutional provision, "that private property shall not be taken for public use without just compensation." This principle applies as forcibly to the streets in this instance, as to private property in other cases. In the case of The Tuckahoe Canal Company v. The Tuckahoe Railroad Company, 11 Leigh, 76, the court says: "It is not perceived that the property of a corporation is less liable to the exercise of the *jus publicum* than the property of a private individual. In both cases the private right must yield to the necessities of the public, and in both the public must make compensation for the loss. This was a case of opposite franchises or easements.

In a case in 3 Hill's N. Y. Rep., 570, the court says: "The

claim set up is an easement, not a right of passage to the public, but to the company who have the exclusive privilege of using the track of the road in their own peculiar manner. The public may travel with them over the track if they choose to ride in their cars; but nevertheless the company are not the public, nor can they be regarded as standing in the place of the public. They are a private company, an ideal individual, and to be treated as an individual." Presbyterian Society in Waterloo v. Auburn and Rochester Railroad Company. That case arose in an effort to subject a public highway to the use of a railroad.

The progress of public improvement, and the increase of trade and commerce may render changes in roads, streets and canals necessary. An easement of one kind may be made to give place to one of a different character, of more enlarged utility. Great and acknowledged public improvements lead to corresponding changes in the rights to be affected by them, accompanied, however, with the just condition of making compensation.

This case differs from that of the Lexington and Ohio Railroad Company v. Applegate et al, 8 Dana, 289, in two essential particulars. 1st, The corporation there gave its assent to the use of the streets of Louisville by the railroad. 2d, The owners of the lots there claimed compensation. In this case the corporation has not given its assent, and the owners of the lots are not before us. The right to the streets, in this case, being in the corporation of Jackson, they cannot be subjected to the use of the railroad without the consent and contract of the corporation, or without the assessment and payment of damages according to law.

At present we are strongly inclined to the belief that the owners of lots adjacent to the track of the railroad will have no claim to compensation. They have no right of soil in the streets; and the charter of the railroad company restricts the use to such bounds as will not interfere with the passage of the streets. Moreover, the salutary maxim will apply to the company, that "they must so use their own rights as not to injure another." 31 Eng. Com. Law Rep., 97; Dudley's S. Car. R., 138. This point, however, need not be decided. See Barclay v. Howell, 6 Peters, 514.

We have no doubt that the corporation has the power to regulate the mode of propelling the cars within its limits; to say whether steam or horse-power shall be employed; and to prescribe the rate at which they may move. This results from the same principle which authorizes it to control the speed of carriages and of horsemen—the principle of necessary protection to the safety of its citizens and their property.

The defendant having failed in his attempted justification, the judgment is affirmed.

THACHER, J., *dissented:*

Because he believes the company possess the right of way through the streets without any compensation; and because he considers the company has a right to use any species of locomotive power, subject to police regulations, to be established by the corporation of Jackson.

LEGORI *c.* THE STATE, 8 Smedes & Marshall, 697.

RETAILING LIQUORS.

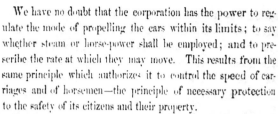

Under the statute of 1842, amendatory of the statute of 1839, " for the suppression of tippling houses," etc., sec. 2, appropriating all the money accruing from the granting of licenses to retail, and from fines for violations of the statute committed within the city of Vicksburg, to that city, the particular place where the offense was alleged to have been committed became a fact and circumstance constituting the offense, and is necessary to be established by proof, as stated in the indictment.

Error to Warren circuit court. COALTER, J.

The opinion of the court contains a sufficient statement of the facts of this case.

Guion & Tompkins for plaintiff in error.

The statute prohibiting the sale of vinous and spirituous liquors in less quantities than one gallon, appropriates to the city of Vicksburg, for the use of a hospital, all fines and forfeitures from a breach of its provisions, within the limits of said city. Acts of 1842, 100, sec. 2.

In cases in which a statute gives the pecuniary penalty for an offense to any particular district or parish, the indictment must charge the offense to have been committed within the particular district or parish, and the proof must correspond with the averment. Stephens' Cr. Law, 154; Archb. Cr. Plead., 40, 96; Barbour's Cr. Treat., 355.

J. D. Freeman, attorney general.

Had the indictment charged the defendant with selling in the county of Warren, the evidence would have sustained the indictment; but, inasmuch as the indictment charges a sale in the city of Vicksburg, it is believed that selling four miles from Vicksburg does not sustain the indictment.

THACHER, J.:

This is an indictment for retailing vinous and spirituous liquors, in less quantities than a gallon, within the city of Vicksburg, and without a license.

The proof upon the trial was, that the defendant below retailed the prohibited article in less quantity than a gallon at a place "four miles out of and from the city of Vicksburg," and upon this proof the jury found a verdict of guilty as charged in the indictment.

The statute of 1842, amendatory to the statute of 1839, "for the suppression of tippling houses, and to discourage and prevent the odious vice of drunkenness," § 2, appropriates all moneys accruing from the granting of licenses to retail, and from fines for a violation of the statute committed within the city of Vicksburg, to that city.

Under this provision of the foregoing statute, the particular place where the offense was alleged to have been committed, became a fact and circumstance constituting the offense, and made it incumbent upon the state to prove it, as stated in the indictment.

Judgment reversed and new trial granted.

SCAGGS *v.* THE STATE, 8 Smedes and Marshall, 722.

HOMICIDE.

In cases of homicide it must appear affirmatively that the accused was present at the trial, or it will be error. The presence of the prisoner cannot be inferred.

Declarations are admitted in evidence as part of the *res gestœ* only upon the presumption that they elucidate the facts with which they are connected, having been made without premeditation or artifice, and without a view to the consequences.

Error to Itawamba circuit court. MILLER, J.

The plaintiff in error was indicted in the court below for the murder of Lewis Smith. The defendant was arraigned on the 14th day of September, 1846, and pleaded not guilty.

On the trial, Isaac Bennett, a witness, testified, that on the morning of the 20th of March, 1846, he saw the defendant about a half a mile from his own house, with blood on his hands. On cross-examination he stated that the defendant was coming directly from his (defendant's) house, and traveling in the direction of his father-in-law's. The defendant asked witness how he came to see the blood on his hands; witness answered that defendant had shown them to him; the defendant then asked the witness what Scaggs said when he showed his hands; to the answering of which question the district attorney objected. The court sustained the objection, and the prisoner excepted.

The defendant was found guilty of manslaughter, and sentenced to imprisonment in the penitentiary for twenty-five years. The defendant then moved for a new trial, which was overruled by the court, and the prisoner excepted, and brings the case to this by writ of error, and assigns the following errors:

1. The case was tried in the absence of the prisoner.

2. There is no entry in the record in relation to the commencement of the trial.

3. It appears that the court, having been moved and seduced by the excellent learning to be found in Howard and Hutchinson's Digest, gave in charge about three pages of the penitentiary code from that instructive book.

4. The court erred in excluding from the jury certain evidence adduced on the trial, and in overruling the motion for a new trial.

Harris & Harrison for plaintiff in error.

The record contains no statement of the fact that the accused was in court from the 14th until the 19th day of September. The *venire* was made returnable on the 17th, the day of the trial.

The act of 1846 does not apply to criminal cases. Taylor v. Manley, 6 S. & M., 305.

The court should have admitted the evidence which was rejected, and erred in overruling the motion for a new trial. Phill. on Ev., Cow. & Hill's notes, 157, 158, 590, 591, 592, 594, 595 ; 1 Greenl. Ev., §§ 108–110 ; Roscoe Cr. Ev., 22, 23.

J. D. Freeman, attorney general.

The statute of 1846, providing that the judge shall not charge the jury unless requested so to do ; or by the second section, unless the charge be reduced to writing, does not apply to criminal cases. The charges in the record are not excepted to, and under the previous statute cannot be a part of the record unless incorporated by a bill of exceptions. 3 S. & M., 295, 614, per SHARKEY, C. J.

There are no exceptions taken to the proceedings as regards the special *venire*, and hence they are presumed to be regular.

THACHER, J. :

This was an indictment for murder, preferred in the circuit court of Itawamba county.

An inspection of the record presents to view several irregular proceedings, but it becomes unnecessary to remark at length upon them all, for the purpose of the present decision of this case, or its future progress.

The error which first protrudes itself to notice is the circumstance, that it does not appear that the prisoner was present during the whole of the trial of the indictment. The only evidence of his presence at all, is contained in a bill of exceptions, where he is stated to have asked some questions of a witness, but he does not appear to have been confronted by the witnesses against him, which was his constitutional right. Const. Art. 1, § 10. It must appear in this class of crimes, that the accused was present during his trial, or it will be error. The presence of the prisoner cannot be inferred, but must appear affirmatively, and for all that appears in this record, the questions directed to the witness by him, might have been propounded in writing.

In view of a future trial, an observation is called for upon another point insisted upon for the plaintiff in error. In the examination in chief upon the trial, a witness for the state deposed that on the day upon which the crime is charged to have been committed, he met the accused a half a mile from his house, and that he had blood upon his hands; and that upon cross examination, the witness stated, that the accused was coming from his own house at the time spoken of, and directed his attention to the condition of his hands. The court thereupon refused, upon a question on behalf of the accused for the purpose, to permit the witness to state what the accused said when he showed the blood upon his hands. This statement was properly rejected. It was not sought to be let in as a part of a confession, and it could not be admitted as a part of the *res gestæ* or transaction. Declarations are admitted in evidence as part of the *res gestae*, only upon the presumption, that they elucidate the facts with which they are connected, having been made without premeditation or artifice, and without a view to the consequences.[*] Stark. Ev. 1, 49. It was the accused who called the attention of the witness to the blood upon his hands, and it was reasonable to presume, that he had premeditated his explanation of its cause, when it was also shown that he was half a mile from the spot where the crime was alleged to have been committed, and had sufficient time to determine upon the explanation he would give concerning the circumstance. The explanation, it is true, might have contained nothing but the truth, but it was not of that impulsive character, which distinguishes declarations at the time of the transaction. To have permitted the question to have been answered, would not have been short of permitting the defendant below to make evidence for himself. The State v. Slack, 1 Bailey, 330.

The judgment of the court below is reversed, and the cause

[*] State v. Hildreth, 9 Iredell, 140; State v. Scott, 1 Hawks, 24; Campbell v. State, 23 Ala., 44; State v. Tilley, 3 Iredell, 424; Gardner v. People, 3 Scam., 83; Bland v. State, 2 Carter, 608; 1 Arch., Cr. Pro. and Pl., 429; Newcomb v. State, 37 Miss., 383; Corbett v. State, 31 Ala., 329; Tupper v. Commonwealth, 1 Metc. (Ky.), 6; Golden v. State, 19 Ark., 590; State v. Jackson, 17 Mo., 544; Bland v. State, 2 Carter, 686; State v. Wisdom, 8 Porter, 511; Wharton Am. Cr. Law., 692.

remanded for a *venire de novo* in this court, for the purpose of a new trial.

MORRIS v. THE STATE, 8 Smedes & Marshall, 762.

FORGERY.

Where an indictment contains four counts, and the jury find the accused guilty as to the three last, the verdict is sufficient to warrant a judgment. Swinney v. State, supra 376, cited and approved.

Evidence of a supposed attempt, by the defendant, three years previous to the trial, and the finding of the indictment, to utter forged bank notes, is illegal evidence on the trial of an indictment for a similar offense.

Where a party is found guilty on three counts of an indictment, and acquitted upon one, and a new trial granted, the new trial should be had upon the three counts on which he was found guilty.

Error to Lowndes circuit court.   ROGERS, J.

The plaintiff in error was indicted in the court below, at the April term, 1846, for forgery. The indictment contained four counts: 1st. "Making and forging a promissory note, commonly called a bank bill," reciting the same, "with intent to defraud the Bank of the State of North Carolina;" 2nd. With "uttering and publishing as true, a forged promissory note, commonly called a bank bill, with intent to injure and defraud the Bank of the State of North Carolina," reciting the same; 3rd. With "having in his possession a forged promissory note of the Bank of the State of North Carolina with intent to utter and publish the same, knowing it to be forged." The fourth count was similar to the third.

The defendant demurred to the indictment, because the defendant's christian name was not set out; it did not conclude against the form of the statute, and was not a common law offense; it did not allege that the Bank of the State of North Carolina was a corporation or a company, by the laws of the United States, or of this state, or of any other state, government or country, the forgery of which is made punishable by the laws of this state, etc. No disposition appears to have been made of this demurrer. At the October term, 1846, the defendant was arraigned, pleaded guilty, and was convicted on the second, third and fourth counts of the indictment. The defendant moved in arrest of judgment, on the grounds, 1st. Because the court permitted improper evidence to go to the jury. 2d. Because the jury found contrary to the law and evidence. 3d. Because there was no finding or verdict on, or disposition made of the first count in the indictment. 4th. Because the indictment was insufficient in law, and will not support a judgment of the court for errors apparent upon the face of the record. 5th. Because the record does not show that any such bill of indictment was ever returned into court by the grand jury a true bill as to three counts, upon which the defendant has been found guilty by the jury. The court overruled the motion, to which the prisoner excepted ; and filed his bill of exceptions, and sued out a writ of error to this court to have the judgment of the court below reversed.

In the bill of exceptions it is stated that Orrall Brown testified that about three years before the trial, defendant passed to him, in Columbus, Mississippi, some money in bills, purporting to be on the Northern Bank of Kentucky ; that afterwards, suspecting that the bills were not genuine, he followed the defendant to Aberdeen, and requested him to give him other money for them, which he did ; stating at the same time, that he, defendant, supposed the bills to be genuine. Witness did not know whether the bills were genuine or not. The defendant objected to this evidence going to the jury, but the objection was overruled by the court, and the opinion of the court excepted.

The prisoner was sentenced to ten years' imprisonment in the penitentiary.

Harris & Harrison for plaintiff in error.

1. The name of the prosecutor is not marked upon the indictment. 3 How., 27, 433.

2. The sentence does not set forth the time from whence the imprisonment shall date. Kelly & Little v. State, 3 S. & M., 518.

3. The sentence is for forgery ; of which offense the prisoner was not convicted. This is the only offense mentioned, and being expressly referred to, necessarily excludes any other.

4. The bills offered in evidence were variant from those set

out in the indictment. None of the precedents set out the forged instrument in that way. See 3 Chitty Cr. Law, 1065, 1071, 1072, 1075 ; Archb. Cr. Pl., 351, 353 ; 8 Leigh, 733.

5. The judgment should be reversed because there was no disposition made of the demurrer to the indictment.

6. The return expressly limits their finding to the offense of forgery.

7. The motion in arrest should not have been overruled.

In the present case the verdict is partial and the judgment of the court is general. There was no evidence of any kind to support the conviction upon the third and fourth counts, or that the prisoner ever saw, or had anything to do with the bills described in said counts. The testimony only relates to one particular bill.

The first count cannot support the judgment because the jury did not find upon it. The second count cannot because it is bad. It does not bring the offense within the statute. It does not allege that it was a " negotiable " note, issued, or purporting to have been issued, by a " corporation " or company duly authorized by the United States, or one of the states, or where the corporation was situated. The People v. Davis, 21 Wend., 309 ; How. & Hutch., 705, § 36.

There is the same objection to the third and fourth counts. The indictment should be certain not only to a common intent, but against every intendment to the contrary.

J. D. Freeman, attorney general.

1. The crime of forgery is a felony and is punishable as such. How. & Hutch., 726, § 24.

2. The statute provides that it shall be the duty of the district attorney to mark on all bills of indictment the name of the prosecutor ; How. & Hutch. Dig., 669, § 30 ; but no penalty is attached for the neglect of this duty. The object of the statute is to protect the state against frivolous prosecutions ; and in cases of inferior offenses to tax the prosecutor with costs. How. & Hutch., 600, § 5. No penalty is attached to a neglect of this duty by the grand jury, and, as the common law provides no remedy, the statute is merely a direction to the grand jury, which they may disregard with impunity. 5 Rand., 669.

3. A presentment is a bill charging a criminal offense against one or more individuals preferred on the volition of the grand jury alone, and is only signed by their foreman. 1 Chitty Cr. Law, 162. An indictment is a criminal prosecution, based on the written accusation of either a private or a public prosecutor, and preferred by the grand jury, and by them endorsed on the back "a true bill" and returned into court. Archb. Cr. Pl., 589; 2 Hawk. P. C., ch. 25, § 1; 1 Chitty Cr. Law, 324; 5 Rand., 674.

4. The law does not require impossibilities, and if there were no private prosecutor the district attorney would not be authorized to mark one on the indictment. This court will presume that the proceedings of the court below are correct unless the contrary is shown. The presumption of law, therefore, is that there was no private prosecutor. It is not essential to the validity of an indictment, or presentment, that the same should be signed by the district attorney. 1 Chitty Cr. Law, 324, note a. The constitution of the United States requires only that an indictment, or presentment, shall be preferred by a grand jury. Art. 7, § 5. The statutes of this state do not require the district attorney to sign his own name to any presentment or indictment. He is simply required to "appear and prosecute for the state, in their respective districts, in all criminal prosecutions," (How. & Hutch., 278,) "and to attend the deliberations of the grand jury," etc., "and give them the necessary information touching the law and the facts of each case," etc. Laws of 1844, 91. If, therefore, the district attorney signs his own name to an indictment, it is a voluntary act, and an assumption of the responsibility of the prosecution. It is well settled by adjudications in other states, on legal principles alone, that the failure to have marked on it the name of the prosecutor, does not vitiate the indictment. See 5 Randolph, 669. At common law an indictment could only be quashed for a defect appearing in its caption, or on the indictment. The name of the prosecutor, under our statute, forms no part of the caption, or of the indictment.

5. The sentence of the court, even if admitted to be defective in not stating the time from which the imprisonment is to commence, does not affect the verdict, for the defendant will be returned to the circuit court for a re-sentence.

6. The motion in arrest of judgment was properly overruled. See 1 Wheeler's Cr. Cases, 195 ; 2 Binney, 332 ; 3 Johns., 299 ; Roscoe Cr. Ev., 462.

7. The prisoner pleaded not guilty, which was a waiver of the demurrer undisposed of ; and it disposed of the demurrer as effectually as if the court had sustained or overruled it.

8. The statute continues all cases undisposed of, without any order of the court.

THACHER, J. :

This is an indictment preferred by the grand jury of Lowndes county against A. Morris, charging him in four counts : 1st. With the forgery of a bank-note of the Bank of the State of North Carolina. 2d. With uttering and publishing as true a forged bank-note of the Bank of the State of North Carolina. 3d. With having in his possession certain forged bank-notes of the Bank of the State of North Carolina, with the intent to utter the same. 4th. Comprising allegations, similar to those of the third count.

The verdict of the jury was, that the prisoner was guilty upon the second, third and fourth counts, without an express finding upon the first count.

The objection to this verdict, that it is imperfect in not containing an express finding upon the first count, was examined in the case of Joel Swinney v. The State, *ante*, 576. And, in that case, we held that such a finding was sufficient to warrant a judgment, and that it should be considered as tantamount to an acquittal upon the first count.[1]

In regard to the evidence adduced upon the trial, it is observable that, while the fourth count charged the defendant with having in his possession, with the felonious intent to utter, a bank-note of the Bank of the State of North Carolina numbered "417," and, while a note of that description was presented in evidence to the jury, there was no proof adduced, that the note

[1] Bishop Cr. Law, 850 ; State v. Tweedy, 11 Iowa, 350 ; Brennan v. People, 15 Ill., 511, 517 ; Stoltz v. People, 4 Scam., 351 ; Brooks v. State, 3 Humph., 25 ; Weinzorpflin v. State, 7 Blackf., 186 ; Kirk v. Commonwealth, 9 Leigh, 627. *Contra* : State v. Sutton, 4 Gill, 494. See also, 1 Bishop Cr. Procedure, 837 ; 1 Stark. Cr. Pl., 346–350 ; United States v. Tweedy, 1 McLean, 429 ; Jones v. State, 13 Texas, 168 ; State v. Smith, 5 Day, 175 ; Wharton Am. Cr. Law, 431, and cases.

was found in the possession of the defendant, and yet the jury found a verdict of guilty on that count.

An objection, taken to the verdict and judgment, is urged, that the court permitted improper evidence to go to the jury, and in looking through the record, we find that the court permitted evidence to go to the jury, of a supposed attempt by the defendant, three years previously to the trial and the finding of the indictment, to utter some forged bank-notes of the Northern Bank of Kentucky. This was manifestly illegal evidence,[1] besides having a strong tendency to prejudice the minds of the jury against the defendant.

Upon the whole, we think the plaintiff in error entitled to a new trial, which must be confined to the second, third, and fourth counts, he having been acquitted upon the first count.[2] Campbell v. The State, 9 Yerg., 333; 1 Chitty C. L., 637.

Judgment reversed, and new trial awarded.

LEWIS *v.* THE STATE, 9 Smedes & Marshall, 115.

HOMICIDE.

Although the rule was formerly different, the court now possesses the power to excuse a juror, when he states voluntarily, without being asked, "that he had conscientious scruples against capital punishment." The rule is, that the court may set aside incompetent jurors, at any time before evidence is given.

Two considerations unite in the admission of dying declarations: The necessity of the case, and the situation of the declarant. The danger of impending death is an equivalent to the sanction of an oath. And the same rules apply, in these cases, to slaves as to white persons.

The presumption of law is in favor of the proper religious culture in slaves, and their belief in revelation and a future state of rewards and punishments; and unless the contrary is shown the declarant will be presumed to have had such belief.

It must be established as a previous fact, before dying declarations can be admitted, that the declarant was sensible of his approaching dissolution.

The fact that the deceased, after the wound was inflicted, cried, "Oh my people!" does not indicate the apprehension of approaching death.

It is the belief of the declarant that his wound is mortal, and of his future accountability, that renders the declarations admissible.

The conduct of a juror, in conversing, writing, and receiving notes from a third person not of the jury, during the progress of the argument of the prisoner's counsel, even when his affidavit is read in excuse, is very reprehensible, and improper.

[1] Wharton Am. Cr. Law, 1457; ib., 631-2-3-4-5; ib., 639, 647-8-9, 712, and cases cited.

[2] Wharton Am. Cr. Law, 550; State v. Morris, 1 Blackf., 37; Esmon v. State, 1 Swann, 14; State v. Kittle, 2 Tyler, 471; Wharton Am. Cr. Law, 3056-7-8, 3230.

Error to Warren circuit court. COALTER, J.

The plaintiff in error was indicted in the court below for the murder of David, a slave, and being tried was found guilty.

During the empanelling of the jury, William A. Haynes, one of the *venire*, summoned in the case, was called and sworn, and tendered by the court to the district attorney, who, being satisfied with the juror, turned him over to the prisoner, who accepted. The said Haynes, of his own motion, told the court he had conscientious scruples against capital punishment. The defendant insisted on accepting him as a juror in the case, but the court refused to have Haynes sworn, and dismissed him, and the defendant excepted.

On the trial, Lawrence Clarke, a witness for the state, and master of the deceased slave, David, testified that on the night of the 8th day of July, 1846, in the county of Warren, about ten o'clock, he was aroused from his sleep by a cry of distress, and hurrying about half a mile he found his slave, the deceased, injured badly; that the deceased said, "Oh my people," seemed like he wanted to see his people, but said nothing to indicate his apprehension of immediate death.

Daniel McGill, a witness for the state, testified that he was a practicing physician; that he was called to see the deceased slave on the night of the 8th of July, 1846, and saw him on the morning of the 9th. The slave was then dead. He examined the body, and found a ragged cut on the right jaw of the deceased; the bone was not hurt; several small shallow stabs and cuts were on his shoulders and back, and one stab, the fatal wound, was inflicted on the left side, between the eighth and ninth ribs, which reached the spine and divided the aorta. That such a wound must necessarily have caused death; it might produce it in a few minutes, and life might endure for an hour or two. Upon this preliminary proof, the district attorney offered to prove by Lawrence Clarke, what the deceased said about the injury he had received. The defendant objected to dying declarations being introduced on the showing made; the court overruled the objection, and permitted Clarke to go on and prove the declarations of the deceased; and the defendant excepted.

On the hearing of a motion for a new trial, the counsel read the affidavits of S. B. Wall, R. H. Smith, and R. H. Tompkins, which stated in substance, that pending the trial of the cause, and while the counsel for the defendant was addressing the jury, one of the jury, Henry Strong, was engaged for a very considerable length of time, first in a conversation, and then in a written correspondence with a person not of the jury, receiving from him and apparently reading several notes. The district attorney then offered to read the affidavit of Henry Strong, which was in substance, that the correspondence referred to in the affidavits filed by the defendant did take place between himself and Harper R. Hunt, while the counsel for the defendant was addressing the jury; but that correspondence did not relate to the case under trial, but was in relation to a matter of private business between himself and Hunt. The prisoner by his counsel objected to the reading of this affidavit, but the court overruled the objection and allowed it to be read.

The court overruled the motion for a new trial, and the prisoner excepted, filed his bill of exceptions, and brings the case to this court by writ of error.

CLAYTON, J.:

Several errors are alleged to have occurred upon the trial of this cause, to the prejudice of the prisoner.

The first related to the rejection of William A. Haynes as a juror. This person, after having stated that he had formed and expressed no opinion in the case, was tendered to the prisoner as a juror, when he voluntarily stated to the court that he had conscientious scruples about finding any man guilty of murder, and could not conscientiously take the oath. The court thereupon discharged him, without challenge, either upon the part of the state or of the accused. This is claimed to be error.

It is admitted by the counsel of the prisoner, that this would have been good cause of challenge on the part of the state if taken before the juror was tendered to the prisoner. Although the rule was formerly different, we think, at this day, there can be no doubt the court possessed the power which it exercised on this occasion. It was the duty of the court to see that an impartial jury was empanelled and that it was composed of men above all exception.　When the proposed juror stated his objections, it was right to respect them, and to procure another who was not restrained by such feelings from the discharge of his duty and the administration of the law.　Otherwise, an undue advantage would be afforded the prisoner.　In the People v. Damon, 13 Wend., 354, the rule is said to be, that the court may set aside incompetent jurors at any time before evidence is given.[1]　See Fletcher v. State, 6 Humphreys, 249.

The next objection is to the admission of the dying declarations of the deceased.　It may be well to observe in the first place, "that by statute, all the laws in force for the trial of a free white person for a capital offense, are declared to be in force for the trial of slaves for offenses declared capital by the laws of this state."　Several reasons are urged for the exclusion of this testimony.　The first is, that by the provisions of our statute, every slave who gives testimony in a court must first be charged before he is examined as to the consequences attached by law to his giving false testimony; that this is in addition to the oath; and as dying declarations are admitted, because the law presumes the situation of the party imposes as solemn an obligation to speak the truth as an oath, they stand only in place of the oath. Where another sanction is added, they cannot supply the place of that sanction.　This reasoning has failed to convince us.　Two considerations unite in the admission of such evidence.　First, the necessity of the case, and next, the situation of the declarant.　The danger of impending death is regarded as equivalent to the sanction of an oath.　The same necessity which justifies dispensing with the oath, will also justify dispensing with the charge directed to be given by the statute.

It is also objected, that there ought, in the case of slaves to be some evidence of a sense of religious accountability, upon which the validity of all testimony rests; and that the same presumption of such religious belief cannot be indulged in reference to them, as in regard to white persons.　As to the latter, it is said, the presumption is in favor of their proper religious culture, and belief in revelation and a future state of rewards and punishments; as to slaves, it is contended, the presumption does

---

[1] See Wharton Am. Cr. Law, 3020, and cases.

not arise, because of a defect of religious education. It is true, that if the declarant had no sense of future responsibility, his declarations would not be admissible. But the absence of such belief must be shown. The simple elementary truths of Christianity, the immortality of the soul, and a future accountability, are generally received and believed by this portion of our population. From the pulpit many, perhaps all, who attain maturity, hear these doctrines announced and enforced, and embrace them as articles of faith. We are not inclined to adopt the distinction.

It is lastly insisted that the preliminary showing of the declarant's knowledge of his situation, of his sense of impending death, was not sufficient to justify the admission of his declarations. The law is, that to authorize their introduction, it must be established as a previous fact, that the declarant was sensible that he was on the verge of dissolution.[1] This rule was stated explicitly in the case of McDaniel *v.* The State, 8 S. & M., 401.

In this case the preliminary proof was, that the deceased, when first discovered, after the wound was inflicted, exclaimed, "O my people;" but said nothing else, which indicated the apprehension of immediate death. This showing was not sufficient. It indicated alarm and suffering, but showed no sense of approaching dissolution. It is the belief of the declarant that his wound is mortal, and that his account with time is to be speedily closed, that renders the declaration admissible. It matters not how this belief is manifested, whether by words or conduct, or by an accurate perception of his true situation; yet its existence must be shown in some way. This kind of evidence forms an exception to the general rule: it is only admissible under peculiar circumstances; and, unless satisfied that they exist, it is our duty to exclude it. 1 Greenl. Ev., 192, *et seq.*

For this reason, a new trial will have to be granted. But if, on the next trial, stronger evidence on this point should be produced, such as to satisfy the circuit judge that the declarant was

[1] King v. Commonwealth, 1 Va. Cases, 78; Woodsides v. State, 2 How., 655; Campbell v. State, 11 Ga., 353; Nelson v. State, 9 Humph., 9; Hill v. Commonwealth, 2 Gratt., 594; Roscoe Cr. Ev., 30; 1 Phill. Ev., 289, 292; Peake's Ev., 15; 1 Greenl. Ev., 156, *et seq.*; Rex v. Van Butchell, 3 C. & P. 631; Rex v. Wilborne, 1 East. P. C., 358; 1 Leach, C. C., 503, n.

sensible of his true situation, and that his end was at hand, then the declarations will be admitted, otherwise not.

Another objection is taken, growing out of the misconduct of one of the jurors. He was engaged in conversing, and in writing and receiving and reading notes from a third person, not of the jury, during the progress of the argument of the prisoner's counsel to the jury. His affidavit was permitted to be read, to show that the correspondence and conversation were about a wholly different matter, and did not touch the subject of trial.

This conduct was highly reprehensible, and should have subjected the juror to punishment. Whether it would avail of itself to set aside the verdict, need not be determined. Yet the trial by jury should be preserved free from all extraneous and improper influences. Confidence in the administration of justice can only be preserved by removing even the shadow of suspicion from those in whose hands it is entrusted. See Hare v. The State, 4 How., 193.

The judgment is reversed and new trial granted.

BOLES *v.* THE STATE, 9 Smedes & Marshall, 284.

HOMICIDE.

Instructions couched in the language of the statute are proper, and should be given.

On a trial for murder it is material to instruct the jury what, under the law, constitutes murder.

The circuit judge is not bound to give instructions in the precise language as asked by counsel. He may modify them so as to make them conformable to his own views of the law.

Error to Warren circuit court. COALTER, J.

The plaintiff in error was indicted in the court below for the murder of one Donohoo.

On the 1st day of May, 1847, the prisoner was arraigned, and, on a plea of not guilty, was found guilty, and sentenced to be hung. He moved the court for a new trial: 1st, Because the court overruled a challenge for cause to a juror; 2d, The court erred in giving instructions to the jury; 3d. The verdict was against the law and evidence. The motion was overruled, and the defendant filed his bill of exceptions, and brings his case to this court by writ of error. The instructions given for the state, and those asked by defendant, which were refused, are contained in the opinion of the court.

CLAYTON, J. :

This was a conviction for murder in the circuit court of Warren county. The case comes to this court for various alleged errors. It will not be necessary to notice all of these.

On the trial, the court, at the request of the district attorney, gave the following charges to the jury :

1. " If they believe that, at the moment Boles killed the deceased, there was no reasonable ground to apprehend danger to his life, or great bodily harm, and no provocation sufficient to reduce the crime of killing, they must find the defendant guilty of murder."

2. " It is not necessary for the jury to believe that the defendant previously harbored the design to kill the deceased; if he killed him even upon a sudden passion, without provocation, such as the law recognizes as sufficient to palliate the crime of killing, and without reasonable ground to believe his life in imminent danger, or in imminent danger of great bodily harm, they must find the defendant guilty of murder."

The counsel for the prisoner then asked the court to charge the jury, " that unless the jury find from the evidence that Boles, with a premeditated design, or in some act dangerous to others, evincing a depraved mind, regardless of human life, killed Donohoo, they cannot find a verdict of guilty for murder."

The charges asked and given upon the part of the state were intended to show that the killing, in this instance, was not a case either of justifiable or excusable homicide. The charge asked, by the counsel of the prisoner, was intended to show what was necessary to constitute the crime of murder. It was couched in the language of the statute, and was improperly re-

fused.   On a trial for murder, it was certainly material to instruct the jury, what, under the law, constituted murder.   They
could then have applied the law to the facts.   If any explanation were necessary, it might have been made.

The circuit judge, in such case, is not bound to give or refuse
the instructions in the precise terms asked by counsel on either
side.   He may modify the charges asked on both sides, so as to
make them comportable to his own views of the law.   They
will thus be presented in a consistent form, and rendered more
intelligible to the jury.

For this error the cause will be reversed and a new trial
granted.

McCANN v. THE STATE, 9 Smedes & Marshall, 465.

HOMICIDE.

An officer of the court should always be placed over the jury, to prevent any one
from having any communication with them; and when they depart from the bar
they should be attended by a bailiff sworn for that purpose.   But it is not unusual
that officers are sworn at the commencement of the term for that purpose.

If the irregularity in a jury has a tendency to affect the rights of parties, their verdict must be set aside.   The evil to be guarded against is improper influence, and
when an exposure to undue influence is shown, and it is not shown that it failed of
effect, then the presumption is against the purity of the verdict.

Where the jury for a portion of the time during the trial, and after retirement,
were not under the care and charge of proper and sworn officers of the court, or
bailiffs sworn for that purpose, would be error beyond controversy.

Irregularity in the jury is not proper ground for a motion in arrest of judgment.

Error to Noxubee circuit court.   DAWSON, J.

The plaintiff in error was indicted in the circuit court of
Lowndes county for the murder of Andrew Toland.   A trial
was had in Lowndes county, and the jury being unable to agree
were discharged.

A change of venue was obtained to Noxubee county, where
the prisoner was again tried on June 26th, 1847, and found
guilty of murder.   The prisoner then entered a motion to set
aside the verdict, to arrest the judgment on the grounds that the
officer who had charge of the jury was not sworn specially to

take charge of them, but was merely acting under the direction of the sheriff. In support of his motion, the prisoner's counsel read the affidavit of the officer to that effect. The motion was overruled and the prisoner excepted. The prisoner then moved for a new trial, which being overruled, the prisoner excepted and brings his case to this court by writ of error.

Henry Gray and *G. W. L. Smith* for plaintiff in error.

J. D. Freeman, attorney general.

THACHER, J.

This is an indictment for murder preferred by the grand jury of Lowndes county. The trial took place in Noxubee county, by a change of venue under the statute, and resulted in a verdict of guilty. A motion in arrest of judgment was made, based upon the affidavit of an individual who had charge of the jury in the case for one half the time during the trial, and a large part of the night of their retirement to deliberate upon their verdict, by which it appears that he was not sworn as bailiff in the case, but acted merely by the direction of the sheriff. It appears that this individual was not a sworn officer of the court, nor sworn to discharge the particular duty which he undertook to perform, and that no officer had charge of the jury at the time he was so employed. No irregularity or miscarriage is charged upon the part of the jury, but the record is entirely silent as to their conduct. This motion in arrest of judgment was overruled in the circuit court.

According to the forms anciently established at trials, an officer of the court should always be placed at the box where the jury sit, to prevent any one from having communication with them; and when they depart from the bar, they should be attended by a bailiff sworn for that purpose. 2 Hale's P. C., 296; Buller's N. P., 308. The form of the oath administered to the bailiff who takes charge of the jury when they retire to consider of their verdict, is as follows: " You shall swear that you shall keep this jury without meat, drink, fire or candle; you shall suffer none to speak to them, neither shall you speak to them yourself, but only to ask them whether they are agreed." 2 Hale P. C., 296; Bac. Abr. Juries, G; 1 Chit. C. L., 632. In the case of Rex v. Stone, 6 T. R., 530, the form of oath permitted the bailiff to speak to the jury, but not "touching any matter relative to the trial."

In many courts, however, at the present day, it is not unusual that officers are sworn at the commencement of the term to take charge of all juries in civil cases, and probably there is no reason for greater caution in criminal cases. Commonwealth v. Jenkins et als. Thach., C. C., 131. And so in regard to the restrictions upon the jury as to meat, drink, etc., they will be found to have been much modified, provided such refreshments are taken in moderation and not at the expense of a party in the cause. 21 Vin. Abr., 448, Trial, (G. g.)

The trial by jury so justly prized, should be scrupulously preserved inviolate, as guaranteed by the constitution, and protected against encroachment in all its essential attributes, and every change or modification of form should be admitted only when found to be absolutely necessary to meet the changes of society and the times. Its very forms, being designed to protect it from innovation, are said, in 4 Black. Com. 320, to be sacred and not to be dispensed with. The rule that requires a jury, after being empanelled, to be kept free from every improper communication or intrusion, was established to render more certain the formation of an impartial and secret verdict. Accordingly, anciently, great strictness was used in relation to the conduct of jurors, and but little consideration indulged for their comfort or convenience. In more recent times, the conduct of jurors has been viewed in different lights, and construed with different degrees of strictness, both as regards the jurors themselves and its effect upon their verdict. 1 Cow., 221, note ; Commonwealth v. Roby, 12 Pick., 496. In the case of the Commonwealth v. Roby, Chief Justice Shaw, speaking of the effect of an irregularity of the jury or of other persons employed in the various departments and various duties connected with the trial, propounds the rule that, if the irregularity is of such nature that it does not, and in its tendency cannot, affect the rights of a prisoner or other party, whatever other consequence may follow upon such irregularity, it shall not avoid the verdict, because it has no tendency to affect that verdict injuriously to the party against

whom it is found. Thus, some modern authorities can be found
of instances where juries have separated without authority of
court, or jurors have separated from their fellows, or persons
have intruded upon juries in their retirement, in which the irregularity has been held not to impair the verdict. 1 Dev. &
Bat., 500; 1 Black., 25; 3 Cow., 355; 12 Pick., 496. But
these are mostly cases where evidence excluded the presumption
that there was either influence, partiality, or undue excitement
on the part of the jury—cases of a mere exposure to undue influences, but in which that exposure has been affirmatively
shown to have produced no consequences of any kind. The effect of such an exposure, however, of which no explanation is
given as to the extent of its influence, presents a subject of different consideration. Under such circumstances, the jealousy
with which the purity of verdict is watched, becomes immediately aroused; for the latest authorities hold that, if the irregularity has a tendency to affect the rights of the party, it is sufficient
to warrant its being set aside. Such a conclusion may be legitimately deduced from the opinion in the case of the Commonwealth v. Roby, 12 Pick. Nor is this a new doctrine, for
it was said by all the judges in Lord Delamere's case, 4 Harg.
St. T., 232, that "an officer is sworn to keep the jury, without
permitting them to separate, or any one to converse with them,
for no man knows what may happen; although the law requires
honest men should be returned upon juries, and without a
known objection they are presumed to be *probi et legales homi-
nes*, yet they are weak men, and, perhaps, may be wrought upon
by undue applications." The evil to be guarded against is improper influence, and when an exposure to such an influence is
shown, and it is not shown that it failed of effect, then the presumption is against the purity of the verdict.

In the case before us, the jury, for a portion of the time
during the trial and after their retirement, were not under the
care and charge of proper and sworn officers of the court, or
bailiffs sworn for that purpose. Such a deviation from the rules
is stated in the case of Jones v. The State, 2 Blackf. R., 479,
to be an error about which there can be no controversy, and that
such is the fact, is plainly deducible from the foregoing principles.

There were other points relied upon in the argument of this case, but the one upon which it has turned was chiefly pressed. There does not seem to have been any other error in the proceedings, and no good reason now exists for a minute examination of these points. It must be observed, in conclusion, that this is not technically a case for a motion in arrest of judgment.

The judgment must be reversed, and a new trial awarded.

KEITHLER *v.* THE STATE, 10 Smedes & Marshall, 192.

MURDER—ACCESSORY.

The duty of the district attorney is to prosecute offenders; but in his absence the state has a right to employ other counsel, and the duty performed by them will be valid.

The legislature has power by the constitution, to provide for the filling of all vacancies; and if the absence of the district attorney cause even a temporary vacancy it may be provided for by legislation.

No offense except perjury and subornation of perjury will disqualify or render a person incompetent to be sworn and testify as a witness in any cause; but such conviction may, in all cases, be given in evidence to impeach the credibility of the person so testifying. That he was an accomplice, does not render him incompetent as a witness against his principal.

The record of the conviction of the principal is evidence against the accessory. It is competent to prove the conviction of the principal and all its legal consequences; but not evidence of the fact of the guilt of the accessory.

The judge of the circuit court has a right to modify instructions asked by counsel, so as to make them conform to his own view of the law. And if a party object to such modifications, he must embody them in his bill of exceptions.

The charge or modification must be in writing, unless by consent of the parties to the contrary; and, in the absence of any objections on the record, such assent will be presumed.

The testimony of an accomplice should be received with great caution by the jury, but it is impossible to say that he should not be believed. The jury are to determine his credibility from his manner and other surrounding circumstances.

A voluntary confession of an accomplice is entitled to little weight; and if a different statement afterwards, under oath, when circumstances have changed his condition, it will be for the jury to say whether they will disbelieve him on account of such discrepancy.

When an accomplice, under sentence of death, without hope of pardon, it will be supposed that all motive to falsehood had ceased to exist.

It is the duty, but not an essential one, that the district attorney should sign the bill of indictment; but the absence of his signature does not affect the validity of the indictment.

If S. has already formed the murderous design, and K. encourage him to carry it out, by stating falsehood, or otherwise, K. is guilty as accessory.

Error to Hinds circuit court. COALTER, J.

The grand jury of Hinds county at the November term of the circuit court, 1846, found an indictment against Jack Fountain Silas, as principal, and Henry Keithler as accessory, of the murder of Benjamin G. Sims, on the 6th of July, 1846. The indictment was signed " J. E. Sharkey, district attorney, *pro tem.*, 3d judicial district."

A change of *venue* was obtained to Claiborne county, in the case of Silas, the principal, and Keithler was tried at the May term, 1847, of the circuit court of Hinds county. The state was represented by Fulton Anderson, district attorney of the district; the prisoner pleaded not guilty; a jury was empanelled and the case tried, and the prisoner, after a trial of two days, was found guilty and sentenced to be hung.

The other facts of the case will be found at length in the opinion of the court.[1]

SHARKEY, C. J. :

The several points made in the argument of this case, will be disposed of in the order adopted in the assignment of errors.

First. The indictment is said to be defective, because it is not signed by the district attorney for the district, but by an attorney who acted under the appointment of the court, the district attorney being absent. It is contended that as the district attorney is an officer elected under the constitution for the discharge of certain duties, his place cannot be supplied by temporary appointment in his absence, and that the law authorizing such appointment is unconstitutional. We do not think so. We are not prepared to say that the legislature may not provide that ministerial duties may be performed by a person appointed according to the law in the absence of the incumbent. The duty of the district attorney is to prosecute offenders against the criminal law. He acts as counsel for the state, and in his absence the state has a right to employ other counsel, and the duty so discharged is valid.[2] The constitution declares that a compe-

[1] [The evidence, confessions, etc., are set forth at length in the original report of this, in 10 S. & M. Reports, 192; but the present compiler feels justified in leaving it out altogether, as it is sufficiently stated in the opinion of the court.]

[2] Wharton Am. Cr. Law, 474; Reynolds v. State, 11 Tex. 120; Isham v. State, 1 Smeed, 112; 1 Archbold Cr. Pr. & Pl., 330; State v. Cox, 6 Iredell, 44; Eppes v. State, 10 Tex., 474.

tent number of district attorneys shall be elected, whose term of
office shall be prescribed by law.   This provision is very general,
leaving everything with the legislature, except the election.   It
is by law, then, that the district attorney is required to attend
the circuit courts and prosecute, and the same law may very
well provide for prosecuting, when he shall be absent.   The
legislature has power, by a provision in the constitution, to provide for filling of all vacancies not therein provided for.   Article
5, § 13.   If the absence of the district attorney causes even a
temporary vacancy, under this provision it may be provided for
by the legislature.

On this point the case of Byrd v. The State has been cited,
but it does not sustain the counsel.   It, in fact, decides the question the other way, by deciding that the district attorney may
withdraw and leave the prosecution to others.   On the position
taken, it would be impossible to prosecute a district attorney ;
he would be entirely exempted from offense.

Second, It is said the court erred in admitting Silas, the principal, who had been convicted and was under sentence, to testify.
The statute furnishes the answer to this objection.   It provides
that no conviction for any offense, excepting perjury and subornation of perjury, shall disqualify or render such person incompetent to be sworn and to testify in any cause, matter or proceeding, civil or criminal ; but such conviction may in all cases be
given in evidence to impeach the credibility of the person so
testifying.   H. & H. Dig., 725, § 18.   The language of this
statute is not to be understood literally, as a difficulty might
arise from it.   It says *conviction* shall not disqualify.   Mere
conviction never did disqualify ; it is the judgment that disqualifies ; though it is usually said by law writers that conviction
disqualifies, and hence the language of this statute. [1]   See 1
Phillips Evid., 30.   The legislature intended no doubt to remove
a legal disability, and the statute must be so construed.   That
he was an accomplice, constitutes no objection to his being a
witness. [2]   1 Phillips, 30.   As the statute removes the infamy,

[1] See Wharton Am. Cr. Law, 761, and notes. See also 4 Bishop Cr. Law, 363,
note 3.

[2] 1 Greenl. Ev., 379–383; Swift's Ev., 146; Wharton Am. Cr. Law, 145.

a principal may now testify against the accessory.[1] People v. Whipple, 9 Cow., 707; 1 Phil., 40.

Third, The next objection was made to the admissibility of the record of the conviction of Silas. That the record of the conviction of the principal is evidence against the accessory will surely not be doubted.[2] It was evidence to prove the conviction of Silas and all the legal consequences, though of course not evidence of the fact of the guilt of the prisoner. But this record is said to be defective in the caption and in the certificate of the clerk. After a very careful examination, we do not perceive any valid objection to it. It is sufficient in these particulars, both in form and substance. See third vol., Notes to Phillips Evid., 820, note 582.[3]

Fourth, It is also assigned for error, that the court erred in giving the instructions asked by the state, and in modifying those asked for the prisoner. The district attorney asked but one instruction, to wit : That it was immaterial whether Silas conceived the design to kill Sims before his interview with the prisoner or not. If Keithler encouraged him in that design, by falsely stating to him threats made by Sims, or by persuading him to kill Sims, Keithler is guilty. This charge was undoubtedly proper.

The counsel for the prisoner asked thirteen instructions, and the court gave all except two, the ninth and eleventh, and they were given with modifications. But how far they were modified, does not appear, and we cannot, of course, undertake to say, whether the modifications were correct or not. The charges, as they were asked, are set out in the bill of exceptions, but the modifications are not. That the court had a right to modify its instructions, has been decided at the present term.[4] For anything that appears, the modifications may have been favorable to the prisoner, and this is probably the case, as it appears by the bill of exceptions that the prisoner's counsel did not object, because they were given verbally. Some controversy arose after the jury had retired about the instructions, when the prisoner's

[1] George v. State, 39 Miss., 570; Josephine v. State, Ib., 613.

[2] Wharton Am. Cr. Law, 111; State v. Duncan, 6 Iredell, 236; Commonwealth v. Knapp, 10 Pick., 477.

[3] See case and authorities cited in note 2 *supra.*

[4] Boles v. State, 9 S. & M., 284. See also cases cited therein.

counsel asked the court to reduce its modifications to writing, which was done, and thereupon the counsel stated, that no objection would have been made to the instructions in that form, but the modifications were understood differently. A request was made that the jury might be called to hear the instructions as written down read to them, which the court refused, saying they were literally the same that had been verbally given. The counsel requested that the written modifications might be sent to the jury room, which was also refused. The argument predicated on this state of things is, that the court had no right to give its instructions verbally. The law of 1813 prohibited the circuit judges from charging the jury unless the counsel differed as to the law and should ask a charge on some point to be distinctly specified. H. & H. Dig., 493, § 53. A subsequent law provided, that the judges should not charge the jury unless the counsel differed and a charge should be asked on some point to be distinctly stated in writing, and it prohibits the judge from charging as to any other point. H. & H. Dig., 482, § 9. This law does not require the judge to put any modifications that he might choose to make in writing. It would be too rigid to say that any modification, however slight, shall be reduced to writing, or the judgment will be reversed. If a party should object to such modification, he should embody it in a bill of exceptions, so that it may be seen whether it was to his prejudice. The law of 1846 requires, that all charges and modifications of charges shall be in writing, and, at the request of either party, the jury may take them to their room. Even if this law should extend to criminal cases, but it is not so understood, there is a provision in it which covers this case. The charge or modification must be in writing, unless *by the consent of both parties.* The bill of exceptions shows this consent, or rather it shows that the prisoner did not object that the modification was made verbally. In the absence of any objection appearing on the record, assent would be presumed. We cannot presume that the court violated the law. This then was not a question raised on the trial. The court was not asked to reduce the modification to writing until after the jury had retired; that was too late. Objections should be made at a time when they can be obviated.

It was said in argument that the tenth instruction is to be considered as having been refused, because the word "refused" is written on the margin. The body of the bill of exceptions must control; and there it is said all the instructions were given, except two, the ninth and eleventh, which were modified.

This brings us to the only remaining point, which is it is necessary to consider, the refusal of the court to grant a new trial, which was moved for, because the verdict was contrary to the instructions and against the evidence. Undoubtedly this court may grant new trials when there is a great preponderance of evidence against the verdict. But there is no such preponderance here. On the contrary, the evidence sustains the verdict, if the main witness, Silas, is to be believed. It is therefore resolved into a question of credibility. It was insisted in argument that Silas was unworthy of belief, because of his having made contradictory statements in his several examinations and confessions, and therefore that a new trial should be granted. The question of credibility is one which belongs so exclusively to the jury, that it would be a delicate point for a court to touch it. True, the testimony of an accomplice should be weighed with great jealousy and distrust by a jury, but it is impossible to say, as a question of law, that he should not be believed. The jury are to determine that from his manner, his consistency, and other attending circumstances. They are to judge how far his testimony has been corroborated, or they may believe him if they choose without corroboration. We are disposed, however to give the prisoner every benefit which can result to him from a thorough sifting of the evidence, so far as we can do so consistently with our duty.

Silas was introduced as a witness, and in the course of his examination, his voluntary confession, made when he was taken before the court of inquiry, was introduced. His testimony before the committing court in the case of Keithler, was also introduced; and lastly, his confession made since his conviction. The object was to impeach his credibility from his own contradictory statements. As might be expected, there are discrepancies. In every instance, he implicated Keithler. His statements do not vary in charging him with being the instigator and cause of the offense.   His voluntary confession does contain statements which are afterwards contradicted.   He then stated that Sims had cut his finger with a knife.   This he afterwards contradicted.   He also said that he had shot Sims but once; this, too, is contradicted, both by his subsequent statements and by Anna Sims.   He also said that he offered to speak to Sims before he shot him, and this is contradicted, and perhaps he contradicts himself in other points.   When he was under examination as a witness on the final trial of Keithler, he stated that his mind was confused from long confinement, and he concludes his testimony by saying, that he had not stated the one-tenth or one-hundredth part of what passed between him and Keithler; that the murder of Sims was a continued subject of conversation.   A voluntary confession is entitled to but little weight, as it is but natural that one accused of crime should endeavor to palliate his guilt by excuses.   And if a different statement should be afterwards made under oath, when circumstances have changed the condition of the party, it will be with the jury to say whether they will disbelieve him on account of such discrepancies.   We cannot think that this would be an unerring indication of false swearing.

The published confession of Silas, made after his conviction, is more in detail than any person's statement.   It was evidently written by another, as he could not write.   Variations might naturally be expected under such circumstances, and yet in the main, it corresponds with his testimony.

In his testimony, given before the committing court, on the trial of Keithler, he says, that Keithler first mentioned the killing of Sims to him on the evening he (Silas) left Sims.   In his subsequent examination, he said it was on the next day.   He then also stated, that he received the cut on his finger from Sims, and with these exceptions, his testimony is not materially variant from his subsequent statements.   He is contradicted in one particular by Anna Sims, a daughter of the deceased, twelve years of age.   She says she was but forty or fifty yards off when Silas shot her father, and that he saw her.   He persists in saying she was not there.   It is possible he may not have seen her.

These contradictions doubtless had their due weight with the

jury. But it is proper to observe, that when he was called to testify against Keithler, he was under sentence of death, and as he says, without any hope of pardon. He testified, therefore, with the certainty of execution before him, when we must suppose all motive to tell a falsehood had ceased to have an influence.

Let us in the next place examine whether his statements, so often repeated in regard to the guilt of Keithler, are corroborated by the other witnesses; for although he may have weakened the strength of his testimony by his contradictions, yet if he is corroborated in the main fact, his testimony was still entitled to weight with the jury.

Philip Alston, a witness on the part of the state, went to the house of Sims immediately after the occurrence. Whilst he was there, Keithler was walking the gallery, and being called in, was asked by Mrs. Sims, if he had seen Silas. He replied, that he had seen him half an hour since riding toward Raymond with Bankstone. He was also asked by her, why he did not arrest him. He replied, that he knew nothing of the matter, until he came to the house. Let us contrast these statements of the prisoner with the testimony of another witness. Bankstone, a witness on the part of the state, heard the firing, and went over to Sims, and after having learned what was the matter, he went to the mill to arrest Silas. He then found Keithler, and told him what had occurred, and requested him to assist in arresting Silas. He replied that he would rather not, and wished Bankstone to get some other person. But upon being pressed to assist, he said he would tell Silas to give himself up, and accordingly started towards Silas on a trot, and met him at a point behind the shop, out of sight of the witness, who was some distance behind. What passed between them the witness did not know; but they met him, when Silas remarked, you have come for me. Keithler's answers to Mrs. Sims, in view of these facts, are certainly calculated to create suspicion. He knew all about the arrest of Silas, and yet he replied evasively, saying, that he had seen him half an hour since riding towards Raymond. He had been informed by Bankstone at the mill what had occurred, and yet he told her he knew nothing of it, until he came to the house. Why did he manifest so much reluctance in arresting

Silas? And that a private conversation passed between them behind the shop is clear, from the remark of Silas to Bankstone. Silas surrendered by the advice of Keithler.

These circumstances are inconsistent with the conduct of one who was acting without some secret motive, and desirous to detect the guilty. But he also stated to Bankstone, as a reason for his reluctance, that Sims had threatened Silas' life the day before. Now hear his statement made in presence of Sims. He was called in by Alston, and asked to state what threats he had ever heard. He replied, that the only threat he had ever heard Sims make was, that if he caught Silas prowling about his negro quarters at night, he must abide the consequences. This does not correspond to his statement to Bankstone. If he could state to Bankstone, that such a threat had been made, when it was untrue, does it not prove, that threats had been the subject of conversation between Keithler and Silas? and we shall see hereafter that such was the fact.

The testimony of Mount proves, that Keithler wished to give a false coloring to the affair. Mount, on Thursday evening, spoke of the murder, as being a cruel and unprovoked one. Keithler remarked that the affair was not so horrid. The witness was surprised at the reply, and asked Keithler, if he had heard any threats. He answered, that Sims had threatened, that if he ever caught Silas on the plantation, he would shoot him. The witness asked, if the threat was not, that if he ever caught Silas prowling about his negro quarters at night he would shoot him. He replied that such was not the threat. At this moment, Keithler was called into the presence of Sims by Alston, and asked what threats he had heard, when he gave an answer differing from his statement to Mount, but a few moments before. To Mount he wished to palliate the offense, but was forced to tell the truth in presence of Sims.

The testimony of A. Jones is also entitled to much weight, as he relates facts substantially as Silas has done. On the evening that Sims was killed, he went to the mill, and shortly afterwards Silas rode up; they had some conversation at the mill, in which Silas told him he expected to have some difficulty with Sims. Witness went up into the mill where Keithler was; Silas

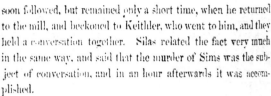

soon followed, but remained only a short time, when he returned to the mill, and beckoned to Keithler, who went to him, and they held a conversation together. Silas related the fact very much in the same way, and said that the murder of Sims was the subject of conversation, and in an hour afterwards it was accomplished.

The testimony of young Dewson, who lived at the mill, is also important. Keithler and Silas slept together in the same room with the witness, and were generally together, and held many private conversations. On one occasion, when Keithler and Silas were lying under a shed together, he heard Silas say, "It will be all right to-morrow," when Keithler answered, "You have promised that frequently, and it is not done yet." This occurred on Tuesday night. Silas mentions the circumstance, and says the answer had reference to the murder of Sims. This young man also heard Silas remark, late at night whilst in bed, "Somebody has promised me a horse and bridle to kill or beat Sims." This witness establishes beyond doubt a very close and confidential intimacy between Keithler and Silas. Such as to render it more than probable that Silas had communicated his design to Keithler, even if he had conceived the plan without Keithler's aid or advise. But when the other circumstances are considered, it is difficult to resist the conclusion that the prisoner was an adviser in the scheme.

We shall close our remarks on the testimony with that given by Amos R. Johnson. Silas sent for him to the jail, and wished him to appear for him before the court of inquiry. He stated, that Sims had threatened his life, and he could prove this by Keithler. Johnson went in search of Keithler, and after some time met him coming from towards the jail, where he had probably been to see Silas. In answer to Johnson's inquiries he stated, that he could prove the threats, but did not wish to testify before the committing court, for fear it might give offense to Mrs. Sims. He wished to wind up his business at the mill, and would testify before the circuit court, and his testimony would clear Silas. He was subpœnaed but did not attend. An attachment was taken out for him, and about the same time he was arrested on the charge and brought to town. Standing under a tree, he beckoned to Johnson, and said to him : " They had me up before Sims the other day and examined me, but that was not a court, and I was not bound to state the truth there." On the examination Keithler was introduced as a witness for Silas, but did not testify as he had told Johnson he would, when Silas, springing up from his seat, propounded this question, " Henry, did you not tell me at the mill, on Tuesday evening, that Sims had said that day, ' that he would kill me on sight, without giving me time to wink ?' " After some hesitation, the prisoner replied, " Why, Silas, you know that is not so." Silas, under excitement, repeated the question, and Keithler denied that he had so told him at the mill, but said that Sims had that day (Tuesday) used the expression, " I will kill Silas on sight, without giving him time to wink." Now, let it be borne in mind, that Sims was killed on Wednesday, or rather the wounds were then inflicted. Silas testified that Keithler had communicated threats on Tuesday. Keithler told Bankstone that Sims had threatened Silas' life the day before (Tuesday). Silas, in the manner above stated, asked him if he had not told him at the mill of Sims' threat. Keithler at first denied, but subsequently stated that Sims had made such a threat. Can any other conclusion be drawn from these circumstances, than that Keithler had made false representations to Silas, and that with a view to induce him to perpetrate the crime. There is something in the testimony of every witness that was examined, that tends to fortify the testimony of Silas, and when every circumstance is duly weighed, his testimony is corroborated as to the guilt of Keithler. We have entered into this investigation of the evidence, to show that Silas was not entirely unsupported in his statements. Whilst there were powerful reasons to question his credibility, the verdict was not given without corroborating evidence, and must stand.

Judgment affirmed.

After the delivery of the foregoing opinion, Messrs. *Davenport* and *Wharton* filed an elaborate petition and argument for a re-argument of the cause, which was refused, and the following opinion delivered by SHARKEY, C. J. :

The judgment of the circuit court in this case was affirmed on a former day of the term, and an application has been made for a re-argument which is based upon supposed errors in the decision. The points relied on for a re-argument have been discussed at some length, and the benefit of a re-argument has thus virtually been had.

The accused had been convicted of murder, and we were reluctantly compelled to affirm the judgment. The magnitude of the case had its due weight in the original investigation. Every point made in the record was very fully and deliberately considered by each member of the court. We should not, of course, have pronounced the judgment without being entirely satisfied of its correctness. No new questions are presented, and we have examined again the points pressed for a re-argument, and regret to say, that we find no reason for changing our opinion. On the contrary, we are strengthened in the conviction which induced us to affirm the judgment, and on that account do not regret that a petition for a re-argument was presented. The grounds relied on will be briefly noticed.

It is again insisted that the indictment was defective, because it was signed by a district attorney *pro tem.*, who had been appointed by the court. We held, the court had the power to make the appointment, and think so still. We did not then wish to take the ground that no signature to the indictment was necessary save that of the foreman of the grand jury, preferring to sustain the practice as it has existed in accordance with the statutes on that subject. But we now remark, that we know of no law in this state which requires the signature of the district attorney to an indictment. The common law certainly does not; and if there be no statute which does, then it is not required at all. An indictment derives its validity by the endorsement of the grand jury, "a true bill," over the signature of their foreman. Thacher's Crim. Cases, 284; Archbold's Crim. Plead., 58; 1 Chitty's Crim. Law, 316-324.

The case of The State v. Byrd is supposed to sustain a different doctrine. It was there remarked that it was the duty of the district attorney to sign the indictment; but it was not said to be an indispensable duty. The question was not involved, and the remark was only made in argument.   With great propriety the same remark might be made again.   It has been the invariable practice for district attorneys to sign indictments, and we still think it a correct one.

A case in 9 Yerger has been cited.   The decision seems to be predicated on a practice, which has grown out of their statute. No indictment is permitted to go to the grand jury, unless the district attorney, after a conference with the prosecutor, shall recommend it.   Statute Laws of Ten., 385.

The same objection was taken to an indictment in North Carolina, and the court decided the point directly, that it was not necessary that the prosecuting attorney should sign the indictment.   That the common law did not require it, and there was no statute which did.   If it was not necessary that this indictment should be signed, of course a useless signature did not vitiate it.   Carolina Law Repository, 493.

The second point is, that Silas was improperly permitted to testify, because the statute only renders competent one who has been convicted, but not one on whom judgment has been pronounced.   We adhere to our construction of this statute.   Judgment amounts to conviction, and conviction of felony and other crimes disables a man to be juror, witness, etc.   Tomlin's Law Dictionary, 414.   See also, Roscoe's Criminal Evidence, 123. We cannot doubt but that the legislature used the word "conviction" in its broadest sense, as one under judgment.

The third ground taken is, that the following charge was erroneous, to wit : " It makes no difference to the merits of this case, whether Silas conceived the design to kill Sims, before his interview with Keithler, or not.   If Keithler encouraged him in that design, by falsely stating to him threats of Sims, Keithler is guilty."   We are always to consider of charges in connection with the evidence before the jury.   We do not understand the language of this charge, as conveying the idea that it is supposed to embrace.   If Keithler was ignorant of Silas' design, then he could not be said to have encouraged him in that design. A knowledge of the design is therefore implied in the language used.   So, at least, we understand it.   The idea which the charge seems to us to convey is this : It is not material that

Keithler should have originated the design. If Silas had previously formed it, and Keithler encouraged him to carry it out, by stating falsehoods or otherwise, he is guilty. The court said to the jury, "if Keithler *encouraged him in that design.*" In what design? The design of killing Sims. This identifies Keithler with the design of course. If Keithler had merely stated falsehoods, without knowing of the design, he could in no sense be said to have *encouraged that design.*

Bradley *v.* The State, 10 Smedes & Marshall, 618.

Assault with Intent to Commit Man-slaughter.

An indictment that charges an "assault and battery with a deadly weapon upon a certain slave, 'with intent to commit manslaughter,'" can only be construed to charge an aggravated assault.

Evidence of a single witness, that the defendant was seen with a knife in his hand, in pursuit of a slave, when he was stopped by the witness, and that he made threats against the life of the slave, is insufficient to warrant a conviction for an assault with intent to kill.

Error to Monroe circuit court. Dawson, J.

The plaintiff in error was indicted in the court below, at the April term, 1847, for having "with a dirk knife, being a deadly weapon, cut, beat, bruised, maimed, and ill-treated, with intent, in and upon one Isham, a slave of William Cozant, wilfully and maliciously, and feloniously, to commit manslaughter."

The case was tried, and the prisoner found guilty; and the court sentenced him to jail for a period of two years.

One McWilliam, the only witness for the prosecution, testified that he saw the prisoner run after the negro, about ten steps behind him, with an open knife in his hand; witness called upon the slave to jump the fence; upon which the prisoner stopped the pursuit, stating that the slave might then escape, but he would catch him and have his blood; the prisoner waited until the witness came up to him. This was all the testimony.

The prisoner sued out a writ of error and brings his case to this court for reversal.

THACHER, J.

This is an indictment preferred by the grand jury of Monroe county against John Bradley. The indictment charges the accused with an assault and battery with a deadly weapon, upon a certain slave, " with intent to commit manslaughter."

This indictment can be construed only to be an indictment for an aggravated assault. It is not an indictment for an assault with an intent to kill, by which is understood and has been held, an intent to murder.

The evidence, that of a single witness only, shows, that the defendant below was seen with a knife in his hand in pursuit of the slave, when he was stopped by the witness, and that he then made threats against the life of the slave.

The evidence is entirely insufficient to warrant the conviction, and the judgment of the circuit court was erroneous.

The judgment must be reversed, and a new trial awarded in Monroe Circuit Court.

THE STATE *v.* WOFFORD, 10 Smedes & Marshall, 627.

FORFEITURE OF RECOGNIZANCE.

The judges of the courts of this state, by the constitution, by virtue of their offices, are conservators of the peace. And within the duties and powers of general conservators of the peace is included the power to commit all breakers of the peace, or to bind them in recognizance to keep it, or to answer for offenses committed against it.

Appeal from the Marshall circuit court. ADAMS, J.

In this case a recognizance was taken by the vice chancellor, conditioned that James Wofford should appear at the next term of the circuit court to answer a charge of stealing a slave. Wofford did not appear; judgment *nisi* was taken, and, on return of the *scire facias*, the recognizance was quashed, on motion of the sureties, on the ground that the vice-chancellor had no jurisdiction to take the recognizance, and the district attorney appealed.

J. D. Freeman, attorney general.

The law establishing the vice-chancery court, makes the vice-chancellor a conservator of the peace. As such, he is clearly authorized to take a recognizance in a criminal case, otherwise his authority to conserve the public peace would be inoperative.

THACHER, J.:

The single question presented in this case is, whether the vice-chancellor is authorized by law to take the recognizance of a person charged with a criminal offense. The act of the legislature, establishing an inferior court of chancery in the northern part of the state, (Acts of 1842, ch. 3, § 3,) constitutes the vice-chancellor a conservative of the peace. This is but a legislative iteration of the constitution, which provides that the judges of all the courts of the state shall, in virtue of their offices, be conservators of the peace. Const. art. 4, § 22. Within the duties and powers of general conservators of the peace, from the earliest periods, have been included the power to commit all breakers of the peace, or to bind them in recognizances to keep it, or to answer for offenses committed against it.

The judgment of the court below must be reversed, the motion directed to be overruled, and the cause remanded.

JONES *v.* THE STATE, 11 Smedes & Marshall, 315.

ASSAULT WITH INTENT TO KILL.

An indictment for assault with intent to kill, without alleging an assault upon a particular person with an intent to kill that person, is defective, and may be taken advantage of by motion in arrest of judgment.

Where a motion in arrest of judgment is overruled in the court below, and sustained in the appellate court, on the grounds of a defective indictment, the prisoner must be remanded for a new indictment.

Error to Jasper circuit court. DAWSON, J.

The plaintiff in error was indicted in the court below for an assault with intent to kill, in the following words of the indictment to wit: "That William Jones, late, etc., on the first day of May in the year of our Lord eighteen hundred and forty-five, in the county aforesaid, with force and arms, etc., with a certain gun, then and there loaded with powder and divers leaden shot, which he, the said William Jones, in both hands then and there had and held, at and against one Cornelius L. Mixon, then and there being, feloniously, wilfully, maliciously, and unlawfully, did shoot with intent, then and there, and thereby feloniously, wilfully, maliciously, and unlawfully, and of his malice aforethought, to kill and murder, contrary," etc. The prisoner pleaded not guilty; was tried and convicted. He made a motion in arrest of judgment, which was overruled; and he excepted and sued out a writ of error to this court.

THACHER, J.:

This is an indictment for an assault with an intent to kill, framed under the statute, (H. & H., 698, § 39,) which runs against any person shooting at another with intent to kill such other person.

The point made here is upon a motion in arrest of judgment for defects in the indictment overruled in the circuit court. The indictment alleges that the said William Jones, etc., "with a certain gun, then and there loaded with powder and divers leaden shot, which he, the said William Jones, in both his hands, then and there had and held, at and against one Cornelius L. Mixon, then and there being, feloniously, wilfully, maliciously and unlawfully, did shoot with intent, then and there, and thereby feloniously, wilfully maliciously, unlawfully and of his malice aforethought, to kill and murder, contrary to the form of the statute," etc.

The objection is, that the intent is not sufficiently averred in this, that the act is not alleged to have been done with the intention of killing the said Mixon or any other person.

The statute (H. & H., 698, § 33) quoted above, specifies the intent to kill the person shot at, as one of the intents made essential to constitute the offense. Such being, probably, the main intent in this case, the indictment should have charged that intent. [1] Rex. v. Gillow, Moody, 85; Rex v. Duffin, Russ. & Ry., 365.

[1] Wharton's Precedents, 242; State v. Patrick, 3 Wisc., 812; Wharton Am. Cr. Law, 1263, 1288; 6 Archbold Cr. Pr. and Pl., 69; 1 Bishop Cr. Proc., 277; State v. Marshall, 14 Ala., 411.

The indictment is uncertain. There is no allegation of an intent to kill any particular person. In Rex v. Holt, 7 Car. & Payne, 518, the indictment, framed under the statute 9 Geo. 4, c. 31, § 11, 12, was for shooting " at one John Hill, with intent to murder the said John Hill." The jury found the prisoner guilty of shooting at Mr. Hill, with intent to do Mr. Lee some grievous bodily harm. The court ordered a verdict of not guilty to be recorded. To come, therefore, within this statute, we think the accused must be charged with having shot at a certain person with intent to kill that person.[1]

The indictment is vicious, and the motion in arrest of judgment should have been sustained in the circuit court.[2]

The judgment of the circuit court is reversed, and judgment is arrested in this court upon this indictment, and the proceedings in the circuit court set aside. 1 Chit. Crim. L., 304, 443, 663 ; Barb. Cr. Trials, 331 ; H. &. H., 725, § 19.

But the accused cannot be set at liberty, but the same proceedings must be had again under a new indictment in the circuit court of Jasper county, to the jail of which county he must be remanded, if he make default in giving bail. H. & H., 669, § 27 ; ib., 725, § 19.

LOFTIN, et al., *v.* THE STATE, 11 Smedes & Marshall, 359.

DEFAULTING ROAD OVERSEER.

In criminal cases no appeal lies from the circuit court to the high court of errors and appeals. Such case can only be brought up by writ of error.

A writ of error cannot be entertained in the appellate court unless there has been a judgment in the court below.

Error to Lauderdale circuit court. DAWSON, J.

Asa Loftin was indicted at the September term, 1847, of the court, as an overseer of the road, for not keeping it in repair. He pleaded not guilty. At the March term, 1848, when the trial was had, after stating that the cause was submitted to the

[1] Vide note (¹) p. 419.
[2] See note (¹) p. 419.

jury, the record states, " that the jury retired to make up their verdict, and returned, in open court, in the presence of the prisoner, the following verdict: " We, the jury, find the defendant guilty, as charged in the bill of indictment;" and the defendant, by his attorney, prayed an appeal to the high court of errors and appeals; and the defendant, and John W. Coates, acknowledged themselves indebted to the State of Mississippi in the sum of two hundred dollars each, to be levied of their goods and chattels, lands and tenements, conditioned that the said Asa Loftin make his appearance in the county of Lauderdale at the court-house thereof, in the town of Marion, at a circuit court to be held on the first Monday in September, 1848; and from day to day, and from term to term, thence to abide the decision of the high court, and not depart from thence until properly discharged by due course of law.

There was no appeal-bond in the record; but a writ of error, purporting to be issued by Benjamin F. Parke, clerk, under the seal of the Lauderdale circuit court; but no fiat of a judge for its issuance.

THACHER, J.:

This is an indictment preferred by the circuit court of Lauderdale county, Hon. A. B. Dawson, presiding judge, against Asa Loftin, as a delinquent overseer of a public road, under the statute in such case made and provided.   H. & H., 458, § 62.

The defendant below pleaded not guilty, but the jury returned a verdict of " guilty," whereupon the said defendant prayed an appeal to the high court of errors and appeals, and tendered an appeal bond, conditioned for his appearance at the circuit court of Lauderdale county, on the first Monday in September, A.D. 1848, to abide the decision of the said high court of errors and appeals, and from thence not to depart until discharged by due course of law.   The said circuit judge allowed this appeal, and accepted the bond tendered thereon.

The above proceeding is entirely erroneous, and has been so held by an early decision of this court.   No appeal lies from the circuit to the high court of errors and appeals in criminal cases, and the same can only be reversed in this tribunal by virtue of writs of error. The State v. Twomey, 5 How., 50. The bond also taken by the circuit court is a nullity, not being warranted by law. Besides, the proceeding is erroneous in another respect. The circuit court neglected to pronounce judgment upon the verdict of the jury, and there being no judgment in the case, there is, consequently, nothing to appeal from, even if an appeal would lie. The writ of error in the record cannot be entertained in the present condition of the case, because no case of this kind can be allowed a writ of error until a final judgment in the circuit court, and only upon the fiat of a competent officer. H. & H., 538, § 40; 1 S. & M., 163; 2 ib., 27; 3 ib., 588.

This cause, therefore, must be dismissed from this court, and remanded to the circuit court of Lauderdale county, with instructions to the judge of that court to pronounce the sentence and judgment of the law upon the verdict of the jury; when the defendant can make his application for a writ of error to the proper quarter, if he so elect. 5 H., 291.

WILLIAMS *v.* THE STATE, 12 Smedes & Marshall, 58.

BETTING ON ELECTIONS.

It is not necessary that a person to be guilty as principal, should perpetrate an offense with his own hands. If it be committed through the medium of an innocent agent, the employer though absent when the act is done, is answerable as principal; and if the agent be aware of the consequences of the act and answerable for it, he becomes a principal in the first degree, and the principal accessory before the fact.

In all offenses below the degree of felony, there can be no accessories either before or after the fact. Those, who in felonies would be accessories before the fact, are, in offenses below that degree, principals, and must be proceeded against as such. This rule holds in regard to the highest and lowest of such offenses.

Where a bet is made on the result of a presidential election, it is competent to establish the result of the election by parol testimony.

In legal acceptation, United States treasury notes are not money; and if the indictment charge the bet to have been made with them as valuable things, their value must be proved to warrant a conviction.

Error to Hinds circuit court. COALTER, J.

At the June term, 1845, of the circuit court of Hinds county, the grand jury indicted Sidney S. Erwin and Daniel O. Williams, for betting two hundred dollars on the result of the presidential election, which took place on the first Wednesday in December, 1844. The case was dismissed as to Erwin, and in November, 1846, a trial was had on the plea of not guilty by Williams. It was proved by Samuel H. Charles, that some weeks previous to the presidential election of 1844, he had been requested by Williams to effect a bet for him with Erwin on the result of that election, saying to him, at the time, that he presumed that Erwin, in the event of Mr. Clay being elected president, would be pleased to attend his inauguration; and he (Williams), if Mr. Polk should be elected, would be gratified at being present at Mr. Polk's inauguration; and proposed that if Mr. Clay were elected, he (Williams) should pay Erwin's expenses to Washington; and if Mr. Polk were elected, Erwin should pay Williams' expenses there.

The witness received from Williams, for the purpose of the bet, four United States treasury notes, each of the denomination of fifty dollars, which, after arranging the bet with Erwin, were put up with two hundred dollars of Erwin's in the hands of a third person; that the presidential election occurred as stated in the indictment, and resulted there as stated; after the result had been ascertained, Williams received back his stake with the two hundred dollars of Erwin's. This was all the testimony.

Williams excepted to the parol proof of the result of the election. The court, on the part of the state, gave the following instructions, to wit:

1. That if they believed from the evidence that Williams, in making the bet, offered four fifty dollar treasury notes, as two hundred dollars, and Erwin, with whom he was making the bet, made no objections to treasury notes as money, but received them as money, that would be sufficient to satisfy the charge of betting two hundred dollars.

2. If the parties intended to bet money, and the four treasury notes, deposited by Williams, were intended to represent that amount of money, and were accepted by him as money, and Erwin bet money against them, the allegation is sustained, even if the treasury notes had no intrinsic value.

The following instructions were asked for by the defendant and refused:

4. If the jury believe from the evidence that the defendant did not make this bet himself, but procured to make it for him, they must acquit him, under the indictment.

5. The charge in the indictment being that money was bet, if the jury believe that the proof only shows that United States treasury warrants were bet, they cannot find against the defendant.

The defendant was found guilty, and he brings his case to this court by writ of error.

THACHER, J.:

This is an indictment framed under the act of February, 1839, entitled, "An act farther to discourage and suppress gaming." Hutch. Code, 951, Art. 11.

The indictment charges that Daniel O. Williams did wager and bet with, and against one Sidney S. Erwin, the sum of two hundred dollars, upon the result of an election of a president of the United States of America, had and held on the first Wednesday in the month of December, A. D. 1844.

The evidence of Samuel H. Charles, established that some weeks previous to said election, he was requested by Williams to effect a bet for him with said Erwin, on the result of said election; that he afterwards received from said Williams four United States treasury notes, each of the denomination of fifty dollars, which, after arranging the terms of the bet with said Erwin, together with two hundred dollars supplied by said Erwin, were placed in the hands of a third person; that the said presidential election did occur, as charged in the indictment, the result was made known, and that Williams did receive back his said treasury notes, together with the said two hundred dollars supplied by said Erwin.

The act under which this indictment was framed, runs against any person who "shall wager or bet, or promote or encourage the wagering, or betting of any money, or other valuable thing, upon any cock-fight, or duel, or upon the result of any election of any kind whatever."

The conviction in this case is claimed to be illegal and erroneous for various reasons.

In the first place, it is contended that the evidence establishes that Williams did not himself make the bet, but procured it to be done for him by another, which should relieve him from this indictment. It is not necessary that a person to be guilty as principal, should perpetrate an offense with his own hands, for, if it be committed through the medium of an innocent agent, the employer, though absent when the act is done, is answerable as a principal; and if the agent be aware of the consequences of the act, and answerable for it, he becomes a principal in the first degree, and the employer an accessory before the fact. Such is the law in the commission of felonies; but, as in all offenses below the degree of felony, there can be no accessories, either before or after the fact; those, therefore, who, in felonies, would be accessories before the fact, are, in respect to offenses below that degree, principals, and must be proceeded against as such. This rule holds in regard to the highest and lowest of such offenses. 4 Black. Com., 36; 1 Hale, 616.

It is also insisted, that it is not competent to establish the result of the said presidential election by parol evidence. This point is not, we think, well taken, for various reasons, and among others, because such a matter of great public interest is universally known throughout the land, and can, therefore, be proved or disproved with absolute certainty by parol proof.

It is likewise relied upon, however, that, while the indictment charges a bet of money to the amount of two hundred dollars, the evidence shows the bet upon the part of Williams to have been four United States treasury notes, each of the denomination of fifty dollars, and it is insisted, that in this particular the *probatum* does not correspond with the *allegatum*. This point we deem to be well taken. In legal acceptation, such notes are not money, and even if the indictment had charged the bet to have been made with them, as valuable things, their value must have been proved, to have warranted a conviction. 1 Nott & McCord, 9; 12 Wend., 547; 2 Leach, 1036, 1090; 2 Car. Law Rep., 269.

As upon this latter principle the instructions of the circuit court to the jury held a different doctrine, we accordingly reverse the judgment, and direct a new trial to be had in the case.

Judgment reversed, and a new trial awarded.

BARNEY et al. v. THE STATE, 12 Smedes & Marshall, 69.

GAMING.

An accused has the right to challenge, by plea in abatement, the competency of the grand jury by whom the indictment against him is preferred.

Indictments, not found by at least twelve good and lawful men, are void at common law, and if any one of the grand jury, who find an indictment, be within any one of the exceptions in the statute, he vitiates the whole, though ever so many no exceptionable persons joined him in finding it.

The statute of this state (H. & H., 490, § 44) requires, among other qualifications of jurors, that they should be either freeholders or householders.

Error to Amite circuit court. POSEY. J.

At the March term, 1847, separate indictments were preferred by the grand jury of Amite county against George H. Barney, Jacob Halfin, Augustus W. Forsyth, William R. Carter, Edmund Drayfus, and David Jewett, for playing for money at a game of cards, commonly called "poker." At the preceding term of the court, each of them pleaded in abatement to the respective indictments found against them, for the want of legal qualifications in one of the grand jurors, Alexander Dixon, by whom the indictments were found.

The grand jury presented the indictments on the third day after their empanelment. The district attorney demurred to the plea, and the demurrer was sustained. The prisoners then, respectively, plead not guilty; were tried and found guilty, and sentenced; and each sued out a writ of error to this court; and the cases were all submitted together.

THACHER, J. :

This is an indictment under the act of February 9, 1839, entitled "An act further to discourage and suppress gaming." Hutch., c. 951, art. 11.

To this indictment preferred by the grand jury of Amite county, the accused pleaded in abatement, "That one Alexander Dixon was then and there a member of the said grand jury, and that said Alexander Dixon was not then and there at the finding of said indictment by the said grand jury, either a freeholder or a householder within the said county of Amite," etc. To this plea the district attorney filed a demurrer, and assigned for cause, that the plea did not allege, that the said juror, Alexander Dixon, was at the time of empanelling the said grand jury, neither a householder nor a freeholder; and that the accused, by not challenging the said juror, Alexander Dixon, at the time of the empanelling of said grand jury, waived all right to question, after that time, the qualifications of said juror. This demurrer was sustained in the circuit court, and upon judgment of *respondeat ouster*, the accused pleaded not guilty, and upon a trial, conviction and sentence ensued.

In the case of Dowling v. The State, 5 S. & M., 664, we stated, that it had been held in Massachusetts, "that objections to the personal qualifications of grand jurors, or to the legality of the returns, cannot affect any indictments found by them, after they have been received and filed by the court; but that such objections, if any exist, must be made before the indictments are found, and may be received from any person, who is under a presentment for any crime whatsoever; or from any person present, who may make the suggestion as *amicus curiæ*." The English forms and practice of stating in the caption of every indictment, that it was found by twelve good and lawful men, is not there preserved, but the language is simply, "The jurors for the commonwealth, upon their oath, present," etc., and hence if any irregularity should happen, it might be made a subject of inquiry upon a suggestion to the court, for in that state the grand jury is constituted under its superintendence, and must be understood to have the legal number of qualified men. The rule in Massachusetts was not, however, adopted by us in the case of Dowling v. The State, nor can it be under our forms and practice, which follow, in this particular, the English modes. On the contrary, in McQuillen v. The State, 8 S. & M., 587, where the question was directly made, we decided, that an accused has the right to challenge, by plea in abatement, the competency of the grand jury, by whom he is indicted. This privilege arises not alone from the legal principle, that indictments not found by twelve good and lawful men at the least, are void and erroneous at common law, and, therefore, some mode must be left open for ascertaining the fact, but is well sustained as a method of insuring to accused persons a fair and impartial trial. Such persons are not present, when the grand jurors are empanelled, perhaps have not been made subjects of complaint or even suspicion. It certainly would not be right to estop a party from pleading a matter, to which he could not otherwise except.

The interest of an accused under indictment, with the grand jury, commences at the time of the finding of the indictment. This is the point of time when, as to him, the legal number of qualified men must exist upon the grand inquest. Indictments not found by at least twelve good and lawful men, are void at common law. Cro. Eliz., 654; 2 Burr, 1088; 2 Hawk. P. C. 307. It is said by Hawkins, P. C. B. 2, ch. 25, § 28, that, if any one of the grand jury, who find an indictment, be within any one of the exceptions in the statute, he vitiates the whole, though ever so many unexceptionable persons joined with him in finding it. Chitty, in his Cr. Law, vol. 1, p. 307, lays down the same doctrine, if it be discovered after the finding. The statutes of this state require, among other qualifications of jurors, that they should be either freeholders or householders. H. & H., 490, § 44. Hence, we think the demurrer of the district attorney in this case should not have been sustained.

The judgment must be reversed, and the demurrer directed to be overruled in this court, and we remand the case for further proceedings.

BUTLER *v.* THE STATE, 12 Smedes and Marshall, 470.

FORFEITURE OF RECOGNIZANCE.

All recognizances entered into by persons charged with a criminal offense, must be made returnable to the term of the circuit court next to occur by law after the time that the said recognizances are taken.

A recognizance, taken, conditioned for the appearance of the accused at a time when no court is held, is void.

The recognizance being void, all the steps based upon it are also void, and it is competent for the court to vacate it at any time.

Error to Warren circuit court. COALTER, J.

On the 6th of March, 1846, Miles C. Folkes, mayor of the city of Vicksburg, recognized William Mayhew, Joseph Butler,

J. J. Rawls, Robert Wilson, Frederick Rogers, Henderson Markham, and W. J. Fotheringham; Mayhew in the sum of fifteen hundred dollars, and each of the others in the sum of two hundred and fifty dollars; the condition of which was, that the said William Mayhew should be and personally appear before the circuit court of Warren county, to be held at the court house thereof, on the third Monday of April, 1846, to answer the State of Mississippi, on a charge of exhibiting a faro bank, being interested in the loss or gain thereof, in the city of Vicksburg, on or about the 15th day of January, 1846; and that he should not depart therefrom without the leave of the court, but should continue to attend said court from day to day and from term to term, until legally discharged.

On the 16th of June, 1846, this recognizance was forfeited, and judgment *nisi* entered, because of the non-appearance of the parties on that day.

On the 3rd of August, 1846, a *scire facias* issued, reciting the recognizance, the judgment *nisi*, and the order for *scire facias*.

On the 17th of April, 1848, a motion was entered to quash the recognizance, because, 1st. It was returnable to a term of the court unknown to the law; and 2d. The defendant had no notice that a forfeiture would be taken at a term subsequent to the one named in the recognizance. The court overruled the motion, and the defendants excepted. Butler alone sued out this writ of error.

W. C. Smedes, for plaintiff in error.

J. D. Freeman, attorney general.

THACHER, J.:

On the 6th day of March, 1846, the mayor of Vicksburg took a recognizance from Mayhew, Butler and others, conditioned that Mayhew should appear before the circuit court of Warren county, to be held on the third Monday of April, 1846, to answer the state on a charge, etc. On the 16th day of June, 1846, this recognizance was forfeited in the circuit court, and judgment *nisi* entered thereon, and *scire facias* issued on the 3rd day of August, 1846; and upon which execution issued on the 7th day of November, 1846, Butler having made no answer.

On the 17th of April, 1848, a motion to quash the recognizance was overruled.

All recognizances taken from persons charged with a criminal offense, must, by our statutes, be made returnable to the term of the circuit court next to occur by law, after the time that the said recognizances are taken. So, at common law, recognizances in cases of felony were to be certified to the general goal delivery. Hawk. P. C., ch. 15., § 85, note.

This recognizance was taken, conditioned for the appearance of the accused at a time when no court sat by law. The change of the time of holding the terms of the circuit court of Warren county, to the second Monday in April. 1846, did not take effect until the 1st day of July, 1846. Laws of 1846, ch. 26, § 5, p. 187. The recognizance was therefore void.[1] The Commonwealth v. Bolton: 1 Serg. & Raw., 328; The State v. Sullivant, 3 Yerg., 284. Besides, this recognizance appears to have been made for the appearance of the accused on the third Monday of April, 1846. This is an additional defect.

The recognizance having been void, all the steps based upon it were void also, and it was likewise competent for the court to vacate the recognizance at any time.

The judgment of the circuit court is reversed, and the recognizance is here declared void, together with all the proceedings thereon.

SAM (a slave) v. THE STATE. 13 Smedes & Marshall, 189.

HOMICIDE.

It must appear from the record that the court is held at the proper place within the county; and it is error for the court to sit at any other place; and a plea in abatement alleging these facts, when sustained, is sufficient to quash the indictment.

CASE AT BAR. The caption of the indictment stated that the court was held at Tallula, the prisoner plead that Tallula was not at that time the county seat; to which the state demurred: held, that the demurrer admitted that the court was not holden at the place designated by law, and that the indictment should, therefore, be quashed.

The belief of a juror that he can do justice can have but little influence in determining his competency. The presumption of law is against his competency, when a decided opinion as to the guilt or innocence of the prisoner has been formed.

[1] 1 Archbold Cr. Pr. & Pl., 190, notes; People v. Mack, 1 Parker, 567; State Treasurer v. Danforth, Brayt., 140.

Error to Warren circuit court.   COALTER, J.

The plaintiff in error was indicted on the first Monday in April, 1848, at the court-house, in Tallula, in the circuit court of Issaquena county, for the murder of Absalom H. Barrow. At the October term next, the *venue* was changed to Warren county.   At the April term, 1849, of the Warren circuit court, a special *venire* for fifty jurors was ordered, returnable on Tuesday, the 8th day of the term ; on that day Charles L. Buck, Esq., for and on behalf of the state appeared, and on motion and by consent the plea of not guilty was withdrawn, and the defendant filed two pleas in abatement, the substance of which is stated in the opinion of the court, to which the district attorney demurred, and the demurrer was sustained.   The prisoner was then arraigned and plead not guilty.   At the next term of the court the prisoner was tried and found guilty, and sentenced to be hung.

The following are the bills of exceptions taken by prisoner, and noticed by this court, viz :

3d. To the action of the court overruling the challenge for cause to Thomas Rigby, tendered as a juror, who stated, " that he had not heard the witness, but had heard the cause talked of ; had formed and expressed his opinion ; his mind was made up from rumor ; thinks he could decide the case from the testimony, free from the bias on his mind, but thinks it would require some testimony to remove the impression."

5th. To the action of the court overruling the challenge for cause to Baptiste McCombs, one of the jurors tendered to the prisoner who stated, " that he had heard the argument of counsel, in the case of Jack, who was tried on the day before as an accomplice of the prisoner ; heard their statements of the testimony, the witnesses being the same in each case ; did not hear the witnesses themselves ; has formed and expressed an opinion ; it would require testimony to remove it, but thought he could give an impartial verdict on the testimony."

CLAYTON, J. :

The first question to be noticed in this case arises on the two pleas in abatement of the defendant.   The first is, that at the term of the court at which the bill of indictment was found, the court was not held in the court-house of Issaquena county. The second is, that Tallula, the place at which said court was holden, was not at that time the county seat of the said county. To each of these pleas a demurrer was filed.

The act of 1846 establishes Tallula as the seat of justice of Issaquena county. An act passed in January, 1848, authorizes the board of police of that county "to remove the then location of the county seat of said county" to some other place which they might select. Pamp. Acts, 220. The indictment in this case was found in April, 1848. Whether the board of police had in fact changed the location of the county seat before that time, is not shown by any testimony in the record. But the demurrer admits the fact that the court was not holden at the proper place within the county. The same is taken to be the established law in Kelly et al. v. The State, 3 S. & M. 524. The caption of the indictment in this case states, that the court was holden at Tallula. If it were not for the act of 1848, this state of facts would have existed, the caption of the indictment would have shown that the court was holden at the place appointed by law, and the demurrer to the plea would have admitted the reverse. But this difficulty is obviated by the statute of 1848. It was error in the court to sit at any other place than the one designated by law; and as it stands admitted upon the record that it did so, the judgment upon the second plea in abatement should have been, that the indictment be quashed. Had issue been taken on the plea, the question would then have rested upon the fact.

Another error assigned is the admission of two jurors upon the trial, who are alleged to have been incompetent by reason of partiality. Although the case must be reversed on another point, yet, as this was elaborately discussed in the argument, we have thought it but proper to give our opinion upon it.

The objection to each of the jurors is very much the same. The one had formed his opinion from the rumors he had heard; the other from the arguments of counsel to which he had listened on the previous day, upon the trial of an accomplice of the prisoner for the same offense, and in which the witnesses were the same. Each stated he had formed and expressed an opinion ; one said his mind was clearly made up from rumor ; each thought he could decide the case from testimony, free from bias, but both thought it would require some testimony to remove the impression from their minds.

The great value of the trial by jury consists in its fairness and impartiality. A right of trial by such a jury is secured to every one who may be accused, by the constitution. It is the duty of the court to see, that an impartial jury is empanelled, and that it is composed of men above all exceptions. Lewis v. The State, 9 S. & M., 119. In a civil case this court reversed a judgment, because one of the jury had expressed a strong opinion before the trial, but had denied it when questioned. The court remarked, "that the sanctity of the trial by jury requires, that the jury should be impartial and unbiassed." Childress v. Ford, 10 S. & M., 30. The same reason applies with much greater force in a capital case.

This rule appears to be simple, yet it is often found to be difficult in its application. A man is impartial whose mind is not inclined either to the one side or to the other. He is partial when it has taken a direction either in favor of or against a prisoner. That direction may be so slight as to constitute no impediment to the arriving at a just conclusion. It may be so strong as not to let the judgment have fair scope, and to close the avenue to the admission of a conviction opposed to the preconceived opinion. In the one case the juror would be competent, in the other not. It is the nature and character of the opinion on which his competency must depend ; not the source from which the opinion has been formed, nor its having been expressed or concealed. The belief of the juror that he can do justice can have but little influence in determining his competency. The presumption of law is against his competency, when a decided opinion as to the guilt or innocence of the prisoner has been formed.

The supreme court of Tennessee thus laid down the rule: " If it appear to the judge who, under our system, is the trier of the competency of the juror, that he has heard the circumstances of the case, and believing the statements he has heard to be true, has formed, or has formed and expressed an opinion, that is, has made up his mind as to the guilt or innocence of the prisoner, he ought to be rejected." McGowan v. The State, 9 Yerg., 193: Payne v. The State, 3 Humph., 376. The court manifestly felt the difficulty of laying down any rule which would be free from ambiguity, but adopted this as the best definition of the principles on which the question of impartiality must turn.

We cannot but be sensible of the same difficulty. If a juror were offered who had already heard all the testimony and made up his mind from it beyond all doubt, he would be incompetent. On the other hand, if one were offered who had formed only an hypothetical opinion from rumor, and who at the same time declared that he could render an impartial verdict, it would be equally clear that he was competent. Between these two extremes there is a wide space, in which it is perhaps impracticable to lay down any very definite general rule. The juror ought to be equal between the parties; if he be not, the verdict is liable to some degree of suspicion, and the purity of the administration of justice be thus called into question. Every case, however, must depend in some degree upon its own peculiar facts. Circumstances may exist which would render a departure from a rule necessary and unavoidable, which, in a different state of case, would be inflexibly adhered to. In some cases of very great notoriety and of general concern, it might be impossible to find men in the vicinage who had not formed some opinion of the matter. The recent Astor Place riots and murders in New York, referred to in argument, are of this character. In such cases, some modification of the doctrine may be imperatively required. The rule must yield to the necessity, but only so far as the necessity demands. 1 Burr's Trial, 419. Yet the more nearly we approach the point of entire freedom from preconceived opinion, and of complete equality between the parties, the more nearly we approach the perfection of the system of trial by jury.

In this case, there was no necessity for any exception to the general rule, which requires the juror to be indifferent. We do not think these jurors came up to that standard. They both stated it would require testimony to remove the opinions they had formed. They did not, therefore, stand equal between the parties, for if they did, they would require testimony to convict, whereas, if their opinion were adverse to the prisoner, they would, now require testimony to acquit. This reverses the benign rule of law, which presumes innocence until guilt be proven.

We shall not attempt to lay down a rule of universal application upon a subject so hard to place within precise limits.

In consequence of the error in the decision upon the demurrers to the pleas in abatement, the judgment will be reversed, the indictment quashed, and the prisoner remanded to the county of Issaquena for farther proceedings according to law.

CICELY (a slave) v. THE STATE, 13 Smedes & Marshall, 202.

HOMICIDE.

It is well settled that it is competent for the circuit judge, in criminal prosecutions, as well as in civil cases, to modify the instructions requested on either side, so as to make them conform to his own views of the law.

The legal test of the sufficiency of evidence to authorize a conviction, is its sufficiency to satisfy the understanding and conscience of the jury; and a juror ought not to convict unless the evidence excludes from his mind all reasonable doubt of the guilt of the accused.

As an abstract proposition, the force of circumstantial evidence to warrant a conviction, ought in no case to be inferior to that which is derived from the testimony of a single witness, the lowest degree of direct evidence. And the direct testimony of a single witness ought not to authorize a conviction, unless it were in itself sufficient to exclude from the mind of the jury every reasonable doubt of the guilt of the accused.

Error to Jasper circuit court. HARRIS, J.

In October, 1848, the grand jury indicted Cicely, a slave of Andrew McAlpin and Thompson Wells, administrators of Achilles Wells, for the murder of Anne Longon.

The prisoner was arraigned, and upon the plea of not guilty, was convicted and sentenced to be hung. The prisoner made a motion for a new trial, which was overruled, and she sued out a writ of error and brings the case to this court.

The substance of the evidence adduced upon the trial, the instructions of the court, and all the main facts of the case, will be found in the opinion of the court.

Heyferon, Street and *Evans,* for plaintiff in error,

Cited 1 Starkie Ev., 510 ; ib., 478, 502, 515.   They reviewed the facts of the case *in extenso,* insisting that they did not sustain the verdict ; they were not sufficient to establish beyond a reasonable doubt.

D. C. Glenn, attorney general,

Insisted that the proof disclosed a case of guilt of unexampled atrocity.

On the refusal to give the instructions asked by the prisoner, he cited and commented on 2 Phill. on Ev., (Cow. & Hill's Notes), 393, n. 323, 325 ; 2 Wheeler's Cr. Cases, 451 ; 1 Wash. C. C. Rep., 372 ; 1 Wheeler's Cr. Cases, 131 ; 3 Starkie Ev., 504, 505.

SMITH, J. :

This was an indictment for murder, tried in the circuit court of Jasper, upon which the prisoner, a slave, was convicted.

The only questions which require the consideration of this court arise upon the instructions which were requested by the counsel of the prisoner, and the decision of the court below on the motion for a new trial.

1. The first instruction is as follows, to wit : " If the jury, after weighing the evidence, have a reasonable doubt that the prisoner (the negro girl Cicely) is guilty of killing Mrs. Longon, they are bound by law to find her not guilty."   This instruction was given with the following explanation or modification, to wit : " To warrant the jury in finding the prisoner guilty, there should be evidence before them sufficient to satisfy their minds of her guilt beyond a reasonable doubt.   That which amounts to mere possibility only, or to conjecture or supposition, is not what is meant by a reasonable doubt.   The doubt, which should properly induce a jury to withhold a verdict of guilty, should be such a doubt as would reasonably arise from the evidence before them ; and if such a reasonable doubt should arise from the evidence, the prisoner should have the benefit of that doubt."

The objection urged is, that the judge refused to give the instruction without the explanation, or, as it is insisted, without the modification above quoted. It is well settled that it is competent for the circuit judge, in criminal prosecutions, as well as in civil cases, to modify the instructions requested on either side, so as to make them conform to his views of the law. Walker v. McDowell, 4 S. & M., 118 ; Boles v. The State of Mississippi, 9 ib., 284. The object of the court was to explain and render intelligible to the jury in what, according to the law, consisted a reasonable doubt. The explanation was correct, and did not vary the rule laid down by the instruction, as it was presented.

2. The second instruction was as follows, to wit : " That, unless the jury are as well satisfied from the evidence of the guilt of the accused, as they would be from the testimony of a single witness testifying directly to the fact, they should acquit." This instruction was refused.

The evidence adduced on the trial of this issue was entirely indirect or circumstantial ; and the object of this instruction was to institute a rule for the direction of the jury more definite than the principal which requires an acquittal, in case a reasonable doubt of the guilt of the accused should arise from the evidence.

It is said, 1 Stark. Evid., 577 (7 Am. ed.) " That the legal test of the sufficiency of evidence to authorize a conviction, is its sufficiency to satisfy the understanding and conscience of the jury. That a juror ought not to convict, unless the evidence excludes from his mind all reasonable doubt of the guilt of the accused." This is, doubtless, the true and only practical criterion by which the force of evidence in criminal prosecutions, sufficient for conviction, is to be determined. For, what circumstances will produce the requisite degree of certainty or conviction in the mind of the juror, can never be the subject of any general definition. Absolute, metaphysical and demonstrative certainty in the proof is never required. But it is undeniably true, as an abstract proposition, that the force of circumstantial evidence, to warrant a conviction, ought, in no case, to be inferior to that which is derived from the testimony of a single witness, the lowest degree of direct evidence. It is equally true that the direct testimony of one witness ought not to authorize a conviction, unless it were, in itself, sufficient to exclude from the mind of the juror every reasonable doubt of the guilt of the accused. To say that the jury should acquit, unless they were as well satisfied from the evidence of the guilt of the prisoner as they would be by the testimony of a single witness testifying directly to the fact, is only saying, in a different form, that they ought to acquit unless every reasonable doubt were excluded by the evidence.

This instruction was, in effect, embraced by the previous one. The objection, however, to this instruction is, that it applies a rule which is neither practical nor altogether safe. Under the operation of this rule, the juror would be compelled to act not upon the direct effect which the evidence had produced on his mind. He would be not only required to inquire into the state of his mental convictions to a certain whether the evidence offered in support of the prosecution had excluded from his mind all reasonable doubt; he would be forced to go farther, and to institute a comparison between the degree of conviction produced by the evidence and that which would be the result of the testimony of one direct witness; for that would be the standard by which he would have to determine the degree of certainty in the proof, which would authorize a conviction or require an acquittal. We have daily experience that the same evidence, in judicial proceedings, does not invariably produce the same degree of conviction in different minds. Hence, we may well conclude, that the legitimate force of the direct evidence of a single witness would be differently estimated by persons whose minds were differently constituted. The practical application of the principle contained in the instruction would, in effect, be to adopt a standard for estimating the force of this species of evidence, which would differ with the varying mental organization of each juror. Its practical effect, in all probability, would be, on the one hand, to lead to convictions in cases where, by the use of the more intelligible and safe rule, acquittals would follow; and, on the other, to produce acquittals where, by the same test, the parties would merit conviction. Upon this view of the subject, although we do not deny the abstract verity of the legal proposition contained in the instruction, we think it was properly refused.

3. The propriety of the decision of the court in overruling the motion for a new trial must be determined by the sufficiency of the evidence to sustain the verdict.

The issue was one purely of fact; and from the character of the evidence, peculiarly in the province of a jury. The evidence, as above remarked, was entirely circumstantial. The numerous facts and circumstances from which the jury were to infer the guilt or innocence of the accused, were deposed to by witnesses whose integrity, whose character for veracity, accuracy of observation and general intelligence were, we may suppose, known to the jurors. Upon the oral examination before them, they were in a condition to know whether these witnesses were influenced by any bias, by any preconception of the prisoner's guilt; or whether they deposed from a distinct and lively recollection of the incidents of the transaction, or from a vague remembrance, where the party testifying is but too liable to mistake·the impressions made upon his memory by the statements of others for his own preconceptions; and to confound inferences from facts with the facts themselves. Looking at the testimony through the medium of a record, we possess none of these advantages. Those tests which are used instinctively by the juror, in determining the degree of credit to be attached to the statement of any witness, cannot be applied by us. Hence, however sacred the obligation may be which rests upon the courts to protect the humblest individual from the errors or mistakes of a jury, an appellate tribunal will always with reluctance disturb a verdict involving merely a question of fact. And hence, also, the rule, that a verdict will always be permitted to stand, unless it is opposed by a decided preponderance of the evidence, or is based on no evidence whatever. Dickson v. Parker, 3 How. 219; Fisher v. Leach, 10 S. & M., 313; Leflore v. Justice, 1 ib., 381; Nye v. Grubbs, 8 ib., 643.

The counsel for the prisoner insist, that the verdict is entirely unsupported by evidence; at most, that the finding of the jury is against a decided preponderance of the evidence. A reference to the testimony will enable us to place the subject in its proper light. Mrs. Anne Longon, the victim of the alleged crime, her two infant children, and the prisoner, who was the servant of the family, constituted the entire household of Dr. Longon. On the night of the 12th of April last, the first witness, James E. Watts, was aroused from sleep and informed that Dr. Longon and his family were murdered. The witness rose from his bed, and providing himself with a light, in company with three other persons, proceeded to the scene of the murder. Arriving at the gate, which opened into the inclosure of Dr. Longon, the witness proposed to his companions that they should examine for tracks; and on entering the gate they discovered, about midway between that point and the house, the body of Mrs. Longon, which lay dead, with her feet upon the edge of the walk leading from the gate to the house, and her body resting upon the flower-bed which bordered it. Upon entering the gate, witness and companions proceeded cautiously and examined carefully for traces which they hoped might lead to a discovery of the perpetrator of the deed. Upon this examination, they discovered "foot prints" pointing from the house to the gate. They were the tracks of a person barefoot. Near the corpse were slight signs of a scuffle, and several "barefoot prints" of the same description. One was discovered at the back of the corpse on the flower-bed. The deceased was barefoot and in her night-clothes, and her death was caused by a severe wound on the head, behind the right ear, inflicted, as witness supposed, by some heavy weapon, such as the poll of an axe. From the body to the house were seen "foot-prints," as if they were made by two persons; one set corresponding with those found between the body and the gate, and the other supposed to be those of the deceased. No other traces or tracks were observed. It was possible for a person, by using great caution, to get into the house without leaving any traces of his ingress. The doors of the house were unprovided with shutters; one was defended by a quilt, and on entering, witness discovered on the right side of the door a large broad-axe. This axe had been, a few days before, used in hewing the walls of the house. It was, when seen, bloody. The corpse of Dr. Longon was on a bed upon the floor; the head was severed from the trunk, with the exception of a small portion of skin in the rear of the head. A murdered infant lay at the foot of the bed, its head and face crushed. Another child was lying on the right arm of the murdered man, severely wounded. At the moment of the murder, it was supposed to be sleeping in the arms of the deceased, and from the position of the father and child, it was inferred that the same blow which had inflicted the wound on the one, had deprived the other of life. The floor, particularly near the bed, was covered with blood, the walls were sprinkled with the same material, and bloody foot-tracks were left on the floor.

Witness, after making these observations, proceeded along the road in the direction of Mr. Brown's, which was distant about one mile and a half. He continued to examine with the same circumspection for any traces of the murderer, and in the road he found foot-prints which appeared to correspond with those first seen in the walk; they pointed in the direction of Brown's. From the length of the steps, and the impressions made in the sandy parts of the road, witness inferred that they were made by a person in a walk. Half way between Longon's and Brown's, witness met prisoner, who in answer to his question, said, " that five robbers, three white men and two negroes, had come to Dr. Longon's the night before (it then being daylight) to get his money, and had killed him and his family. That after they had killed him and his family, Mrs. Longon and herself ran out of the house and were pursued by the robbers, who overtook Mrs. Longon and killed her, where she lay ; but that prisoner outran Mrs. Longon and escaped, and ran over to Mr. Brown's. The robbers threw a stick at her as she passed through the gate at Dr. Longon's." At this time witness had no suspicion of the guilt of the prisoner.

Witness returned to Dr. Longon's house with the prisoner, who went in. The murdered and wounded children were sent to the house of the witness. They were accompanied by the prisoner and witness, who followed in the rear ; and he did not see the prisoner have either of the children in her arms. It was not until after arriving at his house, that witness began to suspect the prisoner. He then scrutinized her person and appearance. " There was blood on her left sleeve, which looked as if it had been wiped off, or rubbed off with something ; and the front part of her dress was spattered with blood, having many specks and spots on it." The attention of those present was directed to the blood on her dress; which being observed by the prisoner, she immediately commenced picking an old wound or sore on her finger, as if with the intention of making it bleed. Her purpose was prevented. Prisoner was then asked to account for the blood on her dress. She replied "that it came from the sore on her finger." Witness was confident it did not proceed from that source. Immediately afterwards she said "it came from the quilt, which Mr. Williams had sent her for in the morning."

The prisoner was then conveyed back to Dr. Longon's for the purpose of further examination, and with the view of comparing her tracks with those discovered at the place of Mrs. Longon's murder. Her tracks were found to correspond with those first discovered in the morning, and with those seen in the walk, near where the corpse of Mrs. Longon lay. She exhibited a good deal of reluctance to have her feet compared with the tracks.

We have recited at some length the testimony of this witness, who seems to have been cool and impartial, and is manifestly observant and intelligent. His testimony establishes the fact of the homicide, conveys a distinct idea of the scene of this shocking tragedy, and proves many of the facts and circumstances from which our conclusion of the guilt or innocence of the accused is to be deduced. Several other witnesses were examined, three of whom coincide precisely, in substance, with this witness. They detail many other facts, which form important links in the chain of evidence on the part of the prosecution, and facts and circumstances relied upon by counsel, as conducive to establish the innocence of the accused. We will only extract such parts of their testimony as may have an important bearing on the issue, or refer to them in the course of our observations.

James Watts, the second witness, states, that after the prisoner had been taken into the house at Dr. Longon's, he discovered something concealed in her dress above the waist. Upon being asked what it was, she replied that it was her money, and refused to give it up upon the demand of the witness. It was taken from her, and proved to be a purse containing between seven and eight dollars.   Prisoner said the money was her own; that Dr. Longon had given her two dollars of the money and the purse, two days previously, for a purpose which the witness declined to state, and that the remainder of the money was acquired in a similar way from other persons.   Upon being asked how much money the purse contained, she answered eleven dollars. Prisoner said, during this conversation, that there were three negroes and two white men who entered Dr. Longon's house; that when they came she was awake, and saw them enter.   At another time she said she was asleep, and did not see them enter; that the robbers kindled a light on the hearth, and informed Longon that they wanted his money.   Longon got up and said he had no money.   The robbers replied that he had, and must give it to them.   They bid him then to lie down, or made him lie down, and killed him.   After having been taken into custody, she said that when the robbers were about to kill Dr. Longon, the night before that, he gave her some money and informed her that he owed some debts about Gordonsville, and requested her to pay them.

James E. Newsom testified that he examined the bloody footprints in the house, and believed they were made by a person barefoot, and while the blood was yet warm and uncongealed; that some of these bloody tracks corresponded in size and shape, with those of the prisoner.   "The toes not making any impression, because they extended beyond where the blood was." The pantaloons of Dr. Longon were found near the head of his bed, and "one of the pockets was stained with blood, as if done by a bloody hand thrust into it;" that blood in spots appeared high up on the wall; that everything in the house was bloody, and that a person might approach the house in any direction, save that of the gate, without leaving traces of his ingress.

James Williams testified that he remained in the house, washing the children and dressing them; that whilst so engaged, prisoner came in from Brown's, who was then directed by him to bring something in which to wrap the children; that prisoner went to an out-house and brought him a quilt or a sheet, which he used for that purpose; that witness walked about in the room;

that everything was bloody; that he did not notice the bloody tracks; that she may have had hold of some of the bloody clothes; and did not recollect to have seen the prisoner with any of the children in her arms; that there was but one room in the house, in which the prisoner and family slept.

William Judge deposed that the purse exhibited on trial was seen by him in the possession of Dr. Longon, the week previous to his death; that he had examined the purse in consequence of a proposal to swap; the purse then contained only two or three dimes, and when exhibited on trial had no visible stains of blood on it.

Mr. Perry, a witness called on the part of the defense, testified that he was at Brown's when prisoner arrived there on the night of the murder; it was about three o'clock in the morning; witness informed the inmates at Brown's that some robbers had murdered Dr. Longon and family; prisoner lingered at the negro quarters about fifteen minutes, before she went to the house, and when she entered she stopped near the door; she was asked to come near the fire, where witness and others were standing; she did not advance to the light, but retreated into a dark corner of the room, out of the light; she made contradictory statements about the murder, and witness suspected her guilt at Brown's; did not observe blood on her dress; prisoner, in speaking of the murder, said, that Dr. Longon had suspected that robbers would come, from the barking of the dogs, and had placed a broad-axe near the head of his bed; he saw prisoner carry one of the children as far as the gate in front of the house; thought the child was wrapped in something lying on the bed; the child was bloody, and he did not observe the blood on her dress, until she returned from the house of Mr. Watts.

John Johnson, a witness called on the same side, says, he examined the bloody foot-prints on the floor of Dr. Longon's house, and says they resembled a stocking foot-print, as the toes were not distinctly marked.

From this statement of the testimony, the facts which militate against the accused, and lead to conclusion of her guilt, are:

1. Her presence at the commission of the homicide, and the

perfect means which were at her command, for the accomplishment of her object.

2. The fact, that from the door of the house, in the walk, to the spot where the corpse of Mrs. Longon was found, during the night, after cautious and careful examination, there were discovered but two sets of tracks or "foot-prints," one of which was supposed to be those of the deceased, and the other corresponded with those of the accused.

3. The fact, that at the place where the homicide was committed, the traces of a scuffle were visible, and the prints of feet were discovered, which corresponded with the tracks of the accused.

4. The fact, that from the point at which the corpse was found, to the gate, there was found but one set of tracks, and they corresponded with those of the accused.

5. The prisoner's declining to advance into the light at Brown's, where the witness Perry was standing with others, and her retreat into a dark corner.

6. The statement prisoner made to witness, James E. Watts, in the road between Longon's and Brown's, before any suspicion of her agency in the murder had arisen in the mind of the witness. She stated, that after the robbers had killed Longon and his family, Mrs. Longon and herself ran out of the house, and were pursued by the robbers, who overtook Mrs. Longon and killed her where she lay; but that she outran Mrs. Longon and escaped, and ran over to Brown's.

7. The stains of blood upon the front of her dress. Witness says, "There were many specks and spots upon it."

8. The blood-stain upon the pantaloon-pocket of Longon, coupled with her possession of his purse, secreted, and her ignorance of the amount of its contents.

9. The improbable version she gave of the whole transaction, and her palpably contradictory statements.

The question which naturally presents itself is this: Can all of these facts, distinctly proven, stand, and yet the prisoner be guiltless of the homicide.

It is, in the first place, objected, that the presence of the prisoner, who would necessarily have been there, whether guilty or innocent, creates no presumption of her guilt; and that the absence of any sufficient motive for the commission of so dreadful a crime, is a circumstance strong in her favor. It is difficult to estimate the force of any motive, which may arise in any given case. We have evidence from painful experience, that a desire to possess the wealth of another has often constituted the operative motive for the perpetration of the deepest crimes. The prisoner may have been ignorant of the amount of money which Longon possessed, or the glittering contents of the purse may have presented a temptation which she did not resist. We are forced to infer that the acquisition of the purse, with the attendant circumstances, formed at least a part of her motive.

Again it is urged, that the existence of the foot-prints, in the walk from the door to the point where the dead body was found, and from thence to the gate, is in harmony with prisoner's statement, and must have existed if her statement were true. This assumption is directly rebutted by the facts. If Mrs. Longon were slain by the robbers, who rushed from the house in pursuit of the fugitives, there must have been other tracks made in the walks besides those of the two persons in flight, and the place where the blow was struck and the victim fell, which bore evidence of a scuffle, would also have been eloquent of the presence of her murderers.

It is also insisted, that the stains of blood upon her dress, as that circumstance may be accounted for in various ways, consistent with the innocence of the accused, creates no presumption of her guilt. Her own explanations are unsatisfactory and untrue. It did not proceed from the old wound on her finger, as she at first stated and afterwards denied. It is highly improbable, that these stains were contracted from the quilt which the witness Williams had sent her for to wrap the children in. The stain on the sleeve of her dress may have proceeded from that source, or have been contracted by carrying the children; but, how are we to account for the " many specks and spots " on the front of her dress? From the testimony of Newsom, it is inferable, that the blood at the time when the children were sent to Watts' house, appearing in different parts of the house, where the murder of Longon and child was committed, was congealed. If these stains had been contracted from the bed - furniture in which the children were enveloped, they would have appeared like the stain on the sleeve, as if produced by rubbing against a bloody article. The "specks and spots" upon her dress were probably produced by the blood gushing from the veins or arteries of the murdered victim. The conduct of the accused at Brown's can only rationally be accounted for upon the supposition of conscious guilt. "She retreated into a dark corner," after having lingered some time at the negro quarter, before she told her tale. Judging from the emotions of horror and fear, with which an innocent female would have been oppressed, who had witnessed such a scene as the prisoner described, we may well suppose she would have rushed to the light and sought protection from the friendly persons whom she saw there. Then, why did she retreat into a dark corner? To this question, there is but one satisfactory answer to be given ; she feared that an exposure to the light would detect the evidence of her participation in the murder.

Again, it is insisted that the fact of the purse of Longon having been found upon her person is no evidence of her having murdered Mrs. Longon ; that she might have obtained the purse and the money in the manner related by her, or have received it from the person who committed the homicide on Longon. Her ignorance of the amount of money it contained is a strong argument against the truth of her statement, which she in fact contradicted after she was taken into custody. If, say the prisoner's counsel, she did actually take the purse from the pantaloon pocket, it would probably have been blood-stained, as the hand that withdrew it was bloody, and the purse was unstained. If the hand of the prisoner grasped the handle of the axe with which the blow on Longon was inflicted, the back of the hand would have received the blood, which, upon the stroke, flowed from his arteries. This supposition accounts for the manner in which the pocket was stained, " as if," says the witness, " a bloody hand was thrust into it." Again, say the counsel, if the prisoner took the purse from Longon's pocket, she must have returned into the house, after having pursued and overtaken Mrs. Longon in the walk, and would consequently have left " foot-prints " pointing to the house. The evidence shows that the house could be approached in any direction save that of the gate, without leaving signs. If the prisoner had returned into the house by passing along the walk, after murdering Mrs. Longon, she would have left additional and conclusive evidence of her guilt. We may suppose, therefore, that she would naturally, after passing out at the gate, return in some other direction. And this view is strengthened by the discovery of her tracks immediately in the rear of the house. The evidence of James E. Watts renders it highly probable, if not certain, that the broad axe was used in the slaughter of Longon. It was bloody, and but one blow was given, which severed the head and some of the fingers of Longon, and wounded his child, which witness supposes to have been, at the moment, asleep in his arms. The instrument must have been broad, or this effect could not have been produced by a single blow. It would have been strange, if five persons in concert had entered the house for the purpose of doing robbery and murder, without suitable implements to effect their purposes. The statement of the prisoner, in reference to this point, is not unimportant. To Perry she said, that Longon had suspected that robbers would come that night from the barking of the dogs, and had placed a broad-axe near the head of his bed. Why such a suspicion, from so ordinary an occurrence, in the midst of a peaceable community ? The jury might well have inferred that this was only an attempt to forestall any suspicion against herself, which might arise from the position of the axe where she knew it was left.

These facts, all of which are independent, could not exist in harmony with the assumption of the innocence of the accused. One circumstance, in addition to those, the objections to which we have above noticed, is this,—and to our minds it is strongly indicative of the guilt of the prisoner. She says, that after the robbers had killed Dr. Longon, Mrs. Longon and herself ran out of the house, and were pursued by them, " who overtook and killed Mrs. Longon where she lay ; but that she outran Mrs. Longon and escaped, and ran over to Mr. Brown's." If the statement of four witnesses be true, this statement was false ; but its falsehood is not the most damnatory feature. It supposes a knowledge of a fact which the darkness and the flight of the prisoner rendered impossible. It was evidently an effort to give a statement of the transaction which would comport with her assumed innocence. The prisoner might have imagined that Mrs. Longon had been slain by her pursuers; but how did she know that the corpse lay where the murder was committed, if she ran over to Mr. Brown's after having escaped?

In cases depending upon indirect testimony, where the facts or circumstances established by direct proof point strongly to the guilt of the accused, his relation of the occurrence is frequently a matter of great importance. His statement, if true, may explain facts of a doubtful character which otherwise would tend strongly to the conclusion of his guilt; and if it be reasonable and consistent in itself, should always have weight with the jury. On the other hand, if it be unreasonable or contradictory, and proved to be false, it must, upon acknowledged principles, increase the presumption of his guilt. In the case at bar, the evidence, strong, if not conclusive, derives great weight from the strange account which she gave of the occurrence, from the contradictory statements, and from the fact that her relation, in part at least, is proved to be false. Ignorant or weak-minded persons, innocent of the charge, when opposed by circumstances that question their innocence, not knowing that a true account of the matter would be their surest protection, frequently resort to prevarication and falsehood, with a hope of delivery. But in the case under examination there is good reason to believe that the false and contradictory statements of the prisoner were the result of the guilt in which she was involved. Upon the whole, looking at the testimony with that degree of scrutiny and caution, with which circumstantial evidence should be received in a prosecution for a crime of this magnitude, we think the verdict was right, and, therefore, affirm the judgment.

JOLLY *v.* THE STATE, 13 Smedes & Marshall, 223.

HOMICIDE.

The general rule is, that no words of reproach, or provoking or insulting language, or actions short of an assault, will furnish excuse for a homicide, even when committed at the time of the killing.

When the manner of the homicide is not fully shown, a known character for violence of temper and dangerous desperation in the deceased may serve to raise presumption in favor of the prisoner. But the general character for insolence cannot furnish an excuse.

Error to Wilkinson circuit court. HARRIS, J.

The plaintiff in error was indicted, and convicted of the manslaughter of a slave named Jim, the property of John L. Downs. His motion for a new trial being overruled, he sued out this writ of error.

Farrish, Davidson & Barbee, for the plaintiff in error,

Cited State *v.* Tackett, 1 Hawks, N. C. R., 210, 217, 218; 8 Peters, 658; 1 Blackf., 205; Van Ness *v.* Packard, 2 Peters, 144; State *v.* Buchanan, 5 Har. & Johns., 356; Wilford *v.* Grant, Kirby, 117; Pawlett *v.* Clarke, 9 Cranch, 333.

D. C. Glenn, attorney general,

Argued the case orally, and cited Hutch. Code, 954; ib., 514, § 16, 32; 2 Hawks, 210.

SHARKEY, C. J.:

The prisoner was indicted for murder, committed on the body of a slave called Jim, the property of John L. Downs. He was convicted of manslaughter in the fourth degree, and sentenced to two years' imprisonment in the penitentiary. An exception was taken during the progress of the trial, to the rejection of evidence, and on this point alone the case must turn; for, although a motion was made for a new trial because the verdict was contrary to evidence, yet there is nothing in that ground which could justify a reversal of the judgment.

Thomas Woodsides was introduced as a witness for the prisoner, and asked, "if the boy Jim, previous to his death, was insolent and impudent to white persons." An objection was made to this question, which was sustained, and the witness was not permitted to answer.   The propriety of this decision is the question to be determined.

The general rule is, that no words of reproach, or provoking or insulting language, or actions short of an assault, will furnish a sufficient excuse for a homicide, even when spoken or committed at the time of the killing;[1] and much less will a general insolent or insulting habit excuse the killing of the person addicted to such habit.   When the manner of the homicide is not fully shown, a known character for violence of temper, and dangerous desperation in the deceased, may serve to raise a presumption in favor of the prisoner; but in this instance, there was no effort to prove that the negro was dangerous.   His general character for insolence could not have furnished an excuse.   Such character will not justify the killing of a negro.   We need not pass on the effect of insolent language used by a negro, at the time the killing occurs, as no such question is raised; there is no evidence that the negro was even insolent at the time he was killed. Nor was there any such act of violence, on the part of the negro, as to jeopardize the safety of the accused, or to show a violent character in the negro.

The case of the State v. Tackett, 1 Hawks, 210, is relied on, as an authority for reversing the judgment.   The defendant in that case was convicted of murder, and the manner of the commission of the homicide, or the circumstances attending its commission, were not fully shown, the evidence being only circumstantial.   The prisoner offered to prove, that the deceased was a turbulent man, and that he was insolent and impudent to white people.   The court held, that this testimony should have been admitted, because, said the court, "it might, in connection with the threats, quarrels, and existing causes of resentment, he had against the prisoner, increase the probability, that the latter had acted under a strong and legal provocation."   There had been

1 Wharton on Homicide, 168; Keling, 135; 1 Hale, 466; Foster Cr. Law, 290; U. S. v. Travers, 2 Wheeler's Cr. Cases, 504; Commonwealth v. York, 9 Metc., 93; State v. Tacket, 1 Hawks., 210; Allen v. State, 5 Yerg., 453; Jacobs v. State, 3 Humph., 493; King v. Commonwealth, 2 Va. Cases, 98; Wharton Am. Cr. Law, 270; 1 Hale P. C., 456; U. S. v. Wiltberger, 3 Wash. C. C. R., 515; Rex v. Campbell, 4 Boston Law R., 131; State v. Merrill, 2 Devor, 269; Ray v. State, 15 Ga., 223; Rapp v. State, 14 B. Monroe, 614; People v. Freeland, 6 Cal., 96; State v. Starr, 38 Mo., 270; People v. Butler, 8 Cal., 435; State v. Shippey, 10 Minn., 223.

several quarrels, and even a fight, between the prisoner and the deceased, and besides, there was proof of threats made against the life of the prisoner by the deceased; and it was only in connection with these circumstances, that the court held the evidence admissible. The circumstances attending the homicide were moreover unexplained, and hence it was deemed proper, that the evidence should have been admitted, because from it the jury might indulge a presumption favorable to the prisoner. But, in this case, the circumstances are wholly different; the manner of committing the homicide is fully explained, and there had been no previous threats or quarrels, between the deceased and the accused. There was no ground for the jury to draw an inference, that the deceased, by insolence, provoked the commission of the act. The record before us propounds this question in effect: Is it competent, on a trial for murder of a slave, to prove, that the slave was generally insolent and impudent to white persons, although he was not so, at the time of his death, to the individual who caused it? We respond in the negative, and it follows, that the court was right in excluding the evidence.

Judgment affirmed.

Morgan *v.* The State, 13 Smedes & Marshall, 242.

Assault with Intent to Kill.

It is a universal principle of evidence, that a man shall be understood to intend that which he does, or which are the natural consequences of his acts.

Where a general felonious intention is sufficient to constitute the offense, it is no ground of excuse where a party who intended to commit one felony has committed another.

The specific intention of killing the particular person alleged to have been shot at, is an essential ingredient of the offense charged in the indictment, and proof of a general felonious or malicious intention is not sufficient. It is incumbent on the state to prove the specific intent charged.

Error to Lawrence circuit court. Harris, J.

The plaintiff in error was indicted in the court below for an assault and battery with intent to kill one James Foster. He was tried and found guilty. He made a motion in arrest of judgment for various alleged defects in the indictment, which was overruled.

Several instructions were given and refused on both sides, and a bill of exceptions was sealed by the prisoner, who, after being sentenced, sued out this writ of error.

G. P. Fonte, for plaintiff in error,

Cited Hutch. Dig., 960, ch. 64, § 33 ; 2 Starkie Ev., 739, (n.) R.

Swift, on same side,

Cited 1 Chit. Cr. Law, 282 ; 2 Starkie Ev., 740 ; 1 East. P. C., 412, 413.

D. C. Glenn, attorney general,

Cited 2 How. R., 655.

Smith, J. :

The indictment in this case, upon which William Morgan, the plaintiff in error, was tried and convicted, was framed under the 33d §, chap. 64, of the act of 1839, Hutch. Dig., p. 960. The first clause of that section creates and defines the offense with which the party was charged, and is in the following words, viz : " Every person who shall be convicted of shooting at another with the intent to kill, maim, etc., such other person, shall be punished by imprisonment in the penitentiary for a term not exceeding ten years."

Upon the trial of the issue, the prisoner, by his counsel, requested the court to charge the jury, " that under this indictment, it is necessary for the prosecution to prove, that said defendant shot at Foster (the person on whom the assault was alleged to have been committed) with the intent to kill said Foster, before the defendant can be legally convicted." This instruction was refused, whereupon the counsel for the state requested the court to charge the jury as follows :

1. " That if the jury believe from the evidence that the prisoner shot into the crowd with the intention of killing any one in the crowd, but not with the intention of killing Foster, and that the shooting was not at the time in the necessary self-defence of the prisoner, they should find him guilty."

2. " That if the jury believe that Morgan shot at Loftin with a premeditated design to kill him, Loftin, and that said shooting was

not in the necessary self-defence, although he missed Loftin and shot Foster, they should find him guilty, though he entertained no malice towards Foster."

The correctness of these instructions presents the first question for the consideration of this court; and it is obvious that if the former be correct, the latter must be erroneous.

It is a universal principle of evidence, that a man shall be understood to intend that which he does, or which is the natural and necessary consequence of his act. Hence, in the absence of any explanatory testimony, we should be bound to presume that the prisoner intended to perpetrate the assault charged upon the person of Foster; and to hold the offense as charged clearly made out. But the instructions asked for, as well by the state as the prisoner, clearly show, that evidence had been adduced on the trial which tended to establish the fact, that Loftin, and not Foster, was the object of the assault. The instructions, then, did not propound abstract propositions which could in nowise affect the verdict of the jury.

It is a well-understood rule of law, where a general felonious intention is sufficient to constitute the offense, that it is no ground of excuse where a party who intended to commit one felony has committed another. 2 Starkie Ev., p. 416, 5 Am. Ed.; East. P. C., 514.

In the case at bar, the malicious intent might be clearly inferred from the character of the weapon used; and if the alleged attempt had been consummated in the death of Foster, the prisoner would have been guilty of murder, although he entertained no malice as to him. This principle, however, is applicable only to cases where one felony is contemplated and another committed. But the offense of which the prisoner stands convicted is, we apprehend, no felony by the laws of this state. If, however, the offense here charged be in fact a felony, nevertheless, this rule does not apply; for an essential ingredient of the offense, created by the section of the statute above quoted, and charged in the indictment, is the specific intention of killing the person shot at. In the case of Jones v. The State of Mississippi, 11 S. & M., 317, this court expressly recognizes this construction of the act. They say this statute "specifies the intent to kill the person shot at as one of the intents made essential to constitute the offense." The same construction has been given by the English courts to the statute of 9 Geo. 4., ch. 31, § 11 and 12, which is similar to our own; (Rex v. Holt, 7 Carr. & Payne, 518;) and we hold it to be correct.

If, then, the specific intention of killing the particular person alleged to have been shot at, be "an essential ingredient of the offense charged in the indictment," proof of a general felonious or malicious intention was not sufficient. It was incumbent on the state to prove the specific intent as charged. 2 Starkie Ev., p. 416, note S, 5th Am. Ed.; 7 Carr & Payne, 518. The charge requested by the prisoner's counsel was correct, and the court erred in refusing it.

An exception is taken to the decision of the court below on the motion in arrest of judgment. But on looking into the indictment, we do not think it obnoxious to the objections insisted on by counsel. It is true that it is very inartificially drawn, and somewhat obscure. In substance, however, we deem it sufficient. But for the error above pointed out, we reverse the judgment of the court below, and award a new trial in the circuit court of Lawrence county,

---

COON *v.* THE STATE, 13 Smedes and Marshall, 246.

LARCENY OF A SLAVE.

A slave who has absconded from the possession of his owner is nevertheless in his constructive possession; and the master might maintain trespass for any injury done to the slave during the period of his absconding.

If a person lose his goods and another finds them, and converts them to his own use, not knowing the owner, it is no larceny; but if he knew the owner, or had the means of knowing him, it would be larceny.

A negro, by the laws of this state, is *prima facie* a slave. If a person, therefore, who is not the owner, take a runaway negro into his possession, with the intent of feloniously converting him to his own use, knowing or having the means of knowing the owner, it is larceny.

Statements or confessions must be delivered to the jury precisely as they were made; certain facts cannot be detailed to the jury and others withheld. It is for the jury to give such weight to the whole as in their opinion it merits; but they may believe one part and wholly disregard the rest.

The proof of the *venue* must be established to warrant a conviction; but, like other facts, it may be proved by circumstances. Where, therefore, from all the circumstances established in the case, the jury found that the *venue* was correctly laid, it is sufficient, and their verdict cannot be set aside on that account.

Error to Wilkinson circuit court. POSEY, J.

William C. Coon was indicted and tried at the December term, 1848, of the court below, for the larceny of Cæsar, the slave of James A. Stewart. He was found guilty, and his motion for a new trial being overruled, he embodied the evidence in a bill of exceptions, and brings his case to this court by a writ of error.

The opinion of the court contains all the evidence.

Farish & Gildart, for plaintiff in error,

Contended, 1. That the jury erred in disregarding, in the absence of any proof to the contrary, the statement of Coon that he bought the slave from John H. Scott. 2 Phill. Ev., note 224, p. 247, 248.

2. There is no *venue* proved. They reviewed the proof on this point, and cited 1 Chitty Cr. Law, 146 ; How. & Hutch., 723 ; Vaughan v. State, 3 S. & M., 553.

D. C. Glenn, attorney general.

1. This court will not interrupt the verdict, unless a great preponderance of testimony appear against it. See 5 S. & M., 21; ib., 400 ; ib., 22 ; 4 How., 90 ; ib., 122; ib., 231 ; 5 ib., 495.

2. Larceny may be committed of runaway slaves. Randall v. State, 4 S. & M., 351 ; 2 Leach, 952 ; 17 Wend. 460 ; 2 Russ. on Crimes, marg. p. 177, p. 194, and cases cited ; 3 Halst., 324.

3. As to the *venue.* 1st. The defendant confessed that he had taken the slave from Wilkinson county, and thereby finds the *venue.* 2d. That the title to personal property draws to it the possession ; that title in the negro was proven in James A. Stewart, his residence in Wilkinson at the time of possession and title ; a loss of it in Wilkinson, and a discovery of the property in the possession of Coon, unexplained and under suspicious circumstances. 3d. That slaves are a peculiar species of property, unknown to the common law, and, in indictments touching them, the Latin technicalities are wholly inapplicable, but we act upon the broad language of our statute, " whoever

shall steal slaves, the property of another, without his consent, shall be imprisoned in the penitentiary not less than ten years." How. v. Hutch., 709, 710 ; State v. Mooney, 8 Ala. R., 330.

SMITH, J. :

This was an indictment for negro stealing. It was tried in the Wilkinson circuit court, and resulted in the conviction of the plaintiff in error.

No objection was made to the instructions given by the court, and no exception taken to the admission of any evidence which was submitted to the jury. A motion was made for a new trial, which, being overruled, a bill of exceptions was filed to the decision of the court on the motion, and the evidence spread upon the record.

The slave, who was the subject of the larceny charged, at the time of the alleged taking, was a runaway ; and it is insisted that the fact of the possession of the slave in a neighboring state was no evidence of a felonious taking within the State of Mississippi. A slave who has absconded from the possession of his owner is, nevertheless, in his constructive possession. He might maintain trespass for any injury done to the slave during the period of his absconding. "If one lose his goods and another find them, and convert them to his own use not knowing the owner, this is no larceny ; but if the latter knew the owner, or had the means of knowing him, it would be larceny." A negro, by the laws of this state, is *prima facie* a slave. If a person, therefore, who is not the owner, take a runaway negro into his possession, with the intent of feloniously converting him to his own use, knowing, or having the means of knowing, the owner or master, it would be larceny. This is settled in the case of Randall v. The State of Mississippi, 4 S. & M. 349.

The next objection is in effect this, that the jury rejected or disregarded that part of the prisoner's confession which was favorable to him, and gave weight to that which tended to criminate him.

The rule is well settled that statements or confessions of the party to be affected, must be delivered to the jury precisely as they were made ; that certain facts cannot be extracted and de-

tailed to the jury and other parts withheld. It is for the jury
to give such weight to the whole, as in their opinion it merits,
and although the whole of the statement or confession must be
considered together, yet the jury may unquestionably on this, as
on every other point of evidence, believe one part and disregard
the other. 2 Phil. Ev., n. 224, p. 247. If, therefore, the jury
did disregard the part of the confession in which the prisoner
states that he purchased the slave, alleged to have been stolen by
him from Scott, it was no error.

The next objection is, that there was no proof of the *venue.*
This is an important objection, for unless it were proved that the
larceny was committed within the county of Wilkinson, the
court had no jurisdiction, and the finding of the jury was void.

The proof of *venue*, like the proof of any other fact, may arise
from circumstances established by the evidence. Leaving out of
view, for the present, the confession of the prisoner made to the
witness Smith, at Mobile, in the State of Alabama, let us see
what is the amount of the evidence.

James A. Stewart, the owner of the slave, testified that the
slave ran away from his plantation in Wilkinson county, in February, preceding the trial ; that he had never given the negro
permission to go to Mobile, and did not know of his being there
until after the arrest of Coon ; that the prisoner had always, from
infancy, resided in Wilkinson county, and that he had heard of
the negro being in the county about two weeks before the arrest
of prisoner at Mobile. This latter statement was clearly incompetent evidence, but as there was no objection made to its admission, the jury were authorized to give what weight to it they
saw proper.

The witness, Jas. A. Smith, stated that he knew Coon well ;
that he had conversed with him two weeks before he saw him in
confinement at Mobile, in Wilkinson county ; that the prisoner
pretended not to know him, and passed in Mobile under the name
of William Jones, a name which the witness had never before
known the prisoner to assume ; that a man named Stocker said, in
the presence of the prisoner and witness, that prisoner had given
him a due-bill, using the name of William Jones ; that he had
found prisoner and the negro alleged to have been stolen by

Coon, in jail at Mobile; and that, when they were brought back to the jail in Wilkinson, Coon, in reply to a question asked by J. S. Cohen, said that Cohen had arrested him and the negro in Mobile; that Cohen had informed witness, that Coon, on his arrest in Mobile, said that the negro had been bought by him from a Kentucky horse-drover.

This evidence was sufficient to fix the possession of the stolen slave upon the prisoner, and under very suspicious circumstances. He had given his due-bill, using a fictitious name; passed generally under the name of Jones, and had, with the slave in his possession, been arrested and confined in jail. The jury would then have had to inquire whether the felonious taking occurred within the county of Wilkinson. The stolen slave was heard to be in the county two weeks before Coon's arrest in Mobile. He had, from his infancy, constantly made that county his home. About the same time he was seen in the county. The witness, Smith, knew him well, and had conversed with him. Two weeks from that time, the prisoner is seen at Mobile, with the slave in his possession under such circumstances, which, if unexplained, would amount to a strong presumption that he had stolen the property. These were certainly potent facts, from which the jury might have inferred that the theft was committed in Wilkinson county. But it may yet be urged that they do not exclude the fact that the felonious possession was acquired in a neighboring county, in an adjoining state. But his statements or confessions to the witness, Smith, would seem to dispel all doubt, at least to create such strong proof of his guilt, as should, perhaps, induce this court not to disturb the verdict of the jury; particularly as the question for them to decide, and which they did decide, was one of pure fact, lying fully within the range of their appropriate duties.

On arriving at Mobile, the witness, Mr. Smith, as the agent of Mr. Stewart, found the prisoner in jail, under an arrest upon a suspicion of having committed a theft of the negro man Cæsar. He also found the negro in custody. After having seen the negro, he went to see the prisoner, who pretended not to know him at first. The witness stated to Coon, " that he had come to get the negro that had been stolen from James A. Stewart."

Coon replied " that he had not stolen the negro, but had bought him from a man named John H. Scott, who lived in Wilkinson county. Upon being told by Smith that he had never known or heard of John H. Scott, prisoner said Scott was a horse-drover, who was sometimes in Wilkinson, and sometimes in Amite county. Prisoner desired to be taken back to Wilkinson, " because he could not get a fair trial in Mobile; that they had arrested him upon the charge of stealing the negro in question." While there, the prisoner informed witness that he had sold .the negro to some one in Mobile, for $850. Davis and Lewis, who from their positions, were likely to know whether such a person as John H. Scott was a resident of Wilkinson, swear that they know of no such person, either as a resident or otherwise.

These statements of the prisoner were before the jury, with the opposing evidence of Davis and Lewis. It was for them to give such weight to the whole of the statements, as, in their judgments, they merited. It was their duty to consider them together; but if they did, in fact, give credit to such parts of the statements of the prisoner, which, in their opinion, were sustained by other evidence in the cause, or disregard such other parts as were opposed by the testimony of the witnesses, they exercised but a legitimate function of their office. We believe the evidence warranted the conviction, and affirm the judgment.

STOUGHTON v. THE STATE, 13 Smedes & Marshall, 255.

HOMICIDE.

The high court of errors and appeals cannot notice the instructions given or refused in the court below, unless they are embodied in a bill of exceptions.

In cases of homicide, where the wound is inflicted in one county and the death takes place in another, the indictment must be preferred in the latter, or it will be void.

Error to Perry circuit court. DAWSON, J.

The opinion of the court contains all the material facts of the case.

F. Anderson, for plaintiff in error,

On the point of the jurisdiction of the circuit court of Perry county, to try the offense, cited and commented on 1 Hale P. C., 425, 426. This authority is not sustained by reference to any decisions, and is not supported by the reasoning of the author. 1 Hawk. P. C., 93, 94 ; 2 ib., 301, 302, 303, § 40 ; 2 Hale P. C., 262 ; ib., 162, 163 ; 1 East's P. C., ch. 5, § 128, 361 ; 2 Hale, 66 ; 2 Pick., 550 ; 2 Eng. St. at Large, 422 ; 4 Black. Com., 303.

D. C. Glenn, attorney general,

Contended that congress made the common law in force in the Mississippi Territory. 2 Stewart, 362. English statutes, passed before the emigration of our ancestors, which are in amendment of the law and applicable to our situation, constitute a part of our common law. 3 Peters, 559 ; 1 Mass., 61 ; 2 ib., 535 ; 13 ib., 354 ; 1 Dallas, 67, 75 ; 8 Pick., 309 ; 9 ib., 532 ; 3 Greenl., 162 ; 6 ib., 55 : 3 Gill & Johns., 62 ; Charlton, 167 ; Coxe, 338, note.

SHARKEY, C. J.:

The prisoner was convicted in the circuit court of Perry county of the murder of J. A. Harvey. He moved for a new trial, because the verdict was contrary to law and evidence, and because the court erred in refusing charges asked by the prisoner, and in giving those asked by the district attorney. On these points we need make no comments. Indeed, on the charges we could not ; they are not presented by bill of exceptions, but noted by the clerk as having been given or refused. The law of 1846 which provides for so noting charges that may be given or refused, and makes them part of the record, without bill of exceptions, applies only to civil cases. Hutch. Code, 893.

The case must turn on a different point ; the wound was inflicted in Perry county, where the prisoner was indicted, but the death occurred in Harrison county. In such cases there is an express statutory provision, requiring that the indictment should be found in the county where the death occurs. Poindexter's Code, 314. This statute seems to have been overlooked in the subsequent compilations, though it is not repealed ; at least we have found no act repealing it. It simply provides, that the in

dictment found in the county in which the death may happen,
shall be good and valid in law. The better opinion seems to
have been, that by the common law, when the blow was given
in one county and the death happened in another, the offender
was not indictable in either. This, however, was a point that
gave rise to doubts. The difficulty was obviated by the statute of
Edward VI., which made the offense triable in the county where
the death happened. Our statute was passed with the same object. It does not, it is true, say the prisoner shall not be tried
in the county where the stroke was given: and if it could be
clearly shown that he was triable there by the common law, perhaps the statute might be regarded as giving the additional
power to try him in the county where the death happened, without interfering with the jurisdiction as at common law. But as
the question was, to say the least of it, doubtful at common law,
the statute must be regarded as the only law on the subject.
The indictment was, therefore, improperly found in Perry county, for which reason it must be quashed,[1] and the prisoner remanded to Harrison county for indictment and trial.

MᴄGᴜɪʀᴇ ʋ. Tʜᴇ Sᴛᴀᴛᴇ, 13 Smedes & Marshall, 257.

Sᴇʟʟɪɴɢ Lɪǫᴜᴏʀ ᴛᴏ Sʟᴀᴠᴇs.

The essential ingredient of the offense of selling liquor to a slave consists in the
want of the permission of the master, and such want of permission must be proven
to warrant a conviction.

The material allegations of the indictment, or those which charge the facts constituting the offense alleged, must in every case be sustained by sufficient proof.

Error to Hinds circuit court. Wᴀʟᴛᴇʀ, J.

C. Scott & D. W. Adams for plaintiff in error.

D. C. Glenn, attorney general.

[1] Wharton Am. Cr. Law, 1052, 1053; Wharton on Homicide, 254; Hawks, P. C.,
b. 2, c. 25, § 26; 1 Chitty Cr. Law, 178; 3 ib., 732; State v. Orrill, 1 Dev. 139; Commonwealth v. Linton, 2 Va. Cases, 205; Riley v. State, 9 Humph., 646; State v.
Foumer, 1 Chev., 106; Nash v. State, 2 Greene (Iowa), 286; Rex v. Burdett, 4 B. &
Ald., 95, 175; 2 Hawkins P. C., 302; 1 Stark C. P., 5, 6; Turner v. State, 28 Miss,
684; Riggs v. State, 26 Miss. 51; 1 Archbold Cr. Pr. & Pl., 892.

Smith, J. :

This was a conviction under the statute of 1842, prohibiting the sale of vinous or spirituous liquors to slaves, without the permission of the owner, master, or overseer.

It was proved on the trial, that the plaintiff in error, during the month of July, 1847, sold spirituous liquors to a slave, the property of Captain Garland. The only witness, who was examined, stated, that " he did not see or know of any permission which the said slave had from his owner, to purchase the liquor."

The case comes before us on several alleged errors committed by the court in granting and refusing the instructions, which were requested by the district attorney and the defendant. It will be unnecessary to notice all of these.

For the prosecution, amongst other instructions, the court charged, " that the permission of the master, owner, or overseer is a matter of exculpation of a positive nature ; and the failure of the defendant to introduce any proof of such permission will authorize the jury to infer, that there was no such permission."

When an offense has been proved to have been committed by an unknown person, the agency of a party in the commission of the offense charged, may sometimes be inferred from acts which in themselves are perfectly innocent and legal. Thus, where goods, proved to have been stolen, are found in the possession of the party charged with the theft, the possession, under certain circumstances, will raise a presumption of his guilt. In such a case, to avoid the consequences which the law attaches to this presumption, it would be incumbent on him to introduce explanatory or exculpatory evidence. But upon no principle of sound logic could the existence of an offense be inferred from the commission of an act to which the law has not attached the character of a crime. The instruction inverts this rule. The mere vending of spirituous liquor to a slave is no violation of this statute. It only becomes criminal, when done without the permission of the master, owner or overseer. The essential ingredient of the offense consists in the want of such permission. Hence the court manifestly erred in giving this instruction.

For the prisoner, the court was asked to charge, " that it was incumbent on the state to prove all of the material facts constituting the offense, as charged in the indictment, otherwise the jury will acquit the prisoner."

This instruction contains a plain legal proposition. We know of no exception to the rule, that whatever it is material to aver in an indictment, it is necessary to prove; that the material allegations of the indictment, or those which charge the facts and circumstances, which constitute the particular offense alleged, must be sustained by sufficient proof to authorize a conviction. On a trial for any offense, it is certainly material to instruct the jury in regard to the cardinal principles which should regulate their finding. In refusing this instruction the court also erred.

It is insisted by the attorney general, that although the court may have erred in the charges granted or withheld, yet, as the verdict is fully sustained by the evidence, it should not be disturbed. We have quoted above, the whole of the evidence, and the observations before made show that it was insufficient.

Let the judgment be reversed, and the cause remanded.

————

Moore *v.* The State, 13 Smedes & Marshall, 259.

Robbery.

An indictment is defective if the name of the prosecutor is not marked on it. Cody v. State, 3 How., 27; Peter v. State, ib., 433.

If an indictment is defective because the name of the prosecutor is not marked on, it is too late to remedy it by amendment after trial. The law of amendments does not apply to criminal cases.

Error to Adams circuit court. Willis, J.

Guion & Baine, and *Miles & Battaile*, for plaintiff in error, Cited, Cody v. State, 3 How., 27; ib., 433; and contended that a fatal defect in an indictment could not be cured by amendment.

D. C. Glenn, attorney general, Cited, Hutch. Code, 1005, § 65; 1 Chitty Cr. Law, 298.

Per Curiam:

The prisoner was found guilty on an indictment for robbery.

Two questions are presented by the record.   First, is an indictment defective, because the name of the prosecutor is not endorsed on it, according to the directions of the statute? and, Second, can such endorsement be made after verdict, and pending a motion in arrest of judgment?

The first question is settled by the decision of this court in two cases: Cody v. The State, 3 How., 27; Peter, a slave, v. The State, ib., 433.   In both of these cases the indictment was held to be defective, but the persons were remanded for further proceedings.

The second question is certainly clear.   If an indictment be defective, because the name of the prosecutor is not endorsed, it is too late to remedy the defect by amendment after trial.   The law of amendments does not apply to criminal cases.   The reason on which this statute is said to be founded would seem to require, that this endorsement should be made before the indictment goes to the grand jury.   It seems to constitute part of the duty of the district attorney in preparing the indictment.

Judgment reversed, and cause remanded to the circuit court for a new indictment.

HEWARD v. THE STATE, 13 Smedes & Marshall, 261.

HOMICIDE.

The statute of limitations declares, that no person shall be prosecuted, etc., for any offense, wilful murder, arson, forgery, counterfeiting, and larceny excepted, unless the indictment, presentment, or information for the same be found within one year next after the offense shall be committed.   An indictment for murder includes an indictment for manslaughter, and the statute will apply precisely as though the prisoner had been indicted for manslaughter.

A motion in arrest must be made on the grounds of defects appearing on the face of the record; the fact that the offense was committed twelve months before the finding of the indictment is no ground for such motion.

An instruction that charges the jury that if the offense did not amount to murder, but only to manslaughter, and was committed more than a year before the finding of the indictment, they must acquit the defendant, is correct, and should be given.

Error to Carroll circuit court.   ROGERS, J.
J. M. Duffield for plaintiff in error.
D. C. Glenn, attorney general.

PER CURIAM:

At the May term, 1849, of the circuit court of Carroll county, the prisoner was indicted for the murder of William T. Durham. The offense was charged in the indictment, as having been committed on the 22d of May, 1848, which was only two days before the finding of the indictment. The jury found the prisoner guilty of manslaughter in the third degree, and he thereupon moved in arrest of judgment, because the offense was committed twelve months before the finding of the indictment.

The statute of limitations declares that no person "shall be prosecuted, tried or punished for any offense, wilful murder, arson, forgery, counterfeiting and larceny excepted, unless the indictment, presentment or information for the same be found or exhibited within one year next after the offense shall be done or committed. Hutch. Code, 1004.[1] The form of the indictment being for murder, does not preclude the prisoner from the benefit of this statute. An indictment for murder embraces within itself an indictment for manslaughter, and the statute will apply precisely, as though the prisoner had been indicted for manslaughter alone.

But how is this objection to be brought up on a motion in arrest of judgment? Such a motion can only be sustained for matter apparent on the face of the record. If the offense be laid in the indictment more than twelve months before the time it is found, then perhaps, the objection might be reached by such a motion. The statute forbids prosecution, trial or punishment, and the court should not punish, if the defect appears upon the record. But it does not in this instance. The indictment lays the offense on the 22d of May, and it was found on the 24th of the same month. True, the bill of exceptions states, that it was in proof, that the offense was committed more than twelve months before the finding of the indictment; but

[1] The Revised Code of 1857, page 604, act 247, provides that, "No person shall be prosecuted for any offense, murder, manslaughter, arson, forgery, counterfeiting, robbery, larceny and rape excepted, and ... the prosecution for each offense shall be commenced within two years next after the commission thereof: *Provided*, That nothing herein contained shall be so construed, as to bar any prosecution against any person who shall abscond or flee from justice in this state, or shall absent himself from the jurisdiction of the court, or so conduct himself that he cannot be found by the officers of the law, or that process cannot be served upon him."

the bill of exceptions was taken to the overruling the motion ; the fact did not otherwise appear of record. The error of the court, on such a motion as this, must be apparent from what existed on the record when the decision was made, and not from what was placed on it afterwards.

The most that we can do is to award a new trial, because the court refused to charge the jury, that if the offense did not amount to murder, but only to manslaughter, and was committed more than a year before the finding of the indictment, they must acquit the defendant. The charge requested propounds the law correctly, and should have been given.

The statute contains a proviso, that its provisions shall not extend to any one who has fled or absconded, to avoid a prosecution ; but no question was raised on the exception. Perhaps it would have been incumbent on the state to bring up the exception, but in what manner this should be done we need not now decide.

Judgment reversed and cause remanded.

***

Anthony (a slave) *v.* The State, 13 Smedes & Marshall, 263.

Assault and Battery with Intent to Kill.

There is a plain distinction between express and implied malice ; the one is characterized by a sedate, deliberate intention and formed design, evidenced by external circumstances ; the other is the offspring of sudden impulse.

It is a general rule that all indictments upon statutes, especially the most penal, must state all the circumstances which constitute the definition of the offense in the act, so as to bring the defendant precisely within it. They must also pursue the precise and technical language employed in the statute in the description of the offense.

The evidence and the verdict must both be confined to the charge in the indictment, otherwise the administration of the law becomes uncertain, and the prisoner is deprived of the protection which a knowledge of the precise charge is calculated to throw around him.

Error to Lauderdale circuit court. Dawson, J.

No counsel is marked for plaintiff in error.

D. C. Glenn, attorney general.

Cited Hutch. Code, 521 ; 1 Chitty Cr. Law, 233.

CLAYTON, J.:

This was an indictment, under our statute, against the prisoner for an assault and battery upon a white person, with intent to kill. He was found guilty and sentence of death pronounced upon him; whence the case comes to this court.

The first statute which relates to this offense is very general, and declares it to consist of an assault and battery upon a white person, with intent to kill. Hutch. Code, 521, § 52. A subsequent statute is more definite, and, by way of amendment, enacts that this clause, when the killing does not actually occur, shall be so construed as to render the proof of malice aforethought express, necessary to subject the person therein named to capital punishment. Ibid, 532.

In this case the indictment charges the offense to have been committed " feloniously, wilfully and of his malice aforethought." It is objected in behalf of the prisoner, that sentence of death was improperly pronounced upon him, because the indictment does not charge the act to have been done with express malice.

There is a plain distinction between express and implied malice; the one is characterized by a sedate, deliberate intention and formed design, evidenced by external circumstances; the other is the offspring of sudden impulse. 1 Russell on Crimes, 387. It is only against offenses of the former description that the statute is directed.

It is a general rule that all indictments upon statutes, especially the most penal, must state all the circumstances which constitute the definition of the offense in the act, so as to bring the defendant precisely within it. They must, also, pursue the precise and technical language employed in the statute, in the definition or description of the offense. 1 Chitty, Crim. Law, 280–283. This rule was not followed in this case. The most material word in the constitution of the offense is omitted. If the defendant had pleaded guilty to this indictment, or filed a demurrer to it, sentence of death could not have been pronounced against him, because the statute itself directs, that where implied malice only is shown, the punishment shall be by stripes within a certain limit. Upon conviction by a jury, no greater punishment could be inflicted. The indictment contains no charge of that species of malice, which alone authorizes capital punishment.

The finding of express malice by the jury cannot vary this result. It is beyond the issue. No such matter was presented by the pleadings, and the verdict to that extent was unauthorized. The evidence and the verdict must both be confined to the charge in the indictment, otherwise the administration of the law becomes uncertain, and the prisoner is deprived of the protection which a knowledge of the precise charge is calculated to throw around him. He might be charged with one crime, and convicted of another wholly distinct and far more penal. The judgment must be reversed.

Our only hesitancy has been as to the course to be pursued after the reversal. An examination of the various statutes has led us to the conclusion, that the circuit court had jurisdiction of the less offense. How. & Hutch., 164, et seq., § 38, 43 and 46. The indictment was good to that extent. We therefore proceed to reverse the judgment, and to give the judgment which the court below should have given.

Bond *v.* The State, 13 Smedes & Marshall, 265.

Selling Liquor to Slaves.

Instructions granted for the state, not excepted to at the time they were given, nor made grounds for a new trial, will not be considered on error to the high court of errors and appeals.

If, from the evidence, the jury should be of opinion that permission is given to a slave by the master, mistress, owner, or overseer, to buy liquor, then the offense is not committed, though the permission is given to the slave and not to the sellers. But if they should be of opinion that permission was not given to buy, but that the slave was sent to ascertain and fix the fact that the defendant would sell without permission, and the sale took place under these circumstances, then the offense is consummated.

An employer's delivery of an article to a slave, and afterwards standing by to detect the offender who may trade with the slave, does not legalize the trading.

Error to Yazoo circuit court. Perry, J.

The opinion of the court contains a sufficient statement of the case.

[No counsel is marked for the plaintiff in error.]

D. C. Glenn, attorney for the state, argued the case orally.

SMITH, J.:

The plaintiff in error was convicted in the circuit court of Yazoo county, of the offense of selling spirituous liquor to a slave without the permission of the master or owner.

Exceptions were taken at the trial to the introduction of evidence offered in behalf of the prosecution. These, however appear to have been abandoned, as they have not been pressed upon the consideration of the court.

The instructions granted at the instance of the prosecuting attorney will not be noticed. They were not excepted to at the time, and have not been made a ground for the motion for a new trial, which was made in the court below and overruled. Hence, the only question which we have to consider of, is the propriety of the decision on the said motion.

The finding of the jury in this case, necessarily embraced two propositions: 1, That the defendant did in fact sell spirituous liquor to a slave. 2. That the sale was made without the permission of the master, owner, or overseer.

In reference to the first, we think the evidence was sufficient to warrant the conclusion drawn by the jury. The proofs were such as to leave no reasonable doubt on their minds that the liquor was furnished to the negroes by the defendant or delivered to them by his direction, in payment of the articles deposited at his house on the preceding night.

In regard to the second, the question is not so easily settled. In relation to this point, the testimony of Chew, the only witness for the prosecution, was, that this witness accompanied two of his negroes, late at night, to a place near the house of the defendant, the negroes taking with them peas and potatoes to sell to him. This was done by the permission of the witness. The articles were delivered to a negro woman in the employment of the defendant. This was done by the direction of a person in the house, who had been aroused by the negroes, and whom the witness, from his voice, believed to be the defendant. This person said to the negroes. "Leave your things, go away, and return in the morning or some other time, and I will settle with you." Witness with the negroes returned on the next morning, between daylight and sunrise; he saw the negroes enter the defendant's house and come out of it, after remaining a short time, bringing with them whisky and tobacco, which they had procured from some one in the house.

Here was a plan laid for the detection of the defendant, and the conclusion cannot be resisted, that in making the sale, he designed to violate the statute. The question, then, which we have to determine is, whether the permission given to the negroes to sell the articles, and the presence of the master during the transaction, which were unknown to the defendant, had the effect to legalize the sale; or, in other words, were the jury, from the proofs before them, authorized to find that the sale was made without the permission of the master, according to the proper construction of the statute?

This question, arising upon facts very similar to those above detailed, was presented to this court in the case of Jolly v. The State, 8 S. & M., 145. The proofs in that case showed that several persons, suspecting the defendant of a violation of the statute under which this conviction was had, went in the night near to his house, and sent a negro belonging to one of them with money and a jug and told him to get some whisky. The witnesses were concealed. The defendant sold the whisky to the negro. The court, in commenting upon these facts, remarked: " In this case the question arises, Was the permission given to the slave to buy, or was it merely an experiment to see if the defendant would sell without permission? In other words, was it not a plan to detect the defendant in a violation of the law, by seeing him sell spirituous liquor without a permission to the slave to buy? The true point is, whether the master was willing that the slave should buy the liquor of the defendant and gave him permission to do so. This point is for the determination of the jury. If, from the evidence, they should be of the opinion, that permission was given to the slave by the master, mistress, owner or overseer, to buy the liquor, then the offense is not committed, though the permission were given to the slave and not to the seller. But if they should be of opinion, that permission was not given to buy, but that the slave was sent to ascertain and fix the fact that the defendant would sell without permission, and the sale took place under these circumstances, then the offense was consummated."

The principle of this case is, that the permission given to buy the liquor, though given to the slave and not the vendor, will legalize the sale; but that the mere presence of the master, mistress, owner or overseer, and their knowledge, or witnessing the transaction, will not have that effect. In the case under examination, the permission was to sell the articles which the slaves had in their possession to the defendant, and not to receive in payment whisky, money, or any other specific commodity. It cannot, therefore, be said that permission was given to buy the liquor.

In the case of The State v. Anone, 2 Nott & McCord, 27. cited by this court in Jolly's case, a broader and more comprehensive construction was given to a statute similar to this. The witness, upon whose testimony Anone was convicted, was the overseer of the slave. He had given corn to the negro and had sent him to Anone's store for the purpose of detecting him in trading illegally. He witnessed the transaction, but did not interfere or forbid the trade. These facts were held to be no justification or excuse. The court said, "It has long since been decided that an employer's delivery of an article to a slave, and afterwards standing by for the purpose of detecting an offender who may trade with the slave, does not legalize the trading." The decision in that case rests on the ground, that the permission intended by the statute was, where the master or owner in reality designed to allow his slave to trade, and for the ordinary purposes of such trafic, and not where the object is merely to detect an offender against the law.

In the construction which the courts of South Carolina have given to the statute, the illegal intention of the purchaser or vendor is made the principal subject of consideration. The delivery of an article by the master to his slave, to be sold for the purpose of detecting the vendor, and his presence at the sale, is held to be no excuse to the purchaser, unless, by some intimation given by the master, the vendor may fairly infer his assent.

In cases similar to the one under examination, it is obvious that the delinquent can never claim exemption on the ground of the innocency of his intentions.   No one can be convicted upon this construction unless he shall have at least designed to violate the statute.   There is, therefore, no objection on the ground that it would operate oppressively, and the manifest policy of this interpretation commends it strongly to the favorable consideration of our courts.   But whether we test the finding of the jury in this case by the principle recognized in Jolly v. The State, or by the law as laid down in the case cited from Nott v. McCord, we cannot say that it was unauthorized by the evidence.   We therefore affirm the judgment.

SEAL *v.* THE STATE, 13 Smedes & Marshall, 286.

GAMING.

The laws against gaming will not need a strict construction, for the reason that they are remedial and not penal; hence, reasonable certainty is all that the law requires in regard to this offense.

If the contrary does not fully appear from the record, it will be presumed that the grand jury who found the indictment was legally constituted.

The proper manner to take advantage of a defective indictment is by a plea in abatement.

Where the record states that the proceedings took place "in the circuit court of Harrison county, at a regular term thereof begun and held at the court-house of said county in Mississippi city, on the first Monday in March, 1848," it is sufficient.

If a defendant knows of a want of qualification of a juror at the time he is sworn, he waives all objection by failing to challenge him at that time.   If he does not know it, he should make an affidavit of the fact on his application for a new trial.

Error to Harrison circuit court.   HARRIS, J.

The plaintiff in error was indicted in the court below for gaming, and was found guilty.   The other facts of the case fully appear in the opinion of the court.

R. Seal, in proper person.

Cited Carpenter v. State, 4 How. 168; H. & H., 490; 5 How., 32; 8 S. & M., 297.

D. C. Glenn, attorney general,

Cited 1 Chitty Cr. Law, 388; 8 How. R., 28; S. & M., 598; State v. Friar, 3 How. R., 422.

Clayton, J.:

This was an indictment in the circuit court of Harriso
county for gaming.

The defendant moved to quash the indictment, because it di
not affirmatively appear by the indictment or its caption tha
the grand jury was properly constituted.

Secondly, because the indictment does not sufficiently describ
the term of the court, or the house in which the court wa
holden.

We may set out with the remark, that the statute provide
that all laws against gaming are remedial and not penal; hence
a strict construction will not be applied.

The first objection taken is, that " neither the caption nor the
indictment shows with sufficient certainty that the grand jurors
were selected and chosen from the county of Harrison." The
statement in the caption in this particular is as follows: " The
venire being returned into court, executed by the sheriff, the
following jurors appeared and answered to their names, to wit,
etc. Whereupon the following named persons of the same were
duly drawn, elected and empanelled, sworn and charged as a
grand jury for the term."

In the case of Carpenter v. The State, 4 How., 168, which is
relied on in support of the objection, the record states " the grand
jurors of the State of Mississippi, duly empanelled, charged and
sworn, returned into court," etc. It was held that this might
be true, and yet the grand jury might not have been selected from
the proper county.

The law requires the assessor, once in every year, to return
to the circuit court a list of the freeholders and householders,
citizens of the United States, within his county, who are liable
to serve as jurors. From this list, the jurors are drawn by lot,
either before the circuit court or the probate court, and a
venire then issues, containing the names so drawn. From those
thus summoned, the grand jurors are selected by lot. Hutch.
Dig., 886; McQuillen v. The State, 8 S. & M., 597.

Reasonable certainty in the proceedings is all that the law
requires in regard to the offense of gaming; there is, at least,
that degree of certainty in this case, that the indictment was

found by good and lawful jurors of the county. The *venire*, the service and return by the sheriff of that county, their being empanelled and sworn from the *venire*, exclude all reasonable doubt as to the proper constitution of the jury. These circumstances certainly authorize a presumption in its favor until something improper be shown.

In those cases in this court in which bills of indictment have been quashed on account of objections to some of the grand jury, the want of qualifications in the jurors has been pointed out and made apparent by plea in abatement. McQuillen v. The State, 8 S. & M., 587; Barney v. The State, 12 ib., 72; Kincaid v. The State, M S. Had there been, in fact, any objecttion to the grand jury in this case, it is not unreasonable to suppose that it would have been shown in that mode.

The next objection is, that the indictment does not sufficiently describe the term of the court, or the house in which the court was holden. The record states in its caption that the proceedings took place " in the circuit court of Harrison county, at a regular term thereof, begun and held at the court-house of said county in Mississippi city, on the first Monday in March, 1848." This description is entirely sufficient, and it would be difficult to make it more specific without unnecessary prolixity.

An application was made for a new trial, because one of the jurors who tried the case was an alien. The affidavit of the juror to that effect was read to the court; but there was no affidavit of the defendant that he was ignorant of the fact when the juror was sworn. If the defendant knew of this want of qualification of the juror at the time he was sworn, he waived all objection by failing to challenge him at that time. If he did not know it, he should have made affidavit of that fact, in aid of his application for a new trial. Booby v. The State, 4 Yerg., 112.

How far a failure to make inquiry as to a juror's competency, at the time he is presented, may operate as a waiver of objection, we need not now inquire.

The judgment is affirmed.

BOLES *v.* THE STATE, 13 Smedes & Marshall, 398.

MURDER.

Where the court, without the consent of the parties interested, **excuses a competent juror** on account of the sickness of his wife, it is an **unwarrantable exercise of** power by the court, and sufficient grounds for a new trial.

Where a person who was not a sworn officer, is allowed to go **into the jury-room** during the trial, or after the jury have retired to consider their **verdict, it is a good** reason for a new trial.

When a jury is shown to have been *exposed* to improper influence, **it is sufficient;** and it is unnecessary to show that improper influence was exercised.

Error to Hinds circuit court. COALTER, J.

The plaintiff in error was tried and convicted **of murder for** the second time, and his case was once before in this court, **and** was reversed and remanded to the court below. See **9 S. & M.,** 284. The opinion of the court contains a sufficient **statement** of the case.

A. R. Johnston, for plaintiff in error.

1. On the discharge of the juror, cited Hutch. Code, 1007, art. 7, § 1.

2. As to the conduct of the jury, cited Hare v. State, 4 How., 187; Commonwealth v. Robes, 12 Pick., 496, Commonwealth v. McCaul, 1 Va. Cases, 271; McLain v. State, 10 Yerg., 241; Knight v. Inhabitants of Freeport, 13 Mass. R., 218; Perkins v. Knight, 2 N. H., 474; People v. Douglass, 4 Cow., 26; Brant v. Fowler, 7 Cow., 562; McCann v. State, 9 S. & M. 465; McQuillen v. State, 8 ib., 596.

S. A. D. Greaves, on same side,

1. On the first point, cited Rawls v. State, 8 S. & M., 599; State v. Shaw, 3 Iredell, 532.

2. On the second point, cited Nelms v. State, supra; Const. of Miss., art. 7, § 1.

D. C. Glenn, attorney general.

1. There have been two concurring verdicts of **guilty in this** case. See v S. & M., 284; 5 B. Monroe, 20; 1 S. & M. 412. As to the propriety of new trial generally in the case, see Jones v. State, 1 Kelly, 618; Patteson v. Ford, 2 Grattan, 24, 25; Weinzorpflin v. State, 7 Blackf., 198.

2. As to irregularities of the jury as grounds of new trial, see 5 Missouri, 525 : 11 Leigh, 683, 714 ; 4 Humph., 27 ; 10 Yerg., 529 ; 5 Iredell, 58 ; 12 Pick., 496 ; 3 Bibb., 8 ; 7 S. & M., 45.

3. The excusing and discharge of the special *venire* by the judge for proper reasons, as shown, is no error. It was an exercise of a discretion which judges are bound to use.

Sharkey, C. J. :

The prisoner was indicted and found guilty of the murder of one Donaho. A motion was made for a new trial for the following reasons : 1st. Because the verdict of the jury is contrary to law and evidence ; 2d. That the court improperly released and dismissed two of the jurors who had been summoned under the special *venire*, against the consent and remonstrance of the prisoner ; and 3d. Persons, not of the jury, were permitted to visit and mingle with the jury, after the cause had been submitted to them and they had retired to consider of their verdict. We shall confine our remarks to the second and third reasons assigned for a new trial.

A bill of exceptions, taken during the progress of the trial, shows this state of facts : In making up the jury, the name of Jesse D. Granberry was regularly reached on the list of jurors summoned. The juror was examined (on his *voir dire*, as we must suppose), and stated that he had not formed or expressed an opinion as to the guilt or innocence of the accused, and entertained no conscientious scruples as to the punishment of death for murder. The juror stated to the court that his wife was confined to her bed by sickness, and a physician had been called in to attend her, for which reason he desired to be excused. The counsel for the prisoner objected, and the district attorney also refused his assent, but the court, notwithstanding, excused the juror from serving.

There can be no justification for such an exercise of power. A list of the *venire* is to be furnished the prisoner two entire days before the trial. This is to give him an opportunity of selecting a jury from the list furnished. A prisoner has not a right to be tried by such a jury as he might select from the body of the county, but he has a right to make his selection from the list furnished him, as far as it is practicable for him to do so by exercising the right of challenge for cause, or his right of peremptory challenge. When he can no longer challenge, he must take them as they stand upon the list. And when a juror is tendered, the prisoner has a right to him, if he is competent; the court cannot set him aside without a cause which goes to his competency as a juror. Granberry was tendered to the prisoner, for so we must understand the bill of exceptions, as he could not have been examined without being tendered. He was found competent as a juror, and the prisoner was anxious to take him. He had a right to have him, of which he could not be deprived by the court under the circumstances. It is very probable the court might properly set aside a juror who was physically or mentally incompetent, but there was no such emergency in the present case. The juror merely desired to be excused because of the sickness of his wife. He did not even say that his presence at home was necessary. Doubtless it was not, or he would not have been in attendance. Even if a proper excuse would have justified the discharge of the juror, this was not of that character.

On the next point, the material facts are that the jury were placed in charge of an officer, who took them to the jury-room in the court-house. By agreement of the prisoner, they were afterwards taken to the Oak Tree Hotel, where they could get refreshment, and there to be kept until they could agree. At the hotel they were taken to the public table, where they ate with the boarders, being seated at one end of the table, with the officers between them and the guests. Rooms were provided for them at the hotel, and at their request a barber was sent for to shave some of them, and cut their hair. The barber was in the room more than an hour, and whilst there, another deputy sheriff called the officer, having charge of the jury, out of the room; he left it, closing the door behind him, and conversed with the other deputy. He left the jury-room for a few minutes, and during his absence, left the jury in charge of the other deputy. There was no evidence of tampering, either by the barber or by the guests at table; on the contrary, the officer stated that he heard no one speak to them on the subject of trial, though the barber might have done so by whispering, or he might have conveyed written communications to them. On this state of facts, it is sufficient to refer to Hare's Case, 4 How., 187,[1] as decisive of this case. But it has been argued, that the verdict should stand, unless tampering or improper influences be shown. This would be a very unsafe rule. The prisoner, who is in confinement, would not be able, one time in a hundred, to show that a verdict had been procured by improper means, although such may have been the case. The rule of the common law is, where the jurors depart from the bar, a bailiff must be sworn to keep them together, and not suffer any one to speak with them. This is a plain, practical and safe rule. It cannot be mistaken, and is easily followed. Any departure from it is a violation, and leads to confusion and difficulty, in which there is no rule of law to guide us. Each departure may make a new case for the discretion of the court, for, when there has been a departure from the given rule, the verdict must depend upon the discretion of the court. Can the court rule that it is no harm for one person to be with the jury? The law does not say so, and if one may be there, perhaps, in the opinion of the court, two would do no mischief. Then again, if a stranger may be with the jury a few

---

[1] Commonwealth v. Roby, 12 Pick., 496; Commonwealth v. McCall, 1 Va. Cases, 271; McLain v. State, 10 Yerg., 241; 13 Mass., 218; Perkins v. Knight, 2 N. H., 474; People v. Douglass, 4 Cow., 26; Brant v. Fowler, 7 Cow., 562; McCann v. State, 9 S. & M., 465; McQuillen, v. State, 8 ib., 506; Eastwood v. People, 3 Park., 25; Lewis v. State, 9 S. & M., 115; People v. Hartung, 4 Park., 265; Nelms v. State, 13 S. & M., 500; 4 How., 187; 10 Yerg., 141; Wesley v. State, 11 Humph., 502; Wiley v. State, 256; 7 Cow., 562; 12 Pick., 496; 1 Va. Cases, 271; 13 Mass., 220; Pope & Jacobs v. State, 36 Miss., 121; Organ v. State, 26 Miss., 83; Caleb v. State, 39 Miss., 721; Overbee v. Com., 1 Rob., 756; Cornelius v. State, 7 Eng. (Ark.), 782; Hines v. State, 8 Humph., 597; Riley v. State, 9 Humph., 644; Luster v. State, 11 Humph., 169; State v. Prescott, 7 N. H., 287; State v. Fox, 1 Ga. Decisions, 35; State v. Peter, ib., 46; Commonwealth v. Wormley, 8 Gratt., 712; Farren v. State, Warden, 54; Peiffer v. Commonwealth, 15 Penn. State; Wharton Am. Cr. Law, 3111, *et seq.;* ib., 573, 591; Co. Lit., 227; Bac. Abr. Juries, G.; Cochran, 7 Humph., 544; State v. Populus, 12 La. An., 710; Browning v. State, 33 Miss., 48; State v. Hornsby, 8 La. Ann., 554; State v. Crosby, 4 Rob., 434; State v. O'Conner, 5 La. Ann., 398; Archbold's Cr. Pr. & Pl., 633. In the cases here cited, the courts hold that it is only necessary that by the separation of the jury they were *exposed* to improper influences, while in Vermont, Connecticut, New York, North Carolina and Missouri, it is incumbent on the prisoner to show something more than the mere separation of the jury, to set aside the verdict. State v. Camp., 23 Vermont, 551; State v. Babcock, 1 Conn., 401; State v. Miller, 1 Dev. & Batt., 500; Wiatt v. State, 1 Blackf., 25; State v. Barton, 19 Mo., 227; State v. Harlow, 21 Mo., 446; State v. Igo, 21 Mo., 469; State v. Whitney, 8 Mo., 165. See also Com. v. State, 3 Texas, 31.

minutes or an hour, the court must settle a question of time. How long may he be with them without vitiating the verdict? There is no rule of law by which these things can be determined. If the common law rule be followed, there is certainty, but if not, there is uncertainty. And if a prisoner must show that the verdict is vicious, it is needless to pretend to hold to the forms of law, it may be made up in the street or in the court-yard, and it is good. The case of Hare received deliberate consideration, and is believed to propound the law correctly.

Let the judgment be reversed, and the cause remanded.

KIRK *v.* STATE, 13 Smedes & Marshall, 407.

NEGRO STEALING.

The neglect to mark on the indictment the name of the prosecutor, is a fatal objection.

Every error which would be fatal on demurrer, or in arrest of judgment, will be sufficient to procure a reversal.

Wills, after probate, are required to remain in the court of probates, and an authenticated copy is made evidence in all the courts of this state.

Error to Panola circuit court. ROGERS, J.

The facts of the case will be found in the opinion of the court.

F. Anderson, for plaintiff in error.

Insisted that there were fatal defects in the record, which he pointed out; and among others, no prosecutor is marked on the indictment.

D. C. Glenn, attorney general.

CLAYTON, J.:

This was an indictment in the circuit court of Panola, for negro stealing. Upon the trial, the defendant was found guilty, and sentenced to confinement in the penitentiary for ten years. A motion was made for a new trial, which was overruled, and the case thence comes to this court.

One only, of the errors assigned, is sufficient to reverse the judgment. There is no prosecutor marked upon the indictment.

According to several decisions of this court, that is a fatal objection. Moore v. The State, ante, 259.

The only question as to this was, whether, in a case in which the writ of error was sued out to the refusal to grant a new trial, the objection could be taken in that stage of the proceedings. It would appear to have been thus taken in the case of Cody v. The State, 3 How., 27. And as the statutes of jeofails and amendments do not extend to criminal proceedings, it follows, that every error which would have been fatal on demurrer, or in arrest of the judgment, will be sufficient to procure its reversal. 1 Ch. Crim. Law, 751. The judgment must be reversed, and the indictment quashed, and the prisoner remanded to the county of Panola for a new indictment.

An objection was taken to the admission of a certain will in testimony upon the trial, which it may be important now to determine, as the point will probably arise on the next trial again. The objection is, that the will was admitted to probate upon insufficient testimony, and that the original should have been produced, or its absence accounted for, before the copy could be read.

Both these objections are conclusively disposed of by the statutes. One witness is sufficient to a will of personalty. Hutch. Code, 649. Wills, after probate, are required to remain in the court of probates, and an authenticated copy is made evidence in all the courts of the state. Ib., 650.

Judgment reversed.

CAIN *v.* THE STATE, 13 Smedes & Marshall, 456.

BETTING ON AN ELECTION.

The statute which requires the clerk to put down the charges given or refused, and make them a part of the record, does not apply to criminal cases, except they are embodied in the bill of exceptions.

The time for the presidential election is fixed by law, and is therefore sufficiently certain, and need not be averred in the indictment.

Where the parties agreed that a present of a coat should be made to the defendant in the event of a certain result of the election, but if otherwise, the defendant was to make a present of a coat to the other party, and it was in proof that the election was held and the bet paid in money, it was a mere evasion, and is sufficient to justify a verdict of guilty against the defendant.

Error to Franklin circuit court. POSEY, J.

Dempsey B. Cain was indicted, for betting on an election, in the court below; the indictment contained two counts. On the first there was a verdict of acquittal; on the second, which charged that the defendant, "on the 1st day of October, 1848, did bet a certain valuable thing, to wit, a certain fine coat, upon the result of a certain election to be holden on the 7th day of November, A.D. 1848, (according to law,) in the State of Mississippi, for six electors for said state to vote for a president and vice-president of the United States of America," he was found guilty.

The substance of the testimony adduced on the trial is as follows:

Willis Byrd testified that he and the defendant did not bet on the result of the election of six electors, but that he promised, in the county of Franklin, on the day charged in the indictment, to make a present to the defendant of a nine or ten dollar coat if Cass got two thousand more votes than Taylor, and if Cass did not get that majority, defendant was to make a present of a nine or ten dollar coat to witness; that he voted for six electors, and that there was an election at which the electors were voted for at Jones's Precinct, where he voted; that Cass and Taylor were candidates for president, and the persons for whom the six electors to be elected were expected to vote; that there was nothing up in the hands of the stake-holder at the time, and that defendant afterwards, in Adams county, paid him nine dollars; that this was in lieu of the present he expected to receive, on account of it being conceded that Cass did not get two thousand votes in the State of Mississippi more than Taylor. The way it was determined who had the present to pay, was by knowing the majority received by the electors in the state; and there was a dispute about the amount of the present.

The state then introduced a writ of election, directed to the sheriff of that county, directing him to hold an election of six electors for president and vice-president, and proved by the sheriff that an election was held on the day mentioned in the indictment.

The court gave certain instructions for the state and refused those asked by the prisoner; but the instructions were not embodied in the bill of exceptions, though copied by the clerk into the record.

The defendant moved the court for an arrest of judgment because the indictment did not charge that the election had been holden. This motion was overruled. He then moved for a new trial, which was also overruled. The court fined him twenty dollars and costs, when he sued out this writ of error.

Cassidy & Sanders, for plaintiff in error,

Cited Hutch. Code, 951, 953; 1 Chitty Cr. Law, 662; 4 Black. Com. 325; 3 Burr, 901; 1 East, 146; Foster, 194; 3 Inst., 41; 2 M. & S. 386; 2 Leach, 594; 1 Chitty Cr. Law, 382, 114.

D. C. Glenn, attorney general.

Insisted that the indictment was sufficiently certain, and the proof conclusive of guilt.

PER CURIAM.

The plaintiff in error was indicted for betting on the election of 1848, for electors for president and vice-president. Several reasons are urged for the reversal of the judgment, which we cannot notice. The statute which requires the clerk to take down the charges given or refused, and make them a part of the record, without bill of exceptions, does not apply to criminal cases. We therefore pass over the alleged error in this particular.

A motion was made in arrest of judgment, because the indictment does not charge that the election was holden. The indictment charges, that the bet was "upon the result of a certain election to be holden on the seventh day of November, in the year of our Lord one thousand eight hundred and forty-eight, according to law in said state, for six electors," etc. The election is provided for and directed to be holden by a public law. The event was therefore sufficiently certain, and it was not necessary to charge that it had occurred. The statute on which the indictment is founded, is declared to be a remedial, and not a penal statute. The object of this provision must have been to get rid of the general rule, which requires that penal statutes should be construed strictly.

A new trial was moved for on the evidence. It was in proof, that the parties mutually agreed that a present of a coat should be made to the defendant, if the Cass electors obtained a majority of two thousand votes, but if they did not, the defendant was to make the other party a present of a coat. This was mere evasion. It was in proof that the election was afterwards holden, and the bet was paid in money. There is no pretence for holding the verdict to be against law or evidence.

Judgment affirmed.

Brantley v. The State, 13 Smedes & Marshall, 468.

Assault with Intent to Kill.

Under the statute, Hutch. Code, 963, § 22, upon an indictment for an offense consisting of different degrees, the jury may find the defendant not guilty of the offense charged, but guilty of an inferior degree of such offense, and such a conviction will be a bar to another indictment for the same offense.

An indictment, charging in one count an assault with intent to kill, and a second count charges an assault and battery, is good, and the jury may acquit the accused as to the first count, and find him guilty as to the second.

When no exceptions are taken in the court below to the grand jury, the prisoner cannot, after plea of not guilty, and conviction, for any defects in that body, be entitled to a new trial in the high court of errors and appeals.

Error to Yalobusha circuit court. Rogers, J.

James R. and William Brantley were indicted in the court below for an assault with intent to kill one Jefferson Russell Trible, in the first count of the indictment, and in the second for an assault and battery upon the said Trible.

The defendants demurred to the first count, and the demurrer was overruled. A trial was had on the plea of not guilty, and a verdict of not guilty as to the first count, and guilty on the second, was brought in by the jury. A motion for a new trial was made and overruled. The court fined them one hundred dollars each, and they sued out a writ of error and bring their case to this court.

Acee, for plaintiffs in error,

Cited Hutch. Code, 960, § 33; Hilderbrand v. State, 5 Mo. R., 548.

D. C. Glenn, attorney general.

CLAYTON, J. :

This was a bill of indictment preferred in the circuit court of Yalobusha county, against the defendants. It contains two counts, the first of which charges them with an assault and battery, with intent to murder; the second, with an assault and battery only. There was a demurrer to the indictment, which was overruled. The defendants were then tried, acquitted upon the first count, and found guilty upon the second.

It is insisted, that this joinder of counts is error, for which the judgment should be reversed. There seems to have been some want of uniformity in the decision on this point at the common law, and in the different states of the Union. See 1 Chit. Cr. Law, 250, and notes. But, in this state, there is a statute which clearly governs the case. Hutch. Code, 983, § 22. But, at common law, such an objection could not have been made available, either upon demurrer, or in arrest of judgment, but only upon a motion to quash, or to compel the prosecutor to elect on which count he would proceed. Chitty, 248.

By the statute referred to, it is provided, "that upon an indictment for an offense consisting of different degrees, the jury may find the defendant not guilty of the offense charged, but guilty of an inferior degree of such offense, and such conviction shall be a bar to any other indictment for any degree of the same offense." § 22 and 23. If, for example, there had been but the first count in this indictment, the jury might have found the defendant not guilty of the assault with intent to kill, but guilty of the assault and battery. The second count can do no harm, because, although the jury found upon it, they only found what they might have done, under the statute, without such count. At most it was but surplusage, and ought not to be allowed to vitiate. But we think there is now no impropriety in the joinder.

The other objections made to the indictment are not available, especially as they are directed against the first count, and the defendants were acquitted upon that, and found guilty on the second.

No exceptions were taken to the grand jury in the court below, either by plea or otherwise. We cannot in this court, after a plea of not guilty and trial without objection, go back to look for defects in the organization of that body.

The evidence in the case is rather of an unsatisfactory character. It shows that some suspicion was cast upon the principal witness for the prosecution. But the jury gave him credit, and it is not our province to say they did wrong in this respect.

The judgment is affirmed.

McCann v. The State, 13 Smedes & Marshall, 471.

Murder.

Circumstantial evidence has been received in every age of the common law, and it may rise so high in the scale of belief as to generate full conviction. When after due caution this result is reached, the law authorizes its ministers to act upon it.

What circumstances will amount to proof, can never be matter of general definition; the legal test is the sufficiency of evidence to satisfy the understanding and conscience of the jury. It is sufficient if they produce moral certainty, to the exclusion of every doubt; even direct and positive testimony does not afford grounds of belief of a higher and superior nature.

In cases depending upon circumstantial evidence, a number of links often concur in forming the chain. It cannot be said what bounds are to circumscribe the inquiry. All which may tend to elucidate the transaction should be admitted.

A jury may believe that part of a confession which charges the prisoner, and reject that part which is in his favor, if they see sufficient grounds for so doing.

The union and concurrence of various detached circumstances may produce full conviction, when either of them standing alone might leave room for much doubt.

An objection taken to an indictment, because it charges the offense as at common law, whilst the punishment is inflicted by statute, cannot prevail.

Error to Lowndes circuit court. Rogers, J.

At the September term, 1848, of the court below, the grand jury returned into court, through their foreman, an indictment against James McCann, for murder, and John F. Toland for being accessory to the murder of Andrew Toland.

The indictment contained two counts. The first against McCann, charging him with the murder of Andrew Toland by shooting him with a pistol on the back of the head, on the 1st day of April, 1847. It is in the common law form, and concludes, "against the peace," &c.

The second count charges John F. Toland as accessory before the fact.

McCann was arraigned at the same term of the court, and pleaded not guilty; and it was ordered that Toland be tried separately, on his motion.

At the March term, 1849, the defendant was tried, and the following is the evidence adduced on the trial:

James J. Toland, a witness for the state, deposed, that on the 14th of April, 1845, on Monday night, in Lowndes county, Andrew Toland was killed; the body was found on Tuesday morning; he saw the body, ten or twelve feet from the road, the left foot over the right one; he was lying on his back; from his eyes down all his face was gone; his head was connected with the body by the skin on the back part of his neck; all the face bones and neck bones were gone; all the brains eaten out of the skull by the hogs; the hogs were eating the body when found; knew it was the body of Andrew Toland from the clothing and the bones of his feet; deceased was his uncle; the body was found about eleven miles from Columbus, near Profitsfield, on the right of the Gilmer road, near Cross' lane, some two or three hundred yards from the mouth of the lane, in a thicket of bushes. Witness was acquainted with the Gilmer road; it leaves the Robinson road beyond Westport; Whitfield's plantation is on it, four miles from Columbus; Mills' house is to the left of the road, seven or eight miles, and Gilmer's plantation to the right, ten miles from Columbus; Cross' plantation is to the right, and Profit's on the left side of the road; McGowan's is on the same road, twelve miles from Columbus; Lyon resides west of the road, about a mile from the Gilmer road. The McCann road intersects the Gilmer road at the corner of McGowan's field; there is a road running off from the Gilmer road, just this side of where the body was found, towards McCann's, by Lyon and Smith's lane, and a path turns off at the corner of Smith's field through the woods, which leads into the McCann road, which leads to McCann's house. A map of the road was shown to witness (which was copied in the record), and he proved its correctness. Newsom lived about a quarter of a mile from Mills', to the left of the road, and a thick wood was between the house and road; woods all the way from Gilmer's to where the body was found, and about three hundred yards beyond to Cross' lane, from that and on to McGowan's lane, about a mile; about one and a half miles to where Toland lived; near where the body was found, there was the mark of a ball on the sapling six feet from the ground; the ball struck the sapling diagonally from the road; knocked the bark off and fell to the ground. Hamilton's lane is six miles from Columbus, Rowland's over six miles; it is three quarters of a mile from Gilmer's to where the body was found. Witness knew the body and helped to lay it out, and has never seen Andrew Toland since. The face was entirely gone, and there was a wound in the back of the neck; it looked like a slit three quarters of an inch long, when the skin was stretched, but when the skin was put its natural position it looked like a hole; he thought it was a bullet hole; his hat was powder-burnt and had blood on it; there was plenty of blood under his head, in his clothes, and on the ground. No other wounds were on the body except where the hogs had broken the skin on his fingers. The soil was red potash land. There was a saddle on the ground with blood on the right stirrup leather. Witness thought that single ball would not carry away all the face, but that the hogs had eaten it; the hogs could not have made the wound in the back of the neck, they could not have gotten to it to make it. He saw no bones that the hogs had chewed; don't think that a ball could have blown the face away; he thought a musket loaded with twenty or thirty-buck-shot could have done it. The skull was sound above the eyes, and the head was held on the body by the skin of the back of the neck; a good many persons were on the ground when witness got there; he left home about twelve o'clock. He said further that a part of the skull bone on the right side was detached.

John P. Krecker testified, that he saw McCann, the prisoner, Frank Toland, an Irishman named Kinch, and another by the name of Mallory, eight or ten days before the murder, on the

Columbus bridge, in conversation together, some twenty or thirty feet on the bridge. Kinch was leading a horse; witness did not hear the conversation between them. McCann had his back towards witness; he put his hand in his pocket, and when he saw witness looking at him, he pulled some papers out of his pocket and put them into another pocket, again put his hand into his pocket, and pulled out something, and turned his back on witness; he saw Frank Toland take something out of his pocket like a powder gourd, put it to his mouth and pulled out the stopper, and poured something into McCann's hand; supposed it was powder; he thought their actions strange. The bridge was a retired place; they stood about there some twenty or thirty minutes. Witness was bridge keeper, and called to them to pay the toll. Kinch and Mallory passed on over, and Toland and McCann returned and paid toll. Witness saw and knew McCann four or five days afterwards; did n't know every one that crossed the bridge; he has often seen men pour powder out of a gourd into their own hands, but never into another's. The gourd was about the size of an orange. The singularity of their conduct attracted his attention. He said it was unusual for persons to act as they did.

Samuel T. Sappington testified that between nine and twelve o'clock on the day that Andrew Toland was said to have been murdered, Toland and McCann came to his grocery, and remained until about three o'clock in the afternoon. They were a great part of the time in a billiard room up stairs in a conversation together, at that time the billiard room being a private place. About one o'clock a young man by the name of Bird invited them to dine with them at Mr. Fletchall's. Toland at first refused to go, because he said his father was in town, but afterwards went. Witness did not know what they were doing up stairs; they appeared to be transacting business; they were very friendly, and frequently visited his house. Witness saw a pistol in his grocery that day or a day or two before; didn't know who left it; neither of the two shown was the one.

E. B. Gaston testified that he saw the prisoner with Frank Toland, the day before the news of the death of Andrew Toland reached town, near Sappington's, in an alley between the drug store of Lineeum and the cabinet shop, some ten or twelve feet from the street; saw them from his store through the window. From their gesticulations, witness thought they were quarrelling, and came to his door to see, and found them very friendly, with their arms around each other's necks.

Henry Sullivan testified that he was ferryman at Columbus. On the day of the murder McCann crossed the ferry going home, about two hours by sun. Andrew Toland, the deceased, crossed about one hour by sun, and Frank Toland when the sun was some twenty minutes high, or about sunset. Witness does not recollect all who crossed the ferry that day; Mr. Mize and several others crossed. He recollects about old Mr. Toland, Frank Toland, and McCann crossing, it being called to his mind so soon afterwards. Mr. Toland spoke to him about it, and he expected to be called to testify about it; didn't recollect whether McGowan's wagon crossed that day, nor all who crossed, it is so long ago: McCann, J. F. Toland, and Andrew Toland crossed the river, going in the direction of the Gilmer road.

Sanditer testified that he was in Columbus the day the old man was killed; was riding along the Gilmer road with Riddle, when McCann overtook them at Whitfield's lane, and rode with them some three or four miles; they stopped at Mills' and got water; saw deceased near Rowland's, riding behind a wagon; after riding about a quarter of a mile from Mills', McCann turned off about dark to go down to Newsom's; he overtook them about sundown; witness and Riddle kept the Gilmer road, and went some five or six miles beyond Prairie Hill; all passed the wagon together about seven miles from Columbus; McCann drank water at Mills'; from Mills' to Newsom's is some two or three hundred yards; they rode pretty much together, sometimes scattering; McCann was a little ahead when they parted; Newsom's is about one hundred yards from the road, with woods between the road and the house; don't think McCann said anything about supper. About a mile from Newsom's, at Gilmer's gate, a man passed them at full gallop; he was dressed in black, and had a cap on. Witness didn't recollect anybody being with old Mr. Toland when they passed him; he was riding just behind the wagon; they crossed the ferry when the sun was an hour or an hour and a half high; no other white person overtook them that night after they passed the gate.

Riddle testified that he thought it was in the spring of 1845; a gentleman rode up to them some three or four miles from Columbus; said his name was McCann; they rode on together to Mills' and got water; went on together to Newsom's, where McCann said he was going to get supper, and asked witness if he would go down and get some, too; he saw old Mr. Toland at Hambleton's gate; there were several of them together; witness left town about an hour by sun; McCann overtook him where the sandy land meets the prairie, and they rode on to Newsom's together; they rode some four or five miles an hour; he thought old Mr. Toland rode not half so fast, that he was traveling slow behind a wagon; McCann told his name when he came up; he had whiskers and wore a black hat. After McCann left them, a man rode by them very fast; he was a small man with a cap on; they passed old Mr. Toland's house that night as they went on, but saw no horse standing in the yard.

Robert Profit testified that he saw old Mr. Toland on the morning of the day of the murder; he met him in the road coming from Columbus, riding a small sorrel sway-back mare; he stooped considerably and rode in that way; he heard the report of a gun or rifle an hour or a half an hour after dark, in the direction his body was found; it is nearly half of a mile from witness' house to the place; he met deceased at the northwestern corner of witness' field, and about half a mile behind him met McCann, coming toward Columbus; first saw McCann in the narrow lane between Cross' and McGowan's; they passed the residence of the deceased that morning, but did not stop; before they got to the house they saw Frank Toland and his mother standing in the yard in apparently close conversation; when he rode opposite the house they parted; Frank was dressed in black with a cap on. Old Mr. Toland was dressed in a light summer coat and a broad-crown hat; McCann was riding a pretty good-sized sorrel horse, not very tall, but good sized; witness saw the body and examined it; all except the top, the head had disappeared; there was a wound on the back of the neck marked with powder, the hat was powder-burnt; saw the ball-mark on the tree six feet from the ground; he saw no other wound on the body; he could see no other wound on the body; could see no appearance of horse tracks on the ground; other people were there before witness; the body was thirty or forty feet from the road, in a clump of post oak bushes; there were tracks to the right of the road along the road, but none traceable that turned out of the road. Witness was on the jury of inquest, and no accusation was made against any one. The coroner's jury met on the ground about twelve o'clock, and commenced their investigations about dark, and got through about ten o'clock P. M. The wound was about one inch long, and appeared as if made by a bullet; when the head was down the wound was round, the hogs had eaten the face away; all the face bones were gone; nothing was left but the skull. Witness heard the report of a gun about a half an hour or an hour in the night; there was no horse in the yard when witness passed Mr. Toland's in the evening.

Josiah S. Morehead testified that he saw the body of Andrew Toland, after he was killed, near the road-side at Profit's fence; he saw hogs eating him; he was riding along the road coming to town; first saw the hat, and got down to take it up, when his horse scared, and thus he first discovered the body; he saw the prisoner and his father that morning, four or five miles from there, going to witness' father's house; he stopped to talk with them; they were going to witness' father to get bail, the grand jury having found a true bill against them for an assault with intent to kill; prisoner appeared to hurry his father, and urged him to go on; when witness picked up the hat, he saw that there was blood and smoke on it, and blood in the road under witness' feet; he saw where the body was dragged, as if to throw it between the logs, and then drawn to the thicket, the body lying on the back, with the hands on the back.

George E. Lyon testified that he lived a mile and a half from Cross' lane; heard the report of a gun a while after dark, about a half an hour or an hour, in the direction the body was found; some ten or twenty minutes after heard a horse running from that direction; the horse was galloping, but witness did not see it; went in south-westerly direction through Smith's lane, and turned off at a corner of a field through a woods path that intersects the McCann road; prisoner lived with his father at the time; witness was at his shop at the time about fifty yards from the road; Smith's lane is one half a quarter long; report of gun was loud; he heard it distinctly; witness thought it was some one shooting turkeys; it was a moonlight night, with flying clouds; one not acquainted with the road, would not have taken that direction.

James Whitfield testified that he was on the inquest; saw the hat, a new chip one, and powder-burnt; deceased had an old round-top hat in one of his pockets; the wound on the back of the neck was powder-burnt, and the skin black and dark.

O. H. Millican testified that he was on the inquest; saw the ball mark on a small tree, and a twig cut therefrom on the side next the road, about on a level with the mark; witness examined the wound on the back of the neck; the face was all gone.

John Cross testified that Morehead found the body and came and told him; he went to see it, and then went to inform the neighbors; did not get back until after dinner; the body was lying on the back, with the feet from the road; was present before the jury; no one was accused of the murder at the time.

—— Morehead testified that the prisoner was at his house between seven and eight o'clock the morning the body was found; he appeared natural and staid an hour or three quarters; he came with his father, and wanted his father to go, after sitting a few minutes; after a while he again wished his father to go; the father told him "not to be in a hurry—it is not often we get with our friends;" the bottle was handed round, and the old man took two drinks; prisoner said again, "Let us go; if you don't, I will," and got up, and looked out to where the horses were tied; witness couldn't say why prisoner wished to get his father off; has seen the old man pretty merry.

Joseph Morehead testified that he saw prisoner at his house the next day after the murder; he appeared to be uneasy; got up and went to door and looked up and down the lane twice. Witness took the bottle out and treated the old man. McCann lived four miles from witness. Prisoner twice asked his father to go, and then said, with an oath, if he would not go he would leave him.

Henry N. Jones testified that he examined the wound on the body at the back of the neck; it was powder-burnt; the flesh was about the thickness of a man's hand; some powder-burn inside of the wound, and a blackness about where the ball struck and entered. Witness saw the tree where the ball struck.

Nich. Morgan testified that he heard the report of a gun in the direction where Toland was killed; shortly after the report he heard a person riding up Smith's lane; first heard the riding in the lane between Lyon's and Smith's fields; heard Lyon's dogs break out; the rider turned off into the woods at the corner of Smith's field intersecting the McCann road, in the direction of McCann's house; from where the horse turned off at the corner of Smith's field to the neighborhood road leading out to McCann's is not very far; a stranger would hardly have seen the neighborhood road; witness was about half a mile from the place of killing, when he heard the gun distinctly; the sound of the report was ordinary; could not see the horse distinctly; saw a glimpse of him and some one on him; witness could not tell whether the report was that of a pistol or not; the night was still and calm.

Henry Quarles testified that on the day the body was found, he saw McCann going westwardly; he looked like he was going off; had no saddle-bags that witness recollects; it was three or four miles from Cross' lane, between twelve and two oclock; his brother Pat was with him; they were going through the woods and riding fast for going through the woods; witness had not then heard of the death of Andrew Toland, but heard it an hour afterward.

Jeremiah Dowsing testified that some day or two after the murder, he heard some one at Noxubee turnpike about two o'clock at night calling out; from the voice he thought it was McCann; he did not see him; had known him before; said he wanted to buy corn and fodder for his horse; that he had been lost in the swamp; Noxubee turnpike is ten or twelve miles from Prairie hill.

Wiley Ross testified that during the second week of the Carroll circuit court, at Carrollton, he saw the prisoner; but did not recollect the day. Witness had business with Mr. Gilder; he went into Judge Johnson's office and went up-stairs, and as he struck the landing, the prisoner rose up from a bed where he was lying behind Mr. Gilder; prisoner put his hand into his bosom and backed into a corner; witness saw the butt-end of a pistol in his bosom; Gilder said witness was no officer; witness had a paper in his hand for Mr. Gilder; witness asked what it meant, and Mr. Gilder said that old Mr. Toland had been killed, and McCann had left on account of it. In the mean time prisoner had returned to the bed and knelt down on it. Witness put his hand on McCann and told him, if he had killed Toland, he had better leave. He replied that he had not killed him, but was accused of it, and in proof that he had not killed him said, that Toland's children had given him money and weapons to leave, and promised to write to him. He further said that Mr. Toland had been found killed and nearly eaten up by the hogs; that it would be very hard for him to prove his innocence, as he was the last man seen by an overseer that night behind Toland, near Cross' lane, before Toland was killed. Witness told him he had better leave. Prisoner sold his horse in Carrollton. It was after twelve o'clock when witness first saw him, and the sun was about two hours high when he left on foot, with his saddle-bags on his arm, and took the road to Williams' Landing. It was agreed that the day when witness saw McCann, was Thursday, second week of Carroll circuit court, 1845.

Elijah W. Smith testified that he first saw the prisoner aboard the stage on the Jackson and Memphis road, in the county of Lafayette. Witness pursued and overtook him at the dinner-stand, eight miles from Oxford, towards Memphis. Witness went in, took hold of him, and arrested him for James McCann, when he replied that it was not his name, that he had never known anybody of that name, that his name was Wilson or some such name; that he did not wish to be detained; that he was on his way to Tennessee to see his relations. Witness searched his pockets and found receipts in the name of James McCann, and had the same name on his shirt; witness told him he would have to go back with him, and on their way back, three miles from Oxford, he acknowledged that his name was McCann; said he had heard Toland was killed, and that he did not know he could prove himself clear. At first he wanted to go back to Lowndes county; he was examined and committed to prison in Oxford. When witness went to take him back to Columbus, he seemed to change his mind and wished to be tried in Oxford, stating as a reason why he did not want to go back, that it would be a damned long tedious case. He requested witness to write to Frank Toland, or let him write. When arrested, he had a pair of pistols (shown in court and identified by witness), and powder and ball.

Champion testified that he saw the prisoner in custody of Smith, when taking him back to Lowndes county, at Pontotoc; his cousin was with him, and knew McCann. Witness spoke to prisoner, and told him they had him in a tight place. He replied that he thought not, and asked what people said about it. Witness replied that they said he had killed Toland. Prisoner said he knew he was accused of it, and that was the reason why he left. Witness' cousin remarked to prisoner that it was strange he left before he was accused; to which the prisoner made no reply.

L. W. Ward testified that he was one of the jury of inquest. He saw the body lying twenty-five or thirty feet from the road, head towards the road, the skirts of his coat in the rear of his head; the coat was a Kentucky jean one, with velvet collar. Witness was acquainted with deceased; he was fifty or sixty years old. Witness didn't recollect seeing marks where the body was dragged; it was after twelve when he came to the ground.

James McGowan testified that he heard the report of the gun or pistol on the night of the killing; it was near a mile from where the body was found to his house; it was about three-quarters of an hour after daylight; he heard the report distinctly; it was nearly all prairie between where the body was found and witness' house; thought a gun could be heard distinctly that distance. Witness was sitting on his portico at the time, and thought it was some one shooting turkeys. He went on the ground about eleven o'clock, saw the mark on the tree where the ball struck; told some one to search about the root of the tree for the ball, and it was picked up by some one in witness' presence (a ball was shown in court which he thinks the same); didn't recollect seeing McCann or Toland on the day of the death; he heard but the one report of a gun or pistol that night.

This was all the testimony on the part of the state.

For the defendant, —— Riddle testified that he was traveling with the prisoner the night of the killing, and saw no pistol or gun on him; did not see any weapon on him.

Henry N. Jones testified that he saw no pistol on the prisoner; was not close to him; he rode past witness; did not think of pistols; supposed he might have had pistols and witness did not see them.

Patrick McCann testified that he was the brother of prisoner; had seen one of the pistols shown him; gave it to the prisoner the day he started away; had it in his trunk four or five days before; got it from Frank Toland to give to Chandler; was at home the night of the murder; prisoner returned about half an hour after dark; didn't know that Frank Toland was at witness' father's house the day the body was found, but saw him riding by the field where witness was at work planting corn or plowing. Witness spoke to him, but held no conversation with him; it was about ten o'clock; prisoner was away from home with his father at the time; he started away from home two or three hours after witness saw Toland; witness went with him to go to Wallace's; prisoner said he was going away; they rode sometimes through the woods; he told witness he was going away because he was indicted for an assault with intent to kill, and he did not intend that they should make him give security; he did not say where he was going when they parted; he bade witness good-bye; he rode a chestnut-sorrel horse; he started from home the day of the killing, after breakfast, to go to town; witness' father was at home when prisoner and he left; Frank Toland and prisoner were very friendly, like most young men, and once went to South Carolina together. Witness was not intimate with Frank Toland, but was acquainted with old man Toland.

—— McCann testified that he was a brother of prisoner; was at home the night of the killing; prisoner returned home about half an hour in the night.

Walter Troup testified that he went to old Mr. McCann's the day the body was found; was within one hundred and fifty yards of the house, and saw a gentleman riding towards the house; it was about twelve o'clock; he had black clothes and a cap or low-crown hat on; he was afterwards satisfied it was Frank Toland. Witness was then talking with Patrick McCann, who was then plowing near the stable in the field. Witness' business was with old Mr. McCann, and Patrick told him he was not at home. Witness was not nearer than three hundred yards to the person who was so going to the house, and left before he got to it. He saw a gentleman sitting, at that time, in the passage, but did not know who it was.

This was all the testimony.

Numerous charges were asked and given on both sides, and are found in the record, but not embodied in the bill of exceptions, and are not considered by the court.

The jury found the prisoner guilty. His counsel moved for a new trial, assigning various grounds, which was overruled, exceptions taken, embodying the evidence as heretofore set out.

The prisoner then moved in arrest of judgment, because, 1st, The indictment was insufficient; and, 2d, Because there was a misjoinder of counts and alleged offenders; the motion was overruled, and the prisoner sentenced to be hung.

Sharkey, J. C., on McCann's application, ordered this writ of error.

Clayton, J.:

This was an indictment in the circuit court of Lowndes county for murder. The prisoner was convicted upon circumstantial evidence, and has brought his case to this court for revision.

There are but three acts of the circuit court complained of by bill of exceptions; one, the admission of certain testimony; the others, the refusal to give two charges asked by the counsel of the defendant. Upon these we shall remark in conclusion, and shall first consider the refusal to grant a new trial.

This point has been pressed with great earnestness, and it has been insisted with much zeal, that the verdict is without any sufficient testimony.   The inconclusiveness of circumstantial proof, and the danger to be apprehended from convictions upon that species of evidence, have been dwelt upon with much force.

It is certainly true, that great care and caution should be used in the investigation of such testimony.   This is true also of every other kind.   All human testimony may be false.   Our own perceptions may be wrong; our own senses may deceive us.   Whilst this should teach us caution in the forming of our opinions and deliberations in adopting conclusions, it should not make us carry our doubts too far, because we should thereby be rendered unfit for all the practical duties of life.   Such is the state of things which surround us in life, that in all which concerns ourselves and our highest interests, we are compelled to act upon testimony, and often upon that testimony which circumstances afford.   The same rule is carried into judicial proceedings.   Circumstantial evidence has been received in every age of the common law, and it may rise so high in the scale of belief, as to generate full conviction.   When, after due caution, this result is reached, the law authorizes its ministers to act upon it.

After a careful review of the subject, Starkie lays down the only rule which can be regarded of practical application. " What circumstances will amount to proof," he says, "can never be matter of general definition; the legal test is the sufficiency of the evidence to satisfy the understanding and conscience of the jury." " On the one hand, absolute. metaphysical and demonstrative certainty is not essential to proof by circumstances. It is sufficient if they produce moral certainty, to the exclusion of every reasonable doubt; even direct and positive testimony does not afford grounds of belief of a higher and superior nature." 1 Stark., 577.

We shall proceed, in connection with this rule, to consider the evidence most material in this cause, without dwelling on some of the facts which have a more remote bearing.   It is in proof, that on the day of the murder the deceased went from his residence to the town of Columbus, a distance of twelve miles; that he rode a small horse, and from age stooped forward as he rode; that on his way home he crossed the ferry at Columbus, about an hour before sunset; that, in point of fact, he never reached home alive, but his body was found the next day in a small clump of bushes, some thirty or forty feet from the road, and rather more than a mile from his house; there was a wound in the back of the neck, occasioned by a ball from a gun or pistol; there was powder in the inner surface of the wound, and the skin around it, as well as a straw or chip hat which he wore, were blackened with smoke and powder; the face, from the eyes down, had been eaten up by hogs, but no other part of the body had received much injury; the body had been dragged into the bushes thirty or forty feet from the road; there was an impression made by a ball upon a tree near the spot, some six feet from the ground, on the side next the road, and the ball was found at the foot, bruised and flattened; the skull above the eyes was sound, except that a part of the bone on the right side was detached; there was a saddle found on the spot, with blood upon the right stirrup leather; there were several traces of blood on the ground and the clothes; the murder was committed on a private road leading to the house of the deceased, a little distance from the public road; a report of a gun or pistol was heard by several of the neighbors, about half an hour or an hour after daylight down; the body was found about ten or eleven o'clock the next day; a jury of inquest was held, which terminated its sitting about ten o'clock at night, and up to that time no one was accused of the murder.

It was in proof, that the prisoner lived with his father near the deceased; that he also went to Columbus on the day of the murder, starting after the deceased did; that he was seen there on several occasions during the day, in company with J. F. Toland, a son of the deceased; that they spent a great part of the day together in a billiard room attached to a grocery, in which there was no other person at the time; that they were not engaged at play, but apparently upon business; that upon being invited to dinner, young Toland at first declined, saying that his father was in town, and that he did not wish to be seen by him, but that he afterwards consented to go.

That the prisoner crossed the ferry about two hours before sunset, consequently about an hour before the deceased; about sunset the prisoner overtook two witnesses, Sandifer and Riddle, some five miles from Columbus, and rode with them three or four miles; he was riding a horse of good size; he conversed freely with the witnesses and told them his name; about seven miles from Columbus they overtook the deceased, who was riding very slowly in the rear of a wagon; at the house of Mills, near by, eight miles from Columbus, they got some water; a short distance from that point, the prisoner said he was going to Newsom's to get supper, and asked Riddle to go with him; Newsom lived about one hundred yards from the road, and there were thick woods between the road and his house; the witness did not go; McCann left them, but whether he went to Newsom's does not appear from the evidence; about a mile from Newsom's, near Gilmer's gate, a man passed these two witnesses at full gallop, whom they did not recognize, but who, from other testimony, is shown to have been J. F. Toland; after they passed Gilmer's gate, they were not overtaken by any other person; the road to the residence of old Mr. Toland leaves the Gilmer road a short distance beyond his gate; the murder was committed on this road, not very far from the Gilmer road, in a wood which extends from Gilmer's to the spot where the body was found; near this place there is a road leading from the Gilmer road to McCann's.

There is no direct trace of the prisoner, except in his own declaration, after he left Sandifer and Riddle, until he reached his father's house some half hour after dark, according to the testimony of his brother. The murder occurred near Cross' lane, one and a half miles from McCann's. Some ten, or twenty, or perhaps thirty minutes after the report of the gun or pistol, Lyon, who lived near the road leading from the Gilmer road to McCann's, heard a horse galloping, and observed that he left the road and took an unfrequented path, not likely to be known by any except those who lived near, leading through the woods in the direction to old Mr. McCann's. Nicholas Morgan makes the same statement, with the addition that he saw a rider on the horse.

The next day the body was found, and a jury of inquest held, as already stated. During the same morning J. F. Toland went to the house of old Mr. McCann. Towards two o'clock of the same day, the prisoner was seen in company with his brother, some three or four miles from his house. They were riding rapidly through the woods, and prisoner appeared to be going off. His brother states, that he went with him several miles, and that they traveled sometimes in the road and sometimes in the woods; that the prisoner told him he was going away, because the grand jury had found a true bill against him, for an assault with intent to kill. A witness states, that a day or two after the murder, he heard some one at the Noxubee turnpike, about two o'clock at night, calling out, and from the voice thought it was McCann. He did not see him, but had known him before. He wanted to buy corn and fodder for his horse, and said he had been lost in the swamp. This was twelve or fifteen miles from the place of the murder. The next place he was seen, so far as the proof shows, was at Carrollton. He there exhibited great apprehension of being arrested. He told a witness that he had not killed old Mr. Toland, but he was accused of it; that the body had been found nearly eaten up by the hogs, and that it would be very hard for him to prove his innocence, as he was the last man seen by an overseer that night behind Toland, near Cross' lane, before Toland was killed. He also stated, that Toland's children had given him money and weapons to leave, and had promised to write to him. The same evening he left Carrollton on foot, having sold his horse. A few days afterwards he was arrested in the county of Lafayette, and voluntarily stated after his arrest, that he had heard that Toland had been killed, and that he did not know he could prove himself clear. Before his arrest he had denied his name, said that his name was Wilson, and that he was on his way to Tennessee, to see his relations. After his arrest, and whilst on his way to Columbus, a witness at Pontotoc remarked to him that he was in a tight place; he replied that he thought not. To another remark, he said he knew he was accused of killing Toland, and that was the reason he left.

There was no proof that the prisoner had any pistol or other arms on the day of the murder.

These are the most material facts to be gathered from the testimony on both sides. We shall proceed to consider their effect, in order to determine whether they sustain the verdict of the jury.

There is an absence of all effort on the part of the prisoner, to explain two circumstances in the early part of the transaction, which have some bearing in the case. The first is the failure to show where he was, from the time he crossed the river, until he overtook Sandifer and Riddle at sunset. The other is, that he did not show whether he went to Newsom's to supper, as he said he intended to do. These are considerations of great force against him. 1 Stark., 574, 575. They seem to indicate that he crossed the river before the decedent, so as to be sure that he should see him, and that having waited until he passed, he pursued his way homeward; that having overtaken the deceased upon the road, he again stopped, until he got in his rear, where he remained until the commission of the deed.

It is almost certain that the murder was committed with a pistol; the smoke and powder upon the surface and edges of the wound, and upon the hat, show that it was fired in immediate contact with the person. The blood upon the right stirrup-leather, which was the side next the woods, connected with the impression upon the tree, goes to show that he was shot upon his horse, and the range of the ball likewise shows that the person who fired was on horseback. The impression of the ball upon the side of the tree next the road, and the finding of the flattened ball at the foot of the tree, prove that the shot did not proceed from a person concealed in the woods. It is very certain that the ball could not have killed him, after it struck the tree and fell upon the ground. It is a fair conclusion, then, that the pistol was fired by some one on horseback in the road, very near to the decedent, who was higher than the deceased, bending forward on his small horse, and that the ball entered the neck, passed through the lower part of the head, and came out on the right side, detaching a portion of the bone, and having nearly spent its force, struck the tree, and fell at its foot. As it was after night, the murderer had to be near his victim to be sure of his aim. It will be remembered that the prisoner rode a good sized horse, and if he perpetrated the deed from his saddle, was elevated enough above the decedent to give the ball the direction it took. Soon after the report of the gun, the rapid galloping of a horse was heard, going from the direction of the place of the murder towards the house of old Mr. McCann; a rider was seen upon him, and he took an unfrequented by-path through the woods, which led in a more direct course to the house than the road. It is not shown that any one else went to the house that night. The prisoner reached home, according to the testimony of his brother, about half an hour after dark, which was about the time of the report of the gun, according to the other witnesses. If there were any certainty as to the precise time of these several incidents, and the exact moment was fixed at which each took place, then it would be established that the prisoner was at home when the deed was committed. All experience, however, proves that but little reliance can be placed upon the recollection of witnesses, as to the exact moment of any occurrence. Men generally take so little note of the passing of time, that an approach to accuracy is all that can be expected. The killing took place about a mile and a half from McCann's. It is clear that but little time was spent at the spot by the murderer. The body was dragged a few paces from the road, and no attempt was made either to bury it, or carefully conceal it. The saddle and hat of the deceased were left where they fell. There was no appearance of the trampling of a horse, as if he had been tied and detained. It was the work of only a moment or two, followed by immediate flight, to avoid detection. A rapid gallop, such as Lyon and Morgan described, would have carried a person from the scene to McCann's certainly in fifteen minutes. The early hour at which the prisoner reached home almost precludes the belief, that he stayed at Newsom's to supper, if indeed he went there at all.

These are the circumstances as developed up to the time of the killing, and however much they point to the guilt of the prisoner, they may leave room for a reasonable doubt. But the evidence does not close here. By far the strongest portion has been furnished by the conduct and declarations of the prisoner, subsequent to the deed.

There are no circumstances which require comment on the morning after the murder, until the interview with J. F. Toland. That interview appears to have prompted his immediate flight. He stated at Carrollton, that the children of Toland had furnished him with money and weapons to leave.   He saw none of the children, so far as the evidence discloses, except Frank.   If he had no agency in the act, it is not at all probable, that he could have been bribed, or induced by Frank Toland, as has been argued, to fly before he was accused.   A consciousness of innocence would have led him to abide the issue, and to see whether time would not disclose the real perpetrator.   But he fled on the instant, and he must be content to bear whatever weight this circumstance furnishes against him.   The consequences of his own act must fall on his own head.   He was on his way before two o'clock of that day.   The jury of inquest did not return their verdict until ten o'clock of that night, and up to that time, no whisper had been heard that he was accused or suspected.   His fears induced flight before the voice of accusation was raised.   The excuse, which he offered to his brother for leaving, was, that an indictment had been found against him and his father, for an assault and battery with intent to kill. But he had been the previous day to Columbus, the county town, and had not been disturbed.   It does not appear that any process had issued upon the indictment, or that there was any necessity from that source for such sudden flight.

It was probably on the night of the same day, that he was at the Noxubee turnpike.   He had been lost in the swamp, as he stated; for the reason, probably, that after parting with his brother, he still endeavored to make his way through the woods.

His conduct at Carrollton is not easy to reconcile with a belief of his innocence.   He exhibited great fear of being arrested; put his hand upon his pistol, and threw himself into a defensive attitude, when a stranger entered the room in which he was. He then stated the fact of the killing, and of the finding of the body eaten up in part by the hogs, and said he had left, because he was the last person seen behind the old man, near Cross' lane, before he was killed, and that it would be hard for him to prove himself clear.   This declaration is decisive of his fate.   It brings him to the very theatre of the murder, at the time it was committed, and if he did not do the deed himself, it is almost certain, that he would have seen the person who did.   He might then have saved himself by disclosing the real murderer.   How

did he know that he was the last person seen behind the old man before he was killed, unless he was the real murderer himself? And this statement clears up all the doubt, which might otherwise have existed from the different opinions of the witnesses, as to the time of the act.

By his own confession he was not at home, but near Cross lane, behind the old man, when drawing to the very scene of the murder. The declaration, thus made, to give an appearance of innocence to the circumstances of his flight, puts the seal of guilt upon his act.

In Lafayette county he denied his name, in order to elude arrest, but after he was apprehended, he voluntarily made the same explanation in substance which he had made at Carrollton. It was repeated at Pontotoc, and to a remark that it was strange he had fled before he was accused, he made no reply.

He has in this way furnished the most undeniable evidences of his guilt. If the jury has acted upon them, he has no human being to blame but himself, and his doom is upon his own head. They place his guilt beyond all reasonable doubt. They are entirely consistent with that conclusion, but utterly at war with all experience and with all our knowledge of the ordinary motives of human conduct, if we are to believe him innocent.

The case does not call for any elaborate attempt to define the limits of the power of this court in granting new trials in criminal cases, upon the testimony. Doubtless, it is a power which may be exercised where the jury has gone wide of the mark, and found a verdict against the decided preponderance of the testimony. But it is a power which should be exercised with great caution, because our constitution and laws have provided the trial by jury as the safeguard and protection of the lives and liberties of the citizen on the one hand, and of the safety and interests of the commonwealth on the other. It is placed by the constitution beyond the reach of legislative interference. This safeguard would be shorn of half its strength, if it might be withdrawn or disturbed by the courts, unless in a case of palpable error or of gross abuse. This is not a case of such a character. On the contrary, after carefully considering all the testimony, and listening to all which the ingenuity of counsel could suggest, we are not at all prepared to say that, if we had been on the jury, we should have come to a different conclusion. To set the verdict aside under such circumstances, would be an unwarrantable invasion of their province.

There were but three exceptions taken during the progress of the trial. The first was to the admission of the testimony of John P. Krecker. This witness stated, that some eight or ten days before the murder he saw the prisoner and J. F. Toland in conversation on the Columbus bridge, some twenty or thirty feet within the bridge. Witness did not hear the conversation; the prisoner had his back towards witness; put his hand in his pocket, and when he saw witness looking at him, pulled some papers out of his pocket and put them in another pocket; again put his hand into his pocket and pulled out something. J. F. Toland took something out of his pocket that looked like a powder-gourd, put it to his mouth, and pulled out the stopper, and poured something into prisoner's hand which he supposed to be powder. The part of the bridge on which they were was a retired place; they remained about twenty or thirty minutes.

In cases depending upon circumstantial evidence, a number of links often occur in forming the chain. It cannot be said what bounds are to circumscribe the inquiry. All which may tend to elucidate the transaction, should be admitted. 1 Starkie's Ev., 561, *et seq.* The proof of the guilt of McCann, in some degree, depended upon establishing a combination between him and J. F. Toland. Apart from such combination, no motive is shown to have existed to lead to the perpetration of the crime. With such combination a motive is furnished, dark and hideous, it is true, and one which, for the honor of human nature, we should be glad to deem incredible, but which the records of crime show sometimes have found place in the bosom of the child, and have prompted to the murder of the parent. This circumstance, then, separated only by an interval of ten days from the fatal tragedy, might be an important aid in fixing the relation of the parties and in disclosing their real intentions and purposes. We cannot, therefore, say its admission was erroneous.

The other exceptions relate to the refusal of the court to give certain charges asked by the counsel of the prisoner. The first of these instructions was as follows: "That all the declarations of the prisoner brought out by the state are to be taken together, as well those in his favor as those against him, and that the portions favorable to him are to be regarded by the jury as being true, unless impossible in their nature or inconsistent with other evidence in the case." This was refused, and the following given in its place: "That in confessions by a prisoner all must be taken together, as well that which is in his favor as that which is against him, but that the jury are the sole judges of the truth of confessions, and can receive a part and reject a part." The instruction, as given, propounds the law correctly. A late writer on evidence thus lays down the rule: "If, what the prisoner said in his own favor is not contradicted by the evidence offered by the prosecution, nor improbable in itself, it will naturally be believed by the jury; but they are not bound to give weight to it on that account, but are at liberty to judge of it like other evidence by all the circumstances of the case." 1 Greenl., 263, § 218. Roscoe says: "It must not be supposed that every part of a confession is entitled to equal credit. A jury may believe that which charges the prisoner, and reject that which is in his favor, if they see sufficient grounds for so doing." Crim. Ev., 51; 1 Stark. Ev., 283; Clewes' Case, 4 Car. & P., 221; 3 Phil. Ev., 927; Coon v. The State, ante, 246.

The remaining charge excepted to was as follows: "In criminal cases the mere union of a number of independent circumstances, each of which is inconclusive in its nature and tendency, cannot afford a just ground for conviction, unless the combination is conclusive." This was given in lieu of one asked by the counsel of the defendant, which laid down the converse of this proposition.

The instruction as given is not liable to objection. The union and concurrence of various detached circumstances may produce full conviction, when either one of them standing alone might leave room for much doubt. 1 Stark., 570.

An objection was taken to the indictment, that it charges the offense as at common law, whilst the punishment is inflicted under the statute. This objection cannot prevail. Vance v. Commonwealth, 2 Virg. Cases, 162; ib., 378; White v. Commonwealth, 6 Bin., 179; Commonwealth v. Searle, 2 ib., 339; Mitchell v. The State, 8 Yerg., 514.

These are all the points made in the argument which it is deemed necessary to notice. A careful examination of the testimony and of the points involved has disclosed to us no error in the proceedings of the court below. It only remains to say that the judgment is affirmed.

Mr. Potter, in behalf of the prisoner, filed a petition for a re-hearing upon the point, principally, of the error in the refusal of the instruction asked by the prisoner's counsel with reference to his confessions.

The re-hearing was refused and the prisoner sentenced to be hung.

NELMS *v.* THE STATE, 13 Smedes & Marshall, 500.

HOMICIDE.

MURDER.

It is generally conceded that an opinion formed or expressed on common rumor does not disqualify a juror. But if an opinion be formed and expressed on information derived from a reliable source, the juror is objectionable. An opinion from having heard the evidence, or from having conversed with the witnesses, is of that nature.

An examination before the magistrate on trial of *habeas corpus* cannot be read for the purpose of discrediting a witness, unless it be read over to and signed or approved by the witness at the time it was made.

Where a conversation was had with the deceased previous to his dying declarations, on the subject of the transaction which caused his death, it is important that such conversation should be made known to the jury, to show that it varied from the dying declarations; and it is error to exclude it.

A juror may be received to testify to any improper conduct of the officer who has the jury under his charge.

Error to Marshall circuit court. MILLER, J.

The plaintiff in error was indicted in the circuit court of Panola county, at the May term, 1848, for the murder of Jesse Price.

He obtained a change of venue to Marshall county, where at

the July term he was tried. The jury found him guilty on the 6th day of August. He moved for a new trial, which was refused, and he sealed a bill of exceptions embodying the evidence, and sued out this writ of error. The prisoner was sentenced by the court below to be hung on the 14th of September, 1849. CLAYTON, J., *dissenting.*

Estelle, Tarpley and *Barton,* for plaintiff in error,

Argued the case orally, in which they made the following points:

1. That the statement of the juror was admissible. McGowan's case, 9 Yerger, 193; 3 Humph., 376; 4 ib., 196, 276.

2. The refusal of the court to allow the notes of the vice-chancellor to be read to impeach a witness was error. 2 S. & M., 58.

3. On the subject of the dying declarations, and the exclusion of the testimony to impeach them, cited Greenl. Ev., 193; 4 Starkie Ev., 461; 2 H. & McH., 120; Rex v. Pike, 3 C & P., 598; 2 Phill. (C. & H.), 611.

4. That the affidavits of the jurors were admissible. They did not impeach their own conduct, but that only of the officer.

5. That the misconduct of the officer was sufficient to vitiate the verdict. 10 Yerger, 241; 4 Humph., 38, 289; 7 Cow., 562.

6. The jury found contrary to the law and the evidence.

D. C. Glenn, attorney general.

Argued the case in reply; and on the various points raised referred to the following authorities:

1. As to the competency of the juror, Sam. v. State, *supra,* 189; 2 Leigh, 769; 3 ib., 785; 9 ib., 651, 661; 3 Stewart, 454; 2 Va. Cases, 375; 4 How., 330; 5 Rand., 660, 665; 5 How., 730.

2. As to the exclusion of the proof to contradict the witness. 1 Greenl. Ev., § 463.

3. As to the dying declarations of Price. Archb. Cr. Pl., 156; 24 How. St. Tr., 753; 1 Greenl. Ev. 509.

4. On the motion for a new trial. 3 How., 429; 1 Greenl. Ev., § 460, and note; 2 Ev. Pothier, Ob., 256, (294,) App. no. 16.

5. With reference to misconduct of jury, 5 Pickens, 296; 3 How., 426; 4 Humph., 251; Stewart v. Small, 5 Mo., 535; 1

Chitty Cr. Law, 632, 633, 334 ; Graham on N. T., and cases cited.

6. As to the verdict being against the evidence. The case presents a conflict of testimony, and the appellate court will never interfere in a criminal, or in a civil case, unless it is manifestly against the evidence, or palpably without evidence, or unless the evidence greatly preponderates against it. Patton v. Ford, 2 Gratt., 245 ; Hill v. Commonwealth, 692, 693 ; Weinzorpflin v. State, 7 Blackf., 198 ; Sims v. State, 2 Bailey (S. C.), 35 ; Jeffreys v. State, 3 Murph. (N. C.), 480 ; Jones v. State, 1 Kelly, 618 ; Cassels v. State, 4 Yerg., 149 ; McCune v. State, 2 Rob. Va. ; 2 Erskine's Speeches, Defense of Rights of Juries, 152–209.

SHARKEY, C. J. :

The prisoner was indicted and found guilty of the murder of Jesse Price. He brings up his case on eight bills of exceptions, seven of which were taken on points ruled during the progress of the trial, and the last to the decision of the court in overruling a motion for a new trial, in which the testimony is set out, and seven reasons assigned in support of the motion.

The several points raised were thoroughly investigated by counsel, and the arguments on both sides were so lucid and forcible, that the labor of deciding is rendered comparatively light.

The first exception was taken to a refusal to sustain a challenge for cause to a juror. When called to answer questions, he stated, that he had formed and expressed an opinion from what he heard one Mansfield say some of the witnesses had told him, though the juror had not heard any of the witnesses say anything on the subject; that his opinions were not such as would influence his verdict, but he would be governed by the evidence.

This point is not, certainly, free from difficulty. The question is one of very frequent occurrence, and the decisions are numerous, though entirely consistent. It is a question on which it seems difficult to lay down a definite and precise rule, which can be applied as a test in all cases. The great principle is, that every man who is accused has a right to demand a trial by an impartial jury of his country; a jury whose minds are free from prejudice and from bias. Cases may arise in which it is next to impossible to procure a jury of this description, but even in such cases, the nearer we can approach to the principle, the better. It seems to be generally conceded, that an opinion formed and expressed on common rumor, will not disqualify a juror. Strictly speaking, this is a departure from the true principle, but it is a departure which may be rendered necessary in certain cases. It should be avoided, however, if possible. The mind which has received impressions from any source, cannot be said to be entirely free and impartial, since the false impressions must be removed before the true one can be made. It may often happen that a crime may be of such a character, as to become a matter of general notoriety throughout a whole county. In such cases it may be absolutely necessary to take jurors who have formed an opinion on mere rumor. But, if an opinion be formed and expressed on information derived from a reliable source, the juror is certainly objectionable. An opinion from having heard the evidence, or from having conversed with the witnesses, is of that character. And an opinion formed on the information of one who heard the witnesses testify, or speak of the subject, may be equally a ground of objection, if the juror had confidence in the statement he received. An opinion so formed is not based on common rumor.[1] In Vermilyea's case (6 Cow., 562), Judge Woodworth said it was good cause of challenge, that a juror had formed and expressed an opinion from a knowledge of the facts. The juror had heard the testimony on a former trial, and was held incompetent. And in the same case, reported in 7 Cow., 108, it was said that the mind of the juror should be in a state of neutrality as to the person and the matter to be tried. In the trial of Aaron Burr, Chief Justice Marshall said it was one of the clearest principles of natural justice that a juryman should come to the trial of a man for life with a perfect freedom from previous impressions, and he accordingly held that jurors who had formed opinions from newspaper publications and common rumor, were incompetent. On this ground many of the jurors were set aside,

[1] Wharton Am. Cr. Law, 3004.

and many of them had formed opinions only from current rumor.
1 Burr's Trial, 370.   In Mather's case, (4 Wend., 229), a juror
was set aside who had formed and expressed an opinion from
newspaper publications, and from common rumor, although he
declared that he was prepared to weigh the evidence and decide
accordingly.   In this case all the authorities are reviewed, and
the rule settled, on what was regarded as the weight of authority.
In McGowan v. The State, 9 Yerg., 184, the court laid down
this rule, that if the juror has heard the circumstances of the
case, and believing the statements to be true, has formed, or
formed and expressed, an opinion, he is incompetent.   In that
instance the juror had formed his opinion, not, as it was said,
upon rumor merely, but from a detail of circumstances by persons in whom he confided.   This question was very fully considered at the present term in Sam v. The State, when jurors
were held incompetent who had formed decided opinions, one
from common rumor, and the other from having heard the case
argued by counsel.   In the case of Johnson v. The State, Walker R., 392, it was decided that an opinion formed on common
report, did not disqualify the juror, though the court evidently
regarded the point as worthy of great consideration, and leaves
the inference that an opinion formed otherwise than on common
report, would be sufficient cause of challenge.   On these authorities, and in view of the principles above noticed, we do not feel
prepared to approve the decision of the court in holding that the
juror was competent.

The second bill of exceptions raises this question : Was it competent to discredit a witness by introducing his statement made
on the trial of a *habeas corpus*, as taken down by the vice-chancellor, before whom the trial was had?   The statute does not
make it the duty of the judge on such a trial, to take down the
evidence, unless one of the party desire it, and then he is only
required to take down the material facts.   Hutch. Code, 1001.
We do not think an examination taken down under the statute
can be read for such a purpose, unless it is read over to, and
signed or approved by the witness.   1 Phil., 293.

The third bill of exceptions relates to the declarations of deceased made *in extremis*.   They were made under all due solem-

nity. The deceased declared that he knew he could live only a few hours at most, perhaps not more than an hour. The declarations were made to Ostun, who asked the deceased who shot him. Deceased replied "that Nelms shot him;" when some one, standing by, asked if it was Samuel H. Nelms, to which deceased replied "Yes." The question was repeated, and deceased indicated assent by a forward inclination of the head. The witness, Ostun, was then asked "If deceased did not so express himself as to convey the idea that it was a mere opinion, and not a thing within the actual knowledge of the deceased?" and he was asked also, "What Jesse Price had said to him before on the subject?" To these questions the district attorney objected, and the objections were sustained. The question is, Should the court have permitted the witness to answer these questions

Evidence of this description is classed under the head of hearsay evidence, though, perhaps, it stands somewhat on a different footing. The awful situation of the party in prospect of immediate dissolution, is supposed to be as powerful on the conscience as the obligation of an oath. Such evidence is only admissible under a rule of necessity, and constitutes the only case in which evidence is admissible against the accused without an opportunity of cross-examination. The leading rules in regard to the admissiblity of such evidence are laid down in Note 453 to Phillips' Evidence, and in 2 Starkie's Evidence, 366, 367. It is said the court must try the competency of the deceased and the jury his credibility. Various questions may arise after the court shall have admitted the evidence. The jury may question its credibility, and consider its effect. As it is given and received under peculiar circumstances, great caution is called for in the application and use of such evidence. To this end, it is important that all attending circumstances should be well weighed by the jury. The degree of self-possession, of observation and recollection of the deceased, should be ascertained. The state of mind arising from a sense of his critical situation, added to his suffering condition, may produce indistinctness of memory, and all these may tend to shake the confidence of the jury. It is said by an eminent writer, citing

2 Starkie, 366, that "sometimes the declaration is a matter of judgment, of inference and conclusion, which, however sincere, may be fatally erroneous. The circumstances of confusion and surprise, connected with the object of the declaration, are to be considered with the most minute and scrupulous attention ; the accordance and consistency of the facts stated with the other facts established in evidence, is to be examined with peculiar circumspection." There is great force in these remarks. It may often happen that the party, without being perfectly certain, would ascribe the act to some suspected person, when, if the grounds of his suspicion could be known, they would be unsatisfactory. An enmity, which had been but recently exhibited by threats, would be very likely to lead the mind of a wounded person to a thorough conviction that the wound had been inflicted by the person who made the threat, and he might, consequently, speak of it as a fact. Hence the necessity for that degree of caution which is said to be necessary in the use of such evidence. The object of the first question seems to have been to ascertain the true meaning of the deceased. Usually the opinions of a witness are not admissible ; but the peculiarity of this description of evidence, the absolute necessity for confining it within proper limits, might, under certain circumstances, seem to require a departure from the strict rule. If the declarations had been equivocal or ambiguous, perhaps the impression made on the mind of the witness who heard them, might have been a proper subject of inquiry. It seems to be sufficient if the substance of the declarations be given.[1] 11 Ohio Rep., 424. A witness who is called to prove what a deceased witness swore on a former trial, need only state the substance, and such testimony very much resembles the proof of dying declarations. To give the substance is but to give the ideas conveyed to the mind of the witness, which he clothes in his own language. But there is no occasion for a resort to proof of the substance of what the dying man stated, since the witness gives the language used. The meaning of that language can be determined by the jury. We

[1] Wharton Am. Cr. Law, 682; Starkey v. People, 17 Ill., 17; Ward v. State, 8 Blackf., 101; Wharton Am. Cr. Law, 679.

do, not, therefore, feel prepared to say there was error in refusing to permit the witness to answer the first question; but, in view of the foregoing rules, we are well satisfied that there was error in refusing to allow him to state what the deceased had said to him on the same subject at another time. If such previous conversation was had, which gave a different version of the transaction, it was important that the jury should have known what was said. To exclude it from them was to exclude the means of trying the credibility of the evidence, a question which it was indispensably necessary for them to consider of. They could not otherwise justly weigh the declarations; it was compelling them to take them without the attending circumstances, and, perhaps, depriving them of the means of judging with that circumspection which the law requires. Important light may have been thus shut out.

We shall touch but one other question. Several of the jurors were introduced to testify in support of the motion for a new trial, who stated that two of the officers who had them in charge spoke of the enormity of the offense, by saying, that it was a worse case than Dyson's, and one of them said that public opinion was against the accused. To my mind this presents a very satisfactory and even a conclusive reason for a new trial. The purity of trial by jury must be strictly guarded. The verdict, when rendered, should command entire confidence; whatever may detract from that confidence, must weaken the security which is felt by the community in this mode of trial. I adhere to the doctrine laid down in Hare's case, 4 Howard, 187, which seems to me to apply here. The officer is required by the nature of his duty, as well as by an oath, not to speak to the jury himself on the subject of their deliberations, or to permit others to do so. This ceremony is a mockery, if a violation has no other effect than to subject the officer to punishment. If he may speak to them himself, he may permit others to do so, and the door is thus thrown open to tampering, and the safety of trial by jury is invaded to an alarming extent. The duty of the officer is prescribed for the protection of the accused. If improper influences have been employed, it is but a poor boon to say to him, that the officer is liable. The officer may be willing to incur the punishment for the sake of gratifying his wishes, or for reward. One who thus violates his duty and his oath, should be subjected to the severest possible penalties, but that does not purify the verdict; it should be set aside. It is dangerous to permit a verdict to stand which is liable to suspicion. The jury should not know the opinion of any one; and more especially should they be kept in ignorance of public opinion, which is often the result of prejudice.

The general rule is, that a juror shall not be allowed to impeach the verdict by disclosing his own misconduct, or his motive, or opinion, or that of his fellows; but this is a different question. The jury are not involved in the misconduct of the officer; that is a matter over which they have no control. A juror may be received to testify to improper attempts of a party to the suit to influence the minds of the jury.[1] Chews v. Driver, Coxe's Rep., 166. On the same principle we should be allowed to state the misconduct of the officer, who may be the instrument of the party.

Judgment reversed, and cause remanded.

WASH *v.* THE STATE, 14 Smedes and Marshall, 120.

RAPE.

In criminal prosecutions no alleged error in the instructions to the jury will be noticed, unless they are embodied in the bill of exceptions, and thus made a part of the record.

The same indictment against the same individual may contain counts for several felonies of the same degree, and it is no ground for either demurrer or motion in arrest of judgment; hence, if several felonies of the same degree be included in the same indictment, and there be a general verdict, judgment may be given on any or all the counts, according as they may be supported by the evidence.

It is an irregularity to charge distinct felonies in different counts of the same indictment. But this does not constitute a ground for a motion in arrest of judgment.

In prosecutions for misdemeanors, where there is a general verdict of guilty, and there is any good count in the indictment, it will be referred to that and supported.

Error to Warren circuit court. SMITH, J.
The facts sufficiently appear in the opinion.

1 2 Graham & Waterman on N. T., 380; Wharton Am. Cr. Law. 3155.

R. H. Tompkins, for plaintiff in error, argued the case orally.

D. C. Glenn, attorney general.

1. There were no exceptions taken to the judgment of the court, overruling the motion in arrest and for a new trial. Objections thereto cannot now be heard in this court. Code, 855, 856.

2. The instructions of the court were not excepted to, or placed before this court by bill of exceptions. The law making instructions given or refused, a part of the record, does not apply to criminal cases. The statute of 1846, Code, 893, applies only to the trial of civil suits.

3. A memorandum by the clerk, that exceptions were had to various opinions of the court, which, however, it seems, were never signed and sealed, is insufficient. 1 S. & M., 326; 3 ib., 533; 7 How., 346.

4. The offense charged is fully proved by the only bill of exceptions taken.

5. The only error charged, which this court can notice, is the ruling of the court, in regard to the ownership of the prisoner; and on this point cited, 10 Mo., 232; 1 Hawks, 24; 2 Bailey, 67; Riley's Law Cases, 298, 299; 8 S. & M., 584, and cases cited.

SMITH, J.:

The prisoner at the bar was tried in the circuit court of Warren, upon an indictment, which charged, first, the commission of a rape upon Catharine Windridor, an infant under the age of ten years; and, second, an attempt to commit a rape upon the same party, described as a "free white female child, under the age of twelve years." The jury returned a general verdict of guilty, and the court pronounced sentence of death upon the prisoner.

Three exceptions are taken to the proceedings in the circuit court, one of which will not be noticed. It is the objection to the charge of the court. It is settled, that in criminal prosecutions, no alleged error in the instructions to the jury will be noticed, unless the party objecting excepts, and, by means of a bill of exceptions, places the objectionable charge on the record.[1] This the plaintiff in error neglected to do.

Pending the trial before the jury, the plaintiff in error offered to read, in evidence, a bill of sale for the prisoner, from one Werlein to Buchanan and Steigleman, and also offered Steigleman as a witness to prove that the prisoner was the joint property of himself and Buchanan. The court excluded the bill of sale and the testimony of Steigleman. In this it is insisted the court erred.

Steigleman is described in the indictment as the owner of the prisoner, Evidence was adduced by the prosecution, tending to show that Steigleman was the owner, sufficient to authorize the jury to find that fact. The evidence rejected was offered by way of rebuttal, or to disprove the allegation of ownership contained in the indictment.

The question which would naturally first present itself, is, whether it is essential to warrant the conviction of a slave charged with the commission of a capital offense, to prove his ownership as laid in the indictment. But as we are informed, that a more thorough argument of this question is desired, and as we can decide the point raised by the exclusion of the evidence on other grounds, we will defer any expression of opinion on the subject.

By the common law, it was necessary to insert in the indictment the name of the owner of the goods alleged to have been stolen, and to prove the ownership as charged, for the reason, that a restitution would be ordered of the stolen property, if found, to the owner. We may safely apply the rules, in reference to the proof of the ownership of stolen goods, in prosecutions for larceny, to the subject under consideration.

When goods, the subject of larceny, are the joint property of two or more persons, it is sufficient, if they be described in the indictment as the property of any one of the joint owners. Arch. Cr. Pl., 160. And where goods are stolen from the possession of a bailee, they may be described as the property of either the bailor or bailee. 2 Haile, 181 ; Rex v. Remnant, R. and R., 136 ; 2 East, P. C., 658. Upon these principles the

1 Nelms v. State, 13 S. and M., 500 ; and cases cited.

evidence excluded, so far from contradicting the averment of ownership, was sufficient to sustain it. Hence, as the introduction of the evidence could in no respect have benefitted the prisoner, he was not injured by its exclusion.

The indictment, as we have seen, contains two counts. The first was framed under the statute, Hutch. Dig., 959, § 22, defining the crime of rape. The second was predicated on the 55th section of the act concerning slaves, free negroes, and mulattoes, Hutch. Dig., 521. This latter statute makes it a capital offense for "any slave to attempt to commit a rape on any free white woman, or female child under the age of twelve years." By the former, the punishment attached to the actual commission of the offense is only imprisonment in the penitentiary for a term not less than ten years. By the statute, Hutch. Dig., 983, § 21, it is provided, that no person shall be convicted of an assault with intent to commit a crime, or any other attempt to commit an offense, when it shall appear, that the crime intended, or the offense attempted, was perpetrated by the accused person, at the time of such assault, or in pursuance of such attempt.

It is insisted in argument, that one of the counts in the indictment is bad. Hence, that as the verdict was a general finding of guilty on both charges, the court could not pronounce a judgment subjecting the prisoner to the punishment attached to the highest of the offenses charged.

The objection is pointed at the second count, and if it be well taken the judgment should be reversed, and a new trial awarded. The argument of counsel, however, shows that it is not an exception to the count itself, but to the finding of the jury upon it. It is not pretended, that the offense created by the 55th section of the statute concerning slaves, free negroes and mulattoes, is not properly and sufficiently charged; but it is said, that the statute (Hutch. Dig., 983) above referred to, interposed and prevented the conviction of the prisoner upon that count, as it distinctly appeared from the evidence in the cause, that the attempt to commit a rape, the offense charged, was actually perpetrated by the prisoner.

Without going into a minute examination of the testimony,

the whole of which appears in the bill of exceptions, it is sufficient to observe, that we do not think that the evidence established an actual commission of a rape, but only an attempt to perpetrate the offense. Hence, the finding of the jury upon the count under consideration was sustained by the evidence.

In the case at bar, the indictment charges two distinct felonies of different degrees, and assuming that both counts are good, was it competent for the court, by its judgment, to subject the prisoner to the penalty attached to the highest offense? Or, in other words, could the court pronounce any judgment whatever? In propounding the question, we have stated another exception to the judgment in this case.

The same indictment against the same individual may contain counts for several felonies of the same degree, and it is no ground for either demurrer or motion in arrest of judgment. State v. Crank, 2 Bailey, R. 66 ; Chitty Cr. L., 252, 253. The reason of this rule is obvious. The same plea may be tendered to, and the same judgment may be given on all the counts. It follows, hence, that if several felonies of the same degree be included in the same indictment, and there be a general verdict, judgment may be given on any or all of the counts, according as they may be supported by the evidence. But in the case under examination distinct felonies of different degrees are included in the indictment.[1]

It appears to be settled, that it was irregular to do so. A prisoner ought not to be charged with distinct felonies in dif-

1 Wharton Am. Cr. Law, 3047; U. S. v. Furlong, 5 Wheaton, 164; Miller v. State, 5 How., 250; Commonwealth v. Holmes, 17 Mass., 337; Edgerton v. Commonwealth, 5 Allen, 514; Commonwealth v. Nickerson, 5 Allen, 519; Guenther v. People, 10 E. P. Smith, 100; Price v. State, 2 Tenn., 254; Pole v. State, 2 Tr. Com. Rep., 494; State v. Davidson, 12 Vermont, 300; Kane v. People, 3 Wend., 363; Commonwealth v. McKisson, 8 Serg. & R., 420; West v. State, 2 Zabriskie, 212; Bullock v. State, 10 Ga., 47; Roberts v. State, 4 Ga., 8; State v. Jennings, 18 Mo., 435; Buch v. State, 1 Ohio St. R., 15; Baron v. State, 1 Parker, C. C., 246; People v. Stein, ib., 202; Isham v. State, 1 Sneed, 111; Shaw v. State, 18 Ala., 547; Bailey v. State, 4 Ohio (N. S.), 440; Buford v. Commonwealth, 14 B. Monroe, 24; Commonwealth v. Hawkins, 3 Gray, 463; U. S. v. Potter, 6 McLean, 186; Munly v. State, 7 Md., 132; U. S. v. Burns, 5 McLean, 23; State v. Burke, 38 Maine, 574; Hazen v. Commonwealth, 23 Pa. St. R., 355; Baker v. State, 30 Ala., 521; Josselyn v. Commonwealth, 6 Metcalf, 236; Jennings v. Commonwealth, 2 Pick., 356; Bennett v. State, 8 Humph., 118; Parker v. Commonwealth, 8 B. Monroe, 80; Hartman v. Commonwealth, 5 Barr, 60; Stone v. State, 1 Spencer, 404; U. S. v. Burroughs, 3 McLean, 705; State v. Miller, 7 Iredell, 275; State v. Connelly, 3 Rich., 337; Grant v. Astley, Doug., 730; Peake v. Oldham, Comp., 275; Rex v. Barfield, 2 Burr, 986.

ferent counts of the same indictment. But this irregularity
does not constitute a ground for a motion in arrest of judgment.
If the objection had been made before prisoner pleaded, it might
have been good ground for quashing the indictment; and even
after the case had been put to the jury, the court, upon the application of the prisoner, might have compelled the prosecuting
attorney to his election, as to which charge he would proceed on.
Rex v. Young, et al. 3 Durnf. & E., 106; Arch. Cr. Pl., 56;
Rex v. Strange, 34 Eng. Com. R., 341. In the last case cited,
which was an indictment under the statute of 7 Will. 4, and 1
Victoria, the offense of stabbing and cutting with intent to
murder, with intent to maim, and with intent to do grievous
bodily harm, were all included in the same indictment; and notwithstanding the judgment is, by the statute, different, being for
the offense charged in the first count capital, and for the others
transportation, an application to compel the prosecutor to elect
on which count he would proceed, was refused.

The statute, Hutch. Dig. 959, was not intended by the legislature to apply to the commission of the prohibited offense by a
slave. This intention is manifest, when we regard the character
and degree of punishment attached to the crime of rape, and
the penalty denounced against a bare attempt, by a slave, to
perpetrate the offense upon a free white woman, or a female
child under the age of twelve years. We are not permitted to
indulge the supposition, that the legislature designed to punish
the same individual capitally, for a mere attempt to commit a
rape, but if he should succeed in perpetrating the offense, to
subject him only to imprisonment in the penitentiary. The
completion of the act of rape, necessarily includes an attempt
to commit it; but rape by a slave, upon a free white woman, or
female child under the age of twelve years, is not made an
offense by the statute law of this state. Hence, the first count,
framed under the statute above referred to, was bad. It remains
then to be seen whether the second count, which is valid, will
sustain the verdict in this case. In disposing of this, we shall
settle the remaining objection to the judgment. It is well settled
in this state, that in prosecutions for misdemeanors, where there
is a general verdict of guilty, and there is any good count in the

indictment, it will be referred to that and supported. Kliffield
v. The State, 4 How. 304; Friar v. The State, 3 ib., 422; Miller v. The State, 5 ib., 250; Brantley v. The State, 13 S. & M.,
468. The reason is, because the jury, on the law and the facts,
have found the prisoner's guilt; and enough appearing on the
record to enable the court to see his crime, and to award the
appropriate legal punishment, there is nothing to prevent the
rendition of judgment. The same rule applies in civil cases by
express statutory enactment. How. & Hutch., 591, § 12. We
do not find, however, that this rule has been applied in any case,
where the defendant was capitally charged. But there can be
no good reason, why it should not be sanctioned, as well in
capital cases as in prosecutions for misdemeanors. In England
the rule is applied to both; 1 Chitty, Cr. L., 249; although a
different principle is recognized there in civil cases. In South
Carolina, the same rule governs in both classes of offenses
State v. Crank, 2 Bailey, R., 66.

Let the judgment be affirmed.

BAKER v. THE STATE., 23 Miss. Rep., 243.

UNLAWFULLY KEEPING A TAVERN.

Except in capital cases, the court has no authority to entertain a challenge to the
array of the *venire facias*; or award a special *venire*, only when there is none of the
regular *venire* in attendance on the court; and an indictment found by a grand jury
selected from the special *venire* is void.

Error to Yalobusha circuit court. ROGERS, J.

The facts of the case as presented by the record are, that at
the March term of the circuit court of Yalobusha county, Miss.,
1850, a presentment was found by the grand jury of said county
against James Baker, for unlawfully keeping a tavern without
license for that purpose. At the October term, 1850, of said
circuit court, the defendant Baker appeared and answered the
charge, and filed the following plea in abatement, because Clary,
one of the grand jurors, had not been regularly drawn.

" State of Mississippi, Yalobusha county, Circuit Court, October term, 1850.

" And the said James Baker comes and defends the wrong and injury, when, etc., and says that he ought not to answer the bill of indictment against him found by the grand jury at the last April term of this honorable court, for the reasons hereafter mentioned, to wit: That Nathan Clary, one of the grand jurors, by whom said indictment was found and returned into said circuit court, at the said April term thereof, was not, at the time he so acted, and at the time said indictment was found and returned, duly and legally qualified to act as such grand juror; in this, he, the said grand juror, had not then and there been drawn by the clerk and sheriff of the county of Yalobusha aforesaid, either at a regular term of said circuit court, next preceding the said April term of said circuit court, there in open court, or by the said clerk and sheriff, and in the presence of the judge of the probate court of the county of Yalobusha aforesaid, sixty days next before the said April term of the said circuit court of the county of Yalobusha aforesaid, as a juror liable to serve for the first week of the aforesaid circuit court at the said April term thereof, then and there, from a list of the names of the freeholders, being citizens of the United States, and householders of the county of Yalobusha aforesaid, returned either in term time of said circuit court, or to the clerk thereof, in vacation, at his office, by the assessor of taxes of the county of Yalobusha aforesaid; nor was he, the above-named grand juror, then and there summoned as a person liable to serve as juror, for the first week of said April term of said circuit court of Yalobusha county aforesaid, then and there, by virtue of a special writ of *venire facias*, then and there awarded by the said circuit court, at the said April term thereof, directing the said sheriff of said county of Yalobusha to summon persons there liable to serve as jurors, at the said April term of said circuit court, for the first week thereof. Nor were all, or the above named one there summoned as such juror, for the first week of said April term of said court, then and there, by virtue of an order of said court; nor had all and every one of the jurors of the regular panel of the jurors summoned and in attendance at the said term of said court, for the first week thereof, nor had the regular panel of the jurors summoned and in attendance upon said court, at the said term thereof, as liable to serve as jurors, for the first week, been gone through with, then and there to constitute a grand jury, to serve at the said term of said court, by lot, when the name of the said grand juror above named was drawn by lot, to serve as grand juror for the said term of said circuit court ; nor was the above named grand juror summoned by the sheriff of said county, from the by-standers then and there liable to serve, as a juror, for the first week of the said term of the said court, and this he is ready to verify ; wherefore he prays judgment of said indictment, and that the same may be quashed."

The plea was sworn to and issue taken on it.   The court over-ruled the plea, and the defendant (Baker) was convicted; from which decision of the court the defendant prayed a writ of error.

S. P. Caldwell for plaintiff in error.

D. C. Glenn, attorney general.

SMITH, C. J. :

In this case a *venire* had been drawn, returnable to the term of the circuit court at which the indictment was formed, by the clerk and sheriff, in the presence of the probate judge.   A suffi-cient number of this *venire* were proved to be in attendance on the court to constitute a grand jury.   For some reason, not dis-tinctly set out in the record, the court set aside the whole panel, and ordered a special *venire*, returnable forthwith.   From the jurors summoned under the special *venire*, the grand jury which preferred the indictment was selected.

A plea in abatement, setting up an illegal organization of this grand jury, raises the only question in the case.

If the court was correct in rejecting the *venire facias*, which issued on the 14th March, 1850, the special *venire*, from which the grand jury were drawn who found the indictment, was legally ordered.   Consequently, no valid objection could be raised to the organization of the grand jury.

By the statute of February 27, 1836 (Hutch. Code, Dig. 888, art. 10, § 2), it is made the duty of the circuit judges. " If, at any regular or special term of the circuit courts there shall not be in attendance any of the regular jurors summoned to such term, forthwith to award a special *venire facias*," and from the jurors summoned, by virtue of such writ of *venire facias*, "to organize a grand jury and petit jury."

The authority to award a special *venire*, except in a peculiar class of cases, in which parties are capitally charged, is confined to cases in which there are none of the regular *venire* in attendance upon the court. It seems clearly not to have been the intention of the legislature to vest in the circuit court, under this provision of the statute, the authority to decide upon the legality or the illegality of any act connected with the drawing of the names of the persons who are to constitute the *venire;* the issuance of the writ, by virtue of which they are to be summoned, or the mode in which they may be summoned. By the first section of the statute above quoted, the authority of the circuit court, as it then existed, to entertain challenges to the array, and motions to quash the *venire facias*, is expressly repealed.

In the case under examination, the *venire facias*, as it is alleged, illegally issued, in consequence of the irregular mode by which, and the improper time at which, the drawing took place. Let that be granted. What then? The circuit court could not entertain a challenge to the array, or quash the *venire facias*, for any cause whatever. And we apprehend that the *venire facias* could not have been properly treated as a nullity by the court.

The record shows, that persons summoned by virtue of the first *venire facias*, were in attendance on the court. The single condition, therefore, on which the court could rightfully have awarded a special *venire*, did not exist. It was a void act. Hence, the grand jury who preferred the indictment were illegally constituted. The plea, therefore, presented a valid defense to the indictment, and should have been sustained.

Judgment reversed, and indictment quashed.

COPELAND v. THE STATE, 23 Miss. Rep., 257.

PERJURY.

On trial of the indictment for giving false testimony as a witness, an affidavit of the accused is not admissible as evidence. In such case, the accused should have been indicted for the perjury of making a false affidavit.

Error from Jones circuit court. HARRIS, J.

This was an indictment for perjury. The offense alleged in the indictment, consisted in his falsely swearing to the correctness of an account introduced by him as an offset in the trial of a suit against him, before a justice of the peace, while giving testimony as a witness in said suit.

The proof showed that he was not sworn as a witness on the trial, but that he made oath to the truth of an affidavit asserting the correctness of the account. The affidavit was introduced as evidence on the trial for perjury in the circuit court, and read to the jury.

The accused was convicted, and sentenced to two years' imprisonment in the penitentiary.

H. F. Simrall for plaintiff in error.

There is a palpable distinction made in all the authorities between an indictment for false swearing to a written paper, and false testimony given upon a trial.

Proof applicable to the last indictment will not sustain the former. See 3 Wheeler's Rep., 180.

D. C. Glenn, attorney general,

FISHER, J.:

At the October term, 1850, of the circuit court of Jones county, the plaintiff in error was convicted of perjury, and sentenced to two years' confinement in the penitentiary of the state. A motion was made in the court below for a new trial, on the ground that the verdict of the jury was not sustained by the evidence, and upon the further ground of newly-discovered evidence since the trial. The court overruled the motion, and the counsel for the prisoner took a bill of exceptions to the judgment of the court in overruling the motion, and have prosecuted a writ of error to this court.

The indictment charges, " That on the trial of a certain issue before Benjamin C. Duckworth, a justice of the peace of Jones county, in a certain cause wherein Robert Tromborough was plaintiff, and the said Samuel Copeland defendant, the said Copeland appeared as a witness in his own behalf, and took his corporal oath before the said justice of the peace that the evidence which he, the said Copeland, should then give, touching the matters in question between the said parties, should be the truth, the whole truth, and nothing but the truth."

That upon the issue joined as aforesaid, it then and there became, and was a material question, whether a certain account in favor of the said defendant and against the said plaintiff for $15.80 had been paid ; that said account was offered by the defendant as an offset against the demand of the plaintiff ; that the said prisoner being sworn as aforesaid (omitting the formal part) before the said justice, did depose and swear, etc., that the account offered as an offset was just and true, still owing, etc.

We have stated the substance of the indictment so far as it relates to the oath of the prisoner, and the matter in controversy before the justice of the peace ; the charge is, that the prisoner appeared as a witness in his own behalf, etc. From this we must infer that he gave his testimony orally in the usual way on the trial ; and this brings us to the question whether the evidence introduced before the jury was proper or sufficient to sustain the verdict.

The proceedings before the justice were introduced on the trial of the prisoner, amongst which appears a copy of an affidavit in these words :

" The State of Mississippi, Jones county. Personally appeared before the undersigned justice of the peace, ' who deposeth and say' on oath that the within account is just and true, still owing and due, and that he has received no part thereof, or any person for him.

his
" SAMUEL × COPELAND.
mark.

" Sworn to and subscribed before me this 5th day of January, 1850.   B. C. DUCKWORTH."

The magistrate certifies that this affidavit is a true copy from the original in his office, " and that the affidavit was made on the trial before him, and duly taken by the prisoner on the aforesaid trial." This is every particle of evidence relating to the oath taken by the prisoner. It no where appears on the record that the account was offered, as an offset, on the trial of the issue before the justice. But the question we desire to notice is, whether the party accused could be introduced as evidence under the indictment. It is unnecessary to cite authority to sustain the position that an indictment must set forth, in a certain and definite manner, the offense with which the party is charged, and that proof can only be introduced to sustain the charge thus made in the indictment. The charge in this case is, that the party was sworn as witness in his own case, and while thus testifying, committed the perjury set forth in the indictment. The affidavit was not evidence which could be introduced on the trial of the issue, except by consent of parties, and this consent is neither charged nor proved; we are bound, therefore, to infer from the indictment that the accused gave his evidence orally. If it is intended to convict a party of perjury, in falsely swearing to an affidavit, the indictment must sufficiently charge the fact that the affidavit was made by the accused, otherwise it cannot be introduced as evidence. In the case of The People v. Robertson, 3 Wheeler, 191 the court said, that "All indictments for perjury upon an affidavit, state the charge in one or two ways; either that he did corruptly say, depose, swear and make affidavit in writing, or that he did procure and exhibit a certain affidavit in writing." If the indictment must contain a charge that an affidavit was made when the perjury was committed in that manner, it follows that without such a charge in the indictment, an affidavit could not be introduced as proof to authorize a verdict of guilty.

We are, therefore, of opinion that the court erred in refusing the new trial.

Judgment reversed, and cause remanded; new trial granted.

CLARKE *v.* THE STATE, 23 Miss. Rep., 261.

MAYHEM.

A prosecuting attorney has the discretion to quash an indictment or enter a *nolle prosequi* at any time before the jury is empanelled and the prisoner arraigned for trial.

The statute of limitations does not run in favor of fugitives from justice.

When, after an offense has been committed, an act of the legislature changes the punishment, the accused, on conviction, has the option to select the punishment prescribed by the new or old law.

Error from Wayne circuit court. WATTS, J.

G. W. L. Smith for plaintiff in error.

D. C. Glenn, attorney general.

Cited H. & H., 739, § 10 ; 2 Rob. Va. R., 800 ; 1 Leigh, Va. Rep., 569.

YERGER, J. :

The plaintiff in error was indicted at the October term, 1850, of the circuit court of Wayne county, for an assault and mayhem committed upon Richard Dodd, by cutting out his eyes with a knife. On the trial, the proof clearly established the fact of mayhem, which it appears was committed in the year 1833. The proof also showed that immediately, and in less than a year after the commission of the crime, the plaintiff in error fled and absconded from justice, and was not within the county of Wayne, where the crime was committed, until within twelve months before the indictment on which he was tried was found against him. At the April term, 1834, of the circuit court of Wayne county, an indictment for this offense was found against defendant, and *capias, alias capias, pluries,* etc., were issued against him repeatedly, and all were returned " not found." The indictment found in 1834 was quashed by the court, at the instance of the district attorney. The defendant was convicted and sentenced to punishment, according to the provisions of the act of 1822, which was in force when the offense was committed by him. Three errors are assigned for the prisoner.

1. It was error in the district attorney to quash the indictment founded in 1834. In this we are unable to see any error. It was a matter entirely discretionary with the district attorney, who had the power to enter a *nolle prosequi,* or quash the indict-

ment, if he saw fit to do so, until the defendant was arraigned and put upon his trial on that indictment. What effect the act of quashing an indictment, after a prisoner is arraigned and a jury empanelled to try him, might have under that clause in the constitution, which says that "No one shall be twice put in jeopardy for the same offense," we need not now determine. Certainly until after arraignment and the empanelling of the jury, the power of quashing an indictment rests in the discretion of the district attorney, and is not an act of which the defendant can complain, it not being to his prejudice.

2. It is said that a new trial should have been granted to the prisoner, because the offense of which he was charged was committed more than twelve months before the indictment was found against him. To this it is sufficient to reply, that, in our opinion, the proof clearly showed that the defendant came within the proviso of the act which declares, that it "shall not extend to any person or persons absconding or fleeing from justice."

3. It is said the court erred in not arresting the judgment, because the law in relation to mayhem and its punishment had been changed since the commission of the crime for which the prisoner was convicted, and that this change of the law amounted to a statutory pardon. This position is not tenable. The act of 1839, which changed the law on the subject of mayhem, and provided for its punishment by imprisonment in the penitentiary instead of the pillory and fine, by which it was formerly punished, expressly enacted, that "No offense committed and no penalty or forfeiture incurred, previous to the time when this act shall take effect, should be affected by this act," except that when punishment, forfeiture or penalty shall have been mitigated by this act, its provisions shall be applied to the judgment to be pronounced for offenses committed before its adoption.

This provision clearly shows that the legislature did not intend that the penitentiary code should amount to a statutory pardon for offenses committed before its adoption. The only change which it made in the law, was to commute or change one form of punishment for another, substituting the more mild for the severer punishment inflicted before its passage. We think that in every case of offenses committed before the adoption of the penitentiary code, the prisoner has the option of selecting the punishment prescribed in that code, in lieu of that to which he was liable before its enactment.   But inasmuch as this record does not show that the prisoner claimed a commutation of his punishment, we are of opinion that the court acted properly in sentencing him to punishment, according to the law in force when the offense was committed by him.

Let the judgment be affirmed.

LAMBETH *v.* THE STATE, 23 Miss. Rep., 322.

HOMICIDE.

The guilt or innocence of the accused is in no degree dependent upon the question of his or the deceased's title to the land or fence, which had caused the dispute between them and ended in the killing of deceased. If either killed the other with a deadly weapon in order to prevent a trespass in the removal of the fence, such homicide would be murder in the absence or proof that would tend to rebut the presumption of malice arising from the weapon used.

The competency of dying declarations is exclusively for the consideration of the court, and having once decided on its competency, it then becomes the province of the jury to decide upon its credibility, who are at liberty, in doing so, to consider all the circumstances under which they were made, and give to the evidence only such merit as they may think it deserves.

Where the court has admitted the dying declarations as competent evidence for the jury, the law raises a presumption that they were made by the party under a due sense of impending dissolution.

It is proper for the court to modify instructions as asked by counsel, so as to make them conform to his own views of the law, yet, it is the safer rule, to give instructions as asked by the accused, provided the court believes them to be the law, and if any explanations are necessary, to give them afterwards.

Objections to the admission of dying declarations must be made on the trial; it is too late to object on error.

The Bill of Rights, which declares that "the accused shall be confronted by the witnesses against him," does not apply to the admission of the dying declarations of the deceased, in cases of homicide.

Dying declarations are not entitled to the same degree of credibility, as if the deceased had sworn to the same facts in open court, as a witness; and an instruction to that effect is erroneous.

Lovick Lambeth, the plaintiff in error, was indicted and arraigned before the Madison Circuit Court, for the murder of John Tate. A change of *venue* was granted, and he was tried and convicted at the November term, 1850, of the circuit court of Yazoo county, of the crime alleged.

It may be proper to state that Lambeth was indicted jointly with Isaac and James Mayfield, who were acquitted. Lambeth fled, but came back and took his trial separately. Darling Rollins, first witness, testified that he had known Tate fifteen years, was hired by Tate, and worked for hire, at fifty cents a day, on the 4th March, 1850. On the morning of that day, Tate told witness to take the negroes, and reset a fence then in dispute between Tate and Lambeth, beginning at the east end of the line, and northeast corner of the Shular field. He ran the fence for some distance westward, and then ran it south, below witness' house. After breakfast, Tate came out where he was, with a double-barrelled shot gun. Witness said if he had come sooner, he would have had a chance at some partridges. Tate made no reply. Witness and Tate were at the south-west corner of the Shular field, and just then Lambeth passed, going towards Canton. He told Tate he had forbade his moving the northern string of fence. Tate said, "Pass on, I want nothing to do with you." Lambeth said he was going to Canton, and would stop Tate before night, and passed on, turning to the right around the field, and went back through the woods, in the direction of his own house. Witness told Tate he had better go home; he said he would not, that he would not interfere with Lambeth. Witness urged him, saying some devilment was going on, and he thought Lambeth would shoot him. Soon he heard guns firing, and caps bursting, in the direction of Lambeth's house, which was about five hundred yards from the field; thought he heard three guns fire. Witness was putting up stakes; said to Tate, "Yonder comes a crowd of them now;" they were in full view up the road, and coming down to the mouth of the lane, towards me and Tate. Don't know that Tate turned his head. Just then Magruder rode up. Witness begged him to stay, that he feared a difficulty, but he would not. Lambeth and the Mayfields neared the mouth of the lane; Lambeth turned off there, and went towards the north-east corner of the field, where the negroes were moving the fence, and the Mayfields came down the lane where witness and Tate were; they, starting to the negroes, met the Mayfields at witness' house. Tate shook hands with one or both; they appeared friendly. Israel said to Tate, "What in the devil is all this fuss about?" Tate said, "Nothing only that fence," pointing to it; that he never did Lambeth any harm, or said anything against him. They stepped into witness' yard; his wife called him, and told him to keep out of any difficulty. Said he must do his work. At this moment heard Tate say to the Mayfields the line had been correctly run. Witness talked to his wife some time, Tate and the Mayfields going towards the fence in a line east of north; they walked eighty yards; Tate turned and waved his hand to witness, as if calling him, but Tate and the Mayfields continued their direction some thirty yards further. Tate again beckoned to witness, who was at his house. Witness went and came up to them as they were crossing a drain, two hundred and fifty yards from the house. As they crossed it, the Mayfields turned rapidly off to the left. Tate kept up the drain towards the negroes. Witness turned to the left also, not comprehending the movement of the Mayfields; Tate walked some forty yards up the drain; saw Lambeth step from behind a tree, and ask Tate what he wanted. Tate said, "Nothing from you, Lambeth." Lambeth said, "D—n you, I'll shoot you," and raised his gun; Tate wheeled to the left, and made for a tree they had passed, but Lambeth fired on him before he succeeded. Tate had his gun in the hollow of his left arm, and right hand on the breech, when shot. One of the Mayfields, when he was shot, said, "There, by God, Tate drew his gun first!" but he did not. Lambeth was about to fire again; witness raised his hand, and said, "Don't, you have killed him." When Tate was shot, he tried to shoot at Lambeth, but could not; walked a few steps, tried again, and failed. Witness was five steps from the Mayfields, about twenty-five from Tate, and the same from Lambeth, when the shooting happened. Tate walked about fifty yards and fell. Witness asked for help of the Mayfields, who refused it, and went to and off with Lambeth. Lambeth stood behind a tree about two feet through, the largest about; no obstruction between Lambeth and Tate when Lambeth fired, or between Lambeth and the path up which Tate had come. An ignorant negro carried Tate's gun home; did not know how to let a hammer down; examined in the evening; found both hammers down, a cap on the gun. This was 4th March, 1850, eight or nine o'clock A. M. On the 26th February, 1850, Lambeth came to the field; said what sort of writing was that he sent him? Tate said, "Such as I wanted; Lambeth, you old devil, did you think I would receive such a small sum of money?" Tate was moving a tree cut on his land, but part of it had fallen on Lambeth's land. Lambeth forbade him. Tate said, "Ill do it or die;" fastened a chain to it, and told his negro to drive on. Lambeth drew his gun and threatened to shoot. Tate said, "Shoot and be d——d!" and walked off, when Lambeth said, "You old devil, I'll get you in a few days."

Cross-examined.—Witness reproved Lambeth, who said he had no idea of shooting Tate. Tate told witness that county surveyor had run a line, and the fence was on Lambeth's land, but he did not believe it, as one Gillespie run the line in 1837, but it was on his land. The evening of the shooting, witness gave a negro woman a six-barrel revolver; did not belong to him, but found it in his trunk. Saw Lambeth some moments before Tate was shot; don't know that Tate saw him. Saw Tate going towards Lambeth in speaking distance; did not warn him of danger; formerly told Tate Lambeth would shoot him, as he "saw shoot in his eye," the 26th February. Tate did not cock his gun or present it at Lambeth when he was shot.

Rev. Thomas McGruder.—Says a portion as Rollins; Tate said he would have difficulties about his road; asked him to stay, but he would not. Tate said he must do then the best he could, but he could not be run off his own land. Witness rode on towards Canton; soon reached an eminence; looked back; corroborates Rollins down to his, Tate's and the Mayfields' reaching Rollin's house. Witness then went on; heard gun fire; turned back toward the Shular field; saw three men enter the road going from where he found Tate's body; heard a female cry for help; started to the house, met Rollins and some negroes; said Tate was shot, Rollins was excited; told Rollins 'twas no use to send for help; proposed to go and see Tate; found him pale, ghastly, and weltering in his blood; thought him dying;

had some religious conversation ; asked him what was the matter ?   Said "Lambeth had shot him ; that he made no effort to shoot Lambeth till he shot him ;" fainted, thought him dead ; revived.   Soon Esq. Carstarphen came, and soon we called some wagoners to help us ; asked them where they lived, that they might be needed as witnesses ; did not hear a conversation between Tate and Carstarphen, as stated by the latter, but such might have been and he not hear it, while he was talking to the wagoners ; found no gun near Tate when he came to him ; soon took Tate to the house, when he left.

Carstarphen says, on March 4, 1850, met four men, Lambeth, the two Mayfields, and another, where a road meets the main Canton road at right angles, walking fast.   Lambeth said, " Good morning, squire."   Heard a woman cry " Stranger ;" said Lambeth had shot Tate ; asked aid.   Went back to where he saw Lambeth and the Mayfields,· round the north string of fence ; came up to Tate ; badly hurt, thought mortally.   Tate fainted. Came to, and made this statement, that he did not know Lambeth was there till he poked his head from behind a tree, and said, " Stop ;" that he dropped his gun.   Lambeth : " What will you have of me to-day ?"   Tate : " Nothing from you."   Lambeth ordered him again to stop, and shot him.   Tate said this before and after he fainted ; McGruder and Rollins were there at the time.

Dr. P. O'Leary.—Says he is a regular M. D. ; describes Tate's wounds.   All came in the direction from the right side of Tate ; of these he died.   Those under the arm would have struck the arm had it been down ; but if Tate was running or walking rapidly, they might have missed the arm.   Range of wounds from right side to spine.   His statements corroborated by several witnesses.

Jonathan Coleman.—Says he was on his way to Canton, on the morning of the 4th March, 1850.   Passed Lambeth's house short distance ; was hailed by Lambeth, who was going towards his own house, and was some fifteen or twenty steps from the road when he hailed.   Stopped, and asked Lambeth if he was going to town.   Said no ; that Tate was moving his fence, and he was going to get the boys and stop him.   Lambeth said Tate had cocked his gun on him in the lane, and seemed to be excited.

Mrs. Mary Rollins states in substance as D. Rollins. When Tate waved his hand to Rollins, he was on the side of the drain next the house. Tate then had his gun on his right shoulder, and also when he passed her house. Heard gun fire; ran out; saw Rollins beyond drain, his hand raised; did not hear him say anything. Shortly saw Lambeth and the Mayfields start from the outside of the fence, in the direction towards the main Canton road. Cross-examined, and said that at her house she heard Tate tell the Mayfields "The line was correctly run." Did not hear the Mayfields propose to get the county surveyor to run it again. Day windy and blustering; but thinks she would have heard it. She could, though she might not hear. She then corroborates the first part of Carstarphen's proof, on cross-examination. Saw Tate's woman with pistol; laid it on her bed; made her put it into a trunk to be out of reach of the children. Supposes she got it out of Tate's clothes the day he was shot.

Thomas H. Gillespie says he was county surveyor in 1837 and '38. State asked if he then run a line between Lambeth's and Tate's land. Before answer, defense asked him if he had any personal knowledge of the length of the lines run by him in the survey. He said, no; except as he learned from his chain-carriers, who were sworn. He did not know that they made true or false report of the distances. Defense then objected to his proof; overruled, and exception taken. States how and when he made his survey. That Tate called on him "last Spring," (i. e., 1850,) to get the county surveyor, and run the line. Tate said he had no confidence in Holliday's survey. Witness then retraced his old lines, and found the disputed fence on Tate's land. That Shular, who once owned Tate's land, put up the fence from rails off of Tate's land. Witness stated these facts after Rollins had been cross-examined.

Several witnesses then said Tate fired a gun like most men, the butt to his right shoulder, his left hand on the barrel, and his right on the trigger. Tate was a peaceable man, but a brave and determined one, where he thought his rights were involved.

John Simms says he was with Tate the day he died, April 3,

1850. Was in full possession of mind, and satisfied of approaching death, and while so situated made a declaration, which is in substance as follows, as it was taken down in writing at the time by the witness :

" I sent Rollins to move the fence ; while so doing, Lambeth came by and passed me, turned, and asked me if he did not tell me not to remove those rails. I said I had moved part, and would move the rest. He swore he would put me up for it ; would put me in the penitentiary ; that he was going to Canton to do it ; passed on, turned at the forks of the road, and at the house rounded the fence, leaving the field on the right, and went home ; then heard caps bursting, guns firing, and concluded he was preparing for me. During this time I was staking for the negroes to put up the rails, and was nearly done, when I saw Lambeth and the Mayfields coming down the road. McGruder came up, pointed out the men to him ; told him Lambeth had his gun ; asked him to stay ; he would not. Asked Rollins to stick by me, but he said he would have nothing to do with it. Went towards negroes ; met the Mayfields, friendly, shook hands. They asked what had got into me and Lambeth. Said I did not know ; had never said a harm word about Lambeth. They said it could be settled without going any further. I said I did not know how. They talked on the same way. James asked me to give up my gun. I said ' not to a crowd that was after me.' He said, if I would, Israel would go and get Lambeth's. I said if they wanted it settled, they ought to have taken Lambeth's gun before he came up ; that I was certain not to meddle with him when he had no gun. Thus talking, we went towards my hands, I suspecting Lambeth was there, but not seeing him. Then we crossed the drain ; the Mayfields stepped quickly off to the left ; I halting, not understanding their movements. Lambeth spoke from behind a tree, asked what I wanted. I looked up, saw he had his gun drawed ; told him I would have nothing from him. He told me not to come any further, or he would kill me. I looked around, saw an old tree, tried to get behind it ; he shot me before I succeeded, and got behind the tree again. 3d April, 1850.—Wednesday evening, fifteen minutes after three."

Witness said Tate shot as other men; describes the usual mode. Saw Tate's gun, after he was shot, with hammer down. Cross-examined, and said Tate died at half-past five that evening. That early on 4th March, Tate came to his house with a double-barrel gun, and procured witness to load and charge it with great care; so much so, that he asked if there was any further difficulty between him and Lambeth. He said no. After standing and talking some time, Tate started off, saying he intended moving that fence that day.

Israel P. Mayfield, for defense, says, he and his brother James were at the shop "when they received some information from their mother, which caused them to go straight to Lambeth's house." Met him between his yard and gate with his gun; asked him what was the matter; Lambeth said he had started to Canton, found Tate's hands removing his fence; forbade it. Tate cocked his gun, told him to pass on; wanted to talk to Tate, but was afraid to stop; Tate looking as if he would shoot him off his horse if he did; said he intended to stop the removal; asked Lambeth to leave his gun; he said Tate had a gun, and he was not safe without his, but he would not shoot Tate for a million, the world, and would not go in shooting distance of Tate; asked witness to say so to Tate, and settle the difficulty. They went up to the mouth of the lane. Lambeth then asked them to go up the road to Tate and settle the difficulty, to tell him if he would put down his gun, he would his, to meet and settle it by words; if not, then fight it out, "fist and skull." Lambeth said he would go on to where the negroes were at work and stop them. They, Israel and James, went on and met Tate at Rollins' house; shook hands friendly. Witness said, "What the devil is this fuss about?" Tate said, "Nothing much, except that fence," pointing to it. Witness proposed to get the surveyor and have the line run, and thus settle it. Tate said, "The fence was his; he would remove it that day or do worse." The line had been correctly run. All, Tate, Rollins, witness, and James, had stepped into Rollins' yard, whose wife called him. They passed on, Tate leading the way. As they passed the house corner, witness said, "Mr. Tate, for God's sake, stop; don't go where Lambeth is. Yonder he

stands with his gun ; you see him as plain as I do," and pointed
to Lambeth.   Tate said, "He didn't care where Lambeth was,
or what in the h——ll he had."   They then walked on some
seventy or eighty yards towards Lambeth.   Tate stopped, and
beckoned Rollins on.   Witness told Tate that Lambeth had told
him to tell him to put down his gun, and he would his ; that he
would not shoot him for the world ; to meet and settle it without guns ; if not, to settle it "fist and skull."   Witness asked
Tate to put down his gun, and Lambeth would his.   Tate said
he would not put down his gun to settle a difficulty with any
man.   James proposed to Tate to give up his gun, and witness
said, "Yes, Mr. Tate, do so ; if you don't want to give it to
James, call your overseer and give it to him, and I will go and
get Lambeth's gun, and carry it three hundred yards off, and go
clear off."   Tate said, "he did n't care what Lambeth did with
his gun ; that he would not give up his gun to settle a difficulty ;
that he carried his gun to settle it, and with his gun he would
settle it."   During this they halted, Tate beckoned Rollins on,
who was sixty or seventy yards off.   Tate started on, cocked
his right hand barrel ; told witness and James to walk on ahead
of them.   We turned a little to the left—all crossed the drain
nearly at the same time, a few feet below Tate.   We were half
way between Rollins' house and the drain at the second halt,
when Tate cocked his gun.   After crossing the drain, Tate did
not halt, but turned to the right in a different direction from
Lambeth, and towards his negroes.   Witness went on the way
they were walking, which led to Lambeth.   Tate went up the
drain towards his negroes, and eight or ten steps till he found
a tree, cocked his other barrel, carried it presented, and seemed
to keep the tree between him and Lambeth.   As he reached it,
believes he rested his gun by the left hand side of the tree.   Lambeth told him to stop ; not to come on further till he told what
he wanted.   Tate asked Lambeth what he wanted.   Lambeth
said, "Nothing with you, Tate."   Lambeth then asked Tate
what he wanted.   Tate said, "Step out from behind that tree
and I'll show you what I want."   Tate then seemed to be drawing back his gun, as if to place it on the other side of the tree ;
took a step or two backwards, and turned as if stepping to the

other side of the tree, and, in so doing presented his right side
to Lambeth, who shot him.   For the time witness left Rollins'
house till Tate put his gun by the tree, Lambeth stood leaning his left side against the tree, leaning his gun butt on the
ground.   He then picked up his gun, stepped behind the
tree, and fired from the other side.   Tate presented his gun
first.   It is one hundred and twenty or thirty yards from
where Tate passed the drain to where Lambeth was standing.
Tate told witness that all, save a few panels of fence, was
on Lambeth's land.   Witness is brother-in-law of Lambeth,
indicted for the same offense, and acquitted.   Denies that he or
James said " There, by God, you see that Tate drew his gun
first," or such like words, as Lambeth fired.   Says Rollins was
not over the drain when Lambeth fired.

James Mayfield corroborated Israel.

John Simms stated that the surveyor of Madison ran the
line between Lambeth and Tate, at their request.   Lambeth,
Tate, and witness carried the chain.   By it the fence half way
was entirely on Lambeth's land when it struck the line, and run
upon it at the rail top to the end of the line.

The state then called John Henry, S. G. McGruder, wagon-
men, B. Sutherland, Montgomery, Hicks and Phil. Rayford;
all of whom said, from the general character of the Mayfields,
known to them, they would not believe them on oath, and had
come to this opinion since the killing.

The defence then called Bowman and twenty-four others, who
deposed to the exact contrary, and would not believe them on
oath.

The following are the instructions asked by the counsel for the
state :

1st. That every killing is presumed malicious, and is murder,
unless the contrary is proven.   (Granted.)

2d. Malice is presumed, from the use of a deadly weapon.
(Granted.)

3d. If there is premeditation, however short, the killing is
murder.   (Granted.)

4th. If Lambeth designed killing Tate for moving the fence, and Tate died of his wounds, it is murder, unless done in self-defense.

5th. Lying in wait and threats, are evidence of malice express, previous, and defendant must disprove them. (Granted.)

6th. Although Tate might be wrongfully removing the fence, it did not justify his killing, and, if killed in pursuance of a design, it is murder. (Granted.)

7th. The jury can compare and weigh testimony, and give it such weight as they may deem it entitled to. (Granted.)

8th. The statements of accused are evidence, but the jury may give them such credit as all the facts and circumstances of the case show them to be entitled to. (Granted.)

9th. The dying declaration is entitled to the same verdict as if sworn to in court. (Granted.)

10th. Refused, and qualified as below.

11th. The declaration is presumed to be made under a "solemn and religious sense," unless the contrary is shown. (Granted.)

Defendant objected to the 7th, 9th, 10th, and 11th charges. The defendant asked seven charges; four were given, three were refused, and those were, —

Charge 4. A long hypothetical string of supposed facts, not in evidence, and conclusions therefrom. (Refused.)

Charge 5. Refused, as asked, and given as qualified below.

Charge 6. Refused, as asked, and given as qualified below.

Qualification of defendant's 5th charge :—In considering the dying declarations of Tate, the jury may take into consideration the condition of the deceased, his state of mind, and all the circumstances by which he was surrounded at the time such declaration was made.

Qualification of state's 10th, and defendant's 6th charge :—To warrant the jury in finding the defendant guilty, there should be evidence before them to satisfy their minds beyond a reasonable doubt. That which amounts to mere possibility only, or to conjecture, or supposition, is not what is meant by reasonable doubt. The doubt which should properly induce a jury to withhold a verdict of guilty should be such a doubt as would reasonably arise from the evidence before them ; and if such reasonable doubt should arise from the evidence, the prisoner should have the benefit of that doubt.

The jury found Lambeth guilty. A new trial was moved for, because,

1. Illegal testimony went to the jury.

2. The 7th, 9th, and 11th charges were not law.

3. The 4th, 5th, and 6th defence charges were refused.

4. The verdict was contrary to the evidence.

The court overruled the motion, to which opinion exception was taken, and the case comes into this court.

W. R. Miles for plaintiff in error.

The plaintiff in error was indicted for murder in Madison county. A change of venue was prayed for, and the trial took place in Yazoo. He was found guilty. A motion was made for a new trial, because,

I. The court erred in suffering illegal testimony to go to the jury.

II. In granting the 7th, 9th, and 11th instructions asked for by the state.

III. In refusing to grant the 4th, 5th, and 6th instructions asked by the defendant; and,

IV. Because the verdict was contrary to the evidence.

1. That the court erred in admitting Gillespie's evidence is quite plain. He was called to speak of a dividing line, running from east to west, through a section of land, midway between its external boundaries. He stated that, in order to find the starting point, he had commenced at the north-east or south-east corner of the section, and run half a mile. From that point he had run due east; that in measuring the half mile he had no personal knowledge of the distance travelled, and put his stake down at the point where the chain-bearer said it should be.

This is all believed to be hearsay evidence of the broadest kind. All he knew he derived from others. He does not know whether they gave him true or false information. And if the chain-bearers spoke falsely in 1837, when they indicated the half-mile point to the witness, although that false information might have cost the plaintiff his life, the witness would not be answerable to the charge of perjury. The law as laid down by elementary writers, and adjudged cases, requires the witness to speak from his "own knowledge;" and I am not aware of any exception to this universal rule in favor of "surveyors."

It is now said by the state that Gillespie's evidence, even if wrongfully admitted, furnishes no ground for reversal; for that the question of title to the ground on which the fence stood does not connect itself with the guilt or innocence of the plaintiff. But this is not true.

If, therefore, Gillespie's evidence had been excluded, there would have been no testimony in regard to the ownership of the fence, except the survey of Holliday, which gave it to Lambeth. And the jury might, and in all probability would have acquitted, or at least reduced the offense to manslaughter. For there is scarcely a man in this state who would not shoot down another who was forcibly tearing down his fence and moving it off his land.

It has been a matter of grave doubt, whether the court can instruct at all at the instance of the state. For as the jury in criminal cases are judges of both the law and the fact, and may at their election acquit against the instructions of the court, it would seem to follow that the court had no power to instruct them for the purpose of procuring a conviction. For if the court have a right to instruct, it is a legal right. If it be a legal right, the court has power to enforce obedience. But we know the jury may, and often do, acquit against the instructions. In such cases the court has no power to enforce its decision on the instructions; and it therefore follows that the court has no right to give them.

Supposing, however, the court pursues the right, I submit that it has not propounded the law correctly on the seventh, ninth, and eleventh instructions. In the seventh instruction, the court tells the jury among other things, that they are "to compare it (the testimony of Israel and James Mayfield) with the testimony of other witnesses, and the facts established in the case," etc. Now what does this mean? So far as the comparison of their testimony with that of other evidence in the case is concerned, I make no objection. But what is meant when the jury are told to compare the testimony with the "facts established in the case ?" What were the "established facts of the case ?" I had thought the jury had been empanelled for the express purpose of "establishing the facts of the case." Now, until the verdict was returned, it would seem that they remained unestablished. The testimony of the Mayfields and that of the principal witness on the part of the state stood opposed, and that upon the most vital and important points. An effort had been made to discredit their testimony. Their good character for truth had been attacked by seven and sustained by twenty odd witnesses. Standing thus opposed by the state's principal witness, standing thus attacked, and sustained, and the question being who was to be believed, the Mayfields or Rollins, the court informed the jury that it was their duty not alone to compare all the testimony, and determine what weight was due the evidence on both sides, but also to compare the testimony of the Mayfields with that of Rollins, (whose testimony constituted the "established facts of the case,") and then decide upon the weight to be given to each. In other words and in plain English, the jury were told that there were certain "facts established in the case" by the state; that these established facts admitted no contradiction; that though they might wish to credit the Mayfields, they could not do it, for that would be to destroy the effect of the "established facts" proved by Rollins; and they must therefore believe Rollins, first, as having "established the facts of the case;" and then, secondly, disbelieve the Mayfields because they did not believe with him !

I. It violates that clause of the constitution which gives the accused the right to be confronted by the witness against him.

II. It instructs upon the weight of testimony, etc.

III. It is not law, if the 1st and 2d objections to it should be overruled.

1. Upon this point I need only refer to the constitution. Its language is too emphatic and direct for argument. U. S. Const., art. 8, sec. 6 ; Miss. Const., art. 1st, sec. 10. This is in direct conflict with the common-law rule, allowing death-bed declarations to be read in evidence. They cannot both stand together. One must give way. Which shall it be ? The constitution or the common-law rule ? We shall see.

2. It is a direct instruction upon the weight of testimony. The jury are told exactly how much "credit and force" they are to give to Tate's dying declaration. They have no discretion at all. If the state meant any thing in asking an instruction upon the "credit and force" of testimony, it must have been what the language implies. Is not the force of the testimony and the weight of the testimony the same? Testimony has force according to its weight, no more, no less; without weight, testimony has no force. With little weight, testimony has little force. And with great weight testimony has great force. To instruct the jury, therefore, that certain testimony is entitled to the same "credit and force" as certain other testimony, the credit and force of which is fixed, is palpably to instruct upon the weight of testimony. It is for the court to decide upon the admissibility of the evidence; it is for the jury, under the circumstances, to judge of the effect of it. 2 Starkie, Ev., 460 [edition of 1830); 1 Greenl. Ev., 191, § 160.

3. Independent of the foregoing reasons, the instruction is fatally erroneous.

Supposing the dying declarations of the deceased to be competent, it does not follow that they are entitled to the same weight, credit, or force, as other testimony regularly given in court. On the contrary, it has always been held, until this case, that they are not. They want several important additions to bring them up to the common level of testimony regularly sworn to in court. The common law makes such declarations competent. The rule is, that the sense of approaching dissolution is substituted for an oath, inasmuch as it is supposed a man *in extremis* will not speak falsely. Roscoe's Crim. Ev., 22.

But the obligation of an oath is not the only thing necessary. Not only the truth, but the whole truth is required. An examination in chief of a witness, although bringing out the truth so far as the witness speaks, not unfrequently leaves half the truth untold. This is well understood; and is matter of every day experience. And hence it has been well said, that a searching cross-examination is quite as important to get at the whole truth as the sanctity of an oath. 1 Greenl. Ev., 192, § 162; 2 Stark. Ev., 460 (ed. of 1830); 13 S & M. 507.

In all the authorities cited, it will be seen that this class of testimony stands on ground peculiar to itself, and falls far short of testimony rehearsed in open court. It is incomplete. It is subject to be greatly biased by feelings of anger or ill-will, and lacks the great essential of a cross-examination; and is therefore to be received with great caution. 1 Stark., 101 (ed. of 1830].

A single remark will dispose of the 11th instruction granted for the state.

No judge or writer of any reputation has ever held, that the law "presumes" death-bed declarations to be made under a "solemn and religious sense." No respectable authority sustaining this instruction can be produced. It is, therefore, a manifest interpolation upon the law.

The 4th instruction asked for by the defendant ought to have been granted; it propounds the law correctly and was predicated upon testimony before the jury. By refusing it, the court told the jury, that even if they should believe the Mayfields (upon whose testimony this instruction was founded), they must still convict the defendant.

Upon defendant's 5th instruction, which was refused, I only ask that the court will compare it with the authority, 1 Greenl. Ev., 192, § 162. If the 6th instruction does not state the law correctly, I have read law to little purpose. The refusal to give it was an error the most gross and flagrant.

The court gave an instruction instead of defendant's 5th; and also one as a qualification to defendant's 6th.

I am not disposed to quarrel with the instruction given in lieu of the defendant's 5th, as not being good law. I admit it to be sound so far as it goes. But it stops short at asserting a general rule denied by no one, and does not touch the principle asserted in the defendant's instruction.

The misnamed "qualification" of the defendant's 6th is utterly objectionable. As a "qualification" it might do very well. But the learned judge first refused the rule as asked by the defendant, and then, with great judicial gravity, "qualified" it.

For all these reasons, I think the verdict should be set aside, and a new trial granted. The admission of Gillespie's evidence;

the instructions granted for the state; the refusal of those asked for by the defendant; each and all, are erroneous.

But, independent of all these reasons, the verdict is contrary to the evidence, and a new trial should be granted on that ground.

I do not mean that there is no evidence to support the verdict, or that it is palpably against the evidence; but I insist it is against the preponderance of testimony (the "reasonable doubt" included), and should not, therefore, be permitted to stand.

In connection with this point, I ask the court to reconsider its decision in the case of Cicely v. State, 13 S. and M., 213, wherein the rule is made the same in criminal as in civil cases. With great respect, I submit that the law, as settled in that case, is erroneous, and should be corrected.

The authorities referred to in 13 S. & M., 213, are all civil cases, and therefore furnish no rule for a criminal case.

But the cases cited and relied on by the attorney general, in Nelm's and McCann's cases, in the same volume, are of a somewhat different character, and require a brief notice.

The case of The State v. Jeffreys, 3 Murph. N. C. R., 480, is the first in point of time. What is there said upon the point is but a dictum of the court, no new trial having been asked for.

State v. Sims, 2 Bailey S. C. R., 29, is the next in point of time; and in that case the whole opinion is so plainly against the law, as to strip it of all weight and respect.

McCune's case, 2 Rob. Va. R., 772–790, follows next in date, and then, although the indictment was for murder, the jury reduced it to the second degree, and it, therefore, ceased to be a capital case, and the rule as to reasonable doubts could not apply.

Hill's case, 2 Grattan Va. R., 603, was a capital case, and the court relied entirely on the opinion in McCune's case for authority, and here is a palpable departure in principle.

The case in 1 Kelly R., 618, was for larceny; and the one in 7 Blackf. 198, for rape.

It will thus be seen, that out of all the authorities cited, there is but one capital case, where the point was directly made and decided, and that is made to depend upon an authority not in point.

It follows that, if the jury are bound to acquit upon a "reasonable doubt," it is also the court's duty to grant a new trial, if they convict over a reasonable doubt. Can any man peruse this record without a reasonable doubt of the defendant's guilt?

Simms had loaded Tate's gun at his request, and when afterwards requested to put down his gun by Mayfield, and settle the matter without its going any further, he replied, he "did not know how" else it could be settled.

Tate was never known to carry a gun or weapon before. At this time he was armed with both gun and pistol. He saw Lambeth and the Mayfields approaching him, and with his gun on his shoulder went directly where Lambeth was; and this, too, within a short time after hot and angry words had passed between Lambeth and himself. Rollins, the state witness, makes one statement, the two Mayfields make a different statement. Dr. O'Leary's testimony in regard to the wound sustains the Mayfields and contradicts Rollins. The credibility of the Mayfields was attacked by a few witnesses, and sustained by a great number. Their testimony would certainly acquit Lambeth, as would that of Rollins alone, certainly convict him.

In the face of all this, how is it possible for any man to say, there is not a "reasonable doubt" of the guilt of the accused.

D. C. Glenn, attorney general.

1. The evidence fully sustains the verdict of the jury. The evidence of Rollins and the declarations of Tate make a clear case of murder. In much of the statements of each they entirely coincide, are partially borne out by the other state witnesses and witnesses for the defense, the position of the ground favors the truth of what they swear, and such part of the defendant's proof as conflicts with theirs, is confused, improbable, and unworthy of belief.

It is clear that Lambeth found Tate moving his fence, ordered him to stop, and threatened him if he persisted. Tate did persist. Lambeth went home, saying he would get the boys and stop him. The Mayfields were soon summoned, and came. Caps were burst and guns fired as a "preparation" to force

Tate to desist. Soon Lambeth, armed with his gun, and the boys, re-appear. The boys go to Tate, and Lambeth makes his way to the shelter of a wood at the northeast corner of the Shular field, near where the negroes were at work. Much conversation ensued between the boys and Tate. They swear that they preached peace to Tate, begged him to give up his gun, and promised him to take Lambeth's gun from him if he would. Tate says they were only seeking to disarm him, which he refused to permit. The probability of the truth of either statement is well determined by a single reflection. If the Mayfields desired peace and fair play and to settle the difficulty amicably, why did not they first disarm their friend and brother-in-law, Lambeth? This they could easily and should have done. But how was it? The removal of the fence was the *casus belli* of the parties. Right where this was going on they station Lambeth, armed with his gun. They then, two of them, friends of Lambeth's, brothers-in-law, who had been summoned by him for the fray to the scene of action, approach Tate and ask him to surrender his means of defense, in the face of the man who had threatened him. The belief is far more reasonable that they were seeking to lull Tate's vigilance, to throw him off his guard and to disarm him, so as to place him at the mercy of Lambeth.

The accounts which the Mayfields give of the actual shooting is confused and unintelligible to me, and is contradicted by the position of the ground and the proof of all the witnesses. They saw Tate cock both barrels of his gun ; presented it, and took his position by a tree ; that he sat his gun on the left side of a tree ; this was the north side. Lambeth was leaning his left side against his tree, which, of course, made him face south, looking west and south at the parties. Tate, they say, seemed to be drawing back his gun from the left to the right side of the tree, and in so doing, stepped back some two feet, which exposed him to Lambeth, who moved around to the left of his tree and fired. Is this probable or natural? If Tate sought the tree and reached it, and placed his gun on the left hand side of it, would he have been crazy enough to have drawn back his gun, and stepped out two feet in the clear to the right, when his

adversary was on the same side ready to shoot? This voluntary and most unnecessary exposure of himself by Tate is a trick
of the Mayfields; it was intended, as far as could be, to meet
and satisfy the proof of the wounds which show all the shot in
the right side running diagonally towards the spine; the probability is, that Lambeth was on the left of his tree the whole
time, for the reason that he could not fire from the right side,
unless he exposed his whole body, while on the left he was
almost unexposed.   There he stood, and from thence he fired,
as Tate ran, the shot running southwest from side to spine.
This seems credible, and was the fact, as Tate and Rollins
swear. If the Mayfields say truly, Tate was a raving maniac.
Warned of his danger, to advance one hundred and fifty yards
with his gun cocked and presented in a threatening manner,
in the face of an armed man under the protection of a tree, and
who, he was told, would shoot him; then himself seek cover of
a tree, to set down his gun, and then, for no reason that can
possibly be assigned, under the eye and in the reach of an
enemy, armed and seeking his life, he surrenders the cover he
had found, steps out, and permits himself to be shot down, with
his gun in his hand, and it not even raised! This is rather too
much; like the fish story, it throws discredit over all their
statements. Now, it is clear that the Mayfields, in their evidence, posted Tate's gun on the left of his tree, just to make
him pull it over to the right, in order to give plausibility, to afford some shadow of excuse for his stepping backward two
steps, and letting Lambeth kill him. The truth is, that if Tate
had got to the tree, as stated, the natural place for his gun was
the right side, and from that side he could fire, and at no exposure, just as Lambeth's proper place was the left side of the
tree. But the whole statement is awkward, and bears the mark
of perjury on its face, and besides is disproved by Tate and Rollins, who swear positively, and whose account is reasonable and
true.

But the deed is done. Tate is shot; he lies "pale, ghastly,
and weltering in his blood." Rollins, affrighted, calls for aid.
He implores help from the Mayfields. Where, now, are the
peace-makers who but now were so friendly to the dying man?

Do they offer the sympathy which so unhappy an event called for, even admitting that poor Tate was wrong? Nothing of the kind; their work was finished. Silently, but naturally, the confederates came together again, and swiftly sped them from the scene of their murder. If the deed was justifiable, there were the Mayfields to prove it, ready and on the ground. Why not wait, why not face their friends and neighbors, and say, it is a sad affair, but necessity required it? The instinct of truth would so have irresistibly held them; but not so; an inward monitor spake of guilt, of a planned and preconceived murder; their victim was before them in his blood; conscience whispered, and suddenly they left, as the Scripture hath it " The wicked flee when no man pursueth;" 'tis the sound of the driven leaf that scareth them.

The credibility of the Mayfields was strongly assailed by the state, and well sustained by the defense. On that point " honors are easy." The proof of Tate and Rollins was not assailed.

I shall reserve further comment on the testimony for an oral argument. Thus much has been said to show the verdict was borne out by the evidence.

2. I have shown the evidence supports the verdict. I therefore invoke the application of the rule so solemnly laid down by this court, which is sustained by authority, and borne out by principle, that this court will not disturb the verdict unless it is palpably against the evidence, or manifestly without evidence. McCann v. State, 13 S. & M., 497; Cicely v. State, ib., 213.

3. It is held to be a maxim of law, that it is peculiarly the province of a jury to determine in cases where there is a conflict of testimony. Such is here the case. If Tate and Rollins are to be believed, Lambeth is guilty. If the Mayfields, he is not. The jury have discredited the latter, and found him guilty. This is an additional and powerful reason why the verdict should not be disturbed. Keithler v. State, 10 S. & M. 228; Whart. Am. Crim. Law, 643, and many authorities cited.

4. Is there any error of law in the proceedings?

The 1st, 2d, 3d, 4th, 5th, 6th and 8th charges on the part of the state were not objected to, and no objection can now be raised. The 10th was refused. So there only remains of state charges the 7th, 9th and 11th.

Charge 7th only asserts the well known power of a jury to compare and weigh testimony, and give it such weight as it may be entitled to. Coon v. State, 13 S. & M., 262 ; McCann's case, ib., 497 ; Ciceley's case, ib., 213.

Charge 9th simply asserts, *in hæc verba*, the rule laid down by the chief justice, "that the awful situation of a dying man is supposed to be as powerful on the conscience as the obligation of an oath." Nelms v. State, 13 S. & M., 506.

Charge 11th is but the sense and spirit of the case just cited, and of all law on the subject of dying declarations. Ib.

The 1st, 2d, 3d and 6th charges for defendant were given. No question arises on them.

Charge 4th was refused. The facts, in part, are imaginary; in some portions, are true ; these are mingled together, and with the facts are then bundled into law by scraps in such a way as to confuse and mislead a jury. The gist of the charge is clearly embodied in the 1st, 2d and 3d charges given. Just so in McDaniel's case, 8 S. & M., 419. In regard to the 5th, 6th and 7th charges, these were refused, and refusal sustained by Mr. J. Clayton. See 2 Stew. & Port., 193 ; 1 Greenl. R., 135 ; 4 Chit. Gen. Pr. 40 ; 4 Hamm., 389 ; 1 Denio, 524 ; 7 J. J. Marsh, 194.

Charge 5th, qualifying defendant's, is not law, or if so, it is so stated as to mislead. It is qualified in the very language and plain sense of charge 9, in Nelm's case, 13 S. & M., 506.

Charge 10th, qualifying state, and 6th defence. Either of these charges may be law ; still the judge has a right to refuse, so he give the law in another form.

A circuit judge is not bound to give charges in the exact language asked, but may modify them in conformity with his own views of the law. Boles v. State, 9 S. & M. 288.

The right under the Act of 1846 is again asserted in the Keithler case, 10 S. & M., 227 ; and finally in Ciceley's case, 13 ib., 210, the very modification of the very charge in hand was given and was sustained.

Lastly. The objection to Gillespie's proof was properly overruled. The testimony of any surveyor or other public officer, as to acts which the law makes it his duty to perform, is conclusive. If this objection was good, no survey could ever be proven. I cannot see much importance in it any way. No matter to whom this fence belonged, a trespass in moving it did not justify a killing. McDaniel v. State, 8 S. & M. 419.

Fully as I have looked into this case, I can see no error in law or of fact which authorizes the defendant to ask for a reversal. Not often does justice, in this our day and time, reach high offenders against the criminal laws of the land. When it has done so, as in this instance, after long and earnest investigation, a fair and impartial trial, the rights, safety and interests of the many appeal as powerfully to the court as the misfortune of the accused.

Surely in this case has justice been fairly done in all things; so must the defendant bide his doom and answer the offended laws of his country.

A. H. Handy, on same side.

I. The testimony of Gillespie was properly admitted, because, 1. The prisoner had offered evidence in the first instance, in relation to the subject matter, in his cross-examination of the witness Rollins, with a view to disparage Tate. He could not object to further testimony on the same point to which he had opened the door. 2. Gillespie's testimony as to the survey and bounds of the land is not hearsay evidence, so far as the measurement was reported to him by the chain-bearers. He was acting as county surveyor, in his official capacity, and the chain-carriers were persons recognized by law, whose sworn duty it was to report the distances as measured. Their reports to the surveyor, during the survey, were part of the *res gestæ*, and therefore original evidence. They were official acts, and therefore presumed to have been done correctly. So of the survey itself, which could be made only by the aid of the chain-bearer. 3. But even if improperly admitted, all prejudicial effect of it was prevented by the 6th instruction given at the instance of the state, which, in effect, told the jury to disregard all this evidence. The question was not one of property, for all such evidence was inadmissible for such purpose. 8 S. & M., 419. But the point of the evidence was to show unjustifiable conduct on the part of Tate in claiming the land. It was a question of motive and provocation to which the question of property was merely collateral, and that being introduced first by the prisoner, it was certainly proper to show the reason on which Tate acted. And to that extent alone was the testimony admissible in any point of view.

II. The 7th instruction at the instance of the state is clearly law. 1 Stark. Ev., 580, 581; McCann v. State, 13 S. & M., 471; Cicely v. State, ib., 202; Coon v. State, ib., 252.

So the 9th instruction. 1 Greenl. Ev., § 157–160; Rosc. Cr. Ev., 34; Whar. Am. Cr. Law, 179; 13 S. & M., 506; 8 ib., 419.

So of the 11th instruction at the instance of the state. The dying declarations had already been received and admitted as evidence by the court. The question of admissibility was a preliminary one for the court. After that had been settled by the court, it is presumed that the preliminary proof, on which alone such declarations could have been admitted in evidence, had been made, and then the only question for the jury was as to their weight under the particular circumstances of mind, feelings of anger, revenge, or, on the contrary, of calmness, justice, etc., etc., in which the defendant was, at the time of making them. 1 Greenl. Ev., § 160; Whart. Am. Cr. Law, 179.

These instructions, together with the qualifying instruction given by the court, placed the whole subject of the dying declarations and their weight fully and properly before the jury. And the 5th instruction asked by the prisoner was unnecessary, and calculated to embarrass and mislead the jury. That instruction submitted to the jury the preliminary question already decided by the court, and left the question of what was a " religious sense " of impending dissolution to the uncertain, and possibly conflicting and irreconcilable opinions of the jury. That was a question of law already decided by the court. There was no evidence of Tate's religious belief. And the presumption of law in this land and age of christian enlightenment is, that every man is a believer in the fundamental principles of the christian religion, a future state of accountability, and of rewards and punishments.

Then, no injury could have been done by the refusal of this instruction asked by him, because, in addition to the general rule given at the instance of the state, all the circumstances under which the declarations were made, were fully submitted, to be weighed and considered by the jury, by the instruction given by the court in its stead, and in qualification of the instructions given at the instance of the state.

III. The 4th instruction asked by the prisoner was properly refused. So far as it could properly have been given, it was fully covered by the 1st, 2d, 3d, and 7th instructions given at his instance. These instructions contain a full expression of the law operating to his justification. The court was not bound to give instructions in every variety of form suggested by counsel. If the law was substantially and plainly given, it was sufficient. Cicely's case, 13 S. & M., 210 ; Keithler's case, 10 ib., 227 ; Boles' case, 9 ib., 288 ; 10 ib., 25.

This instruction is fully covered by the other instructions given for the prisoner, unless it was intended to convey the idea that Lambeth had a right to shoot Tate, if Tate was merely going with his gun on his arm or in his hand, in the direction where Lambeth was, and knew that Lambeth was there, it being near where Tate's negroes were at work and where he was obliged to go in superintending them. This seems to be the bearing of the charge, and if so, it was properly refused. It was, at all events, of doubtful import, and calculated to mislead and embarrass the jury. So far as it was not already covered by the 1st, 2d, 3d, and 7th instructions for the prisoner, it is erroneous, and should not have been given ; and so far as it is embraced by these or other instructions, it is superfluous and was properly refused. 10 S. & M., 25.

The 5th instruction asked by the prisoner and refused, and the 10th instruction asked by the state and refused, should undoubtedly have been given. But the instruction given in lieu of them, fully embraces everything contained in them. It fully and clearly recognizes the principle that the prisoner is entitled to the benefit of all reasonable doubts, and defines what such reasonable doubts are in law. The instruction is in the very language in which the rule is laid down in Cicely's case, and it is not possible to conceive but that it conveyed to the minds of the jury a clear and distinct idea of the rule, that the prisoner should have the benefit of all reasonable doubts resting upon their minds from the evidence. Although the instruction, as given, does not positively state this rule, yet it so clearly and fully recognizes it in stating the proper qualifications to it, as to place the rule itself as distinctly before the mind as the most positive statement of it could do. And it would, indeed, be strange to hold that the court below erred in giving the law to the jury, under like circumstances, in the very terms in which it is laid down in this court.

As to the court's instructing the jury on the weight of evidence in the state's 11th instruction, the court simply declares the presumption of law arising from the dying declarations which have been admitted in evidence. And the authorities fully sustain this instruction to this extent. Whar. Am. Cr. L., 179; 1 Greenl. Ev., § 160. But even if this instruction stated the rule as to the dying declarations too strongly, all possible prejudice to the prisoner was prevented by the qualifying instruction given by the court, which left the weight and influence of the dying declarations entirely to be considered by the jury. 2 S. & M., 17.

The points insisted on, that dying declarations are not admissible in criminal cases, in virtue of the 10th section of our bill of rights, and of the 6th amendment to the Federal Constitution, which guarantee to the prisoner the right to be " confronted with the witness against him," and that the jury are the conclusive judges both of law and fact in criminal cases, need no reply except a reference; on the first point to Woodsides v. State, in this court, 2 How., 264, and on the second, to the opinion of Judge Story, in United States v. Battiste, 2 Sumner, 240.

YERGER, J.:

The plaintiff in error was found guilty in the Yazoo circuit court of the murder of John Tate. He seeks to set aside that verdict, and reverse the judgment upon several different grounds. In stating the result to which our minds have come, it will not be necessary to notice all the evidence in the cause or all the points made by counsel in behalf of the accused. Such evidence only will be referred to as may be necessary to elucidate the points decided by us. Darling Rollins was the first witness introduced in behalf of the state, and from his testimony it appears, that a dispute had arisen between the deceased and the accused, in relation to the boundary line between their respective tracts of land; and that during the day on which the slaves of the deceased were engaged in removing a fence situated on the disputed land, he was shot by the accused, and died from the effects of the wounds. Upon his cross-examination the witness stated, that Tate had previously told witness, that R. J. Holliday, then surveyor of Madison County, had run the dividing line between Lambeth and himself; and that by that demarkation and line, the fence in dispute was left on Lambeth's land, but that in the same conversation he had further stated, that he did not believe Holliday's line was correct, because Gillespie, in 1837 or 1838, had surveyed the same land, and by his survey the fence in dispute was on Tate's land. Gillespie was subsequently introduced by the state and proved, that in 1837 or 1838 he did run the dividing line between the tracts, and by that survey the fence in dispute was on Tate's land. Before Gillespie's testimony was given, a preliminary question was asked him by the counsel for the accused, namely, whether he had any personal knowledge of the length of the lines run by him in that survey. To which he replied, that he knew nothing of the distance of any of the lines, except what he learned from the chain-carriers, who were sworn chain-carriers; and he did not know, whether, what they told him, was true or false. Defendant's counsel then objected to his testimony in relation to the survey made by him, but the objection was overruled, and the testimony admitted, and the admission of this testimony is assigned as error.

During the progress of the trial, John Simms was introduced as a witness by the state, and proved that on the 3d of April, 1850, the day on which Tate died, witness was with him; that Tate was then in full possession of his mental faculties, and while in that condition, and when satisfied that he was about to die, he made a declaration in regard to his murder, which was reduced to writing at the time by the witness. The statement was then given in evidence without objection. After the testimony closed, many instructions were asked for by both parties, and several on both sides given and some refused. Among others given in behalf of the state, the defendant excepted to the 9th and 11th instructions, and the giving of those is assigned as error.

The court refused to give the 5th and 6th instructions asked for by the defendant's counsel, but gave others in lieu of them, and this is likewise alleged to have been erroneous.

During the argument of this case, the objection to Gillespie's testimony was earnestly pressed upon the court. We confess we cannot view this point in the same light with the prisoner's counsel. In the first place, we may remark that the guilt or innocence of the accused is in no degree dependent upon the question of his or Tate's title to the land or fence in dispute between them. Had Lambeth attempted to remove the fence, the law would not have excused his homicide by Tate in preventing the removal, although the fence were the rightful property of Tate; of course the converse of this proposition is equally true. If either killed the other with a deadly weapon, in order to prevent a trespass in the removal of the fence, such homicide would be murder, in the absence of proof that would tend to rebut the presumption of malice arising from the weapon used; and in the absence of such proof, the kind of weapon used determines the intent, and fixes the degree of guilt.[1] McDaniel v. State, 8 S. & M., 418. Hence, in considering the questions of the guilt or innocence, the correctness of Gillespie's survey, or whether he knew it or not to be correct, is immaterial. If his testimony had been offered in a suit about the boundary of the land, we are not prepared to say that it should have been rejected. It is true, he stated that he knew nothing of the length of the lines, except from the statements made at the time of the survey by the sworn chain-carriers. The survey was made by Gillespie, and the length of the lines fixed by him in the same manner that other surveys are usually made, and the

[1] Wharton on Homicide, 233; 1 Hale, 473, 486; 1 East P. C., ch. 5, § 58, p. 290; Archbold Cr. Pr. & Pl., 846, notes; ib., 805; Foster, 291.

length of lines determined. He had the same knowledge of the distance run by him that surveyors generally have. The mode adopted by them in surveying land, is to put down the distance as it is communicated from time to time by the chain-carriers, and these statements, made at the time of the survey, would seem to be admissible when referred to by the surveyor, rather as a part of the *res gestæ* of the survey, than as hearsay evidence of statements by the chain-carriers.

But Gillespie was not introduced to prove Tate's title to the land in controversy, or the correctness of the survey made by him. On the cross-examination of Rollins by the defendant, he stated, that Tate had said the dividing line between Lambeth and himself had been run by Holliday, by which survey the fence in dispute was on Lambeth's land; but that he did not believe that survey was correct, inasmuch as Gillespie had previously surveyed it, and by his survey it was on Tate's land. It was competent, after this testimony was given on cross-examination, to introduce Gillespie as a witness, to prove the fact, that he had made the previous survey, as stated by Tate. And in this point of view, we think the evidence was admissible, whether the survey was correctly made or not.

Secondly. Did the court err in giving the 11th instruction asked by the state. It is in these words, " The presumption of law is, that the declarations of Tate, made when he believed he was about to die, and shortly before his death, were made under a ' solemn and religious sense' of approaching dissolution, and the jury must consider said declarations as made under such sense, unless the contrary is proved." By our law, the dying declarations of a party are only admissible on a trial for homicide, where the death of the deceased is the subject of the charge, and the circumstances of the death are the subject of the dying declarations. A preliminary fact, essential to be proved before their admission is, that they were made under a sense of impending dissolution. [1] This preliminary proof, and the proof of the

[1] 1 Archbold Cr. Pr. & Pl., 449; 1 East P. C., 354, 358; Rex v. Woodcock, 1 Leach, 652; Rex v. Wilborn, 1 East P. C., 358; Rex v. Van Butchell, 3 C. & P., 629; Com. v. Williams, 2 Ashmead, 69; 1 Greenl. Ev., 158; 2 Russ. on Crimes, 752; Hill's case, 2 Grat., 594; Nilson v. State, 7 Humph., 542; Moore v. State, 12 Ala., 764; Brakefield v. State, 1 Sneed, 215; Starkie v. People, 17 Ills., 17; Robbins v. State, 8

circumstances under which the declarations were made, are to be shown to the judge, who is the exclusive judge of their admissibility, in the same manner as the preliminary proof of documents and the competency of witnesses is always addressed to the court.[1] 1 Greenl. Ev., § 156, 160.

The awful situation of the party making the declarations and his belief in his immediate and impending dissolution, are considered by our law as equivalent to the sanction of an oath.[2] If the declarant, by reason of infancy, or imbecility of mind, tender age, or a disbelief in a future state of accountability, would have been excluded as a witness while living, his dying declarations would, for like causes, be rejected by the court. An oath derives the value of its sanction from the religious sense of the party's accountability to his Maker, and the deep impression that he is soon to render Him his final account. The danger of immediate and impending death, and the belief of the party therein, is, by our law, considered equivalent to this sanction. It follows as a necessary consequence of the rule which admits dying declarations made under such circumstances, that the law must presume them, in the absence of proof to the contrary, to have been made under "a solemn and religious" sense of impending dissolution; that is, under a serious sense, that the party would be soon called to account for the truth or falsehood of the statements, in the same manner as the law will presume, in the absence of evidence to the reverse, that every witness placed upon the stand and sworn to testify, believes in the existence of a God and a state of accountability in the future, for the commission of crimes perpetrated here. 1 Greenl. Ev., § 157. In this connection it is proper to notice the action of the court in overruling the motion for the defendant's 5th instruction, by which the court was requested to charge the jury, that unless the dying declarations of Tate were deliberately

---

Ohio St. R., 131; Brown;v. State, 32 Miss., 483; Kilpatrick v. Commonwealth, 7 Casey, 198; Commonwealth v. Densmore, 12 Allen, 535; Rex v. Pike, 3 C. & P., 589; Rex v. Crockett, 4 C. & P., 544; Rex v. Hayard, 7 C. & P., 187; Montgomery v. State, 11 Ohio, 424; State v. Poll, 1 Hawks, 442; Dunn v. State, 2 Pike, 229.

[1] See cases cited in note * supra.

[2] Archbold Cr. Pr. & Pl., 449; 1 East P. C., 354; 2 Russ. on Crimes, 752; Wharton Am. Cr. Law., 669; 1 Greenl. Ev., 158.

made under a "solemn and religious sense" of impending dissolution, they were entitled to but little weight.

We have just attempted to show, that where the court has admitted the "dying declarations," as competent evidence for consideration of the jury, the law raises a presumption, that they were made by the party in a state of mind indicated by this instruction ; unless the court was satisfied that they were made so, it would have been his duty to have excluded them from the jury, and not permitted them to have any weight in the formation of the verdict. The competency of this kind of testimony we have before seen, was exclusively for the consideration of the court. Having once decided that it was competent that the party was in the frame of mind required by the law, to authorize the admission of his dying declarations, the power of the court over that question was determined. It then became the province of the jury to decide upon its credibility, who were at liberty, in doing so, to take into consideration all the circumstances under which the declarations were made, including those already proved to the court, and to give to the evidence only such credit or force as, upon the whole, they might think it deserved.[1] 1 Greenl. Ev. § 160. We are of opinion, therefore, that the court did not err in refusing defendant-in-error's 5th instruction.

Again, will this court reverse the judgment because the circuit court refused to give the defendant's 6th instruction ? That instruction was in the following words : "If from all the evidence the jury entertain any reasonable doubts of the guilt of Lambeth, they cannot find him guilty, but must acquit him." As a legal proposition, this instruction was certainly correct, and we are at a loss to ascertain an adequate reason inducing the judge to refuse it. On its refusal, the jury were instructed in lieu of it, that "To warrant the jury in finding the defendant guilty, there should be evidence before them sufficient to satisfy their minds beyond a reasonable doubt. That which amounts to mere possibility, or conjecture, or supposition, is not what is meant by a reasonable doubt. The doubt which should properly induce a jury to withhold a verdict of guilty, should

[1] Vide cases cited supra.

be such a doubt as would reasonably arise from the evidence before them, and if such a doubt should arise from the evidence, the prisoner should have the benefit of that doubt." This instruction is in the precise language used by the circuit judge, in the case of Cicely v. State, 13 S. & M., 210. In that case, however, it was given by the circuit judge as an explanation of the words, "reasonable doubts." After he had given an instruction asked for by the accused, similar to that refused in this case, we think the court, in the case of Cicely v. State, adopted the safe and proper rule, that is, to give the instruction and afterwards to give the explanation, if it deemed that the instruction needed explanation. It is the safer course, and one which in criminal trials the circuit court ought to adopt, to give the instructions asked by the accused, provided the court believes them to be law, and if any explanations are needed in the opinion of the court, they can be afterwards given.

This brings to the consideration of the last proposition which we deem it necessary to notice in this opinion. Did the circuit court err in giving the 9th instruction asked for by the state? We think it did. That instruction was as follows: "That the dying declarations of Tate, written by the witness Simms and offered in evidence, are entitled to the same credit and force before the jury as if the statements had been regularly sworn to in court before the jury." In connection with this point the counsel for the prisoner elaborately argued that the dying declarations of the deceased ought not to have been admitted, because the admission violated the 10th article of the bill of rights, which declares that in all criminal prosecutions " the accused shall be confronted by the witnesses against him ;" and we have been earnestly invoked to review the former opinions of this court on this question. It would probably be sufficient to state in reply that these declarations were admitted without objection, and, therefore, it is too late to make it in this court for the first time. If, however, the objection had been made in the court below, it would in our opinion have been wholly untenable. This view of the law has been so often held by the courts of other states, having clauses in their constitutions similar to that in our bill of rights, and this court has decided so repeatedly that these declarations are admissible, even if our minds could be brought to doubt upon this point, we would not feel at liberty to disturb a principle so often settled and acquiesced in for so long a time. In Woodside v. State, 2 How. R., 665, decided in January, 1837, this question was fully discussed, and in an elaborate opinion delivered by the present chief justice, this objection to the dying declarations was pronounced untenable, and the admission of them was held in no wise to conflict with the bill of rights. If this were a new question, now arising for the first time, we could not entertain a doubt of the correctness of the principle as now settled. The admission of these declarations was established as a rule of evidence by the courts of the common law, are almost coeval with the foundations of that law itself. The general principle of the common law, on the subject of evidence, with few exceptions, has always been that "hearsay evidence" could not be admitted. But simultaneous with the adoption of this rule, an exception was made to it in the case of the "dying declarations" of the deceased, on the trial of the party charged with his murder. This exception to the rule was made upon the ground of an overruling public necessity for preserving the lives of the community by bringing man-slayers to justice. It would often happen that there was no third person present to be an eye-witness to the fact, and the usual witness in other cases of felony is himself destroyed. 1 Greenl. Ev., § 156. When the bill of rights was adopted by the framers of our constitution, they were aware of this rule of evidence of the common law. They found it adopted into, and forming a part of the jurisprudence of our country. The object they had in view in adopting the clause referred to, was not to introduce a new, or abolish an old rule of evidence. Their intention was not to declare or specify the nature, character, or degree of evidence which the courts of the country should admit. Their aim was simply to reassert a cherished principle of the common law which had sometimes been violated in the mother country in political prosecutions, leaving to the courts to decide, according to the rules of law, upon the nature and kinds of evidence which a witness, when confronted with the accused, might be permitted to give. The dying declarations are not the witness against the accused. They are only evidence against him which the witness confronted with him is permitted to introduce. The party testifying is the witness alluded to in the bill of rights. What testimony he shall be allowed to give is, in our opinion, regulated by the principles of the law and the practice of the courts, unaffected by the bill of rights.

But in our opinion the 9th instruction was erroneous because the language was calculated to mislead the jury in respect to Tate's declarations, which, under any circumstances, are at least but hearsay testimony, and subject to the objections which apply to that kind of evidence ; nothing but an imperative sense of public necessity ever justified their admission. Hence the courts constantly declare that they should be received with great caution. It is true, some authorities lay down the rule, that "A sense of impending death is equivalent to the sanction of an oath ; and that the persons whose statements are thus admitted, are considered as standing in the same situation as if they were sworn."

In thus laying down the rule, nothing further was intended by the writers than to assert the ordinary principle of the law on this subject, to wit : that for the purpose of admitting these statements to the consideration of a jury, the law substitutes the situation of the party making them in lieu of the oath which is usually required, and so renders the evidence competent. But the degree or weight to be given to such statements is left for the consideration of the jury, and depends upon a variety of circumstances which may tend to increase or diminish them. Among these circumstances are the mental and physical condition of the deceased when the declarations were made ; his memory, the extent to which disease may have impaired his recollection, and the accuracy with which the witness who testifies to the declarations, repeats the language used by the deceased. When statements are regularly sworn to in court before a jury, there are methods by which the jury can test the truth or falsehood of the statements, which cannot be applied by them to testimony given in any other way. Hence, the provisions before referred to in the bill of rights, that the accused shall be confronted with his witnesses. In addition to the solemn sanction of an oath administered to the witness and which impresses him with the necessity of speaking the truth, as he will hereafter be held to account for it, there is a salutory and restraining fear of punishment for perjury if a false statement is made; and when the witness is thus confronted with the accused before the jury, the accused has the power of cross-examination, a power as essential to the eliciting the truth as the sanction of an oath itself, as thereby an opportunity is afforded to ascertain facts omitted in the statement which may be essentially important to the truth of the narrative. 1 Greenl. Ev., § 162; 2 Pothier on Obl., 255 (Mr. Evans' note); 2 Starkie's Ev., 263.[1] At the same time, from a personal observation of the witness, from his manner of testifying, from his willingness or unwillingness to answer questions, from the clearness of his statements or the hesitancy with which he speaks, the jury is called to judge of the truth of his statements, in a manner which gives a weight and force to testimony, which evidence given in no other way should receive.

If, then, the court, by the 9th instruction, intended to charge the jury, that the same weight and force was to be given to Tate's statements as if Tate himself had been a witness in the court, it was certainly erroneous; and whether such was the meaning of the court or not, the language used would bear such a construction, and the jury may have so considered it, inasmuch as Tate could not have regularly sworn in court before them in regard to these statements, except as a witness. But the instruction, in our opinion, is objectionable in another point of view. The jury is directed to give to the statement of Tate, written by Simms, the same degree of weight and force as if it had been made directly by Tate in their presence; thus giving to secondary evidence the same weight which is due to direct testimony. Although the witness Simms intended to communicate accurately the statements made to him by Tate, and the circumstances under which they were made, it is impossible for him to communicate the tone and manner of Tate in making

[1] See also Phill. & Ames on Evidence, 305, 306; 2 Johns., 85, 96; Rex v. Ashton, 2 Lewin Cr. Cases, 147, per Alderson, B.

these statements. It is impossible for the witness to do more than convey to the jury the impression made on his own mind at the time. Every day's experience teaches us that we cannot and ought not to rely with the same confidence upon what is communicated to us, as upon those things which we see and hear ourselves; nor are such statements entitled to the same weight and force, however anxious the informant may be to communicate accurately what he has seen and heard; he can only give the impressions that were made upon his own mind; and if, from any cause, that impression is inaccurate, is incorrect, he will, of course, make an inaccurate and false impression on the mind of the party to whom the communication is addressed. We do not think, therefore, that Tate's statements, written out and offered in evidence by Simms, were entitled to the same weight as if Tate had been regularly sworn in court before the jury; because, in the latter case, the jury could have judged for themselves, by personal observation, in relation to Tate's mental and physical condition, how much his mind had been affected by his wounds and impending death; to what extent his memory and recollection had been impaired thereby; how far the passion of anger or feelings of revenge operated upon his mind and affected the truth and accuracy of his statements. In short, they could have decided in regard to these things, by impressions made immediately on their minds, and not made mediately upon them by information derived from another. It is, therefore, our opinion, that the statement of Tate, if sworn to regularly in court, before the jury, would have been entitled to greater weight and force, than when communicated to them by the witness Simms. Let the judgment be reversed, a new trial granted, and the cause remanded.

THE STATE *v.* BORROUM et al., 23 Miss. Rep., 477.

UNLAWFUL TRADING WITH SLAVES.

. The court is presumed to know the ordinary meaning of words, and is to construe them, when used in pleading, according to that sense.

Where the indictment states that the accused bought "seventy-five pounds of cotton" from a slave, the offense is as sufficiently charged as if it contained the additional averment that the same was a " product or commodity."

Error to Lafayette circuit court.　Miller, J.

The opinion of the court and the briefs of counsel contain a sufficient statement of the facts of the case.

J. W. Thompson for the state.

The bill of indictment charges that defendant, Wesley Bruce, bought of a slave seventy-five pounds of cotton, without the authority of the master, &c., in writing.　See Acts, December, 1850, p. 100, § 1.　The district attorney, in framing the bill of indictment, uses the word " cotton" (not in the statute), instead of the term " produce" or " commodity," and it is insisted for this reason, the bill of indictment is not sufficient.　Is not the word " cotton," used in the bill of indictment, equivalent to " produce" or " commodity?"　If so, this indictment is sufficient.　Arch. Cr. Pl., 52.　It is safest to pursue the words of the statute, though not essential.　The general rule is, to pursue the words of the statute.　But when the pleader departs from the general rule, he must be careful to keep within the true and well known limits of the exceptions to such general rule.　Where a statute declares the doing of certain acts for and with a certain intent and purpose, as in the case of " clipping," " rounding," or filing the coin of the realm (5 Eliz., ch. 11, § 2), the intent must be specially alleged ; but where a statute declares that the stealing of a certain thing or of certain things, by name, shall be felony, the judges would not enlarge the circle of crime by including things not named by any construction whatever, but adhered to the very words and letter of the statute ; as in the case of 2 and 3 Edw. 6, ch. 33, where only " horse," " gelding," and " mare," were named, the judges, under this statute, would not extend the meanings by any, the very least intendment, so as to embrace any other subject matter of larceny beyond what is expressed by the very words of the statute.　This strictness, it is well known, was always observed *in favorem vitæ*, only in its strictest sense.　The legislative power only could rightfully say what should, and what should not be a crime.　But such is not the question here.　Our statute of 1850, p. 100, § 1, makes the purchase of any produce or commodity from a slave a misdemeanor, not a felony; and the only question is, whether the subject matter (cotton) of this offense is sufficiently described. The sale of any " commodity" to a slave, without authority, etc., is an offense.   Cotton is a " commodity;" therefore, the sale of cotton to a slave without authority, etc., is an offense.   " Commodity" and cotton are equivalent terms, or cotton is contained within and embraced by the term " commodity."   The bill of indictment in all other respects is good.   Great strictness was intended to be dispensed with.   See second section of same statute, p. 101.

This statute is unlike the statute against the exhibition of deadly weapons.   In reference to the exhibition of deadly weapons, if the instrument charged to have been exhibited be not one of those enumerated in the statute, it must be shown by suitable averments wherein it was deadly.   Not so of " produce," or " commodity."   A gun, for instance, is not a deadly weapon without being loaded with gunpowder and ball, while cotton is a commodity in any condition, and needs no averment to show or convey the idea that it is a " commodity."   So of the word or term " produce."   It is believed that the bill of indictment in this cause was perfectly drawn, and that the rule of criminal pleading here should not be more strict than the English rule; and surely the rule in England is, that if you do use a word not in the statute, the word must be of similar import, or be equivalent to or embraced in the word used in the statute.   In dropping the word here used in the statute, one is adopted in its stead that most clearly is equivalent to it or legitimately embraced by it; and if this is so, the bill of indictment may be upheld by the principles of that rule just quoted, which is of the strictest class.

D. C. Glenn, attorney general,

Cited the following authorities: State v. Noel, 5 Blackf., 548; Peek v. State, 2 Humph., 78; State v. Foster, 3 McCord, 442; United States v. Bachelder, 9 Gall., 15; State v. Hickman, 2 Hals., 299; State v. Little, 1 Verm., 331; United States v. Gooding, 12 Wheat., 460.

H. A. Barr for defendants in error.

The indictment set out in the replication to which the demurrer was sustained, does not charge Bruce with any misdemeanor or crime known to the laws of this state.

The act of 1850 makes " the buying, selling, or receiving from a slave without permission, etc., any corn, fodder, hay, meal, spirituous liquors, or other produce or commodity," a high misdemeanor. Acts of 1850, p. 100. The word cotton is not embraced in the act. And it is not alleged in the indictment that cotton is a product or commodity. The court must know judicially from an inspection of the indictment that an offense is charged. Most of us in this country know, as a matter of fact, that cotton is a product and a commodity. But a court cannot draw upon its knowledge of facts to ascertain that cotton is a product or commodity. No court knows judicially that cotton is a product or commodity ; for there is no law declaring it either a product or commodity. It was, therefore, necessary that the indictment should allege that cotton is a product or commodity. If the indictment had alleged that cotton is a product or commodity, the court would know it judicially, and could pronounce that a misdemeanor had been charged against Bruce ; because the charge would be within what the law pronounces a misdemeanor.

Hence, it is necessary not only to set forth all the circumstances which constitute the statutable definition of the offense, but also to use the precise and technical language of the statute. 1 Chitty's Crim. Law, 286 ; Anthony v. State, 13 S. & M., 264.

Not even the fullest description of the offense, were it even in the terms of a legal definition, would be sufficient ; the very expressions of the statute must be used. Chitty's Crim. Law, 282.

An indictment charging a party with making an assault, etc., with a drawn knife, with intent to kill, etc., was held insufficient. The court says it should be alleged that the knife was a deadly weapon ; that all the circumstances which made up the statutable definition of the offense should be set forth, and that the precise and technical language of the statute must be pursued. Ainsworth v. State, 5 How., 245.

J. F. Cushman for defendants in error.

The court below quashed the bill of indictment, because there was not a sufficient description of the article alleged to have been sold by the negro to Bruce, the real defendant. The charge in the bill of indictment, that the defendant purchased cotton of the negro, when cotton is not mentioned in the statute, cannot be considered as equal or equivalent to produce or commodity, unless the court knows, in a judicial manner, that cotton is a commodity or produce. It is a well established principle of law, " That the facts of the case necessary to make it appear judicially to the court that the indictors have gone upon sufficient premises, should be set forth ; but there should be no unnecessary matter, or any thing which on its face makes the indictment repugnant, inconsistent or absurd." See 1 Bouv. Law Dict., p. 670. The same certainty is required in an indictment for goods, as in trespass for goods, and rather more certainty, for what will be a defect of certainty in a count, will be much more defective in an indictment. 2 Hale's P. C., 183 ; 2 Strange R., 1226 ; 2 Ashmead's R., 105.

The act of 1850, not having specified cotton as one of the articles that negroes were prohibited from selling without special permission, unless cotton is averred in the indictment to be a product or commodity, this court has no more right to know that such article is a commodity or product than it has to know any other fact in the case, unless it is proven by the record. The act under which this indictment was found is a very penal statute, and must be construed strictly, as all penal statutes are by the courts. It is not the province of the courts to enlarge the circle by including things not named in the statute. I apprehend the judgment of the court below was correct.

YERGER, J. :

An indictment was found in the circuit court of La Fayette county against Wesley Bruce, under the 1st section of the act of 6th March, 1850, for suppression of trade and barter with slaves. The words of that section are : " Any person or persons who shall buy, sell or receive of, to or from any slave or slaves, any corn, fodder, hay, meal, spirituous liquors, or other produce or commodity whatsoever," etc. The indictment charged that Bruce did " buy and receive of, and from, etc., seventy-five pounds of cotton," etc. Bruce gave a recognizance with the defendants in error as his sureties for his appearance. He forfeited the recognizance, and a *scire facias* was issued to the defendants to appear and show cause, etc. They pleaded to the *scire facias* that Bruce had never been charged with any crime or misdemeanor by indictment, information, or presentment of a grand jury, at or before the issuance of the writ, etc. To this plea the district attorney replied setting out the indictment. The counsel for defendants in error demurred to the replication upon the ground that the indictment charging a purchase of cotton was not sufficient, it not being named in the statute. The circuit judge sustained the demurrer, from which the state has brought a writ of error. It will be seen that the statute names specifically certain articles, and then uses the general language, "any produce or commodity whatever." Is cotton a product or commodity? If so, it is certainly within the language. But it is said it should have been described in the indictment as a "product or commodity." If it were so in fact, it was embraced by the statute, and the court could know judicially whether the general words used in the act embraced the specific article named in the indictment or not. The court is presumed to know the ordinary meaning of words, and is to construe them when used in pleading according to that sense; and hence we conclude, that when the indictment stated that "seventy-five pounds of cotton" were purchased, the offense was as sufficiently charged as if it had contained the additional averment that the same " was a product or commodity," because that averment would not have rendered any more certain and definite the nature of the offense, than the language used had already done.

Judgment reversed, and cause remanded for further proceedings.

THE STATE *v.* JOINER, 23 Miss. Rep., 500.

DEFAULTING PUBLIC OFFICER.

In a proceeding by the state upon the official bond of a defaulting public officer, a general statute of limitations or the neglect or delay of the public officers in commencing proceedings, is no defense.

A disabling statute does not apply to a state unless made applicable by its express terms.

Error to Monroe circuit court. WATTS, J.

The facts of the case are sufficiently stated in the opinion of the court.

D. C. Glenn, attorney general.

Cited Parmiloe v. McNutt, 1 S. & M. 179.

Guion & Bains for plaintiff in error.

SMITH, C. J.:

This was a proceeding by motion on the official bond of Watson C. Joiner, as collector of taxes for the county of Noxubee, instituted pursuant to the directions of the 51st section of the statute regulating the collection of the public revenue.

The defendants demurred, and insist that the motion on its face shows that the state is not entitled to recover, because, 1. The statute requires the auditor of public accounts, within sixty days after defalcation on the part of a tax collector, to certify to the attorney general or district attorney for the proper district, the amount due from the defaulting collector, who is immediately to institute proceedings against such defaulter; whereas, the motion on its face shows that the defalcation occurred on the 1st March, 1843, and that the proceedings were not instituted until the 15th September, 1849. 2. Because it is apparent from the face of the motion, that it was barred by the statute of limitations.

The proper method of presenting the defense relied on by the defendants, would have been by plea; but to the mode adopted, no objection was made in the court below.

There may have been neglect on the part of the auditor of public accounts, or of the district attorney; in the one for not certifying within sixty days the amount due by the collector, in the other for not immediately instituting proceedings as the law directs. But the delay or neglect on the part of the officers of the state certainly constitutes no ground of defense on the part of the principal in the bond, unless the statute of limitations applies.

And it is settled that a general statute of limitations does not affect the state. Parmilee v. McNutt, 1 S. & M., 179. The statute of 1844, sec. 9, Hutch. Code, 831, relied on, does not, by express terms, include the state. It must, therefore, be held to apply exclusively to actions brought by individuals or third persons, as it is a settled rule of construction that the state shall never be subjected to the provisions of a disabling statute, or affected in any of its privileges, unless the intention to do so is clearly expressed in the law.

The court below, therefore, should have given judgment for the state on the demurrer.

Let the judgment be reversed, and cause remanded for further proceedings.

GREEN *v.* THE STATE., 23 Miss. Rep., 509.

RAPE.

A count in an indictment charging in the usual form an assault upon a woman, and attempt to ravish, is not bad for duplicity in charging that in said attempt, the accused did forcibly choke and throw down the woman. The latter allegation is only descriptive of the assault.

A conviction without proof of the *venue* is void.

Error to Pike circuit court. HARRIS, J.

The opinion of the court contains a sufficient statement of the facts of the case.

J. T. Lamkin for plaintiff in error.

The indictment charges the criminal act to have been committed on Eliza *Conely;* the proof is, that the act was committed on Eliza *Conerly.* 2 Russ. on Crim. Ev., 714–716 ; Roscoe, Crim. Ev. 97, 98 ; R. & R., 351 ; 5 Taunt., 814 ; Whart.

Am. Crim. L., 72, 156–158 ; 1 Chitty Pl., 216 ; 7 Serg. & R., 469.

That the defendant is "a slave," is a material averment, and must be proved. Hutch. Dig. ch. 37, art. 2, sec. 55 ; Wharton's Am. Crim. L., 156, 158, and authorities therein.

Therefore the refusal of the court to instruct the jury, that "If they believe it is not in evidence that the defendant is a slave, he ought not to be found guilty," is error. Boles v. State, 9 S. & M., 284. And the error is not cured by the court offering to give another, even though of the same import, as that other was not given, and the decision in Keithler v. State, 10 S. & M., 226 does not therefore apply.

There is no evidence on the record that the act was committed in the county charged in the indictment. Vaughan v. State, 3 S. & M., 553.

The attempt to commit a rape is nowhere proven or alluded to in the testimony. 1 Stark. Ev. 512 ; Whart. Am. Crim. L., 169, 316 ; 6 Yerg. 345.

There is a palpable preponderance of testimony against the identity of the defendant as the perpetrator of the criminal act charged. Lefore v. Justice, 1 S. & M., 381 ; Sims v. McIntyre, 8 ib., 324 ; Keithler v. State, 10 ib., 228 ; Fisher v. Leach, 10 ib., 316 ; Graham on N. T., 368.

The indictment is bad for uncertainty and duplicity ; or the charge, if well laid, is assault and battery for "forcibly choking and throwing down the prosecutrix." 1 Chitty's Crim. L. 169, 171, 172, 175, 231, 255 ; Miller v. State, 5 How. 250 ; Whart. Am. Cr. Law, 81, 82, 96, 97 ; 1 Chitty Pl., 292 ; 2 Mass. R., 163 ; 9 Wend. 193 ; 7 Serg. & R., 474, 475 ; 6 Am. Cr. L., 11, 26 ; U. S. Dig., Sup. 5, p. 151, § 164.

D. C. Glenn, attorney general.

1. The point raised by the first bill of exceptions is, that the name of the party is written in the bill of indictment "Conely" instead of "Conerly," as it should be. The law is, that if the sound of the name is not affected by the misspelling, the error is not material. 2 Ch. Crim. Law, 203, and cases cited.

2. The second bill is the refusal of the court to charge the jury as asked. The court was right. The peculiar phraseology

of the charge was intended to mislead the jury, that it was technically "not in evidence" that the boy was a slave. Under our law, negroes are *prima facie* slaves by statute and by decisions of high court. It is true that the jury were bound to believe, from the evidence, that the boy was a slave, but it was not bound to be in evidence before them. His presence and appearance proved it, and if the allegation of slavery was contravened, the *onus* was upon the defense to make it appear. Until this is done, the presumption of law is, and the fact arising from such legal presumption is, that every negro is a slave. Again, if the position insinuated in this charge be correct, the trial of slaves for criminal offenses, instead of being trials of guilt and innocence of the charge, will really be trials to ascertain whether the negro is bond or free. I ask the court to consider this.

3. The court overruled the motion for a new trial. The evidence is embodied in the bill of exceptions. Mrs. Conerly says she believes the assault was committed on her by Green, and her proof is almost complete, except she cannot unequivocally identify the defendant. Caroline Conerly saw defendant that evening, and swears that the person who assaulted her mother had on the same kind of clothes as the defendant, and swears to her belief that it was Green. The proof of the two negroes shows that it was Green's declared intention to make an assault on some white woman that night, and his own declarations show he could intend no one but Mrs. Conerly. He was proved to have dogs with him that evening; and Mrs. Conerly says there was a dog with the person who assaulted her. The defendant's evidence amounts to but little, and while the proof is not as positive as I could wish of the "*corpus delicti*," yet it was matter for the jury, and they have found a verdict. I insist that this court ought not to disturb it. The rule of the court is, not to interfere, unless the preponderance of evidence is very great against the verdict. See 7 How., 340. The court will please note the fact, that this is the second time a jury have found the defendant guilty on this charge.

4. Motion in arrest. The indictment follows the exact words of the statute, and this being a statutory offense, it is sufficient.

The statute says, if "any slave shall attempt to commit a rape," and the indictment says that defendant "did attempt to ravish and carnally know" this party.　This is the technical charge of a rape.　3 Ch. Crim. Law, 810, 812; 7 Blackf., 164.　The allegation made in the indictment of choking and throwing down the party assaulted, is merely by way of aggravation or description, making no part of the offense, and if improper, may be rejected as surplusage.　1 Chitty's Crim, Law, 173, 233.

On the whole, it seems as if the judgment below must be affirmed.

SMITH, C. J.:

This was an indictment for an attempt, by plaintiff in error, who is a slave, to commit a rape upon a free white woman.　It was tried in the circuit court of Pike county, when verdict and judgment were rendered against the prisoner.

A motion for a new trial was entered in the circuit court and overruled.　To the decision overruling the motion, a bill of exceptions was filed; by which means the whole of the evidence adduced on the trial was placed on the record.

Several exceptions to the validity of the judgment are pressed upon our consideration.　But from the view we have taken of the case, we deem it necessary to notice only the objections to the indictment, and the decision overruling the motion for a new trial.

1. It is objected that this indictment is defective for duplicity; that the prisoner is charged with two distinct offenses in the same count; it is also contended that the indictment is void for uncertainty.　If the count is not double, there is no pretence for the charge of uncertainty.

The offense charged in the indictment is described in the following terms, namely, that the prisoner "with force and arms, in the county aforesaid, in and upon one Eliza Conerly, (being then and there a free white woman,) feloniously did make an assault on her, the said Eliza Conerly, then and there feloniously did attempt to ravish and carnally know, by force and against her will, and in said attempt did forcibly choke and throw down the said Eliza Conerly," etc.

It must be perceived by a bare inspection that there are not two distinct and separate offenses charged herein. The last allegation, which is made the point of attack, is evidently no more than a description, somewhat more minute, of the manner of the assault, before averred to have been made. By no rule of construction can this allegation be held to charge an assault and battery distinct from the previously alleged attempt at rape. For if separated from this allegation, it conveys no meaning whatever, as it stands in the indictment, it forms no part of the description of the offense, and was with propriety treated as surplusage by the court. 1 Ch. Cr. L., 173, 232.

2. In passing upon the exception to the decision on the motion for a new trial, we shall not examine the evidence in reference to the guilt or innocence of the prisoner, but solely in regard to venue.

As we have before said, the whole of the evidence is certified in the record. And after a careful examination, we find no proof that the offense of which the prisoner was convicted, was perpetrated in the county of Marion as alleged in the indictment.

This proof was essential. 1 Ph. Ev. 515; 3 ib. 703, n. 381. The prosecution, from inability or inadvertence, having failed to produce it, the finding of the jury and the judgment of the court were void.

Let the judgment be reversed, the cause remanded, and a new trial awarded in the circuit court.

Ike *v.* The State, 23 Miss. Rep., 525.

Assault and Battery with Intent to Kill.

Indictments upon statutes, particularly of a highly penal character, must state all the circumstances which constitute the definition of the offense, in the act. They must also be clear and certain to every intent, and pursue the precise and technical language employed in the statute in the description of the offense.

Express malice is not an essential ingredient in the offense of assault and battery upon a white person by a slave with intent to kill. Hence it is unnecessary to allege it in the indictment or prove it on the trial.

Error to Adams circuit court. Posey, J.

The facts of the case are stated in the opinion of the court and the briefs of counsel.

L. Sanders, Jr., for plaintiff in error,

Contended that the indictment was not in accordance with the statutory requirements.   Hutch. Code, 521, sec. 52 ; ib., 532, sec. 1, 2.

Indictments must have a precise and sufficient certainty.   4 Black. Com., 206.   The indictment ought to be certain to every intent, without any intendment to the contrary.   Cro. El., 490 ; Cro. Jac., 29.

It is contended, malice must be proved before conviction, and it was not proven on the trial.

D. C. Glenn, attorney general.

But a single point arises in this case.   The plaintiff in error was convicted of an assault with intent to kill William Shillings, his overseer, while inflicting legal chastisement upon him, under the proviso of the 1st section 1829, Code, 532.   Sentence of death was pronounced upon him.   It was moved in arrest of judgment, the indictment does not allege that the chastisement was being inflicted by said William Shillings, at the time of the commission of the said stabbing with intent to kill.   The words of the indictment are as follows : " Upon one William Shillings then and there did make an assault, in resistance then and there of legal chastisement, the said Shillings being then and there a white person, and then and there the overseer of said Ike."   I cannot perceive the uncertainty complained of.   The resistance to legal chastisement by the slave, is by the " then and there" of the commission of the assault on William Shillings, indissolubly connected therewith so as to show, to a sufficient certainty, that the assault was in resistance of chastisement by Shillings, and to preclude every other intendment, which satisfies the general language of the statute.   2 How., 661, 662 ; Cro. Jac., 639 ; 1 Ld. Raymond, 1467, 1468 ; 1 Leach, 529 ; Doug., 525.

Again, the offense was a statutory one, and the offense is described in the very language of the act.

This, with properly connected averments, is sufficient.

SMITH, C. J. :

This was an indictment in the circuit court of Adams county, for an assault and battery upon a white person with intent to kill. The prisoner, who is a slave, was found guilty, and sentence of death pronounced upon him; whence the cause comes into this court.

There are but two acts of the court complained of; one, the decision of the judge overruling the motion in arrest of judgment; the other, the judgment subjecting the prisoner to capital punishment.

The first statute in reference to the offense charged, directs "That if any slave or slaves shall at any time commit an assault and battery upon any white person, with intent to kill, every such slave or slaves, so committing such assault and battery with intent to kill, as aforesaid, and being thereof convicted, shall suffer death." Hutch. Code, 521, sec. 52.

This statute was modified by the act of 1829, by the first section of which it is provided, that in case of assault and battery upon white persons, by slaves with intent to kill, but where the killing does not actually occur, the statute above quoted "shall be so construed as to render the proof of malice aforethought express, necessary to subject the person or persons therein named to capital punishment; provided, no proof of express malice shall be required where the assault and battery is committed by a slave upon his or her master, employer, or overseer in resistance of legal chastisement."

The indictment was framed under these statutes, and it is insisted that it does not contain a sufficient description of the facts and circumstances which constitute the offense therein denounced.

It is a well settled rule, that indictments upon statutes, particularly of highly penal character, must state all the circumstances which constitute the definition of the offense in the act, so as to bring the defendant judicially within it. They must also be clear and certain to every intent, and pursue the precise and technical language employed in the statute in the description of the offense.[1] Chit. Crim. Law, 280, 283; 13 S. & M., 264.

[1] Wharton's Am. Cr. Law, 364; Respublica v. Trier, 3 Yeates, 451; U. S. v. Batchelder, 2 Gall., 15; State v. Hickman, 8 Halst., 299; State v. Little, 1 Vermont, 331; Whiting v. State, 14 Conn., 487; State v. Williams, 2 Strob., 474; Comisa v. State, 3 Kelly, 419; U. S. v. Dickey, 1 Morris, 412; State v. Click, 2 Ala., 26; Resp. v. Bush,

If the indictment under consideration be tested by these rules, we think that it will not be found objectionable.

The objection brought particularly to our notice refers to the allegation of the time at which the assault and battery were committed. It is contended, that it is not shown with sufficient certainty that the assault was made upon the prosecutor at the precise time when he was in the act of chastising the prisoner. It is essential to the constitution of the offense charged, that the assault and battery should have been committed in "resistance to legal chastisement," which was being inflicted at the time by the overseer. Hence, if it is not so averred, the indictment is defective. The charge is in the following words: The prisoner, "upon one William Shillings, in the peace, etc., feloniously, wilfully, and of his malice aforethought, did make an assault, in resistance then and there of legal chastisement, the said William Shillings being then and there a white person, and then and there the overseer of the said Ike," etc.

In this averment we are unable to perceive the alleged uncertainty. The language of the act is pursued, and the facts and circumstances which constitute the offense, are charged with such certainty as to exclude every other intendment.

In the next place it is objected that sentence of death was improperly pronounced upon the prisoner, because the indictment does not charge the assault and battery with intent to kill, to have been committed with express malice.

The first statute, which relates to the offense with which the prisoner is charged, as we have seen, is very general. The offense is made to consist in an assault and battery by a slave upon a white person with intent to kill. The subsequent statute is more

2 Texas, 455; Drummond v. Resp., ib., 156; State v. Seamons, 1 Iowa, 418; Com. v. Hampton, 3 Gratt., 590; State v. Hereford, 13 Mo., 3; Buckley v. State, 2 Greene, 270; State v. Bullock, 13 Ala., 413; State v. Ladd, 2 Swan, 226; Sodano v. State, 25 Ala., 64; Cook v. State, 11 Ga., 53; Com. v. Chapman, 5 Wharton, 427; State v. Blease, 1 McMullin, 472; State v. Gibbons, 1 Southard, 51; State v. Calvin, Charlton, 151; 1 Hale, 517, 526, 535; Staunf., 180 b.; Foster, 423, 424; Hard., 2; Dyer, 304; Kelly, 8; Com. Dig. Just G., 1; 1 Chitty on Pl., 357; Moore, 5; 1 Leach, 264; 1 East, P. C., 419; 2 Hale, 170, 189, 190, 193; 3 Dyer, 368; 2 Lord Raymond, 791; 2 Burr, 679; 1 T. R., 223; U. S. v. Lancaster, 2 McLean, 431; People v. Allen, 5 Denio, 76; State v. Pratt, 10 La., 191; State v. Foster, 8 McCord, 442; State v. O'Bannon, 1 Bail., 144; State v. La Preux, 1 McMullin, 488; State v. Noel, 5 Blackf., 548; Chambers v. People, 4 Scam., 351; State v. Duncan, 9 Port., 260; State v. Mitchell, 6 Mo. 147; State v. Helm, ib., 263.

specific, and directs that this clause, where killing does not actually occur, shall be so construed as to render the proof of malice aforethought express, necessary to subject the person charged to capital punishment. But by the proviso in the first section, its enactments do not apply to the offense when committed upon the master, employer, or overseer of the slave, and " in resistance to legal chastisement." The effect of the amendatory act was to render the offense defined and made capital by the original statute, capital only in cases where the assault and battery were committed in resistance of legal punishment, upon the master, employer, or overseer of the slave charged, unless done with malice express. In all other cases, that is, where there was no express malice, and where the offense was not committed in resisting the legitimate authority of the master or overseer, the punishment prescribed was repealed.

We do not concur in the construction which it is insisted should be placed upon the second section of the amendatory statute. It does not conflict with the preceding section. Hence, it cannot be held to repeal, or in any wise to modify the punishment which would attach under the original act as amended by that section. It was the evident intention of the legislature to apply a milder punishment in lieu of the more rigorous penalty which was repealed, and not to create a new offense, or to modify the punishment prescribed by the preceding enactments.

If we are right in this construction of the statutes, express malice is not an ingredient in the offense of which the prisoner was convicted. Hence, it was unnecessary to allege it in the indictment, or to prove it on the trial.

It is insisted that a different rule was laid down in the case of Anthony v. State, 13 S. & M., 263. We do not think so. In that case the defendant, who was a slave, was indicted for an assault and battery upon a white person, with intent to kill. There was no averment in the indictment that the offense was committed upon the master, employer, or overseer, in resistance of legal punishment, nor was the offense alleged to have been committed with express malice. The jury found that the offense was committed with express malice, and sentence of death was pronounced. This court reversed the judgment, holding, correctly, that the averment of express malice was necessary to authorize the infliction of capital punishment, notwithstanding the finding of express malice by the jury.

The distinction between that case and the case at bar is so obvious that it is scarcely necessary to point it out. In the one, the statute required proof of express malice. Express malice, therefore, was an essential ingredient in the constitution of the offense. Hence, it was not only necessary to charge it, but to prove it on the trial, in order to warrant the infliction of capital punishment. In the other, proof of express malice is dispensed with. The description of the offense is complete, when it is shown by proper averments that the prisoner committed the assault and battery upon the prosecutor, with intent to kill, in resistance of legal chastisement.

Let the judgment be affirmed.

Portis *v.* The State, 23 Miss. Rep., 578.

GAMING.

It is essential to the validity of the indictment, that the grand jury by whom it is preferred, should not only possess the requisite qualifications, but that they should also be drawn and empanelled according to law.

The circuit court has the power to cause a bystander to be sworn in the place of a grand juror who is sick or absent. But where the court discharged a grand juror on account of the sickness of his family, and appointed another in his stead, such substituted person is an illegal grand juror and vitiates the whole.

Error to Tippah circuit court. MILLER, J.

The facts of the case as shown by the record are, that Addison Portis, at the March term, 1850, of the circuit court of Tippah county, was indicted by the grand jury of said county for playing a game of cards for money. At the September term of the said circuit court, 1850, the defendant (Portis) appeared and pleaded four pleas to said bill of indictment, in abatement. 1st. That after the jury at the March term, 1850, of said circuit court had been called, and one of the grand jurors of the thirteen drawn, and the balance of the *venire* had been apportioned as petit jurors, it being the second day of the term,

Waldrop, one of the grand jurors, applied to the court to be discharged from further service, on account of the sickness of his wife; and he was thereupon discharged, and C. A. Green was sworn as a grand juror in his stead, which juror was taken from the by-standers, and was not one of the *venire facias.* The three first pleas of the defendant involve the question of the authority of the court to discharge a grand juror on account of the sickness of his wife, and when a juror is discharged, that the vacancy must be filled out of the balance of the *venire* then serving as jurors.

The fourth plea involves the question of the legal organization of the whole grand jury, and denies that the assessor of taxes had returned a list of the householders of the county, as it was his duty to do under the statute, out of whom a grand jury must be drawn; and that there was in fact no legal grand jury to find the indictment against defendant, and prays it might be quashed. These pleas were all demurred to by the state, and the demurrers sustained, and upon a plea of not guilty the defendant was convicted, when a writ of error from the judgment of the court below, sustaining said demurrer, was prayed to this court.

Price & Jackson for plaintiff in error, filed an elaborate brief, and relied chiefly on the following authorities, to show that the decision of the court below sustaining the demurrer to the pleas was erroneous. Rawls v. State, 8 S. & M., 599; McQuillen v. State, 8 ib., 587; Barney v. State, 12 ib., 68; 1 Morris, R., 192.

D. C. Glenn, attorney general.

Contended, the opinion of the court below was correct, and cited the following authorities. Hutch. Code, 886; ib., 879; ib., 887; 2 Wheelen's Cr. Cases, 473–476; 2 Gall. R., 364; King v. State, 5 How., 732; Dowling v. State, 5 S. & M., 664; Planter's Bank v. Sharp., 4 ib., 85; 13 ib., 287, 288.

J. W. Thompson, on same side.

SMITH, C. J.:

This was an indictment for a violation against the statute against gaming, tried in the circuit court of Tippah. The defense relied on was presented through several pleas of abatement to the indictment.   These pleas were judged insufficient by the court, and the defendant was convicted on the issue of not guilty.

The exceptions taken to the proceedings in the circuit court are, that the court erred in sustaining the demurrer to the defendant's last plea ; that the court erred in discharging a member of the grand jury by whom the indictment was preferred, after he had been chosen, empanelled, and sworn as such, for the reason assigned in the record ; and that the court erred in ordering the sheriff to summon a substitute from amongst the by-standers to supply the vacancy occasioned by the discharge of the original.

1. The last plea alleges in substance, that the names of the individuals composing the *venire,* from which the grand jury was chosen by lot, were not drawn by the clerk and sheriff from lot number one, which by the statute of 1830, the clerk of the circuit court was bound to keep, and in which the names of all freeholders and householders of the county, liable to serve on juries, should be deposited.

The demurrer admitted the truth of the facts averred in the plea, which, if well pleaded, doubtless constituted a valid defense to the action of the indictment ; as it is essential to the validity of the indictment that the members of the grand jury by whom it was preferred, should not only possess the requisite qualifications, but that they should also be drawn and empanelled in accordance with the directions of the statute.[1]   McQuillen v. State, 8 S. & M., 587 ; Barney v. State, 12 ib., 68.

We think the plea was technically correct.   Hence the court erred in sustaining the demurrer.

2. On the second day of the term, after the grand jury had been organized and charged, one of their number who had been regularly drawn, empanelled, and sworn as such, upon his own application was discharged, and a substitute ordered to be summoned by the court from the by-standers.   The reason assigned by the juror for the application was the indisposition of his wife.

This action of the court is the subject matter of the next ex-

[1] Wharton Am. Cr. Law, 472; State v. Duncan, 7 Yerg., 527; State v. Bryant, 10 Yerg., 271; State v. Brooks, 9 Ala., 10; Rawle v. State, 8 S. & M., 599; State v. Symonds, 36 Me., 128; Vanhook v. State, 12 Tex., 469; Jackson v. State, 11 Tex., 261; but see State v. Mahan, 12 Tex., 283; Wharton Prec. 1158.

ception. The question involved is one of great impression in this court and of some practical importance. Counsel have not furnished us with references to adjudicated cases upon this point, if, indeed, they are to be found.

If the circuit courts possess the authority to discharge a grand juror for the cause appearing in the record, they necessarily possess an unlimited discretion over the subject; for the reason given for exercising the discretion in this particular case involved neither the legal incapacity nor the mental or physical inability of the juror. It does not even appear that the illness of his wife was of such character as to require his presence at home.

The authority exercised in this instance is claimed for the circuit courts as a power necessarily incident to them as courts of oyer and terminer. The learned counsel for the state have, however, not produced any direct authority in support of this position, and we are unable to deduce an argument in favor of the doctrine from the power exercised by these courts in reference to petit jurors.

The courts of oyer and terminer in England and the circuit court of this state, by virtue of their character as such, doubtless possess the power to adjourn or dismiss the grand jury whenever they deem it proper to do so. But it is apprehended that the power to suspend the functions of a grand jury by discharging them, is clearly to be distinguished from the authority to discharge a part or the whole of its members, and the consequent right to cause others to be sworn in their stead. The capriciousness or vicious exercise of the power in the one case would doubtless constitute a public wrong, but it could not impair the integrity of grand juries; but in the other, the power in its full extent, as claimed for the courts, might be, and probably would be used as radically to affect their organization and thereby seriously to impair the sanctity and purity of this invaluable institution.

In our examination of this subject we have not been able to discover a single case in which this power was claimed or exercised by the courts in England or this country as resulting from their common law authority. The books are silent on the subject, and we presume, for the reason that the power did not exist. We dissent from the proposition.

The statute laws of this state have not, certainly, in direct terms vested the circuit courts with an unlimited jurisdiction on this subject. They have not, in fact, expressly clothed them with the power to discharge a grand juror for any cause whatever, unless the provision which empowers them to cause a grand juror to be sworn in the place of one who is sick or absent, be held to convey such authority in these specified cases.

The cases in which the courts have power to cause substituted jurors to be sworn, are designated in the statute. The cases are, where the grand juror, after he has been empanelled and sworn, has died, is sick, or absent. The specification of the occasions on which this power may be exercised by the courts, upon a plain principle, would seem to exclude the authority of the courts to supply vacancies occurring in grand juries from any other cause. We have seen that the circuit courts, by virtue of their common law power as courts of oyer and terminer, do not possess a discretionary right to discharge grand jurors after they have been empanelled and sworn. If, then, the conclusion be just, that the authority of the courts " to cause other grand jurors to be sworn," is limited by the statute to the cases specified, it follows that the legislature could not have intended to vest in them an unrestricted discretion over the subject. For it would be absurd to suppose that the legislature designed that a circuit judge should possess the power to discharge, at his discretion, any number of the members of a grand jury which have been regularly empanelled and sworn, and yet deny to him the authority to cause the vacancy thereby occasioned to be supplied.

It is manifest, if the court were correct in the case under consideration, that the general power is unrestricted. If it were lawful for the judge to discharge one member of the grand jury without cause, he might, with equal propriety, so far as the mere question of power is concerned, discharge any number on his own mere motion and with as little cause. The practical results of this doctrine are too manifest to require elaboration, and too much opposed to the spirit of the laws regulating the organization of juries to be sanctioned by this court.

But it does not follow, that by this unauthorized act of the court the grand jury were rendered invalid. If the action of the court had ceased here, no such result would have followed. For, after the discharge of the juror in question, a sufficient number to constitute a legal grand jury remained; the body would have preserved its organization, and possessing all the requisites of a legally constituted grand jury, its acts to all intents would have been valid.

But the court, as we have seen, having acted without authority, manifestly could not, by such illegal and void act, acquire a right to cause the substitute to be sworn in the place of the discharged grand juror. The admission, therefore, of this person upon the panel of the grand jury and his participation in their deliberations vitiated the whole body. It could not then be said that it was a grand jury drawn and empanelled in accordance with the directions of the law. Hence, upon the well-settled doctrine of this court, all of its acts were void.

There remains another objection. It is, that the court improperly ordered the grand juror who was sworn as a substitute, to be summoned by the sheriff from amongst the by-standers.

It is argued that this juror should have been selected by lot from the remainder of the original *venire* then in attendance upon the court.

We do not concur in the validity of this exception. The statute is indefinite on the subject. It has not prescribed the mode in which jurors in such cases shall be selected. The method adopted by the court in this case is the one which we believe has been uniformly pursued, and has been, at least indirectly, sanctioned by this court.

Let the judgment be reversed, and the indictment quashed.

MORMAN v. THE STATE, 24 Miss. Rep., 54.

HOMICIDE.

PENITENTIARY CODE — INTENT — VERDICT — ACQUITTAL.

The 33d and the 36th sections of the 3d article of the Penitentiary Code, Hutch. Code, 960, 961, 965, have created separate and distinct classes of offenses; and under an indictment for an assault, with intent to kill and murder, a conviction for an assault with intent to commit manslaughter cannot be sustained.

Nor will such conviction be aided by the 22d section, article 8th of said Code, that section relating only to that class of offenses which the statute makes to consist of different degrees; and where a conviction of a degree inferior to that charged in the indictment will be sustained.

Where an evil intent is necessary to constitute an act a crime, it must be alleged in the indictment and proved in the same manner as any other material fact; and an allegation of shooting with intent to kill A will not be sustained by proof of shooting with intent to kill B.

A charge in an indictment of an assault with intent to kill and murder, is negatived by a verdict of an assault with intent to commit manslaughter, and the verdict is an acquittal of the prisoner of the offense charged in the indictment, and a bar to further prosecution for the same offense.

Error to Yalobusha circuit court.   ROGERS, J.

The facts of the case are contained in the opinion of the court.

E. S. Fisher & Thomas for plaintiff in error.

D. C. Glenn, attorney general.

Morman was indicted for an assault, with intent to commit manslaughter. He was convicted of an assault, with intent to commit manslaughter. This was correct. Hutch. Code, 983, § 22; ib., 960, § 33.

The evidence presents a case of a most aggravated and cowardly assault to take life. The proof is clear and unequivocal.

YERGER, J.:

At the October term, 1851, of the circuit court of Yalobusha county, the plaintiff in error was indicted for an assault and battery with a deadly weapon, with intent to kill and murder. He was found guilty of an assault, with an intent to commit manslaughter. A motion was made in arrest of judgment, which motion was overruled, and the prisoner sentenced to the penitentiary for four years.

The indictment was framed under the thirty-third section of

the third article of the Penitentiary Code, which is in these words : " Every person who shall be convicted of shooting at another, or of an attempt to discharge any kind of firearms, or any air-gun at another, or of any assault and battery upon another, by means of any deadly weapon, or by such other means or force as was likely to produce death, with the intent to kill, maim, ravish, or rob such other person, or in the attempt to commit any burglary, larceny, or other felony, or in resisting the execution of any legal process, shall be imprisoned in the penitentiary for a term not exceeding ten years." Hutch. Code, 960.

By the thirty-sixth section of the third article of the same law, it is further provided that " every person who shall be convicted of an assault with an intent to commit any robbery, rape, manslaughter, or any other felony, the punishment of which assault is not hereinbefore described, shall be punished by imprisonment in the penitentiary for a term not exceeding ten years," etc. Hutch. Code, 961, 985.

It will thus be seen that the statute in the foregoing sections has made a difference between an assault and battery with a deadly weapon, with the intent to kill, etc., and a mere assault, with the intent to commit manslaughter or other felony, and has fixed a different punishment to the two offenses.

When it is recollected that the prisoner was indicted for an assault and battery, with the intent to kill and murder, and that he was convicted of an assault, with intent to commit manslaughter, it will be seen that he was convicted of another and different offense than that charged in the indictment.

It is said that the 22d section of tit. 8 of the Penitentiary Code, Hutch. Code, 983, will sustain the verdict in this case. It is in these words : " Upon an indictment for any offense consisting of different degrees, the jury may find the accused not guilty of the offense in the degree charged in the indictment, and may find such accused person guilty of any degree of such offense inferior to that charged in the indictment, or of an attempt to commit such an offense."

This section of the law is obviously applicable only to that class of offenses which, under the statute, consists of different degrees, and in which the conviction is for the same offense, but in a different degree, from that charged in the indictment, and is very far from authorizing a verdict for a different crime or offense than that of which the accused is charged.

Nor will the common-law rule that "where the accusation includes an offense of inferior degree, the jury may discharge the defendant of the higher crime and convict him of the less atrocious," uphold this verdict.

It has been uniformly holden, that where the evil intent accompanying an act is necessary to constitute such act a crime, the intent must be alleged in the indictment, and proved; and the intent with which the act was done must be proved to be the same with that charged. Thus, for instance, where, in an indictment on 43 George 3, c. 58, where the intent laid in several counts was to murder, to disable, or to do some grievous bodily harm, and the intent found by the jury was to prevent being apprehended, it was held bad, and that the intention should be stated according to the fact. 1 Chitty, C. L., 233; Russ. & Ry., C. C., 365. So, in burglary, if the entry be alleged to have been made with intent to commit a specific felony, the indictment is not sustained by evidence of any entry with the intention to commit another kind of felony. 2 East, P. C., Rosc. Cr. Ev., 328.

And in this state it has been held, under this statute, where the prisoner was indicted for shooting, with the intent to kill A, he could not be convicted by proof of shooting, with intent to kill B. Morgan v. State, 13 S. & M., 242; 11 ib., 317. In the case of Morgan v. State, the court says: "It is incumbent on the state to prove the specific intent as charged." See also 7 Carr. & Payne, 518; 3 Johns. R., 511; 2 Stark. Ev. (5th Am. ed.), 416, 419.

In the case at present before us, the finding of the jury negatived the intent as charged in the indictment. That intent was averred to be "to kill and murder." The intent found by the jury was to "commit manslaughter," another and distinct felony from that charged. The variance is, therefore, fatal, and the judgment must be arrested. We do not express any opinion on the question, whether on an indictment for an assault and battery, with the intent to kill and murder, or commit another felony, the jury may find a verdict for an assault, with the intent to commit such felony.

In this case, the verdict of the jury is an acquittal of the prisoner from the offense charged in the indictment, and will bar another prosecution against him for the same offense. In arresting the judgment, it is proper that he should be discharged.

Let the judgment be arrested and the prisoner discharged.

FISHER, J., having been consulted by the plaintiff in error, gave no opinion.

––––––

BRIDGES *v.* THE STATE, 24 Miss. Rep., 153.

EXHIBITING A DEADLY WEAPON.

A judgment upon a *scire facias* which does not recite the original judgment correctly, is erroneous.

Error to Covington circuit court. HARRIS J.

The facts are contained in the opinion of the court.

FISHER, J. :

Willis Bridges was indicted by the grand jury of Covington county for exhibiting a deadly weapon in a rude, angry and threatening manner. At the October term, 1847, of the circuit court of said county, he entered into a recognizance giving the plaintiff in error as security for his appearance to the April term, 1848, of said court. At the November term, 1848, of said court, the accused failing to appear, judgment *nisi* was entered against him and his bail, *scire facias* ordered, etc. The *scire facias*, after reciting the recognizance entered into, proceeds as follows : " And whereas the said Willis Bridges failed to appear, on being found guilty, to receive the sentence of the court, thereupon, according to the condition of said recognizance, whereby the same became forfeited, and a judgment was accordingly rendered by said court *nisi* on the 9th day of November, 1848."

This writ was executed on the plaintiff in error, who appeared and filed two pleas: 1. That there was no such recognizance as recited in the *scire facias.* 2. That there was no such judgment *nisi,* as recited in the writ of *scire facias;* upon both of which issue was taken to the court and decided against the defendant below.

We will only notice the question presented by the second plea. Judgment was entered against the accused, that he forfeit his recognizance because he failed to appear and answer the indictment pending against him. The *scire facias* says that he failed to appear, on being found guilty, and receive sentence. The variance in the two judgments is too palpable to require comment.

The judgment reversed, and judgment rendered in this court on the second plea for the plaintiff in error.

BOLES *v.* THE STATE, 24 Miss. Rep., 445.

HOMICIDE.

A prisoner indicted for a capital offense, has an unquestionable right to select his jury from the whole number of those summoned by virtue of the special *venire facias,* and of whose names a list had been furnished to him, provided a sufficient number could be regularly obtained therefrom.

It is not competent for the circuit court to discharge a person summoned under the special *venire,* in a capital case, without good and sufficient cause. The court says: "Upon the principles of reason and common sense, it is manifest that a circuit judge has no authority, without sufficient cause, to discharge a juror specially summoned for the trial of a capital felony." And further, "To dispense with a juror, summoned upon the special *venire* in capital cases, without cause and against the consent of the accused, would be an unwarrantable exercise of authority by the judge presiding."

In an attempt to impeach the judgment of the circuit court, the record should distinctly show the facts upon which the charge of error is predicated, otherwise the action of the court will be presumed to be strictly in accordance with law.

To dispense with the attendance of persons summoned on the special *venire,* who failed to attend when called, is not error, provided the jury has been completed from those summoned and in attendance.

To dispense with the attendance of such persons, is not a discharge of them, and they may be called again, if the jury should not be completed from those summoned and in attendance, and their attendance enforced, under the discretion of the court, by proper process.

That persons not freeholders or householders, were summoned on the *venire,* is no ground for challenge to the array, or to quash; nor is it sufficient cause for reversal.

Upon cross-examination of a witness, greater latitude is allowed than on an examination in chief, and leading questions are admissible.

The answer of the accused to a question asked subsequent to the commission of the offense, is no part of the *res gestæ*, and was properly excluded from the jury.

Where the accused has been indicted, tried, convicted and sentenced in one county, and upon a reversal of the judgment has obtained a change of venue to another county, and is put upon his trial there, it is error to allow the affidavit upon which the venue has been changed, or the record of the former trial and conviction, to be read in evidence to the jury.

Error to the circuit court of Hinds County.   BARNETT, J.

The accused was indicted at the October term, 1846, of the Warren county circuit court, for the murder of one Donnahoo. He was tried and convicted at the May term, 1847. Upon error to the high court a new trial was granted. At May term, 1848, the venue was changed to Hinds county, and at May term, 1849, a trial and conviction was had. Upon error to the high court, a new trial was again granted, and at May term, 1852, he was again tried, convicted and sentenced ; to this judgment the present writ of error was taken.

In making up the jury, six of those summoned on the special *venire* failed to appear when their names were called. The prisoner objected to the further call until the attendance of those absent could be enforced. The court overruled the objection, and the call proceeded. To this the prisoner excepted. The jury was completed from the remainder of the panel summoned on the special *venire*.

Among those summoned on the special *venire*, appeared the name of John W. Jones. When this name was called, one James W. Jones appeared, and proving to be a competent juror, was peremptorily challenged by the state. The prisoner stated to the court that the name of James W. Jones was not on the copy of the panel furnished to the prisoner. Jones was called back, and stated that he had been summoned by the sheriff as a juror in the case, and had told the sheriff that he signed his name J. W. Jones. The accused demanded the production of John W. Jones, and objected to a further call without him. The objection was not sustained, and the call proceeded.

Four of the panel summoned were incompetent, being neither freeholders nor householders.

On cross-examination of a witness, (Carlisle,) the state put this question, " Was not the intoxicated condition of the deceased such that, unless he had leaned for support on the post, or some other support, he could not have stood up?" To this question the prisoner objected; the court overruled the objection, and the witness answered, "I considered the deceased *very drunk* and quite overpowered by liquor."

The prisoner having introduced one McElwee as a witness, who stated that on the day of the killing, he saw the prisoner running, pursued by one E. E. Bruner (a witness who had testified on the part of the state), who had a pistol in his hand, and exclaimed, "Stop, you old rascal, or I'll shoot you," the state re-introduced said Bruner in rebuttal of this portion of McElwee's statements, and who denied having a pistol in his hand at the time referred to, or having used the expressions attributed to him by McElwee.

The state then asked Bruner the following question : "When you had overtaken the prisoner, or while pursuing him, what did you say to him?" He replied, "that he asked the prisoner why he did so?" and, in opposition to the remonstrance of the state, further stated that the prisoner replied, "that he would allow no man to follow him round town." This part of the answer was excluded from the jury.

The state then read to the jury the record of the trial, conviction and sentence of the prisoner in the circuit court of Warren county, the judgment of the high court of errors and appeals granting a new trial, and the affidavit of the prisoner upon which the *venue* was changed. To which the prisoner objected and excepted.

The errors assigned are as follows :

1. Because the court dispensed with the attendance of James W. Farr and five others, persons summoned as jurors on the special *venire*, and refused the application of the prisoner for an attachment against said jurors.

2. Because the juror, John W. Jones, was not presented, though returned on the special *venire*, and James W. Jones placed on the *venire* in his stead.

3. Because the special *venire* contained the names of four persons summoned as jurors, who were neither freeholders nor householders.

4. Because the court below permitted a leading question to be propounded to the witness, John C. Carlisle.

5. Because the court below, in the examination of the witness, Bruner, permitted him to relate part of the declarations of the accused touching this offense, and rejected that portion of such confessions favorable to the accused.

6. Because the court permitted the district attorney to read the affidavit of the accused for a change of *venue*, and the entry of such change as contained in the minutes of Hinds circuit court.

7. Because the court permitted the district attorney to read to the jury the record from the Warren circuit court, reciting a former conviction for this offense.

Amos R. Johnston for plaintiff in error.

Upon the power of the court to dispense with absent jurors, summoned on the special *venire*, counsel cited: Hutch. Dig., 1007, art. 7, § 1; ib., 1003; and as to the copy of the *venire*, Boles v. The State, 13 S. & M., 399.

As to the summoning of disqualified persons by the sheriff, on the panel, defendant cited, Byrd v. The State, 1 How. R., 163.

Questions propounded to witness, Carlisle, are leading ones, and objectionable. Toomy v. The State, 8 S. & M., 104; 1 Greenl. Ev., § 434; 1 Starkie Ev., 169.

The state was permitted to call for and obtain part of the statement of accused at the time of the homicide, and excluded the balance. This was error. The whole conversation ought to be given. 1 Greenl. Ev., §§ 201, 218; Torrance v. Hurst, Walk. R., 403; Roscoe Cr. Ev., 51.

The constitution of Mississippi intended to preserve the trial by jury inviolate with all the common-law incidents of the institution. See Constitution, art. 1, § 28.

D. C. Glenn, attorney general,

Insisted in reply to many points made by counsel for accused, that something must be permitted to the discretion of the court below; Barb. Cr. Law, 356, 357; 13 Wendell, 351, 355; 4 Taunt., 309.

It was insisted that the proof of a former conviction and reversal, and the change of *venue*, was proper and essential, as the legal history of the case. Accused was indicted eight years ago; and the record should show, that in the mean time, the state has done its duty in the prosecution, or else the party is entitled to his discharge. See Byrd's case, 1 How. R.; Lowper case, 3 ib.; Nixon's case, 2 S. & M., 503.

SMITH, C. J.:

This was an indictment tried in the circuit court of Hinds, upon which William H. Boles, the plaintiff in error, was convicted of the murder of one Donnahoo.

A motion was made for a new trial, which was overruled, and the case having been removed into this court, we are asked to reverse the judgment for errors alleged to have occurred during the progress of the trial below.

We will proceed to consider the objections pressed upon our attention in the order in which they were discussed.

1. The three first bills of exceptions present this state of facts: In making up the jury the names of James W. Farr, Hugh Sheridan, James Staughton, Peter Barr, H. E. Windley and Elijah Peyton, were regularly reached on the list of jurors, summoned by virtue of the special *venire facias*, which issued in the case. These persons, upon being called, did not answer to their names; whereupon the prisoner, in each instance, and before the succeeding name was called, objected to a further call of the persons summoned as jurors, until the juror called and failing to attend, should be attached, or his attendance otherwise procured. The objection in each case was disregarded, and the call of the special *venire* proceeded with. This action of the court, it is alleged, was unauthorized and illegal. By the statute, (Hutch. Code, 1007, art. 7, § 1,) it is directed that whenever any person shall have been arraigned, charged with an offense the punishment of which is death, it shall be the duty of the court forthwith to award a special *venire*, by which the sheriff is required to summon from the county any number which may be directed by the judge of said court, not exceeding one hundred jurors. From the persons thus summoned, the jury by whom the award is to be tried, are to be taken, unless the *venire* should be exhausted before the jury is completed. In the event that a

sufficient number of competent and impartial jurors to constitute a jury cannot be selected from the special *venire*, recourse must be had to the regular panel, and the *tales* jurors summoned for the day.

By another provision of the statute, (Hutch. Code, 1003,) the party under an indictment for a capital felony is entitled to a list, to be furnished at least two entire days before the day of trial, of the jurors summoned by virtue of the special *venire facias*. These directions of the statute are of the highest importance. They are designed to ensure to persons criminally charged the full benefit of a trial by an impartial jury of the country, as guaranteed in the bill of rights. Courts, therefore, charged with the administration of the criminal jurisprudence of the state, will be solicitous to enforce intelligently and with firmness and fidelity, every provision of the statute regulating the trial by jury. Hence, if in the course pursued by the court upon the point under consideration, the rights of the accused have in anywise been violated, it will be for us to apply the corrective.

It will not be contested that the prisoner was entitled to a trial by jury selected from the persons summoned under the special *venire facias*, and of whose names a list had been furnished to him, provided a sufficient number of competent jurors be, according to the rules regulating the empanelling of juries, obtained therefrom. The objection is, that the action of the court tended to impair this right of the prisoner. It is argued, that if a judge under such circumstances has a right to dispense with the attendance of any number of the *venire* from which the jury should be selected, he may, with equal propriety, dispense with the whole, and thus be enabled to defeat the manifest intention of the statute, and thereby deprive a party capitally charged of rights solemnly guaranteed by the constitution. This court has never held that it was competent for a circuit judge to discharge a person summoned under the special *venire* in a capital case, without sufficient cause. In the case at bar, when before this court on a former occasion (13 S. & M., 401), the contrary doctrine seems to have been intimated. It was then said: "A list of the *venire* is to be furnished the prisoner two entire days before the trial. This is to give him an opportunity of selecting a jury from the list furnished. A prisoner has not a right to be tried by such a jury as he might select from the body of the county, but he has a right to make his selection from the list furnished him, as far as it is practicable for him to do so, by exercising the right of challenge for cause, or his right of peremptory challenge." On the same occasion, it was further held, that a juror who had been tendered to the prisoner, could not, against his consent, be discharged; this court saying, that the "prisoner had a right to have him, of which he could not be deprived under the circumstances. It is very probable, that the court might properly set aside a juror who was physically or mentally incompetent, but there was no such emergency in the present case." Indeed, without the aid of authority, upon the principles of reason and common sense, it is manifest that a circuit judge does not possess the authority to discharge without sufficient cause, a juror specially summoned for the trial of a capital felony. And the violation of principle would be equally great, although the injury might not be so obvious, if the exercise of an unrestrained discretion over the subject were confined to a single instance, instead of being extended to an indefinite number of the *venire*. Concurring with counsel, that to dispense with a juror summoned upon the special *venire* in capital cases, without cause, and against the consent of the accused, would be an unwarrantable exercise of authority by the presiding judge, we nevertheless think the action of the court under consideration was unexceptionable.

The record in the case at bar does not show that the special *venire* was exhausted before a jury had been selected, and that recourse was therefore necessary to the regular panel, or to *tales* jurors summoned for the occasion. As the effort is to impeach the judgment of the court, the facts, upon which the charge of error is predicated must be shown distinctly by the record to exist; as upon an unvarying principle, unless that be done, the action of the court will be held to be in strict accordance with the law. We must assume, therefore, that the jury, which was empanelled, and by whom the prisoner was tried, were taken from the special *venire*. But it is assumed, that the prisoner had a right to select the jury from the whole of the special *venire*. Hence, it is argued, that the court, by dispensing with the jurors above named, infringed that right, as the accused was compelled thereby to select his jury from a part, and not from the whole panel. The argument is not borne out by the record. When those persons were called, and failing to attend, the prisoner objected to a farther call of the *venire*, unless the attendance of the absent jurors should be procured by attachment or otherwise, the court disregarded the objection and proceeded with the cause. The record does not show that they were discharged, nor does it affirmatively appear, that an application was made for an attachment to bring them before the court. If, after the state and prisoner had failed to obtain a sufficient number of competent jurors from those of the special *venire*, in attendance upon the court, an application for an attachment to compel the attendance of the absentees had been refused, a very different question would have arisen. In such a case we apprehend, the accused, as a general rule, would have a right to demand the process of the court to compel their attendance. But even here, something must necessarily be left to the discretion of the court, as we may readily suppose the existence of circumstances, which would justify a refusal. Then, upon the facts presented by the record, of what has the prisoner a right to complain? We answer, nothing. The absents jurors were not discharged. The exigency did not arise in which the prisoner could demand an attachment, as the jury was empanelled before the special *venire* was exhausted. The right to select the jury from the whole number summoned was not abridged; at most, the right of the accused to select from the absent jurors was postponed, until it could be ascertained, whether a jury could be constituted of those, whose names stood posterior on the list, which was precisely what the representative of the state, with the sanction of the court, would have had the power to do, if they had been present.

2. The next exception is of a similar character. It is presented by the fourth bill of exceptions, from which it appears, that John W. Jones was returned, as summoned by the sheriff on the special *venire*. Upon the call of the *venire*, James W.

Jones answered to that name, and upon examination, being found to be a competent juror, was peremptorily challenged by the state. Afterwards it was ascertained, that the name of James W. Jones was not upon the list of the names of the jurors returned as summoned. It appears, that James W. Jones was in fact summoned, but it does not appear that John W. Jones was not. The prisoner's counsel demanded the production of John W. Jones, and upon his non-appearance, objected to proceeding with the call of the *venire*. The court overruled the objection, and proceeded with the cause. What we have above said is a sufficient answer to this exception.

3. It appears from the record, that four persons were summoned as jurors, who, upon their appearance at the trial, were examined on oath, and found to be neither freeholders nor householders; whereupon they were severally discharged by the court. This proceeding does not appear, from the bill of exceptions, to have been regarded as objectionable. It was undoubtedly correct; but it is now insisted, that, as it was the duty of the sheriff, in obedience to the mandate of the special *venire facias*, to summon as jurors for the trial of the prisoner, only such persons as were duly qualified, his omission to do so, or rather his having returned upon the panel, persons disqualified to sit as jurors, was an infringement of the prisoner's rights.

By the statute, Hutch. Code, p. 888, art. 10, it was enacted, that thereafter, no challenge to the array should be sustained, nor should any *venire facias* be quashed, by any court, for any cause whatever, except in capital cases, in which the special *venire* might be quashed, for partiality or corruption in the officers executing the writ. The fact, that disqualified persons were summoned, if it constituted a defect in the special *venire*, could not, therefore, be objected to by a challenge to the array, and was no ground to quash, unless upon proof of partiality or corruption in the sheriff. There is no charge of partiality or corruption against the officer, and it is difficult to perceive, why an alleged defect, which, if admitted to exist, constituted no ground for quashing the special *venire*, should be a sufficient reason for reversing the judgment. We apprehend, that it could not have been the intention of the legislature to subject a party criminally charged, to trial by a jury illegally constituted, and whose finding would consequently be erroneous.

4. The next objection is, that an illegal question was allowed to be propounded to, and answered by a witness, examined on the trial.

John F. Carlisle was produced as a witness, and examined in chief by the prisoner. Upon his cross-examination, the following question was asked by the district attorney, to wit: "Was not the intoxicated condition of the deceased such, that unless he had leaned for support on the post or some other supporter, he could not have stood up?" The objection is, that this was a leading question; and doubtless it is. 2 Ph. Ev. 401; Turney v. State, 8 S. & M., 104. But, as we have seen, the question was propounded to the witness on his cross-examination. Upon cross-examination, a much greater latitude is allowed, than upon the examination in chief, and it is settled, that upon such examination, leading questions are admissible. 2 Ph. Ev., 406; 4 ib. 723; note, 373. In permitting the question to be asked, there was, therefore, no error. Nor do we think the court erred, in refusing to allow the answer of the prisoner to the question addressed to him by the witness Bruner, to be given in evidence. The answer of the prisoner was properly excluded upon a plain principle. It is not contended, that it was admissible as a part of the *res gestæ;* and no attempt had been made on the part of the state to introduce the statements or confessions of the prisoner.

5. We will, in the last place, direct our attention to the exception taken to the admission of certain evidence introduced in behalf of the prosecution.

The crime charged was committed, as alleged, in the county of Warren; in which the prisoner was indicted, and, in the first instance tried and convicted of murder. The judgment rendered upon that conviction was reversed by this court, and the cause was sent back to that county for a new trial. Afterwards the venue was changed, and the case transferred to the circuit court of Hinds county. On the trial in the latter county, the affidavit made by the prisoner for the purpose of obtaining a change of venue from the Warren circuit court, and the record of the conviction and sentence of the prisoner therein, were offered as evidence to the jury. The prisoner objected, but his objection was overruled, and the affidavit and record were accordingly read by the prosecuting attorney.

The affidavit for a change of venue made by the prisoner could not conduce to prove the issue submitted to the jury. It was wholly irrelevant, and therefore inadmissible. But the irrelevancy of this testimony was not the strongest reason why it should have been rejected. Its obvious tendency was to prejudice the minds of the jurors, and thereby render them less capable of a calm and impartial examination of the evidence. It presented to them the prisoner in the odious attitude of a man, who, charged with a capital offense, was so hateful, or whose guilt was so strongly suspected, that a fair trial could not be had in the county where the offense was committed.

The same objections apply, but with greater force, to the introduction of the record of the conviction and sentence. The fact, that a jury of the county of Warren, on a previous trial of the prisoner for the same offense, upon the same indictment, had found him guilty of the offense charged, was certainly not legitimate evidence to establish his guilt before a jury in the county of Hinds. The fact, that the judge, who presided on the trial, after a review of the evidence, refused the prisoner's application for a new trial, and pronounced sentence upon him, was equally inadmissible as evidence in the cause. The effect of this evidence, under any circumstances, must have been unfavorable to the prisoner, and in a doubtful case might have proved fatal to him.

We think the court erred in the admission of this evidence; and, therefore, reverse the judgment, award a new trial, and remand the prisoner.

VAN BUREN, (a slave,) v. THE STATE, 24 Miss. Rep., 512.

BURGLARY.

The signing and sealing of bills of exception is clearly a ministerial and not a judicial act, and the statute, (Hutch. Code, 890,) providing that bills of exception may, under circumstances, be signed by the attorneys of the court, is constitutional.

Where confessions were made on one day, under the influence of fear from previous whipping, and a threat of further punishment, and were repeated the day following to another person, (the master of the accused,) such repeated confessions are properly presumed to have been made under the same fear and apprehension, and ought not to be given in evidence on the trial.

In the case of Peter, (a slave,) v. The State, cited by the court, they say, "that after the fact is known, that either the influence of hope or fear existed, superinducing the confessions, explicit warning should be given to the prisoner of the consequences of a confession, and it should be likewise manifest that the prisoner understood such warning, before his subsequent confessions could be given in evidence.

Error to the Circuit Court of Hinds County.   BARNETT, J.

The plaintiff in error was indicted for burglary, was convicted, and sentenced to be branded and whipped.   The further facts are sufficiently stated in the opinion of the court.

Guion & Wharton, for the plaintiff in error, contended that the confessions of the prisoner were improperly admitted as testimony, being made under the influence of fear, threats and compulsion; and cited the case of Peter v. The State, as decisive of the one at bar.

The statute authorizing counsel to sign bills of exception in cases in which the judge refuses to do so, is constitutional.   It is objected, that the judge so refusing may be proceeded against by impeachment.   Grant it,—but the inquiry recurs: What remedy does that afford the injured party, who is entitled to have the history of the trial certified to this court?

D. C. Glenn, attorney general.

The act of 1842 is unconstitutional, and there is no bill of exceptions in the record.   See Constitution, Art. 4, § 10, 11, 12, 13, 14 and 15; Brier v. Williamson, 7 S. & M., 15; 2 How., 856; 3 ib., 252.

YERGER, J.:

The bill of exceptions in this case was signed and sealed by two attorneys of the court, according to the provisions of the Act of 22d February, 1840, Hutch. Code, 890.

It is insisted by the attorney general, that this act of the legislature is unconstitutional, because it confers upon the attorneys those powers and attributes which belong to the judge, and is therefore an infringment upon the judicial prerogative. If this argument be correct, we must disregard the bill of exceptions, as a nullity, and affirm the judgment of the court below; as the only error assigned by the prisoner's counsel, refers to the action of the court set out in the bill of exceptions.

The practice of taking bills of exceptions seems to be entirely a statutary regulation, and was originally established by the Statute of Westminster, 2, (13 Edward 1,) ch. 31, which enacted that "if the party write the exception, and pray that the justices may put their seals to it for testimony, the justices shall put their seals, and if one will not another shall. And if the king, on complaint made of the justices, cause the record to come before him, and the exception be not found in the roll, and the party show the exception written with the seal affixed, the justice shall be commanded to appear at a certain day, to confess or deny his seal; and if the justice cannot deny his seal, judgment shall be given according to the exception, as it may be allowed or disallowed." Tidd's Pr., 862.

According to the further provisions of the statute, if the judges refuse to sign the exceptions, the party aggrieved had a writ, founded on the statute, commanding them to put their seals. This writ contains a surmise of an exception taken and overruled, and commands the justices, if it be so, that they put their seals, upon which, if it be returned by the judges, that it is not so, an action lies for a false return, and thereupon the surmise is tried, and if it be found so, damages are given; and upon such recovery there issues a peremptory writ. Tidd's Pr., 864. The sole object in allowing bills of exceptions is, to perpetuate for the use of the appellate court a full and complete history of the facts occurring *in pais* during the progress of the cause in the inferior court. It is made a part of the record, for the inspection and use of the superior court, to enable it to proceed to judgment in correcting any errors that may have occurred in the court below. In the mere signing and sealing of a bill of exceptions, no judgment of the court is required, no act of the judicial mind is demanded. It is purely ministerial in its character, and might be as readily performed by the clerk as recording the verdict of a jury, nor can we see that any judicial function is exercised in preparing a history or statement of the case as it occurred in the court below.

We have no doubt that it would be perfectly competent for the legislature to abolish altogether the practice of taking bills of exceptions, and to substitute in its place any other mode deemed appropriate to bring before the higher court evidence of the action which took place in the inferior court; and accordingly we find that, to some extent, this has been done by the act of the 3d March, 1846, (Hutch. Code, 893,) which provides " that charges given or refused by the court, shall be so noted at the time, by the clerk, and when so noted and endorsed form a part of the record in the high court, without any bill of exceptions."

We are, therefore, clearly of the opinion that the act of the legislature directing the method of taking bills of exceptions, which was resorted to in this case, is constitutional, and that the bill of exceptions in this record is properly taken according to the provisions of that act.

This brings us to the consideration of the errors assigned by the counsel for the prisoner. We do not deem it necessary to refer to more than one, as in our opinion the judgment must be reversed on that ground.

Thomas Cooper was offered as a witness for the state, who proved that he had hired the defendant from Birdsong, to whom he belonged ; that going into his stable at night, on the 15th of December, he perceived that his horse had been ridden, and supposed, from his appearance, that a bag of potatoes had been carried on him. Suspecting the prisoner to have ridden the horse, he called him up next morning and charged him with the fact, and also with having carried off a bag of potatoes. This the prisoner denied. He then whipped him, but obtained no confession. In the evening he again took him up, and threatened to whip him again, when he confessed what articles he had, to wit : two jugs of whisky and two loaves of sugar, and where they could be found, and accompanied the witness to the place and showed him the articles. The witness then asked him to state when and where he had obtained them, when, the witness says, he voluntarily and without any threat, confessed that he had taken them the night before from the store of Birdsong and Gory, which he entered by means of a false key. On the next morning, Tuesday, the witness informed Birdsong, the master of the slave, of these facts, and on the evening of that day Birdsong accompanied witness home, when the slave being called before them, witness said to him : " Van, here is your master, who has come for the things you took ;" and thereupon the prisoner, without any threat made or any promise given or reward offered, voluntarily confirmed the confession he had previously made to the witness. This confession, thus made on Tuesday to Birdsong and the witness, the court permitted to be given in evidence, although objected to by the prisoner's counsel.

No objection is made to the admission of that part of the evidence of the witness detailing the conduct and action of the prisoner in pointing out the whisky and sugar. These are facts which it was certainly competent to prove. So much, however, of the confession made to the witness on Monday, as related to the time and manner in which the prisoner alleged he had obtained the articles, ought to have been and was properly excluded by the court, as it was manifestly obtained under the influence of fear, arising from the previous whipping and the threat of further punishment. The confession made the next day to witness and Birdsong, the court permitted to go to the jury, and we think erroneously.

In the case of Peter, (a slave,) v. The State, 4 S. & M., 31, confessions obtained under very similar circumstances were held to be inadmissible; the court remarking that, after the fact is known, that either the influence of hope or fear existed, superinducing the confession, explicit warning should be given to the prisoner of the consequences of a confession, and it should likewise be manifest that the prisoner understood such warning before his subsequent confessions could be given in evidence.

We think the judgment should be reversed, and a new trial granted.

JOHN (a slave) *v.* THE STATE, 24 Miss., 569.

HOMICIDE.

Under the statute, approved March 9th, 1850, it is not necessary to allege in the indictment the name of the owner of any slave guilty of any crime punishable with death.   But if the ownership is alleged, it must be proven on the trial.

It is incumbent on the prosecutor to prove, on the trial, every fact and circumstance set out in the indictment which is material and necessary to constitute the offense charged.   And every averment in the indictment not necessary to constitute the offense may be rejected as surplusage.   But this rule does not apply to allegations, which, however unnecessary, are nevertheless descriptive of that which is material.

Error to Hinds circuit court.   TOMPKINS, J.

The facts in substance, are, that Mr. Banks, the first witness introduced, proves that, as a physician and surgeon, he examined the body of the negro killed, who was found dead near a wagon on the road; was sure he was killed by choking with a rope that was then found around his neck; had heard that negro killed belonged to Feguno Lowe, but did not know it.   The dead negro's pockets had been rifled after death; there were cuts on the hands and fingers.   He saw defendant, John, on the same day of the killing, after his arrest, and examined the wound in his head, and thought it was made by some sharp instrument, and defendant said it was inflicted by a blow from one of the wagon wheels in helping the negro that was killed to get his wagon out of the mud the night before; but witness did not think the wound could have been inflicted that way; and upon examining defendant's mouth, one tooth had been knocked out, and blood was streaming from it.   Defendant said he had received the wound a day or two before on the railroad, and these wounds, in witness's opinion, had not been inflicted more than twelve hours; witness could not say to whom the dead negro belonged.

Dr. Williams testified, that John told him that two of the depot boys had killed Austin, but did not say he knew it, and John said he was at the wagon the evening before, when it was stated he got wounded on the head; witness knew nothing of the man killed.   John was hired to work on the railroad, but left the morning of the killing.

H. Moseley was at the coroner's inquest, and saw the rope

around the neck; saw the wounds on the fingers. He heard John say, after arrest, that he knew a man had been killed, but he did not do it; heard him say before the examining court, that he (Austin) was killed by Jim Saunders and Henry Simmons; a shirt was exhibited, but did not know that John ever had it on, or who the dead negro belonged to, who seemed to have been very stout.

George (a slave) stated, that about supper time, on the night the wagon was stalled, he came across John and old Jim, who helped the man to get his wagon out of the mud and up the hill; and then he, witness, started home, and old Jim back to Clinton, and John went along after the wagon, and did not see John again until after arrested.

Alfred (a slave) stated, that he saw John on the railroad on the evening the murder was committed, and asked him where he was going, and John told him to go to hell; but did not see John again until he came to the shanty, about an hour before daybreak the next morning; he was very muddy, and witness and John slept together in the shanty. John did not go to work in the morning, but said he was sick, and went to bed; at dinnertime he saw blood on the shirt-collar and bosom of John's shirt, and knows that to be the shirt exhibited to the jury; he could not positively say John was not at the shanty on the night the murder was supposed to have been committed.

Davy (a slave) stated, he and John both worked on the railroad and slept in the same shanty, and he did not see John in the shanty that night until he came in, about an hour before day; John then said he was sick. John told witness a short time before that, while at work together, that he thought he ought to kill somebody; but he thought this a mere foolish remark. Next morning, when witness heard a man had been killed, he told Mr. T. that he had better examine John; but on looking into the shanty, found he was not there, and witness did not see John again until he was arrested.

Willis (a slave) states, at about one o'clock on the night the murder was committed, John came to the shanty where they both slept, and John called Nathan out to take a drink with him, and Nathan soon returned, but John went off, and he did not see him any more until about one hour before daybreak next morning; that, on the day the inquest was held over the body, he saw a number of persons going towards the dead body, and John asked him, witness, where all these people were going to, when he replied that they were going to have a jury and make all the railroad hands go before them and put their hands on the dead body, and that blood would follow the hand of the murderer; that John then took off his cap and asked Nathan to take care of it, took his hat, jumped over the fence near the shanty, and went off, running some at first; and this took place on the day John was arrested, and John did not go to work on that day. Witness knew Austin, the negro killed, and heard him say he belonged to Mr. Lowe; that Austin had been coming to the depot ever since the railroad was built, hauling cotton and other freight, and he had seen Mr. Lowe with him, controlling and managing him as his own.

This was all the evidence for the state.

The defense then introduced Jack, (a slave,) who stated, that on Thursday night, about midnight, he, being then run away from those to whom he was hired, met John in the road, from one to two hundred yards from the wagon, and between it and Clinton; that he had come across the field and got into the road near where he had met John, and he, witness, was going towards the wagon to get something to eat, but that just after he met John, and while they were standing together, he heard some noise in the direction of the wagon, heard some one say, "Boys, my head is cut; I'll give up;" that he asked John what was the matter; to which he replied, they were quarrelling and fighting down there, he believed; that witness did not know whether John had been to the wagon or not; that he and John came on towards town, and when they got to the railroad, John went towards the shanty, and he in the opposite direction. Jack and John belonged to the same master, (Baxter,) and Cook only controlled them.

The error chiefly relied on in this court is, the refusal of the circuit court to grant the following instructions, asked by the counsel for the prisoner:

"Unless the jury are satisfied beyond a reasonable doubt, from the proof adduced and allowed to go before them by the court, that the defendant John is the property of John D. Cook, as alleged in the indictment, they must find a verdict of not guilty."

The prisoner was convicted of murder; a new trial was moved for and overruled, and this writ of error prayed by the counsel for the prisoner.

G. P. Foute for plaintiff in error.

The allegation in the indictment of the ownership of the slave (the accused) is material and absolutely necessary. The ownership of the deceased slave must also be alleged and proved. See Archbold's Criminal Pleading, pp. 34, 35, 38, 39, 40—45, and notes p. 100; 2 Russ. on Cr., 706, on subject of surplusage, etc.; 3 McLean's R., 233. See also Hutch. Code, 540—542, art. 24. This is the statute which entitles the owner or master of the slave to half his value, upon his conviction and execution. This statute is also the same (differing only in some minor particulars) with the statute of Alabama upon the same subject.

In the absence of any decision of our own court, as to the effect which this statute should have in all indictments of slaves for capital offenses, I submit that the ruling of the supreme court of Alabama should have great weight. On this point, see the case of Flora (a slave) v. State, 4 Porter R., 111; and State v. Marshall (a slave), 7 ib., 302. (The opinion of the court in the last case contains the statute of Alabama, Clay's Dig., 474, § 19.)

These cases, I insist, are conclusive upon the point, that the allegation must be made and proved. Our statute (art. 24, above referred to) makes the necessity still stronger, for it declares that no non-resident owner of any slave shall be entitled to the benefit of the act. This would seem to render it necessary and material, that not only the ownership of the slave should be alleged, but the citizenship of such owner.

Upon general principles of law and common sense, I also insist that such an allegation is material and necessary. This indictment is found under the statute, Hutch. Code, 521, § 55, providing for the punishment of slaves for certain offenses therein named.

A slave, by our law, is declared and held as personal property. An offense, therefore, committed by or against him, is an offense by or upon the property of the master or owner.

The property in him, therefore, is not only necessary to identify him, but is a part of his existence, his estate or condition, the way in which he is known and described by law, and in common parlance. The very meaning and essence of the term "slave" indicates property in another than himself. It is thus contradistinguished from all other terms implying any other kind of servitude. If by the policy and requirements of our law, in all writings, conveyances, bills of sale, and every other known method for conveying title in him, "John" is to be described as belonging to, or the property of A. B., it would seem that an indictment which seeks to deprive A. B. of the life of his property, should describe and prove him to be such property.

But if it is not a material and necessary allegation to be made in the indictment, yet being made, can it be regarded as surplusage, or must not the allegation be proved as laid?

The allegation, though unnecessary, must be proved. Russell on Crimes, 706, 707, 708, and cases there cited; also authorities first above cited.

1 Chitty on Pleading, 263, lays down the rule, that matter which is wholly foreign and irrelevant, can only be rejected as surplusage. "If the prosecutor choose to state the offense with greater particularity than is required, he will be bound by the statement, and must prove it as laid." 3 McLean's R., 233, 234, and Rex v. Dowling, 5 T. R., 311, therein cited.

But if mistaken in the foregoing positions, the proof in this case shows a fatal variance between the allegation and proof of ownership in both the slaves, the accused and deceased. The indictment alleges that the slave John (the accused) is the property of John D. Cook; when John D. Cook, introduced as a witness on the part of the defendant himself, testifies that John is not his property, but belongs to a man by the name of Baxter, who lives in North Carolina. There is no proof at all as to the true ownership of the deceased (Austin). See Archbold's Crim. Plead., marginal page 100, 101; also 15 Maine R., 476, and authorities cited upon the foregoing points. Ruff. & Hawk. R., 32, etc.

D. C. Glenn, attorney general.

The point in this case arises on two charges given for the state, that it was unnecessary to prove the ownership of the accused, or deceased negro.

The court was correct. Ownership had nothing to do with the charge ; it is no part of the offense. It was equally criminal to kill the slave of one man as another ; and the slayer is equally guilty if he be the property of A. or B. The accused has no further interest in having it stated than for purposes of identity. For such a defect in proof, an acquittal being had, a plea of *autrefois acquit* would be good, and this incontestably proves that the title of ownership of the slave is not of essence of the offense of killing or being killed by him. If averment is made, it may be rejected as surplusage, and the verdict cures the defect if any there be. See generally on the negro question, Pye's case, 2 East Cr. Law, 785 ; Ch. Cr. L., 168, 169 ; ib., 211, 213, 214, 215, 232, 233 ; 3 ib., 1087 ; 2 Hawk. Pl. Cr. Ch., 25, § 71, 72 ; 10 Missouri R., 232 ; 8 S. & M., 584, and cases cited ; 1 Hawks R., 34 ; 2 Bailey R., 67 ; Riley's Law Cases, 298 ; ib., 299.

SMITH, C. J. :

This was an indictment for murder, tried in the circuit court of Hinds county. It was alleged in the indictment, that the plaintiff in error was the property of John D. Cook. Austin, the subject of the homicide, was likewise a slave, and stated to belong to Figune Lowe. The jury found a verdict of guilty ; a motion was made for a new trial, which was overruled, and the case hence comes into this court.

The exceptions chiefly relied on for a reversal of the judgment refer to the refusal of the court to give the third and fourth instructions requested on behalf of the prisoner, and the decision of the court on the motion for a new trial. The first of these instructions is in the following words, to wit : " Unless the jury are satisfied beyond a reasonable doubt, from the proof adduced and allowed to go before them by the court, that the defendant John is the property of John D. Cook, as alleged in the indict-

ment, they must find a verdict of not guilty." The second instruction laid down the same rule, in reference to the alleged
ownership of the deceased.

We will proceed to inquire, in the first place, whether the
court erred in refusing to grant these instructions.

By the statute approved the 9th of March, 1850, which was
prior to the commission of the offense charged in the indictment,
it was enacted, that "it should not thereafter be necessary to
allege in the indictment the name of the owner of any slave
guilty of any crime punishable by the laws of this state with
death."

The history of this statute is familiar to the bar. It was believed by many members of the profession, that it was necessary
to warrant the conviction of a slave charged with a capital felony, that the name of the owner should be alleged in the indictment and proved as averred. The decision of this court
on that point had not been made; to dispel all doubt on the
subject the act was passed. Whatever may have been the previous rule, the effect of this statute is clearly to dispense with
the necessity of the averment of ownership in indictments against
slaves for capital offenses; and, of consequence, of the proof
of ownership; for unless the averment is made, the proof
would be unnecessary. But, we apprehend, the recognized rules
of criminal pleading were not designed by the legislature to be
changed, except so far as it was made necessary by them, to
allege the ownership of a slave capitally charged. In a case,
therefore, in which the allegation of ownership is contained in
the indictment, it becomes a question whether such averment is
to be regarded as impertinent or foreign to the charge, and,
therefore, to be rejected as surplusage, or as unnecessary and
immaterial, but being made, requires to be proved as alleged.

The general rule in regard to the proof of indictments is, that
it is incumbent on the prosecutor to prove at the trial every fact
and circumstance stated in the indictment which is material and
necessary to constitute the offense charged.[1] On the other hand,

[1] Wharton Am. Cr. Law, 623; 1 Greenl. Ev., 74; 3 Ib., 24; Commonwealth v.
McKie, 1 Lead. Cr. Cases, 347, note; 1 Archbold Cr. Pr. & Pl. 385; 4 Esp., 136, 139,
144; 2 East P. C., 993; 4 Black. Com., 356; 1 Leach, 300, 393, n. a; 2 T. R., 201, n. a;
3 Camp., 401; 2 Stark. R., 155; Commonwealth v. Kimball, 24 Pick., 366; Common-

every fact and circumstance laid in the indictment, which is not
a necessary ingredient in the offense, may be rejected as surplusage, and need not be proved at the trial.[1]   Archb. Crim.
Plead. 39.   These rules are well recognized; but in their application to particular cases it is not unfrequently somewhat difficult to distinguish between allegations which are material and
necessary, and those which may be totally disregarded as proof.
Phillips, in his Treatise on Evidence (vol 1, p. 500), lays down a
rule by which the immateriality of matter alleged in the indictment may be tested.   " If," says he, " an averment may be
entirely omitted without affecting the charge against the prisoner, it will be considered as surplusage, and may be disregarded
in the evidence."   But this test is held applicable only to averments which are not only unnecessary in themselves, but foreign
to the charge.   As an illustration of this rule, the case of the
King v. Minton may be referred to.   In that case, which is cited
in 2 East P. C., 1021, the defendant was charged with having
committed arson in the night time, and it was proved on the
trial that the offense was committed in the day; he was convicted, and the conviction was holden good, for the reason that
the averment, which charged the offense to have been committed
in the night, was unnecessary and foreign to the charge, and,
therefore, might be disregarded in the evidence.   So, upon the
same principle, in Rex v. Holt, 5 T. R., 446, it was holden, upon
an information for a libel with intent to bring the proclamation
of his majesty into contempt, that an averment that divers ad-
dresses had been presented to the king on the occasion of such

---

wealth v. Dana, 2 Metc., 329; 2 Leach, 594; People v. Townsend, 3 Hill, 479; Commonwealth v. Hope, 22 Pick., 1; State v. Noble, 15 Maine, 476; Commonwealth v.
Tuck, 20 Pick., 356, 364; U. S. v. Vickery, 1 Har. & Johns., 427; Commonwealth
v. Pray, 13 Pick, 359; U. S. v. Howard, 3 Sum. 12; State v. Cassedy, 1 Richardson,
91; State v. Morrison, 2 Iredell, 9; Commonwealth v. Arnold, 4 Pick., 251; Commonwealth v. Gable, 7 Serg. & R., 423; Addison, 171, 173; 11 Mass., 93; 2 Camp.,
583; 2 East P. C., 782; 8 East, 192; 3 Camp., 10, 12; 2 Hale, 29.

[1] Wharton Am. Cr. Law, 622; Leach, 536; 1 T. R., 322; Com. Dig. Pleader, c. 28,
29, F. 12; 4 Coke, 412; Mod., 327; People v. Lohman, 2 Barb. S. C. R., 235; State
v. Copenburg, 2 Strobh., 273; State v. Brown, 8 Humph., 89; State v. Cozens, 6 Iredell, 82; State. v Wilder, 7 Blackf., 582; U. S. v. Howard, 3 Sumner 12; State v.
Noble, 3 Shep., 476; 2 Russ. on Crimes, 786; State v. Palmer, 35 Maine, 9; Jilliard
v. Commonwealth, 2 Casey, 170; State v. Bailey, 11 Foster, 521; State v. Carrigan,
24 Conn., 296; State v. Elliott, 14 Texas, 423; Wharton Cr. Law, 592, 599; Leach,
127, 536; Rex v. Morris, 1 Leach C. C., 109; 1 Archbold Cr. Law, 282; 2 Hale, 182.

proclamation, was disconnected with the charge and did not require proof.

But this rule has never been held to apply to allegations which, however unnecessary, are nevertheless connected with, and descriptive of that which is material; or, in other words, to averments which might with propriety have been dispensed with, but, being inserted in the indictment, are descriptive of identity of that which is legally essential to the charge. 3 Phil. Ev., 668, Cow. & Hill's ed.; Arch. Cr. Plead., 101; U. S. v. Porter, 3 Day, 286.[1]   As, for example, an indictment for stealing a black horse will not be supported by proof that the horse was of some other color, for the allegation of color is descriptive of that which is legally essential to the offense, and cannot be rejected. 2 Starkie Ev., 1531. So also on this principle, upon an indictment under the statute of 57 Geo. 3, c. 90, for being found armed with intent to destroy game in a certain wood, called the Old Walk, in the occupation of a person named; it was holden, it appearing that the wood had always been called the Long Walk, and never the Old Walk, that although it was unnecessary to state the name of the close where the occupation was stated, yet, being stated, it was material, and could not be rejected. Rex v. Owen, 1 Moody C. C., 118; Rex v. Craven, 1 Russ. & R. 14; Rex v. William Deely, 1 Moody, C. C., 303.

Let us apply this rule to the question whether the averment that the prisoner was the property of Cook, could be treated as surplusage, and, therefore, disregarded in the evidence.

As we have seen, this allegation was unnecessary. The ownership of the prisoner was in no respect an ingredient in the offense charged, which was complete when it was shown that one human being was wilfully, feloniously and maliciously killed by another human being. But, the fact of the ownership being alleged, it

---

[1] See also Wharton Am. Cr. Law, 626; Rex v. Plestow, 1 Camp., 493; State v. Clark, 3 Foster, 439; Wharton Am. Cr. Law, 629; State v. Canney, 19 N. H., 135; Dick v. State, 30 Miss., 631; State v. Langley, 34 N. H., 529; U. S. v. Howard, 3 Sumner, 12; Commonwealth v. Atwood, 11 Mass., 93; Commonwealth v. Tuck, 20 Pick., 356, 364; State v. Noble. 15 Me., 476; Commonwealth v. Hope, 22 Pick., 1; U. S. v. Brown, 3 McLean, 233; 1 Bishop Cr. Procedure, 233; Commonwealth v. King, 9 Cush., 284; Rex v. Woolford, 1 Moody & R., 384; State v. Johnson, 6 Jones (N. C.), 485; State v. Weeks. 30 Maine, 182; U. S. v. Kean, 1 McLean, 429; State v. Jackson, 20 Me., 29; Dick v. State, 631.

became a part of the identity of the prisoner; quite as much so
as the name under which he was indicted.   It was, at least, a
statement of an unnecessary particular, but in connection with,
and as descriptive of, that which it was essential to allege.   If
so, it comes within the principles of the cases above cited;
and we do not feel authorized to say that it was unnecessary to
prove it.

But it does not follow, because the averment of ownership
could not be disregarded in the evidence, that proof in the
strictest sense was required.   The rule seems to be, in regard to
averments of this character (that is, averments in reference to
matter which it is unnecessary to allege, but, being made, it becomes necessary to prove them), that precise proof is never required except when the subject of the averment is a record, a
written agreement, and, perhaps, an express contract.   Gould
Pl., 164, 165.   This is the doctrine in reference to the pleadings
in civil proceedings.   The same rule applies in criminal cases,
except that in the latter, courts will be more strict in requiring
proof of matters alleged than in the former.   United States v.
Porter, 3 Day's R., 286.

If this rule was applicable to the proof in regard to the
averment of ownership, the third and fourth instructions were
improper.   They laid down the rule, that, before the jury
could convict the prisoner, they should be satisfied beyond a
reasonable doubt of the fact of ownership, as charged in the
indictment.   This was requiring too high a degree of evidence
in reference to a question of property, even admitting the necessity of strict proof in regard to the ownership of the prisoner.   We think, therefore, that the court did not err in refusing to give the said instructions.

We will now proceed to notice the question arising upon the
decision of the circuit judge in overruling the motion for a
new trial.

We do not deem it necessary, it might, perhaps, be improper,
to go into a minute examination of the testimony upon which
the prisoner was convicted.   It is sufficient to remark, that the
whole of the evidence offered in support of the charge was
circumstantial; that no fact distinctly proved was, in itself, suf-

ficient to raise more than a very slight presumption, if any at all, of the guilt of the prisoner; and that all of the circumstances proved on the trial, when united, were, upon well-recognized principles, insufficient to create such a presumption of his guilt as would warrant a conviction.

We, therefore, reverse the judgment, remand the prisoner, and award a new trial in the court below.

Murphy et al. *v.* The State, 24 Miss. Rep., 590.

Trading with Slaves.

So much of the 2d section of the act of March 6th, 1850, "to suppress trade and barter with slaves," as declares that "the name of the slave, or of his owner, or the kind or quantity of the produce or commodity bought or sold, need not be stated," is in direct conflict with the 10th section of the bill of rights which secures to every accused, the right "to demand the nature and cause of the accusation against him; and an indictment under this act, that does not allege these facts, is defective and must be quashed.

It is not absolutely necessary to state in the indictment for trading with slaves, the name of the owner of the slave, but the article or commodity bought or sold, must be stated; and on the trial the state should be confined in the proof of the offense to the day named in the indictment.

Error to Madison circuit court.   Perry, J.

The indictments in these cases were found for violations of the act of the legislature of the 6th March, 1850, "to suppress trade and barter with slaves."

In the two cases against Murphy, the indictment charged, "that Daniel W. Murphy, late of the County of Madison aforesaid, on the 1st day of October, a. d. 1851, at the county of Madison aforesaid, did then and there unlawfully sell spirituous liquors to a slave, without the consent in writing of the master, owner or overseer of said slave."

The indictment against Allman stated neither the name of the slave nor the name of his master, owner, overseer, or employer, nor the commodity alleged to have been sold.

Murphy pleaded in abatement, that Lewis Finley, one of the grand jurors who found the bill, was interested in the penalty or fine to be inflicted under said indictment. The plea was demurred to, and the demurrer sustained. He then moved to quash the indictment, as being uncertain, and giving to the defendant no sufficient notice of the nature and cause of the charge brought against him ; which motion was overruled.

The jury returned a verdict of guilty, and the defendant moved in arrest of judgment, and for a new trial; both which motions were overruled.

William Vincent, the sole witness for the prosecution, testified in substance, that about the latter part of November, or the 1st of December, 1851, he saw a negro man enter the storehouse of the defendant, and speak some words to him, which witness did not hear, when defendant pointed to a barrel with a tumbler upon it, and the negro went to the barrel, drew some liquid in the tumbler, and having drank it gave the defendant half a dime.

Witness did not know positively what was in the barrel, or whether it was spirituous liquor or not ; but some month or so before had drawn whisky out of a barrel sitting in the same place, and very much like the barrel from which the negro drew the liquid that he drank. Witness did not know the name of the negro, or his master or employer.

The evidence of the defendant consisted of several orders from various persons to sell liquor to negroes, the orders being without date.

The testimony was of a similar character in both the cases against Murphy.

A. H. Handy, for plaintiff in error.

Contended, 1. That the act of 1850, ch. 31, justifying this indictment, is in palpable conflict with the 10th section of the constitution of this state, art. 1, which secured to the accused the right to be notified of the " nature and cause of the accusation against him ;" that this indictment, and the statute authorizing it, violated that right, because, though notice was given of the " nature " of the offense, that is, selling spirituous liquor to a slave, no notice was given of the " cause " of the accusation, which must consist of the specification of the person with whom the offense is charged to have been committed. This is necessary, in order 1st. That the accused may know the offense charged against him, and come prepared with evidence to meet it; 2d. That he may not be accused of one offense, and tried for another; 3d. That he may not be again tried for the same offense; and therefore, that the charge may be so distinctly specified so as to enable him, if again charged with the same offense, to plead the former acquittal or conviction. Wharton's Crim. Law., 81, 82.

These requisities of certainty must appear in the record, for the only evidence to support the plea of *autrefois acquit* is the record. 1 Arch. Crim. Pl., 84, 85, 119.

2. There is a total absence of all proof on the trial to show any particular slave, with whom the offense was committed. It was, therefore, impossible for the accused to produce the only evidence which this statute permits as a justification, "the original order in writing of the master," etc., because he had no notice whatever as to the particular slave, either by the indictment, or by proof on the trial. If such a prosecution can be sanctioned, it is only necessary, to insure a conviction, to leave the accused in ignorance of who was the "master, owner, or employer" of the slave, and no human skill or wisdom would be able to avoid a conviction, however innocent the accused may be. If the accused produces written orders, how is their effect destroyed? By alleging that the order produced is not applicable to the particular case. But why is this? It is because there is a total failure to indicate in any manner the persons from whom the accused is to show his justification. And thus the citizen is deprived of his liberty and property, without any notice of the "cause of the accusation," cut off from all possibility of justification, and liable to be prosecuted and punished *ad infinitum* upon the very same cause of offense, deprived of the power of ever showing by the record his former acquittal or conviction.

J. J. Davenport, for Allman, on same side.

D. C. Glenn, attorney general.

Yerger, J.:

The defendant was indicted in the circuit court of Madison county, under the act of 6th March, 1850, "to suppress trade and barter with slaves."

The first section of the act declares "that any person who shall buy, sell, or receive of, to, or from any slave or slaves, any corn, fodder, hay, meal, spirituous liquors, or other produce or commodity whatsoever, without the consent in writing of the master or employer of such slave or slaves, shall be held guilty of a high misdemeanor," etc.

By the second section it is enacted, that in indictments for the offenses named in the first section, it shall not be necessary to charge the kind or quantity of the produce or commodity so bought, sold, or received; nor the name of the slave or of the owner of the slave; and that, on the trial, it shall not be necessary to prove the name or ownership of the slave; but it shall be sufficient to prove, that the buying, selling, or receiving was from, to, or of a negro or mulatto.

The third section declares that on the trial the accused shall only be permitted to prove the consent by the production of the original writing and parol or other evidence of its authenticity.

The counsel of the plaintiff in error contends, that so much of the second section of the act as declares that the name of the slave or his owner, or the kind or quantity of the produce or commodity, need not be stated in the indictment, violates the provision in the tenth section of the bill of rights, declaring that "in all criminal prosecutions the accused shall have a right to demand the nature and cause of the accusation against him."

It cannot be doubted that the legislature had the constitutional power to declare it criminal to commit any of the acts enumerated in the first section of the statute. Nor do we doubt that it might have conditionally prohibited all trade and barter with slaves, whether with or without the consent of the owner. But the possession of these powers would not authorize the denial to the accused of any right guaranteed to him by the constitution, in order to make full defense when charged with violating this law.

The constitutional provision, that every man charged with a crime has a right "to demand the nature and cause of the accusation against him," was intended to secure to the accused such a specific designation of the offense laid to his charge as would enable him to make every preparation for his trial necessary to his full and complete defense. We, therefore, think, that under it the accused is entitled to demand " such a certain description of the offense charged and statement of the facts by which it is constituted as will fully identify the accusation, lest the grand jury should find a bill for one offense, and the defendant be put upon his trial for another, without any authority; and also that the defendant may know what crime he is called upon to answer, in order that he may be prepared with his evidence, and that his conviction or acquittal may insure his subsequent protection, should he again be questioned on the same ground ; and that he may be enabled to plead a previous conviction or acquittal of the same offense in bar of any subsequent proceedings against him."

The indictment ought, in our opinion, to describe and identify the offense with such a degree of certainty that the accused and the court may know, that the offense for which he is put upon his trial, is the same offense with that for which he stands indicted, in order that he may plead in bar a previous conviction or acquittal. An indictment which does not contain this degree of certainty, does not communicate to the accused " the nature and cause of the accusation" against him in the manner contemplated and designed by the bill of rights. Nor has the legislature the power to dispense with such a degree of certainty in indictments.

Do the provisions of the second section of this act dispense with this requisite certainty in indictments framed under it ?

The mischief that act was designed to remedy, was trade and barter with slaves, without the consent of those having the management and control of them. The mere act of trading with a slave is no offense against the law. To make it criminal, it must be done without the consent in writing of the master, owner, etc.

But according to the provisions of this statute, every act of dealing with a slave is presumed to be done without authority, and is *prima facie* a violation of the law. Whenever the party accused is proved to have bought, sold, or received any article or produce, or any commodity from a negro or mulatto, the *onus* of exculpation is thrown upon him. He must, then, in order to discharge himself, prove either that the negro or mulatto was not a slave, or if a slave, that the dealing was with the written consent of the master, etc.   This consent, according to the statute, can only be proved by the production of the original writing.

The accused may also defend himself by showing that, although he did receive a commodity from a slave, yet, in fact, the slave only acted in that instance as the agent of the master.

It is most obvious, then, that, unless the particular act of trading or receiving is stated with sufficient certainty to inform the accused for what he is to be tried, he may be totally unable to defend himself by plea of a former acquittal or conviction, because he would be unable to identify the two charges as relating to the same offense.

Entertaining these views, we have come to the conclusion, that indictments framed in the general manner indicated in the second section of the act do not furnish to the accused " the nature and cause of the accusation against him," in the manner contemplated by the constitution.   They cannot, therefore, be sustained.   We do not think it absolutely necessary to state in the indictment the name either of the slave or of his owner, etc. But it is necessary where the name of the owner, employer, etc., is not given, that the article or commodity should be stated ; and that on the trial the state should be confined in its proof of the offense to the day named in the indictment.   It is true that, as a general rule, it is not necessary to prove the offense to have been committed on the day named in the indictment.   But this rule is subject to exceptions, one of which is, that the state shall be confined to that day, if it is necessary to identify the offense.

In Archbold's Cr. Pl., the rule on this subject is stated in the following language : " When the precise date of any fact is necessary to ascertain and determine with precision the offense charged or the matter alleged in excuse or justification, the slightest variance between the pleadings and evidence in that particular will be fatal."   Arch. Cr. Pl., 90.   Of course, where the name of the owner, employer, etc., of the slave is given, there would not be any necessity to name the commodity, or on the trial to confine the state to the day named in the indictment, as the offense would thereby be sufficiently identified to enable the party to make his defense.

In the present case, the specific article sold is named in the indictment, and the court did not, therefore, err in refusing to quash the indictment or arrest the judgment.   But the evidence did not establish the guilt of the accused, and a new trial should have been granted.   We, therefore, reverse the judgment, and remand the cause for a new trial.

Judgment reversed, a new trial awarded, and cause remanded.

Let the same order be entered in the next case.

In Valentine Allman v. The State, judgment of the court below is reversed ; and this court, entering such order as should have been rendered in the court below, proceeds to arrest the judgment on the verdict of the jury.   The indictment in that case does not give the name of the master, etc., or specify the article or commodity sold to the slave.

SARTORIOUS *v.* THE STATE, 24 Miss. Rep., 602.

RECEIVING STOLEN GOODS.

The misconduct of a witness for the state in answering an illegal question, put by the state, after it had been objected to by the accused, when the answer is promptly ruled out by the court, is no ground for a new trial ; unless it were distinctly shown that the answer thus made had a sinister influence on the verdict of the jury.

Witnesses who have been ordered by the court to withdraw from the court-room during the examination of witnesses, but who still continued present and heard the examination, will not ordinarily be examined.   But it rests in the sound discretion of the judge whether they shall be examined or not.   The safest rule seems to be not to reject such evidence altogether, but to admit it, subject to such remarks as the circumstances may warrant.

The party examining a witness in chief should interrogate him as to all material matters in the first instance ; if he omits a material question it cannot be put on examination in reply.   New questions unconnected with the subject of the cross-examination, or which do not tend to explain it, cannot be put in reply.   Such is the general rule, but it rests in the sound discretion of the court, to determine whether the facts of a particular case, do or do not warrant a departure from it.   This court will interfere with the exercise of this discretion, only in cases where the injury arising from a departure from the rule is manifest and great.

On a trial for receiving goods, knowing them to be stolen, it is error to charge the jury " that the discovery of the goods in the possession of the defendant, (they having been proved to be stolen,) shortly after they were missed, and the denial by the defendant that he had any such goods in his possession, is presumptive evidence that he received them, knowing them to be stolen." It assumes as a fact proved, that the goods alleged to have been bought by the prisoner, were stolen. It was in effect, a charge upon the weight of testimony. Besides, the presumption arising from the facts would be that the accused had stolen the goods himself, and not that he had received them knowing they had been stolen.

It was error to charge the jury that "if they believed from the evidence, that the articles were purchased under their value, it is a presumption of the guilty knowledge of the defendant." The rule embraced in this instruction is too broad and comprehensive, and is indefensible upon reason or authority.

The denial of a party, having in his possession stolen goods, that he has such goods in his possession, is presumptive proof of his guilty knowledge; but if it be shown that such denial of possession was the consequence of misunderstandings, such denial ceases to raise a presumption of guilt.

A party must plead to the indictment before he can be put upon his trial, and such plea must be shown by the record.

Error to Hinds circuit court.   BARNETT, J.

At the October term, 1849, of Warren county, the plaintiff in error was indicted for buying certain stolen articles, being copper pipe worth $15, a stop-cock worth $10, three brass boxes worth $15, and pieces of casting worth $10, knowing them to be stolen. He was tried at the April term, 1850, and the jury returned a verdict of "guilty," which verdict was set aside, a new trial granted, and the venue changed to Hinds county.

At the May term, 1850, of the Hinds county circuit court, he was again tried; and, the jury being unable to agree, were discharged by consent.

The plaintiff in error was again put upon his trial, at the September term, 1851, and found guilty. The motion for a new trial was overruled, and the bill of exceptions thereto embodied the testimony in the case, the exceptions taken during the progress of the trial, and the instructions of the court.

S. Zimmerman, for the state, proved that he went to the store of defendant about the first of July, 1849, to search for articles missed from the foundry of Messrs. Peck & Redding; that Peck accused the prisoner of having seen them in his possession, which prisoner denied; and that, after searching the premises, the articles were found in the defendant's store-room, packed in a barrel. The witness identified the articles as the property of Peck & Redding; he had handled them often, and they were in his charge at the time they were taken, and they were taken without his knowledge or consent. He proved the articles to have been worth about the amounts charged in the indictment. Peck was very much excited at the time he questioned the prisoner; an officer named Casey was present, who told prisoner he had a search warrant; prisoner is a foreigner, but speaks English well enough to be understood, and understands what is said to him.

The district attorney asked this witness, if he " knew of other stolen goods having been found on the premises of the prisoner ?" to which question the defendant's counsel objected, and, while the objection was being made, the witness answered, " Yes, to my sorrow," in opposition to the remonstrances of counsel. The court immediately instructed the jury not to regard this answer of witness. At the time the articles were found, the prisoner said he purchased them from a white man, some days before the search.

Lockwood and Peale, for the state, proved substantially the same that was proved by Zimmerman.

Samuel Rothschild and John Bracy, for defendant, proved that they were in the employ of the defendant; that they were present when the articles alleged by the state to have been stolen, were bought by defendant; that he bought them from a white man; that they saw him receive and pay for them, and take a receipt; that he gave about thirty dollars for them. Defendant dealt in such articles; they were brought to his store in the day time, on a dray, in baskets and barrels. They knew them to be the same articles that were found on defendant's premises, because there were none other in the house when these were bought from the white man, and they had assisted to pack them in the barrels in which they were found. These, together with several other witnesses, proved that the prisoner was a foreigner, and understood the English language very imperfectly. The state then offered to re-examine Zimmerman and Lockwood, who had remained in the court-room, and heard the testimony of defendant's witnesses, though they had been placed under the rule, and ordered to remain out of hearing. Defendant objected to their being examined; the objection was overruled, and exception taken; witness Zimmerman then proceeded to state, that, on the trial before the committing court, the prisoner had said, that he had bought the articles from two white men; when defendant was charged with having the stopcock, he denied it, and said, "he had nothing of Peck's in his store."

The district attorney asked the witness how he happened to go to the store of defendant to look for the stolen articles, when he was proceeding to state what a negro had confessed, when he was interrupted by the counsel for the defendant, and instructed by the court not to tell any thing the negro told him. But the witness persisted in going on, and said, "that he had gone there because a negro had confessed that he had stolen the articles, and sold them to the prisoner."

The court immediately instructed the jury to disregard this statement.

Lockwood, on his re-examination, stated that Peck had told him that his stopcock was stolen, and he had reason to believe, was at the store of the defendant. The counsel for the defendant objected to this testimony, and the objection was overruled.

The errors assigned were—1st. The record does not show that the defendant was arraigned, or pleaded to the indictment. 2d. The evidence is against the verdict. 3d. The court below should have granted a new trial, on account of the statement improperly made by witness Zimmerman to the jury, of what a negro had told him; and also on account of his statement, that other stolen goods had been found in the possession of the defendant. 4th. The court erred in allowing witness Lockwood to testify as to what Peck had told him. 5th. The court erred in giving the 1st, 2d, and 7th instructions, asked on the part of the state. 6th. The court erred in refusing to give the 7th, 11th and 14th instructions, asked on part of the defense. 7th. The court erred in allowing the state's witnesses, who had been placed under the rule, and who had failed to abide by it and stay out of the court-house, to be recalled and examined.

The charges given on the part of the state, and assigned as error, are—1st. That proof that the articles alleged in the indictment were bought by the defendant, knowing them to be stolen, may be made, as well by the circumstances in the case, as by direct testimony. 2d. The discovery of the goods in the possession of the defendant shortly after they were missed, they having been proved to be stolen, and the denial of the defendant that he had any such goods in his possession, is presumptive evidence of the fact that he received them knowing them to be stolen.   The 7th is, that if the jury believe from the evidence that the articles were purchased under their value, it is a presumption of the guilty knowledge of the defendant.

The instructions asked by the defendant, and refused by the court, are as follows :

7th. " The jury must take all the circumstances into consideration ; and even should they believe that the defendant denied the possession of the goods, yet if the jury believe that such denial was not the result of conscious guilt, but of misunderstanding, or apprehension of consequences, then such denial affords no evidence of guilty knowledge."

11th. " It is essential that the circumstances should, to a moral certainty, actually exclude every supposition but that of the guilt of the prisoner ; and that the jury should be so fully convinced by the evidence, that they would be willing to act upon that conviction, in matters of the highest importance to their own interest."

14th. " Manifestations of warmth and zeal beyond what the occasion calls for, over-forwardness in testifying that which will benefit the party by whom he is called, are tests by which the jury may, with the other evidence in the case, estimate the true character of the witness, and the value of his testimony."

The record does not show that the prisoner was arraigned, or pleaded to the indictment.

F. Anderson for plaintiff in error.

The first error assigned is fatal, and entitles the prisoner to a new trial.

The second instruction given for the state, besides assuming to be true what was an essential point to be made out by the state, and charging the jury upon a matter of evidence, announces, as a rule of evidence, a proposition the reverse of true.   The facts stated would not raise a presumption that the prisoner received the goods knowing them to be stolen, but that he stole them himself; and if the jury believed the prisoner guilty of larceny, they were bound to acquit him of the charge in the indictment.

The 7th instruction asked for the defense was good law, and applicable to the case. See Barbour's Cr. Pl., 173, 174; 1 Starkie, 448, 451; Roscoe Cr. Pl., 123.

D. C. Glenn, attorney general.

The court will not interfere with the verdict of the jury; the facts are sufficient to sustain it. Nelm's case, 13 S. & M., 500; McCann's case, ib., 471.

The objections, if well founded, amount to mere irregularities. The court below must possess some discretion, and this court will not interfere unless that discretion is grossly abused. Barbour's Cr. L., 127.

The charges I will not discuss. One or more are doubtful law; and I leave to the court to approve or reject them.

SMITH, C. J.:

The plaintiff in error was tried and convicted in the circuit court of Hinds county upon a charge of having purchased stolen goods, the property of Redding & Peck, with a knowledge that said goods were stolen. A motion was made for a new trial, which was overruled. The bill of exceptions filed to the decision of the court overruling said motion, contains the evidence adduced on the trial, and sets out the exceptions taken by the prisoner during the progress of the trial, and the instructions which were granted or refused at the instance of the state or the prisoner.

The exceptions brought to our attention in the argument are numerous. We shall, however, notice only such as are mainly relied on, and which present questions of practical utility.

1. It is insisted, that a new trial should have been granted, in consequence of the misconduct of a witness offered on the side of the prosecution.

It appears that, on the examination in chief of the witness referred to, the district attorney asked him what induced them to suspect that the prisoner had the stolen articles in his possession. Objection was promptly made to the legality of this question; but in defiance of the remonstrance of the prisoner's counsel, and while the objection was being urged before the court, the witness proceeded to state, "that he had been informed by a negro man, who confessed that he had stolen the said articles, that he had sold them to the prisoner." The court immediately instructed the jury that the answer of the witness was not evidence, and that they should not regard it in making up their verdict.

This conduct of the witness was certainly very reprehensible, and should have been properly noticed by the court. But we do not think it was ground for a new trial. Certainly not unless it were distinctly shown that the statement thus made to the jury had a sinister influence upon their verdict. It is difficult to imagine in what method such fact, if it existed, could be proved; and hence, we are compelled, from the nature of the transaction, to regard the subject as committed exclusively to the discretion of the circuit court.

2. The jury having been empanelled and sworn, upon the motion of the district attorney, the witnesses in attendance, as well for the prisoner as the state, were ordered to withdraw from the the court-room. The evidence for the prisoner having closed, the district attorney proposed to examine a witness called for the prosecution, and who, with the rest, had been put under the rule, for the purpose of rebuttal. This witness, after his examination in chief, had remained in the court-room, and had heard the examination of the whole of the witnesses for the prisoner. His examination was objected to by the prisoner's counsel; but the objection was overruled, and the witness examined. This, it is insisted, was error.

The rule on this question appears to be settled. A witness who has been ordered to withdraw, but who continues in court in violation of the order, will not ordinarily be examined. It rests, however, in the sound discretion of the judge, whether such witness shall be examined or not.[1]   "This (says Phillips)

---

[1] 1 Archbold Cr. Pr. & Pl., 574; Laughlin v. State, 18 Ohio R., 99; Parker v. McWilliams, 6 Bing., 683; 4 Moore & Payne, 483; Beamon v. Ellce, 4 Carr. & Payne, 585; Rex. v. Colley, 11 Moody & Salk., 329; Woods v. Pheran, Peck, 371; 1 Greenl. Ev., 432; Chandler v. Horne, 1 M. & Rob., 423; State v. Brookshire, 2 Ala., 303; Atty. Gen. v. Bulpit, 9 Price, 4; 4 Moore & Payne, 480; Thomas v. David, 7 C. & P., 350; McLean v. State, 16 Ala., 672; Lee Anon. 1 Hill, 254, 256; State v. Sparrow, 3 Murphy, 487; Dyer v. Morris, 4 Mo., 214; Keath v. Wilson, 6 Mo., 485; Pleasant v. State, 15 Ark., 624; Horter v. State, 2 Carter, 435.

seems to be the safest and justest course, not to exclude his evidence altogether, but to admit it, subject to such remarks as the circumstances may warrant; for otherwise an innocent party, possibly both parties, might be made to suffer a serious injury from the carelessness of a witness, or perhaps from his ill designs or ill-will. A reluctant or hostile witness might thus accomplish his purpose and defeat the party." 2 Phil. Ev., 396, Hill and Cow., Ed.; 4 ib., 711, note 361.

In the State of North Carolina, according to the case of State v. Sparrow, the courts have not even the discretion to prevent the examination of a witness who has violated the order of the court to withdraw, and has remained and heard the testimony of the other witnesses. 3 N. Carolina R., 487.

3. Two of the witnesses for the prosecution, Lockwood and Zimmerman, on their examination in reply, were permitted by the court to testify as to the facts not strictly in rebuttal of the evidence adduced by the defendant, nor in explanation of the testimony in chief offered by the prosecution. This was objected to on the trial, and is now assigned as error.

On the examination in chief, the party calling a witness is bound at his peril to interrogate him as to all material matters in the first instance; and if any material question is omitted, it cannot be put upon the examination in reply. No new question can be put in reply, unconnected with the subject of the cross-examination, and which does not tend to explain it. This is the general rule, which courts of original jurisdiction have found it expedient to adopt. But it rests with them, in the exercise of a sound discretion, to determine whether the facts and circumstances of a particular case do not warrant a departure from it. Hence, an appellate court will never interfere with the exercise of this discretion, except, perhaps, in an extreme case, where the injustice caused by the departure from this rule is manifest and great. In permitting the re-examination of these witnesses as to facts not in reply or rebuttal, the court therefore exercised a discretionary authority; and it does not appear that any injustice was done. 4 Phil. Ev., p. 701, note 360.[1]

[1] 3 Brod. & Bing., 297; 2 Russ., 634; 1 Archbold Cr. Pr. & Pl. 579; People v. Mather, 4 Wend., 229; 1 Greenl. Ev., 431, 467; 2 Phill. Ev., 910, 878; Law v. Mer-

4. It is insisted that the court erred in giving several of the instructions applied for by the district attorney, and in denying others which were requested in behalf of the prisoner.   The following instruction, which was the second one given for the prosecution, is amongst those to which objection is made, to wit : " The discovery of the goods in the possession of the defendant, (they having been proved to be stolen,) shortly after they were missed by Lockwood, and the denial by the defendant that he had any such goods in his possession, is presumptive evidence that he received them knowing them to be stolen."

There are two obvious objections to this instruction.

1st. It assumes as a fact proved, that the goods alleged to have been bought by the prisoner were stolen.   The averment that the goods were stolen, was as necessary an ingredient in the offense charged as the allegation that the prisoner had purchased them with a knowledge of the theft.   It was, in effect, a charge upon the weight of testimony, and a clear invasion upon the peculiar offices of a jury.

2d. It lays down an incorrect rule in regard to the presumption which would legally arise in the case assumed in the instruction.   Generally, the fact that a party is found in the possession of stolen property recently after the commission of the larceny, is not a circumstance from which it can be legally inferred that the party found in possession received the property with a knowledge that it had been stolen.   On the contrary, proof of such fact, connected with other circumstances, would be presumptive evidence that the party himself had committed the larceny.   This is the presumption which would generally arise ; but it is conceded that there might be cases where recent possession of stolen goods, united with other circumstances, would warrant the presumption of a felonious reception, and not of a larceny of the goods.   And it was so held in the State of New York, in the case of The People *v.* Teal, 1 Wheeler's Cr. Ca., 199.   But in the case assumed by the instruction, that is, admitting it to be proved that the prisoner, within a short time after the goods were stolen, was found in possession of

rills, 6 Wend., 268 ; 9 Cowen, 65 ; Weber *v.* Kingsland, 8 Bosw., 430 ; 2 Phill. Ev., note 570, 584 ; Beal *v.* Nichols, 2 Gray, 262 ; Commonwealth *v.* Wilson, 19 Barb. (N. Y.), 510.   [These are leading cases. ED.]

them, and that he denied having such goods in his possession, it is evident that the presumption would arise that the prisoner had committed the larceny, and not as charged by the court, that he had received them with a knowledge of the larceny.

The seventh instruction for the prosecution is also excepted to.   It is as follows: " If the jury believe from the evidence that the articles were purchased under their value, it is a presumption of the guilty knowledge of the defendant."

The purchase of stolen goods by a party similarly charged, under circumstances calculated to awaken suspicion, and at a price greatly below their value, would, doubtless, constitute grounds of presumption that the party purchased with knowledge.   The rule laid down by the instruction is too broad and comprehensive, and is indefensible upon reason or authority.

5. The following instruction was requested by the prisoner, and refused by the court, to wit: " The jury must take all the circumstances into consideration, and if they believe that the defendant denied the possession of the goods, yet if they believe that such denial was not the result of conscious guilt, but of misunderstanding or apprehension of consequences, then said denial is no evidence of guilty knowledge."

The denial of the party having in his possession stolen goods, that he has such goods in his possession, is holden to be presumptive proof of his guilty knowledge, for the obvious reason, that if he were ignorant of the larceny, and had come by the possession fairly, he could have no motive for concealment. When, therefore, it is shown that the denial of the possession was the consequence of misunderstandings, such denial ceases to be a presumptive proof of the guilt of the party charged. There was evidence before the jury that the prisoner was a foreigner, and that he spoke and understood the English language imperfectly.   Hence, there was some probability that he might not have understood what articles he was charged with having in his possession.   The instruction contained a plain proposition, the truth of which was indisputable, and was warranted by the facts in proof before the jury.   It was error, therefore, in the court to refuse to give it.

6. The record does not show that the prisoner was arraigned, or

that he pleaded to the indictment.   In trials for minor offenses, a formal arraignment in practice is generally dispensed with. In such cases, where the defendant has pleaded to the indictment, an arraignment will be presumed.   But a party, before he can be put on his trial, must plead to the indictment.   In civil proceedings, it is error to submit a cause to the jury without an issue in fact having been made up by parties.   In prosecutions for offenses, it must be equally erroneous to put a party upon his trial unless he has taken issue upon the charge by pleading to the indictment.

Having determined to reverse the judgment for the errors above noticed, it has become unnecessary and improper to examine the question, whether the evidence adduced on the trial was sufficient to warrant the verdict of the jury.

Let the judgment be reversed, the prisoner remanded, and a new trial awarded in the court below.

STOKES AND JOHNSON *v.* THE STATE, 24 Miss. Rep., 624.

GAMING.

The duties imposed by law upon the assessor of taxes in this state cannot be performed by an agent; and there is no statute which authorizes the assessor to act by deputy.

A grand jury composed of members who do not possess the requisite qualifications, or who have not been drawn, summoned, or empanelled in the manner prescribed by law, have no power to find a valid indictment.

A list of the persons liable to jury service, returned by a person acting as deputy assessor of taxes, is invalid, and a valid grand jury cannot be drawn from it.

Error to Holmes circuit court.   PERRY, J.

The opinion of the court contains a statement of the facts of the case, where also will be found the instructions given and refused.

D. C. Glenn, attorney general.

1. The replication and issue, in short, is conclusive on plaintiffs in error.   The court below admitted the proof complained of; and this court, in the absence of contrary proof, will presume it did so correctly.   2 Howard, 774 ; 3 ib., 205, 422.

2. So much of the indictment as relates to the amount bet, is surplusage, and may be rejected. The fact of gaming is the gist of the proceeding. See H. C., 951, § 1, 7.

3. Upon the facts in the bill of exceptions the assessment was legal. 1 Missouri, 219; 9 ib., 183; 3 Hill, N. Y., 194.

SMITH, C. J. :

This was an indictment under the statute of 1839, for the suppression of gaming, tried in the circuit court of Holmes county. The defendants pleaded severally in abatement of the indictment. The pleas contain precisely the same averments; and allege as abatable matter, that the assessor of taxes for said county, did not, within one year previous to the finding of the indictment, return into the said circuit court in term time, nor to the clerk thereof in vacation, according to the statute, a list of the householders and freeholders of said county, liable under the statute to perform the service of jurors within said county; nor did the said clerk record in a book, kept for that purpose, a list of the names of the householders and freeholders so taken and returned as required by law, from which the grand jury who found the said indictment were drawn; nor was the said grand jury drawn from any "box" containing a list of the names of persons taken and returned in conformity to law. Issue was taken upon these pleas, and determined against the defendants, who thereupon pleaded not guilty, and on trial were convicted and sentenced.

On the trial of the issues joined upon the pleas in abatement, it appeared from the evidence that the list of the names of the persons from whom the grand jury were selected, was not made out and returned by the assessor for said county, but by one West, who assumed to act as the deputy or agent of the assessor; who subsequently, and probably after the grand jury by whom the indictment was preferred, were drawn and empanelled, approved and ratified the acts of his deputy or agent.

Upon the case thus made before the jury the defendants requested the court to charge the jury as follows: "That if they believe from the evidence, that the list of persons from whom the grand jury were drawn who found the indictment, was made out and returned to the circuit court of Holmes county by West,

and not by Denton, the assessor of said county, and said list was
so made out and returned in the absence of said Denton, then
the law is for the defendants." This instruction was refused,
and the jury were charged that "although the jury may believe
that Denton did not return a list of persons liable to jury service, yet if they shall believe from the evidence that West returned said list as agent for Denton, and Denton afterwards
ratified the act of West, the jury will find that the return was
properly made."

It is manifest that the duties imposed by law upon the assessor
of taxes in this state, cannot be legally performed by a private
agent; and there is no statute which authorizes the deputy to
act as deputy. As Denton, therefore, had no authority to appoint a deputy, and could not legally act in the performance of
his official duties by a private agent, the list of persons qualified
and liable to perform the service of jurors, as made out and returned by West, could not be made legal or valid by the subsequent approval and ratification of the assessor. But was the
grand jury taken from the list, for that reason, illegally constituted?

In McQuillen v. State, it was holden that a grand jury, composed of members who do not possess the requisite qualifications,
or who have not been drawn, summoned or empanelled in the
manner prescribed by law, have no power to find a valid indictment. A grand jury, say the court, does not, by our law, consist of thirteen or more men congregated by the mere order of
the court, or by accident in a jury box; but it consists of a requisite number of competent individuals, selected, summoned
and sworn according to the forms of law; and if the law be not
followed, it is an incompetent grand jury. The same rules were
recognized as settled law in the case of Rawls v. State, 8 S. &
M., 599, in which it was said that the forms of the law must be
followed in forming the grand jury, and that an indictment found
by an incompetent grand jury, may be quashed upon plea. Both
these cases have since been held to lay the law down correctly.

The statute, Hutch. Dig., 886, contains specific directions as
to the mode of constituting the grand jury. They are to be
selected by lot, from the householders and freeholders of the

county, a list of whose names have been made out and returned
in the manner prescribed, by the assessor of taxes. Upon the
authority of the cases above cited, it is not sufficient that they
are citizens, householders or freeholders liable to jury service.
It is essential that they should also be selected, empanelled
and sworn according to law. It is clear, upon the settled doctrine of this court, that a grand jury could not be legally constituted of persons, however qualified as jurors, who were not
drawn but summoned upon the order of the court. If it is important that they should be selected by lot, it is equally so that
they should be taken from the list returned by the assessor. The
same reason which makes it imperative upon the courts to observe the direction of the statute in the one case, requires our
obedience in the other. "These restrictions have been imposed
for wise purposes. They are guards thrown around the liberties
of the citizen. They constitute an important part of the right
of trial by jury." If we were authorized to disregard this direction of the statute, we might dispense with an observance of any
other provision. It is useless to comment on the result. The
effect might be entirely to break down its provisions.

It follows, from these observations, that the issue upon the
plea in abatement should have been determined in favor of the
plaintiffs in error. The court, therefore, erred in its instruction
to the jury.

PACE v. THE STATE, 25 Miss. Rep., 54.

FORFEITURE OF RECOGNIZANCE.

A recognizance is an obligation of record entered into before a court or officer duly
authorized for that purpose with condition to do some act required by law.

The sheriff is only authorized to take a recognizance from a person whom he may
arrest on the process of a circuit court of law, charged before such court with any
crime or misdemeanor, not punishable with death.

Error to Newton circuit court. WATTS, J.

The opinion of the court contains the facts of the case.

E. Rush Buckner, for plaintiff in error.

D. C. Glenn, attorney general.

Fisher, J. :

This was a writ of error to the judgment of the circuit court of Newton county, rendered upon a *scire facias* against the plaintiff in error, as bail for one George W. Buchanan.

The question for decision is, whether the obligation upon which the judgment was rendered, is a bond or recognizance ; and if a bond, whether a forfeiture could be taken and judgment rendered thereon, as in the case of a recognizance.

A recognizance is an obligation of record entered into before a court or an officer duly authorized for that purpose, with condition to do some act required by law. 2 Bl. Com., 341 ; 2 Bou. Law. Dic., 413.   The instrument in the record under this authority, cannot be treated as a recognizance, but only as a bond.

The principal, Buchanan, was admitted to bail by Judge Dawson, in the sum of two thousand dollars, with four securities in the sum of five hundred dollars each.   The bond in question was not taken or approved by the judge making the order for bail ; but by the sheriff, who clearly had no authority under the statute to take even a recognizance.   He is only authorized to take a recognizance from a person whom he may arrest on the process of a circuit court of law, charged before such court with any crime or misdemeanor, not punishable with death.   Hutch. Code, p. 444, § 13.

Under the authorities, we are of opinion, that the court below erred in overruling the demurrer to the *scire facias*, and rendering judgment against the plaintiff in error.

Judgment reversed, and judgment final on the demurrer for the plaintiff in error.

The State v. Borroum, 25 Miss. Rep., 203.

Forfeiture of Recognizance.

The parties to a recognizance, cannot, after the defendant's failure to appear, interpose objections to recognizance, on account of the insufficiency of the grand jury. Objections to the grand jury must be made by the defendant by plea in abatement.

Where the *scire facias* is demurred to on account of a variance between it and the judgment *nisi*, the demurrer should be sustained and the defendants discharged.

Error to La Fayette circuit court.　MILLER, J.

This was a *scire facias* issued from the circuit court of La Fayette county upon a forfeited recognizance given by Wesley Bruce for his appearance at the next term of said circuit court, to answer a charge of trading with a negro slave without legal authority, in which D. P. Borroum, Sims McNeely, and Nathaniel G. Dacus were his securities. The defendant Bruce failed to make his appearance at a term of the court as required by his recognizance, and a *scire facias* was issued against the securities upon the forfeited bond, to which the defendants, Borroum et al., pleaded that said Bruce had never been charged with any crime or misdemeanor known to the laws of the state, to which the district attorney, on the part of the state, replied, setting out the bill of indictment which had heretofore been found against Bruce for the offense charged; to which replication the defendants rejoined, that the grand jury, by whom the said bill of indictment was found, was illegally organized, to which the district attorney demurred, and upon a joinder in the demurrer the court overruled the demurrer and gave judgment for the defendants. The district attorney, on behalf of the state, prayed a writ of error.

D. C. Glenn, attorney general.

J. W. Thompson, on same side, cited and commented on 1 Arch. Cr. L., 447, 448; Gould's Pl., 227; ib. ch. 5, § 2–4.

J. F. Cushman, for defendants in error, cited in reply and commented on Gould's Pl., 40, 41, § 35, 38; 3 Black. Com., 301; Barb. Cr. Law, 343; Gould's Pl., 43; 1 How., 139; Gould's Pl., 453; Black. Com., 310; 6 Com. Dig., 154, (F.); Co. Litt., 304.

The *scire facias* does not recite correctly the charge alleged in the bill of indictment. The charge in the indictment is, "unlawfully did buy and receive of and from a negro slave named Ellick, which said negro was then the property of David M. Brown, seventy-five pounds of cotton," etc. The *scire facias* recites, that he made default to answer a charge of "unlawfully buying seventy-five pounds of cotton," without setting forth the name of the slave or his owner. This certainly is such a variance as will sustain the decision of the court below, and the same point has been adjudicated by this court in the case of Bridges v. State, 2 Cush., 153.

According to the well-settled rules of pleading, a demurrer goes back to the first defect in the pleading, and this, I think, is shown to be error and justifies the decision of the court below on the pleadings.

H. A. Barr, on same side.

YERGER, J.:

This case was before us in January, 1852. It is now presented upon a demurrer by the state to the rejoinder of defendants.

By the rejoinder the defendants seek to avoid the recognizance, because, as they aver, the grand jury which found the indictment against Bruce, was not duly and legally organized.

Without deciding whether the defendants are precluded by the state of the pleadings from making this defense, it is sufficient to remark, that in our opinion the defendants could not at any time have avoided the recognizance for any defects in the organization and qualification of the grand jury.

The defendant in the indictment could only have questioned the sufficiency of the grand jury by a plea in abatement, and that plea could only have been interposed by him on his appearance in court to answer the charge against him. If upon his appearance he had entered the plea of " not guilty," he could not afterwards have made objections to the grand jury. The right to object to its legal sufficiency is the personal right of the defendant in the indictment, a right, of which he could only avail himself by appearing to answer the charge and insisting upon it by plea. In our opinion the parties to a recognizance, who are intended to compel the appearance of the accused, have no right after his failure to appear, to interpose objections to the proceedings, which objections, if true, would not render the proceedings absolutely void, but only erroneous and voidable upon the appearance and plea of the accused.

The demurrer to the rejoinder was well taken, and judgment should have been entered on it for the state, but for the rule, that a demurrer reaches back to the first error in the pleadings.

There is a manifest variance between the recognizance, the judgment *nisi*, and the *scire facias*. The accused, Wesley Bruce, was recognized to appear and answer a charge by indictment of "unlawfully buying and receiving from a certain negro slave, named Ellick, who was the property of David M. Brown, seventy-five pounds of cotton without," etc. The *scire facias* recites, that he was called and made default to answer "a charge of unlawfully buying from a negro slave seventy-five pounds of cotton."

The recognizance only bound the parties for the appearance of Bruce to answer a charge of buying and receiving from a particular specific slave, whereas the *scire facias* recites a recognizance for his appearance to answer a charge of buying from a slave generally and without identity. For this variance the demurrer must be sustained to the *scire facias*, and the judgment below affirmed.

EX-PARTE DYSON, 25 Miss. Rep., 356.

HOMICIDE.

BAIL.

By the constitution of this state, all prisoners, before conviction, are bailable by sufficient securities, except for capital offenses, where the proof is evident or presumption great. [1]

The circuit courts of this state now possess and may exercise the power of bailing after conviction in all cases not capital, whenever a sound discretion will warrant it. *Semble.* In cases of misdemeanor, whenever the party obtains a writ of error and *supersedeas*, this discretion ought always to be exercised in favor of bail.

In cases of bail each case must depend upon its individual merit. And, after a full inspection of the case, if the court does not find the existence of those special circumstances which ought to exist, bail will be refused. [2]

This was an application by James H. Dyson, who had been

[1] Street v. State, 43 Miss., 1.

[2] In the case of Street v. State. 43 Miss. R., 1, the subject of bail is fully discussed. The case of Dyson is there cited and explained, and the practice on *habeas corpus* in cases of bail, together with the discretionary powers of the court hearing the *habeas corpus*, are fully set forth in a very comprehensive and elaborate opinion by SIMRALL, J.

convicted of manslaughter in the circuit court of Panola county, and sentenced to fifteen years in the penitentiary, to be discharged on bail until his case can be re-argued in this court, having had the sentence of the circuit court confirmed by the high court ; on application a re-argument was granted.

Watson & Estelle, for prisoner, filed no brief in the papers.

D. C. Glenn, attorney general.

The demandant stands convicted of manslaughter, and sentenced to fifteen years imprisonment in the penitentiary. He sued out a writ of error to this court and a *supersedeas*. The cause coming on to be heard, the judgment of the court below was affirmed. A petition for rehearing has been filed, and has been granted, and the case stands for a re-argument.

I oppose the application now made in the case. I will not deny the power of the court to grant the bail. I presume it is regarded as settled.

I, however, deny that the demandant has an absolute right to bail after conviction. The constitution I do regard as having made it the sworn duty of this court to turn loose every convicted felon in this state, except where he had slain his fellow-man. It uses the word " offenses." Is the word " offense" used when a man has been convicted, or does it not refer to cases where a party is charged and not convicted? Chief Justice Henderson, of North Carolina, in 2 Haws, 447, says that this clause " relates entirely to prisoners before conviction." It seems to me that this is the true position.

The court, then, has the power to bail, but the prisoner has only a conditional right to bail, not an absolute one. As Judge Henderson says, then, the middle course is the true one, " to leave it to the sound discretion of the judge before whom the appeal is taken."

Being, then, a matter of discretion, the only question is, Does this case demand its exercise? I think, for various reasons, it does not.

1. Because the demandant stands convicted of a felony second only to murder, and condemned to an infamous punishment, fifteen years in the state prison.

2. Because, upon solemn argument, this judgment has once been affirmed by this court.

3. Because the facts show a case of enormous guilt on the part of demandant, and upon the law there is only a possibility of a reversal of his conviction on two points only out of thirteen assigned as error.

4. Because, from the magnitude of the offense, the severity of the punishment, and the alarming doubts of the final issue of the case growing out of its past history, showing two adverse judgments, in all human probability, and looking at the matter as reasonable men, we must infer that the inducement to the demandant to flee the justice which seems impending over him will be very great; nay, will it not be irresistible?

5. Because there is no written precedent in the state which sustains the demandant. The case of Davis would only sanction bail in cases of "fine and imprisonment," and only then "where there are peculiar circumstances incident to the case;" and it is held, that "the court should exercise the power with great caution, and only in minor offenses." Davis' case, 6 Howard, 399.

6. Because I believe, in the strong language of Chief Justice Henderson, that "to compel the defendant in all cases of appeal, even for the most petty misdemeanors, to go to jail but by permission of the prosecuting officer, would render useless the right of appeal; and an indiscriminate right of going at large, upon giving bail, after an appeal, would be rendering the criminal law a dead letter."

Yerger, J.:

James H. Dyson was indicted for murder in the circuit court of Panola, at the May term, in the year 1852, was convicted of manslaughter in the first degree, and sentenced to imprisonment in the penitentiary for fifteen years. A writ of error was prosecuted by him to this court, and, after argument, the judgment of the circuit court was affirmed, two of the judges being of opinion that there was no error in the record, and one of them believing that there was. An application for a re-argument was made, and a re-argument granted, the judgment of affirmance being set aside. This re-argument cannot be had until the October term of this court, and an application is now made by the prisoner to be discharged on bail, till his case can be re-argued in this court.

By the constitution and laws of this state, "all prisoners, before conviction, are bailable by sufficient securities except for capital offenses, where the proof is evident and the presumption great." Const., art. 1, § 17. The right of a prisoner to bail, after conviction, is not regulated by the constitution or, by statute, and is governed by the rules and practice of the common law. It seems to be fully and clearly established, that the court of king's bench could bail in all cases whatsoever, according to the principles of the common law; the action of that court not being controlled by the various statutes enacted on the subject of bail, but regulated and governed entirely by a sound judicial discretion on the subject. 2 Hale's P. C., 129; 4 Co. Inst., 71; 2 Com. Dig., p. 6, tit. (f. 3); 1 Bacon's Ab., 483, 493; 2 Hawk. P. C., 170; Cowp. R., 333.

In the exercise of this discretion, the court in some instances admitted to bail, even after verdict, in cases of felony, whenever a special motive existed to induce the court to grant it. 1 Bac. Abr., 489, 490; 2 Hawk. P. C., 170.

In this state it has been held, that the circuit courts now possess and exercise the power of bailing after conviction, in all cases not capital, whenever a sound discretion will warrant it. In cases of misdemeanor, whenever a party obtains a writ of error and *supersedeas*, we think this discretion ought to be always exercised in favor of bail.[1]

But in felonies not capital, while we admit the power of the circuit judges to take bail after conviction, we think it should be exercised with great caution, and only where the peculiar circumstances of the case render it right and proper.[2]

We do not deem it advisable, in this opinion, to enumerate the circumstances which in our judgment would warrant the exercise of the power to bail. Each case must depend on its own

---

[1] Hurd on Habeas Corpus, 446.
[2] Hurd on Habeas Corpus, 446; Davis v. State, 6 How., 399.

intrinsic merits, and we could not undertake to specify all cases in which it would be proper to bail.

In the case before us, we have not been able to find any special circumstances which should induce us to allow bail. The evidence of indisposition and ill health introduced, did not, in our opinion, establish such danger of loss of life from the prisoner's confinement as would justify us in bailing him, nor does the record contain any other peculiar facts, which render it proper to exercise the power.

While denying bail to the prisoner on this application, we would wish to be understood, that it is not done on the ground that he will be refused a new trial, as that is a question which can only be determined on the re-argument of this case. Bail is denied in this case, because, upon a full inspection of the record, we do not find the existence of those peculiar circumstances which ought to exist, in order to warrant the exercise of the power by us.

Bail refused, and prisoner remanded.

Hurt *v.* The State, 25 Miss. Rep., 378.

Homicide.

The verdict of a jury, on the trial for murder, finding a person guilty of manslaughter, operates as an acquittal of the charge of murder, and will be a bar to a second prosecution for the same offense.

An indictment is defective in substance, when the court cannot pronounce the proper sentence of the law upon a verdict finding the accused guilty.

Error to Hinds circuit court. Barnett, J.

The plaintiff in error, John Hurt, was indicted in the circuit court of Hinds county, to which indictment several pleas in abatement were filed by defendant (Hurt), alleging the illegal organization of the grand jury which found the indictment, because some of the said jurymen who found the bill of indictment were summoned from the bystanders and were not of the regular *venire*. All of these pleas were demurred to by the state, and the demurrers sustained. Hurt was tried at the March term, 1853, of said court, on the plea of not guilty, and he was

convicted of manslaughter in the third degree.   He then moved
for a new trial, which was refused, and prayed for this writ of
error.

T. J & F. A. R. Wharton for plaintiff in error.

The verdict of the jury has fixed the grade of the offense as
manslaughter in the third degree.   This, and not the finding of
the grand jury, is the criterion.

If, therefore, the court should be of the opinion that the grand
jury was illegally organized, and should reverse the judgment
of the court below and quash the indictment, we insist that the
plaintiff in error should be discharged, as the record shows that
more than twelve months have expired since the commission of
the offense.   He could not be indicted again for murder, having
been already tried for that, and by a conviction of manslaughter
acquitted of murder.   This principle has been recognized by
this court in Swinney v. State, 8 S. & M., and in Howard v.
State, 13 ib., 261.   He could not be indicted for manslaughter,
because of the statute of limitations.

It is insisted that the plaintiff in error was convicted improperly, as the acts of the grand jury are all null and void, unless it
was organized according to law.   Admit this, and we demand
his discharge, because illegally detained in custody.

On the point of having been tried and put in jeopardy twice.
Wharton's Am. Cr. Law (2d ed.), 198–205 ; State v. Norvell,
2 Yerg., 24 ; 4 Scam., 168 ; 1 Humph. R., 253 ; 6 ib., 410 ; 4
Black. Com., 329.

D. C. Glenn, attorney general.

I refer to and rely on the following authorities in reply to
counsel for the accused ; 12 Met., 387 ; 1 English, 187 ; 13 Johns.,
351 ; 3 Grattan, 623 ; 1 Stewart, 31 ;   Lord Raymond, 422 ; 1
Walker, 204 ; Wharton's Am. Cr. Law, 194, 202.

FISHER, J.:

The plaintiff in error was indicted at the March term, 1851,
of the circuit court of Hinds county, for murder.   He appeared
at the same term of the court and filed certain pleas in abatement, alleging the illegal organization of the grand jury to the
indictment ; to which pleas the district attorney demurred, which

demurrer was sustained by the court. The prisoner afterwards having pleaded not guilty, was put upon his trial, at the March term, 1853, of said court, and was by the jury found guilty of manslaughter in the third degree. From the judgment rendered upon this verdict, he prosecuted a writ of error to this court, assigning at the hearing the action of the court in sustaining the demurrer to the pleas in abatement as error, which having been considered as well assigned, the judgment of the court below has been reversed and judgment rendered here, overruling the demurrer and quashing the indictment. It is now insisted that the verdict of manslaughter is an acquittal of the charge of murder; and inasmuch as the statute of limitations will bar another indictment and prosecution merely for manslaughter, the prisoner is now entitled to his discharge.

The attorney general urges in opposition to this motion that the reversal of the judgment on the verdict of manslaughter annuls the whole proceedings upon the trial below as well for as against the prisoner; and that the indictment having been avoided by pleas in abatement, he can be again indicted for the crime of murder.

A verdict of a jury finding a party put upon his trial for murder guilty of manslaughter in the third degree, must of necessity operate as an acquittal of every crime of a higher grade of which he might have been convicted under the indictment upon which the issue was made; otherwise the party, after undergoing the sentence for manslaughter, might be put upon his trial for the charge of murder, which would thus be only postponed and not decided by the verdict of manslaughter.

The jury in such case, in contemplation of law, render two verdicts, one acquitting the accused of the higher crime charged in the indictment, the other finding him guilty of an inferior crime. They must first determine his guilt or innocence upon the charge made by the indictment, before proceeding to consider whether he is guilty of an inferior crime. The verdict of manslaughter is as much an acquittal of the charge of murder as a verdict pronouncing his entire innocence would be; for the effect of both is to exempt him from the penalty of the law for such crime.

But it is said that such verdict only operates as an acquittal, while it is permitted to stand as part of the action of the court below ; and as it has been set aside by this court upon the prisoner's own application, the cause must be treated in all respects as if no trial had taken place. In support of this position authorities have been cited, holding that, when the judgment upon a trial for murder is arrested, the party may be remanded and again indicted for the same crime. The authorities, doubtless, announce the law correctly, but they have no application to the question under consideration. The judgment is only arrested in any case when the verdict is against the party. He would certainly never move, neither would the court for a moment entertain such motion in arrest of the judgment when the verdict was in his favor. Here the verdict of the jury acquitted the party of the crime expressly charged in the indictment, and at the same time exempted him from the penalty of the law for its supposed commission. He could not move in arrest of judgment on this part of the verdict, because the judgment corresponding, in contemplation of law, with the verdict in this respect, must also have been one of acquittal of the charge of murder. Whether this judgment was in fact pronounced by the court, as ought to be the practice, or attached by mere operation of law to the verdict, it was bound to be in the party's favor, and it could not, therefore, be arrested or set aside on his motion.

The same may, in effect, be said with regard to the action of this court upon the writ of error, which brought to its consideration only the judgment and proceedings of the court below, prejudicial to the accused. This was the final sentence upon the verdict of manslaughter, as no other threatened his liberty or in any manner affected his rights. He sought relief against no other. The judgment of reversal could extend only to such judgment and matters as the writ of error brought to our consideration. A judgment, acquitting the party of murder, not being one which could be embraced in this writ of error, for the same reason could not be embraced in our judgment. Hence, it stands unaffected by our action, as the judgment of the court below on a charge of murder. It may be true that no formal judgment of acquittal was entered, but we hold that the sentence of the court upon the verdict of manslaughter was of itself a complete acquittal of all higher crimes of which the party might have been convicted under the indictment. It will not do to say that the reversal of the sentence against the party also destroys the verdict and judgment by operation of the law in his favor. The former, being against the party, could be made the subject of revision upon a writ of error to this court. The latter, being in the party's favor, was final, conclusive, and irreversible. Neither he nor the state could ask a revision of such judgment upon a writ of error to this court, and having no power to revise it, we have no authority to reverse or annul it. It still stands, therefore, wholly unaffected by our action upon the writ of error. To this our mind is clear upon principle; but the question has been directly adjudicated by the supreme court of Tennessee and settled in a well considered opinion as we have stated the rule. Slaughter v. State, 6 Humph., 410.

It is not necessary that we should go into examination of the principles involved in the other question made by the attorney general. It may be admitted, for the sake of the argument, that the indictment was voidable, and still, under the record, the prisoner would be entitled to his discharge. The indictment purports to have been by a grand jury organized by the court. The record shows that the prisoner was arraigned and regularly tried upon the charge therein contained, and that he was acquitted of the charge of murder upon the facts and testimony introduced before the jury. The statute is decisive of the question and was no doubt enacted to relieve against such cases. It is in these words, to wit: "No person shall be held to answer on a second indictment for any offense of which he has been acquitted by the jury upon the facts and merits on a former trial, but such acquittal may be pleaded by him in bar of any subsequent prosecution for the same offense, notwithstanding any defects in the form or the substance of the indictment on which he was acquitted. How. & Hutch., p. 690, § 5; ib. 725, § 20. An indictment is defective in substance when the court cannot pronounce the proper sentence of the law upon a verdict finding the accused guilty. In such case the judgment is arrested, and the party, according to the authorities, remanded for another indictment.   While this may be the law and the universal practice of the courts upon a verdict of guilty, it by no means follows that the law or practice ought to be the same upon a verdict of not guilty. The party has gone through the legal form of a trial, and has by it established his innocence, and hence the wisdom of the statute in providing for such cases.

Let the prisoner be discharged.

PRESTON v. THE STATE, 25 Miss. Rep., 383.

HOMICIDE.

Charges given or withheld by the court, in criminal cases, are not necessarily a part of the record. Hence, they will not be noticed by the appellate court unless they are embodied in a bill of exceptions. But papers, which are not legitimately parts of the record, when transcribed into the record, and referred to by counsel, in his bill of exceptions, will be noticed, when there is no doubt of their identity.

A high degree of sudden and resentful feeling will not alone palliate an act of homicide committed under its influence. It is essential that the excited and angry condition of the party committing the act, which would entitle him to a milder consideration of the law, should be superinduced by some insult, provocation, or injury, which would instantly produce in the minds of ordinary men the highest degree of exasperation.

Error to Greene circuit court.   WATTS, J.

The plaintiff in error, Preston, was convicted of the murder of David Turner, at the May term, 1852, of the circuit court of Greene county.   Many instructions were asked and given for the state and the accused; but the following one (the 4th), which was asked by the counsel for the defence, was refused by the court, and excepted to by accused : " If the jury believe from the evidence, that the prisoner killed the accused on a sudden heat, though voluntarily ; that he had been greatly provoked, and had received other great indignities, and acted under passion, the law pays that regard to human frailty as not to put a hasty and a deliberate act on the same footing.   And after being greatly provoked, or having received other great indignities, though no absolute necessity for the act, yet it is not murder, but manslaughter, there being no previous malice."

The jury found the accused guilty of murder. A full statement of the facts of the case will be found in the opinion of the court. The accused made a motion for a new trial, which was overruled by the court below, and he then prayed a writ of error to this court.

A. *Burwell*, for plaintiff in error.

The instruction referred to is clearly proper, and should have been given, unless wholly inapplicable to the case before the court. On the part of the state, (see third instruction for state,) the jury were told by the judge, in substance, that killing with a deadly weapon, in all cases, is murder, and the refusal of the court to give the fourth instruction asked by defendant, so pointed this instruction, that the jury were not left at liberty to find any other verdict, without flying directly in the face of the instructions. Take the instructions together, and on what principles was the defendant tried? It seems to me, on the hard rule sometimes laid down in the text books, that killing with a deadly weapon is murder, and that insults, however grievous, will not in any case reduce the killing in the heat of passion, there being no previous malice, from murder to manslaughter, if a deadly weapon is used.

But it is said, that the law may be so abstractly; but the case justified the refusal of the fourth, and the giving of the other instructions. This mode of argument seems to me to take for granted the very issue to be tried, and which it was the province of the jury to try, according to correct principles of law laid down by the court. The main issue is "malice aforethought." Can this court undertake to say how far the jury were misled by the instructions? or what their verdict would have been under a proper exposition of the law?

It is proved in the case, that the defendant was an honest man; this was ruled out, it is true. It is then shown, that the deceased had accused the defendant of stealing and other offences. The defendant called on deceased, and they both said, "they could stand it no longer," and the deceased having on his shot-bag, stepped back, and the defendant fired and killed him. Now, what is the fair application of the words used, "I can stand it no longer;" and what was the subject of discussion be-

tween these men ?   It must have been the previous accusations
of theft, etc.   The defendant, as an honest man, may have been
suddenly fired with indignation, and seeing the man who had
unjustly accused him, with a part of his armor on, step back,
the defendant may have (in the heat of passion, without previous
malice, but under the impression that deceased was about to
procure the gun, without which the shot-bag was a very useless
appendage) used a deadly weapon, and though not justifiable,
may not be guilty of murder.   It surely is not for the court to
say, that the evidence must make out a case in which the instructions will entitle the party to a verdict ; or that, if the instructions had been given, the party ought still to have been
convicted.   The rule is, that the instructions must be wholly inapplicable, such as could not possibly affect the result, or it will
be error to refuse to give them.   The correct practice is stated
in Lambeth v. State, 23 Miss. 356.   The court will not determine whether the instruction is intimately or remotely connected
with the case, or that it will have a certain effect on the minds
of the jury.   To do so, would be to usurp their province.   I
ask the accused may have a trial according to the correct rules
of law.

   D. C. Glenn, attorney general.

SMITH, C. J. :

   The prisoner at the bar was tried in the circuit court of
Greene county, and convicted of the crime of murder.   A motion was made for a new trial, which was overruled ; and sentence of death was pronounced.   The bill of exceptions filed to
the judgment of the court on the motion, contains the evidence
adduced on the trial.   The instructions which were given or refused, are transcribed into the record, and are referred to in the
bill.   The objection mainly relied on by the counsel for the
prisoner, refers to the fourth instruction requested by the defendant, and refused by the court.   That instruction is in the following words, to wit : " If the jury believe, from the evidence,
that the prisoner killed the deceased on a sudden heat, though
voluntarily ; that he had been greatly provoked, and had received other great indignities, and acted under passion, the law

pays that regard to human frailty as not to put a hasty and a deliberate act on the same footing. And after being greatly provoked, or having received other great indignities, though no absolute necessity for the act ; yet it was not murder, but manslaughter, there being no previous malice."

This instruction was the only one requested by the prisoner, and which was denied by the court. And it is insisted by the attorney-general, that neither this charge, nor any instruction given at the instance of the district attorney on the trial below, can be noticed by this court.

The ground of this objection is, that the charges objected to were not made part of the record by bill of exceptions taken at the time, nor embodied in the bill filed to the decision on the motion for a new trial.

It is settled, that charges given or withheld by the court in prosecutions for crimes or misdemeanors, are not necessarily a part of the record. Hence, that they will not be noticed by this court, unless they are placed there by means of a bill of exceptions. This rule applies, generally, to all proceedings in the lower courts, which are not by law made matters of record. But it has been repeatedly held by this court, that papers, which are not legitimately parts of the record, if transcribed into it by the clerk, will be noticed if referred to by so apt a description in the bill of exceptions, that there can be no doubt as to their identity. If this rule were rigidly applied in the case at bar, we should be bound to hold, that no notice could be taken of any of the charges given or withheld on the trial below. But as it is probable, that the instructions were originally copied into the bill of exceptions, and omitted in the transcript before us by the mistake or inadvertence of the clerk, we will consider the objection urged to the refusal of the court to give the instruction above quoted.

It is laid down, that the law having a regard for the frailty of human nature, will not put an act done upon a sudden impulse and in the heat of passion, on the same footing in regard to guilt, with a deed deliberately performed. The indulgence shown by the law in such cases, proceeds on the supposition, that the reason or judgment of the party perpetrating the act has been temporarily suspended or overthrown by the sudden access of violent passion. But a high degree of sudden and resentful feeling will not alone palliate an act of homicide committed under its influence. It is essential that the excited and angry condition of the party committing the act, which would entitle him to the milder consideration of the law, should be superinduced by some insult, provocation, or injury, which would naturally and instantly produce, in the minds of ordinarily constituted men, the highest degree of exasperation. Cases are given in books to illustrate the principle. In Blackstone's Commentaries it is said : " If a man be greatly provoked as by pulling his nose, or other great indignity, and immediately kills the aggressor, though this is not excusable *se defendo,* since there is no absolute necessity for doing it to preserve himself; yet it is neither murder, for there is no previous malice; but is manslaughter." So, also, if a man takes another in the act of adultery with his wife, and kills him upon the spot, it is not at common law ranked in the class of justifiable homicide, but is held to be manslaughter in the lowest degree. 4 Black. Com., 192.

It is, therefore, true, that an act of homicide committed under the influence of sudden, great, or violent resentment, will be looked upon by the law with less disfavor than a similar deed perpetrated with deliberation; but it is equally true, that the cause of provocation must be one deemed by the law sufficient.

Taken by this rule, the court did not err in refusing the instruction above quoted. The terms employed were too broad and unqualified. A man might be subjected to great indignities, and be greatly provoked, and still not stand acquitted of murder, if he should instantly slay the aggressor. But the principal objection to the charge is, that it left to the jury to determine not only the degree of provocation under which the prisoner acted, but the sufficiency of the cause of that provocation. The instruction would have left the character of the provocation, insult, or injury to which he was subjected, to be determined by each juror according to no fixed standard, but according to his peculiar tastes or habits of thought.

This charge was, in substance, contained in the eighth instruction asked for by the prisoner, which was given. That charge is as follows : " It is true, if a man kill another, without any or instant or considerable provocation, the law implies motive, and the homicide is murder ; but if the provocation were great, and such as must have greatly provoked him, the killing is manslaughter only."

This instruction certainly laid down a rule for the guidance of the jury, sufficiently favorable to the prisoner. But if it were conceded, that the instruction was correct as stating a general or abstract principle of law, it may, nevertheless, have been perfectly proper for the court to refuse it. The rule on the subject is, that the court is not bound to charge on abstract questions of law, or to state legal principles to a jury, however true they may be, which are not applicable to the facts nor pertinent to the questions raised by the evidence submitted to them. And accordingly it is contended by the attorney general, that the said instruction, for that reason, was properly withheld.

To determine the validity of this objection, we must recur to the evidence adduced on the trial, and which is contained in the bill of exceptions.

Nancy Turner, who was the wife of the deceased, testified, that the killing took place in Greene county, in this state, about one hour before sundown ; that she and deceased were sitting under a tree in the back yard, in conversation, when the prisoner came to the gate, hallooed, and called Turner, who went to him ; witness followed soon afterwards ; when she came in view of them they were talking ; prisoner on the outside of the fence and Turner on the inside. Witness could not understand what they said, for they were conversing in a low tone of voice ; only heard prisoner say to Turner, that he could not stand it ; and Turner answered, that he could not stand it either. Turner then stepped one or two paces, turning his left side to the prisoner, in the direction witness was coming ; the prisoner stepped back one or two paces, threw up his gun, and fired, and so soon that she could not speak. Witness was near enough to catch the deceased in her arms as he fell. The deceased called her by name, said he was gone, and instantly expired. The deceased was shot in the left arm, which was broken ; the ball penetrating the body under the arm-pit. No one was present but witness, the deceased, and the prisoner. This is the substance of Mrs. Turner's evidence delivered on her examination in chief. On the cross-examination, no additional fact of any importance was elicited in regard to the circumstances of the meeting between the deceased and the prisoner.

Nancy Green testified that the killing happened on the evening of the 27th of December, 1851, in Greene county; witness was in the kitchen and heard some one call; she went to the door; saw Turner pass through the yard to the fence; she did not understand what they said, only that he could not stand it, and Turner said, I neither can stand it. Turner stepped towards his wife, and Preston shot him; Turner was on the inside of his fence, and Preston on the outside, near the gate. When Preston shot, Turner immediately fell into his wife's arms, and Preston then turned and ran off. Upon cross-examination, this witness stated no additional material fact connected with the killing.

These two persons were the only witnesses of the transaction. By their testimony alone, we are to determine whether the instruction prayed for and refused was relevant to the facts of the case. The testimony is very short. The facts are simply and clearly stated, and leave no ground for the assumption, that such a provocation was offered to the prisoner, which, according to the law applicable to the case, could palliate the act which he then committed.

We hold, therefore, that the court did not err in refusing to give said instruction.

In regard to the motion for a new trial, we deem it unnecessary to go into a minute examination of the evidence. It is sufficient to remark, that upon the most favorable view of the question for the prisoner, we are unable to perceive any ground upon which we could be warranted in granting a new trial.

We are compelled, therefore, however painful the duty, to affirm the judgment.

GARRARD *v.* THE STATE, 25 Miss. Rep., 469.

SELLING INTOXICATING LIQUOR TO SLAVES.

Where none of the evidence is embodied in the record, and the indictment is sufficient, it will be presumed that the verdict of the jury is correct, and will not be disturbed.

Error to Madison circuit court. PERRY, J.

The facts of the case are contained in the opinion of the court.

A. H. Handy, for plaintiff in error.

D. C. Glenn, attorney general.

YERGER, J.:

The plaintiff in error was indicted in the circuit court of Madison county, for selling spirituous liquors to a slave without the consent in writing of the master, owner, overseer, or employer. A motion to quash the indictment was overruled. So likewise was a motion in arrest of judgment. There was no motion made for a new trial, and consequently we have none of the evidence before us. The indictment in this case is similar to that in Murphy *v.* State, which we held to be sufficient. The court, therefore, committed no error in refusing to quash the indictment, and overruling the motion in arrest of judgment. Murphy's case was reversed, not because the indictment was bad, but because the evidence did not establish the guilt of the accused. The language employed by the court was this : "In the present case, the specific article is named in the indictment, and the court did not, therefore, err in refusing to quash the indictment or arrest the judgment. But the evidence did not establish the guilt of the accused, and a new trial should have been granted."

Applying the principles laid down in Murphy's case to the present, we must affirm the judgment of the court below. Because in this, as in that case, the specific article sold is named in the indictment, and the court, therefore, did not err in refusing to quash the indictment or arrest the judgment ; and, in the present case, none of the evidence is before us. We must presume the verdict to be correct.

Let the judgment be affirmed.

ALGHERI v. THE STATE, 25 Miss. Rep., 584.

HOMICIDE.

While circumstantial evidence is in its nature capable of producing the highest degree of moral certainty, yet experience proves that it is a species of evidence, in the application of which the utmost caution and vigilance should be used.

It is the exclusion of every other hypothesis, which invests mere circumstances with the force of truth. Whenever the evidence leaves it indifferent which of several hypotheses is true, or merely establishes some finite probability in favor of one hypothesis rather than another, such evidence cannot amount to proof, however great the probability may be.

Error to Harrison circuit court. HARRIS, J.

The facts of this case are, that Barnardo Algheri was indicted in the circuit court of Harrison county for the murder of Bartolo St. Andrew, who was found dead in the town of Biloxi, with two wounds on his left breast, and one in his back beneath the left shoulder blade, which seemed to have arrested the instrument. The wounds were examined by a physician, and were declared to be inflicted with a slender pointed instrument of not exceeding a half an inch in breadth, which had penetrated four or five inches. The wounds were mortal, and appeared to have been made with the spear of a sword-cane, or some such instrument. Two or three days after the murder was committed, the prisoner (Algheri) was brought to Biloxi by the deputy sheriff, who found in his possession when taken, a sword-cane, which was fourteen inches long and slightly bent at the point. The body of deceased was disinterred for further examination and the spear or sword-cane of prisoner inserted in the wound on the back which came in contact with the breast bone, which bone was examined and appeared to have been struck by some pointed instrument; upon examination, the other wounds in the body corresponded with the size of the instrument shown; it was further proven, that on the night the murder was committed, a number of persons collected round the body, and on the statement of one Guin, the sheriff arrested one George Young as the supposed murderer of St. Andrew. Witness Henley stated, that on the night of the murder, witness Guin and Nixon had been supping together at an oyster saloon, and had risen from supper and walked out together about nine o'clock, and soon Nixon and

Guin went in the direction of the Magnolia Hotel, which was near the scene of the murder, and in a few minutes after the parties separated, the cry of murder was heard in the direction his companions had gone ; and when he approached the dead body, he found Guin and Nixon standing over it, and witness asked Guin and Nixon who committed the murder, when Guin said he saw the man killed, and deceased was fleeing from the murderer, who did not stop after deceased fell, but immediately fled ; and he (Guin) pursued him a short distance, but the man turned upon him and presented some sort of a weapon, which arrested his (Guin's) progress ; and the man turned and continued his flight, and he lost sight of the man near the premises of Capt. Goos ; and he (Guin) took the man to be George Young ; that the man wore a cap and had on a colored shirt.

George Young, when arrested, was found in an oyster-house in a direction opposite to that in which the person described by Guin was seen fleeing ; and Young exhibited no emotion when arrested but astonishment ; and no weapon was found upon his person but an old pocket knife with a short blade ; his dress was a glazed cap, a dark-colored shirt, and shoes without heels. Young was discharged upon examination by proof that clearly established he was at another place at the time the killing took place. That thirty yards from where the body was found there were signs of scuffle on the ground, and from that point to where the body was found, there were tracks of two persons' feet on the sand, and one appeared to have been made with shoes without heels. Prisoner (Algheri) was arrested in Hancock county on board of a steamboat, and was much frightened when brought to Biloxi and delivered to the sheriff, and a crowd of persons assembled to witness his landing. Prisoner told the sheriff that the sword-cane he had belonged to James Stromley, which Stromley denied.

Gabriel Mazean testified that he knew the deceased, who kept a grocery and oyster-house near the Magnolia Hotel in Biloxi ; that he saw the prisoner with two others, and the deceased together, on the same evening the murder was committed ; they were in witness' grocery between five and six o'clock on that evening, and drank together. While there, a quarrel ensued between them; the prisoner (who is a native of the isle of Sicily) and the two others, accused the deceased of something which he denied; the three seemed to be against the deceased, and the prisoner seemed most excited against him, and quarelled with him most; and they shortly after separated; the prisoner and the two others (who were Italians) going towards the house of James Stromley, and the deceased went towards the house of the deceased, which was about fifty yards west of witness' house. He saw no more of the prisoner and his companions until 8 o'clock the same evening, when they came to his door from the direction of Stromley's, and, while passing, he saw prisoner have in his hand a sword-cane, exactly similar to that exhibited in court, and which he believes to be the same cane; prisoner tapped witness on the breast with the cane and said to him "Adieu," as he passed with the two other men. The moon shone very brightly at the time; prisoner had on a cap, and the cane was such as witness had never seen before; they were going in the direction where deceased lived; and after the lapse of ten or fifteen minutes, witness heard the cry of murder in the direction prisoner and his companions had gone. The body of deceased was found about one hundred yards west of witness' house, and deceased lived about fifty yards west of him. The prisoner and his companions disappeared from Biloxi that night, and the other two men have never been heard of or seen since about that place, nor was prisoner to be found there that night after nine o'clock.

Daniel Goos testified that on the night the murder took place he was alarmed by the barking of his dog, and went out of his house, found two persons in his yard, and one ran away, and the other, who was about the size of prisoner, told him if he would let him off he would not come there again; thinks the man had on a cap, but did not know him, and next morning he saw where the men had crossed some dirt thrown up out of a well, and one of them must have had on shoes without heels. The man who spoke to him did so in broken English; he was not George Young, for he was an American, and he knew Young well. Witness knew nothing of the killing until next morning. It was also in proof, that, on the night the killing took place, three men in company were seen going in the direction of the house of deceased, when in a few minutes the cry of murder was heard in the direction of the house of deceased.

James Stromley knew deceased and prisoner, and saw him on the night the murder was committed about nine o'clock, but not afterwards, until brought back to Biloxi in custody of the sheriff; and heard prisoner and deceased quarrelling about one or two weeks before the killing took place; that deceased had insulted prisoner, but they were friendly afterwards up to the time of the killing, so far as he knew. Prisoner wore a cap on that night. It was in proof, that, at the time of the quarrel, deceased had chased the prisoner with an oyster knife.

Richard Nixon testified that on the night the killing took place, John L. Henley, Guin and witness supped together at an oyster saloon, and thinks it was about nine o'clock when they left the saloon; they walked towards the Magnolia House, and Guin was somewhat under the influence of spirits; that Henley left them, and soon after they saw two men running, and one of them made a blow at the other and then ran off, and the other man ran ten or fifteen steps and fell; and saw another man running with the man who stabbed deceased, and Guin followed after them a short distance, when he returned, and they both examined the body of the dead man. Guin told witness he knew the man who killed St. Andrew, and said it was George Young, and said the two men who ran towards Goos' went through a puddle of water. The sheriff immediately went in search of George Young and arrested him; his pantaloons were wet when arrested. Young proved an *alibi*, and was discharged. This was all the testimony.

The jury found the accused guilty of murder, when his counsel made a motion for a new trial, which was refused, and the accused prayed a writ of error to this court.

John D. Freeman for plaintiff in error.

There is no prosecutor marked on the indictment, and it must, therefore, be quashed. Cody *v.* State, 3 How. 27; Peter *v.* State, ib., 433.

The record does not state on what day of the term the accused was arraigned, if at all. The statement of the arraignment should have been made in the form in which it is averred. 1 Chit. Cr. L., 415–419.

No special *venire facias* issued or was returned into court, and there is no return of the sheriff that there was any good and lawful men summoned by him to try the prisoner only. Hutch. Co., 1007 ; People v. McKay, 18 Johns., 212 ; Commonwealth v. Hoofnagle, 1 Brown, 201 ; 1 Chitty's Cr. L., 515–517. The jury were not sworn in the form prescribed. Ib. 552–555. The verdict was not rendered in the presence of the prisoner. Ib., 636.

The evidence is circumstantial, and the prisoner was not identified as the murderer ; and another person was believed to have committed the offense. The evidence does not exclude the hypothesis that any other person might have committed the offense. For these, and many other reasons, the cause should be reversed.

D. C. Glenn, attorney general.

YERGER, J. :

The plaintiff in error was indicted for murder, and was convicted. The evidence in the case was entirely circumstantial. And although its tendency is to create an impression in the mind unfavorable to a belief of the innocence of the accused, it is not sufficiently strong, in our opinion, to warrant his conviction.

While circumstantial evidence is, in its nature, capable of producing the highest degree of moral certainty, yet experience and authority both admonish us that it is a species of evidence in the application of which the utmost caution and vigilance should be used.

A distinguished writer on the law of evidence has said, that " it is always insufficient, where assuming all to be proved, which the evidence tends to prove, some other hypothesis may still be true, for it is the actual exclusion of every other hypothesis which invests mere circumstances with the force of truth. Whenever, therefore, the evidence leaves it indifferent which of several hypotheses is true, or merely establishes some finite probability in favor of one hypothesis rather than another, such evi-

dence cannot amount to proof, however great the probability
may be." 1 Stark. on Ev., 572. We do not deem it proper to
comment upon the evidence, as the case will be reversed, and
the prisoner again tried. In our opinion, however, the circumstances proved in this record against the accused, did not warrant his conviction. We, therefore, reverse the judgment and
remand the case.

ABRAM *v.* THE STATE, 25 Miss. Rep., 589.

HOMICIDE.

The recital in the indictment that the grand jury " was duly elected, empanelled
and sworn," cannot supply the omission of it in the record.

The authority of the grand jury to find the indictment must appear in the record,
and the bill becomes no part of the record until it is acted upon and returned into
open court, in the manner prescribed by law.

Error to Copiah circuit court. HARRIS, J.

The accused (Abram) was indicted for murder in the circuit
court of Copiah county, and he was, at the June term, 1852, of
said court, found guilty of the charge alleged in the indictment,
and upon a motion being made for a new trial, and refused by
the court, the plaintiff in error brought the case to this court by
writ of error.

Peyton & Sturges for plaintiff in error.

1. Every caption of an indictment should show that the indictors were of the county for which the court was holden. 5
Bac. Abr., 93 (Amer. edit., 1844). If the caption does not state
that the grand jury are of the county for which the court had
jurisdiction to inquire, the whole will be vicious. 1 Chitty's
Crim. Law, 327, 333.

2. The record must show that the indictment was taken upon
oath, and if this allegation be omitted, the indictment cannot be
sustained. Ib., 333; Cody v. State, 3 How., 27. Jurors have
no authority to find a bill of indictment unless they have been
sworn ; and the court say, in the case of Cody v. State, that the

authority of the jury to find the indictment must be contained in the record. 3 How., 30.

3. It must appear upon the record, that the bill of indictment was found by at least twelve jurors, or it will be insufficient. 1 Chitty's Crim. Law, 838; Cro. Eliz., 654; 2 Hale, 167; Hawk., 126; Faulkner's case, 1 Saunder's R., 248, note 1; Andr., 230; 5 Bac. Abr., 93 (Amer. edit., 1844); Carpenter v. State, 4 How., 163. The court say in the case of The Thomases v. State, that it is the business of the caption of an indictment to state with sufficient certainty, not only the style of the court, the judge then presiding, but the time and place when and where it was found, and the jurors by whom it was found. 5 How., 32. It is believed, therefore, that there is wanting in this record a statement of the facts essential to confer jurisdiction on the court below.

D. C. Glenn, attorney general.

1. The error assigned in regard to the caption of the indictment is unfounded in point of fact.

2. The error assigned, that it does not appear that the grand jury were sworn, is also unfounded in fact.

3. The error assigned, that the record does not show that there was a legal grand jury in point of numbers, is untenable; because no objection was made to the grand jury in the court below, and it is too late after a party pleads not guilty and goes to trial on the merits, to object here; and because the statement in the record, that the grand jury found the bill, concludes the party, because there could be no grand jury, unless there was the legal number requisite to such a jury. Brantly v. State, 13 S. & M., 468; Dyson v. State, MS.

YERGER, J.:

The judgment in this case must be reversed. It does not appear by the record that the grand jury were sworn. It has been repeatedly held that this is a fatal defect.[1] There is a recital in the indictment, that the grand jury " were duly elected, empanelled and sworn." But the court in the case of Cody v. State, 3 How. R., 29, say: " The recital of this fact in the bill of in-

---

[1] Archbold Cr. Pr. & Pl., 585; Stokes v. State, 24 Miss., 621.

dictment, cannot supply the omission of it in the record. The record may aid the indictment, but not *e converso*. For the authority of the jury to find the indictment must be contained in the record, and the bill becomes no part of the record until it is acted upon and returned into court in the manner prescribed by law."

Let the judgment be reversed, and the cause remanded.

EX-PARTE ADAMS, 25 Miss. Rep., 883.

CONTEMPT OF COURT.

HABEAS CORPUS.

The right of all courts of justice to punish, by fine and imprisonment, for contempt of their authority, is an inherent right pertaining to them, and which they would have power to exercise independent of any statute.

The judgment of a court of competent jurisdiction, acting within the scope of its jurisdiction, is binding upon all the world until its judgment has been reversed or set aside by itself or some superior tribunal having authority for that purpose.

Every order of commitment must show a previous conviction. Therefore a naked order of the court, that a person be imprisoned until he signifies his assent to answer questions to the grand jury, without showing a previous conviction for contempt, is void, and the person should be discharged from custody.

The only question in this case arose on a writ of *habeas corpus*, which was obtained by George H. Adams, to be released from imprisonment; and in his petition he alleged that he was illegally held in custody by John P. Oldham, the sheriff of Hinds county. The sheriff answered, that he held the prisoner in custody by virtue of an order made by the circuit court of Hinds county, until he signifies his assent to the court to answer questions to the grand jury of said county, or until the adjournment of said grand jury at the July term, 1852, of said court. A motion was made to discharge the prisoner.

J. A. Guion, for motion.

D. C. Glenn, attorney general, and *C. E. Hooker*, contra.

YERGER, J.:

In this case George H. Adams obtained a writ of *habeas corpus* from the Honorable Richard Barnett, returnable before me, on a petition and affidavit, that he was illegally held in custody by John P. Oldham, the sheriff of Hinds county. In answer to the writ, the sheriff has returned that he holds the petitioner in custody by virtue of an order made by the circuit court of Hinds county, which order is in the following words: "Ordered, that George H. Adams be sent to jail, and remain there until he signifies his assent to the court to answer questions to the grand jury, or until the final adjournment of said grand jury at this term of the court."

The questions which have been argued by counsel, are of very great importance, involving, on the one hand, the right of the citizen to freedom from unlawful and arbitrary imprisonment, and on the other, the power of the courts of the country to punish by imprisonment or fine for contempts committed against them and their authority. For the state it is insisted, that as a judge, sitting to try a question on *habeas corpus*, I have no power to examine into the validity of the order of commitment, but must, upon the return made by the sheriff, remand the prisoner.

By the provisions of our statute, on the subject of *habeas corpus*, it is declared, that "whenever any person detained in custody, charged with a criminal offense, shall by himself, or some other person in his behalf, apply to the supreme court, or any circuit court of law, or court of chancery in this state, or to any judge thereof in vacation, for a writ of *habeas corpus ad subjiciendum*, shall show by affidavit or other evidence, probable cause to believe that he is detained in custody without lawful authority, it shall be the duty of the court or judge to whom said application is made, forthwith to grant the writ," etc. Hutch. Code, 999. By the fourth section of this statute, it is made the duty of the "court or judge before whom the prisoner may be brought, to proceed without delay to inquire into the cause of his imprisonment, and either discharge him, admit him to bail, or remand him into custody, as the law and the evidence shall require." Ib., 1000. The same remedy by *habeas corpus* is given by the 18th section of the statute, to "persons restrained of their liberty under any pretence whatever." By the 15th section the judge or court is prohibited from discharging any person suffering imprisonment under lawful judgment, founded on a conviction of some criminal offense. Hutch. Code, 1002. It is contended by the district attorney, that the prisoner is lawfully imprisoned for a contempt of the authority of the court, in refusing to answer a question asked him by the grand jury. For the prisoner it is insisted that the question asked him was improper and illegal, and that he was not bound by the laws of the land to answer it.

On this branch of the case two questions arise. First, Has the circuit court power to imprison a party for contempt? Second, If so, can a party be discharged from the judgment of that court directing an imprisonment for a contempt, by a direct proceeding on *habeas corpus?*

In regard to the first point, it may be stated, that the legislature has declared that the "circuit courts shall have power to fine and imprison any person who may be guilty of a contempt of the court while sitting, either in the presence or hearing of such court; provided, that such fine shall not exceed one hundred dollars, and no person for such contempt shall be imprisoned for a longer period than the term of the court at which the contempt shall have been committed." Hutch. Code, 737. See, also, p. 861, §§ 108, 109, which provides, that a witness who refuses to testify shall be committed to prison by the court, there to remain without bail or mainprise until he shall give evidence.

Indeed, the right of all courts of justice to punish by fine and imprisonment for contempts of their authority, is an inherent right pertaining to them, and which they should have lawful power to exercise independent of any statute. [1]

Conceiving the point indisputable, then, that the circuit court has the power to fine or imprison for contempt, I am brought to the second proposition, to wit: Can a party be discharged from the

[1] Hurd on Habeas Corpus, 412; Brass Crosby's case, 3 Wils., 183; Kearney's case, 7 Wheaton, 38; Yates' case, 4 Johns., 318; McLaughlin's case, 5 Watts & Serg., 275; Johnson v. Commonwealth, 1 Bibb, 602; *Ex-parte* Alexander, 2 Am. Law. Reg., 44; *Ex-parte* Nugent, 7 Penn. Law. Journ., 107; State v. White, T. U. P. Charlton, 123; *Ex-parte* Hickey, 4 S. & M., 749; State v. Tipton, 1 Blackf., 166; Clark v. People, 1 Breese, 266; Bickley v. Commonwealth, 1 J. J. Marshall, 575; Grist et al. v. Bowman et al., 2 Pray, 182; Matter of Smithurst, 2 Sandf., S. C., 724; Lockwood v. State, 1 Carter, 161; State v. Woodfin, 5 Iredell, 199; *Ex-parte* Williamson, 4 Am. Law Register, 27; *Ex-parte* Nugent, 1 Am. Law Journal, (N. S.,) 111.

judgment of that court directing his imprisonment for contempt by proceeding on *habeas corpus.*

There is no principle more fully established in our jurisprudence than this, to wit : The judgment of a court of competent jurisdiction, acting within the scope of its jurisdiction, is binding. and conclusive upon all the world, until its judgment has been reversed or set aside by itself or by some superior tribunal having authority for that purpose. Upon an application by *habeas corpus* to discharge a party from a commitment for contempt, the only question which the judge trying the writ can ask himself is this : Did the court which made the order of commitment have jurisdiction over the party and over the subject matter? If it did not, then the judgment would be *coram non judice* and void, and the party would be entitled to his discharge. But if the objection be not that the court had no jurisdiction of the case, but acting in the bounds of its authority, it made an erroneous application in its judgment of the law, then, I conceive, that sitting as a judge to try the writ of *habeas corpus*, it would not be competent for me to enter into the inquiry, whether the judgment was erroneous or not. This principle will be found to pervade all the decisions made in this country and in England upon this subject.

In a very early case of Bross Crosby, mayor of London, (3 Wilson, 188,) which was an application to the court of common pleas for a *habeas corpus* to bring up the body of the lord mayor, who was committed for contempt by the house of commons, the writ was granted, on the return, the causes of commitment were set out. It was argued for the prisoner, that the house of commons had no authority to commit for a contempt, and if they had, that they had not used it rightly and properly, and that the causes assigned were insufficient ; but the whole court was of opinion, that the house of commons could commit for a contempt, and that the court could not revise its adjudication for error. Lord Chief Justice DeGrey, on that occasion, remarked, " When the house of commons adjudged anything to be a contempt or breach of privilege, their adjudication is a conviction, and their commitment in consequence is an execution, and no court can discharge a person that is in execution by the judgment of any other court ; this court can do nothing when a person is in execution by the judgment of a court having competent jurisdiction. In such case, this court is not a court of appeals." Again, he remarked : " The court of king's bench, or common pleas, never discharged any person committed for a contempt, in not answering in the court of chancery, if the return was for a contempt. If the admiralty commits for a contempt, or one to be taken up on *excommunicato capiendo*, this court never discharges the persons committed."

In the celebrated case of Paty and others v. The Queen, occurring in the time of Queen Anne, reported in 2 Lord Raymond, 1105, being a writ of *habeas corpus*, sued out in the court of queen's bench, for their discharge from a commitment for contempt, by the house of commons, that court held that it had no authority to inquire into the sufficiency of the cause of commitment. In this case it is true, the justly distinguished Lord Holt was of opinion that parties were entitled to be liberated. But he was overruled by the other eleven judges. In remarking on this case, Lord Campbell, a jurist remarkable for his learning and ability, as well as his liberal principles, uses the following language : " Holt was carried away by excusable indignation, to hold that they were entitled to be liberated ; but he was properly overruled by the other judges, on the ground that the court had no power to examine into a commitment by either house of parliament." Campbell's Lives of L. C., vol. 4, 165. It is worthy of remark, too, that the opinion of Holt, Ch. J., proceeds rather upon the ground of a want of power or jurisdiction in the house of commons, in the case before him, than an erroneous judgment and application of the law where it had unquestioned jurisdiction.

Blackstone, on this subject, has stated the rule of law in the following language : " All courts, by which I mean to include the house of parliament, and the courts of Westminster hall, can have no control in matters of contempt. The sole adjudication of contempt, and the punishment thereof, belongs exclusively, and without interfering, to each respective court. Infinite confusion and disorder would follow, if courts could, by writs of *habeas corpus*, examine and determine the contempt of others."

See case of Paty and others. This whole subject underwent a very elaborate investigation in England, in the late case of Stockdale v. Hansand, 9 Adol. & Ellis, 1 (36 E. C. L. R.), and the opinion of the judges accorded with that already announced by me, to wit : " Where a commitment for contempt is made by a court of competent jurisdiction, there is no authority to discharge the party, upon the grounds that the court erred in its judgment of the law."   In the opinion of Justice Patteson, the following language was used : " When a person is committed for a contempt by the house of commons, the court cannot question the propriety of such commitment, or inquire whether the person had been guilty of contempt, in the same manner as this court cannot entertain any such question, if the commitment be by any other court having power to commit for contempt. In such instance, there is an adjudication of a court of competent authority in the particular case, and the court which is desired to interfere, not being a court of error and appeal, cannot entertain the question whether the authority has been properly exercised. Upon an application for a writ of *habeas corpus*, by a person committed by the house, the question of the powers of the house to commit, or of the due exercise of that power, is the original and primary question propounded to the court, and arises directly. Now, as soon as it appears that the house has committed the person for a cause within their jurisdiction, as, for instance, for a contempt, so adjudged to be by them, the matter has passed *in rem adjudicatam*, and the court before which the party is brought by *habeas corpus* must remand him."

Similar language was used by the other judges. Such, then, is the rule established by the English courts on this question. Have the courts in the United States varied the rule ? Upon as full an examination as I have been able to give this question since it was submitted to me, I cannot find that they have.

In New York, in the case of J. V. N. Bates, 4 Johns. R., 318; the rule was laid down as it had been by the English judges. In the opinion in the case of Kent, Ch. J., he reviewed the English cases, and remarked, that " there was not an instance in the English law of a judge in vacation undertaking to decide upon the legality of a commitment in execution by the judgment of any court of record, and much less of a court of the highest degree." He even extended the rule so far as to hold, that if, upon the return of a writ of *habeas corpus*, awarded in vacation, it appears that the prisoner stands committed by a judgment of a court of record or other court of competent authority, the judge is bound immediately to remand the prisoner, and he has no power to examine and decide touching the legality of the judgment or the jurisdiction of the court. These questions belong to the cognizance of the supreme court, as possessing general appellate powers, and as having supreme control of all inferior courts. While I most respectfully dissent from one position taken by the chief justice, to wit, that a judge, on trying the *habeas corpus*, " cannot examine the jurisdiction of the court," yet I feel confident that the other position is fully sustained by the law, to wit, " If the jurisdiction be admitted, the judge has no power to decide touching the legality of the judgment, or whether it be erroneous or not." In relation to a judgment made by a court without jurisdiction, the chief justice stated in the same opinion, that " a proceeding without jurisdiction is void and a mere nullity."

The power to discharge on *habeas corpus* from a commitment for contempt, came up before the supreme court of the United States, in *Ex-parte* Kearney, 7 Wheaton's R., 43, and in that distinguished tribunal where Story then held a seat, and John Marshall presided, it was unanimously held, Judge Story delivering the opinion of the court, that a " writ of *habeas corpus* is not deemed a proper remedy where a party was committed for a contempt by a court of competent jurisdiction, and, if granted, the court could not inquire into the sufficiency of the cause of commitment, and they are bound to remand the party unless they were prepared to abandon the whole doctrine, so reasonable, just and convenient, which has hitherto regulated this important subject." The law has been ruled in the same way in Indiana, in Kentucky, in Georgia and in Tennessee. 1 Breese, 266; 1 Black, 166; 1 J. J. Marsh, 575; Charlton, R., 136; 5 Yerger.

The argument has been pressed very earnestly, that unless the power to discharge on *habeas corpus* exists, an arbitrary and irresponsible power may exist in the courts of the country by which the rights and liberties of the citizens may be taken away without remedy. The same argument was used before the supreme court of the United States, in *Ex-parte* Kearney, before referred to. But that court replied, " where the law is clear, this argument can be of no avail, and it will probably be found that there are also serious inconveniences on the other side. Wherever power is lodged it may be abused. But this forms no solid objection against its exercise ; confidence must be reposed somewhere, and if there should be an abuse, it will be a public grievance, for which a remedy may be applied by the legislature, and it is not to be devised by courts of justice."

In the decision made by Judge Thatcher, in *Ex-parte* Hickey, 4 S. & M., 751, I do not find any thing which conflicts with the view of the law taken by me in that case. Judge Thatcher discharged Hickey, among other reasons, upon the ground that the circuit court had no power or jurisdiction to commit for contempts not committed in the presence of the court. The power to commit in that case was denied, but, I apprehend, if the power had been admitted, the judge would not have decided that he had any right to examine whether it had been erroneously exercised or not. Indeed, I think the power to discharge on *habeas corpus* from a commitment for contempt, ordered by a court of competent jurisdiction, is expressly taken away by the *habeas corpus* act itself, which, among other things declares, that a person shall not be discharged out of prison who is suffering imprisonment under lawful judgment, founded on a conviction of some criminal offense. Hutch. Code, 1002.

It would not be pretended, if the petitioner had been convicted by the verdict of a jury of a misdemeanor, and sentenced by the court to imprisonment therefor, that I could discharge him, on the ground that erroneous and improper charges were given by the court, or that illegal and improper evidence was admitted against him ; every person would admit that I could not enter at all into such an investigation, and it could only be done by an appellate court. Yet the supreme court of the United States declares there is no distinction, in principle, between that case and a judgment of imprisonment against a party for contempt, for when a court commits a party for contempt, their adjudication is a conviction, and their commitment in consequence is execution. *Ex-parte* Kearney, 7 Wheat., 43. If, then, it should appear from the return to a writ of *habeas corpus*, that the party was imprisoned by the judgment of a court of competent jurisdiction, for a contempt committed in its presence, I would feel precluded by the statute from discharging the prisoner.

It is true, the high court of errors and appeals has held that on a writ of error and *supersedeas* being awarded in a criminal case not capital, they may admit the prisoner to bail, to appear and abide the judgment of the appellate court. Whether a writ of error would lie from a judgment of imprisonment for contempt in this state, has never been decided. In some states it has been held, that a writ of error would lie. In others, that it would not. Should it be held, that it would lie in this state, I presume the party would be bailable till trial and judgment, as in other cases of criminal convictions.

From a review of the law applicable to this case, I am satisfied, if it appeared from the return that the prisoner was imprisoned by the judgment of the circuit court of Hinds county, for a contempt of the authority of that court, that I could not enter into an examination in this proceeding, whether the questions asked the witness, and refused by him to be answered, were legal or not. I think that would be a question which could only be received, if it could be received at all, by an appellate tribunal, and I would therefore be bound to remand the prisoner. But the return set out in this case is, in my opinion, insufficient to justify his imprisonment. It does not appear from that return that there has been any conviction or judgment of the circuit court of Hinds county, that Mr. Adams was guilty of a .contempt. The order set out is, that "George H. Adams be sent to jail, and remain there until he signifies his assent to the court to answer questions to the grand jury," etc. It was formerly held, that a judgment for contempt, which did not set out the particular case on which it was founded, was a nullity, and that a party was entitled to be discharged from it. But the more recent cases laid down the rule, that the judgment will be sufficient, if it express on its face that it was for a contempt generally, and that the specific cause need not be set out. Iredell, R., 36 ; E. C. L. R., 1.

But it is clear, that a general order to imprison a party, unless he has been convicted either by a jury or by the court, is a mere nullity. The law requires, that, before a sentence of imprisonment shall be passed against a party, he should be first convicted of an offense. In ordinary cases this conviction must be by the verdict of a jury. In cases of contempt, it may be by the judgment of the court. Still, in either case, the record must show a conviction. Now, it will be seen from this return, that there is no judgment of imprisonment for a contempt generally, or for a contempt in refusing to answer questions. There is not any conviction or adjudication by the court, that Mr. Adams had been guilty of a contempt. Without such judgment, the court had no right to commit him to prison, nor the sheriff to detain him. It is true, and was admitted on the argument, that Mr. Adams did refuse to answer questions asked by the grand jury, and it may be true, that the court considered that a contempt for which he deserved imprisonment, but no such judgment has been rendered in the case, and however many contempts the prisoner may have committed, it is not lawful to imprison him until convicted thereof by the judgment of the court, which judgment and conviction must appear by the record. For this reason, I direct that he be discharged from custody.

RIGGS *v.* THE STATE, 26 Miss. Rep., 51.

HOMICIDE.

All the facts and circumstances which constitute a criminal offense must be stated with precision and certainty in the indictment. And every material circumstance in regard to time and place must be averred with sufficient certainty to exclude every other intendment.

It is indispensable that the indictment should aver that the murdered man died in the county in which the indictment was preferred.

A juror cannot be allowed to testify to facts that will avoid his verdict.

Any irregularity, or exposure to undue influence, of a jury, or misconduct of the officer in charge of them, will vitiate their verdict.

Error to Monroe circuit court.   ROGERS, J.

James Riggs was indicted in the circuit court of Monroe county for the murder of Joel E. Hunt, and at the March term, 1853, of said court, sentence of death was pronounced against him by the court, after conviction by the jury.

The following causes of error are assigned by the plaintiff in error for reversal of the judgment of the court below:

1st. Because the indictment does not allege that the deceased (Hunt) died in the county of Monroe, where the accused was indicted and tried.

2d. The jury, while sitting in the case, ate at a public table of a hotel with a crowd of guests, and the landlord and servants of the hotel were freely admitted into their room. A private room, apart from the one they occupied, was prepared for the jury, in which was put intoxicating drink, into which they went separately to drink. The officer in charge went to sleep at ten o'clock, and left the jury in the room with the door unlocked. The jury had cards, liquor, and a fiddle, all of which they used during the night. The next morning, one of the jurors, without the consent of the officer in charge of them, separated from the balance and paid a visit to his family.

Three other grounds of error were assigned, but the court gave no decision on them, and it is unnecessary to state them. The defendant prayed a writ of error to this court.

W. F. Dowd for plaintiff in error.

The time and place must be added to every material fact in the indictment. The death of the deceased in the county where the offense is charged to have been committed, is a material fact, without which the prisoner cannot be lawfully convicted. Arch. Crim. Pl., 84; ib., 381; Stoughton v. State, 13 S. & M., 225.

The jury ate at the public table with a crowd of guests. The landlord and servants of the Walton House were freely admitted into their room. A private room, apart from the one they occupied, was prepared for them, with intoxicating liquors, into which they went separately to drink. The officer in charge goes to sleep at ten o'clock, leaving the jury up in the room, and the door unlocked. Cards, liquor, and a fiddle had been previously prepared for them. The game and the midnight revel engaged a large portion of their attention, while deliberating on a verdict involving the life of a fellow man and the destiny of an immortal soul.

One of the jurors on the next morning, without the knowledge of the officer, separated from his fellows and paid a visit to his family.

Every barrier and safeguard which the common law, founded in profound wisdom, and matured by the experience of ages, has thrown around the jury-box, to protect it from corruption and contamination, has, in the trial of this cause, been broken down.

If such practices are to receive the sanction of the courts, the trial by jury, hitherto so celebrated for its purity and impartiality, will become equally famous as a mere engine of cruelty and an instrument of murder, armed with irresistible power.

The case is much stronger than any of those to which I now refer the court. Commonwealth v. McCall, 1 Va. Cases, 271; Overbee v. Commonwealth, 1 Rob., 756; McLane v. State, 10 Yerg., 241; Roby v. Commonwealth, 12 Pick., 496; Hare's case, 4 How. Miss. R., 187; Bolles' case, 13 S. & M., 400; Morgan v. State, Opinion Book, 629, 630.

D. C. Glenn, attorney general.

A motion was made to arrest the judgment, because it was not alleged in the indictment that Hunt died in Monroe county. If this defect existed, it would be fatal. But it does not exist. The indictment avers as follows: "Of which said mortal wounds the said Joel Hunt did then and there" (that is, in Monroe county) "languish, and languishing did live for about the space of twenty hours, and did then die." There is no uncertainty or defect here. The languishing, living, and death are plainly connected and pointed to by the "then and there," which, by natural and proper meaning, refers to all of them. Ike v. State, 1 Cushm., 525; Johnson's case, Walker R., 392; 1 Leach, 529; Douglass, 212; 4 Co., 41, 43; Dyer, 69 a; 2 Lord Raym., 1467, 1468; State v. Cherry, 8 Murph., 7; 2 How., 661.

Smith, C. J.:

The plaintiff in error was tried and convicted of murder in

the circuit court of Monroe county. Upon the return of their verdict by the jury, the prisoner moved the court for a new trial and in arrest of judgment. These motions were overruled, and sentence of death was pronounced upon the prisoner, who has brought his case into this court upon the bills of exception filed by him during the progress of the trial in the court below. From the view we take of the case, it will be unnecessary to notice in detail the various exceptions taken to the judgment of the court.

The objections mainly relied on by the plaintiff in error, are based: 1. Upon the alleged invalidity of the indictment; and 2. Upon the misconduct of the jury during their retirement to consider of their verdict.

1. It is said that the indictment is defective and illegal because it does not allege with sufficient certainty the place at which the party charged to have been murdered died.

The facts and circumstances which constitute the offense charged must be stated with precision and certainty. And every material circumstance, in regard to time and place, must be averred with that degree of certainty which is sufficient to exclude every other intendment.[1] Arch. Crim. Plead., 34–381; Chit. Crim. Law, 280, 283. Let us apply this rule to the indictment under consideration.

The description of the act with which the prisoner is charged as a felony is contained in the following averment, to wit: "That the said James Riggs, with a certain knife which he then and there in his right hand had and held, the said Joel E. Hunt, in and upon the right shoulder, and in and upon the right side of the body, and in and upon the right side of the belly of him the said Joel E. Hunt, then and there feloniously, wilfully, and of his malice aforethought, did strike and thrust, giving to the said Joel E. Hunt, etc., the mortal wounds, etc., of which said mortal wounds the said Hunt did then and there languish, and languishing did live for the space of about twenty hours, and did then die."

[1] Wharton Am. Cr. Law, 365, et seq.; Wharton's Prec., 1061–2; People v. Taylor, 3 Denis, 91; Briggs v. People, 8 Barb., 547; State v. Philbrick, 1 Red., 401; Kit. v. State, 1 Humph., 167; 2 Hawk., c. 25, § 57; Bac. Abr. Indictment, G. 1; Cowp., 683.

Every valid charge for murder necessarily contains three distinct propositions: 1, That the person slain was murdered; 2, that the party charged perpetrated the deed; and 3, that the felony was committed within the county where the indictment was found. In the indictment before us, it is seen that no averment of place is affixed to the time when the subject of the alleged murder is stated to have died. After the reception of the wounds which caused his death, he "languishing did live for the space of about twenty hours, and then did die." It is manifest that, tested by the rule above laid down, this averment is insufficient. The fact that the murdered party did not die within the county of Monroe is not necessarily excluded, or rather it does not appear by direct averment and with certainty, that he died within that county. This fact it was indispensable that the indictment should aver.[1] For although the mortal wound may have been there inflicted, if the death, in fact, occurred in another county, by express statutory provision the circuit court of Monroe had no jurisdiction of the offense. Poindex. Code, 814.

2. On the hearing of the motion for a new trial, which was based in part upon the alleged misconduct of the jury, and that some of them, after they had been committed to the charge of an officer, separated from their fellows, several witnesses were examined, amongst whom two of the jury were permitted to depose to facts which tended to inculpate themselves and some of their associates. This was improper, and in plain violation of the settled rule on the subject. But, excluding their testimony, which was not objected to in the court below, enough

---

[1] Archbold Cr. Pr. and Pl., 892, notes. At common law, the party committing a criminal offense, must be indicted in the county where the offense was committed. But in the case of homicide, if the wound was given in one county and death happened in another, it was said by some that the party was not indictable at all, because the offense was not complete in either county, and the jury could inquire of only what happened in their own county. 1 Hawk. P. C., 94; 1 East, 361. The common opinion is that the prisoner may be indicted where the stroke was given, for that alone is the act of the party of which the death is but a consequence. Riley v. State, 9 Humph., 466. By our statute, "Where the mortal stroke, or other cause of death occurs or is given or administered in one county, and the death occurs in another county, the offender may be tried in either county; and so, also, if the mortal stroke or cause of death occurs, or is given or administered in another state or country and death happens in this state, the offender shall be tried in the county where death happened." Rev. Code of 1857, 613, art. 146. See Archbold Cr. Pr. and Pl., as to rule in different states, p. 892, note (1).

appears from the testimony of the other witnesses to require us, in conformity with the doctrine recognized in repeated decisions of this court, to set aside their verdict.

Irregularities on the part of juries empanelled and charged with the trial of felonies, and misconduct in the officers having them in charge, have become of such frequent occurrence that we deem it incumbent upon us to suggest respectfully to the learned judges who preside in our circuit courts, that the corrective which they hold in their hands should be promptly and rigidly applied. It is manifest that if these evils, which appear to be greatly on the increase, are not arrested, it must become in the end a vain effort to bring to just punishment any violation of the laws of the land.

Let the judgment be reversed, the indictment quashed, and the prisoner remanded to the circuit court of Monroe county, to await the future action of the court.

LEATHERS *v.* THE STATE, 26 Miss. Rep., 73.

ASSAULT WITH INTENT TO KILL.

The statute in relation to grand juries was manifestly intended to apply to the circuit courts of all the counties then in existence, or that might be afterwards created by statute.

A grand jury composed of members who have not been drawn, summoned, or empanelled according to law, is illegal, and all their acts are void. Therefore where the clerk and sheriff draw a *venire* composed of forty persons, instead of the number required by law, an indictment preferred by a grand jury selected from such *venire*, is invalid.

Error to Pontotoc circuit court. MILLER, J.

The defendant was indicted in the circuit court of Pontotoc county for an assault with intent to commit murder, and he filed several pleas in abatement to the bill of indictment, and among them he pleaded, in substance, that thirty-six persons were not drawn and summoned, as directed by law, to serve as jurors for the first week of the term of the circuit court of Pontotoc county, from which, by law, the grand jury for said term were to be selected ; but that forty persons were drawn and summoned, from whom the grand jury who preferred the bill of indictment were drawn or selected at said term of the court.

This plea was demurred to and the demurrer sustained. The defendant was convicted, and he prayed a writ of error to this court.

Price & Jackson for plaintiff in error.

The circuit court act of 1833, § 8, Hutch. Code, 888, directs the number of jurors to be drawn for the first week of the terms of the circuit courts; and further directs that out of these jurors, thirty-six in number, the grand jury shall be drawn. This act was passed some three years before the counties of the Chickasaw cession were organized; but we take it for granted it is equally applicable to them, by construction of law, as it is to the older counties. If it is not, then there is not and has never been any legal method of constituting juries in these counties. This statute prescribes distinctly the number of jurors to be drawn for the first week, thirty-six, and with equal distinctness enacts that out of these thirty-six the grand jurors shall be drawn. The second and third pleas in this case aver, that the demurrer to them admits, that forty instead of thirty-six jurors were drawn for the first week of the term at which this indictment was found; and that out of these forty, the grand jury who found this bill were drawn.

Surely, so palpable a departure and violation of the plain directions of the statute vitiates the grand jury in its organization, and annuls all its action. There is no mystery in the enactment; it is easy to understand, and easy to comply with. No discretion is vested anywhere to increase or reduce the number of jurors to be drawn and summoned. That number is definitely fixed by the statute itself; and a circuit judge, or a sheriff and clerk have no more right to vary from it, than they have to dispense with it altogether. It will not do to say that the greater number, forty, included the lesser thirty-six; and that therefore the law was complied with. The statute goes on to enact, that from the thirty-six jurors, not from any greater number, to be summoned for the first week, the grand jury shall be drawn. If departures from this simple enactment are to be tolerated, and the whole thing opened to the arbitrary discretion of judges or inferior officers, then the statute has failed of its purpose, and there is no other security for the citizen than the will and caprice of the officers of the law. If those officers can increase the number of the *venire* to any, the slightest, extent, they can increase it till all the persons whose names are liable are included. If they can increase it at all, equal authority can be found to limit and reduce it, even below the number requisite to constitute a grand jury. To tolerate such departures from the statute, would be to defeat its purpose and to subvert its whole policy, which are to mark out distinctly the manner in which the tribunals shall be organized which are invested with the high powers of putting in jeopardy the lives, liberties, and rights of citizens. The whole reasoning of this court in the several cases which have been before it, from McQuillen v. State down to the case of Stokes and Johnson, sustains these views, and shows a proper determination to permit no relaxation of the wholesome guards thrown by law around the citizen for his protection.

G. T. Swann, on same side.

To show the error of the court below in overruling the pleas in abatement tendered by the prisoner, it is conceived that the cases of Rawls v. State, 8 S. & M., 559, and McQuillen v. State, 8 S. & M. 587, are conclusive to show the validity of these pleas.

It is insisted, also, that this court, in looking into the whole record, will quash the indictment and discharge the prisoner, because,

1st. The indictment does not sufficiently and distinctly allege any assault upon the person of any one, nor that it was done with a deadly weapon. Ainsworth v. State, 5 How. 242 ; Jones v. State, 11 S. & M. 315.

2d. The name of the prosecutor is not endorsed on the indictment. The memorandum written on the indictment no more designates the person named as prosecutor than it does as a witness. For this it is defective and cannot support any sentence. Cody v. State, 3 How., 27 ; Peter v. State, ib., 433 ; Kirk v. State, 13 S. & M., 406 ; Moore v. State, ib., 259.

3d. Any new indictment that may be framed for the same offense charged in this, will show on its face that the prosecutor is

barred by the statute of limitations; and if the prisoner should
be found guilty by a jury, a motion in arrest for this cause will
be sustained.   Howard v. State, 13 S. & M., 262.

This court will, therefore, refuse to remand the prisoner, to
subject him to a new indictment which must be bad if it charges
the time of the alleged offense truly.

J. F. Cushman, on same side.

D. C. Glenn, attorney general.

SMITH, C. J.:

The plaintiff in error was convicted of an assault with intent
to commit murder on an indictment framed under the 33d section, ch. 64, of the statute of 1839, Hutch. Dig., 960. Numerous objections are urged to the validity of the judgment rendered in the circuit court, all of which, with the exception of
that which arises on the third plea of defendant in abatement to
the indictment, we deem it unnecessary to notice. That plea was
demurred to and the demurrer was sustained.

The said plea in substance avers that thirty-six persons were
not drawn and summoned, as directed by law, to serve as jurors
for the first week of the ensuing term of the circuit court of
Pontotoc county, and from which, by law, the grand jury for
said term were to be selected; but that forty persons were drawn
and summoned, and from whom the grand jury, who preferred
the bill of indictment, were in fact selected.

The exception to the judgment on the demurrer is based upon
the provisions of the 8th section of the statute of March 2d,
1833, Hutch. Dig., 888, which directs that " in the several counties of this state, except the county of Monroe, where the term
of the circuit court continues more than one week, the sheriff
and clerk shall draw for the first week, in the manner now prescribed by law, thirty-six jurors, out of which the grand juries
shall be drawn and shall serve for one week, except the grand
jurors who shall serve until they are discharged by the court."

The circuit court for the county of Pontotoc may by law be
held for the term of two weeks.

It was said by the attorney general, in the argument at bar,
that the county of Pontotoc was not created until many years

after the enactment of said statute. That there is no statutory provision by which the act above quoted is made to apply to the counties thereafter to be organized; and hence it should not be held to regulate the drawing and empanelling juries for counties subsequently created. In reply to this it is sufficient to observe that the said act is general, except as to the county of Monroe, and was manifestly intended by the legislature to apply to all the circuit courts to be holden in the counties then in existence, or which might thereafter be created by statute.

In McQuillen v. State it was holden that a grand jury, composed of members who have not been drawn, summoned, or empanelled in the manner prescribed by law, have no power to find a valid indictment. A grand jury, said the late chief justice, does not, by our law, consist of thirteen men, congregated by the mere order of court or by accident, in a jury box; but it consists of the requisite number of competent individuals, selected, summoned, and sworn according to the forms of law; and if the law be not followed, it is an incompetent grand jury. The same doctrine has since been repeatedly recognized as the settled law of the state. Rawls. v. State, 8 S. & M., 599; Stokes v. State, 24 Miss. R., 621.

It cannot be doubted that the act of the clerk and sheriff, in drawing forty persons instead of the number prescribed by law, was a palpable violation of the statute; and if it should be held valid, an end at once is put to the authority of the law which prescribes the mode in which grand juries are to be constituted. For, if the officers charged with the duty and who are empowered to select by lot, draw forty persons from whom the grand jury may be chosen instead of the legal number, they may, with equal propriety, draw any number, either greater or less, which their caprice may direct. And if the specific directions of the law may be violated in one respect, why not in any or every other? But the same reason which makes it imperative upon the courts to observe the directions of the statute in one case, requires our obedience in every other. The various regulations which have been adopted in regard to the constitution of juries, we apprehend, were designated for wise purposes. They are all intended as guards to protect the liberty of the citizen, and should be held to constitute an important part of the right of trial by jury. Holding this view of the subject, we are compelled to reverse the judgment, to overrule the demurrer, and to quash the indictment.

ORGAN *v.* THE STATE, 26 Miss. Rep., 78.

ASSAULT AND BATTERY WITH INTENT TO KILL.

The *venire* does not necessarily constitute a part of the record, unless placed there by being embodied in the bill of exceptions.

It is not competent for the prisoner to question the sufficiency of the *venire* on error, when he has raised no objections to it in the court below, by motion or plea in abatement, but has pleaded in bar and been convicted.

Any separation of a juror from his fellows, or from the superintendence of the bailiff is *prima facie* evidence of irregularity; and his affidavit is inadmissible to justify his conduct during the separation.

Error to Hinds circuit court. BARNETT, J.

Madison Organ was indicted in the circuit court of Hinds county, for an assault and battery, with intent to kill J. M. Currie, and at the September term of said court, 1852, he was found guilty as charged in the indictment. A motion was made for a new trial, but refused by the court below.

The jury separated before they rendered their verdict in the case, by William S. Mullen, who was one of them, leaving the other eleven jurors without permission of the court, as they were about retiring to their room to consider of their verdict, and passing by a number of persons in conversation in the courthouse and going out of the house, and he was absent two or three minutes, whilst the balance of the jurors, under charge of the proper officer, went up-stairs, and left Mullen behind, but he joined them in a short time. The affidavit of the juror, Mullen, was introduced to show that he did not talk with any one about the case, or hear any one talk about the case while absent from the other jurors.

The defendant prayed a writ of error to this court.

Grafton Baker, for plaintiff in error.

Every step essential to a regular conviction, in cases highly penal like this, should appear by the record of the proceedings to have been properly taken.

What the law requires to be done, and to appear of record, can, if done, only be made to appear by the record itself, or an exemplification of the record. It is perfectly immaterial whether the act required, be or be not performed, if it do not appear of record. Elliot v. Piersol et al., 1 Peters, 340; Dakin v. Hudson, 6 Conn., 224.

Apply these principles to the record in this case, and it is clear this conviction cannot stand.

By the second section of the act prescribing the mode of drawing and empanelling juries, the names of the jurors drawn are required to be entered by the clerk on the minutes of the court. Hutch. Dig., 886. This does not appear by the record to have been done.

By the 5th section of the same act, the clerk is required to issue " a *venire facias* according to law," and the sheriff shall " summon the jurors named in such *venire facias*," etc. Neither of these acts appears by the record to have been performed. A record imports absolute verity, and the legal presumption is, that the circuit court caused a record to be made of every step which was actually taken in the progress of the cause.

And hence it is that the non-performance of an act, or the non-existence of a fact, where the performance in the one case, or the existence in the other, should by law appear of record, may be proved by the record. So if a material matter does not appear by the record which the law requires so to appear, the just inference is, that it did not exist or take place. Thornton v. Slatford, 1 Salkeld, 284. These principles apply to this record; it clearly appears that no *venire facias* in the case was issued, served, or returned.

The circuit courts of this state are courts of oyer and terminer. 1 How., 241. No issue of fact can be tried before them without a precept, a *venire facias*, to summon a jury; and such precept should be good in form and substance, and returned duly executed. 1 Chit. Cr. Law, 508, 509; 2 Hale, 260, 261; 3 Bacon, 730; Peck, 140–166; 18 Johns., 212.

No court is authorized to put any citizen on trial for a capital or infamous crime, unless a grand jury of the proper county, organized as the law directs, has preferred a formal charge against him.   Thomas v. State, 5 How., 32.   The record does not show that the grand jury was regularly organized.

D. C. Glenn, attorney general.

1. The first error assigned is, that the court below permitted a witness to testify in detailing his evidence, to an exclamation made by a by-stander, " that Organ had stabbed Miller."   I do not conceive it well taken.   This exclamation was made use of the moment the stabbing occurred.   The witness was forced to state it in the natural order of his evidence.   It was to some extent a part of the *res gestæ.*   Its admissibility was to be determined by the discretion of the judge.   The main point in such matters is, whether the exclamation which here came incidentally into proof, was contemporaneous with the main fact under consideration, and whether it was so connected with it as to illustrate its character.   I think it was.   In Lord George Gordon's case, the cries of the mob were received as part of the *res gestæ,* and showing the character of the principal fact.   This case, though not similar, is somewhat analagous to the one just cited.   1 Greenl., § 108, and note, and cases therein cited.

2. A juror separated from his fellows for two minutes.   It is shown by his own affidavit and that of a brother juror, that no one spoke to him.   This evidence was objected to, but was received.   This was proper.   2 Yerger, 60 ; 7 Humph., 544.

This is not a capital case.   The state has shown affirmatively that the juror was not tampered with ; this is sufficient.   8 Humph., 597 ; 7 N. H., 290 ; 4 Cowen, 26 ; 1 Conn., 401 ; 1 Dev. and Batt., 500 ; 1 Blackf., 25.

Handy, J.:

The first, second, and third errors are assigned to the *venire facias* for the grand jury, the return on it, and the oath administered to the grand jury when it was organized in the circuit court. No motion to quash was made, nor plea in abatement filed, presenting any of these objections, but the prisoner appeared and pleaded in bar to the indictment.

The *venire* does not constitute a necessary part of the record, unless some objection has been taken to it in the court below, and it is introduced into the record by bill of exceptions, for the purpose of having its validity examined in this court.   Boyd v. State, 1 How., 253.   Its absence from the record is, therefore, no ground of error.

Nor is it competent for the prisoner to question its sufficiency in this court, when he has raised no objection to it either by motion or plea in abatement, in the court below, but has pleaded in bar, and been convicted.   Brantley v. State, 13 S. and M., 468.

It is also urged, that the court erred in refusing to exclude from the jury the exclamation of the witness Obannion, as to the prisoner having stabbed another person than the party named in 'the indictment.   None of the circumstances connected with that exclamation are set forth in the bill of exceptions.   Nothing appears but the isolated expression, and the bill of exceptions does not show that this was all the testimony of the witness.   Other facts and circumstances might have been stated by the witness necessarily connected with the *res gestæ*, and making the exclamation proper evidence.   Experience shows that witnesses are not unfrequently in the habit of stating much irrelevant matter in giving their testimony, and also, that many things which, taken disconnected from all the facts and circumstances proved by the witness, seem to have no relevancy to the cause, when taken in connection with the whole evidence, have a most important bearing.   In the absence, then, of all other testimony, this court cannot properly determine whether this evidence was improperly admitted, and will presume that the court below acted properly in refusing to exclude it.   Otherwise, it would be in the power of any party on trial, to isolate from the entire evidence any portion of it, seeming, when alone, to be wholly foreign to the *res gestæ*, except to its admission, and have the judgment against him reversed in this court, when, upon the whole evidence, it would appear that the court below acted with perfect propriety.

It is next objected, that after the case had been submitted to the jury, and they had left the bar to retire to their room to deliberate on their verdict, one of them separated for a few minutes from his fellows, and was out of the presence and supervision of the bailiff. This presents a point of much diversity of opinion among the most learned courts of the Union.

On the one hand, it is held to be incumbent on the accused to show something more than the mere separation of the jury to set aside the verdict. This is the rule in New Hampshire, in Connecticut, in North Carolina, and in Indiana. 7 N. H., 290; State v. Babcock, 1 Conn., 401; State v. Miller, 1 Dev. and Batt., 500; Wyatt v. State, 1 Blackf., 25.

On the contrary, it is held in Virginia and in Tennessee, that if the separation was such that the juror might have been improperly influenced by others, it is sufficient ground for setting aside the verdict. Commonwealth v. McCall, 1 Va. Cases, 271; Overbee v. Commonwealth, 1 Rob., 756; 10 Yerger, 241. The reason of this rule seems to be fully sanctioned in Massachusetts, in 12 Pick., 496, and this court has acted in conformity to it. Hare v. State, 4 How., 187; Boles v. State, 13 S. and M., 398.

We are satisfied that this is the sound and safe rule. In dispensing with the ancient rigor in the treatment of juries, which tended to operate coercively on their judgment, the most enlightened courts have ever firmly adhered to the necessity of keeping the jury together. Any departure from this practice, which is not sufficiently explained to exclude the possibility of undue influence in the particular instance, must lead to the greatest uncertainty in the rule, the most unsafe judicial discretion in its application, and the destruction of public confidence in the solemnity of trials by jury. If any separation is to be allowed, without incurring the imputation of irregularity, for what length of time and for what purposes may it be? How frequently may it be practiced, and to what distance may it extend? By what means are communications between the juror and other persons which may take place, and which must necessarily be secret, to be disclosed?

These considerations show the looseness and dangerous uncertainties to which the practice would lead, and the soundness of the rule, that every separation of the juror from his fellows and the bailiff, should be treated as vitiating the verdict, unless it be affirmatively proved by competent evidence that the juror has been guilty of no improper conduct.

This leads us to consider the last question, whether it is proper to admit the juror himself as a witness to prove the propriety of his own conduct.

We think such a practice of the most evil tendency. If there have been corrupt communications between the juror and others, they must from their nature be secret, and, in almost every case, impossible of proof by other testimony. Any juror who would be guilty of corruption, would not scruple to purge his conduct of all suspicion by the most comprehensive swearing, and then the only security for justice would be the right of the judge to examine his credibility; and as there would probably be no evidence to impeach his veracity, and no circumstances going to show that he was tampered with, it would rarely, if ever occur, that the judge would treat his testimony as false. Thus the verdict, however corrupt, is established beyond the possibility of correction.

We think, therefore, that the regularity and purity which should characterize judicial proceedings are best promoted by establishing the rule, which, though rigid, is the more plain and easy of application, that any separation of the juror from the presence of his fellows, and the superintendence of the bailiff, is *prima facie* evidence of irregularity, and that his affidavit is inadmissible to justify his conduct during the separation.

For these reasons, we reverse the judgment, and grant a new trial.

Botto *v.* The State, 26 Miss. Rep., 108.

ILLICIT RETAILING OF INTOXICATING DRINKS.

The law gives to the city of Vicksburg all the fines and license money for retailing vinous and spirituous liquors within the corporate limits. And, therefore, an indictment charging a sale within the county of Warren, is not supported by proof of a sale on a wharf-boat in the city of Vicksburg.

Error to Warren circuit court. BARNETT, J.

The opinion contains the facts of the case.

W. C. & A. K. Smedes, for plaintiff in error.

VOL. I.—44.

Cited Hutch. Code, 271, § 4; ib., 270, § 2; Legori v. State, 8 S. & M., 697.

D. C. Glenn, attorney general.

Fisher, J. :

The defendant below was convicted at the May term, 1853, of the circuit court of Warren county, of retailing spirituous liquors in less quantity than one gallon without a license.

The indictment charges, in general terms, that the retailing was in the county of Warren. The proof shows, that it was on a wharf-boat, in the city of Vicksburg.

Upon this evidence, the jury founded a verdict of guilty, and the court pronounced judgment.

It is true that evidence was introduced on the trial showing that Vicksburg was in the county of Warren. But this, coupled with other evidence, was insufficient to authorize a verdict of guilty. The jury should, in their investigation, have been confined to the issue made by the indictment, that the defendant retailed spirits in the county of Warren, without a license from the Board of Police of said county. He was not required to have such a license to authorize him to retail within the city of Vicksburg. The power to grant the license belonged alone to the city, which was entitled not only to the tax, but also to all fines for a violation of the law within corporate limits.

Under the evidence, the city would be entitled to the fine; but under the indictment upon which the court had to pronounce the judgment, the fine would take a different direction. There was no evidence to sustain either the verdict or judgment in this respect. If the law was violated, it was in the city of Vicksburg; and the indictment should have so charged, and the evidence so established the offense. The indictment was only good, if at all, for an offense committed at some other place in the county of Warren, and the evidence could establish no more than the indictment charged. 8 S. & M., 697.

Judgment reversed, new trial granted, and cause remanded.

STRINGFELLOW *v.* THE STATE, 26 Miss. Rep., 157.

HOMICIDE.

A leading question is one which directly suggests the answer which is desired, or which embodies a material fact and admits of an answer by a simple negative or affirmative, though neither be directly suggested. But if the object of the question is to direct the mind of the witness to what is material; and if it relate to matter merely introductory, it should not be objected to although in form it be leading.

The prisoner's confession, when the *corpus delicti* is not proved *aliunde*, is insufficient to warrant a conviction.[1]

Error to Issaquena circuit court. BARNETT, J.

Richard Stringfellow was indicted in the circuit court of Issaquena county for the murder of Decatur Whitley, and at the November term, 1852, of said court, the accused was found guilty of murder, and sentenced to be hung. The defendant by his counsel, moved the court for a new trial, because of the introduction of illegal testimony by the state, and also for the refusal by the court to give certain instructions asked by the accused on the trial; all of which are fully set out in the opinion of the court.

The court below refused to grant the accused a new trial, when he prayed a writ of error to this court.

F. Anderson and *C. L. Buck* for plaintiff in error.

1. The question and answer embraced in the first bill of exceptions were illegal, because the question was a leading one, and because neither the letter was produced, nor the handwriting of the letter proved. Turney v. State, 8 S. & M., 104.

2. The question objected to, as shown in the third bill of exceptions, was illegally permitted to be asked of the witness, because it was a leading question.

4. The question and answer embraced in the fourth bill of exceptions were illegal for the same reasons, and the additional reason, that the question was intended and calculated to bring out, and did bring out in answer, hearsay evidence; and it also assumed as proved what was not proved, and what the witness did not know, namely the death of Decatur Whitley. Turney v. State, 8 S. & M., 104.

5. The venue was not proved by competent evidence.

1 Pitts v. State, 43rd Miss., 472.

6. The court erred in the instructions given and refused, as the following authorities show :—1 Greenl. Ev., 261 ; 2 Phil. Ev., 232, n. 203 ; ib., 234, n. 204 ; Guild v. State, 5 Hals. R., 185 ; 2 Stark. Ev., (Tit. " Murder,") 509 ; 3 Greenl. Ev., 121 ; State v. Long, 1 Hayw. R., 524 ; 2 Hale, Pl. Cr., 290 ; 5 Humph., 383 ; 1 South., 231 ; 2 Russ. Cr. (last ed.), 824.

D. C. Glenn, attorney general.

I only refer the court to the following cases on the points presented :

1. For questions objected to as leading, see 1 Greenl. Ev., §§ 434, 435, 447.

2. For proof of venue, see Coon v. State, 13 S. & M., 246 ; 1 Greenl. Ev., §§ 100, 101, 103, 106, 128.

3. For weight of confessions generally, Whart. Am. Cr. Law, 253 and note ; 1 Greenl., §§ 214, 215.

4. For proof of *corpus delicti*, 3 Greenl. Ev., § 30 ; ib., 181.

5. For sufficiency of confession to convict of homicide, without corroborating circumstances, Cowan's case, 7 Ired., 239 ; Henry's case, 2 Dev. & Batt., 396 ; Weir's case, 1 Dev., 363.

6. The court will not interfere with the action of the jury, unless flagrantly wrong. McCann v. State, 13 S. & M., 476 ; Nelms v. State, ib., 500 ; Cicely v. State, ib., 202.

SMITH, C. J. :

The plaintiff in error was indicted and tried in the circuit court of Issaquena county, and convicted of the murder of Decatur Whitley. The bill of exceptions filed to the decision of the court overruling the motion for a new trial embodies the whole of the evidence submitted to the jury. Several exceptions were taken to the rule of the court in reference to the admission of evidence on the trial. The charges of the court, and its refusal to instruct the jury as requested by the counsel for the plaintiff in error, are made the grounds of exception. The bills of exception filed to these various acts of the court present the questions which it becomes our duty to examine and decide. The questions arising upon the introduction of evidence naturally present themselves first for our consideration.

During the examination in chief of a witness called on the

part of the prosecution, the following question was propounded by the prosecuting attorney : " Did you ever receive a letter purporting to be from Decatur Whitley, and if so, at what place was it written and dated, where postmarked, and when did you receive it ?" To which the prisoner's counsel objected, without stating the ground of objection. The court disallowed the exception, and permitted the witness to answer. The witness answered as follows, to wit: That he had received a letter purporting to have been written by Whitley. It was postmarked at Ashton, and was dated on the inside from the island of Bunch's Bend Cut-off. That he did not remember the date of the letter. It was received by him about three weeks before he came to Mississippi, in the latter part of October or the first of November. The answer was excepted to, but the objection was overruled, and it was permitted to go to the jury.

It is now insisted that the question was a leading one, and the answer thereto illegal and incompetent evidence.

A leading question has been defined to be one which directly suggests the answer which is desired, or which embodies a material fact and admits of an answer by a simple negative or affirmative, though neither the one nor the other be suggested.[1] 2 Phil. Ev., 401 ; 1 Greenl. Ev., 434-5-6-7. But in the examination of a witness, if the object be to direct his mind with the more expedition, to what is material, and if the question propounded relate merely to introductory matter, it should not be objected to, although in form it be leading. Hence, it is not unfrequently a matter of great difficulty to distinguish between those questions which are not to be tolerated because they are leading, and those which are such in form, but in effect are only calculated to lead the mind of the witness to the subject of in-

1 Snyder v. Snyder, 6 Binn., 483; Harrison v. Rowan, 8 Wash., 580; Parkin v. Moon, 7 C. & P., 408; Alison's Practice, 545; Tait on Ev., 427; Turney v. State, 8 S. & M., 104; Roscoe Cr. Ev., 130; Kemmerrer v. Edelman, 11 Harris, 143; Wilson v. McCullough, ib., 440; Lee v. Tinges, 7 Maryland, 215; Sexton v. Brock, 15 Ark., 345; Willis v. Quinsby, 11 Foster, 485; Bartlet v. Hoyt, 33 N. H., 151; Floyd v. State, 30 Ala., 511; Mathis v. Buford, 17 Tex., 152; Hofler v. State, 16 Ark., 534; Spear v. Richardson, 37 N. H., 23; Dudley v. Elkins, 39 N. H., 78; Allen v. State, 38 Ga., 395; Page v. Parker, 40 N. H., 47; Pelamourgis v. Clark, 9 Iowa, 1; Shields v. Guffey, 1 ib., 522; Hopper v. Commonwealth, 6 Grattan, 684; Roscoe Nisi Prius Ev., 171; 2 Russ. on Cr., 913; Nicholls v. Dowding & Kemp, 1 Stark N. P. C., 81; 2 Eng. C. L. R., 305; People v. Mather, 4 Wend., 231; 1 Archbold Cr. Pr. & Pl. 577; Peake's Ev., 196.

quiry. So in the case under consideration, if the question be determined by the test above laid down, it is, at least, very doubtful whether it should be held objectionable on the ground that it is leading; but if tried by the principle recognized in Turney v. State, 8 S. & M., 104, it would seem exceptionable on that account. In that case, after a witness, who had previously testified that about the 1st of December, 1854, the defendant had committed a rape upon her, she was asked, on her examination in chief, by the district attorney, " If the defendant then, or at any subsequent time, said anything in relation to this matter, to dissuade you from disclosing it? State when, and where, and what he said." Again. " If defendant, in any of his antecedent conversations, offered property or any other advancement to you, in order to attach you to him, say so." And again the witness was asked, " If any time subsequent to this transaction, the defendant said anything about what punishment the laws of Mississippi would inflict on him or you, or both? State all." These questions were, after mature deliberation, held by a majority of this court to be leading; and because they were permitted to be propounded to the witness, the judgment of the circuit court was reversed. It is obvious that if these were leading questions, the one under consideration was improper.

The following questions, set out in the second and fourth bills of exception, are objected to on the same grounds, to wit: 1. " If he (witness) was induced to leave Alabama and go to Mississippi by reason of a letter received from Decatur Whitley?" 2. " Did you carry property from Bunch's Bend in Issaquena county, as the property of Decatur Whitley, deceased?" The answers to these questions are set out in the bills of exception, and are objected to as illegal and incompetent testimony.

It is obvious that the latter question was illegal. No direct evidence had been adduced to prove that a homicide had been committed upon the person of Decatur Whitley, or that the killing occurred within the county of Issaquena. If the prosecution failed to establish either of these facts, the acquittal of the prisoner would necessarily ensue. It was therefore indispensable to prove, not only that Whitley was dead, but that he had been killed in the county of Issaquena. If it could be proved that Whitley had been murdered, and that about the alleged time of the murder he was in the county of Issaquena, the jury might infer that the deed was there perpetrated. If the fact that the witness had carried property, as the property of the deceased, from that place to Alabama, conduced to prove that he was at the time alleged in that county, the question was clearly leading, and it was particularly objectionable because it assumed a fact not proven, that is, the death of Whitley.

Another and a more serious objection to the first and last questions which we have been considering, arises when they are looked at in a different point of view. The matter intended to be extracted by these questions was irrelevant, and therefore incompetent evidence in the cause. By the first question, the witness is asked if he had ever received a letter purporting to be from Decatur Whitley? If so, at what place was it dated, and where postmarked? Supposing the witness to state, as in fact he did, that he had received a letter purporting to be from Whitley, and that it was dated at the place and near the time when the alleged homicide occurred, it will certainly not be contended that such an answer was competent evidence. If it were admitted to have been competent to give parol evidence of the contents of the letter, without first proving that it was in the handwriting of Whitley, or accounting for its non-production, the answer of the witness would not ascend upon the roll of testimony, even to the dignity of hearsay evidence. But let it be assumed that the letter was proved to be in the handwriting of Whitley, and that it was dated from the island of Bunch's Bend Cut-off. Upon such admission, a fact would be established from which the jury might legitimately have drawn the conclusion that the letter was in point of fact written by Whitley whilst upon the island; but it could not certainly warrant the presumption that he was there at any other point of time, and more especially at the date of the alleged murder. If the fact had been conclusively proved, by direct evidence, that Whitley was, within some short time before the alleged homicide, upon the island, the presumption might have been feebly indulged that he remained there until its occurrence. But to make the answer of the witness, assuming that the letter was in the handwriting of Whitley, conduce to prove the question at issue, it would be essential to base the latter presumption, that is, that Whitley was in fact upon the island at the time when the alleged homicide was committed, upon the presumption that he was upon the island at the date of the letter, inferred from the fact that the witness had received a letter in the hand-writing of Whitley, bearing date at the island. This would certainly be extending the doctrine of presumptions beyond the limits recognized by either reason or authority.

The same observations are applicable, to some extent, to the last question and answer. The fact that the witness had carried property from Bunch's Bend in Issaquena county to Alabama, as the property of Decatur Whitley, deceased, might constitute the basis of a presumption, that the property so transported was, in truth, the property of the deceased, but it could not warrant the inference that Whitley was ever in the county, not having been otherwise proved to have been there, much less could it, upon any principle of law, or logic, sustain the conclusion, that he was there at the date of the alleged murder.

The questions which come next in order, arise upon the exceptions taken to the instructions of the court.

On the part of the defense the court was requested to instruct the jury as follows, to wit: 1. "Although the jury may believe from the evidence in the cause, that the prisoner confessed to the negro King that he had killed Decatur Whitley, yet if that confession is unsupported by other proof that said Whitley was killed, they must find the prisoner not guilty." 2. "That the best evidence that Decatur Whitley was killed, is the testimony of some one who saw him when killed, or who has seen his dead body; and unless the jury believe, from the testimony in the case, that some one who has testified before them saw Whitley killed, or his dead body, they will find the defendant not guilty." These instructions were disallowed by the court.

The court was further requested to instruct the jury, 1. "That if they believe from the evidence that the prisoner made any confessions or admissions of guilt, such confessions or admissions are to be received by them with great caution, and, unless supported by other proof in the cause, are not sufficient to convict."

This charge the court refused to give; but gave the following as a modification of it, to wit: "That if the jury believe from the evidence that the prisoner made any confessions or admissions of guilt, such confessions or admissions are to be received by them with great caution, and unless fully believed by the jury, are not sufficient to convict." 2. "That before the jury can convict the defendant, it must be proved conclusively that Decatur Whitley was killed, and that the extrajudicial confessions or admissions of defendant that he killed him, unless supported by other proofs in the cause, are not sufficient to convict." This instruction the court also refused to give; but gave the following as a modification thereof, to wit: "That before the jury can convict, it must be proved conclusively that Decatur Whitley was killed, and that the extrajudicial confessions or admissions of defendant that he killed him, ought to be weighed by the jury with great caution, and unless sufficient to satisfy them that Whitley was killed, and by defendant, they ought to acquit."

Without pausing to consider the minor objections which were urged against these instructions, we will at once proceed to the examination of the main question which they present; that is, Whether the extra judicial confessions of a prisoner charged with a capital felony is sufficient, without any proof whatever, independent of the confession of the *corpus delicti*, to authorize a verdict of guilty?

It is well settled by the law of England, that a voluntary and unsuspected confession of guilt, whether made in the course of conversation with private individuals, or under examination before a magistrate, is clearly sufficient to warrant a conviction whenever there is independent proof of the *corpus delicti*.[1] Will. Circum. Ev., 61. According to some elementary writers,

[1] 5 Halstead, N. J. R., 163, 185; Haywood, 455, 524; 1 Greenl. Ev., 217–219, 220; 3 ib., 30; Rex v. Benditt, 4 B. & Ald., 123; Pitts v. State, 43 Miss., 472; Bergen v. People, 17 Ills., 427; 3 Parker Cr. R., 401; 2 Hawk. P. C., ch. 46, § 18; Brown v. State, 32 Miss., 433; 1 Leach Cr. Law, 311; 1 Phill. Ev., 532; Brown v. State, 33 Miss., 433; Tyner v. ——, 5 Humphreys, 383; Roscoe Cr. Evi., 38, *et seq.*; People v. Hennesey, 15 Wend., 147; Keithler v. State, 14 S. & M., 192; Stephen v. State, 11 Ga., 225; People v. Badgeley, 16 Wend., 63; State v. Fields, Peck Rep., 140; State v. Gardiner, Wright, 392; 1 Archbold Cr. Pr. & Pl., 406; Roscoe Cr. Ev., 29. See Russ. on Cr., 825; Wharton's Am. Cr. Law, 683; Burrill on Circ. Ev., 498, 499; Rex v. Eldridge, Russ. & Ry., 440.

confession a'one is sufficient to warrant conviction, without any such evidence. By Russell, in his Treatise on Crimes, it is said, that such confessions are admissible in evidence as the highest and most satisfactory proof, because it is fairly to be presumed, that no man would make such a confession against himself if the facts confessed are not true. And that the first authorities have now established that a confession, if duly made and satisfactorily proved, is sufficient alone, without any corroborating evidence *aliunde*, to warrant a conviction. 2 Russ. on Cr., 824. The text in Roscoe's work on Criminal Evidence is to the same effect (p. 28). Foster and Blackstone maintained a different opinion; the latter holding that confessions, even in cases of felony at common law, were the weakest and most suspicious of all testimony, very liable to be obtained by artifice, false hopes, promises of favor or menaces, seldom remembered accurately, or reported with precision, and incapable, in their nature, of being disproved by other negative testimony. 4 Bl. Com., 357.

The cases cited in support of the text in Roscoe and Russell, are, Wheeling's case, 1 Leach, 311; Eldridge's case, Faulkner's case, White's case, and the case of King v. Tippet, reported in Russ. & Ry. Upon examination it will be found, that in each of these cases, with the exception of that of Wheeling's, there was, independent of the confession, some corroborating circumstance which tended to prove the commission of a felony. Russ. on Cr., 834 (n. b); 1 Greenl. Ev., 279, n. In reference to Wheeling's case, it is observed in Greenleaf's Evidence, that "it is too briefly reported to be relied on." The whole statement of that case in 1 Leach, 311, is, that "it was determined that a prisoner may be convicted on his own confession, when proved by legal testimony, although it is totally uncorroborated by any other evidence." It is manifest that this statement may mean, that where the commission of a felony is proved by evidence *aliunde*, a prisoner may be convicted on his confession, notwithstanding there be nothing to corroborate his confession as to his agency in the commission of the felony. It does not, therefore, appear that it has ever been expressly decided that the naked confession of a prisoner alone, and without any other evidence, is sufficient to authorize a jury to convict.

In the valuable treatise on circumstantial evidence, the author, commenting on this subject, and referring to the cases cited by Russell and Roscoe, observes, " that, according to some authorities, confession alone is a sufficient ground for conviction, even in the absence of any such independent evidence (that is evidence tending to establish the *corpus delicti*); but the contrary opinion is most in accordance with the general opinions of reason, justice and humanity, the opinion of the best writers on criminal jurisprudence, and the practice of their enlightened nations. Nor are the causes adduced in support of the doctrine in question very decisive, since in all of them there appears to have been some evidence, though slight, of confirmatory circumstances, independently of the confession."

In the United States, the very few adjudicated cases on the question under consideration, are not harmonious. In the State of North Carolina, State v. Cowan, 7 Ired., 239, it was decided, that a prisoner may be convicted on his own unbiassed confession without corroborative evidence establishing a felony. The supreme court of the State of New Jersey appears to have adopted the contrary doctrine, and to have held that the naked confession of the prisoner was not sufficient to justify a verdict of guilty. State v. Aaron, 1 South., 231 ; Guild's case, 5 Hal., 163.

This question is one of the first impression in this court, and its importance has induced us to bestow upon it the greatest deliberation which circumstances would permit. We believe the doctrine which holds that, in capital felonies, the prisoner's confession, when the *corpus delicti* is not proved by independent testimony, is insufficient for his conviction, best accords with the solid principles of reason, and the caution which should be applied in the admission and estimate of this species of evidence. We hold, therefore, that the court erred in refusing to instruct the jury, that the extra-judicial confession of a prisoner, without proof *aliunde* of the commission of a felony, and of the death, was insufficient to warrant his conviction.

As we reverse the judgment for the errors already noticed, it will be unnecessary to examine the remaining exceptions.

LAURA *v.* THE STATE, 26 Miss. Rep., 174.

CONSPIRACY.

The doctrine of merger does not apply to the offense of conspiracy of slaves to murder a white person. Nor was the statute (Hutch. Digest., 983, § 21) which declares "that no person shall be convicted of an assault with intent to commit a crime, or any other attempt to commit an offense, when it shall appear that the crime intended, or the offense attempted, was perpetrated at the time of such assault, or in pursuance of such attempt," designed to apply to this class of cases.

No fact which enters into the essence of the offense, save that of criminal intention, can properly be denominated an assault with intent to commit a crime. It is a separate, distinct offense created and defined by statute.

No person can be subjected to punishment for any offense, unless a conviction be had upon an indictment found by a grand jury of the county in which the offense was committed.

In regard to matters which, by law, should appear in the record, no presumption can be indulged which would either contradict the record or supply a defect. Therefore the record must show that the indictment was regularly-found and returned into court, according to law.

Error to De Soto circuit court. MILLER, J.

The plaintiff in error, a slave, was indicted in the court below for conspiracy and plotting, with two other slaves, the murder of John D. Watkins, and was convicted and sentenced to death.

The record contained a copy of the indictment, but it was not referred to as the one upon which the conviction was had, nor did it identify the indictment as a copy of the one returned into court by the grand jury that indicted the prisoner. A motion was made for a new trial but refused by the court below, and the prisoner sued out this writ of error.

T. W. White, for plaintiff in error,

D. C. Glenn, attorney general.

SMITH, C. J.:

This was a conviction in the circuit court of De Soto upon an indictment framed under the statute concerning slaves, free negroes, and mulattoes. Hutch. Dig., 520.

The following objections are taken to the judgment of the court below, to wit:

1. The record does not show that the indictment on which the prisoner was tried and convicted, was returned into court by the grand jury.

2. The court erred in not quashing the indictment.

3. The court erred in not granting a new trial; and

4. That the court improperly overruled the motion in arrest of judgment.

The second objection is untenable for the reason assigned. There is no ambiguity or uncertainty in the averment charging the prisoner with a conspiracy to murder a free white man.

Nor do we think the fourth exception well taken. It is our opinion that the doctrine of merger does not apply to the offense of which the prisoner was convicted. And further, we think the provisions of the 21st section of the statute (Hutch. Dig., 988) which declare " that no person shall be convicted of an assault with intent to commit a crime, or any other attempt to commit an offense, when it shall appear that the crime intended or the offense attempted was perpetrated by the accused person at the time of such assault or in pursuance of such attempt," were not designed to be applied to cases like the one under consideration.

The offense charged in the indictment was neither an assault to commit a crime nor any other attempt to commit an offense. The prisoner was charged with conspiring to murder a free white man. That offense is complete, whenever the acts which constitute it have been performed by the party. No fact which enters into the essence of the offense, save that of criminal intention, can be properly denominated an assault with intent to commit a crime or an attempt to commit an offense. It is a separate, distinct and independent offense, created and defined by statute.

The reason, moreover, fails when the act is applied to a slave charged with an assault with intent to commit murder upon a free white person ; as a bare assault of that character, committed by a slave, is visited with the highest punishment known to the law. In the case of a free white person, the reason upon which the rule was founded is obvious. In case of the conviction of a white person for an assault, with the intention of murdering the party assaulted, the punishment is by confinement in the penitentiary, whereas the consummation of the design, by the party making the assault, would subject him to capital punishment.

It is unnecessary to notice the exception taken to the decision on the motion for a new trial. We will therefore proceed in the last place to notice the first error assigned.

No person can be subjected to punishment for any offense, unless a conviction be had upon an indictment found by a grand jury of the county in which the offense was committed.

The record before us contains no statement which shows, directly and positively, that the indictment under which the trial took place was found and returned into court. This, it is indispensable, the record should show by a distinct statement which establishes the identity of the indictment found by the grand jury with that which is contained in the record. In the case before us this is a question left by the record to be decided by inference. From the known and settled practice of the courts, and the presumption that, in all cases where it is a matter of presumption, their proceedings are regular, we might infer that the indictment in the record was, in fact, found and returned into court by the jury. But in regard to matters which, by law, should appear in the record, no presumption can be indulged which would either contradict the record or supply a defect.

As much as we regret the impunity of crime, arising from the neglect or incapacity of persons engaged in the administration of the law, and as little as we feel disposed to regard objections to form, we are nevertheless bound in cases which, like the present, are of a highly penal character, to enforce with strictness the rules which the laws of the state have imposed.

Let the judgment be reversed, the indictment quashed, and the prisoner remanded to await the future action of the circuit court of De Soto county.

JONES *v.* THE STATE, 26 Miss. Rep., 247.

LARCENY.

No definite length of time after loss of goods and before possession shown in the accused, seems to be settled, as raising a presumption of guilt. Where the goods are bulky, or inconvenient of transmission, a greater lapse of time is allowed to raise the presumption of guilt, than if they were light and easily conveyed.

In prosecution for larceny of a saddle or the like, after the lapse of nearly a year, the mere fact that the chattels were found in the possession of the accused, creates no presumption of guilt, and such possession without evidence *aliunde* to establish the charge is not sufficient to put the accused on his defense.

Error to Lauderdale circuit court. WATTS, J.

William Jones, the accused, was indicted in the circuit court of Lauderdale county, for stealing a saddle, the property of William C. Burton. It was proven that the saddle was found in the house of Elijah C. Jones, some time in May, 1853, but it had been taken from the shop of Burton, in December, 1852, and it was proven that William Jones, the accused, brought the saddle to the house of E. C. Jones in the month of July or August, 1852.

The defendant proved that he was an honest man, and had heretofore sustained a good reputation in the community where he lived. The defendant, on the trial of the case, asked the court to give the jury the following instructions, which were refused:

1st. "That the possession of the thing stolen must be shown to be in the defendant shortly after the taking; and if the state has not shown that the defendant had possession of the saddle until four or five months after the taking of the saddle, such possession does not raise any presumption of the guilt of the defendant having the saddle in possession in August, 1852."

4th. "To raise a presumption of guilt of the defendant, from the fact of the property being found in his possession, it must have been so recently after the taking from the owner; and if the jury believe from the evidence, that the saddle was not found in the possession of defendant until four months or more after the taking, such possession does not raise any presumption of the guilt of the defendant whereon to find a conviction."

The defendant excepted to the refusal of the court to give the above instructions. The jury found the defendant guilty, as charged in the indictment; and having moved the court for a new trial, which was refused, the defendant prayed a writ of error to this court.

Chandler & Baldwin, for plaintiff in error.

D. C. Glenn, attorney general.

HANDY, J. :

Apart from the testimony of the witness, Sarah Jones, the only proof of the larceny in this case consists of the evidence that the article lost was found in the possession of the accused. That witness, it is true, states that the accused brought the article to the house where he resided. But she proves that this took place several months before the property is proved to have been lost by the owner; and if her testimony could have any weight, it must have produced an acquittal.

The evidence shows that the goods were not found in the possession of the accused until the lapse of five or six months after the taking; and the question here presented, is, whether such possession, found after such a lapse of time, of itself raises a presumption in law of a felonious taking by the accused.

No definite length of time, after loss of goods and before possession shown in the accused, seems to be settled, as raising a presumption of guilt. Where the goods are bulky, or inconvenient of transmission, or unlikely to be transferred, it seems that a greater lapse of time is allowed to raise the presumption than when they are light and easy to pass from hand to hand, and likely to be so passed; because, in the one case, the goods may not have passed through many hands, and the proof to justify the possession may, therefore, be more simple and easy; but in the latter case, the goods may, very probably, have come to the accused through many persons, and their transit, from the smallness of their nature and value, be much more difficult to be proved.[1] Roscoe Crim. Ev., 18; 3 Greenl. Ev., § 32.

Yet, all the cases hold that the possession must be recent after the loss, in order to impute guilt; and this presumption is founded on the manifest reason, that, where goods have been taken

---

[1] Rex v. Partridge, 7 C. & P., 551; State v. Bennett, 3 Brevard, 514; Comst., 693; Cocklin's case, 2 Lewin C. C., 235; State v. Jones, 8 Dev. & Batt., 112; Rex v. Adams 3 C. & P., 600; Hall's case, 1 Cox C. C., 231; Regina v. Cruttenden, 6 Jur., 267; Anon, 7 Monthly Law Mag., 58; 2 Russell on Crimes, 123, 124, 125; 2 East P. C., 656; 1 Phill. on Ev., 168; 2 Hale, 289; 2 C. & P., 459; State v. Iredell, 9 Iredell, 140; Warren v. State, 1 Iowa R., 106; State v. Floyd, 15 Mo., 349; Archbold Cr. Pr. & Pl., 397, *et seq.*; 4 Stark. Ev., 841; Wharton Am. Cr. Law, 728; Bishop Cr. Procedure, 696, *et seq.*; Hughes v. State, 8 Humph., 75; Hall v. State, 8 Ind., 439.

from one person and are quickly thereafter found in the possession of another, there is a strong probability that they were taken by the latter. This probability is stronger or weaker in proportion to the period intervening between the taking and the finding; or it may be entirely removed by the lapse of such time as to render it not improbable that the goods may have been taken by another and passed to the accused, and thus wholly destroy the presumption.

In prosecutions for larceny of chattels like that in this case, it has been well held, that after the lapse of such a period of time as in this case, the mere fact that the chattels were found in the possession of the accused, created no presumption of criminality; and that such possession, without other evidence of any kind to establish the charge, is not even sufficient to put the party on his defense.[1] Rex v. Adams, 3 C. & P., 600; 3 Greenl. Ev., § 32; State v. Williams, 9 N. C., 140.

We recognize the soundness of this rule, and accordingly are of opinion that the first and fourth instructions, asked on the part of the accused, should have been granted.

The judgment is, therefore, reversed, and a new trial awarded.

McCARTY v. THE STATE, 26 Miss. Rep., 299.

HOMICIDE.

It is not necessary that the record should set out the oath prescribed to the jury.[2] Dyson v. State, 26 Miss., 362.

If the record show that an "officer was sworn to take charge of the jury," it is sufficient.[2] Dyson v. State, 26 Miss., 362.

Where the organization of the court at the term the trial took place is fully shown by the caption of the record, it is not necessary to show the caption of a previous one.

The name of the same juror appearing twice on the *venire*, without any collusion or improper design, and without any injury shown to have been done the prisoner by it, is no ground of error.

The regular *venire* is a matter of record, accessible to the accused, and he is not entitled to a copy of it. But by the statute, he is entitled to a copy of the special *venire*.

[1] See note 1 p. 704 *supra*.

[2] The first two points decided in this case are more fully discussed in the case of Dyson, 26 Miss. R., 362. *Infra*, p. 710.

It is the duty of the court to see that a competent, fair and impartial jury is empanelled, and nothing can interfere with this duty but the right of the parties of peremptory challenge, or of challenge for cause good and sufficient in law, to be judged of by the court.

The high court of errors and appeals will give no countenance to objections to the grand jury, when no complaint was made in the court below, and the accused submitted himself to trial, and was convicted.

If a party be present with the intention of giving assistance, if necessary, in the killing, he would be an aider and abettor, and a principal in the second degree, though his assistance might not be called into actual requisition. Presence and intention to aid in killing amount to participation.

Error to Warren circuit court. BARNETT J.

Alexander McCarty was indicted, together with several others, in the circuit court of Warren county, for the murder of William McCay, and on the 11th day of June, 1853, he was convicted of manslaughter in the first degree, and sentenced by the court to twenty years' imprisonment in the penitentiary of the state.

The defendant made a motion for a new trial, assigning various grounds, which are stated in the opinion of the court. The first instruction given to the jury, to which the defendant excepted at the time, as well as a sufficient statement of the facts of the case, are set forth in the opinion of the court. The motion for a new trial was overruled, and the defendant prayed a writ of error to this court.

Anderson & Buck, for plaintiff in error.

The oath administered to the jury, namely, "The truth to speak in and upon the premises," was illegal, and the verdict was therefore void. 1 Chit. Cr. L., 551; Pile v. State, 5 Ala., 72; Jones v. State, 5 ib., 666; 1 How. 215; Arthur v. State, 3 Tex; 2 Eng. 59; 1 Green, 106.

The record shows what judge presided when the prisoner was indicted. 5 How. 20; 1 Chit. Cr. L. 331.

The record shows that the jury were permitted to retire during the progress of the cause, under charge of an officer sworn only "to take charge of the jury." That was error. 2 Hale, P. C., 296; 1 Chit. Cr. L., 632; 8 Leigh, 745; 8 S. & M., 587; 9 ib., 465; Boles v. State, 13 ib.; 2 Comst., 373; 11 Johns., 442; 2 Blackf., 475; 4 How., 187; 12 Pick., 496.

D. C. Glenn, attorney general.

HANDY, J.:

The errors assigned in this cause are as follows :

1. That an improper oath was administered to the jury.

2. That the record does not show what judge presided when the prisoner was indicted.

3. That the record shows that the jury, on their retirement, were under the charge of an officer who was merely " sworn to take charge of them."

4. That the trial should have been suspended on prisoner's motion, because one of the jurors on the special *venire* was twice named therein.

5. It was error to require the juror Lum to be tendered to the prisoner, after he had been challenged for cause by the state, the prisoner not objecting.

6. That prisoner was entitled to regular service of a list of the panel of regular petit jurors, after the special *venire* was exhausted.

7. It does not appear by the record that the grand jurors who found the indictment were competent jurors.

8. That the first instruction asked by the state is erroneous.

The first and third grounds of error have been disposed of, and held to be untenable, in the case of Dyson *v.* State,[1] at this term.

The second ground of error we do not think well taken. The circuit court for each county of the state is a tribunal established by law, and can be held only by the judge properly assigned to the circuit to which the county belongs, unless under special circumstances which constitute an exception, and which, if they exist, must appear on record. If the record states that a circuit court was held at the time and place appointed by law, in and for the particular county, it could only be held by the appropriate judge, and this must be judicially known and considered by this court, unless something varying the regular course of that court is shown. A different rule may be possibly applicable to courts of special and limited jurisdiction. We think it therefore questionable whether the organization of the court, even as it appears in the caption of the indictment, is not suffi-

[1] 26 Miss. R., 362, *infra*, p. 710.

cient. But, under the statements of the record in this case, the organization of the court is fully shown by the caption to the record, and it is not necessary that the caption to the record of a previous term should be shown.

As to the *venire facias* containing the name of the same juror twice, it does not appear that any prejudice was occasioned to the prisoner by it, or but that it was the mere mistake and inadvertence of the sheriff, without any collusion or improper design, and without any real injury shown to the prisoner. Under such circumstances, a mere informality of such a character is not ground of error. 12 East R., 230;[1] 7 Wend., 417; Whart. Am. Cr. Law, 923.

Nor do we think that the prisoner was entitled to a copy of the names of the regular *venire*, after the exhaustion of the special *venire*. The regular *venire* was a matter of record, and entirely accessible to any one interested in the proceedings of the court, and therefore bound to be taken notice of for all legal purposes. The statute goes no further than to give the accused the right to a copy of the special *venire*, doubtless upon the supposition that a sufficient number of jurors would be ordered to enable the parties to select the jury. To extend the right of special notice further would be to give a right which the statute had not given, and which, by its silence, cannot be presumed to have intended to be given. It would be without the sanction of law, and lead to the greatest delays in trials, as the same right might, with equal reason, be claimed as to all talesmen, and thus all law and justice be defeated.

The objection to the juror Lum is equally untenable. When a juror is objected to for cause, it is the duty of the court, under

---

[1] Wharton Am. Cr. Law, 3218; Mix v. Woodward, 12 Conn., 262; Cole v. Perry, 6 Cowen, 584; 4 Barn. & Ald., 430; 5 Cowen, 289; 7 Cowen, 282; 2 Graham & Waterman N. T., 153; State v. Lamon, 3 Hawks, 175; 1 Archbold Cr. Pr. & Pl., 621, 622, 623. Mistakes or omissions in empanelling jurors, where such mistakes and omissions have no tendency to injuriously affect the interests of the accused, are no ground for a new trial. Com. v. Roby, 12 Pick., 496; People v. Vermilyea, 7 Cow., 382; U. S. v. Gilbert, 2 Sumner, 19; King v. Hart, 4 Barn. & Ald., 430; People v. Ransom, 7 Wend., 417; State v. Hascell, 4 N. H., 352; Com. v. Norfolk, 5 Mass., 435; State v. Underwood, 4 Iredell, 96; People v. Griffin, 2 Barb. S. C., 427; Fenalty v. State, 7 Eng., 630; State v. Lyttle, 5 Iredell, 58; Benton's case, 2 Dev. & Bat., 196; U. S. v. Cornell, 2 Mason, 91. When, however, the irregularity affects the verdict against the accused, a new trial will be granted. State v. Powell, 2 Halst., 244. See 2 Graham & Waterman N. T., 159, *et seq.*

the practice which obtains in this state, and in many other states of the Union, to examine into the sufficiency of the objection, and this, whether the adverse party consents to the objection or not; for otherwise, however insufficient the cause alleged might be, it would be the duty of the court to reject the juror. If a party challenge a juror for cause altogether immaterial, as that he were a planter or a mechanic, a rich or a poor man, the adverse party assenting, it would be the duty of the court to set aside the juror as incompetent, under the position here urged. This places the empanelling the jury altogether in the hands of the parties to the suit, who, by equal reason, might consent to place the most palpably illegal men upon the jury. But the argument is fallacious. It is the duty of the court to see that a competent, fair, and impartial jury is empanelled, and nothing can interfere with this duty but the right of the parties of peremptory challenge, or of challenge for cause good and sufficient in law, to be judged of by the court.

As to the objection to the sufficiency of the grand jury, we do not think it valid. But even if it would be when properly taken, this court will give no countenance to such objection, when no complaint was made of it in the court below, and the accused submitted himself to trial, and was fairly tried and convicted. Such is the settled rule established by this court. Brantley's case, 13 S. & M.; 3 How., 432; Organ v. State, at this term.

The last objection is to the first instruction granted at the instance of the state, as follows: "That if the defendant was present at the time of the killing of deceased, with the intention to aid and abet in the murder of deceased, they must find him guilty as charged in the indictment."

This instruction is clearly sound law, as a general rule, and it is not pretended that the evidence did not justify it in this case. It is said, that the presence of the accused at the killing of the deceased with the intention to aid and abet in murdering him, and he was murdered, would not make the accused a principal in the second degree; that it requires participation to constitute such character. If by this it is meant that there must be an actual part taken by the accused in the fact of killing, it is not supported by reason or authority. If a party be present, with the intention to give assistance, if necessary, in the killing, he would be an aider and abettor, and a principal in the second degree, though his assistance might not be called into requisition; because he would give encouragement to the deed. Presence and intention to aid in the killing have, therefore, very justly been held to amount to participation.[1] Arch. Cr. Pl. and Ev., 4; Rex v. Borthwick, Dougl., 207; Commonwealth v. Knapp, 9 Pick., 496; 1 Russ. Cr., 26, 27; Whart. Am. Cr. L., 28, (1st ed.)

We are of opinion, that there is no error in the record, and that the judgment should be affirmed.

A petition for re-argument was filed by the plaintiff in error in this case, but the court refused to grant it.

DYSON *v.* THE STATE, 26 Miss. Rep., 362.

HOMICIDE.

The record, in criminal cases, must show that the jury were sworn, but it need not set out the form of the oath prescribed to them by the court, McCarty v. State, 26 Miss., 299; and if the swearing of the jury is improper in any respect, it must be made a part of the record by bill of exceptions. But where the oath is set out and is incorrect the verdict will be set aside.

Until the contrary appear, it will be presumed that the jury were sworn according to law.

The statement in the record that the jury "were sworn the truth to speak in the issue joined," is sufficient to show that they were sworn according to law.

If evidence is proposed, which, of itself, appears irrelevant to the issue on trial, and is objected to, the party offering it is bound to show its relevancy either by explanation to the court as to its bearing on the case, or by introducing other evidence connecting it with the *res gestæ*, and opening the door to its admission.

Bare fear of danger or great bodily harm, unaccompanied by any overt act indicating a present intention to kill or injure, will not warrant a person in killing another. There must be actual danger at the time. There must be an overt act on the part of the deceased to carry out his threats to warrant his killing, or the danger of such design must be imminent, pressing and unavoidable.

The acts of public officers, especially judicial tribunals acting within their jurisdiction, are valid, and done rightly until the contrary is proven.

[1] Archbold Cr. Pr. & Pl., 62, 63; State v. Hardin, 2 Dev. & Batt., 407; State v. Town, Wright (Ohio) R., 75; State v. Coleman, 5 Porter, 32; Brennnan v. People, 15 Ill., 511; Foster, 350; 2 Hawk. P. C., c. 29, §§ 7, 8; Reg. v. Howell, 9 C. & P., 437; Rex v. Hargraves, 5 Car. & P., 170; 1 Hale, 439; Connaughty v. State, 1 Wisc., 189; Wharton Am. Cr. Law, 116, *et seq.*; Rex v. Moyre, 1 Leach, 314; Rex v. Borthwick, 1 Doug., 207; 1 Leach, 66; 1 Russ., 31; 1 Hale, 155; Rex v. Goggerly, Russ. & Ryan C. C., 343; Rex v. Owen, 1 Moody C. C., 96.

The high court of errors and appeals will not take cognizance of points not presented in the court below; [1] and the rule applies with greater force where the point is one of fact, and was raised and abandoned.

Every fact incidental to the proceedings in the circuit court, not required by law to be incorporated in the record must be presumed to have been properly done.

Error to Panola circuit court. MILLER, J.

James H. Dyson was indicted in the circuit court of Panola county for killing Samuel H. Nelms, and was found guilty of manslaughter in the first degree, and sentenced to fifteen years' imprisonment in the state penitentiary. It was proven that Nelms was riding along the road leading from the town of Panola to his house. Jennings Estell, about sixteen years of age, was the only person in company with him. When within a mile of his own house, the accused (Dyson), who had previously taken his position about fifteen yards from the road, in a sink-hole in a ravine, shot Nelms with a gun as he passed, who fell from his horse. Dyson then walked up to where Nelms was lying badly wounded, and said to Nelms, " You were going to kill me." Nelms said, " I was not." Dyson then said, " You tried to get Jones to kill me." Nelms answered, he " had not." Dyson then presented his gun to Nelms' head, who turned, as he lay on the ground, and said, " Good-bye, Jennings." The gun fired and killed Nelms dead immediately, and the muzzle of the gun was so near him that the powder burnt his coat and shirt and blistered his skin.

The defendant offered in justification of this act of killing, threats made by Nelms against him (Dyson).

The proof was in substance, that John R. Dickens, a few days before the killing, heard Dyson say to Nelms, " You made a difficulty with me, and I don't want a difficulty with you." Nelms replied, " God damn you, I don't want any difficulty with you either," and added, " Mr. Dyson, you have treated me damned badly."

W. B. Killebrue says, as Nelms and he were sitting in the court-house yard, Dyson came in sight; Nelms looked up, and said, " Here comes the damned son of a bitch now. I will have him in less than ten days where he won't bother me or any one else. I have got my triggers set for him." It looked

[1] 3 How., 214; 4 ib., 90; 6 S. & M., 197.

to him as if Dyson might have heard what Nelms said as he passed on.

Another witness says he heard the above, and told Dyson of it; says he heard Nelms say if Jones would attack Dyson, and Dyson denied his charges, he (Nelms) would settle it. This, also, witness told Dyson.

It was also in proof that Nelms told the witness that Turner had told him he was in danger from Dyson, and Nelms said he would give Dyson a fair fight.

Thomas B. Turner says Nelms told him Dyson was a damned rascal, and he would give Dyson a fair fight.

James M. Jones proved that Nelms never urged him to get into a difficulty with Dyson.

Anthony Foster and John R. Dickens and some others, proved that Nelms was a man of violent character.

The opinion of the court contains all the instructions commented on by the court.

The court below having refused to grant a new trial, Dyson prayed a writ of error to this court.

Watson & Estelle for plaintiff in error.

The errors relied upon for reversing the judgment of the court below, will be stated and considered in the order in which they occurred.

1st. The jury by whom the prisoner was tried was not duly and legally sworn.

That the record must show affirmatively that the jury was legally sworn. 1 How., 24, 30, 497; 4 S. & M., 110, 112.

On this subject the language of the record is: "Thereupon came a jury of good and lawful men, to wit (naming them), who being elected, tried and sworn the truth to speak in the issue joined, and having heard the evidence," etc. This oath was an insufficient one. For the proper form of the oath which should have been administered to the jury, see Hutch. Code, 879, § 132; 1 Chitty Cr. L., 551, 552.

Nothing can be presumed in support of the record. 1 How., 30. The record undertakes to recite the precise oath which was administered to the jury, and the oath recited being insufficient for this cause, the judgment must be reversed. The jury should have been sworn well and truly to try the issue joined between the defendant and the State of Mississippi, and a true verdict give according to the evidence.

The oath, as administered, did not inform the jury between whom the issue was joined which they were to try; nor did it require them a true verdict to give according to the evidence. The oath was defective, therefore, in two material particulars. This objection is believed to be fully sustained by the case of Holt v. Mills, 4 S. & M. 110, 112.

2d. On the bills of exception to the ruling of the court excluding testimony. 4 S. & M., 207.

3d. The court erred in giving to the jury the first, second, fourth and seventh charges, which were given for the state, and also in the explanation which it gave of defendant's sixth charge.

As expounded by the court in this case, the law of self-defense is practically annihilated. A person may legally assail another for injuries threatened when there shall be reasonable grounds to apprehend a design to do some great personal injury, and there shall be imminent danger of such design being accomplished. Hutch. Code, 957, § 3. So, too, a man may kill another who has threatened his life to prevent such other person from carrying this threat into execution. But these obvious and plain legal propositions are denied by the charges of the court in this case.

The error in the fourth and seventh charges consists in the fact that these charges make it essential that an actual felony should be about to be committed, or a design to do some great personal injury, in order to justify the killing in self-defense; whereas the law gives the right of self-defense upon a reasonable apprehension of these things.

On the law of self-defense, see Barb. Cr. Tr., 40, 41 ; 1 Russ. on Cr., 451, n.; 4 Ired., 415, 417 ; Granger's case, 5 Yerg.

The fifth charge asked by the state should have been refused.

This charge, in connection with the other charges given by the court, left to the jury no discretion whatever, but required them, under the penalty of perjury, to find a verdict against the defendant. No one can carefully read over the various charges and explanation of charges given by the court, without discovering that the jury, as to their verdict, were placed under something like *duress*.

On contradictory charges, 13 S. & M. 40.

4th. The silence of the record as to the disposition that was made of the jury on the trial of the defendant, on the adjournment of the court on the evening of the 24th of May, and also on the evening of the 25th, is a fatal objection to the judgment of the court below.

The trial by jury in criminal cases, and the rights of criminals generally, are most scrupulously guarded by the constitution and laws of the state.

By the tenth section of our declaration of rights, it is declared that, in all criminal prosecutions, the accused cannot be deprived of his life, liberty or property but by due course of law. It is also declared, by express legislative enactment, that no person shall be punished for any offense unless he shall have been duly and legally convicted thereof. Hutch. Code, 954, § 7.

On this subject the decisions of this court have sustained fully the meaning and spirit of the constitution and laws of the state, and in no single instance has this court weakened or impaired those principles of the common law, which were designed as the shield and safeguard of the personal rights of Englishmen.

It has been decided that the record must show affirmatively, that the court, trying an accused, was held at the place appointed by law, 4 How. 163 ; 5 ib. 20.

That the caption of the indictment must state with sufficient certainty the style of the court, the judge presiding, the place at which the indictment was found, and the, jurors by whom it was found. 5 How. 20.

That the record must show, affirmatively, that the accused was present during the trial. 8 S. & M., 722.

The record must show, affirmatively, that the accused pleaded in person, after due and legal arraignment. 8 S. & M., 587, 595.

From the foregoing decisions, it will be seen that this court has never indulged in any inference or presumption to sustain the action of a circuit court in a criminal trial, where such action involved the legality of the proceedings of the court in reference to a matter of judicial duty touching the rights of the accused.

In several of the states of the Union it is held to be in the discretion of the court to permit the jury charged with a criminal case to disperse or separate during the trial (15 Ohio, 72); whilst in this state, the separation of the jury without the consent of the accused, has uniformly been held to be error, for which a verdict against the accused will be set aside.   13 S. & M., 898.

In Virginia, it is held, that before jurors, elected by the prisoner, have been sworn, and the jury fully made up, they need not be committed to the care of an officer, 11 Leigh, 714. Whilst in this state it is held, that in a criminal case, where a juror is elected, he must remain under the care of the court before, as well as after, he is sworn, 8 S. & M., 587.

It has been also held, that no special oath need be administered to a sheriff, to whom a jury, in a criminal case, is committed during the trial, 8 Leigh, 745.   Whilst in this state it has been repeatedly decided, that it is the duty of the court to swear an officer to take charge of the jury.   4 How., 196; 13 S. & M., 402.

In several of the states it is held, that after judgment, no advantage can be taken of the want of a prosecutor; whilst the contrary is the settled law of this state, as established by the decisions of the court.

There are many matters not entering necessarily into the record of a criminal case, as to which, until the contrary is shown, the action of the court will be presumed to have been correct.   This principle explains all the cases on this subject relied upon by the state.

But this principle has never been applied by this court to any matter constituting a necessary part of the record, or which, upon the principles of the common law, it was necessary that the record should show affirmatively; as that the court was held at the proper place; that the grand jury and petit jury were sworn; that there was a prosecutor marked; that the prisoner was in court during the trial.

The law is, not only that the jury shall remain in charge of the court or a sworn officer, but that the record shall show affirmatively that this was the case. To the care and custody of the jury the law applies the same rule that it does to the place where the court was held; to the swearing of the grand and petit jury; to the name of the prosecutor; and to the personal presence of the prisoner during the trial. The fact must not only exist, but the record must show it. 6 Term R., 246; 1 Chitty Cr. L., 632; 2 Hale P. C., 296.

The cases in 11 Blackford, 20, and 8 Leigh, 745, do not go to the extent of sustaining the judgment in this case. In those cases the record contained the statement that the jury was committed to the care of the sheriff, with instructions, etc. And in the absence of this express statement, it is certain that those cases would have been reversed. 2 Black., 475; 8 Leigh, 745.

Even the case in 2 Gillman, 551, concedes the common law rule; and the decision there made is placed on grounds to which this court can give no countenance without a departure from the principles and spirit of its previous decisions. 4 How., 187, 196; 8 S. & M., 587, 596; 9 ib., 465, 467, 468, 469; 13 ib., 259. See 2 Metcalf, 18, 19; 18 Johns., 212, 217, 118.

The following references are to cases in which the very question under consideration was decided. 2 Cain, 373; Johns., 2 Blackf., 475.

In Bennett's case, 8 Leigh, 745, in which the record states that the jury was committed to the care of the sheriff, who was charged, etc., but omits to state that he was sworn, the majority of the court who sustain the judgment, place their decision on the ground of the practice in Virginia; whilst the minority, who were for deciding the case on principle and authority, were for the reversal of the judgment. The dissenting opinion in this case is able and lucid, and the attention of the court is respectfully invited to it.

In Hare's case, 4 How., 193, Chief Justice Sharkey, in delivering the opinion of the court, quotes with approbation from 12 Pick., 496, this language:

" It is a well-settled rule of practice incident to all jury trials, that, after the jury are charged and have left the court to consider of their verdict, they are to be kept by themselves, without refreshment and without communication with others, until they have agreed. Any departure from this rule is an irregularity."

In the same case the chief justice says : " It is the duty of the court to swear an officer to take charge of the jury ; his oath is, that he will not speak to them or permit others to do so."   4 How., 196.

In McQuillen's case, 8 S. & M., 587, the record shows that a portion of the jury was selected, though not sworn, when the court adjourned until the next day, and the record then proceeds :

" And thereupon the persons selected as jurors were charged according to law, and required to be in attendance the next morning, at ten o'clock."   Page 589.

After this the jury was sworn, without objection, and a verdict of guilty found against the defendant.

A motion was then made for a new trial, but it does not appear from the case as reported, whether or not one of the grounds of this motion was that the persons elected as jurors on the first day, were permitted by the court to disperse until the next day. This was one of the errors, however, assigned in this court, and it was sustained.

The court say : " It is thirdly assigned that seven of the jurors were tendered to the prisoner, and elected, and permitted to disperse until the next day, without having been sworn, and that they were not sworn until the next day when the panel was completed.   The record shows this to have been the fact, and it is a palpable error.   When a juror is elected, he must remain under the care of the court or an officer, before as well as after he is sworn, and it is error to permit the jury to disperse without the consent of the prisoner."

Passing over a few sentences, the court add : " Perhaps the prisoner had a right to object to them the next day, before they were sworn ; if so, they should have been retendered to him. But even if he had such rights, it did not cure the error in permitting them to disperse."   8 S. & M., 596.

The case is submitted as an authority directly in point.   If, when the record shows that the jurors were charged according to law, and required to be in attendance the next morning at 10 o'clock, it shows, in the absence of all other proof, that the jurors were permitted to disperse; much more is it shown by the record under consideration, which shows that the court adjourned from day to day, without making any disposition of the jury, and which states affirmatively, that on the evening of the third day of court, "the jury not agreeing, were committed to the care of their officer, and were adjourned over until tomorrow."

At the close of the first day, the record says: "The day being expired, this cause is continued till to-morrow."

On the next day, the record says: "Thereupon came the jury impanelled and sworn on yesterday," and proceeds thus: "The cause being fully argued, the jury retired to consider of their verdict."

And on the next day, the record states, among other things: "And also came the jury, etc., who, not agreeing, were committed to the care of their officer, and were adjourned over until to-morrow."

Now, on this state of the record, is there room for the inference or supposition, that the jury, on the first and second adjournments of the court, was committed to the care of a sworn officer?

The statement that, on the evening of the third day, the jury was committed to the care of an officer, leaves the implication a necessary one, that prior to this time no such disposition had been made of it; and, in this connection, it is an important consideration, that one of the grounds assigned in the court below for a new trial is, that "the jury were not kept together as the law requires." This objection having been thus raised in the court below, when it was competent for the court to have changed or amended its record, so as to make it conform to the truth of the case, can it now be supposed by this court that the record does not show the entire action of the court below in the premises?

In Carpenter's case, 4 How., 167, it was urged upon the court to presume that the circuit court, in which the accused had been convicted, was held at the proper place, when the record was silent on the subject; but to this it was replied by Mr. Justice Smith, who delivered the opinion of the court:

"It (that is, the place where the court was held,) is not directly expressed, and no presumption can be indulged which contradicts the record; nor are we warranted in the assumption of any fact which is not necessarily included in that which is expressed."

Now, apply this rule to the present case, and the presumption that the jury from the first were regularly committed to the charge of a sworn officer, is certainly cut off. That the jury was thus disposed of during the adjournment of the court, for the first two days, is certainly "not necessarily included in that which is expressed."

In McCann's case, 9 S. & M., 465, Mr. Justice Thacher, in delivering the opinion of the court, states the practice of criminal courts "according to the forms anciently established at trials;" and gives the form of the oath administered to the bailiff who takes charge of the jury when they retire. He suggested it as probable that it might be held sufficient for the officer to be sworn at the commencement of the term, to take charge of all the juries, and then adds:

"'The trial by jury, so justly prized, should be scrupulously preserved inviolate, as guaranteed by the constitution, and protected against encroachments in all its essential attributes; and every change or modification of form should be admitted only when found to be absolutely necessary to meet the changes of society and the times. Its very forms being designed to protect it from innovation, are said, in 4 Black. Com., 320, to be sacred, and not to be dispensed with." 9 S. & M., 468.

Now, in 6 Term R., 531, the form of the proper entry of the swearing of the bailiffs to take charge of the jury, and of the disposition made of the jury on the adjournment of the court, is given, and these forms all the common law authorities require to be substantially observed; but in this case, the forms of the law, which has ever been held to be the evidence of what the law is, are proposed to be wholly overlooked, or to be supplied by intendment or presumption.

In McCann's case, 9 S. & M., 469, the case of Jones *v.* State,

2 Blackf., 475, is quoted, in the opinion of the court, as an authority to be followed.   This case in Blackford, it will be remembered, arose upon a record which was silent as to the disposition made of the jury by the court on its adjournment; and this silence was held to be fatal to the judgment.

In Boles' case, 18 S. & M., 402, Chief Justice Sharkey, in delivering the opinion of the court, says : " The rule of the common law is, where the jurors depart from the bar, a bailiff must be sworn to keep them together, and not suffer any one to speak with them.   This is a plain, practical and safe rule.   It cannot be mistaken and is easily followed.   Any departure from it is a violation and leads to confusion and difficulty in which there is no rule of law to guide us.   Each departure may make a new case for the discretion of the court, for, when there has been a departure from the given rule, the verdict must depend upon the discretion of the court."

The truth of this language is fully verified by the experience of several of the states.   In Ohio, New Hampshire, Vermont, Virginia, and some of the other states, this doctrine of the discretion of the courts, with reference to jury trials, is prevailing and growing.   But in this state, so far, this doctrine has found no foothold or countenance ; and it is certainly to be hoped that, if it is ever introduced, it will not be by " judicial legislation," but by legislation proper.

It is respectfully submitted that, if in this case the presumption can be indulged that the jury was from the first committed to the charge of a sworn officer, when the court adjourned for two evenings without making any entry on its minutes about the jury, and when it is nowhere stated in the record that any officer ever was sworn to take charge of the jury, or that the jury ever was committed to the sheriff (from the third day onwards, the language of the record is, that " the jury was committed to their officer," without saying who this officer was or that he was sworn), the precedent will be set for presuming in future, where the record is silent, that the court was held at the place appointed by law ; that the jury in every case was sworn ; that in every criminal case there was a prosecutor ; and that the prisoner was duly arraigned and was in court during the whole time

of the trial.   The court is no more required to see to these matters, than it is to see to the proper care and custody of the jury
during the progress of a criminal case.   Nor can any reason be
assigned for requiring the record to state affirmatively any one
of the foregoing matters, which does not apply with equal force
to the care and custody of the jury.

  D. C. Glenn, attorney general.

  1. It is not "made to appear" that the court erred by any
thing contained in the bill of exceptions.   The rule of presumption, therefore, makes good the proceeding below.   Briggs v.
Clark, 7 How., 457 ; Robinson v. Frances, 7 ib., 458 ; Smith v.
Berry, 1 S. & M., 321 ; Pender v. Felts, 2 ib., 535.

  2. The bill of exceptions does not show or set out the testimony which was rejected by the court below.   Harris v. New-
man, 5 How., 654 ; Bone v. McGinley, 7 ib., 671.

  Witness Turner was asked if he knew anything of an attack
made on the defendant, by one Jones, the day before Nelms was
killed ; and if so, to state what took place on that occasion.

  The bill of exceptions does not show how such proof was pertinent to the issue joined, and it was properly ruled out as being
irrelevant.   State v. Wisdom, 8 Porter, 511 ; Stone v. State, 4
Humph., 27 ; and many others.

  Several witnesses who had deposed to the violent character of
the deceased, were asked if they had communicated their knowledge to the accused.   The court refused to allow them to answer.

  The question asked was not an admissible one.   On the trial
of an indictment for homicide the general rule is, that the character of the deceased is not in evidence.   In some one or two
instances, when the nature of the offense committed was very
doubtful, the general character of the accused has been drawn
into evidence.   But the rule undoubtedly is, that the character
of the deceased can never be made a matter of controversy, except when involved in the *res gestæ ;* for it would be a barbarism
to allow A. to give as a reason or excuse for killing B., that B.
was a savage and riotous man.   The state was forbid to prove
murder was a familiar thing to Dyson as an excuse for hanging
him.   So the defendant may prove that he was acting in self-

defense in this particular case, or he may exhibit whatever provocations were given him at the time by the deceased ; but he cannot set up general reputation as a defense. State v. Field, 13 Maine R., 248 ; Com. v. York, 7 Law R., 507 ; State v. Tilley, 3 Ired., 424 ; and many others.

3. On the charges only two points arise :

Threats against Dyson by Nelms were in evidence before the jury.   The defense attempted is, that it appeared from the threats that Dyson's life was in danger from Nelms, and consequently that, to save his own life, he was compelled to take the life of Nelms ; and, therefore, the homicide was excusable or justifiable.

The law on this subject, as it exists in Mississippi, is as follows :

It is so when committed in defense of a person, "when there shall be a reasonable ground to apprehend a design to commit a felony or do some great personal injury, and there shall be imminent danger of such design being accomplished."   Code, 957.

At common law the same doctrine was thus expressed and explained at the same time :

"But a bare fear of any of these offenses, however well founded, as that one lies in wait to take another's life, unaccompanied by any overt act indicative of such intention, will not warrant him in killing that other by way of prevention.   There must be an actual danger at the time."   1 East Cr. L., 271, 272, 293, 294 ; Russ. Cr., 513, 517.

The same is found in Foster, Hale, Hawkins, Chitty, and Blackstone, in the same language.

It is also expounded and practically applied in cases where threats were proven and self-defense set up as an excuse ; cases far less hideous in their general features than the one at bar.   State v. Scott, 4 Ired., 409 ; Wiltberger's case, 3 Wash. C. C. R., 522 ; 3 Eng., 451 ; 8 Humph., 671 ; 2 Hill S. C. R., 619.

In this case I will even admit the correctness of the law laid down in the celebrated case of Grainger, 5 Yerg. R. There the party was excused on the score of ungrounded fears and cowardice in the presence of an apparent assailant.   The case at bar is simply one of cold-blooded and deliberate assassination.

The facts of this case will uphold the charges of the court. They show the commission of the most deliberate murder which record of crime has for a long time furnished.

Exception is taken to the charge given by the court for the state. The substantive meaning of this charge is, that jurors should regard the law as expounded to them by the court. Of course, the jury have the power to disregard the law in their finding, as they have the power to disregard the evidence in the case. If so, however, they disregard the obligation of their oaths.

This subject has been carefully examined by Judge Story. He says that, if he thought the jury were the proper judges of law in criminal cases, he should feel it to be his duty to abstain from the responsibility of giving the law in charge to them upon any such trial. That he holds it the most sacred constitutional right of every party accused of crime, that the jury should respond as to the facts, and courts as the law of the case, and they cannot act otherwise without a violation of their sworn duty. This is most certainly the doctrine of common sense, and safest for the state, the accused, and general purposes of justice. U. S. v. Battiste, 2 Sumn., 243; Com. v. Knapp, 10 Pick., 477; U. S. v. Shive, 1 Bald., 512.

I contend, this court will not entertain these questions now, as the same were not raised in the court below by motion in arrest, demurrer, or otherwise.

In many cases this court has so held. I will cite them before assigning a general rule for the rule in this case:

In the case of Loper v. State, 3 How., 432, the record showed that the prisoner, on his trial below, was not served with a copy of the indictment and a list of the *venire*, two days before his trial, as is expressly commanded by law. The point was raised in the high court. It said, " as the prisoner made no objection in the court below, he cannot object here." Such was the decision of this court in Johnson's case, Walker, 396, and Shæffer's case, 1 How., 288.

In the case of Brantley, 13 S. & M., exceptions were taken to the grand jury in this court. Judge Clayton says : "No objections were taken to the grand jury in the court below by plea or otherwise. We cannot, in this court, after a plea of not guilty and trial without objection, go back to look for defects in the organization of that body."

In Walker, 540, C. J. Turner says : "We can only reverse for errors which were excepted to, and none other."

In 4 How., 90, the court says : "It is a general rule, subject to very few exceptions, that a party shall not be permitted to assign for error in the appellate court, matter not insisted on in the court below." The court says : "This principle was adopted in Randolph v. Goss, 3 How., 214, and it will be adhered to as one which is essential to maintain the true purposes of an appellate jurisdiction, and prevent injustice and oppression." Neely v. Planters' Bank, 4 S. & M., 116 ; Sessions v. Reynolds, 7 ib., 730 ; Doe v. Natchez Insurance Company, 8 ib., 197 ; Ferguson v. Oliver, ib., 332 ; Rabe v. Fyler, 10 ib., 440 ; Talbert v. Melton, 9 ib., 9.

I have examined nearly every important case relied on to support the point, and I find they do not conflict with my position, as in every instance the objection was made in the court below, and thus came before the appellate tribunal in a shape proper to be decided.

It was so in each of the following cases, in which points similar to these under discussion were raised. 3 Halst., 298 ; 5 ib., 348 ; 2 Bay., 451 ; Peck. R., 165, 166, 308 ; McCord, 301 ; 1 Murph., 181 ; 5 How., 20 ; 2 Humph., 451 ; 5 Cow., 283 ; Hare's case, Carpenter's case, Boles' case, in this state.

But one case makes the points as here made, and decides them against the state. It is the case of Jones v. State, 2 Blackf., 475. I submit this case is not an authority.

I meet its authority and utterly overturn it by the sound and powerful reasoning contained in the following cases in other states. McKinney v. People, 2 Gilm., 551 ; Pate v. People, 3 ib., 657 ; McClure v. State, 1 Yerg., 218.

As to the general correctness of the rule, in regard to the caption of the indictment, see, in addition to the foregoing cases,

State v. Wasden, 2 Tay., 163 ; Kirk v. State, 6 Mis., 469 ; Waccalakshee's case, Morris, 332.

And as to the neglect of the care of the jury, see in same way, 8 Leigh, 745 ; 7 Blackf., 20 ; 11 Ohio, 474 ; 13 ib., 492 ; 15 ib., 72.

In regard to the oath of the jury, see Judah v. McNarree, 3 Black. R. ; Clifton v. Mann, ib. Citing a criminal case, State v. Jones, 5 Ala., 72 ; State v. Pile, 5 ib., 666 ; 1 How., 215 ; " Code ;" Thacher Crim. C., 118.

In conclusion, I maintain that, in the language of Judge Trotter, " in order to preserve the true purposes of an appellate tribunal, and to prevent oppression and injustice," this court will refuse now to listen to all these objections not raised in the court below. Give the state some repose ; let at least that be considered as rightly done, of which no one was ever heard to complain. Under our system we give the accused every advantage compatible with bringing him to trial at all. Every presumption is in his favor, and every doubt weighs for him.

He has his counsel and his witnesses, and every avenue to a successful defense is thrown wide open. He can plead in abatement, demur, and move in arrest of judgment. He can take his exception at every step in the cause, and fix judicially every fact which he conceives to his prejudice. He can move for a new trial, and on its refusal can embody all his evidence and have a trial, *de novo*, in the appellate court.

To the state, no error is allowed, or appeal given. Though an ignorant judge may set at defiance the law, or a corrupt jury set at defiance both the law and the evidence, yet the state is powerless. From a community, by its own courts, is withheld every privilege which is extended to an individual, though he has broken and outraged every law common to the whole.

I ask, then, under all these circumstances, if it is not most unequivocally to encourage and invite a fraud upon all the privileges which the benign spirit of our law has secured to the accused, a fraudulent tampering with the courts of the country at this stage and in its forum, to allow exceptions, such as those now urged, to prevail over the demands of justice ?

All I ask is that this court will carry out and give full weight

to the principles expressed by Judge Trotter in the case of Loper, and by Judge Clayton in the case of Brantley, and uphold
the sound and conservative doctrine of Judges Lockwood and
Treat of Illinois, and Judge Catron of Tennessee.

HANDY, J.:

This case has been submitted on the re-argument very fully
and elaborately, and we shall confine our present examination to
the points therein presented in behalf of the plaintiff in error.

1. It is insisted, in the first place, that it appears by the record that the jury were not properly and legally sworn.

The opinion of the court on this point delivered on the former
argument, seems to proceed on the assumption that the full oath,
as administered to the jury, is stated in the record, or intended
to be stated, a view which we have not been able to take. And
had the oath administered been properly and fully shown in the
record, and contained nothing more than is embraced in the
statement of it in the record, we should be strongly inclined to
hold it insufficient. It would not embrace the important duties required of the jury, and would be a wide departure from
the just and comprehensive oath so necessary to injoin upon
them the faithful discharge of their solemn responsibilities,
which, for ages past, has been sanctioned by wisdom and experience, and has received almost universal adoption at the present
day. But we cannot think that the oath here was intended to
be set out in the form or entire substance in which it was administered, or that it was necessary to set it out for the purposes
of the record of proceedings in the court below.

It is not the duty of the clerk, in making up the record of the
proceedings in a cause, to set out the oath administered to the
jury. All that is required of him, in this respect, under the
law as settled by this court, in reference to courts of general jurisdiction is, that the record should show that the jury were
sworn according to law.[1]　1 How., 24; 3 ib., 497. And we are

---

[1] Archbold Cr. Pr. & Pl., 624; Harriman v. State, 2 Greene (Iowa), 270; Patterson
v. State, 2 Eng., 59; Warren v. State, 1 Greene (Iowa), 106; Bell v. State, 5 Eng.,
536; Sanford v. State, 6 Eng., 328; State v. Jones, 5 Ala., 666; State v. Pile, ib., 72;
State v. Rollins, 2 Foster, 528; Russell v. State, 10 Tex., 288; Archbold, 542; 1
Bishop Cr. Procedure, 918; Bivens v. State, 6 Eng., 465; Drake v. Brander, 8 Tex.,
351; Arthur v. State, 3 Tex., 403; Pierce v. State, 12 Tex., 210; Wrocklege v. State,
1 Iowa, 167.

not disposed to extend this rule beyond its strict limit. If he
undertakes to state other things connected with the administration of the oath, these additional statements would be unofficial
and not properly a part of the record.   The general rule in relation to acts of this character will be found in the cases referred
to in 3 Phil. Ev. (Cow. & H. ed.), 1045, 1046, 1083.   The statement of the oath administered, is no more a part of the duty of
the clerk, than it is his duty to incorporate it in any document
or deposition offered in evidence in the course of the trial.   In
the case of Barfield et al. v. Impson, 1 S. & M., this court says:
"We cannot notice a mere certificate of the clerk that this or
that evidence was introduced; the certificate of the court is required."   And in Abbott v. Hackman, 2 S. & M., 510, it is
said: "This court is bound to presume the judgment of the
court below correct, unless, from a review of the grounds of such
judgment, certified to by the court, manifest error is apparent."
4 How., 222; ib., 431.   If a document offered in evidence in
the cause cannot be made a part of the record by the mere act
of the clerk, much less could his mere statement of its substance
be treated as a part of the record, and that is what is here attempted.

If, then, the swearing of the jurors is improper in any respect,
the objection must be presented by bill of exceptions, and unless
it is so presented, if sufficient evidence appears of record to
show that the jury were sworn, it must be presumed that they
were *legally* sworn.   This principle is distinctly held in the
cases in this court just cited; and in Barfield et al. v. Impson,
the court says: "That (the bill of exceptions) affords the only
evidence which we can recognize, of what takes place upon the
trial; and we are bound to presume the proceedings of the court
below to be correct, unless by the bill of exceptions we are furnished with evidence to the contrary."   This rule we think altogether applicable to the present objection.   It is the true rule
in relation to courts of general common law jurisdiction, but it
does not apply to courts of special and limited jurisdiction; and
for this reason, the case of Holt v. Mills, 4 S. & M., does not
sustain this objection.   That was a case of unlawful detainer, a
matter of special and statutory jurisdiction, in which the oath re-

quired to be administered is prescribed in the statute. Moreover, the oath actually administered is fully set out in the record, and shown not to be in conformity to the statute. And the court says, " in this proceeding, if the oath is set out, and is not such as the law requires, the verdict cannot stand."

In the present case, it appears manifest that it was not intended by the clerk, as it was no part of his duty, to set out the oath in the manner and form used in administering it to the jurors. The statement is by way of recital, thus : " And thereupon came a jury of good and lawful men, to wit," etc., " who being elected, tried, and sworn the truth to speak in the issue joined," etc., referring to what had previously taken place, in order to show that an oath had been administered, rather than to state its form or substance. It is a memorandum relative to a proceeding in the case, made after the fact had transpired, and not the record of the very thing done at the time, and in the manner and form in which it was done.

Great strength is given to this view of the subject, by referring to the practice and precedents touching it. It is conceded that in England, the form of oath, as contended for by the counsel for plaintiff in error, is adopted. It also prevails in practice in Virginia and Maryland. 3 Rob. Va. Prac., 174; 2 Harris, Ent., 282. Notwithstanding this, and though this form of oath has been duly administered in empanelling the jury, yet, when the record of the proceedings is being made, the entry of swearing and empanelling the jury is made nearly in the very terms contained in this record. Blackstone has the entry as follows : " Who being elected, tried, and sworn to speak the truth of and concerning the premises." 4 Black. Com. Appendix. Robinson has it thus : " Who being elected, tried and sworn the truth of and upon the premises to speak." 3 Rob. Pr., 177. Harris has it thus : " Who are sworn to say the truth in the premises." 2 Harris, Ent., 293. The distinction between the fact of the oath actually administered to the jurors, and the reference afterwards made to it as a part of the history of the case by the clerk in making up the record, is clearly shown by these precedents ; and they are certainly authorities of high character.

Justified by these precedents, a practice has grown up in this state to make up the records of jury trials after the manner of the record in this case; a practice in violation of no principle, and in keeping with the proper office of the clerk in making up records of such proceedings. The records of this court show, that this mode of making up such records, has become the established practice of the state. It has ripened into general usuage without objection, and the instances are numerous where men have suffered the extreme penalty of the law under its operation. If it were unsupported by precedents from other states, this court would hesitate long before it would hold, considering the nature and office of such an entry in the record, that for such an inaccuracy, if it should be one, the trial in the court below should be treated as illegal and nugatory. But, sanctioned as it is by precedent, and no right of the accused or rule of law being sufficiently shown to be violated, we cannot hesitate to say that it constitutes no ground for reversing the judgment below.

Again, no objection to the oath, as administered, was made in the court below; and the very universality of the adoption of the form urged by plaintiff's counsel as the proper and legal oath, renders it almost certain, that if it had been so materially departed from on the trial in this case, as is inferred from the reference to it in the record, objection would have been made to it.

But it is urged, that the record must affirmatively show that the jury were regularly sworn, and that such has been the ruling of this court.

It is undoubtedly true, that the record must affirmatively show those indispensable facts, without which the judgment would be void, such as the organization of the court; its jurisdiction of the subject matter, and of the parties; that a cause was made up for trial; that it was submitted to a jury sworn to try it (if it be a case proper for a jury); that a verdict was rendered, and judgment awarded. Out of abundant tenderness for the rights secured to the accused by our constitution, to be confronted by the witnesses against him, and to be heard by himself or counsel, our court has gone a step further, and held that it must be shown by the record that the accused was present in court pending the trial. This is upon the ground of the peculiar sacredness of this high constitutional right. It is also true, as has been held by this court, " that nothing can be presumed for or against a record, except what appears substantially upon its face." But this rule has reference to those indispensable requisites necessary to the validity of the record, as a judicial proceeding, and can have no application to those incidental matters, which transpire during the progress of the proceeding in court. For otherwise, what would be the limit to the rule? There could be none short of requiring every thing that was connected with the trial, the summoning of the jury, the facts touching the examination and empanelling of each of them, the summoning of witnesses, their oath, the course of their examination; in short, every matter, however trivial, to be set forth in the record. No such details are required by justice or law. If irregularities occur in relation to any of them, the party aggrieved is not without remedy. He can introduce them into the record by bill of exceptions; but otherwise the rule is, as to all incidental acts which transpire on the trial, *omnia præsumuntur rite et solemniter esse acta, donec probatur in contrarium.* See instances of this application of this rule to judicial proceedings in Best on Presumptions, 79.

In addition to this view, the bill of exceptions, taken upon overruling the motion for a new trial, states that after the defendant had been arraigned, a jury was " selected and sworn to try the issue joined," etc. This statement in the defendant's own bill of exceptions, taken together with his failure to raise any objection on the trial to the oath administered to the jurors, when the oath alleged to have been administered would have been so unprecedented, greatly strengthens the legal presumption, and must remove all doubt from the mind that a formal and sufficient oath was administered, and that the present objection is an afterthought, founded on the mere reference by the clerk to an act previously and formally done.

2. The second error assigned is the exclusion of the question propounded to the witness Turner, inquiring what took place on the occasion of an attack made by one Jones, on the defendant, on the day Nelms was killed.

Upon its face, this question has not the most remote connection with the point in issue, the killing of Nelms by Dyson. The bill of exceptions presenting the objection, shows nothing but the questions asked and overruled, and contains nothing from which a connection could possibly be justly inferred. This court cannot, then, presume upon the possibility, that the question might have some pertinency to the cause. As it was presented, it was clearly irrelevant, and the defendant has failed to show its relevancy by anything either in the special bill of exceptions in relation to it, or in the general bill of exceptions setting out the whole evidence. No connection whatever, anywhere appears between the attack of Jones upon Dyson, and the killing of Nelms by Dyson. If, as is contended, the witness might have proceeded in answering the question to connect Nelms with Jones, in the attack upon Dyson, and then to show the connection of that transaction with the killing of Nelms by Dyson, is it not strange that the witness was not interrogated afterwards, and in some form, whether Nelms was connected with the attack of Jones upon Dyson? This inquiry would have been unobjectionable, and it is not to be supposed that all effort to prove facts alleged to be so important in the defense, would have been abandoned simply because a question not showing the connection of the evidence with the case on trial, had been rejected. This court cannot know what the testimony proposed to be brought out was; but for all that appears in the record, we cannot say but that the court acted correctly in sustaining the objection.

But it is said that the objection was improperly sustained because it was general. The ground of the objection or the reasons urged in support of it are not stated, but it is not in every instance necessary to state the reason for an objection to a question; for it may be so palpably illegal as not to require reasons to be stated against it. No settled practice seems to be established as to the manner in which objections in such cases should be made. But if an objection be made, and either allowed or overruled, the ruling of the court below will be sustained in the appellate court, if in any point of view regarding the whole record, the question allowed or overruled was legal and proper, or illegal and improper, as the case may be. It is true that a party is not compelled to adopt any particular order in the introduction of his testimony. But if evidence is proposed, which of itself appears to be foreign to the issue on trial, and it is objected to, it is incumbent on the party offering it to show its relevancy, either by explanation to the court as to its bearing on the case, or by introducing other evidence connecting it with the *res gestæ*, and opening the door to its admission. Otherwise the most prejudicial testimony might go to the jury, the effect of which it might be impossible fully to destroy by instructions of the court to disregard it. And for obvious reasons, the rule confining the evidence strictly to the point in issue, is more rigidly applied in criminal cases.[1] 2 Russ. on Cr., 772.

It will not do to say that the evidence may be shown, by subsequent developments, to be immediately connected with the *res gestæ*, for of this the court can know nothing, unless brought to its notice by a proper showing of its connection.

3. Again, it is urged that the court erred in granting the 7th instruction asked in behalf of the state, and in qualifying the 2d instruction in behalf of the defendant. The 7th instruction is as follows: "That a bare fear that a man's life is in danger from the violence of another, however well founded, and whatever may be the character of the man feared, as that such man lies in wait to take away the life of the party, unaccompanied by any overt act indicating an intention immediately to kill such party or to do him some great personal injury, will not warrant him in killing that other, by way of precaution, if there is no actual danger at the time of killing; that both the design to commit a felony, or to do such person some great personal injury, and the imminency of the danger of such design being carried into execution, must both exist to warrant the man thus in fear of his life to kill, and that imminency of danger means danger at the time of the killing."

The explanation of defendant's 2d charge is as follows: "In explanation of defendant's 2d charge, that although a party is not bound to retreat in some cases, and may pursue his adver-

---

[1] 1 Greenl. Ev., 65; Roscoe Cr. Ev., 73; 1 Deacon's Dig. Cr. Law, 459, 460; 2 East P. C., 735, 1201; 1 Phil. Ev., 505; Rex v. Watson, 2 Stark, 116, 155; Lord Melville's case, 29 How. St. Tr. 876; Russ. on Cr., 588; U. S. v. Brittain, 2 Mason, 464, 468.

sary until he is out of danger, yet this only applies when there is immediate danger of a felony, or some violence being committed by the party killed."

Without an extended recital of the evidence on the trial, it is sufficient for the present purpose to say that the testimony on the part of the prosecution characterized the killing of which the defendant stood charged, as premeditated, malicious and aggravated to an extraordinary degree, the defendant lying in wait and shooting the deceased as he passed unsuspectingly along the highway. The only evidence in justification or mitigation of the deed, consists of proof that the deceased had had a grudge against defendant; had made threats against his life; was a violent and desperate man, and that defendant's life was in danger at his hands. It therefore became necessary for the court to declare the law arising upon the facts alleged to constitute a justification or extenuation of this deed, and I see nothing in the rulings of the court in doing so, in violation of law or sound policy.

By the rules of the common law, in order to justify the killing, bare fear of danger or great bodily harm, unaccompanied by any overt act indicating a present intention to kill or injure, would not warrant a party in killing another. There must have been actual danger at the time. 1 East, Cr. Law, 271, 272.

Our law renders the act justifiable: "When committed by any person in the lawful defense of such person, or of his or her husband, wife, parent, child, master, mistress or servant, when there shall be a reasonable ground to apprehend a design to commit a felony, or to do some great personal injury, and there shall be imminent danger of such design being accomplished." Hutch. Code, 957, § 3.

The only modification of the common law made by this statute, consists in the justification extended to the accused "when there shall be reasonable ground to apprehend a design to commit a felony or to do some great personal injury," instead of the old rule requiring "actual danger at the time." But it is not the intention of the legislature to dispense with the necessity of showing some overt act indicating a present intention to kill or do some great personal injury, and that the danger thus indicated, was imminent at the time of the killing. It was intended to alter the rule of the common law so far as to justify a party acting conscientiously upon reasonable fears, founded on present overt acts to all appearances hostile, although there was really no actual danger. If this were not so, what is to constitute "reasonable grounds of apprehension?" By what limit is this dangerous rule to be defined? Must this reasonable ground of apprehension be founded on a present and immediate emergency, unavoidable to the party, or may it consist of mere fear, which though reasonable, all danger may be avoided? Are we to refer the reasonableness of the grounds of apprehension to the judgment or feeling of the party implicated, and not to a just and dispassionate standard? The peace of society and the security of life require that "the reasonable grounds of apprehension," as justifying homicides, should be limited as strictly as possible to the right of self-defense, and this seems to have been properly regarded by the court below in the instructions under consideration.

In substance, the entire instructions in the case, as given by the court, contain the following principles:

First. That, in order to justify killing, there must be some overt act indicating a present intention to kill the party, or to do him some great bodily injury.

Second. That the danger of such design being accomplished must be imminent, that is to say, immediate, pressing, and unavoidable at the time of killing.

Third. That mere fears of a design to commit a felony or to do some great personal injury to the party, though honestly entertained, unaccompanied by any overt act indicating a design immediately to commit the felony or to do the injury, will not justify the killing.

And this exposition of the law meets my approbation as the law of this case, and the sound and salutary rule for the protection of society.

4. The last objection presented for our consideration is, that the jury were allowed to separate after they were sworn, and during the time they were deliberating of their verdict, and were not kept together.

By reference to the bill of exceptions, taken upon the motion for a new trial, it appears that there is no evidence tending to show a separation of the jury, or any act of impropriety on their part, nor is there any thing shown calculated in the least to impeach or cast suspicion upon their verdict. But it is insisted, that, inasmuch as the record shows that the jury were several days deliberating of their verdict, and it does not affirmatively appear by the record that they were duly kept together, during all that time, under the charge of a properly sworn officer, this is sufficient to set aside the verdict; that the disposition made of the jury must be shown by the record, and makes a necessary part of it; otherwise the verdict is erroneous.

We do not think this position well founded, either on principle or sound authority.

We have already adverted to those acts of the court which are required to appear affirmatively of record, by which it appears that every incidental act connected with the trial, and which transpires during its progress, is not necessarily to be incorporated in the record. If this were not true, every important fact, without which a verdict and judgment could not be rendered, must positively appear on the record; the swearing of witnesses, the evidence to support the verdict, and every minute act which the convenience or necessities of the jury would require to be done in the course of a greatly protracted trial. It is said that these are matters *in pais*, and, therefore, not a part of the record. But we cannot perceive how the swearing witnesses, or the fact of the admission of evidence, or the evidence itself as admitted, are matters *in pais*, but the disposition made of a deliberating jury is matter of record. They are equally acts of the court, and the former are more strictly matters of judicial action than the latter, and at least equally necessary to a proper and legal judgment. And it may be remarked in reference to all the instances of judicial action, adduced by the counsel for the plaintiff in error, necessary to appear of record, that they are examples either in relation to the organization of the court, or its jurisdiction of the subject-matter or of the person, or held by this court to be matters of so solemn a judicial nature, or of such high constitutional right, as to form an exception to the general rule.   These instances have been above alluded to, and we are not disposed to extend exceptions to the rule further than has already been done by this court.

It is a firmly established and wise maxim of the law in relation to the acts of public officers, and especially of judicial tribunals acting within their jurisdiction, that all things shall be presumed to be done rightly until the contrary is proved.   This is a rule of convenience, because it dispenses with unnecessary prolixity, and the incorporation of immaterial matter in the record.   It is a rule of justice and safety, because it prevents advantage being taken of acts that have been legally and formally done, but the recital of which in the record might be inartificial, and tend to prevent justice by informality ; and we know of no class of judicial duties to which the reason and propriety of the rule has more just application than to criminal trials, which, from their nature, constantly give rise to strange and novel proceedings.

The justice of applying this principle to the objection under consideration, is forcibly shown by the history of this case, as it appears of record.   In the court below, the objection was to the fact of separation.   No suggestion or showing whatever was made, on the motion for a new trial, that the fact then alleged was true ; and if it was made, it must have been shown not to be true, for the defendant's counsel omitted all notice of it in the bill of exceptions.   It must, then, have been abandoned or disproved on the motion for a new trial.   Nor was it pretended in the court below, as this court is asked to presume, that the jury were not under the charge of a duly sworn officer.   That court was most competent to pronounce whether that suggestion was true or not in fact, and the silence of the bill of exceptions upon that point again creates a strong presumption that no such irregularity existed, and, therefore, that no complaint was made of it.   Under these circumstances, it would subserve any thing else than the purposes of justice or law, for this court to indulge the presumption that the court below had committed so gross an outrage upon propriety, in a case of life and death, as not to place the jury under proper and legal custody.

But, although the defendant abandoned the charge of separation or want of proper custody of the jury, in the court below, or it is shown to be unfounded, yet the objection here rests upon the silence of the record, and we are asked hence to infer, that the irregularity existed. This objection is entitled to less favor, than if no objection as to the separation or custody of the jury had been made in the court below; for it not only encounters the general presumption in favor of the regularity of the proceedings of that court, but also that arising from the fact that the alleged irregularity was there objected to, and either abandoned or shown to be unfounded. The objection, therefore, now founded on the mere silence of the record about an incidental fact in the trial, certainly comes with a very bad grace. Had it been urged in the court below, it doubtless could have been corrected to suit the views of the defendant according to the fact. It is the settled law of this court, that it will take no cognizance of points not presented in the court below; 3 How., 214; 4 ib., 90; 8 S. & M., 197; and the rule applies with greater force where the point is one of fact, and was raised and abandoned in the court below. The only exceptions to this rule which this court has indulged, or which now receive its sanction, are cases where the record shows that the court was not properly constituted, or that it had not jurisdiction of the subject-matter or person, or that some judicial act so absolutely essential and indispensable to the validity of the proceeding as to be shown, in due form, to have been performed, does not appear to have been done. We do not consider the action of the court, in relation to the disposition of a jury, such a judicial act, but an incidental step in progress of the cause, which will be presumed to have been duly and legally done until the contrary is shown.

Opposed to this view, two decisions from the state of New York, and one from the state of Indiana, have been brought to our notice. 2 Caines R., 373; 11 I. R., 442; and 2 Blackf., 475. The first two cases relate to proceedings of courts of special and limited jurisdiction, upon *certiorari* from justices of the peace. In such cases, the courts of New York seem to hold that they cannot intend that any thing was done which is not stated in the justice's return, because he is required to state all his proceedings and the whole history of the case. This is the proper rule in reference to courts of special and limited jurisdiction, but it does not apply to courts of general common law jurisdiction. 2 Phil. Ev., (Cow. & Hill,) 305 ; 3 ib., 1013. In the case in Indiana, it is broadly held that, as the law requires the clerk to send up a full and complete transcript of all the proceedings in the court below, the court must conclude that nothing more was done than is certified to have been done. Whatever may be the law in Indiana upon this point, the position declared in the case referred to cannot be recognized by this court as sound law. On the contrary, it has been constantly held by this court, that every fact incidental to the proceeding in the circuit court not required by law to be incorporated in the record must be presumed to have been properly done. Upon this principle, it will be presumed that the jury are good and lawful men ; that they have been duly summoned and empanelled ; that the witnesses, if any were produced and examined, were sworn ; that there was sufficient evidence to support the verdict and judgment ; and, as in this case, that the jury were legally and properly disposed of, unless the contrary be made to appear. But according to the case in Indiana, every judgment in this state, in which the record did not show affirmatively that these things had been done, could be declared erroneous, and reversed ; and this court would have to retrace its steps from its earliest organization, and establish a new rule, alike unsound in practice and unsupported in principle.

This court has always manifested a sedulous anxiety to preserve the purity of trials by jury, especially in criminal cases, by setting aside verdicts, where it was shown affirmatively that the jury were not in charge of a sworn bailiff, or that strangers had been with them, or where one had separated from his fellows out of the charge of the bailiff, although no tampering or improper influence was shown to have been practiced, declaring that the mere possibility of improper influence or irregular conduct is sufficient to vitiate the verdict. In this case there is no pretence of any such impropriety in fact, but it is insisted that we must presume that the court below failed to perform its duty in having the jury properly disposed of on its retirement, on the solemn issue of life or death, a presumption in violation of established principle and the settled law of this court.

After a careful examination of the objections urged to the proceedings below, upon a re-argument of this case, we are of opinion that they show no sufficient ground for reversing the judgment.

The judgment is therefore affirmed.

JESSE (a slave) *v.* THE STATE, 28 Miss. Rep., 100.

ARSON.

As a general rule, an indictment framed under a statute must follow the precise words in charging the offense, that the statute uses in its description. But where the words in the statute do not embrace every ingredient necessary to constitute the crime, the full offense must be charged by the use of such words as are necessary and proper under established rules of law to characterize it.

An indictment for arson must charge that the burning was done maliciously, otherwise it is defective and should be quashed.

Every error in charging an offense which would be fatal to the indictment on general demurrer or on motion in arrest of judgment, may be urged in error, and is ground for reversal.

Error to Carroll circuit court.   HARRIS, J.

The facts of the case are sufficiently set forth in the opinion of the court and the briefs of counsel.

J. Z. George for plaintiff in error.

The indictment is fatally defective, because it does not charge, either directly or by necessary implication, that the burning was malicious. As a preliminary question to this, it is necessary to determine whether, upon the one hand, the statute upon which these proceedings are based (Hutch. Code, 521, § 55) creates a distinct statutory offense, prescribing a definition of all the facts which constitute the crime; or whether, upon the other hand, the statute merely refers to a common law offense by its popular name, and provides a penalty for its commission; or whether it defines the offense by terms constituting a legal conclusion instead of prescribing a definition of the facts which in law constitute the crime.

If either of the two latter hypotheses be correct, then the indictment should be drawn as at common law ; if the first be correct, then it should follow substantially the words of the statute. Whar. Am. Cr. Law, 134.

I insist that the statute cannot, with any propriety, be construed to create an offense, containing a definition of all the facts which constitute it. There are eleven distinct offenses mentioned in the section of the statute under consideration, for the commission of either of which by a slave, the penalty is death. It is manifest that the legislature did not intend in the section under consideration, to define the facts constituting the offenses therein mentioned. If such be the intention of the legislature, they were singularly unfortunate in making that a capital offense which may be done or committed, as a most innocent transaction, although attended by every fact or circumstance mentioned in the statute. For a slave may, by his master's direction and consent, burn his master's own barn, not situated where, by any possibility, any damage or loss could arise to any third person.

Again, if we look at the context, the intention to prescribe a punishment for crimes, instead of a definition of them becomes more manifest. It will not, I presume, be contended that under the same section, a slave could be lawfully indicted, " that," etc., " he attempted to commit any capital crime ;" or " that," etc., " he was, voluntarily, accessory before the fact in a capital offense ;" or, " that," etc., " he was guilty of a capital crime ;" or, " that" etc., " he was guilty of any other crime made capital by law," without charging what particular crime and the facts necessary to constitute it. Yet, if these phrases constitute a definition of the facts constituting the several offenses, such indictment would be good.

Under such an indictment, a slave might be tried either for murder, arson in the first degree, or treason, without any notice which of these several offenses were intended to be alleged against him. And if he should be so fortunate as to be acquitted upon the charge selected for his trial by the district attorney, under the indictment, he might afterwards, under a similar one, be tried for the same offense without any possibility of pleading and proving by the record his former acquittal.

I conclude, then, that the statute does not furnish us with a definition of the facts constituting the crime for which defendant stands indicted, but that we must look to the common law for such definition, and for the rule by which the indictment must be framed.

Arson is the wilful and malicious burning of the house or outhouse of another.   Whar. Am. Cr. Law, 584 ; 4 Black. Com., 220.   At common law it is necessary to aver that the offense (of burning) was committed wilfully and maliciously as well as feloniously.   2 East, P. C., 1033 ; 1 Hawk., P. C., 140 ; Whar. Am. Cr. Law, 537.   In an indictment under the statute of 9 Geo. 1, it is necessary to aver that the burning was malicious, although the statute does not contain these words, for the malice is the essence of the offence.   2 East, P. C., 1033.

This indictment does not contain the word malicious, and is, therefore, fatally defective at common law, unless the above authorities are wrong, and unless it be unnecessary to aver in an indictment the fact which constitutes the essence of the crime, or that without which it is no crime at all ; a position which is simply absurd.   But if I should be mistaken in supposing that this indictment must be tried by the standard of the common law, instead of by the statute, I insist that it is defective in not containing the statutory definition.

"Where the words of the statute are descriptive of the offense, the indictment should follow the language of the statute. It is necessary that the defendant should be brought within all the material words of the statute, and nothing can be taken by intendment." Whar. Am. Cr. Law, 132, 133. "It is a general rule that all indictments upon statutes, especially the most penal, must state all the circumstances which constitute the definition of the offense in the act, so as to bring the defendant precisely within it.   They must also pursue the precise and technical description of the offense.   This rule was not followed in this case.   The most material word in the constitution of the offense is omitted."   Anthony v. State, 13 S. & M., 264.

If tried by this standard, the indictment is defective.   The language of the statute is, "If any slave shall be guilty of burning any dwelling-house, barn, etc., he shall, on conviction, suffer death." The indictment avers that "he wilfully and feloniously did burn," etc. It is only by a most strained construction that the definition of any offense can be ascertained from the language of the statute. If the court decides to resort to the language of the statute for a definition of the facts and circumstances which constitute the offense, I insist that the word guilty is of most material effect in ascertaining that the statutory definition is a crime at all.

The statute says, " If a slave shall be guilty," etc. The word guilty is in this connection all-important, because it signifies, *ex vi termini*, a breach of a legal duty, and a violation of law, and it is the only word in the statute which defines or denotes a criminal act, for, as before remarked, the remaining words of the statute define no act which may not be perfectly innocent. The word guilty does not serve merely as a kind of legal *vinculum* to connect the agent with the act done, it also connects him with every other fact, material and moral, which is necessary in law to accompany the act in order to constitute it a crime.

If a man be indicted for a malicious homicide, the verdict of guilty not only establishes that he committed the homicide, but that he perpetrated it under such circumstances as, in law, constituted the crime of murder. So if one be indicted for a malicious burning, the verdict of guilty not only ascertains the fact of the burning, but also the legal malice, which renders it unlawful. The word guilty, universally, in law, implies a violation of law,—a commission of an act, or omission of a duty, under circumstances which render the commission or omission unlawful. When it is said, " that the law is made for the protection of the innocent by a due punishment of the guilty," and that it is better that ninety-nine guilty persons should escape than one innocent should be punished — the term " guilty" is not asserted of persons who do or have done acts which may or may not be unlawful according to circumstances, but of those who actually do or have done acts attended by such circumstances as render them illegal.

The burning of a barn is innocent or criminal, lawful or unlawful, according to the attendant circumstances. The legislature has failed to define these circumstances, except so far as they may be implied in the term "guilty." That term, then, must be used in the indictment, as *generalissimum nomen*, including within itself the legal definition of those facts which constitute the crime, or, discarding the general name, the pleader should have averred specially those facts which are implied in the term "guilty." This he has failed to do, and I confidently conclude that the indictment, whether tried by the statute or the common law, is fatally defective.

The next question is, whether the defendant, having failed to demur, to move to quash, or in arrest of judgment in the court below, can take advantage in this court of the error complained of. This question is settled by a deed of adjudication of this court. The court say, "The only question as to this was, whether in a case in which the writ of error was sued out, to a refusal to grant a new trial, the objection could be taken in that stage of the proceeding." It would appear to have been thus taken in Cody v. State, 3 How., 27. And as the statute of jeofails and amendments does not extend to criminal proceedings, it follows that every error which would have been fatal on demurrer or in arrest of judgment, will be sufficient to procure its reversal. 1 Chit. Cr. Law, 7511 ; 13 S. & M., 406. In that case the error was that no prosecutor was marked on the indictment at all.

The next error complained of is, the giving of the third instruction asked in behalf of the state, which is as follows: "A free and voluntary confession of guilt made by a prisoner, whether in the course of private conversation with private persons, or upon examination before a magistrate, is admissible in evidence as the highest and most satisfactory proof, because it is fairly to be presumed that no man would make such a confession against himself if the facts confessed were not true."

I object to this instruction on two grounds: 1st, That as a legal proposition it is not true; 2d, That it is a charge upon the weight of testimony.

1. Notwithstanding the contrariety of opinion among foreign judges and text writers as to the weight due to confessions, it is no longer an open question in this state, if two direct adjudica-

cations of this court, holding the very reverse of the principle announced in the third instruction, be competent to settle it. See Keithler v. State, 10 S. & M. ; Stringfellow v. State, 26 Miss., 157.

The evidence of verbal confessions of guilt is received with great caution. 1 Greenl. Ev., § 214. "Of all kinds of evidence, that of extrajudicial and casual declarations is the weakest and most unsatisfactory ; such words are often spoken without serious intention, and they are always liable to be mistaken and misremembered, and their meaning is liable to be misrepresented and exaggerated." 1 Starkie on Ev., 549, *et seq.*

Judge Blackstone, speaking of confessions, says : "And even in cases of felony at common law, they are the weakest and most suspicious of all kinds of testimony ; ever liable to be obtained by artifice, false hopes, promises of favor, or menaces, seldom remembered accurately or reported with due precision, and incapable from their nature of being disproved by negative evidence." 4 Blackstone, Com., 357.

The voluntary statement of a prisoner is of little weight. Keithler v. State, 10 S. & M.

This court in Stringfellow's case, after reviewing the decisions and the text writers on this subject, come to the conclusion in conformity with the authorities cited above. The court say : "We believe that the doctrine which holds, that in capital felonies the prisoner's confessions, when the *corpus delicti* is not proved by independent testimony, is insufficient for his conviction, best accords with the solid principles of reason, and the caution which should be applied in the admission and estimate of this species of evidence."

Now, if confessions, free and voluntary, are the highest and most satisfactory proof, it is a little singular that this court should discard that kind of evidence, being the highest and most satisfactory, and require proof of the *corpus delicti*, by the lower and less satisfactory proof of the testimony of an eye-witness to the act of killing, or of a person who had seen the dead body. For if confessions are the highest and most satisfactory proof, all other evidence is less satisfactory.

As there is no statute of frauds and perjuries in criminal

cases (unless the constitution, as to proof of treason, be one), I infer that the court, in deciding that the confessions of a prisoner are insufficient to prove the *corpus delicti*, did not act in obedience to a positive law, prohibiting that particular fact to be proved in that particular manner; but that they held that confessions, on account of their intrinsic weakness, are incapable of producing a satisfactory belief that the fact is so, or in other words, that they required higher and more satisfactory proof of the fact to be established.

We are not left entirely to inference as to the true position of the court in this respect, for they assign as a reason for their opinion, " the caution which should be applied in the admission and estimate of that species of evidence."

2. The instruction is liable to objection on another ground, namely, it charges the jury on the weight of evidence.

" It is surely not competent for the court to charge the jury on the weight of evidence; this must be left to the jury to determine."   " The weight of evidence is the influence or effect which it has in establishing a fact, or in enabling the jury to draw a conclusion."   Perry v. Clark, 5 How., 499.

If the jury be told by the court that certain evidence is the highest and most satisfactory proof of guilt, they are certainly charged as to the influence or effect which the proof should have in establishing the fact of guilt; for, if the proof of be the highest effect in establishing the fact to be proved, it is so in enabling the jury to draw a conclusion.

The second instruction given on behalf of the state is also error; it is as follows: " If the jury believe that the proof shows that the defendant burnt such a building as the one described in the first instruction, it will be your duty to convict him."

This assumes that the burning of the barn is *per se* a crime, whether it be done wilfully and maliciously or accidentally. This, as a legal proposition, is monstrous, repugnant to the common ideas of justice of all mankind, whether civilized or barbarous, and utterly unfounded in any decision or dictum of any judge or justice, from the high dignitary who sits in the highest court in Christendom to the contemptible retailer of judicial wares in the presiding genius of a *pri pondre* court.

The instruction is indefensible as modified by an instruction on the part of defendant, to the effect that the burning must be wilful.   It must also be malicious.   4 Blackstone, 220 ; 2 East, P. C., 1033 ; Whart. Am. Cr. Law, 534.

The judgment should be reversed for another reason ; there is no evidence in the record that the defendant is a slave.   Under the indictment it was necessary to prove that the defendant was a slave, as charged.   The slavery of defendant is one of the ingredients of the crime and is that which makes it capital. The crime, as charged, consists of two facts, one of the malicious burning, the other the slavery of the defendant.   If either fact does not exist, the defendant is not guilty.   It then becomes the duty of the state to prove both facts.   This, I presume, will not be controverted.

It may be insisted that the proof of color would raise a presumption of slavery upon which the jury would be authorized to act, and that such proof may be made by witnesses testifying to the fact, or the personal inspection of the jury.   Waiving for the present the fact that there is no proof in the record on this subject, I insist that the rule cannot be applied in this case.

That presumptions of slavery or freedom arise from color in civil cases has been decided in this and other southern states. See Fox v. Lamburn, 3 Halst., 275 ; Gentry v. McInnis, 3 Dana, 382 ; Hall v. Mullen, 5 Harris. & Johns., 190 ; Hooke v. Page, 3 Mumf., 379 ; Gober v. Gober, 2 Hayw., 170 ; Burke v. Joe, 6 Gill & Johns., 336 ; Hudgins v. Wright, 1 Hen. & Mumf., 141 ; Thornton v. De Moss, 5 S. & M., 609.

The supreme court of Alabama has held other proof to be necessary.   State v. Marshall, 8 Ala. R., 302.

It would be a violation of well-settled legal principles, to extend this rule to criminal cases.   The accused, as he stands, is presumed in law to be innocent until his guilt is proved.   No presumption of guilt can arise, except as a legal inference from certain acts which the proof connects him with as the agent or author, as the presumption of malice arising from the use of a deadly weapon or the administration of poison, or of intent, from the principle that a party is presumed to intend the ordinary and natural consequences of his own acts.   In these cases it will be recollected that the presumption arises alone upon proof of such acts as the party commits either by himself or another, or is legally responsible for.

It is submitted, that no principle exists by which a presumption of guilt can arise from the proof of a fact for which the defendant is in no way responsible, and from the nature of things cannot be.

D. C. Glenn, attorney general.

1. Upon the objections to the indictment I refer to the decision in Sarah's case, 28 Miss., 267.

2. I insist the objection comes too late here, in not being made below. Loper's case, 4 How.; Brantley's case, 13 S. & M.

3. The 2d charge is qualified by all the law given to the jury.

4. The charge on confessions is upheld by the author in Whar. Am. Cr. Law, 252, and cases cited.

HANDY, J.:

This was an indictment in the circuit court of Carroll county, under the 55th section of the statute of 1852, Hutch. Dig., 521, concerning slaves, free negroes, and mulattoes. The indictment charges that the plaintiff in error, "on the 5th day of June, 1854, with force and arms, in the county aforesaid, did then and there wilfully and feloniously set fire to and burn up and consume with said fire a certain barn situate in said county," etc., "contrary to the statute in such cases made and provided," etc. The accused pleaded not guilty, and on the trial a verdict and judgment of conviction were rendered, from which the case is brought here.

The first and principal ground of error alleged is, that the indictment is essentially defective in not charging that the act of burning was committed maliciously, and, therefore, that no judgment can be pronounced upon or supported by it, and it must be quashed.

The offense charged is founded upon the statute above mentioned, which provides, that "if any slave shall be guilty of burning any dwelling-house, store, cotton-house, gin or outhouse, barn or stable, or shall be accessory thereto, every such slave shall, on conviction, suffer death."

It is not denied on the part of the state that malice is of the essence of the crime of arson at common law, and that the same ingredient must enter into offenses of house-burning created by statute. But it is insisted that in the latter class of cases it is sufficient to charge the offense in the indictment by the terms used in the statute.

While this is true as a general rule, we apprehend that it only applies where the description of the offense in the statute, taking into consideration its nature and the natural and legal import of the terms used in designating it, is such as to convey a certain, clear, and full idea of the offense intended to be created, and to embrace every ingredient necessary to constitute it, though the words employed be not the same as would be required in indictments for similar offenses at common law. In such a case no prejudice can be done to the accused by following the words of the statute. But if the words used in the statute do not, in view of the nature of the offense and the recognized principles of law, describe the offense so as to convey to the mind a full and clear idea of every thing necessary to constitute the crime, in such case the full measure of the offense must be charged, by the use of such words as are necessary and proper under established rules of law to characterize it. The difference is simply that between offenses which are fully and clearly defined in the statute and such as are described generally. In the former, the description contained in the statute is sufficient; in the latter, the offenses must be charged agreeably to the rules of the common law. It depends upon the nature of the offense and the terms in which it is described in the statute, whether the one or the other of these rules will apply to the particular case. Whar. Am. Cr. Law, 132, and cases cited.

In the present case, it is manifest that the words used in the statute do not show any thing which, as described, it can be supposed the legislature intended to punish. No term is employed conveying the idea of malice or criminal intent; and yet it is obvious that it was not intended to punish the mere burning of the houses enumerated, without it should be done with a malicious intent.   It is plain, therefore, that the legislature have not adverted to the full measure of the offense, and that it was not intended to do so, but to provide generally for its punishment, leaving the proper description of it to be supplied according to the settled rules of law when persons should be charged under the statute.   We are, therefore, of the opinion that the statute does not dispense with the averment of malice, and that the indictment without such averment showed no offense in law.

The next question is, whether the plaintiff in error, after having pleaded in bar to the indictment and made no question as to its sufficiency in the court below, can avail himself of a fatal defect in it in this court, and have it quashed.   This point was decided in Kirk v. State, 13 S. & M., 407, and we think correctly.   We think it well settled that every error in substance, in charging the offense, which would have been fatal to the indictment on general demurrer or on motion in arrest of judgment, may be urged in error and is ground for a reversal; for otherwise this court would be called on to pronounce judgment against a party who is not charged with any offense in law.

The cases of Loper v. State, 3 How., 429, and Brantley v. State, 13 S. & M., 468, are urged by the attorney general as opposed to this view.   But there is no conflict.   The case of Loper holds that the accused may waive the right to a copy of the indictment and of the special *venire* secured to him by law, and the case of Brantley holds that exceptions to the organization of the grand jury will not be entertained in this court after plea of not guilty and conviction in the court below; and the principle held in both cases is, that the objections will be considered as waived, if not made in the court below; but these are questions pertaining rather to the regularity and formality of the proceeding than to its substance and indispensable requisites. Here the error is radical and fatal to the conviction.   It is nothing less than a judgment of death against an individual for an offense, which, as charged, is no crime in law; and if the judgment were affirmed, this court would have to pronounce judgment of death anew against him, when no crime is alleged against him.   It appears to us, therefore, clear, that in cases like this it is proper to examine the indictment, and though not questioned in the court below, if it appear to be fatally defective in substance, that it should be quashed here.

The judgment is therefore reversed, the indictment quashed, and the prisoner ordered to be kept in custody for a new indictment.

Sarah (a slave) v. The State, 28 Miss. Rep., 267.

Attempt to Murder by Poison.

To prepare poison with intent to kill a person, and the crime of administering such poison for a like purpose, are two different offenses. Yet there can be no objection to an indictment on the ground that these two offenses are charged in it against the same person.

In England it is held to be irregular where two distinct felonies are charged in the same indictment, but in the United States the courts have held that distinct felonies of the same character, though differing in the degree of punishment, may be charged in the same indictment against the same person.

The words "persons in this state" in the statute against poisoning, were intended to designate the jurisdiction of the offense, and not as descriptive of the persons against whom the crime might be committed. And an indictment not alleging that the person attempted to be poisoned, was "a person of this state," is not deficient on that ground.

In order to show that the alleged act of administering the poison came within the meaning of the statute, it is essential to allege the manner in which the poison was administered.

The word "administer" used in the statute, does not mean that the article given in order to effect the felonious intent, must be given under the pretense that it is a medicine. The intention of the legislature was to punish any preparation, giving, or administration of any substance known as a medicine, with intent to kill.

The compelling the prosecutor to elect which count of the indictment on which he will proceed, is a matter in the discretion of the court, and a refusal to do so is no ground of reversal.

In an indictment for a statutory offense it is sufficient to describe the offense in the words of the statute. But this rule can only apply in cases in which there is a sufficient description of the offense intended to be created by the legislature.

In all cases of felony in which malice is the gist of the offense, malice must be averred in the indictment, otherwise it will be defective and the judgment arrested on motion. HANDY, J., dissenting.

Error to Warren circuit court. BARNETT, J.

C. L. Buck for plaintiff in error.

1. To sustain an indictment under the 53d section of Hutch. Code, 521, it must appear in proof that the poison or medicine was prepared or administered by the defendant under the pretense that it was a medicine; and proof that the defendant

merely prepared or administered poison "with intent to kill," will not sustain the indictment. The latter offense is punishable under the succeeding section of the same page. No adjudicated case can be found upon the question, as there has been found no statute similar to it. It is, however, submitted, that the section explains itself, and requires nothing more than a perusal to show the error of the court below. If it be contended that section 55 protects the conviction, it will be apparent to the court that there was not a single averment in the indictment necessary to sustain it under the latter section. The proof in the cause is, that "a deadly poison" and not "a medicine" was prepared and administered by the appellant.

2. The judgment below must be reversed, and the indictment quashed, because there is no averment in either of the counts that the persons for whom the poison was prepared and administered to, were "persons in this state." The section provides, that "if any slave shall prepare, exhibit, or administer to, any person in this state, with intent to kill such person," etc.

In the first count, there is an entire omission of this essential averment. To "prepare medicine, with the intent to kill" any person out of this state, is no offense under this section, and this count is, therefore manifestly defective. It may be contended in argument, that this omission is supplied in the second count, as it is there charged that the poison was administered in this state, and that, therefore, the persons to whom it was administered were "persons in this state." It will, however, require neither argument nor authority to this court to sustain the principle of law declared, as well in all the elementary books, as in adjudicated cases, and every material allegation must be accompanied with time and *venue*, and must be positively averred, and that inference is never sufficient in the statement of either. The *venue* and time here stated relates to the "administering" of the poison, a fact that required a distinct and positive averment itself. We can only infer that the parties to whom the poison was administered were "persons in this state," from the averment that the poison was administered here. This is clearly error. See Chitty Cr. Law, 231; 1 Sess. Cas., 159, 416; 2 ib., 8, 8; 2 Stra., 900; 1 Salk., 317; 3 Mod., 53; 2 Hawk., ch. 25,

§ 60 ; 1 Lord Raymond, 1363 ; also to the decisions of this court.

It is absolutely necessary to charge in the indictment under the statute, that the parties for whom the poison was prepared, and administered to, were "persons in this state." Chitty Cr. Law, 280 ; ib., 282, note; 2 Hawk., ch. 25, § 84, 112 ; Chitty Cr. Law, 284, 285 ; 13 S. & M., 263. The indictment must be quashed because there is no allegation that the poison was prepared with intent to murder. This averment is absolutely requisite. The word "murder" is a technical one, which cannot be omitted in indictments for murder, and to use the word "kill" is insufficient. 1 Russ., 470 ; 3 Chitty Cr. Law, 737 ; Archb. Cr. Pl., 49. It is true the statute uses the words "to kill ;" but the offense to be punished was evidently doing the act with intent to kill and murder, as the mere act of killing does not necessarily imply any offense. If the word "kill" only be used in an indictment for homicide, the party can only be convicted of manslaughter. See Russell, Archbold and Chitty on Criminal Law.

The words "malice aforethought" are wholly omitted in both counts, and are yet absolutely necessary. Russell on Crimes, 470 ; 1 Dyer, 69. Without these words, every law-book upon the subject declares, that a party cannot be convicted of murder. Archbold expressly, as well as Russell, lays down this doctrine. Our own statute lays down this rule, that there can be no murder without premeditated malice. If, then, without the use of these technical words in the indictment a party cannot be convicted of the crime itself, surely, without them, the prisoner cannot be convicted of the attempt to commit it. The offense created by our statute, and under which the present indictment is framed, is an attempt to kill and murder with "malice aforethought." The allegations in the indictment and the proof must come fully up to this, or else they are insufficient. The word "feloniously," it is true, is used, but this is insufficient. Manslaughter is a felony. 1 Russ., 470. The word "feloniously" does not imply "malice aforethonght," the last being the ingredient in homicide which divides manslaughter from murder, and raises the offense to the highest degree. These objections should have sustained the motion in the court below to quash. The motion to quash, when made, reaches every objection to the indictment, and the motion in this case is because the indictment is insufficient ; and second, because felonies were improperly joined in the indictment. This motion was overruled, and exceptions taken. But the objection is good on demurrer, or motion in arrest of judgment. There is no question on this point. Chitty Cr. Law, 661, 664, 752, 754 ; Dyer, 69 ; Archbold, 51–54 ; Hawk., 468, § 4 ; Hale's P. C. At common law every defect reached by demurrer, was good on motion to arrest, etc. In England, this principle was, to some extent, changed by statute. But we have no statute upon the subject, and the rule with us is unchanged. This point has been settled by our own courts. In Kirk v. State, 13 S. & M., 407, the court expressly decides that every objection to an indictment that may be reached by demurrer, can be reached by motion in arrest of judgment.

The second count in the indictment is either double or it is contradictory ; it charges, first, an administering and then a mingling of the poison with coffee, with intent that it should be administered. This can be reached on motion to quash, or motion in arrest of judgment. But the court below overruled both motions, and this court will correct the error.

The court below erred in refusing defendant's instructions, and giving those asked by the state. The latter use the words " with intent to kill," and omit the " murder." Moreover, to sustain the indictment, the proof must show the poison was prepared or administered under pretence of its being a medicine. This the proof wholly fails to establish.

The court below erred in overruling the motion to quash, because two distinct felonies were charged in the indictment, and also in refusing to compel the state to elect on which count it would proceed. It is not the statement of the same offense, or different degrees of the offense in the indictment, which is the legitimate office of several counts ; but each count charges a separate, distinct and independent felony, thereby placing the party upon trial for two offenses at the same time. This is contrary to all rule and practice in criminal proceedings. See

Chitty Cr. Law, 248; 1 Leach, 510, 511; 8 East, 41; 2 Campbell, 131; 8 Wend., 211; 2 Hale, 173; 2 Leach, 1103; 12 Wend., 425; Galloway's case, Ry. & M., C. C. R., 234; 7 Serg. & Rawle, 469; Wash. v. State, 14 S. & M., 120; Brantley v. State, 13 ib., 468.

D. C. Glenn, attorney general.

SMITH, C, J.:

The prisoner was convicted in the circuit court of Warren county, under the provisions of the fifty-third section of the statute of 1822, Hutch. Dig., 521.

The indictment contains two counts. The first count charges the willful, malicious, unlawful and felonious preparation of a certain medicine, namely arsenic, alleging the said arsenic to be a deadly poison, and that the prisoner well knew that arsenic was such deadly poison, " with intent there and then to kill" the persons named in the indictment, " contrary to the form of the statute," etc. The second count charges the " willful, malicious, unlawful and felonious" administration to certain persons named in the indictment, of " a certain medicine commonly called arsenic, the said arsenic being then and there a deadly poison, by then and there mixing and mingling the said arsenic in certain coffee which had been prepared for the use of the said" persons, " with the intent, then and there, that the said coffee should be administered to them for their drinking the same, and the said coffee, with which the said arsenic was so mixed and mingled as aforesaid, afterwards, namely, etc., in the county aforesaid, was delivered to the said" persons, " then and there to be drunk; and said persons, not knowing said arsenic to have been mixed and mingled with said coffee, did afterwards, namely, etc., in the county aforesaid, take, drink and swallow, etc., a large quantity of said arsenic, so mixed and mingled with said coffee" by the prisoner " with the intent then and there to kill the said" persons, " contrary to the form of the statute," etc.

In the court below, before trial, a motion was made to quash the indictment, and after verdict the prisoner's counsel moved in arrest of judgment. There was also a motion made for a new trial, which was overruled. Hence the cause is brought before us by writ of error.   The grounds relied on in support of these motions are now urged as reasons for reversing the judgment.

First, it is insisted, that the indictment should have been quashed, because the prisoner was charged with two distinct, separate and independent felonies.

The statute under which the conviction was had, provides that " if any slave, free negro or mulatto, shall prepare, exhibit or administer to any person or persons in this state, any medicine whatsoever, with intent to kill such person or persons, he or she so offending shall be judged guilty of a felony, and shall suffer death."   It is manifest, that distinct and separate offenses have been created by this act.   To prepare any medicine with intent to kill any person, is a separate and distinct offense from the crime of administering such medicine for a like purpose.   This is clear, for the evidence, which would sustain an indictment for the preparation by a slave, free negro or mulatto, of medicine with the intent to murder any person, would not be sufficient to convict, where the party is charged with the administration of any medicine for the same purpose.   It must, therefore, be conceded, that the indictment charges the prisoner with two distinct felonies.

But does it follow, hence, that the refusal of the court to quash the indictment is ground for reversing the judgment ?

The rule is well settled that, in point of law, there is no objection to the insertion of several distinct felonies of the same degree in the same indictment, against the same offender.[1]   1 Chitty, Cr. Law, 253 ; Kane v. The People, 8 Wend., 203 ; 12 ib., 425 ; Wash. v. The State, 14 S. & M., 120.   But while this is the acknowledged doctrine, both in this country and England, it is held in the courts of the latter country to be irregular, in

1 Wharton Am. Cr. Law, 414, *et sequitur ;* Baker v. State, 4 Pike's Ark., 56 ; People v. Rynders, 12 Wend., 425 ; Edge v. Commonwealth, 7 Barr, 275 ; Coulter v. Commonwealth, 5 Metc., 532 ; State v. Kirvy, Miss., 317 ; Mills v. Commonwealth, 1 Harris, 631 ; Hoskins v. State, 11 Ga., 92 : Engleman v. State, 2 Carter, (Ind.,) 91 ; U. S. v. O'Callahan, 6 McLean, C. C. R., 569 ; Johnson v. State, 29 Ala., 62 ; Orr v. State, 18 Ark., 540 ; Young v. Rex, 3 T. R., 105 ; Rex v. Jones, 2 Camp., 132 ; Rex v. Saunders, 2 Burr., 984 ; Rex v. Kingston, 8 East, 41 ; Archbold Cr. Pr. & Pl., 310 ; Commonwealth v. Tuck, 20 Pick., 356 ; State v. Brady, 14 Vermont, 353 ; State v. Crocker, 3 Harr., (Del.,) 554 ; State v. Grisham, 1 Hayw., 12 ; State v. Flye, 26 Me., 312 ; People v. Austin, 1 Park. Cr. R. 154 ; State v. Patterson, 1 W. & M., 305 ; Commonwealth v. Manson, 2 Ashmead, 131 · State v. Hogan, Charlt., 474.

cases of felony, to charge upon the prisoner more than one distinct offense at one time in the same indictment. And if the joinder of more than one distinct felony in the same indictment be objected to before plea, the court will quash the indictment, lest it should embarrass the prisoner in his defense, or prejudice him in his challenge to the jury. But this appears to be regarded not as a right, strictly speaking, of the accused, but as a matter submitted to the discretion of the court, which it might exercise as a measure of prudence for the safety of the accused. [1] Chitty, Crim. Law, 253; King v. Strange, 34 Eng. Com. L. R., 341. In the case last cited, which was an indictment under the statute of 7 Will. 4, and 1 Victoria, the offense of stabbing and cutting, with intent to murder, with intent to maim, and with intent to do grievous bodily harm, were all included in the same indictment; and notwithstanding the judgment is by the statute different, being for the offenses charged in the first count capital, and for the others transportation, the court even refused to compel the prosecutor to elect on which count he would proceed.

The courts in many of the states of this confederacy have gone a step further, and hold that distinct felonies, of the same character, though differing in the degrees of punishment attached by law to their perpetration, may be charged in the same indictment against the same person. Wharton's Crim. Law, p. 149.

In the case at bar the felonies charged in the indictment differ neither in character nor in the punishments attached to their commission. They manifestly refer to the same transaction, and depend necessarily to some extent on the same evidence. I am, therefore, of opinion that the joinder of the two felonies charged in the indictment was not good ground for quashing it.

Secondly. It is contended that the indictment should have been quashed, because there is no averment in either of the

[1] Archbold Cr. Pr. & Pl., 310; Young v. Rex, T. R., 96; Wharton Am. Cr. Law, 414, 422; Kane v. People, 9 Wend., 203; Wright v. State, 4 Humph., 194; Weinzorpflin v. State, 7 Black., 186; State v. Hazzard, 2 R. I., 474; State v. Jacobs, 10 La. R., 141; Ketchingham v. State, 6 Wisc., 426; Commonwealth v. Hills, 10 Cushing, (Mass.,) 530; Donnelly v. State, 2 Dutch., (N. J.,) 463, 601; Lozier v. Commonwealth, 10 Gratt., 708; Rex v. Austin, 7 C. & P., 769; Rex v. Hartall, ib., 475; Rex v. Wheeler, ib., 170; Regina v. Pulham, 9 C. & P., 281; People v. Costello, 1 Denio, 83; State v. Hogan, R. M. Charlton, 474; Dowdy v. Commonwealth, 9 Gratt., 737; State v. Jackson, 17 Mo., 544; Mayo v. State, —— 32; Cash v. State, 10 Humph., 111, 114; 1 Bishop Cr. Law, 206.

counts, that the persons for whom it was administered, were "persons in this state."

In my opinion this exception is based upon a misconstruction of the statute.

That construction assumes that it was the intention of the legislature, by the words "in this state," to designate the persons for whom, or to whom, to prepare or administer medicine with intent to kill, the statute declared to be a felony. That is, that the medicine must be prepared for or administered to a person within the state at the time of the alleged offense. Hence, that these words constitute an essential part of the description of the offenses created by the act.

It cannot be imagined that the legislature deemed it necessary to declare that it was their intention to confine the operation of the law to acts performed within her jurisdiction; as it will certainly not be contended that it was not known to it, that the statutes of this state could not extend to offenses committed without her jurisdiction. A medicine or a poison might be prepared for a person, not at the time of the preparation within the state, but neither could it be administered to any one, in such a way as to violate any law of the state, unless the person who might be the subject of the felony were, at the time of the administration of the medicine or poison, within the jurisdiction of the state. If, therefore, the words, "in this state," employed in the statute, are understood as characterizing the persons against whom the offense must be committed, they are useless and unmeaning. But if these words are held to refer not to the persons against whom the offense may be committed, but to the felonious act itself, they are intelligible and proper, and the intention of the legislature becomes manifest. It appears to me too evident to admit of question, that by the proper and legal construction of the statute, these words were intended to designate the jurisdiction in which the offenses are prohibited, and not as descriptive of the persons against whom they might be perpetrated. Upon this interpretation of the act, the counts in the indictment, in reference to this exception, are unobjectionable.

Thirdly. It is insisted that the second count in the indictment charges the prisoner with two distinct felonies; and for that reason the court below erred in overruling the motion to quash.

This objection is untenable. In the count under consideration it is averred, that the prisoner mixed and mingled the medicine with coffee, which had been prepared for the use of the persons intended to be killed; but the alleged act of mixing the medicine with the coffee is not charged as an act of felony. It is stated as a part of the means or manner in which the administration of the medicine was effected. This was not only proper, but essential, in order to show that the alleged act of administering the medicine came within the meaning of the statute.

Fourthly. It is contended that a new trial should be awarded, upon the ground that the proof did not show that "the poison or medicine was administered under a pretence that it was a medicine." The statute affords no pretence for this exception. It declares, that "if any slave, free negro or mulatto shall prepare or administer to any person or persons, any medicine whatever, with intent to kill," etc. According to the evidence, arsenic was administered, which is not only a medicine, but a poison, and such is the case with many articles used as medicines, depending upon the quantity in which they are given. The word "administer," as used in the statute, does not mean that the article given, in order to effect the felonious intent, must be given or administered under the pretence that it is a medicine. The manifest intention of the legislature was to punish any preparation, giving, or administration of any substance known as a medicine, with intent to kill.

Fifthly. It is insisted that the court below erred in refusing to compel the prosecutor, upon the application of the prisoner's counsel, to elect upon which count of the indictment he would proceed.

We have seen[1] that it was no objection to the indictment, that it charged the prisoner with two distinct felonies in separate counts; although it rests with the court as a matter of prudence and discretion to order the indictment to be quashed for that reason, when the objection is made before plea.[2] The same an-

---

[1] *Supra;* notes [1] 755 [1] 756.   [2] Ibid.

swer may be given to this objection; it was a matter of discretion with the circuit court, and is, therefore, no ground upon which the judgment should be reversed.[1]   Rex v. Strange, 34 Com. L. R., 341; People v. Rynders, 12 Wend., 425; Oone v. Hope, 22 Pick. R. 1.

Sixthly. It is contended that the court below erred in overruling the motion in arrest of judgment.

Neither count of the indictment charges the alleged felony to have been committed with malice aforethought. This, it is insisted, is a fatal defect.

The words used in the statute are, "with intent to kill." In Bradley v. The State, 10 S. & M., 618, it was holden that an indictment for an assault with intent to kill, means an indictment for an assault to commit murder, according to the understanding of this court; therefore the words above quoted from the statute, mean "with intent to commit murder." Hence, the gist of the offense charged in the indictment is willful malice.

It is unquestionably true, as a general rule, that in an indictment for an offense created by statute, it is sufficient to describe the offense in the words of the statute. But, it is manifest, that this rule can only apply in cases, in which there is a sufficient description of the offense intended to be created by the legislature. It is a mistake, says Justice Earl, (Blease v. The State, 1 McMul. R., 479,) to suppose, that it is always sufficient to allege the offense in the mere words of the statute; for where it consists of several acts, they should be averred with the same particularity, as at common law. The rule, adopted in this court,

1 Wharton Am. Cr. Law, 414; Baker v. State, 4 Pike's Ark., 56; Edge v. Com., 7 Barr, 275; Coulter v. Com., 5 Metc., 535; State v. Kirvy, Miss., 317; Mills v. Com., 1 Harris, 631; Hoskins v. State, 11 Ga., 92; Engleman v. State, 2 Carter, (Ind.,) 91; U. S. v. O'Callahan, 6 McLean, C. C. R., 569; Johnson v. State, 29 Ala., 62; Orr v. State, 18 Ark., 540. In misdemeanors the joinder of several offenses will not, in general, vitiate the prosecution in any stage. Wharton Am. Cr. Law; Young v. Rex, 3 T. R., 105; Rex v. Jones, 2 Camp., 132; Rex v. Saunders, 2 Burr., 984; Rex v. Kingston, 8 East, 41; Harman v. Com., 12 S. & R., 69; Com. v. Gillespie, 7 S. & R., 476; U. S. v. Peterson, 1 W. & M., 305; People v. Costello, 1 Denio, 83; Weinzorpflin v. State, 7 Black., 186; Com. v. Demain, Brightly, 441; U. S. v. Porter, 2 Cr. C. C. R., 60. In cases of felony, where two or more distinct offenses are contained in the same indictment, it may be quashed, or the prosecutor be compelled to elect on which charge he will proceed. Wharton Am. Cr. Law, 416; Kane v. People, 9 Wend., 203; Wright v. State, 4 Humph., 194; Weinzorpflin v. State, 7 Black., 186; State v. Hazard, 2 R. I., 474; State v. Jacob, 10 La., 141; Kitchingham v. State, 6 Wisc., 426; Com. v. Hills, 10 Cush., 530; Donnelly v. State, 2 Dutch., (N. J.,) 463, 601. See Wharton Am. Cr. Law, 423.

is, that indictments, especially upon highly penal statutes, must state all the circumstances, which constitute the definition of the offense in the act, so as to bring the defendant precisely within it. [1]   Anthony v. State, 13 S. & M., 262.

It follows, necessarily, from this doctrine, in all cases of felony, in which malice is the gist of the offense, that the malice must be averred in the indictment; otherwise it will be defective, and the judgment arrested on motion.   We believe there is not a recognized exception to this rule either in England or this country.   And this is the case, whether the offense exist at common law, or be one of statutory creation.   Thus, in murder, where the death has been caused by the administration of poison, or by any other means, however indicative of a malicious intent, it is essential to charge the act to have been done with malice aforethought; and no other words will suffice.   So, in an indictment under the statute of 9 Geo. 1, which made it felony for any person to burn any dwelling-house, out-house, barn, stable, etc., it was holden necessary, that there should be an averment of willful malice, although the statute did not contain the words " willful and malicious ;" for the reason, that malice was of the essence of the offense.   2 East, P. C., 1033.

The statutes of 7 Will. 4 and 7 Vict., provide, that whoever shall administer, or cause to be administered, any poison or other destructive thing, " with intent to commit murder," shall be guilty of a capital felony.   The only material difference between these statutes and the one under consideration consists in the use of the words, " with intent to commit murder," instead of

---

[1] Wharton Am. Cr. Law, 364; State v. Foster, 3 McCord, 442; State v. O'Bannon, 1 Bail, 144; State v. La Preux, 1 M'Mull., 488; State v. Noel, 5 Black., 548; Chambers v. People, 4 Scam., 351; U. S. v. Lancaster, 2 McLean, 431; State v. Duncan, 9 Port., 260; State v. Mitchell, 6 Mo., 147; State v. Helm, 6 Mo., 263; Ike v. State, 23 Miss., 525. For a very liberal view on this point see Com. v. Fogerty, 8 Gray, 489. See, also, State v. Gibbons, 1 South., 51; State v. Calvin, Charlton, 151; 1 Hale, 517, 526, 535; Staunf., 130 b; Foster, 423, 424; Hard., 2; Dyer, 304; Kelyng, 8; Com. Dig. Jus., G. 1; 1 Chitty on Pl., 357; Moore, 5; 1 Leach, 264; 1 East, P. C., 419; 2 Hale, 170, 189, 190, 193; 1 Eliz., c. 1, § 25; 3 Dyer, 363; 2 Lord Raym., 791; 2 Burr., 679; 1 T. R., 222; U. S. v. Lancaster, McLean R., 431; People v. Allen, 5 Denio, 76; Com. v. Hampton, 3 Gratt., 590; State v. Pratt, 191. If the indictment profess to recite the statute, a material variance will be fatal, or if the statute do not support the verdict, it must fail. Wharton Am. Cr. Law, 365; Butler v. State, 3 McCord, 383. Defects in the description of a statutory offense will not be aided by verdict (2 East, 333), nor will the conclusion, *contra formam statuti*, cure it. Lee v. Clark, 2 East, 333; 2 Hale, 170; Rex v. Jukes, S. T. R., 536; Com. Dig. Information, D. 3.

the words, " with intent to kill," employed in the latter. But, according to the construction of this court, the words " with intent to kill" mean " with intent to commit murder." The precedents of indictments, under the English statutes, all show, that it was deemed essential to charge the offense to have been committed with malice aforethought. And we apprehend, that it is not to be doubted, that an indictment, framed under those statutes, would be holden, in an English court, to be fatally defective, without such an averment.

The statute, ch. 64, § 33, Hutch. Dig., 960, declares it to be an offense punishable by imprisonment in the penitentiary, for any person to shoot at another, " with intent to kill such other person ;" and the statute of 1822, ch. 37, § 55, Hutch. Dig., 521, makes it a capital offense for any slave " to burn any dwelling-house, store, cotton-house, gin or outhouse, barn or stable." But, in neither of the offenses created by these statutes, is willful malice made an ingredient, by express words. It will not, however, be denied, that malice is the very gist of each of these offenses. For, it is not to be doubted, that the legislature did not intend to punish a person for shooting at another in just self-defense, although such person intended to kill the assailant ; or to punish a slave for setting fire to and burning his master's stable or outhouse at his master's command. These statutes furnish examples, which show conclusively, that wherever a malicious intent is an essential ingredient in the constitution of an offense created by statute, although it is not so made by the express words of the act, the indictment will be invalid, unless it contain an averment of the malicious intent. For, if indictments, framed under these statutes, would be valid, because they contain a description of the offense in the language of the statute, the consequence would be, that the jury would be compelled to convict, and the court to pronounce judgment, however innocent the accused might be of any intent or act held criminal by the law.

We are unable to perceive a distinction, in reference to the question under consideration, between the statute, under which the prisoner is charged, and the statute above referred to. For, in neither is malice, by express words, made an ingredient in the offense therein defined.   Hence, if it be necessary, in order to warrant the conviction of a slave for setting fire to and burning a stable, to charge the act to have been done with malice, it must, upon principle, be equally essential to charge the administration of poison with intent to kill, to have been done with malice aforethought, before the accused can be legally convicted of a capital offense.

The indictment in the case of Anthony v. The State, above referred to, was framed under the statute of 1822, ch. 64, § 36, Hutch. Dig., 521; as amended by the act of 1825, Hutch. Dig., 532, art. 8, § 1.   By the original act, it was made a capital felony for any slave to commit an assault and battery upon any white person, "with intent to kill."   The amendatory act provides, that the foregoing act, "when the killing does not actually occur, shall be so construed as to render the proof of malice aforethought expressly necessary, to subject the person or persons therein named to capital punishment."   The indictment charged the offense to have been committed "feloniously, willfully, and of his malice aforethought."   The jury, upon the evidence submitted to them, found the accused guilty, and that the act was committed with express malice, and sentence of death was pronounced.   Upon the removal of the cause into this court, the judgment was reversed, upon the ground of the insufficiency of the indictment, to authorize the punishment of death.   The court say, the indictment contains no averment of that species of malice (that is, express) which alone authorizes capital punishment.   This is a direct decision upon the question under consideration.

According to these views, both counts in the indictment were defective.   The court, therefore, erred in overruling the motion in arrest of judgment.

Let the judgment be reversed, and the prisoner remanded to be proceeded against in the court below.

HANDY, J., dissenting:

I am unable to concur in the conclusion of a majority of the court, that the indictment in this case is insufficient; and I will briefly state the view I take of the subject.

The indictment is framed under the 53d section of the act of 1822, Hutch. Dig., 521, which provides, that, " if any slave, free negro or mulatto, shall prepare, exhibit or administer to any person or persons in this state, any medicine whatsoever, with intent to kill such person or persons, he or she so offending shall be judged guilty of a felony, and shall suffer death." It contains two counts ; one charging the preparation, and the other the administration of the poison, which acts are severally charged to have been done " knowingly, wilfully, maliciously, unlawfully and feloniously," and " with the intent to kill" the persons concerned.

The objection taken to the sufficiency of the indictment is, that it contains no charge that the poison was prepared or administered with intent to murder, or of malice aforethought ; and although the indictment charges the acts to have been done wilfully, maliciously, feloniously and with intent to kill, yet it is urged that malice is a necessary ingredient in the offense, and that in such cases it is necessary to charge in appropriate legal terms that the offense was committed with malice aforethought.   This is undoubtedly the rule in relation to offenses at common law, and the authorities cited by the counsel for the plaintiff in error have reference to that class of offenses. But the crime, in this case, is the creature of statute, and must be regulated by the principles applicable to statutory offenses. The rule is thus accurately stated in a recent useful and practical work upon criminal law : " It is a well-settled rule, that in an indictment for an offense created by statute, it is sufficient to describe the offense in the words of the statute, and if in any case the defendant insists upon a greater particularity, it is for him to show, that from the obvious intention of the legislature, or the known principles of law, the case falls within some exception to such general principle."   Whart. Am. C. L., 132. This principle is well sustained by reason and authority.   United States v. Batchelder, 2 Gall., 15 ; State v. Chick, 2 Ala. R., 26 ; State v. Blease, 1 McMul. R., 475.   When the legislature have created an offense and clearly described its essential qualities, it is to be presumed that it was intended to dispense with the common law requisites pertaining to offenses of a like nature, and to mark out and characterize the crime intended to be punished ; and in an indictment for such an offense, it is clear that it is sufficient to describe it in the terms of the statute, because the legislature has fully pointed out the nature and description of the crime intended to be punished. They have made both the crime and its punishment.'

This principle appears to be decisive of the point in question, for the indictment follows the language of the statute in describing the nature of the offense, unless this case can be brought under some exception to the general rule.

Counsel has relied upon the precedents in Archbold's Crim. Pl. of indictments for attempts to poison, under the English statutes, in which the offense is charged to have been committed "of malice aforethought." These precedents do not appear ever to have had judicial sanction upon the point in question, and may, in many instances, not improperly be ascribed to a disposition to adhere to ancient forms, which superabound in redundancy and circumlocution. But the English statute is very different from ours. Its provisions are against persons who shall administer poison "with intent to commit the crime of murder." The use of the common law term, "the crime of murder," may require that an indictment in such a case should charge the offense with all the ingredients necessary at common law to constitute the crime of murder. But where the offense and the terms used in designating it are purely statutory, no such principle could apply, and the offense would stand as to its nature and essential ingredients, a new creature of law, to be judged of by the principles of reason and justice inherent in it, and not by the forms of the common law.

Let us apply this principle to the present case. The offense is one created by statute. Its character and essential qualities are fully but simply described in the statute. The provision is, that if any slave shall prepare or administer medicine to any person in this state with intent to kill, such slave, upon conviction, shall suffer death. Here the criminal act and the malicious intent are necessary to constitute the offense. When the act is charged to have been done, and with intent to kill the persons affected by it, the terms used convey the idea clearly and irresistibly to the mind, that the act was done from previous malice. This necessarily results from the nature of the act, for it is impossible to say that a sane man could administer poison to another wilfully, maliciously and feloniously, with intent to kill him, without conveying the idea irresistibly of previous preparation, deliberation and malice. There is no room for sudden heat or impulse in such a case, and from the very nature of the act, any idea but that it was done with previous malice, must be excluded as completely as though the vocabulary of technical expletives were exhausted. In the present case, the statute has designated the offense in such a manner that both the act and the motive are set forth in the description of it in the act. And if there was anything wanting in it to make up the full measure of the offense, it is supplied by the terms in which it is characterized in this indictment, which, although they would not be sufficient in a common law offense, are sufficient in the case of an offense created and defined by statute. The charges in the indictment are plain and not to be mistaken, sufficiently full and comprehensive to bring offenders to punishment, but, at the same time, sufficiently explicit to give them ample notice of the nature, cause and extent of the accusation.

I concur in the conclusions of the court upon the other points considered, and am of opinion that the judgment below is correct and should be affirmed.

MURPHY v. THE STATE, 28 Miss. Rep., 637.

TRADING WITH SLAVES.

Although it has been held[1] that sec. 2 of the act[2] prohibiting trade and barter with slaves, which dispensed with the averment and proof of the kind of produce or commodity bought or sold, is invalid under sec. 2 of the bill of rights, yet, an indictment under this statute containing the necessary averments, is valid, and should be sustained.

As a general rule, in civil as well as criminal cases, a person who is interested in the event of a suit or prosecution, is incompetent as a witness. But where the statute gives a reward for the conviction of offenders, or the witness as informer is entitled to a part of the fine imposed by statute on the accused; on the grounds of

[1] Murphy v. State, 24 Miss. R., 590.   [2] Act of March 6th, 1850.

public policy, and for the purpose of bringing offenders to justice, such interested person is a competent witness in behalf of the prosecution. FISHER, J., *dissenting.*

As a general rule, every material averment in the indictment must be proved; but it is unnecessary to prove the offense to the whole extent charged. It is sufficient to prove so much of the indictment as to show that the accused has committed the offense charged.

The jury was instructed that "if the slave came out with spirituous liquor which he did not take into defendant's house, the defendant's knowledge is presumed; *Held,* that the instruction was correct.

The identity of the slave nor his ownership is in anywise an ingredient in the offense of trading with slaves. But being alleged it is necessary that they should be satisfactorily proved.

Error to Madison circuit court. HENRY, J.

The plaintiff in error was indicted under the law approved March 6th, 1850, entitled, "An act to suppress trade and barter with slaves, and for other purposes." The indictment was found at the October term of the court below, 1854, and avers, "that Daniel W. Murphy, late of the county aforesaid, yeoman, on the 18th day of April, A. D., 1854, with force and arms at the county aforesaid, unlawfully, did then and there sell spirituous liquors, namely, whisky, rum, gin and brandy, to a certain slave named Allen, owned by Robert Love, without the consent in writing of the master, owner, overseer, employer or mistress of said slave, contrary to the form of the statute," etc.

The case was called for trial on the 17th of October, 1854, and the prisoner pleaded not guilty, and was put upon his trial. Thereupon the district attorney called as a witness, Henry R. Coulter, the prosecutor, and marked as such on the back of the indictment, who being sworn, the district attorney propounded a question to him, as to his knowledge of the charge in the indictment; defendant objected to the answering of said question by said Coulter, and to said Coulter's competency as a witness in the cause on account of the direct interest which said Coulter had in the result of said prosecution, the statute directing that one half of all the fines collected under the provisions of said act should be paid to the prosecutor. The court overruled this objection, and allowed the prosecutor to testify in the cause. To this ruling of the court defendant excepted. Witness then proceeded to state, that on the morning of April 18th, 1854, he was standing about three hundred feet from Murphy's store, when he saw a mule-team wagon of Judge Robert Love, loaded with

cotton, stop near him, with its driver, whom he thought was
Judge Love's Frank, but who, he learned afterwards from Judge
Love, that it was Allen, whom he knew was a slave of Judge
Love; the wagon stopped near where witness was standing; the
driver of the wagon took out of the wagon a bottle without a
stopper, and witness tried to take it from him, but failed to do
so; said driver jerked away from him, and went with his bottle
into the house of said defendant's store; witness saw said driver
enter the front door of said Murphy's said store, and after being
there for some time, the said driver returned to his wagon with a
bottle under his coat, and put the bottle back into the wagon.
Witness proceeded to the wagon, took out the said bottle, and
found whisky in it, which witness thought was the same bottle
the driver had taken away with him.

Judge Robert Love, a witness for the state, testified, that he
had and owned a mule-team wagon, and a driver named Allen,
on the 18th day of April, 1854, and that said driver was engaged
in hauling cotton about that time.

The defendant offered to prove by John B. Hemphill, the district attorney, who was in attendance on the grand jury which
found and presented said indictment, that Henry R. Coulter,
prosecutor, was the sole witness before the grand jury, and on
whose testimony alone said bill of indictment was found; but
the court ruled said proof to be illegal, and would not allow said
Hemphill to answer said question or to be sworn in the cause for
that purpose, to which ruling of the court, defendant excepted.
Defendant did not introduce any evidence to the jury.

The following instructions were asked by the defendant and
refused by the court:

2d. " The indictment charging the offense to be that the defendant did unlawfully sell spirituous liquors, namely, whisky,
rum, gin and brandy, unless the jury believe from the evidence
that the defendant did sell rum, whisky, gin and brandy, the
law is for the defendant, and they will find him not guilty."
This instruction was modified and amended by the court as follows: " But if the slave came out with spirituous liquor which
he did not take in, the defendant's knowledge is presumed."

4th. " Even if the jury should be satisfied that the slave got whisky out of defendant's house, yet, unless the jury believe from the evidence that defendant knew of his so getting the whisky, the law is for the defendant, and the jury will find the defendant not guilty." To the refusal of this instruction, and the modification of the court of the second instruction, defendant excepted.

The jury returned a verdict of guilty. Defendant below moved in arrest of judgment, because there was no valid law or statute to found a judgment upon under a verdict rendered with such testimony and instructions. The court overruled the motion in arrest of judgment, and the defendant excepted. The defendant then made a motion for a new trial, because; 1, the jury found contrary to the law and evidence; 2, because the court erred in refusing defendant's instructions; 3, because the court erred in allowing the prosecutor to be a witness, he having a direct interest in the result of the prosecution, as regulated by sec. 5, of the law of 1850; 4, because the court refused to let the district attorney answer the question whether Henry R. Coulter, the prosecutor, was not the only witness sworn before the grand jury, and upon whose testimony the indictment was found. Which motion for a new trial the court overruled; and the defendant having embodied the testimony in his bill of exceptions tendered the same to the action of the court in overruling said motion, and the same was signed, sealed, and enrolled, according to the statute.

Franklin Smith, for plaintiff in error.

The defendant was modest enough not to ask that the jury must be satisfied before they could convict, or that the defendant did sell the commodity, or was present when it was sold; but he was content to ask that unless they were satisfied from the evidence that defendant knew of the commission of the offense, they must find for the defendant. But the court charged in this case (in which there is not a scintilla of proof that the defendant was in the store at the time, or where he was), that the presumption was that he knew of the negro getting the commodity which he had in his hands when he came out of the store, and that he got it in his store. History reads some sad lessons to the judicial mind as to what Draconic laws have been put upon the statute book to enforce some supposed "necessity" of "state" (the tyrant's plea), or to sacrifice, in its diseased condition, to popular odium, some of its supposed enemies, and to punish even the innocent to get at the guilty, on that same "tyrant's plea of necessity." But the just judge of all ages has defied alike the depraved mandates of the excited populace, and the cruel behests of the tyrant, and vindicated the august position of God; asks only, what is law, and here in America, especially, what says the written constitution?

That the legislature has gone too far in sec. 3 of the laws of 1850, pp. 101, 102, we think that even a slight investigation of first principles will show. In every age and country of the civilized world, where the common law has been known, its humane maxims that crime "must be fully proved," and that "every person is presumed to be innocent until he is proved guilty," are household words, known to the tyro and the citizen, as well as to the wisest of the bar—incorporated into jurisprudence, interwoven into the very net-work of society—truths as startling to deny, next to the denial of a future state of rewards and punishments, and of the soul's accountability to God. Early and late, at the first dawn of legal science, in the reigns of the worst Tudors and Stuarts, before the American revolution and since, up to the last page put to press by the last author—these truths of the common law of England and America have never been doubted or called into question in the countries named until the passage of the law of 1850 in this ultra republican state of Mississippi. See Wills on Circumstantial Ev., 120, 121, 145; 3 Greenl. Ev., 29, 30. Where has a contrary opinion prevailed? In countries of the civil law? In countries of extorted confessions by thumb-screws and the rack, the iron boot and the boiling lead—places where the poor wretch is presumed guilty, and on that presumption is tortured until he confesses; in the dungeon of the bastile, and in the tyrant's state prison, "where hope never comes that comes to all." It was in one instance made to sully the pages of the statute law of old England, but it was driven from it in disgrace, amid the execrations of all honest men. It was that horrid law, which makes the blood curdle in the veins at its recital, which presumed the mother of an illegitimate child, when it died, guilty of infanticide, unless she could prove by one witness at least, that the child was born dead. Wills on Circumstantial Evidence, 125. The crying injustice of condemning men in advance, of holding them guilty unless they proved themselves innocent, has been immortalized by Virgil, where he makes the common sybil lead his hero through his fabled hell. On his way to the Elysian plain, the horrid sounds of Tartarus, surrounded by a triple wall, salute his ears; the clank of iron, the rattling of chains, the groans of anguish, the reverberations of the lash! Affrighted, he asks of his conductress, the meaning of those sounds, who the culprits, by what manner of punishments afflicted? The sybil replies, that "no pure spirit can ever enter those accursed abodes. There the Cretan Rhadamanthus holds his dreadful courts—he first punishes, and then hears the crimes, compelling the prisoner to confess," etc.

"Nulli fas casto sceleratum insistere limen. . .
Gnossius hæc Rhadamanthus habet durissima regna
Castigatque auditque dolos; subigitque fateri," etc.
　　　　　　　　　　　　　　　　—[6th Ænead.

Now, what does this law of 1850, sec. 3. ch. 31, pp. 101, 102, do, but pursue the Rhadamanthian system? If a negro (in a county where two-thirds of the population are such) is seen going into a store and come out with an article which he might have purchased in it, the owner of the store is presumed guilty, and will be thrown into prison until he proves himself innocent; and that he may never be able to do this, the district attorney is allowed to select any day in three hundred and sixty-five, to prove that a negro was seen going into a store and come out.

Is this according to the republican system established by our constitution? We think not. Among the sacred rights guaranteed in the declaration of rights in this state which, in the conclusion of that declaration, are "excepted out of the general powers of government, and shall for ever remain inviolate," is the right by sec. 10, to demand "the nature and cause of the accusation," "to be confronted by the witnesses against him," to have compulsory process for witness in his favor, and in all prosecutions by indictment or information, a speedy and "public trial by an impartial jury," of the county where the offense was committed; nor can he be deprived of his life, liberty, or property, " but by due course of law." Sec. 3, of the law of 1850, ch. 31, pp. 101, 102, does not confront a man with the witnesses against him; it condemns him without any witness; it does not give him a trial; the question of his guilt is not before the jury (as in other cases to be tried by them), on the evidence adduced; but he is already pronounced guilty before the trial begins. He is deprived of his liberty on each charge, from one to twelve months (see sec. 1, ch. 31, Laws of 1850, p. 100), not by due course of law; for due course of law, at the time the constitution was framed, required that " crime should be fully proved," and not presumed. These views are susceptible of the clearest demonstration, by authority as well as reason. The number proper to constitute the tribunal called "jury" is nowhere defined in our constitution, and yet it is a term susceptible of the clearest definition, by reason of the common law when the constitution was adopted. To dispense with the necessity of proof is just as great a stretch of power as would be the legislative dispensing with the number of twelve men on the jury; and we have authority for saying that, if the legislature were to prescribe as a jury a less number than twelve men, the law would be unconstitutional. Byrd v. State, 1 How., 177; 1 Tuck. Black., 60; 1 Thomas' Coke, 8.

The counsel for the prisoner requested in the court below, that the jury might know that the defendant must have had some knowledge of the offense to make him guilty. Even in the trial of the mob cases in 1780, Erskine took as the foundation of the defense of the deranged Lord George Gordon the maxim of the law for ages, the maxim of reason and of common sense, "*Actus reum non facit nisi mens sit rea.*" This maxim is nullified under this law. It is not only the keeper of the store that is to be punished, but, as in this case, the owner of the store. Now, the presumption of law is, that the owner would not violate the law; that he carries on an honest traffic; that, as retailing was not allowed, if the negro got any thing in the store, he must have got it (by watching his opportunity when the owner was absent) from some other person present. Under this

law, though the defendant might have been asleep in another
house, or he might have been otherwise absent from his store, so
that it would be impossible to have presumed his presence; yet,
unless he can prove that he was so absent on the particular day
selected by the district attorney, he is made guilty of an offense
which is itself presumed, and loses his liberty. It ought to be
proved that he was present, that the deed was done, that he did
it, that he was present when another did it, or at least that he
knew of the crime and did not prevent it, but directly, indirectly, or tacitly connived at it. Unless these positions be correct,
what becomes of the first principle of the law? "*Nemo punitur pro alieno delicto.*" "*Nemo punitur sine injuria facto
seu defalto.*" 2 Co. Inst., 287. In such way · is a man to be
punished by due course of law, for his own offenses proved and
established; and until proved and established he is to be presumed innocent. No man can be said to have "a trial" of his
case when he is already condemned without the production of
a particle of proof to fix a crime upon him. Under this sec. 3,
he has not a trial under the law on evidence, but remote facts
only are proved from which the crime is to be presumed. And
then a presumption is raised on that presumption that he did it,
and his trial thus becomes a mockery, because in violation of the
first principles of a fair "trial." He is not to be proved guilty, but
he is to be taken as guilty in the outset, on the presumption of a
crime being committed; and secondly, on the presumption that
the prisoner did it, in outrage of the due course of law, which
presumes him innocent until proved guilty. By section twenty-
eight of the declaration of rights, "the right of trial by jury
shall remain inviolate;" under the instructions founded on this
law the jury being compelled to presume every thing against
the prisoner, he has no more opportunity to be tried by jury
than if the jury had been abolished. The law had as well have
said, if a negro be seen going down the street, all persons there
inhabiting must prove themselves innocent, or else they shall be
presumed guilty. The fact of the negro going into a store is a
perfectly innocent act; but as the negro was found with a commodity coming out, it is not to be presumed that he got the
commodity himself, or got it from some person other than the

defendant, but a crime is to be presumed, and the owner to be presumed the guilty agent. The innocent act is established, it is undoubted, it is undisputed; the consequences of guilt are not found by the jury on the evidence, but are found fastened by the law. Such proceeding is palpably unconstitutional, and has been pronounced so in similar cases by this court. Smith's Admr. v. Smith, 1 How., 102–105. The trial by jury must remain inviolate, and the party cannot be deprived of his liberty, only by due course of law. Flournoy v. Smith et al., 3 How., 62–65. The ablest courts will not allow constitutional rights to be frittered away by ingenious sophistries, but will adhere to the plain letter and the meaning attached thereto when the constitution was framed. Thompson v. Grand Gulf Railroad and Banking Co., 3 How., 247–250; Marbury v. Madison, 1 Cranch., 137; 1 S. C. U. S. Condensed Reports, 267, 284, 285.

The fearful consequences of declaring a state law unconstitutional were hurled at Chief Justice Marshall with great fierceness by a daring man, in the case of Craig et al. v. State of Missouri, 4 Peters, 410, 438. But the venerable and upright judge, in declaring the law unconstitutional, mildly replied to all the "sound and fury" about the consequences of the court's so doing, "These are considerations which address themselves to those departments which may with perfect propriety be influenced by them." "This department can listen only to the mandates of law, and can tread only that path which is marked out by duty." 4 Peters, 438. In Craig v. State of Missouri, a man was most unconscionably seeking to take advantage of an unconstitutional law. The person may be vile; the principles to be struck down on his account may be sacred and of incalculable value to all the citizens as a community; and the only question for a just court is, What are the mandates of (constitutional) law? What is the path marked out by duty? Whenever the legislature is to look to who are good or bad citizens, apart from the crime itself, and make that apply to particulars which will not admit of universal enforcement, our liberties are at an end. In many respects this is an infamous, iniquitous, tyrannical law, worthy of the worst days of the Stuarts and of the worst of the judges. A rigid enforcement of this would sweep it from the statute book in six days after the legislature met. . .

Section three of the act is unconstitutional, because it makes a difference between the man whose store is also his dwelling-house and the man who has his store separate from his house. In the latter case the dwelling is the owner's castle and is respected; crime is not presumed against its inmates. The offense has to be made out under the first section of the act as in other criminal cases, by being "fully proved." In the case of a person who has a dwelling and store in the same house, it is made a crime against him for a particular class of persons to be seen entering his house, though such persons are the lawful inmates of every dwelling-house in the state. A difference is set up between different classes of citizens; against one set crime has to be "fully proved;" towards the other set, crime may be presumed against the person charged, on the presumption that a crime has been done by somebody. This difference between classes of citizens falls directly under the condemnation of the declaration of rights, and is scouted with reprobation by the solemn adjudications of this court. Smith's Admr. v. Smith, 1 How., 102–105. Striking at bad citizens may do for tyrants and their tools, but pure and enlightened courts never allow the constitutional rights of freemen to be crushed away on any such plea.

John Wilkes, a member of the British house of commons, was a man of very bad private character (had he been a man of good character, Dr. Johnson says, he would have dethroned George III.); he was sent to the tower under the warrant of the secretary of state. He demanded of the court of King's bench, through his counsel, his liberty by writ of *habeas corpus*, on the ground that the publication of a libel (which was the offense alleged) was not a breach of the peace, and that the privilege of parliament exempted him in all cases except in treason, felony, and breach of the peace. The state was in a diseased condition at the time (1763), and the necessity of enforcing the law was very great. But the able judges of the King's bench looked only to the cause without regard to persons, and based their unanimous decision on the constitutional rights of the citizen, as if the purest man in the kingdom stood there before them.   Chief Justice Pratt delivered the opinion of the court, and said in the conclusion of the opinion, " I cannot find that a libeller is bound to find surety of the peace, nor ever was in any case except one, namely, the case of seven bishops, where the judges said that surety of the peace was required in the case of a libel ; Judge Powell, the only honest man of the four judges, dissented, and I am bold to be of his opinion, that case is not law ; but it shows the miserable condition of the state at that time ; upon the whole it is absurd to require surety of the peace or bail, in the case of a libeller, and, therefore, Mr. Wilkes must be discharged from his imprisonment." The King v. Wilkes, 2 Wilson R., 160.

In the case of the State v. Borgman, reported in a note to 2 Nott & McCord R., 34–37, the views herein taken will be found in the main sustained, especially as to the constitutional necessity of connecting by proof the defendant with the crime, either by proving that the defendant participated in, or did the act, or was present when it was done, or tacitly approved of, or instigated it by his recognition of the act in permitting another habitually to do it in his employment, with his knowledge.

In this case, it is not proved that the defendant was in his store, knew of the crime, or that he had a clerk or negro through whom he transacted his business.

It is evident from the proof that the district attorney designed to punish the defendant by aid and through the rigor of section three, as the keeper or owner of a storehouse. But as it has been said of persons designing certain bequests in a will, and failing to express their wish *voluit sed non dicit*, so it may be said here of the district attorney, *voluit sed non fecit*. The word storehouse nowhere appears in the indictment, nor any thing like it. The statutory, indispensable words, " or keeper or owner of such storehouse," nowhere appear.   The presumptions of section three can be of no service against any one except against persons " owning or keeping a storehouse, warehouse, tippling-shop, or other place fitted up or kept for trading." § 3, p. 101. It is only against " a person owning or keeping such storehouse," etc., that the going in and coming out of a negro with something he might have purchased therein, is " presumptive evidence" of guilt. § 3, p. 102.

No matter what the proof was in this cause, yet to bring the party within the purview of the provisions of section three, it is altogether essential that the language of the statute " creating the offense," should have been pursued. The court charged on section three ; the case was pressed under section three by the state, and the proof was made to fit section three. Yet it is very evident from the averments of the indictment, that the presumptions of section three were all illegally applied, and to have had advantage of " presumptive evidence " against the defendant, it should have charged that the defendant was the owner or keeper of a certain storehouse, and that the slave did bring out of such storehouse a certain commodity, which said defendant sold to said slave in said storehouse, without permission, etc., *contra formam*, etc., etc., so that the court might see that the proof sustained the charge, and that judgment and punishment were applied where the law prescribed, and to do this there must appear on the record the offense charged in the language of the statute. 1 Chitty Cr. Law, 168, 169, 171, 281–283 ; Anthony v. State, 13 S. & M., 264, 265 ; Starkie Cr. Pl., 252, 253.

From the averments in the indictment, the court is constrained by the rules of criminal pleading, and the benefits of a fair trial, as provided in the authorities last referred to, to make the case fall under section first, and not under section three. Murphy's house is not averred to be " a storehouse ;" the defendant is not averred to have been keeping or owning such storehouse at the time of the commission of the offense. Is the testimony, then, sufficient in this case to convict any citizen in the state independent of all considerations of his being " a storehouse owner or a shop-keeper ?"

D. C. Glenn, attorney general.

1. The law under which the indictment in this case was found is a stringent police regulation, it is true, to preserve a peculiar class of our population, and when once promulgated is as binding as any other law. The court silently ignore this objection to this law in 24 Miss. R., 590.

2. When it is plain the infliction of a fine or penalty is intended as punishment in furtherance of public justice, rather than as an indemnity to the party injured, or to secure a mere pecuniary benefit to the prosecutor, and that the detection and conviction of the offender are the objects of the legislature, the case will be within the exception, and the person benefited by the conviction, will, notwithstanding his interest, be competent. 1 Greenl. Ev., 412 ; 3 McLain, 53, 299 ; 16 Peters, 203 ; 1 Bald., 90 ; 9 Barn. & Cress., 556.

SMITH, C. J. :

The plaintiff in error was indicted and convicted under the act of the 6th of March, 1850, " to suppress trade and barter with slaves."

Several exceptions are now urged to the validity of the judgment.

1. It is insisted that the court below erred in overruling the motion in arrest of judgment. The reason assigned in support of that motion, denies the constitutionality of the act, under which the indictment was framed.

The same objection was made in Murphy v. The State, 24 Miss. R., 590. In that case, the question arose on a motion to quash the indictment, which was framed under the same statute. On that occasion, this court entertained no doubt of the constitutional power of the legislature to declare that it would be criminal to commit any of the acts enumerated in the first section of the statute, and consequently to provide for the punishment of the offenders in the mode provided. It was held, also, that indictments for the offenses defined in the first section, " framed in the general manner indicated in the second section," would be invalid, inasmuch as an indictment thus framed, and which would consequently contain no allegation of the character or quantity of the produce alleged to have been sold or received, nor of the name of the slave with whom the illegal traffic was had, nor of the name of the owner of such slave, would violate the right secured by the tenth section of the bill of rights to the accused, to demand the " nature and cause of the accusation against him."

In the case at bar, the date of the offense, the character of the commodity, the name of the slave and his owner are alleged in the indictment.   There can, therefore, be no doubt, under the previous decisions of this court, that the motion in arrest of judgment was properly overruled.

2. On the trial, Henry R. Coulter, the prosecutor, whose name was endorsed on the indictment, was offered as a witness for the prosecution.   His examination was objected to by the defendant on the ground that he was interested in the event of the suit.   The objection was overruled, and the defendant excepted.   The competency of this witness is the next question for our consideration.

The first section of the act, under which the plaintiff in error was convicted, provides, that upon the conviction for any of the offenses therein defined, the party convicted " shall be fined in a sum not less than fifty dollars, nor more than five hundred dollars."   The fifth section directs that " one half of all the fines collected under the provisions of this act, shall be paid to the prosecutor, and the other half to be appropriated to the common school fund of the county."

It is very manifest, under these provisions, that the witness examined on the trial below, had a direct interest in the result of the prosecution.   The question arising here is : Did that interest render him incompetent as a witness for the prosecution ?

It is unquestionably true, as a general rule, in civil as well as in criminal cases, that a person interested in the event of a suit or prosecution, is not a competent witness.   Thus, where a penalty is imposed by statute, and the whole or a part is given to the informer or prosecutor, who becomes entitled to it forthwith upon the conviction, he is not, at common law, a competent witness for the prosecution.   Roscoe Cr. Ev., 126 ; Greenl. Ev., 472, § 403.   But there are many recognized exceptions which are said to be as old as the rule itself.   Thus, it is stated as a clear exception, that where a statute can receive no execution, unless a party interested be a witness, then he must be allowed. This exception to the general rule is based upon the presumption, that the rules of the common law are laid aside by the statute, that it may have effect, which would be otherwise wholly defeated. Gilbert Ev., 114. So cases of necessity, where no other evidence can be reasonably expected, have been from the earliest periods recognized as another exception. Thus, for example, in prosecutions for robbery, the person robbed is a competent witness for the prosecution, although he will, upon conviction of the offender, be entitled to a restitution of his goods. Greenl. Ev., 480, § 412. Another exception is that of a person who is to receive a reward for or upon the conviction of the offender. A person thus situated, is universally recognized as a competent witness, whether the reward be offered by the public or by private persons. " The case of a reward (says Mr. Justice Bayley) is clear on the grounds of public policy, with a view to the public interest ; and because of the principles upon which such rewards are given. The public has an interest in the suppression of crime, and the conviction of criminals. It is with a view to stir up greater vigilance in apprehending, that rewards are given ; and it would defeat the object of the legislature by means of those rewards to narrow the means of conviction, and to exclude testimony which would be otherwise admissible." Rex v. Williams, 17 Com. Law R., 440.

Where a penalty, given by statute, is recoverable on the indictment itself, so that the person entitled to the penalty is not driven to a suit, his title thereto gives such an interest as will render him incompetent as a witness. But if the act by which the penalty is given to the informer, prosecutor, or other person, contemplates his being a witness, his competency is of course continued ; and it is clear, that it is not necessary there should be an express legislative declaration to that effect, but that the court may infer such intention from the language of the statute or its professed objects. Cases of this description are recognized as another exception to the rule at common law. Murphy v. United States, 16 Peters R., 211 ; Rex v. Trasdale, 3 Esp. R., 68 ; Howard v. Shipley, 4 East R., 180.

It is insisted in behalf of the state, that the case at bar falls within the principle of this last exception ; that there has been, although no express words to that effect are contained in the statute, " a legislative capacitation given" to the prosecutor.

In Rex v. Williams, it was said by Mr. Justice Bayley, " Where it is plain that the detection and conviction of the offender are the objects of the legislature, the case will be within the exception, and the person benefited by the conviction will, notwithstanding his interest, be competent." This language was quoted with entire approbation by Judge Story in Murphy v. The United States; and the rule is laid down in almost the same terms in Greenleaf's Evidence, 480, § 12.

It is very manifest, if this rule is to determine the question under consideration, that the prosecutor, notwithstanding he had a direct and certain interest in the event of the prosecution, was a competent witness. For it cannot be doubted, that the detection and conviction of offenders were the objects of the legislature, and not the private benefit of the prosecutor. But, if this rule is applied as the test of the competency of persons who are to be benefited by the conviction of offenders, there is no case in which a person, having a direct and certain interest in the event of the prosecution, unless rendered incompetent by express legislative declaration, would not be competent. For the manifest reason, that the presumption is not to be entertained, that the legislature would create an offense and impose a penalty with any other view than the public good, or that the penalty would be given to the informer or prosecutor for any other purpose than that of promoting the detection and conviction of offenders. The rule, as laid down in Rex v. Bayley, does not appear to be sustained by the cases cited in the opinion of the court, and is not defensible upon principle. And although it has received the approval of some high authorities in this country, we are not prepared to give it our sanction; as it is evident that its recognition and application would effectually annul the unquestioned principle of the common law, that where the penalty is recoverable on the indictment itself, and the informer or prosecutor is not driven to a suit, he is, in consequence of his title to the penalty, rendered incompetent as a witness.

The question then is: Can it be implied, from the particular provisions and policy of the act, that the legislature intended to make the prosecutor a competent witness in prosecutions for offenses under the act?

The statute against bribery, 2 Geo. II., ch. 24, § 8, provided, that any offender against the act discovering, within a certain time, any other offender within the act, so that the person so dis- -covered be thereupon convicted, the discoverer not having been before the time himself convicted of the offense, shall be indemnified and discharged of all penalties and disabilities incurred under the act; that is, he should have the benefit of using the verdict against the other offender for his own indemnity. Under the particular provisions and policy of that statute, it was held, that the discoverer was a competent witness for the plaintiff in an action for the recovery of the penalty imposed by the act. In the language of Lord Ellenborough, " a parliamentary capacitation was given to the witness through whom the fact is discovered, and who might otherwise at common law have been incapacitated." Howard v. Shipley, 4 East R., 180. In Rex v. Trasdale, which was an indictment on the 21 Geo. III., ch. 37, § 1, for exporting machines used in the manufactures of that country. By the statute, the offender, upon conviction, was to forfeit the machines, etc., and also £200. The forfeitures, where not otherwise provided, were to go to the informer. The informer was called as a witness, and objected to on the ground of interest. The objection was overruled by Lord Kenyon, who considered the term " informer" in 21 Geo. III., as equivalent to the term " person discovering" in 2 Geo. II., ch. 24, § 8; and as it had been decided, that the legislature must have intended, that the person designated as the " person discovering" in the one case should be a witness, it must be taken it had the same intention as to the person designated by the word "informer" in the other. 8 Esp. R., 68; 17 Com. L. R., 448. Both of these cases were cases of secrecy, and the detection and punishment of the violators of these statutes deemed of great importance to the public. The terms " discoverer" and " informer," as employed in the English statutes, implied a personal knowledge of the criminal act sought to be detected and punished. Hence, the courts were doubtless justified in holding, that the witnesses were made competent by a parliamentary declaration; for, if the witnesses offered on those occasions had been excluded on the ground of their interest in the event of the prosecution, the provision would have been rendered nugatory and useless.

It would have been holding out inducements to persons to discover offenses committed in violation of the statute, and to inform upon the offenders, when, by the operation of the common law rule, the discoverer and informer would be excluded from the rewards proffered by the statutes themselves.

But, it is insisted, that the term "prosecutor" does not generally and necessarily imply a knowledge of the criminal act charged in the indictment; hence, that the rule laid down in the English cases above cited ought not to be applied to the case at bar.

The illicit traffic with slaves is an evil, in this community, of great magnitude. Acts in violation of the statute on the subject are committed in secret, generally at night, and always in the absence of the owner of the slave, who is the person most seriously affected. The history of the legislation on this subject, and of the criminal jurisprudence, furnish unmistakable evidence of the difficulty encountered in the detection and punishment of offenders under the existing laws. The consequent impunity with which illegal trading with slaves was carried on, not less than its ruinous consequences, led to the adoption of the statute, remarkable for its stringent provisions, under which this indictment was framed. Whilst, therefore, it may be conceded, that the prosecutor is not presumed, necessarily, to have a personal knowledge of the offense charged, and hence, that the term is not used in our statute in a sense equivalent to the term "discoverer," as employed in the English statute against bribery, nevertheless we cannot doubt, from our view of the particular provisions and policy of the statute, that they amount to a legislative declaration, that the person prosecuting for an offense, under the act, may be a witness against the party charged. A different construction, instead of advancing the objects of the act, would narrow the means of the detection and punishment of offenders, by taking away the inducement held out by the legislature, with the view of stirring up greater vigilance, in bringing them to justice; for it is manifest, if the expectation of sharing the penalty consequent upon conviction is the operative motive with the prosecutor, and the provision is based upon that supposition, it is unreasonable and illogical to expect that any person would act the part of an informer or prosecutor, without hope of being remunerated. For that reason, as well as from the character of the offense, and the secrecy with which it may always be committed, it is greatly to be apprehended, if the prosecutor should be excluded as a witness, that the statute itself will fail of any beneficial execution. We feel fully justified, therefore, in holding that the objection to the competency of the witness was properly overruled.

3. The court was requested by the defendant to charge the jury, " that unless they believed from the evidence, that the defendant did sell whisky, gin, rum, and brandy, the law is for the defendant, and the jury will acquit him." The refusal of the court to give this charge is excepted to. The indictment charged the illegal sale of whisky, gin, rum, and brandy to a slave.

The general rule is, that every material averment in the indictment must be proved; but it is generally unnecessary to prove the offense to the whole extent charged. It is invariably sufficient to prove so much of the indictment as shows that the defendant has committed a substantive crime therein specified. Rex v. Hunt, 2 Camp. R., 585 ; Swinney v. The State, 8 S. & M., 576. Proof, therefore, that either whisky, gin, rum, or brandy was sold to the slave by defendant, would have authorized a conviction. There was, hence, no error in withholding the instruction.

4. The court was further asked to charge that " even if the jury were satisfied that the slave got whisky out of defendant's house, yet, unless the jury believe from the evidence, that defendant knew of his getting the whisky, the law is for the defendant, and the jury will find the defendant not guilty."

This instruction was given, qualified by adding to it the following words : " But if the slave came out with spirituous liquor, which he did not take into the defendant's house, the defendant's knowledge is presumed."

The charge, as modified, was correct. It is in strict accordance with the fifth clause of the third section of the act ; which, upon the proof before the jury, raised the presumption of the defendant's guilt, as charged in the indictment, upon the proof made, that the slave obtained the whisky from the store of the defendant. If the ownership of the slave was sufficiently established, the jury, in the absence of all opposing testimony were bound to convict, unless the provisions of the third section of the act are void. In our opinion they are not so. Those provisions may be extremely unwise and impolitic. They are certainly rigorous and harsh; but we are not prepared to say with counsel, that the legislature, in the enactment of them, transcended their constitutional authority.

5. It is, in the last place, objected that the court erred in overruling the motion for a new trial.

According to the rule of evidence laid down by the third section, the proof was complete of the commission of an offense, when it was shown by the testimony that a slave had obtained the whisky from the store of the defendant. Neither the identity of the slave nor his ownership was in anywise an ingredient in the offense for which the defendant was indicted. But, being alleged, it was necessary that they should be satisfactorily proved. It is clear, however, that the same strictness is not required in the proof of an averment of that character, which is requisite in the establishment of the *corpus delicti*, except in cases where the subject of the averment is a record or a written agreement. Applying this rule, we think the verdict ought not to be disturbed.

Let the judgment be affirmed.

HANDY, J., concurred.

FISHER, J., dissenting:

It is admitted that the prosecutor, according to the rules of the common law, was an incompetent witness against the accused. The question, then, arises: How has the prosecutor been rendered competent? The majority of the court say, by the statute. But the statute is entirely silent on the subject. The word "prosecutor" occurring but once in it, and then so as to disqualify him as a witness.

It is the right of every person put upon his trial for the alleged commission of a criminal offense, that none but competent witnesses should be introduced against him. This is a right secured by the common law, and a statute which attempts to abridge or interfere with such right, must receive a strict construction, by which is understood a construction according to its letter. But if it be entirely silent in this respect, there is nothing to construe, and the statute does not, of course, speak at all on the subject.

The same may be said in regard to penal statutes, or statutes which create offenses. They must be strictly construed; that is to say, they must not be extended by implication beyond the "legitimate import" of the words used, so as to embrace cases not clearly described by such words.

Remedial statutes may receive a liberal, or, in other words, an equitable construction, by which the letter of the act "is sometimes restrained and sometimes enlarged, so as more effectually to meet the beneficial end in view, and prevent a failure of the remedy." And hence, it is often said, that such a case, though not embraced by the letter, is nevertheless embraced by the equity of a particular statute. A remedial statute may, therefore, speak both by its words and by its equity. But a penal statute, having no equity, can, of course, speak only by its words, and if they are not in such statute, it does not speak at all on the subject, and hence the rule of the common law, whatever it is, remains unchanged.

My opinion, therefore, is that the witness should have been excluded.

TURNER *v.* THE STATE, 28 Miss. Rep., 684.

HOMICIDE.

Under the statute of 1822, Hutch. Code, 814, where a person receives a wound in one county and dies in another county, the indictment should be preferred in the county where the death occurs; and it must be proven that deceased did die in the county where the indictment is found.

Error to Yazoo circuit court. HENRY, J.

J. M. Moore for plaintiff in error.

1. The statute requires the assessor to return to the court "a list of the names of all freeholders, being citizens of the United States, within his county, and householders," etc. Hutch. Code, 886, § 1.

No person can be subjected to punishment for the same offense unless a conviction be had upon an indictment found by a grand jury of the county in which the offense was committed. Laura v. State, 26 Miss., 176.

The record must affirmatively show those indispensable facts, without which the judgment would be void. Dyson v. State, 26 Miss., 383.

In regard to matters which, by law, should appear in the record, no presumption can be indulged which would either contradict the record or supply the defect. Laura v. State, 26 Miss., 176.

2. The record does not show that the grand jury were regularly elected and empanelled, etc. The record must show that the grand jury were duly elected and empanelled, etc., and its omission cannot be cured by the recital of it in the indictment. Abram v. State, 25 Miss. 589.

3. The record does not show otherwise than by a recital by the clerk, that the bill of indictment was endorsed by a prosecutor. Hutch. Code, 1005, § 69 ; Cody v. State, 3 How., 27 ; Peter v. State, ib., 433.

4. The record must show the accused was served with a copy of the bill of indictment and the special *venire* summoned to try the cause. Hutch Code, 1003, § 49.

5. The evidence should show that the deceased died in Yazoo county, or the court is without jurisdiction. Green v. State, 23 Miss., 509. It is indispensable that the indictment should aver that the murdered party died in the county in which the indictment is found against the accused. State v. Orsell, 1 Dev., 125 ; Riggs v. State, 26 Miss., 51. The prosecutor must prove any fact and circumstance stated in the indictment which is materially necessary to constitute the offense charged. John v. State, 24 Miss. 569.

6. The evidence of the attending physician clearly shows that the deceased died of a fatal disease prevailing at the time, and that the nurse or attendant, without his knowledge, and in violation of his practice, administered remedies which were highly injurious. " It is clear, " says Mr. Alison, " that if death be not owing to the effects of the wound, but to a supervening

accident or misfortune, though induced by the first violence, the prisoner cannot be convicted of homicide." Roscoe Cr. Ev., 703 ; Campbell & McMillan's Cases ; Alison's Prin. Cr. Law of Scotland, 147, and cited in Roscoe Cr. Ev., 705.

7. There was no evidence before the jury which identified the prisoner, nor was there any proof that the deceased was one of the parties engaged in the rencontre.

8. The reading of the bill of indictment only until the case was submitted to the jury, was in gross violation of criminal practice, and was of itself a good cause for a new trial. 4 Black. Com., 355.

D. C. Glenn, attorney general.

Smith, C. J. :

The plaintiff in error was tried upon an indictment for murder in the circuit court of Yazoo, and convicted of manslaughter in the second degree. The evidence adduced on the trial is contained in the bill of exceptions taken to the decision of the court on a motion for a new trial.

The errors assigned are, 1. That the record does not show that the grand jury, by whom the indictment was found, were selected, summoned, and empanelled in the mode prescribed by the statute ; and 2. That a new trial should have been granted, because the verdict was not sustained by the evidence.

1. In reference to the last exception, it is very clear that the proof was insufficient. There was no evidence offered, either direct or circumstantial, which showed that the death occurred in the county of Yazoo, in which the bill of indictment was preferred. This was essential to give the circuit court of that county jurisdiction. For, by the statute of 1822, Hutch. Code, 314, it was expressly provided, where a party having received a wound in one county, dies in consequence of such wound in another county, in the state, that the indictment should be found in the county where the death occurs, and not in the county in which the wound was inflicted. [1] Stoughton v. The State, 13 S. & M., 255.

In the case cited, the proof was, that the wound was inflicted

[1] See Riggs v. State, 26 Miss., 57 ; Rev. Code of 1857, 613, art. 246.

in Perry county and the death occurred in Harrison county. The indictment was found in Perry county, and this court reversed the judgment and quashed the indictment, upon the ground that the circuit court of that county could take no jurisdiction of the offense. In the case at bar, the evidence does not show that the death did not occur in Yazoo. It failed to show that the death did occur there. Under these circumstances, although the judgment must be reversed and the verdict set aside, it would be improper for this cause to quash the indictment, for it may be true, in point of fact, that the death did occur in Yazoo county, in which event the court, of course, had jurisdiction.

2. The first exception is untenable. In our opinion the record shows with sufficient certainty that the grand jury were selected and empanelled in the manner directed by the statute.

Judgment reversed, and prisoner remanded for a new trial.

Green v. The State, 28 Miss. Rep., 687.

Homicide.

Where the record of the trial of an indictment for murder shows that the grand jury returned into open court an indictment against the defendant for murder with no further description of the indictment, and immediately follows an indictment for murder and the arraignment and plea of defendant, the trial by a jury and other proceedings in the case, all bearing the same style of parties, the same designation of offense, the same number and the same circumstances of identity as the indictment, it is held that the record sufficiently identifies the indictment as that returned into court by the grand jury. A *venire facias* is no part of the record, unless made so by bill of exceptions. 1 How. Miss., 253.

After a party has pleaded in bar to an indictment, and been convicted, it is too late to urge objections to the constitution of the grand jury. Wh. Am. Cr. L., 863; 13 S. & M., 468. Such objections must be pleaded in abatement, or they will be considered as waived. Leathers v. State.

Every homicide is presumed to be murder, until the contrary appears from facts or circumstances proved. Malice is implied from the nature and character of weapon used.

If a party enter into a conflict with a deadly weapon, not intending to use it, but only resort to it in the heat of conflict, and death ensue, the offense is manslaughter. But if he intends from the first to use it, if necessary, to overcome his adversary, and do use it, and kill his adversary, it is murder. And this, although the slayer habitually carried the weapon. The court may modify instructions asked by either party before giving them to the jury. The phrase "great personal injury" in our statutes is equivalent to "great or enormous bodily harm," or danger of loss of life or limb.

Error to the circuit court of Marshall county. R. MILLER, J.

George N. Green was indicted in the circuit court of De Soto county, at the November term thereof, for the murder of William L. Mormon; and subsequently the *venue* was changed to Marshall county, where Green was convicted of murder and sentenced to be hanged.

The facts of the case are in substance, as shown for the state, that a short time previous to the killing, which took place on Sunday, the 19th of September, 1852, Green went to the house of Suddith, who was his neighbor, and asked S. if he had ever heard Mormon say that he had directed Eddings to kill his, G.'s, oxen, and S. replied that he had not; and G. asked S. what he should do, who replied that he could not tell G., and advised him to consult some one who had more knowledge. This conversation took place on Saturday, and S. invited G. to come over to his house on the next day, which was Sunday, with his, G's, nephew, Shultz, who S. wanted to ride a colt; and on Sunday G. and Shultz came; and during the time they were at S.'s house, G. spoke again about the killing of his oxen, and declared that he would have revenge on M., and he would whip Eddings, and during the time G. was at S.'s house, he saw a bowie knife or pistol in G.'s pocket. While G. was at the house of S., Mormon and Eddings came there, and M. and G. spoke to each other rather angrily, and they all remained until after dinner, saying several times he would not eat with such damned rascals, and it was supposed M. heard the remark, as he blushed in the face. Late in the evening M. and Eddings started home, leaving G. at S.'s, and defendant (G.) soon after they left, said he would give a gallon of whiskey, or five dollars, or something for his mule; that he (G.) had a settlement to make with M. and Eddings that evening. S. advised G. that he had better not and to go home; but G. replied that he would drink their hearts' blood; and S. went to water his horses, and while he was gone G.'s mule returned, which had been ridden off by another person; and G. rode up to the fence around the house of Mormon, who was in his cotton patch, and called to M., who went to the fence, and they talked a few minutes, but their conversation was not heard by any others, and as M. was in the act of getting over the fence, G. jumped from his mule, ran up, and took hold of M., and G. stabbed him several times with his bowie knife; when M. stepped off six or eight steps, sat down, and died in a minute or two. No arms or weapons of any kind were found on M., nor was he seen to have any in the conflict.

Shultz testified for defendant that he was seventy-five or one hundred yards off and did not see the commencement of the difficulty, but when he got to where it took place Mormon had G. down and hold of the hair or back part of his head, and was striking him on the left side, and he saw Eddings running from M.'s house, with a pistol in his hand, towards where the fight took place.

Three or four witnesses testified that they would not believe Shultz on oath, and that they knew his general character for veracity. The opinion of the court contains the instructions objected to by the defendant.

The jury found the defendant Green guilty of murder, and he was sentenced by the court to be hung. The court having refused him a new trial, he prayed this writ of error.

J. R. Chalmers, for plaintiff in error.

I. The record does not show affirmatively and distinctly that the bill of indictment found in the papers is the bill of indictment found by the grand jurors against Green. M. S. Opin., Laura v. The State.

II. The court below erred in not arresting judgment, for the following reasons:

1st. It does not appear of record that John Robertson, the foreman of the grand jury, took the oath prescribed as such, in the presence of all the other members of the grand jury. Hutch. Code, 878, 128.

2d. It does not appear of record that the grand jury ever returned the bill of indictment into open court. 3 Gilm. 71; 8 Yerg., 166; 7 Humph., 155; 1 Chit. 324; 2 Stra. 1026.

3d. It does not appear of record that defendant pleaded to the bill of indictment in open court. Rev. Const., art. 1, 10; 8 S. & M., 725.

4th. It appears of record that more than the legal number of persons required to constitute a grand jury were summoned and in attendance, and that out of these thirty-six were drawn. Hutch. Code, 887, 6, 7 ; M. S. Opin., Leathers v. State.

III. The court below erred in giving the fifth instruction for the state : " That every killing is presumed to be malicious and amounting to murder, until the contrary appears from circumstances of alleviation, excuse, or justification ; and that it is incumbent upon the defendant to make out such circumstance to the satisfaction of the jury, unless they arise out of the evidence produced against him."

Malice is an essential ingredient in murder, and therefore must be clearly proved and not presumed.   1 Russ., 385, 386 ; 3 Greenl. Ev., 29 ; Coffee v. State, 3 Yerg., 283 ; McDaniel v. State, S. & M. 401 ; 4 Black., 199–201.   Burden of proof never shifts in criminal cases.   Commonwealth v. Dana, 2 Met., 329 ; Commonwealth v. Kimball, 24 Pick., 389.

IV. The court, without being requested either by the defendant or the district attorney, gave in modification of the defendant's second, third, sixth and seventh instructions for the defendant, the following, namely : " That if the jury believe from the evidence that the defendant went into the fight having upon his person a deadly weapon, intending from the first to use the same, if necessary to enable him to overcome his antagonist, and did in the fight use the same and kill his antagonist, he is guilty of murder, although he habitually carried the weapon.

" That if the defendant entered into the conflict with a deadly weapon drawn, intending to use it, he is guilty of murder.   But if he did not enter into the fight intending to use the weapon, and only resorted to it in the heat of conflict, he is only guilty of manslaughter.

" That by great personal injury the law does not mean slight blows with the fist, or injury by any other means not calculated to endanger the life or limb of the party."   State v. Tackett, 1 Hawks, 219 ; State v. Yarborough, ib., 78 ; State v. Hill, 4 Dev. & Batt., 491 ; United States v. Travers, 2 Wheel. Crim. Case, 508 ; 5 Yerg., 453 ; 3 Humph., 493.

V. The fifth instruction of the state, " That malice is implied by law from the nature and character of the weapon used ; and that the use of a deadly weapon in a fight, and not in necessary self-defense, is in law evidence of malice." The use of a deadly weapon does not authorize a court to pronounce upon the intent, because an indignity offered to the person, coupled with a breach of the peace, will extenuate a homicide to manslaughter, although a deadly weapon is used. And there may still be a question for the jury, whether it is manslaughter in the first or in a lower degree. State v. Tackett, 1 Hawks, 219; State v. Yarborough, ib., 78; State v. Hill, 4 Dev. & Batt., 491; United States v. Travers, 2 Wheel. Crim. Case, 508; Rex v. Phillips, 2 Cow., 830; Reg. v. Mawgridge, Kelly, 125; ib., 135; Lanure's case, 1 Hall, P. C., 455; Reg. v. Sherwood, 1 Cor. & K., 556; Rex v. Stedman, Foster, 292.

F. Anderson, on the same side, made an elaborate argument.

D. C. Glenn, attorney-general, in addition to an extended oral argument,

1st. Upon the technical points raised in the argument, I rely on the reasoning of C. J. Henderson, in Kimbrough's case, 2 Dev. N. C. R., 431.

2d. Objections to the constitution of the grand jury. Byrd's case, 1 How., 153; Commonwealth v. Chauncey, 2 Ashm., 90; McQuillen's case, 8 S. & M., 587.

3d. In support of the fifth and sixth charges, I cite State v. Powell, 2 Halst., 244; York's case, 9 Met., 93; C. J. Shaw, and the elementary books and cases cited by him; McDaniel's case, 8 S. & M., 401; 1 Greenl. Ev., 24, 34; 9 Ired., 436; 17 Ala. R., 596.

4th. Right of judge to modify his charges Cicely's case, 13 S. & M., 202.

5th. In support of third modification, I rely on Oliver's case, 17 Ala. R., 596. The reasoning and the law cited by the court in this case, abundantly vindicate the charge. I invite a careful scrutiny of both. Tackett's case, 1 Hawks, 219, was decided in regard to killing of a slave; and the court says the law is different where the killing of a white man is concerned. I am not prepared to say this is a just or proper distinction. But whether it is or not, it deprives this case of all weight, as an authority in the case before the court.

HANDY, J. :

This was an indictment for murder, in the circuit court of De Soto county, from which there was a change of venue to Marshall circuit court, where the prisoner was tried and convicted of murder. Many objections are urged to the proceedings in the court where the indictment was found, and in the court where the case was tried, as sufficient grounds for reversing the judgment. These objections we will proceed to examine.

First. It is said that the record does not sufficiently show that the indictment appearing in the record, is the indictment found by the grand jury against the prisoner. The record contains the following entry :

" No. 400.   The State v. George N. Green.

" This day the grand jury, under the care of their proper officer, by the hands of their foreman, John Robertson, returned into open court a bill of indictment against George N. Green, the defendant in this case, for murder, indorsed by the foreman of said grand jury ' a true bill.' "

Then immediately follows the indictment, answering the description of it contained in this entry, and indorsed and numbered in the same manner as the entry. Immediately following is an entry of the case, with the same number and style of parties above stated, showing the arraignment on the indictment and the plea of not guilty. The same circumstances of identity, the number of the case, the style of the parties, and the designation of the offense, appear in various other proceedings taken in the case, until it was removed to Marshall county for trial. If it was not sufficiently certain, from the fact of the indictment immediately following the entry of its return into court by the grand jury, that the indictment thus appearing in the record was the bill found by the grand jury, all reasonable doubt upon the point must be removed by these additional evidences of identity.

Secondly. It is insisted that the court below erred in not sustaining the motion in arrest of judgment.

The first ground of this motion is founded on a mistake of fact. It is, that the record does not show that the foreman of the grand jury took the oath prescribed by law in the presence of the other members of the grand jury. This is distinctly and with all necessary certainty stated in the record.

The second ground is met by a like answer. It is, that it does not appear by the record that the grand jury returned the indictment into open court. The entry above stated shows that this is founded upon a misapprehension of fact, or an improper construction of the language used. The just and fair construction to be given to it is, that the grand jury came into court under the care of their proper officer, and by the hands of their foreman returned the indictment into open court. The third ground of the motion was, that it does not appear that the prisoner pleaded to the indictment in open court, or that the change of venue was ordered in open court. But the record shows quite a different state of facts: that the prisoner was brought to the bar of the court, and arraigned on the indictment, and pleaded not guilty, and on another day he appeared in proper person in court, and on his motion, supported by his oath, etc., the change of venue was ordered. The last ground of the motion was, that it appears by the record that more than the legal number of persons required to constitute the grand jury were summoned and in attendance, and that out of these the grand jury were drawn. This is not a sufficient ground upon which to arrest the judgment. The *venire* did not constitute a part of the record. Byrd v. The State, 1 How., 253. It cannot be noticed unless made a part of the record by bill of exceptions, taken under a proper state of case in the court below. Moreover, after the party has pleaded in bar to the indictment and been convicted, it is too late to urge objections to the constitution of the grand jury by motion in arrest of judgment. Whart. Am. Crim. Law, 863; Brantly v. The State, 13 S. & M., 468. Such objections, being proper subjects for pleas in abatement, will be considered as having been waived, and all benefit of them lost. In the case of Leathers v. The State, relied on in support of this objection, the point was presented by plea in abatement. But numerous decisions of this court, hold that such an objection cannot be supported after a plea in bar and a conviction upon the merits of the case.

The next and principal ground of error insisted upon is, that the instructions of the court upon the law of the case were erroneous. Before considering these instructions, it is necessary to take a view of the evidence in reference to which they were given.

James Suddith, a neighbor of both the deceased and the prisoner, testified, that on Friday previous to the Sunday on which deceased was killed, the prisoner spoke to the witness in relation to the deceased directing Eddings to kill the prisoner's oxen, and consulted him as to what he ought to do ; and witness advised him to consult some one better acquainted with such matters, which he agreed to do. Witness saw him again on Saturday, and invited him to come over to witness' house on the next day, with prisoner's nephew, John Shultz, whom witness wanted to ride a colt. They came accordingly, and Shultz rode the colt ; and while they were riding out during the day, the prisoner spoke of Eddings having killed his oxen, and said he would have revenge on Mormon and would whip Eddings. When he stooped witness saw the point of a bowie knife or pistol on him, and he was in the habit of wearing weapons. When they reached witness' house, they found Mormon and Eddings there, and prisoner and Mormon spoke to each other, the witness thought angrily. When dinner was ready, witness invited them all to dinner ; the prisoner declined, saying he would not eat with such rascals, using profane language, which Mormon heard. The prisoner then went to the workshop in the yard, and witness went there and again invited him to dinner ; but he declined, repeating the abusive language before used. Late in the afternoon Mormon and Eddings left to go home ; soon after which prisoner said he would give a gallon of whisky or five dollars if he had his (prisoner's) mule ; that he had a settlement to make with Mormon and Eddings, and intended to make it that evening. Witness advised him not to do so, but to go home. He replied he could or would drink their hearts' blood. Witness then parted with him and went some distance to water his horses, and while at the watering place heard a noise in the direction of Mormon's house, and while returning to his house met his wife, who told him that the prisoner had killed Mormon. When parting with the prisoner, he rode to the watering-place and watered his horses, and returned directly home, the watering-place being about three-quarters of a mile from witness' house. Prisoner in coming to witness' house, always came by Mormon's house, which was the nearest way.

Andrew J. Eddings testified, that Mormon was killed on the 19th of September, 1852, by the prisoner; that about noon of that day deceased and witness went to Suddith's and found prisoner and Shultz there; prisoner and deceased had some conversation, and seemed friendly. Deceased and witness left there late in the afternoon, prisoner and Shultz remaining. After witness and deceased reached home, prisoner rode up to the fence, and they talked a few moments; witness heard their voices, but not what was said. Deceased was in the act of getting over the fence, and prisoner jumped off his mule and ran up and took hold of the deceased; he drew his bowie knife, which witness saw as he approached deceased, and took hold as deceased got off the fence to the ground. Witness started to them as soon as he heard their voices, and then saw the prisoner draw his knife from his bosom. They struggled together, standing on their feet, and, four or five yards from the fence, prisoner stabbed deceased in the side, who went off six or eight paces, and sat down at the root of a tree, and when witness got to him he was dead. Prisoner ran off after his mule. When prisoner rode up to the fence, he came in a rapid gait, Shultz following about seventy-five or one hundred yards behind him. While the parties were struggling, there was nothing to obstruct witness' view of them. Shultz was some seventy yards from where the fighting took place. Witness did not see the prisoner pressed down and the deceased over him. A misunderstanding had occurred between witness and the prisoner, caused by the witness shooting three of prisoner's oxen that had broken into his cornfield. Deceased was not present when this was done, but he and the prisoner met shortly afterwards, and angry words passed between them. Witness and deceased were cropping together, but the plantation belonged to deceased, and witness lived with him. Deceased and witness had no arms, and there were none about the house; deceased was searched for arms after his death, and he had none about him. He was about twenty-five years of age, and stouter than the prisoner.

McMahan testified, that he knew the premises, and that there was nothing to obstruct the view from the house to the place of killing, and that he saw marks of struggling close to the fence, and the parties seemed to struggle from the fence.

Several witnesses proved that they examined the body after death, and found two wounds on the left side, one in the soft part of his body, just above the hip bone, and the other between his short ribs, sufficient to produce death, and several cuts in the clothes, which did not take effect upon the body.

The prisoner then introduced John Shultz, who testified that he did not see the fight when it began, but saw it about the time it ended; when he came up, that deceased had the prisoner down by the hair on the back of his head, and was striking him in the left side; deceased fell, and prisoner ran off after his mule; saw Eddings come running from the house to them, with a pistol in his right hand and the barrel lying on his left; he put it up before he got over the fence, and he did not get over until the fight was done and prisoner had gone after his mule. Witness was twenty or thirty yards from them when he saw them fighting. When he first heard hallooing he thought it was the prisoner calling him to ride on, he being then about three hundred yards off. He further stated, that when he had first said that he had not seen the prisoner the evening of the killing, he had told a lie, because his grandmother told him to say so, as his uncle, the prisoner, was in danger; but she told him, when sworn, to tell the truth. He did not see any knife in prisoner's hands during the fight, but saw him have the bowie knife presented in court on the same evening, after the fight. Witness was fourteen or fifteen years old.

Four witnesses were introduced by the state, who testified that the witness Shultz was not worthy of credit on oath; one witness for the prisoner, that his character for veracity was tolerably good, and another, that he had never heard it doubted.

This is the substance of all the testimony.

The first instruction given by the court and alleged to be erroneous, is the fifth instruction at the instance of the state, as follows: "That every killing is presumed to be malicious, and amounting to murder, until the contrary appears from the cir-

cumstances of alleviation, excuse, or justification; and that it is
incumbent upon the defendant to make out such circumstances
to the satisfaction of the jury unless they arise out of the evidence
produced against him." The rule here stated is fully justified by
the decision of this court in the case of McDaniel v. The State, 8
S. & M., 417,[1] and this instruction is more favorable in its terms
to the accused, than the instruction there referred to, with the
addition held by the court to be necessary in declaring the true
rule. There, the late learned chief justice says, " in cases where
the killing is proved and no accompanying circumstances appear in the evidence, the law presumes the killing was done
maliciously."

After adverting to other circumstances, affording presumptive evidence of malice, he adds, " These presumptions of law,
if unopposed, may amount to full proof of the fact. They stand
until the contrary is proved, or until such facts are proved as are
sufficient to raise a contrary and stronger presumption." The
same principle is sanctioned by courts and jurists of the greatest
learning and ability in England and the United States; Commonwealth v. York, 9 Met., 93, and the authorities cited in the
learned opinion of Chief Justice Shaw; 3 Greenl. Ev., 14; 1
Stark. Ev., 452. If anything is to be considered as settled by
sound judicial reasoning and authority, this doctrine must be so
regarded. Exception is also taken to the sixth instruction given
at the instance of the state in the following words: " That
malice is implied by law from the nature and character of the

[1] 1 Archbold Cr. Pr. & Pl., 846; 1 East P. C., 215; 4 Black. Com., 200; Riley v.
State, 9 Humph., 646; Bratton v. State, 10 Humph., 103; Haile v. State, 11 Humph.,
154; State v. Lipsey, 3 Dev., 485; State v. Sisson, 3 Brev., 58; State v. Tilley, 3 Ire-
dell, 424; Mitchum v. State, 11 Ga., 615; Boles v. State, 9 S. & M., 284; State v.
Town, Wright, 75; Mitchell v. State, 5 Yerg., 340; State v. McFall, Addis., 255;
People v. McLeod, 1 Hill., 377; State v. Turner, Wright, 20; McDaniels v. State, 8
S. & M., 401; State v. Tilley, 3 Iredell, 424; Ann v. State, 11 Humph., 159; People
v. Kirby, 2 Parker, 78; State v. Johnson, 3 Jones, 266; 1 Hale, 455; 4 Black. Com.,
200; 1 Hale, 474; 1 Hawk. P. C., c 29, § 12; 1 East P. C., c 5, § 18; Wharton Am.
Cr. Law, 710; Com. v. York, 9 Metc., 93; Foster, 255; 1 East P. C., 340; State v.
Peters, 2 Rice Dig., 106; Conner v. State, 4 Yerg., 137; State v. Irwin, 1 Haywood,
112; People v. McLeod, 1 Hill, (N. Y.), 277; U. S. v. Connell, 2 Mason, 91; Com.
v. Drew, 4 Mass., 391; Resp. v. Bob., 4 Dallas, 146; State v. Zellers, 2 Halst., 220;
State v. Merrill, 2 Dev., 269; State v. Smith, 3 Strobh., 77; Rex v. Martin, 3 C. & P.,
211; Rex v. Pitts, C. & M., 284; Rex v. Cheeseman, 7 C. & P., 455; Rex v. Shaw, 6
C. & P., 372; Com. v. Webster, 5 Cush., 320; Riggs v. State, 30 Miss., 635; Wharton on Homicide, 34, 39; Bird v. State, 14 Ga., 43; Price v. State, 36 Miss., 531;
Wharton Am. Cr. Law, 710, 944, 1112.

weapon used, and that the use of a deadly weapon in a fight, and
not in necessary self-defense, is in law evidence of malice." The
general principle contained in this instruction is sanctioned by the
authorities above cited. 8 S. & M., 417; 9 Met., 103; and 1
Greenl. Ev., 34; 17 Ala. R., 601; Wharton Am. C. L., 368.
But it could not prejudice the accused, because, first it was
directed alone to the point of implied malice, whereas the evidence went beyond all reasonable doubt to show express malice.
If it could have had any effect upon the minds of the jury, it
tended to direct them rather to the implied and uncertain evidence of malice, than to that which was direct and positive to
the point.

Secondly. Whatever prejudicial effect might have been occasioned by the instruction as it originally stood, was removed by
the instruction subsequently given by the court upon the point
of the use of the deadly weapon, as follows: " If the defendant entered into the conflict with a deadly weapon drawn, intending to use it, he is guilty of murder; but if he did not
enter into the fight intending to use the weapon, and only resorted to it in the heat of conflict, he is only guilty of manslaughter." " That if the jury believe from the evidence that
the defendant went into the fight having upon his person a
deadly weapon, intending from the first to use the same if necessary to enable him to overcome his antagonist, and did in the
fight use the same and kill his antagonist, he is guilty of murder, although he habitually carried the weapon." These qualifications, and the original instructions, undoubtedly contained a
correct statement of the law upon the point embraced by them,
and the accused could not have been prejudiced by them. Many
other instructions upon both sides were given by the court,
which tended still further to declare the whole law applicable to
the case in all its bearings, and to prevent any prejudice to the
accused. But it is objected in behalf of the prisoner, that the
court had no authority to modify charges already given by
qualifications and additions. It is the duty of the court to declare the law arising upon the case upon the pleadings and
evidence whenever thereto requested by either of the parties.
If the law upon any point in the case is incorrectly or imper-

fectly stated by the counsel in asking the instruction, it is the province and duty of the court to declare the law to the jury upon the question as fully as may be necessary to enable them to apply the true rules of law governing the case to the facts submitted for their determination.   This power exists whenever the counsel for the parties differ upon any point, or whenever the court is requested to charge the jury upon any point of law arising in the cause ; otherwise the main duty and province of the judge would be rendered nugatory.   In this case, the points upon which the additional instructions were given by the court, were distinctly presented by the instructions asked by both parties.   The court was of opinion, and we think correctly, that those instructions, though generally correct, did not state the law upon the points in question as fully as was necessary under the particular facts of the case, so gave it more fully and distinctly to the jury.   We think this was clearly within the power and duty of the court.

The last ground of error insisted upon in behalf of the plaintiff in error, is the following instruction : " That by great personal injury the law does not mean slight blows with the fist, or injury by other means not calculated to endanger the life or limb of the party."

This instruction was given in qualification of the following instruction given at the instance of the accused : " Killing is justifiable when done in lawfully protecting oneself from great personal injury, imminent and designed by another, and there is imminent danger of such design being accomplished."

It is not easy to perceive what proper bearing this last instruction had upon the case presented by the evidence.   The evidence showed clearly that the accused having just before expressed his malicious intent against the deceased, went to his abode armed, called him from his employment, and upon deceased answering his call and coming to him, that he met him at the fence, and so soon as the deceased had gotten over the fence, that he drew his bowie knife and commenced the attack upon him.   This is fully proved by the witness Eddings, corroborated by the witness McMahan, who testifies that the marks of struggling were close to the fence, and that the struggling was from the fence. And this testimony is entirely uncontradicted; for the witness Shultz states that he did not see the fight when it commenced, but only about the time it ended. The instruction under this state of facts was a mere abstract proposition, which had no proper application to the case, and should have been refused. But if it could possibly have been applicable to the case under any proper view of the evidence, it was proper for the court to instruct the jury as to the import in law of the terms "great personal injury," and this was plainly the object and probable effect of the qualification given. The expression, of itself, is very uncertain and indefinite, and unless explained and interpreted by reference to the legal principles appertaining to the subject, it is not easy to ascertain what construction might be placed upon the terms by the jury. Its uncertainty is well calculated to produce doubt and diversity of opinion upon it with the jury. It was, therefore, proper for the court to define the expression so far as might be necessary to enable the jury to understand it clearly and to apply it to the facts of the case, if, in any respect, it could properly have any application to them. In doing so, the court appears to have stated the general rule correctly in reference to the principles of the common law which the legislature must have had in view in enacting the statute in which the terms in question are employed. Tested by these principles, the terms "great personal injury" must be understood to be equivalent in import to the terms "great bodily harm," or "danger of loss of life or limb," or "enormous bodily harm," as defined by the rules of the common law, to constitute a justification or excuse for homicide. This construction was properly given by the court in this case, if the point involved could have had any effect upon the case. If, therefore, the proposition asked in behalf of the accused to be given in charge to the jury were pertinent to the case, this qualification was properly added; if it was not pertinent, as we think was the case, the qualification could do no injury to the accused; and being a proper modification of a general abstract rule given at his instance, he cannot complain that the correct rule was declared by the court. We have thus examined all the grounds of error urged in behalf of the plaintiff in error;

and after a careful and patient consideration of them, together with the evidence and all the rulings of the court, we are brought to the conclusion that there is no error in the proceedings and judgment of the court below.

The judgment is, therefore, affirmed.

A petition for a reärgument was filed in this case by the counsel for appellant, but the court refused to grant a reärgument.

Smith *v.* The State, 28 Miss. Rep., 728.

The record is the only evidence of the organization of the grand jury, and whether the proper oath was administered or not, is never ground for a plea in abatement, and such plea should be disregarded by the court.

Where the issue on a plea in abatement is an immaterial one, and the plea is quashed by demurrer, the defendant should be allowed to plead over.

Error to Clarke circuit court.   WATTS, J.

Freeman & Dixon for plaintiff in error.

D. C. Glenn, attorney general.

FISHER, J. :

The defendant in the court below pleaded in abatement to the indictment, that the grand jury were not sworn according to the provisions of the act of 1830 (Hutch. Code, 887), to which the district attorney replied that they were sworn according to the provisions of the act of 1822, setting out the form of the oath. To this replication the defendant demurred; which demurrer being overruled, the defendant filed a rejoinder to the replication, upon which issue was taken and the cause submitted to a jury, who returned a verdict in favor of the state, that is to say, that the grand jury were sworn according to law.

This whole proceeding is palpably absurd, and requires no comment. It is, perhaps, the first and only instance in the history of the jurisprudence of the state, where a jury were empanelled to ascertain the fact whether a grand jury were sworn according to the requirements of the law. The record, which shows the empanelling of the grand jury, is the only evidence which can be introduced to prove or disprove this fact; and whether the proper oath was in fact administered or not, or administered in the proper manner, can never be made the subject of a plea in abatement, but must be ascertained by an inspection of the record, which, in this instance, shows that the grand jury were sworn according to law.

The plea, therefore, presented an immaterial issue, and should have been disregarded by the court.

After the jury returned their verdict, the defendant moved for leave to file the plea of not guilty, which was refused by the court, and a final judgment was accordingly entered against the defendant. If the plea in abatement had presented a material issue, this action of the court would have been right. But as the plea was a nullity, and as the issue formed upon it could settle nothing, the application of the defendant to plead, should have been treated as though there had been no other pleading in the cause; or, in other words, the issue being an immaterial one, the court should have awarded a re-pleader, when the defendant could have had the full benefit of his motion.

The judgment must, therefore, for this error be reversed.

SUMRALL v. THE STATE, 29 Miss. Rep., 202.

AFFRAY.

The annual list of jurors returned by the assessor of taxes does not annul or supersede the lists previously returned, but is intended to return the names of such persons as may have been previously omitted, or have since become liable to jury duty. Therefore, a person whose name did not appear on the list last returned, but did appear on the one next before the last, and was drawn from box number one, is a competent grand juror.

In misdemeanors, where the issue on a plea in abatement is decided against the accused, he will not be allowed to plead over, but it is otherwise in cases of felony.

Error to Perry circuit court. McNAIR, J.

Charles A. Smith, for plaintiff in error.

D. C. Glenn, attorney general.

HANDY, J.:

This was an indictment in the Perry circuit court, against the plaintiffs in error for an affray.

The defendants below pleaded in abatement, that one of the grand jurors, who was a member of the grand jury which found the indictment at May term, 1854, was not drawn from a list of the names of persons in the county liable to serve as jurors taken and returned by the assessor within one year next preceding the finding of the indictment, as required by the act of December 16, 1830 ; nor was said juror drawn in any other mode authorized by law.

Upon this plea issue was taken, and it was found against the defendants, and judgment was rendered thereon, the defendants not being permitted to plead over to the indictment.

The first question arising upon the record, is as to the regularity of the drawing and organization of the grand jury.

It appears by the bill of exceptions, that a list of the persons within the county liable to serve as jurors, was duly returned by the assessor on the first day of December, 1853, wherein the name of Archibald Graham, the juror named in the plea, does not appear, that being the only list taken and returned within one year next preceding the finding of the indictment at the May term, 1854. But a list was duly taken and returned on the 16th October, 1852, more than a year previous to the finding of the bill, upon which the name of the juror appears.

The plea raises, 1st. Whether it is necessary, under the act of 1830, that the jurors for each term of the circuit court should be drawn from a list returned within one year next preceding the finding of the indictment ; and 2d. Whether, if the name of a person, being a member of the grand jury, be not on the list returned within the year, but appears on a previous list returned, such person is a competent juror.

These questions are free from difficulty, when we consider the provisions of the act of 1830, and the object intended to be accomplished in passing it.

The object of the act manifestly was to regulate the mode of drawing juries, with an especial view to equalizing the duty of serving on juries among all persons within the county liable to such service. To that end, a list of all persons liable to such duty is required to be returned, and when the first list is returned, the names appearing on it are required to be entered on a book kept for that purpose, and also to be written on separate slips of paper, which are to be put in a box numbered one, from which the requisite number of jurors for each term shall be drawn; and the names of such jurors so drawn, as shall be required to serve at the terms to which they shall be summoned, shall be put in a box numbered two, until the entire names in box number one shall be exhausted. Thus the feature of rotation is established.

In order that all persons within the county not on the original list, and who may from time to time become liable to serve as jurors, may be subjected to that duty, it is provided that a list of such persons shall be returned once in every year, and that such names as are thus annually returned and not included in previous lists, shall be added to the general list of jurors, and be put in box number one, to be drawn out in the same manner and subject to the same rules as those persons originally returned.

These are the general features of the system, and in view of them, it is clear that the idea that the jurors for each term are to be drawn from a list returned next preceding, is without just foundation. The spirit and intention of the statute are, that the jurors shall be drawn from box number one, which contains the names of the persons generally in the county liable to jury service. The object of the annual list is not to annul or supersede the lists previously returned, but to return the names of such persons as may have been previously omitted, or may have become, from any cause, subject to the duty since the previous return. If, therefore, the name of any person already returned, be omitted in the annual list (as was the case here), or the name of an improper person be returned in the annual list, or if the assessor should wholly fail to return an annual list, as required by law, it will not vitiate the list of jurors, provided they are regularly drawn from the box number one, because the persons so drawn have been legally returned and enrolled as competent jurors, and it is no objection to their competency that other persons who should have been added to the list, in order that they might bear their part of the burden of such service, have not been regularly returned. The question is: Have those persons, who have been duly drawn from the box as jurors, been duly returned and entered as persons liable to such duty? And if this be answered in the affirmative, it would be absurd to say that they were illegal jurors, except so far as the individuals should be found deficient in the legal qualifications, to be tried by the court when they should be empanelled as a jury.

If this view were not correct, the greatest inconvenience and confusion might frequently occur by the errors or delinquency of the returning officers, and the administration of justice be delayed or defeated by a narrow and literal interpretation of the statute in violation of its true spirit and intent. It would be to apply a regulation which was merely intended to subject all persons in the county liable as jurors to the performance of that duty, and thus equalize the burden among the people, in such a manner as to render illegal persons duly returned, drawn and empanelled, and thereby to embarrass and defeat the very system intended to be established.

The second question presented by the record, is, whether the defendants were entitled to plead over upon the replication to the plea in abatement being found against them.

It is held that where an issue in fact is joined by replication and found for the plaintiff in cases of misdemeanor, the judgment is final. 1 Chitt. Pl., 464; Com. v. Barge, 3 Penn. Rep., 264. The rule is otherwise upon an issue of law on the plea, or in case of a felony. 1 Arch. Cr. Pl., by Waterman, 116.

The judgment is affirmed.

Drrro et al. *v.* The State, 30 Miss. Rep., 126.

Forfeiture of Recognizance.

It is immaterial to the question of liability of the accused, arising from his failure to appear in court, according to the tenor of his recognizance, that the issue upon the indictment is still pending. He is bound to appear according to the recognizance, in order to be regularly put on trial for the offense for which he was indicted.

A variance between the *scire facias* and the judgment *nisi* is a fatal defect, sufficient to quash the *scire facias*. So, also, is a variance between the recognizance and *scire facias*, a good defense to the *scire facias*. But the defendant will not be entitled to it unless he sets it up by plea to the *scire facias*.

If the defendant suffers judgment by default, on the *scire facias*, he cannot on writ of error to that judgment bring to notice anything contained in the recognizance.

Error to Carroll circuit court.   HARRIS, J.

James P. Scales, for plaintiff in error.

1. The court had no right to render a judgment by default, while there was a plea filed in the action to which no objection was taken.   Vide 3 S. & M., 120.

2. The record shows that judgment *nisi* was rendered for $100, and judgment final for $150.   The judgment is therefore inconsistent with itself, and of course, erroneous.

3. The *scire facias* recites a judgment *nisi* to have been entered upon a recognizance, conditioned for the appearance of Ditto, on the first Monday of December, 1854; when, in truth, as appears by the record, the condition was, that he should appear on the first Monday of June, 1854.   This variance must be fatal, because the *scire facias* gave to defendant no notice of the *real* recognizance being forfeited, which it was bound to do, that they might have opportunity to answer, and show cause why it should not be final.

D. C. Glenn, attorney general.

HANDY, J.:

This is a writ of error to a judgment rendered in the Carroll circuit court, against the plaintiffs in error, as principal and bail in a recognizance entered into, upon a charge of gaming, and which was forfeited.

The errors assigned are:

1. That the judgment upon the *scire facias*, issued after the forfeiture was rendered by default, when there was a plea filed to the indictment, and was not disposed of.

2. That the judgment *nisi* was for the sum of one hundred dollars, and the final judgment on *scire facias*, was for one hundred and fifty dollars.

3. That the *scire facias* recites a judgment *nisi*, rendered upon a recognizance, conditioned for the appearance of Ditto on the first Monday of December, 1854, when the record shows that the condition was to appear on the first Monday of June, 1854.

The first ground of error is untenable. It was immaterial to the question of the liability of the accused, arising from his failure to appear in court, according to the tenor of his recognizance, that the issue upon the indictment was still pending. He was bound to appear according to his recognizance, in order to be regularly put on trial for the offense for which he was indicted.

The second cause of error is well assigned. The variance between the sum of money for which the forfeiture was taken, and the sum stated in the *scire facias* issued to enforce that judgment, is material; and this objection is not obviated by the fact, that the sum of money for which the judgment *nisi* was taken was erroneous, and not conformable to the recognizance; and that the judgment final was for the sum stated in the recognizance. If the *scire facias* had been in conformity to the judgment *nisi*, and had properly described the recognizance, and had been in other respects regular, it would not be competent for the cognizors to complain that the judgment *nisi* varied in amount from the recognizance, because the error would not be to their injury. But where the *scire facias* is not supported in a material respect by the judgment *nisi*, a judgment final, inconsistent with the judgment *nisi*, is erroneous, and if to a party's prejudice, must be reversed.

Of a like character is the third ground of error. The variance between the recognizance and the *scire facias*, as to the term of the court at which the defendant was bound to make his appearance, is material, and constitutes a good defense to the *scire facias*. But the defendant will not be entitled to the benefit of it, unless he sets it up by plea to the *scire facias;* because, after the judgment *nisi*, and when the *scire facias* has been issued to enforce that judgment, the recognizance is not properly a part of the record of that proceeding, and must be brought before the court by plea of *nul tiel record*, or other appropriate plea. If the defendant suffers judgment by default on the *scire facias*, he cannot, on writ of error to that judgment, bring to notice any thing contained in the recognizance. And such is the attitude of the plaintiff in error in this case.

For the second ground of error, the judgment on the *scire facias* is reversed, and the case remanded for further proceedings.

DOUTHIT *v.* THE STATE, 30 Miss. Rep., 133.

SCIRE FACIAS.

A judgment *nisi* is not final until rendered so by judgment upon the *scire facias*, and it is competent in determining upon the latter judgment, to consider whether the *scire facias* is supported by the judgment *nisi*, which it is merely process to complete and render final.

If the judgment *nisi* and the *scire facias* are insufficient to sustain the final judgment, it will be erroneous and must be reversed, though no objections were made in the court below.

A variance between the judgment *nisi* and the *scire facias*, is fatal to the *scire facias* and the final judgment.

In error from the circuit court of Monroe County. Hon. FRANK M. ROGERS, Judge.

The plaintiff in error, as bail for one Richard B. Douthit, entered into a recognizance, conditioned for the appearance of said Richard B. Douthit, at the term of the court, as prescribed by law, to answer an indictment against him for larceny. The said Richard B. Douthit made default; and judgment *nisi* was rendered against him and the plaintiff in error, his bail. The judgment *nisi*, against the plaintiff in error, recites, that it was for his default in not bringing into court the body of John W. Douthit. A *scire facias* was issued on this judgment *nisi* against the plaintiff, describing the judgment *nisi* as having been entered against him for the default of Richard B. Douthit. Upon the return of this *scire facias* executed, the judgment *nisi* was made final, the plaintiff in error failing to appear and make any defense thereto. From this judgment the writ of error in this cause was sued out.

Reynolds & Kinyon, for plaintiff in error.

There is a fatal variance between the judgment *nisi* and the *scire facias*. The first describes the principal of plaintiff in error as John W. Douthit, the other as Richard B. Douthit. Bridges v. The State, 24 Miss. Rep., 153.

D. C. Glenn, attorney general.

HANDY, J. :

Of the various errors assigned in this cause, we consider it necessary to decide upon but one.

The judgment *nisi* against the plaintiff in error, appears by the record to have been rendered against him in consequence of his failure to bring into court the body of one John W. Douthit, for whom he had become bail upon recognizance, and who had been charged with a felony. The *scire facias* issued upon this judgment, recites and shows that the plaintiff in error had become bound to bring into court the body of one Richard B. Douthit, and on his failure to do so, that the judgment sought to be enforced had been rendered. Upon this *scire facias* a judgment by default was rendered against the plaintiff in error, who thereupon sued out this writ of error.

It is manifest by the record that the obligation of the plaintiff in error, as stated in the *scire facias*, was essentially different from that appearing by the judgment *nisi*, and that the *scire facias* was not supported by the judgment *nisi*. That judgment not being final until rendered so by the judgment upon the *scire facias*, it is competent in determining the latter judgment, to consider whether the *scire facias* is supported by the judgment *nisi*, which it is merely process to complete and render final. And if the judgment *nisi* and the *scire facias* taken as parts of the same proceeding, are insufficient to sustain the final judgment, it will be erroneous and must be reversed, though no objections were taken to the insufficiency of the proceedings in the court below; because upon the whole record the judgment is erroneous.

The variance between the judgment *nisi* and the *scire facias* is essential, and fatal to the *scire facias* and the final judgment.

The judgment is reversed and the *scire facias* quashed.

JENKINS *v.* THE STATE, 30 Miss. Rep., 408.

HOMICIDE.

The record must show that the indictment on which the prisoner was tried was found and returned into court by the grand jury.

In change of venue in criminal cases, it must appear that the record transmitted to the court to which the venue is changed, is the record of the proceedings upon the indictment on which the prisoner was tried.

Error to Jasper circuit court. WATTS, J.

The plaintiff in error was indicted in the Jones circuit court for the murder of a slave. On application, the prisoner obtained a change of venue to Jasper county, where he was tried and found guilty of manslaughter. He made a motion for a new trial, which was overruled; whereupon he was sentenced by the court to twelve years' imprisonment in the penitentiary. Which judgment he sued out a writ of error to this court, to have reversed.

Evans, McDugald and *McMillan,* for plaintiff in error.

D. C. Glenn, attorney general.

FISHER, J.:

The prisoner having been put upon his trial for murder, in the circuit court of Jasper county, was convicted of the crime of manslaughter in the first degree; and from the judgment rendered upon that verdict, this writ of error has been prosecuted.

The indictment appears upon its face to have been found in the county of Jones, and the venue changed to the county of Jasper. Nothing appears in the record to show that the indictment was ever returned into court. Nor does it appear that the record from Jones county is the record of the proceedings had upon said indictment.

Judgment reversed.

DICK et al. (slaves) *v.* THE STATE, 30 Miss. Rep., 593.

HOMICIDE.

In order to render the confessions of a prisoner competent evidence against him, it is not necessary to inform him of his rights, or that he is not bound to confess. All that is necessary is that they must be free from compulsion.

It is too late, after a confession has gone to the jury without objection, for the prisoner to object and move for its exclusion.

A party may be convicted of a crime upon the testimony of his accomplice. His connection with the crime goes to his credibility, but does not affect his competency, and the jury are the exclusive judges as to the degree of weight that his testimony is entitled to.

Error to Yazoo circuit court. HENRY, J.

The proceedings in the court below, necessary to be stated,

are fully set out in the opinion of the court, except the testimony of witness, Peter (a slave). This witness, on the part of the state, testified as follows : "That on the night his master was killed, he went with the prisoners to the house—they made him go with them. Henry went in first, Dick next, and Aleck stayed in the gallery. When they went in, his master (Theophilus Pritchard) jumped out of bed ; that Henry caught hold of him, and threw him on the floor, and choked him until he got tired, then got hold of him (witness) and pulled him down, and made him take hold of his master's neck. He, witness, choked his master, but the breath was nearly out of his body, and he was nearly dead when he first took hold of him. They then took his master up and put him in the bed, laid his hands by his side, and covered him up. This was about two years ago."

George B. Wilkinson and *W. E. Pugh* for plaintiffs in error.

The first error assigned is : The court who tried this cause, erred in overruling the motion to exclude from the jury the evidence of Julius Johnson and Tilman Johnson.

1. Because the confession of each of the prisoners made after the deed was done, was permitted to go to the jury, as evidence to prove the guilt of the others. The confessions or admissions of an accomplice in a felony, made after the commission and completion of the offense, are not competent evidence against a prisoner, even though a previous conspiracy and combination between the prisoner and the accomplice to commit the felony, has been proven. Hunter's Case, 7 Gratt. 642 ; 2 Russ. Crimes, 652, n. 2 ; Stark. Ev. 31.

2. Because these confessions were not voluntarily made, or obtained, even had the prisoners been freemen, much less, as they are slaves, and perfectly under the control of those surrounding them, and in whose custody they were. The man who is born a slave, raised a slave, and knows and feels his destiny and lot is to die a slave ; always under a superior, controlling his actions and his will, can not be supposed to act or speak voluntary and of his free-will, while surrounded by fifteen or twenty of those to whom he knows he is subservient, and by the law bound to obey. Such a being, in his physical, moral, and intellectual faculties, is, and must ever be, more or less subservient

to the will and wishes of the freeman having the control over him; and when in chains, and informed that it would be better for him to confess, is under duress. Place man physically and morally in perpetual slavery, and how, I ask, can the intellectual man be free? Perpetual slavery and free-will are incompatible with each other. They can not exist in the same being at the same time. By our state, the same evidence, and the same rules of law, that govern the trial of a freeman, govern the trial of a slave. If a freeman make confessions while under duress, or after being induced so to do by threats, fear, promises or hope, such confessions can not be given as evidence against him; and the same law that governs the trial of the freeman, governs the trial of the slave.

It will be borne in mind that the prisoners made no confessions until late in the evening, and some of the white men had been there all day; and among the rest, the two Johnsons (the witnesses). Nor did they confess until they were surrounded by eighteen or twenty white men, and after being arrested and chained, and told to confess; it was better for them. Rex v. John Wilson, 1 Holt, 597; 3 Eng. Com. Law R., 190; 2 Stark. Ev., 27, note n; 2 Russ. Cr., 645; Peter v. State, 4 S. & M., 31; Van Buren v. State, 2 Cushm., 512; Rex. v. Stokes, 1 Am. Law Reg., 435.

The court erred in granting the third instruction asked for by the state. Because it does not state if prisoners combined, confederated, or agreed to kill, etc., or some like words; it was not necessary for them all to be present, etc. The design and agreement beforehand is wanting. The instruction is in the words "ready and able;" the word *willing* should have been added.

The court erred in granting the second and fourth instructions for the state; because neither of them confine the jury to the evidence before them as jurors, but permit them to take into consideration their private knowledge, to exercise any outside prejudice, and to carry with them into their retirement, all rumors they may have heard before they were sworn to try this cause. Savenbury v. Harper, 5 Cushm. R., 299, determined by this court in 1854, is in point.

The court erred in refusing the sixth instruction asked by prisoners.

It does not appear that the negro boy, Peter, was either sworn or charged before he was permitted to testify. Hutch. Code, 521, § 59.

The record does not show that the prisoners were valued before sentence of death was pronounced upon them. Hutch. Code, 540, § 2, art. 20.

The judgment of the court is against Pritchard for costs, the record showing that he was dead at the time. It is, therefore, so far, void, and being an entire thing, if void in part is void *in toto*.

D. C. Glenn, attorney general.

1. The confessions in evidence were freely and voluntarily made. Each one made separate confessions, and each confession was properly received.

2. There is no point raised on the instructions needing notice, save the allegation that they do not confine the jury to the evidence. I think this is a mistake. The first instruction does confine them, and it applies to all save the last instruction, which renews the restriction.

3. It need not appear that Peter was sworn or charged before testifying. This court presumes he was.

4. In Jack's case, Miss. Rep., the court say, the assessment of a condemned negro has nothing to do with the record of his conviction.

5. The question of costs raised, has nothing to do with the guilt or innocence of these appellants.

Smith, C. J. :

The plaintiffs in error were indicted and tried in the circuit court of Yazoo county; and convicted of the murder of Theophilus Pritchard. A motion was made for a new trial, which was overruled. Whereupon the prisoners excepted, and filed their bill of exceptions, which contains the evidence adduced on the trial.

The first exception taken to the judgment below is, that the court erred in overruling the motion of the prisoners, " to rule out all the testimony as to the confessions of the prisoners."

To determine the validity of this exception, we must refer to the evidence, as it appears in the bill of exceptions.

Julius Johnson, the first witness called for the prosecution, testified, that " on the morning of the day of the death of Pritchard, the boy Aleck came to his house, and informed him that his master was dead ; that he went over about an hour by sun in the morning, and found Pritchard in bed, with his hands down on his sides, lying on his back, dead ; that from appearances, he had not been dead long : some warmth about his heart. Afterwards, when a *post-mortem* examination was had, there appeared bruised blood on one side of the neck about as large as a dollar, and something like the print of fingers on the neck ; gave no other views or evidence of violence on the body except a scratch or two on the leg, and one of his toe-nails was loose ; that the coroner arrived there in the evening, about an hour by sun ; that there were some sixteen or twenty white men there before any attempt was made, to his knowledge, to get any thing out of the negroes ; or, if so, he thinks they made no confessions until after the coroner arrived ; then Dick confessed to him that he knew his master was killed ; that the boys had laid this plan to kill him ; and that he agreed to it ; but he remained outside the door while the others went in. This confession took place in the yard."

Aleck confessed " he helped kill his master ; said they went in, and his master was asleep ; he woke up and jumped out of bed ; he and the other boys caught him and threw him on the floor, and choked him until he was dead."

Tilman Johnson testified, that he went to Pritchard's room in the morning, and remained there all day ; that in the afternoon all the negroes, or nearly all, except Dick, were in a room together. In talking to the negroes about the death of their master, he said to them all, that it would be better for the guilty ones to confess, that the innocent might not be punished ; that when he made this remark, Aleck and Henry were chained, and he thought Henry was asleep ; but he jumped up, and said, " it was no use to deny it any longer ; and stated that he and the other boys went in and killed their master, by choking him, and then laid him on the bed, as he was found." The coroner and jury were then in the other room of the house, and the negroes were in charge of one, in whose possession the coroner had placed them.

No warning of any kind whatever, was given to the prisoners of their rights,—and that they were not bound to make any confession by which they would criminate themselves.

The confessions of the prisoners, Dick and Aleck, were not made before an officer during the course of a judicial examination. They were made to the witness, with whom they happened to be present. No effort was made by the witness, or any one else, by threats or promises, to induce these parties to confess. The confession of each appears to have been perfectly voluntary. Under these circumstances, it was not necessary, in order to render their confessions competent evidence against the party making them, that they should have been informed of their rights, or warned that they were not bound to make any statement which would tend to inculpate themselves. As evidence, therefore, against the party making them, these confessions were clearly competent.

According to the rule recognized in the case of Peter v. State, 4 S. & M., 31, and in that of Van Buren v. State, 24 Miss., 512, the confession of the prisoner, Henry, was incompetent; and doubtless would have been excluded, if it had been objected to when offered on the trial. But no objection appears then to have been made to its introduction as evidence. It was too late after the confession had gone to the jury, without exception, for the prisoner to object, and move for its exclusion. And, moreover, the force of the exception, if it were conceded that it was made at the proper time, is materially weakened, by the subsequent action of the court.

The judge, at the instance of the defendants, charged the jury, " that the confessions of the prisoners, made while in the custody of the coroner, or his appointees, are not evidence, unless they were first warned that they were not bound to criminate themselves."

If the jury observed this instruction in estimating the guilt of the accused parties, they not only excluded from their consideration the confession of the prisoner Henry, which in our opinion was incompetent evidence, but likewise the confessions of Dick and Aleck, which we think was proper evidence in the cause ; as it was distinctly stated by all the witnesses, that no such warning or caution was given to the prisoners.

Assuming that this instruction was correct (and no objection as to its legality can be heard as coming from the parties at whose instance it was given), and that it was obeyed by the jury, let us see whether there was not other evidence before them which fully sustains the verdict.

The testimony of the witness Peter, who was jointly indicted with the prisoners and acquitted on a former trial, is direct and clear, and establishes every material fact necessary to be proved, in order to fix the guilt of the accused.

Upon his examination, this witness confessed that he was an accomplice in the commission of the crime. This, however, did not disqualify him as a witness ; and as to his credibility, the jury were the exclusive judges. As they gave credit to his testimony, we are bound to hold that the verdict was sustained by sufficient evidence, independent of the confessions of the prisoners.

There are other objections made to the judgment, but as, in our opinion, they are unimportant or untenable, we deem it unnecessary to notice them specially

Judgment affirmed.

HANDY, J.:

I concur in the above opinion.

FISHER, J.:

I disagree as to so much of the opinion as holds, that the judgment must be affirmed as to the slave Henry.

BOVARD *v.* THE STATE, 30 Miss. Rep., 600.

HOMICIDE—INSANITY.

Instructions given to the jury as follows:

1. The law presumes every man to be sane, until the contrary is proven.

2. That if the jury believe, from the evidence, that the accused killed the deceased with malice, and not in necessary self-defense, he is guilty of murder, notwithstanding they may believe he was, at the time of committing the deed, laboring under partial insanity, unless he was, from such insanity, incapable of understanding the nature and consequence of his act, and of knowing that it was wrong, and that he would be punished for it.

3. That insanity, however produced, constitutes no excuse for crime, unless it be so great as to deprive the party of his power to understand the nature of his act, or of his ability to distinguish between right and wrong, and of his ability to understand that he will be liable to punishment if he commits it.

4. That though a party be partially insane, yet he is responsible for his criminal acts, unless it appear that he was prompted or instigated by his madness to perpetrate such act.

5. That if the homicide charged is proven, in the opinion of the jury, the barbarity of the act affords no legal presumption of insanity in the accused.

Held, that these instructions correctly expounded the law in regard to insanity, as a defense for crime.

Error to Yazoo circuit court. HENRY, J.

Young C. Bovard, the plaintiff in error, was indicted in the circuit court of Yazoo county, for the murder of his wife, on the 20th day of November, 1855, and was convicted. The defense relied on was, that the act of homicide was committed whilst the prisoner was insane.

The opinion of the court contains the facts of the case.

John M. Moore, for plaintiff in error, cited and commented on Commonwealth v. Rogers, 7 Metc., 500; The State v. Gardner, Wright, Ohio R., 392; State v. Spencer, 1 Zab. R., 196; 1 Greenl. Ev., §42; Ray, Med. Juris., 413; 1 Copeland, Dictionary of Medicine, 572; 1 Cyclopædia of Practical Medicine, 587.

D. C. Glenn, attorney-general, argued the cause orally.

SMITH, C. J.:

The plaintiff in error was indicted and tried in the circuit court of Yazoo, for the murder of his wife. No question whatever was raised as to the fact of homicide, or the agency of the accused in the commission of the deed. The defense was placed solely on the ground of insanity; and the jury having found the prisoner guilty of the charge, a motion was made to set aside the verdict, and for a new trial. The grounds upon which the motion was based were, first, misdirection in the charges to the jury; and, second, that the verdict was contrary to law and evidence. The same reasons are now urged as a ground for reversing the judgment.

In support of the first ground, it is insisted, that the third, fourth and fifth instructions for the state are erroneous, inasmuch as they "do not properly and fully explain the legal consequences of insanity, and lay down rules for the guidance of the jury, under which the accused might be convicted, although proved by the evidence to have been insane at the time the alleged offense was committed."

The only questions which could properly arise upon the evidence before the jury, were, first, whether the accused labored under a general derangement of his moral and intellectual faculties; second, whether he was affected with partial mania, accompanied with a delusion which was connected with, or embraced in the circle of its operation, the act with which he was charged; and third, if by the proof he was shown to have been either generally or partially insane, whether the insanity was of such a character as to absolve him from responsibility as a moral agent."

A person, in the estimation of the law, to be capable of the commission of a crime, must have intelligence enough to have a criminal intent and purpose; and if his mental capacity is either so deficient that he has no conscience, nor will, nor controlling mental power over his actions; or if through the access of mental disease his intellectual power is for the time completely suspended, he is not to be regarded either as a moral agent or punishable by the law for his acts.

Cases of insanity of such extreme character as these are not easily mistaken. And it is not to be controverted that the prisoner, as shown by the evidence, was not so totally deprived of conscience, will, or mental control over his actions, or that his intellect and capacity were not so utterly deficient, as to be incapable of entertaining a criminal purpose.

But in cases of partial insanity, where the mind, though capable of memory, of reasoning, and of judgment, is clouded and weakened, or so perverted and influenced by insane delusions, as to be compelled, as it were, to act under false impressions and influences, the rule of law, as it is now generally understood, is laid down by Chief Justice Shaw as follows: " A man is not to be excused from responsibility if he has reason and capacity sufficient to enable him to distinguish between right and wrong as to the particular act he is then doing, a knowledge and consciousness that the act he is doing is wrong and criminal, and will subject him to punishment. In order to be responsible, he must have sufficient power of memory to recollect the relation in which he stands to others, and in which others stand to him; that the act he is doing is contrary to the plain dictates of justice and right, and injurious to others, and a violation of the dictates of duty. On the contrary, although he may be laboring under partial insanity, if he still understands the nature and character of his act and its consequences; if he has a knowledge that it is wrong and criminal, and a mental power sufficient to apply that knowledge to his own case and to know that, if he does the act he will do wrong and receive punishment; such partial insanity is not sufficient to exempt him from responsibility for criminal acts." Com. v. Rogers, 7 Met. R., 500.

Without quoting the instructions to which exception is taken, or noticing them in a more special manner, it is sufficient to state that they contain, in very distinct and intelligible terms, the rules laid down by the learned judge in the charge from which we have quoted above. In our opinion, therefore, there was no error committed in giving the instructions which were requested in behalf of the prosecution. Nor do we think there was error in withholding either of the instructions which were requested by the prisoner and refused by the court.

The remaining ground upon which reversal of the judgment is claimed is, that a motion for a new trial was improperly overruled. The question thus presented must, of course, be determined by the evidence submitted to the jury, and we will proceed to notice such of the facts established by the testimony which tend to prove or disprove the insanity of the accused.

The homicide was committed on the night of the 20th of November, 1855. The prisoner was for several years previous to that date a man of intemperate habits; some eight or ten days before the deed was committed he was very much intoxicated, but it was supposed that he had abstained entirely from drink for the five or six days immediately preceding the 20th of November. On the 19th he had been at Benton, which was four miles distant from his place of residence; and on his return he was met by Dr. Woods, who had previously been his physician; he complained of being unwell; he said his right arm was dead and he could not use it; he complained of soreness about the shoulders and neck. Dr. Woods, from a slight examination, thought it might be paralysis arising from intemperance. He was rational, and the doctor observed no symptoms of delirium tremens or any indication of mental derangement of any description about him. On the same day he was at Mr. Quini's, dined there and ate more heartily than usual; Mrs. Quini observed no wildness in his appearance at dinner; he frequently changed the subject of conversation, acted strangely, and walked more rapidly than usual. He went away and returned some time after dark; he then appeared to be under some delusion connected with the subject of religion; he said he had got religion, that his wife had got religion, and was the happiest woman in the world; he had come back to tell Quini and wife of it; he wished them to get religion, also; and insisted upon their getting " down and going through the religious performance;" he prayed, preached, and said he had turned preacher. He frequently ran out into the piazza and seemed to be watching for something; said that they would get religion in a few minutes; that he saw it coming down from heaven.

These acts and declarations, and many others of a similar character, and quite as frantic and absurd, if they were not simulated, undoubtedly show that he was afflicted with partial insanity, attended with delusion, on the subject of religion.

He left Quini's and returned again the same night; the weather was cold, and he went back in his shirt and drawers, without hat or shoes; and behaved in the same way. He was persuaded to go to bed, and was supposed to sleep; he remained quiet for two hours; he then got up and went away. On the following day, the 20th of November, at eight o'clock, he returned to Quini's, and deported himself much in the same manner that he had on the previous night.   He asked for breakfast; said that he had eaten nothing that morning; that breakfast was ready when he left home, but that he could not wait.   He sat down to the table and ate as usual.   On the 19th or 20th, he spoke of his "lame arm," and said that it had got well.   From Quini's, after having remained an hour, he went to the graveyard and assisted in putting down a post; a person being then engaged in paling it in.   He was rational; and, while there, evinced no indications of mental alienation.   At home, in the evening of the 20th, his conversation and conduct indicated that he was under the same delusion under which he appeared to labor in the morning and on the preceding night.   He was kind and affectionate to his wife, and manifested great solicitude on her account.   He showed no dislike or hostility to any one; did not appear to be suspicious of any one; and although he said they would all be dead in a short time, he did not appear to be alarmed on that account.

On the 21st, the day following the commission of the deed, he appeared to be in full possession of his intellectual faculties; he confessed his crime, described its atrocity in the strongest terms, expressed great remorse at having committed the deed, but declined to state his motive for its commission.

Late in the evening of that day he was visited by Dr. Holmes. The doctor was under the impression that he was asleep when he first went in; his pulse was natural, and he thought that the accused was not laboring under any disease whatever.   He had known the accused for many years, and had never seen him with the symptoms of *mania-a-potu* upon him.   On the occasion of this visit, he saw nothing about the accused which indicated insanity.

In reviewing the evidence in the case before us, it is impossible to come to the conclusion that the plaintiff in error, at the time he perpetrated the crime, was affected with a mental malady which involved his entire intellectual faculties; and there are very cogent reasons for rejecting the hypothesis, that his affection was that of delirium tremens.

According to an approved writer on the medical jurisprudence of insanity, this disease—delirium tremens—at its approach is generally attended, amongst other symptoms, with disturbed sleep and impaired appetite; after the symptoms have continued for two or three days, they increase in severity, the patient ceases to sleep altogether, and soon becomes delirious. At first the delirium is not constant—the mind wandering during the night—but during the day, when its attention is fixed, capable of rational discourse. It is not long, however, before it becomes constant, and constitutes the most prominent feature of the disease. This state of watchfulness and delirium continues three or four days, when, if the patient recover, it is succeeded by sleep, which at first appears in uneasy and irregular naps, and lastly, in long, sound and refreshing slumbers. Ray, Med. Juris., 417.

"Almost invariably," says the same author, "the patient manifests more or less feelings of suspicion and fear, laboring under continual apprehension of being made the victim of sinister designs and practices." "One of the most common hallucinations is to be constantly seeing devils, snakes, vermin and all manner of unclean things about him, and peopling every nook and corner of his apartment with these loathsome objects. The extreme terror which these delusions often inspire, produce in the countenance an unutterable expression of anguish, and frequently impels the patient to the commission of suicide."

Assuming this to be a correct description of the course, and constantly attendant symptoms of *mania-a-potu*, it is difficult, if not impossible, to believe that the accused labored under that disease.

The disease, if it ever existed at all, did not manifest itself until the afternoon of the 19th of November; for on that day, at dinner, none of its peculiar and marked symptoms were observable; on the contrary, he was neither irrational nor delirious, and ate more heartily than usual. On the following morning, although, if we judge from the evidence in relation to his conduct during the night, his malady had made most rapid progress, he ate his breakfast with unimpaired appetite, and went, in compliance with his promise, to assist in putting an inclosure around the grave-yard; and whilst there disclosed no indication of irrationality or symptoms of delirium tremens. These facts are irreconcilable with the idea that, if he labored under any mental affection, it was that of delirium tremens.

The total absence of almost every marked peculiarity usually attendant upon this disease, and particularly the short continuance of the attack, and the complete restoration of the accused to his natural, sound and healthy state, within less than thirty hours after its commencement, render this conclusion unavoidable.

There are several facts and circumstances connected with this transaction, as they appear from the evidence, which might well have authorized the jury to doubt whether the accused was at all affected with any form of mental malady.   But conceding that there was no attempt at simulated mania on the part of the accused, and that he in fact did labor under some disease of the mind, which amounted to partial, but very temporary insanity, according to the rule of law which must govern in the case, he is clearly to be held responsible for his act.

There was no proof that the accused had not capacity and reason sufficient to distinguish between right and wrong, in relation to the act which he committed ; or that he had not a knowledge and consciousness that it was wrong and criminal, and that punishment would be inflicted upon him in consequence of its commission ; on the contrary, he was perfectly rational, except in reference to a single class of subjects, about which he seemed to entertain very wild, ridiculous and absurd notions. But there was no proof before the jury which, either directly or by inference, showed that the fancy or delusion under which he labored had any connection as the antecedent or cause with the commission of the offense.   It is not sufficient to absolve from the penalties of the law, that the party charged was partially insane, and that such insanity was attended with delusion.   In all such cases it is essential that it be clearly shown, in order to excuse, that the act was committed under the direct or necessary influence of such delusion.

Judgment affirmed.

NOTE.—The early English authorities on the subject of insanity may be found in 3 Coke Inst., 6 ; 1 Hale P. C., 30 ; 8 Hargrave's State Tr., 322 ; 16 Howell's St. Tr. 695–794.

In Lord Ferrer's case, in 1760, tried by the House of Lords, for murder, we find the first intimation of views that afterwards grew into a decided test, and which might. be expressed thus :

"If the accused, at the time the act charged was committed, knew right from wrong, he was accountable."

It being held, that if the accused had such possession of reason as enabled him to comprehend the nature of his actions, and "could discriminate between moral good and evil," it was sufficient. The defendant was convicted and executed. 19 Howell's St. Tr., 947. See Bellingham's case, 5 C. &. P., 169, and note; Collinson on Lunacy, 630; 54 Ann. Reg., 304, (1812.) Also Tonsley's case, 3 Foster & Fin., 847; also Oxford's case, 9 C. & P., 532; Bowler's case, tried at the Old Bailey, for murder, in 1812; Offerd's case, 5 C. & P., 168. See also 1 C. & K., 129; Stokes' case, 3 ib., 185. See also the opinions of Lord Brougham and the judges, in reference to McNaughten's case, 10 Clark & Fin., 200, quoted in 1 Beck Med. Juris., 793, Ed. 1863; Regina v. Layton, 4 Cox C. C., 149.

In the cases of Regina v. Allnut, before the same judge, in 1848; Regina v. Burton, 3 Cox C. C., 275; and Regina v. Pate, before Baron Alderson, (see Black. Mag., Nov., 1850, p. 559,) the defense that the act was done under an irresistible impulse, which amounted to insanity, was not allowed to vary the rule. The court said, in the last case cited, " that the law does not acknowledge the doctrine of an uncontrollable impulse, if the person was aware it was a wrong act he was about to commit." And that if the jury " were not satisfied that at the time the party was suffering from a disease of the mind which rendered him incapable of judging whether the act was right or wrong," they must convict. This is still the rule in England; Reg. v. Davis, 1 Foster & Fin., 69; Reg. v. Burton, 3 ib., 780; Reg. v. Leigh, 4 ib., 915. The same rule was applied in the case of the State v. Spencer, 1 Zab., 196.

In Regina v. Vaughn, 1 Cox C. C., 80, the test was modified by extending the general knowledge of the accused as to right and wrong, to the particular act charged. As to this modification, see the cases of Pate and McNaughten, *supra ;* also, Carter v. State, 12 Texas, 500; State v. Huting, 21 Mo., 476;

Com. v. Farkin, 2 Parsons, 459; Willis v. People, 32 N. Y., 717. CURTIS, J., in United States v. McGlue, 1 Curtis C. C., 8, says: " The test is the capacity to distinguish between right and and wrong, as to the particular act with which the accused is charged," etc. See also U. S. v. Shultz, 6 McLean, 121.

In the case of Freeman v. People, 4 Denio, 49, a further modification was recognized, in this : " That the knowledge of the party as to right and wrong, meant, not such knowledge in a moral sense purely, but in a legal one. And it may be assumed, from the debates, and from the opinions of the judges in McNaughten's case, (*supra*,) that this is the rule of the modern English authorities ; and also in the United States. See also U. S. v. Clark, 2 Cranch C. C., 158 ; U. S. v. Shultz, 6 McLean, 121 ; People v. Sprague, 2 Parker C. C., 43 ; Vance v. Com., 2 Va. Cases, 132 ; Willis v. People, 32 N. Y., 714 ; McAllister v. State, 17 Ala., 434 ; People v. Hobson, 17 Cal., 424 ; Loeffner v. State, 10 Ohio St. R., 598 ; Fisher v. People, 23 Ill., 283.

The test, so modified, might be expressed thus :

That the accused must have the capacity to distinguish between right and wrong, in a legal sense, as to the act charged.

From all which this general conclusion might be drawn :

That the incapacity to distinguish between right and wrong, in a legal sense, (as to the law of the land, for example,) and as to the act charged, would certainly excuse.

DELUSION.

There are many cases which show that the above test has not guided or governed the administration of the law, where the " knowledge " of the party has been obliterated, or subordinated to some delusion, or mistake, or prepossession, or morbid propensity, the effect of disease of the mind ; or where the party has been impelled to forget the ties of nature, or humanity, to lose all sense of right and wrong, by mental disease, caused, perhaps, by bodily ailment, but not the legitimate consequence of the long continued indulgence of bad passions.

The case of Hadfield, 27 Howell's St. Tr., 1281, is a notable one. He discharged a pistol, loaded with slugs, at the king in the theatre. When arrested he said he knew very well that his life was forfeited—but that he was tired of life—that he did not intend to kill the king, but knew that the attempt would answer his purpose. The evidence tended to show that he labored under the delusion that it was his duty to offer himself as a sacrifice for his fellow men ; and that he must do some act by which he should be visited with the extreme penalty of the law. Erskine, his defender, claimed that this delusion was the cause of his act, and that it rendered him irresponsible. Lord Kenyon concurred with him, and ordered the withdrawal of the prosecution.

In the case of Martin, tried in 1829, the prisoner fired the cathedral at York. He knew the act to be contrary to law—that it was a capital felony, and expected to be hanged for it. He was acquitted as undoubtedly insane—having done the act, as the judges said, " under the insane delusion of producing a public benefit." See 71 Ann. Reg., 301 ; also Regina v. Tyler, 8 C. & P., 616 ; Tonchett's case, 1844, in the Central Criminal Court ; also the case of Brixey, in the same court, 1845. In the latter case, a servant maid, who had for some months been suffering under disordered menstruation ; no one had ever suspected, nor had she given any signs of insanity ; she cut the throat of her master's baby, and immediately rushed into his presence, exclaiming, " Oh what will become of me ! I have murdered the dear baby ! Will you, sir, forgive me ? Will God forgive me ?" She was acquitted on the ground of insanity.

PAROXYSMAL INSANITY.

In the case of Regina v. Vyse, 3 Foster & Fin., 247, a mother poisoned her children whom she fondly loved—the poison having been obtained deliberately, under pretence of killing rats. She was acquitted on the ground of " paroxysmal insanity "—the physician testifying that the impulse to violence may be dormant for weeks or months, and then break out into a suicidal or homicidal act.

Delusion is also admitted as one test of insanity, in the ecclesiastical courts ; Dew v. Clark, 3 Addams, 79 ; Frere v. Peacocke, 1 Robertson, 442.

The case of Com. v. Rogers, 7 Met., 500, cited and quoted by our chief justice, is justly regarded as a leading case on the

same point. To the same effect, see Roberts v. State, 3 Ga.,
310 ; People v. Pine, 2 Barb., (N. Y.,) 571 ; and Regina v. Law,
2 Foster & Fin., 836.

Uncontrollable impulse—moral insanity—that disease of the
mind which takes away the power of choosing between duty and
the act complained of—seems to be recognized in many cases.
State v. Windsor, 5 Harring., 512 ; Reg. v. Bleasdale, 2 C. & K.,
765 ; Com. v. Mosler, 4 Barr, 267 ; Lewis' Cr. Law, 404 ; The
People v. Sprague, 2 Park. C. C., 43 ; Sanchez v. People, 4 ib.,
535 ; Steph. Cr. Law, 91 ; 2 Am. Jour. of Ins. (1846), 261 : U. S.
v. Hewson, 7 Boston Law Rep., 361 ; Scott v. Com., 4 Met.
(Ky.), 227 ; Smith v. Com., 1 Duvall, 224 ; Hopps v. State, 31
Ill., 385 ; Billman's Case, in 1 Whart. Crim. Law, 30 ; Com. v.
Shurlock, Legal Int. (1857), 83 ; Com. v. Smith, ib., (1858), 33 ;
Com. v. Freath, 6 Am. L. Reg., 400 ; see Appendix to Hunting-
don's Trial ; but see Reg. v. Haynes, 1 Fost. & Fin., 666 ; and
State v. Brandon, 8 Jones (N. C.), 136.

Is not the real difference between the impulse of *passion* and
that of a *diseased mind?*

Thus, while the decisions have been fluctuating, and while
there has been an inability to give a definition of insanity satisfactory to all, these conclusions seem to follow : That the accused is not accountable,

1. If he was incapable of knowing that the act charged was
wrong—contrary to the law of the land.

2. If he did the act under a positive *bona fide delusion*, as to
the existence of certain facts, which were wholly imaginary, but
which, if they had existed, would have been a good defense ; or,

3. If he did the act under some uncontrollable impulse, the
result, not of ungovernable *passion*, but of a *diseased mind*.

EVIDENCE.

As to the evidence in regard to insanity—that of *experts* and
non-experts.

It seems that a higher degree of insanity must be shown in
criminal than in civil cases ; 2 Greenl. Ev., § 372 ; but the rule
seems to be the same in both cases, as to what evidence should
be admitted or excluded. Rex v. Watson, 2 Stark., 155 ; Reg.

v. Murphy, 8 C. & P., 297; Rex v. Burdett, 4 Barn. & Ald., 122; Lewis v. Lewis, 9 Ind., 105.

And though the question is as to the insanity of the party at the very time the act was done, yet his conduct and declarations before and after that time may be proved. Peaseley v. Robbins, 3 Metc., 164; Norwood v. Morrow, 4 Dev. & Batt., 442; Vance v. Com., 2 Va. Cases, 132; Grant v. Thompson, 4 Conn., 203; Dickenson v. Barber, 9 Mass., 225; United States v. Sharp, 1 Peters C. C., 118; Bryant v. Jackson, 6 Humph., 199; McAllister v. State, 17 Ala. 434; McLean v. State, 16 ib., 672; Kinne v. Kinne, 9 Conn., 102; People v. March, 6 Cal., 543; Beavam v. McDonnell, 10 Exch., 184; 26 Eng. Law & Eq. Rep., 184; Lake v. People, 1 Parker C. C., 495.

And where *general* insanity is proved to have existed prior to the act, its continuance up to that time will be presumed, and the prosecution must then show the occurrence of a lucid interval. Cartwright v. Cartwright, 1 Phillimore, 100; Jackson v. Van Dusen, 5 John., 144; Armstrong v. Timmons, 3 Harring., 342; Jackson v. King, 4 Cow., 207; The State v. Spencer, 1 Zab., 196; Crouse v. Holman, 19 Ind., 30; Hoge v. Fisher, 1 Peters C. C., 163; and the same may be said of *partial* insanity —Thornton v. Appleton, 29 Maine, 298—unless such prior insanity was caused by some violent disease, in which case the presumption of continuance does not apply, for *cessante ratione, cessat ipsa lex.* Hix v. Whittemore, 4 Metc., 545.

Such a presumption calls for proof of habitual, not occasional insanity. Lewis v. Baird, 3 McLean, 56; Brooke v. Townshend, 7 Gill, 10; Legeyt v. O'Brien, 1 Mil., 334; State v. Sewell, 3 Jones (N. C.), 245; Stewart v. Reddell, 3 Maryland, 67.

Hereditary insanity may be proved both in criminal and civil cases. Regina v. Tuckett, 1 Cox C. C., 103; Baxter v. Abbott, 7 Gray, 71; Regina v. Oxford, 9 Carring. & Payne, 525; Smith v. Kramer, 1 Am. Law Reg., 353; State v. Windsor, 5 Harring., 512; State v. Christmas, 6 Jones (N. C.), 471.

Insanity of brothers and sisters: evidence of this is *competent*, even without proof of ancestral taint, the weight of it being solely for the jury.   People v. Garbutt, 17 Mich., 9 ; Regina v. Oxford, 9 C. & P., 525.

Medical books, containing opinions of medical gentlemen of the highest authority, are inadmissible.   Commonwealth v. Wilson, 1 Gray, 337 ; Ashworth v. Kittridge, 12 Cush., 193 ; State v. O'Brien, 7 R. I., 336 ; Collier v. Simpson, 5 C. & P., 74 ; Cocks v. Purday, 2 C. & K., 270 ; Carter v. State, 2 Carter, 617 ; Melvin v. Easley, 1 Jones, 386.

The reading of such books to the jury would seem to be forbidden.   Regina v. Cranch, 1 Cox C. C. 94 ; Washburn v. Cuddihy, 8 Gray, 430 ; Gehrke v. The State, 13 Texas, 568.

But whether this is not a matter for the discretion of the court ?   Luning v. The State, 1 Chandler, 178.

Professional gentlemen who are acquainted with the disease of insanity, and *who have personally examined the party to whom insanity is attributed*, may give their opinion upon the direct question whether he was insane or not.   People v. Lake, 2 Kernan, 358 ; McAllister v. The State, 17 Ala., 434 ; In Re Vananken, 2 Stock., 186.

But as to whether persons so conversant with insanity (*experts*), and who have heard all the testimony adduced at the trial, but who have never had any personal knowledge of the party, can give their opinion on the sanity or insanity of that party, supposing the facts detailed to be true ;   the practice in America is in favor, and in England against, the admission of such opinion.

The proper mode of eliciting this " opinion," is, in substance, this : Premising that the expert shall have attended the whole trial, and shall have heard *all* the testimony as to the facts and circumstances of the case, and that he is not to judge of the credit of the witnesses, or of the truth of the facts testified by others (which are questions for the jury), the proper question is this : If the symptoms and indications testified to by the other witnesses are proved, and if the jury are satisfied of the truth of them, whether, in his opinion, the party was insane ?   See Commonwealth v. Rogers, 7 Metcalf, 500 ; The People v. Luke, 2 Kernan, 358 ; Same v. Thurston, 2 Parker C. C., 49 ; Sanchez v. The People, 22 New York, 147–154 ; United States v.

McGlue, 1 Curtis C. C., 9 ; Woodbury v. Obear, 7 Gray, 467 ;
The People v. McCann, 4 Parker C. C., 297 ; Wharton's Crim.
Law, 94 ; McAllister v. The State, 17 Ala., 434 ; Clark v. The
State, 12 Ohio, 483 ; Potts v. House, 6 Georgia, 324 ; Terry v.
Townsend, 9 Maryland, 145. See also State v. Windsor, 5
Harrington (Del.), 534 ; Spear v. Richardson, 37 New Hamp.,
28 ; Champ v. The Commonwealth, 2 Metcalfe (Ky.), 17.

The English practice is different. See the cases of Ferrers,
and McNaughten, cited *supra.* Also Rex v. Wright, Russell
and Ryan C. C., 451 ; Regina v. Southey, 4 Foster & Finla-
son, 887 ; Regina v. Frances, 4 Cox C. C., 57. In this case :

Alderson, B., and Cresswell, J. said : " The proper mode is to
ask what are the symptoms of insanity, or to take particular
facts, and assuming them to be true, to ask whether they indicate insanity on the part of the prisoner," etc., not allowing the
witness " to decide upon the whole case."

[The distinction between the American and English practice
is understood to be, that the former does and the latter does not
permit the opinion of the expert on the result of *the very facts*
testified to the jury, (as to whether they constitute insanity or
not,) the objection being that the witness would thereby take on
himself the functions of the jury, in deciding upon the weight
or preponderance of the evidence.]

See further to the same point : Rex v. Searle, 1 Moody & Robinson, 75 ; Rex v. Offord, 5 Carring. & Payne, 168 ; Doe d.
Bainbrigge v. Bainbrigge, 4 Cox C. C., 454 ; the case of Pate,
cited above ; Malton v. Nesbitt, 1 Carring. & Payne, 70 ; Fen-
wick v. Bell, 1 Carring. and Kirwan, 312 ; Beckwith v. Syde-
botham, 1 Campbell, 116 ; Thornton v. Royal Exchange Assurance Co., Peake, 25 ; also Commonwealth v. Rich, 14 Gray,
335 ; Clark v. State, 12 Ohio, 483.

The expert is not permitted to give his *mere opinion*—Clark's
case, *supra* ; Hathorne v. King, 8 Mass., 371 ; White v. Bailey,
10 Mich., 155 ; Dickenson v. Barber, 9 Mass., 225.

The opinion must be a *positive* one—the expert not being
allowed to testify as to his *doubts* of a person's sanity. Sanchez
v. the People, 22 N. Y., 147.

As to what physicians would not be allowed to give their

opinions as experts—as those *e. g.* who had always refused that class of cases—see Baxter v. Abbott, 7 Gray, 72 ; Commonwealth v. Rich, 14 Gray, 335 ; Caleb v. The State, 39 Miss., 722 ; State v. Hinkle, 6 Iowa, 380 ; State v. Knight, 43 Maine, 11.

As to whether witnesses not professional, *non-experts*, but who have, for a long time, personally known the individual charged with insanity, and have had opportunities of observing his habits, manners and conduct, can give their opinion of his sanity, see in the affirmative, Clary v. Clary, 2 Iredell, 78 ; Wheeler & Batsford v. Alderson, 3 Haggard, 574 ; Eagleton & Coventry v. Kingston, 8 Vesey, 449 ; Doe v. Reagan, 5 Blackf., 217 ; Harrison v. Rowan, 3 Washington C. C., 580 ; Baldwin v. State, 12 Missouri, 223 ; Wilkinson v. Pearson, 11 Harrington, 117 ; Dorsey v. Warfield, 7 Maryland, 65 ; Clark v. State, 12 Ohio, 483 ; Grant v. Thompson, 4 Connect., 203 ; Rambler v. Tryon, 7 Sargeant & Rawle, 90 ; Wogon v. Small, 11 Sargeant & Rawle, 141 ; Morse v. Crawford, 17 Verm., 499 ; Lester v. Pitsford, 7 Verm., 158 ; Gibson v. Gibson, 9 Yerger, 329 ; Potts v. House, 6 Georgia, 324 ; Calver v. Haslam, 7 Barbour, 314 ; Baldwin v. State, 12 Missouri, 233 ; Dewitt v. Barley, 13 Barbour, 550 ; Kinne v. Kinne, 9 Connect., 102 ; Dunham's Appeal, 27 Connect., 193 ; McDougal v. McLean, 1 Winston (N. C.), 120 ; Norris v. State, 16 Ala., 776 ; Florey v. Florey, 24 Ala., 241 ; Powell v. State, 25 Ala., 27 ; Cram v. Cram, 33 Verm., 15 ; Fairchild v. Bascom, 35 id., 398 ; Bricker v. Lighter, 40 Penn. St. Rep., 474 ; Pelamourges v. Clark, 9 Iowa, 1.

But see the following cases on the other side : Commonwealth v. Wilson, 1 Gray, 337 ; Poole v. Richardson, 3 Mass., 330 ; Needham v. Ide, 5 Pickering, 510 ; Commonwealth v. Fairbanks, 2 Allen, 511 ; Sears v. Shafer, 1 Barbour, 412 ; Baxter v. Abbott, 7 Gray, 71 ; Wyman v. Gould, 47 Maine, 159 ; Caleb v. State, 38 Miss., 722. See also opinion of Hand, J., in Culver v. Haslam, 7 Barbour, 314, *supra.* Also, Dewitt v. Barley, 5 Selden, 371, in which is cited the case of Wright v. Tatham, 5 Clark & Finnelly, 692 ; and 17 N. Y., 340 ; and Boardman v. Woodman, 47 New Hamp., 120.

The *burden* of proof of insanity, lies on the defendant.

Every man is presumed to be sane till the contrary appears—

and if the defendant relies on insanity as a defense, it is for him
"*to make it clear*," (says Baron Rolfe,) that he was insane at the
time of committing the offense charged.   "If the matter be left
in doubt it will be the duty of the jury to convict." Rolfe, Baron,
in Regina v. Stokes, 3 Carrington & Kirwan, 188; see also,
Attorney General v. Paruther, 3 Brown C. C., 441; Leo v. Lee,
4 McCord, 183; Jackson v. King, 4 Cowen, 207; Hoge v. Fisher,
1 Peters C. C., 163; Jackson v. Van Dusen, 5 Johnson, 144;
The State v. Stark, 1 Strobhart, 479; The People v. Robinson,
1 Parker C. C., 649; Lake v. The People, 1 Parker C. C., 495;
Regina v. Layton, 4 Cox C. C., 149; Regina v. Turton, 6 Cox
C. C., 385; Regina v. Higginson, 1 Carrington & Kirwan, 130;
and Regina v. Stokes, 3 same, 188.   See also, The State v.
Bringea, 5 Ala., 244; The State v. Huting, 21 Missouri, 476;
People v. Myers, 20 Califor., 518; The State v. Spencer, 1 Za-
briskie, 202.

But if "the preponderance of the evidence" be in favor of
the insanity of the prisoner, the jury will be authorized to find
him insane.   Shaw, C. J., in Commonwealth v. Rogers, 7 Metcalf, 500.   See also, Commonwealth v. Eddy, 7 Gray, 583; Loeffner v. The State, 10 Ohio St. Rep., 598; Fisher v. The People,
23 Illinois, 283; Polk v. The State, 19 Indiana, 170; People v.
McCann, 18 New York, 58, reversing the case in 3 Parker C. C.,
272; The State v. Ellick, 1 Winston (N. C.), 56; The State v.
Starling, 6 Jones (N. C.), 366; State v. McCoy, 34 Missouri,
531; The People v. Garbutt, 17 Michigan, 9; Commonwealth
v. York, 9 Metcalf, 94; Campbell v. The People, 16 Illinois,
17; Miller v. The People, 39 id., 458; Fife v. The Commonwealth, 29 Penn. St. Rep., 429; Smyth v. Jefferies, 9 Price,
257.

Principals and accessories.

If a party be charged as principal, and other parties as accessories, and the principal be adjudged insane, the other parties
cannot be found guilty as accessories, though they may be as
principals.   Regina v. Tyler, 8 Carrington & Payne, 616.

The defense of insanity before the grand jury.

If the grand jury find that the accused did acts which would
be murder in a person of sound mind, they should bring in a

true bill—the defense of insanity not being for their consideration. See Regina v. Hodges, 8 Carrington & Payne, 195 ; also,
United States v. Lawrence, 4 Cranch C. C., 514.

[In regard to the question of doubt, as to the insanity of the
accused, on the minds of the jury—and whether, if they have a
reasonable doubt, they should not acquit :

See the cases collected on pages 305, 6 and 7, of Bennett's
work.]

STATEN *v.* THE STATE, 30 Miss. Rep., 619.

HOMICIDE.

Homicide is justifiable where the accused had a reasonable ground to apprehend a
design to commit a felony, or do some great personal injury to his wife, and there is
imminent danger of the design being accomplished.

The accused must be entitled to have rules distinctly declared to the jury.

Error to Yalobusha circuit court. HARRIS, J.

Yerger & Rucks, and *F. Anderson,* for plaintiff in error.

The plaintiff in error was convicted in the circuit court of
Yalobusha county, of manslaughter in the second degree, upon
an indictment purporting to be found in the circuit court of
Tallahatchie county ; it being alleged that the venue was
changed from Tallahatchie county. The judgment must be reversed for several errors :

1. The record contains no evidence, that the circuit court of
Yalobusha county had jurisdiction of the cause. It is true, it is
alleged that the venue was changed from Tallahatchie county,
but the record contains no legal evidence of any order changing
the venue in said cause, nor any legal evidence that any bill of
indictment, or other proceedings, were had in the circuit court
of Tallahatchie county, for the offense of which the plaintiff in
error was convicted.

It is true, there will be found in the transcript, copies of certain orders and proceedings, purporting to have been made and
had in the circuit court of Tallahatchie county, which the clerk

of the circuit court of Yalobusha recites to have been delivered to him by the clerk of Tallahatchie.

These loose memoranda are not certified by the clerk of Talla-ᵢ hatchie county to be copies of the orders and proceedings had in that court. They have no seal of the court attached to them, and do not even purport to be copies of all the orders and proceedings in the circuit court of Tallahatchie county.

2. This court, therefore, cannot regard them as evidence for any purpose, nor could the circuit court of Yalobusha county. The court in Yalobusha county could only have jurisdiction of this cause by a change of venue, regularly made. This fact the record must show affirmatively. 1 Stark. Ev., 189 ; Dyson v. The State, 4 Cushm., 383 ; 1 ib., 502 ; 4 ib., 176.

3. The court erred in giving the seventh instruction, which is in these words: "If the jury believe, from the evidence, that the defendant killed the deceased at a time when there was no danger from the deceased to the defendant's family, or sister, and upon revenge for a supposed insult to his family, in the heat of blood, this is at least manslaughter."

This charge is error, because the defendant was entitled to an acquittal, if he had reasonable ground to apprehend a design on the part of the deceased to commit a felony, or to do some great personal injury to himself, or some member of his family ; and there was imminent danger of such design being accomplished. Hutch. Code, 957.

Under the instruction, as given by the court—although the jury may have believed the defendant had reasonable ground to apprehend, on the part of deceased, a design to commit a felony, or to do some great personal injury to himself or family—they could not have acquitted him ; the charge was therefore erroneous. Dyson v. State, 26 Miss., 388 ; McDaniel v. State, 8 S. & M., 417.

4. The court erred in compelling the prisoner to go to trial, without giving him a copy of the *venire*. He was indicted for murder, and on a previous trial had been found guilty of manslaughter ; but, as the indictment for murder was still in exis'- ence against him, he was put upon his trial for murder ; and the previous acquittal could only avail him by way of defense—by

plea or evidence given of the former acquittal. He was, in fact, on trial for murder, and might have been, and would have been convicted of it, if the facts had warranted a conviction, unless he showed, by way of defense, the former acquittal.

5. The court erred in giving the first instruction, because it assumes, as a fact proven, that the defendant was guilty of the homicide charged, and that this homicide was committed with malice aforethought.

6. The third and sixth instructions for the state should not have been given, unless the court had also charged the jury in reference to the different degrees of manslaughter, as defined by our statute ; there being no crime of manslaughter, as known at the common law, in this state.

7. The tenth instruction was erroneous. It is obnoxious to the same objection as the seventh instruction ; and, by the use of the word " apparent," was calculated to mislead the jury.

8. A new trial ought to have been granted, because the killing, at most, could not exceed manslaughter in the third degree. Hutch. Code, 958.

To constitute manslaughter in the second degree, the killing must be done " *in a cruel and unusual manner.*"

Manslaughter in the third degree, is defined precisely as manslaughter in the second degree, except that the words " dangerous weapon " are substituted for " in a cruel and unusual manner." In this case there is no pretense that the killing was done in " a cruel and unusual manner." On the contrary, the circumstances as proved, show most clearly, in our opinion, a case of excusable homicide ; and if manslaughter can be predicated of it at all, it surely can not be held to be in a degree higher than manslaughter in the second degree.

D. C. Glenn, attorney general.

Argued the case orally ; but no memoranda or brief of his argument have come to the possession of the reporter.

HANDY, J.:

This was an indictment found in the Tallahatchie circuit court, against the plaintiff in error, for murder. At the instance of the accused, the *venue* was changed to Yalobusha circuit court, where he was tried, and found guilty of manslaughter in the second degree, and judgment rendered. The case was thereupon brought to this court and the judgment reversed, and a new trial awarded. Upon this trial a verdict was again found against the plaintiff in error, of guilty of manslaughter in the second degree, and judgment rendered thereon. To this judgment, the present writ of error is prosecuted.

Several questions have been presented in the argument by the counsel for the plaintiff in error, as grounds of error in the proceedings below. These questions are important, and not free from difficulty ; and in all probability, the two members of the court sitting in the cause, would not agree in opinion upon them, and no decision would be made upon them. We, therefore, deem it proper to present no views in relation to those points, but will proceed to consider a material point, which is decisive of the case as it is now presented.

The court instructed the jury, at the instance of the state, as follows :

"If the jury believe, from the evidence, that the defendant killed the deceased at a time when there was no danger from the deceased to the defendant's family, or sister, and upon revenge for a supposed insult to his family, in the heat of blood, this is at least manslaughter.

"If the jury believe, from the evidence, that Hamblin was unarmed at the time the defendant killed him, and there was no real or apparent danger from him at the time of killing, either to Staten himself, or to his wife or sister, or family, then the killing is neither justifiable nor excusable."

Without a particular detail of the evidence, and of the circumstances under which the killing was done, it is sufficient for the purpose of testing the propriety of these instructions, to observe, that there was testimony tending to show that the deceased had entered the bed-chamber in which the wife of the accused (she being sick at the time), and his sister were asleep, and after midnight ; that he aroused the sister by putting his hand on her ; that she told him to go away, and that he went under Mrs. Staten's bed, which was in the same room ; that after a short time, she went into the room where Staten was sleeping, and awoke him, and told him that the deceased was in his wife's room, and he arose and went immediately into his wife's room, and a noise like the falling over chairs was heard; and that shortly afterwards the deceased was seen bleeding, and lived but a short time, being stabbed in several places. There is also evidence tending to show that the deceased took supper that night at Staten's house, and was there after supper, and in the room where Staten's wife was, in company with Staten; but that Staten supposed he had gone home, when he was informed by his sister that he was in his wife's room.

The statute provides that homicide is justifiable " when committed in the lawful defense of a person, or of his or her husband, wife, parent, child, master, mistress or servant, when there shall be a reasonable ground to apprehend a design to commit a felony, or to do some great personal injury, and there shall be imminent danger of such design being accomplished." Hutch. Code, 957.

The instructions above stated do not declare the rule in conformity to this statute. If the accused had a " reasonable ground to apprehend a design *to commit a felony,* or to *do some great personal injury* to his wife, and there was imminent danger of the design being accomplished," he was justifiable in the killing. But the instructions do not give the accused the benefit of the apprehension of danger, in the particulars specified in the statute; and the jury were left free to put whatever construction they deemed proper upon the general terms, " *danger to himself or his wife,*" etc. They might have supposed that it required *danger to life,* in order to justify the killing, and hence concluded that, as there was no evidence of such danger, the killing was unjustifiable; whereas the statute distinctly recognizes *a just apprehension of immediate danger of the commission of a felony, or of some great personal injury or bodily harm,* as a justification. The plaintiff in error was entitled to have the rule thus distinctly declared to the jury; and for the error in this respect in the instructions, the judgment is reversed, and the cause remanded, and a new trial awarded.

FISHER, J., having been of counsel in the court below, took no part in the decision of the cause.

MARSH *v.* THE STATE, 30 Miss. Rep., 627.

HOMICIDE.

Upon the challenge of a juror it is proper for the court to interrogate and try him as to whether he has formed or expressed an opinion in relation to the matter in issue, and to reject him if found to have formed such opinion.

It is the duty of the court to see that an impartial jury is empanelled, and that it is composed of persons above all exception.

Error to Warren circuit court.   GUION, J.

The plaintiff in error was indicted in the court below for the murder of one William J. Sims, was tried by a jury, and convicted of manslaughter in the first degree.

On the trial, the persons who were summoned on the special *venire* as jurors, were called and sworn to answer questions, and were examined by the court as to their competency to try the cause, without their first being tendered to or challenged by either the state or the prisoner.   The court, after such examination, rejected the juror or tendered him, as it had been determined he was incompetent or not.   To this the prisoner objected and tendered his bill of exceptions.

W. A. Lake for plaintiff in error.

The record of this case shows that the prisoner was convicted of manslaughter in the first degree, and sentenced to seven years' confinement in the penitentiary.   A motion was made for a new trial which being overruled, the testimony is embodied, and a bill of exceptions filed.   In the progress of the trial, three bills of exceptions were filed to the empanelling of the petit jury.   They are numbered in the record two, three, and four, and are considered by the counsel of the prisoner as showing manifest error in the selection of a jury by whom he was tried. The objection exhibited by these bills of exceptions is, that John Lyman, John Mixen, and James C. Wright were severally introduced as jurors and sworn to answer questions, and actually questioned as to their qualifications to serve as jurors, without being first challenged by the district attorney.   We think that both in England and America this practice is condemned by the highest judicial authorities of both countries.   Chief Justice Marshall ruled in Burr's trial, "that unless the challenge is made, it will be improper to draw out any expressions from the juror."

But it is needless to call the attention of the court to authorities out of the State of Mississippi, as our own high court have expressly adjudicated the point. See The State v. Flower, Walker R., 318; The State v. King, 5 How. R., 730.

These decisions are full to the point and must be regarded as decisive of it. It cannot be urged that the answers would be the same without a challenge that they would be if the juror were challenged, and that, therefore, the prisoner is not damaged by the omision. The law presumes the prisoner injured whenever there is a failure to give him the benefit of the law applicable to his case. He was entitled to have the persons composing the panel tendered him as jurors, unless they were challenged by the state and their challenge sustained by proper proof. It is the challenge that gives the right to interrogate the persons composing the panel, and the turning away one of the *venire*, because he had said he had both formed and expressed an opinion in reference to the guilt or innocence of the accused when he was not challenged, was as unjust to the prisoner and as much a misapplication of the law as if he had been made to stand aside without interrogation or proof of any sort.

Take, for example, the case of John Mixen, contained in the third bill of exceptions. He was one of the persons returned on the special *venire*. When his name was called, he appeared, and was sworn to answer questions, and was actually examined as to his qualifications by the attorney for the state, and rejected by the court as incompetent to serve on the panel without being challenged at all. Now, if I am right in asserting that the law requires that he should have been challenged before any proof of his incompetency could be heard or adduced, then it follows that he was rejected as a juror, and the benefit of his services denied to the prisoner, without any proof of his incompetency to serve.

In the case of King v. The State, already referred to, the court decided the point with distinctness, although the bill of exceptions did not set it forth distinctly. In this case, the bills of exceptions bring the point before the court with absolute distinctness, and we ask the application of the rule as enunciated in the cases reported in Walker and Howard, above mentioned, and that a new trial may be granted.

D. C. Glenn, attorney-general.

Cited and relied on, Lewis v. The State, 9 S. & M., 115; Sam v. The State, 13 ib., 190; McCarty v. The State, 26 Miss. R., 382; People v. Damon, 13 Wend., 354; 6 Humph, 249. He also argued the case orally, as involving a matter of importance in practice.

HANDY, J.:

The only question raised in this case is, whether it was competent for the circuit judge to examine the jurors summoned to try the accused, and before they were challenged either by the state or the accused, whether they had formed or expressed an opinion as to his guilt or innocence of the charge for which he was about to be tried.

Whatever may have been the rule in England upon this subject, we think that the principles sanctioned by this court fully warrant the course pursued by the court below in this case.

In the first place, the practice is sanctioned by numerous cases, that upon the challenge of a juror, it is proper *for the court* to interrogate and try him as to whether he has formed or expressed an opinion in relation to the matter in issue, and to reject him if found to have formed such an opinion.

It is also held to be the duty of the court to see that an impartial jury is empanelled, and that it is composed of men above all exception. Lewis v. The State, 9 S. & M., 115; Sam v. The State, 13 ib., 190; McCarty v. The State, 26 Miss., 302. In the case of Lewis v. The State, the court below discharged a juror without challenge from either party, and after having examined him and found that he had not formed or expressed an opinion as to the issue, it being ascertained from his own statement made as he was about to be sworn, that he had conscientious scruples with regard to finding any man guilty of murder; and the action of the judge was approved by this court, and held not to be error upon the principle just stated.

If it was proper for the court, of its own motion, to reject a juror under such circumstances, on the ground that it was its duty to see that an impartial jury, composed of men free from all exceptions, was empanelled, surely it was not error for the court to interrogate the juror as to his competency before he was sworn or tendered to and accepted by the parties, and to set him aside when it was shown that he had formed an opinion as to the issue to be tried.

The course adopted in this case has been very generally adopted, as the practice in this state, in trials for capital offenses, if, indeed, it is not the established practice ; and it appears to us to be commended by its decided tendency to secure the selection of jurors, in such cases, as free as possible from all bias or prejudice—an object highly conducive to the just policy of the state, and protective especially of the rights and safety of the accused.

Under such circumstances, and where no injury is shown to have been done to the accused, we are not disposed to hold that the practice is illegal, and that the course pursued by the court below is ground for reversing the judgment.

The judgment is affirmed.

Dick (a slave) v. The State, 30 Miss. Rep., 631.

RAPE.

Where a witness for the state was allowed to testify that the accused had confessed to him that he was guilty of the offense charged against him, and that he had heard him soon afterwards, on the same evening, make other confessions to other persons, the accused has a clear right to cross-examine the witness on that subject, such examination being material to the issue to be tried by the jury.

In an indictment against a slave for an attempt to commit a rape upon a free white woman, it is unnecessary to state that such slave is a negro or mulatto,—such an averment would be immaterial, and need not be made, but if made, it must be proved.

The rule is clearly settled that it is incumbent on the prosecutor to prove on the trial, every fact and circumstance stated in the indictment, material or necessary to constitute the offense charged ; but those allegations in the indictment which are not necessary ingredients in the offense, may be rejected as surplusage, and need not be proved.

If an averment may be entirely omitted without affecting the charge against the prisoner, it may be considered as surplusage, and be disregarded in the evidence. This rule applies to averments which are not only unnecessary in themselves, but foreign to the charge; but it has not been held to apply to allegations which might have been properly dispensed with, but being inserted in the indictment, are descriptive of the identity of that which is legally essential to the charge.

The averment that the accused was a negro was wholly unnecessary, but having been made, it was descriptive of the person of the prisoner, and became a part of his identity, as much so as the name by which he was indicted.

Error to Pontotoc circuit court.   SCRUGGS, J.

J. F. Cushman, for plaintiff in error.

D. C. Glenn, attorney general.

SMITH, C. J.:

This was an indictment for an attempt, by a slave, to commit a rape upon a free white woman, upon which the prisoner was convicted.

A motion was entered for a new trial, which was overruled, and thereupon a bill of exceptions was taken, setting out the evidence, the action of the court in regard to the introduction of testimony, and the charges given or refused.

Several exceptions are taken to the judgment. We deem it, however, unnecessary to notice only those objections, which, in our opinion, are well founded.

A material part of the evidence adduced in support of the prosecution, was the confessions of the prisoner, as testified to by the witness, Murphy. This witness testified that when the accused was brought before him, as a justice of the peace, on warrant for examination, he made known to him the charge against him; and asked him whether he was guilty; and that he acknowledged that he was guilty. The witness also stated that he heard the accused afterwards, and during the same evening, make other confessions to other persons, which was soon after those made to the witness. The accused, by his counsel, proposed to cross-examine the witness in regard to the confessions made to other persons; but the court refused to permit such examination; and the prisoner excepted.

It is manifest that the examination proposed was material to the issue to be tried by the jury. It may have been important to the prosecution. The witness had first deposed to confessions made to himself; and in addition, had stated that the accused had shortly afterwards made other confessions to different persons. If the confessions made to other persons than the witness, were to the same effect as those made directly to the witness, his confession first made, the particulars of which were delivered to the jury, would have been corroborated. They would thus have been placed in possession of more satisfactory evidence of the guilt of the prisoner. On the other hand, it was clearly the right, and might have been of the greatest importance to the prisoner, to cross-examine in relation to those confessions—an imperfect statement, and reference to which, had been made to the jury. That statement or reference, as general as it was, undoubtedly was calculated to injure the prisoner. The jury could have looked upon the confession stated by the witness to have been made to other persons, in no other light than as a deliberate repetition and re-affirmation of the confessions first made to the witness. But if these "other confessions" were different in any material respect from those first made directly to the witness, as might possibly have been the case, the accused was clearly entitled to bring out, by cross-examination, every circumstance that was calculated to destroy or weaken their force as confessions, or to show that those confessions were incompetent evidence against him.

We think the court erred also in refusing the sixth instruction asked for the prisoner.

In that instruction, the prisoner requested the court to charge, that if the jury believed from the evidence, that the prisoner was a mulatto slave and not a negro man slave, as charged in the indictment, they should acquit him.

The provision of the statute is that "if any slave shall attempt to commit a rape upon a free white woman," etc., Hutch. Dig., 521, § 55. If the attempt to commit a rape upon a free white woman, etc., is made by a slave, the offense created by the statute is complete, whether the slave be a negro or mulatto. It was hence unnecessary to charge that the slave alleged to have committed the offense, was either a negro or mulatto. The averment was immaterial; and the question is, whether it is of that class of unnecessary or immaterial averments, which may be rejected as surplusage and therefore need not be proved on the trial.

The general rule, in reference to the proof of indictments, is well understood. As laid down by Archbold, it is incumbent on the prosecutor to prove at the trial, every fact and circumstance stated in the indictment, which is material, or necessary to constitute the offense charged. On the other hand, every fact and circumstance stated in the indictment, which is not a necessary ingredient in the offense, may be rejected as surplusage, and need not be proved at the trial. Archl. Cr. Plead., 39.

However clear and definite general rules may be, difficulty is frequently encountered in applying them to particular cases. Hence, it is often a nice point to determine whether an allegation in an indictment should or should not be totally disregarded in the proof. Phillips, in his work on Evidence, says: "If an averment may be entirely omitted, without affecting the charge against the prisoner, it will be considered as surplusage, and may be disregarded in the evidence," vol. 1., p. 500. This rule, as laid down by Phillips, has been held uniformly to apply to averments, which are not only unnecessary in themselves, but foreign to the charge. The cases of The King v. Minton, cited in 2 East, Pleas of the Crown, 1021; and Rex. v. Holt, 5 T. R., 446, are referred to, as illustrative of this principle. But it has never been held to apply to allegations, which, although they might, with propriety, have been dispensed with, but being inserted in the indictment, are descriptive of the identity of that which is legally essential to the charge. 3 Phill. Ev. 668 (Hill & Cow. Ed.); Archb. Cr. Pl., 101; United States v. Porter, 3 Day, 286; 24 Miss. Rep., 578. Thus, on an indictment under the statute of 57 Geo. III., ch. 90, for being armed with intent to steal game, in a certain wood called the "Old Walk," in the occupation of a person named in the indictment, it appeared that the wood had never been called the "Old Walk," but always the "Long Walk;" and it was holden, that, although it was unnecessary to state the name of the close, where the occupation was stated, yet being alleged, it was material, and could not be rejected. Rex v. Owen, 1 Moody, C. C., 118, 303; Rex v. Craven, 1 Russ. & Ry., 14; 2 Stark Ev., 1531.

The averment, that the prisoner was a negro, was in no respect an ingredient in the offense charged. It might therefore, with propriety, have been omitted. But having been inserted, it was descriptive of the person of the prisoner; it became a part of his identity; manifestly as much so as the name under which he was prosecuted. The averment was connected with and descriptive of that which it was essential to establish by the evidence, that is, the identity of the party charged.

The rule of the English courts on this subject was clearly re cognized by this court, in the case of John, a slave, v. The State, above cited. Applying it to the case at bar, we think the court erred in refusing the instruction.

Judgment reversed, and cause remanded for a new trial.

RIGGS *v.* THE STATE, 30 Miss. Rep., 635.

HOMICIDE.

The statements of a physician, who examined the wounds of the deceased, immediately after they were inflicted, although not an eye-witness of the affray — that the wounds were given in the proper county—and the description of, and reference (by other witnesses) to various localities at and near the scene of killing, which were probably familiar to the jury, are sufficient proof of the venue, particularly when no objection is raised on this account at the trial.

A party indicted for murder may be convicted of any degree of manslaughter, that the evidence warrants; but he cannot be convicted of manslaughter, unless the indictment be found within one year next after the offense shall have been committed.

Express malice is evidenced by a previous threat or former grudge; and it is for the jury to determine whether the threat or grudge is established. If the threat be proved satisfactorily to have been made, and afterwards carried into execution, it will be presumed to have been done with a malicious intent, and it is incumbent on the accused, to show circumstances giving it a different character.

Where express malice is shown, and the person against whom the threat or other evidence of malice was made or existed, be afterwards killed with a deadly weapon, by the person harboring the malicious purpose, no mere provocation at the time of committing the act will relieve it of the character of malicious killing, but it is presumed to be in consequence of the previous threat or grudge.

Where a witness is impeached only by one other witness, and such impeaching witness is afterwards contradicted by another witness, it is the peculiar province of the jury to judge which of them are entitled to credit.

Error to Monroe circuit court. HARRIS, J.

James Riggs was indicted in the court below, for the murder of one Joel E. Hunt, which was alleged in the indictment to have been committed on the 21st day of September, 1852. At the September term, 1854, of said court, he was tried and convicted of murder; a motion for a new trial was made and overruled, and the prisoner sentenced to be hung. A bill of exceptions was filed to the judgment of the court, and the case comes to this court on writ of error.

W. F. Dowd, for plaintiff in error.

1. The record nowhere shows that the offense was committed in Monroe county. John L. Tindall, the only witness who testified on this subject, was the attending physician; he proved that Hunt died of the wounds in Monroe county; proved the character of the wounds inflicted, and says that this conversation with Hunt occurred in Monroe county, just before his death. He did not see the fight, and does not pretend to say in what county the mortal stroke was given. It must be proved either that the mortal stroke was given in one county, and the victim died in the county where the indictment was found, or that the mortal stroke was given, and the victim died in the same county.

At common law, if the offense was committed in one county, and the victim died in another, the prisoner could not be tried in either. McGuire v. State, 13 S. & M., 257. The statute (Poindexter's Code, 314) simply provides, if the offense is committed in one county, and the death happens in another, the prisoner must be tried in the latter. 13 S. & M., 257.

Every material circumstance in regard to time and place must be averred with that degree of certainty, which excludes every other intendment, and must be proved as laid. Arch. Cr. Plead., 34, 381; Chitty Cr. Law, 280, 283; Riggs v. State, 26 Miss., 54; Vaughn v. State, 3 S. & M., 553.

2. The court erred in charging the jury on the application of the state, that if the jury find that " the killing occurred in the year 1852, more than twelve months before the finding of the indictment, they cannot convict the defendant of manslaughter."

The indictment is for murder. Under this indictment, the jury may find the prisoner guilty of any of the grades of manslaughter, without noticing the more aggravated offense. Swinney.v. State, 8 S. & M., 584; 2 Hale, P. C., 302; 1 Chitty Cr.

Law, 640. See also, Howard v. State, 13 S. & M., 261. Any charge calculated to mislead the jury, that is not practical and altogether safe, is erroneous. Cicely v. State, 13 S. & M., 202.

3. The second charge is, " express malice is evidenced by a previous threat or former grudge." This is the foundation of all subsequent charges save one. Express malice is defined to be " when one person kills another with a sedate, deliberate mind and formed design ; such formed design being evidenced by external circumstances, discovering the inward intention ; as lying in wait, antecedent menaces, former grudges, *and* concerted schemes to do some great bodily harm." 1 Russ. Cr. 482, 483 (5 Am. ed.) ; Anthony v. State, 264.

The jury must judge from all the circumstances, whether there was " a *deliberate, sedate mind,* and formed design to do a great bodily injury." By the charge given, the jury were precluded from this investigation. They were told that a single threat, though made in the heat of passion, without deliberation or reflection, which the party may have regretted, and repented of in ten minutes afterwards, is of itself conclusive proof of a *sedate, deliberate mind* and *formed design.* The charge does not say, that a threat is one of the evidences or proofs of express malice. But express malice is *evidenced,* that is, *proved,* by a threat,—whatever may be the nature of the threat, or the circumstances under which it was made. There is no precedent or authority for such a principle. These instructions taken together, amount to this, that if the prisoner made any threat whatever, it is sufficient proof of express malice, and no provocation whatever will relieve him from guilt,—and taken with the eighth charge—the guilt of murder.

The fourth, fifth and sixth charges are too broad ; the state of facts supposed by each might be true, and yet the prisoner be not guilty of murder. Roscoe, Cr. Ev. 681 ; 1 Russ., 440.

4. The testimony, at most, only makes out a case of manslaughter. Hale, P. C., 456 ; Roscoe, Cr. Ev., 737 ; Snow's case, Roscoe, 737, 738 ; Kessell's case, 11 Eng. C. L. R., 441 ; Roscoe, 732, 733 ; 32 Eng. C. L. R., 750.

If the provocation was great, and such as must necessarily have greatly provoked the prisoner, the killing is manslaughter only.   Preston v. State, 25 Miss., 388 ; Copeland v. State, 7 Humph., 479 ; 2 Archb., 224, 1–2–5.

5. If Riggs had reasonable ground to apprehend a design on the part of Hunt, to commit a felony, or do some great bodily injury, he is excusable.   Dyson v. State, 26 Miss., 362.

D. C. Glenn, attorney general.

Argued the case orally, and cited and commented on the following authorities ; Wharton Am. Cr. Law, 360, 361, 368, 369 ; State v. Lane, 4 Ired., 113 ; State v. Martin, 2 ib., 10 ; State v. Johnson, 3 ib., 354 ; State v. Telley, 1 ib., 424 ; State v. Hildreth, 1 ib., 429 ; State v. Scott, 4 ib., 409 ; Storter v. the People, 2 Comst., 197, 202.

Handy, J. :

The plaintiff in error was indicted and convicted in Monroe circuit court, of the murder of one Joel E. Hunt.   A motion was thereupon made in his behalf to set aside the verdict, for several reasons assigned ; which motion was overruled and a bill of exceptions taken, upon which the case is brought here for review.

We will proceed to examine the grounds, upon which it is contended that the judgment should be reversed, in the order in which they are presented by the counsel for the plaintiff in error.

The first of these is, that it does not appear by the record, that the offense was committed in Monroe county, or that it was committed in any other county in this state ; and that the deceased died in Monroe county.

It fully appears, that the deceased came to his death by wounds inflicted by the accused in a combat, which took place between the parties in July, 1852, at the house of one McBeth, some time after supper.   Dr. Tindall testified, that he was called to the deceased about eight o'clock of the night on which the difficulty occurred, and found him suffering from the wounds inflicted by the accused, of which he died shortly thereafter in Monroe county, in this state.   He describes the wounds, and then proceeds to state the declarations made by the deceased in prospect of death, in relation to the circumstances of the difficulty, and concludes by stating that the deceased lived about fourteen hours, and that he was cut with a large knife, and that " this took place in Monroe county, in this state." It is plain, that this last statement was made for the purpose of proving the *venue*, and that it must be understood as referring to the inflic-tion of the wounds, the calling upon the witness as a physician, the declarations of the deceased, and his death from the wounds. After mentioning all these particulars, the witness concludes by stating that " this took place in Monroe county," thereby clearly referring to all the circumstances previously stated by him. It is true, that he did not witness the infliction of the wounds; but he was called to attend to the wounded man immediately after the occurrence, and might have been able to state with certainty, from the freshness of the wounds or from a knowledge of the house, where the difficulty is shown to have occurred, that it took place in Monroe county.

In the testimony of other witnesses, many references are made to localities connected with the scene of the difficulty, the streets and the house in the town; and especially is the house where the difficulty occurred, described. All these circumstances might have afforded conclusive proof of the place, where the wounds were inflicted, to the jury, who were familiar with these localities, and could not fail to recognize them as being in Mon-roe county, which render it unnecessary to prove positively be-fore them, that they were located there. That the localities thus shown by the evidence, as well as the testimony of Dr. Tindall, were ample proof of the venue of the offense, to the comprehen-sion of the jury, is clear, from the fact, that no objection was taken in the court below, to the want of proof on that point. The concluding statement of Dr. Tindall was doubtless intended to cover that very point; and in the attitude in which the ques-tion appears by the record, we are bound to presume, that the localities mentioned by other witnesses were confirmatory of the statement, that the whole occurrence took place in Monroe county.

This objection is, therefore, no just ground for reversing the judgment.

The next objection is, that the court erred in instructing the jury, that if they believed, from the evidence, that the killing occurred in the year 1852, more than twelve months before the finding of the indictment, upon which the accused was on trial, they could not convict the accused of manslaughter.

It is objected that, under this instruction, if the jury thought the accused guilty of manslaughter, they would not have been justifiable in finding a general verdict of not guilty, and that it was therefore equivalent to a direct charge to find him guilty of murder. But we do not consider this a just view of the instruction.

The indictment was for murder, charging that the offense was committed more than twelve months before the bill was found. It is well settled, that, under our laws, a party indicted for murder may be convicted of any degree of manslaughter, that the evidence warrants, but that he cannot be convicted of manslaughter, unless the indictment be found within one year next after the offense shall have been committed. The instruction given by the court simply stated this rule. It instructed the jury as to what they could not do, giving no indication as to what they should do. If they thought the accused guilty of manslaughter, but not of murder, it is not to be supposed, that they could have so misapprehended the instruction as to have been led by it to find what they did not consider a true verdict. It is rather to be presumed, that they would have come to the very natural and reasonable conclusion, that, as they were not justified by the evidence in finding him guilty of murder, and could not, under the rule declared to them, find him guilty of manslaughter, there was no alternative but to find him not guilty, generally. The instruction, in effect, presented the plain issue, that the verdict should either be guilty of murder, or not guilty generally. And it can with no more justice be said to indicate to the jury, that they should find the former, than the latter verdict.[1]

[1] In regard to the limitation of criminal prosecutions, the Revised Code of 1857 provides, that, "No person shall be prosecuted for any offense—murder, *manslaughter*, arson, forgery, counterfeiting, larceny, robbery and rape excepted, unless the prosecution for such offense shall be commenced within *two* years next after the commission thereof. *Provided*, that nothing herein shall be so construed as to bar any prosecution against any person who shall abscond or flee from justice in this state, or shall absent himself in this state, or out of the jurisdiction of the court, or so con-

The third error assigned is, the statement in the second instruction, that " express malice is evidenced by a previous threat or former grudge," and the third instruction, that " when a party kills another upon express malice and by the use of a deadly weapon, no provocation, however great, will free the party killing from guilt."

The testimony contained in the record tends to show a previous threat by the accused against the deceased, founded on a grudge entertained by him.

It is unquestionably true, as the court instructed the jury, that a previous threat or a grudge is evidence of express malice, and it goes to fix the character of the killing afterwards perpetrated, unless circumstances be shown to alter or mitigate it, and to relieve it from the imputation of malice. [2]   It is for the jury to determine whether the threat or grudge is established; but if proved to their satisfaction to have been made, and the threat be afterwards carried into execution by the party taking the life of his adversary by the use of a deadly weapon, the presumption of law is, that the act was done under a wicked and malicious purpose to destroy him, and it is for the party committing the act to show circumstances giving to it a different character. [3]   It is also well settled, that where express malice is shown, and the person against whom the threat or other evidence of malice was made or existed, be afterwards killed with a deadly weapon, by the person harboring the malicious purpose, no mere provocation at the time of committing the act will relieve it of the character of a malicious killing, but it is presumed to be in consequence of the previous threat or grudge. 1 Russ. Cr., 423, 440, 442, (3 Am. ed.)   And it is sufficient to give to the threat such effect, if it appear to have been made deliberately, and not from sudden heat of passion; or the killing be done after sufficient time for passion to subside, and reason to be restored.

duct himself that he cannot be found by the officers of the law, or that process cannot be served upon him."   Page 618, art. 247.

[2] Wray, *Ex-parte*, 80 Miss., 675; Wharton Am. Cr. Law, 727; Moore v. State, 2 Ohio S. R., 500; Jim v. State, 5 Humph., 164; Commonwealth v. Burgess, 2 Va. Cases, 494; Com. v. Smith, 7 Smith's Laws, 697; Com. v. Mulatto Bob, 4 Dallas, 146; 1 Russell on Cr., 482; 1 Hale, 451; 4 Black. Com., 199; 3 Greenl. Ev., 14, 144; 1 Phill. Ev., 476; Rex. v. Greenacre, 8 C. & P., 35.

[3] See cases cited in note (†) *supra.*

As applicable to the testimony in this case upon the point of previous threats, or a grudge on the part of the accused, we perceive no error in the instructions. The rules, as stated, were substantially correct as legal principles, and were pertinent to the testimony upon the points involved in them, that testimony being sufficient to warrant the jury in believing in the existence of a previous threat or grudge.

The last ground of error insisted upon is, that the evidence did not warrant more than a verdict of manslaughter. In order to determine the propriety of this objection, it is necessary to take a view of the substance of the testimony, as it is presented in the record.

The first witness on the part of the state, Dr. Tindall, testifies to the dying declarations of the deceased, giving his statement of the circumstances of the difficulty, which was in substance, that the deceased went to a house and found Riggs there, and asked him where Susan Thomas was, telling him, that he had been using the name of deceased in a manner he would not permit; that the deceased then rose from his chair with a stick in his hand, when the accused struck him with his fists, and the deceased knocked him down twice with a stick; that they fought out of the house into the yard, where the fight terminated; the deceased not knowing that the accused had cut him with a knife, until after the fight had ceased.

This account of the affair is corroborated by the testimony of Emily McBeth, who was present and witnessed the difficulty, and who states some additional particulars. She states, that when the deceased entered the house, he spoke first to the accused, who replied gruffly; that deceased asked the accused where Susan Thomas was, to which he replied by asking if it was any of his business; that an altercation then took place in relation to the woman alluded to, which terminated in the fight; that when some of witness' family remarked, that the deceased was coming, and as he was seen approaching the house, the accused took out his knife and opened it and put it behind him; that when the accused struck the deceased with his fist, the deceased arose from his chair and knocked him down to his knees with his stick. On cross-examination it appeared, that this wit-

ness had no idea of the situation and localities of the house,
where the fight took place; that she did not know North from
South, or East from West, nor whether the sun rises in the East
or in the West, and was exceedingly ignorant. It also appeared
that she stated several particulars of the occurrence, differently
from what she had stated on her examination before the justice
of the peace, when the accused was first arrested and committed,
which examination was read for the purpose of discrediting
her.

Mrs. A. McBeth testified that she saw the accused at her
house on Monday before the killing, and he said that he had
been hunting for the deceased the night before, and that he intended the first time he saw him to stick his knife into him mortally; that witness heard a conversation between the accused
and Nancy Casey, alias Franklin, in which he charged her with
improper intimacy with the deceased, which she denied; but
Riggs then made the threat of violence with his knife against
the deceased.

Pendleton testified that he saw the accused on the evening of
Monday or Tuesday before the killing, inquiring for the deceased
at witness' grocery, but nothing peculiar in his manner was observed; the witness suspected nothing.

Strawhan stated that he saw deceased after the killing, and
helped to undress him; saw the stick supposed to have been
used in the fight; it was a light walking stick; and the deceased
had no arms on his person.

Dr. Tindall testified that the deceased had three wounds, one
in the right shoulder blade, which witness thinks penetrated the
bone; another on the right side cutting the fifth rib in two, and
another in the abdomen; that these wounds caused the death.

In behalf of the accused, Nancy Franklin, alias Casey, was introduced, and stated that the deceased had expressed to her his
intention to have revenge upon Riggs, for taking Susan Thomas
from him; that he afterwards came to Riggs' house, and in the
presence of his wife and the witness, in Riggs' absence, said, he
intended to kill Riggs, and put him out of the way, and take
his wife for his own purposes; that these declarations were made
known by Riggs' wife to him, in witness' presence, about a week

before the killing took place. She denied that she was at Mrs. McBeth's house on Monday or Tuesday before the killing, or that she heard Riggs threaten to stick his knife into the deceased, as stated by Mrs. McBeth, but she states that he said at another time and place, when told that the deceased intended to kill him, that if the deceased attempted to kill him, he would cut him to pieces before he could do it.

Elizabeth Lyons, being called for the state, stated that she heard the last witness repeat the remarks of the accused, and that she did not then say that Riggs had said, that if the deceased attempted to kill him, he would stab him; but that she stated that Riggs, measuring his knife-blade, said, he would put that much of it into the vital parts of the deceased.

It was also proved, by several witnesses, that the accused, when brought before the examining court, refused to state on oath, that he expected to prove by Nancy Franklin, that she communicated to him the threats made against him by the deceased to the wife of the accused and Nancy Franklin.

From this statement of the testimony before the jury, it is manifest that the character of the killing depends upon whether it was done as the result of a previous hostile purpose on the part of the accused; and the determination of that point depends upon the credibility of the witnesses in behalf of the state. The threats of the accused against the life of the deceased are distinctly proved to have been made by Mrs. McBeth, who also states the cause of his malicious feeling. This witness is not impeached or contradicted, except by the testimony of Nancy Franklin, whose testimony is impeached by another witness, who proves that Nancy Franklin made statements of the declarations of the accused, different from those deposed to by her on the trial, and in accordance with the testimony of Mrs. McBeth. It was peculiarly the province of the jury to determine to which of these witnesses they would give credit; and in a case of doubt, we could not say, that they judged improperly upon such a question.[1] But in this instance, we think that

[1] Where there is conflicting evidence on both sides, and the question be one of doubt, a new trial will not be granted. Wharton Am. Cr. Law, 3110; Com. v. Gallagher, 4 Penn. Law, 514; Leake v. State, 10 Humph., 144; Com. v. Flannagan, 7 Watts & Serg., 422; Smith v. Hick, 5 Wend., 48; Cassells v. State, 4 Yerg., 153;

the jury were well justified in giving credit to the two witnesses in behalf of the state.

The deadly purpose of the accused is also proved by the testimony of Emily McBeth, showing that when the accused was aware that the deceased was approaching the house, he drew his knife and put it behind him, preparing for the conflict.

The credibility of this witness is strongly assailed, and not without much reason, as her testimony appears in the record. She appears to be ignorant to a degree that would almost lead to the belief that she affected ignorance in order to avoid the scrutiny of a cross-examination, and in some respects she is shown to have made statements in relation to the occurrence, upon the trial, different from those previously made by her before the committing court. These discrepancies, however, are not irreconcilable, and do not affect the most material features of the occurrence, and may be attributed to the ignorance of the witness, or her want of distinctness of recollection, from the lapse of time between the occurrence and the time of her testifying on the trial. Her statement of the circumstances is corroborated by the account given of them in the dying declarations of the deceased, so far as they both speak of the same things, with the exception that she states, that the deceased was sitting in his chair when the accused struck the first blow; and he states that he had risen from his chair with his stick in his hand when the accused struck the first blow. And her statement about the drawing of the knife is distinctly made, both in her deposition before the committing court and in her testimony on the trial. It is corroborated by the fact that it was in accordance with his previous threats, and that he used the knife in the rencounter.

Although this witness does not appear in a very creditable light, either from her gross ignorance or from the discordant

State v. Jim, 2 Bailey, 29 ; Kirby v. State, 3 Humph., 289 ; Pleasant v. State, 15 Ark., 624 ; State v. Lamont, 2 Wisc., 437 ; Taylor v. State, 4 Ind., 540 ; Winfield v. State, 8 Iowa, 839 ; Jerry v. State, 1 Blackf., 395 ; Douglass v. Tousey, 2 Wend., 352 ; Jeffries v. State, 3 Murphy, 480 ; Mortey v. Montgomery, 2 Bailey, 11 ; Lavall v. Cromwell, Const. R., 593 ; Stanton v. State, 8 Eng., 339 ; Bennett v. State, ib., 694 ; Darby v. Calhoun, 1 Rep. Con. Ct., 398 ; Miller v. McBurney, ib., 237 ; Cohn v. Simmons, ib., 446 ; Caldwell v. Barkley, 2 ib., 452 ; Roberts v. State, 2 Kelly, 810 ; Hudgins v. State, 2 ib., 173 ; Palmer v. Hyde, 4 Conn., 426 ; Laflin v. Pomroy, 11 statements made by her of some of the features of this occurrence, yet we are not authorized to say that the jury were not justified in crediting her statements in any respect. The delicate and important duty of graduating the credit and weight due to testimony is not only the peculiar province of the jury, because it involves inferences of fact especially intrusted to their judgment, but they have the means of aiding their opinion upon the subject in doubtful cases, which an appellate court does not possess. The witness is personally before them, where they can observe his look and manner, his willingness or hesitation to testify, the feeling or indifference he manifests for either party, the degree of his intelligence, and from all these, as well as the facts stated by him, come to a just conclusion as to the degree of credit or weight to be given to his testimony. All these aids to a just and correct conclusion upon the point are lost in the appellate court. We have nothing but the naked, dry language of the record, which conveys a very imperfect idea, not unfrequently, as to whether the testimony is liable to the objection of ignorance, confusion or corruption in the witness. Hence the rule has been well and wisely established, that an appellate court will rarely, if ever, set aside the verdict of a jury founded upon the credit or discredit given by them to the witnesses on the trial, especially when the testimony is conflicting.

Considering the credit of these witnesses, then, as established by the verdict, it is clear that the killing was perpetrated as the result of express malice, and by the use of a deadly weapon, which the accused had concealed and ready to be used when he entered into the conflict with the deceased. And it is clear, beyond doubt, that the killing, under such circumstances, was murder, and not manslaughter. 1 Russ. Cr., 446, (3 Am. ed.) The judgment is therefore not erroneous on this ground.

We have thus carefully considered all the evidence in the rec-

Conn., 440; Trowbridge v. Baker, 1 Cow., 251; Winchell v. Latham, 6 Cow., 682; McKnight v. Wells, 1 Mo., 13; Clasky v. January, Harden, 539; Nelson v. Chalfant, 3 Litt., 165; Lee v. Banks, 4 ib., 11; Johnson v. Davenport, 3 J. J. Marshall, 390; Reed v. Langford, ib., 420; Creel v. Bell, 2 ib., 309; Talbot v. Talbot, ib., 3; Fitzgerald v. Barker, 4 ib., 398; Swain v. Hall, 3 Wilson, 45; Gregory v. Tuffs, 1 Crom., M. & Rosc., 310; 1 Camp., 450; Melin v. Taylor, 3 Hodge, 125; 3 Bing., N. C., 109; Empson v. Farriford, 1 Will. Woll. & Dav., 10; Stanley v. Wharton, 8 Price, 301; Loff., 147; Hankey v. Trottman, 1 W. Bla., 1; 2 Price, 282; 1 Burr, 54.

ord, and the various grounds urged for a reversal of the judgment; and we are brought to the conclusion, that there is no error in the record which would justify a reversal of the judgment.

The judgment is, therefore, affirmed.

JONES *v.* THE STATE, 30 Miss. Rep., 653.

LARCENY.

The possession of property recently stolen will create a presumption that the possessor is a thief; but this is a mere presumption, and the true state of the case may be entirely different, and the party may be enabled to show his innocence by positive testimony.

The possession of stolen goods must be accounted for; but as this cannot always be done by legal evidence, owing to the nature of the goods and the circumstances of the case, it is a matter of no little weight that the conduct of the accused is consistent with the account he gives of his acquisition of their possession.

The fact that he makes no attempt at concealment, but openly exposes the goods where they are subject to be recognized by the owner or others interested, are circumstances that strongly tend to destroy the presumption arising from such recent possession.

When the accused gives a reasonable account of his possession of stolen property, it lies on the prosecutor to show that it is false; but if it is unreasonable or improbable on its face, the accused must prove its truth.

Error to Lauderdale circuit court.   WATTS, J.
Freeman & Dixon, for plaintiff in error.
D. C. Glenn, attorney general.

HANDY, J.:

The plaintiff in error was indicted and convicted of larceny in the court below. A motion for a new trial was made, on the ground that the verdict was contrary to the evidence, which being overruled, the case is brought here; and the only matter for consideration is, whether the evidence was sufficient to support the verdict.

Several witnesses were examined in behalf of the state, but the material facts proved were, that the knife stolen was the property of one Bartle, who loaned it to one Winningham, who placed it under the counter in a store, and in a few days thereafter went to an adjacent county, and when he returned, the knife was gone; that it was about three weeks from the time it was loaned before it was found. When it was found, it was in Jones's possession, in his room, lying openly on the bed, the room being frequently visited by persons of the village; that Jones made no attempt to conceal it, and was not at all disconcerted when the witness took up the knife; and he said that he had got it in North Alabama. Another witness stated, that he found the knife in Jones's box, who showed the box willingly, and invited the witness to examine what he had in it. The articles in it were exposed willingly to persons interested in making the examination; and the room in which the knife lay openly exposed was near to the store, where it had been deposited, and only about seventy yards from the place where Bartle and Winningham resided.

Upon this evidence, we do not think that the mere possession of the article by the accused was sufficient to justify his conviction. It is true that the possession of goods recently stolen, will create a presumption that such possessor is the thief. Yet this is a mere presumption, and the real state of the case may be entirely different, and yet the party be unable to show his innocence by any positive testimony. It is held, that the person in whose possession the stolen goods are found, must account for his possession; yet, as from the nature of the goods and the circumstances of the case, this cannot always be done by legal evidence, it is held to be a matter of no little weight, that the conduct of the accused is consistent with the account given by him of the manner in which the goods came to his possession.[1] Roscoe, Cr. Ev., 20; 2 East P. C., 665. As where he makes no attempt to conceal them, and, on the contrary, openly exposes

---

[1] Rex v. Crownhurst, 1 C. & K., 370; 47 E. C. L. R. In this case Alderson, B., charged the jury that, "In cases of this nature you should take it as a general principle, that when a man in whose possession stolen property is found, gives a reasonable account of how he came by it, as by telling the name of the person from whom he received it, and who is known to be a real person, it is incumbent on the prosecutor to show that the account is false; and if the account given by the prisoner be unreasonable or improbable on the face of it, the *onus* of proving the truth of it lies on the prisoner." See, also, Rex v. Wilson, 26 L. J., M. C., 45; 2 Hale P. C., 289; 3 Greenl. Ev., 31; Wills on Circ. Ev., ch. 3, § 4; Burrill Circ. Ev., 454; 1 Stark. Ev., 512, 513; Regina v. Smith, 2 C. & K., 207; 1 Phill. Ev., 634, *et seq.*; 2 Archbold Cr. Pr. & Pl., 370.

them where they are subject to apprehension by the owner or others interested in them.   These are circumstances tending strongly to destroy the presumption arising from recent possession; and they fully appear in the conduct of the accused in this case.

It is also held, that where a man in whose possession stolen property is found, gives a reasonable account of how he came by it, it is incumbent on the prosecutor to show that the account is false; but if the account given by him be unreasonable or improbable on its face, the *onus* of proving its truth lies on him. Regina v. Crownhurst, 1 C. & K., (47 Eng. C. Law R.,) 370. The reasonableness of his account must necessarily depend, in a great measure, upon his deportment in relation to the article found in his possession, and upon the time and circumstances under which it is found.   If the article be small and such as is easily and quickly transmissible from one person to another, and when it is found in the possession of the accused, it is openly exposed where the owner may readily find it, and will probably discover it, and he makes no effort to conceal it, but gives an account of his possession, which is probable from the nature of the article, these circumstances would be sufficient to destroy the presumption arising from mere possession, and to raise the presumption of innocence.   These circumstances are shown to have existed in this case, and, accordingly, we are of opinion that the evidence was not sufficient to justify the verdict.

The judgment is reversed, and the cause remanded for a new

BROWNING *v.* THE STATE, 30 Miss. Rep., 656.

CONSPIRACY AND HOMICIDE.

On change of *venue* in a criminal case, the clerk should send a transcript of the indictment and record to the court which is to try the cause, and not the original papers.

Before the statements of co-defendants can be given in evidence against each other respectively, there must be a *prima facie* case established by evidence *aliunde*.   1 Greenl. Ev., 111; 2 Stark. Ev., 827; Wharton's Am. Cr. Law, *passim.*

If the combination for illegal purposes be once established, then the acts and words of every person party to such combination, and in furtherance of the common design, is the act of all, and all are alike responsible.

Reasonable doubt is not probability only, or conjecture or supposition; the doubt which should induce a jury to withhold a verdict of guilty should be such a doubt as would reasonably arise from the testimony before them.

Error to Holmes circuit court.   HENRY, J.

John D. Browning and Gaston E. Browning were indicted in the circuit court of Sunflower county for the murder of one John W. Neal. Upon application of the prisoners the *venue* was changed to the county of Holmes. At the November term of the court below, the court having allowed the defendants to sever in the trial, Gaston E. Browning was tried and found guilty of murder. He moved in arrest of judgment, and for a new trial, which motion was overruled, and the court thereupon pronounced sentence of death upon him. The ground upon which the motion in arrest of judgment was made will be seen in the opinion of the court. Numerous exceptions were taken to the proceedings, and the plaintiff sued out this writ of error.

The testimony was entirely circumstantial, and is very voluminous. The only facts necessary to be stated are as follows, to wit:

That on Sunday evening, the 23d day of July, 1854, the deceased, John W. Neal, left the plantation of his employer, James Y. McNeil, between twelve o'clock M. and one o'clock P.M., with the avowed intention of crossing the Yazoo river, at John D. Browning's, and going to a Mr. Pool's and returning home that night, a distance of about eighteen miles in going and returning. He was not seen afterwards by any of the witnesses until on the Tuesday evening following, being the 25th of July, when his dead body was discovered floating down the Yazoo river.

John D. Browning was present when the body was discovered; and a witness was permitted to relate the acts and declarations of John D. Browning, then performed and made, and which tended to implicate him in the murder of Neal. John D. Browning was a justice of the peace, and, as such, officiated the next day as coroner, in holding an inquest over the body of Neal, and his conduct and declarations on that occasion were admitted in evidence against the prisoner.

On Tuesday, the 25th day of July, previous to the discovery of the body of Neal, John D. Browning and the prisoner, and a third party, searched the river for it, and John D. Browning's conduct and declarations at that time were also admitted in evidence. After the arrest of John D. Browning and prisoner, the conduct and declarations of John D. Browning during the pendency of his trial before the committing court were also admitted in evidence; so were declarations made by him about three weeks before the death of Neal. These declarations were not direct confessions of guilt, but were intended to show a knowledge of the circumstances of the murder, inconsistent with innocence, and also to show a motive.

There was no proof of a conspiracy or combination between the prisoner and John D. Browning to murder Neal. The prisoner was the son of John D. Browning, and lived at his house at the time of Neal's death.

The ninth instruction, alluded to and commented on by the court, is as follows :

"Whenever the probability of guilt is of a definite and limited nature, whether in the proportion of one hundred to one, or one thousand to one, or in any other limited ratio, it can not safely be made the ground of conviction."

Thos. Botters and *J. Z. George* for plaintiff in error.

1. The court erred in forcing the prisoner to trial on a copy of the indictment. He was entitled to be tried on the original. The law authorizing a change of *venue* in civil cases, directs that the original papers shall be transmitted. Hutch. Code, 849. This act was passed in 1823. The act afterwards passed in 1831, authorizing a change of *venue* in criminal cases, makes no provision as to the mode in which it shall be done. It does not direct what shall or shall not be transmitted to the court into which the cause is removed. This omission can not be accounted for, except upon the ground that the mode provided in the act in civil cases was intended to be pursued in criminal trials.

2. The court erred in permitting the conduct and declarations of John D. Browning to be detailed in evidence against the prisoner. It is impossible to conceive upon what principle these declarations were admitted. The fact that they were jointly

indicted will not authorize their admission. See 2 Stark. Ev., 329; Wharton Am. Cr. Law, 326. The rule on this subject seems to us to be so well understood and so well defined that it is impossible to mistake it. Before the acts and declarations of one can be admitted in evidence against another, the following conditions must be complied with : First, that there was a conspiracy or combination existing between them for the commission of the crime charged ; Second, that the acts and declarations were done and made in pursuance of the criminal enterprise, and in furtherance of its object ; and Third, that these should have been done and made in point of time subsequent to the formation of the conspiracy, and previous to its completion or abandonment; or, in other words, *pending* the criminal enterprise. See 1 Greenl. Ev., § 98, 111, 283 ; 3 ib., 94; Rosc. Crim. Ev., 76, 77, 78, 79 ; Breese R., 268 ; 2 Burr's Trial, 338, 339; 7 Grat. R. 641.

None of these conditions were complied with. In the first place, there was not a single iota of proof that there was a criminal combination between the Brownings to murder Neal. There is no evidence tending to show this fact, unless it be the declarations of John D. Browning. These were incompetent to show this fact, for the reason that they could not be admitted at all until after, and upon the condition the conspiracy was proven. Upon the second point, the acts and declarations were inadmissible as not having been done and made in pursuance of the original concerted plan to murder Neal, (admitting it to be proven). Not all the acts and declarations of a conspirator are admissible against his associates, even when made pending the criminal enterprise. The rule is restricted to the admission of those acts and declarations done in pursuance of the concerted scheme and in furtherance of its object. What one might say or do, although criminal in itself, yet, if it be outside of the conspiracy, it is not admissible against the others.

But, upon the third point, the reason for the exclusion of the evidence is, if possible, more obvious than in the others. All the acts and declarations of John D. Browning, which were admitted in evidence, were done and made after the death of Neal ; except one conversation which took place about three weeks previously. Some of them occurred even after their arrest. They can not possibly be said to have been made and done during the pendency of the criminal enterprise to murder Neal, for this had been accomplished by his death. See 1 Greenl., §. 111, and authorities above cited.

3. The court evidently erred in granting the third instruction asked for the state. It is substantially copied from the syllabus in Ciccley's case. The syllabus substitutes the word "probability" for "possibility," as contained in the court's opinion. It may be true that a *possibility* of the prisoner's innocence may exist, there being a reasonable doubt of his guilt; but, to say that there is a *probability* of his innocence, and yet no reasonable doubt of his guilt, is manifestly absurd. If authority be used on this point, let Webster's Dictionary decide the matter. This instruction was prejudicial to the prisoner; under it, he was utterly excluded from the benefit of a reasonable doubt.

4. The court erred in refusing the ninth instruction asked for by defendant. This, as a proposition of law, is undeniable, and is copied from the most learned and philosophical law-writer known to the profession (1 Stark. Ev. 574); besides, it announces a vital principle in the application of circumstantial evidence, and one recognized by this court in Algheri's case, 3 Cush., 389. By that case, the doctrine is distinctly asserted that, if the evidence only raises a definite and finite probability in favor of the hypothesis of guilt, it is insufficient. The probabilities in favor of guilt must be indefinite and beyond all human calculation; otherwise it is insufficient. This is all that is announced in the instruction; and the refusal to give it is equivalent to charging the reverse of it to be law.

5. The court erred in refusing to grant a new trial. On this point, counsel reviewed the evidence, but it is unnecessary to set out their argument, inasmuch as the court expressed no opinion on that point.

D. C. Glenn, attorney general.

1. Upon the testimony, this case presents a clearer case of guilt than the case of Cicely or the case of McCann. In fact, the conclusion of guilt is irresistible.

2. The admission of the evidence of John D. Browning was

justified by well-established principles, as proof of *facts* in the
cause, and not as evidence of themselves to fix guilt on Gaston
Browning—as indicatory evidence tending to prove the main fact
in issue.   The authorities relied on are McCann's case, 13 S. &
M., 471, and cases cited, which was maturely weighed and deliberately decided by the whole court.   This was not hearsay evidence.   On each point, I rely on 1 Greenl. § 100, 108 ; 1 Stark.,
§ 563, 567 ; Keithler's case, 10 S. & M., 226, 47, 54, 55, 56, 57,
58, 59, and note ; also, 62, 63, 64, 65.

3. The charge refused was calculated to confuse and mislead
the jury, and moreover, it propounds a rule of numerical and
mathematical expression to be applied to moral probabilities,
which is not safe, nor is it sanctioned by authority.   6 Wills,
Cir. Ev. ; 1 Stark., close of volume.

SMITH, C. J. :

John D. Browning and Gaston E. Browning were jointly indicted in the circuit court of Sunflower county for the murder
of John Neal.   Upon the application of counsel of prisoners,
the venue was changed to Holmes County, in which the trial
took place.   The parties charged were tried separately ; and, .
Gaston E. Browning, whose case is now before us, was convicted
of murder and sentenced accordingly.

After the verdict, the prisoner moved in arrest of judgment.
His motion being overruled, he moved for a new trial ; which,
being also refused, exception was taken to the judgment on the
motion for a new trial, and the evidence embodied in the bill of
exceptions.

The objections now urged apply to various proceedings of the
circuit court.

1. It is insisted that the court erred in overruling the motion in
arrest of judgment.

A certified transcript " of all the orders, records, and papers,
including the indictment," in conformity with the order changing the venue, was deposited with the clerk of the circuit court
of Holmes County.   When the prisoner was about to be put
upon his trial, he demanded the production of the original indictment found by the grand jurors of Sunflower county, and ob-

jected to being tried on the copy contained in the transcript. The objection was overruled, and the trial was proceeded with. This was the ground relied on in support of the motion.

The propriety of this action of the court, depends exclusively upon the construction to be given to the statute, in regard to the change of venue in criminal cases.

The statute on this subject, (Hutch. Dig., 1007, art. 63,) is entirely silent as to the mode in which an order for a change of venue in prosecutions shall be carried into effect. It provides simply that it shall and may be lawful under a proscribed state of circumstances, for any circuit or criminal court, to grant an order for the change of venue. The act in reference to a change of venue in civil cases, directs that the original papers shall be transmitted to the court into which the cause, by the order changing the venue, has been removed,—which are to be accompanied by a descriptive list of those papers. But we cannot hold, in the absence of any intimation by the legislature to that effect, that these directions are to be applied to criminal cases in which the venue has been changed, without authority for that purpose. If not conferred by the legislature, it would clearly be illegal, for the clerks of the circuit courts to part with the original papers or records pertaining to a prosecution therein pending. All that a clerk could do in such cases—and we must infer that it was all the legislature intended to be done—is to transmit to the clerk of the court, into which the cause has been removed, a perfect transcript of all the original papers in the cause, and of the minutes, or records of the court, containing the orders and proceedings of the court in relation to the same, properly certified under the seal of his office. [1]

In Green's case, (not yet reported,) there was a change of

---

[1] The Revised Code of 1857, provides that "Upon the order being made, changing the *venue* in a criminal case, the clerk shall make out a transcript of the caption of the record, also of the proceedings empanelling the grand jury, of the indictment, with the entries or endorsements thereon, and all entries relative thereto in the records of his office, the bonds, obligations and recognizances of the defendants, and all witnesses and all orders, judgments, or other papers or proceedings belonging to or had in said cause; and attach his certificate thereto, under his hand, with the seal of his court annexed, and forward it, sealed up, by a special messenger, or deliver it himself, together with all the original subpœnas in such case to the clerk of the circuit court, to which the trial is ordered to be removed. Rev. Code, 631, art. 299. See also, ib., 621, arts. 300, 301.

venue; and he was, as in the case at bar, tried upon a certified transcript of the indictment. The exception based upon that fact, was not noticed in the opinion of this court affirming the judgment; but, on a petition for re-argument, the question was maturely considered; and it was held to be no ground for reversing the judgment. Our subsequent examination of the subject, has confirmed our conviction of the correctness of the decision then made.

2. It is next objected, that the court erred, on numerous occasions, in the admission of evidence adduced in support of the prosecution.

The cases, or instances, in which it is alleged there was an erroneous admission of testimony in behalf of the state, are very numerous; and it is deemed unnecessary to notice them in detail, as we can fully understand the questions presented by the exceptions to the various items of testimony by a statement of the general character of the evidence excepted to, and the grounds of objection.

The Brownings—father and son—were jointly indicted for the murder of John Neal. They were tried separately; and the younger Browning was first put on his trial. During the examination of the witnesses, many persons called for the prosecution were permitted to testify as to the conduct and acts, occuring after the death of Neal, of the elder Browning; as to statements made by him after the perpetration of the alleged homicide; and in relation to conversations, in which he detailed facts which had happened long anterior to the date of the offense, as well as facts occurring after the deed was perpetrated. All of this testimony was objected to by the prisoner, as incompetent evidence, on the trial of the issue before the jury.

Two positions are assumed in support of the exception to the admission of this testimony.

1. It is assumed, that the testimony referred to was illegally admitted, because, as it is insisted, no proof whatever was offered tending to establish a conspiracy or combination between the plaintiff in error and the elder Browning.

It is not to be questioned, that the mere fact that these parties were jointly indicted for the murder of Neal, would not make the declarations or acts of Browning the elder, evidence in the cause. The principle upon which they could alone be admitted as evidence is, that the act or declaration of one, is that of both united in one common design ; a principle which is wholly unaffected by the consideration of their being jointly indicted. 2 Stark. Ev., 329.

The act or declaration of one wrong doer, is no evidence to affect any other person ; for it is merely *res inter alios acta ;* unless where it is proved that several persons have entered into the same criminal design ; in such case the acts or declarations of any one of them, in furtherance of the common object, are not to be considered *res inter alios*, with regard to the rest of them ; they are all identified with each other in the prosecution of the scheme ; " they are partners," says Starkie, " for a bad purpose, and as much mutually responsible, as to such purpose, as partners in trade are for more honest pursuits ; they may be considered as mutual agents for each other."

The existence of a conspiracy, or of a combination for the commission of a crime, is a fact, which, like all other facts, when it is material to be proved, can only be established by competent evidence. The declaration of a stranger in regard to it would be mere hearsay ; unsustained by any of the legal tests of truth. The mere assertions of a stranger, that a conspiracy existed amongst others, to which he was not a party, would be clearly inadmissible, and it is equally clear, that the confession of the party making the assertion, that he was a party to the conspiracy, would not make the assertion evidence against strangers.

Hence, although in cases in which crime has been jointly committed by several persons, when once a conspiracy or combination has been established, the act or declaration of one conspirator or accomplice in the prosecution of the enterprise, is considered the act or declaration of all, and is evidence against all ; a foundation must first be laid by proof, sufficient in the opinion of the court to establish *prima facie*, the existence of the combination, or to be laid before the jury, as tending to establish such fact, before the acts or declarations of any of the conspirators or accomplices can be given in evidence to charge the others. This, as the general rule, seems to be universally recognized.[1]

Greenl. Ev., § 111; 2 Stark. Ev., 327; Whart. Am. Cr. L., 261, 262; and cases cited by the respective authors.

Tested by this rule, it is manifest that the court erred in admitting the acts and declarations of the elder Browning, as evidence in the cause; there having been no foundation laid by proof, establishing or tending to establish the existence of a concert or combination between him and the party on trial.

But an exception to the rule above laid down, confessedly, at least in its application, of not very ancient date, is recognized by the English courts.

Starkie says: The rule that one man is not to be affected by the acts or declaration of a stranger, rests on the principles of the purest justice; and although the courts, in cases of conspiracy, have, out of convenience, and on account of the difficulty in otherwise proving the guilt of the parties, admitted the acts and declarations of strangers to be given in evidence, in order to establish the fact of a conspiracy, it is to be remembered that this is an inversion of the usual order for the sake of convenience; and that such evidence is, in the result, material so far only as to the assent of the accused, to what has been done by others, is proved. 2 Stark. Ev., 329.

This exception, with some modification, has been sanctioned by Greenleaf in his work on Evidence. He lays it down that sometimes, for the sake of convenience, under peculiar and urgent circumstances, the acts or declarations of one of a company of conspirators are admitted in evidence before sufficient proof is given of the conspiracy; the prosecutor undertaking to furnish such proof in a subsequent stage of the cause. 1 Greenl.

[1] Rex v. Watson, 32 How. St. Tr., 7; Rex v. Brandreth, ib., 857, 858; Rex v. Hardy, 24 Howell's St. Tr., 451, 452, 453, 475; American Fur Co. v. U. S., 2 Peters, 358, 365; Crowninshield's case, 10 Pick., 497; Rex v. Hunt, 3 B. & Ald., 566; 1 East P. C. 97, § 38; 1 Greenl. Ev., 111; Wharton Am. Cr. Law, 702 et seq.; Clawson v. State, 14 Ohio St. R., 234; 1 East P. C., c. 2, § 37, p. 96; 1 Phill. Ev., 447, citing the Queen's case, 2 Brod. & B., 302; 2 Russ. on Cr., 697; State v. George, 7 Iredell, 321; Clayton v. Anthony, 6 Randolph, 285; U. S. v. Cole, 5 McLean C. C. R., 513; State v. Nash, 7 Iowa, 347; Commonwealth v. Brown, 14 Gray, 419; State v. Ross, 19 Mo., 32; State v. Taylor, 3 Brevard, 243; Commonwealth v. Boot, Thacher's C. C., 390; Archbold Cr. Pr. & Pl., 620; The Queen's case, 2 Brod. & B., 302; Rex v. Hammond & Webb, 2 Esp., 719; Rex v. Stone, 6 Vern., 527.

Ev., 127. This rests in the discretion of the judge; and he adds, " that care must be taken that the acts and declarations thus admitted, be those only made and done during the pendency of the criminal enterprise, and in furtherance of its objects."

It is difficult to reconcile this exception to the rule, with the universally admitted principles of the law of evidence, or with the great object of all laws regulating the examination of witnesses and the introduction of evidence, which is to secure a fair and impartial trial of the question at issue. But conceding that the exigencies of the public required the recognition of this principle, and that it will be observed by this court; let us see whether under it the action of the circuit court can be justified.

The offense charged, if committed at all, was unseen by all, save by the parties engaged in its perpetration. The whole transaction was shrouded in secrecy. The very fact of the homicide, as well as the question who were the perpetrators of the deed, depended entirely upon indirect or circumstantial evidence. The charge, as laid in the indictment, presupposes the co-operation of at least two persons in the commission of the offense. It may hence well be conceded, that peculiar and urgent circumstances existed in the cause, which authorized the application of the exception to the rule above stated, if any combination of circumstances could authorize a departure from the prescribed mode. But it should ever be borne in mind, that no man can be asserted to be legally guilty of an offense, unless his guilt shall have been established according to the forms and principles of the law; and that in no case should a disregard of either the law itself or its established forms be tolerated from any considerations of difficulty in the conviction of offenders, or from the supposed manifest guilt of the accused.

According to some adjudged cases, very slight evidence of the existence of a conspiracy or combination in which the accused is implicated, is sufficient to let in proof of the acts and declarations of his accomplices, done or made pending the conspiracy, and in furtherance of its objects. In the case at bar, judging from the record, no attempt whatever seems to have been made by the prosecution to prove the existence of any concert or combination between any persons in the perpetration of the alleged offense.   In fact, no evidence had been offered to prove a *corpus delicti* before the first witness called for the prosecution was allowed to testify in regard to the acts and declarations of the elder Browning.   It does not appear that any reason or cause was assigned for the admission of this evidence before a proper foundation was laid.   Indeed, for aught that appears of record, the acts and declarations of the elder Browning were received and treated as original evidence in the cause, competent and pertinent to the issue to be tried.   Every presumption, however, is in favor of the legality of the proceedings of courts.   We are bound, therefore, to presume, in the absence of any thing to the contrary appearing of record, that testimony in relation to those acts and delarations, was admitted by the judge in the exercise of a wise discretion; and that in allowing it to go to the jury, the conditions of the law were strictly complied with. [1]

But there is an insurmountable objection to the admission of the testimony of many of the witnesses for the prosecution, in relation to certain acts and declarations of the elder Browning. As this objection would apply at all stages of the cause, and be equally tenable, if there had been proof *aliunde* connecting the plaintiff in error with a conspiracy for the murder of Neal, it will be considered in reference to the second ground taken in support of the exception to the admission of evidence.

2. It is insisted that the court erred in overruling the prisoner's objection to the testimony of certain witnesses for the prosecution, who were allowed to depose as to the acts and declarations of the elder Browning, not done or made pending the existence of a combination for the murder of Neal, and in furtherance of such object, but which occurred after the commission of the offense.   The objection applies to portions of the testimony of many of the witnesses who were examined on the trial.

It is not our purpose to determine whether, upon all the evidence as submitted to the jury, the plaintiff in error was guilty

[1] Wharton Am. Cr. Law, 713; Co. Litt., 282; Van Omeron v. Dowick, 2 Camp., 44; Doe v. Evans, 1 Cr. & M., 461; 2 Russ. on Cr., 732; Reed v. Jackson, 1 East, 325; Sutton v. Johnstone, 1 T. R., 503; Lyttleton v. Cross, 8 B. & C., 327; 1 Greenl. Ev., 19; Broom's Legal Maxims, 907; U. S. v. Dandridge, 12 Wheaton, 69, 70; Davies v. Pratt, 17 C. B., 183 (E. C. L. R., 84); Regina v. Brennan, 16 L. J. Q. B., 289.

of the crime charged; but it will not be controverted that without the evidence in reference to the acts and declarations of Browning, the elder, there is not proof sufficient to connect him with the murder. The proofs, therefore, derived from the conduct and statements of the former, and which, in the estimation of the jury, were conclusive of the prisoner's guilty connection with the transaction, were important and material.

We have above stated the ground upon which the acts or declarations of one conspirator or one accomplice—where a crime has been committed by several persons—are admitted in evidence, to charge the others; and the rule in reference to the question under consideration, is too well settled to admit of doubt.

"It is an established rule," says Phillips, "that where several persons are proved to have combined together for the same illegal purpose, any act done by one of the party in pursuance of the original concerted plan, and with reference to the common object, is, in the contemplation of the law, the act of the whole party. It follows, that any writings, or verbal expressions, being acts in themselves, or accompanying and explaining other acts, and therefore part of the *res gestæ*, and which are brought home to one conspirator, are evidence against the other conspirators; provided it sufficiently appear that they were used in furtherance of a common design." 1 Phill. Ev., 200. [1]

And further: "But where words or writings are not acts in themselves, nor part of the *res gestæ*, but a mere relation of some part of the transaction, or as to the share which other persons have had in the execution of a common design, the evidence is not in its nature original. It depends on the credit of the narrator, who is not before the court; and therefore it can not be received." [2] Id., 208.

[1] See also Wharton Am. Cr. Law, 702; U. S. v. Hinman, 1 Baldwin, 292; Martin v. Commonwealth, 11 Leigh, 745; U. S. v. Goodwin, 12 Wheaton, 469; Glory v. State, 8 Eng., 236; Stewart v. State, 26 Ala., 44; Cornelius v. Commonwealth, 15 B. Monroe, 539; Waterbury v. Sturtevant, 18 Wend., 353; State v. Poll, 1 Hawks, 442; State v. George, 7 Iredell, 321; State v. Loper, 4 Shep., 293; Mulone v. State, 8 Ga., 408; 1 Greenl. Ev., 111; Rex v. Watson, 32 Howell's St. Tr., 7; Rex v. Brandreth, ib., 857, 858; Rex v. Hardy, 24 ib., 451, 452, 453, 475; American Fur Co. v. U. S., 2 Peters, 358, 365; Crowninshield's case, 10 Pick., 497; Rex v. Hunt, 3 B. & Ald., 566; 1 East P. C., 97, § 38; Nichols v. Dowding, 1 Stark. R., 81.

[2] 1 Greenl. Ev., 111; Rex v. Hardy, 24 Howell's St. Tr., 703, per Eyre, C. J.; Rex

Acts performed, or declarations made, after the consummation of the object for which the parties combined, can, upon no principle, be considered a part of the *res gestæ ;* much less can an act done, or a declaration made, after the execution of a common design, be regarded as performed or made in the prosecution of such design. The boundary between those acts and declarations of conspirators and accomplices, which are admissible in evidence, and those which are not, is as clearly defined as the rule itself, upon which, in any case, they are admitted. Greenleaf, in terms, lays it down, that the evidence in respect to the acts and declarations of conspirators and accomplices, must be confined to acts and declarations made or done " during the pendency of the criminal enterprise, and in furtherance of its objects ;" and that, " after the enterprise is at an end, whether by accomplishment or abandonment, is not material ; no one is permitted, by any subsequent act or declaration of his own, to affect others. His confession, therefore, subsequently made, even though by the plea of guilty, is not admissible in evidence, as such against any but himself." 1 Greenl. Ev., 127, § 111 ; ib., 280, § 233. The same rule is recognized by the approved writers on the law of evidence. Roscoe Cr. Ev., 80 ; 2 Stark. Ev., 326 ; Am. Cr. Law, 161, 162.

Let it be assumed, then, that there was sufficient evidence to establish the common guilt of the prisoner and the elder Browning ; and, hence, that the prisoner was properly chargeable by the acts and declarations of the latter, done pending the combination and in the prosecution of its objects ; but, tried by this rule, it is manifest that the court erred, in several instances, in the admission of testimony in relation to the acts and declarations of the elder Browning. Many of these acts and declarations, deposed to by the witnesses, were done and made after the perpetration of the alleged offense. In some instances, statements of the elder Browning, made even after he was placed under arrest, were allowed to be detailed to the jury. This was a palpable violation of a rule of evidence, founded upon the purest justice and the plainest principles of reason.

v. Salter, 5 Esp., 125 ; Rex v. Cope, 1 Stark., 144; Cuyler v. McCartney, 33 Barb., 165 ; 2 Starkie Ev. (2d ed.), 236 ; Roscoe Cr. Ev., 386 ; 2 Russell on Cr., 697 ; Rex v. Murphy, cited in Roscoe Cr. Ev., 386.

3. It is insisted, further, that there was error in granting the third charge requested in behalf of the prosecution. The instruction is in the following words : "A reasonable doubt, authorizing an acquittal, must arise from the testimony ; and if the jury are satisfied, from the testimony, of the guilt of the prisoner, beyond a reasonable doubt so arising, they must convict."

"A reasonable doubt is not probability only, or conjecture, or supposition ; the doubt which should properly induce a jury to withhold a verdict of guilty should be such a doubt as would reasonably arise from the testimony before them."

It is possible that there has been a clerical mistake in copying this instruction into the record, by which the word "probability" is substituted for the words "mere possibility," which are contained in the instruction granted in Cicely's case, and held to be correct. However, as the charge stands in the record, it is clearly erroneous.

Where the probabilities are in favor of a party on trial, the jury may nevertheless entertain a doubt of his innocence. But where, in the estimation of the jury, the probability arising from the evidence, is in favor of the innocence of the accused, it is impossible for them not to doubt as to his guilt. If the jury entertained a well founded doubt of the prisoner's guilt, arising from the testimony, the law made it their duty to acquit. The instruction, if it means any thing, reverses this rule. The jury were instructed that "probability only" was not what is meant in law by a reasonable doubt. In effect, that a probability of the prisoner's innocence, arising upon the testimony, was not a legal foundation for a reasonable doubt of his guilt. The instruction imposed upon the jury the obligation to convict, although the evidence might preponderate in favor of the accused.

In regard to the ninth instruction requested by the prisoner, we perceive no error in the refusal of the court to grant it.

It is true, that this charge is a literal transcript of language used by a learned writer in expounding the doctrines of circumstantial evidence. It is manifest, that the proposition contained in the charge was not announced by the author, from whom it was copied, as a distinct principle of law. It was intended as an illustration of the weight which should be given to circumstantial evidence in determining the question in any given case whether such evidence was sufficient to exclude from the mind of the judge or jury all doubt of the guilt of the party sought to be affected by it. The instruction presents an extremely abstract proposition, and was much more likely to confuse the jury than to enlighten them upon the questions under consideration. This was a sufficient reason for withholding the instruction ; especially as the jury had been, at the instance of the prisoner, fully instructed as to the character and weight of circumstantial evidence.

As we reverse the judgment for the errors above noticed, and remand the prisoner for a new trial, it is deemed improper to examine the exception taken to the judgment, on the motion for a new trial.

Judgment reversed, *venire de novo* awarded, and cause remanded.

WRAY, EX-PARTE, 30 Miss. Rep., 673.

HOMICIDE.

All prisoners shall, before conviction, be bailable by sufficient securities, except for capital offenses, where the proof is evident or presumption great.

Bail, in capital cases, is a matter resting in the sound legal discretion of the court ; but if the offense is not shown by proof evident, or great presumption, to be such as deserves capital punishment, bail is not a matter of discretion in the court, but of right in the prisoner.

Express malice is, when one, with a sedate, deliberate mind and formed design doth kill another, which formed design is evidenced by external circumstances, discovering that inward intention, as lying in wait, antecedent menaces, former grudges, and concerted schemes to do him some bodily harm.   4 Black Com., 199.

The declarations of a prisoner, made when he obtained weapons for an anticipated difficulty, that he did not intend to use them unless other parties interfered, and the fact that he did not use them until closely pressed by his antagonist and violently beaten, are sufficient to disprove express malice.   HANDY, J., *dissented.*

When a well founded doubt can be entertained as to the guilt of the prisoner, the proof is not evident nor the presumption great.   HANDY, J., *dissented.*

Error to the judgment of Hon. PHINEAS T. SCRUGGS, Judge

of the Seventh Judicial District, on *habeas corpus*, refusing bail
to Jacob K. Wray.

The material facts of the case will be found in the opinion of
the court and the dissenting opinion of Mr. Justice HANDY.

Fontaine & Bradford and *Harris, Freeman & Goodman*, for
plaintiff in error.

D. C. Glenn, attorney general.

FISHER, J. :

The petitioner, being in custody, awaiting his trial upon an
indictment preferred against him by the grand jury of Pontotoc
county, for the murder of one Clarke S. Brown, applied to the
judge of the seventh judicial district of this state to be admitted to bail ; and the court, after hearing the testimony, as
well on behalf of the petitioner as of the prosecution, refused
the application, and remanded him to the custody of the sheriff
of said county. The object of the writ of error is to revise the
judgment thus pronounced.

We have given to the testimony, as shown by the record, a
patient consideration ; and our minds are forced to the conclusion that under the law which must govern the court in weighing
the evidence, the charge of murder, as made by the indictment, can
not be sustained, and this settles the question as to the prisoner's
right to bail. It is neither required nor proper that we should
intimate an opinion, either as to the innocence of the accused,
if we entertain it, or as to any degree of manslaughter of which
he might be thought guilty. The question is unimportant so
far as the present application is concerned, whether the party be
wholly innocent, or whether the offense, if falling below the
crime of murder, be attended with aggravated circumstances ;
the result in either case is the same ; the party is entitled to his
liberty, and the court has nothing to do but to follow the mandate of the constitution on this subject and admit the party to
bail, on his giving, in the language of that instrument, good
securities. The provision of the constitution is as follows :
" That all prisoners shall, before conviction, be bailable by sufficient securities, except for capital offenses, where the proof is
evident or the presumption great." The inquiry is, whether the

proof in this case is evident, or the presumption great ; that is to say, is the offense, as shown by the whole testimony, one which must, under the law, be capitally punished ; for, if so, while a court might, in the exercise of a sound discretion, admit a party to bail, he could not certainly claim it as a right. But if the offense is not shown by evident proof or *great* presumption, to be one for the commission of which the law inflicts capital punishment, bail is not a matter of mere discretion with the court, but of right to the prisoner.

But we will proceed to state, with as little comment as possible on the testimony, the grounds of our opinion. We have seen, that the constitution requires that the proof must be evident, or the presumption great. *Evident proof*, or great presumption, of what?   That the offense as shown by the testimony, is one which the law denominates as capital.   When is a party committing a homicide guilty of a capital offence?   The answer is, when he is prompted by malice to commit the deed ;— for without malice there can be no murder ; and if in this case there is no murder, there is, of course, within the meaning of the constitution, no capital offense.   As no question can arise, under the testimony in this case, as to implied malice, we will inquire whether there is sufficient proof of express malice, or, in other words, whether the proof is evident, or the presumption, arising from the facts and circumstances, great.   "Express malice is when one, with a sedate, deliberate mind, and formed design, doth kill another; which formed design is evidenced by external circumstances, discovering that inward intention ; as lying in wait, antecedent menaces, former grudges, and concerted schemes to do him some bodily harm." 4 Black. Com., 199.   We will now, in a very brief manner, glance at the testimony ; keeping in view what has already been intimated, that as little of it as is possible to present the point, will be noticed, or made the subject of comment.   Brown, the deceased, was a teacher in the Male Academy at the town of Pontotoc ; two of the prisoner's younger brothers were pupils of this school; the younger brother had been, about a week before the killing, whipped by Brown ; but this does not appear to have been noticed by the prisoner.   About ten o'clock on the day of the killing, which occurred about twelve o'clock, or a few minutes thereafter, the elder of the two brothers was expelled from the school ; and the prisoner, being informed of what had occurred, applied to one or two persons for weapons ; manifesting at the time, both excitement and distress of mind. He stated, it seems, to all who approached, on this subject, that his object was to seek an explanation from Brown, and that if he had to have a difficulty with him, he should not use his weapons, but that if the school-boys, in the language of the testimony, "pitched in," he would use his weapons in defending himself.

After a conference with the president of the board of trustees, and being told by him that he, the prisoner, could go and see Brown, relative to the expulsion of the brother from the school, he repaired to the school-house and inquired for Mr. Brown. Being informed that he was busy, and could not be seen, the prisoner left a message that he would see Brown on his way to his boarding-house to dinner. School being a few minutes thereafter dismissed, Brown, informed of the message left by the prisoner, started to his boarding-house, travelling his usual path, or road. The parties met on this path—appeared to converse a short time, when the prisoner was heard to use an epithet, and was seen almost at the same moment to strike with his fist about the shoulder of the deceased. The deceased was almost at the same instant seen to draw from his side pocket, what the weight of evidence shows to be a whip, and with it, to strike the prisoner a severe blow on the head, felling him almost to the ground. The prisoner, catching to the clothes of the deceased, recovered from the fall, and commenced backing ; the deceased continuing to use this whip, and to follow up the prisoner. The evidence shows that he backed or retreated about thirty yards before getting out his weapon, with which he inflicted the mortal wounds on the body of the deceased. The testimony shows that the whip, in the hands of a strong man, was a formidable weapon, having in the butt-end about two and a half ounces of lead, covered in the usual way. This is as briefly as it can be stated, the substance of the evidence tending to prove malice.

Let it be conceded, that the fact of procuring weapons, going to the school-house, and waiting on the road, must be regarded as a circumstance tending to prove malice, if unexplained. But how is the testimony when accompanied by the whole explanation.

1. The declaration of the prisoner at the time of seeking the weapons, that he did not intend to use them on the deceased.

2. He commenced the difficulty by giving a moderate blow with his fist, thus indicating that his declaration was sincere, and consequently there was no sedate, deliberate mind, or formed design, to kill the deceased.

3. No attempt or effort was made to use his weapon in the difficulty, until the resistance had become altogether disproportioned to the assault, and until he was so closely pressed that he may be supposed to have acted as much, or more, from the instinct of man's nature, than from reason, or in carrying out a former design to kill his antagonist. The worst, under the whole evidence, that can be said against the prisoner, is, that a doubt may exist as to the malice; and if a well-founded doubt can even be entertained, then the proof can not be said to be evident nor the presumption great; and if our decision rested alone on this ground—a well-founded doubt—we should feel ourselves compelled to bail the prisoner.

Judgment reserved, and judgment in this court, admitting the prisoner to bail.

HANDY, J.:

Dissenting, as I do, from the opinion of the majority of the court, reversing the decision of the circuit judge in this case, I will proceed to state very briefly the reasons which, I think, lead to the conclusion, that the evidence in the record shows a clear case of murder.

The material facts of the case, as shown by the record, are briefly these:

The deceased was a school-teacher, in conjunction with a gentleman named Fearnster, in the town of Pontotoc, at whose school two of the brothers of the prisoner were pupils. Brown had punished one of the brothers for improper conduct in the school, and the other had resented it, and acted in such a manner, as to destroy the discipline and government of the school.

Upon consultation between the two teachers, it was determined that the case required expulsion, and accordingly, the pupil who had been guilty of the insubordination, was expelled, and he left the school, with great resentment towards Brown. This occurred on Monday morning, the 11th June, shortly after the school met. About ten o'clock of the same morning, the prisoner, an elder brother of the expelled pupil, came to the office of Drs. Fountain and Cain, in the same town, much excited, and wanted to borrow a pistol from Dr. Fountain, who asked him what he wanted with it, and he would not say. He made the same request of Dr. Cain ; and when asked by him what he wanted with it, replied : " he would see if he would let him have it," and mentioned the name of Brown in connection with the remark. Shortly after this, he went to the printing-office, and asked for a pistol, much agitated, and mentioning the name of Brown, and muttering something which was not understood by the witness. The witness, Heard, cautioned him to act prudently, and not lay himself liable to the law. He went into another room, where the witness had a bowie-knife and a pistol, and had the latter loaded, and came out, having these weapons upon him. As he came out, he said, that if he had a difficulty with Brown, he would use a stick, and if the boys interfered in Brown's behalf, he would use his weapons, to defend himself ; stating, in reply to an offer of a third party, to accompany and assist him in the difficulty, that he did not expect a difficulty. Upon being told, as he came back from the room where he had got the weapons, into the printing-office, that he had better take another pistol, which had been placed there, which was thought to be better than the one he had, he replied, that he was satisfied with what he had. He was next seen talking with Miller, the president of the board of trustees of the academy, who stated that he told the prisoner that he ought to see about his brother's expulsion from the school. Shortly after this, he went to the academy, and called Mr. Fearnster, and was very much agitated, and very angry, and requested to see Brown, in relation to the expulsion. Fearnster advised him to go away, and take time to deliberate and become cool. He urged his request to see Brown, saying that he " *wished to settle the difficulty now*." Upon being told that his seeing Brown would interrupt the school, he requested Fearnster to say to Brown, that he "would see him on his way to town or to dinner, when we will settle the difficulty." He then left, and his request was communicated to Brown, who desired Fearnster's advice, as to the course he ought to pursue; but he declined giving any advice, and they both left the academy together, shortly afterwards.

Brown left the academy, and walked on in the path he always walked, in going to his dinner. The prisoner had stationed himself on this path, and when he saw Brown approaching the place where he was, he accosted him, and the first word that was heard was, that the prisoner told him he had been imposing upon his brother. Brown replied, that he had whipped him upon very reasonable cause, and he would leave it to any reasonable man in the town. The prisoner then called him a damned dog. Brown stepped back, and the prisoner struck him with his fist, Brown's hand then hanging down by his side. Brown then took from his coat pocket a small leather whip, of flexible leather, which he was in the habit of wearing in his pocket, with a leathern handle, at the end of which there was lead, of about two ounces, or two and a half ounces weight. The witnesses speak of it as a small whip, and when they saw it in Brown's hand, some of them thought it a hickory withe. Upon receiving the blow, Brown commenced striking the prisoner over the head with the little end of the whip, and the prisoner striking with his fist, Brown continuing to advance upon him and striking him with the whip, and once when Brown struck him, he fell nearly to the ground; and when he got up, he commenced backing, and endeavoring to draw his weapon, Brown continuing to whip him over the head. So soon as the prisoner drew the bowie-knife, he commenced striking Brown with it, and in a short time Brown fell. The knife was about twelve inches long, and the blade seven or eight inches. Brown died very shortly of the wounds inflicted, which were six in number.

Dr. Fountain dressed the wounds of the prisoner, after the fight. He had a contused wound on the side of the head, extending to the bone, about half an inch long, and nearly as wide, supposed to be made by some blunt instrument; and some bruises on his shoulders and back,—some four or five.

The prisoner is not shown to have had any stick or cane, nor does it appear that there was any interference by the boys, in behalf of Brown.

The question which lies at the foundation of this case is, whether the evidence shows previous malice, on the part of the prisoner.

It seems to be considered by the majority of the court, that in order to constitute malice, it is necessary to show a previous settled purpose, absolutely to take away the life of the deceased, or a threat showing such an intention.

I think such a position wholly unsustained by authority, and unfounded in legal principle.

Malice, which is essential to murder, is defined by Blackstone, to be "any evil design in general, the dictate of a wicked, depraved, and malignant heart," and may exist without any fixed purpose to take the life of the individual. The evidences of this malice towards an individual, are lying in wait, antecedent menaces, former grudges, etc. 4 Black. Com., 199. Roscoe says, "the malice necessary to constitute the crime of murder, is not confined to an intention to take away the life of the deceased, but includes an intent to do any unlawful act which may probably end in depriving the party of life."

Roscoe Crim. Ev., 708, 4th Am. Ed.

Here, it seems to me, there cannot be a reasonable doubt that the prisoner had a previous grudge against the deceased, and that he lay in wait for him; either of which facts would be sufficient to show express malice. Laboring under a feeling of animosity and a desire for revenge for the alleged injury done to his brother, he is diligent in procuring the most deadly weapons—plainly indicating by his declarations, that he intended to seek a difficulty with the deceased. It is most probable that he intended to inflict some corporal punishment upon him, sufficient to disgrace him, and consider that, if submitted to, sufficient revenge for the alleged injury. This is the most favorable construction that can be put upon his conduct. But, if that was his expectation, it is manifest that he did not intend to make the experiment without being amply prepared, if necessary by a vigorous resistance, to take the life of his antagonist.

It is said that his declarations to Heard and Winston that he did not intend to have a difficulty, (by which, I suppose, it is understood that he did not intend to make an assault upon him with his bowie-knife and pistol, and his declining the proffered aid of Winston, who supposed from his conduct that he was about to enter into such a conflict,) show that he had no idea of provoking a difficulty which would end in the shedding of blood.

But this excuse for his conduct is altogether destroyed by his subsequent conduct. It might possibly have been true that, when he left the printing-office, he merely intended to chastise the deceased with a cane, and not to use his weapons, unless the boys interfered in behalf of the deceased. But his subsequent conduct when he called at the academy, his great excitement, and his declaration to Fearnster that he *wished to settle the difficulty then*, his appointing the place to meet the deceased, his conduct when they met, which altogether excludes the idea that he intended anything else than a personal conflict, and his failure to carry out his intention as declared, to use a stick and not to resort to his weapons, unless compelled by the interference of the pupils—all go clearly to show that he intended to bring on a conflict, and, if necessary by resistance, to use the weapons he had provided himself with against the deceased.

In the case of Green v. The State, it was held by this court that, "if the defendant went into the fight, having upon his person a deadly weapon, intending from the first to use the same, if necessary to enable him to overcome his antagonist, and did, in the fight, use the same and killed his antagonist, he is guilty of murder, although he habitually carried the weapon." Decided at April term, 1854, and not yet reported.

It appears to me that the mind cannot hesitate a moment in saying that all the terms of this rule are filled by the evidence in this case.

I take the rule to be sound and well-established that, whenever a party, having previous malice, provides himself with deadly weapons, intending to use them, if necessary, in a conflict, and he *provokes the conflict*, and uses the weapons, and kills his adversary, it is clearly murder. Roscoe Crim. Ev., 724. Whatever may have been his intention when he left the printing-office as to using the weapons, it is clear that he must have changed it; for he did not use the stick as he there said he intended to do, and his conduct after his visit to the academy is susceptible of no other view than that he then intended to bring on a personal conflict at all hazards, though it might end in blood, for which contingency he was fully prepared.

But, it is said that the killing is extenuated, because, in the conflict, he was hard pressed by the blows of the deceased, and only resorted to his weapon to defend himself against the fierceness of his adversary's blows; that the killing must be regarded as the result of that *furor brevis* produced by the violence of the assault upon him, and cannot be ascribed to the original malicious purpose shown by his conduct.

I dissent *in toto* from this view, and I do not think that a case can be found to support it, when the conflict was provoked by the prisoner, who had provided himself with deadly weapons, to be used, if necessary, except in some cases of mutual combat, and when the parties fight on equal terms; as was the case of the State v. Hill, 4 Dev. & Batt. Eq. Cases, 491. The true doctrine upon the subject is thus stated by Roscoe, 724: "It frequently becomes a most important question in the proof of malice, whether the act was done under the sudden influence of such a degree of provocation as to reduce the crime from murder to manslaughter. The indulgence shown to the *first transport* of passion in these cases, says Mr. Justice Foster, is plainly a condescension to the frailty of the human frame, to the *furor brevis*, which, while the frenzy lasts, renders the man deaf to the voice of reason. The provocation, therefore, which extenuates in the case of homicide, must be something that the man is conscious of, which he feels and resents at the instant the fact which he would extenuate is committed; not what time or accident may afterwards bring to light. Whenever death ensues from sudden transport of passion or heat of blood, *if upon a reasonable provocation* and *without malice,* or if upon a sudden combat, it will be manslaughter; if without such provocation, or, if the blood has had reasonable time or opportunity to cool, or *there be evi-*

dence of express malice, it will be murder ; *for, in no instance can a party, killing, alleviate his case by referring to a previous provocation, if it appear by any means that he acted upon express malice.   When the provocation is sought by the prisoner, it cannot furnish any defense against the charge of murder.*"

It appears to me that the circumstances of this case bring it fully within the condemnation of these just and salutary rules ; and, that the rule by which this case could be reduced to manslaughter, would be equally unsustained by authority, subversive of the wholesome penal laws of the state, and dangerous in the extreme to the peace and safety of society.

But the killing, in this case, cannot be reduced to manslaughter, even upon the principles applied to cases of mutual combat ; for, in order to lessen the crime of manslaughter in such cases, it must appear that the accused sought or took no unfair advantage. " To save the party making the first assault, upon an insufficient legal provocation, from the guilt of murder, the occasion must not only be sudden, but the party assaulted must be upon an equal footing, in point of defense at least, at the outset." Roscoe, 738. " But," says Mr. Justice Bayley, " if a party enters into a contest dangerously armed, and fights under an undue advantage, though mutual blows pass, it is not manslaughter, but murder." Whiteley's case, 1 Lewin C. C., 173, cited Roscoe 739. And this case falls fully within these rules.

In any view in which this case can be legally regarded, I think the evidence shows a clear and unmitigated case of murder, and that the circuit judge acted properly in refusing bail to the prisoner.

FOSTER *v.* THE STATE, 31 Miss. Rep., 421.

UNLAWFULLY TRADING WITH SLAVES.

The record should show affirmatively that the grand jury who found the indictment was duly sworn. The formal statement in the indictment itself, that they were sworn, is insufficient.

Error to Madison circuit court.　Henry, J.

No counsel appeared for plaintiff in error.

D. C. Glenn, attorney general.

Fisher, J.:

The plaintiff in error was indicted in the circuit court of Madison county, under the statute of 1850, to suppress trade and barter with slaves, and for other purposes, and was convicted on his trial in the court below.

On looking into the record, we deem it unnecessary to decide the points made by the attorney-general, on behalf of the state, in argument at the bar, as it does not appear by the record, that the grand jury, who found the indictment, were in any manner sworn to inquire in and for the body of the county of Madison. [1]

This is not now an open question in this court.

Judgment reversed and cause remanded.

Scott *v.* The State, 31 Miss. Rep., 473.

Indictment—Practice.

This court will not review the action of a circuit court, overruling a motion for a new trial, or giving instructions alleged to be erroneous, or any other matter assigned for error, unless the same shall have been properly excepted to in the court below.

An indictment under a statute must pursue the words of the statute, and aver all the facts and circumstances necessary to constitute the offense.　13 S. & M., 264; 23 Miss. Rep., p. 527.

In error, from the circuit court of Madison county.　Henry, J.

Lawson and *Tupper*, for plaintiff in error.

The indictment was founded on the statute for cruel or unusual punishment of slaves.　Hutch. Code, 519.

The indictment should have been quashed, because it does not show that defendant was master, or that he was entitled to the

---

[1] The caption of the indictment must show that the grand jury were sworn.　Archbold Cr. Pr. & Pl., 257; Jerry v. State, 1 Blackf., 395; Curtis v. People, 1 Breese, 197; Hoffman v. Commonwealth, 6 Rand., 685; People v. Guernsey, 3 Johns. C., 265; Woodsides v. State, 2 How., 655; State v. Fields, Peck, 140; State v. Hunter, ib., 166.

services of the slave, but simply states that he was overseer; it does not contain the statutory offense; indictments, founded on statutes, must pursue the precise and technical language employed in the statute, in the definition or description of the offense. Anthony v. State, 13 S. & M., 264; Ike v. The State, 28 Miss. R., 527; 4 Porter, 410; 1 Chitty Crim. Law, 250, 282.

It may be urged that the defendants could have been indicted, and the indictment is good, under the first sentence of the paragraph, "That no cruel or unusual punishment shall be inflicted on any slave in this state." We think the whole section must be taken together, and the subsequent part qualifies the first; one of the cardinal rules, for the interpretation of statutes, is to look at the old law for the mischief and the remedy. By the old or common law, all persons, except those having the right to control the slave, were liable to indictment for assault and battery on him. Law of Slavery, 239; State v. Hale, 2 Hawks N. C. R., 582.

The master or other person entitled to his services was not liable to be punished for cruelty. Law of Slavery, 244. State v. Mann, 2 Devereux (N. C.) R., 263.

The mischief was, that those who had the control of slaves could not be indicted for cruel or unusual punishment.

The law afforded a remedy, by subjecting them to indictment, and applies only to them as strangers were before the law liable to indictment. The overseer has an authority, delegated from the master, to control the slaves, and inflict punishment to correct them. The overseer could not be indicted at common law, for chastising the slaves, if the master could not; and that the master could not, see the able opinion in the case of State v. Mann, above cited.

If the overseer be not punishable under the term, "or other person entitled to the service," then his is an omitted case, and, if so, cannot be supplied by the judiciary. Dwarris on Statutes, 53.

To the legislature belongs the power to declare the crime and fix the punishment. Smith Com., 861, 865.

F. Smith, on same side.

The plaintiff in error was indicted on the following statute, to wit :

"No cruel or unusual punishment shall be inflicted on any slave in this state. And any master or other person, entitled to the service of any slave, who shall inflict such cruel or unusual punishment, or shall authorize or permit the same to be inflicted, shall, etc., be fined, etc." Hutch. Code, 519, § 44.

The indictment in this case is sustainable on the first clause of the statute. Supposing the words of the latter clause not to be pursued, the contempt of, or disobedience to, the general prohibitory clause is an indictable offense. Every contempt of a statute which prohibits any thing in general terms, is indictable. Dwarris on Statutes, 9th vol. of Law Library, 33, 34, 89.

1. The attempt to indict under the particular clause, and failing to pursue the words, which make such words as would not be required in drawing an indictment on the general clause surplusage, this is the only effect it could have.

2. In South Carolina, it has been decided that a man is indictable for an assault and battery on another's slave, and that such is a good indictment at common law, according to a well-established canon in criminal law ; if there was a common-law offense prior to the making of the statute, the statutory offense was merely cumulative, and if the indictment be not, from bad pleading, a proper indictment, as a statutory indictment, it will be good as a common-law indictment. The words used in the indictment show, at common law, what would be termed an aggravated assault. Dwarris on Statutes, 9th vol. Law Library, 33, 34.

3. But the statutory words in the latter clause of the statute are sufficiently specific in this indictment ; the indictment alleges that Richard Scott, being then and there the overseer of a certain slave by the name of Bob, unlawfully did, then and there inflict cruel punishment upon said slave, etc.

4. The term overseer, *ex vi termini*, satisfies the statutory definition of "a person entitled to the service of a slave." State v. Borroum et al., 1 Cushm. Miss. Rep., 477, 482.

A motion was made in arrest of judgment. One reason assigned was that the verdict did not show on which count it was founded, there being two counts in the indictment.

It is allowable to include two counts in an indictment, and a general verdict thereon will be sustained. Wilbourn v. State, 8 S. & M., 348 ; Morris v. State, ib., 772.

The only mode the prisoner had to except to the joinder of two counts in the same indictment was, a motion to compel the district attorney to elect which of the counts he would proceed on, on the ground that such election was due to the prisoner, to prevent his being embarrassed on the trial of his case. Brantley v. The State, 13 S. & M, 470.

There was a motion to quash the indictment, but no such ground was taken or stated ; and a point not presented to the court below cannot be adjudicated upon in an appellate court. Dyson v. The State, 4 Cushm. Miss. Rep., 391.

There is no position better commended, or more fully established in the law, than the last.

As to the motion for a new trial : the testimony was fairly before the jury, the credibility of the witnesses known to them ; and there can be no pretence, it appears to me, to say that there is a clear preponderance of evidence against the verdict. There is as strong evidence for as against the verdict ; at least, the requisite state of things to give a new trial does not exist ; there is neither great preponderance of evidence against the verdict, nor is the verdict without evidence at all.

There were five charges asked for by the state, and eight asked for by the defendant. The court granted them all, and fairly presented the law to the jury. Whatever misruling or mistakes were made, it is manifest that on the whole record the law has been administered and justice has been done.

D. C. Glenn, attorney general.

SMITH, C. J. :

The plaintiff in error was indicted, in the circuit court of Madison county, for inflicting cruel punishment upon a slave, in violation of the statute. The indictment contained two counts. The first charged, that the prisoner, being then and there the overseer of a certain slave by the name of Boh, unlawfully did then and there inflict cruel punishment upon the said slave, said slave being then and there the property of Lawson F. Henderson, in the manner following; setting out the character and the manner in which the alleged punishment was inflicted. The second count charged the prisoner with having, at divers times, before the finding of the bill of indictment, unlawfully inflicted cruel punishment upon other slaves of the said Henderson, the prisoner being, at the time, the overseer of the same.

A motion was made to quash the indictment, which was overruled, and the cause submitted to a jury, who returned a general verdict of guilty. A motion was then interposed in arrest of judgment, which being disallowed, the prisoner moved for a new trial. First, Because the court, in behalf of the prosecution, gave erroneous instructions to the jury; and Second, Because the verdict was contrary to law and evidence. This motion was overruled, and the defendant sued out a writ of error to this court.

It is now contended that the conviction and judgment were erroneous, for the following reasons: 1st, Because the court erred in overruling the motion to quash the indictment; 2d, Because the court erred in overruling the motion in arrest of judgment; and lastly, Because there was error in the decision of the court on the motion for a new trial.

1. We shall notice, first, the question raised upon the motion for a new trial.

There was no exception, as shown by the record taken in the court below, to the judgment of the court on the motion for a new trial. This was an indispensable prerequisite to a revision of the question of the alleged invalidity of the decisions on that motion. Hutch. Dig., art. 7, § 1. Nor were the instructions, granted at the request of the prosecuting attorney, excepted to. We cannot, therefore, notice the alleged error committed by the court in granting these instructions, as connected with either the propriety of the finding or the supposed error committed in overruling the motion. We pass, therefore, to the only questions properly presented by the record. These arise upon the motion to quash and the motion in arrest of judgment.

2. The questions presented by these motions are substantially the same, with the exception of the last ground taken in support of the motion in arrest of judgment; that is, that the indictment contains two counts, and it does not appear on which of these counts the verdict was founded; we will consider the subject in addition to the ground above stated; they are that the "indictment was founded on the statute, and does not contain the statutory words necessary to constitute the offense as defined by the statute;" and that the "indictment does not contain any charge that is punishable under the statute, nor does it specify any crime indictable at common law."

The indictment under which the prisoner was convicted is framed upon the statute concerning slaves, free negroes and mulattoes, passed in 1822, the 44th section of which provides that "no cruel or unusual punishment shall be inflicted on any slave within this state. And any master or any person entitled to the service of any slave, who shall inflict such cruel or unusual punishment, or shall authorize or permit the same to be inflicted, shall, on conviction thereof," etc. Hutch. Dig., 519.

The first clause of this statute makes it criminal for any one to inflict cruel punishment on a slave within this state. Generally an act committed in contempt or violation of the general prohibitory clause of a penal statute is indictable at common law. And hence it is contended, in support of the judgment, that as the indictment was framed upon the first clause, it should be sustained as an indictment at common law, although it should be found to be insufficient as an indictment upon the statute. But passing this question, let us notice the exception urged by counsel for the prisoner; that is, that the facts and circumstances which constitute the offense created by the statute, are not, with sufficient certainty, alleged in the indictment.

The rule on this subject is well settled in this court. An indictment upon a statute must state all the circumstances which constitute the definition of the offense in the act, so as to bring the accused judicially within it. It should be clear and certain to every intent, and pursue the precise language of the statute.[1] 13 S. & M., 264; 23 Miss. R., 527.

[1] Wharton Am. Cr. Law, 364; State v. Gibbons, 1 Southard, 51; State v. Calvin,

It is not controverted that the act alleged to have been committed by the plaintiff in error was that which is denounced and intended to be punished, or that the indictment does charge with the requisite degree of precision and certainty the facts and circumstances which amount in law to the offense of cruel or unusual punishment of a slave ; but it is contended that the averments of the indictment do not bring the defendant within the class or classes of persons against whom the penalty contained in the statute is denounced ; in other words, that the defendant is not brought judicially within the act.

It is averred in the indictment that the prisoner, " being then and there the overseer of a certain slave named Bob, unlawfully did then and there inflict cruel punishment upon the said slave, the said slave being then and there the property of one Lawson F. Henderson, in the manner following, to wit," etc.

This description of the party charged with the commission of the offense is sufficient. It brings him judicially within the statute. The term " overseer of a slave," according to its statutory import, means a person who, as agent or employee of another, has a right to command the obedience, and, of course, is entitled to the services of the slave placed under his charge. It was manifestly not the intention of the legislature to confine the punishment prescribed in the act to the owner, master or other persons entitled beneficially to the services of the slave who might inflict cruel or unusual punishment upon him, but to include all descriptions of persons having the charge, management or control of slaves. To exempt overseers from the penalties of the act, upon the ground that they are not beneficially interested in, or do not own the labor of the slaves committed to their charge, would, to a great extent, defeat the benign and salutary purposes of the law. The objections urged, and mainly relied on in the argument, that it was essential that the indictment should allege that the party charged was the master, or was en-

Charlton, 151; 1 Hale, 517, 526, 585; Staunf., 130, b.; Foster, 423, 434; Hard., 2; Dyer, 304; Kelyng, 8; Com. Dig. Just. G., 1; 1 Chitty on Pl., 357; Moore. 5; 1 Leach, 264; 1 East P. C., 419; 2 Hale, 170, 189, 190, 193; 1 Eliz., c. 1, § 26; 3 Dyer, 363; 2 Lord Raym., 791; 2 Burr, 679; 1 T. R., 222; U. S. v. Lancaster, 2 McLean, 431; People v. Allen, 5 Denio, 76; Com. v. Hampton, 3 Gratt., 590; State v. Pratt, 20 La., 191.

titled, as the beneficiary or owner, to the services of the slave, is wholly without foundation.

3. The last exception, that it does not appear on which of the counts in the indictment the verdict was based, is untenable.

The verdict was general. The prisoner was found guilty, therefore, upon each of the counts in the indictment. And as neither of the counts was defective, and might, with perfect propriety, be included in the same indictment, there is no ground whatever for the objection.

Judgment affirmed.

SAM v. THE STATE, 31 Miss. Rep., 480.

HOMICIDE.

Under the constitution of 1832, and the laws in force in 1855, the governor of this state had power to fill vacancies in the office of circuit judge by temporary appointment, till the election and qualification of a judge should occur; and this, although the unexpired term exceeded one year, and no special election had been ordered. Per HANDY, J.

After verdict it appeared that one of the jury had prejudged the case, although he had stated on his *voir dire* that he had formed or expressed no opinion. *Held* that the accused was entitled (under the rule laid over, in Nelson's case, 13 S. & M., 509, and Cotton's case, 31 Miss., 504) to a new trial. HANDY, J., *dissented.*

The credibility of witnesses swearing to a juror's prejudgement of the issue was to be determined entirely by the court to whom the application for a new trial was addressed. The court was to consider the characters and positions of the juror and witnesses respectively, and the manner and circumstances of the juror's statements on his *voir dire*, and from these evidences to determine; and a determination thus made should stand. Per HANDY, J., *dissenting.*

In error from the circuit court of Warren County. YERGER, J.

The prisoner was indicted for murder in the circuit court of Issaquena county, at the November term, A. D. 1855, thereof; which court was holden before the Hon. John M. Moore, who had received a temporary appointment from the governor, to supply the vacancy occurring from the death of the Hon. J. I. Guion. At a subsequent term of the court, holden by the Hon. J. S. Yerger, the prisoner pleaded in abatement to the indictment, that the said term of the court at which he was indicted, was illegal in this, that John I. Guion was elected judge of the district in which that county was situated, in November, A. D. 1853, for the term of four years; that said Guion died on the 10th day of June, 1855, leaving an unexpired term of more than one year; that the governor immediately had notice thereof; that on the 8d day of July, A. D. 1855, he appointed said John M. Moore judge of said district; that the governor did not issue a writ for an election of a successor to said Guion, as required by law, and that said term of the court at which he was indicted, was holden on the 12th day of November, A. D. 1855, after the Hon. J. S. Yerger had been elected judge of said district.

To this plea the state, by the district attorney, filed the following replication: "And the said State of Mississippi, by Richards Barnett, acting as district attorney, for the third judicial district of the State of Mississippi, comes, and for replication to said plea of the said defendant Sam, by him above pleaded, says, that the said State of Mississippi, for anything in the said plea alleged, ought not to be precluded from having or maintaining her aforesaid indictment against the said defendant Sam, or from further prosecuting the same; because the said State of Mississippi says, that true it is, that a vacancy did occur in the office of circuit judge of the third judicial district of the State of Mississippi, (in which said district, said county of Issaquena is included,) by the death of the Hon. J. I. Guion, the late judge thereof, on the 10th day of June, A. D. 1855, and that at the time of the death of the said John I. Guion, there was unexpired, more than one year of the term of office for which said Guion was elected, as alleged in said defendant's plea. And the said State of Mississippi further admits that the governor thereof, on the 8d day of July, A. D. 1855, and after the death of the said Guion, did, as alleged in said plea, have notice of said death, and to fill the vacancy occasioned thereby, did, afterwards, to-wit, on the day and year last aforesaid, duly appoint and commission John M. Moore, Esq., as judge of the third judicial district as aforesaid, and that the said Moore accepted said appointment, and was duly qualified as such judge, and was duly authorized and empowered to hold the circuit courts in and for the several counties of the said third judicial district of the said state, ineluding the circuit court of the county of Issaquena aforesaid, from the time of his being commissioned and qualified as aforesaid, until his successor should be duly elected and qualified according to law ; and that the said John M. Moore, acting under the appointment so made as aforesaid, did, as judge of said third judicial district of the State of Mississippi, on the second Monday of November, A. D. 1855, being the 12th day of said month, and the time appointed by law for holding said court, and before his successor was commissioned and qualified according to law, hold the said term of the circuit court of Issaquena county, as he had authority and right to do, and not contrary to the statute in such cases made and provided, as is alleged in said plea, and at which term of said court so held by said John M. Moore, as aforesaid, the said defendant was indicted as in his plea is alleged, all which the said State of Mississippi is ready to verify. Wherefore," etc.

The defendant moved the court to strike out the replication, which the court refused to do. He then filed his general demurrer to the replication, which being overruled, he pleaded not guilty.

Upon the application of the prisoner, the venue was changed to Warren county ; and at the June term, 1856, of the circuit court of that county, he was tried and convicted of murder. He then moved the court for a new trial, "because one of the jurors—one E. R. Wells—who was empanelled to try him at the present term of the court (and by which said jury he was convicted) had said before he was sworn and empanelled in said cause as a juror, in the presence of witnesses, that said defendant was guilty as charged, and ought to be hung."

On the trial of this motion, he read to the court the affidavits of Charles A. Harris and Charlotte M. Hayes, in which they severally deposed that on the day previous to the trial of the cause, the said E. R. Wells, one of the jurors, who was empanelled to try the prisoner, stated in their hearing, and in the hearing of others, "That if the evidence in the cause should be the same as that given on a previous trial, which he had heard, that the defendant was guilty of murder, and ought to be hung." The prisoner and his counsel each made their affidavits, in which they severally deposed that they knew nothing of the said declarations of the said Wells, until after the trial of the cause. It was further shown that the juror, Wells, was examined on his *voir dire* before he was accepted and empanelled as a juror, and that he then denied that he had formed or expressed an opinion as to the guilt or innocence of the prisoner. The district attorney offered as rebutting evidence, the affidavit of said Wells, in which he deposed that he had not made the statement attributed to him by the witnesses Harris and Hayes; but this affidavit, upon objection by the prisoner, the court ruled as incompetent evidence, and refused to consider it. No other evidence was offered by either party, and the court overruled the motion.

The prisoner sued out this writ of error.

H. A. H. Lawson, for the prisoner, made the following points:

1. A new trial should have been granted, because the prisoner was not tried by an impartial jury. The proof shows clearly that the juror, Wells, had previously expressed an opinion, formed from hearing the evidence, that the prisoner was guilty. See Whart. Am. Cr. Law, 1022; Childress v. Ford, 10 S. & M., 25; The People v. Vermilyea, 7 Cow. R. 128; Sam v. The State, 13 S. & M., 189; Nelms v. The State, ib., 500; Cody v. The State, 3 How. (Miss.), 27.

2. The court in which the prisoner was indicted was illegally constituted. Under the circumstances, the appointment of John M. Moore, Esq., as judge, was void. See Constitution of Mississippi, art. 4, § 13; ib., art. 5, § 13; Hutch. Code, 164.

D. C. Glenn, attorney general.

It is urged that Sam had not a fair trial, because Wells, a juror, declared his opinion before trial, that if the evidence turned out as on a former trial, Sam ought to be hung. This fact is proved by several witnesses, and Sam swears he was ignorant of it until after his trial was over. The juror was offered by the state to prove the reverse, but the court refused to hear his affidavit.

It is true, that when it appears, after the trial, the juror had prejudged the case, it is good ground for a new trial. See 2 Salk., 645; 1 Denio, 281; 1 Wharton State Tr. 606; 7 Cowan, 108; 1 Leigh, 598; 9 Dana, 203; 19 Ohio, 198.

A qualified opinion, however—such as the one in question—dependent on a particular state of facts, will be no ground for a new trial. 2 Virg. Cases, 510, 516; 5 Rand., 655; 7 Watts & Serg., 421; 1 Yeates, 378.

The court should have received the affidavit of the juror. 3 Greenl., 204; 1 Wharton State Tr., 606.

FISHER, J.:

Upon the point, as to the refusal of the court below to grant a new trial in this case, we are of opinion that the court erred. The case we conceive falls clearly within the rule laid down by this court in the case of Nelson v. The State, 13 S. & M., 500; and of Cotton v. The State. The affidavits, supposing them to have received full credit by the court, and nothing appears to the contrary, must be taken and treated as placing the juror in the same attitude in which he would have stood, if he had stated the facts deposed to, himself in open court, when brought forward as a juror, and examined, touching his fitness to sit on the trial of the prisoner.

Judgment reversed, and new trial granted.

HANDY, J., dissenting:

Two questions are presented in this case. First. Whether in case of the death of a circuit judge, whose term of office has more than one year to run, the governor has power to appoint a judge to discharge the duties of the office, until an election to fill the vacancy be held. Second. Whether the court erred in overruling the motion for a new trial based upon the affidavits, showing that one of the jurors who tried the cause had prejudged it, to the prejudice of the prisoner.

1. The 13th section of the fifth article of the constitution provides, that "all vacancies not provided for in the constitution shall be filled in such manner as the legislature after the adoption of the constitution shall provide. An act was passed providing that "whenever any vacancy shall occur in any state office, when the unexpired term thereof shall have more than one year to run, it shall be the duty of the governor when notified of such vacancy to issue a writ of election, requiring an election to be

held to fill the unexpired term of said office in the particular district or in the state, which election shall be held in the case of filling any vacancy in the office of a district officer, on thirty days' notice; and in case of a state or general officer, on sixty days' notice, provided however, that the governor of the state may make a temporary appointment to any office, a vacancy in which occurs, to have effect and be in force until the election so ordered by him shall have been held, and the successor or person elected to the office be duly qualified in the manner prescribed by this act." Hutch. Dig., 164.

The appointment in question in this case having been made in virtue of the proviso of this act, its validity would appear to be clear and unquestionable.

But it is objected. First. That it was the duty of the governor immediately on receiving notice of the death of the incumbent, to order an election to be held, on thirty days' notice, and that the temporary appointment could not extend beyond the period at which the election was required to be held, and until the new judge should be qualified; and that as the notice of the vacancy under consideration, was received by him in June, and the election was not held until November, the appointment was void.

We do not consider this a proper view of the statute. In providing that it should "be the duty of the governor *when* notified of such vacancy," to order the election, the term *when* was doubtless intended to refer to the *condition* upon which the election should be ordered, and not prescribe *the time* when it should be ordered; and it should be understood as if the language was *upon being notified.* This is frequently the sense of the word in technical language.

Again, it is objected that the governor has no power to make a temporary appointment, until he has first issued the writ of election, and fixed the day on which the election shall be held. But the statute does not in terms render the performance of the former duty dependent upon the performance of the latter. It is made the duty of the executive generally to issue a writ of election to fill the vacancy, when the unexpired term shall exceed one year; and, as above shown, this duty must be per-

formed *upon his being notified* of the vacancy.   The proviso
then confers the power to make a temporary appointment, to
continue in force until election *so ordered* shall have been held, .
and the successor qualified.   What is to be understood by the
terms "so ordered?"   They do not mean that the election must
be ordered at the time of his receiving notice of the vacancy, as
is above shown.   It can only, therefore, be understood to mean,
that the temporary appointment shall continue in force until
the election, which the executive in the preceding part of the
act is required to order, shall have been held, etc.

It is certainly his duty to order the election in good faith and
without necessary delay ; and we think, that the spirit of the
law, and of the constitution, required it should be ordered speedily.
He may not perform his duty in this respect with proper diligence. But this does not necessarily render a temporary appointment made by him void.

Nor is the fixing of the day of election previous to making
the temporary appointment necessary, in order to fix the period
for which the appointee shall hold the office.   For if the election
be ordered within such time as a faithful performance of that
duty by the executive requires, the appointee is bound to take
notice of the time so appointed for the election, and also, of the
fact of the election and qualification of his successor ; and it is
not necessary that the period of the election shall be specified
in the commission.

The special appointment must be presumed to have been
made because the governor considered that the emergency of the
public interest required it to be made ; and the power to determine the question of the necessity for the appointment, is conferred upon him by law.   He is also required to order an election to fill the vacancy.   But it appears to me, that neither by
the terms of the statute nor by the reason upon which the two
acts are required to be performed, does the validity of the former
act depend upon the previous performance of the latter.

Another objection is founded on the fifth section of the fourth
article of the constitution, which is, that " all vacancies that may
occur in said court," (that is the high court of errors and appeals,) " from death, etc., shall be filled by election as aforesaid,

provided however, that if the unexpired term do not exceed one year, the vacancy shall be filled by executive appointment." The word "*court*" in this section is sometimes, but erroneously, printed in some prints of the constitution "*courts*." But both the context and the correct prints of the constitution show that the high court of errors and appeals only is referred to ; and as this objection rests solely upon the assumption that other courts were referred to, it is fully answered by the correct print of the constitution.

But, moreover, this provision of the constitution referred to the election or appointment of a judge, to fill the entire unexpired term. If that term exceed one year, it is required to be filled by election, which cannot be held without notice of thirty days. During that period, there would be an *interregnum*, or temporary vacancy in the office, not contemplated or embraced by this section of the constitution, and which the public interest might imperatively require to be supplied ; and this case, not being especially provided for in the constitution, is embraced by the 13th section of article 5th, and the act of 1833, passed in pursuance of that section ; by which the power to make a temporary appointment until the election and qualification of the successor, is conferred upon the executive.

2. In support of the motion for a new trial, the prisoner introduced the affidavits of two witnesses, stating that on a day previous to the trial of the case at that term, they had heard E. R. Wells, one of the jurors who tried the case, and returned the verdict, say that if the evidence on the trial should be the same as that given upon a previous trial of the same case, and which said juror had heard, the prisoner was guilty of murder, and should be hung ; also, the affidavits of the prisoner and of his counsel who defended him on that trial, that they did not know until since trial, that the said Wells, or any of the jurors, had expressed any opinion in relation to the prisoner's guilt.

It appears to be well settled, that if, after the trial, it appears that a juror had prejudged the case, but had stated on his *voir dire* falsely that he had not formed or expressed an opinion upon it, and that the prisoner who was prejudiced thereby, was ignorant of the fact at the time, a new trial will be granted.

Wharton Amer. Crim. Law, (2nd ed.,) 905, and cases there cited ; 1 Graham & Wat. on New Trials, 129.

But a qualified opinion, dependent on a particular state of facts, will not be a ground for a new trial.   As where the juror said, that if the prisoner killed the man, he ought to be hanged. Commonwealth v. Hughes, 5 Rand., 655 ; or that if the prisoner had made the attempt to commit the crime charged against him, he ought to go to the penitentiary.   Kennedy v. Commonwealth, 2 Virg. Cases, 510.

If it appeared by the record that the judgment of the court below, overruling the motion for a new trial, was based solely upon the ground that the opinion of the juror, as shown by the affidavits, was qualified and hypothetical, we could not sanction that view.

It clearly appears, from the affidavits, taking them to be true and entitled to entire credit, that the juror had formed the opinion, *from having heard the testimony* on a previous trial of the prisoner, that he was guilty ; that the opinion must have rested upon his mind at the time he made the declaration ; and, if he spoke truth, it is impossible to conceive but that he had formed an opinion that it would have required testimony to remove ; the opinion expressed could not be said to be dependent upon the fact that the prisoner's guilt should be established, and was therefore not hypothetical ; but it was certain and fixed in the mind, and dependent on its being carried out, only on the fact that the same evidence should be introduced on the trial then to be had, which had been adduced on a previous trial.

But it does not appear by the record, that the motion for a new trial was denied on this ground, nor upon any particular ground.   And, therefore, if there be any ground on which the court might have refused the motion, it must be presumed that the court acted on that ground.

The question of the credibility of the witnesses who had sworn as to the juror's expression of opinion, was to be determined entirely by the court.   It was a matter submitted to its sound, legal discretion.   It was the duty of the judge to consider closely the character and position of the witnesses, which may have been known to him, and the character of the juror, the circumstances under which he may have been elected and empanelled on the jury, and the examination to which he may have been subjected at that time, and to determine from all these facts and circumstances whether the witnesses should be credited. It was competent for him to determine, from these circumstances, as well as from his own knowledge of the characters of the witnesses and of the juror, that they should not be credited. The State v. Duestoe, 1 Bay., 380. If this was not true, any party convicted of crime would readily be able to procure some corrupt witness, whose character was not sufficiently known to the community at large, to cause the proper legal testimony to impeach his credit to be adduced, to come forward and swear, that any one of the jurors had made use of declarations of the prisoner's guilt. These declarations could easily be stated to have been made under such circumstances that no witness could be adduced to disprove them ; and if the affidavit of the juror would not be admissible for that purpose, it might be impossible to counteract the legal effect of the false statement of such a witness, and a most serious blow would be struck at the whole criminal jurisprudence of the country. Every verdict, however just and fairly made, would be liable to be set aside upon testimony not intrinsically entitled to credit ; and the facility with which this might be done, would endanger every verdict. From the nature of the case, therefore, the judge must have the power to scrutinize the testimony, and to settle the question of the credibility of the witnesses. If the court refused the motion upon this ground, it was, therefore, a matter within its legal discretion ; and as every presumption must be indulged in favor of the propriety of the judgment, which is not removed by the record, it must be taken that the court acted properly on this ground.

This presumption is much strengthened, when we consider the fact that the affidavits of these witnesses was in direct contradiction of the sworn statements of the juror, made when he was tried and elected as a juror, so that the question of the credit due to the respective parties must have been directly presented for the determination of the court, and may be very justly taken to have been the formation of its action.

I am, therefore, of the opinion, on the first point, that the judgment is correct, and on the second point, that we should not be warranted in declaring it wrong ; and that the judgment should be affirmed.

Weeks *v.* The State, 31 Miss. Rep., 490.

Homicide.

It is unnecessary for the record to show that the grand jury were summoned at least five days before the commencement of the term of the court, or that the members thereof were over twenty-one and under sixty years of age, or that they were taken equally from each police district in the county.

The legislature, in requiring the sheriff to summon twenty men to serve as grand jurors, did not intend thereby to designate the number of which the grand jury should be composed, but only to provide a body of men, out of whom a grand jury should be selected, and it will not be error, if the whole twenty who are in attendance on the court, be not empanelled on the grand jury.

The indictment, after reciting the state and county and the term of the court, and averring that " the grand jurors of the State of Mississippi, being good and lawful men of the county of W., aforesaid, and being then and there duly elected, empanelled, and sworn," etc., is sufficient to show that the grand jury was composed of duly qualified men.

The return of the sheriff upon a special *venire*, " executed by summoning seventy-five men, as within, to pass as jurors in the case of The State v. H. Weeks," accompanied by a list of the men, is sufficient ; it need not be stated in the return that the jurors are good and lawful men of the county.

A continuance should not be granted on account of the absence of a material witness, unless the affidavit shows that proper efforts were made to secure his attendance, and that they failed.

If the court should improperly refuse to grant an application for a continuance on account of the absence of a material witness, the error will be cured if the witness appear during the progress of the trial and testify in the cause.

In a criminal case, the accused has no right to demand that a change of venue be granted upon his mere *ex-parte* showing, made in accordance with the statute ; the court has the right to examine other witnesses as to the grounds upon which the application is based, and if, upon such examination, the court is satisfied that the accused can have a fair and impartial trial in the county where he was indicted, it is not only his right but his duty to refuse the application.

Error to the circuit court of Winston County.　Henry, J.

The plaintiff in error was indicted in the court below, at the September term thereof, A.D. 1855, for the murder of one Willis Norris, and at the same term was convicted and sentenced to be hung.

The record recites, " that the sheriff returned into open court a list of the following named persons, good and lawful men, citizens of the United States and residents of said county of Winston, summoned by him, according to law, to serve as grand jurors during the present term of the court, to wit :" (here the names of twenty men are inserted). " And the said jurors so returned, having appeared in open court, it was ordered by the court that sixteen of said jurors be drawn and empanelled to serve as grand jurors, etc., and thereupon the clerk and sheriff proceeded to draw said grand jury according to law, etc., whereupon the following named persons were drawn as aforesaid," (naming them). The record then shows that a foreman was appointed, and that the grand jury was regularly sworn and a bailiff appointed and sworn.

The record further recited, as follows : " This day came the grand jury into open court, under the charge of their proper officer, and through their foreman, James W. Wilcox, returned into open court a bill of indictment against the following named person, for the following named offense, to wit :

<blockquote>
" The State of Mississippi   Indorsed a true bill, by
     v.   Murder.   James W. Wilcox,
Harvey Weeks.   foreman of the grand jury.
</blockquote>

" Whereupon the jury retired," etc.

Then follows in the record a copy of an indictment against Harvey Weeks, for the murder of Willis Norris, with the following indorsement thereupon : " Prosecutor George W. Norris, A true bill. James W. Wilcox, foreman of the grand jury."

The statement of the indictment, in reference to the grand jury, is as follows :

<blockquote>
" The State of Mississippi,
     Winston county.
</blockquote>

" In the circuit court of said county, at the September term thereof, in the year of our Lord, one thousand eight hundred and fifty-five.

" The grand jurors of the State of Mississippi, being good and lawful men of the county of Winston aforesaid, and being then and there duly elected, empanelled, sworn and charged to inquire in and for the body of the county of Winston aforesaid, in the name and by the authority of the State of Mississippi, upon their oaths present," etc.

A special *venire* was issued, commanding the sheriff to summon seventy-five good and lawful men of the county " to be passed upon as jurors in the case of the State of Mississippi v. Harvey Weeks." A list of seventy-five persons was appended by the sheriff to the writ, and he thereupon made the following return : " Received and executed by summoning seventy-five men as within, to pass as jurors in the case of The State v. Harvey Weeks."

An application was made by the prisoner for a continuance, for the want of a witness, Wm. Goyne. The affidavit of the prisoner upon which this application was based, after reciting the absence of the witness and the materiality of his testimony, gives as a reason of his non-attendance, " That the prisoner has been confined in the jail of Lowndes county since a short time after his arrest and imprisonment, and has had but little opportunity of conferring with his counsel, or to procure testimony for his defense ;" but it shows no effort to have the witness subpoenaed. The record also shows that this witness was present at the trial and testified on behalf of the prisoner.

The prisoner, before he was put on his trial, made an application for a change of venue. This application was based on his own written affidavit, supported by that of two witnesses, to the effect that, owing to the prejudice in the public mind in Winston county against the prisoner, he could not have in that county a fair and impartial trial for the offense with which he was charged.

The record then recites that, upon the consideration of this motion, H. Goyne (one of the affiants for a change of venue) and three other witnesses " were introduced and duly sworn and examined, touching the change of venue in this case," etc., . . " and that, after a full investigation, the court being fully satisfied from the evidence of these witnesses, that the prisoner could have a fair and impartial trial in said county of Winston, and that no cause exists for a change of venue," refused the application.

The testimony of these witnesses is not set out in the record.

On the trial, the state proved by Mrs. Jane Norris, the widow of the deceased, that some two or three weeks previous to the killing of her husband, there originated a state of unfriendly feeling between her husband and Hiram Weeks, the father, and William Goyne, the brother-in-law of the prisoner; that they abused him, and offered him violence at his own house. That some few days thereafter, and some twelve or fifteen days before the killing, she and her husband met the prisoner, and he refused to speak to them; that on Sunday evening, the 25th day of March, 1855, being the day before the killing, the prisoner and Hiram Weeks, and William Goyne, passed the residence of her husband in company; that on the same evening and before nightfall, Hiram Weeks and William Goyne returned, and stopped at the gate, and "cursed, and abused, and denounced her husband;" that Goyne tried to ride his horse over him, and challenged him to go out from his house and fight; that she interfered, and by her importunities suppressed any "further difficulty;" and Goyne and Hiram Weeks then left.

That on the morning of the 26th of March, 1855, about eight or nine o'clock, the prisoner came to her husband's house; that he walked thither, and was dressed in black; had on a black frock coat and a black fur hat; that prisoner and her husband remained about the house and yard, talking about swapping horses, until about 11 o'clock A.M., when her husband took his ox-cart and went to his new ground, a short distance from the house, to bring a load of wood; that prisoner went with him; that owing to the unfriendly feeling existing between them, and the conduct of Goyne and Hiram Weeks on the day before, she kept a watch on prisoner, both whilst at the house and after he left and went to the new ground; that she saw him with her husband on the new ground; that just before the killing she saw her husband squatted down and Weeks standing near him. They appeared to be in conversation about something. They were in this position at twelve o'clock M., when she went to the door and called her husband to come to dinner. Her husband answered, and she turned round to go back into the house, and had taken but one step, when she heard a gun or pistol fire in the direction of her husband and the prisoner; she immediately turned and saw her husband lying on the ground, and exclaimed that "Harvey

Weeks has killed my husband." She ran immediately to the place where her husband was lying on the ground; he moved his lips and tried to speak, but could not; and died in a few moments. Near her husband, who was shot with a ball under the left nipple, she found a pistol "*barrel*," with a percussion-lock attached under the barrel, and a part of the stock broken. The pistol was peculiar in appearance; she had never seen one like it, and she identified the one in court as the same. She did not see the prisoner after her husband was shot. She did not look for him, her attention being given entirely to her husband; she had a clear and distinct view from the house to where she saw Weeks and her husband just before the latter was shot, but there was timber on either side. She had known Weeks for several years and was well acquainted with him and his size and general appearance; that she could not and did not recognize his features on the new ground when with her husband, the distance being too great; but she did recognize his dress and general appearance, and is perfectly satisfied that the prisoner is the same man who was with her husband that morning whilst at the house. She never saw him afterwards until he was arrested, and was on trial before the committing court.

Margaret Van Laningham, Ellen Weeks and Mrs. Blain were at the house of the deceased on the morning he was killed, and testified as to the prisoner's arrival there, and his conduct when at the house, and his departure with the deceased at about 11 o'clock A. M., to the new ground; the same in substance as Mrs. Norris. These witnesses were engaged in quilting in a room in the house, and did not see either the prisoner or the deceased after they left for the new ground. They stated that they heard the firing of the pistol at 12 o'clock M., immediately after Mrs. Norris had called her husband to dinner, and that Mrs. Norris then exclaimed that "Harvey Weeks has killed my husband." They saw the dead body and the pistol, which they described as Mrs. Norris had done, and recognized when shown in court.

Henry Van Laningham testified, that about ten days before Norris was killed, the prisoner, being a little intoxicated, denounced the Norrises, and swore he could whip the whole family, and any one who would protect them. The next day after this—the witness being Willis Norris' father-in-law—the prisoner came to him and apologized for the remarks he had made about the Norrises in his presence, and said he did not wish to hurt witness's feelings; but he did not retract what he had said, nor express any regret for his remarks, so far as the Norrises were concerned. Witness was one of the jury of inquest, and saw the pistol found by the side of Norris, and recognized the one in court as the same.

Daniel Blain was sent for soon after the killing, and he described the wound on the deceased as the other witnesses, and identified the pistol.

Simon Berry testified, that he lived one and a-half miles from the deceased; that previous to the 26th of March, 1855, the prisoner had hired with him as a laborer, for about four months. That prisoner was absent from his house on Saturday, the 25th March, all day, and did not return until about one or two hours before day-break, on the morning of the 26th. That he heard prisoner, on the morning of the 26th, talking to himself rather loudly in his room. Prisoner said " he would have satisfaction." Witness went in prisoner's room, and saw he was a little intoxicated, though not much. He asked prisoner from whom he was going to get satisfaction? Prisoner replied, that he " had not said who." Prisoner had two pistols in his room, and witness saw him put them on his person, under his clothes. Witness never saw prisoner have any pistols before that time. Witness identified the pistol in court, and which had been shown to and identified by the other witnesses, as one of the pistols in the possession of the prisoner on the morning of the 26th of March. The prisoner left witness' house soon after breakfast; he bid the witness farewell, which was unusual for him to do when he left. The prisoner left all his clothes at witness' house, except those he wore; and he never returned after he left that morning. This witness on cross-examination proved that the prisoner had been angry with a neighbor, but that matter had been amicably adjusted previous to the 26th March, 1855; he also proved that the prisoner was a quiet and peaceable man.

Mrs. Berry, Miss Berry, and the wife and daughter of Simeon Berry, and Mrs. Ellen Berry, his daughter-in-law, were all present at his house on the morning of the 26th of March, and testified, in substance, the same as he did on his examination-in-chief.

R. C. Miller testified that hearing, on the 26th March, 1855, that Willis Norris had been killed, he went to his house, and thence he went in pursuit of the prisoner; that on that evening and night he went to the residence of prisoner's father, and also to the residence of his relatives in the neighborhood, and made inquiries respecting him, but he could not learn any thing about him. That on the morning of the 29th of March, he found the tracks of two horses—one of which, from a peculiarity in the shoeing, was easily distinguishable from other horse-tracks. That he traced these tracks from the house of prisoner's father, for about seventeen or eighteen miles, where he found prisoner's horse tied in a low swampy place in the woods, back of the house of one of his relatives. That he saw there the peculiar track before alluded to, and saw a place where the horse had made it, had been hitched and removed. That before reaching this place he met prisoner's father, who was on horseback. That he could not find or hear of prisoner until the 31st of March, when he came to Louisville (the county seat of Winston county), in company with Hiram and James Weeks.

Samuel Harris was with R. C. Miller in his search for prisoner, and testified in substance the same.

Charlotte Weeks, for the defendant, testified, that she had dinner earlier than usual on the 26th March, 1855, because Wm. Goyne and wife were on a visit at her house, and wanted to get home by 12 o'clock M. That dinner was ready at 11 o'clock A. M., at which time prisoner came there and ate dinner, and remained until late in the evening. That she saw nothing unusual in his appearance that evening. That late in the evening, prisoner and her husband left on horseback; but they went in opposite directions. She did not see prisoner afterwards, until she saw him in jail. Witness is mother of the prisoner. Upon cross-examination, she denied having stated to R. C. Miller, on the 26th of March, and George W. Norris, on the 27th, in reply to a question by them as to where prisoner was, " that she did not know, and had not seen him since the evening of the 25th."

William Goyne, for defendant, testified that he was at the house of Hiram and Charlotte Weeks on Monday the 26th March, 1855; that prisoner arrived there at 11 o'clock A. M., and ate dinner; that he saw nothing unusual in his appearance. Upon cross-examination, stated that he was the brother-in-law of prisoner, and was the same person who had cursed and abused deceased. That he did not see prisoner after 12 o'clock M., on the 26th March, until he saw him in jail. Witness denied having stated to Miller and Hunt, on the 26th March, or subsequently, that he had not seen prisoner since the evening of the 25th.

Mrs. Goyne and Miss Weeks, for defendant, testified the same as last witness, on his examination-in-chief.

J. R. Goyne, for the defendant, testified that William Goyne reached his house on Monday the 26th March—it being about one and a-half miles from Hiram Weeks'—at 12 o'clock, and that they soon after went to the field to plough.

The state then introduced R. C. Miller and two other witnesses, who proved that they were in search of the prisoner soon after the killing, and visited his father's house, and, upon inquiry made of them, the defendant's witnesses, Mrs. Goyne, Mrs. Weeks, Miss Weeks, and William Goyne, denied knowing any thing of him, and stated they had not seen him since the evening of the 25th of March.

All the witnesses who testified as to the time of day, spoke from their judgment and opinion; none of them having verified it by a time-piece. It was proven that Hiram Weeks, father of the prisoner, resided about two miles from the residence of the deceased.

As no question was raised in this court in reference to the instructions given by the court, it is not deemed necessary to set them out.

The jury having found a verdict of guilty against the defendant, he moved for a new trial, which being overruled, he tendered his bill of exceptions, embracing the evidence in the cause; and sued out this writ of error.

Freeman & Dixon, for plaintiff in error,

Filed an elaborate brief, in which they made the following points :

1. The record does not show that the grand jury was legally constituted. It does not show that the grand jury were summoned at least four days before the term of the court ; nor that they were taken equally from each police district. See Session Acts of 1854, p. 468.

2. The act of 1854 requires the sheriff to summon twenty men " to serve as grand jurors for the term." The record shows that the whole twenty were summoned, and in attendance ; but the court, instead of empanelling the whole, required sixteen to be drawn by lot from the number, and constituted them a grand jury. This was error.

3. The indictment does not state that the grand jury " were taken from the body of good and lawful men of the county aforesaid, at the term aforesaid, of the court aforesaid ;" and it is insufficient on that account.

4. The record does not state that the indictment therein contained was returned into court a true bill *at that term, or any other term.* The record merely recites that a bill of indictment was returned against the prisoner for murder, indorsed, etc., and then follows the indictment ; but there is no allegation in the record that this is the *indictment so returned.* Moreover, the indictment copied is not indorsed as the indictment is stated in this record to be indorsed. The indictment copied in the record, has this material indorsement, " Prosecutor, George W. Norris." The one noticed in the record, is stated therein to be indorsed, " a true bill, James W. Wilcox, foreman of the grand jury."

5. The return of the sheriff on the special *venire,* is insufficient, because it does not state that he summoned the within-named jurors ; nor that they were good and lawful men of the county, householders, or freeholders, and citizens of the United States. Besides, it appears that the clerk selected the names, and the sheriff only summoned them. This was clearly error.

6. The court erred in refusing to change the *venue.* The prisoner had done all that the statute required of him, to procure a change of *venue.* In a criminal case, when the statutory

provisions are complied with, it is compulsory on the court to change the *venue;* but in civil cases the rule is different, for then the statute expressly provides that the court may hear witnesses on both sides. Why this difference in the provisions of the two statutes, unless a different rule, based on the distinct and different provisions of each, was intended to be established?

7. The court erred in refusing the application for a continuance. The affidavit was sufficient.

8. The evidence is insufficient to convict the prisoner; and on this point they reviewed the evidence at length.

D. C. Glenn, attorney general,

Argued the case orally.

HANDY, J.:

The plaintiff in error was tried and convicted at the September term, 1855, of the circuit court of Winston county, for the murder of one Willis Norris; and the case is brought to this court upon a bill of exceptions, taken to the action of the court below in overruling a motion for a new trial.

Several objections have been raised and urged here, to the regularity of the summoning of the grand jury which found the indictment; the constitution of the grand jury; the return of the indictment into court; the sufficiency of the indictment with reference to its showing that the grand jury were composed of duly qualified men; and the sheriff's return upon the special *venire* as to his summoning the jury.

We have examined the record with reference to these several objections, and are satisfied that they are untenable.

An exception was taken to the refusal of the court to continue the cause on the application and affidavit of the prisoner. But from the statement of the affidavit, it does not appear that any effort was made to procure the attendance of the absent witness; and it moreover appears by the subsequent details of the record, the witness actually appeared and testified in behalf of the prisoner. Even, therefore, if he was entitled to a continuance, as he clearly was not upon his affidavit, all ground of objection is removed by the witness's appearing and testifying on the trial.

Another exception was taken to the refusal of the court to change the venue upon the application and affidavit of the prisoner, accompanied by the affidavits of three witnesses, stating that "owing to the prejudice existing against the prisoner in the county of Winston, he could not have a fair and impartial trial in that county." It appears that, in considering this application, the court examined one of the affiants and several other witnesses, among whom was the sheriff of the county, under oath, as to the grounds of the application; and being satisfied from the evidence that the prisoner could have a fair and impartial trial in the county, the application was refused.

It is now insisted that the court was bound to act in the matter upon the affidavits of the prisoner and others offered by him, and it was error in the court to examine other witnesses in order to determine whether he could have a fair and impartial trial in the county.

The provision of the statute is, that "it shall and may be lawful for any circuit court or judge thereof in vacation, to change the venue in a criminal case to any adjoining county, on a sufficient showing made by the prisoner on oath, supported by the testimony of one or more credible witnesses, that he cannot have a fair and impartial trial in the county where the offense is charged to have been committed." Hutch. Code, 1007, Art. 6.

In giving the right of a fair and impartial trial to the accused, it is manifest that the statute contemplates that, whenever a change of *venue* shall be applied for, to that end, it shall be determined by the court whether there is just ground for the application. Public justice as well as private right must be considered as equally within the contemplation of the statute, giving this power to the court. Its language confers power on the court to grant the application, but it is not imperative; and the exercise of the power must necessarily be a matter within the sound discretion of the court. And, although the court would have full power to grant the application upon the mere showing mentioned in the statute, without further inquiry or proof; yet cases may arise in which justice and right might require that the court shall not receive such testimony as conclusive ground for granting the application. It might be suggested in behalf of the state, that the witnesses whose affidavits were introduced to sustain the application, were not worthy of credit, or that they were incapable of forming a correct judgment upon the matter stated by them, or that the state of public opinion in the county was clearly not to the prejudice of the accused. If this were the true state of the case, it would be a flagrant perversion of justice to grant the application; and the true state of facts could only be ascertained by a proper examination of witnesses whose situation and means of knowledge upon the subject would entitle their testimony to full confidence. Hence the nature of the power conferred upon the court must require that, whenever the ends of complete justice render it necessary, the court should exercise the power to inquire and determine whether it is proper that the application should be granted; and if, upon such investigation, the court is satisfied that the reasons alleged for the application have no just foundation, the application should be refused, and it follows, that the right of a change of venue, upon a mere application of the prisoner, supported by the affidavit of himself, and one or two more witnesses, is not a matter of absolute right, beyond the power of the court in the exercise of its sound legal discretion.

In the present case, it appears that the court examined one of the affiants upon whose testimony the application was made, and several other witnesses, upon the subject matter of the application. Neither the testimony of these witnesses, nor the reasons which caused their introduction, appear upon the record. And, as it was competent for them to be introduced and examined, and as their testimony might fully have justified the court in determining that the reason stated by the prisoner and his affiants as the ground of the application, was unfounded, it must be presumed that the testimony was sufficient to justify the action of the court in refusing the application.

No particular objection is made to the instructions given to the jury; those asked in behalf of the state as well as those asked on the part of the prisoner, having all been given; and the principles of law applicable to the contested points in the case, were thereby very fully and fairly presented to the jury.

The only point in the case which appears to have been contested on the trial, was that of an *alibi* attempted to be proved in behalf of the prisoner. The widow of the deceased and four other witnesses proved that the prisoner was near the deceased about the hour of twelve o'clock M., on the day on which he was killed. On the contrary, several witnesses on his part state that the prisoner was at his father's house, about two miles from the place where the deceased was killed, from eleven o'clock on that day until late in the evening. But other witnesses testify that several of these witnesses in behalf of the prisoner, and who are his near family relations, had previously declared when pursuit was made, after the killing, that they had not seen him since the day before the deceased was killed. The question of credibility of the witnesses was, therefore, directly presented for the consideration of the jury, upon proper instructions by the court upon the point ; and the verdict is conclusive of that question.

In all other respects, the evidence goes fully to sustain the verdict ; and after a careful examination of the whole record, we are of opinion that there is no error in the judgment, and that it must be affirmed.

Judgment affirmed.

COTTON *v.* THE STATE, 31 Miss. Rep., 504.

HOMICIDE.

A man who from common rumor has formed an opinion as to the guilt or innocence of a party indicted for murder, which it would require testimony to remove, but who on his oath states that he feels as free to act in the matter as if he had never heard of the case, is incompetent. Nelms v. State, 13 S. & M., 500, cited and approved as authority.

A court in this class of cases should never give the jury any instructions which, even by remote construction or bare possibility, may limit or cramp the free action of the jury in considering the evidence before them.

To excuse one person in taking the life of another, on a plea of self-defense, there must have existed at the time of the killing a reasonable ground to apprehend a design on the part of the deceased to commit a felony or some great personal injury upon the accused, and at the same time immediate danger of its accomplishment. The reasonable ground to apprehend the design, *and* the imminent danger, must both exist, and the homicide must have occurred, all at one and the same time.

As a means of determining the fact of the reasonable apprehension of design and danger, the peculiar character of the hostile party is as much a fact for the consideration of the jury as any other fact in issue.

But it may occur, in an extreme case, that although there be no actual danger at the moment, the danger may be increased by delay, or by allowing the hostile party to escape and arm himself; and hence upon this subject a court can, with safety or propriety, lay down only general, and not universal, rules.

If incorrect instructions be asked, the court may modify or correct them before giving them to the jury. But if correct, and asked, they should be given without modification or amendment.

Error to the circuit court of Yazoo county. HENRY, J.

John Cotton, the plaintiff in error, was indicted in the circuit court of Yazoo county, for the murder of one John Smith. At the February term, A. D. 1854, of said court, he was tried and convicted of murder, and sentence of death pronounced against him, which judgment this court, on a writ of error, reversed, and awarded the prisoner a new trial. At the November term, A. D. 1855, of said court, the prisoner was again tried and convicted, and judgment of death was pronounced against him.

From this last judgment he prosecuted this writ of error.

The first, second and third bills of exception taken by the prisoner on his trial, relate to the action of the circuit court in overruling his challenges for cause, to three jurors, and requiring him to accept or peremptorily challenge them. By the first, it appeared that when the name of James Blundell, one of the special *venire*, was called, he was accepted as a juror by the state and tendered to the prisoner. Blundell being interrogated by the prisoner's counsel, answered that he had formed an opinion in reference to the guilt or innocence of the accused; that his opinion was formed from having heard persons speak of the matter; that he did not know that he had ever spoken with any of the witnesses on the subject, and that the opinion that he had formed was such that it would require evidence to remove it. Whereupon the prisoner challenged Blundell for cause. The court then asked Blundell "if his opinion was fixed, or that it was formed from rumor?" He replied that it was formed from rumor. The court then asked him, "if his mind was free to act on the testimony as if he had heard nothing about the case?" He replied "that it was." The court then overruled the prisoner's challenge for cause, and tendered Blundell to him as a competent juror. The prisoner then challenged the juror peremptorily, and excepted to the ruling of the court.

2. In substance the same questions were propounded by the prisoner and the court to James Sherrod, another one of the special *venire*, who had been accepted by the state and tendered to the prisoner, and the same answers were given. The court ruled as in the case of Blundell, and the prisoner challenged Sherrod peremptorily, and excepted.

3. The same course was pursued in reference to J. J. Billington, who made the same answer as the other two ; and further, he stated in answer to an interrogatory propounded by the court, that his opinion was not fixed, but hypothetical, and that he could render an impartial verdict on the evidence.

The evidence for the state was in substance as follows :

Greenberry Anderson stated, that in July, A. D. 1852, he, with several others, was in the store of one Frawley, in Yazoo city, in company with John Smith, the deceased; that the prisoner came in the room and he and Smith exchanged salutations. Prisoner then told Smith that he wanted to speak with him, to which Smith replied, "certainly." Prisoner then walked out, and Smith followed ; both turned down the street and went about sixteen feet from the door of the store-room of Frawley. Witness soon after heard Smith say, "I did not say it." Cotton replied, "that he believed Smith was a liar, and did say it, and that he could whip him." Smith then said, "If you think so, pitch in." These words were spoken in an angry manner, and witness thinking there was about to be a fight, went out into the street, and immediately heard a blow struck by one the parties, but he could not tell which one of them struck it. Smith was standing on the sidewalk, with his back toward the houses, and the prisoner was walking backward across the street, in a direction from Smith. Witness then approached to within a few feet of the parties, on a line which would have led him between them ; he then stopped ; he then heard the prisoner say three several times, "draw it." Witness looked at Smith, "but did not see him draw any thing." While prisoner was saying "draw it," witness saw him pull a pistol out of his pocket and shoot Smith. This was about dark, and in Yazoo county, where Smith died on the same night. Witness went up to Smith after he was shot and carried him across the street and laid him down in a house; he saw no weapons on him. Smith had blood on his mouth, which looked as if he had been struck.

Upon cross-examination, witness stated that it was very dark that night; there was no moon, and it was a little cloudy; that it was so dark that he could not distinguish Cotton except by his voice; that he could not see what Cotton was drawing from his pocket until the pistol was fired; that he was nearer to Cotton than to Smith; that Smith was standing with his left side toward witness, and that he could not see his right hand, and did not know what he was doing with it; that Cotton was going backwards until he fired; that it was not more than two or three minutes from the time Cotton and Smith left the store, until the pistol was fired.

Dr. Leake, for the state, described the character of the wound of Smith, and stated that it caused his death.

This was all the evidence; the prisoner offered none.

The second instruction given on behalf of the state, was as follows:

That if the jury believes from the evidence that the accused killed Smith, the deceased, and no accompanying circumstances appear in the evidence to excuse the act, the law presumes the killing was done maliciously, and that they will find him guilty of murder.

The other instructions given on behalf of the state, which are necessary to be noticed, are fully set out in the opinion of the court.

The first, second and third instructions given on behalf of the prisoner, with the modifications of the court, are as follows:

1. That unless the jury believe from the evidence that the prisoner killed John Smith from a premeditated design formed beforehand to effect his death, or the death of some other person, they cannot find him guilty of murder.

The court refused to give this instruction as asked, but added to it the words, "but if it was premeditated the law does not regard how short beforehand the time was," and with this addition, gave it.

2. That to kill a human being with a premeditated design, the mind must have acted in regard to the killing before the killing was committed; and the mind must have settled down, resolved and determined to kill and murder; and that the killing was done with a deliberate mind and formed design of so doing.

Which the court refused to give as asked, but added thereto the same modification as the one to the first instruction, and then gave it.

3. That if the jury believed that Cotton killed Smith on a sudden quarrel, without a premeditated and formed design so to do, they must not find him guilty of murder.

To which the court added, " unless he sought the quarrel and used a deadly weapon ;" and, with this addition, gave it.

To all which modifications and additions, so made by the court, the prisoner excepted.

Other instructions were asked by the prisoner, and given by the court, but it is unnecessary to set them out.

W. E. Pugh, for plaintiff in error.

Filed an elaborate brief, and cited and commented on the following authorities :

On the point that the court erred in overruling the challenge for cause, of prisoner, to Blundell, Sherrod and Billington.　Sam v. The State, 13 S. & M., 189 ; Nelms v. State, ib., 500.

On the law of homicide.　Whart. Am. C. L., 393, note ; Shorter v. People, 2 Comstock R., 197 ; 27 Miss. R., 379 ; 2 Stark. Ev., 46 ; Roscoe Crim. L., 290 ; 1 Bay R., 351 ; 2 Wend. R., 497 ; 23 Miss. R., 322.

On the point that the grand jury was defective.　M'Quillen v. The State, 8 S. & M., 597 ; 2 Pick. R. 550 ; 12 S. & M., 68 ; 23 Miss. R. 580.

D. C. Glenn, attorney general.

FISHER, J. :

The prisoner having been convicted at the last November term of the circuit court of Yazoo county, of the crime of murder, has brought this case for revision into court.

The errors assigned relate :—First. To the action of the court in empanelling the jury by whom the prisoner was tried. Second. To the instructions given on behalf of the state; to certain modifications of the instructions asked on behalf of the prisoner; and, Third. To the action of the court in overruling the motion in arrest of judgment. These several errors will be noticed in the order in which they have been assigned by counsel.

As to the first assignment. A juror being tendered by the state to the prisoner, was asked if he had formed or expressed an opinion as to his guilt or innocence. Answering that he had formed such opinion, the juror proceeded further to state that his opinion thus formed, was such that it would " require testimony to remove it," whereupon the prisoner's counsel challenged the juror for cause; but the court proceeding further to interrogate him, the juror stated that his opinion was formed from rumor, and that he felt as free to act in the matter, as if he had heard nothing about the case; thereupon the court held the juror competent, and forced the prisoner either to accept the juror, or to challenge him peremptorily.

The same state of facts apply to two other jurors tendered by the state to the prisoner. This point underwent elaborate consideration by this court in the case of Nelms v. The State, 13 S. & M., 500; and the facts of that case, if not identical, are certainly not stronger than the facts of the case at bar. The juror in that case was held incompetent; and recognizing that decision as authority, we are compelled to hold that the jurors tendered to the prisoner were incompetent, and should not have been forced upon him by the court.[1]

[1] Wharton Am. Cr. Law, 3004; King v. State, 5 How., 730; State v. Johnson, 1 Walker, 392; Nelms v. State, 13 S. & M., 500; People v. Mahony, 18 Cal., 180; Burtine v. State, 18 Ga., 534; Rice v. State, 7 Ind., 332; Bradford v. State, 15 ib., 347; McGregg v. State, 4 Blackf., 101; Romaine v. State, 7 Ind., 63; Morgan v. Stevenson, 6 Ind., 169; State v. Sater, 8 Iowa, 420; Commonwealth v. Webster, 5 Cush., 295; Commonwealth v. Gee, 6 ib., 174; Baldwin v. State, 12 Mo., 223.

GENERAL RULE AS TO PREADJUDICATION OF JURORS.

A previous opinion formed on rumor does not disqualify a juror; but one formed on hearing information from a witness, either directly or through another person, does render a juror incompetent. Nelms v. State, 13 S. & M., 500; and see The State v. Johnson, Walker R., 392; King v. State, 5 How., 730. If upon examination a juror is found to have formed an opinion as to the issue to be passed upon, he may be set aside before either party has an opportunity to challenge him. Marsh v. State, 30 Miss., 627; and see Sam's case, supra.

It is ground for a new trial, that, after a juror was summoned, and before trial, he said he did not see how he could clear the defendant should he be on the jury, but

Next, as to the instructions of the court. It is said that the second instruction limited the investigation of the jury to the crime of murder or to the defense of excusable homicide, and they were not permitted to take into consideration the defense of manslaughter, which, so far as the crime of murder is concerned, may be regarded as a defense to the prisoner. The instruction was, no doubt, intended to leave the jury free to investigate, according to the testimony, the degree of crime of which the accused, if guilty at all, was really guilty; but it must be admitted at the same time that the instruction, if taken strictly according to its language, might warrant the construction given to it by counsel, and might have confined the jury to an investigation too limited. The jury, no doubt, without the instruction, would have clearly understood their duty, and the question is, whether it tended to cramp their action? In answering this question, we think it barely possible that the instruction could have produced such an effect. Our conclusion upon this point, therefore, is that, while the instruction was wholly unnecessary, and while we are of opinion that it did not in the least influence the jury, and we would not, therefore, reverse the judgment if this were the only error, yet the safer rule, unquestionably, is that, where the court undertakes to give even unnecessary instructions in this class of cases, the instructions should not be framed, so as even by remote construction to limit the free action of the jury in considering the testimony before them.

It is next said that the court erred in giving the fourth instruction, which was as follows: "That to render the homicide justifiable by the law, on the ground of self-defense, it must appear from the evidence that Cotton, the accused, acted con-

he would be bound to find him guilty,—in a case, where, on the preliminary examination he denied having formed or expressed an opinion. Cody v. State, 3 How., 27. That a juror has impressions as to the guilt of the prisoner, derived from hearing the testimony in another case, is not sufficient to disqualify him. "To disqualify," it was observed, "the juror must have formed and expressed an opinion, or have such acknowledged prejudice or bias as would disable him from doing justice, according to the evidence between the state and the accused." Noe v. State, 5 How., 330. Though no general rules of competency can be fixed, each case depending on its peculiar circumstances, it may be stated generally, that a juror is incompetent to sit in a case on which his mind is so far prejudiced as to require evidence to annul the opinion he has formed. Sam v. State, 13 S. & M., 189. Even though the opinion is formed from rumor, it disqualifies, if evidence is required to remove it. Alfred v. State, 37 Miss., 296; Ogle v. State, 33 Miss., 383.

scientiously upon reasonable fear, founded upon present overt acts of Smith, the deceased, to all appearances hostile, threatening a felony or some great personal injury ; and the danger of such felony being accomplished or great personal injury being inflicted, to all appearances must be immediate, pending, and unavoidable at the time of killing, though there really might be no actual danger."

The party interposing the plea of self-defense, on a trial for murder, must be understood as undertaking to show that in the perpetration of the deed he acted under a necessity, either actual or apparent, forced upon him by the party killed ; for if such were not the case, his defense cannot avail him any thing, or certainly not further than to mitigate the crime. The very defense presupposes danger to the party's life or person, except in cases where he may act in defense of the life or person of another. When he assumes the defense, he at the same time undertakes to establish the danger, or what is the same thing, what appeared to be danger. The question presented by this instruction is, in what manner must the danger exist to justify the party in taking the life of his adversary? The law says that there must be reasonable ground to apprehend a design to commit a felony, or do some great personal injury, and imminent danger of such design being accomplished. Hutch. Code, 957. Reasonable ground to apprehend the design and imminent danger of its accomplishment must both exist at the same time. What is reasonable ground to apprehend such design must always be as much, or, indeed, more a question of fact for the jury than a question of law for the court ; for, while it is true that, in regard to inanimate subjects, where the fact is the same, the law must also be the same, this is not true, even as a general rule, in this class of cases. The hostile demonstrations of two men may in every respect be the same ; yet the party threatened may be placed in imminent peril from the conduct of one and feel not the slightest danger from the other. A design to commit a felony or to do some great personal injury may be apprehended in the one case and it may have no existence whatever in the other. One may excite fear and the greatest apprehensions of danger, while the same demonstra-

tions on the part of another may only excite mirth and ridi-
cule.   The question is in both cases the same — was there
imminent danger to the life or to the person of the party
threatened ?   As a part of the means of arriving at the truth
of this fact, the peculiar character of the hostile party is as
much a fact for the consideration of the jury as any other fact
in issue ; and the jury must determine from the hostile demonstrations whether there was such danger of *this party's*
executing his felonious design as to justify the party killing ;
in doing so, although there may have been no actual danger
from the deceased at that very moment of time, the question
in such case is, whether, by the delay, the danger is not increased ; as, for instance, suppose the party threatened is in
the upper story of a building, and the ground to apprehend
the design to take his life or do great personal injury, is there
for the first time discovered, and his adversary leaves for the
purpose of arming himself and taking a favorable position at
the foot of the stairs, with the known and avowed purpose of committing the deed while the party is descending to make his way
out of the building, would a few moments, or even ten minutes,
make any difference in the killing in such a case ?   The very act
of allowing the hostile party to escape might prove fatal to the
party threatened and deprive him of all means of self-defense.
It may be said that this is putting an extreme case.   Grant
it.   It nevertheless serves the purpose for which it was intended,
of showing the impropriety of laying down a rule, within the
operation of which the court declares a person, without regard
to the peculiar circumstances of the case, must bring his defense,
in order to be successful.   Whether the danger must be immediate or unavoidable at the time of killing to justify the party
in the act, must depend upon the facts and circumstances of the
case.   This is the only general rule which a court can with any
safety lay down on the subject.   The jury must of necessity be
the judges whether reasonable ground to apprehend the design
contemplated by the law existed, and whether there was imminent danger, from all appearances, that such design would be
executed.   In arriving at their conclusion on this subject, they
are expected to avail themselves of such knowledge as they

possess in regard to human transactions from their intercourse with society. The right of self-defense is not derived from the law. All the law attempts to do on the subject is, to prescribe rules of caution and prudence to be observed by persons before exercising the right, by ascertaining whether the danger exists and whether it is imminent; and, as already remarked, whether it must be immediate and impending at the very time of killing, will depend upon the facts and circumstances surrounding the transaction.

But it is not necessary to pursue this subject further, and we proceed next to notice the seventh instruction, as follows: " That if the accused was armed with a deadly weapon, and sought and brought about the difficulty with the deceased, and killed the deceased, in the difficulty, with such weapon, he is guilty of murder." The fact of a man being armed with a deadly weapon, though he may be the aggressor in a difficulty, amounts to nothing, unless he provided himself with the weapon, with a view to using it if necessary in overcoming his adversary. It may be a man's habit, as it is unquestionably his right under the law of this state, to carry a deadly weapon, and whether he is permitted to use it or not, must depend upon the nature of the difficulty in which he may be involved. A man may begin a difficulty, intending to inflict no violence, or next thing to none, on his antagonist, and may be so closely pressed as to be forced to use his weapon in self-defense. The rule is stated thus by Blackstone: " If the slayer has not begun the fight, or (having begun) endeavors to decline any further struggle, and afterwards being closely pressed by his antagonist, kills him to avoid his own destruction, this is homicide, excusable by self-defense." 4 Bl. Com., 184. In such case, the party having commenced the difficulty, he can only use his weapon in self-defense, or take the life of the other party, when the danger is immediate or impending, and unavoidable.

The first and second instructions, asked on behalf of the prisoner, simply announce, as a legal proposition, that to make out the crime of murder, it must appear that the prisoner " acted from a premeditated design, formed beforehand, to effect the death of the deceased." These instructions ought to have been given as asked, as they were entirely free from objection. The court may modify an instruction to make it correct, but if it be already correct, it ought to be given as asked by counsel.

The qualification of the court, made to the third instruction, is clearly erroneous. The instruction is, in substance, that if Cotton killed Smith, not in pursuance of a premeditated design, but on a sudden quarrel, the crime of murder is not made out. The modification made is, " unless Cotton sought the quarrel and used a deadly weapon." The question was, whether malice prompted the accused to kill. He interposed, as his defense, by the instruction, "*no design to kill*, and that the killing was on a sudden quarrel." The court say to him that this is no defense, not even to mitigate the crime, if you sought the quarrel and used a deadly weapon. Now, he may have done both, without being guilty of murder ; for he may not, by seeking the quarrel, have intended the slightest personal injury to the deceased, and he may, from sudden provocation, have used his weapon, or he may have been forced to do so in self-defense, although he was the aggressor in the quarrel.

The modification amounts to this, that although there must be a formed design to take life, to constitute murder ; yet such design is not necessary where the party killing seeks the quarrel, and uses a deadly weapon.

There must be proof of malice, in some form ; the seeking of the quarrel, and using the deadly weapon, may be evidence for this purpose. But this is what the defendant below was endeavoring to meet, by showing no design to take life, because the killing occurred on a sudden quarrel. The modification virtually declares this to be no defense, if the party sought the quarrel.

We will briefly dispose of the error last assigned—the motion in arrest of judgment.

The *venire* from which the grand jurors were taken, contains their names in full ; but their Christian names, that is of some of them, are abbreviated on the minutes of the court ; as, for instance, the name of Fountain Barksdale appears in full on the *venire*, and it is F. Barksdale on the minutes. We do not think this error can prevail, when the record shows that the grand jurors were taken from the persons whose names appear on the *venire*.

It is next said that one of the grand jurors was excused, and the record does not show upon what ground. The record shows that the excuse was, by the court, considered sufficient. This must be treated as a legal excuse.

Judgment reversed, *venire de novo* awarded, and cause remanded.

THE STATE *v.* BROWN, 32 Miss. Rep., 275.

SHERIFF'S POWER TO BAIL OFFENDERS.

A party in custody of the sheriff under indictment for felony, and in whose case a mis-trial has been had, and the jury disagreed, must be considered as remaining in custody till legally discharged; and the sheriff has authority, under the act of 1822, (Hutch. C., p. 444, § 13; Rev. C. 1857, p. 127, art. 129,) by virtue of an order of the court, to take bail or recognizance at any time before such legal discharge.

In error from the circuit court of De Soto county. Hon. P. F. SCRUGGS, Judge.

D. C. Glenn, attorney general, argued the case orally.

H. W. Walter, for defendant in error, argued the case and submitted a brief, in which he made the following points and cited the following authorities, viz:

1. The sheriff had in his hands no process authorizing him to take the recognizance. Overraker v. The State, 4 S. & M., 738; The State v. Pace, 3 Cushm., 54.

2. The sheriff is an officer of official and limited power, and a recognizance taken by him must show on its face the authority by which it was taken. Hutch. Code, 443, 1009; 4 Humph., 213, 226; 3 Cushm., 54, 607; 6 Wheaton, 119; 3 Grattan, 82, 214; 11 Mass., 446; 2 Kelly, 865; 2 S. & M., 200; 4 Texas, 419; 1 Stew. & Port., 465.

HANDY, J.:

This was a *scire facias* upon a recognizance of bail entered into by a party who was indicted for a felony, and the defendant in error, his bail, taken by the sheriff of the county in which the indictment was found. It appears that after the indictment was found, a *capias* was issued against the accused, which was executed; and, that a trial was had upon which the jury could not agree, and were discharged; and the record shows that "the sheriff was thereupon ordered by the court to admit him to bail in the sum of five hundred dollars and good security in like amount." This order appears on the proceedings of the court, under date of the 8th of June, 1853; and, in pursuance of it, the sheriff took the recognizance on the 13th of June, 1853, of the accused and the defendant in error, and, at the November term, 1853, a judgment of forfeiture was taken, both against the principal and the defendant in error.

The defendant in error demurred to the *scire facias* issued on this judgment; which was sustained, and judgment rendered for the defendant; to which the state prosecutes this writ of error.

The controlling question in the case is, whether the sheriff had authority to take the recognizance.

It is held in Pace v. The State, 25 Miss., 54, that, under the provisions of the act of 1822, Hutch. Code, 444, § 13, the sheriff is only authorized to take a recognizance of bail from a party whom he may arrest on the process of a circuit court.

In this case it appears that the accused had been arrested under such process, and, for aught that appears in the record, was in custody under that arrest at the time of the mis-trial. He must be considered as in custody under the original arrest until it be shown that he was duly discharged. The order made by the court after the mis-trial was, in effect, an order of re-commitment until the defendant should give bail; and he was not discharged until he was bailed in virtue of the recognizance taken by the sheriff. He was, in the meantime, in custody under the original arrest by virtue of the process from the circuit court, and in such cases the sheriff has authority by the act above-mentioned to take recognizances.

The act of 1846, Hutch. Code, 1009, art. 12, has reference to persons committed to jail by the order of any judge, justice of the peace, or other officer, and not to one committed under process issued from a circuit court. But, if that statute apply to the case, the order made by the court was a sufficient authority to the sheriff to take the recognizance.

There appear to be no substantial merits in any of the other grounds of demurrer relied upon by the defendant.

The judgment is reversed, and the cause remanded for further proceedings on the *scire facias.*

JORDAN *v.* THE STATE, 32 Miss. Rep., 382.

HOMICIDE.

A confession of guilt by the accused cannot be given to the jury in evidence against him on a trial for murder, unless it appears that such confession was entirely voluntary. The prisoner has the constitutional right to remain silent as to his guilt; and hence, if a confession be extorted or induced by violence or threats of violence, or by hope of reward or immunity from punishment, it cannot be given in evidence to the jury.

The state, itself, being restrained by the constitution from compelling an accused party to testify against himself, the courts can give no countenance or sanction to such compulsion when exercised by private persons. Hence, all that may be thus wrung from the accused must be rejected.

In error from the circuit court of De Soto County. SCRUGGS, J. *Clapp & Strickland* for prisoner.

The grounds of error relied upon in this case are these:

First. The admission of the confession of the accused, which was obtained by threats and violence. Second. The overruling of the motion for a new trial.

1. That the confession of the accused was not under the circumstances admissible in evidence; see Barb. Cr. L. 419–21. It violates the last clause of the 10th section of the 1st. art. of the constitution.

.   .   .   .

There is no proof of *malice,* express or implied, without which the offense was not murder.

The only pretext for the charge of *express* malice is the testimony of Benton, a slave, which was not to be relied on as true; and even if true, proves nothing but an idle braggadocio, such as may at any time be overheard in the conversation of negroes, who have but the intellect of children, without their moral culture. There was no threat on the part of the defendant *to take life*, but simply to use such means as were necessary to make his escape, if he should run away and be arrested.

Malice cannot be implied either from the relative position of the parties, (the defendant not being a *felon*,) nor from the use of a deadly weapon. This can only be implied where there was a design to take life. Cotton v. The State, Opinion Book, 152. The object for which the deadly weapon was used is open for explanation. It is not enough that the evidence against the accused goes to show his guilt. It must be inconsistent with the reasonable supposition of his innocence. 3 Greenl. Ev., 31. The knife may have been obtained by defendant to procure food or resist the attacks of dogs. The circumstances warrant the inference that the defendant never had the knife which is referred to in the proof, but that it was pretended to have been found by the slave, Allen, and there is a strong probability that the homicide was in fact accidentally perpetrated by Mallory himself. Had there been no charges given by the circuit judge, the verdict of the jury was manifestly contrary to law and the evidence, and should have been set aside.

But the court incorrectly charged the law. The last clause of the first charge given for the state excludes the idea of explaining the intent with which a deadly weapon is used, and is contrary to the rule laid down in Cotton v. State.

The third and fourth charges on behalf of the state, and the last charge volunteered by the court in explanation or modification of the charges given on behalf of the defendant, proceed upon the idea that the law applicable to the arrest of felons applies to runaway slaves, and therefore misled the jury.

Looking to the peaceful and tractable disposition of the defendant, as shown by the proof, and reviewing all the circumstances connected with the homicide, the case is one appealing powerfully to the justice as well as the mercy of the court.

In addition to authorities cited, see Jennings v. Fundeberry, 4 M'C., 161 ; Richardson v. Dukes, ib., 156 ; Witsell v. Earnest and Parker, 1 N. & M'C., 182 ; Copeland v. Parker, 3 Iredell, 513.

D. C. Glenn, attorney general, argued the case orally.

FISHER, J. :

This was an indictment found by the grand jury at the June term, 1856, of the circuit court of De Soto county, charging the prisoner with the murder of a slave named Aaron, upon which the prisoner was convicted and sentenced at that term of the court.

It is first assigned as error, that the court below erred in permitting certain statements or confessions of the prisoner to be given in evidence before the jury. One Mallory being introduced as a witness on the part of the state, testified that after the killing of the slave Aaron, and after the arrest of the prisoner, he, witness, and one Williams, went to the prisoner, and attempted to draw him into conversation in regard to the killing of Aaron ; that the prisoner refusing to answer their questions, they told him that if he did not talk they would kill him ; the witness having a pistol then cocked in his hand, with which he threatened to shoot the prisoner ; and the other a stick, with which he threatened to strike, and did strike the prisoner one blow. Under the influence of these threats, and violence thus inflicted, the prisoner proceeded to state the time and place, when and where he lost his knife, describing it at the same time. The court admitted this evidence to go to the jury, upon the statement of the district attorney, that he expected to show, by other testimony, that, upon search being made, a knife corresponding with that described was found at or near the spot indicated by the prisoner. It is insisted by counsel, that the knife found upon this search does not correspond with that described by the prisoner, and that the court therefore erred in admitting the testimony. Counsel is, doubtless, right in his construction or view of the testimony, as well as the rule of law, that the place of finding, and knife found, must both agree with the description given by the accused, and, if a discrepancy appeared as to either or both, the court should have excluded the testimony. We prefer, however, not to rest our decision on this point, upon this ground, as it would seem to sanction, at least to some extent, the legality of the testimony, as well as to give countenance to the unauthorized mode by which it was procured.

If there is a principle which may be regarded as settled, in the criminal jurisprudence of this country, it is, that the accused has the right under any and all circumstances, to maintain his silence in regard to the commission of the crime alleged against him, and the rule which protects him against a full confession of guilt, if it appeared that the confession had been extorted by violence, also protects him against testimony which could only be dicovered, or made available through the instrumentality of such confession, for otherwise the rule could always be successfully evaded. The rule which excludes the whole confession must necessarily exclude all its parts. That which protects a man against the principal thing, must, of course, protect him against its incidents. The rule which secures a man against lawless violence, must, of necessity, to be efficacious, secure him against the consequences of such violence. It is no answer to say that the confession was true ; the question, and the only question which can be considered is, whether the confession was voluntary, extorted by threats or violence, or induced by the hope of reward, or immunity from punishment. It was not only the right of the party accused, to preserve his entire silence in regard to the killing, but to resist force by force, to compel him to act otherwise, if it had been in his power to employ such force. So far from the means employed to procure the confession being sanctioned by law, it is not even within the power of any branch of the government, as at present organized, to give to such means any legal validity whatever. He could not be compelled by any of the government authorities to give evidence against himself, and an express statute, authorizing such a course of proceeding, would be simply a nullity under the constitution. It will certainly require no argument to show that there can exist in this state no rule of the common law, in regard to a particular subject, when an act of the legislature on the same subject would be nugatory. To state the proposition is to decide it. Let us then apply the principle to the case at the bar. Can it be contended for a moment, that a confession extorted by a threat of violence, extending to even

the life of the accused, would be admitted as evidence against
him, merely on the ground that the violence was threatened by
private individuals, and not by the officers of the government.
If it is true that a person, though accused of crime, is still protected by law, upon what principle can it be contended, that his act
shall bind him, if it shall appear that the act was the result of
force, employed by persons in violation of this right? Must all,
or only a part of that which was wrung from him be treated as
if it had never been uttered? There can certainly be but one
answer to these inquiries. The state being powerless as to this
mode of procuring testimony, can give no countenance or sanction to a similar mode, when employed by individuals. The
power which restrains the state, equally restrains her citizens in
this respect. To hold otherwise would not unfrequently expose
the accused to the excited passions or fury of that class of population who in all countries are the subjects upon whom the
criminal jurisprudence of the government can be most beneficially employed.

We are therefore of opinion, that the court below erred in admitting the testimony.[1]

.　　　　.　　　　.　　　　.　　　　.　　　　.

Judgment reversed and *venire de novo* awarded.

[1] Before any confession can be received in evidence in a criminal case, it must be
shown that it was voluntary. Wharton Am. Cr. Law, 219; Archbold Cr. Pr. & Pl.,
120, 127; 2 Russell on Crimes, 825; 1 Greenl. Ev., 219; 1 Phill. Ev., 401; 2 East
P. C., 659; Rex v. Tyler, 1 C. & P., 129; Rex v. Enoch, 5 C. & P., 539; Rex v.
Court, 7 C. & P., 486; People v. Ward, 15 Wend., Roscoe Cr. Ev., 37 *et seq.* If any
inducement by promise of favor or by threat be held out to the prisoner—as by telling
him "he had better tell all he knew" (Rex v. Kingston, 4 C. & P., 387; Rex v.
Gardner, 18 Law J., 1 M., 2 C. & K., 920); "I'll forgive you if you will tell the truth,"
(C. & M., 584); "it is of no use to deny it, as every body knows you did it" (Rex
v. Mills, 6 C. & P., 146); Archbold Cr. Pr. & Pl., 127. In Alabama, where it was
proved that a slave was arrested, tied and left by his master in charge of a third person, to whom he immediately after made a confession, proof that the master "had
always been in the habit of tying his slaves when they were charged with any matter,
and whipping them until they confessed the truth, and that he had frequently treated
the prisoner in the same way," was held admissible in order to determine whether
the confession was induced by hope or fear. Spencer v. State, 17 Ala., 193; see
Franklin v. State, 28 Ala., 9. In the same state, a slave's confessions to his master
were excluded because the latter said to him: "Boy, these denials will only make
the matter worse;" and the repetition of them before the examining magistrate in
the presence of the master was also ruled inadmissible, the magistrate having neglected to caution him as to their effect. Wyatt v. State, 25 Ala., 9. In the case of
Dick v. State, 30 Miss., 593, supra p. 811, where a white person remarked, in the
hearing of a slave who was charged with the murder of his master, that "it would

WILLIAMS *v.* THE STATE, 32 Miss. Rep., 389.

HOMICIDE.

Jurors in capital cases should always be entirely impartial between the state and the accused; and it is the duty of the court to see that the jury is composed of men above all exceptions in this respect.

A large class of the community doubt the expediency of capital punishment, others have a strong repugnance to it. And some few individuals sincerely entertain conscientious scruples against it. It is the latter class who are disqualified from serving as jurors in capital cases, "provided only, however, that their scruples are such as would prevent them from finding a verdict according to the evidence." The disqualification of this class is too firmly settled to admit of controversy.

The jury are not to decide questions of law in criminal, any more than in civil cases. In this country, as well as in England, the courts are the judges of the law us much in criminal as in civil cases. The court here adopts the language of Judge Story,[1] in the case of U. S. *v.* Battisto, 2 Sumner, 243. But the court is authorized to instruct the jury only in writing, at the request of the parties, and upon contested questions of law applicable to the issue.

---

be better for the guilty to confess, that the innocent might not be punished," it was held that a confession thus obtained was admissible.

Where a previous confession is obtained by improper means, any subsequent confession given on its basis is inadmissible. Roscoe Cr. Ev., 45, 46; Moore v. Com., 2 Leigh, 701; State v. Guild, 5 Halst., 163; Case of Bownhas et al., 4 Rogers, Rec., 136; Case of Stage et al., 5 ib., 177; Case of Milligan et al., 6 ib., 69; State v. Roberts, 1 Dev., 259; Peter v. State, 4 S. & M., 31; Van Buren v. State, 24 Miss., 572; Com. v. Knapp, 10 Pick., 477; Com. v. Harman, 4 Barr, 269; Whaly v. State, 11 Ga., 123; Com. v. Taylor, 5 Cush., 505; Conley v. State, 12 Mo., 462; State v. Nash, 12 La., 895; State v. Fisher, 6 Jones Law, 478; Simon v. State, 36 Miss., 636; 2 Russell on Crimes, 826; 1 Greenl. Ev., 221; Maynell's case, 2 Lewin's Cr. Cases, 122; Sherrington's case, ib., 123; Rex v. Cooper, 5 C. & P., 135; Wharton Am. Cr. Law, 694; Deathridge v. State, 1 Sneed, 75; 2 Russ. on Cr., 832.

But the presumption of a continuing influence may be repelled; and then a subsequent confession becomes admissible. Rex v. Sexton, 6 Peters, 83; such presumption may be removed by the length of time intervening between the threats and the examination, from proper warning of the consequences of such confession, or from any other circumstances that might be reasonably considered sufficient to dispel the fears induced by the threats. Peter v. State, 4 S. & M., 31; Com. v. Knapp, 10 Pick., 477; State v. Roberts, 1 Dev., 259; State v. Gould, 5 Halst., 163; 1 Greenl. Ev., 221; Wharton Am. Cr. Law, 694; 2 Russ. on Crimes, 824, 836; State v. Hash, 12 La. Ann., 895; State v. Carr, 37 Vermont, 191; 2 Stark. Ev., 36.

[1] STORY, J., in summing up, to the jury said: "Before I proceed to the merits of this case, I wish to say a few words upon a point suggested by the argument of the learned counsel for the prisoner, upon which I have had a decided opinion during my whole professional life. It is, that in criminal cases, and especially in capital cases, the jury are judges of the law as well as of the fact. My opinion is that the jury are no more judges of the law in a capital or other criminal case, upon the plea of not guilty, than they are in every civil case tried upon the general issue. In such of these cases their verdict when general, is necessarily when compounded of law and of fact; and includes both. In each they must necessarily determine the law, as well as the fact. In each they have the physical power to disregard the law, as laid down to them by the court. But I deny, that in any case, civil or criminal, they have the moral right to decide the law, according to their own notions or pleasure. On the contrary, I hold it to be the most sacred constitutional right of every party accused of a crime, that the jury should respond as to the facts, and the court as to the law. It is the duty of the court to instruct the jury as to the law; and it is the duty of the jury to follow the law as it is laid down by the court," etc.

In error from the circuit court of Marshall County. SCRUGGS, J.

T. W. Harris, for plaintiff in error.

D. C. Glenn, attorney general.

SMITH, C. J., delivered the opinion of the court:

The plaintiff in error was tried in the circuit court of Marshall county upon an indictment for murder, and convicted of manslaughter in the second degree. A motion was made in arrest of judgment and for a new trial, which being overruled, the prisoner excepted, and prosecutes this writ of error to reverse the judgment entered against him.

Several grounds are taken in this court upon which it is insisted that the judgment should be reversed and a *venire de novo* awarded. In proceeding to notice them, we shall pursue the order in which they are presented in the record.

The first exception relates to the rejection of certain persons as jurors. Henderson Kirk having been examined by the court and pronounced competent, was put upon the state. Whereupon the district attorney asked him, " if he was opposed to capital punishment." The question was objected to by the prisoner's counsel ; but the objection was overruled. Kirk responded to the question in the affirmative, and stated, further, " that he had conscientious scruples upon the subject of capital punishment ; that they would bias his judgment, and he would prefer being excused." The state then challenged him for cause, and the court sustained the challenge.

John B. Norfleet was also, after having been examined by the court and pronounced competent as a juror, turned over to the representative of the state, who propounded the same question to him. The question was likewise objected to by the prisoner, and his objection overruled. Norfleet thereupon answered, that " he did have conscientious scruples on the subject of capital punishment, and that it would be against his conscience to render a verdict by which a party would be subjected to the punishment of death ; but that he thought he could do justice as between the state and accused." Whereupon he was challenged for cause by the state, and the challenge was sustained by the court.

We perceive no objection to the course of examination pursued. Although the judge expressed himself satisfied of the competency of the persons produced as jurors, they were neither tendered to, nor accepted by the prisoner, but were turned over to the district attorney for the purpose, we presume, of further examination. In all cases of this character it is the duty of the court to see that an impartial jury is empanelled, and that it is composed of men above all exception. 9 S. & M., 119. And although objections to jurors on the ground of conscientious scruples, usually assume the shape of a challenge on the part of the prosecution, the court may set aside the juror of his own motion; and in the United States v. Connell, 2 Mason, 91, this was done without even swearing or affirming the jurors. In the People v. Damon, 13 Wend., 351, the rule is laid down, that the court may set aside incompetent jurors at any time before evidence is given.

But the objection mainly relied on, involves the question of competency. It is insisted that in neither instance was the juror rendered incompetent by reason of the conscientious scruples declared and entertained by him.

A large class of the community doubt the expediency of capital punishment, others have a strong repugnance to it, while some few individuals sincerely entertain conscientious scruples against it. It is this latter class which have been held disqualified from serving as jurors, in cases in which a verdict of guilty would be followed by capital punishment, "providing only, however, that their scruples are such as would prevent them from finding a true verdict according to the evidence." And it is now too firmly settled to admit of controversy that conscientious scruples entertained by a person which would prevent him from *assenting*, or agreeing to a verdict, which would subject the accused to capital punishment, although justified by the evidence, disqualify him as a juror. Lewis v. State, 9 S. & M., 115; People v. Damon, 13 Wend., 351; Com. v. Lesher, 17 Serg. & Rawle, 155; Jones v. State, 2 Black., 475; Martin v. State, 16 Ohio, 364; Williams v. State, 3 Kelly, 453.

The reason upon which this rule is founded is, that such scruples entertained by a juror, incapacitate him as such, in the performance of his part in the due administration of the law.

He must violate his conscience or disregard the obligations which the laws of his country attach to the relation in which he stands. There is no third course by which he can escape from these alternatives.   If placed on the jury he is compelled either to violate his oath or his conscience, and a man who would do either, is unfit to serve as a juror.

The conscientious scruples against capital punishment, entertained by Kirk, would, as he stated under oath, bias his judgment; the question then is, was Kirk rendered incompetent as a juror by reason of those scruples?

If sworn as a juror, the question which he would have to decide, was, whether the evidence adduced on the trial proved beyond a reasonable doubt the facts alleged in the indictment, constituting the offense.   That was purely a question of fact to be determined by the evidence.   And, it is said, as the subject of inquiry for the jury was entirely distinct from the question whether the state could rightfully impose the penalty of death as a punishment for crime, and from the question, whether the juror would, in any case, without a violation of his religious obligations, consent to a verdict which would be followed by capital punishment, any scruples which the juror might entertain on these subjects, as they could not influence his judgment in weighing the evidence, ought not to exclude him, unless his scruples were of such a character as to preclude him from convicting the accused of a capital offense; that guilt is conclusion of law from facts, judicially ascertained, and in the ascertainment of which the witness who testifies, and the juror who founds his verdict on his testimony, are equal actors; but as it is neither the juror nor the witness, but the law that dooms the culprit to death, no better reason can be offered for excluding the juror than excusing the witness from testifying, on the grounds of conscientious scruples against capital punishment.

These arguments are more specious than solid.   They do not meet the question.   The question is not one of exemption from the discharge of a public duty upon the ground of religious belief or conscientious scruples; it is one which respects the fitness and competency of a person called to act in the capacity of a juror.   Conceding for the purpose of argument, that Kirk's scruples would not influence his judgment in weighing the testimony; they were nevertheless, as he admitted, sufficiently strong to bias his judgment. ·

If, then, according to the argument, his scruples would have no influence upon his mind in the examination of the evidence and the decision of the question of fact submitted to him, on what subject would his scruples operate, and in what way would they bias his judgment, as he admitted they would. Assuredly if they operated at all in controlling his action, it would be by preventing him from consenting to a verdict, however conclusive the evidence might be of the guilt of the accused, which would subject him to the death penalty. It is true, Kirk did not state that his scruples would preclude him from rendering a verdict in any case of a capital felony. But under the view in which the question is argued, it is clear, if his scruples touch him at all, they must of necessity produce that result. At all events, he could not convict the prisoner of murder without violating his conscience. He therefore did not stand indifferent; he was not in a condition in which he could impartially hear and examine, and acquit the innocent and convict the guilty. " He that is of a jury," (says Coke,) " must be *liber homo ;* that is, not only a free man and not bond, but one also that hath such freedom of mind, that he stands indifferent as he stands unsworn." We therefore think that he was properly excluded.

In coming to this conclusion, we have gone a step farther than the courts of this country have gone. The rule on this subject, heretofore generally recognized, is, that conscientious or religious scruples in regard to capital punishment, to disqualify from serving on juries, must be such as would prevent the person entertaining them from finding a true verdict according to the evidence, and compel him to disregard the obligations of his oath as a juror. 2 G. & W. on New Trials, 258. We are satisfied, however, that the rule we have here applied, is founded on sound principles, and necessary to the attainment of the true objects for which trials by jury were instituted.

The action of the court in reference to Norfleet, the second juror called and examined, presents a different question, and one which is not entirely free from doubt. The rule, judicially recognized, applying to his case is, that opposition to capital punishment which would not influence the mind of the juror, but would leave him free to find a true verdict according to the evidence, is no disqualification. This was held in Commonwealth v. Webster, 5 Cush., 295. This and the case before us are not precisely alike. Here the objections of the juror to capital punishment assume the form of conscientious scruples, and hence the reasons for excluding him are the stronger. But he stated that " he thought he could do justice as between the state and the defendant." It is not so clearly perceived how a juror who entertains conscientious scruples against capital punishment, can perform his part in the due administration of the law, when acting as a juror on the trial of a capital felony. If, however, we regard the obligation imposed by the oath of a juror paramount to any supposed moral duty, arising from a belief that the punishment of death is inexpedient and sinful, and he is thus enabled impartially to weigh the evidence, and to find a verdict accordingly, it will not be contended that he is incompetent as a juror. Upon this supposition, he would stand " indifferent as he is unsworn." And we suppose the answers of the juror are the only means by which his impartiality can be determined. If one called as a juror state that he has formed or expressed an opinion in regard to the guilt or innocence of the party charged, from the statements of persons which he believed, such person would not be a competent juror, although he might also state that he thought he could, with perfect impartiality, examine the case and render a true verdict according to the evidence. This is what one might say, and what every honest man should endeavor to do. But he would be incompetent, because he would not stand indifferent between the parties. Having admitted the existence of an opinion, we know that evidence would be required to remove or change it. We could thus reason from an admitted fact, and found a conclusion from the necessary effect of such admitted fact, which would contradict the opinion expressed by the juror as to his impartiality and freedom from bias. But as it is impossible, in any case, to ascertain what effect would be produced, or whether any influence whatever would be exerted upon the mind of the juror, in deciding upon the weight of the evidence, by his scruples in reference to capital punishment, we are compelled to take the statement of the juror as conclusive. Whether such scruples would or would not control or bias his judgment, must, of necessity, be left to him to decide. If, upon an examination of his own heart, he is satisfied that he can fairly and impartially weigh the testimony in the cause, and without bias render a true verdict, we do not think he ought to be excluded. In our opinion, therefore, the court erred in setting aside this juror.

Charges were granted at the instances of the district attorney, and excepted to by the prisoner. Numerous instructions were requested by the prisoner, all of which except one, which we shall notice hereafter, were given. Several of these were subsequently modified or explained by the court. As we must reverse for the error above pointed out, we deem it unnecessary to notice the objections raised in the argument in regard either to the charges given for the prosecution or to the modifications made in those granted for the defense.

The instruction refused by the court, and above referred to, is as follows: " The jury are not only the judges of the facts in the case, but they are also the judges of the law."

In many of the colonies, immediately preceding the revolution, the arbitrary temper and unauthorized acts of the judges, holding office directly from the crown, made the independence of the jury, in law as well as fact, a matter of great popular importance. From this cause, the doctrine embodied in the charge under consideration, grew into recognition, and for some time, after the adoption of the federal constitution, it was generally received. It is unnecessary to notice the course of judicial decisions on this subject. It is scarcely necessary to state, that in no great while after Fries' Case, in which the doctrine was fully recognized by the court, who charged that " the jury are to decide on the present and in all criminal cases, both the law and the facts, on their consideration of the whole case," the courts one after another abandoned the doctrine. In England, it has always been held that the court were as much the judges of the law in criminal as in civil cases. And this doctrine is now undoubtedly sustained by the great weight of authority.

Am. Cr. Law, 896. Our own opinion accords with that of Judge Story, in the case of The United States v. Battisto, 2 Sumner, 243, and we adopt his language in that case as fully expressing the views of this court. We hold, therefore, that there was no error in the refusal of the court to give the instruction.

After the court, at the request of the district attorney and the prisoner, had charged the jury, it proceeded, of his own motion, to charge them generally upon the law of homicide. This proceeding of the court was excepted to, and the charge, which was in writing, placed upon the record. It is now insisted that this proceeding was in violation of the statute, and constitutes a good ground for reversing the judgment.

As an exposition of the law, in our opinion, the charge was unexceptionable. It was a succinct, extremely intelligible, and very accurate explanation of the principles of the criminal law applicable to the case before the jury. But, in our opinion, it was a proceeding unauthorized, and in plain violation of the statute restricting the authority of the circuit judges to charge the jury, in criminal trials, except under certain specified conditions. Hutch. Dig., 888, art. 9, § 14.

The object and policy of the act are declared in the preamble. They are to secure juries, in the discharge of their appropriate functions, from any improper influence on the part of the court, and thereby the better to preserve the sanctity of the trial by jury. And to these ends the legislature, according to the construction of the statute, which, we think, the proper one, has declared that any judge, before whom any issue of the fact is tried, shall charge the jury only upon contested questions of law applicable to the issue, and at the request of one of the parties, or their counsel, distinctly specifying, in writing, the point of law in regard to which the instruction is asked.

We are bound to believe that no officer of the state would designedly transcend the authority vested in him by law; and in this particular case, that the learned judge proceeded upon reasons which were satisfactory to himself. But upon this interpretation of the statute, it is impossible to justify the course pursued by the court.

Judgment reversed.

HANDY, J., delivered the following dissenting opinion:

I cannot agree to the opinion of a majority of the court upon the point of the competency of the juror Norfleet.

That juror, upon examination, stated that he had conscientious scruples upon the subject of capital punishment, and *that it would be against his conscience to render a verdict by which a party would suffer death; but that he thought he could do justice between the state and the defendant.*" Upon objection on this ground by the state, he was held incompetent, and discharged.

It is true, that under the rule held in most of the states of this Union upon the subject of the competency of jurors, this juror would have been competent. But a different and much more stringent rule has been held by this court in excluding jurors in cases of homicide, who were not free from all exception, than has been adopted by those courts. The courts which hold the rule which renders this juror competent, also hold a juror to be competent who has formed or expressed an opinion as to the guilt or innocence of the accused, but who states that his mind would be as free to decide upon the evidence that might be adduced before the jury as if he had never heard anything of the case. But this question has often been presented to the court in behalf of prisoners, and the rule has always been held, and is now considered as entirely settled, that such juror is incompetent, because the juror must be above all exception. Nelms v. The State, 13 S. & M., 500; Cotton v. The State, 31 Miss. R. 504. In this last case, the juror stated, on his examination, that he had formed an opinion of the case *upon rumor,* and *that he felt as free to act in the matter as if he had heard nothing about the case.* Yet this court reversed the judgment below, and held that the juror was not competent, because he was not above all exception—in which opinion I concurred, *solely on the ground that it was a settled rule* under previous decisions of this court. I am unable to comprehend how it is that, upon any just principle, the rule thus established does not apply to the present case. That rule is, that the juror must be entirely free from all bias or preconceived opinion from any cause, and " *above all exception.*" It must apply with as much force to any abstract principle involved in his action as a juror, and which would warp his judgment and incline him to resolve everything in the evidence in a way that would relieve him from the necessity of doing violence to his conscience, as to the question whether the facts did or did not establish the guilt of the accused. If there is any difference in principle between the two cases, the juror who entertains conscientious scruples which would necessarily incline him to favor the accused, is clearly the more obnoxious to the objection of not being " above all exception ;" for, in the other case, the previously formed opinion may be controlled by the evidence. It is an opinion or impression formed upon a supposed state of facts. That is the very subject of trial, and to which the evidence and the whole investigation are directed ; and there is every opportunity to remove his first impressions, and it is to be presumed that he will render a true verdict upon the evidence and law of the case, by which his action would be wholly controlled. But in the case of a juror who would be acting against his conscience in finding a verdict which would inflict capital punishment, there would necessarily be a bias proceeding from a principle of moral duty which could never be removed upon the trial, because its correctness and moral force could never be the subject of proof and judicial investigation in the trial of the cause. The opinion, therefore, must have its full sway upon the juror's judgment, without any opportunity of correcting or removing it ; and, hence, it appears to me to be impossible to hold that such juror could be wholly free from bias and above all exception, without reversing the rule that is considered as settled in this court.

Suppose the juror in this case had stated, on his examination, that he could not conscientiously render a verdict of acquittal of any one who had taken the life of his fellow man, but that in the case in which he was called, " he thought he could do justice between the state and the defendant ;" and that juror had been received upon the panel and a verdict for murder had been found in the case. Could this court have hesitated a moment in reversing the judgment? I presume not ; nay, I suppose it would have been considered an outrage upon the settled law of this court ; and yet I am incapable of perceiving any distinction between that case and the one under consideration. There is in each of them a bias of judgment upon an abstract principle, which must, more or less, influence the juror in considering the evidence, and incline him to find pretexts by which he can render a verdict consistently with his previous views of principle and duty; and it appears to me most obvious, that equally, in both cases, it is impossible to say that such a juror was " above all exception."

I therefore think that the ruling of the court below was most manifestly right in excluding the juror.

HAYNIE *v.* THE STATE, 32 Miss. Rep., 400.

PRACTICE—EVIDENCE.

The high court of errors and appeals refuse to revise the action of the circuit court in giving or refusing instructions asked in a criminal case, because the instructions, being no part of the record, were not made so by exceptions tendered at the trial.

A bill of exceptions to the judgment overruling a motion for a new trial, brings before the appellate court, for review, the motion and the reasons by which it was sustained; the evidence; and the judgment. The exception in such cases may contain a transcript of the instructions, but do not properly bring them up for revisal.

On trial of an indictment for illegal traffic in ardent spirits, the excuse being a sale " for medical purposes," the declarations of the vendee made at the time of the sale, are not sufficient to establish that the liquor was for medical purposes.

In error from the circuit court of Lafayette County. SCRUGGS, J.

The facts will be found in the argument of the counsel for plaintiff in error, and the opinion of the court.

J. F. Cushman, for plaintiff in error.

The appellant (Haynie) was indicted in the circuit court of Lafayette, at the October term, 1855, for a violation of the act of February, 1848, which prohibits the sale of vinous and spirituous liquors in less quanties than five gallons within five miles of the University of Mississippi; at the April term of said circuit court the said Haynie was found guilty, and sentenced to one month's imprisonment in the county jail, and to pay a fine of two hundred and fifty dollars. The only witness for the state was William Trigg, who testified that as many as fifteen times, with-

in the year before this indictment was found, he had bought
spirituous liquors in less quantities than five gallons from Haynie, at his drug store, who was druggist in the town of Oxford,
within five miles of the University of Mississippi.   Witness further said, that Haynie always asked him, when he purchased
the liquors, if he, witness, desired it for medical purposes, before
he let him have it, and witness always said he did want it for
medical purposes ; that he, witness, never purchased two bottles
in one day, and witness did not use the liquors purchased for
medical purposes; that he, witness, did not know that Haynie
knew for what purpose they were used, or that they were not
used for medical purposes.   Witness testified that he was a single
man, and has generally enjoyed good health, which he presumes
Haynie knows; and that he, witness, never told Haynie that he
wanted the liquor for other than medical purposes.

This was all the testimony in the case.   The appellant, Haynie, had no witnesses ; but he asked the court to give the following charge to the jury, which was refused ; and a motion
was made, after conviction, which was overruled, and at the
time excepted, and the charge incorporated in the bill of exceptions.

" The defendant, Haynie, is not responsible for what the witness, (T.,) did with the liquors after he had obtained them, if,
at the time Haynie did not know that witness wanted them for
any other than medical purposes."

The state, also, among others, asked the following charge to
the jury, which was excepted to in the appellant's motion for a
new trial ; but the exception was overruled, and the charge incorporated in the bill of exceptions :

" If the jury believe that the defendant sold the liquor to
Trigg on his representations that it was for medical purposes, it
devolves on the defendant to prove that the liquor was for medical purposes ; and if he has failed to do this, the jury will find
him guilty."

It certainly cannot require argument to prove that the charge
given by the court for the state, which was excepted by the appellant, was erroneous ; for the statute under which the indictment was found does not require a druggist, when he sells from

his drug store liquors for medical purposes, to prove that such liquors were used for that purpose. Acts Leg., 1848, (Hutch. Code, 237.) If it did require such proof, no sensible man would sell spirituous liquors from his drug store in Oxford, as it would be the next thing to an impossibility for him to follow the purchaser, and watch him all the time, to see what he did with it. Besides, such an act would contravene that long established and humane rule of criminal law, which presumes every one innocent until they are proven to be guilty. It was error to have refused appellant's charge. The statute does not require a druggist to foresee what is to be done with the liquor, when he sells, as in this case, for medical purposes. Hutch. Code, 237, § 1.

The appellant certainly ought not to be made to suffer because the witness for the state chose to make false representations as to the use he intended to make of the liquor, when he sold it within the strict letter of the law, for medical purposes, as the witness proves.

D. C. Glenn, attorney general

SMITH, C. J.:

This was a conviction under the act of 1848, declaring it to be unlawful for any person to sell vinous or spiritous liquors, in any quantity less than five gallons, within five miles of the University of Mississippi; provided, however, that the act shall "not be construed to prohibit the sale of vinous and spirituous liquors from any drug store, for medicinal purposes."

The grounds relied on for a reversal of the judgment are:
1st. The refusal of the court to instruct the jury as requested by the defendant. 2d. The jury found contrary to law and the evidence.

Both of these questions arise upon the motion for a new trial, which was made and overruled in the court below.

The act of March 3d, 1846, which provides that "when charges or instructions are given or refused, the same shall be noted at the time by the clerk as given or refused, and when so noted or endorsed, shall be a part of the record, without any bill of exceptions, either on appeal or writ of error to the high court of errors and appeals," is expressly confined to civil suits in the circuit courts.   Hutch. Dig., 893, § 1, 2.

The statute of the 29th of June, 1822, is the only act which authorizes a party on trial for any criminal offense, when he feels himself aggrieved by any charge or decision of the court, to except thereto, and to tender a bill of exceptions, which, when signed and sealed by the judge, is declared to be a part of the record.   It follows hence, that, unless this is done, no decision made, or charge given, pending a prosecution, will become a part of the record in the case; and consequently, although the clerk may note such charge or instruction as having been given or refused, and transcribe it as a part of the record, the court cannot judicially take notice of it.

It does not appear from the record before us, that the action of the court in reference to the giving or refusing of any instructions requested by either party, was excepted to on the trial. This, according to the plain construction of the statute, was essential, before such action of the circuit court could be made the subject of revision in this.   It is clear that an instruction which is given, or one which is refused, is no more a part of the record than the arguments of counsel on the evidence offered at the trial.   And it is settled that no matter, which is not necessarily a part of the record, can be made such, except through the medium of a bill of exceptions.

The proper office of a bill of exceptions tendered to the decision on a motion for a new trial is, to place upon the record the motion, and the reasons assigned in support of it; the judgment on the motion, and the evidence, or the substance of the evidence adduced on the trial.   But a very loose and irregular practice has crept into use, and has been sanctioned by the decisions of this court.   Matter foreign to the legitimate objects of a bill of exceptions to the granting or overruling a motion for a new trial, has been allowed by that means to be introduced into the record.   This practice is commended by its convenience, but the confusion and uncertainty which it occasions are sufficient to condemn it.   A further departure from the rule of practice laid down by the statute is not to be tolerated.

We cannot, therefore, notice the instructions, which appear

from the endorsement of the clerk to have been either granted or withheld, and which are transcribed into the bill of exceptions tendered to the decision overruling the motion for a new trial. If the bill had stated that the defendant did, at the time the instructions were granted or refused, except to the ruling of the court, although he did not tender a formal bill of exceptions, it would, perhaps, have been sufficient. But no such statement is contained in the bill.

But if the defendant had, in fact, excepted, formally, to the refusal of the judge to grant the charge requested by him, and the instruction given at the instance of the district attorney, the result would not be different. The charge granted for the prosecution was unquestionably correct; and conceding that the defendant's instruction which was refused, was proper, and should have been given, the verdict ought not to be set aside, as it was manifestly correct upon the evidence.

Judgment affirmed.

FISHER, J., dissented, as follows:

I dissent from so much of the opinion of the majority of the court, as holds that it was necessary to take a special exception to the refusal of the court to give the defendant's instruction. My opinion is, that the bill of exceptions taken to the decision of the court overruling the motion for a new trial, brings before this court every matter which the court below could consider on that motion.

The court could certainly, on the motion for a new trial, correct its own error, either in giving a wrong, or in refusing a correct instruction, whether the exception was specially taken at the time or not. The court, then, having committed an error, and having the power to correct it, and failing to do so, the question is, can such refusal be made the ground of an exception; and if of an exception, can it not be made a ground of error in this court? I think it can.

MASK et al *v.* THE STATE, 32 Miss. Rep., 405.

HOMICIDE.

On application in a capital case for a change of venue on account of alleged public excitement and prejudice, it is competent for the state to examine witnesses to disprove the existence of such excitement and prejudice; and in such case the defendant has a right to cross-examine the state witnesses. Wheeler v. State, 31 Miss. Rep., 490.

In the examination of witnesses it is the general rule that the cross-examination, like the examination in chief, may be co-extensive with the issue, and not confined to matters brought out by the examination in chief. HANDY, J., dissented.

The weight and number of authorities sanction the rule that a party has no right to cross-examine a witness except as to facts and circumstances connected with matters stated in his direct examination, unless it be to open the way to impeach his credit. HANDY, J., dissenting.

In error from the circuit court of Marshall county. SCRUGGS, J.

Pleasant M. Mask was indicted as principal, in the first degree, and James Mask, Thomas Wooley, and Henry Wooley, as principals in the second degree, for the murder of Susan E. Smith. At the July term, 1855, of the circuit court of Marshall county, the three first were tried, and Pleasant M. Mask was convicted of murder and sentenced to be hung; James Mask was convicted of manslaughter in the second degree, and sentenced to the penitentiary for five years; and Thomas Wooley was convicted of manslaughter in the fourth degree, and was fined $250 and sentenced to confinement in the county jail for three months.

Before the parties were put upon their trial, or any steps were taken in relation thereto, James Mask and Thomas Wooley each moved the court for permission to sever on the trial. In support of their motions the parties severally made and read their affidavits, in which each stated that he had no connexion with the murder with which Pleasant M. Mask was charged, and that he believed that he could not have a fair and impartial trial if tried in connexion with said Pleasant M. Mask. The court overruled the motions, and refused to permit the parties to sever, to which they excepted.

Pleasant M. Mask, then, before any steps were taken for the formation of the jury, moved the court for a continuance. In support of this motion his affidavit was read, in which he stated in substance that, since the indictment was found against him, which was during the present term of the court, he had been confined closely in jail, and had no opportunity of preparing for his defense; that he was too poor to employ counsel, and that counsel had not been employed for him by others until within the last few days; that since the indictment was found he has had not time to procure the attendance of any witness who did not reside in Marshall county; that he understands that one Jonas Smith is to be introduced as a witness against him by the state; that he has been informed, and believes, that John Robinson, who resides in Tippah county, and Frederick Hubbard, who resides in Tishomingo county, are well acquainted with said Smith's character, and have been for a long time, and that they will prove that he is unworthy of credit; that he cannot prove this fact so satisfactorily by any other witness in attendance; and that they are not absent by his consent or procurement; that he expects to have them in attendance at the next term of the court; and that this application is not made for delay, but that justice may be done.

Before the court acted on said motion, the defendant asked leave to amend his affidavit, by adding that he did not know that he could prove the facts by the witnesses therein named until the 23d day of the (then) present month, which was two days before the motion was made for a continuance. The court refused leave to amend as requested, and overruled the motion for a continuance. To all of which the defendant excepted.

The defendant, Pleasant M. Mask, then, before the special *venire* was called, or any steps taken to empanel a jury, moved the court for a change of venue. In support of this motion the defendant read his own affidavit, supported by the affidavits of five others, as required by the statute. The district attorney, for the purpose of traversing these affidavits, called several witnesses, and proposed to examine them. The defendant objected, upon the ground, that the state had no right to traverse the affidavits, and that he was entitled to a change of venue upon his *ex-parte* showing, made in pursuance of the statute. The court overruled this objection, and the district attorney then examined the witnesses in relation to such excitement and prejudice in the county against the prisoner as would prevent his having a fair and impartial trial in Marshall county. These witnesses testified that there was no such excitement or prejudice against the prisoner as would prevent his having a fair and impartial trial in that county, and that they believed he could have such trial. The defendant then proposed to cross-examine said witnesses in relation to the testimony that they had given in their examination in chief; but the court, upon the objection of the district attorney, would not permit any cross-examination whatever of said witnesses. The defendant then asked each of the witnesses " if, at the time of his arrest, and also at the time he was committed to jail on the charge for which he was then indicted, there had not been an attempt by some of the citizens of Marshall county to execute him by ' mob law,' and were not the officers who had him in custody compelled to hurry him to jail to prevent such execution ?" The court refused to permit the witnesses to answer these questions, and the prisoner excepted.

After the jury were empanelled, and during the progress of the trial, one Jonas Smith, a witness for the state, testified that immediately after the deceased was shot, and before the parties had left the scene of the killing, the defendants and said Henry Wooley (who was also indicted with them, but was not on his trial) were near to each other—nearer than witness was to either of them, and near enough to hear all that was said. The district attorney then asked witness if he heard either of the parties, at the time they left, say anything ? The defendants objected to witness answering the question, and the court overruled the objection and permitted the witness to answer. Witness then answered, "that he heard Henry Wooley say to his (witness's) daughter, Sarah Jane, as he was leaving, ' If you do not hold your mouth, I will blow your damned brains out.' " The defendants excepted to this action of the court, and also to the refusal of the court to exclude said answer from the consideration of the jury upon the motion.

In the further progress of the trial, Jane Norris, a witness for the state, testified, that about nine o'clock of the morning of the day on which deceased was killed by the defendants, a Miss Wooley, and Mrs. Mask, the wife of defendant, Pleasant M. Mask, " came along the public road by her house ; they were going from the direction of Pleasant M. Mask's house toward old man Wooley's, and were laughing and talking; when they were opposite her house they stopped and looked towards the house, and were all in a crowd together." She was then asked by the state, "If she heard any of them say anything, and if so, what?" To this question the defendants objected, but the court overruled the objection and permitted the witness to answer it. The witness, in reply, stated, "She heard one of the party—she does not know which—say, 'that if they did not get the d—d rascal that day, they would get him.'" To this action of the court in overruling their objection; and also to the refusal of the court to exclude said answer from the consideration of the jury upon their motion, the defendants excepted.

In the further progress of the trial, the state introduced one Robert Walker, and examined him in relation to the locality of the various roads in the neigborhood in which the killing took place, and also in relation to the road on which he saw the defendants traveling on the evening of the killing, and the direction in which they were going; and also in relation to declarations made by them as to which of the roads they would travel. The defendants, on cross-examination of said witness, asked him, "if he had seen the wound of which the deceased died, and what was its size, nature and character?" The state objected to witness answering said question, because he had not, in his direct examination spoken of the wound. The court sustained the objection, but stated to the prisoners, that after the state had closed her testimony they might recall said witness, make him their witness, and examine him to that point, to which ruling of the court the prisoners excepted.

In the further progress of the trial the state asked Louis Deshong, (a witness for the prosecution,) if James Norris had prosecuted Pleasant M. Mask before a justice of the peace for stealing corn, and were Smith Lyons, and the witnesses R. J. Smith and William Smith witnesses against him on that trial? The witness answered that Mask had been so prosecuted, and that the persons named were witnesses against him.

It is necessary to state that the testimony of the state tended to show an attempt on the part of the defendants to kill or do some injury to R. J. Smith, who was the father of the deceased, and William Smith, who was her brother, and that she was killed whilst the parties were so engaged in carrying out this enterprise, and that the quarrel was in relation to what they had said about Pleasant M. Mask stealing corn.

In the further progress of the trial, and after the state's testimony had closed, and the defendants had introduced a portion of their testimony, the defendants, James Mask and Thomas Wooley, offered to prove by Mrs. Mask, wife of Pleasant M. Mask, that there was no conspiracy on their part to do any act connected with the murder of the deceased. The state objected, and the court refused to permit Mrs. Mask to be examined for any purpose whatever. To which ruling of the court the defendants excepted. The defendants moved for a new trial, which was overruled, to which they tendered a bill of exceptions. They also moved in arrest of judgment because the jury had convicted them of different offenses. This motion was also overruled, and they excepted.

This writ of error was sued out by Pleasant M. Mask and James Mask.

Clapp & Strickland, for plaintiffs in error.

H. W. Walter, on same side.

The first error which I shall notice, grows out of the refusal by the court below to change the venue. It is found in the third bill of exceptions.

The court below not only erred in refusing to change the venue, but it committed two additional errors in order to consummate the first.

The law provides that it shall and may be lawful for the circuit court to change the venue in criminal cases, " on a sufficient showing being made by the prisoner on oath, supported by the testimony of one or more credible witnesses, that he cannot have a fair and impartial trial in the county where the offense is charged to have been committed." Pleasant Mask made that showing on oath in the very language of the statute. This oath showing was supported not only by one, but five witnesses. It was then the duty of the court below to grant the change. No discretion was allowed it. What is meant by the statute in using the term, "sufficient showing on oath?" Simply the affidavit of the prisoner that he believed he could not get a fair and impartial trial, and then supporting that affidavit by that of one or more credible witnesses. This is the sufficient showing on oath, and no discretion was left to the court. It is like the plea in the imparlance term; whenever legal on its face it operates a continuance. An affidavit, complying in terms with the language of the statute, and supported by other affidavits, is a sufficient showing, and the venue should have been changed; and the refusal to do this, constituted error number one, as disclosed by this bill of exception.

If this view be correct, then the court committed error number two, in permitting the affidavit of Mask to be traversed, to as great an extent as it would have erred had it permitted a hearing of a traverse of a plea, at the imparlance term. The affidavits, like the plea, sufficient on their face, admitted of no denial then. Suppose, however, that we are mistaken on this point, and that the court below had discretion as to the deficiency,—still these affidavits, like those for a continuance of a case, (certainly they are of a higher grade and importance,) are not traversable. This point is too well settled by both practice and precedent to admit of a doubt.

In McDaniel v. The State, 8 S. & M., the court say that the court below could look only to the facts stated in the affidavit. Suppose however, that we may be wrong in both the foregoing opinions, and that it was a matter within the discretion of the court; yet even this discretion can be reviewed by this court. It is true that this court will seldom interfere, yet it sometimes does, and therefore the discretion of the court below is not beyond the control of this court. In Marshall v. Fulgan, 4 How., 216, it was held that a refusal to hear an application for continuance, was error.

In Franks v. Wanzer, 3 Cushm., 121, this court again said that, "if flagrant and manifest injustice were done by an ill-directed and capricious exercise of such discretion, we are not prepared to say that it would not be our duty to apply the corrective." This court then reversed the judgment of the court below.

These cases at least show that this court does not regard the discretion of the court below as entirely beyond correction. How stands the case at bar? We had made the showing required by law. Of itself, and without contradiction, it was sufficient to change the *venue,* even in the judgment of the court below. This is shown by the traverse of the case we made. If our case was not sufficient, why traverse, why rebut it? and if traversed, why not permit us to avail ourselves of, and put on the record all the testimony? Why refuse a cross-examination altogether? If this court has heretofore reversed, because a judge in a civil case refused to hear an application, would they not in a case involving life, reverse, because the court refused to hear the whole of the evidence offered to support the application? Suppose, even in a civil suit, that a court would hear but part of an affidavit for continuance, would not this court, in accordance with its decision in 4 Howard, reverse it? How much more certainly would reversal follow in a matter of death! Not only did the court do this, but in the language of Franks v. Wanzer, 3 Cushm., 121, it committed flagrant and manifest injustice in refusing a cross-examination of witnesses—a judgment without a precedent since the days of Lord Jeffreys. The great test of credibility was wholly disregarded. The only safeguard against perjury was beaten down. The avenues of prejudice were open without a guard. Not only was the law, in its humanity, annulled, but the very constitution itself was assailed. It delares that the accused shall be confronted by the witnesses against him. Not merely that he shall look upon and listen to them, but that he shall use, when desired, the great test of truth, a cross-examination. Even this was denied the prisoner, Pleasant Mask, and he was forced to remain for trial in the midst of an infuriated populace, who would have respected neither his personal rights nor those of the jury, had they acquitted him. He was forced to trial in the midst of such a population; and James Mask suffered equally with the effects of that undue excitement. But we must again repeat, that the matter of changing the *venue* is one not left to the discretion of the court below; that when a showing is made by affidavit of the accused, that he cannot have a fair trial, supported by one or more competent witnesses, the *satisfactory* showing is made, and the court must grant it.

Whilst this court has not directly decided whether a change of *venue* is matter of discretion, yet it has in several cases, alluded to the subject in such manner as shows it would take jurisdiction. For instance, when the *venue* is changed, the order granting it must appear upon the record. Sanders v. Morse, 3 How., 101. That after trial no objection can be taken to the order for a change of *venue.* 4 How., 90. That the affidavit for change of *venue* must be made part of the bill of exceptions. Grant v. Planters' Bank, 4 How., 326 ; and that, when a party has obtained a change of *venue,* he cannot question its regularity. Soper v. The State, 3 How., 429. But this court has gone still further ; and in Carbrough v. Yalabusha County, 3 S. & M., reversed the order of the court making the change, because that change was illegal. If this court can, for any cause, reverse, then it can, for all causes, take jurisdiction, and even though it might be a matter of delicacy to disturb the judgment below, no question is purely a matter of discretion in the circuit judge, over which this court exercises a revisionary power, *for any purpose.*

(We respectfully call the attention of the court to the fact, that the law in reference to change of *venue* in civil or criminal cases, is essentially different. In the former (Hutch., 850), the judge is required to hear evidence from both parties ; in the latter, no such permission is granted. In criminal cases, the prisoner is warring against the excitement of the populace. That populace is not permitted to be heard, and thus gratify its prejudice, the very thing the change of *venue* is to defeat. The legislature has, therefore, wisely declined giving the court the right to hear testimony from both parties in a criminal case, the populace being one party, and the prisoner another to this issue. This is here (somewhat out of place) urged in support of our second position.)

The court below erred in stopping the cross-examination of Robert S. Walker. The state asked the witness several questions as to what he had seen of defendants on the day of the killing. The defendants cross-examined as to this, and then further asked the witness if he had seen the wound of which deceased died, and what was its size, nature, and character ? This question the court told the witness not to answer, as he had not alluded to this subject on his examination in chief; and the court told the prisoners that after the state had closed its testimony, they might call the witness, *make him theirs*, and then examine him on this point.

We submit that the court erred on this point. The rule is this, viz. : " a party may cross-examine as to the *res gestæ*, though it may be new matter." In England this rule has never been questioned. It is universally recognized and supported. Morgan v. Brydges, 2 Starkie R., 314 ; Rex v. Brook, ib., 472 ; 1 Phillips Ev., 273.

The supreme court of Pennsylvania, in a case in 16 S. & R., adopted a different rule, but reversed it, and in Markley v. Swartzlander, 8 Watts & Serg., 172, employed the language above quoted. The English rule was sustained in Moody v. Rowell, 17 Pick., 490 ; Jackson v. Varrick, 7 Cow., 283 ; Fulton Bank v. Stafford, 2 Wend., 483. The rule is universal in England and equally so in the state courts in this country. The supreme court of the United States is the only exception. The answer to this question might have been highly important. It certainly was pertinent to the issue. One of the witnesses says the deceased died of that wound. Walker could have proved its character, and then proof would have been admissible, that such a wound as described could not have produced death. Proof might also have been made that the pistol of Mask was loaded with such character of shot, as could not have produced such a wound. The question was pertinent to the issue. We might have been willing to have made this proof from the witness of the state, but not from our own witness. His answer would have been conclusive on the state. As its witness, his credit could not have been impeached ; as ours it might. The court below refused us this benefit, for it expressly refused permission to cross-examine him *as the witness of the state ;* but said we might recall him and *make him our witness.* This was in violation of the rule as uniformly established in England, and with equal uniformity held by the *state* courts in this country ;

the supreme court of the United States being the only exception.

The court erred in giving the 7th charge asked by the prisoners, *with the addition annexed*. The charge asked for was that "the jury must be satisfied from the evidence and the evidence only, that a conspiracy existed, and they cannot infer it from any thing not in proof before them." This unquestionably is law, but the court added the following, viz. : "A conspiracy does not imply a previous meeting and formal agreement of the parties. It is sufficient if they were present with a common felonious intent."

Our legislature has declared that for the better preservation of the sanctity of the trial by jury pure and uninfluenced, no judge "shall charge the jury on points or principles of law, applicable to the case before them, unless the parties to such issue or their counsel differ in opinion as to the same ; or one of the parties or counsel shall ask the charge of said judge to be given upon some point in controversy in said issue, which shall be distinctly specified in writing by the party asking such charge ; and the judge shall charge no other point than that to which his opinion is required." Hutch. Code, 888. Such is the law, and in making additions to the 7th, 9th, and 10th charges of defendants, the court violated this law. As the 7th charge was the first to which the court below made an addition, we will confine our remarks to it, and these remarks will be applicable to all the additions to the other charges.

The 7th charge is unquestionably sound law. There was no issue in the court below as to its legality. The court should have given it. In the next place, the charge was distinctly reduced to writing, and should have been given or refused. In the last place, the jury were by the instruction told that they could only regard the evidence in the case. This was the point in the charge, and yet the court below told the jury what constituted conspiracy, and thus charged on a point "to which his opinion was not required." In civil cases, (Hutch. Code, 891), the law permits the court to add in writing a charge. This is applicable to civil cases only, but in criminal cases, "for the better preservation of the sanctity of trial by jury pure and uninfluenced," the court shall not charge. It is true that this court (*obiter dictum*) said in Bowles v. The State, 9 S. & M., 284, that the judge is not bound to give or refuse the charge in the precise terms asked by counsel, but may modify the charges asked on both sides, so as to make them conformable to its own views of the law. We respectfully submit that this was an unguarded remark by this court, (it was certainly not pertinent to the point under consideration,) and is not law. It might be true in a civil, but not in a criminal case. Concede for argument's sake that this may be true in criminal cases. The *dictum* is, that the court may *modify* the charge. This is all—*modify*. What modification to the 7th charge is the addition to it? The charge is, that the jury can look to the evidence only in forming their verdict. The addition tells the jury what a conspiracy is. The charge tells the jury the range of their investigation; the addition tells them what the law terms a conspiracy. It is as much a modification as the change of a dwelling-house to a steamboat would be.

This very addition is fully embraced in the charges of the state, and if the course pursued by the court below is tolerated, a prisoner can be crucified by having the state's charges *seriatim*, tacked on each of his charges. The purity of trial by jury would be fearfully tarnished.

We respectfully submit, that the fifth charge given by the state is too broad, and was calculated to mislead the jury. It allows nothing for human passions. The insult by words may be such, for a moment, as completely to unsettle the judgment, and would reduce the killing to manslaughter.

Again, the court below erred in giving the ninth charge asked for by the state, and in refusing to arrest the judgment. The charge, and the refusal to arrest, present the same error. The whole case, as to James Mask and Thomas Wooley, is based on their conspiracy to commit a felony on R. J. Smith, the brother of the deceased. The admission of the testimony of Mrs. Norris, and of L. Deshong, was permitted. If the conviction of James Mask and Thomas Wooley, did not follow from conspiracy, then this testimony was clearly illegal. But the whole case, as to them, was based on the fact, (as attempted to be established,) that a conspiracy did exist to commit a felony on R. J. Smith.   As co-conspirators then, the court could not charge that one of them could be acquitted, one found guilty of one offense, and the third of a still different one.   The court having charged this, and the jury having found them all guilty of different offenses, the judgment should have been arrested. It is certain, that neither James Mask nor Thomas Wooley did the act that produced death.   How, then, were they responsible? By entertaining a criminal intent in common with Pleasant Mask for an offense not committed, (the injury to R. J. Smith,) and the act of Pleasant, in committing another act, not contemplated by them, viz.: the killing of Miss Smith.   The criminal intent is one part of the offense, the commission of the act another.   The criminal intent was nothing; but became a grave offense when consummated by the act of their co-conspirator. How is it possible, then, that mere co-conspirators, not themselves acting, can be guilty of a different offense from the actor?   How can one be acquitted, another be found guilty of one offense, and another, still, of a different one?   The criminal intent is the power of attorney by which the agent acts.   This delegated power is general, and binds the principal to the full extent in all acts committed under it.   And yet the principal, under this charge, may be bound for nothing, or for a part of the act, or for the full act.   This will not do.   The criminal intent is the power by which the principal is bound for the whole conduct of the actor, or he is bound for nothing.   As there is no agency in crime, but all are alike bound or alike free, you cannot say to the actor, you are guilty of one offense, and to the co-conspirator, you are guilty of another.   The doctrine of relation or privity in the act applies to all.   The same offense could not be murder in Pleasant Mask, and but manslaughter as to the others.   His act bound them—his act was theirs.   It is impossible, therefore, that this act, as to him, could be murder, as to them, manslaughter.

H. H. Chalmers, for the state.

This is an appeal from the circuit court of Marshall county, where the plaintiffs before this court were indicted, together with Henry and Thomas Wooley, for the murder of Susan Elizabeth Smith.

Henry Wooley, before the finding of the true bill, fled to parts unknown, and made his escape. Thomas Wooley was convicted of manslaughter in the fourth degree; sentenced to three months in the county jail, and has already served out his time. Pleasant M. Mask and James Mask, his brother, were convicted respectively of murder and manslaughter in the second degree, and sentenced accordingly. From that verdict and judgment, they have taken their appeal to this court, and assign various errors apparent upon the record, for which they contend that they should have a new trial.

First. Because the court below refused to grant them a severance of their cases.

In overruling the prisoners' motion for a severance, I respectfully submit that the court below did not err, or even if it did, it is not such error as will entitle the appellants to a new trial. The accused assigned no cause in their motion for a severance and the affidavits accompanying it, save the general one, that they believed it would be prejudicial to their interests to be tried jointly; because, I suppose they wished to avail themselves of the testimony of each other. Was this a sufficient reason to deprive the state of the right, which she unquestionably has, to insist upon the exclusion of the testimony of one codefendant in favor of another? And even if it were sufficient, is not the granting or the refusal of a severance a matter wholly within the discretion of the court below, and one over which this court will hesitate to take control? In the case of the United States v. Gibert et al., 2 Sum., 63, Judge Story uses the following language: "Now, this" (the granting of a severance) "has been long since settled by the supreme court of the United States, to be a matter not of right, but of sound discretion, to be exercised by the court." See also United States v. Marchant, 12 Wheat., 480. "Where the reason assigned for separate trials was, that the prisoners might use the testimony of each other in their defense, it was held that this would not justify the court in the exercise of its discretion." Wharton Criminal Law, 918, and authorities there cited.

The second error, assigned by appellants, is the refusal of the

court below to grant them a continuance of their case to the
next term of the court.

This cause of error, like the first, is not one for which this
court will grant a new trial.   In the case of Babcock v. Scott,
1 How. (Miss.) R., 100, Judge Smith holds the following language : "I am not aware that it has ever been holden that a
refusal to grant a continuance is error.   This power is committed entirely to the discretion of the judge."   See also Berry v.
Hale, 1 How., 315 ; Wharton Crim. Law, 830.

The third error assigned by appellants is, the refusal of the
court below to grant a change of venue.   And this point, too,
like the first and second, I submit, is a matter entirely within the
discretion of the court below.

A change of venue, in criminal cases, is a thing unknown in
the common law, and owes its origin entirely to statutary enactments.   Upon this point our *statute*, whatever may have been
heretofore the practice of circuit judges, is clear and explicit.

" From and after the passage of this act, it shall and may be
lawful for any circuit court in this state," etc.   The language
used " *shall be lawful*," without doubt implies that it is left entirely to the discretion of · the court below.   The prisoners
applied for a change of venue, because they said they could not
get a fair trial in Marshall county ; and two witnesses swore that
they did not believe they could.

In the exercise of the discretion entrusted to him by the
statute, the court below had a half-dozen witnesses, from all
parts of the county, examined, who swore that there was no
undue or unusual excitement against the prisoners ; that, in their
opinion, they could have a fair trial there, and that the witnesses
introduced by the accused were their relations.   Upon this
showing, Judge Scruggs overruled the motion for a change of
venue, as he had an unquestionable right, by the statute, to do.

Is this court prepared to grant the prisoner a new trial in
consequence of such action ?   An affidavit of one indicted for
a capital offense, stating that he believed he could not obtain an
impartial trial, because a subscription for his arrest was had in
the district, was held, in South Carolina, not a sufficient cause
for change of venue.   State v. Williams, 2 M'Cord, 383.

The fourth ground of error alleged by the accused is, that the witness, Jonas Smith, was permitted to testify as to a remark made by Henry Wooley, who was not upon his trial.

Henry Wooley was one of the four persons who, in conspiracy together, as charged by the state, went to the house of the father of deceased. He was indicted, together with the other three, but made his escape. After the shooting of Miss Smith by Pleasant M. Mask, and just as the party were leaving the scene of action, he pointed his rifle at Sarah Jane Smith, who was weeping and screaming over the body of her murdered sister, and told her to "shut her mouth, or he would blow her damned brains out."

To the giving in of this testimony the defendants objected, though upon what ground it is difficult to perceive.

If there was a conspiracy among the accused, (and that there was, there is scarcely room for a shadow of a doubt,) Henry Wooley was certainly one of the conspirators, and as such, whether he was on trial or not, any acts or declarations of his, made at the time of the perpetration of the deed, are clearly admissible. Whart. Crim. Law, 261, 263.

The court is too familiar with the principle, that any act or declaration of one of the conspirators, done or said in the transaction of the preconcerted plan, is the act or declaration of all, and is evidence against all, to require more than a passing reference to it. Russell on Crimes, 510; Barbour Criminal Treatise, 228.

The fifth error, on account of which the appellants ask a new trial, is, that the witness, Mrs. Norris, was permitted to testify as to the remark overheard by her, as three of the accused, in company with two ladies, were passing her house, on the morning that Miss Smith was killed.

Mrs. Norris is the wife of James Norris, whose corn Pleasant M. Mask had been charged with stealing, about which the whole of this most unfortunate difficulty had arisen. It had been proved, that the first question asked by Pleasant Mask, when he rode up to Smith's house, was for Norris.

On the morning of that day, as Mrs. Norris was standing in front of her house, the two appellants before this court, and

Thomas Wooley, together with Mrs. Mask and Miss Wooley
came along the road.   In front of her house Mrs. Norris saw
them pause and look towards the house, and one of them, she
could not say which, remarked, "If we don't get the d——d rascal
to-day, we will get him."   Her husband was in sight, going
towards the field, with a gun on his shoulder.   We submit, that
in view of the facts in the case, the testimony went properly to
the jury.   It was their province to determine how much weight
it was entitled to.   The state is attempting to prove a conspiracy, on the part of the accused, to commit a felony upon the
elder and younger Smith; in the perpetration of which, Miss
Smith was killed.   The ground of their animosity against the
Smiths was, that they had given evidence against P. M. Mask,
in the corn-stealing charge, upon which he had been prosecuted
by Norris.   This remark, overheard by Mrs. Norris, was evidently made by one of the accused.   Counsel will scarcely contend that it came from Mrs. Mask or Miss Wooley.   It went
directly to show a formed and expressed intention among the
prisoners to do some great bodily harm to some one; the probabilities all are, that that some one was Norris or the Smiths.
The jury was the proper judge of those probabilities.   The evidence of a conspiracy must, from the nature of the case, be
always vague and circumstantial, and to lay down a strict and
arbitrary rule to the state, would always defeat the proof
of one.   Whart. Crim. Law, 695 ;   Russ. on Crimes, 511 ;
2 Starkie Evidence, part 1, p. 330;   Barbour Crim. Treatise,
228.

The defendants rely, sixthly, upon an error alleged to have
been committed by the court below, in permitting the witness,
Louis Deshong, to testify as to the charge of corn-stealing having
been brought by Norris against Mask ; and the Smiths having
been witnesses upon the trial before the magistrate.

Whilst we admit, that the fact that this charge had been
brought, and that the Smiths testified as to its truth, was not
strictly a part of the "*res gestæ*" of the killing; yet, as establishing the fact of the malice, and giving a clue to the formation of the conspiracy, it is all-important.   Without some testimony as to antecedent transactions between the parties, it would

have been difficult to show any motive by which the accused were actuated.

Malice, like conspiracy, must be inferred; and may be inferred from a great many extraneous circumstances, not directly connected with the perpetration of the deed; and with a view to show a preconceived grudge, and give a clue to the formation of the conspiracy, we submit it to the court, if the questions asked Deshong were not admissible.

The seventh cause of error assigned by the prisoners, why a new trial should be awarded them is, that the witness, R. J. Walker, was not permitted to answer a question put to him by defendants' counsel.

The witness was introduced by the state and examined as to the roads running in different directions through the country where the deed was committed. He was handed over to the accused for a cross-examination, and was asked by them, " if he had ever seen Miss Smith's wound, and what was its nature, size and character." The district attorney objected to the question, and the court sustained the objection.

All writers upon the evidence, after giving the general rules for its introduction and rejection, conclude, by giving great latitude to the exercise of the sound discretion of the courts. Many questions of a delicate nature, they leave altogether to the judgment of the presiding judge.

In 1 Monroe, 118, 119, the court, after setting forth the manner in which testimony should be introduced, go on to say : " We say *generally*, for it will often be found necessary and proper for the presiding court, for good reasons, to depart from them to attain complete justice ; and when they ought or ought not to be varied, must in a great measure be left to the sound discretion and prudence of the inferior court. And this court (an appellate court) ought never to interfere for such departure, except injustice is done by that departure."

Has any injustice been done the prisoners by the rejection of the testimony in this case ? Does it in any way affect the substantial justice of the verdict, that Walker was not permitted to speak of Miss Smith's wound ? Had not the nature, character and *effects* of that wound been already proven beyond cavil or question ? Will this court set aside the verdict of the jury upon this ground ?

And, again, this question was asked the witness on cross-examination—was altogether a new fact, about which he had not spoken, and to which he had not alluded, and it was evidently put with a view afterwards to discredit him. The authorities upon this subject are full and explicit. "It is here to be observed, that a witness is not to be cross-examined as to any distinct, collateral fact, for the purpose of afterwards impeaching his testimony by contradicting him." Starkie Evidence, 189.

A witness cannot be cross-examined as to any distinct, collateral fact, for the purpose of afterwards contradicting him." Barbour Crim. Treat., 389 ; Roscoe Crim. Ev., 128–139.

But I take the broader position that the refusal of the court to allow the witness to answer this question, was right, because it was a question asked upon cross-examination, and having no connection with any thing deposed to by him in his examination in chief. I am not aware that this question has ever been brought before this court before ; and it is not a new one in the judicial history of the country. Barbour, in his "Criminal Treatise," p. 399, lays down the broad proposition—"The questions upon the cross-examination should all be such as arise out of the evidence given by the witness in his examination in chief, or are calculated to elicit the witness's title to credit." And the rule is now considered by the supreme court of the United States to be well established, that " a party has no right to cross-examine any witness except as to facts and circumstances connected with the matters stated in his examination in chief, and if he wishes to examine as to other matters, he must do so by making the witness his own and calling him as such in the subsequent progress of the cause." Greenleaf Evidence, 522, § 446. See also 14 Peters Reports, 461, from which Greenleaf extracts the preceding sentence. Also, 16 Serg. & Rawle, 77, where the the same doctrine is declared.

Judge Scruggs, in the court below, suggested to the defendants the very course which Judge Story, in 14 Peters, lays down as the proper one, viz., to recall the witness at a subsequent stage of the case, make him their own, and examine him as to any thing they saw proper. They declined doing so. Will this court now set aside the verdict of the jury and award them a new trial, because of the exclusion of evidence, which could not possibly have had any material influence upon the verdict, and which they could most easily have introduced, had they wished it?

The accused demand a new trial, eighthly, because Mrs. Mask, the wife of one of the defendants, was not permitted to testify in behalf of the other two.

The law upon this point is ample and clear. Says Greenleaf, "Nor is she, (the wife of one co-defendant,) a witness for a co-defendant if her testimony, as in the case of a conspiracy, would tend directly to her husband's acquittal." 1 Greenleaf Ev., 406, § 335.

"So upon an indictment for a conspiracy, the wife of one defendant cannot be called as a witness for another." Roscoe Cr. Ev., 138; also 2 Starkie Ev., part 1, p. 330; Whart. Cr. Law, 294.

The appellants assign as the ninth error on the face of the record, on account of which they should have a new trial, the overruling by the court below of their motion for a new trial.

Their motion was based upon several grounds, some of which have already been considered. Among the rest (merely *pro forma*, it is to be supposed), they allege that the verdict of the jury was contrary to law and evidence. I can say with safety and without fear of exaggeration, that dark as are the criminal annals of our state, such an awful and unprovoked murder as the record sets forth in this case, never disgraced them before. By its side the offenses of McCann and Dyson fade almost into insignificance. They except too to the charges of the judge. These charges are many in number, and in matter range through the whole science of criminal law. In them I see nothing illegal or calculated unjustly to prejudice the defendants' case. The last cause, for which they moved a new trial in the court below, was, that one Joseph Walker, the clerk of the court, and a physician by profession, administered to one of the jurors a dose of medicine without the permission of the judge. The juror was taken dangerously ill with cholera-morbus in the night;

the officer in charge applied to Dr. Walker; he sent him a preparation in which it was proved there was an infusion of brandy, of which medicine the juror took a table-spoonful that night; brought it into court with him next morning, and during the argument of counsel took several more doses.

As to whether counsel for the accused mean to insist that Dr. Walker and the sheriff should have allowed the unfortunate juror to have died, without any medicine at all, or whether they would intimate that the brandy contained in it rendered him unable to render a correct verdict, I must refer the court for information to the gentlemen themselves.

The tenth and last error assigned by the accused, is the overruling by the court below of their motion in arrest of judgment.

This motion was based solely upon the fact, that the jury had found them guilty of different offenses.

There was certainly no error in this. By the statute in this state, a jury can find a criminal guilty of any less grade of the same offense for which he is indicted; and certainly where two men are tried jointly for the same offense, the jury can determine that one is guilty of a higher, and the other of a lower degree of crime, according to the share which each took in the perpetration of the deed.

D. C. Glenn, attorney general, argued the cause orally.

Fisher, J.:

This was an indictment returned by the grand jury into the circuit court of Marshall county, charging the defendants below with the murder of one Susan Elizabeth Smith.

The first error assigned relates to the defendants' application for a change of the venue to some other county of the district. The application appears to have conformed to the requisitions of the statute. The court, however, permitted the prosecution to introduce and examine several witnesses, with a view of making a counter showing, and upon hearing their testimony refused the application, to which action of the court the counsel for the defendants excepted. This point has recently been decided by this court in the case of Weeks v. The State, holding that such testimony could be introduced. But it is said that the court erred in refusing to permit the defendants' counsel to cross-examine the witnesses. It appears by the record that the court refused any cross-examination whatever to be made. The rule on this subject is almost without exception, and is founded in both reason and the clearest principles of justice, that an examination in chief of a witness by a party, carries with it the right to a cross-examination by the adverse party; the object being to elicit the whole truth in regard to the particular subject of investigation before the court. We perceive nothing in the nature of this investigation to authorize in disregarding the rule. The witnesses doubtless intended to express nothing but an honest opinion in regard to the state of public opinion in the county; but this opinion, though potent in their estimation, might have been worth nothing in the sound and discriminating judgment of the court, when tested by the facts and circumstances brought out on a cross-examination. We are therefore of the opinion that the court erred on this point.

It is next assigned as error that the court erred in refusing to permit the counsel of the defendants to cross-examine a witness introduced on the part of the state as to matters not immediately connected with the direct examination. The witness stated, that on the day of the killing he saw the defendants in a certain road leading in the direction of the house of the father of the deceased, and that he overheard a certain conversation among the parties in relation to the road. The counsel for the defendants asked the witness on cross-examination if he had examined the wound of which the deceased died, and if so, to state its size and character. Upon objection being made, the court refused to permit the witness to answer this question, but stated to counsel that he could, at the proper time, if he so desired, make the witness his own and examine him as to this matter.

The general rule as laid down in all the elementary writers is, that the cross-examination, like the examination in chief, may be co-extensive with the issue, and that it is not confined merely to matters brought out by the direct examination. The object of the testimony was, no doubt, to form a link in the chain of evidence to establish malice or a conspiracy by the defendants; and conceding, for the sake of argument, that it could rise to this importance, it still would be but evidence taken by itself of an intention to commit murder, and not of the actual commission of it.   Now, suppose the cross-interrogatory had been answered, the size and character of the wound given, and that it had appeared from the nature of the wound that the defendants could not have inflicted it with any weapon which they or either of them had about their persons or within their reach at the time, would not the force of the testimony elicited by the state have been completely destroyed.   It is the doing of an unlawful act that gives the state the right to prove an unlawful intent, and hence, if the parties were not guilty of the act itself, to wit, the homicide, or concerned with others who were guilty, though they may have intended to do the act, yet their unexecuted intention, while it may have been highly criminal, could not be treated as murder, or as any other grade of homicide.   What, then, would the proof, taken as a whole, establish?   The prosecution might say that we have by our testimony, taken by itself, created a presumption of malice ; that is to say, an intention to commit murder.   The defendants might reply, if you have, the same witness proves that we could not have committed the murder.   Whatever force, then, there might be in the first presumption, it would be destroyed by the second.

The testimony thus goes to the jury as a whole, and the question is, What fact does it tend to establish?   The answer is at once—none.   Because the presumption of malice is rebutted by the other presumption that the parties could not have committed the deed.

We have treated the cross-interrogatory as having been answered for the purpose of illustrating the principle and of showing that, while it may frequently be convenient to confine a party to the matter embraced in the direct examination, yet it is a rule founded in good and safe policy to allow the cross-examination the same latitude which is allowed to the examination in chief.   Circumstances will generally suggest to the judge presiding at the trial when there should be a departure from the rule.   It is not deemed necessary to notice the conflict which is said to exist in the authorities on this subject.   The conflict has no doubt arisen from the fact that courts have sometimes misunderstood the object of a cross-examination, and have treated the testimony thus elicited as the defendant's evidence instead of treating it as a part of the testimony of the party introducing the witness.   When the state introduces a witness on the stand, he is there for the purpose of telling the whole truth of the matter relevant to the issue, and whether what he states is in response to the questions propounded by the prosecution or by the defendants, it is the testimony of the state, and as such must be received, weighed, and considered by the jury.   It is not the case of a confession and avoidance, for the reason that murder, when confessed, cannot be avoided except by a plea of acquittal or former conviction.   Nor is it the case of a party endeavoring to prove himself innocent, but of the state endeavoring to prove him guilty ; and in making this proof, he is only insisting that the witnesses shall state what they are required by their oath to state—the whole truth relevant to the issue then under investigation.

In regard to the various other questions involved in the case, we are of opinion that the court committed no error.   If we were to go into an examination of each question, we would be compelled to comment to some extent upon facts which ought to be left for the consideration of the jury, untrammelled by any opinion of this or any other court, as it is their province alone to weigh the evidence.

For the reasons already stated the judgment will be reversed, and a *venire de novo* awarded.

Smith, C. J., concurred.

Handy, J., dissented, as follows :

I cannot concur in the opinion of the majority of the court upon the point of the refusal of the court below to allow the examination of the witness, Walker, proposed on the part of the prisoners, as upon cross-examination.

It appears that that witness had been called and examined by the state, and testified merely that he had seen the prisoners on the day when the killing took place, riding together, and the direction from which they came, and that one of them inquired of the others, at a particular point, which was the way to go. The prisoners thereupon proposed to interrogate the witness whether he had seen the wound of which the deceased died, and what was its size and character? No connection between this alleged cross-examination and the statements of the witness in chief was shown or suggested, nor does it appear that the object of the cross-examination was to lay the foundation for impeaching the credit of the witness. The question presented, therefore, is, whether a witness called by one party and examined in chief upon a distinct and isolated fact, may be examined by the other party by way of cross-examination upon points not embraced in the examination in chief, but pertinent to the general merits of the case.

A difference of opinion upon this point exists between courts whose opinions are entitled to the greatest respect. In Massachusetts it has been held that a witness who has been sworn and examined as to an isolated fact, may be fully cross-examined as to the whole case. Moody v. Rowell, 17 Pick., 499. And the same rule appears to be sanctioned in England, in the case of Rex v. Brooke, 2 Stark. Rep. (3 Eng. Com. Law Rep.), 472. On the contrary, the weight and number of authorities sanction the rule that a party has no right to cross-examine a witness except as to the facts and circumstances connected with the matters stated in his direct examination, unless it be to open the way to impeach his credit. Harrison v. Rowan, 3 Wash. C. C. Rep., 580; Ellmaker v. Buckley, 16 S. & R., 72; Floyd v. Bovard, 6 Serg. & Watts, 75; Philadelphia and Trenton Railroad Company v. Stimpson, 14 Peters, 448.

I consider this latter rule as founded on the sounder reason, and as establishing the better practice.

Cross-examination, *ex vi termini*, must relate to what has been stated by the witness on his examination in chief and it could not properly be denominated cross-examination when it extended to new matter about which the witness had given no testimony. Suppose the first witness introduced by the plaintiff testifies only to an isolated fact, as, for example, the execution of a document relied on by the plaintiff as evidence. Would it be competent for the defendant to anticipate the merits of the case to be developed by the plaintiff, and, by way of cross-examination, to examine the witness as to matters which he sup-

posed to be involved in establishing the plaintiff's case, and go
into the merits of the whole case? Such a course would scarcely
be sanctioned or tolerated by any court. And why? Because
it would tend to subvert the regular order of presenting the case,
and lead to confusion. And the same principle would seem to
apply to the examination of every witness by either party in any
stage of the cause; and this is shown by the general rule of
practice in the examination of witnesses. That rule is, that the
party calling the witness examines him in chief; the adverse
party then cross-examines him, and the party calling him then
re-examines him, if necessary, for the purpose of explanation of
the matters of the previous examination, and he is then dismissed. But if, upon cross-examination, the witness could be
examined as to new matter not embraced in his examination in chief, this rule of proceeding must be abandoned. For
the party by whom the witness was called would certainly have
the right to cross-examine as to the new matter, and the other party
would have the right, upon general principles, to re-examine.
This would occasion two examinations of the same witness by
each party, and the party not calling him would have the closing
examination, which is contrary to principle and the established
rules of procedure. That principle is, that a party calling a
witness and examining him as to a particular matter, takes the
affirmative of the matter proposed to be proved by him, and
the witness is to be regarded as then introduced and before the
court only for that purpose. The cross-examination is by way
of response to the special matter proved and for the purpose of
disproof or explanation of it. And the same principle which
governs the pleadings between the parties should regulate the
exhibition of the proof upon the trial. And as each pleading
should be strictly in answer to that to which it applies, so the
cross-examination of each witness should be confined to the matter testified in his examination in chief, in order to produce certainty and distinctness in ascertaining the facts to be proved.

This course, while it is sanctioned by the rules of logical proceeding, can be productive of no prejudice to a party desiring
to prove by the witness other matters than such as are embraced
in the examination in chief; for it is well settled that he may

afterwards introduce him as his own witness to prove any matters pertinent to the merits of the cause, and that the adverse party having called him, is thereby precluded from objecting to his competency or from impeaching his credibility.

It is no just objection to this view of the subject that the party, against whom the witness is originally called, should not be compelled to introduce him as his own witness to the new matter, and thereby preclude himself from impeaching his credit. For, if he would rely upon the new matter proved by the witness, it would be against his interest to impeach him, and it is to be presumed that, if he wished to impeach him, he would not introduce him to prove material facts in his case.

In nearly all the cases which are cited in the books to show that a witness called and examined as to a single fact, may be cross-examined as to the whole case, it will be found, on close examination, that they hold merely that, when a witness is examined as to one fact or point in the cause, he is a witness for all purposes pertinent to the issue, *so far as to preclude the party introducing him from discrediting him, or from objecting to him on the ground of interest.* This is the extent of the rule held in Fulton Bank v. Stafford, 2 Wend., 285 ; Varick v. Jackson, ib., 200, 201 ; Morgan v. Bridges, 2 Stark Rep., 314 ; Murrill v. Inhabitants of Berkshire, 11 Pick., 273, 274 ; Webster v. Lee, 5 Mass., 336. And it will be perceived in these and other cases of the same character that the term " *cross-examination* " is used in a very loose and general sense to signify the right of the adverse party to avail himself of the testimony of the witness introduced on the other side generally, and not with reference to the mode in which the testimony of such witness is to be brought out. And none of these cases present the case of an effort, upon cross-examination, to bring out testimony not pertinent to the matter testified to by the witness in his examination in chief.

The case of Moody v. Rowell, above cited, is the only direct adjudication which I have been able to find sustaining that position, and believing it to be not well founded in principle or sustained by authority, I cannot accede to its correctness.

I am therefore of opinion that the ruling of the court below upon this point is correct.

Brown *v.* The State, 32 Miss. Rep., 433.

Homicide.

Dying declarations are admitted as evidence only in cases of homicide.

The party offering declarations of this character must first prove that they were made under a sense of impending death, and when the deceased had given up all hope of surviving. Such a condition is presumed to silence all motives of falsehood, and induce the mind by the most powerful consideration to speak the truth.

But even then, the accuracy of the memory, and coolness of the judgment are, in general, to some extent impaired by wounds or disease. So that it is generally impossible to make as full, clear and accurate a statement as if in an undisturbed and healthful condition.

Statements made by deceased after the mortal stroke, but before giving up hopes of recovery, and reduced to writing by others, and afterwards, when deceased was conscious of approaching death, sworn to by him, as his dying declarations, are admissible as evidence. But if from such writing part of what deceased said, be omitted, and it appears that the narrative is incomplete, it should be rejected.

Confessions of an accused person are not the highest and most satisfactory proof of guilt.

Distinction should be made between confessions deliberately made, and those made in casual conversation.

Erroneous instructions to the jury in a criminal case are no ground for reversal of the judgment unless excepted to in the court below.

In error, from the circuit court of Tippah county. Scruggs, J.

Bird R. Brown, the plaintiff in error, was indicted in the circuit court of Tippah county, for the murder of one John Tatum. At the September term, A. D. 1856, he was tried and convicted of manslaughter in the second degree, and was sentenced to the state penitentiary for five years.

It appeared that the deceased was shot on the evening of the 11th day of May, A. D. 1854, and died on the 23d day of the same month.

It was proven that some short time before the killing, unfriendly feelings existed between the prisoner and the deceased, and that a violent altercation took place between them on the 9th of May, 1854, at the house of the defendant's father, in which the defendant applied to the deceased epithets grossly abusive and insulting; that the deceased soon afterwards, in referring to this altercation, alluded to the insults, and threatened that he would kill the accused unless they were withdrawn; that these threats were communicated to the accused before the killing. It was also proven that the accused made conditional threats against the deceased. On the evening of the 11th of May accused was at a mill in the neighborhood with a negro boy and unarmed; he left the mill about three o'clock for home. It was also shown that on the same evening the accused, with the negro boy, passed near to a spring at which the deceased's wife and daughter were washing, and that he was armed with a gun. Soon afterward the wife and daughter of deceased went to his house, and deceased soon thereafter took his gun and went into the woods, as his family stated, for the purpose of hunting his oxen and squirrels. Deceased's wife and daughter denied that they had informed him that they had seen Brown pass the spring; but it was proven on behalf of the defendant that deceased stated after he was shot that they did so inform him. It also appeared in proof that the accused and the negro boy with him, were hunting oxen at the same time they were seen passing the spring.

Dr. J. W. Carter, a witness for the state, who was sent for on the evening of the 11th of May, to dress the wounds of deceased, and who attended on him until his death, upon cross-examination by defendant, stated: That deceased, on the evening he was shot, stated to witness that he (deceased) was in the woods hunting his oxen; that he had a rifle-gun with him; that he saw Bird R. Brown, the prisoner, passing by him in the woods, and that deceased called to Brown to stop; that deceased went up to where Brown was and asked him why he was talking about him; that he ought to wait for older people to talk about him first; that in the course of the conversation deceased told Brown he had stolen a gun, or had as well have stolen a gun; that Brown gave him the d——d lie.

Witness further stated, that when he went to the house of deceased, on the morning the dying declarations were taken, H. B. Robinson was there; that Robinson was going forward to take the declarations in presence of, and in the room where deceased was lying; witness objected to this, because he feared it would affect deceased injuriously. Witness directed Robinson to go into another house near by, and that he did so; that deceased made no statement to Robinson in his, witness's, presence about the facts of the case, and of the meeting of defendant and deceased in the woods, nor as to how the shooting occurred. Witness further stated, that he and Robinson consulted together, as to whether they should ask the deceased whether he did or did not snap or present his gun at Brown, for the purpose of putting his reply in the dying declarations; that on witness's suggestion they concluded it was not necessary, because it was matter for the defendant himself to establish. Witness had heard that defendant had said that deceased snapped or presented his gun at him, and therefore he, witness, asked deceased if such was the fact, to which deceased replied, that he did not snap or present his gun at defendant, "for he knew he had no cap on the tube."

Witness further stated, " that he had heard deceased tell over the circumstances of his and defendant's meeting in the woods, from time to time, after he was wounded, and that he told Robinson to write the declarations down as he, witness, should repeat them to him from memory, and that he, witness, would go from the house where the declarations were being written down, to the room where deceased was lying, and ask deceased questions as to any matters that witness had any doubts about; that in this way the declarations were taken—he, witness, repeating from memory what deceased had told him from time to time, soon after he was wounded up to Saturday before he died, and that on Monday following, Robinson wrote the statements down as witness recited them to him." Witness further stated, that he went two or three times to the room where deceased was lying, to ask him questions about the facts, and to bring back the answer of the deceased; but that he does not know and cannot state what facts he inquired about of deceased, on these occasions; that he is not able to state what facts are written down in the dying declarations, from what deceased told him before deceased was convinced he would die, nor can he tell what facts are stated in said declarations, from what deceased told him after deceased thought he would die, but that the larger part of the facts embraced in the dying declarations are those which deceased told witness of, before he thought he would die.

Witness further stated, that he repeated the declarations of deceased just as he had repeatedly told him. He further stated, that he and Robinson left out and omitted some things that deceased had said in relation to the way in which deceased and defendant met in the woods, and the quarrel between them; because they thought them unnecessary. The witness being asked if he had told Robinson, while he was writing down the declarations, that deceased had told him, witness, "that he (deceased) called to defendant as he was passing him in the woods, and went up to him," answered that he did so repeat it to Robinson; and being further asked if it were so written down in the dying declarations, answered that he could not state from memory what was in the dying declarations, and that they would speak for themselves." Witness further stated, that when the dying declarations, drawn up as before stated, were read over to deceased, he was weak and feeble, and spoke only in a whisper, his throat being much disordered.

H. B. Robinson, for the state, testified that he was sent for by deceased to take his ": depositions" the night before the declarations were taken, but did not go until next morning, which was on the day before he died. Witness further stated that deceased told him in part what occurred between deceased and defendant when they met in the woods, and when the shooting occurred; that this was done on the morning the declarations were written, and in presence of Mr. Adams. The witness also identified the paper containing the dying declarations of deceased, and hereinafter copied. Witness concurred with Dr. Carter as to the mode in which the declarations were written down. He also stated, that, after finishing writing them out, he carried them to deceased, and read over to him, and called his attention to them; that deceased was then in his senses, and said that the declarations were right and as correct as he himself could state them under oath. Witness then administered an oath to deceased to the truth of the declarations.

On cross-examination, the witness was asked if the deceased

told him any of the facts connected with the deceased and the defendant's meeting in the woods, and the facts that occurred at the time of the shooting; to which witness answered, "that the deceased did—that the deceased told him what was written in the dying declarations, as far as that he, deceased, 'had not put a cap on the tube.'" Witness was further asked if he had not told Melton Young, at his office in Ripley, some eight or ten days previous to the commencement of the September, A. D. 1856, term of the circuit court, "that all that deceased had told him, as to the facts of the meeting of defendant and deceased in the woods, when the shooting occurred," was "*that the deceased and defendant met in the woods alone,* and that just as deceased made the statement to witness, Dr. J. W. Carter stepped in and objected to any further conversation." Witness, in answer thereto, denied having made the statement.

Melton Young was afterwards introduced on behalf of defendant, and testified that Robinson had made the statement to him as contained in the interrogatory propounded as above.

Polly Adams, for the state, among other things, stated that she was present when the dying declarations drawn up by Robinson were presented and read over to deceased; "that Dr. Carter came into the room and told deceased to arouse up and collect his senses; that the doctor slapped him about a little to awake him, and then H. B. Robinson read over to him the dying declarations."

The state then offered in evidence the dying declarations drawn up by Robinson; the prisoner objected, but his objection was overruled, and the prisoner then excepted to the opinion of the court. The instrument read as follows:

"State of Mississippi, }
    Tippah county.   }

"Personally appeared John Tatum, senior, before me, Harris B. Robinson, an acting justice of the peace in and for said county, and made oath in due form of law; deposeth and sayeth that on the eleventh day of May, in the year 1854, on his own land, a short distance from his own dwelling, he did then and there fall in company with one Bird R. Brown, the said Tatum, having just discharged his rifle at a squirrell, and had loaded his gun, but had not put on the cap on the tube; he the said Tatum resting the butt of his gun on a log. Whilst in this position, there was a dispute arose between them, standing face to face, some 8 or 10 feet apart. After some conversation, Brown gave Tatum the damed ly repeatedly; the said Brown then said he intended shooting of him; after pausing a half a minute or more, he accordingly did shuit, discharged one barrell of his shot-gun, and the said Tatum received some several shot in his neck and shoulder. Question ast by Robinson: Tell me what position you was in when you was shot? Answer: We was face to face, until I discovered him, the said Brown, in the act of shooting; I then rather srunk back, turning myself to the rite when I received the shot. Question: What did Brown do? Answer: He went of amediately up the hill, calling back unto a negro boy who had bin in company with him, to come on, for he had kill the damed old raskell, leaving me, so I saw him no more.

his
" JOHN + TATUM, [L. S.]"
mark.

" Sworn and subscribed before me on the 22 day of May, 1854. Given under my hand and seal, day and date above written.

" HARRIS B. ROBINSON, [L. S.]
" *Justice of the Peace.*"

Jesse Allen, for the state, testified that soon after the shooting the defendant came to his house and staid all night, and they had a conversation in relation to the difficulty. Witness did not recollect all that the defendant said. He stated that the defendant told him that the first difficulty was about dogging hogs; that deceased came to his father's house, where defendant lived, and abused his father and mother and himself very much. That the day the shooting took place, he was out in the woods hunting his oxen, and as he was going up a little valley or branch bottom, he heard a rifle-gun fired, which he knew was Tatum's gun; defendant then turned up on the side of the hill, and was passing by where deceased was, who called to defendant to stop ; that he did so, and that deceased then went to defendant and put his gun across his arm as if he was putting a cap on the tube as he went along towards him. He then came up to defendant and commenced abusing him, and called him a thief, and then he gave the deceased the d——d lie ; that deceased said he would not take that from any man, and presented his gun at defendant, and snapped it twice at him. Defendant saw there was no cap on the tube of deceased's gun, and that he knocked the gun off one side and fired. Witness asked defendant why he fired when he saw there was no cap on the gun, and defendant replied that he was " agitated."

Witness was asked, on cross-examination, if he was certain that defendant had used the words he had repeated about " *seeing* there was no cap on the tube." He replied he could not be positive, but that he believed his first statement was correct, though it is possible he might be mistaken. Witness was then asked if defendant did not tell him (instead of what witness had sworn) that defendant " had, upon reflection, thought that deceased had no cap on his tube ;" to which witness replied that it might be so, but that he did not think so. His first statement was according to his recollection.

The testimony was conflicting as to whether the declarations of the deceased read in evidence were made under a belief of impending death. Several witnesses, on behalf of the prisoner, testified to declarations made by the deceased after he was shot, contradictory of the statement contained in the paper drawn up by Robinson. Several other witnesses were also examined, both by the state and the defendant, in relation to matters material to the issue, but the foregoing is all that is deemed necessary to set out in order to a correct understanding of the opinion of the court.

Numerous instructions were given, both at the instance of the prosecution and the defense, but only the 14th given for the state is necessary to set out, and that is copied in the opinion of the court. After the court had instructed the jury at the instance of both parties, he, of his own volition and without being requested by either party, instructed the jury generally on the law in relation to homicide. These charges are contained in the bill of exceptions taken to the judgment of the court overruling the prisoner's motion for a new trial, but there is no statement or recital in the bill of exceptions that any exception was taken to the action of the court in that respect, except that it was assigned in the motion for a new trial, as cause for the granting of the same, that the court had erred in giving certain instructions asked for by the state, and in charging the jury generally of his own volition, and without being requested so to do, as before stated.

The defendant's motion for a new trial being refused, he excepted, and sued out this writ of error.

John W. Thompson and *Hugh R. Miller*, for plaintiff in error.

D. C. Glenn, attorney general.

Smith, C. J. :

The plaintiff in error was tried upon an indictment for murder, in the circuit court of Tippah county, and convicted of manslaughter in the second degree. Several errors are assigned as causes of reversal. They respect the admission in evidence of the dying declarations of the deceased ; the charges granted at the instance of the district attorney, and certain instructions, which were requested by the prisoner, and refused by the court ; the general charge delivered, of his own motion, by the judge, and the judgment overruling the motion for a new trial.

We shall notice, first, the alleged error in the admission of the dying declarations of the deceased.

Declarations of this character are a species of hearsay evidence ; and are admitted under an exception to the general rule which rejects all evidence of that nature. They are permitted, only, in cases of homicide ; and from considerations of necessity. The general principle on which this species of evidence is received is, that they are declarations made when the party is at the point of death, having given up all hope of surviving. A sense of impending death is presumed to silence every motive to falsehood ; and to induce the mind, by the most powerful considerations, to speak the truth. The obligation thus created is regarded by the law as equal to that imposed by a positive oath in a court of justice. [1]   Rex v. Woodcock, 2 Leach Cr. Cases, 567. That such declarations were made under a sense of impending death, is essential to their admissibility, and that they were so made is a preliminary fact to be proved by the party offering them.   1 Greenl. Ev., § 158.

The accuracy of the memory and the coolness of the judgment of a person *in extremis,* are, in general, to some extent impaired by his wounds or the disease under which he labors. And although by his situation he is placed under a strong obligation to speak the truth, and freed from every motive to falsehood, it is impossible, generally, that he should be as well qualified to make a full, clear, and accurate statement of the facts of the transaction, to which he speaks, as he would be if his body and mind were both in an undisturbed and healthful condition. A person in that situation is liable to be impressed and easily influenced by the feelings and suggestions of those around him. Consequently, he is the more apt to confound the impressions thus created in his mind, and inferences drawn from the circumstances of the transaction, with the facts themselves.   And, it is to be considered that the acts of violence, to which the deceased may have spoken, were in general likely to have occurred under circumstances of confusion and surprise, calculated to prevent their being accurately remembered, and leading to the omission of facts important to the truth and completeness of the narrative.   Moreover, the party to be injuriously affected by such declarations is deprived of the privilege of cross-examination. It is, therefore, the dictate of reason and common sense, that declarations of this character in all cases and under any circumstances, should be admitted with caution, and weighed by the jury with the greatest deliberation.   1 Greenl. Ev., § 162.

According to some of the decided cases, it is sufficient if the substance of the declarations be proved, and consequently that it is not essential to the admission of such evidence that the precise words of the deceased should be proved.   11 Ohio R., 424. But for very obvious reasons, declarations *in articulo mortis,* which are partial, and incomplete statements of the facts of the

---

[1] DYING DECLARATIONS.—The general principle on which this species of evidence is admitted is, that they are declarations made in extremity.

transaction should not be allowed to go to the jury. Am. Cr. Law, 249. For similar and additional reasons, dying declarations, however formally drawn up, and complete upon the face of them, should be rejected, if, from the preliminary examinations, it satisfactorily appeared that they were made under the suggestion of improper influences; or, through the agency of others, are so drawn up as to present a partial, incomplete or false statement of the facts of the transaction.

We shall not pause to inquire whether the deceased, at the time the paper purporting to be his dying declarations was read, subscribed and sworn to, acted under a sense of impending death, but will proceed directly to the objection mainly relied on; which is, that the declarations were not written under the immediate dictation of the declarant nor in his presence, and that important and material facts connected with the alleged homicide were intentionally omitted by the parties who drew them up.

Dr. J. W. Carter and H. B. Robinson were the agents in this transaction, and were examined as witnesses for the prosecution. We shall extract such portions of their testimony, as have immediate reference to the question before us.

Dr. J. W. Carter testified that he was a practicing physician, and was called in to see the deceased on the evening of the 11th of May, 1854, and "found deceased wounded with shot, which seemed to pass from the left side to the opposite side, cutting the skin of the throat over the windpipe, and lodging in the right shoulder." The deceased died from the effects of the wounds, on the 23rd of May, 1854. On Sunday night, (the 22d of May) witness conversed with the deceased about his prospects of recovery. Witness told him that his family desired "to know how he felt on the subject of death, and about his business;" deceased replied, that "there were some matters of business which he had thought he would have arranged before that time, but that he disliked to disturb his family." Witness then thought deceased's case a very doubtful one; but deceased then expressed no opinion as to whether he would live or not. Witness did not remember whether this conversation was before or after deceased had the spasm on Sunday night (22d), but it is certain that it was on that night; deceased said nothing to witness on Sunday night after he had the spasm as to whether he thought he would die or not. "That, when the dying declarations were read over to him and signed, he (deceased) was weak and feeble, and spoke only in a whisper, his throat being much disordered."

On cross-examination, this witness further testified that the evening after deceased was shot, he stated to witness that he was in the woods hunting oxen ; that he had with him a rifle gun ; that he saw defendant passing by him in the woods, and that he called to defendant to stop ; " that deceased went up to where defendant was ;" " that in the course of conversation deceased told defendant he had stolen a gun, or had as well have stolen a gun ;" " that defendant gave deceased the d—d lie ;" that when witness went to the house of the deceased on the morning the dying declarations were taken, H. B. Robinson was there. " Robinson was going forward to take the declarations in the presence of, and in the room where deceased was lying ;" witness objected to this, and " directed Robinson to go into another house near by to take the dying declarations." Robinson · did so. " Deceased made no statement to Robinson in witness' presence about the facts of the case, of the meeting of the deceased and defendant in the woods, nor of how the shooting occurred." Deceased made no statement in the presence of witness to Robinson " as to whether deceased thought he would live or not." Witness and Robinson " consulted as to whether they should ask deceased whether he did or did not snap or present his gun at defendant, for the purpose of putting his reply in the dying declarations ; that on witness' suggestion they concluded it was not necessary, because it was matter for the defendant himself to establish." Witness had heard the deceased tell over the circumstances of his and defendant meeting in the woods, " from time to time after he was wounded," and told Robinson to write the declarations down, as witness recited them to him. " Witness then went two or three times to deceased to ask him questions as to any matters that witness had any doubt about ; in this way the declarations were taken." Witness " would repeat from memory what deceased had told him from time to time, soon after he was wounded, up to Saturday before he died, and · then Robinson wrote the statements down as witness recited them to him." Witness went two or three times to deceased to ask him questions about the facts, and to bring back the answers of the deceased, "but did not know and could not state what facts he inquired about on these occasions." Witness could not state " what facts are written down in the declarations" from what deceased told him before he was convinced he would die, nor could he "tell" what facts are stated in the declarations from what deceased said after he thought he would die; but that the larger part of the facts embraced in the dying declarations were communicated to witness before deceased " thought he would die." Witness "gave in or repeated the declarations of deceased just as deceased had repeatedly told them to witness," and " that Robinson wrote them down just as witness recited the same to him." That witness and Robinson " left out and omitted some things" which deceased said, " that they thought were unnecessary, about the way they (deceased and defendant) met in the woods and the quarrel between them." To the question whether witness " told Robinson while he was writing down the delarations, that deceased told him that he (deceased) called to defendant as he was passing him in the woods, and went up to him," he answered "that he did so repeat it to Robinson." And upon being further asked " whether it was so written down in the dying declarations," replied " that he could not state from memory what was in the declarations, and that they would speak for themselves."

Robinson testified that he was sent for by deceased to take his "depositions" the night before they were taken, but did not go until the next morning. Upon inquiring for what purpose he had been sent for, deceased replied, to take his depositions. " That deceased told him, in part, what occurred between deceased and defendant when they met in the woods, and when the shooting occurred." That before the declarations were reduced to writing, deceased said to witness " he was very low ; " " that the doctors had got scared and had given him out ; and that he was going to die." The paper purporting to be the dying declarations of the deceased lay there. Dr. Carter would bring to him the facts as stated by deceased, and witness would write them down. After finishing the writing, they took it to deceased and called his attention to it, and read it over to him; deceased was entirely himself, and said it was right; that it was correct as he could state it under oath. The deceased was sworn to the statement, and his mark, at his request, was affixed to it.

On cross-examination, witness being asked, "if the deceased told him any of the facts connected with deceased and defendant's meeting in the woods, and of the facts that occurred at the time of the shooting," answered, "that deceased did; that deceased told him what was written in the dying declarations, as far as that he, deceased, had not put a cap on the tube."

Mrs. Adams, a witness for the prosecution, testified that she heard the deceased tell Robinson that he was going to die, and wanted him to take his dying declarations; that they were read to the deceased; "that Dr. J. W. Carter came into the room and told deceased to arouse up and collect his senses, and that the doctor slapped deceased about a little, to awake him."

The paper, identified by Robinson as the dying declarations of the deceased, was read in the following words, to wit: "Personally appeared, John Tatum, before me, Harris B. Robinson, etc., and, having made oath in due form of law, deposeth and saith, that on the 11th day of May, in the year 1854, on his own land, a short distance from his own dwelling, he did then and there fall in company with one Bird R. Brown; the said Tatum having just discharged his rifle-gun at a squirrel, and had loaded his gun, but had not put the cap on the tube; he, the said Tatum, resting the butt of his gun on a log; whilst in this position, there was a dispute arose between them, standing face to face, some eight or nine feet apart; after some conversation, Brown gave to Tatum the damned lie repeatedly; the said Brown then said, he intended shooting of him; after pausing a half minute or more, he accordingly did shoot—discharged one barrel of his shot-gun—and the said Tatum received some several shot in his neck and shoulder. Question asked by Robinson: Tell me what position you were in when you were shot? Answer: We were face to face, until I discovered him, the said Brown, in the act of shooting; I then rather shrunk back, turning myself to the right, when I received the shot.　Question : What did Brown then do ?　Answer : He went off immediately up the hill, calling back unto a negro boy, who had been in company with him, to come on, for he had killed the damned old rascal, leaving me ; so I saw him no more.''

The evidence showed, that feelings of animosity existed between these parties, and that mutual threats were made.　That the threats made by the accused were communicated to the deceased prior to the rencontre in the woods ; and that the negro boy was the sole witness of the transaction.　This latter fact was well known to Dr. Carter, whose report, made from memory, of deceased's declarations, was reduced to writing by Robinson. These persons must have known, that if the wounded man died, his declarations which they drew up, would determine the fate of the accused.　The deceased's dying declarations, in the absence of any contradictory evidence, would establish conclusively the commission of the homicide by the defendant ; and these parties well knew that, if, in fact, any circumstance of justification, excuse, or palliation existed, in connection with the meeting in the woods, there was no means by which they could be proved, except by these very declarations.　Under these circumstances, the safety of the accused required it ; and humanity and justice demanded, that they should contain a fair, full, and complete account of the facts and circumstances of the transaction.

When we compare the declarations composed, and prepared upon consultation, for the deceased, with the circumstances of the meeting in the woods, as detailed by the declarant himself to Carter, it is impossible not to perceive that the statements contained in the paper read to the jury, are partial, incomplete, and flagrantly unjust to the accused.

It was in proof that the accused and the deceased were unfriendly towards each other ; they had quarreled, and mutual threats had been made.　The deceased had said that he would take the life of the accused, unless the accused retracted an insult which he had given to him.　Under these circumstances, it was of vital importance to the accused, and essential to truth and the justice of the case, that it should be shown, if such were indeed the fact, that the interview in the woods was not sought by him ; that he did not begin the colloquy, and was not the first to use abusive, degrading and insulting language. On the contrary, the dying declarations, drawn up in the manner stated in the testimony, showed that the meeting took place on the land of the deceased and near his dwelling ; and that the accused, without the slightest provocation, first outraged the deceased by gross insults, and then deliberately discharged the contents of his gun into his body.

The declarations were not dictated by the deceased, nor reduced to writing in his presence. They were drawn up from Carter's recollection of the statements made to him, at different times, by the deceased. And when we turn to Carter's testimony, it is manifest that they were not the same account or history of the transaction which was given to him by the deceased, and repeated on several occasions. For according to the testimony of this witness, the deceased stated to him that the accused was passing by in the woods, and, perhaps, unconscious of the presence of any one, when deceased called to him to stop—went up to him—commenced the quarrel—and charged the defendant with the commission of a larceny. Further, that witness and Robinson omitted and left out of the written statement, some things about the way the parties met in the woods, and the quarrel that ensued, which had been communicated to Carter by the deceased. This seems to have been done designedly, and under the impression that any facts connected with the interview, which would excuse or palliate the homicide, were matters of defense, which it devolved upon the accused to establish.

It seems clear, therefore, that the statement read to the jury, as the dying declarations of the deceased, ought not to be regarded as such, and should have been excluded, unless they were made so by the subsequent act of the deceased in swearing to and subscribing them.

By swearing to the declarations which were drawn up and read to the deceased, he adopted them as his own. And no sufficient reason can be urged, why such an act of recognition and adoption should not render declarations of this character admissible as evidence, where the declarant acted under a sense of impending death, and was in a condition fully to understand the contents of a document thus prepared ; and did, in fact, fully comprehend the statements contained in it.

But in this case there are strong reasons for believing that the deceased did not fully understand the declarations as read to him, or that his faculties were so much impaired by the wounds under which he suffered, that he was incapable of remembering with distinctness or stating with accuracy the facts and circumstances of the rencontre which resulted in his death. It is true that Robinson testified that he was entirely himself when the declarations were read. But Mrs. Adams states, that when Dr. Carter came into the room, he told the deceased " to arouse himself and collect his senses," and " slapping him about a little, to wake him." And when we consider that the statement, sworn to by him as his dying declarations, was materially different from the account he gave of the affair to Carter, the conclusion is not to be resisted that he either did not understand what was read to him, or did not remember what had transpired at the meeting between himself and the accused in the woods.

In addition, there are circumstances even calculated to excite suspicions as to the propriety of the motives under which Carter and Robinson acted ; and to authorize the presumption that an improper influence was exercised over the deceased, whose mind and memory, it is reasonable to suppose, were clouded or impaired by the mortal wounds under which he was laboring. These persons acted upon consultation ; and for reasons, which it is difficult to reconcile with their innocency, excluded from the statement, which they drew up, every circumstance connected with the meeting in the woods, which was at all exculpatory of the accused. They must have known that such facts did exist, and that unless they were brought to light through the dying declarations of the deceased, there was no possible way of proving them on the trial of the accused.

We think, therefore, that under all the circumstances disclosed, the court erred in admitting this evidence.

The charges granted at the instance of the prosecuting attorney and the prisoner are very numerous. Some of the instructions given in behalf of the prosecution are relied upon as a ground of reversal. The refusal of the court to give certain charges in behalf of the accused is also assigned for error.

We have no hesitation in saying that the 14th instruction, granted in behalf of the prosecution, was erroneous. That instruction is in the following words: "Confessions made by a person charged with an offense, when made voluntarily, and not obtained by force, fraud or threats, are regarded by the law as the highest and most satisfactory character of proof. If, therefore, the jury believe from the confessions of defendant, as given in evidence, that the defendant shot Tatum, the deceased, at a time when he knew that Tatum had no power to do him any injury, then such shooting was unlawful, and defendant is guilty of either murder or manslaughter, according to his intention at the time of shooting."

The confessions of prisoners are received in evidence upon the presumption that a person will not make a false statement which will militate against himself. And while the elementary writers, and the courts, have not entirely agreed upon the weight to be given to this species of evidence, it is admitted by all that it should be received with great caution. "For," says Blackstone, who maintained that confessions in cases of felony were the weakest and most suspicious of all testimony, "they are very liable to be obtained by artifice, false hopes, promises of favor, or menaces; seldom remembered accurately or reported with precision, and incapable in their nature of being disproved by other negative evidence." 4 Com., 357. Subject, however, to the proper caution in receiving and weighing them, "it is generally agreed that deliberate confessions of guilt are amongst the most effectual proofs in the law." 1 Green. Ev., § 215. But that they are to be "regarded as the highest and most satisfactory character of proof" has never been the doctrine of this court. And it was held in Stringfellow's case, that, without proof, *aliunde*, of the *corpus delicti*, the extrajudicial confessions of the prisoner were not sufficient to warrant his conviction. 26 Miss. Rep., 137.

The charge, therefore, gave too great weight to this species of evidence. It is objectionable also, because it does not draw any distinction between confessions deliberately made, whether judicial or otherwise, and statements or confessions made in casual conversations. It was further objectionable for the reason that it referred directly to the evidence of a particular witness, who testified to a statement made by a prisoner in a conversation with himself, and who admitted that he might be mistaken as to the precise words of the accused; giving to an admission the import of which was not remembered with absolute certainty, all the weight which is due to confessions formally and deliberately made by a party charged with a crime. It wears very much the appearance and was calculated to have the effect of a charge against the prisoner on the weight of evidence.

But for this error, or any other which may have occurred in the instructions to the jury, we would not be authorized to reverse the judgment, as no special exceptions were taken in the court below in conformity with the directions of the statute of the 11th of March, 1856, Session Acts, 86.

For the first error noticed, we reverse the judgment, remand the cause, and award a *venire de novo.*

BROWNING *v.* THE STATE, 33 Miss. Rep., 47.

HOMICIDE.

The refusal of the court to grant a continuance on the affidavit of the defendant, that material witnesses are absent, when the state admits as true the facts expected to be proved by such witnesses, is no ground of error.

A mistake in the copy of the special *ventre*, by which the Christian name of a juror is slightly changed by mistake or inadvertence, is not error, especially when no objections are made before the trial.

The circuit court, into which a criminal case has been removed by change of venue, must try the defendant upon a certified copy of the indictment, and not upon the original. Browning v. State, 30 Miss., 656.

The court is not bound to instruct the jury in mere abstract propositions of law, which would mislead rather than enlighten the jury.

The declarations of a messenger sent by the prisoner to a third party, if made with reference to the object of his visit, are admissible in evidence against the prisoner, if it be shown that they were made by his authority. SMITH, C. J., *dissenting.*

The admission of improper evidence when the defendant sustains no injury thereby, is no ground of error, or for setting aside the verdict. SMITH, C. J., *dissenting.*

What circumstances will amount to proof, can never be a matter of general definition; the legal test of its sufficiency to authorize a conviction, is its power to satisfy the understanding and conscience of the jury. Absolute metaphysical demonstration is not essential to proof by circumstances. It is sufficient if they produce moral certainty, to the exclusion of every reasonable doubt. Cicely v. State, 13 S. & M., 211; McCann v. State, ib., 440. As to the case at bar, SMITH, C. J., *dissented.*

To judge of the weight of circumstantial evidence, is peculiarly within the province of the jury, and, therefore, a verdict on such evidence, unless it is opposed by a preponderance of testimony, or palpably without evidence to support it, will always stand. As to the case at bar, SMITH, C. J., *dissented.*

Where the jury in a capital case, the trial of which lasted four days, lodged in a room at a public hotel, separate from the other guests, ate their meals at the table with the guests and boarders, but in a body at one end of the table, with an officer stationed between them and the other guests, were served at the table by the landlord and servants, were under the vigilant care of two sworn officers, could easily hear the conversation going on at the table, but none of the witnesses examined on the application for a new trial heard the case mentioned in the hearing of the jury, *Held,* that as the jury were always kept together, and under the supervision of a sworn officer, it is not to be presumed that any undue influence was exercised over them ; and that the manner in which they were fed, though an irregularity, was insufficient to vitiate the verdict. FISHER, J., *dissented.*

The refusal of the court to grant a new trial, asked for on the grounds of irregularity in the jury, and the want of evidence to sustain the verdict, was assigned as error; and on the hearing of the cause on writ of error, SMITH, C. J., and HANDY, J., were of opinion that the irregularity in the jury was insufficient to vitiate the verdict, from which decision, FISHER, J., dissented, while HANDY, J., and FISHER, J., (SMITH, C. J., dissenting,) decided that the evidence supported the verdict. On motion to set aside the judgment of affirmance in the case, it was held, That as the same majority of the court did not agree on both grounds for refusing the new trial, the judgment of affirmance should be set aside, and the judgment of the court below reversed and the cause remanded. HANDY, J., *dissented.*

Error to Holmes circuit court. HENRY, J.

The plaintiff in error was indicted with his son, Gaston E. Browning, for the murder of John W. Neal. The indictment was found in Sunflower county, but on application of the defendants the venue was changed to Holmes county, where there was a severance had, and at the November term, 1855, of the Holmes circuit court, the plaintiff in error was tried, convicted and sentenced to death.

Before the jury was empanelled, the defendant applied for a continuance, on account of the absence of several witnesses which he deemed material for his defense. In support of his application, he made an affidavit setting forth what he expected to prove by each of the witnesses who were absent. The district attorney admitted that the facts which the prisoner expected to prove by the absent witnesses were true, and should be so considered by the court and jury on the trial, and thereupon the court refused the application and forced the prisoner to go to trial, and the prisoner excepted.

On calling the special *venire,* the name of J. J. Cowsett appeared on the list, and one John J. Cowsett appeared and answered to the name. In the copy of the *venire* furnished the prisoner, the juror's name was written Joseph J. Cowsett, and the juror stated upon his examination that his father's name was Joseph J. Cowsett, but that he (the juror) was summoned.

The defendant then objected to proceeding any farther, because he had not been furnished with a true copy of the *venire.* The state consented for the juror to stand aside; the court overruled the objection; whereupon the prisoner excepted.

After the jury had been empanelled and sworn, the district attorney offered to read to the court and jury a copy of the indictment against the prisoner and Gaston E. Browning, regularly certified in the record from the circuit court of Sunflower county, to which the prisoner objected, and demanded that the original should be produced and read. This objection was overruled and the district attorney read the copy of the indictment to the jury. The district attorney then produced in court a paper which he stated was the original indictment, and which, on comparison with the copy read to the jury, differed in this, that in that portion of the copy which describes the mode in which the deceased was murdered, the word "neck" is omitted. The prisoner then objected to the reading of said copy because it was not a true one. This objection the court overruled, and the prisoner excepted.

The substance of the evidence, as disclosed on the trial is as follows:

The deceased, John W. Neal, was engaged at the time of his death as overseer on the plantation of Hill and McNeill, in Sunflower. The last time he was seen by any of the witnesses was at said plantation, on the 23d day of July, 1854. On that day he ordered dinner earlier than usual, with the intention of going by prisoner's house and crossing at his ferry and to visit a Mr. Pool, and return home that night. Deceased left home between twelve and two o'clock that day; he took a gun with him, which he said he wanted to sell or have cut off. He rode a clay-bank-colored horse, and wore an overcoat. He was in good spirits, and talked a good deal about the prospects of a good crop on the plantation. He said just before he left, that it was possible that he would not return home that night, and that if he did not he would go by Sidon (a small town on Yazoo river), and bring home with him, on Monday morning, some files which were needed on the plantation. One witness accompanied him on his road on Sunday evening about one mile, and returned immediately back to Mr. Cole's, about one mile from the house on the plantation, and two miles from where he left Neal, and when witness arrived at Cole's it was about three o'clock. This witness never saw deceased wear any bandages such as shown in court. A negro boy was sent after the files which Neal was to bring home with him ; witness directed the negro to go by Browning's.

The distance from McNeill's plantation to Browning's house, on the Yazoo river, was about six miles, and about two miles from Browning's to Pool's.

On Monday morning the horse which Neal rode on the evening before was in the possession of Gaston Browning, on the road leading from McNeill and Hill's plantation to the house of the prisoner, and about one mile distant from the latter place. At this point,Gaston Browning and some others were at work on the road. The horse was not carried to Browning's house until Monday evening, when Gaston returned from working on the road.

On Tuesday morning, the negro who had been sent after the files arrived at Browning's, and stopped there, and informed the prisoner and his family that Neal had left on the preceding evening, carrying his gun with him, and had not returned.

On Monday morning the skiff of the prisoner was found in Yazoo river, lodged, as it seemed, to a tree or limb, and about one mile below the prisoner's house, and near to that bank of the river on which he resided Prisoner's family were informed of this, and a negro boy and James Browning were sent to bring it up.

On Tuesday morning, after the arrival of the negro sent for the files, the prisoner and Gaston Browning solicited G. J. Petty to assist in searching the Yazoo river for the body of Neal, stating that they supposed he was drowned, and giving as a reason for such belief that Neal's horse had been found on Monday morning, about one-half mile back of Browning's house, in the swamp; that the negro had informed the family that Neal had left home on Sunday evening, and had not been heard of since; that the skiff had been found as before stated, and that Neal, when crazy, at Browning's house, the winter before, had threatened to drown himself in the deep hole in the river where the skiff had been found. Petty and the two Brownings went in Browning's skiff down to Pool's, who lives on the opposite side of the river, near where the skiff was found; and Gaston went after Pool and asked him to assist in searching for Neal, telling Pool that the prisoner had sent him for that purpose, and also to get him to take his ferry-flat and assist in the search. Pool took his flat and he, and the Brownings, and Petty searched the deep hole where the skiff had been found, and where the prisoner said he supposed Neal was drowned. No trace of the body being discovered, and Pool deeming it very improbable that Neal was drowned, the search in the ferry-boat was discontinued, and Petty and the Brownings, at the suggestion of the prisoner, went in a skiff down the river to a plantation called Shell Bluff, about three miles from J. D. Browning's. At this place the prisoner stated to N. S. Fields, who was overseer, and to J. C. Fields, who resided there, that he was searching for Neal's body; that he supposed he was drowned, giving the same reasons as he had given to Petty; and he further stated to them that Neal had made a will, giving $300 to Mrs. Browning, and the balance of his estate to the prisoner; that he had told Neal that he did not want his property, and if he did not want any of his relations to have it, he ought to give it to the public schools; and that Neal was deranged at the time, and said he was going to drown himself; this happened the winter before. Browning asked Fields to keep a negro looking for the body, and to let the neighbors who lived on the river below know about the matter. Browning also said that McNeill, one of Neal's employers, had requested him to attend to his business, in the event anything should happen in his absence, and that he was going out to the plantation that evening. The prisoner, Gaston Browning and Petty started back up the river about eleven o'clock. After dinner the prisoner sent his son

Gaston up the river to the house of the sheriff of Sunflower county, to carry an attachment, and from that place to McNeill and Hill's plantation to look after their business. About the same time Petty, who lived about a quarter of a mile from Browning, started to work on the road leading to McNeill and Hill's plantation, The prisoner also started with Petty, saying before he started, that he was going to the plantation to take charge of their business, as requested. Petty parted from the prisoner before they reached the fork in the road, where one road led to McNeill and Hill's, and the other to Shell Bluff. It was shown, however, by witnesses for the state, that Mercer had written a letter to B., on Tuesday morning, requesting him to come down the river, and swear in some appraisers, and that Pool, who was at Browning's on Tuesday morning before Browning left, in reply to a statement of Browning that he had received that letter, but would have to go to McNeill and Hill's plantation, advised Browning to send Gaston out to the plantation, and to go himself and swear in the appraisers, and that the road to the place where the appraisers were to be sworn in, led by Shell Bluff. Soon after he parted with Petty, the prisoner arrived at Shell Bluff, as he stated, on his way down the river to swear in the appraisers. About five minutes after he arrived at Shell Bluff, the negro stationed on the bank of the river to watch for the body of Neal, reported that he saw a body floating down the river. The prisoner and J. C. Fields were then in the house at Shell Bluff, and at so great a distance from the body that J. C. Fields could not distinguish it, but the prisoner stated, upon the negro making the report, " that it was the body of Neal ; he could swear to it." The body was floating on the face and belly, and very deep. Browning and the negro boy got into a skiff and rowed into the river. Browning attached a fishing-line to the body, and had the boat rowed about one hundred yards below the landing. As soon as the skiff and the body were fastened to the bank, the prisoner commenced untying the ropes about Neal's body, but failing to untie them he came out on the shore, and asked N. S. Fields (who had arrived about the time the body was landed) for his knife, which Fields gave him. Browning then went to the end of the skiff farthest from the bank, and commenced to cut the ropes around Neal's body. Fields protested against this, saying that the body ought not to be interfered with until a coroner's inquest should be held over it. Browning said he was a sworn officer, and had a right to cut the ropes, and that he wanted to get Neal's key. Browning then hitched the knife under the ropes, and in trying to cut them, raised the body so as to enable Fields to see that there was a bag of bricks attached to it. Fields remarked to Browning that he saw the bag of bricks, and Browning then cut the rope which attached it to the body, and it fell into the river where the water was about four feet deep. Browning then commenced unbuttoning Neal's coat, and said he wanted to get Neal's pistol. Upon being asked how he knew Neal had a pistol, he said that Neal owned one and always carried it. Prisoner then took a pistol from one side of Neal's breast. N. S. Fields then saw a knife on the other side of Neal's breast, and told Browning to take that up also. Browning replied that he did not think Neal had a knife. Fields said he saw one on his breast, and Browning then took it up. Browning also took from Neal's pocket his pocket-book, and then came out of the skiff, and asked N. S. Fields to have a coffin made, and that they should proceed to bury him, saying that the body would be so offensive by the time a jury could be collected, that the law would not require the men "to sit on it." The two Fields objected, and one of them started off to summon the neighbors, and the prisoner and the other Fields remained on the premises. Some of the neighbors arrived that evening, and during the night a physician was sent for, who also arrived during the night. Before daylight of the next morning, when only eleven men besides the physician had arrived, Browning insisted on holding the inquest then, taking the doctor for the twelfth juror, and giving as a reason that the body would become still more offensive. This proposition was declined by the company present. On Wednesday morning the inquest was held, Browning, who was a justice of the peace, acting as coroner.

The body, when discovered, had on the usual clothing, and also a heavy winter overcoat, which was buttoned up to the chin; gloves were on the hands, and drawn up over the cuffs of

the coat; strings of baling twine were around the gloves, over
the wrists, and around the pantaloons, just above the ankles,
but neither the feet nor the hands were tied together. The
collar of the overcoat was turned up, and a twine string tied
around it. There were two bandages, made of towels, about
fourteen inches wide, around the body, under all the clothes;
one of these extended from the hips up the body, its entire
width; the other was over the breast, extending down and meeting the other. They were both buttoned in front, and also tied
with twine strings. The holes through which the twine strings
were tied, seemed to have been cut with a knife. The twine
strings were each of them short, only passing through two holes
in the bandages, one on each side of the buttons. The button-
holes in one of the bandages were worked, as if intended for
ordinary use. The lower bandage was fastened by straps of
towels, running around the thighs, and tied in each groin in a
very large knot. The upper bandage was fastened over the
shoulders by similar straps, which were all tied into a large knot
on the back of the body, at a place where it was thought by the
witness that Neal could not have tied them. A twine string
was also tied around the neck, and in the swollen condition that
the body then was, it was very tight, and slightly imbedded in
the flesh. The body was not taken out of the water until Wednesday morning. One of the witnesses who assisted in taking
it out, stated that he then noticed that the neck was very limber,
and hung to one side. The body was then much swollen, and
decomposition had proceeded to a considerable extent. One of
the eye-balls was protruded, and lay on the cheek; the other
was also protruded. There were four bruises on the head, one
on the temple, and three on the occipital portion of the head.
The bruises were small and round, and about the size of a silver
dollar. The skin was not broken at either of the bruises, nor
at any other place on the body. The witness, Dr. Dodd, took
off the scalp, and found coagulated blood under the skin, beneath the bruises; he also removed, with a saw, a part of the
skull, and it was not fractured externally or internally. He
did not think that the blows caused the death of Neal.
While making the examination, witness noticed that the neck

was limber, and he then said he thought it was luxated. He saw coagulated blood about the chest, also on the calves of the legs and on the thighs—that is, "those parts appeared bruised." Witness thought at the time that Neal had been hung, and that the discoloration of the chest was produced by a determination of the blood to that part while hanging. Upon cross-examination, he stated that his opinion that Neal was hung was based on the fact that the neck was dislocated. The brain was in a softening condition, so that no correct examination could be made of it. In Neal's mouth was some tobacco, which had been chewed but very little, also some bread crumbs.

P. A. Davis, a witness for the state, was one who assisted in examining the body at the inquest. He turned the head round without moving the rest of the body, and remarked that his neck was broken. The prisoner was standing by ; the witness looked up at him as he made this remark, and the prisoner turned pale and leaned over the bank of the river.

As the body was being taken out of the water some one remarked that he believed Browning was the murderer, or was connected with it, from his looks. Browning was pale and excited. Most of the jury looked pale. The body was very offensive. During the inquest, Browning remarked that he thought Neal had been murdered by negroes.

Browning remarked to N. S. Fields, on Wednesday, that he had had a settlement with Neal, and had paid him the balance found due, which was $42.62. After the inquest was over, Browning opened Neal's pocket-book ; in it were a sovereign, half-eagle, and quarter-eagle, and some silver coin ; there was also what was thought by one witness, the impression of a $20 gold piece. The pocket-book of Neal was produced in court, and a $20 gold piece and a new silver half-dollar were compared with the impression referred to ; the former was found to be a little too large, and the latter very slightly too small to fill it.

Soon after the body was buried, Browning said to the company present that he would go out to McNeill and Hill's plantation to see about their business. Some of the jury proposed to go with him, but he objected, saying that he was afraid that in the present excitement their negroes might be interfered with, or that they would be frightened and run off. Several of the jury, however, went with him. When they got there, Browning, in the presence of the others, endeavored to unlock Neal's trunk but could not do it; thereupon Mercer took the key and opened it without difficulty. In the trunk were found some valuable papers and Neal's will, all of which were, by the persons present, delivered to Browning and his receipt taken for the same.

The prisoner and Gaston E. Browning were arrested for the murder of Neal on Friday, July 28th, 1854. On that evening or the next day—it does not appear which—the prisoner's house was searched, together with his whole premises. When it was proposed to search his premises, he did not object, but wrote to his wife to permit a full and thorough search. His house was situated on the west side of Yazoo river, which, at that place, runs from a direction a little east of north to a point of the compass a little west of south. A public road ran between his yard-fence and the river, leading up the river bank to the residence of H. H. Southworth. This road unites at right angles with another road at the south-east corner of Browning's yard; this latter road leads directly from the river, and is called the Sunflower road. From Browning's house to the road leading up the river, the distance is about twenty-five feet; from the Sunflower road to an old house used as a saddle house, the distance is sixteen feet. The saddle house is an open entry between two rooms; there is a gate opening into the Sunflower road, nearly opposite the entry. Browning at that time kept a public house for the entertainment of travelers; he also kept a public ferry across the Yazoo river, where the Sunflower road touched the bank. Southworth's residence is about three hundred and fifty yards north-east of Browning's house, and on the road leading up the river. Southworth's negro-quarters were about the same distance below Browning's house and also on the river. Browning's brick-kiln was about forty yards from his house up the river, and in the direction of Southworth's and between the road and the river.

Upon the search, there was found in the saddle house, a hemp rope about twelve feet long; this had a noose at one end of it, which hung out from the rope at right angles. On the rope near the noose were found several hairs, corresponding exactly in color and length with Neal's hair; there were also several spots of what seemed to be blood on the rope, and that portion of it upon which the spots were, seemed to have been washed or dragged through the water. A small piece of towel was also found which corresponded in appearance with the bandages around Neal's body. A bunch of twine was also found, much tangled and cut, so as to have a great many ends to the pieces of twine. A very minute search was made, but nothing else was found, except Neal's saddle and bridle, which were on his horse when in the possession of Gaston Browning on Monday. The saddle and bridle were in the saddle house, and the rope referred to was not all concealed, but lying on the floor of the saddle house. On Saturday, some of the witnesses examined Browning's skiff, and in it they found some spots of blood, which seemed to have been washed or rubbed.

On Wednesday, the prisoner and several of the neighbors examined his brick-kiln. It was found, by comparing them, that the bricks in the sack exactly fitted places in the kiln from which bricks had recently been taken. N. S. Fields stated that there were some human foot-prints about the kiln, but he could not discover more than one which was perfect and entire. It was made by a coarse shoe or boot, of medium size, say No. 8 or 9; that Neal had on when found, thick boots of medium size, say No. 9 or 10. Neal's boots were too large for witness, and the track at the brick-kiln was also larger than witness's.

During Browning's trial before the committing court, one witness visited a maple tree situated about four hundred yards west of Browning's, and about fifty yards north of the Sunflower road. The tree was in a thicket, and about twelve feet from an old trail leading from the Sunflower road. This witness saw tracks in this trail, but saw none immediately around the tree, where leaves were on the ground. He also saw " a mark on the tree."

J. C. Reeves, a witness for the state, visited this tree the day after the trial of the prisoner before the committing court. There was a fork in the tree about thirteen or fourteen feet from the ground. He climbed the tree, and, in the fork, saw a slight indentation as if made by something drawn through. On visiting the tree a second time in company with J. Y. McNeill, about two weeks afterwards, they found some hairs of light color corresponding with Neal's; they also, at that time, saw a rotten chunk near a small bush, broken, and both ends turned up, and, in the place where the chunk was broken, was an indentation which fitted one end of a large gum stick lying near by. This gum stick was about five feet long, two inches in diameter at one end, and three inches at the other end. There were some marks on the tree about seven feet high, as if made by a knife; witness could not tell whether it was fresh or not; and that he did not find any hairs at all on his first visit. McNeill proved, in addition to the evidence of Reeves, that there seemed to have been a good deal of trampling about the tree.

Another witness, who visited the tree about the 8th of August, noticed "that in the fork was an impression about the size of a walking-stick, a slight indentation of the bark, and, on each side of the fork, it was a little frazzled."

J. Y. McNeill, for the state, testified that Neal had a rifle-gun; it was rather long, half-stocked, of medium size bore, and steel-mounted; the spring keeping the tallow box closed was defective, so that in hunting or other use the lid would sometimes open; the stock of the gun was dark.

E. B. Redus, for the state, testified that he was at Browning's about a week before he started to the trial in November, 1854. He had his washing done there at that time. He and William Browning went up stairs—William a little ahead of him. As they got to the top of the stairs, William Browning stepped forward quickly, and picked up a rifle-gun, and carried it to a corner of the room, and set it up by a clothes press. As he stepped forward and took hold of the gun, he remarked, "I wonder what in the h—ll this gun is doing here!" It was leaning up against a bed. The gun was a rather long one, and was half stocked; it had a percussion lock, and was steel-mounted; the tallow box was open; the stock was dark. Witness saw the breech of the gun, and about a foot in length of the barrel above the lock; he saw a small portion of the upper end of the barrel of the gun over William Browning's shoulder. He afterwards went back, and did not find the gun where William put it, or anywhere else. William Browning in carrying the gun had it in such a position as to have the triggers on the under side. Witness did not see the lock; it was on the left-hand side of the gun. The tallow box was on the right-hand side; it was round, and its lid was about the size of a half-dollar. Witness could not tell whether the rifle had a single or double trigger. Witness did not think he had said on Gaston's trial that he could not tell whether it was whole or half-stocked, nor did he say on that trial that he only saw the upper end of the ramrod of the gun over Browning's shoulder. He did not remember whether the ramrod projected beyond the muzzle or not. Witness was not sure that the lock was on the left-hand side of the gun; he did not see it or notice it. He remembered seeing the cock; it was a percussion gun.

Thomas Botters, for the defense, testified that he acted as counsel on the trial of Gaston Browning. He cross-examined E. B. Redus, touching the description of the gun he saw, and he distinctly remembered that Redus then said he only saw the upper end of the ramrod over William Browning's shoulder, and did not see any of the muzzle of the gun, and that he further stated, that he could not tell whether it was a whole or half stocked gun. The remarkable fact that Redus only happened to see the end of the ramrod impressed itself on witness' mind as improbable.

W. B. Helm and Wm. Carthian, who were also counsel for Gaston Browning, corroborated the statement of Thomas Botters. So also did J. M. West, a witness for the state, but understood Redus to say that he saw the muzzle down to the first thimble over Wm. Browning's shoulder. Upon cross-examination he stated, "that he was not sure he said down to the first thimble; something was said about a thimble;" witness could not say positively whether he said he saw from the muzzle to the first thimble, or from the lock to the first thimble from it.

M. F. Nesbitt, the prosecutor, for the state, testified that he heard Redus give in testimony on the trial of Gaston Browning. Redus stated, that he saw about a foot of the lower part of the barrel; he understood Redus to say the gun was half stocked.

William Browning, a son of the prisoner, testified on his behalf, that the gun referred to by Redus was brass mounted, and belonged to the prisoner.

J. Y. McNeill, for the prisoner, stated that the lid of the tallow-box on Neal's rifle was two and a half or three inches long, and that it was not so wide as long; it was made in the usual proportions. He thought it opened at the end of the stock by placing the finger nail under the lid and raising it. The lock of the rifle was on the right side, the tallow box was on the left side. Witness was not sure as to the shape of the tallow-box.

There was only one plantation or residence on the road from McNeill and Hill's to Browning's, and it was proved that the only white person on that place was absent in the swamp, surveying, from ten o'clock A. M. to four o'clock P. M., on Sunday the 23d of July, 1854. It was shown that Neal left home between twelve and two o'clock of that day. Pool and Dunaway arrived at Browning's on that evening about two o'clock, and remained there about one hour and a half. Metz crossed the river at Browning's ferry on the same evening at three o'clock, and saw Pool and Dunaway at Browning's. Petty and Davis passed Browning's about one half hour by sun, going from Southworth's dwelling to his quarters. None of these parties saw anything of Neal or his horse. Pool and Dunaway saw all the family at home, and saw nothing unusual or suspicious in the conduct of any of them. Petty, when he passed with Davis, saw Gaston Browning. Dunaway crossed over the river in Browning's skiff on Monday morning; the skiff had water in it and looked like it had been washed.

After the prisoner had been arrested, and on the morning after the search had been made, the prisoner, who was then on his trial before the committing court, called John W. Boyd to him, when the following conversation occurred, as related by Boyd: "The prisoner asked me if we had discovered anything about his premises. I told him not much, and yet it might be a good deal. He then asked me if his children and negroes were scared. I told him they were not. He asked me if we found out anything from Ed, his negro boy, about a twenty dollar gold piece; I told him we had not; he then said Ed had found on Monday morning, a twenty dollar gold piece, in the ferry flat; that Ed brought it to him, and he gave it to his wife, and told her to put it away till the excitement was over, and if any one called for it, he could then have it.

After the prisoner was arrested, Neal's body was disinterred; and Dr. Fisher, who was present at the examination then made, testified that Dr. Loyd cut into the neck, and put his fingers into the incision, and moved the parts about; the neck was then luxated.   Witness thought that Neal's death was caused by luxation of the neck.   Witness also examined the sack attached to Neal's body and containing the bricks before referred to.   He made out the letters E. Sm · ⁻h; he took the dot for the dotting of an *i*, and the dash for the crossing of a *t*.   E. Smith once lived in Sunflower county, and had recently died, and the place for landing his freight was Browning's.

The prisoner proved by his sons, William and James Browning, that he and Gaston Browning were at home on Sunday evening and during the night; that Neal never left there on that evening or night; and that they had not seen him since about two weeks before his death.   Upon the rope found in the saddle house being shown them, they denied having any knowledge of it; but it was shown by two witnesses, that they had acknowledged, when the prisoner was on trial before the committing court, that the rope was the prisoner's ox-rope.

John Garrell, for the prisoner, testified that he was at the plantation of McNeill and Hill, in the latter part of January, 1854; that Neal was then strangely affected; was drinking more than usual; that soon after twelve o'clock, Neal got into a skiff on a large lake, in front of the house, and remained there till midnight.   He threatened to drown himself, and proposed to witness to will him all his property, after paying his debts; that witness frequently persuaded Neal to get out of the skiff, and come to the house, but he refused.   It rained hard, and Neal stayed out in the skiff during all the time it was raining, and when he came into the house he was very wet, and he asked witness if he could come in; he asked if there was any other person in the room, and, upon being told that there was not, he came.   While he was in the skiff, Dr. Curtis and Mr. Cole came to the house, and witness sent word to Neal that Dr. Curtis wanted to see him. Neal sent word back for Dr. Curtis to communicate to witness what he had to say to him. He seemed to be afraid of some person. He referred to a difficulty he had previously had at Sidon, and said he had no friends. Witness endeavored to persuade him that he had as many friends as his antagonist in that matter. The next day, the witness and Neal went to Browning's and both stayed all night there; two strangers stayed there the same night. When supper was announced, witness went out to get a drink of water; Neal followed him, and witness asked where he was going; he said he was going after water. The company then went into supper, except Neal; after supper was over, the prisoner and witness went out to hunt for Neal; they found him in the ferry-boat, in the end farthest from the shore. Witness and prisoner endeavored to induce Neal to come out, but he would not come. The prisoner and witness then went to the house, and Mrs. Browning went down to the boat to try and get him out. Neal seemed to be afraid of the strangers; and the witness and Browning endeavored to persuade him that the strangers would not hurt him, but could not succeed. As soon as Neal discovered Mrs. Browning coming, he turned loose the ferry boat, and floated down the river; the prisoner and witness followed, and overtook Neal about two hundred yards below the house; they then persuaded Neal to go back, but he would not go. They landed the ferry boat, and Neal then spoke of drowning himself; witness told him to "pitch in," he would see it well done. Witness did not think Neal intended to drown himself. Neal got out of the ferry boat, and remained all night on the bank of the river; it was a very cold night, and some of Browning's family sent Neal some fire, and he camped out. Neal could not be persuaded to leave his camp until about ten o'clock the next morning. He conducted himself very well the balance of the day; he drank a good deal during that day. Witness was unable to account for his strange conduct. Witness left Browning's that evening and never saw Neal afterwards. Witness informed Browning of Neal's conduct at the plantation the day previous to their arrival at Browning's house.

J. Y. McNeill, on the subject of Neal's derangement, testified as follows: "I was Neal's employer in 1854. In February, on my way from my residence in Claiborne county to the plantation in Sunflower county, I found Neal at Browning's in a deranged state. When he first came to where I was, and began to converse, he seemed sane, but he soon showed symptoms of derangement, especially when I spoke of his going home. He seemed to think there was some person out there waiting to arrest him. On ascertaining the condition of his mind, I advised Browning to keep him at his house for a few days; that I thought he would get better, and that he ought not to permit any one to converse with Neal on the subject of his derangement. Browning told me that Neal had been there about a week. A few days after my arrival, I went to Browning's after Neal, and he came home with me. During the summer, Neal did not appear to be deranged, but he had lost his wonted energy, and seemed suspicious of every one who came to the place."

McNeill further testified that on Thursday before Neal died, he left his plantation in Sunflower county to visit Claiborne county; that he came to Browning's to take a steamboat; whilst there the prisoner asked him how Neal was getting along; witness replied, "Not very well, and if he did not do better he should discharge him when he came back." The prisoner then remarked that he did not think Neal could get employment in the neighborhood; witness replied, he did not think Neal wished to do so, but that he thought he would go to North Carolina where his relations were. Browning spoke of his son Gaston, and indirectly, as witness thought, as an overseer; he also mentioned in the conversation something about Neal's will; witness understood him to say that Neal had made a will, giving Mrs. Browning $300, and himself the balance, after paying his debts.

This witness stated that at the time of Neal's death, a lawsuit was pending between witness and one Stoneburner, in which Neal was the only witness for McNeill; that after Neal's death the suit was decided against witness for the want of Neal's testimony; that in June before Neal's death, Neal told witness that Stoneburner had said to him, "Damn you, you will be killed;

I won't do it, but some one else will." Stoneburner, at the time of Neal's death, was living at Mr. Marye's, about four miles from witness' plantation, and about twelve miles from Browning's; that Stoneburner had some negro carpenters; that some three or four weeks before his death, Neal showed witness a memorandum showing that Browning owed him $240.

H. S. Cole testified that Stoneburner was at his house all day Sunday, the 23d of July, 1854, and left there about sundown; and Boyd, who was overseer for Mayre, stated that Stoneburner got home about sunset, and stayed there all night.

Wm. Duberry, for the prisoner, testified, that on the Tuesday evening on which Neal's body was discovered, he crossed the river at Browning's, and after he crossed over, he saw Browning's little boy bring a turtle up the river in the skiff and land it, and that it was then bleeding at the mouth. James Browning, on this point, stated the same as Duberry.

The statement in the prisoner's affidavit for a continuance, as to what he expected to prove by Dr. Richards, and which was admitted by the state to be true, is as follows: "That he, Richards, was present at the second inquest held over the body of Neal; that he is a physician by profession, and will state that, owing to the inartificial manner in which the examination of the body was made by the physician in attendance, it is extremely doubtful whether the dislocation of said Neal's neck was not produced by the persons who made the first examination of said body."

It was proven by F. C. Mercer, that Neal had some $300 in money, a few weeks before his death, which he said he was going to send to M. F. Nesbitt, to loan out for him, and that among his money were some $20 gold pieces.

Jacob Metz crossed Browning's ferry about twelve o'clock on the Sunday night before referred to; he called for the ferry-man to let him over, and recognized the voice of the prisoner calling his boy Ed, and commanding him to set Metz over; witness also observed that Browning's skiff was not at the landing, where it was when he crossed in the evening.

The prisoner proved, by several witnesses, a good character

for truth and honesty, and for peace, from the year 1836, up to the time that he was charged with the murder of Neal.

The same instructions were given and refused in this case as in the case of Gaston Browning.[1]

The jury having returned a verdict of guilty, the prisoner moved for a new trial on the following grounds:

1st. Because the court erred in forcing the prisoner into trial, after he had made his affidavit for a continuance, because the state admitted the truth of the affidavit.

2d. Because the court erred in forcing him to trial, when he had not been furnished with a true copy of the special *venire*.

3d. Because the court erred in permitting the district attorney to read to the jury what purported to be a copy of the indictment.

4th. Because the court erred in refusing the 14th instruction asked for by the prisoner (being the same as the ninth, in Gaston's case).

5th. Because the court erred in permitting illegal testimony to go to the jury.

6th. Because the jury found contrary to the law and the evidence.

7th. Because, while they had the case under consideration, they were permitted, and did board and eat, from day to day, at the public hotel, with all the guests and boarders, separated only by an officer sitting between them; and said jury were exposed to, and might hear the conversation of said guests and boarders, and were waited on and served at said public table by the landlord and servants at said hotel; and there were ample means and opportunities for communication with said jury by means of and through said landlord and servants.

Upon the trial of this motion, Daniel W. Beall, for the prisoner, testified as follows: "I am one of the proprietors of the hotel kept at this place (Lexington). The jury that tried John D. Browning during the present term, were lodged and fed at said hotel during the trial, which lasted four days; when at the hotel, before and after meals, and at night, they were kept in a room separate from the rest of the boarders and guests. They

[1] See 30 Miss. R., 651, 658.

got their meals at the public table, and usually at the same time with the other guests; they always occupied the west end of the table, six on each side; between them and the other guests I always had provided a chair and plate on each side, to be occupied by an officer, or left vacant. The jury were usually conducted to the table by two or three officers, one officer preceding them; they were conducted from the table in the same manner. I noticed that the officers took unusual precaution to prevent any one from speaking to, or having any communication with the jury. I did not see the jury in the dining-room at any time, when there was not an officer sitting or standing by them. The jury could hear the conversation of the guests sitting nearest to them, when carried on in an ordinary tone of voice. On several occasions the jury got their meals after the other guests had eaten. My servants and myself served the jury at the table. I did not speak to any of the jurors, nor did any of the servants, as far as I know; I charged my servants not to speak to the jury, and so did the sheriff. I don't think the case elicited more interest than such cases usually do."

Cross-examined: "I did not speak nor hear any one else speak of the case in the hearing of the jury; during most of the time they were eating, I was at a carving table in a remote part of the room from the jury. I thought once of noticing for conversation about the case, and did notice for awhile, but did not hear any thing said about it. I feel certain it was not mentioned at the table in my hearing. About twenty witnesses in the case were boarding at the hotel, and got their meals at the same table with the jury."

P. C. Richardson, for the prisoner, stated that he, on one occasion, inadvertently took one of the seats intended to be left between the jury and the guests; and that soon afterwards the jury came in, and one of them took the seat next to him, and thus situated they ate that meal; an officer stood behind them all the time. The guests and boarders were usually talking during meals; the jury could hear those who were nearest to them. Witness did not hear the case spoken of at the table.

J. M. West, the sheriff, for the state, testified, that he assisted in taking charge of the jury, in the case of John D. Browning.

There was no conversation about the case in his hearing at the table where the jury ate. "I was particular to listen and notice for it. I usually, while at meals, remained by the juror next to the other guests, and on the north side of the table. I sometimes walked to the west end of the table to assist in waiting on the jury; there were usually two or three officers in charge of the jury in the dining-room; never less than two. The servants and Beall, with myself and bailiff, waited on the jury; the servants were ordered, and Beall instructed, not to speak to the jury. There was usually conversation going on among the guests, but not about the case; it would have attracted my attention. When I was at the extreme western end of the table, a word or so about the case might possibly have been uttered by guests nearest the jury, without my hearing it; but nothing like a regular conversation could have occurred. When I was at the western end of the table, there was always another officer about the jurors next to the guests."

Being cross-examined, he stated: "It was possible that a servant, in waiting on the jury, could have handed to a juror, a written communication, without my seeing it; and it is also possible that a servant might have whispered a word or so in the same way, though I think it very improbable, as I was on the lookout; of course I could not look at all twelve of the jury at once. I was at every meal with the jury, except once at breakfast."

Samuel C. Johnson, for the state, stated that he acted as bailiff to the jury in the Browning case, and was with them at every meal they ate, except one. He usually stood or sat between the jury and the guests, on the south side of the table. He heard no conversation about the case in the hearing of the jury, and saw no communication between any one and the jury, directly or indirectly. He thought he saw Richardson, at one meal, occupy a seat next to the jury, or the one next to it.

James M. Haynes, for the state, testified that he was a regular deputy sheriff, and after conveying the prisoner to the jailer, upon the adjournment of court, he usually went to the hotel, where he arrived, sometimes before the jury finished their meals, and sometimes afterwards. He heard no conversation about the case in their hearing.

This was all the testimony on the motion. The court over-ruled it, and the prisoner excepted, and sued out this writ of error.

Thomas Botters and *J. Z. George*, for plaintiff in error.

D. C. Glenn, attorney-general.

HANDY, J.:

The plaintiff in error was indicted, together with his son, Gaston E. Browning, in the circuit court of Sunflower county, for the murder of John W. Neal. The venue was changed to Holmes circuit court, where the parties were tried separately, and were both found guilty of murder. The case of Gaston E. Browning has recently been decided here, and the judgment reversed, upon grounds which are stated in the opinion of the court.[1]

After the verdict, in the case now under consideration, the prisoner moved to set it aside and for a new trial, upon sundry grounds, which motion, being overruled, a bill of exceptions was taken, embodying all the evidence adduced on the trial, and the rulings of the court in the cause; and, upon these arise the questions, which are here to be considered.

We will proceed to examine the several grounds, upon which it is insisted that the verdict should be set aside, the judgment reversed, and a new trial granted.

1. It is said, that it was error not to grant the continuance moved for by the prisoner on his affidavit setting forth material facts, which he could establish by certain witnesses, who were absent, and that it was not sufficient, that the prosecution admitted the facts, as stated, to be true. This is no ground of error. Domingues v. State, 7 S. & M., 475. Under the admission, the prisoner was entitled to treat the facts stated in his affidavit as absolutely true, according to their force and effect, as stated; and supposing, that he stated the facts not more nor less strongly than the truth, it is not to be presumed that he was prejudiced by their admission.

2. The next ground of error is, that the prisoner was not furnished with a true copy of the special *venire* summoned to try

[1] Supra, p. 860.

him, the copy furnished him containing the name of Joseph J. Cowsett, when in the original *venire* it was J. J. Cowsett, and the juror summoned and called was John J. Cowsett.

This objection comes within the rule laid down in McCarty *v.* The State, 26 Miss., 301. The mistake in the copy must have been through inadvertence, and one which might quite easily occur under the circumstances, without an improper design, and no injury is shown to the prisoner in consequence of it. In addition to this no objection was made to proceeding with the trial at the time, and it was too late to raise such an objection after the verdict.

3. The third and fourth grounds of the motion have been considered in the case of Gaston E. Browning, and held to be insufficient.

5. The fifth objection is founded on the admission of the declarations of Gaston E. Browning, made after the death of Neal, to which the prisoner objected on the trial. The only declarations of this character, which appear to have been objected to, are those mentioned by the witness Pool, and are in substance, that on Tuesday morning, after Neal's death, Gaston came to the witness's house, and told him, his father, the prisoner, had sent him to get witness to take his ferry-boat down the river, and help them to look for the body of Neal. This was objected to, but the testimony was admitted, and we do not consider it error under the circumstances. The declarations objected to, were clearly immaterial, because it was not denied, that the prisoner was searching in the river for Neal's body, which he insisted was there by drowning. And when the witness went to where the prisoner was, he found him searching for the body, in accordance with the message he had sent to the witness. If, therefore, these declarations of Gaston were material, the circumstances tended strongly to show, that they were made by the authority of the prisoner, and should be taken against him. But, they are immaterial, and are mentioned by the witness as the commencement of his knowledge of the transaction, it being impossible that the fact stated could have any effect upon the case.

The next objection to the verdict is, that it is contrary to the evidence. This point has been urged with great earnestness and ability by the counsel for the plaintiff in error, and has received that anxious deliberation, which its importance, as well as the strange and mysterious character of the case, in most of its details, demanded.

The principal facts of the case appear to be briefly as follows :

The deceased was the overseer on a plantation in Sunflower county, lying about seven or eight miles from the prisoner's residence in the same county, which is near the Yazoo river. On Sunday, the 23d of July, 1854, the deceased left the place where he resided, declaring his intention to go by the prisoner's house to Mr. Pool's, who lived on the opposite side of the river, and to return either that evening or on the next morning. He left on horseback, clad in ordinary summer clothes, taking his blanket coat, on which he rode, and a rifle gun, which was very long, and which he said he took to get it cut off. He left between twelve and two o'clock, in the daytime, and it is not shown, that he was seen afterwards alive. He was temperate at the time, and did not appear to be laboring under any mental affliction. He did not return as he promised. On Monday afternoon, his horse was found in the possession of Gaston, who said he had found him in the woods near the prisoner's house. A negro was sent on Tuesday, from the plantation, where the deceased had resided, and, in passing by Browning's, told him that Neal had not returned home. The prisoner said that he had drowned himself, and summoned persons to search the river for the body. He said he knew that he had drowned himself, because he had said he would drown himself ; and his horse, saddle and bridle, had been found the preceding day in the woods back of his place. On Tuesday morning, the prisoner, with Gaston and one of the state's witnesses, whom he had requested to go upon the search, went to search the river for the body. A skiff belonging to prisoner was found in the river on Monday morning, loose, and the prisoner said he supposed Neal had drowned himself there. They searched that place, but did not find the body, and went below to a place called Shell Bluff, where he requested one of the witnesses to station a negro to watch for the body, and to warn the people below to watch for it, and returned up the river to prisoner's house. He said, while at Shell Bluff, that he was going that evening to take charge of the McNeill place, where Neal had been, as he had promised McNeill to do so in case it became necessary. After remaining at prisoner's house, until about three o'clock P.M., he and the witnesses, who had searched the river with him, started thence and rode together three or four hundred yards on the Sunflower road, which leads to McNeill's, the witness understanding that he was going to McNeill's, and the witness left him and turned off to attend to negroes under his charge, and the prisoner rode on. Shortly after this, he was at Shell Bluff, and he had been there but a few minutes, when the negro, stationed to watch for the body, came to prisoner and another witness, and reported that the body was floating down the river. Prisoner and the witness went to the landing, and saw the body at a long distance in the river, prisoner asserting positively, that it was Neal's body. Prisoner and the negro went after the body in a skiff, and brought it to the bank. It was lying with the face and belly down, and sunk quite deep, and had on a blanket coat over the other clothes, and there were ropes tied around the body outside the clothing. Prisoner went to the end of the skiff, and commenced untying and cutting the ropes around the body. Two witnesses protested against his interfering with it, but he claimed the right to do so, as a justice of the peace. In cutting the ropes, he raised the body so as to enable the witness to see a sack of bricks, which was tied to the body, which he cut off, and it sank to the bottom. He then proceeded to unbutton the coat (the witness still objecting, and he claiming the power to do so as before), and took the key, pocket-book, pistol and knife of the deceased from the body, and desired witness, who lived at the place, to have a coffin made and proceed to bury it, because he said it would be so offensive before a jury could be assembled, that the law would not require an inquest upon it. The witnesses objected, and one of them proceeded to give notice to the neighbors, and the body remained in the water until the inquest was held.

The prisoner insisted that the inquest should be held by eleven men, taking the physician for the twelfth, urging, as a reason, that it would be so offensive by the morning as to render the inquest impracticable. The others objected.

The body, when examined, was found to have twine strings tied around the wrists and around the ankles outside of the clothes, and under the clothes were two wide towel bandages, tied and buttoned around the body. There were found three or four bruises on the occipital part of the head, which must have been made by a round or blunt instrument, as the skin was not broken, though the blood was coagulated; but they were not sufficient to produce death. There were also bruises on the breast and on the calves of the legs. The physician who examined the body at the first inquest, states that the neck was luxated, and that that was the cause of the death. Another physician, who examined it on the second inquest, is of the same opinion; while a third physician, who was present at the latter inquest (it was conceded by the admission of the facts stated in the prisoner's affidavit), would prove that, owing to the inartificial manner in which the examination of the body had been made by the physician, it was extremely doubtful whether the dislocation of the neck was not produced by the persons who made the first examination. One of the jurors of the first inquest states, that whilst the jury were examining the body, he turned the head around without moving the body, and remarked that the neck was broken. Prisoner was standing near, and witness looked at him as he made the remark, and the prisoner turned pale and leaned over the bank of the river.

During the inquest, the prisoner seemed to be aware that he was suspected; and when the last juror arrived, which was not until late on Thursday night, he proposed again that the inquest should proceed, for the reason previously stated by him; but the others objected, and it was not held until daylight. In the meantime, he told this juror that he supposed the deceased was murdered by negroes.

After suspicion had arisen against the prisoner, search was made about his premises, and a rope was found in a house in his yard with appearances of blood upon it, with a knot and noose, around which were hairs corresponding in color and appearance with the hair of deceased. Appearances of blood were discovered on the skiff, which seemed to have been rubbed or washed. On Monday morning, the skiff appeared to have been washed out.

The deceased is shown to have had a twenty-dollar gold piece and other money a few days before his death. When the prisoner took the pocket-book from the body, it had some money in it, and had an impression in it which looked like one made by a twenty dollar gold piece; but on producing the pocket-book at the trial and applying a twenty dollar gold piece to the place, it was found that the coin was a little too large for the impression, and a new silver half dollar was found a little too small to fit it.

It was in evidence that after the search of the prisoner's house, he asked one of the witnesses if they had discovered anything about the premises; to which it was replied, "Not much, and yet it might be a great deal." He asked if the children and negroes were searched, to which the witness said "No." He asked if they found out anything from Ed (his negro) about a twenty-dollar gold piece. Witness said they had not. He then said Ed had found on Monday morning a twenty-dollar gold piece in the ferry flat, and brought it to him, and he gave it to his wife, and told her to put it away until the excitement was over, and if any one called for it he could then get it.

It was in evidence that one of the witnesses, who was at the prisoner's house shortly after Neal's death, had occasion to go up-stairs, and that he saw a gun, which, from the partial view he got of it, corresponded with the description of Neal's gun, which he had with him when he left his place of abode. The testimony is somewhat conflicting as to the description of the gun as given by the witness corresponding with that of Neal. But it is in evidence that the prisoner's son, who was with the witness when he saw the gun, stepped forward quickly and took the gun, which was leaning against a bed up-stairs, and put it away, expressing anger and surprise that the gun was there. The witness afterwards went back, but did not find the gun where the prisoner's son had put it, or anywhere else. The prisoner's son proves that the gun alluded to was his father's, and of quite a different description from that given by the other witness.   It does not appear that Neal's gun was ever found or accounted for, nor was the gun, as described by the prisoner's son, produced and identified. ·

In connection with the statements of prisoner in relation to Neal having drowned himself, he also said that Neal had told him that he intended to leave Mrs. Browning about $300, and the balance to the prisoner, after paying his debts, but that he told Neal that he did not want his property, and that he had better leave it to a public school.   It was proved that Neal was intimate with the prisoner, and had great confidence in him; that he had been laboring under partial mental derangement from the use of ardent spirits in the winter of 1854, but had recovered, and was in his right mind in the summer, and was temperate in his habits.   McNeill, his employer, states that he was not deranged, but had lost his wonted energy, and seemed to be suspicious of every one who came to his plantation.   This witness states that he was at the prisoner's house on Thursday before the death, and prisoner asked him how Neal was getting along, and he replied not very well, and that if he did not get along better, he would discharge him.   Prisoner said he did not think he could get employment in the neighborhood, and spoke of his son Gaston indirectly, as he thought, as an overseer.   He also mentioned Neal's will; and witness understood him to say that Neal had made a will giving Mrs. Browning $300 and the balance of his property to him after paying his debts.   And it appears, by other testimony, that, after the inquest, he objected to other persons going to McNeill's, on the ground that he was afraid the negroes might be frightened and run off.   It also appears that Gaston went to McNeill's place on Tuesday evening, and said that he had come to take charge of McNeill's business; that Neal was drowned.

Several of the witnesses for the prosecution state that they saw no blood on the skiff.   A witness for the prisoner proves that he crossed the river between eleven and twelve o'clock on Sunday night, and that the prisoner was then at home.   He crossed the ferry in the ferry-boat.   When he crossed the previous afternoon, about three o'clock, the skiff was at the ferry;

but it was not there when he returned and crossed at night. He saw nothing strange about the ferry.

The prisoner's son testified that the prisoner was at home all day Sunday; that Gaston got home shortly after dinner; that they ate supper about dark, and prisoner went to bed soon thereafter, and Gaston and witness soon after their father; that Neal did not come there that day or that night, so far as he knew. Testimony was offered for the purpose of discrediting this witness. Another son of the prisoner also stated that Neal was not at the prisoner's house on Sunday or Sunday night. Testimony is also adduced to discredit this witness. This witness and another account for the blood on the skiff by stating that it was caused by cutting a hook out of a turtle's mouth in the skiff.

Several witnesses testified to the good character of the prisoner before this charge was made against him.

These being the material facts which appear to have any important bearing on the case, it is insisted, in behalf of the plaintiff in error, that they are not sufficient to support the verdict in either of two points of view: 1st, That they are insufficient to show, with necessary legal certainty, that Neal came to his death by the violence of another, and that he was not drowned by his own act; 2d, That they are not sufficient to warrant the conclusion that the prisoner participated in the murder.

Before proceeding to consider these points, it is proper to recur to the rules of law by which the sufficiency of the evidence is to be tested. The evidence in the cause was entirely circumstantial, and the rule in such cases is thus stated in Cicely v. The State, 13 S. & M., 211: " That the legal test of the sufficiency of evidence to authorize a conviction is its sufficiency to satisfy the understanding and conscience of the jury; that a juror ought not to convict unless the evidence excludes from his mind all reasonable doubt of the guilt of the accused." And in the case of McCann v. The State, ib. 490, the following rule is laid down, cited, as the one just quoted was from Starkie, as the only one which can be regarded as of practical application :

What circumstances will amount to proof can never be matter of general definition; the legal test is the sufficiency of the evidence to satisfy the understanding and conscience of the jury." On the other hand, absolute " metaphysical and demonstrative certainty is not essential to proof by circumstances. It is sufficient if they produce moral certainty, to the exclusion of every reasonable doubt." In Cicely's case, such evidence is held to be peculiarly within the province of the jury, from its character, because it is always solemnly to be weighed and acted upon by their understandings and consciences, and is, from its very nature, the subject of inferences and conclusions in their minds. And the rule is there stated to be " that a verdict will always be permitted to stand unless it is opposed by a decided preponderance of the evidence, or is based on no evidence whatever."

Applying these rules to the verdict and the evidence with respect to the first point, we cannot say that the verdict was unwarranted by the evidence.

There is scarcely a circumstance shown in the case that renders the hypothesis that the deceased drowned himself at all probable. The only fact tending to establish such a result is his declaration made during the previous winter, and whilst he was laboring under partial derangement of mind, that he intended to drown himself. And the testimony tended to show that he had recovered from that attack, and had been temperate, and was sane on the day of his death, and had evinced nothing of mental derangement for a considerable length of time. The presumption of law is, that he was sane, and there is nothing to destroy that presumption as applicable to his condition when last seen.

It is not contended that there is any evidence that he was drowned by others, nor is it insisted upon, with any confidence, that the evidence shows that he committed suicide otherwise than by drowning.

The circumstances against the hypothesis that he drowned himself, and in favor of that, that he came to his death by violence inflicted by others, are clear and strong. The bruises on the occipital part of the head, which could not have been inflicted by himself; the bruises on his breast and calves of his legs ; the luxation of the neck, which was discovered by one of the jurors when the body was examined; the coagulated blood about the neck, which increased from the surface of the skin to the vertebrae, and which showed that the death was produced by luxation of the neck; the opinion of two physicians who examined the body (one at the first inquest and the other at the second), that the death was caused by hanging or strangling and luxation of the neck; the improbability that Neal should get bricks from the prisoner's brick-kiln, which was near his house, and make all the preparations which he must have made in order to drown himself in the condition in which his body was found, and go by the prisoner's house to the ferry or the river and not be discovered by some one of the prisoner's family, who all profess not to have seen him; the strangeness of his tying twine strings around his neck and both of his wrists and ankles, which no man about to drown himself would be likely to do, or could easily do, but which might readily and naturally be done by another who wished to sink a dead body about to be thrown into a river; and lastly, the declaration of the prisoner, after it was manifest, from an examination of the body, that the deceased had been murdered, that he had been murdered by negroes.

Against these circumstances, the only evidence that has any force is the affidavit of the prisoner, stating what he could prove by Dr. Richards; which was admitted as evidence by the state. Giving to that testimony all its force as absolutely true, it would only show that it was, in his opinion, extremely doubtful whether the dislocation of the neck was not produced by the inartificial manner in which the examination at the first inquest was made. Two other physicians, one who made the first examination, and another who attended at the second inquest when Dr. Richards was present, are of opinion that the luxation of the neck was caused by hanging, and state satisfactory reasons for their opinion. And one of the jurors remarked about the dislocation of the neck, whilst the jury were examining the body. From these and all other circumstances above referred to, we think that the jury were well warranted in coming to the conclusion, that the neck was broken, and that the death was produced in that manner.

But if it were conceded with reference to the point under

consideration, that the luxation of the neck was produced by the inartificial examination of the body, it would not follow that the deceased did not come to his death by strangulation or hanging, which, according to standard medical authorities, might produce death without causing luxation of the neck.

Let us next consider the circumstances in evidence, tending to show that the prisoner was implicated in the crime.

1. The evidence presented to the jury a motive to commit the act, which it was their province to graduate. That was, the expectation of succeeding to Neal's property, and the hope of securing the place filled by him on McNeill's plantation for his son Gaston. The testimony of McNeill shows, that these things were upon his mind but a few days before Neal's death.

2. The prisoner was the first to declare and insist that Neal had drowned himself, and to make the search for the body. His conduct about the search and inquest was deeply suspicious; his positiveness that Neal was drowned, his alacrity in searching the river for the body without a particular inquiry at Neal's residence about him; his having a negro placed below on the river to watch for it; he going above; his arrival at the place where the negro was watching immediately before the body came floating down; his positiveness that the body was Neal's, when it was at too great a distance to be identified, and nearly under the water, lying on the belly, with a blanket coat on, in the month of July; his persisting in cutting the ropes around the body, against the remonstrances of the others present, which might very rationally have proceeded from the motive of cutting the sack of bricks tied to the body, and bricks, that may have been tied to the wrists, ankles and neck of the body, by the strings there found, as a means of preventing detection; his anxiety to bury the body speedily and without inquest; and his further insisting on an inquest without a full jury; and at night; his paleness and alarm, when it was mentioned, in making the inquest, that Neal's neck was broken; his declaration to Burns (after being apprehensive that Neal was believed to have been murdered, and that he was suspected), that Neal had been murdered by negroes; his declarations to Fields, before he left Shell Bluff on Tuesday morning, and to Petty after he had returned

home and dined, that he was going to McNeill's place that evening, and his starting apparently with that purpose, but instead of going there, got to Shell Bluff shortly before the body was discovered floating down, having turned off from his road to McNeill's, after Petty left him; his objecting to the jury of inquest going to McNeill's; his proceeding to take charge of McNeill's place, and Gaston going there for that purpose on Tuesday, before he knew that Neal's body was found; and his statements in relation to the twenty-dollar gold piece, that his negro Ed found it in the ferry-boat on Monday morning, and brought it to him, and he gave it to his wife, telling her to put it away until the excitement was over, and then that the owner could have it. It would appear that this last incident all took place on Monday morning, and before there was any excitement about Neal's death. At all events, his statements evince a restless anxiety to account for the gold piece, when the testimony shows that Neal had recently had such a coin in his possession, and when he knew, that the pocket-book had been opened by him in the presence of suspecting witnesses, who had seen it and might have discovered the impression of the coin in it.

3. The rope was found on the prisoner's premises, in an out-house close by his dwelling-house, having on it the appearance of blood, and hairs corresponding in color and appearance with Neal's, also a noose and knot at one end, where the hairs were found.

4. The skiff was at the ferry landing of prisoner on Sunday afternoon, about three o'clock, but was not there, when the witness Metz recrossed, about eleven or twelve o'clock that night. It was found next morning down the river, and appeared to have been washed out. Several of the witnesses saw marks of blood upon it, which had been rubbed or attempted to be washed out.

5. It appears that Neal's gun was never found; and there was evidence tending to show, that it was seen by one of the witnesses in an upper room of the prisoner's house. On the contrary, the prisoner's son proved, that the gun seen by the witness was of quite a different description from that of deceased, and

that the gun seen belonged to the prisoner. The witness for the state testified, that he had afterwards looked for the gun where he saw it, but could not find it there or elsewhere. The gun alleged to be the prisoner's was not produced on the trial, nor its absence accounted for.

In the most of the above particulars, the evidence was without material conflict as it is stated; but, upon some of them, there was testimony in behalf of the prisoner, either tending to contradict or to explain that in behalf of the state. This was the case with regard to the identity of the gun and the impression in the pocket - book. The first point involved a question of credibility of the witnesses, and it was not material to give force to the prisoner's declarations about the gold piece, that its impression should appear in the pocket - book, for the deceased might have had the coin in his pocket-book and without leaving any impression, or the impression made might have been diminished in size by the shrinking of the pocket-book, after it had been soaked for many hours in the water and then dried. But the force of the circumstances connected with this coin arises from the prisoner's declaration about the excitement, made with reference to the coin, before any suspicion of Neal's death had been excited.

These numerous facts and circumstances all indicate that the prisoner was implicated in the death of Neal. If the jury gave entire credence to the testimony of the witnesses, who deposed to them, which was their especial privilege, it is impossible for the mind to come to the conclusion, that the verdict was without testimony to support it, or that it is clearly against the preponderance of the evidence; and that is the question which we are called upon to decide. The evidence is sufficient to show a motive in the prisoner to commit the deed, a course of conduct inconsistent with his innocence in nearly all his actions after its discovery, with evidence of guilt traced to his premises; and, after the full and fair instructions given by the court in his behalf, we cannot say that the evidence was not sufficient to satisfy the understanding and conscience of the jury, to the exclusion of every reasonable doubt. For the question with us is not, whether the verdict is clearly right, but is it manifestly wrong.

The only remaining objection to the verdict is founded upon the fact, that the jury, during the time when they were deliberating upon the case, took their meals at the public table at a hotel, where they were exposed to influence from the conversation of persons generally, at the table, and where improper communications might have been made to them.

The testimony to support this objection is, first, that of Beall, one of the proprietors of the hotel, who states that the jurors always occupied the west end of the table, six on each side, with a place on each side to be occupied by an officer in charge of them 'or left vacant; that they were usually conducted to and from the table by two or three officers, who used unusual precautions to keep any one from having communication with or speaking to the jurors. Witness did not see the jury at any time in the dining-room, when there was not an officer sitting or standing by them. They could have heard the conversation of guests at the table. Witness and his servants waited on them at the table; witness did not speak to them, nor did the servants, to his knowledge; witness and the sheriff had both charged them not to do so; did not hear any one else speak of the case in their hearing; witness was the greater part of the time at a carving-table, in a part of the room remote from the jury. There was an officer always in the dining-room where the jury were. The case was never mentioned at the table in his hearing. There were about twenty witnesses in the case who took their meals at the same table with the jury.

The sheriff testified that there were never less than two officers in charge of the jury in the dining-room of the hotel. He was with the jury at every meal except one, and there was no conversation with them in his hearing; that he was attentive in noticing the jury, and was generally with the juror next to the guests, though he sometimes went to the other end of the table where they were sitting, to wait on them. The witness and Beall and the servants waited on the jury. When he was at one end of the table, attending to the jury there, it is possible a word or two might have been uttered to those at the other end by the guests near them; and when he was at one end an officer was at the other. A servant might have said a word or handed a note without witness seeing it; but he thinks that very improbable, as he was on the watch.

Johnson was a bailiff having the jury in charge, and was with them every meal except one, and usually stood or sat between them and the guests; heard no conversation about the case, and saw no communication between any one and the jury, directly or indirectly.

From this testimony it appears that the jury were all kept together, without any separation, and though they took their meals at a public table, at a hotel, where other guests were seated, they were always under the charge of a sworn officer, and generally, if not always, under strict vigilance. The case is, therefore, different from any one in which it has been held by this court, that the verdict was vitiated by improper conduct, as by persons being admitted to them in the absence of a sworn officer, or when one or more of the jurors separated from his associates, and was out of the sight or supervision of the officer. It is not to be presumed, that when the jury were always kept together, and under the direct supervision of a sworn officer, that any undue influence was exercised upon them, because, considering the probability of detection, and the severe consequences to be visited upon them, it is not to be supposed that others would attempt or that the jurors would admit any improper influence to be addressed to them.

The present case, therefore, comes within that class of irregularities, which are contrary to the proper forms of proceeding, but not sufficient to vitiate the verdict. Hare v. The State, 4 How., 194.

It is much to be regretted that irregularities of this nature are of so frequent recurrence in the circuit courts, notwithstanding the rules, which have been repeatedly held by this court, and which, if followed and rigidly enforced against officers and jurors, by exemplary punishment, would prevent all such irregularities. And, it is much to be regretted, that the learned circuit judges appear to be so little disposed to prevent violations of such established and salutary forms as are necessary to the validity and purity of judicial proceedings, by the exercise of the ample powers with which they are clothed. This evil, which is so often presented for our consideration, can be easily prevented by prescribing rules, by which juries will be kept from all possibility of communication with others, and by enforcing such rules inflexibly, by proper punishment of all violations of them. Such rules may cause personal inconvenience, but they are necessary to the proper administration of justice, and to the purity of judicial proceedings, for which every citizen is bound to yield his personal convenience when necessary.

Let the judgment be affirmed.

Smith, C. J., concurred in the opinion of Mr. Justice Handy upon all the points discussed, except as to the sufficiency of the evidence to sustain the verdict. On this point the chief justice delivered an elaborate oral opinion, in which he reviewed all the evidence, and declared it to be his conclusion, that the evidence was insufficient to sustain the verdict.

Fisher, J., also concurred in the opinion of Mr. Justice Handy, except as to the last point discussed. He was of opinion that it was error to permit the jury to take their meals at the hotel, under the circumstances stated in the record.

Under the foregoing opinions, a judgment of affirmance was entered in this court. Afterwards, the counsel for the prisoner entered a motion to correct the judgment, so as to reverse the judgment below, upon the ground that two of the judges were of opinion that there was error in the record, and that a new trial should be granted.

This motion was argued by

Thomas Botters and *W. B. Helm* for the prisoner, and *D. C. Glenn*, for the state.

Fisher, J.:

This is a motion to correct the judgment entered in this case, by changing the judgment of affirmance into a judgment of reversal, so as to make it consistent with what is alleged to be opinions of a majority of the court.

To understand correctly the point presented for consideration, it will be necessary to refer briefly to the respective opinions of each member of the court. The most important points involved in the case, arose in the court below, on the motion for a new trial.　It was first insisted, that the verdict finding the prisoner guilty, was not sustained by the evidence, and

Second. That the jury, during the four days of the trial, took their meals at the public table in the town of Lexington, and were, without stating specially the grounds, exposed on such occasions to improper influences.

Upon the first point, two members of the court were of opinion that the testimony was sufficient to uphold the verdict.　The chief justice dissented on this point.　Upon the other point, the chief justice and Judge Handy were of opinion that there was nothing shown in the conduct of the jury, while at the hotel, to authorize the court in disturbing the verdict.　This being the attitude of the court, a judgment of affirmance was entered, on the ground that the law presuming the judgment of the court below to be correct, it could only be reversed upon a majority of the court agreeing that there was error in the judgment, or proceedings connected therewith.　The question, in every case decided in this court, is error or no error in the judgment of the court below.　The party assigning error assumes the affirmative of the proposition ; and hence, if a majority of the court do not agree as to such proposition, to wit : That there is error ; the judgment must be affirmed, for the reason, that the presumption in favor of its correctness has not been rebutted.

But it must, at the same time, be borne in mind, that when it is said that the majority of the court must agree upon error, it is not necessary that the majority should agree upon the same point, unless such point could of itself constitute a distinct assignment of error ; for it is not every point that may be argued by counsel, or be considered by the court, that could be assigned as error here.　Such points are considered, because they tend to support the assignment, supposing it to be formally made.　The question, therefore, is whether the two points already noticed, to wit : the insufficiency of the evidence to sustain the verdict, and the alleged improper conduct of the jury, could each constitute a separate assignment of error in this court.　If a verdict respond to the issue, whatever may be the want of evidence to sustain the jury in their finding, it must stand until set aside by the court, upon a motion for a new trial, or upon some other legal proceeding. Such a thing as assigning as error, that a verdict was not sustained by the evidence, when no motion had been made in the court below, to set the verdict aside for this reason, was never known in this court, or even attempted by the most inexperienced practitioners. How, then, does this court apply the corrective in such case, to wit : in case of an erroneous verdict ? I mean erroneous, when compared with the evidence. I answer, in but the one way, by deciding that the court below erred in refusing to grant the new trial. Under what assignment of error, then, must the question of a wrong verdict be considered ? I answer, under the assignment that the court below erred in permitting such verdict to stand, and to constitute the basis of its judgment ; or, in other words, erred in refusing to sustain the motion for a new trial. Those matters, which could only be considered by the court below, on such motion, must enter into this assignment of error in this court. The court could only weigh the evidence upon the motion for a new trial, and in this way test the correctness of the verdict. The same may be said in regard to the misconduct of the jury. This question could only be considered upon the motion for a new trial, and it was but an additional reason urged upon the court for this purpose. Both points, the want of evidence and the misconduct of the jury, tended to establish the same proposition, to wit : a wrong verdict. The object was to show a wrong verdict. Two members of the court have agreed as to this point, that the verdict was wrong, and that the court below erred in permitting it to stand. Why, then, have not the majority agreed upon error in the judgment ? The chief justice says the verdict was clearly wrong, and that the court below erred in not setting it aside. I say the same thing—wrong verdict and error of the court in sustaining it, but base my opinion upon a different ground from that assigned by the chief justice. Do we not both agree, however, in the error assigned, or at least the only error which could, under any known rule, be assigned, that the court erred in pronouncing the judgment of death upon the prisoner, upon a verdict, which we both say was manifestly wrong ? It is not necessary that our process of reasoning should be the same, or that we should each attach the same importance to the same points involved; it is sufficient if we agree upon the error or substantial matter, to wit: Was the verdict manifestly wrong, was the act vicious, and has the court sustained such act? The majority agree in this result—a wrong verdict and error in the court below in not setting it aside. Such being my view of the question, I am of opinion that the motion ought to be sustained, and that the correction accordingly be made.

In coming to this conclusion, that I may not be misunderstood, I again repeat that I hold that a majority of the court must, in every case brought into this court, agree upon error, before reversing the judgment of the court below. But when I make this declaration, I, at the same time say, that the error must be something which could, under proper rules of practice, be assigned as error.

The want of evidence to sustain a verdict, or improper conduct in the jury finding it, can neither be assigned as error in this court. They both, or either, may prove that the court below, whose duty it was to set the verdict aside, erred in refusing to do so. We only know the error in the verdict through the action of the court in sustaining it. We do not say in such case that the verdict is reversed, but that the judgment upholding the verdict is reversed, and a new trial shall be granted.

HANDY, J., dissenting:

This case is now presented again, upon the motion of the plaintiff in error, to correct the judgment entered here, and to have a judgment of reversal entered.

The ground of this motion is, that in the opinions expressed in the decision of the case, a majority of the court considered that there was error in the record, one member of the court, (Judge Smith,) thinking that the evidence was not sufficient to sustain the verdict, and in which opinion he dissented from Judge Fisher and myself, and Judge Fisher being of opinion that the verdict should have been set aside and a new trial granted, by reason of the jury being permitted to take their meals with the guests at the public table of a hotel, and in which opinion he dissented from the two other members of the court.

It thus appears, that although two of the members of the court are of opinion that the judgment should be reversed, yet they do not agree that there is any error in any specific decision or ruling of the court below ; and when the various grounds of error assigned were considered by the court *seriatim*, a majority of the court were, and still are, of opinion that there is no error in any specific decision or ruling of the court.

It appears to me, therefore, clear, that the decision must be, that there is no error in the record for which the judgment should be reversed.

When a judgment is reversed in this court, it is the duty of the court to state in writing the reasons for the decision, in order that they may be a guide to the inferior court, to prevent the recurrence of the errors found to exist in the subsequent trial of the case, and in order to settle the rule of law involved in the case, for the benefit of all the citizens of the state, and in all similar cases in which it may arise, for the action of the citizen, or for the government of the courts. It requires a majority of the court to agree upon some specific rule or point of law which has been erroneously decided in the inferior court ; and, although a majority of the court may not agree in the reasons which led each of their minds to the conclusion that any specific rule or point of law has been erroneously decided, yet it is necessary that a majority should concur in the opinion that there is error in one and the same rule or point of law, as held by the court below. Otherwise, if the case goes back for a new trial, and the same point arises, the decision of the court below would necessarily be the same as was previously made, because the judge would be bound to know that this court had held that there was no error in that particular decision ; and the same rule of action would be observed by all other courts in the state whenever the same question might arise.

Otherwise, if upon a new trial of this case in the court below, the prisoner should be convicted upon the same evidence which appears in this record, and a motion for a new trial should be made upon the ground that the testimony was not sufficient to warrant the verdict, the court below would be bound to overrule it, because this court, which has the power to declare the law of the case, has, by a majority, decided that the verdict should not be set aside upon that ground.   And the same result would take place, if, upon another conviction, the conduct of the jury should be the same as appears in this record; for that is held by a majority of the court not to be error.   If the case should be again brought to this court in the same condition in which it is now presented; what would be the decision?   It appears to me impossible to avoid the conclusion, if the members of the court adhere to their present opinions, that the court below had committed no error upon either of these points, and, therefore, that the judgment should be affirmed, because it has been solemnly declared by this court that there is no error upon either of these points.   And, if that judgment should then be reversed, it would be but the very case now before us, and in which it is held that, although a majority of the court determine that there is no error in either of these rulings, yet the judgment must be reversed; the result of which is that the judgment is reversed when there is no error.   And such would be the strange and anomalous attitude of the case *ad infinitum,* as often as it should be tried below, and brought here under the same state of facts.

But it is said that the motion for a new trial, on account of the insufficiency of the evidence to support the verdict, and on account of the misconduct of the jury, presented but a single proposition which could be assigned for error here; that the error assigned was, that the court overruled the motion for a new trial; and, although the members of this court may differ as to the reasons why they think that the motion was erroneously overruled, yet if a majority think that it should have been sustained, one member upon one of the grounds stated in the motion, and the other upon the other ground, that the judgment must be reversed.

The error of this reasoning, I think, consists in this: the grounds upon which the motion for a new trial in the court below was made, are specified in the record.   Each ground is separate and distinct from the others, involving points of law, and either of them, if decided in favor of the prisoner, would have entitled him to a new trial.   Although the assignment of errors be general, that the court erred in overruling the motion for a new trial, yet when the case comes to be considered by this court, each specification is the subject of separate and distinct deliberation, as each involves a separate and distinct point of law, properly arising in the case, and necessary to be settled upon its own merits. Though the assignment or charge of error be general, it necessarily refers to the specifications of grounds contained in the motion in the court below ; and before the judgment can be reversed for error in overruling the motion, it must be determined by this court that the court below erred in its ruling upon some one specification. The court might not agree in the reasons upon which the several members founded their opinion, but there would and must be an agreement of opinion upon the single point, that the particular specification was sustained, and that on that ground the new trial should have been granted. After deciding upon the first specification, the second is considered, and unless there be a majority of opinion, that the new trial should have been granted on that ground, there will be no error as to that. And so each specification is taken up and considered and determined, *seriatim*, whether or not there be error in the ruling upon that point. And though there be a minority of the court of opinion upon each specification that there is error, yet if no two of the members concur as to error upon some specific point ruled by the court below, the fact that two of them think that there is error, one upon one specification, and another upon another, will not cause a reversal, because a majority of the court consider that there is no error upon any specific point or rule of law presented as ground of error.

Under our present practice, no assignment of errors is made here in legal form ; but they are assigned in argument as they appear upon the record. It is, however, said that the question under consideration must be treated as if there had been a general assignment of error, that the error overruled the motion for a new trial. We are referred to the record to see what that motion is, and find it based on sundry grounds, any one of which, if sustained, would carry the motion. The generality of the assignment does not amalgamate points and questions of law which are in their nature distinct, and which this court must pronounce upon as legal questions in deciding the case. Suppose, on the trial, the court below had granted these instructions at the instance of the state. The assignment of error here, on that ground, under the strict rule which formerly prevailed here upon the subject, would be a general one, that the court erred in granting the instructions for the state. And in considering that assignment, the first instruction comes up, and two members of the court think that there is no error in it, the third member considering it erroneous. It is then settled that there is no error as to that. The second instruction is then considered, and two members are of opinion that there is no error as to that, one of the majority upon the first instruction thinking that there is error in it. It is then settled that there is no error as to the second instruction. The third is then considered, and determined by a majority of the court to be proper, the member who agreed with the majority upon the two other instructions, dissenting upon this. It would be settled that there was no error in the third instruction. It would therefore clearly be the judgment of the court, that there was no error in any of the instructions. And how is it possible, that the general mode of assigning errors could make error in that which was not error in itself, or that several propositions which in themselves were distinct and separate, and ascertained to be correct and proper, could be rendered erroneous by being considered together?

I consider this motion as settled by the rule held by this court in the case of Bell v. Morrison, 27 Miss., 68, where the court was divided in opinion upon two points in the case, but there not being a majority holding that upon either of the points there was error. The first impression of the court in that case was, that the judgment should be reversed, there being a majority of that opinion, as in this case; but upon motion and after argument, the decision was that the judgment should be affirmed, which was accordingly done, because there was not a majority of the court holding that there was error in any of the points decided by the court below. The same rule is held in Alabama, in Cook v. Drew, 3 Stew. & Porter, 392.

When, therefore, it is the duty of the court to determine whether there is error in the points of law held by the court below, and this court is of opinion that there is no error in such rulings, I cannot understand upon what principle it is that the judgment can be reversed.

I am, therefore, of opinion, that the judgment be entered, as in law I consider it to be, affirmed.

Note.—This case was decided at the April term, A. D. 1856.

This case and that of Gaston Browning had acquired so much notoriety in the county of Holmes, to which the venue had been changed in the first instance, that it was deemed advisable, both by the counsel for the prosecution and for the defense, to petition the legislature for an act changing the venue to Carroll county. This was accordingly done, and the case of John D. Browning was tried at November term, 1857, of the circuit court of Carroll county, when there was a mistrial. At the April term, A. D. 1858, he was again tried and acquitted. He was defended by W. Cothran, W. B. Helm, J. K. Clinton and J. Z. George, and prosecuted by E. C. Walthall, district attorney, and W. Brooke and Richard Nelson.

At the July special term, A. D. 1858, of the said court, Gaston E. Browning was tried and acquitted. He was defended by Messrs. Cothran, Helm and George, and prosecuted by E. C. Walthall and R. Nelson.

END OF VOL. I.

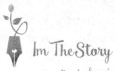

Im TheStory

personalised classic books

"Beautiful gift., lovely finish. My Niece loves it, so precious!"

Helen R Brumfieldon

★★★★★

UNIQUE GIFT

FOR KIDS, PARTNERS AND FRIENDS

Timeless books such as:

Kids

Alice in Wonderland · The Jungle Book · The Wonderful Wizard of Oz
Peter and Wendy · Robin Hood · The Prince and The Pauper
The Railway Children · Treasure Island · A Christmas Carol

Adults

Romeo and Juliet · Dracula

Highly Customizable

Change Books Title

Replace Characters Names with yours

Upload Photo dot inside page

Add Inscriptions

Visit

Im TheStory .com

and order yours today!